THE DEBATE OVER CORPORATE
SOCIAL RESPONSIBILITY

THE DEBATE OVER CORPORATE SOCIAL RESPONSIBILITY

STEVE MAY, GEORGE CHENEY, AND JULIET ROPER

OXFORD
UNIVERSITY PRESS

2007

OXFORD
UNIVERSITY PRESS

Oxford University Press, Inc., publishes works that further
Oxford University's objective of excellence
in research, scholarship, and education.

Oxford   New York
Auckland   Cape Town   Dar es Salaam   Hong Kong   Karachi
Kuala Lumpur   Madrid   Melbourne   Mexico City   Nairobi
New Delhi   Shanghai   Taipei   Toronto

With offices in
Argentina   Austria   Brazil   Chile   Czech Republic   France   Greece
Guatemala   Hungary   Italy   Japan   Poland   Portugal   Singapore
South Korea   Switzerland   Thailand   Turkey   Ukraine   Vietnam

Published by Oxford University Press, Inc.
198 Madison Avenue, New York, New York 10016

www.oup.com

Oxford is a registered trademark of Oxford University Press

Library of Congress Cataloging-in-Publication Data
The debate over corporate sodcial responsibility / [edited by]
Steve May, George Cheney, and Juliet Roper.
p. cm.
Includes bibliographical references and index.
ISBN 978-0-19-517882-1; 978-0-19-517883-8 (pbk.)
1. Social responsibility of business.   I. May, Steven, 1961–   II. Cheney, George.
III. Roper, Juliet.
HD60.D35 2007
174'.4—dc22   2006022343

Printed in the United States of America
on acid-free paper

Foreword

GILBERT LENSSEN

President of the European Academy of Business in Society

In addition to the excellent historical overview the editors of this book provide, I would like to draw attention to the shifts that have taken place in the debate on corporate social responsibility (CSR) during the last decade. In the 1990s, corporate attention was focused on external and internal communication of the firm's policies and commitments on CSR. It was often in the remit of external relations or corporate communications managers. Similarly, the academic literature focused largely on communication with stakeholders internally and externally. Corporate social responsibility also became part of the narrative on "globalization."

This was challenged by the allegation that firms handle CSR as a postmodern public relations exercise with much spin and without real substance. The focus then switched to the substance of economic analysis of the so-called business case for CSR and sustainability.

In firms, CSR and sustainability departments were founded. In the academic literature, case studies, surveys, and meta-analyses of the relationship between corporate social performance and corporate financial performance took the limelight. This era was epitomized by the publication of meta-analytical studies on this relationship and case studies undertaken by the International Institute for Management Development (IMD) in Lausanne, Switzerland, on a large scale in several global industry sectors as part of a project titled the Business of Sustainability, supported by the European Academy of Business in Society.

What becomes clear from that work is the following:

1. Despite the economic evidence of a considerable potential for (self-interested) responsible corporate action—which is clearly documented for companies and whole industry sectors alike—this opportunity is far from utilized.
2. Despite efforts to link CSR to competitiveness—including at the macrolevel of countries and regions such as the European Union—policy makers and scholars in competitiveness studies have difficulty viewing CSR as integral to the effective and sustainable functioning of markets and business environments.

For example, a senior executive from a large global firm, recently interviewed by a research team of which I was part, noted that "we do not seem to have the language to create and connect the different narratives within the firm and within society. The interconnections are missing." What came to my mind was Jean-François Lyotard's metaphor of postmodernity: the archipelago of unconnected islands of different cultures of which the coherence only becomes visible at a meta-level, high up in the air over the archipelago.

As such, we might be heading toward a new era with a communication focus on studying the debate over CSR, with a view to the following:

1. To apply historical analysis to the rise of CSR to understand how it takes its place (or not) within the history of ideas in political economy, politics, moral philosophy, institutional economics, and management
2. To perform critical rhetorical analysis on the discourses in the debate over CSR in search of dichotomies and oppositions stemming from the 19th century Victorian era: public–private, local–global, and virtue–vice, among others
3. To perform narrative analysis of CSR and how these narratives have evolved with a view to identify traces of fashion, utopia, apologia, fiction, and the social imagination
4. To apply critical theory to the questions of power, influence, and interests that are at stake and possibly concealed by the polemics on CSR
5. To apply phenomenology to CSR as a movement with different meanings, in different guises and on different agendas in business, society, and government

Therefore, this book by reputable scholars in communication studies could not be more timely. It makes some fine contributions to the objective set out above by digging beneath narratives and arguments and performing some social and political archeology on CSR.

The analysis of the grand as well as the small narratives is present in this book, history of ideas and neomarxist critical theory sit side by side, and the diversity of perspectives (e.g., business ethics, sustainable development, global responsibility, corporate citizenship) and the different dimensions of analysis (e.g., social, environmental, ethical, economic, legal) are given a place. Contributions on business alternate with contributions on organizational processes between business and society.

Readers should ask themselves whether this all adds up to something of coherence, or is it rather a masterpiece in postmodern plurality, which in itself might be worthwhile as an aesthetic achievement. I might even suggest a subtitle for this book, "from business ethics to organizational aesthetics," because if we go back to the profound observation by the senior executive interview mentioned above, we must ask ourselves whether and how we—as academics—meet the needs of those who want to advance the debate over, and substance of, CSR. Moreover, if we have a new drive for a communication approach to CSR, are we offering coherent insights into the ways of constructing a new language and new narratives to deal with the complexity and ambivalence that CSR poses?

I believe this book has made an excellent start with this drive. I congratulate the editors and authors for their courageous endeavor.

Acknowledgments

As in the case of many scholarly endeavors, this book could not have been completed without the support of numerous other individuals. In many respects, an edited volume is a joint accomplishment among the editors, the authors, and the publishers. This book has been a creative collaboration among the editors, and it also required the contributions of many colleagues who produced the chapters contained in it. Although we do not name each of the authors individually, we do want to acknowledge their efforts to produce chapters that we believe are insightful, informative, and forward looking. The case authors' own varied interests and perspectives have helped represent a diverse set of responses to today's corporations. We hope that the chapters promote healthy dialogue and constructive change regarding the current and future role of corporations in all of our lives.

In addition, we appreciate the support of Oxford University Press in the development of this book. In particular, we thank John Rauschenberg for his ongoing support of the project. We also want to acknowledge Robert Milks, Sara Needles and Trish Watson for seeing the book through its completion. Jennifer Buckle provided helpful proofreading and copyediting at earlier stages of the book. We appreciate the helpful and constructive suggestions provided by the following reviewers: Maribeth Metzler, University of Cincinnati; Mette Morsing, Copenhagen Business School; Bryan Taylor, University of Colorado–Boulder; and Dean Ritz.

Steve thanks Geriel for her ongoing support and encouragement and Arcadia for her constant reminder that our futures matter. He also thanks the Arthur W. Page Center at the Penn State College of Communications for their support during the final stages of the book. George thanks Sally Planalp for her continuing love and support and especially for her patience with his recovery from overcommitment. Juliet acknowledges her children, Katherine, James, and Alexander, as representatives of the generation that carries the burden of our irresponsibility. Finally, we express gratitude to all those who work for social justice and environmental sustainability around the world, recognizing that business as usual will probably mean no planet as usual.

Contents

Foreword   v
  Gilbert Lenssen, The European Academy of Business in Society (EABIS)

Contributors   xiii

Overview   3
  George Cheney, Juliet Roper, and Steve May

I. Introduction

1. Why Corporate Social Responsibility: Why Now? How?   15
   Jill J. McMillan

2. A New Generation of Global Corporate Social Responsibility   30
   Michael Stohl, Cynthia Stohl, and Nikki C. Townsley

3. Progressing from Corporate Social Responsibility to Brand Integrity   45
   Malcolm McIntosh

II. Cases and Contexts

4. Facing Corporate Power   59
   Jem Bendell and Mark Bendell

5. Corporate Citizenship: The Dark-Side Paradoxes of Success   74
   Sandra Waddock

6. Corporate Social Responsibility in Scandinavia: A Turn Toward the Business Case?   87
   Mette Morsing, Atle Midttun, and Karl Palmås

7. Corporate Social Responsibility in Asia: A Confucian Context   105
   Glen Whelan

8. Corporate Social Responsibility and Public Relations: Perceptions and Practices in Singapore   119
   Krishnamurthy Sriramesh, Chew Wee Ng, Soh Ting Ting, and Luo Wanyin

9. Corporate Social Responsibility in Mexico: An Approximation from the Point of View of Communication   135
   Mariela Pérez Chavarría

III. Legal Perspectives

10. Legal Versus Ethical Arguments: Contexts for Corporate Social Responsibility   155
    Matthew W. Seeger and Steven J. Hipfel

11. Corporate Deception and Fraud: The Case for an Ethical Apologia   167
    Keith Michael Hearit

12. Regulation: Government, Business, and the Self in the United States   177
    John Llewellyn

13. Can Corporate Personhood Be Socially Responsible?   190
    Dean Ritz

IV. Economic Perspectives

14. How to Read Milton Friedman: Corporate Social Responsibility and Today's Capitalisms   207
    James Arnt Aune

15. Corporate Social Responsibility as Oxymoron: Universalization and Exploitation at Boeing   219
    Dana L. Cloud

16. Toward an Accounting for Sustainability: A New Zealand View   232
    Stewart Lawrence

17. Consumer Activism and Corporate Social Responsibility: How Strong a Connection?   241
    Brenden E. Kendall, Rebecca Gill, and George Cheney

V. Social Perspectives

18. Corporate Governance, Corporate Social Responsibility, and Communication   267
    Stanley Deetz

19. Corporate and Institutional Responses to the Challenge of HIV/AIDS: The Case of South Africa   279
    Grant Samkin and Stewart Lawrence

20. Business, Society, and Impacts on Indigenous Peoples   292
    Marcus Breen

21. Activism, Risk, and Communicational Politics: Nike and the Sweatshop Problem   305
    Graham Knight

VI. Environmental Perspectives

22. Corporate Environmentalism   321
    Connie Bullis and Fumiko Ie

23. Greening of Corporations? Eco-talk and the Emerging Social Imaginary
    of Sustainable Development   336
    Sharon M. Livesey and Julie Graham

24. Discourses of Sustainability in Today's Public Sphere   351
    Tarla Rai Peterson and Todd Norton

25. Green Marketing and Advertising   365
    Worawan Yim Ongkrutraksa

26. Sustainable Development Discourse and the Global Economy:
    Promoting Responsibility, Containing Change   379
    Shiv Ganesh

27. The Behavior of Corporate Species in Ecosystems and Their Roles
    in Environmental Change   391
    Douglas Crawford-Brown

**VII. Commentary on Corporate Social Responsibility:
The Contributions of Communication and Other Perspectives**

28. Is Sustainability Sustainable? Corporate Social Responsibility, Sustainable Business,
    and Management Fashion   405
    Theodore E. Zorn and Eva Collins

29. Corporate Social Responsibility and Public Policy Making   417
    Charles Conrad and JéAnna Abbott

30. The Case of the Subaltern Public: A Postcolonial Investigation of Corporate Social
    Responsibility's (O)Missions   438
    Debashish Munshi and Priya Kurian

31. The Discourse of Corporate Social Responsibility: Postmodern Remarks   448
    Lars Thøger Christensen

32. Corporate Social Responsibility/Corporate Moral Responsibility: Is There a Difference
    and the Difference It Makes   459
    Patricia H. Werhane

Index   475

Contributors

ABOUT THE EDITORS

George Cheney (Ph.D., Purdue University, 1985) is Professor of Communication at the University of Utah, Salt Lake City, where he also serves as Director of Peace and Conflict Studies. In addition, he is Adjunct Professor of Management Communication at the University of Waikato, Hamilton, New Zealand. Cheney's teaching and research interests include identity and power at work, democracy and labor, quality of work life, professional ethics, the marketization of society, and the rhetoric of war and peace. He has authored, co-authored, or co-edited six books and has published more than 80 journal articles, book chapters, and reviews. Recognized for both teaching and research, he has lectured, taught, and conducted research in Western Europe and Latin America, in addition to the United States and New Zealand. He is a past chair of the Organizational Communication Division of the National Communication Association and is a senior associate editor for *Organization*. He has consulted for organizations in the public, private, and non-profit sectors and is a strong advocate of service learning in the community beyond the university.

Steve May (Ph.D., University of Utah, 1993) is Associate Professor in the Department of Communication Studies at the University of North Carolina at Chapel Hill. He is also currently a Leadership Fellow at the Institute for the Arts and the Humanities and an Ethics Fellow at the Parr Ethics Center. In addition, he serves as an ethics researcher and consultant for the Ethics at Work program at Duke University's Kenan Institute for Ethics. His research focuses on the relationship between work and identity, as it relates to the boundaries of public/private, work/family, and labor/leisure. Most recently, he has studied the challenges and opportunities for organizational ethics and corporate social responsibility. His most recent books include *Case Studies in Organizational Communication: Ethical Perspectives and Practices* (2006) and *Engaging Organizational Communication Theory and Research: Multiple Perspectives* (2005). In addition to his publications in journals, he is also a past Forum Editor of *Management Communication Quarterly*.

Juliet Roper (PhD, University of Waikato, 2000) is Professor of Management Communication at the Waikato Management School, University of Waikato, Hamilton, New Zealand. Roper is currently the Sustainability Convenor for the Waikato Management School, representative for the school's membership of the European Academy of Business in Society, and founder of the Asia Pacific Academy of Business in Society. She was a 2006 finalist for the Faculty Pioneer Award for External Impact from the Aspen Institute and World Resources Institute. Her research and teaching interests include public relations, influences on public policy, dialogue, and government and corporate discourses on sustainability and social responsibility. She is co-author of *The Politics of Representation: Election Campaigning and Proportional Representation* (2004) and has had articles published in U.S. and European journals, including *Journal of Public Relations Research*, *Public Relations Review*, *Journal of Applied Communication Research*, *Journal of Public Affairs*, and *Corporate Governance*.

ABOUT THE CONTRIBUTORS

JéAnna Abbott (LL.M., J.D., M.B.A., M.H.M., C.H.E.) is the Spec's Charitable Foundation Professor in Corporate Social Responsibility at the Conrad N. Hilton College of Hotel and Restaurant Management at the University of Houston, where she teaches hospitality, business law and ethics, negotiations, convention planning, and event management at the graduate and undergraduate levels. She is also Adjunct Professor at the University of Houston Law Center, where she teaches negotiations. Abbott completed her law degrees at the University of Houston and her M.B.A. at the University of Chicago. She is presently pursuing another graduate degree at Texas A&M University in Organizational Communication. Her present research interests are in conflict resolution and corporate social responsibility. Abbott is also the editor of the *Journal of Convention & Event Tourism*.

James Arnt Aune (Ph.D., Northwestern University, 1980) is Professor of Communication at Texas A&M University. He is the author of two books, *Rhetoric and Marxism* (1994) and *Selling the Free Market: The Rhetoric of Economic Correctness* (2001), which won the 2003 Diamond Anniversary Book Award from the National Communication Association. An edited volume, *The White House and Civil Rights Rhetoric*, was published in 2005. He has published a number of articles in rhetoric and law journals, including *Quarterly Journal of Speech*, *Rhetoric & Public Affairs*, and *Hastings Constitutional Law Quarterly*. His main research interests are in the theory and history of public controversy over legal and economic issues. He serves on the Board of Directors of the Rhetoric Society of America and is current editor of *Free Speech Yearbook*.

Jem Bendell (Ph.D., University of Bristol, 2003) is an Associate Adjunct Professor of Management at the University of Griffith Business School and Senior Strategic Advisor with WWF. He has been involved in, has advised on, has analyzed, and has written about corporate and nongovernmental organization responses to the challenges of globalization for 10 years. His research interests concern the systemic transformation of markets toward sustainable development. With two books on cross-sector relations, a column in the *Journal of Corporate Citizenship*, and more than 30 other publications, he is one of the world's leading commentators on partnerships for sustainable development. As director of the progressive professional services company Lifeworth, he worked with many international organizations, including the International Labor Organization, the World Health Organization, and the Joint United Nations Programme on HIV/AIDS. His work on the future of corporate responsibility, *Barricades and Boardrooms* (2004), was published by the United Nations Research Institute for Social Development.

Mark Bendell (Ph.D., University of Cambridge, 1997) is Senior Lecturer in Communications and Social Science, University of Chester, United Kingdom. He received a First Class honors degree from the University of Cambridge in 1991, and his Ph.D. in Social and Political Science. He has published in the fields of corporate social responsibility and identity politics. His publications have appeared in the *Journal of Corporate Citizenship*. Forthcoming outputs include *Decoding Discrimination* (2005) and "Policies of Empire," forthcoming in *Globalisation*. He is working with Dr. Catrin Smith on women's use of media in carceral settings.

Marcus Breen (Ph.D., Victoria University of Technology, Melbourne, 1997) is Associate Professor in the Department of Communication Studies at Northeastern University, Boston. His interests include media and cultural studies and the political economy of international business and social and economic development through information and communication technologies. He is the editor of *Our Place Our Music: Aboriginal Music. Australian Popular Music in Perspective* (1989) and *Rock Dogs: Politics and the Australian Music Industry* (1999). His published research has appeared in journals such as *Popular Music*, *Cultural Studies*, *Cultural Studies Review*, *Ethicomp*, and

Computer Mediated Communication and as book chapters.

Connie Bullis (Ph.D., Purdue University, 1984) is Associate Professor of Communication at the University of Utah, Salt Lake City. Her teaching and research have focused on organizational communication and environmental communication. She has taught and studied environmental sustainability as it pertains to organizations. She is a past president of Western Communication Association, where she catalyzed a sustainability initiative.

Lars Thøger Christensen (Pd.D., Odense University, 1993) is Professor of Communications at the Department of Marketing and Management at the University of Southern Denmark. Previously he was Research Professor at the Copenhagen Business School, where he established the CBS Center for Corporate Communication. His research and teaching interests include critical and postmodern approaches to the broad fields of marketing, organizational, and corporate communication. In particular, his research has centered on issues of identity, issues management, integration, advertising, and transparency. In addition to five books, his research is published in *Organization Studies, European Journal of Marketing, Consumption, Markets & Culture, New Handbook of Organizational Communication, Handbook of Public Relations, Communication Yearbook,* and elsewhere. Currently, he is writing a book with Mette Morsing that challenges the prevailing discourses of corporate communication. Christensen's contribution to the chapter in this volume was made possible by a grant from the Danish Social Science Research Council.

Dana L. Cloud (Ph.D., University of Iowa, 1992) is Associate Professor of Communication Studies at the University of Texas–Austin. Her research and teaching interests include Marxist theory, feminist theory, public sphere theory, critical organizational communication, social movements (particularly labor), cultural studies, and visual rhetoric. Her work has appeared in *Quarterly Journal of Speech, Critical Studies in Media Communication, Management Communication Quarterly, Western Journal of Communication,* and *Rhetoric & Public Affairs,* as well as in numerous edited collections. She has authored one book, *Control and Consolation in American Culture and Politics: Rhetorics of Therapy* (1998), and is working on another book about dissident unionists at the Boeing Company. She is a longtime member of the International Socialist Organization.

Eva Collins (Ph.D., George Washington University, 2002) is Senior Lecturer in the Strategy and Human Resource Management Department at Waikato University, Hamilton, New Zealand. Her teaching and research have focused on sustainability practices of business, business climate change strategies, and voluntary environmental programs. Her work has appeared in the *Journal of Communication Management, Australian Journal of Communication, Business Strategy & the Environment, Journal of Cleaner Production,* and *Electronic Journal of Radical Organisation Theory.*

Charles Conrad (Ph.D., University of Kansas, 1980) is Professor of Organizational Communication and Organizational Rhetoric in the Department of Communication at Texas A&M University and immediate past editor of *Management Communication Quarterly.* His research focuses on the interface among organizational discourse, power, and politics and has appeared in the *Quarterly Journal of Speech, Journal of Applied Communication Research, Communication Monographs,* and *Management Communication Quarterly.* He is currently involved in research on the processes through which organizational discourse influences public policy making in the United States and Canada, primarily related to health care issues.

Douglas Crawford-Brown (Ph.D., Georgia Institute of Technology, 1982) is Professor in the Departments of Environmental Sciences and Engineering and in Public Policy Analysis, and Director of the campuswide Carolina Environmental Program, at the University of North Carolina at Chapel Hill. Trained initially in physics and nuclear science, he currently teaches and carries out research in the areas of environmental modeling, risk assessment, and the application of scientific models in the assessment and selection of environmental policies. His writings include more than 140 journal articles on these topics, as well as a series of four books on environmental risk assessment and epidemiology. He has served on a wide range of advisory committees in areas related to risk and the environment, including committees established by the

U.S. Environmental Protection Agency, World Trade Organization, Department of Energy, European Commission, National Institutes of Health, International Life Sciences Institute, and Chemical Industry Institute of Toxicology.

Stanley Deetz (Ph.D., Ohio University, 1973) is Professor of Communication and Director of Peace and Conflict Studies at the University of Colorado–Boulder. His research focuses primarily on relations of power in work sites and the way these relations are produced and reproduced in everyday interaction. Normatively, this work attempts to produce governance structures, decision processes, and communicative micropractices that lead to more satisfying work experiences and more inclusive, collaborative, and creative decisions. His books include *Leading Organizations Through Transitions* (2000), *Doing Critical Management Research* (2000), *Transforming Communication, Transforming Business* (1995), and *Democracy in an Age of Corporate Colonization* (1992). He has published around 100 essays in scholarly journals and books regarding stakeholder representation, decision making, culture, and communication in corporate organizations and has lectured widely in the United States and Europe. He is a Fellow of the International Communication Association (serving as its president during 1996–1997), is a National Communication Association Distinguished Scholar, and has held many other elected professional positions. He is also an active consultant for companies in the United States and Europe.

Shiv Ganesh (Ph.D., Purdue University, 2000) is Senior Lecturer at the University of Waikato, Hamilton, New Zealand. His research projects involve issues of power, identity, and practice in nonprofit and nongovernmental organizations in the context of globalization. His research has been published in such journals as *Communication Monographs*, *Management Communication Quarterly*, and *Journal of Communication Inquiry*. He is co-author, with George Cheney, Ted Zorn, and Lars Thøger Christensen, of the book *Organizational Communication in an Age of Globalization: Issues, Reflections, Practices* (2004). His current projects involve studies of nonprofit coalitions, grassroots decision making, and activism over outsourcing.

Rebecca Gill is a doctoral student in the Department of Communication at the University of Utah, Salt Lake City. Her research interests lie at the intersections of organizational communication, gender, and the media and address quality of work life and work-life trends, specifically focusing on work-life relationships for women and women entrepreneurs, as well as mediated representations of women in the public sphere.

Julie Graham (Ph.D., Clark University, 1984) is currently Professor of Economic Geography at the University of Massachusetts–Amherst. Her research focuses on rethinking and reenacting economy and on fostering alternative organizations and practices of development. Under the pen name J. K. Gibson-Graham, which she shares with Katherine Gibson of the Australian National University, she has co-authored many articles and several books, including *The End of Capitalism (As We Knew It): A Feminist Critique of Political Economy* (1996), soon to be released in a new edition alongside its sequel, *A Postcapitalist Politics* (2006).

Keith Michael Hearit (Ph.D., Purdue University, 1992) is Associate Professor of Communication and Associate Dean of the Lee Honors College at Western Michigan University in Kalamazoo, Michigan. He teaches courses in organizational communication, public relations, corporate advocacy, and crisis management. His research focuses on noncommercial forms of external organizational communication by corporations, particularly in those instances when companies are accused of wrongdoing. In addition to his book, *Crisis Management by Apology: Corporate Response to Allegations of Wrongdoing* (2006), he has published articles in the *Handbook of Public Relations*, *Communication Studies*, and *Public Relations Review*, as well as contributed chapters in a number of edited books. Hearit is active in the National Communication Association, Association for Journalism and Mass Communication Education, and the Central States Communication Association.

Steven J. Hipfel (J.D., Indiana University, 1982; M.A., University of Evansville, 1990; LL.M., George Washington University, 2000) is environmental legal counsel at the U.S. Navy's Office of the Chief of Naval Operations. He is also a graduate of the U.S. Army Command and General Staff College (1997) and U.S. Naval War College (1993).

He has taught at several universities and colleges, including the U.S. Naval Academy, where he also served as legal counsel. His research and publications have centered on water pollution issues. In addition to serving as an active duty naval officer, he has served as a Special Assistant U.S. Attorney. Prior to entering public service, he was a law firm partner advising corporate and commercial clients on employment and labor matters.

Fumiko Ie is a doctoral student in the Department of Communication at the University of Utah, Salt Lake City. She holds a master's degree in interpersonal communication from the University of Utah and is pursuing a Ph.D. in organizational communication. Her scholarly interests include linkages between interpersonal and organizational communication, organizations' environmental messages, and discourse among Japanese temporary workers.

Brenden E. Kendall is a doctoral student in the Department of Communication at the University of Utah, Salt Lake City. His research interests coalesce around organizational communication, environmental communication, quality of work life and time politics, and social movements.

Graham Knight (Ph.D., Carleton University, Ottawa, Canada, 1978) is Chair of the Department of Communication Studies & Multimedia, McMaster University, Hamilton, Canada. His recent research interest has been the controversy over sweatshop labor practices and how this has been framed in corporate and activist communication strategies. Recent publications have appeared in the *European Journal of Communication, Journalism Studies, Management Communication Quarterly, Communication & Critical/Cultural Studies, Australian Journal of Communication*, and *International Review for the Sociology of Sport*.

Priya Kurian (Ph.D., Purdue University, 1995) is Senior Lecturer in the Department of Political Science and Public Policy at the University of Waikato, Hamilton, New Zealand. Her research interests include environmental politics and policy, science and technology politics, and development studies, with a particular focus on issues of gender, race, and culture. She is the author of *Engendering the Environment: Gender in the World Bank's Environmental Policies* (2000) and co-editor of *Feminist Futures: Re-imagining Women,*

Culture and Development (2003, with Kum-Kum Bhavnani and John Foran) and *International Organizations and Environmental Policy* (1995, with Robert V. Bartlett and Madhu Malik). Her work has appeared in a number of journals, including *Ethnic & Racial Studies, Policy & Politics, Feminist Media Studies, Public Relations Review, Cultural Politics* and the *Asian Journal of Public Administration*.

Stewart Lawrence (Ph.D., University of Waikato, 1990) is Professor in Accounting at the Waikato Management School, University of Waikato, New Zealand. Research publications have been in the areas of performance measurement and control in public sector organizations, particularly in the health sector. He has published in journals such as *Accounting, Auditing & Accountability, Critical Perspectives on Accounting, Accounting Forum*, and *Health Policy*. He is co-author of *Accounting at Work: in Business, Government and Society* (3rd ed., 2004, with S. Lawrence, H. Davey, and M. Low). Current projects include sustainability practices of small and medium-sized enterprises in New Zealand and communitarian models of accountability.

Sharon M. Livesey holds a J.D. from Northeastern University. Her research on business and the natural environment and partnerships between businesses and eco-advocacy groups has been published in *Management Communication Quarterly, Journal of Business Communication*, and *Organization & Environment*.

John Llewellyn (Ph.D., University of Texas, 1990) is Associate Professor of Communication at Wake Forest University in Winston-Salem, North Carolina. His research interests include public relations, corporate social responsibility, institutional rhetoric, and urban legends. His writing has appeared in *Society, Public Relations Quarterly, Research in Corporate Social Responsibility & Performance*, and the *Journal of Communication*.

Malcolm McIntosh (Ph.D., University of Bradford, 1989) is Professor of Human Security and Director of the Applied Research Centre in Human Security (ARCHS) at the University of Coventry in England from August 2006. He is a writer, commentator, and educator on corporate responsibility and sustainability, and has been a Special

Advisor to the United Nations Global Compact. He is Visiting Professor at the universities of Bath, Nottingham, and Stellenbosch. He was Founding Editor of the *Journal of Corporate Citizenship* and is the General Editor for 2007–8, and is a former director of the Corporate Citizenship Unit at Warwick Business School in the United Kingdom. He has published numerous books and articles on corporate citizenship and other topics.

Jill J. McMillan (Ph.D., University of Texas, 1982) is Professor Emerita of Communication at Wake Forest University in Winston-Salem, North Carolina. Her research and teaching interests include organizational communication, group communication, communication pedagogy, rhetorical criticism, organizational rhetoric, and deliberative democracy. Her research has appeared in such venues as *Presidential Studies Quarterly, Quarterly Journal of Speech, Journal for the Scientific Study of Religion, Communication Education, Southern Communication Journal, Journal of Higher Education, Journal of Applied Communication, Communication Yearbook*, and *Higher Education Exchange*. She has recently completed a longitudinal study, sponsored by the Kettering Foundation, with Dr. Katy J. Harriger of the Wake Forest University Department of Political Science, that tracks the development of political attitudes among college students and how early introduction to deliberative skills and repeated opportunities to deliberate affect the citizenship skills that students develop over time. Their study will be fully reported in a forthcoming book, *Speaking of Politics: Preparing College Students for Democratic Citizenship Through Deliberative Dialogue.*

Atle Midttun (Ph.D., University of Uppsala, 1987) is Professor at the Norwegian School of Management, Director of the Centre for Corporate Citizenship, and Co-director of the Centre for Energy and Environment. He holds a Ph.D. in economic sociology. Midttun has worked and published extensively in several fields, including energy and environmental policy/economics, corporate social responsibility, industrial policy, innovation policy, business strategies, and regulation. He has had visiting scholarships/professorships at several leading universities, recently including visiting Scholar at the University of California–Berkeley Haas School of Business (2003–2004), visiting Professor at Université Paris Sud Faculté Jean Monet (2002), and visiting Professor, University of Michigan Business School/School of Natural Resources (2000–2001).

Mette Morsing (Ph.D., Copenhagen Business School, 1993) is Associate Professor and Director of CBS Center for Research into Corporate Responsibility at Copenhagen Business School. Morsing's research interests include corporate communication in a broad sense, corporate social responsibility, ethics, organizational identity, and image and reputation management. She has published a number of books and articles on these issues in, for example, *Corporate Reputation Review, Journal of Corporate Communication*, and *Corporate Communications: An International Journal*. Her latest authored book is *Beyond Corporate Communication* (2005) with Lars Thøger Christensen and her latest co-edited book is *CSR: Reconciling Aspiration with Application* (2006) with Andrew Kakabadse. She is a member of board the Øresund Environment Academy, a member of the management committee of the European Academy of Business in Society (EABIS), and a vice-chair of the academic board of EABIS.

Debashish Munshi (Ph.D., University of Waikato, 2000) is Associate Professor in the Department of Management Communication at the University of Waikato, Hamilton, New Zealand. His research scrutinizes the core function of managerial control, particularly in public relations and diversity management strategies of business organizations. His research brings theoretical perspectives from such other disciplines as cultural studies, media studies, postcolonial studies, and subaltern studies into the study of management in organizations. He has guest edited special issues of the *Australian Journal of Communication* and *Public Relations Review*, and his work has also been published in a range of other journals such as *Business Communication Quarterly, Asia Pacific Public Relations Journal, Feminist Media Studies, Cultural Politics,*, and *Review of Communication*.

Chew Wee Ng (B.A., Nanyang Technological University, Singapore, 2005) is Marketing Executive of Singapore Press Holdings in Singapore.

Todd Norton (Ph.D., University of Utah, 2006) is an Assistant Professor in the Edward R. Murrow School of Communication, Washington State

University. His research focuses on the organizational dimensions of the environmental policy domain, with principal attention to the roles of power and discourse in stakeholder processes. He is especially interested in the tensions involved in stakeholder participation and contestation in federal land-management processes. He has collaborated on inter-disciplinary projects funded by the Department of Energy and National Science Foundation. In 2005–2006, he received the David C. Williams Memorial Graduate Fellowship from the University of Utah College of Social and Behavioral Sciences for his dissertation *Grand Staircase-Escalante National Monument: Organizing Land Politics*. His publications appear in the *Southern Communication Journal*, *Quarterly Journal of Speech*, and *Proceedings of the Conference on Communication & the Environment*.

Worawan Yim Ongkrutraksa is a doctoral candidate at Tokai University, Kanagawa, Japan. She is a lecturer on the Faculty of Communication Arts, Chulalongkorn University, Bangkok, Thailand. Her research and teaching interests include international advertising and social advertising for corporate image (green advertising). Her works have appeared in *BU Academic Review* (Bangkok University), *Regional Studies* (International University of Kagoshima), and *Association for Consumer Research Asia-Pacific Conference Proceedings*. She gained her Master of Arts in media studies from the New School University, New York, New York, and Master of Letters in mass communications/advertising from Tokai University. She was a Monbusho scholar (Japanese government scholarship) and a recipient of the Yoshida Hideo Memorial Foundation Research Scholarship (Dentsu Inc.).

Karl Palmås (Ph.D., London School of Economics & Political Science, 2005) heads the Centre for Business in Society at Gothenburg University. His research and teaching interests revolve primarily around the study of corporations and their societal role using theories and methodologies adopted from science and technology studies. Palmås is one of the contributors to a recent anthology on new theoretical approaches to studying corporate social responsibility and has previously published a book on social enterprise. He tends to work with ethnographic methods and currently researches the links between corporate social responsibility and the concept of "risk" in a large multinational corporation. He is also involved in a project that experiments with "new social partnership" models aimed at facilitating research and development efforts for underserved markets. He is also engaged in the development of social enterprise models and practices.

Mariela Pérez Chavarría (completing dissertation in Organizational Communication at the University of Málaga in Spain) is Professor of Organizational Communication, Corporate Image, and Public Relationships at the Tecnológico de Monterrey, Campus Monterrey, México. Her research and teaching interests include language, corporate identity, and intercultural and organizational communication. She is co-author of two books and has published research, articles, and essays in such communication journals as *Razón y Palabra* and *World Futures*. She is a member of the Mexican Association of Organizational Communicators and the International Communication Association.

Tarla Rai Peterson (Ph.D., Washington State University, 1988) holds the Boone & Crockett Chair of Conservation Policy at Texas A&M University and is Adjunct Professor in the Department of Communication at the University of Utah, Salt Lake City. Her research focuses on how the intersections between communication, environmental policy, and democracy constrain sustainable development. She seeks to provide a theoretically rich analysis of environmental policy development and implementation that is useful to citizens in nominally democratic regimes. She has been a co-principal investigator on research grants funded by the National Science Foundation, the U.S. Department of Energy, and the U.S. Environmental Protection Agency. Her most recent book is *Green Talk in the White House: The Rhetorical Presidency Encounters Ecology* (2004). She also has published *Sharing the Earth: The Rhetoric of Sustainable Development* (1997) and articles in a variety of professional journals, including *Communication & Critical/Cultural Studies*, *Conservation Biology*, *Quarterly Journal of Speech*, and *Journal of Wildlife Management*.

Dean Ritz (M.A., University of Montana, 2004) is an ethics educator and consultant in Seattle, Washington. His ethics work appears in the journals *Ethical Space* and the *New College of California Law Review*, as well broadcast on public radio with his syndicated show *Ethically Speaking*. His principal research interests and activities revolve around contemporary community-based organizing and the potential guidance offered by historical social and legal efforts to secure and expand universal human rights.

Grant Samkin (D.Compt., Accounting Science, University of South Africa, 1997) is Senior Lecturer in the Department of Accounting at the University of Waikato, Hamilton, New Zealand. His research publications have been in the area of accounting education, accounting history, and sustainability. He has published in *Advances in Public Interest Accounting*, *South African Journal of Accounting Research*, and *South African Journal of Education*. Samkin is the co-author of *New Zealand Financial Accounting* (3rd ed, 2006, with C. Deegan). Current projects include the use of learning portfolios in an undergraduate financial accounting class and a historical examination of the rise of the accounting profession from the perspective of the consumer-controlled model of occupation control.

Matthew W. Seeger (Ph.D., Indiana University, 1982) is Professor and Chair of the Department of Communication at Wayne State University in Detroit, Michigan. His work on organizational communication and ethics has appeared in the *Journal of Organizational Change Management*, *Encyclopedia of Public Relations*, *Communication Studies*, *Southern Communication Journal*, *Journal of Applied Communication Research*, *Management Communication Quarterly*, *Journal of Business Communication*, *Journal of Business Ethics*, and several edited books. He has published two books, *Ethics and Organizational Communication* (1997) and *Communication and Organizational Crisis* (2003). His commentaries on organizations, ethics, and leadership have appeared in both the *Detroit Free Press* and the *Detroit News*.

Krishnamurthy Sriramesh (Ph.D., University of Maryland, 1992) is Associate Professor at the School of Communication and Information at the Nanyang Technological University, Singapore. In November 2004, he received the prestigious Pathfinder Award from the Institute for Public Relations (U.S.) for "original scholarly research contributing to the public relations body of knowledge." He co-edited *The Handbook of Global Public Relations:*

Theory, Research, and Practice, (with Dejan Vercic) in 2003, which won the National Communication Association's PRIDE award for the best book in public relations published in 2003. He also edited *Public Relations in Asia: An Anthology* (2004). He is Associate Editor of the *Journal of Communication Management* and on the editorial board of the *Journal of Public Relations Research* (U.S.), *Public Relations Review*, *Journal of Communication Studies* (India), and the *Journal of Information & Knowledge Management* (Singapore).

Cynthia Stohl (Ph.D., Purdue University, 1982) has been a member of the Department of Communication at the University of California–Santa Barbara since January 2002. Prior to joining the UCSB faculty, she was the Margaret Church Distinguished Professor and Head of the Department of Communication at Purdue University. Professor Stohl's research focuses on the relationships among new communication technologies and internal and external communication processes as they manifest in global collaborations. Her most recent work addresses a diversity of global network and collective action organizations, including human rights nongovernmental organizations, membership-based organizations, and terrorist organizations. She is currently a co-principal investigator on a National Science Foundation grant titled "Technological Change and Collective Association: Changing Relationships Among Technology, Organizations, Society, and the Citizenry." Her most recent articles appear in *Communication Monographs*, *Communication Theory*, and *Management Communication Quarterly*.

Michael Stohl (Ph.D., Northwestern University, 1974) is Professor and Chair of the Department of Communication at the University of California–Santa Barbara. Prior to his appointment at UCSB in 2002, he was Dean of International Programs (from 1992) and Professor of Political Science at Purdue University in West Lafayette, Indiana, where he had taught since 1972. His research focuses on violence, terrorism, and human rights, and he is the author and editor of more than 100 scholarly publications that have appeared in journals across the social sciences, including *Communication Monographs*, *Journal of Conflict Resolution*, *International Studies Quarterly*, *Journal of Peace Research*, *Contemporary Sociology*, *American Journal of Political Science*, and *Political Psychol-*

ogy. His current research focuses on networks of global organizing focusing on both terrorists and human rights advocates.

Soh Ting Ting (B.A., Nanyang Technological University, Singapore, 2005) is Category Executive for Unilever Singapore Pte Ltd. in Singapore.

Nikki C. Townsley (Ph.D., Purdue University, 2002) is Assistant Professor in the Department of Communication at the University of Colorado–Boulder. Her ethnographically informed research focuses on the interconnections among gender, work, organization, and the nation-state; life history and biography, and globalization. She is particularly interested in the relationship between discourses of contingent labor including temping, outsourcing, and offshoring, and individuals' experiences of alternative work arrangements. Her work appears in the journals *Management Communication Quarterly*, *Organization*, and *Western Journal of Communication*.

Sandra Waddock (D.B.A., Boston University, 1985; M.B.A., Boston University, 1979) is Professor of Management at Boston College's Carroll School of Management and Senior Research Fellow at Boston College's Center for Corporate Citizenship. She is currently a visiting Scholar at Harvard University's John F. Kennedy School of Government. She was editor of the *Journal of Corporate Citizenship* from 2003 to 2005. She has published extensively on corporate responsibility, corporate citizenship, and inter-sector collaboration. She and co-author Sam Graves won the 1997 Moskowitz Prize for their research on socially responsible investing. In 2005, Waddock received the Faculty Pioneer Award for External Impact from the Beyond Grey Pinstripes program. Her latest book is *Leading Corporate Citizens: Vision, Values, Value Added* (2002). She received the Faculty Pioneer Award for External Impact from the Aspen Institute and World Resources Institute in 2005, was a Fellow of the Ethics Resource Center in Washington from 2000 to 2002, and is a founding faculty member of the Leadership for Change Program at Boston College.

Luo Wanyin (B.A., Nanyang Technological University, Singapore, 2005)is Information Analyst with the Ministry of Defense in Singapore.

Patricia H. Werhane (Ph.D., Northwestern University) is the Wicklander Chair of Business Ethics in the Department of Philosophy and Director of the Institute for Business and Professional Ethics at DePaul University in Chicago with a joint appointment as the Peter and Adeline Ruffin Professor of Business Ethics and Senior Fellow at of the Olsson Center for Applied Ethics in the Darden School at the University of Virginia in Charlottesville. She has been a Rockefeller Fellow at Dartmouth, Arthur Andersen Visiting Professor at the University of Cambridge, and Erskine Visiting Fellow at the University of Canterbury (New Zealand). Werhane has published numerous articles and is the author or editor of 16 books, including *Ethical Issues in Business* (7th ed, 2001, with T. Donaldson and Margaret Cording), *Persons, Rights and Corporations* (1985), *Adam Smith and His Legacy for Modern Capitalism* (1994), *Moral Imagination and Managerial Decision-Making* (1999), and *Employment and Employee Rights* (2003, with Tara J. Radin and Norman Bowie). She is the founder and former editor-in-chief of *Business Ethics Quarterly*, the journal of the Society for Business Ethics. Werhane is a member of the academic advisory team for the newly created Business Roundtable Institute for Corporate Ethics housed at the University of Virginia. Her current research projects include an examination of best practices in American corporations and a study of women in leadership.

Glen Whelan (Ph.D. Deakin University, 2004) is Lecturer in Business Ethics at Middlesex University. He was previously a postdoctoral scholar and lecturer in the International Centre for Corporate Social Responsibility at the Nottingham University Business School. His current research projects include a study of Buddhism and consumerism, an investigation into the distinction between 'moral markets' and 'moral managers', and the application of Austrian economics to organization studies. More generally, his research and teaching interests include the philosophy of commerce and enterprise; comparative philosophy, cross-cultural understanding, and international business; and the epistemological foundations of human action and the social sciences.

Theodore E. Zorn (Ph.D., University of Kentucky, 1987) is Professor in the Department of

Management Communication, University of Waikato, Hamilton, New Zealand. He teaches and conducts research on organizational change-related communication. Zorn is past editor of *Management Communication Quarterly* and past chair of the organizational communication division of the National Communication Association. He has recently published research in *Journal of Applied Communication Research*, *Management Communication Quarterly*, *Australia Journal of Communication*, and *Business Communication Quarterly*.

THE DEBATE OVER CORPORATE
SOCIAL RESPONSIBILITY

Overview

GEORGE CHENEY

JULIET ROPER

STEVE MAY

Corporate social responsibility (CSR) risks the same practical and linguistic fate as other trends in business and popular culture. "Green marketing" is but one fairly recent example. By being applied to a host of situations, the term "corporate social responsibility" can lose its cutting edge. When it is used in disingenuous ways, it suffers cooptation. Through sheer overuse, the term becomes analogous to worthless currency. We are fully aware of these possibilities, just as we are of critiques from the Left and the Right. From the perspective of neoliberal economics, CSR is wrong-headed: a violation of the principles of free enterprise and a confusion of roles of the private, governmental, and nonprofit sectors. From the Left, CSR is viewed as at best a public relations strategy for complacency and control; at worst, an illusion arising from an oxymoron—a misunderstanding of the social potential of the corporate form (Doane, 2005; Frankental, 2001). From either perspective, as well as from several between them, CSR has enough of a history of debate and discussion behind it to merit a wide-ranging and nuanced treatment. That is what this book is about.

When we set out on this project four years ago, we saw this range of perspectives before us, yet we did not appreciate fully the subtleties of arguments for and against CSR, nor were we aware of the diversity of cases around the world that aim to make the most powerful global institution, the corporation, more responsive to human needs.

With the diversity of chapters in this volume, we have tried to bring together in one place just such a range of thought about CSR. We therefore offer an array of viewpoints, present a variety of cases, and examine diverse parts of the world.

Our own bias should already be apparent. We believe that unchecked corporate power is problematic for democratic society, despite the ease with which capitalism and democracy are equated in Washington, London, Tokyo, Canberra, and other capitals today. In fact, the interrelations of capitalism and democracy merit far closer attention than they are given by the mainstream media or even by most scholars (Almond, 1991). At the same time, we maintain that it would be a mistake to paint all corporations with the same brush, thereby failing to see substantive differences in their goals, structures, practices, and relationships to national governments as well as multilateral institutions such as the World Trade Organization (WTO). Important initiatives are afoot within and outside of corporate boundaries to question de facto corporate public policy (in organizations such as the WTO), to broaden relationships between corporations and their multiple stakeholders, to apply consumer pressure toward social responsiveness, to use union leverage to assert the human rights of employees, and to convert what sometimes begin as the mere window dressings of corporate philanthropy and nods to community projects into meaningful and sustained efforts.

This volume includes within its pages timely commentaries by scholars and practitioners from a variety of continents, disciplines, and political viewpoints. If the contributors all share one goal, it is to probe in an informed and systematic way the potentials for positive social change in, through, and around the modern corporation.

A HISTORY OF CORPORATE SOCIAL RESPONSIBILITY

The desire to create positive social change in the corporate world is not necessarily a new phenomenon, although current social, political, economic, and ideological conditions inflect it in specific ways today. Questions regarding the nature, scope, and impact of organizations have been present in various forms for centuries, ranging across the "classical," medieval, mercantile, industrial, and corporate eras. Although seldom acknowledged, the corporate form and the modern labor union both grew out of late medieval guilds. In both cases, organizations were established to transcend individual persons in time, space, and power and thereby challenge the hegemony of Church and State. As large-scale commercial enterprises grew, some became wedded to the state and were explicit instruments of empire. This is what happened with the Dutch and then the British "Indies" companies, which not only supported control of Indonesia and India, respectively, but actually made such control possible in the seventeenth through nineteenth centuries. Meanwhile, with the possibilities brought by the Industrial Revolution, the factory system moved production away from the craft model and toward large-scale, highly differentiated, and often inhumane workplaces of the kind to which Karl Marx responded in the mid-nineteenth century.

As Charles Conrad and JéAnna Abbott note in chapter 29 of this volume, along with the ebb and flow of actions and reactions, control and resistance, between corporations and their critics, the history of CSR has been a somewhat cyclical one. As a result, we believe that it is particularly important to briefly summarize some of the debates regarding CSR that have emerged historically and to locate the issue in today's context.

By most accounts, CSR is, in many respects, a product of industrialization and, more recently, globalization. As today's mega-companies began to emerge in the 1870s, their activities increasingly affected other realms of society. With the growth of petroleum, railroads, and other corporations toward monopoly status in the late 1800s, public debate regarding the appropriateness of their actions intensified. For example, as a result of public pressure in the 1890s, the U.S. government passed a series of laws attempting to control major corporations. During this same period, increased globalization coupled with colonization meant that corporate behavior crossed national boundaries. In fact, the period from about 1870 to World War I is frequently characterized as the peak of economic globalization. Laws passed in the United States and in Western Europe addressed emerging business issues such as the formation of trusts, use of child labor, and safety in a range of industries. From 1900 through 1920, under the banner of the Progressive Era, additional legislation was passed. Much of this effort, however, settled on governmental regulation as a weaker version of what populists of the day demanded: societal transformation.

Industrialists of that Progressive Era found themselves in the awkward position of advocating a system of factory labor that, by many critics' standards, was proving to be a detriment to society. In response, many large corporations developed "industrial welfare programs," deemed a "citizenship theory of labor relations," in order to curb growing public dismay over the negative impact of industrialization on community and family life. These programs—like many company towns—provided for the education, recreation, and socialization of workers, seeking to produce simultaneously good workers and good citizens (May, 1993).

According to historian Roland Marchand (1998), these and other corporate programs were always about *legitimation* as much as they were about community or public service. Thus, by the 1920s, corporations began to portray themselves as indispensable and responsive both in their internal communication to employees and in their external public relations campaigns. Central to this effort was the use of the family and neighborhood metaphors to demonstrate corporations' interconnectedness with the body social (see also Christensen, Morsing, & Cheney, in press). This was one way that corporations expressed their social embeddedness.

The Great Depression through to World War II saw further interest in social controls in various fields, including labor protection, banking reform, and public utility controls. Such legislation was accompanied by passionate policy-related debate by the public on each specific issue, as well as on the more general nature of the corporation–society relationship. A view that came to be known as "corporate social responsibility" emerged as a coherent position shortly after World War II. A postwar emphasis on free enterprise laid the foundation for a project that both endorsed capitalism and sought to humanize it by expecting corporations to serve social ends (Terris, 2005). Although several of the contributors to this volume question the very fundamental assumptions of "free enterprise" capitalism, particularly in an era of widespread corporate globalization, it is nevertheless important to acknowledge the early roots of CSR.

One of the earliest conceptions of CSR was developed shortly after World War II by Howard R. Bowen, an economics professor at Williams College in Massachusetts. According to Bowen (1953), America's postwar prosperity produced a new set of expectations for corporations, and as a result, he sought to outline the social responsibilities of business, arguing that "[w]e are entering an era when private business will be judged solely in terms of its demonstrable contribution to the general welfare. . . . The acceptance of obligations to workers, consumers, and the general public is a condition for survival of the free enterprise system" (p. 52). For Bowen, businesses were expected to produce social goods such as: (1) higher standards of living; (2) widespread economic progress and security; (3) order, justice, and freedom; and (4) the development of the individual person.

Others, such as management scholar Keith Davis, were advocating an even more expansive understanding of CSR, relating it to a treatment of corporate power. Davis (1960) proposed the "Iron Law of Responsibility," which suggested that the "social responsibilities of businessmen need to be commensurate with their social power" (p. 71). He further argued that the absence of social responsibility would lead to a gradual erosion of social power on the part of businesses. For Davis, CSR created social goods whose impact must be understood within the whole social system. Davis's argument assumed a somewhat consistent level of corporate social power, yet that level has varied internationally, in accordance with the sociopolitical context and the resultant social expectations of corporations.

In the United States, one of the common means to fulfill social responsibilities was through corporate philanthropy, which at the time had become a normative part of the social fabric. Concurrently, government regulators (e.g., the Federal Communications Commission, the Federal Trade Commission) and public interest groups (e.g., American Civil Liberties Union, Sierra Club) also emerged, holding corporations to a new level of accountability. Later, between 1969 and 1972, four of the major regulatory agencies in the United States—the Occupational Safety and Health Administration, the Equal Opportunity Commission, the Consumer Product Safety Commission, and the Environmental Protection Agency—were founded to create greater disclosure and transparency of corporate actions.

During the 1970s, the debates regarding the responsibilities of corporations changed somewhat. The focus shifted from corporate responsibility to corporate *responsiveness*, thus emphasizing what companies could do to better the world rather than what companies could do to ensure their own survival (Makower, 1994). This move was partly in response to threats of U.S. government taxation on "windfall" profits of industries such as petroleum (Crable & Vibbert, 1983). The result, according to some observers, was a new emphasis on political action, public affairs, lobbying, and public relations directed toward "strategic philanthropy" and "cause-oriented" marketing. This proactive posture quickly spread to other industries and other nations. During this period, "corporate social responsibility" became so fashionable that its acronym (CSR) could stand alone. In some cases, the concept became a strategy by which companies attempted to turn public relations problems into public relations assets.

It was into this responsibility–responsiveness debate that Milton Friedman (1970) entered, with his now classic essay in the *New York Times*, "The Social Responsibility of Business Is to Increase Its Profits." According to Friedman, the doctrine of CSR required accepting that "political mechanisms, not market mechanisms, are the appropriate way to determine the allocation of scarce resources" (p. 122). For Friedman, such an approach was more firmly grounded in socialism than in capitalism; therefore, he was highly critical of expanding the responsibilities of business beyond making money for shareholders.

Friedman, then, was primarily concerned with the economic outcomes of business decision making. He believed that the greatest good would occur for all if businesses made decisions based on increasing shareholder value. His essay has been widely used to support the common business adage that one's first duty is to increase shareholder value. Friedman does suggest, though, that an executive should try "to make as much money as possible, while conforming to the basic rules of society, both those embodied in the law and those embodied in ethical custom" (Friedman, 1970, p. 32). Aside from this minor caveat, though, he explains that acting in a socially responsible manner—at the expense of shareholders—is akin to spending someone else's money for the social interest. The person is, in effect, imposing a tax of his or her choice in the process. He argues that it is best to trust market mechanisms when making decisions. A focus on social responsibility, according to Friedman, is a "fundamentally subversive doctrine" in a free society.

By contrast, scholars such as Archie Carroll (1979) acknowledged the profit motive of corporations but also extended their responsibilities to encompass the "legal, ethical, and discretionary expectations that a society has of organizations at a given point in time" (p. 500). Carroll and others moved discussions of CSR beyond the economic bottom line and legal compliance to the range of contemporary social issues that may concern the public at any historical moment.

The sociopolitical context of much of Western Europe has seen a much greater regulatory role for governments than was the case in the United States, where there has long been a strong culture of individualism and, with that, individual responsibility for one's own welfare. The social-democratic practices of Europe expected corporations to be responsive to social needs and demands and expected governments and trade unions to exert control over corporate actions in the social interest. Thus, corporate responsibility in Western Europe historically was voluntary and required a multistakeholder approach rather than a purely shareholder-oriented one (Crane & Matten, 2004).

In the 1980s, authors in the United States such as Thomas M. Jones (1980) and R. Edward Freeman (1984) expanded the discussion to a broader set of stakeholders, such as employees, customers, suppliers, distributors, competitors, and communities. At this time, however, there was an ideological shift away from neo-Keynesian confidence in governments' power to regulate economies toward *laissez faire*, free market, neoliberal economics. Introduction of the new ideology was effected through widespread deregulation of financial markets as well as privatization of state-owned enterprises such as those associated with public transport, telecommunications, and energy. Health and education sectors were also restructured to conform to a market model. With the structural changes came a change in the relationship between governments and corporations, with far less government regulation and investment in the social good. Many developing countries had market deregulation forced upon them by the structural adjustment policies of the International Monetary Fund and the World Bank, as a condition of receiving loans. Others opened their markets as a condition of joining the WTO. However, the extent to which neoliberalism was embraced across the world has varied. Outside of the United States, its most radical adoption was in the United Kingdom, New Zealand, Argentina, and Mexico. Nations such as France and Germany retained much of their more socialist orientation in terms of the relationship between government and civil society and in consumer expectations regarding corporate compliance to social norms (Maignan, 2001).

Distinctive models developed, for example, in Japan and China, primarily because of very different social and cultural structures. Whereas in Western Europe the process of deregulation that went hand in hand with the rise of *laissez faire* economics entailed a shrinking of influence of the state, in Japan the government retained the central, interventionist power it had always held. Furthermore, far from the tendency toward individualization, Japanese business and society retained its tradition of working within the socially imposed constraints of a network of trust, rather than legally imposed contracts. These relationships extend to state institutions, maintaining the key imperative of harmony, or *wa* (Gray, 1998).

China's political history differs from that of Japan, although many of the cultural traditions are comparable. Chinese business and society also continue to operate within a close network system (*guanxi*), which has a basis of trust and loyalty. Confucian principles, including loyalty, honor, and societal harmony, are still seen as guiding many of China's business relations (Roper & Hu, 2005; Zhang, 1999; see also Whelan, chapter 7 this volume). China's blend of communism and capitalism since the late 1970s has been carefully controlled by its government (Stiglitz, 2002), defying Western demands for rapid deregulation and privatization, yet being spectacularly successful in terms of production and high employment.

By the late 1980s, the negative social impacts of neoliberalism were becoming apparent in those countries that had undergone radical transformation. Unemployment rose, the gap between rich and poor grew dramatically, and environmental damage incurred by corporations operating outside their home countries increased. One of the most devastating effects of neoliberalism was through financial deregulation, coupled with the development of computer technology. This allowed investors to move capital freely from one country to another, creating economic instability around the developing world, bestowing unprecedented power upon corporations over governments (Castells, 2000; Grossman, 1998), and reducing the voice and influence of civil society. Some developing nations that sought to meet the strict standards of the World Bank and International Monetary Fund for inflation control and privatization found themselves with increasing rates of poverty and widespread social unrest.

It was from this time, during the early to mid-1990s, that increasing numbers of corporate scandals and associated societal discontent with corporate behavior and with neoliberalism itself began to emerge. Royal Dutch Shell, for example, found itself at the center of two highly embarrassing crises in 1995: the public outcry, spearheaded by Greenpeace, at Shell's attempted sinking of the Brent Spar oil storage platform in the North Sea; and the hanging of activist Ken Saro-Wiwa and eight associates by the Nigerian government. The activists had been protesting against environmental damage caused by oil extraction and the government's failure to return oil revenue for community development (Schwartz & Gibb, 1999). Shell was blamed for not intervening to stop the execution. The company suffered particularly from the Brent Spar incident as it sparked consumer boycotts of Shell products. In Germany alone, Shell experienced drops of up to 40% in sales.

In 1999, organized demonstrations against globalization and the WTO began in London in June, followed by the more widely publicized uprising in Seattle in November, and later in other cities across the world. Center-left governments also recognized the failed legitimacy of *laissez faire* economics, with the adoption of "Third Way" (Giddens, 1998) policies, calling for a better balance between government, the economy, and civil society.

It is not surprising, then, that according to most scholars of CSR (see, e.g., Carroll, 1999), the 1990s was a decade of intensified discussions of CSR. Scholars and critics alike further expanded their understanding of CSR to develop more nuanced arguments regarding corporate social performance, sustainability, stakeholder theory, green marketing, citizenship theory, and business ethics, among others. Public discussions relevant to CSR revolved around executive compensation, downsizing, and the transition to global labor. Most of the debates in the 1990s sought to come to terms with the profound effects of globalization.

Most recently, the "corporate meltdown" of a number of high-profile U.S.-based corporations (e.g., Enron, Adelphia, Arthur Andersen, WorldCom, Tyco) has reinvigorated the debates regarding CSR. According to Conrad (2003), the crisis was the result of "massive financial and status-related incentives combined with declining external constraints combined to create a fraud-inducing system, which in turn provided organizational actors with ready rationalizations/legitimations of practices that 'pressed the envelope' or worse" (p. 16). Regardless of the reasons, however, the current historical context is likely to prompt additional debates regarding the role of corporations in our society, including a range of related terminology used to describe, study, and act upon the phenomenon.

TERMINOLOGY

The title for this book highlights the term "corporate social responsibility," as does the preceding discussion. However, over time and in different contexts, other terms have been adopted—sometimes synonymously, sometimes with (strategically) significant differences in meaning. The terms "sustainability" and "sustainable development" are the most prominent examples. Generally speaking, we see all of these terms as part of a cluster of concepts that give greater specificity to the domain of business ethics. That is, each of the terms is employed to signify certain perspectives on doing business, serving as a contrast to the traditional neoliberal view (perhaps best exemplified by economist Milton Friedman) that the only responsibilities of business are to make a profit and to operate according to the law. What is particularly interesting regarding the range of terms used alongside or instead of CSR is that their meanings are contested and shifting.

This reminds us to pay close attention to the dynamics of language and visual imagery themselves, for they are neither transparent nor mirrors of reality. As we have seen in politics worldwide over the past quarter-century, a term that is at one time associated or even wedded to one kind of ideology (say, of the Left) may well become attached to a very different ideology (say, of the Right) in the following decade. For example, consider what happened in the United States and the United Kingdom in the 1980s, when the symbol of "revolution" was appropriated by conservative parties from liberal ones. Definitions and terms are not static, despite our desire to fix labels and identities in an elusive yet compelling search to say "what something really is." From the standpoint of communication, then, the debate over CSR (or anything else) must be considered in part with respect to the emergence, rise, and fading of certain labels, certain images. This is not so much a question of fads or fashions as it is part of the fundamental operation of language and visual symbols in a society that is cluttered with terms and images shouting for attention.

Such postmodernist insights about language do not mean that we give up the cause of definition, however. Within the term "corporate social responsibility" itself, words are separately challenged, according to context. Is it too limiting to use "corporate" rather than the more widely applicable "business"? And, then, what about the even broader term "organization," as covering all sectors of society? Still, are corporations of particular interest because of their size, scope, and financial power? What of governmental agencies, nongovernmental organizations, and cross-sector partnerships? The World Business Council for Sustainable Development has affiliated branches in many countries, while the European Academy of Business in Society is a large and growing organization comprising corporate and academic partners. The U.S.-based Business for Social Responsibility organization provides yet another example. It would appear, then, that "*business* social responsibility" could be equally applied.

The "social" aspect of our term has been variously challenged. As recently as December 2005 at the European Academy of Business in Society annual colloquium in Warsaw, the term "corpo-rate responsibility" was declared by a prominent corporate member to be preferable to the previously more commonly applied CSR. His rationale was that the word "social" is too narrow and points to philanthropy, which doesn't really address their aspirations. That view is echoed in chapter 32 by Werhane in this volume in her discussion of discretionary versus moral responsibilities. Some see the absence of "environmental" in the CSR set as a drawback (see Willard, 2002). On the other hand, many others see the word "social" as *implicitly* inclusive, relating to all aspects of society, including environmental and (intra)organizational, offering an inspired counterpoint to the usual understandings of "economic" (see Cheney, 1999).

"Responsibility" raises ethical versus legal questions, at least, and is an issue also explored in depth in chapter 32. The nature and scope of responsibility lie at the core of our discussions here. It is the very essence of the difference between collective and individualist perspectives on society and our place on the planet, now and in the future. The term "citizenship," which now often appears in the context of "corporate citizenship" rather than its previous application to the notion of individual civic roles, also denotes responsibility. Yet the literatures on "corporate citizenship" and on "organizational citizenship behaviors" have both been criticized for their conservative, even complacent biases.

The second set of terms within our cluster, "sustainability" and "sustainable development," used by different authors in this volume, are frequently used interchangeably with corporate or social responsibility. However, they are also arguably more widely challenged. Sustainable development commonly requires equal attention to the economic, social, and environmental impacts of development, to the extent that they do not reduce the ability of future generations to enjoy those same resources (World Commission on Environment and Development, 1987). This is reflected in the notion of the triple bottom line, promoted by John Elkington (1998) and now increasingly a part of corporate reporting. The heart of the debate here is to what extent any form of development, particularly economically driven development, can actually be sustainable. Deep ecologists say not at all. At the other end of the spectrum, adherents of weak sustainability believe that sound economic stewardship will in itself result in social and environmental sustainability, a view that continues to privilege the economic.

Other criticisms of the "sustainable development" terminology are based in the assertion that it is in practice and in research too closely linked to environmental concerns and actions, putting social imperatives in the background (Sharma & Ruud, 2003). Yet, for many, sustainable development comes under the umbrella of (social) responsibility: society is dependent upon its environment, social and natural, and if a responsible attitude is not assumed, development cannot be sustainable.

We are not attempting to argue for one term over another. Indeed, many would argue that terminology does not matter as long as actions and results are consistent with the overall agenda of ethical business. The histories of and contests over various terms are taken up in more detail in several chapters in this book. As we stated above, it is the shifting rationales behind the usage of terminologies that is interesting, especially when such shifts are strategic in intent. If not strategic, many shifts are at least reflective of the normative nature of CSR (de Bakker, Groenewegen, & den Hond, 2005). Most important of all, however, is whether or not, and to what extent, the language is backed up by action or, to put it another way, that one practice seems to fit in a reasonably coherent way with others. In this volume, Livesey and Graham in chapter 23 and Christensen in chapter 31 maintain that at least some degree of cause–effect relationship between the language of sustainability and practice is likely because of the constitutive dimension of language. If this is so, then there will be a strategic sensitivity to the language chosen.

The issues surrounding the choice of terms are complex. The evolution and interrelationship of the terms themselves are important to understand business ethics in multiple contexts, to explore a range of possible responsible and irresponsible actions, and to consider how initiatives are shaped, contained, or suppressed.

AUDIENCE

One of the reasons we have sought to explicate the importance of the political and historical context of, and terminology surrounding, CSR is that our intent is to reach a broad set of readers interested in the range of complex, contested issues that are at the heart of wide-ranging discussion regarding corporations at all levels of our cultures. Thus, we hope the book will effectively reach both academic and nonacademic readers, maintaining the book's scholarly integrity while opening up discussion for a much wider range of audiences. The volume is likely to be of primary interest to scholars of CSR, business ethics, sustainability, globalization, and economic development. Yet, it should also be relevant for policy makers and businesspersons, among others. If successful, the diversity of perspectives and recommendations offered by our contributors will further stimulate and strengthen both the debates and practices surrounding CSR among a wide range of interested parties. In that respect, we hope that the collection of chapters is provocative and engaging, producing new understanding, judgment, and action regarding CSR.

Specifically, the book can serve several purposes for a variety of readers. First, it can be used in upper division undergraduate- and graduate-level courses on business ethics and related themes (e.g., corporate law, nonprofit leadership). Currently, business schools in many parts of the world are advancing programs in ethics, values, responsibility, and citizenship. Also, such courses are now regularly found in departments of philosophy, political science, economics, and sociology, in addition to management and communication. In communication curricula, for example, such courses are frequently offered as "special topics" seminars as follow-ups to survey courses in organizational communication. In management, such courses fall under the headings of business ethics and "business and society." In sociology, we find such courses under the headings of organizational and industrial sociology and "social institutions." Many law schools now have cross-listed courses with business and philosophy, which provides another venue for the proposed text. This book is also appropriate for courses on globalization in any discipline. These are but a few examples in the academic context.

However, we believe that the book is written in an accessible style, making it attractive to many educated professionals in law, business, and government. As a result, the book may also be appropriate for a growing number of international associations devoted to business ethics and CSR. Finally, the book is also ideally suited for informed practitioners, such as business, government, and nonprofit leaders. In short, the book should be of great interest to scholars, policy makers, business leaders, and others interested in the contours of the debate over what role large-scale corporate commerce should take in the future of the industrialized world.

PREVIEW

We have asked contributors to consider the following question: Should business strive to be socially responsible and, if so, how? This book updates and broadens the debate over this question—and others related to it—by bringing together in one volume a variety of practical and theoretical perspectives on CSR. Moreover, it draws from experiences and examples from around the world, including but not limited to recent corporate scandals and controversies in the United States and Europe. *The Debate over Corporate Social Responsibility* is perhaps the single most comprehensive volume available on the question of just how "social" business ought to be.

In order to address the debates circulating within and around CSR, this volume includes contributions from the fields of communication, business, law, sociology, political science, economics, accounting, and environmental studies. A number of the chapters examine closely the basic assumptions underlying the philosophy of socially responsible business. Others present cases from various regions of the world. Still other chapters speak to the practical challenges and possibilities for corporate social responsible in the twenty-first century.

For example, the chapters in part I provide an overview of and an introduction to the historical and contemporary reasons for examining the movement for CSR. This part explores past as well as contemporary corporate scandals, argues for the importance of addressing CSR issues today, and internationalizes the discussion. It also explains the merits of a communication-based perspective for analyzing the history, development, and future of CSR.

Part II explores a range of cases and contexts, based on our belief that a full understanding of the nature and scope of CSR is dependent upon exploring the unique features of different types of organizations in different contexts. The part develops, in greater detail, an understanding of the origins, evolution, and practices of the modern corporation. By many standards, the corporation has become the primary institution in modern society, often eclipsing the state, family, community, religion, and education in its power. As a result, corporate influence in both work and non-work realms of life is far-reaching. Acknowledging that the corporation is a complex and important institution, part II identifies specific cases that illustrate how corporate activities have been treated in various parts of the world. This analysis thus engages the different forms of capitalism as well as the specific trajectories of CSR movements and associations.

Part III incorporates insights from recent developments in legal philosophy, especially those dealing with the status of the corporate "person" in society. Thus, this part explores issues such as rights, obligations, and precedents from some of the most important legal cases and discussions of the past few decades. Our purpose is *not* to offer a legal *history* but rather to highlight key cases and debates that feature specific concerns such as corporate free speech, responsibility to community, and obligations to employees. Even more important, this section draws a connection between legal and ethical perspectives, considering the deeper ethical implications of typical legal "framings" of corporate rights and responsibilities. Finally, part III explores governmental rules and regulations, from a communication perspective, considering how they frame, as well as promote or hinder, CSR.

In part IV, several contributors examine the economic dimensions of CSR, from the level of firm and industry accounting practices to macro-concerns of the relationships between financial institutions, government, and business. Similar to part III on legal perspectives, part IV is not strictly economic but relates economic to sociosymbolic aspects of the issues of CSR, with particular attention to the role of communication in constituting a range of economic discourses that enable or constrain organizational actions. As such, several chapters in this part emphasize the interplay of the material and the symbolic realms, including framing the CSR debate within the context of contemporary corporate capitalism and strategies of resistance against it.

Contributors to part V investigate the concept of social capital, its importance to government, society and business alike, and the extent to which social justice not only is served but also is considered in corporate policy. Social capital is founded upon trust within societies and organizations that facilitates cooperation and minimizes friction. Corporations have a responsibility to be socially accountable both internally toward their employees and externally in their impacts on their immediate communities and more broadly in their impacts on society as a whole.

Part VI explores the environmental dimension of CSR, looking at environmental conditions such as pollution (e.g., air, water, noise, solid waste, nuclear waste, toxins), resource depletion (e.g., species, fossil fuels, minerals), and growth. Also, this part examines the fact that, in some countries and for some organizations, it has become more politically expedient, and therefore more fashionable, to declare a company "green" and to argue for "sustainability" than to pursue an even broader "social" agenda. Given these developments, part VI also explores "green marketing," considering its strengths and its weaknesses as a substantially diluted movement. As in preceding parts, particular attention is paid to the role of communication in creating, maintaining, and transforming social movements related to the environment and CSR.

The book concludes with part VII. Given that previous parts of the book, written from other standpoints, have explored communication-based and rhetorical insights, this part develops those ideas further and thus serves as the capstone of the book. This concluding part of the book bridges microlevel (e.g., deception and fraud) and macrolevel (e.g., symbolism and markets) concerns with a series of commentaries from noted scholars who represent diverse viewpoints. These noted commentators draw upon their own expertise, using popular management, public policy, postcolonial, postmodern, and philosophical-ethical perspectives to reconsider and reimagine the future prospects and forms of CSR.

REFERENCES

Almond, G. (1991). Capitalism and democracy. *Political Science and Politics, 24,* 467–474.

Bowen, H. R. (1953). *Social responsibilities of the businessman.* New York: Harper & Row.

Carroll, A. B. (1979). A three-dimensional conceptual model of corporate social responsibility performance. *Academy of Management Review, 4,* 497–505.

Carroll, A. B. (1999). Corporate social responsibility: Evolution of a definitional construct. *Business and Society, 38,* 268–295.

Castells, M. (2000). Information technology and global capitalism. In W. Hutton & A. Giddens (Eds.), *Global capitalism* (pp. 52–74). New York: New Press.

Cheney, G. (1999). *Values at work: Employee participation meets market pressure at Mondragón.* Ithaca, NY: Cornell University Press.

Christensen, L. T., Morsing, M., & Cheney, G. (in press). *Challenging corporate communication.* London: Sage.

Conrad, C. (2003). Setting the stage: Introduction to the special issue on the "corporate meltdown." *Management Communication Quarterly, 17,* 5–19.

Crable, R. E., & Vibbert, S. L. (1983). Mobil's epideictic advocacy: "Observations" of Prometheus-bound. *Communication Monographs, 50,* 380–394.

Crane, A., & Matten, D. (2004). *Business ethics: A European perspective.* Oxford: Oxford University Press.

Davis, K. (1960). Can business afford to ignore social responsibilities? *California Management Review, 2*(Spring), 70–76.

de Bakker, F., Groenewegen, P., & den Hond, F. (2005). A bibliometric analysis of 30 years of research and theory on corporate social responsibility and corporate social performance. *Business & Society, 44*(3), 283–317.

Doane, D. (2005). The myth of CSR: On philanthropy. *Global Policy Forum.* Retrieved December 19, 2005, from http://www.globalpolicy.org/socecon/tncs/2005/1104myth.htm.

Elkington, J. (1998). *Cannibals with forks: The triple bottom line of 21st century business.* Gabriola Island, Canada: New Society.

Frankental, P. (2001). Corporate social responsibility: A PR invention? *Corporate Communications: An International Journal, 6,* 18–23.

Freeman, R. E. (1984). *Strategic management: A stakeholder approach.* Boston, MA: Pitman.

Friedman, M. (1970, September 13). The social responsibility of business is to increase its profits. *New York Times Magazine,* pp. 32–33, 122, 126.

Giddens, A. (1998). *The third way: The renewal of social democracy.* Cambridge: Polity Press.

Gray, J. (1998). *False dawn: The delusions of global capitalism.* New York: New Press.

Grossman, R. (1998). *Challenging corporate power.* Retrieved September, 7, 2000, from http://www.zmag.org/intgrossman.htm.

Jones, T. M. (1980, Spring). Corporate social responsibility revisited, redefined. *California Management Review,* pp. 59–67.

Maignan, I. (2001). Consumers' perceptions of

corporate social responsibilities: A cross-cultural comparison. *Journal of Business Ethics, 16,* 943–962.

Makower, J. (1994). *Beyond the bottom line: Putting social responsibility to work for your business and the world.* New York: Simon & Schuster.

Marchand, R. (1998). *Creating the corporate soul: The rise of public relations and corporate imagery in American big business.* Berkeley: University of California Press.

May, S. (1993). *Employee assistance programs and the troubled worker: A discursive study of power, knowledge, and subjectivity.* Unpublished Ph.D. dissertation, University of Utah, Salt Lake City.

Roper, J., & Hu, H. (2005, December 4–7). *Modern Chinese Confucianism: A model for Western human capital development?* Paper presented at the European Academy of Business in Society, Warsaw, Poland.

Schwartz, P., & Gibb, B. (1999). *When good companies do bad things: Responsibility and risk in an age of globalization.* New York: John Wiley & Sons.

Sharma, S., & Ruud, A. (2003). On the path to sustainability: Integrating social dimensions into the research and practice of environmental management. *Business Strategy and Environment, 12*(4), 205–214.

Stiglitz, J. E. (2002). *Globalization and its discontents.* New York: W.W. Norton.

Terris, D. (2005). *Ethics at work.* Waltham, MA: Brandeis University Press.

Willard, B. (2002). *The sustainability advantage.* Gabriola Island, British Columbia: New Society Publishers.

World Commission on Environment and Development. (1987). *Our common future* (Brundtland report). Oxford: Oxford University Press.

Zhang, W.-B. (1999). *Confucianism and modernization: Industrialization and democratization of the Confucian regions.* London: Macmillan Press.

I

INTRODUCTION

1

Why Corporate Social Responsibility?

Why Now? How?

JILL J. MCMILLAN

There may have been a time when "social responsibility" meant truly caring in both symbolic and material ways for one's fellow human beings—across the backyard fence, at the community center, in church, or at the bowling ally—but a realistic review of history suggests that those communal ties have been uneven and unstable now, and in fact, we may simply be witnessing what Bellah, Madsen, Sullivan, Swidler, and Tipton (1985) describe as the "latest phase of that process of separation and individuation that modernity seems to entail" (p. 275). Certainly, America was colonized by those who had "come loose" from the old European structures, and yet the colonists brought with them notions of social obligation and group formation that served to ground communal life in the new land. Bellah et al. argue that only gradually did it become clear that "every social obligation was vulnerable, every tie between individuals fragile" (p. 276). So it should not have surprised us as it appeared to when Robert Putnam's (2000) exhaustive research revealed that Americans at the start of the new century were essentially "bowling alone"—that slowly, inexplicably, we had in large measure abdicated many of our responsibilities to one another. Of particular interest to the readers of this volume, and for reasons that I develop in this chapter, the institution that stepped into that vacuum of social responsibility was the modern business organization.

It was an uneasy fit from the start, like a rambunctious youngster in uncomfortable, dress-up clothes. Business, which historically has traded in financial and human capital, suddenly found itself as the chief repository of *social capital* (Hanifan, 1916; Putnam, 2000)—the connection, reciprocity, and trust that bind society rather than separate it through power, hierarchy, and competition (Kohn, 1986). It is not clear that it was a job that the corporate world wanted or ever knowingly signed on for (Marchand, 1998), although there are many cases of corporations and other business organizations assuming the role with a variety of motives. Today no CEO worth his or her salt would fail to recognize the moniker *corporate social responsibility* (CSR), or *business social responsibility*, and most have a plan for it. And yet the paradoxical, even oxymoronic quality of this assignment for social stewardship remains.

We have gathered together in this volume explorations of that paradox, and in this chapter, I address these questions: Why corporate social responsibility? Why now? And how? To that end, I argue (1) that the modern corporation has accepted a role of social responsibility that it is ill-suited to enact, (2) that the shared traits of corporate discourse are inappropriate to promote CSR, and (3) that a reconsideration of *ethos* as *participation* and *place* offers a more appropriate frame for corporate credibility and voice.

ENACTING CSR:
THE ILL-FITTING ROLE OF
SOCIAL RESPONSIBILITY

First, J. Roberts (2003) reminds us that "the corporation is an idea, an imaginary entity, without substance or sensibility and therefore incapable of anything like responsibility. Instead, corporate responsibility will always depend upon people using their frail and vital sentience and following the path that this assigns" (p. 263). Thus, we come to regard organizations, as McMillan and Hyde (2000) argue, by the *collective* actions that human beings take and the words they make: "Not only do organizations 'act' in ways that *character-ize* them, we also come to know them by what they say (and do not say)" (p. 38). And this "doing" and "saying" is no small thing in that it constructs a group's legitimacy and ultimately its survival (Katz & Kahn, 1978). The strength of that legitimacy is one thing when prospective customers are deciding to do business with a company or to purchase its product; it is quite another when the company assumes the moral authority to oversee the construction of the "good life" for the planet and its inhabitants (Boyd, 2000; Coombs, 1992; Suchman, 1995). In the following section, I make two arguments: first, that the modern corporation, *as constituted*, is unfit as a carrier of social responsibility because its *raison d'être* is too narrow for the values of social responsibility *and* it has usurped the influence and neutralized the aid of other institutions better suited for altruism; and second, that even if corporations had tacit social legitimacy to operate unilaterally, and especially to play by the economic rules of shareholder privilege, the recent "corporate meltdown" demonstrates a moral lapse that has betrayed even that social contract and has elicited "calls for substantive reform from virtually every quarter of U.S. society" (Conrad, 2004, p. 312).

CORPORATE COLONIZATION:
ITS NARROW MISSION AND
LIMITED PARTNERSHIPS

Many have argued, as did Milton Friedman (1988), that "responsibility" for a business is to "make money" (as long as the law is not broken) and that to chastise it for being other than it is, is simply inappropriate and unfair. From a purely techni-

cal standpoint, one would be hard-pressed to argue. However, the production and distribution of *social* capital defy such logic. Take, for example, the capitalist system, which Greider (2003) admits is "ingeniously supple and complete, self-sustaining and forward looking" but, for purposes of social responsibility, contains one critical drawback: as a matter of principle, it is inherently incapable of taking society's interests into account.

> The company's balance sheet has no way to recognize costs that are not its own, no reason or method to calculate the future liabilities it causes but that someone else will have to pay. The incentives, in fact, run hard in the opposite direction. The Firm will be rewarded with greater returns and higher stock prices if it manages to "externalize" its true operating costs. It does this by pushing the negative consequences off on someone else: the neighbors who live downstream from a factory's industrial pollution or its own workers, who lose job security and pension rights, or the community left with an empty factory, shattered lives, a ruined environment. (p. 39)

This is not to say that corporate altruism is impossible. In fact, Greider (2003) acknowledges the strong presence of corporate reformers: "a scattered and eclectic lot, mostly operating beneath the media's attention and not yet taken seriously by the citadels of business and financial power" (p. 27). The philosophical disconnect between corporate and social good, which I explore more fully later, simply means that corporate reformers have to work that much harder to unite what seems like the incompatible interests of the two.

Furthermore, society has lost the countervailing influence of institutions whose missions are more expansive and attuned to the wider social good. Deetz (1992) is one of many who argue that the corporate sector has become the "primary institution in modern society, overshadowing the state in controlling the direction of individual lives and influencing social development" (p. 17). This "colonization" of the contemporary life world (see, e.g., Boggs, 2000; Deetz, 1992; Habermas, 1984, 1987; Morgan, 1986; Perrow, 2002; Schiller, 1995) has replaced "religious, familial, educational, and community institutions in the production of meaning, personal identity, values, knowledge, and reasoning" (Deetz, 1992, p. 17).

Given America's fervent commitment to capitalism and the Protestant work ethic, this corporate takeover of meaning might not have seemed so surprising. In fairness, there was also some appeal; for example, early childhood care and socialization could be handed over to daycare centers, community value education could be done in school, care for the elderly could be relocated to nursing homes, and the wisdom and support of friends could be replaced by a therapist. And there was still the state to provide "a safety net for those who were damaged or disadvantaged in the single-minded pursuit of economic efficiency" (J. Roberts, 2003, p. 255). What we did not count on was that the institutions delivering those services would also succumb to market rationality that required them ultimately to measure success, despite the altruism of their commitments, by one single criterion: the bottom line. Especially when the state began to relinquish its caretaker role and organizations began to assume it, the slavish devotion to that economic imperative and, in particular, to shareholder's privilege seemed narrow and fundamentally at odds with notions of a wider social welfare (see Deakin & Konzelmann, 2003; Gioia, 2003).

While the context thus far has been domestic corporations, the pursuit and impact of economic efficiency and corporate rationality are writ large only in "transnational" and "global" corporations (see Karliner, 1997, p. xiii). In fact, in terms of social and political influence, Barnett and Muller argue that domestic corporations may be no match for their international counterparts:

> The global corporation is the most powerful human organization yet devised for colonizing the future. By scanning the entire planet for opportunities, by shifting its resources from industry to industry and country to country, and by keeping its overriding goal simple—worldwide profit maximization—it has become an institution of unique power. (quoted in Karliner, 1997, p. 1)

Surely, when the global marketplace operates at its best, it has the potential, as President John F. Kennedy so eloquently remarked, to "lift all boats" with it and, as such, to function as a critical vehicle for building social capital. However, some worry (Boggs, 2000; Rodrik, 2000; Soros, 1998) that when "corporate hegemony" is allowed to go unchecked, what results, argues Boggs (2000), are "highly uneven forms of growth, sharpened class divisions, social dislocation, and mounting ecological crises" (p. 74). These problems pervade the U.S. brand of capitalism, and they impede the progress of a truly just form of globalization.

Therefore, pursuing a narrow mission and without the influence of the countervailing institutions, such as churches, small businesses, strong local civic organizations, and schools, the modern organization has also assumed the oversight of social responsibility. Financier and philanthropist George Soros (1998) worries that such an ill-fitting combination foretells the possibility of a double whammy: that both human values, such as peace, justice, and freedom, *and* the global economy may be imperiled. At the very least, relinquishing social moral authority to corporate agents alone seems akin to leaving the rooster in charge of the hen house.

THE CORPORATE MELTDOWN

Even if it were possible, as Greider (2003) argues, that society has come to "accept this tension" between a corporate rationality and social responsibility as an "inescapable condition of living prosperously" (p. 38), the recent siege of corporate malfeasance goes beyond the pale. When the Enron scandal broke, optimists declared that we were dealing with just "a few bad apples." Instead, it seems that Enron better demonstrated the "cockroach theory"—that seeing one indicates there may be many more lurking nearby. Joining Enron as highly visible offenders were WorldCom, Arthur Andersen, Global Crossing, and recently HealthSouth, but further evidence of the pesky buggers was yet to come: trials ensued for Credit Suisse First Boston investment banker Quattrone and former Tyco chairman Kozlowski, hedge-fund trader Steven Markovitz copped a plea to making improper "market timing" trades, Alliance Capital admitted trades similar to those of Markovitz, Prudential Securities (now Wachovia) and Merrill Lynch dismissed employees for improper fund trading, and JPMorgan Chase paid $25 million to settle charges that it violated rules concerning initial public offering of stocks (Sloan, 2003, p. 55). On the day in March 2005 that Bernard Ebbers, WorldCom CEO, was convicted for his role in the company's $11 billion accounting fraud, the Securities and Exchange Commission filed new cases against the former CEO and other leaders of Qwest Communications for defrauding investors by overstating the company's growth for the past decade . . . and the list goes on. In short, the economic system that Protestant theologian Emil Bruner called "irresponsibility developed into a system" (quoted in Greider, 2003, p. 35) had seriously run amuck, and its meltdown extracted from the corporation a serious price tag: the public legitimacy that secures customers and stakeholders and affords a corporation its right to occupy space on the planet.

In the aftermath (or what we hope is its aftermath) of the most serious of the corporate crises, a 2003 Gallup poll reported that CEOs ranked below funeral directors and lawyers. Dan Ryterbank, managing director of Frederic W. Cook & Company, expressed the sentiment of many: "I have not bought a single stock in 2002 and I don't plan to in 2003 because I don't trust anybody. . . . Who knows where the next scandal will come from?" (Naughton, 2002, p. 49). Congress responded to the outrage of citizens like Ryterbank by passing the Sarbanes-Oxley Act in 2002, which was designed to impose on companies stricter accountability and greater transparency, but the continuation of scandals since its passage suggests either that those problems were preexisting or that, as some argue, the act may be incapable of providing long-term deterrents to fraud in public companies (Green, 2005, pp. 66–68).

With some recent evidence of economic recovery, the news for corporations has been slightly better. Still, in a fall 2004 poll by GolinHarris, the rising expectations of consumers concerning corporate citizenship were unequivocal. Forty-four percent of Americans believe that corporate citizenship is "heading in the wrong direction"— while less than one quarter (24%) believe the opposite. This represents an 8-point swing (41% and 29%) respectively from the same poll the previous year, indicating that even in a slightly improving economy, Americans increasingly distrust companies' abilities to be good corporate citizens. More than two-thirds of consumers (69%) say that corporate citizenship is "important to their trust in business," and 52% are "inclined to start or increase their business due to corporate citizenship" (GolinHarris, 2004). So despite some encouraging signs in the economy, the public has neither forgiven nor forgotten, and shareholder advocates argue that it will take years for inves-

tors to truly trust again. Carolyn Brancato of the Conference Board agrees: "The scandals have cut the heart out of confidence" (Naughton, 2002, p. 55).

In summary, the modern corporation stepped into a vacuum created when citizens and informal groups vacated the social space previously devoted to caring for each other and for the society in some fairly routinized and systematic ways. In part this was due to the shrinking welfare state in many industrialized countries. In part, the move reflected an attempt at a social form of "rebranding." In part, corporate social efforts responded to demands of employees and consumers. Nevertheless, many businesses and other organizations found themselves in over their heads: (1) the corporate rationality by which they are constituted is designed to build financial not social capital, and the influence of countervailing social institutions has been co-opted and neutralized, as well; (2) just when corporations should have been ratcheting up public evidence of caring, connection, and concern, they experienced a serious institutionwide breakdown of character and ethics that struck a devastating blow to corporate credibility. Thus, corporate *actions* have failed to demonstrate the corporation's fitness to oversee social responsibility. In the next section, I explore how the corporate *voice* fails to pass muster, as well.

SPEAKING CSR: THE INADEQUACY OF MANAGERIAL DISCOURSE

While it would be a mistake to underestimate the material impact of this rising corporate power— real consequences in terms of, for example, misused political power, environmental degradation, exploitation in the workplace, and corporate arrogance and insensitivity to social concerns—it is the case that organizations convey this power symbolically (Conrad, 2004; Cyphert & Saiia, 2004). Indeed, Kuhn and Ashcraft (2003) argue that in the degraded corporate climate that has come to light, organizational communication has gained "particular salience" because of the communicative nature of the questionable practices that have surfaced: "deceptive messages, unscrupulous leadership, inappropriate collaboration, questionable cultural norms, the formation of consent and so forth" (p. 21). In particular, it has been interesting to hear the offending organizations "explain" and "justify" their misdeeds.

The "corporate voice" we have heard represents a contested notion, raising thorny issues about reification, responsibility, representation, and accountability (Cheney & McMillan, 1990; McMillan, 1987, 1988), and yet we know that organizations do indeed create an "identity" for themselves (Cheney & Christensen, 2001), largely constructed, as mentioned above, by the actions they take and the words they say (see also McMillan & Hyde, 2000). Although this corporate voice is a composite of multiple, ubiquitous organizational rhetors,[1] it is invariably dominated by management, still "largely thought to be management's voice" (Cyphert & Saiia, 2004, p. 250). Thus Deetz (1992) proposes that we describe discourse rendered on behalf of the organization and in its name as *managerialism*: "a 'discursive genre'—a way of conceptualizing, reasoning through, and discussing events" that features a unified identity between management and the corporation, a primary mode of reasoning that features cognitive instrumentality, a favored expressive modality that is money, and a favored site of reproduction that is the formal organization (pp. 222–223).

Clearly, managerialism shapes life in contemporary organizations and beyond, as it functions as a kind of "system logic, a set of routine practices, and an ideology" (Deetz, 1992, p. 222). Bellah, Madsen, Sullivan, Swidler, and Tipton. (1991) recall an admonition of early U.S. statesman Alexander Hamilton that "economic institutions teach and form us as effectively as schools and families do, if not more so" (p. 101). But how does managerialism "sound"? What values does it espouse? By what traits shall we know it? And most important for this chapter: How do the essential characteristics of managerial discourse square with an organization's ability to speak and to enact CSR?

In the discussion that follows, I have chosen the Enron corporation to demonstrate examples of managerial discourse. To those who might see this choice as kicking a company when it is down, I would confess that Enron is certainly a selection of convenience, given the extensive amount of attention that the company has received both in the popular and academic press. It is also the case, however, that Enron touted itself as a paragon of corporate virtue, proudly adhering to the RICE

principles (respect, integrity, communication, and excellence) and, indeed, was named by *Fortune* magazine in 1996 as the "Most Admired Company in America" (Kuhn & Ashcraft, 2003). At the height of its success and power, it is likely that Enron would have been proud to be chosen as an exemplar of archetypal corporate rhetoric. While the following discursive traits clearly represent Enron, this research demonstrates that they are widely shared rhetorical markers of organizations generally.

Managerialism Is Instrumental

Although he has been sharply criticized from the Left, Milton Friedman (1988) probably spoke the truth, and for many more organizations than care to admit it, when he said that the sole responsibility of business is to make a profit and to do so within the bounds of the law. Lasch (1978) argues that organizational leaders who once depended on general culture and a unified worldview in which to ground legitimation now rely on "an instrumental culture . . . purely on the capacity to solve technical problems and thereby to enlarge the supply of material goods" (p. 45). Follow, for example, the shifting visions of Enron executive Kenneth Lay as he publicly constructed an account of company goals, against all comers and against all odds:

1985: To become the premier natural gas pipeline in North America
1990: To become the world's first natural gas major [supplier]
1995: To become the world's leading energy company
2001: To become the world's leading company
2002: To emerge from bankruptcy as a viable, albeit smaller company. (quoted in Boje & Rosile, 2003)

While Lay's words seem arrogant, especially in hindsight, no modern CEO would object to his saying them, especially his attempt to harness what Deetz (1992) calls "market rationality—the monetary steering mechanism for strategic managerial technical reason" (p. 235). After all, if Friedman is right about the corporation's *raison d'être*, then any self-respecting organizational spokesperson would be negligent if he or she failed to foreground what Deetz (1992) calls the "central criteria" for managerial rhetoric: "concerns with economic growth, organizational survival, profit and productivity" (p. 231; see also Deetz, 2003). Although Cyphert and Saiia (2004) call our attention to the changing forms of managerial discourse, for example, broadcast media, the Internet, and interactive technologies, they insist that "such discourse in practice remains typically instrumental" (p. 250). In short, corporations are still held captive by what Estes (1996) calls the "tyranny of the bottom line," and with instrumentality so central in organizational discourse, it appears difficult, if not impossible, to construct the "moral imagination" (Haas, 2003, p. 614; M. Johnson, 1993), not to mention the resources, necessary to serve the wider good.

Managerialism Is Exclusive

In managerial philosophy and discourse, the "profits" to which Friedman (1988) alluded are not constructed for the benefit of stakeholders generally, but rather for the privileged class of organizational shareholders who possess the dominant right to maximum return on their investment and the commitment of management to pursue that goal. Deetz (2003) identifies exclusivity as a "fundamental governance model" of modern organizations: "the presumption of managerial prerogative justified by the support of ownership rights over other social rights" (p. 608). Gioia (2003) calls the privileging of stockholders' property rights "an old and increasingly dysfunctional ground assumption" (p. 435), but according to Seeger and Ulmer (2003), that assumption was still alive and well at Enron:

> The case of Enron . . . illustrates the consequences of attending to a very narrow set of values and stakeholder concerns to the exclusion of all else. Senior Enron managers privileged profits, stock values, and personal wealth even over more traditional business values such as profitability. In doing so, they created a powerfully distorted organizational culture of "Enronians" unable to see outside a set of very narrow and limited interpretations. (p. 78)

We now know that Enron's insistence that it was "there for its stockholders" was somewhat disingenuous as corporate executives lined their pockets while company profits fell and life savings were wiped out. What is important for the purpose of this chapter is that Enron's arguments of "stakeholder responsibility" were not aberrational (see Deakin & Konzelmann, 2003); they are, in fact, the stock and trade of any good organizational rhetor, and one would be hard-pressed to find an annual report that does not bolster the interests and concerns of corporate insiders. Indeed, J. Roberts (2003) argues that to speak otherwise would be to engender "hostility" from investors. However, as I show later in this chapter, in an increasingly interconnected and interdependent world, communitarians question how long corporations will be able to sustain such an exclusionary posture and rhetoric.

Managerialism Is Attributional

As noted above, the problem of accountability (see Starck & Kruckeberg, 2001), at least for those of us who would attempt to "converse with" a corporate rhetor, is inherent in managerialism, and it reaches epic proportions when a corporation is embroiled in scandal. Because the agents of the corporate voice are often ill defined and illusory, as are the "partially overlapping audiences of employees, consumers, competitors, stockholders and the government" (Cheney & McMillan, 1990, p. 103), it is difficult to assign blame. The "actual" agents of corporate decision making often remain "behind the scenes" (Crable, 1990) and become "elusive players in scandal" (Kuhn & Ashcraft, 2003, p. 25).

As a tribute to their great skills of rhetorical invention, however, organizational spokespersons have recognized the advantage of corporate anonymity and also have the fine art of scapegoating down to a science: "Kenneth Lay and Jeffrey Skilling have both publicly argued that they did not know about the wrongdoings at Enron and thus cannot be held culpable for the ethical and legal lapses. They blamed the accounting firm of Arthur Andersen, legal firms, and their subordinates" (Seeger & Ulmer, 2003, p. 77).

Two particularly effective attributions, neither new to corporate discourse (see, e.g., Crable & Vibbert, 1983), were also employed to explain Enron's troubles: the "bad apple" (see Conrad, 2004) and "the market made us do it" (Derber, 1998) strategies. The bad apple strategy bemoans the absence of "executive integrity" (DiTomaso, Parks-Yancy, & Post, 2003, p. 148) and seeks to "track the course of individual avarice and immorality . . . [that] implies a two-pronged solution to enhance accountability: prosecute CEOs and reform business school curricula" (Kuhn & Ashcraft, 2003, p. 24). Of course, what this individualistic perspective also accomplishes is to divert attention from the critical systemic issues that may have given rise to the problem in the first place (Conrad, 2003).

Another universally agreed upon and long-standing culprit is the market, which is reified as if it were a "wholly external determinant force, well beyond human hands" (Cheney, 1995, p. 189). Cheney defines "the market" as a grand symbol, an "ideograph" (McGee, 1980) whose wiles were repeatedly invoked by the participants in Cheney's (1999) study of the Mondragón worker cooperatives.[2] These mantras typified the workers' (*socios'*) regard for the power of the market: "the market that is around us," "listen to the market," "the market's orders to us." At Enron, the market attribution went something like this: responding to the demands for short-term results, management deceived investors through adjusting performance reports. Simultaneously, investors, analysts, and directors looked the other way in the face of positive investment returns. All this, according to Thomas A. Kochan, who writes about the crisis of confidence in corporations, constructed the attribution that it was "market forces pushing U.S. corporations to maximize stock book values to the neglect of other interests" (quoted in Kuhn & Ashcraft, 2003, p. 24).

Attribution not only deflects, it also obfuscates and thus diminishes, corporate credibility. As Kuhn and Ashcraft (2003) note, corporate talk makes use of "diverse and shifting images" so that firms appear alternately as "villains, unwitting accomplices, handy vehicles, and neutral containers" (p. 25). But one mantra that most organizations avoid if possible is culpability. Despite the presence in rhetorical history of corporate apologia (see, e.g., Hearit & Courtright, 2003; Rowland, 2002; Ryan, 1998; Ware & Linkugel, 1973), it is usually employed only after attempts at creative attribution have been exhausted. Ordinary citizens, accustomed to having to take responsibility for their actions, may have difficulty respecting the moral authority of a business community often so unwilling to hold itself accountable.

Managerialism Is Monologic

Historically, the corporate voice has been primarily a one-way communication transfer, and usually from top to bottom or from the top outward; managerialism is impersonal and does not encourage much listening (Cheney & McMillan, 1990). B. M. Johnson (1981) employed a letter-writing metaphor to describe the organization's most fundamental communicative relationship with its constituencies; when the organization speaks, argues Johnson, its messages are addressed "To whom it may concern" and signed "The Organization." From the corporation's perspective, the audience has no name and apparently no voice with which to speak back (Deetz, 2003, p. 607).

Deetz (1992) argues that monologue is simply a function of the need to *control*—the workforce, the environment, the market—equivocality in all forms. McMillan (1990) says that "orders" and pronouncements are simply the most "efficient and cost-beneficial" ways to exercise that control; persuasion, on the other hand, is messy and time-consuming. J. Roberts (2003) worries that corporations have even co-opted business ethics as "an exercise in proclamation: the publishing of admonitions, inducements, and seductions toward ethical conduct" (p. 250), when in fact, the real motive lies in enhancing appearance and market position.

From a communication perspective, the fact that managerialism tends to be asymmetrical means that it also tends to be *closed*—to feedback, to contradictory information, to bad news. And thus it was at Enron. Despite Enron's reputation at one time as a paragon of virtue and the company's public endorsement of the RICE code—respect, integrity, communication, and excellence—these values were "neither modeled by leaders nor integrated into operations, [rather] Enron was obsessed . . . with values relating to business success and profitability" (Seeger & Ulmer, 2003, p. 68). Though the RICE code notes that employees are "trained to report without retribution anything they observe or discover that indicates our standards are not being met," the closed communicative system that came to light was one characterized by secrecy and outright deception (Seeger & Ulmer, 2003, p. 68).

As with other characteristics of managerialism, this monologic quality of discourse is not new. There is a long tradition of warning in the rhetorical literature of organizations: the danger of groupthink (Janis, 1971), when leaders get so myopic that they fail to heed the warning signs and to take corrective measures; the problems of upward distortion (Athanaissiades, 1973; Kassing, 2000; K. H. Roberts & O'Reilly, 1978), when subordinates perceive that it is unsafe or politically unwise to convey to management vital feedback that could improve the company's production or even save its life; and the last resort of whistleblowing (Jensen, 1987), when employees get so desperately committed, for example, Sherron Watkins at Enron, that they risk jobs and reputations to publicly expose the wrongdoings of their companies. In short, it seems that savvy organizational rhetors would have learned how to listen, whether it was the *right* or simply the *smart* thing to do. Since both internal and external stakeholders want to be "heard," it is doubtful that a socially responsible corporate rhetoric will be able to maintain the corporation's largely monologic tradition. Of course, there is the opposite problem that Cheney and Christensen (2001) address, which finds the organization with "an almost compulsive concern" (p. 250) about what their publics are "thinking" and "saying"— so much so that the organization is pulled off its center and is no longer a distinguishable figure against the market ground that surrounds it.

Managerialsim Is Narcissistic

One thing is virtually indisputable: organizations have and will continue to speak highly of themselves. And perhaps they must. If the organization does not "toot its own horn," who will? Horn tooting (or positive identity creation), either loudly rendered or in hushed, subtle tones, is the stuff of legitimation. Cheney and Christensen (2001) have offered us a provocative explanation of how organizational identity is formed; in focusing, almost obsessively, upon customers and stakeholders, organizational rhetoric constructs its audience in self-referential ways that, while appearing to radiate outward to adapt to its environment, actually loops back to form and to celebrate the preferred identity of the organization itself. Thus, the customer and stakeholder who appear to be the object of the organization's desire and service actually become the symbolic raw material of the organization's own persona, a nifty rhetorical move that functions to construct the organization and its critical constituencies as one and the same (Burke, 1969).

Even though self-referential identity is of the organization's own making, it is easy to see how members could lose their moral compass in their own deluded and self-aggrandizing accounts. Boje and Rosile (2003) note that at one point Enron's executive committee suggested that the company motto become "the coolest company on Earth," to which Chairman Lay suggested wrapping its headquarters in a pair of giant sunglasses. Boje and Rosile call this "an act of arrogance and extravagance that presages disaster" (p. 98). In his analysis of an Indian nongovernmental organization, DVLINK, that worked on issues of rural poverty, Ganesh (2003) found similar narcissistic behavior, but offered a kinder, gentler interpretation than the critics of Enron. Ganesh suggests that in developing a system of information and communication technology, DVLINK simply began to inflate its own importance in the effort to wipe out poverty and simply "lost its balance" as a public servant. What Ganesh reminds us, however, is that when companies become egocentric, when they "start to believe their own spin and hyperbole" (Fox, 2003, p. 307), they de facto "distance [themselves] from others"—a move that is critical in the demise of social capital.

So not only has the modern corporation failed to *act* in ways that qualify it as a provider of social responsibility, its voice has been inconsistent with the task, as well. In adopting a set of rhetorical strategies that features instrumentality, exclusivity, attribution, monologue, and narcissism, managerial language has positioned itself in direct opposition to a discourse of connection, reciprocity, and trust that characterizes social responsibility. Various scholars (Cyphert & Saiia, 2004; Gioia, 2003; Heath, 2001; J. Roberts, 2003; Starck & Kruckeberg, 2001) are lining up, however, to suggest that there *are* better ways, some plausible alternatives. Deetz (1992) argues that managerialism is "not necessary"—not the only discursive option available—but rather a choice that has been made over against "other models and logics" (p. 22). In the final section I revisit the ancient concept of *ethos* to consider at least one alternative for rehabilitating CSR.

ESTABLISHING A "MUTUAL DWELLING PLACE": A CONTEMPORARY MODEL OF CSR

By now it seems painfully obvious that the only way for the corporation to *legitimately* enact the role of social responsibility to which it has both implicitly and explicitly laid claim—to move from

CSR as "a kind of public relations whipped cream decorating the corporate pudding" (Bellah et al., 1985, p. 290) to *real* structural reform—is to rehabilitate its damaged institutional image and to find an authentic and credible voice. This rehabilitation is necessary because it falls to the institution that would lead us in the pursuit of social responsibility both to model it and to render its ideas compelling and "contagious" (Weick, 1980).

Rhetorical *ethos* offers a promising antidote to the current "international crisis of confidence in corporations" (Child, 2002), because it concerns itself directly with how people judge words and actions—a process that exposed the crisis to begin with and might rescue us if we let it. Coined and privileged by Aristotle as perhaps "the most effective means of persuasion," *ethos* most commonly is thought to refer to the *character* of a speaker constructed primarily in the act of speaking. Audiences determine the strength of ethos by assessing a speaker's *phronesis* (practical wisdom), *arête* (virtue), and *ennoia* (goodwill) (Jasinski, 2001, p. 229). However, as Cheney, Christensen, Conrad, and Lair (2004) argue, since Aristotle's and Cicero's rhetor was an "educated, propertied, male speaker addressing a homogeneous audience" (p. 79), the translation of ethos to a corporate collectivity has been awkward and inexact. For example, how does one apply the criteria of ethos to a *collectivity* or group—one constructed of many "selves" and realities (Cheney, 1991; Larson & Pepper, 2003)? As J. Roberts (2003) claims, there is no "essential" entity that is "The Organization"; thus, McMillan (1987) suggests that we make use of the Latin term *persona* (mask) to assess the unique repository of symbols with which a particular organization aligns —such ordinary artifacts as its newsletters, work manuals, job descriptions, press releases, and memos. This model works well because it formalizes the *watching* and *listening* and *assessing* that ordinary citizens do routinely that is the symbolic stuff of ethos. Symbolic assessment by stakeholders is especially helpful in determining an organization's character: an organization's decision to "*act* on behalf of an issue of conscience . . . is more than half the battle for institutional character" and the character-building exercise continues as that organization "speaks" its struggle with an issue of conscience "with the world looking on" (McMillan & Hyde, 2000, pp. 37–38).

Not only must the means of judging collective rhetoric be recast, so too must the criteria of corporate *ethos*. The judgment of Aristotle's individual rhetor was straightforward: whether he had something worthwhile and knowledgeable to say, was pleasant and appealing as he said it, and was adequately qualified by reputation or past experience to be heard. Certainly, the spirit of those traditional criteria resonates with such markers as the quality of a company's product and services, whether a company is thought to be "customer friendly," and its success at avoiding egregious or unlawful behavior. Still, those measures seem inadequate for the assessment of a human institution that has virtually *asked* that it be judged on *both* financial and social dimensions.

Recently, rhetorical scholars (Hyde, 2004; Jost & Hyde, 1997; Smith, 2004) have refocused attention on two concepts, *place* and *participation*, which better align with the contemporary social presence of the corporation and offer more utility in the assessment of a corporate *ethos*. Grounding their arguments in the writings of Homer and Hesiod, predating even Aristotle, and employing the more contemporary thinking of Heidegger, these scholars point out that "*[e]thos* means abode, dwelling place . . . the open region in which man dwells" (Heidegger, 1977, p. 233). Further, in pursuit of *ethos*, it is the speaker's (or source's) obligation to make us "at home" and "*give us a place to be*" as we think about and deliberate those things most precious to us. Thus, *ethos* not only constructs a safe and hospitable "dwelling place" (*ethos*; pl. *ethen*) but also invites us into *participation* in that social space "where people can deliberate about and 'know together' (*con-scientia*) some matter of interest" (Hyde, 2004, p. 7). This rendering not only is consistent with Aristotle's confinement of *ethos* to the spaces of public utterance but also reaffirms Arendt's (1959) defense of the *polis* as that "space" in Greek life where all voices were equal, and it reintroduces the option of deliberation as a vehicle for social and political governance.

Some (see, e.g., Beck, 1992, 1999; Haas, 2003; Habermas, 1984, 1987; J. Roberts, 2003) are now suggesting that the modern corporation is just the institution to create such places and to facilitate such participation—the site most central to both personal and social progress.[3] According to Deetz (2003), it is the corporation's "responsibility" (from the Latin *respondeo*, "I answer") to assume the role of "caretaker" of this critical social space, both local and beyond. Similarly, Jost and Hyde

(1997) explain to us that hermeneutics philosopher Emmanuel Levinas identifies the primordial domain of ethics as that space where, in the tradition of Adam, Abraham, and Moses, we answer, "Here am I" to the call of the Other (see also Hyde, McMillan, & Mitra, 1998). Further, there is a spaciotemporal expansion to the organization's unique *response-ability*: rather than simply "taking care" of its own workplace and heeding the call of the Other in its presence—workers, potential recruits, customers, investors—the organization's response must be enlarged to encompass broader social space and "distant others who, although remote in space and time, may nevertheless be part of interconnected sequences of corporate actions and their consequences" (Haas, 2003, p. 613).

Furthermore, in this recast notion of *ethos*, it is the obligation of the corporation to facilitate "collaborative and moral deliberation" (Hyde, 2004, p. xviii), as well—both inside and outside its boundaries. For example, Karl Weick has long been on record with the contention that for people to come to understand what they think about things—"from mergers and acquisitions to euthanasia"—they must first "see what they say about them," and that it is management's responsibility to provide those opportunities of articulation and reflection (Weick, 1980, p. 21). Conrad (1993) agrees: "It is through discourse that individuals develop their own views of morality; through discourse that organizations develop and inculcate core values and ethical codes; and through discourse that incongruities within individual and organizational value sets of different persons are negotiated" (p. 2). Deetz (2003) sums up the discursive agenda of the socially responsible organization: Workplaces must become "*places*" of value debate, providing a forum for "the articulation and resolution of important social conflicts regarding the use of natural resources, the production of desirable goods and services, the development of personal qualities, and the future direction of society" (p. 609) It is in the corporation's "inventive and symbolic capacity to construct dwelling places . . . wherein good (and bad) things happen" (Hyde, 2004, p. 8) and the invitation of Others into that moral conversation that the "*mutual dwelling places*" of ethos are formed (Smith, 2004).

How does this rehabilitated corporate dwelling place redress the problems that have been raised in this chapter? First, the corporate rhetor that tra-

ditionally has been "closed" opens itself to the Other,[4] "acknowledges" the Other, and determines the degree to which the organization is willing to "become authentically bound" with the Other in their "collective destiny" (Hyde, 1994, 2001; Hyde et al., 1998; Zbinden, 1970). The days of patronizing constructions of stakeholders as a "naive and helpless public audience" must give way, argue Cyphert & Saiia (2004), to a discourse of symmetry and partnership—"a model of stakeholder involvement that demands respect, commitment, and risk on the part of corporate rhetors" (p. 251). And when the consequences of corporate action exceed the bounds of time and space, the corporation should engage affected stakeholders in what Benhabib (1992) calls "simulated" conversations, in which the organization attempts to envision itself in the role of the stakeholders and to articulate, to the best of its ability, those stakeholder positions. This simulation is consistent with John Rawls's Veil of Ignorance and with the deliberative model that never terminates a public deliberation without consideration of the "voices absent from the table" (Mathews & McAfee, 2000).

Also, the new corporate rhetor does not just *speak* its self-interested agenda; it *listens*, as well, especially to those most vulnerable to corporate conduct. As Beck (1992) argues, "Wealth accumulates at the top [of society], risks at the bottom" (p. 35). Therefore, the socially responsible organization not only attends to the "aggregate effects of its actions, but also carefully considers the social distribution of those effects" (Haas, 2003, p. 616). Furthermore, the socially responsible organization abandons its traditional monologue. Grunig (2001) proposes that the traditional one-way transfer be replaced by a two-way symmetrical model through which organizations may interact with their publics to build relationships (see also Coombs, 2001) and bring the perspectives of those publics to management's attention. Heath (2001) extends Grunig's dialogic model to recommend *rhetorical enactment* that features a "multidirectional flow of information, evaluation, and opinion [which] privileges all players to assert their ideas, offer value-laden propositions, and propose and interpret recommendations" (p. 50).

As new and diverse perspectives penetrate corporate attention, the goals and content of corporate discourse must also be reconceptualized and reframed. No longer can the exclusive, primarily economic, interests of corporations dominate social discourse. Indeed, just as globalization is altering social arrangements and epistemological assumptions, it is also redrawing "discursive boundaries that have defined corporate organizations" and forcing them to a rhetoric of *corporate ecology* (Cyphert & Saiia, 2004) that considers the "concentration and redistribution of resources to accommodate the modern 'struggle for existence'" that is common to us all (pp. 253–254). In short, argues Heath (2001), organizations need to "*hear* society—to understand and appreciate the opinions that are on the minds of people whose goodwill is vital for the mandate of their organizations" (p. 5).

Furthermore, when the new corporate rhetor fails to live up to this mandate of mutuality, it must take responsibility for its failure. Rather than scapegoating, deflecting, or outright lying, the new corporate rhetor accepts "the consequences of [its] behavior" (Seeger & Ulmer, 2003) and offers an accounting that involves "explaining and justifying actions and may involve a variety of explanations, interpretations, and narratives regarding outcomes" (p. 60). Recall that Benhabib, Beck, and Haas all suggest that if those explanations to affected stakeholders cannot be delivered face to face, they should be "simulated." For these scholars, accountability, even *in absentia*, is better for the organization's soul than no accounting at all. Estes (1996) sums up an alternative model of organizational accountability:

> [W]e need a new scorecard, one that will measure corporate success in terms of the corporation's public purpose. It must show the effects on, the returns to, all stakeholders and not just the returns to stockholders. . . . [W]ith adequate information, stakeholders, acting in their own best interests, will reward responsible corporations and penalize irresponsible ones. (p. 16)

Finally, it is the corporation's vulnerable opening of itself to the Other and the provision of "dwelling places" for consideration of mutual concerns than can free it from its historical egoism. Ganesh (2003) argues that organizational narcissism results from the "simultaneous centralization of self and distancing of others" that emphasizes "legitimacy over accountability" (p. 57). The temptation to disregard communal concerns is understandable, given what Bauman (1993) calls the "floated" nature of organizational responsibility,

that is, distance in space and time between the corporation and those affected by its actions. To bridge that divide, J. Roberts (2003) suggests seeking more venues in which the corporation actually encounters the "face and the voice of the Other" (p. 261). These venues, argues Heath (2001), offer opportunities for the "co-creation, co-management, co-definition of meaning . . . that reconcile strains and alienation and foster mutually beneficial relationships" (p. 35). If personal interaction is impossible, however, or those affected by corporate actions are removed in time and space, Benhabib's simulation may offer the next best alternative. From the perspective of these affected constituents, argues J. Roberts (2003), there is "more at stake and more to be said—more felt urgency that *you the corporation* can come to know the difference *you* are making in *my life* and *my community*" (p. 262; emphasis added). Such feedback functions to "break the mirror" of the organization's narcissistic gaze on its own image.

In summary, a *mutual dwelling place* stands to transform both corporate words and actions by

- replacing corporate monologue with dialogue, transforming the faceless public of the corporation to a "Thou" as opposed to an "It" (Buber, 1958);
- replacing exclusivity with corporate profit/loss accounting that assesses *all* stakeholders, rather than a privileged few (Starck & Kruckeberg, 2001);
- replacing solitary measures of instrumentality with measures of success in terms of human and social capital (Greider, 2003);
- replacing external attribution with corporate accountability and disclosure (J. Roberts, 2003); and
- replacing the corporation's self-adoring gaze with an examination of its image in which what the corporation "sees" is no greater than the least of those that have been adversely affected by its actions, and no smaller that those whom the corporation has lifted up (Ganesh, 2003).

This reappropriated model of *ethos* recasts the role of stakeholders in some profound ways, as well. As a wary public reconsiders its commitment to the institutional world of corporations and, in particular, that institution's leadership role in our common "struggle for existence" (Cyphert & Saiia, 2004, pp. 253–254), the audience of the corporation is empowered to ask some hard questions, as well, and those questions originate *not* in the public relations or marketing departments, but with the stakeholders themselves—all of them:[5]

- To what degree have you "created" and "invited us into" a place where we can "dwell and feel at home" (Hyde, 2004, p. xxi)? (i.e., Is our workplace safe, friendly, and free? Does it promote human potential? How do you care for Mother Earth?)
- To what degree have you offered us the opportunity for "collaborative and moral deliberation" (p. vii)? (i.e., Do you listen to us? Do you care? How broad are your concerns? Do you include us in decision making?)
- To what degree have you worked to "modify the lived and attuned spaces" to feature what is "true, just, and virtuous" (p. xvii)? (i.e., Do you tell us the truth? Do you admit your mistakes? Is the welfare of all of us equal to your own?)

CONCLUSION

My answers to the original questions of this chapter are simple. Why corporate social responsibility? Because individuals have largely abandoned, at least seriously neglected, the role of caring for one another, and corporations have assumed it. Why now? Because we have recently become painfully aware of how ill suited the modern corporation is for the task, lacking both the credibility and the voice of moral authority. How? Recast the traditional criteria used to judge individual ethos with a more fitting and timely corporate ethos that features a transformation of *place* and *participation*. These second-order changes (Bateson, 1973) will not be easy for a corporate culture steeped largely in Friedman's measure of "responsibility," but the organization that steps up to this challenge will fulfill what Smith (2004) calls the "teleological function of ethos" that presses to a higher calling "capable of advancing a cause . . . uplifting an audience . . . and improving a *mutual dwelling place*" (pp. 15–16).

NOTES

1. Cheney, Christensen, Conrad, and Lair (2005) distinguish between the unitary corporate voice, which they term "uni-vocal," and the collective voices of the corporation, which render it "multi-vocal." These authors suggest that the organization must constantly manage the tension between presenting an integrated, uni-vocal message or tailoring it multi-vocally to the needs of various audiences.

2. Cheney's study took place in the Basque region of Spain, where he focused on one of the world's oldest (40 years at the time of his study) and most economically successful worker cooperatives. Cheney gathered data for a total of six and a half months in 1992, 1994, and 1999 (Cheney, 1999).

3. See McMillan and Hyde (2000) and McMillan (2004) for case studies of one institution's experience with providing discursive spaces.

4. Estes (1996) suggests that the Others for corporations include employees, customers, stockholders, suppliers, lenders, neighboring communities, and society at large (p. 25).

5. The debate about whether the "self" of ethos is innate or socially constructed places the source of credibility with the source of the message. Lucas (2006), Smith (2004), and others have argued to the contrary, that despite our talk that seems to assume the source as the proprietor of ethos, credibility in truth resides in the minds and perceptions of the audience. This distinction is not to say that the words and actions of a person or group make no difference in the oft-heard communication phrase "credibility building." Indeed, words and actions are vital—the raw material of credibility. Lucas and Smith simply remind us that the ultimate credibility judgment comes from the hearer and thus is beyond the control of the source. In fact, near the end of the *Rhetoric*, even Aristotle advises: "With regard to moral character: there are assertions which, if made about yourself, may excite dislike, appear tedious, or expose you to risk of contradiction. . . . Put such remarks, therefore, into the mouth of some third person."

REFERENCES

Arendt, H. (1959). *The human condition*. New York: Anchor.

Athanaissiades, J. C. (1973). The distortion of upward communication in hierarchical organizations. *Academy of Management Journal, 16,* 207–226.

Bateson, G. (1973). *Steps to an ecology of mind*. New York: Ballantine Books.

Bauman, Z. (1993). *Postmodern ethics*. Oxford: Blackwell.

Beck, U. (1992). *The risk society*. London: Sage.

Beck, U. (1999). *World risk society*. Cambridge: Polity.

Bellah, R. N., Madsen, R., Sullivan, W. M., Swidler, A., & Tipton, S. M. (1985). *Habits of the heart: Individualism and commitment in American life.* Berkeley, CA: University of California Press.

Bellah, R. N., Madsen, R., Sullivan, W. M., Swidler, A., & Tipton, S. M. (1991). *The good society.* New York: Random House, Inc.

Benhabib, S. (1992). *Situating the self.* Boston, MA: Routledge Kegan Paul.

Boggs, C. (2000). *The end of politics: Corporate power and the decline of the public sphere.* New York: Guilford Press.

Boje, D. M., & Rosile, G. A. (2003). Life imitates art: Enron's epic and tragic narration. *Management Communication Quarterly, 17*(1), 85–125.

Boyd, J. (2000). Actional legitimation: No crisis necessary. *Journal of Public Relations Research, 12*, 341–353.

Buber, M. (1958). *I and thou* (2nd ed., Walter Kaufman, Trans.). New York: Charles Scribners' Sons.

Burke, K. (1969). *A grammar of motives.* Berkley: University of California Press.

Cheney, G. (1991). *Rhetoric in an organizational society: Managing multiple identities.* Columbia: University of South Carolina Press.

Cheney, G. (1995). Democracy in the work place: Theory and practice from the perspective of communication. *Journal of Applied Communication Research, 23*, 167–200.

Cheney, G. (1999). *Values at work.* Ithaca, NY: Cornell University Press.

Cheney, G., & Christensen, L. T. (2001). Organizational identity: Linkages between internal and external communication. In F. Jablin & L. Putnam (Eds.), *The new handbook of organizational communication* (pp. 231–269). Thousand Oaks, CA: Sage.

Cheney, G., Christensen, L. T., Conrad, C., & Lair, D. (2004). Corporate rhetoric as organizational discourse. In D. Grant, C. Hardy, C. Oswick, N. Phillips, & L. Putnam (Eds.), *Handbook of organizational discourse* (pp. 79–103). Thousand Oaks, CA: Sage.

Cheney, G., & McMillan, J. J. (1990). Organizational rhetoric and the practice of criticism. *Journal of Applied Communication Research, 18*, 93–114.

Child, J. (2002). The international crisis of confidence in corporations. *Academy of Management Executive, 16*(3), 145–147.

Conrad, C. (1993). *The ethical nexus.* Norwood, NJ: Ablex.

Conrad, C. (2003). Setting the stage: Introduction to the special issue on the "corporate meltdown." *Management Communication Quarterly, 17*, 5–19.

Conrad, C. (2004). The illusion of reform: Corporate discourse and agenda denial in the 2002 "corporate meltdown." *Rhetoric & Public Affairs, 7*(3), 311–338.

Coombs, W. T. (1992). The failure of the task force on food assistance: A case study of the role of legitimacy in issue management. *Journal of Public Relations Research, 4*, 101–122.

Coombs, W. T. (2001). Interpersonal communication and public relations. In R. L. Heath (Ed.), *Handbook of public relations* (pp. 105–114). Thousand Oaks, CA: Sage.

Crable, R. E. (1990). Organizational rhetoric as the fourth great system: Theoretical, critical, and pragmatic implications. *Journal of Applied Communication Research, 18*(2), 115–128.

Crable, R. E., & Vibbert, S. L. (1983). Mobil's epideictic advocacy: Observation of Prometheus-bound. *Communication Monographs, 50*, 380–394.

Cyphert, D., & Saiia, D. H. (2004). In search of the corporate citizen: The emerging discourse of corporate ecology. *Southern Communication Journal, 69*(3), 241–256.

Deakin, S., & Konzelmann, S. J. (2003). After Enron: An age of enlightenment? *Organization, 10*(3), 583–587.

Deetz, S. (1992). *Democracy in an age of corporate colonization.* Albany, NY: State University of New York Press.

Deetz, S. (2003). Corporate governance, communication, and getting social values into the decisional chain. *Management Communication Quarterly, 16*(4), 606–611.

Derber, C. (1998). *Corporation nation: How corporations are taking over our lives and what we can do about it.* New York: St. Martin's Press.

DiTomaso, N., Parks-Yancy, R., & Post, C. (2003). Structure, relationships, and community responsibility. *Management Communication Quarterly, 17*(1), 143–150.

Estes, R. (1996). *Tyranny of the bottom line: Why corporations make good people do bad things.* San Francisco, CA: Berrett-Koehler.

Fox, L. (2003). *Enron: The rise and fall.* Hoboken, NJ: John Wiley.

Friedman, M. (1988). The social responsibility of business to increases its profits. In T. Donaldson & P. Werhane (Eds.), *Ethical issues in business: A philosophical approach.* Englewood Cliffs, NJ: Prentice-Hall.

Ganesh, S. (2003). Organizational Narcissism: Technology, legitimacy, and identity in an Indian NGO. *Management Communication Quarterly, 16*(4), 558–594.

Gioia, D. A. (2003). Business organization as instrument of societal responsibility. *Organization, 10*(3), 435–438.

GolinHarris. (2004, September 17). Doing well by doing good: The trajectory of corporate citizenship in American business [Annual Survey]. *PR Newswire.* Retrieved March 12, 2005, from http://www.prnewswire.com.

Green, S. (2005, March). The limitations of the Sarbanes-Oxley act. *USA Today, 133,* 66–68.

Greider, W. (2003). *The soul of capitalism: Opening paths to moral economy.* New York: Simon & Schuster.

Grunig, J. E. (2001). Two-way symmetrical public relations: Past, present, and future. In R. L. Heath (Ed.), *Handbook of public relations* (pp. 11–30). Thousand Oaks, CA: Sage.

Haas, T. (2003). Toward an "ethic of futurity": Corporate social responsibility in the age of the risk society. *Management Communication Quarterly 16*(4), 612–617.

Habermas, J. (1984). *The theory of communicative action: Vol. 1. Reason and the rationalization of society* (T. McCarthy, Trans.). Boston, MA: Beacon Press.

Habermas, J. (1987). *The theory of communicative action: Vol. 2. Life world and system.* Boston, MA: Beacon Press.

Hanifan, L. J. (1916). The rural school community center. *Annals of the American Academy of Political and Social Science, 67,* 130–138.

Hearit, K. M., & Courtright, J. L. (2003). A social constructionist approach to crisis communication: Allegations of sudden acceleration in the Audi 500. *Communications Studies, 54,* 79–95.

Heath, R. L. (2001). A rhetorical enactment rationale for public relations: The good organization communicating well. In R. L. Heath (Ed.), *Handbook of public relations* (pp. 31–50). Thousand Oaks, CA: Sage.

Heidegger, M. (1977). Letter on humanism. In D. F. Krell (Ed.), *Martin Heidegger: Basic writings* (p. 233). New York: Harper & Row.

Hyde, M. J. (1994). The call of conscience: Heidegger and the question of rhetoric. *Philosophy and Rhetoric, 27,* 372–396.

Hyde, M. J. (2001). *The call of conscience: Heidegger, Levinas, rhetoric, and the euthanasia debate.* Columbia: University of South Carolina Press.

Hyde, M. J. (2004). Rhetorically we dwell. In M. J. Hyde (Ed.), *The ethos of rhetoric* (pp. xiii–xxviii). Columbia: University of South Carolina Press.

Hyde, M. J., McMillan, J. J., & Mitra, A. (1998). Where art thou? Here I am. *Wake Forest Magazine, 45,* 30–33.

Janis, I. (1971). Groupthink. *Psychology Today, 5,* 43–46, 74–76.

Jasinski, J. (2001). *Sourcebook on rhetoric: Key concepts in contemporary rhetorical studies.* Thousand Oaks, CA: Sage.

Jensen, V. J. (1987). Ethical tension point in whistle blowing. *Journal of Business Ethics, 6,* 321–328.

Johnson, B. M. (1981). *Communication: The process of organizing.* Boston, MA: American Press.

Johnson, M. (1993). *Moral imagination.* Chicago: University of Chicago Press.

Jost, W., & Hyde, M. J. (1997). Rhetoric and hermeneutics: Places along the way. In W. Jost & M. J. Hyde (Eds.), *Rhetoric and hermeneutics in our time* (pp. 1–42). New Haven, CT: Yale University Press.

Karliner, J. (1997). *The corporate planet: Ecology and politics in the age of globalization.* San Francisco, CA: Sierra Club Books.

Kassing, J. W. (2000). Investigating the relationship between superior-subordinate relationship quality and employee dissent. *Communication Research Reports, 17,* 58–69.

Katz, D., & Kahn, R. (1978). *The social psychology of organizing* (2nd ed.). New York: Wiley.

Kohn, A. (1986). *No contest: The case against competition.* Boston, MA: Houghton Mifflin.

Kuhn, T., & Ashcraft, K. L. (2003). Corporate scandal and the theory of the firm. *Management Communication Quarterly, 17*(1), 20–57.

Larson, G. S., & Pepper, G. L. (2003). Strategies for managing multiple organizational identifications: A case of competing identities. *Management Communication Quarterly, 16*(4), 528–557.

Lasch, C. (1978). *The culture of narcissism.* New York: Warner Books.

Lucas, S. (2006). *The art of public speaking* (9th ed.). New York: McGraw-Hill.

Marchand, R. (1998). *Creating the corporate soul: The rise of public relations and corporate imagery in American big business*. Berkeley: University of California Press.

Mathews, D., & McAfee, N. (2000). *Making choices together: The power of public deliberation*. Dayton, OH: Kettering Foundation.

McGee, M. (1980). The "ideograph": A link between rhetoric and ideology. *Quarterly Journal of Speech, 66*, 1–16.

McMillan, J. J. (1987). In search of the organizational persona: A rationale for studying organizations rhetorically. In L. Thayer (Ed.), *Organizations—communication: Emerging perspectives II* (pp. 21–45). Norwood, NJ: Ablex.

McMillan, J. J. (1988). Institutional plausibility alignment as rhetorical exercise: A mainline denomination's struggle with the exigence of sexism. *Journal for the Scientific Study of Religion, 27*, 326–344.

McMillan, J. J. (1990). Symbolic emancipation in the organization: A case of shifting power. *Communication Yearbook, 13*, 203–214.

McMillan, J. J. (2004). The potential for civic learning: "Teaching democracy by being democratic." *Southern Communication Journal, 69*(3), 188–205.

McMillan, J. J., & Hyde, M. J. (2000). Technological innovation and change: A case study in the formation of organizational conscience. *Quarterly Journal of Speech, 86*, 19–47.

Morgan, G. (1986). *Images of organization*. Newbury Park, CA: Sage.

Naughton, K. (2002, December 30). The CEO party is over. *Newsweek, 141*, 55.

Perrow, C. (2002). *Organizing America: Wealth, power, and the origins of corporate capitalism*. Princeton, NJ: Princeton University Press.

Putnam, R. D. (2000). *Bowling alone: The collapse and revival of American community*. New York: Simon & Schuster.

Roberts, J. (2003). The manufacture of corporate social responsibility: Constructing corporate sensibility. *Organization, 10*(2), 249–265.

Roberts, K. H., & O'Reilly, C. A. (1978). Failures in upward communication: Three possible culprits. *Academy of Management Journal, 17*, 205–215.

Rodrik, D. (2000). Sense and nonsense in the globalization debate. In P. O'Meara, H. D. Mehlinger, & M. Krain (Eds.), *Globalization and the challenges of the new century: A reader* (pp. 227–239). Bloomington: Indiana University Press.

Rowland, R. C. (2002). *Analyzing rhetoric: A handbook for the informal citizen in a new millennium*. Dubuque, IA: Kendall Hunt.

Ryan, H. R. (Ed.). (1988). *Oratorical encounters: Selected studies and sources of twentieth-century political accusations and apologies*. New York: Greenwood Press.

Schiller, H. I. (1995). The global information highway: Project for an ungovernable world. In J. Brook & I. A. Boal (Eds.), *Resisting the virtual life: The culture and politics of information* (pp. 17–33). San Francisco, CA: City Lights.

Seeger, M. W., & Ulmer, R. R. (2003). Explaining Enron: Communication and responsible leadership. *Management Communication Quarterly, 17*(1), 58–84.

Sloan, A. (2003). Cleaning up a dirty business. *Newsweek, 142*, 49.

Smith, C. R. (2004). Ethos dwells pervasively: A hermeneutic reading of Aristotle on credibility. In M. J. Hyde (Ed.), *The ethos of rhetoric* (pp. 1–19) Columbia: University of South Carolina Press.

Soros, G. (1998). *The crisis of global capitalism*. New York: Public Affairs.

Starck, K., & Kruckeberg, D. (2001). Public relations and community: A reconstructed theory revisited. In R. L. Heath (Ed.), *Handbook of public relations* (pp. 51–59). Thousand Oaks, CA: Sage.

Suchman, M. (1995). Managing legitimacy: Strategic and institutional approaches. *Academy of Management Review, 20*(3), 571–610.

Ware, B. L., & Linkugel, W. A. (1973). They spoke in defense of themselves: On the generic criticism of apologia. *Quarterly Journal of Speech, 59*, 273–283.

Weick, K. E. (1980). The management of eloquence. *Executive, 6*, 18–21.

Zbinden, H. (1970). Conscience in our time. In The Curatorium of the C.G. Jung Institute, Zurich (Ed.), *Conscience* (pp. 3–39). Evanston, IL: Northwestern University Press.

2

A New Generation of Global Corporate Social Responsibility

MICHAEL STOHL

CYNTHIA STOHL

NIKKI C. TOWNSLEY

The social responsibility of business is to increase its profits . . . to make the most money as possible while conforming to the basic rules of the society, both those embodied in law and those embodied in ethical culture.

Milton Friedman

CR is not new. When Robert Owen joined David Dale in 1800 at his spinning mill in New Lanark he created a school and workers' housing and he provided medical services. In short, he ploughed business profits into improving the lives of employees and their families. And over the course of the next century the Cadburys, Frys, Rowantrees [sic], William Lever and others followed suit. And so it has continued to the present day.

Nigel Griffiths

At its best, CSR is defined as the responsibility of a company for the totality of its impact, with a need to embed society's values into its core operations as well as into its treatment of its social and physical environment. Responsibility is accepted as encompassing a spectrum—from the running of a profitable business to the health and safety of staff and the impact on the societies in which a company operates.

Sir Geoffrey Chandler

Despite the ubiquitous acknowledgment of globalization in virtually all areas of social, political, and economic life, conceptualizations and discussions of ethical and responsible organizing within academic, policy making, and local communities often remain remarkably parochial. Typically, for example, when Americans think about the personification of corporate social (ir)responsibility, Enron's Ken Lay and Jeff Skilling loom large in public consciousness. The enormity of the financial fraud and the extent of human devastation brought forth by the Enron scandal come to mind. Twenty-nine top executives secretly sold millions of dollars in stock options while employees were forbidden to do the same; not to mention, 63% of the 21,000 employees lost their life savings in 401(k) pension plans as a result (Sharp, 2002). The case of Enron yields well-known and compelling examples of corporate communication at its worst, including blaming, secrecy, intimidation, plausible deniability, arrogance, silence, withholding, and conspiracy. For example, Arthur Andersen, Enron's auditing firm, shredded Enron documents while on notice of a federal investigation (Oppel, 2002). Indeed, when people typically think about Enron and corporate responsibility, they focus upon events of the most recent past, post-2001, including California's energy problems, the manipulation of corporate earnings and American stock prices, the collapse of stock and subsequent pension funds, and a pattern of corporate and personal lobbying and political contributions that suggest, at the very least, undue access and influence within the American political process itself.

In this chapter, we reconsider corporate social responsibility (CSR) within a global framework, particularly focusing on its evolution and impact over time. We offer a global perspective that seeks to frame CSR in a more expansive temporal and less elite Western-centric frame. Toward this end, we begin with a brief review of Enron and discuss what a "global CSR perspective" might have told us about Enron long before this decade's debacle. We then explore how a global perspective enables us to see the ways in which the development of the CSR movement mirrors (as well as builds upon) the evolution of the global human rights regime. Like the development of international human rights standards and norms, which, we suggest, are integral to corporate global social responsibility, there are several generations of CSR that continue to explore how to construct and enact more humane and ethical organizational practices. The first generation of CSR is grounded in discussions of responsibilities regarding what *not* to do (e.g., negative responsibilities such as *not* to exploit or cheat). The second generation focuses upon discussions of providing adequate compensation and working conditions (e.g., the right to a living wage), and the third generation addresses proactive and positive responsibilities (e.g., to protect and create a sustainable and just world). Taken together, these generations provide a framework for exploring the evolving nature of CSR, as well as the theoretical and pragmatic challenges of developing

standards and norms for global corporate engagement. The final section unpacks the four dynamic processes that make our framework or approach to CSR truly "global."

ENRON: *PLUS ÇA CHANGE, PLUS C'EST LA MÊME CHOSE*

Most recent accounts of the Enron scandal agree that, until 2001, Enron was held as a model of the highest standards for American business (Cruver, 2002; Eichenwald, 2005; McLean & Elkind, 2003; Swarts & Watkins, 2003). On February 6, 2001, Enron's own website reported, "Enron Corporation was named today the 'Most Innovative Company in America' for the sixth consecutive year by *Fortune* magazine. Enron placed No. 18 overall on *Fortune*'s list of the nation's 535 'Most Admired Companies,' up from No. 36 last year" (Enron, 2001). With the notable exception of economist and columnist Paul Krugman, who raised the possibility in December 2000 of Enron's manipulation of the market and the subsequent California electricity crisis, Enron was the darling of the American media. Thus, when the scandal broke, Americans were surprised. But they should not have been. If we had looked beyond our own borders, Enron's actions, and its betrayal of its responsibilities to stakeholders and to the public at large, would have been obvious and predictable.

Indeed, looking at the actions of Enron in India, Argentina, Brazil, Bolivia, Mozambique, Poland, Dominican Republic, Guatemala, Panama, and Colombia, among others, we see the seeds and growth of corporate irresponsibility as well as an exemplar of the evolving nature of CSR in the global arena. Enron had a history of consistent wrongdoing, and to date, it remains the only company in history to be a subject of a full Amnesty International report (Amnesty International, 1997).[1]

As early as 1991, Enron made a controversial deal with the Indian government to build a power plant in Dabhol, India. From 1992 to 1998, Enron owned 80% of the Dabhol Power Company. General Electric and Bechtel each held a 10% share. The deal initially was lauded by the business press (see *Business Week*, 2001), but rumors emerged from the beginning that the contract was corrupt and full of political improprieties. By 1993, the World Bank had questioned the project's viability, and Indian critics argued the project had been compromised by Enron's "high-handed behavior" (Parry, 2001).

Human Rights Watch (1999) reported that Enron misled the public from the start when the firm boasted it had received no complaints during the legally required solicitation of citizen comments about the proposed project. Yet, by 1995, thousands of Indians protested the Dabhol project on grounds of its negative social, economic, and environmental impacts. By early 1997, demonstrators condemned the displacement of more than 2,000 people, and the misappropriation of Indian land grew in size, frequency, and violence, as well. Both Amnesty International and Human Rights Watch reported that Enron colluded with local police, who followed, arrested, beat, and detained peaceful protestors, holding them without trial. "Protesters and activists have been subjected to harassment, arbitrary arrest, preventive detention under the ordinary criminal law, and ill treatment. . . . [Further,] women, who have been at the forefront of local agitation, appear to have been a particular target" (Amnesty International, 1997, p. 1). In fact, stories of women being dragged from their homes and beaten with batons were common. In January 1999, Human Rights Watch starkly concluded, "Human Rights Watch believes that the Dabhol Power Corporation and its parent company Enron are complicit in these human rights violations. . . . The company, under provisions of law, paid the abusive state forces for the security they provided to the company. These forces, located adjacent to the project site, were only stationed there to deal with protests" (1999). Importantly, Enron's international auditors were also local offices of Arthur Andersen in India and in other non-U.S. locations, where it was engaged in duplicitous, illegal, and unethical practices.

As noted above, Enron's abuses of human rights and political interventions, coupled with its documented ecological abuses (e.g., destruction of indigenous mango and cashew plantations and fisheries, and contamination of rivers and seawater) and disregard for mandated consultation processes and political processes (see Chattarjee, 2001) represented "business as usual" for the company. Thus, the "surprising" behaviors uncovered in 2002 were not aberrant. Unfortunately, it was only when Enron's American-based scandals became exposed that policy makers, the media, and the general public grew enraged (see Wysham & Valette, 2002). A global focus on Enron's and Andersen's business practices abroad might have alerted policy makers and Americans in general to Enron problems many years earlier; a global focus might have cultivated a global consciousness and appropriate CSR practices as a result.

Framing Enron activities and its relations with stakeholders within the global arena illustrates the interdependency among social, political, economic, and environmental dimensions and the evolution of CSR. The Enron scandal is not merely a financial or American-based scandal. In today's global economy, profitability cannot be separated from issues related to political equity, social dignity, and environmental viability, and responsibility cannot be limited to whether or not a corporation violated the letter of the law in a particular country, or even a simple calculation of whether or not it did harm economically. As we describe in this chapter, a new generation of CSR has begun to recognize the futility of compartmentalizing ethics from profitability, as well as local from global (or global from local) business practices and requirements. New discourses reveal the theoretical shifts that have been made as scholars and practitioners attempt to make sense of firms' (social) roles and responsibilities in a global economy.

The Enron case also illustrates the limits of conceiving CSR in negative terms or, in other words, focusing solely on what a corporation cannot do legally. Enron's complicity with India's police force may have been within the letter of the law, but its collusion could also be described as socially *irre*sponsible. The recent movement of CSR to a proactive orientation not only is a result of increased knowledge of such dramatic events but also mirrors and works within a context of evolving global standards of human rights and the increased collaboration of corporations, nongovernmental organizations (NGOs), and governmental organizations in the development, monitoring, and implementation of human rights standards. The discursive and practical connections between human rights and CSR are very powerful. A global CSR is intrinsically related to human rights, as identified in the United Nations Charter, including "the dignity and worth of the human person" and "the equal rights of men and women" (United Nations, 1945). Both human rights and CSR are concerned with, among other freedoms, freedom of speech, freedom from arbitrary arrest, freedom of movement, and the right to earn a living wage for a day's work. Thus, to understand the evolution of global CSR, it is necessary to understand the evolution of the global human rights regime. We now turn our discussion to the ways in which the standards, expectations, and monitoring of human rights have evolved in concert with CSR.

THREE GENERATIONS OF HUMAN RIGHTS

Many scholars have described the evolution of a human rights regime over the last 500 years in terms of three generations of rights (Apodaca, Stohl, & Lopez, 1998; Marks, 2004). The first generation of rights, most familiar and comfortable to the Anglo-American tradition, is concerned with the civil and political rights of individuals. This epoch represents a chain of development that began with the Magna Carta and extends through the English Bill of Rights in 1689, the Declaration of Independence, and the Declaration of the Rights of Man in 1789.

First-generation rights arose to protect the individual from the power of the state and, in doing so, were generally conceived of as *negative* rights or freedoms from state interference. First-generation rights are seen as belonging to the individual and often favor the abstention rather than the intervention of government. These include, for example, the freedom from arbitrary execution, the freedom from unreasonable detention, the prohibition against torture and inhumane treatment, and the right to freedoms of thought and expression.

Milton Friedman's (1970) early conceptualization of CSR, outlined in the quotation at the beginning of this chapter, is consistent with first-generation rights. For him, CSR is about maximizing returns to the general shareholders of a company consistent with the law; the state will not interfere with corporations lest they fail to uphold the charter of profitability. His argument parallels discussions of civil and political rights, in this case, requesting that the corporation, rather than the state, refrain from improper behaviors or the violation of the laws of its own country, such as prohibitions against bribery or participating in violations of basic rights and liberties if business is conducted in countries where such rights and liberties exist. Again, the discourse of first-generation rights largely entails the act of "refraining from"; it remains the province of negative rights.

The second generation of rights developed out of the nineteenth-century class struggle and the development of capitalism and industrialization. Responding to the great social upheavals that accompanied the growth of large-scale industrial enterprises within Western democracies, workers demanded more humane conditions of employment and compensation. While first-generation rights emphasized restraint from the state, second-generation rights demanded state intervention on behalf of claimants. These rights include the right to fair and equitable wages; the right to rest and leisure, including reasonable limitation of working hours and periodic holidays with pay; the right to basic health care; and the right to a safe working environment.

In the quotation at the beginning of this chapter, Nigel Griffiths MP, Minister for Corporate and Social Responsibility (Griffiths, 2004), notes that values articulated in the second CSR generation focus upon the provision of living wages, family benefits, and health care, not only in the jurisdiction in which the corporation has its home but anywhere and with any other organization with which it operates. Like the second generation of human rights, these behaviors are positive contributions, not negative avoidance of behaviors.

It is important to note that in the United States and the United Kingdom, the discourse of first-generation rights extends so far that second-generation ones are still most often viewed as luxuries that should not be satisfied until the first are secured. In Northern Europe, second-generation rights are seen not as subsidiary but rather as coequal, and these differences can be seen in the laws of various countries.[2] Interestingly, second-generation concerns about child labor, women's rights to employment, and sweatshops are often contested by those arguing against CSR movements in terms of the imposition of Western values on other cultures, much as with the discussion of requests to governments within the human rights movement to guarantee these rights. For these critics, the second-generation rights discourse of "intervention" implicitly carries with it histories of colonialism and imperial imposition.

The third generation of human rights is of much more recent vintage, although philosophical precursors may be found much earlier. The third generation focuses on the rights of "mankind," or our collective humanity. Foreshadowed in the aspirational statement of the preamble of the UN Charter (United Nations, 1948), Article 28 of the Universal Declaration of Human Rights declares that "everyone is entitled to a social and international order in which the rights set forth in this declaration can be fully realized." These rights differ significantly from those addressed in the first two generations insofar as they are collective rather than individual rights and can be realized only through global participation, cooperation, and agreement. What rights should be included in the third generation, however, remains highly contested.

The right to live in peace and the right to a healthy and balanced environment are generally high on the list of proposed third-generation rights. Indeed, the foci of this generation continue to evolve through a dialogue of confrontation between the rich and poor nations, a dialogue infused with the legacies of war, colonialism and imperialism, and the extraction and degradation of resources to benefit the North at the expense of the South. Sir Geoffrey Chandler (2001), founder chair of Amnesty International's International Business Group, 1991–2001, and former senior executive Royal Dutch/Shell Group, quoted at the beginning of the chapter, embodies the discourse of third-generation CSR. He argues that corporations should contribute to the growth of the people and societies in which they operate and should attend to the "totality" of outcomes, as well. Just as in contemporary discussions of human rights, the third-generation CSR discourse also faces the challenge of discerning or, perhaps more appropriately, dismantling the "boundaries" of impacts prompted by participating in a global world.

In summary, the evolving generational discourse of human rights parallels the emergence of a global CSR. The shift from rights as individuals to the rights as collectives, as well as from negative to positive rights, mirrors similar attempts to theorize the role of the firm beyond its fiduciary function and geographic boundaries. While profitability has been the litmus test for responsibility in the past (and arguably in some present-day circles, as well), academic and business communities alike have expanded their conceptions of CSR beyond simple support for local communities in which firms operate to a consideration of the totality of a firm's impact globally (see Townsley & Stohl, 2003).

WHAT DOES A GLOBAL CSR PERSPECTIVE MEAN?

We presented the Enron case as just one example of how critical CSR issues, concerns, and behaviors are often obscured or hidden when examined solely at the local or national level. To be sure, the cases of regional neglect are plentiful. The ecological devastation wrought by the shrimp industry in Central America, Shell Oil's involvement in disputes over the development of Nigerian oil resources and its complicity in the executions of several Nigerians, and Nike's involvement with child labor and Southeast Asian sweatshops are just a few other well-known examples of corporate actions that appear "local" but actually transcend national borders as well as permeate the political, cultural, social, and economic spheres of everyday life globally. Overall, we suggest that the emerging generation of CSR carries with it the recognition that a global framework is important for all organizations, both large and small. A global CSR is responsive to the multiple cultures, value sets, and communicative practices of different nations while recognizing that (inter)organizational contexts are no longer bounded by the nation-state.

A global perspective also frames CSR in a more expansive temporal and less elite Western-centric frame. Barnett and Muller (1974) identified several problems regarding corporate behavior in the developing world. These problems included the now familiar manipulative accounting practices so as to reduce local tax burdens for corporations while leveraging (through political bribery and payoffs) huge investment incentives from local governments and communities (e.g., free land, major infrastructure installations, and assistance and guarantees of a quiescent work force). But the predominance of a Western-centric elite typical of conceptualizations in the 1970s and 1980s framed the exploitation of corporations as limited in time and emphasized downward direction, as something rich corporations did in (to) poor nations, not in rich ones. That is, Western corporations were stronger than many governments and social sectors, and thus it was only in underdeveloped nations that we had to worry about CSR. Barnett and Muller (1974) did talk of a future where local communities "might well begin to make the same analysis of their situation as underdeveloped countries are doing" (p. 380), but that call was lost amidst the short-term concern of the domination of rich nations' multinational corporations over poor nations' weak governance structures. A new generation of CSR, however, recognizes that the continued growth and conglomeration of corporations across contexts has altered the relative power of the government, social, and corporate sectors throughout the world and that CSR is just as relevant in corporate relations among rich countries today as it is in the relationships between rich to poor countries of decades ago.

Overall, a global perspective not only provides insight into new models for what constitutes ethical practice in today's complex business economy but also demands richer ways of conceiving of organizations, as well as their role and commitment to society at large. The following section provides an entry into what we conceive of a global CSR framework.

THE EMERGENCE OF A NEW GENERATION OF GLOBAL CSR

Fundamental changes are emerging within the third generation of CSR. This transformation is strongly associated with four previously identified dynamic processes of globalization (see Stohl, 2005):

1. No distinction between "out there" from "in here"
2. "Glocalization" within new and old forms of media
3. Reflection of the complex network of organizational relations across sectors rather than any particular organizations, individuals, or specific interests
4. Recognition of the permeability of public/private boundaries

Third-Generation CSR No Longer Distinguishes "Out There" From "In Here"

One of the most important features of the third generation of CSR is that it embodies dynamic, intense, and extensive communicative, economic, cultural, and political exchanges and practices, producing new discourses of identity and new forms of interconnectedness. To borrow from Giddens's (1991) conceptualization of globalization, third-generation CSR "is not just an out-there phenom-

enon. It is an in-here phenomenon" (p. 367). As stated above, early conceptualizations of CSR represented an individual's freedom from organizational wrongdoing by virtue of the corporation not violating the legal mandates of a particular society at a particular time. Those who fell outside the purview of a particular law or context were not included within the corporation's responsibilities. Boundaries between nation-states were strictly adhered to, and acceptable corporate behaviors were widely variable as a result. On the other hand, a global perspective on CSR changes notions of presence and absence: "it has made the identification and communication of 'inside', 'home' and 'away', 'them' and 'us'—more problematic than ever" (Scholte, 2000, pp. 48–49). In this framework, even when individuals and groups consider themselves separate from or having unique CSR contexts, they establish their position in relation to the global system, what Robertson (1990) calls "relativization."

The instantiation of organizational and national boundaries within the first and second generation of CSR can be seen in many of the pivotal moments in the progressive history of CSR. These events are associated with particular corporations in particular places at particular points in time. It was the 1911 Triangle Shirtwaist Factory fire in New York City that brought the issue of "sweatshops" most prominently to the world's attention in the last century and led to the first U.S. legislation on factory working and safety conditions. The Lockheed bribery scandal in 1976, which involved the corporation bribing foreign officials, including the Japanese prime minister, members of the government of Italy, and Prince Bernhard of the Netherlands, led to the passage of the Foreign Corrupt Practices Act in 1977. Because of the tight connections among the diamond company DeBeers, apartheid in South Africa, and the civil wars in Sierra Leone, a movement to address working conditions in extractive industries was formed. In each of these cases, CSR was conceived within the framework of first- or second-generation CSR—the corporation's obligations not to do things (first generation, do not bribe officials) or to address the rights of individual workers (second generation—the right to a living wage, to free assembly) within a particular context.

The attention of the public to grave and dramatic events, galvanized through popular media, often produces direct, albeit short-term, attempts to confront a CSR issue, including, for example, legislation to create safety standards, outlaw overcrowding, or establish clear responsibility and liability for environmental damages caused. The third-generation CSR movement, however, is communicatively rooted in more than the reporting of events to engage the public, and more than Band-Aid solutions. For many years prior to particular large-scale disasters, there was often no push to address the problems, not because they were hidden from view but because the issue had no lasting resonance with the public and corporations were able to carry on with business as usual. Part of the reason is that the relevant publics did not feel connected to those who were the perceived victims: stockholders did not identify with stakeholders; individuals embraced their local and national identities to the exclusion of the "Other." As early as 1922, Lippmann described public opinion as "[t]he pictures inside the heads of these human beings, the pictures of themselves, of others, of their needs, their purposes, and relationships" (p. 30). Absent is some form of self-reflexive global consciousness; when Americans think about multinationals abroad (if they think about them at all), they tend to conceive of behavior in terms of how corporations are performing "over there" and not in terms of what that means at "home." Rare are those who think about these issues beyond themselves or their communities, or in terms of global constituencies or impacts. But as many populaces are learning, the boundaries between us and them are quickly blurring.

Today, the social and material conditions of globalization make it more and more likely that stable forms of place and identity are replaced with flexible flows drawn across borders. These reflexive changes in identities of peoples and groups moving from local centering to universal concerns implicate third-generation CSR in the constant reexamination of corporate social practices in light of new information and new relationships. Increased global consciousness provides the backdrop for the development of the third generation of CSR, a framework that focuses on collective rather than individual protections and rights, an approach that extends stakeholders beyond national borders and that can be realized only through global participation, cooperation, and agreement.

Third-Generation CSR Is "Glocalized" Within New and Old Forms of Media

Roland Robertson (1992) describes glocalization as the copresence of both universalizing and particularizing tendencies within the global system. The dynamic disembedding of events and institutions and the realignment and restructuring of social interaction across time and space create a communicative dynamic in which global events are interpreted through local culture and local events are interpreted through a global framework. The tempering effects of local/global media coverage (both traditional and new media) on global/local conditions have begun to exert strong influences on the development of CSR. Information about corporate behavior and global issues is no longer within the purview or interpretive frame of any one individual, group, or organization. Digitized technology, the World Wide Web, and collaborative communication systems mean that there is no longer a monopoly of information by any one elite group, and an opening for multiple social actors who heretofore have been denied access to or entry into the discussions and sense making of corporate behavior, standards, and expectations. As such, information technologies have the potential to disrupt global West/non-West, North/South power relationships as well as create "new frontier zones" for rethinking the meanings and practices of global participation (Sassen, 2002).

However, it must be noted that in the context of the modern globalized communication environment, especially the compression of time and space and the rapid diffusion of ideas and knowledge through new technologies, there are many ironies surrounding CSR that continue to reinforce localized rather than glocalized frameworks. Despite ubiquitous, multichanneled, and instantaneous communication due to the availability of satellite, wired, and high-speed broadband capabilities that are capable of literally bringing the world to our desks, our automobile radios, our living rooms, or our cell phones, publics do not yet have the information needed as responsible citizens, nor do people typically make appropriate and timely use of the information that is available. News from abroad is not simply incomplete, it still focuses on the dramatic, violent, and episodic and does not bring into focus structural issues or needed changes, long-term trends, and inappropriate behavior unless it involves significant criminal charges, particularly to home-country corporations and executives. Thus, Union Carbide's environmental and human destruction in Bhopal 20 years ago is known within the United States, but few Americans are familiar with the enormous environmental destruction that Rio Tinto Zinc, a British company, has caused through its mining operations in Indonesia, Papua New Guinea, and elsewhere.

In the absence of immediate, local, and dramatic disasters, large, successful, and well-connected corporations are still able to control much of the "news" the public receives and launch highly successful strategic public communication campaigns. They take advantage of the same media-gathering routines that favor governments, incumbents in election campaigns, and well-liked celebrities with generally benign coverage framed by those that are covered rather than the journalists themselves. Corporations have also learned to use the media, oftentimes confounding news reports with public relations exercises, embracing and reframing CSR as good business. CSR Wire (an Internet news service) advertises itself as "the leading source of corporate responsibility and sustainability, press releases, reports and news" (CSR Wire, 2006). During an interview in *The Economist* (2005), Clive Crook describes how CSR has become big business, including executive programs in CSR, business school chairs in CSR, professional CSR organizations, CSR websites, CSR newsletters, and much more.

At the same time, much of the CSR literature within academic business literature continues to focus on the functionality that a CSR campaign can bring to a firm's success, and or the extent to which CSR publicity can enhance consumer practices. Consultancies have sprung up to advise companies on how to do CSR and how to let it be known that they are doing it. Most multinationals now have a senior executive explicitly charged with developing and coordinating the CSR function. But just as with the third generation of human rights, the existence of standards, and even the publicly acclaimed legitimacy of the framework, does not imply implementation or compliance. The proliferation of CSR discourse globally does not necessarily guarantee global CSR practices.

One of the challenges of third-generation CSR discourse remains the omnipresence of first-generation logic summed neatly in the word "profit"

and critiqued in such films as *The Corporation* (2003) and ENRON: *The Smartest Guys in the Room* (2005). In fact, the latter film explicitly chronicles the Enron debacle and displays the worst of corporate excess and greed using the very video and audio tapes made by the insiders themselves (clearly not anticipating the imminent downfall). It is the continued specter of profit that provides the fodder for documentary makers, activist organizations, and other NGOs as they work to expand their sphere of influence on behalf of a global CSR.

In addition to the films mentioned above, the global reorganization of work, perhaps best portrayed in popular discourse through the practices of outsourcing and offshoring, has become rich material for those visually theorizing the complexities of global CSR. For our purposes, outsourcing entails the dispersion of nonessential business tasks, including, for example, software development and implementation, administration and human resource functions, and customer service, to firms providing these services. The related offshoring entails the outsourcing of nonessential tasks to service providers in distant locales, as witnessed by the expansion of American corporation's offshoring to countries such as the Caribbean, Philippines, and India.

One of the central themes of both outsourcing and offshoring, particularly as portrayed in American media, involves the primacy of loss to industrialized nations' workers and the devaluation, disregard, or nonrecognition of the importance of the loss of cultural practices of indigenous populations. And it is in Thomas Friedman's recent Discovery channel documentary on the call center industry in Bangalore, *The Other Side of Offshoring* (2004), that we begin to witness the seemingly unproblematic celebration of American culture. The film depicts how Indian workers, particularly young women, are not only learning how to serve American customers but also learning to become consumers in their own right. With a new salary in hand, young Indian women are able to circumvent more traditional cultural expectations for their future, including marriage or familial obligations, by pursuing a career. At the same time, a problematic loss of cultural identity is embedded in this pursuit. Not only are they often asked to assume an American name and accent for use in customer service interactions in call center work, but they also learn to shop for American products in newly built malls replete with the global likes of Gap and Nike, not to mention eating practices commensurate with McDonald's or Pizza Hut. Their experiences demonstrate how with outsourcing come new work practices across time and space, as well as hybrid identities that transcend gender and cultural traditions. Yet, these impacts remain seemingly absent from U.S.-based discourse, at least until now.

Importantly, old and new media do have the capacity to open up and glocalize the discourses of outsourcing (see, e.g.,Viewpoint From India, 2006, and Outsource Reporter, 2006). This capacity to consider not just who (if at all) loses jobs and who gains them, but what price all sides pay for the alterations in the very first place, is at the very root of the new generation of global CSR. We can view the impact on India, for example, as Thomas Friedman does by celebrating how much the call center there looks like an American oasis. Or we could explore the impact that outsourcing has on the cultural practices of the indigenous population and the social, cultural, and political consequences that follow. The third generation of CSR goes beyond legal constraints on corporate moves (first generation) and issues related to what corporations must do for the workers who lose the jobs (second generation) and addresses what price societies pay for the jobs, recognizing that there is not necessarily a single winner and loser but a series of winners and losers arising out of the process over relatively short periods of time.

This emerging generation of global CSR considers short-term as well as long-term consequences and confronts the inevitable social dislocations for all constituencies affected by offshoring and outsourcing, as well. Ten years after the signing of NAFTA, when American labor was concerned with the loss of U.S. jobs and the flight of capital to Mexico, we find that the processes of outsourcing and offshoring have not ended in Mexico; nor will they stop in India. We now see that the shift of outsourced manufacturing jobs from the United States to northern Mexico and Central America is resulting, under the force of competition from China, in many Central American plants closing and the shifting of hundreds of thousands of Central American jobs to Chinese factories. The first wave of offshoring and the building of Central American factories created an enormous migration of young people to the new factories. It created whole new cities and a changed demography, a concentration in cities away from the countryside

(see Thompson, 2005). In fact, the global migration of peoples to the "global cities" has also contributed to a whole (invisible) service sector that underpins the global economy, including domestic laborers and hotel/restaurant/retail and sex workers (see Sassen, 2005). Yet, what happens now? Whose responsibility is it to assist them and their new communities? What are the implications at the global level? These are the very questions the third generation of CSR has the potential to address.

Third-Generation CSR Is No Longer the Province of Any One Organization, Particular Individuals, or Specific Interests but Rather Reflects the Complex Network of Organizational Relations Across Sectors

The new generation of CSR is emerging in response to the complex and interdependent nature of contemporary life. Globalization embodies the development, reconstitution, and intensification of communication networks among societies, cultures, institutions, and individuals across time and space. Global social capital is created, maintained, and dissolved in new types of organizational affiliations, public spaces, and loosely coupled networks. There are new forms of organization and models of leadership. As Monge and Contractor (2003) note: "These organizational and social forms . . . are built around material and symbolic flows that link people and objects both locally and globally without regard for traditional national, institutional, or organizational boundaries" (p. 4). Thus, the third generation of CSR must deal with hybrid organizational forms. Privatization has resulted not only in corporate forms addressing the civic needs that traditionally were met by public organizations but also in collaborations between different sectors. This melding of organizational types, structures, and functions creates several challenges for CSR.

For example, even in what have been referred to as the "welfare states," former public services such as health care and (un)employment agencies have opened their doors to private firms and providers. And while there have long been temporary help service agencies or labor market intermediaries besides the state, what some assert is different now is the extent of the mixing of organizational genres: "On the one hand, 'social' organizations now have to emulate the characteristics, norms and behaviors of the market. On the other hand, 'economic' organizations have begun to take on tasks once understood as public sector responsibilities" (Larner, 2002, p. 654). Indeed, the "reconfiguration of social government into an 'advanced liberal' form" continues to challenge the who and what of (corporate) responsibility (p. 660). Tracing the New Zealand state initiative to develop into a global call center region, Larner found that the state and Adecco, the private temporary service agency, together were responsible for the "building of a new industrial training regime" by running call center courses targeted at immigrants, single mothers, and long-term unemployed (p. 660). Her work confirms that of others who have traced the extensive role of temporary service agencies in managing human resources in concert with state agencies (Peck & Theodore, 2000; Townsley, 2002; Vosko, 2000).

The case of global restructuring at Ericsson also demonstrates the complexities of pointing the responsibility finger. Ericsson, a Swedish telecommunications multinational, engaged in a series of successive downsizing in locations across the globe starting in the late 1990s and continuing to the present day. What is fascinating about the unfolding of the restructuring process has been the network of firms—private/public, Swedish/American, and hybrids—that, taken together, constitute responsibility for laid off workers in Sweden. As compared to the United States' "at will" employment law, employees in Sweden have been protected not simply by a cultural ethos that frowns upon layoffs but also by the Security of Employment Act (see, for example, Neal, 1984) that condemns arbitrary dismissals. When economics do necessitate layoffs such was the case with Ericsson, the state, the unions, and other hybrid organizations, both profit and nonprofit, rallied to assist redundant workers in transitioning to alternative "solutions." In fact, this multiagent solution, also referred to as the "Norrköping model" after the southeastern Swedish town where the first round of production was halted, was later heralded as a cooperative, organizing genius of a program (see Townsley & Stohl, 2003).

The merging and restructuring of organizational forms are predicated on the fact that corporations today deal with problems and issues that cannot be addressed successfully by any one or-ganization or even a group of organizations alone (e.g., global warming and environmental protection, AIDS in the workplace, political instability and lawlessness). Thus, it is not surprising that with the broadening agenda and sets of expectations we see greater involvement of NGOs and international governmental organizations in discussions of CSR. There has been a recognition that many issues will not be solved unilaterally, bilaterally, or even regionally but rather require cooperation from these different types of global organizations. The development of corporate codes of conduct reflects this global perspective. In 1977, the Sullivan principles were developed by the Reverend Leon Sullivan. Originally inspired by the desire to counter apartheid and pressure U.S. corporations to behave responsibly in their investments and operations in South Africa, Reverend Sullivan carried the successful approach beyond South Africa and created the Global Sullivan Principles of Social Responsibility, thereby applying an expanded set of standards to global organizations operating anywhere.

Other types of organizations have also begun to invest in CSR. For instance, since 1999, the United Nations has urged corporations and nations to embrace the Global Compact, "a voluntary international corporate citizenship network initiated to support the participation of both the private sector and other social actors to advance responsible corporate citizenship and universal social and environmental principles to meet the challenges of globalization" (United Nations Procurement Service, 1999, ¶ 1). The United Nations' Global Compact is also complemented by NGOs formed to assist the corporate, government, and public sector in monitoring not only the inputs (responsible behaviors) but also the outputs (responsible results and impacts). Transparency International also informs corporations (and everyone else) about the climate for being a responsible and legal corporate citizen around the world. Social Accountability International, founded in 1996, seeks to go to the next level of CSR by creating and implementing voluntary standards through an accrediting process to certify qualified organizations worldwide. In an attempt to legitimate their approach, they have replicated the well-established, respected, and highly credible ISO standards process of the International Standards Institutes originally established for technology, engineering, manufacturing, and agriculture.

Another example of the way third-generation CSR has developed a global framework is to look briefly at movements focused against particular iconic corporations such as Nike, McDonalds, Coca-Cola, and Wal-Mart. These behemoth corporations often make the best targets even though they have the resources to be among the most powerful of opponents. By no means do they have to be the worst offenders in the particular corporate sector in which they operate. What these firms have in common is that the very strength of their branding makes mobilizing networks of consumers against them easier (Klein, 2002). For example, Nike became the corporate symbol (along with a few other apparel makers) for Students Against Sweatshops, UNITE, and various other NGOs interested in fighting sweatshops through boycotts, consumer campaigns, and monitoring activities. Nikewatch, like McSpotlight, Cokewatch, and Walmartwatch, through websites and organized activities both monitor the actions of these corporations and help mobilize a disparate set of NGOs, protest movements, and political activists in settings around the world through their ability to diffuse information and bring many unrelated organizations together.

The establishment of linkages between different sectors of society with third-generation CSR also grew out of a human rights case first submitted to the U.S. federal courts in 1979. *Filartiga v. Pena-Irala* (1980) was filed against a Paraguayan police inspector living in the United States. Pena-Irala was accused of torturing and killing the son of a Paraguayan dissident (Filartiga) in Paraguay. Relatives of the victim won a $10 million judgment, which, although never paid, reestablished the right to connect violations of international law to entities under U.S. jurisdiction. The case was based on the Alien Tort Claims Act passed by the first U.S. Congress 1789, in order to allow cases involving violations of the law of nations, or international law, to be heard in federal court. Using this legal (noncorporate) precedent, in *Wiwa v. Royal Dutch Petroleum Co.* (2000), a case was successfully brought against Shell Oil defendants for the executions of several Nigerians, including prominent author Ken Saro-Wiwa, arising out of disputes over the development of oil resources in the homeland of the Ogoni people. The plaintiffs charged that although it was the government of Nigeria that had tortured and executed the victims, these abuses were "instigated, orchestrated, planned, and facilitated by Shell Nigeria under the direction of the defendants," who were said to have "provided money, weapons, and logistical support to the Nigerian military . . . , participated in the fabrication of murder charges . . . , and bribed witnesses to give testimony" (p. 3). More recently, the U.S. Ninth Circuit Court of Appeals in *Doe I v. Unocal Corp.* (2002) held that a corporation may be liable as an aide and abettor of human rights abuses carried out by the Myanmar government along a natural gas pipeline route being built in Myanmar on the company's "knowing practical assistance [or] encouragement . . . which has a substantial effect on the perpetration of the crime" (p. 5). In the last few years, these judgments against the corporations have produced conflicting responses by corporations. On the one hand, they have lobbied and fought in the courts against the application of the law (a struggle they are currently losing in the post-Enron environment) and have worked diligently to try to counter the attendant publicity, publicity that is much greater because the cases are tried in American courts; on the other hand, they have had in the interim to accept the consequences and to readjust to the realities of their new legal liability.

What is critical here is that what started as a creative use of an old law to seek legal redress has, in the March 2005 settlement of the damages in *Unocal*, developed into an attempt by the corporation to demonstrate third-generation responsibility. The corporation is providing not only compensation for the villagers but also funds "to develop programs to improve living conditions, healthcare and education and protect the rights of people from the pipeline region" (see Lifsher, 2005).

Third-Generation CSR Recognizes the Permeability of Public/Private Boundaries

The intensification of linkages across social domains, embedded in each global dynamic, has greatly influenced the evolution of the third generation of CSR in very compelling ways. We see, for example, exponential growth of NGOs that reflect personal interests, individuals' expressions of social values, and even much of their economic activity. These private-interest, value-based organizations are increasing their participation and involvement in what has traditionally been the governmental or corporate sphere. Volunteers and private citizens with strong ideological commitments work side by side with professional managers who may or may not share their political values and social orientation but who nonetheless collaborate on issues related to their communities and social responsibility.

One of the most significant byproducts of the changing communication patterns and content within and across organizational domains is that it has blurred what were previously taken-for-granted distinctions between public and private experiences and obscured the boundaries among local, national, and global spheres of influence. Industrialization brought with it rigid distinctions and barriers between the private and public domains and the belief that these spheres of action operate independently, each with its own set of autonomous conditions, structures, and strictures, what has often been referred to as the "myth of separate worlds" (Stohl, 1995). Today, not only are experiential and national boundaries becoming less delimited, but also the development of new communication technologies has made private and public domains more porous and more easily crossed than ever before (Bimber, Flanagin, & Stohl, 2005). This disembedding of human interaction from local to distributed contexts, facilitated by the Internet, blogging, and sharing of personal files online, has serious import for the development of CSR. As Bimber et al. (2005) note:

> As individuals are able to move more seamlessly between private and public domains, the structure of public domains themselves is altered. Previous factors defining public-ness, such as the family, the community, and the state, become less influential in circumscribing public domains when people's individual public-private boundaries are weakened. This permits the constitution of public spheres around common interests that may join people in disparate regions of the globe. So indeed we find examples of collective action aimed at the status of poor children in all countries, that favor clean air everywhere, or that advance human rights in many locations. (p. 27)

Third-generation CSR addresses myriad, complex, and overlapping activities and issues that heretofore were considered private, not public, matters. One example of the contemporary blurring of private and public domains is the context of work. The evolving international division of labor is clearly influenced by expanding corporate power, but there remains an informal sector that, while figuratively hidden from much public discourse as well as literally hidden in people's homes, restaurant kitchens, and brothels around the globe, provides the necessary services that allow elite workers to do their work without changing diapers or washing laundry. And it is this informal service sector that poses unique challenges to first- and second-generation CSR.

As Jaggar (2002) argues, global neoliberalism is maintained through a system of Northern creditors and Southern debtors that produces "global indentured servitude" of the South for the North. It is the gendering of the North–South relationship that has produced a complex industry of care, or commodified love. Nannies, sex workers, and maids make up the occupational types most often associated with care work (see Ehrenreich & Russell, 2003). The combination of sex typing of these jobs as "women's work" and the migratory patterns of women who travel the globe for work make the commodified love industry a fertile context for the abuse of women's human rights that is relatively hard to chart and monitor. But it is precisely the dispersed and fragmented nature, as well as multiactor enterprise, that demands a third-generation CSR analysis.

Women increasingly leave their families behind to migrate to jobs that will enable them to send remittances to their homeland, to become the breadwinner in otherwise depressed states. In fact, many governments actually encourage the migratory patterns of female labor for international care work (e.g., nurses, nannies, and sex workers) for just this reason—national income. In addition to the nation-state, corporations also foster gendered labor patterns of care, particularly as ex-patriots and the mobile workforce who travel the globe demand services such as child care and domestic help that then allows them to work on the run and abroad. And while nanny work has expanded greatly from state- and corporate-sponsored programs across the globe, the industry continues to function informally, as well, thus making it more complex to track and trace CSR trends as well as abuses in this hybrid public/private care industry.

CONCLUSIONS

Just as the major advances in human rights can be traced to major upheavals such as the Glorious

Revolution of 1688, the American and French Revolutions of the late eighteenth century, and the devastation of World Wars I and II, many of the advances in the assertion of the need for CSR and the attendant rights and obligations associated with CSR have occurred in the aftermath of major changes, disasters, and confrontations in global and civil society. The dynamic and volatile processes of globalization have strongly influenced the trajectory of CSR at the end of the twentieth and into the twenty-first century.

In this chapter, we have demonstrated how a consideration of CSR within a global framework helps us to better understand its evolution and impact over time. Our discussion of Enron showed how interest in corporate irresponsibility abroad might well have alerted us to the impending troubles to come long before this decade's debacle. Exploring the three generations of CSR, placing the concerns within a global perspective, and recognizing the interconnectedness between domains of social life have enabled us to identify and situate the emerging concerns and potential impacts of the changing nature of CSR. This also revealed some of the theoretical and pragmatic challenges of developing CSR standards and norms within this new global context.

There have been great strides in CSR development in the past few decades. The idea itself has been legitimated, moving beyond simply defining responsibility as upholding the law. But just as with the development of human rights standards, the existence and recognition of the legitimacy of the standards and the claims of the rights does not imply their consistent or continuing implementation or even their continuing acceptance as the appropriate norms. And just as the full blossoming of the human rights NGO community came after the victory of the creation of the Universal Declaration of Human Rights as the NGOs expanded their efforts at monitoring, mobilizing, and acquiring resources to assist in the implementation of rights, we should expect further development of a global CSR regime consisting of activist organizations, governments, and corporations based on a dramatic expansion of their interactions and their work. In the context of globalization and global corporate and NGO actors, it is only with a global perspective and global approach that we can truly understand and approach CSR as scholars and practitioners.

NOTES

1. Noncompliance with environmental standards, violations of loan conditions, dubious and misleading accounting procedures, and political scandals associated with corporate coercion regarding Enron's Cuiaba project in Bolivia, Ecopetrol scandal in Colombia, and Elektro generator project in Brazil, among others, were reported as early as 1994 (see, for example, CEADES, 2002, and Amazon Watch, 2006). For a full accounting of Enron's illegal activities and dubious financial accounting worldwide, see Grimaldi (2002).

2. This primacy of first-generation thinking is visible in U.S. law on human rights, which holds the government accountable for its interactions with foreign governments when such persist in a pattern of gross violations of human rights, by which are meant violations of civil and political rights, not economic, social, and cultural rights (see Carleton & Stohl, 1985). Further, the creation of legal standards for behaviors outside the country such as the Foreign Corrupt Practices Act (1977) was intended to prevent bribery of foreign officials by U.S. corporations, but no legislation exists that requires U.S. corporations to pay a "living or minimum wage" when operating outside the territorial boundaries of the United States.

REFERENCES

Amazon Watch. (2006). Retrieved October 15, 2006, from http://www.amazonwatch.org/newsroom/view_news.php?id=187.

Amnesty International. (1997). The "Enron Project" in Maharashtra: Protests suppressed in the name of development. Retrieved October 1, 2005, from http://web.amnesty.org/library/Index/ENGASA200311997?open&of=ENG-IND.

Apodaca, C., Stohl, M., & Lopez, G. A. (1998). Moving norms to political reality: Institutionalizing human rights standards through the United Nations system. In C. F. Alger (Ed.), *The future of the United Nations system* (pp. 185–221). New York: United Nations University Press.

Barnett, R. J., & Muller, R. (1974). *Global reach*. New York: Simon & Schuster.

Bimber, B., Flanagin, A., & Stohl, C. (2005). Reconceptualizing collective action in the contemporary media environment. *Communication Theory, 15*(4), 365–388.

BusinessWeek. (2001, December 3). Energy crisis. Retrieved February 6, 2006, from http://www.businessweek.com/magazine/toc/01_49/B3760magazine.htm.

Carleton, D., & Stohl, M. (1985). The foreign policy of human rights: Rhetoric and reality from Jimmy Carter to Ronald Reagan. *Human Rights Quarterly, 7*(2), 205–229.

CEADES (Collectivo de Estudos Aplicados al Desarrollo Social). (2002). Enron's Operations in Bolivia. Retrieved October 15, 2006, from http://www.eca-watch.org/problems/americas/bolivia/enron_bolivia .html.

Chandler, G. (2001, Autumn). Introduction: Defining corporate social responsibility. *Ethical Performance Best Practices.* Retrieved February 6, 2006, from http://www.ethicalperformance.com/bestpractice/archive/1001/introduction .html.

Chattarjee, P. (2001, December 17). Enron: Pulling the plug on the global power broker. *Corpwatch.* Retrieved February 6, 2006, from http://www.corpwatch.org/.

Cruver, B. (2002). *Anatomy of greed.* New York: Carrol & Graf Publishers.

CSR Wire. (2006). Retrieved February 6, 2006, from http://www.csrwire.com/about /.

Doe I v. Unocal Corp., Nos. 00-56603, 00-57197, 2002 U.S. App. LEXIS 19263 (9th Cir. Sept. 18, 2002). Retrieved February 6, 2006, from http://slomanson.tjsl.edu/Unocal.pdf.

The Economist. (2005, January 20). The good company [Interview with Clive Crook]. Retrieved February 6, 2006, from http://www.charleswarner.us/articles/EconomistTheGoodCompany.htm.

Ehrenreich, B., & Russell, A. (2003). *Global woman: Nannies, maids, and sex workers in the new economy.* New York: Metropolitan Books.

Eichenwald, K. (2005). *Conspiracy of fools.* New York: Random House, Broadway Books.

Enron, (2001). Enron named most innovative for the sixth year. Retrieved October 15, 2004, from http://www.enron.com/corp/pressroom/releases/2001/ene/docs/15-MostInnovative-02-06-01-LTR.pdf.

Filatiga v. Pena-Irala (2d Cir. June 30, 1980). Retrieved February 6, 2006, from http://www.icrc.org/ihl-nat.nsf/46707c419d6bdfa24125673e00508145/27721c1b47e7ca90c1256d18002a2565?OpenDocument.

Friedman, M. (1970, September 13). The social responsibility of business is to increase its profits. New York Times Magazine. Retrieved February 6, 2006, from http://www.colorado.edu/studentgroups/libertarians/issues/friedman-soc-resp-business.html.

Friedman, T., & Levis, K. (Producers). (2004). *The other side of offshoring* [Documentary]. Available from the Discovery Channel. Retrieved October 2006 from http://shopping.discovery.com/product-56037.html?jzid=40588040-0-0.

Giddens, A. (1991). *Modernity and self-identity: Self and society in the late modern age.* Cambridge: Polity Press.

Griffiths, N. (2004). *Speech by Nigel Griffiths MP, Minister for Corporate and Social Responsibility. Thursday 7 October 2004. 10.5am—DTI Conference Centre.* Retrieved February 15, 2006, from http://www.societyandbusiness.gov.uk/pdf/Internatinal_Strategic_Framework_CSR_7_October .pdf.

Grimaldi, J. V. (2002, February 16). Enron spanned the globe with high-risk projects: Deals lost money but helped hide troubles. *The Washington Post,* p.A1. Retrieved March 1, 2006, from http://www.seen.org/pages/media/20020216_washpost.htm.

Human Rights Watch. (1999).The Enron Corporation: Corporate complicity in human rights violations. Retrieved October 15, 2005, from http://www.hrw.org/reports/1999/enron/.

Jaggar, A. M. (2002). A feminist critique of the alleged Southern debt. In B. Christensen, A. Baum, S. Blättler, A. Kusser, I. M. Marti, & B. Weisshaupt (Eds.), *Knowledge, power, gender: Philosophy and the future of the <condition féminine>* (pp. 19–40). Zürich: Chronos Verlag.

Klein, N. (2002). *No logo: No space, no choice, no jobs.* New York: Picador.

Krugman, P. (2000, December 10). California screaming. *New York Times.* Retrieved February 6, 2006, from http://www.pkarchive.org/column/121000.html.

Larner, W. (2002). Globalization, governmentality and expertise: Creating a call centre labour force. *Review of International Political Economy, 9*(4), 650–674.

Lifsher, M. (2005). Unocal settles human rights lawsuit over alleged abuses at Myanmar Pipeline. *Los Angeles Times.* March 22. Retrieved February 6, 2006, from http://www.truthout.org/docs_2005/032305L .shtml.

Lippmann, W. (1922). *Public opinion.* New York: Harcourt, Brace & Co. Retrieved February 6, 2006, from http://xroads .virginia.edu/~Hyper2/CDFinal/Lippman/cover.html.

Marks, S. (2004). The human right to development: Between rhetoric and reality. *Harvard Human Rights Journal, 17,* 137–168.

McLean, B., & Elkind, P. (2003). *The smartest guys in the room*. New York: Penguin.

Monge, P., & Contractor, N. (2003). *Theories of communication networks*. Oxford: Oxford University Press.

Outsource Reporter. (2006). Retrieved February 1, 2006 from http://www.outsourcereporter.com/.

Neal, A. C. (1984). Employment protection laws: The Swedish model. International and *Comparative Law Journal, 33*, 634–662.

Oppel, R. (2002, February 11). Enron's many strands: The overview. *New York Times*, p. A1.

Parry, S. (2001). Enron's India disaster. *Consortium News.com*. Retrieved April 22, 2005, from http//www.rense.com/general119/enfi.

Peck, J., & Theodore, N. (2000). "Work first": Workfare and the regulation of contingent labour markets. *Cambridge Journal of Economics, 24*, 119–138.

Robertson, R. (1990). Mapping the global condition: Globalization as the central concept. *Theory, Culture & Society, 7*, 15–30.

Robertson, R. (1992). *Globalization: Social theory and global culture*. London: Sage.

Sassen, S. (2002). Towards a sociology of information technology. *Current Sociology, 50*, 365–388

Sassen, S. (2005). The global city: Introducing a concept. *Brown Journal of World Affairs, 11*, 27–43.

Scholte, J. (2000). *Globalization: A critical introduction*. New York: St. Martin's Press.

Sharp, K. (2002, March 3). Price gouging inquiries target Enron. *The Boston Globe*. Retrieved February 6, 2006, from http://www.Kathleensharp.com/BostonGlobeEnron.

Stohl, C. (1995). *Organizational communication: Connectedness in action*. Thousand Oaks, CA: Sage.

Stohl, C. (2005). Globalization theory. In S. May & D. Mumby (Eds.), *Engaging organizational communication theory and research: Multiple perspectives* (pp. 223–261). Thousand Oaks, CA: Sage.

Swarts, M., & Watkins, S. (2003). *Power failure: The rise and fall of Enron*. Cornwall, UK: Aurum Press.

Thompson, G. (2005). Fraying of a Latin textile industry. New York Times, March 25. Retrieved February 6, 2006, from http://www.nytimes.com/2005/03/25/business/worldbusiness/25textile.html.

Townsley, N. C. (2002). *A discursive approach to embedded gender relations in (Swedish) global restructuring*. Unpublished doctoral dissertation, Purdue University.

Townsley, N. C., & Stohl, C. (2003). Contracting corporate responsibility: Swedish expansions in global temporary agency work. *Management Communication Quarterly, 16*, 599–605.

United Nations. (1945). *UN charter*. Retrieved February 6, 2006, from http://www.un.org/aboutun/charter/.

United Nations (1948). Universal Declaration of Human Rights, adopted and proclaimed by General Assembly resolution 217 A (III) of 10 December 1948. Retrieved February 6, 2006, from http://www.un.org/Overview/rights.html.

United Nations Procurement Service. (1999). *Global compact*. Retrieved February 6, 2006, from http://www.un.org/Depts/ptd/global.htm.

Viewpoint From India: An IT Outsourcing Blog. (2006). Retrieved February 1, 2006, from http://blogs.ittoolbox.com/emergingtech/outsourcing.

Vosko, L. (2000). *Temporary work: The gendered rise of a precarious employment relationship*. Toronto: University of Toronto Press.

Wiwa v. Royal Dutch Petroleum Co., Nos. 99–7223[L], 99-7245[XAP 2000 (2nd Cir. Sept. 14, 2000) Retrieved October 15, 2006 from http://www.earthrights.org/files/Legal%20Docs/Wiwa%20v%20Shell/appeal.pdf.

Wysham, D., & Vallette, J. (2002, April 11). How government and international agencies used taxpayers money to bankroll the energy giant's international investments. *CorpWatch*. Retrieved February 1, 2006 from http://www.corpwatch.org/article.php?id=2279.

3

Progressing from Corporate Social Responsibility to Brand Integrity

MALCOLM MCINTOSH

The decade from 1995 to 2005 was significant for corporate social responsibility (CSR). The year 2005 was 10 years since Shell's annus horribilis and their debacle over the disposal of the Brent Spar oil rig in the North Sea and 10 years since they were implicated in the death of Ken Saro-Wiwa, a Nigerian human rights activist who was murdered by his government for protesting about the distribution of revenues from what was perceived to be Shell's damaging extrication of oil from the Ogoni region of Nigeria. This decade also saw the flowering of the Global Reporting Initiative (www.globalreporting.org), out of the CERES Principles (www.ceres.org), the development of workplace management systems certification (SA8000), the birth of AccountAbility (www.accountability21.net) and sustainability management systems assurance (AA1000S) out of the Institute for Social and Ethical Accountability, and the first five years of the United Nations Global Compact (www.unglobalcompact.org). In this chapter, I chart the development of some key ideas and initiatives in the CSR movement in the last decade or so and then suggest a new way forward for a movement that is looking for new directions.

Most pertinent to this chapter is the ongoing debate concerning the links between business profitability and global social progress. While the business benefits of CSR are a topic much debated and written about, it needs to be reiterated over and over again that business operates for the benefits of society, not vice versa. There can never solely be a *business* benefit from CSR—that is the ususal sense—but rather asocietal and ecological benefit in the widest sense. If a minority gain net material wealth in the short term at the gross expense of society and the planet in the short, medium, or long term, what real benefit is that? The only reason to argue the case for the business benefits from CSR is to make the case for business being more socially and ecologically responsible if we are to create a more just and equitable world that uses and shares resources for the benefit of this and future generations.

What, then, is the CSR agenda, and what has it achieved over the last decade or so? This question is linked to a number of significant reports from reputable research organizations that argue the case for CSR and profitability. Next, I discuss some thoughts on the link between capitalism and social progress. This is followed by an exploration of new territory, which argues that the emphasis should move from *corporate* social responsibility to *brand integrity*—but in an expanded sense of the term. Indeed, a link is made between the integrity of decision makers and consumers and the integrity of corporations via the integrity of their brands.

While good progress has been made on a number of corporate responsibility initiatives over the last decade, they have not been as successful as they might have been because we have failed to understand that in the modern global corporation we have created a being over which we have less control than we would like to think. It is recognized that many of its agents have the best of intentions; however, because the corporation itself has a life of its own, these agents have less control than is sometimes recognized. The current rules of incorporation tend to steer the organization away from necessarily delivering social progress and protecting our planetary home. Here, then, in this chapter, is a prescription for the profitable, human-scale corporation that operates in tune with social progress and in harmony with planetary boundaries by connecting with all stakeholders through profound brand integrity.

Having established some of the conditions within which the CSR discourse is conducted, this chapter moves on to a new social responsibility agenda. I argue that while new incorporation rules are an absolute necessity, social responsibility lies with us all, not just the corporation. Here brand and integrity are linked. Brands are in fact owned by us all, although we are accustomed to associating them with narrower private concerns and images. They are ubiquitous and more democratic than corporations. What can be said about *brand integrity*? How might we go about measuring the social and ecological footprint of brands (rather than just corporations), as well as their financial performance? This requires a multidisciplinary approach that draws on complexity and systems thinking as well as social network approaches. Is it possible to apply to such brands as the United Nations, the BBC, and Oxfam the same "loyalty without reason" that is applied to the billions of annual sales of Dove soap, Coke, and M&Ms?

SETTING THE SCENE

The CSR agenda has been described as "a desire and a necessity to humanize the globalization process; to build social and environmental pillars in the global temple of commerce" (McIntosh, Waddock, & Kell, 2004, p. 13). John Ruggie, former Assistant Secretary-General of the United Nations and now Director of the Centre for Business and Government at Harvard University and, since 2005, special advisor to the United Nations Secretary-General on CSR, has pointed out that "[b]usiness created the single global economic space; business can and must help sustain it. And CSR offers one viable and vital approach" (Ruggie, 2003, p. 41). So is the CSR agenda attempting to put capitalism back in line with social progress? This begs the question that the currently dominant model of capitalism is currently out of line with social progress. Has the creation of global markets reached all of the world's peoples? Should we be celebrating a "marketized" world to which everyone has access, where everyone has equal opportunities, where everyone can enjoy clean water and access to the Internet and a choice of 20 fast-food outlets in their neighborhood?

The CSR movement has been resurgent over the last 10 years, and multistakeholder engagement, among business, government, and civil society, has resulted in a significant number of global voluntary corporate citizenship initiatives. Nongovernmental public action, or civil society activism, has been at the heart of the development of a number of these initiatives. The field of CSR and corporate citizenship has developed significantly (Andriof & McIntosh, 2001; Waddock, 2002). There are those who argue that *voluntary* mechanisms have replaced or prevented regulatory initiatives and therefore set back real corporate responsibility. Examples of significant global voluntary corporate citizenship initiatives include ethical workplace management systems certification (SA8000); sustainability management systems assurance (AA1000S); learning platforms based on international conventions on human rights, labor standards, environmental protection, and anticorruption (United Nations, 2005); and the standardization of reporting on corporate financial, social, and environmental reporting (Global Reporting Initiative). These have been referred to as four of the "Global Eight" (McIntosh, 2003a, pp. 86–123).

These particular initiatives have been fostered through "new social partnerships" between business and civil society organizations in multistakeholder dialogues (Zadek & Nelson, 2000). Two strands of research literature have emerged around concepts of partnership and stakeholding. Through multistakeholder engagement, often embodied in new social partnerships, the focus has been on sharing difference and celebrating diverse opinions while attempting to find consensus among different actors. In many cases, this has led to radical reappraisals as participants have learned to *listen* as well as talk (Andriof, Waddock, Husted, & Rahman, 2002;

Kunugi & Schweitz, 1999; Tennyson & Wilde, 2000; Wheeler & Sillanpaa, 1998). So, *has* the world been learning to listen *and* talk? (Cragg, 2003; Leipziger, 2004; McIntosh, 2003a, 2003b; McIntosh et al., 2004).

The global corporate responsibility movement operates in the context of an increasing expansion of trade, albeit substantially between a relatively small group of global, often supraterritorial corporations. Both the corporate world and civil society activists have been aided by dramatic changes in communications technology that have democratized information flows and empowered even the smallest community organization. This trend we see plainly in the network organizations that have arisen in movements as diverse as the environmental movement, global health campaigns, and human rights advocacy.

It is common to argue that the United States is the only superpower, but increasingly the corporate responsibility debate has to recognize growing differentiation between the United States and much of Europe on social and market issues. Also, sitting quietly at every table in every board room, on every university campus, and in every manufacturing plant is the presence of China. Economic realignments are afoot that we are only beginning to understand and these will inevitably affect the way we do business and reform corporate capitalism.

The literature on globalization falls into three camps: the largely analytical (Bauman, 1998; Beck, 2002; Giddens, 2001; Hardt & Negri, 2000), the chiefly celebratory (Micklethwait & Woolridge, 2000), and the highly critical (Ali, 2002; Booth & Dunne, 2002; Chua, 2003; Gray, 2003; Stiglitz, 2002). But while there is an implicit and explicit understanding that the modern world has come about through the expansion of trade, the development of technology, and the growth of global corporations, it is corporations that have increasingly been held to account for the social and environmental impacts of their financial performance (Balkan, 2004; Korten, 1995; Zadek, Pruzan, & Evans, 1997). The cases of Shell, McDonald's, Nike, and Starbucks (discussed elsewhere in this book) are but a few examples.

Issues of *continental* territoriality are juxtaposed by a *global* clash of fundamentalisms between religious and political orthodoxy versus tolerance and conviviality and by rampant consumer consumption versus efforts to establish sustainable capitalism that recognizes Earth's carrying capacities and the delicate nature of human development. Also, the current model has not been wholly inclusive, such that the wealth disparity between the developed and the developing worlds is increasing year after year. How we see the world is changing as we face up to the environmental imperative. Wolfgang Sachs of the Wuppertal Institute has said: "Eventually, the world will no longer be divided by the ideologies of 'left' and 'right,' but by those who accept ecological limits and those who don't" (Sachs, 2005).

CSR AND PROFITABILITY?

CSR is not a new subject for discussion: certainly the discussion that links social responsibility and profitability has not arisen just in the last decade. It is possible to prove that there is a direct link, and there are now many sources that new inquirers can reference. For instance, in 1998 I wrote, in *Corporate Citizenship*: "This book outlines the social responsibility issues facing businesses. The companies profiled (here) have recognized that having a social responsibility strategy has made them more competitive" (McIntosh, 1998, p. xix). An award-winning study published in 2001 by Michael King, then with KPMG, in the *Journal of Corporate Citizenship* said: "The study finds that companies can deliver across multiple objectives. Indeed, aggregate performance of 'sustainable' companies is better than their peers and relevant market indices over a five-year period" (King, 2001, p. 99).

In more recent years, SustainAbility and the United Nations Environment Programme published *Buried Treasure* (2005), in which they identified 10 reasons for believing that the links between sustainable development performance and business success will grow stronger. The Dow Jones Sustainability Index (2005) makes the same point: "Corporate sustainability leaders achieve long-term shareholder value by gearing their strategies and management to harness the market's potential for sustainability products and services while at the same time successfully reducing and avoiding sustainability costs and risks." The World Economic Forum (2005) has conducted similar studies and found that:

[t]he *Business Case for Corporate Citizenship* explains that good corporate citizenship can

provide benefits . . . and identifies ways that increased corporate citizenship can improve business performance. Real-life examples of the consequences for companies that have invested in or ignored key aspects of corporate citizenship are also presented.

A more specific study conducted by Claude Fussler and colleagues from the World Business Council for Sustainable Business on the link between signatories to the United Nations Global Compact and profitability concluded in 2004:

> It is a fact that if I had bought the 76 shares of the GCS76 in October 2001 instead of the shares of a larger group I would be 1.1% better off at the end of 2003. As a group, the Global Compact signatories created more value. The goals of sustainability, the challenges of social responsibility and leadership's inspiration by principles higher than the sole profit motivation—they all foster business excellence. (Fussler, 2004, p. 282)

However, as accurate and convincing all these and other studies are at proving a direct link between CSR and profitability, the research also indicates specific characteristics of companies that have been proactive on CSR. First, these companies tend to be in sectors that have become targets of protesting consumer, community, or environmental activist groups. In the 1970s and 1980s this involved the chemical industry, in the 1990s the extractive industries, and perhaps now in the 2000s pressure is particularly focused on the pharmaceutical sector. Second, proactive CSR companies specifically tend to have inspired, values-led senior management in the board room—leadership from the top. Third, they engage in sophisticated and well-financed stakeholder engagement; in other words, they tend to be more "intelligent" by virtue of establishing methodologies for listening and responding to a wide range of stakeholder concerns. Fourth, as a result of the above, these proactive CSR companies have become part of the ongoing dialogue about voluntary and regulatory CSR initiatives around the world. They are as active in the debate as are trade unions and civil society groups. But the debate continues, and a firm link is still to be made between CSR and the delivery of the United Nations Millennium Goals.

CAPITALISM AND SOCIAL PROGRESS?

The promise of the CSR advocacy is that it will civilize corporate behavior so that there is an alignment between capitalism and social progress. While recognizing that some companies were making great efforts in this direction, United Nations Secretary-General Kofi Annan also said, when addressing global business leaders meeting in New York in July 2004 to discuss progress on the United Nations Global Compact: "Symbolism is good, but substance is even better" (Annan, 2004).

In September 2004, the World Bank issued a report on just this issue, which said:

> The growing integration of societies and economies has helped reduce poverty in many countries. Between 1990 and 2000 the number of people living on less than $1 a day declined by about 137 million. Although global integration is a powerful force in reducing poverty, more needs to be done. . . . [Two] billion people are in danger of becoming marginal to the world economy.

So, some progress is being made, perhaps because of new global corporate citizenship initiatives like the United Nations Global Compact, which asks companies to "embrace, support and enact, within their sphere of influence, a set of core values in the areas of human rights, labour standards, the environment, and anti-corruption" (United Nations, 2005).

CHANGE ISSUES

But is the CSR movement asking companies to lead social change on social and environmental issues? Recent research on behavior change in the United Kingdom related to sustainable development published by the U.K. government shows an alarming failure to educate people on these issues. Only one-third of the U.K. population has heard of sustainable development, and only 8% are able or willing to explain it. If companies are being called upon to embed, for instance, the 10 principles of the United Nations Global Compact on human rights, labor standards, and environmental protection in their workforce, are we asking them to do what government has failed to do across wider society? (Department for Food, Environment and Rural Affairs UK, 2005). Similar findings can be found across Europe.

So how is business progressing on these issues? According to the international Association of Certified Chartered Accountants (ACCA) in September 2004: "Businesses worldwide are failing to produce enough sustainability reports, while governments are doing little to encourage such reporting. There are still only 1,500 to 2,000 companies producing reports worldwide. The majority of companies still have to recognize the business case for reporting and starting to engage their stakeholders."

Is this perhaps because the challenges of sustainable development, human rights, and labor standards are not uppermost in the minds of CEOs? Also in September 2004, the U.S. Conference Board (business membership and research organization) reported that a global survey of CEOs showed that they had four challenges, none of which included the CSR agenda: sustained growth; speed, flexibility, and adaptability to change; customer loyalty and retention; and stimulating innovation and creativity and enabling entrepreneurship (Conference Board, 2004).

A clear differentiation occurs between those companies that are proactive in CSR and others. The proactive groups have tended, until this point, to be global and have similar characteristics, which were outlined above. The exception to this is the set of U.N. Global Compact signatory companies, 60% of whom now come from countries that are not members of the Organisation of Economic Co-operation and Development and are not the usual supporters of CSR initiatives. But apart from the proactive group, there are three other groups of corporate "citizens": those from the informal and illegal sectors that actively avoid paying taxes, compliance, and incorporation; the vast majority of the small to medium sized enterprise sector who try hard to comply with the law and establish good relations with their local customers; and a group of discretionary companies that are in compliance with all aspects of the law but have also chosen to be proactive in one or more areas of CSR, such as the environment or human rights (McIntosh et al., 2004). These categories are not necessarily exclusive, and there are some companies that have been radically proactive on CSR issues, such as Enron, Parmalat, and Shell, who have subsequently been found wanting on issues of transparency and integrity in the board room.

Interestingly, while there is differentiation in the originating culture in which a corporation is based, when it comes to issues of integrity there may be no difference between one board room and another. As Roger Adams of ACCA has said:

> Immediately after Enron, the widely held European view was that the US "rules based" culture acted as an incentive to commit fraud rather than as a deterrent against it. We heard a great deal in the UK about the superiority of "principles based approaches". But ultimately, fraud pays no heed to the existence of either rules or principles. (Adams, 2004)

However honest and upright board members of major corporations are, it may be that they serve false corporate masters that bend toward delivering profit at the expense of caring for communities and planet. It is not that these board members do not recognize that society and business are best run on a vision of value *and* values; it is that the former predicates and dominates discussion on the viability of the corporation. Commercial barrister Warren Evans and others have argued that this is because on a fateful day in October 1856, "*artificial personality* was born, and the foundation of modern corporations was laid down" (Evans, 2003, p. 98). Why is it, he asks, that corporations have unlimited mortality and can expand to unlimited size when real personalities, you and I, cannot? Have we not created a monster (Evans, 2003, p.98)? Joel Bakan, co-author of the book and the film *The Corporation*, goes further and talks about "the psychopathic nature of modern business, in which the lunatics have taken over the asylum and have big plans for us all" (Bakan, 2004, p. 1).

But the news from board rooms suggests not that it is the people in the board room that are psychopaths but that the business model tends toward psychopathology. Yve Newbold served on the boards of many significant U.K. organizations. She reports that:

> People are surprised when I tell them that in twenty years in the boardroom (nine at Hanson Plc as Company Secretary, seven at BT and three at Coutts Bank UK as a non executive

director) not once do I recall a discussion on the moral or ethical implications of any decision made by those boards. . . . [But she continues] That is not to say either that the decisions taken during those years were unethical or that the people making them lacked an ethical frame of reference in deciding as they did. It was simply that the language of the boardroom was finance and the focus was primarily the interests of the shareholder. (Newbold, 2002, p. 13)

Boardroom discussions tend, because of the necessity to remain financially viable, to serve investors with a single bottom line, despite efforts to give equal worth to a "triple bottom line" of financial, social, and environmental performance and impact. The company that lays waste an area of land or lays off its workforce can stay in business if it remains financially viable, assuming it is in compliance and has credit, customers, suppliers, and some employees. But the reverse is not true.

INTEGRITY AND THE WHOLE PICTURE

Economist Kenneth Galbraith said in 1978: "Nothing disguises the reality of economic life more than that there is a single theory of the firm. . . . There is also confusion between the market and the corporation, they are not the same . . . they are all parts of the political economy" (Galbraith & Salinger, 1978, p. 37). More recently, in 2004, Klaus Leisinger from the Novartis Foundation, when writing of the links between business and human rights, said that it was

> a feature of modern society to differentiate into a variety of functionally specialized subsystems, such as economy, law, politics, religion, science, and education. . . . The quality of cooperation of the different subsystems determines the degree of possible synergies and allows for the whole (society) being more than the sum of its parts (subsystems). (Leisinger, 2004, p. 77)

So, let me introduce here the multidimensional concept of integrity. Integrity is an enormously useful reference point because it encapsulates the morality of individual decision makers as well as the well-being of the corporate body. The *Oxford English Dictionary* says that integrity has three linked meanings: the quality of being honest and

morally upright, the state of being whole or unified, and soundness of construction. It is the soundness of construction on the part of both the individual and the corporation that is most interesting because in our society there is a tendency to reduce things to their component parts and to fail to see the whole or to contextualize situations.

THE CORPORATION HAS A LIFE OF ITS OWN . . .

The emphasis must be on seeing corporations as entities in their own right over which we do not have as much control as we would like to think. When viewed as a complex adaptive system, with biocharacteristics, the corporation can be seen to have a life of its own. We have given it life by virtue of incorporation law, which created *artificial personality*. The problem of controlling such an organ is that its behavior will necessarily be self-serving. As corporate governance expert Robert Monks wrote in 1988:

> The basic program of the corporations as self-seeking entities wars against the interests of human beings. Yet the living "complexity" of corporations—their tendency towards multiplicity, spontaneity, accommodation, adaptability, transformation, and metamorphosis—links corporations to us humans . . . for we too are complex adaptive systems. (p. 190)

Many will recognize that surviving corporations are dynamic, seemingly chaotic, innovative, opportunistic, and transitory. In the field of CSR, these corporations have a range of complex noncorporate relationships involving diverse values within various social networks where the key dynamic is trust and love as social glue and where people and environment have worth. From this comes a nondeterministic view of the corporation where there is no clear view of the future. Multistakeholder engagement can be viewed as a form of complex behavior where dialogue is a form of organization, or an organizing principle, in itself. Doreen Massey (1999) has suggested that instead of thinking of organizations (and I would suggest, brands) as places, it would be more helpful to think of them as ideas or "as articulated moments in networks of social relations and understandings" (p. 27).

For those wishing to hold corporations accountable, there are significant issues in complex modeling for sustainability. First is the problem of data collection when the boundaries of organizations are amorphous, changeable, and connected to all other notional boundaries. Second is the issue of inherent uncertainty, paradox, and surprise derived from uncertain science, or the public's lack of understanding and trust of science, and the interface with the intangible values that derive from consulting with diverse stakeholder groups. Perhaps society has now decided that there is an imperative for social development and environmental sustainability as iterated in international public policy.

So, the first goal is to recognize corporations as self-organizing systems. The second goal is recognition of public policy objectives on economic, social, and environmental challenges. And the third goal is coordinating the interface between corporations as self-organizing systems and public policy objectives for sustainable business. This is a significant challenge to the current way of seeing and doing things both in the everyday world of business and in the current CSR discourse.

THE NEW BUSINESS AND RESPONSIBILITY AGENDA?

To summarize, we need human-scale organizations that have, at their heart, planetary imperatives, that are servant leaders (where the corporation serves society rather than vice versa), that marry value *and* values, and that put integrity and trust at the heart of the decision-making process. This means that there needs to be a greater emphasis on accountability and assurance and a rewriting of the rules of incorporation; but, first there must be an emphasis on learning and education in business and across society as a whole. As the old African saying goes, "To build a country first build a school." The same applies to our global corporations.

The sustainable human-scale corporation is founded on sustainable conditions: small ecological footprint, enhanced social equity, and extended sense of futurity. Sustainable incorporation, therefore, involves long-term life and appropriate size (rather than immortality and unlimited size) and a balance of power among (and accountability to) a range of stakeholders.

We must be aware that currently we fail to see the corporation in the whole, which means that very often one hand of the corporation takes away what the other promises. As President Lula of Brazil said at the United Nations Global Compact Leaders Summit in 2004: "Business must refrain itself from taking away by its lobbying activities what it offers through corporate responsibility and philanthropy."

REINVENTING BRAND INTEGRITY

Where transgressions of human rights, labor standards, and environmental protection have been detected, corporations have been targeted as easily identifiable culpable parties in the supply chain from producers, often in developing countries, to consumers, often in the developed countries. While the primary focus has been on corporations, there has been less focus on product supply chains or on brands (Hertz, 2001; Klein, 2001). It may be that all stakeholders need to take ownership of these issues by acknowledging that brands are "owned" by all stakeholders. Consumers *and* corporations, as well as producers, suppliers, newsrooms, research students, and governments, are culpable in failing to deliver publicly agreed social and environmental goals.

Brands are a part of everyday life. Brands are existential; they are here and everywhere. Brands are the way we live, the way we identify ourselves. They are amorphous and belong to all of us and no one. Brands that have a direct interface with consumers are more valuable than the corporations that nominally own them. The world's most valued brands are Coca-Cola, Microsoft, IBM, GE, Intel, Disney, McDonald's, Nokia, Toyota, and Marlboro. The vast majority of the world, whether rich or poor, come into contact with one or more of these brands on a daily basis or are regularly affected by their use.

We need to understand more broadly and deeply the social and ecological impact of brands. This involves looking at global supply chains; global trade issues; the interface between government, corporations, and nongovernmental organizations; and the ecological footprint of brands. Viewing the debate from the perspective of brands paints a new picture of a complex network of relationships among ideas, interest groups, and products.

On any given day, average people come into contact with some 1,500 brands, and when they go to the supermarket (in a developed economy), they will be confronted with up to 50,000 (Stark, 2004). They create loyalty to brands through the establishment of superbrands or lovemarks. The director of Unilever's Marketing Academy, Thom Braun (2004), writes: "Values are at the heart of branding. . . . Brand values should not just be 'attachments' to a product or service, but rather the driving force for what the brand can dare to become." The CEO of Saatchi & Saatchi, Kevin Roberts (2004), prefers "lovemarks": "[T]rustmarks come after brands; lovemarks come after trustmarks. . . . Think about how you (business) make the most money. You make it when loyal users use your product all the time. That's where the money is. So having a long-term relationship is better than having a trusting relationship" (Roberts, 2004, p. 69).

Seduction is everything in marketing (Barthes, 1957/1993; Baudrillard, 1979/1990). Blind tests show that consumers prefer the taste of Pepsi to Coke, but people buy Coke by preference. Brand marketing theory and practice are intimately connected with identity, lifestyle, freedom, and security (Stark, 2004). In *Corporate Religion*, Jesper Kunde (1978) writes: "[T]he highest position a brand can reach is that of Brand Religion for the target group" (p. 3). In 1956, Roland Barthes (1957/1993) wrote, regarding the launch of the new Citroen Pallas DS saloon car: "Cars today are almost the exact equivalent of the great Gothic cathedrals: I mean the supreme creation of an era, conceived with passion by unknown artists, and consumed in image if not in usage by a whole population which appropriates them as purely magical objects" (p. 88).

Corporations are the nominal owners of brands, but greater control is exercised by consumers and other stakeholders. Corporations realize their mistakes when they corrupt their own brands, as in the case of Coke's changed recipe in the 1990s. Similarly, Monsanto became a dirty word in Europe in the 1990s through the company's mishandling of sensitivities regarding the issue of genetically modified foods.

A new approach to the subject of CSR is needed that moves the emphasis from the corporation to society as a whole, but not by putting the responsibilities in *another* place, but in *all* places. The way to do this is to examine those things that now affect and implicate all of us every day: global brands. This does not relieve the corporation of its responsibilities to increase total *stakeholder* value, which includes providing financial value to the shareholder, but it shifts the focus of the debate from the organizational and sectoral setting to the delivery of goods, services, and dreams. Central to this is a new understanding of nongovernmental public action as evidenced through activism, consumer choice, passive resistance, and stakeholder engagement.

The corporation is but one part of the delivery of goods and services that society uses. Accusing corporations of abnegating their responsibilities toward the communities in which they operate and toward the planet is too easy. It is an example of the way in which issues are broken down into their component parts, to look for a mechanical fix to a disaggregated problem. Looking at the whole may be more difficult to handle but may, in the end, help produce more practical and useful solutions. This approach crosses national boundaries; it reaches into our most intimate moments; it follows brands from cradle to death, from raw material to disposal, from design concept to consumption, from corporations to cathedrals.

A MULTIDISCIPLINARY APPROACH TO BRAND INTEGRITY

The most highly valued consumer brands are worth more than the corporations that own them. Coke, McDonald's, Mercedes, and Microsoft are some of the best-recognized global brands, but there are also other more mundane brands that can be found in most homes around the world—Dove soap and Colgate toothpaste, for example.

Theory and practice of corporate responsibility have tended to focus on the responsibility of corporations. Brands are more difficult to account for, more amorphous in their ownership. As Kevin Roberts (2004) of Saatchi & Saatchi writes, "the best brands enjoy 'loyalty beyond reason'" (p. 57). Global supply chain management, economies of scale, distribution, logistics, and brand management are at the heart of the most profitable retail corporations. The supply chain for Unilever's Dove soap stretches from poor palm oil farmers to consumers globally—rich and poor.

Much has been written about the ecological footprint of cities, industrial sites, and products, but not so much on brands per se. Taking Unilever's Dove soap as an example, we can begin to build a rich picture of complex relations among stakeholders, the raw materials, and the use and disposal of the product via manufacture, processing, packaging, marketing, retailing, and international trade and governance issues. Unilever sources the raw materials here and there, sells everywhere, and manufactures in some places but not in others. Much of this depends on international trade regulations. In 2000, Unilever was one of the first companies to associate itself with the United Nations Global Compact. Principle 1 of the compact states: "Businesses are asked to support and respect the protection of international human rights within their sphere of influence"; principle 2: "Businesses are asked to make sure their own corporations are not complicit in human rights abuses." The questions that arise are: What is the sphere of influence of a business? How might we better understand the limits to accountability and responsibility? At what point do responsibilities become societal rather than corporate? At what point does responsibility lie with the company and at what point with the individual and the government? Does knowing human rights abuses are committed in a territory in which a company has operations, or even sells, imply complicity with those abuses (Leisinger, 2004; Mendes, 2004)?

The burgeoning interest in multidisciplinary approaches and complexity theory helps link the disparate aspects of this research focus on brands. A holistic approach to the economic, psychological, management, ecological, and governance aspects of global brands is needed to make progress in each of these separate areas. The field of corporate responsibility has become mired in the atomization of indicators for corporate performance on social and environmental impacts. Complexity theory helps us see brands as complex adaptive systems that may have a life of their own. Brands have diffuse ownership and multiple reputations. A product such as Dove soap has a multiplicity of lives but key essential "meanings" that plug into our most basic social, emotional, and spiritual needs: hygiene, smell, seduction, price, packaging—love, peace, and happiness (Cilliers, 1998; Gergen, 2001; McIntosh, 2003b; Monks, 1988). The ubiquity of brands across global socioeconomic and socioecological groups has been at the forefront of the development of the global economy from Dove soap to Toyota cars to Coke.

Just as interesting is the analysis of global social networking where it is possible and common for individuals to connect around an idea or a brand and disperse as quickly as they congregate. Indeed, the congregation may never be physical, but electronic. Thomas Rheingold (2004) calls these groups "flash mobs"—a "new form of social interaction." They can also be thought of as "liquid relationships." The web of life has come alive and been significantly democratized by the technology of communication (Castells, 2001).

This is the future of nongovernmental public action, encountered through virtual ideas groupings such as Al Qaeda and Amnesty International, but also through the collective purchasing choices of consumers worldwide. What Osama bin Laden understands about the world is similar to what Kevin Roberts from Saatchi & Saatchi and Unilever's marketing director know about seduction, brainwashing, co-option, and manipulation.

Advocates for the poor as well as the corporate responsibility movement need to study these new phenomena and, in particular, the disaggregation of societies, where, through the establishment of virtual communities, many people in the developed world are choosing to physically live alone. The current research seems to show that there are some common features across the developing and developed world that support the idea that brand integrity is going to become a much more prominent issue. Particularly in the United States, but also elsewhere, a meaningful life is defined as a spiritual life. This is part of people trying to make sense of an increasingly cluttered and complex world. Today, self-reliance has been defined by technology. What some refer to as the "attention economy" means that it is possible to access vast amounts of information, to contact people instantly, and remain constantly in touch.

The themes that seem dominant, and that relate to global brands (Coke, Dove, Toyota, etc.) and global groupings (Al Qaeda, Amnesty International, the Olympics), are designs and concepts that reach across humanity and transcend other human concerns, such as local politics and family relationships; values and spirituality in life; living the simple life; and finding balance between work and play.

For corporations and other brand holders, such as the United Nations, the BBC, and the Olympic Games, the implications are clear: the public in the shape of consumers, activists, employees, and others have a great awareness of the values that a particular brand or corporate entity embodies. They are increasingly aware of all aspects of products from sourcing to manufacturing to use to disposal.

Now that we have global technological communications literacy in the developed world, nongovernmental public action in all forms will hold all established actors (government, corporations, and respected civil society groups) to account. John Elkington and Julia Hailes published *The Green Consumer Guide* in 1988, and it sold a million copies in the United Kingdom alone. A similar book, by Alice Tepper Marlin, originally published a year later, sold a million copies in the United States. This desire for consumer information was matched by other publications from the Consumers Association and the Ethical Consumer. New Consumer's *Changing Corporate Values* continued the drive for changing corporate behavior through the empowerment of consumers—a real form of nongovernmental public action (Adams, Caruthers, & Hamil, 1991). Now the public has access to vast amounts of information. But while the availability of products with organic, fair trade, and ethical trade labeling has increased significantly all over the world, the ability of consumers to understand, digest and, most important, believe in this labeling shows signs of having reached a plateau.

By painting rich pictures of the impact of certain brands, it is possible to make the connection between the emerging new literature on global communications connectivity and social networking and brand integrity. How can both these labels, the old and the new, build brand integrity and increase their sales to publics who purchase on the basis of value *and* values in an information-rich world?

If the hypothesis is correct that brand recognition is about loyalty beyond reason and that public policy is increasingly formulated on the basis of human rights, labor standards, environmental protection, *and* liberalized markets, then a possible future is that consumers globally will look both at the Dove label and at the symbol of the bird of peace with an olive branch in its beak, alongside some form of labeling that confirms that none of the globally agreed principles of corporate citizenship and sustainability have been transgressed in its production.

In a similar vein, by way of conclusion and taking the project forward, it is necessary to look at some of the more successful globally recognized social and ecolabeling (Forest Stewardship Council, Marine Stewardship Council, Soil Association) and speculate on the possibility of future global brands that uphold the sort of principles enshrined in the United Nations Global Compact—such as the Olympic Games, the BBC, the United Nations, and Oxfam.

How about: "UN—just do it!"

REFERENCES

Adams, R. (2004, March 8). *ACCA*. Retrieved October 10, 2005, from http://www.accaglobal.com/news/centenary.

Adams, R., Caruthers, J., & Hamil, S. (1991). *Changing corporate values*. London: New Consumer/Kogan Page.

Ali, T. (2002). *The clash of fundamentals*. London: Verso.

Andriof, J., & McIntosh, M. (Eds.). (2001). *Perspectives on corporate citizenship*. Sheffield, UK: Greenleaf.

Andriof, J., Waddock, S., & Husted, B. (2003). *Unfolding stakeholder thinking: [Vol. 2] Relationships, communication, reporting and performance*. Sheffield, UK: Greenleaf.

Andriof, J., Waddock, S., Husted, B., & Rahman, S. (2002). *Stakeholder thinking: Theory, responsibility and engagement*. Sheffield, UK: Greenleaf.

Annan, K. (2004, June 24). Address to Global Compact Leaders Summit, United Nations, New York [Speech]. Retrieved June 10, 2006, from http://www.unglobalcompact.org/NewsAndEvents/event_archives/global_compact_leaders_summit.html.

Association of Certified Chartered Accountants. (2004). *Towards transparency: Progress on global sustainability reporting*. Retrieved September 9, 2004, from www.accaglobal.com/publications/as_index/archives/issue17/.

Bakan, J. (2004). *The corporation*. Vancouver, Canada: Viking.

Barthes, R. (1993) *Mythologies*. London: Vintage. (Originally published 1957)

Baudrillard, J. (1990). *Seduction*. New York: St Martin's Press. (Originally published 1979)

Bauman, Z. (1998). *Globalization: The human consequences*. New York: Columbia University Press.

Beck, U. (2002). *What is globalisation?* Cambridge, UK: Polity Press.

Booth, K., & Dunne, T. (2002). *Worlds in

*collision: Terror and the future of global order.*London: Palgrave Macmillan.

Braun, T. (2004). *The philosophy of branding.* London: Kogan.

Castells, M. (2001). *The Internet galaxy.* Oxford: Oxford University Press.

Chua, A. (2003). *World on fire.* London: Heinemann.

Cilliers, P. (1998). *Complexity and postmodernism.* London: Routledge.

Conference Board. (2004, September). . Retrieved November 11, 2006, from http:// www.conference-board.org/cgi-bin/MsmGo .exe?grab_id=62&EXTRA_ARG=&SCOPE =MembersOnly&host_id=42&page_id= 7015680&query=2004+september& hiword=september+2004+SEPTEMBERS+.

Cragg, W. (2003). *Compendium of ethics codes and instruments of corporate responsibility.* Toronto, Canada: Schulich School of Business, York University.

Department for Food, Environment and Rural Affairs UK. (2005). Retrieved November 25, 2006, from http://www.sustainable-development.gov.uk/taking-it-on/background.

Dow Jones Sustainability Index. (2005). Retrieved October 10, 2005, from http:// www.sustainability-indexes.com/htmle/ sustainability/corpsustainability.html.

Elkington, J., & Hailes, J. (1988). *The green consumer guide: From shampoo to champagne—high-street shopping for a better environment.* London: Victor Gollancz.

Evans, R. W. (2003). The rise of the "abroids." In R. W. Evans, R. Shah, D. Murphy, & M. McIntosh (Eds.), *Something to believe in* (pp. 98–103). Sheffield, UK: Greenleaf.

Fussler, C. (2004). Responsible excellence pays. In M. McIntosh, S. Waddock, & G. Kell (Eds.), *Learning to talk* (pp. 276–288). Sheffield, UK: Greenleaf.

Galbraith, J. K., & Salinger, N. (1978). *Almost everyone's guide to economics.* New York: Bantam.

Gergen, K. J. (2001). *The saturated self.* New York: Basic Books.

Giddens, A. (2001). *The global third way debate.* Cambridge, UK: Polity Press.

Gray, J. (2003). *False dawn.* London: Granta.

Hardt, M., & Negri, A. (2000). *Empire.* Cambridge, MA: Harvard University Press.

Hertz, N. (2001). *The silent takeover: Global capitalism and the death of democracy.* London: Arrow Books.

Husted, B. (2002). *Unfolding stakeholder thinking: [Vol. 1] Theory, responsibility and engagement.* Sheffield, UK: Greenleaf.

King, M. J. (2001). Sustainability: Advantaged or disadvantaged? Do organisations that deliver value to all stakeholders produce superior financial performance? *Journal of Corporate Citizenship, 3,* 99–125.

Klein, N. (2001). *No logo.*London: Flamingo.

Korten, D. (1995). *When corporations rule the world.* London: Earthscan.

Kunde, J. (1978). *Corporate religion.* London: Financial Times, Prentice-Hall

Kunugi, T., & Schweitz, M. (1999). *Codes of conduct for partnership in governance: Texts and commentaries.* Tokyo: United Nations University.

Leipziger, D. (2004). *The corporate responsibility code book.* Sheffield, UK: Greenleaf.

Leisinger, K. (2004). Business and human rights. In M. McIntosh, S. Waddock, & G. Kell (Eds.), *Learning to talk: Corporate citizenship and the development of the UN Global Compact.* (pp. 72–100).Sheffield, UK: Greenleaf.

Lula, P. (2004, July 24). Speech to United Nations Global Compact Leaders Summit, United Nations, New York. Retrieved November 11, 2006 from http://www .unglobalcompact.org/NewsAndEvents/ event_archives/global_compact_leaders_ summit.html.

Marlin, A. T. (1994). *Shopping for a better world: The quick and easy guide to socially responsible supermarket shopping.* New York: Council on Economic Priorities (CEP).

Massey, D. (1999) Imagining globalization: Power-geometries of time-space. In A. Brah, M. Hickman, & M. Ghaill (Eds.), *Global futures: Migration, environment and globalization* (pp. 27–44). New York: St Martin's Press.

McIntosh, M. (1998). *Corporate citizenship.* London: FT Pitman.

McIntosh, M. (2003a). *Living corporate citizenship.* London: FT Pitman.

McIntosh, M. (2003b). *Raising a ladder to the moon: The complexities of corporate social responsibility.* London: Routledge.

McIntosh, M., Waddock, S., & Kell, G. (Eds.). (2004). *Learning to talk: Corporate citizenship and the development of the UN Global Compact.* Sheffield, UK: Greenleaf.

Mendes, E. (2004). Operationalising the Global Compact with a focus on the human rights principles: Learning to walk the talk. In M. McIntosh, S. Waddock, & G. Kell (Eds) *Learning to talk: Corporate citizenship and the development of the UN Global Compact* (pp. 101–113).Sheffield, UK: Greenleaf.

Micklethwait, J., & Woolridge, A. (2000). *A future perfect.*London: Heinemann.

Monks, R. A. G. (1988). *The emperor's nightingale.* New York: Perseus.

Newbold, Y. (2002). In M. McIntosh (Ed.), *Visions of ethical business* (pp. 11–13). New York: PricewaterhouseCoopers.

Rheingold, H. (2004). *Smart mobs: The next revolution.* New York: Perseus.

Roberts, K. (2004). Lovemarks. New York: Powerhouse Books.

Ruggie, J. (2003). The theory and practice of learning networks: Corporate social responsibility and the Global Compact. In M. McIntosh, S. Waddock, & G. Kell (Eds.). Learning to talk: Corporate citizenship and the development of the UN Global Compact. (pp. 32–42). Sheffield, UK: Greenleaf.

Sachs, W. (2005). www.wupperinst.org 2005. Retrieved 10 October, 2005, from www .footprintnetwork.org/newsletters/footprint _network.

Stark, M. (2004). *2004: The consumer context.* Retrieved March 19, 2004, from www .kevinsaatchi.com.

Stiglitz, J. E. (2002). *Globalisation and its discontents.*London: Penguin Allen Lane.

SustainAbility/United Nations Environment Programme. (2005). *Buried treasure.* Retrieved November 11, 2006, from http: //www.sustainability.com/insight/article .asp?id=141.

Tennyson, R., & Wilde, L. (2000). *The guiding hand: Brokering partnerships.*London: Prince of Wales Business Leaders Forum / United Nations Staff College.

United Nations. (2005). Global compact. Retrieved November 8, 2006, from http: //www.globalcompact.org/AboutTheGC/ TheTenPrinciples/index.html.

Waddock, S. (2002). *Leading corporate citizens.* Columbus, OH: McGraw-Hill Irwin.

Wheeler, D., & Sillanpaa, M. (1998). *The stakeholder corporation.* London: FT Pitman.

World Bank. (2004, September). Retrieved September 10, 2004, from http: //www.worldbank.org/data/wdi2002.

World Economic Forum. (2005). Retrieved November 8, 2006, from http://www .weforum.org/en/initiatives/ corporatecitizenship/The%20Business% 20Case%20for%20Corporate%20Citizenship/ index.htm.

Zadek, S., & Nelson, J. (2000). *Partnership alchemy: New social partnerships.* London: AccountAbility and the Copenhagen Centre.

Zadek, S., Pruzan, P., & Evans, R. (1997). *Building corporate accountability: Emerging practices in social and ethical accounting—auditing and reporting.* London: EarthScan.

II

CASES AND CONTEXTS

4

Facing Corporate Power

JEM BENDELL
MARK BENDELL

The turn of the millennium saw the return of great street protests in Western cities. Seattle, Prague, Genoa: no longer were these just city names but also battle cries, signifying the mass mobilization of people concerned with the problems facing humanity. While these protests grabbed the attention of the corporate media, they were not unique, as people mobilized across the world in various ways to challenge the dominant political economics of the time (Kingsnorth, 2003). Whether protesters were focusing on the actions of the International Monetary Fund, World Bank, and World Trade Organization, or issues of "third world" debt, climate change, and free trade, the power of large corporations was never far from the debate (Starr, 2000). Social activists were facing and defacing corporate power in increasing numbers. This was not lost on those who observed the emergent social movements, then dubbed "antiglobalization" or "anticapitalist" by different commentators. Pictures of chanting youths framed by clouds of tear gas were used in glossy trade magazines and corporate brochures, alongside arguments that the readers should avoid becoming a target themselves by embracing corporate social responsibility, which even warranted its own acronym—CSR. From barricades to boardrooms, people were increasingly talking about the role of the corporation in society.

These protests came at the end of a decade when voluntary associations of people in what is often called "civil society" had increasingly turned their attention to the activities of corporations. In this chapter, we explore that corporate turn within civil society, in ways that may help future research into the interface between private and public interests in society. We do this by defining and exploring differing perspectives on corporate power held by different groups in civil society and the differing tactics these perspectives inform. We discuss some of the insights from a decade of novel engagements between business and civil society, and whether the differing perspectives on corporate power are mutually exclusive or whether there is possibility of convergence. We highlight how civil groups are now turning their attention to the financial markets and offer some initial ideas on the implications of this for our understanding of corporate power and the future of business–society relations.

Management literature on business–society relations has not often considered these broader issues of corporate power and implications of shifting societal relations for democratic governance. Analyses of the increasing importance of contemporary corporations' relations with nonprofit organizations, charities, or campaign groups have tended to focus on the instrumental challenge of how participants might manage them better, to corporate advantage (Hartman & Stafford, 1997; Neal & Davies, 1998; Peters, 1999; Winter & Steger, 1998) or mutual advantage (Long & Arnold, 1995; Murphy & Bendell, 1997; Stern & Hicks, 2000;

Zadek, 2001) Apart from Peter Newell (2000), this literature has not often cross-fertilized with the disciplines of international relations or development studies. This chapter makes a small contribution to addressing this lacuna in the literature, by beginning an exploration of what various actors in society think of corporate power, and what they are trying to do to influence it. We conclude with recommendations for future research that would employ sociological theories of power to understand business–society relations, and help understand what might constitute the responsible use of power.

CIVIL SOCIETY

People have come together, voluntarily, to work toward progressive change in their local and extra-local communities throughout history. At various times in the history of Western political thought, the term "civil society" has been used to describe the realm of networks and associations that result. The term is contested, with some suggesting that it usefully describes all forms of association, whatever their purpose, and others being more explicit about the role of shared values in making it a category of social importance (Edwards, 2003). For this chapter, "civil society" is used to describe the sphere of associational life formed by people coming together for a primary purpose other than commerce or attaining governmental power.[1] Hence, the term "civil groups" refers to formal or informal organizations and networks that are both not for profit and nongovernmental. "Not-for-profit" implies not only that the organization itself does not repatriate profits to owners, but also that the organization does not aim to represent the interests of for-profit organizations.

When analyzing and commenting on the actions and relevance of these civil groups, much management theory uses the term "stakeholder." This reflects the existence of stakeholder theory and a starting point that places the organization— most often a corporation—at the center of analysis. From this perspective, stakeholders are relevant due to their relationship with the corporation. This leads to models of stakeholder salience, for example, where stakeholders are rated for their ability to influence the corporation (Mitchel, Aglre, & Wood, 1997). This highlights the instrumentalist assumptions that shape much work on business–

society relations. Our analysis is of the relevance of corporations to the associational life and aspirations of civil society, not the other way around. In conclusion, we offer some insights into the implications of our analysis for corporate management, but it is not our main task and is why we employ the term of "civil society."

A common theme of much commentary on civil society as the twentieth century drew to a close was that "it" was increasing. Take these statistics on some subsets of civil society: membership of seven major environmental groups in the United States grew from 5.3 to 9.5 million between 1980 and 1990 (Cairncross, 1995), while in 1999 the "nonprofit sector" in 22 countries employed 19 million full-time paid workers, together turning more than $1.1 trillion annually, and more than 100,000 full-time paid employees and 1.2 million full-time volunteers were working for international civil groups in France, Germany, Japan, Netherlands, Spain, and United Kingdom (Salamon et al., 1999). The 1990s witnessed a continuing boom in the number of these groups, with around one-quarter of the 13,000 international nongovernmental organizations in existence in 2000 having been created after 1990 (Anheier, Glasius, & Kaldor, 2001). To some, this suggests a "global associational revolution" (Salamon et al., 1999), creating a "globalization from below" (Giddens, 1999, p. 8). This associational revolution has been occurring at the same time that traditional forms of political participation, as indicated by the membership of political parties and trade unions, and election turnouts, has fallen in most Western democracies (Patterson, 2002).

THE CORPORATE TURN

Today, corporations are everywhere. The number of transnational corporations (TNCs) has risen nearly 10-fold since 1970, and their turnovers dwarf that of many national economies. One-third of world trade occurs between factories and offices of TNCs (International Labour Organization, 2000, p. 8). On one hand, their involvement in processes meeting basic needs, such as food, shelter, medicines, and infrastructure, makes them directly relevant to billions of people worldwide. On the other, their ability to escape state-based regulation, and even dictate that regulation, has given rise to growing concerns about their accountability. It is not surprising, therefore, that civil groups should consider how corporations influence the lives of their members or the achievement of the issues they work on. A significant turn toward corporations by civil groups in the West can be identified as beginning in the early 1990s (Bendell, 2000). This growing ubiquity is key to this turn, as is an apparent increase in corporate impunity.

Civil groups have turned to corporations both directly and indirectly. First, some groups turn to them as a subject of analysis and criticism and call for action from the corporations themselves. This has occurred due to frustrations with limited success in influencing governments and intergovernmental processes on social and environmental regulations and the weak enforcement of those regulations (Murphy & Bendell, 1997).

The 1990s witnessed an explosion of civil group engagement with corporations. Many early forms of engagement were confrontational. Some groups focus on single issues or single companies. Although a number of anticorporate campaigns such as the International Baby Food Action Network (http://www.ibfan.org/) and the Coalition Against Bayer-Dangers (http://www.cbgnetwork.org) had been running since the late 1970s, the growth of the Internet in the 1990s has supported a new era in such activism: the Internet has become a weapon of mass dissemination. The launch in 1992 of McSpotlight (http://www.mcspotlight.com), a website dedicated to providing information on problems with the McDonald's fast-food business, was indicative of things to come (O'Neill, 1999). Key to these new tactics of naming and shaming corporations is the importance of corporate branding. Intangible assets, such as reputation, brand, strategic positioning, alliances, and knowledge, had come to comprise a large percentage of most companies' total market value—perhaps accounting for one-quarter of the world's financial wealth in 1999 (Clifton & Maughan, 1999).

Civil groups also began engaging corporations in cooperative ways, to help improve corporate practices in relation to the issues of concern to the civil groups. For example, in 1991, the environmental group World Wide Fund for Nature UK (WWF-UK) began coordinating a group of companies in the United Kingdom that agreed to sourcing all their wood purchases from well-managed forests. This involved coordinating information exchange, providing advice on forest issues, and

systems of supply chain assessment. WWF-UK helped establish the Forest Stewardship Council to provide a mechanism for the certification of wood from well-managed forests. Within a few years, civil groups working on social issues, such as Oxfam, were similarly engaged in advising companies on what they should be doing on such issues as workplace practices in their supply chains. In 1997, this work evolved into the Ethical Trading Initiative, the same year that a number of other multistakeholder initiatives were founded, one of the most notable being the Global Reporting Initiative (Bendell, 2004).

Some civil groups direct their calls for action at governments and intergovernmental bodies, not the corporations. What is new to this is how civil groups are not just advocating enforcement or lobbying for regulations on specific social or environmental practices of corporations, but pushing for changes in the general frameworks of law governing corporations as a whole.

As we explain below, the first approach is now understood as part of a "corporate responsibility movement"; the second approach, as part of a "corporate accountability movement" (Hamann, Acutt, & Kapelus, 2003; Richter, 2001). It is our contention that differing views of corporate power play a part in influencing whether civil groups are involved in corporate accountability or corporate responsibility.

CORPORATE POWER

What is corporate power? To begin with, we need to clarify what is meant by "corporate," a definitional issue often overlooked by management analysts. Corporations were invented at the end of the sixteenth century as a means of managing colonial trade. Originally, they were created—chartered—by a number of European governments to undertake activities that the governors determined to be in the interests of the state. In the following centuries, their legal form slowly changed as they were given more freedom to pursue economic activities of their own choosing. Today, in most countries, to create a corporation (a process called incorporation) means the establishment of a legal identity, distinct from the people who run it. It becomes a legal person (as opposed to a natural person). There are a variety of advantages to those involved. First, unlike us, the corporation is not certain to die, so inheritance tax is avoided. Second, it has some civil and legal rights and so can go to court. Third, by being a legal person, it can limit liability or, in other words, shield those who run the business from some of the responsibilities of their actions. These advantages are, however, also partly the cause of some of the problems associated with corporations today (Bendell, 2004).

Corporate power is the power that arises due to the organizational form called a corporation. What is this power? The concept of power has been researched and theorized for hundreds of years and is never far from debates about personal agency and social change (Clegg, 1989). Mobilizing the various sociological theorizations of power is beyond the scope of this chapter. Simply put, power can be understood as that which makes us or helps us to do or not do, to say or not say, to think or not think, to feel or not feel. Those poststructuralist critiques that question whether there are indeed any structures in society do not negate the validity of using such a term as "corporate power" but encourage us to consider this as a description of a complex set of power relations and capabilities that arise due to the existence of corporations. Many critics of corporate power write about this complexity, especially when attempting to describe how the corporation influences discourse and meanings in society. For example, Jonathon Rowe (2001) suggests that the "American corporation" has become "more than just a mode of business" but also "an agenda, the organizing principle for an entire society—the embedding in the institutional matrix of the single-minded quest for monetary gain" (p. 1).

Corporate power has been argued to express itself in most societies in a number of ways, from influence over government, to political culture, to professional and popular culture. One mechanism for influencing governments is lobbying. Leslie Sklair (1998) documents how corporations "work, quite deliberately and often rather covertly, as political actors, and often have direct access to those at the highest levels of formal political and administrative power with considerable success" (p. 286). John Braithwaite and Peter Drahaus (2000) demonstrate how corporations and their lobbying groups are able to maneuver on the international scene in order to generate the rules they wanted and undermine those they perceive as problematic.

Campaign financing is also a key means of influence, which varies in different countries. For example, politicians in the United States must spend many millions of dollars to have a chance of becoming a presidential candidate, and then more on the race itself, the majority of which comes from corporations and rich business people (Palast, 2002).

Industrial location is another mechanism of influence. If certain corporations do not attain the policies they want, then they can often locate their operations elsewhere. By the early 1990s, academics described "the stateless corporation in which people, assets, and transactions move freely across international borders" (Snow, Miles, & Coleman, 1992, p. 8). An overriding imperative of appearing attractive to TNCs, and thus the financial markets, shapes a paradigm of policy making in governments (Strange, 1996). The argument is not so much that the state is in retreat, but that it is on the march in support of corporations.

The mass media is another mechanism of corporate power, influencing political culture as well as culture more broadly. Forty percent of all the world's media are controlled by five TNCs (Simms, Bigg, & Robins, 2000). Being managed to generate advertising revenue, this creates a pressure for quickly boosting ratings and airing adverts to the highest bidders. Thus, people experience increasingly sanguine audio, print, and televisual media with constant messages to consume more products and services. In non-Western countries, television beams images of a consumer utopia into millions of homes, helping create demand for products that provide a symbolic connection to that unreal utopia (Saddar, 2000).

Despite the endeavors of committed journalists, the corporate media generally filters the news agenda in five ways (Chomsky & Hernan, 1994). First, the business interests of the owner companies influence reporting. Second, media managers need to please (and certainly not upset) current and potential advertisers. Third, journalists often rely on press releases from organizations with a commercial interest in influencing the media. This reliance is increased as profit objectives regulate the amount of time most journalists have to research. Fourth, journalists that "rock the boat" are liable to professional criticism and sometimes litigation. A fifth filter identified by Chomsky and Hernan (1994) is a blind acceptance of neoliberal economic ideology, such that many journalists are bemused by, and disinterested in, fundamental critiques of the economic system.

Corporations affect discourse beyond their influence on, and as, the media. Financial and professional pressures on different types of agencies, working on all manner of issues, influence the way people decide between different ideas and actions. For example, research on the monitoring of codes of conduct demonstrates how commercial auditing companies are influencing the professionalization of such practices in ways that promote their own financial interests (Bendell, 2001).

One aspect of the discourse of business that is particularly relevant to this discussion is the idea that business is apolitical. Before the mid-1990s, most managers expressed this perspective and an opinion that their duty as professionals is not to be swayed by subjective and emotional concerns about what, they thought, are nonfinancial matters. Less dominant today, this view means that most managers considered social and environmental issues as not their responsibility but that of government (Bendell, 2000). This view is despite the fact that the modern corporation and globalizing capitalism are political creations and that the private sector has significant power over the political agenda, as described above.

PERSPECTIVES ON CORPORATE POWER

We have argued that corporate power is an important aspect of contemporary societies and that civil society has awoken to this by engaging directly or indirectly with corporations. The future direction and implications of these new cross-sector engagements for the role of corporations in society will depend, in part, on how civil groups regard the power of those corporations. This hypothesis, as well as the contention that involvement in corporate responsibility or corporate accountability reflects differing perspectives on corporate power, is why civil group perspectives on corporate power are important to understand.

The following discussion draws upon research conducted for the United Nations on the "corporate accountability movement," which, *inter alia*, explored perspectives on corporate power held by Western civil groups that were engaging directly or indirectly with corporations, and the tactics these perspectives informed. This involved documentary analysis of the publications and websites of such groups, as well as semistructured inter-

views and e-mail correspondence with staff members and supporters of those groups (Bendell, 2004).

This research revealed that the level of reflection on corporate power by civil group members varies significantly: some obviously have considered it, whereas others have not and so their perspective on it had to be drawn out. At the one extreme is the Stakeholder Alliance, whose slogan is "Confronting Corporate Power with Stakeholder Power." At the other, many of those who are involved in collaborative work with corporations had not reflected on corporate power, and an invitation to them to talk about it was unusual for them. As Tracey Swift, then with the organization AccountAbility, explained, "there is a small cadre of people working in this area who see it's all about power. But yet we are not really working on power, as there is no funding for this sort of thing—it's not what people want to hear."[2]

The research was also used to generate a typology of perspectives on corporate power and tactics for influencing it. The shifting, contextual, and often contradictory nature of reality means that hard and fast definitions and correlations between activists, their goals, and their strategies for achieving them are somewhat arbitrary. It is a necessary evil for anyone attempting to make sense of the diversity of groups in civil society, to end up with a somewhat reductionist worldview of the people who are part of it. With this in mind, four broad perspectives on corporate power could be identified and are offered as explanatory tools.

For some, corporate power presents an *opportunity*, if it can be directed to better use. A member of one large environmental group working in partnership with dozens of companies said, "[W]e have to find new allies with the power and influence to create real change, and fast."[3] Similarly, a member of a British development charity explained, "some of these retailers now have huge market share, and if we can work with them to influence what goes on in their supply chains, then we'll be able to have more impact on working conditions."[4] Many civil groups present themselves as having this perspective, as they seek to collaborate with companies on cross-sectoral collaborations. Examples include Conservation International, Rainforest Alliance, Comic Relief, and Save the Children.

For others, corporate power is regarded as an *obstacle*, a problem in a specific case because it is being used in ways that hinder their particular social or environmental objective. Another member of the same development charity explained that "many corporations have not been helping workers in the developing world, by always seeking the cheapest suppliers and driving down prices, while backing the political agenda that doesn't allow us to discriminate between products on the basis of the conditions under which they were made."[5] A variety of civil groups point the finger at companies as being obstacles to their specific campaign objectives, well-known examples including Friends of the Earth, Action Aid, and Médecins Sans Frontières.

With both of these perspectives, people were not inclined to speak or think of corporate power as one phenomenon, because they regard the power as being different depending on the corporation in question. Others have developed a wider and more categorical critique of corporate power, considering that it is an *obstruction*, a general systemic problem arising because of the logic of capital accumulation driven by stock markets, which leads to externalizing costs, and shaping discourse in ways that will always hinder social and environmental objectives. Civil groups such as the World Development Movement have for some years expressed this more fundamental critique of corporate power. In recent years, more civil groups have expressed this perspective, including many like Friends of the Earth that previously criticized specific companies, not corporate power as a whole. They state, "[T]he growing scale of multinationals has consolidated their power and influence while greatly increasing distance between corporate leadership and the communities and lives that their activities affect" (Friends of the Earth International, 2002, p. 1).

A fourth attitude to corporate power could be identified, where it is regarded as an *obscenity*. Such people consider it morally wrong for corporations to have their power no matter how it is used, because they consider human self-determination, freedom, and democracy to be fundamental and therefore that the most powerful institutions in society should be democratic, or controlled via democratic means, as a matter of principle. A number of civil groups work with this agenda in mind. Notable examples include the Program on Corporations, Law, and Democracy, founded to "contest the authority of corporations to govern" (http://www.poclad.org); CorpWatch, founded to "foster democratic control over corporations" (http://www.corpwatch.org); and Corporate Europe Observatory, founded for "targeting the threats to

democracy . . . posed by the economic and political power of corporations" (http://www.xs4all.nl/~ceo/). Activists that identify with the global social justice movement, described in the introduction, often have this view of corporate power as an obscenity. During a protest against the G8 in 2001, one explained, "[C]orporations don't just provide, they try to make us need their shit. When you put it all together, they want to run our lives for their own ends, not ours."[6] Ultimately, this view of corporate power identifies it as something that requires complete transformation as an end in itself.

CIVIL SOCIETY TACTICS

The different perspectives on power underpin a range of tactics for engaging corporations and corporate issues. The research supported the classification of tactics that are used by various civil groups that engage with corporations either directly or indirectly. Some groups use a variety of these tactics, and some do not conceptualize their work directly in terms of corporate power.

Tactic 1—Remove It

Some civil groups attempt to remove corporate power from their life, community, or country completely. Examples include the campaign for nationalization of corporations, the expulsion of natural resource companies from certain regions, or the prohibition of certain forms of for-profit activity. In the United Kingdom, the privatized company running the rail network, Railtrack, was the target of campaigns for renationalization, after the company turned significant profits while there was a poor safety record contributing to fatal crashes.

Tactic 2—Redefine It

Some civil groups attempt to redefine what a corporation is and how it is permitted to exist under law. Examples include the campaign for rechartering corporations in the United States. Unocal became a focus for such campaigns, particularly in relation to its activities in Burma.

Tactic 3—Reduce It

Some civil groups attempt to reduce corporate power by breaking up corporations. Examples include the use of competition law to break up monopolizing companies. In the past, antitrust laws led to the breakup of companies such as United Fruit, which became the Chiquita and Standard Fruit companies. In recent times, competition law has been used not to break up companies but to regulate how companies can operate, such as Microsoft in the European Union, or restrict new mergers and acquisitions. These are small measures compared to what many civil groups call for.

These three tactics—to *remove*, *reduce*, or *redefine* corporate power—address the existence of the corporation itself, including its form and function. Such tactics are used particularly by those who consider corporate power to be an obstruction or obscenity, as defined above, and are working toward what could be called "corporate reductability."

Tactic 4—Restrain It

Some civil groups attempt to restrain corporate power with rules governing the behavior of corporations. Examples include lobbying for new environmental and labor laws and penalties, and also civil activism. For example, in 2003 a coalition of U.S. groups, including the union federation AFL-CIO, Amnesty International USA, Earth Rights International, Global Exchange, Oxfam America, and Sierra Club, launched the International Right to Know (IRTK) campaign, which calls on the U.S. government to require companies based in the United States or traded on U.S. stock exchanges (and their foreign subsidiaries and major contractors) to disclose information on the environmental impacts, labor standards, and human rights practices of their overseas operations (International Right to Know, 2003). The 200 groups backing the IRTK campaign argue that the United States should extend its right to know laws geographically to cover U.S. activities abroad, and qualitatively to also cover important nonenvironmental issues. Another, international example is the Publish What You Pay campaign, launched in 2002 by the Open Society Institute and Global Witness with a coalition of more than 70 other civil groups. It seeks to tackle the problem of international oil, gas, and mining companies paying billions of dollars a year to the governments of many countries in the global South, such as Angola and Nigeria, but where "few of these countries' citizens benefit from this financial windfall

... because of government corruption and mismanagement" (Publish What You Pay, 2003). They call for the G7 governments to require transnational resource companies to publish the net taxes, fees, royalties, and other payments made in countries where they operate (Publish What You Pay, 2002).

Tactic 5—Redress It

Some civil groups attempt to redress the negative impacts of corporations. Examples include litigation against corporations for compensation and punitive damages, and also taxation. Prosecuting corporations in their home country for abuses committed in other countries, by their subsidiaries, is a new dimension to this (Ward, 2002). In the United Kingdom, courts can hear cases if they determine that the plaintiff will not receive justice in other courts. Prosecutions have been brought against two British companies, Cape and Thor, on behalf of workers suffering from work-related ill health in South Africa.

Tactic 6—Resist It

Some civil groups attempt to resist the expression or extension of corporate power, in a particular instance or generally. Examples include campaigns against multilateral trade and investment agreements and also campaigns against high-profile branded companies over specific issues. These often involved boycotts and media-friendly stunts that put executives in the awkward position of having to answer questions from journalists about their company's activities. Demonstrations at corporate offices, retail outlets, or annual general meetings are another tactic used against companies. Some campaigners buy shares in order to table controversial motions at their annual general meetings. Some high-profile examples include Shell, over the North Sea oil platform Brent Spar (and then the Ogoni in Nigeria); brands such as Nike and Gap, over working conditions in their supplier factories; and Monsanto, over genetically modified foods (Klein, 2000).

These three tactics—to *resist*, *restrain*, or *redress* corporate power—seek to counterbalance the power of corporations. Such tactics are used particularly by those who consider corporate power to be an obstacle or obstruction, as defined above, and who are working toward corporate accountability. The term "corporate accountability" is often used interchangeably with other terms such as "corporate responsibility" and "corporate citizenship." The meaning of the word "accountability" aids this inconsistency in understandings of corporate accountability. For example, the *Merriam-Webster* dictionary allows for both views of accountability, defining it as "the quality or state of being accountable; especially: an obligation or willingness to accept responsibility or to account for one's actions" (*Merriam-Webster*, 1992, p. 556). Peter Newell (2002) argues that "the term implies both a measure of answerability (providing an account for actions undertaken) and enforceability (punishment or sanctions for poor performance or illegal conduct)" (p. 92).

Tactic 7—Redirect It

Some civil groups attempt to redirect corporate power into more socially and environmentally beneficial ways of working, often as the second step to resist tactics, and often as the indirect outcome of all other previous tactics, as corporations begin to operate differently in response. Examples include responsible or ethical investing, and corporate coalitions on social and environmental issues. Some civil groups and corporations have formed partnerships to develop new products, techniques, or management practices. Codes of conduct and certification schemes, often as part of multistakeholder initiatives, grew significantly during the 1990s (Bendell, 2000; Utting, 2002; Zadek, 2001). One pioneering multistakeholder initiative is the Forest Stewardship Council, which aims to provide a credible guarantee to consumers that wood products come from well-managed forests (Murphy & Bendell, 1997). Another is the Global Reporting Initiative, which is developing a widely endorsed reporting framework for social and environmental issues.

Tactic 8—Reinforce It

Some civil groups attempt to reinforce corporate power in specific or general cases. Examples include efforts to expand certain corporate activities and freedoms that are seen as beneficial to society. Working with corporations to increase their provision of products and services to the financially poorer regions of the world, suggesting that they can profit from poverty alleviation, is one

example of this thinking (Prahalad, 2004). However, quite often it appears that the argument that a particular activity will benefit a corporation or corporations in general appears to be a tactical argument to encourage action, or even an unintentional byproduct of the other tactics mentioned above.

These last two tactics—to *redirect* or *reinforce* corporate power—address the challenge of encouraging more beneficial impacts from corporations. Such tactics are used particularly by those interested in promoting voluntary corporate responsibility, which is often called CSR or corporate citizenship. For them, the argument that if corporations work toward their particular social or environmental objectives it could increase corporate power, is functional in encouraging a greater response.

The tactics are not exclusive to particular perceptions of corporate power. Note, for example, that voluntary corporate responsibility initiatives that are driven by civil groups are acting as mechanisms through which parts of civil society exert a power over business. Therefore, they do not necessarily add to, or avoid challenging, corporate power. The definition of tactics is not meant to classify activists and civil groups, because many adopt a mix of tactics depending on circumstances. For example, after initially resisting corporate power, many civil groups have sought to redirect it by establishing multistakeholder initiatives and voluntary codes. In any case, organizations often express multiple perspectives on corporate power. One reason for this is the diversity of personal opinions in organizations. For example, although the organization AccountAbility is not particularly critical of power, while working there Tracey Swift said she saw "corporate accountability as concerned with balancing up the hegemony of power exerted by corporations. For me, this is a question of increasing the voice and power of people so that corporations cannot treat them with impunity."[7]

Another reason for organizations exhibiting various perspectives on corporate power is that they are not mutually exclusive. For example, one can regard corporate power as an obstacle to a particular problem, a systemic obstruction to solving problems generally, and as a moral obscenity. Moreover, even with such a perspective, one might consider that corporate power presents an opportunity if it could be channeled in support of efforts to control corporate power.

DIVERGENCE OR CONVERGENCE?

How civil groups with these different perspectives and tactics might relate to each other is an important question for both the civil actors and managers of corporations, as well as policy makers and analysts. Before concluding, we briefly explore the possibilities for divergence or convergence of the different perspectives and tactics.

Identifying different perspectives on corporate power helps us to understand why some civil groups criticize voluntary corporate responsibility initiatives and some work with corporations on such initiatives. The concern is that for very limited changes in corporate practice, their position of power in society could be reaffirmed. Critics of the sufficiency of corporate changes induced by civil society, or "civil regulation" (Bendell, 2000), point to a number of limitations. First, they are said to be of "defective scope." With more than 60,000 TNCs in the world, some question whether corporate responsibility initiatives will only ever be patchy and partial, driven by the whims of Western activists, media, consumers, and investors (Utting, 2002). Second, voluntary responses from corporations are seen as maintaining a "democratic deficit," where the agenda is driven by certain groups in the West and not the (supposed) intended beneficiaries in the global South (Bendell, 2005). Peter Newell (2000) argues that those civil groups engaging with business have "neither the mandate nor the legitimacy to represent broader publics," and thus civil regulation is no replacement for state or international regulation (p. 913). A third criticism concerns the "distraction effect" of voluntary initiatives. This is not about what voluntary initiatives can achieve or not achieve, and the power relations involved, but what they might stop from being achieved. This is because some companies point to voluntary action as evidence that they do not need state regulation, suggesting that the development of corporate responsibility adds weight to the neoliberal policy paradigm. As increasing numbers of people from civil groups, governments, and academia are involved in corporate responsibility, some suggest this might distract them from the main tasks at hand (Bendell, 2004).

This analysis could imply that the actions of different civil groups, arising from different perspectives on corporate power, will be divergent and reduce the effectiveness of each approach. However, there is some evidence that the opposite may be true. For example, there are complex relations between laws and voluntary corporate responsibility standards, with voluntary standards often being incorporated into contracts or leading to differing levels of government inspection in ways that are mutually reinforcing (Ward, 2003). Meanwhile, the existence of more critical civil society pressure adds to the rationale for companies to engage with less critical civil groups, as it creates more reputational risk that must be responded to. This benefits the groups who regard corporate power as an opportunity. But do these groups do anything that might help the agenda of the more critical civil groups? It is still quite early to say, and more research is required, but there is already some evidence that the approach of some groups and corporations involved in voluntary corporate responsibility is beginning to converge with those pursuing a more critical corporate accountability agenda.

Our hypothesis on why this is possible is twofold. First, people in those corporations who have moved furthest for the longest period of time in adopting voluntary responsibility measures are learning about the commercial limits of their efforts. Second, rather than retreating into an old paradigm of business that ignores wider societal responsibilities, corporate leaders have awakened to their influence and to a purpose wider than the narrow self-interest of their company and themselves. This is leading to new strategies that are beginning to recognize the importance of addressing power imbalances in society. We briefly explore each proposition.

In many cases, the commercial case for responsibility has proved elusive. This is for four key and connected reasons. First, leading on social or environmental issues does not diffuse reputation-damaging criticism and can sometimes lead to more negative attention. For example, Frey (2002) notes that "by virtue of its slogans and its actions" the oil company British Petroleum "tried to seize the moral high ground and so is judged by a different standard" (p. 99). For the media, hypocrisy is a much better story than mere malpractice. The clothing company Nike also experiences continual campaigning despite investing more in voluntary corporate responsibility measures than its direct competitors. What most proponents of voluntary corporate responsibility have failed to realize is that the key issue was corporate power, not just corporate practices. To illustrate, two of the highest profile corporate responsibility issues in the 1990s, deforestation and child labor, have existed for thousands of years. They became issues of corporate responsibility because enough people believed that other organs of society, such as communities, religions, and governments, were no longer strong enough to act on these issues alone. If corporate power is what made these issues reputationally damaging for companies, then any voluntary initiative addressing these issues might further develop corporate power, and therefore compound the root of the business problem.

A second reason for problems with the commercial case for responsibility is that companies investing in above-compliance behavior can be undercut by less concerned competitors and therefore either reduce profit margins or risk losing market share. This can occur because consumers are not rewarding companies enough for their social responsibility, through brand loyalty or by paying a premium, while governments are not enforcing penalties on companies that do not perform to equivalent standards. Nike's vice president of corporate responsibility, Hannah Jones, explains that "premium brands are in a lonely leadership position" because "consumers are not rewarding us" for investments in improved social performance in supply chains.[8]

The third reason is that solving some social and environmental challenges is material to companies, as they impinge on production processes and consumption patterns, yet they cannot be solved without improved performance from all companies. Depletion of fish stocks due to overfishing, for example, will not be solved by an individual company changing its practices—the whole fishing industry needs to change in order to protect the future of the industry. The commercial impacts of climate change on the insurance industry, agriculture, water supply, among other aspects of economic life, will not be addressed by an individual company voluntarily reducing its carbon emissions: all must act. It is the same for HIV/AIDS, because the impact on workforces cannot be effectively managed by individual companies but requires prevention measures involving the wider economy and society (Bendell, 2003).

For these reasons, it is not that surprising that the performance of investment funds that consider extrafinancial social, environmental, and governance issues is mixed. That such funds outperformed the norm until 2001 was more because they tended to be overweight in technology stocks during the boom of the 1990s rather than because of any competitive advantage derived from responsible behavior. "Unethical" stocks have remained strong. "Look at any public information on [defense] stocks like Lockheed Martin or General Dynamics. You'll see that they outperformed the S&P 500 Index by wide margins over the past 15 years," argued MutualFunds.com (cited in Lifeworth, 2003).

Faced with the evaporation of the win–win proposition that the business case for responsible commerce is widespread enough to make voluntary above-compliance behavior a sensible corporate strategy, corporate executives face a difficult choice. One option is to return to the old paradigm of business, which regards social and environmental issues as the concern of government alone. However, a decade of voluntary corporate responsibility conversations has generated a shift in the sense of what it means to be in business. Although academic debates are still had between supporters of shareholder models, on the one hand, and stakeholder models, on the other, in some societies a conceptual shift is under way in the minds of business people: the question of how people live their values at work is now a valid one. No longer is it assumed in mainstream (Western) business that to be professional means not to consider the social and environmental impacts of one's work. It is our experience, from being involved in this area for 10 years, that increasing numbers of people hope or believe they should be able to do well in business by having a positive impact on society (Bendell, 2004).

Given this, another response is being pursued by some business people. The CEO of AccountAbility, Simon Zadek, who is a leading practitioner in the corporate responsibility field, illustrates this thinking when in 2003 he explained that "we have to move beyond what individual, enlightened companies choose to do. This must include the amplification of the corporate community's progressive role in changing the framework conditions, including difficult policy areas covering international trade and investment, public subsidies, intellectual property and competition policy" (cited in Bendell, 2004, p. 32). Nike illustrates this new approach well. Hannah Jones says that, whereas the company has previously looked at how to solve problems for themselves, now they are exploring how to create systemic change in the industry as a whole. Consequently, Nike's latest corporate responsibility report describes a main goal "to effect positive, systemic change in working conditions within the footwear, apparel and equipment industries" (Nike, 2005, p. 1). This involves the company engaging labor ministries, civil society, and competitors around the world to try and raise the playing field so that all companies have to attain better standards of social and environmental performance. They have moved from arguing that a business case for more responsible practice exists to exploring how to engineer that business case, by changing the signals coming from regulators, consumers, competitors, and investors. Like other companies, they have realized that the responsibility of one is to work toward the accountability of all.

This resonates with previous analysis of the concept of corporate citizenship (Bendell, 2000). One aspect of the concept of citizenship relates to being active on issues of public concern. However, another aspect of the concept relates to membership of a political community. As individual citizens, people give up certain freedoms, such as the freedom to kill, drive fast, and so on, in order to benefit from others not having such freedoms. This is done by subordinating oneself to a political community. If this concept is applied to such organizations as TNCs, then the question must be what political community they are subordinate to, what freedoms they are relinquishing, and what benefits there are for them in return, especially given that these corporations are no longer properly governed by nation states. This idea of corporate citizenship has not yet taken hold in either academia or society. Peter Newell (2002) notes that most expressions of corporate citizenship did not extend to an integrated view of rights and obligations, "relying instead on charitable acts subject to philanthropic whim" (p. 95). Yet the trends described in this chapter suggest that a fuller understanding or citizenship may spread among the corporate community.

As it spreads, various forms of corporate communications, from government relations to marketing and advertising, become important tools for driving systemic change in markets. Already, some companies are reconsidering their stance on questions of government regulation. For example, Jules Peck of WWF-UK explains that leading companies are "showing signs of discontent with trade asso-ciations that do not adequately represent their interests. For many pioneering companies, environmental regulation or economic instruments would reinforce their competitive position by pushing other companies to internalize more of their environmental costs."[9] Corporate lobbying is becoming increasingly central for understanding a corporation's social responsibility (Bendell & Kearins, 2005). One example is the recommendation on sustainability reporting from the main accountancy body of the United Kingdom that "reports should disclose the lobbying positions an organization takes on key public policy issues" (Association of Certified Chartered Accountants, 2003, p. 18).

What these shifts in corporate responsibility strategies may mean is that in the future we will witness a new type of partnership between business and civil groups that aim at changing the framework conditions of markets, including government regulations. This gives rise to a paradox where those who are concerned about corporate power are now presented with new allies—from the corporate world. How this paradox is managed may determine the future of corporate power in a globalizing world.

THE CAPITAL TURN

There are signs that after a decade of the contemporary corporate turn in civil society, more civil groups are realizing that in order to change the way business does business, we have to change the way money makes money. After facing corporate power, civil groups have realized that the real power lies behind the corporation, in those who own them or govern them through ownership of stock. Consequently, attention is turning to the role of the financial markets as the origin of, and therefore potential solution to, social and environmental problems. One example in the United States is the Corporate Sunshine Working Group, which is alliance of investors, environmental organizations, unions, and public interest groups working to enforce and expand Securities and Exchange Commission corporate social and environmental disclosure requirements.[10] In 2002, a meeting of civil groups in the Italian village of Collevecchio drafted the first civil society statement on the role of financial sector and sustainability. More than 200 civil society organizations signed up to it, and two years later an international network of nongovernmental organizations from 10 different counties, called BankTrack, was launched to act on the agenda it established (http://www.BankTrack.org). In 2005, a number of civil groups, including Amnesty International, Greenpeace, Oxfam, and WWF, launched the Fair Pensions campaign to campaign for changes in pension fund management that would allow them to reflect the values and long-term concerns of pension fund holders (http://www.fairpensions.org.uk). These initiatives indicate the beginning of a "capital turn" within civil society, which may become more significant for companies and society than the previous corporate turn.

Some parts of the financial services industry are responding positively to concerns about their social and environmental impacts. Some institutional investors are realizing the lesson mentioned earlier: that major problems such as AIDS, climate change, and poverty actually pose threats to long-term business success, and to combat them will require all companies to respond, not just a few companies that seek an ethical profile. Many investing institutions, such as pension funds, are so large that they own a broad cross section of an economy, and so many of the costs externalized by some companies in their portfolio are picked up by other companies in the same portfolio, thereby negatively affecting the value of the fund as a whole. As "universal owners," institutional investors could therefore seek a change to the way their assets are managed and redefine what it means to exercise fiduciary duty to include a broader range of factors (Hawley & Williams, 2000).

This analysis implies that a new whole-systems theory of value and valuation could arise that takes into account a company's influence and reliance on the well-being of the whole world economy. A number of initiatives are signposts for what may emerge in the future if this theory of value develops. Frank Dixon of Innovest Social Investors has developed a new approach to assessing the social and environmental performance of companies that focuses on the political activities of companies and thereby "encourages firms to proactively work with others to achieve system changes that hold them fully accountable."[11] Another signpost is the launch of the Enhanced Analytics Initiative, where asset managers and asset owners with more than €380 billion in assets under management are actively supporting better sellside research on extra-

financial issues concerning society, the environment, and corporate governance. They have committed to allocate individually a minimum of 5% of their respective brokerage commissions to sell-side researchers who are effective at analyzing material extrafinancial issues and intangibles (http://www.enhanced-analytics.com). Farsighted fiduciaries looking after trillions of dollars of assets have also backed the Carbon Disclosure Project and the Extractive Industries Transparency Initiative, both of which encourage more corporate reporting on extrafinancial issues.

It is possible that the thinking on what constitutes voluntary responsible behavior in the financial world may develop in the same way that it is currently developing in the corporate world, and so questions of power and accountability will arise. This will require us to consider issues of economic democracy and, specifically, the obligations that society should place on those who enjoy certain rights and freedoms, such as the property rights embodied in financial instruments. Ultimately, we may begin to consider how to ensure "capital accountability," which means the regulation of capital by those who are affected by it (Bendell, 2004). Given that, although capital is not owned evenly, it is owned diffusely, and in the final instance by individuals, we see that corporate power reveals itself as the personal power of individuals. Corporate power becomes "'defaced,'" not in the sense of protests targeting corporate brands, but in terms of the dissolution of a fixed face of power into an amorphous mass of aspects of ourselves. Facing corporate power means that many of us have to face ourselves. Thus, the question becomes one of our own accountability for the demands we place on institutions managing our savings, and the lack of accountability that we have to those affected by those demands.

CONCLUSIONS

Many civil groups do not make the connections between their different efforts and are unaware of the history of struggles against corporate power (Broad & Cavanagh, 2000, p. 167). This attempt at describing the diversity of perspectives on corporate power and tactics for engaging with that power that exist within civil society may help people in civil society to understand their work in new ways. It is worth remembering that whether we work in or for academia, business, government, or civil groups, we can all be part of civil society, if we associate together for collective goals.

Our analysis highlighted this unity. The initial distinction between civil society, on the one hand, and corporations, on the other, became blurred as, paradoxically, individuals in the business and financial sectors become potential allies in efforts to check corporate power. For-profit organizations may continue to be understood usefully in terms of a sector of society distinct from government and from voluntary associations of people that do not seek profits, but individuals within those companies can identify and operate beyond the roles ascribed to them by their employers and participate in social movements. This poses a challenge to mainstream views of civil society as a sector of organizations, rather than as a way of describing the collective pattern of values-based participation in society by individuals.

In addition, our exploration of how corporate power is being faced by civil groups and the consequent "capital turn" of civil society leads to a questioning of the location of that power and whether the best analytical "face" of power is the corporation, financial institutions, or individual owners of capital. This reflects poststructural debates about difficulties in defining the nature of power and locating its origin and points of application (Hayward, 2000). Because our research was an initial exploration of perspectives on corporate power, it did not employ theories on power to support a deconstruction of perspectives on power. More analytical work is needed to explore the nature of power in and around corporations, drawing upon different sociological theories for understanding power. Given our concern for the accountability of organizations and individuals in society, this future research could usefully explore what might constitute the responsible exercise of power. This is a question often sidestepped by poststructuralist approaches that regard power as pervasive and unplaceable, yet it is one that we must engage with if we seek to be relevant to how private and public interests interface in society today.

NOTES

1. This is a null definition, defining what the primary purpose is not, rather than what it is. A positive definition for "civil society" is important but beyond the scope of this chapter.

2. Interviewed confidentially by Jem Bendell, London, June 2002.

3. Interviewed confidentially by Jem Bendell, London, June 2002.

4. Interviewed confidentially by Jem Bendell, London, June 2002.

5. Interviewed confidentially by Jem Bendell, London, June 2002.

6. Interviewed confidentially by Jem Bendell, Genoa, July 2001.

7. Interviewed by Jem Bendell, London, June 2002.

8. Remarks in a speech to the Ethical Trading Initiative Conference, May 2005.

9. Correspondence with Jem Bendell, November 2002.

10. Investors also began looking at how they could lobby progressively. In the United Kingdom, the Climate Change Working Group of the London Responsible Investors Network established a subgroup to look at opportunities for the city to engage with government on public policy. Meanwhile, the Corporate Sunshine Working Group began campaigning for the Securities and Exchange Commission to expand its environmental and social disclosure requirements.

11. Correspondence with Jem Bendell, July 10, 2005.

REFERENCES

Anheier, H., Glasius, M., & Kaldor, M. (2001). Introducing global civil society. In H. Anheier, M. Glasius, & M. Kaldor (Eds.), *The global civil society yearbook* (pp. 3–22). London: London School of Economics.

Association of Certified Chartered Accountants. (2003). *ACCA UK awards for sustainability reporting 2002: Report of the judges.* London: Certified Accountants Educational Trust.

Bendell, J. (Ed.). (2000). *Terms for endearment: Business, NGOs and sustainable development.* Sheffield, UK: Greenleaf Publishing.

Bendell, J. (2001). *Towards participatory workplace appraisal: Report from a focus group of women banana workers* [Occasional Paper]. Bristol, UK: New Academy of Business.

Bendell, J. (2003). *Waking up to risk: Corporate responses to HIV/AIDS in the workplace* (Programme Paper 12). Geneva: United Nations Research Institute for Social Development (UNRISD).

Bendell, J. (2004). *Barricades and boardrooms: A contemporary history of the corporate accountability movement* (Programme Paper 13). Geneva: United Nations Research Institute for Social Development (UNRISD).

Bendell, J. (2005). In whose name? The accountability of corporate social responsibility. *Development in Practice, 15*(3–4), 362–374.

Bendell, J., & Kearins, K. (2005). The "political bottom line": The emerging dimension to corporate responsibility for sustainable development. *Business Strategy and the Environment, 14*(6), 372–383.

Braithwaite, J., & Drahaus, P. (2000). *Global business regulation.* Cambridge: Cambridge University Press.

Broad, R., & Cavanagh, J. (2000, May). *The corporate accountability movement: Lessons and opportunities.* Paper presented at the WRI Conference, Washington, DC. Retrieved July 12, 2003, from http://www.wri.org/iffe/corporat.htm.

Cairncross, F. (1995). *Green, Inc.: A guide to business and the environment.* Washington, DC: Island Press.

Chomsky, N., & Hernan, E. (1994). *Manufacturing consent: The political economy of the mass media.* London: Vintage.

Clegg, S. (1989). *Frameworks of power.* London: Sage.

Clifton, R., & Maughan, E. (1999). *The future of brands: Twenty-five visions.* London: Macmillan.

Edwards, M. (2003). *Civil society.* London: Polity Press.

Friends of the Earth International. (2002). *Towards binding corporate accountability: FOEI position paper for the WSSD.* London: Friends of the Earth International. Retrieved July 12, 2003, from http://www.foe.co.uk/pubsinfo/briefings/html/20020730133722.html.

Frey, D. (2002, December 8). How green is BP? *New York Times,* section 6, p. 99. Retrieved July 2002 from http://www.nytimes.com/2002/12/08/magazine/08BP.html?tntemail0.

Giddens, A. (1999). The role of the third sector in the third way. *CAF Focus, 2,* 8.

Hamann, R., Acutt, N., & Kapelus, P. (2003). Responsibility versus accountability? Interpreting the world summit on sustainable development for a synthesis model of corporate citizenship. *Journal of Corporate Citizenship, 9,* 32–48.

Hartman, C. L., & Stafford, E. R. (1997). Green alliances: Building new business with environmental groups. *Long Range Planning, 20*(2), 184–196.

Hawley, J. P., & Williams, A. T. (2000). *The rise of fiduciary capitalism: How institutional investors can make corporate America more democratic.* Pittsburgh: University of Pennsylvania Press.

Hayward, C. R. (2000). *De-facing power.* Cambridge: Cambridge University Press.

International Labour Organization. (2000). *Sustainable agriculture in a globalised economy.* Geneva, Switzerland: International Labour Organization. Retrieved July 12, 2003, from www.ilo.org/public/english/dialogue/sector/techmeet/tmad00/tmadr.htm.

International Right to Know. (2003). *International right to know: Empowering communities through transparency.* Washington, DC: Author.

Kingsnorth, P. (2003). *One no, many yesses: A journey to the heart of the global resistance movement.* London: Free Press.

Klein, N. (2000) *No logo.* London: Flamingo.

Lifeworth. (2003). *The Lifeworth 2002 annual review of corporate responsibility.* Retrieved July 12, 2003, from http://www.jembendell.com/lw2002/summer1.html.

Long, F., & Arnold, M. B. (1995). *The power of environmental partnerships.* Orlando, FL: Harcourt Brace & Co.

Merriam-Webster. (1992). *Collegiate dictionary & thesaurus.* 8th Edition, Springfield, MA: Author.

Mitchel, R. K., Aglre, B. R., & Wood, D. J. (1997). Toward a theory of stakeholder identification and salience: Defining the principle of who and what really counts. *Academy of Management Review, 22*(4), 853–886.

Murphy, D. F., & Bendell, J. (1997). *In the company of partners: Business, environmental groups and sustainable development post-Rio.* Bristol, UK: Policy Press.

Neal, M., & Davies, C. (1998). *The corporation under siege.* London: Social Affairs Unit.

Newell, P. (2000). Managing multinationals: The governance of investment for the environment. *Journal of International Development, 13,* 907–919.

Newell, P. (2002). From responsibility to citizenship: Corporate accountability for development. *IDS Bulletin, 33*(2), 91–100.

Nike. (2005). *Nike corporate responsibility report, 2005.* Portland, OR: Author.

O'Neill, K. (1999). *Internetworking for social change: Keeping the spotlight on corporate responsibility* (Discussion Paper No. 111). Geneva, Switzerland: United Nations Research Institute for Social Development (UNRISD).

Palast, G. (2002). *The best democracy that money can buy: An investigative reporter exposes the truth about globalisation, corporate cons, and high finance fraudsters*. London: Pluto Press.

Patterson, T. (2002). *The vanishing voter: Public involvement in an age of uncertainty*. New York: Alfred A. Knopf.

Peters, G. (1999). *Waltzing with the raptors: A practical roadmap to protecting your company's reputation*. Chichester, UK: John Wiley & Sons.

Prahalad, C. K. (2004). *The fortune at the bottom of the pyramid: Eradicating poverty through profits*. Philadelphia, PA: Wharton School Publishing.

Publish What You Pay. (2002, June 13). *George Soros and NGOs call for rules to require corporations to disclose payments* [Press Release]. Retrieved July 12, 2003, from http://www.publishwhatyoupay.org/english/pdf/releases/pwyp_130602.pdf.

Publish What You Pay. (2003). Homepage. Retrieved July 12, 2003, http://www.publishwhatyoupay.org.

Richter, J. (2001). *Holding corporations accountable: Corporate conduct, international codes, and citizen action*. London: Zed Books.

Rowe, J. (2001, July/August). Is the corporation obsolete? *Washington Monthly*. retrieved July 12, 2003, from http://www.wwdemocracy.nildram.co.uk/democracy_today/corp_obsolete.html.

Saddar, Z. (2000). *The consumption of Kuala Lumpur*. London: Reaktion Books.

Salamon, L. M., Anheier, H. K., List, R., Toepler, S., Sokolowski, S. W., et al. (Eds.). (1999). *Global civil society: Dimensions of the nonprofit sector*. Baltimore, MD: John Hopkins University Press.

Simms, A., Bigg, T., & Robins, N. (2000). *It's democracy [gone?] stupid: The trouble with the global economy—the United Nations' lost role and democratic reform of the IMF, World Bank and the World Trade Organization*. London: New Economics Foundation.

Sklair, L. (1998). Debate transnational corporations: As political actors. *New Political Economy, 3*, 284–287.

Snow, C. C., Miles, R. E., & Coleman, H. S. (1992). Managing 21st century network organizations. *Organizational Dynamics, 21*(Winter), 5–21.

Starr, A. (2000). *Naming the enemy: Anti-corporate movements confront globalization*. London: Zed Books.

Stern, A. J., & Hicks, T. (2000). *The process of business environmental collaborations: Partnering for sustainability*. Westport, CT: Quorum Books.

Strange, S. (1996). *The retreat of the state: The diffusion of power in the world economy*. Cambridge: Cambridge University Press.

Utting, P. (2002). *Regulating business via multistakeholder initiatives: A preliminary assessment in voluntary approaches to corporate responsibility. Readings and a resource guide*. Geneva: United Nations Non-Governmental Liaison Service (NGLS) and United Nations Research Institute for Social Development (UNRISD).

Ward, H. (2002, May). *Corporate accountability in search of a treaty? Some insights from foreign direct liability* (Briefing Paper No. 4). London: Royal Institute for International Affairs (RIIA).

Ward, H. (2003). *Legal issues in corporate citizenship: Paper prepared for the Swedish partnership for global responsibility*. London: International Institute for Environment and Development (IIED).

Winter, M., & Steger, U. (1998). *Managing outside pressure: Strategies for preventing corporate disasters*. Chichester, UK: John Wiley & Sons.

Zadek, S. (2001). *The civil corporation*. London: Earthscan.

5

Corporate Citizenship
The Dark-Side Paradoxes of Success

SANDRA WADDOCK

STRATEGY-CREATING
TENSIONS OF OPPOSITES

Understanding corporate citizenship is a difficult proposition at best, made more so because understanding and performance can differ depending on circumstances and context. In many parts of the world, normal business operations, strategies, and conduct are increasingly being challenged by protests against globalization and global companies. Companies' performance on human rights, labor standards and working conditions, corruption, exploitation of natural resources, marketing practices, and local community impacts, among others, increasingly calls into question corporate integrity and stakeholder and ecological responsibility. In many ways, it is the successful companies whose practices most frequently fall under the critical scrutiny of outside watchdogs, nongovernmental organizations, and activists, while less successful or less visible (particularly nonbranded) companies seem to proceed largely under the radar screen.

In this context, simple efforts to deflect criticism by, for example, donating to charities or engaging in volunteerism (the typical U.S. corporation's historical response to the need to establish its corporate citizenship) fail to establish companies as good social actors or provide credibility to their efforts to establish themselves as corporate citizens. In part, the questions arise because of the very strategies and operating practices that have resulted in financial, economic, and market success. Something more than charitable contributions and image-building initiatives is needed when a company's corporate citizenship depends not just on external perceptions of its explicit social contributions but on its business model and practices.

No one could doubt the strategic and financial success of such companies as Wal-Mart, Starbucks, Microsoft, Home Depot, and CVS. Each of these and numerous other large, high-growth, high-flying companies has succeeded with strategies that have allowed them to achieve enormous scale economies and significant clout with respect to their suppliers and employees, domination over competitors, and customer loyalty. Yet there is a dark side to their successes, a dark side that results from the very seeds of that success. That dark side involves the impacts that extremely successful companies such as these have on the societies and communities in which they are embedded and the amount of power that they wield over their stakeholders in the very process of achieving success.

In a slightly bigger context, something is dreadfully wrong with the system when successful corporate strategies result in social ills just by virtue of their success. The better some companies perform, the more discouraged and concerned some people are about the quality of life, the sustainability of the planet, and the set of values that are driving societies. Yet this seems to be the reality of the economic model and corporate incentives that dominate today's world. Although obviously not applicable in every situation, it is relatively easy to identify situations in which the very success of a company's corporate strategy results in negative social and ecological consequences. Add in the amassing of significant power, wealth, and control of resources by interests focused narrowly and solely on economic gains for the few; throw in a materialistic orientation in which entire cultures are bent to the will of those who focus predominantly on the consumption of more and more material "goods," oh, yes, at the lowest possible price, with the lowest possible wage scales, and the most efficient use of company assets; and all of this takes place in a world where the multinational corporations that exhibit these characteristics, in many instances, control more resources than do whole nations and where their reach extends many corners of the planet. Notably, it is in this context of global economic might that both the reality and the rhetoric of corporate citizenship have arisen.

Many business leaders argue that good corporate citizenship is about businesses meeting their "social" responsibilities and being proactive or interactive about engaging with society's numerous stakeholders and social needs. Of course, it is important to be proactive with respect to such issues, rather than simply waiting until there are accusations, issues, or problems to deal with and then reacting to cope with those problems. These leaders suggest, as many companies do on their websites, that there is deep recognition within the company that corporate responsibility matters—and that every effort is being made so that the company does not just appear to be but actually is responsible, as the following examples of Novartis and Cisco Systems illustrate:

Novartis

At Novartis, corporate citizenship—or corporate social responsibility—is a top priority. As a corporation, Novartis wants to act the same way as responsible and conscientious individuals would act in their community. We do everything we can to operate in a manner that is sustainable—economically, socially, and environmentally—in the best interest of long-term success for our enterprise. (Novartis, n.d.)

Cisco Systems

Cisco strives to be a good citizen worldwide. Our culture drives us to set high standards for corporate integrity and to give back by using our resources for a positive global impact. We pursue a strong "triple bottom line" which we describe as *profits, people,* and *presence.* Profits are one traditional and valuable metric which helps measure our financial performance. People are equally important. Strong, mutually beneficial relationships with partners, customers, shareholders and the people who work for, with and near us are essential to our business. The third bottom line—presence—measures our standing in, respect for and contribution to global and local communities. We believe companies with strong triple bottom lines are the most sustainable, responsible and successful. We hope the information in the pages of this web site demonstrates our commitment to a strong triple bottom line (Cisco, n.d.).

A list of similar corporate citizenship (corporate responsibility, corporate social responsibility) statements could go on for quite some time. Emphasis on corporate citizenship (and its synonyms) has grown exponentially since the mid 1990s when the term first began gaining popularity. The intriguing question behind this explosion of corporate interest in responsibility was posed by a participant in a recent conference at Wingspread: "Corporate citizenship is the symptom, but what is the problem?" Just what is all of the corporate attention to corporate citizenship designed to accomplish? Is it possible that corporate critics are correct in their assertions that corporate citizenship is merely a smokescreen designed to divert attention from the real impacts and even harms inflicted on society and nature by corporate activities? Or do corporate citizenship initiatives in their various guises represent real efforts by companies to meet their social obligations and real recognition of their embeddedness in (and subservience to) the interests of society and the planet?

This chapter explores what we can call the paradox of corporate citizenship, as posed above. That is, it explores the paradoxical dark underbelly created by strategic success in corporations and their efforts to implement voluntary corporate social responsibility initiatives to demonstrate their good corporate citizenship. This exploration looks at the tensions of corporate citizenship and responsibility that are created, not when there are crises, scandals, or misdeeds, but when the very success of the company's strategy is itself the source of concern.

PARADOX: THE DARK SIDE OF CORPORATE CITIZENSHIP

Viewed from the perspective of paradox, corporate citizenship not only highlights the light side of corporate involvement in society—doing real social good—but also potentially reveals a hidden dark side. In some respects, corporate citizenship efforts can represent, at least to critics, part of an overall effort to disguise or at least mitigate the dark side of corporate strategies and their successes that arise directly from the power and resource commanded by many, particularly large transnational, companies today. Here is the tension: we have created a system in which success means continual growth and expansion, a focus on efficiency within the company (and externalizing costs wherever possible to society), and control over resources, markets, customer preferences and choices, and employees (to name a few factors).

This system has resulted in huge multinational companies (MNCs), many of which are larger than the entire national economy of small countries. At the same time, there is little or no effective system of global or local governance over MNCs that can ensure that they are subordinated to the interests of the societies that they are intended to serve. The best that can be said is that a voluntary responsibility assurance system is at the very early stages of emerging and that a few countries have promulgated new laws requiring various types of disclosure (Waddock, 2006). For the most part, however, financial analysts, investors, and corporate leaders applaud voluntary approaches to corporate citizenship and seek to avoid more regulation of their activities.

Critics, of course, have long noted the problems associated with corporate dominance over societal interests. Business leaders have responded—largely through their corporate citizenship initiatives. It is in these initiatives that the paradox arises. Think for a minute of the contrast inherent in the good works that many companies undertake for their communities, combined with the negative community impacts of so-called big box superstores on local communities. The favorite whipping boy in this regard, of course, is Wal-Mart, whose hugely successful strategy of efficiency aimed at "low prices—always" attracts customers searching for those low prices, and which responded heroically in many respects to the disaster in the southern

United States wrought by Hurricane Katrina, but which simultaneously devastates local downtown shopping districts, pays low wages to contingency (part-time) workers, and creates incentives for more people to get into their cars and drive to shop. The result is what some observers and critics term "sprawl-mart," or greater suburban sprawl (Multinational Monitor, 2004); outraged communities; more than a million relatively low-paid workers, many of whom are "contingency" or part-time workers; huge discrimination lawsuits; and tremendous pressures on suppliers for efficiencies that drive sometimes already-poor human rights and labor practices even lower. Customers, of course, are happy with the low prices. I explore Wal-Mart's situation in more detail below.

As with similarly successful companies in other industries (e.g., Starbucks, Home Depot, CVS, Microsoft), it is Wal-Mart's very success that has created the considerable downside unintended consequences for community, employees, workers in supply chain companies, the natural environment, and even whole societies that fear the homogenization that a Wal-Mart brings. Companies like Wal-Mart command enormous resources, great market clout, the capacity to pressure suppliers, and the political savvy to overcome many obstacles to strategic success. Effectively, they make choices for consumers about what they will be able to buy and even, in some cases, screen products that are not to their liking. But is a world dominated by the likes of Wal-Mart—or any economic engine like it—really the world we want to live in and leave behind for our children? That is the fundamental question that faces us today.

In a world dominated by economic interests, corporate power combines with the decidedly short-term thinking that seems characteristic of today's financial markets and is inherently part of what Frederick (1995) termed "economizing." The attendant power aggrandizing (Frederick, 1995) means not only that successful companies tend to become enormously large, but also that they command significant market power and resources to use for their own purposes rather than the good of all. Add in the seemingly endless series of scandals that show that self-regulatory and self-governance efforts do not always work, and you arrive at the paradox of corporate citizenship.

THE DARK SIDE ELEMENTS OF CORPORATE CITIZENSHIP

Several fundamental issues are embedded in the paradox of corporate citizenship raised by disconnects between intent and practice: (1) the short-term orientation on which both companies and financial markets operate and the long-term societal issues that short-term thinking creates, (2) an overly narrow focus on corporate citizenship as explicitly doing good while ignoring other effects of company behavior, (3) the gap between the rhetoric and reality of many companies' corporate citizenship, and (4) the reality that most corporate citizenship agendas, even when quite broadly stated, fail to deal with the significant risks, impacts, and practices of companies that result from their business models.

Taken together, these issues represent the dark underbelly of corporate citizenship—and provide plenty of fodder for corporate critics and critics of the corporate responsibility movement (Crook, 2005; Derber, 2004). In what follows I explore these dark-side elements, while recognizing that for many companies (or what I have elsewhere termed "leading corporate citizens"), their corporate citizenship initiatives are real, profound, and honorable. For at least a fraction of companies, however, dark-side implications need to surface lest we be saddled with an overly optimistic view of the possibilities of corporate citizenship.

Short-Term Orientation

Corporations and the financial markets that they serve are notoriously short-sighted. On one hand, short-term thinking forces companies to be efficient, using their resources wisely, producing positive results for shareholders, products and services for customers, and jobs for employees. On the other hand, sometimes short-term thinking leads directly and indirectly to very "dark-side" effects: the ebb and flow of layoffs, lack of investment in "human resources" (i.e., people), and the constant forming and reforming of companies that is involved in the waves of mergers, acquisitions, and restructurings, all of which have wrought havoc on employee loyalty in recent years. Over years of corporate and political rhetoric about free markets, efficiency, and the need for profits to sustain our material bents, we have come to accept these

dark-side effects—and even sometimes fail to recognize their negative impacts on people as individuals and on communities as important parts of society.

Short-term thinking places significant demands on companies to always have to make a business case, that is, the case for profitable outcomes, for undertaking much of any long-range activity, including investment in people, products, research and development, and market research about real social needs. While it is clear from recent meta-studies (e.g., Margolis & Walsh, 2003; Orlitzky, Schmidt, & Rynes, 2003) that there are no necessary trade-offs between being responsibility and good financial performance, it is also clear from a short-term perspective that irresponsibility can also produce good results at times. The performance of tobacco companies (selling products that in their normal use kill people) makes this reality clear. The clear imperative embedded in U.S. law is an emphasis on profitability through whatever means are feasible, with little regard for consequences typically labeled as externalities.

Indeed, even a reasonable business case for corporate citizenship in the broader sense (beyond simply "doing good" through charity and encompassing operational practices; Waddock, 2006) can be insufficient grounds for constructive action on the part of companies. Most business leaders have fully bought into the notion of maximizing shareholder wealth at all costs and focusing on this quarter's earnings, because the financial markets expect returns. Further, some things are valuable of their own accord, whether or not they are profitable, as recent emphasis on human rights, codes of conduct, and ecological sustainability (among other factors) suggests (although more prominent in Europe than the United States, according to Rifkin, 2004). These things relate to human values that go well beyond materialism to tap into something else in human nature that aspires to connection, love, and even transcendence.

Still, short-term thinking infects decisions on just about everything that companies touch, particularly in the United States, though increasingly elsewhere, as well. It played no small role in the numerous scandals that have hit the United States and Europe during the early 2000s, as company leaders attempted to "improve" their near-term results to satisfy intense demands from financial markets, or to line their own pockets without regard for the company, employee, customer, investor, or societal consequences. Further, it is entirely possible that companies look (and are) strategically and financially successful in the short term while their managers are doing unethical, or at least highly problematic, things to attain those results and that can backfire, sending the company into ruin (e.g., Enron, WorldCom). The paradoxes inherent in this tension combine with corporate leaders' apparent desire to govern themselves in this difficult context.

The spillover effects of short-term thinking have been obvious and include the emergence of a social context and broken social contract in which loyalty to or from companies is unfashionable, at best, whether it is from the investor or employee side. Yet we know, from such studies as Collins and Porras's *Built to Last* (2002) and Collins's *Good to Great* (2001) that truly great (responsible?) companies engender loyalty from their investors and their employees (not to mention their customers), in part because they are thinking beyond the next quarter.

An Overly Narrow Focus for Corporate Citizenship

One aspect of the short-term orientation is the suspicion by corporate critics that some (many) corporate citizenship initiatives are simply efforts to downplay some of the realities of today's corporate practices and short-termism through image manipulation. In this view, corporate citizenship activities attempt to create the appearance of (and some actual) investment in the social good, while allowing companies to avoid the real responsibilities for the impacts that their short-term oriented practices have on employees, customers, investors, and the natural environment.

Combine short-term thinking with a mindless growth-at-all-costs mentality, emphasizing free trade and market building that rides roughshod over local and regional interests (Cavanagh et al., 2002), add the increased recognition of the importance of reputation to branded companies, and it is perhaps no wonder that corporate citizenship (responsibility) rhetoric and practice have emerged as a key phenomenon of the modern corporate landscape. By this reading, corporate citizenship efforts, particularly the dominant ones aimed at doing explicit social good though charitable contributions of either money or in-kind services and goods, are efforts to put a good public face on the company while it continues business as usual. When, however, business as usual involves such practices as outsourcing from sweatshops, paving over vast tracts of land for parking lots, creating even more incentives for people to drive to shop, fostering consumption of scarce or nonrenewable resources, harming the ecological environment, producing useless, unnecessary, and even harmful products, and so on, critics, environmentalists, and community activists become outraged.

Numerous companies today highlight their voluntary (good) corporate citizenship and social responsibility in public forums such as their websites, in triple-bottom-line reports, and through their public statements. Studies seem to confirm that there is a neutral to possibly slightly positive correlation between corporate responsibility and financial performance (e.g., Margolis & Walsh, 2003; Orlitzky & Benjamin, 2001). The notion is that companies can "do well by doing good," following what Waddock and Graves (1997a, 1997b) call the "good management hypothesis," that is, that being responsible is simply good management.

Yet the reality of corporate citizenship is rather more nuanced—and considerably more problematic. Sometimes, as noted above, the very strategic and financial success of firms results in negative consequences for society—or at least the consequences are negative in the eyes of critics. So, in response, many companies have developed corporate citizenship, corporate social responsibility, and corporate giving programs. It is in the focus of these corporate citizenship initiatives that part of the paradox lies. Despite the broad expressions of corporate citizenship articulated by Cisco and Novartis, which emphasize a holistic conception of the company's relationships with its stakeholders, nature, and society, more typical expressions of corporate citizenship (particularly in U.S. companies) are considerably more narrow, encompassing community relations and philanthropy, but not going much further. MasterCard's statement is typical of this focus: "MasterCard's corporate citizenship efforts focus on supporting organizations that focus on youth, with a particular emphasis on programs that address educational needs; help youth access technology; and international initiatives that benefit youth" (Mastercard, 2006).

Arguably, voluntary corporate citizenship initiatives such as these provide a hoped-for way for companies to show their good heartedness to their many stakeholders beyond investors. Corporate citizenship, from this perspective, represents the efforts of business leaders to voluntarily and openly "do good" in society in the hopes of building trust and a good reputation among customers, employees, and investors, as well as activists, communities, and government. At the same time, skeptics and critics view such narrowly focused corporate citizenship initiatives as mere window dressing, intended to draw attention away from the other, sometimes negative, consequences of large powerful corporations in society. That disconnect brings us to another paradox of corporate citizenship: the rhetoric/reality gap.

The Rhetoric/Reality Gap

In the context presented above, it is perhaps unsurprising that critics question how much corporate citizenship rhetoric is for real (e.g., Derber, 2002, 2004). Company leaders who have good intentions can feel caught in a conundrum of trying to look good to investors and employees in a social context where demands that they act as "good citizens" have dramatically escalated in recent years, but where short-term financial performance pressures seem endless and where the business imperative is to be efficient by externalizing costs whenever possible. More sophisticated customers, socially oriented investors, and activists have developed the skills to publicize perceived problems broadly and damage hard-won reputations. Fueled by global connectivity, growing awareness of pressure tactics such as shareholder resolutions, and, in some instances, laws that are increasingly focused on various forms of disclosure and transparency in different parts of the world, companies are being pressured to act responsibly.

There may be some justification to the views of critics who claim that corporate citizenship largely represents an effort to cover up the dark side of capitalism, at least in some cases. This perspective seems reasonable if we compare the actual behaviors and impacts of certain (but certainly not all) companies with their stated corporate citizenship objectives. For example, consider the following statements about corporate citizenship from company websites:

1. "We believe that good corporate citizenship means helping to meet the world's growing demand for energy in an economically, environmentally and socially responsible manner" (ExxonMobil, 2004).

2. "Our business is built on relationships— with our customers, partners, investors, employees, and with the communities where we live and work. We are committed to keeping those relationships strong by communicating openly about our business practices, being transparent about our performance, and remaining accountable for our conduct. We know that our decisions have significant ramifications for other companies and for people and communities worldwide. We take that responsibility very seriously" (Microsoft, 2005).

3. "Citizenship defines our role in local and global communities and how we strive to conduct business responsibly in a changing world. Being a good corporate citizen includes listening to, understanding, and responding to our stakeholders about their needs regarding [our] policies and operations. Stakeholders are people or groups who affect, or are affected by, [our] business activities. Our relationship with them is at the heart of our citizenship because they define what it means for [us] to create value. They are the ones who will determine when [the company] fulfills its mission to become the world's most valued company to stakeholders" (Pfizer, 2005).

These sentiments are brought to you by (1) the company responsible for the *Exxon Valdez* oil spill in Alaska for which reparations are still not fully made, which has refused to admit the reality of concerns about global warming, and is one of the world's largest producers of oil and gas; (2) the company accused of strong-arming its allies and suppliers to ensure its relative monopoly status; and (3) the company whose popular pain killer Celebrex is said to cause heart attacks but that refused in 2004 to take it off the market (notably unlike its direct competitor Merck, which withdrew its similar drug Vioxx for that reason). Behavior and the rhetoric about values do not seem in these and many other instances to be well matched to the values that can be observed by watching the actual practices of companies. More insidious even than the rhetoric/reality gap, however, is the lack of recognition of negative social impacts that derive from successful business mod-

els, the final and perhaps more important paradox discussed here.

Impacts from
the Business Model

Interesting examples of highly successful companies
can be found—companies that have achieved wealth
and competitive success beyond their founders' wild-
est dreams but whose corporate citizenship is
strongly questioned by at least some critics. Some
of these very companies are now being accused of
being bad social actors, in part because of the very
successes they have experienced and, of course, because of the power they have accumulated as a result of that success. The tensions inherent in this
situation are epitomized by *Fortune* magazine
awarding in 2004 the designation of "most admired" (and largest retail) corporation to Wal-Mart.
In the very same issue, the magazine carried a
thoughtful article by Jerry Useem titled "Should We
Admire Wal-Mart?" that lays out the tension starkly:

> There is an evil company in Arkansas, some say.
> It's a discount store—a very, very big discount
> store—and it will do just about anything to get
> bigger. You've seen the headlines. Illegal immi-
> grants mopping its floors. Workers locked in-
> side overnight. A big gender discrimination suit.
> Wages low enough to make *other* companies'
> workers go on strike. And we know what it does
> to weaker suppliers and competitors. Crushing
> the dream of the independent proprietor—an
> ideal as American as Thomas Jefferson—it is the
> enemy of all that's good and right in our nation.
>
> There is another big discount store in Ar-
> kansas, yet this one couldn't be more different
> from the first. Founded by a folksy entrepre-
> neur whose notions of thrift, industry, and the
> square deal were pure Ben Franklin, this com-
> pany is not a tyrant but a servant. Passing along
> the gains of its brilliant distribution system to
> consumers, its farsighted managers have done
> nothing less than democratize the American
> dream. Its low prices are spurring productiv-
> ity and helping win the fight against inflation.
> It is America's most admired company.
>
> Weirdest part is, both these companies are
> named Wal-Mart Stores, Inc. (Useem, 2004,
> p. 118)

Ironically, as the paragraphs above make clear, it
is the very success of Wal-Mart's business strat-

egy that has resulted in significant questions about
its corporate citizenship, where that term is defined
to mean the impacts that the company's strategies
and operating practices have on stakeholders and
the natural environment (Waddock, 2006). And
it is questions like the ones raised by Useem about
Wal-Mart that are actually at the heart of many
current debates about corporate citizenship.

Many companies are caught in a conundrum
similar to the one that faces Wal-Mart. On the one
hand, they are trying to be effective global competitors strategically by using efficiency-oriented
economizing strategies (Frederick, 1995), combined with a continual growth orientation to satisfy investors' needs for profit "maximization"
(see, e.g., Rowell, 2003; Strategic Direction, 2004).
They are under significant pressure from their
investors and the financial community to continually enhance performance and growth opportunities. Companies viewed as successful constantly
grow their revenue and sales bases, selling more
products and services to ever wider and more
dispersed markets. To achieve success in highly
competitive markets, many companies develop operating practices that externalize hidden or even
unrecognized costs to society, while creating ter-
rific shareholder returns.

Such companies may be using strategies that
disregard the consequences of their goods and services or corporate practices on local communities,
whole societies, and nature, in their quest to gain
more market, financial, and customer-based power,
creating problems for other stakeholders (Bianco,
Zellner, Brady, & France, 2003). Let us explore the
corporate citizenship impacts of one dominant company—perhaps the most visible icon of this societal problem: Wal-Mart. Note here that corporate
citizenship is defined not merely as the discretionary activities to do social good (e.g., Carroll, 1979,
1998) but as the impacts of the company's strategies and operating practices on its stakeholders and
on nature (Waddock, 2006).

Wal-Mart is the world's largest company; in
2002, it represented 2.5% of U.S. gross domestic product (Hoch, 2004). Known for its efficiency, the company has also been subjected to
many questions about its corporate citizenship. A
listing of the titles of some critical articles about
Wal-Mart illustrates the range of some of the concerns related to the company's successful strategy
(see appendix 5.1). For example, the company
pays relatively low wages to a largely contingent

workforce (Malch, 2004) and has been known to use harsh management tactics to achieve its efficiency goals (Saporito, Boston, Gough, & Healy, 2003). Those wages can discourage other employers from paying living wages locally and thereby create what one observer called "the Wal-Martization" of the economy, causing employees in *other* companies to protest the incursion of a Wal-Mart into their territory (Holmes & Zellner, 2004; Tsao, 2002). The employment of part-time workers at marginal wages creates situations where employees need to use food stamps and other tax-based resources simply to live.

Wal-Mart's strategy also affects the natural environment, which not only deteriorates the greenscape with huge paved-over tracts of land (some of which are abandoned when the company consolidates into larger facilities) but also forces customers to drive long distances to do basic shopping that used to be done in local downtowns, worsening urban sprawl (Multinational Monitor, 2004; Sanson, 2004). Local culture and character are homogenized into one faceless low-prices-always mentality, while local stores, particularly in neighboring communities to the Wal-Mart facility, suffer or simply go out of business (Davidson & Rummel, 2000; Multinational Monitor, 2004; Pearson & McGee, 2000; Stringer, 2004). Consumers, of course, benefit, at least in the short term while they still have jobs and money to spend, before their jobs are outsourced by suppliers, who must become as efficient as Wal-Mart simply to do business with the giant retailer (e.g., Fishman, 2003). And all of these impacts hardly take into account Wal-Mart's status as the "world's biggest target," its determined antiunion stance and the huge discrimination lawsuit filed against it on behalf of 1.6 *million* women (Bergdahl, 2004; Daniels, 2004), or the constant criticisms of its supply chain and employee practices (Saporito et al., 2003).

Wal-Mart is not alone in evidencing negative corporate citizenship effects that result directly from their successful strategies. Nor is it alone in being subjected to the negative reputational impacts as critics have become more vocal and the negative by-products of company strategies have become more evident. At least one observer, in fact, claims that the reputational problems for Wal-Mart represent a serious "mid-life crisis" for the company (Malch, 2004). Other powerful companies, for example, Home Depot, Starbucks, Microsoft, Staples, Borders, and Barnes & Noble, have developed similarly successful retail strategies that have resulted in stunning competitive success—at significant costs to other stakeholders (at least so critics claim), especially smaller competitors, local communities, and the environment. Nike's successful efforts to become a design and marketing company, leaving the manufacture of its footwear to suppliers working on a cost-competitive basis in developing nations, resulted in all kinds of accusations of human and labor rights abuses in its supply chain. Think, for example, about the criticisms that Starbucks, now seemingly ubiquitous in some cities, has faced about its sourcing practices, which are no worse than and quite possibly better than those of its competitors. But it is the largest company, and hence its practices are more noticeable and leave a larger footprint than do those of smaller competitors.

Thus, possibly the most insidious paradox of corporate citizenship derives from the reality that in many instances is the very success of a company's business model that creates problems for society, nature, or stakeholders. Numerous observers consider the current economic model to be broken, especially with respect to its societal impacts (e.g., Bakan, 2004; Cavanagh et al., 2002; Handy, 2002; Korten, 1995, 1999). As noted above, the dominant economic logic emphasizes short-term profitability; has an overly narrow orientation toward owners who, as Handy (2002) points out, are really only investors; and emphasizes dominance and growth of the company at the expense of most stakeholders.

CORPORATE SOCIAL RESPONSIBILITY AS FAILED ANTIDOTE

Traditional approaches to corporate citizenship, based on an understanding of corporate *social* responsibility (Carroll, 1998; see Waddock, 2004, for an elaboration of definitions) or performance (Wood, 1991) that aims at the discretionary and philanthropic things that companies do to enhance their reputations, do not seem sufficient to solve the real problems of corporate citizenship that derive from strategic success, as detailed above. Consider that leaders in these companies seem narrowly focused on economics and efficiency (economizing; Frederick, 1995), rather than treating other stakeholders (and nature) with respect. For example, here are Sam Walton's (Wal-Mart's founder) "Three Basic Beliefs," on which Wal-Mart was built, which are posted on the Wal-Mart website:

> Sam Walton built Wal-Mart on the revolutionary philosophies of excellence in the workplace, customer service, and always having the lowest prices. We have always stayed true to the Three Basic Beliefs Mr. Sam established in 1962:
>
> 1. Respect for the individual
> 2. Service to our customers
> 3. Strive for excellence (Wal-Mart, 2005).

There is nothing wrong (and indeed, much right) with these statements as a business model, but his set of beliefs also comes closest to a public articulation of Wal-Mart's corporate citizenship philosophy that can be found on the website. The company does detail specifics of its employee, diversity, environmental, and community-related practices, which have received awards listed on a separate webpage (see appendix 5.2 for the highlights as of 2005). Tellingly, given its community-related controversies, Wal-Mart has established a foundation, the theme of which is: "We're committed to the communities we serve. We live here, too, and we believe good, works" (Wal-Mart Foundation, 2005a, 2005b). For what it calls "good works," that is, its philanthropic programs, Wal-Mart states the following philosophy:

> Wal-Mart's Good Works community involvement program is based on the philosophy of operating globally and giving back locally. In our experience, we can make the greatest impact on communities by supporting issues and causes that are important to our customers and associates in their own neighborhoods. We rely on our associates to know which organizations are the most important to their hometowns, and we empower them to determine how Wal-Mart Foundation dollars will be spent. Consequently, our funding initiatives are channeled directly into local communities by associates who live there. (Wal-Mart Foundation, 2005b)

While laudable in its own right, the activities of any foundation or charitable giving program alone cannot and do not constitute good corporate citizenship (defined in the broad sense) for a company whose impacts are as many and as broad in scope

as Wal-Mart's. Something more is needed to balance the interests of society against those of economy, something that is unlikely to happen based on companies' goodwill alone, simply because their incentives are focused on short-term profitability and share price. *Societal* welfare depends on healthy companies, to be sure, but it also depends on good treatment of employees and other stakeholders, as well as products and services that add true value for customers and do not detract from ecological sustainability. Doing this well—meeting the real demands of corporate citizenship—means that society itself (through governments) must specify the standards to be met—and ensure that companies actually live up to those standards.

It is increasingly clear that the corporate citizenship agenda is being misinterpreted—and perhaps misused—by companies as a smokescreen to hide the real negative impacts of some of their practices, the ironic fruits of success for the company that result in problems and externalities imposed on societies. Even as conservative a magazine as *The Economist* has recognized these realities:

> [P]rivate enterprise serves the public good only if certain stringent conditions are met. As a result, getting the most out of capitalism requires public intervention of various kinds, and a lot of it: taxes, public spending, regulation in many different areas of business activity. It also requires corporate executives to be accountable —but to the right people and in the right way. (Crook, 2005)

As long as corporate citizenship/responsibility is narrowly interpreted to mean specific "do good" activities and, indeed, as long as societies rely on the voluntary goodwill of managers to behave in responsible ways when the incentives of profitability push them in other directions, there will be problems and externalities that derive directly from the successes of companies, just as illustrated with Wal-Mart.

CONCLUSION

Most companies are simply trying to succeed by playing by the current rules of the game, which allow them to externalize many of their real costs to society without much regard for the true consequences of their actions and strategies (see also

Handy, 2002). So, arguably, none of these companies' leaders is ill-intentioned. All are trying to meet the expectations that have deliberately been placed on them by (in this case American) society: to maximize profits in the best interest of shareholders, as well as to achieve competitive success for their companies and career success for themselves. In focusing on these goals, however, corporate leaders too often overlook or ignore the societal and ecological implications of their actions and of their successes. As Bakan's explosive book (and related movie) *The Corporation* (2004) points out, the actions that companies take bear significant resemblance to those of a sociopath. And to control a sociopath, we need to take more severe measures than can be found in the activities we now call corporate social responsibility.

APPENDIX 5.1: HEADLINES ILLUSTRATING CONCERNS ABOUT WAL-MART

- "Welcome to Wal-World: Wal-Mart's Inexhaustible March to Conquer the Globe" (Rowell, 2003)
- "Taking on Sprawl-Mart: Sprawl-Busting, Community to Community" (Multinational Monitor, 2004)
- "There's Big—and There's Wal-Mart: Winners on a Huge Scale" (Strategic Direction, 2004)
- "Wal-Mart's Woman Problem" (Daniels, 2004)
- "Being the World's Biggest Target" (Bergdahl, 2004)
- "Is Wal-Mart Too Powerful?" (Bianco et al., 2003)
- "Can Wal-Mart Get Any Bigger?" (Saporito et al., 2003)
- "Are Chain Stores Ruining the Landscape of America?" (Sanson, 2004)
- "Wal-Mart's Surge Leaves Dead Stores Behind" (Stringer, 2004)
- "Wal-Mart Cuts the Union" (Cray, 2000)
- "Retail Changes Associated with Wal-Mart's Entry into Maine" (Davidson & Rummel, 2000)
- "Survivors of W-Day: An Assessment of the Impact of Wal-Mart's Invasion of Small Town Retailing Communities" (Pearson & McGee, 2000)

APPENDIX 5.2: WAL-MART STATEMENTS OF CORPORATE RESPONSIBILITY

Wal-Mart Stores: Commitment to the Community

Overview

Wal-Mart Stores, Inc. believes each Wal-Mart store, SAM'S CLUB and distribution center has a responsibility to contribute to the well being [sic] of the local community. Our more than 3,400 locations contributed more than $150 million to support communities and local non-profit organizations. Customers raised an additional $75 million with the help of our stores and clubs.

Philosophy

Wal-Mart's Good.Works. community involvement program is based on the philosophy of operating globally and giving back locally. In our experience, we can make the greatest impact on communities by supporting issues and causes that are important to our customers and associates in their own neighborhoods. We rely on our associates to know which organizations are the most important to their hometowns, and we empower them to determine how Wal-Mart Foundation dollars will be spent. Consequently, our funding initiatives are channeled directly into local communities by associates who live there. (Wal-Mart, 2005)

Wal-Mart's Commitment to People

Under "Our Commitment to People" Wal-Mart lists a series of awards and recognitions it has received. Similarly, the company lists a series of facts about its employment policies under the rubric: "Our Commitment to Responsible Employment."

Our Commitment to People

- "Wal-Mart Stores, Inc. is the leading private employer of emerging groups in the United States. More than 160,000 African American associates and more than 105,000 Hispanic associates work for Wal-Mart Stores, SAM'S CLUBS and Wal-Mart's logistics facilities nationwide.

- "Wal-Mart Stores, Inc. received the 2002 Ron Brown Award, the highest Presidential Award recognizing outstanding achievement in employee relations and community initiatives.
- "The National Hispana Leadership Institute recognized Wal-Mart with the 2002 National Leadership Award for its support of leadership and development programs for Latinas.
- "The NAACP presented Wal-Mart with the NAACP 2000 Pacesetter Award for corporate leadership.
- "The National Action Network presented Wal-Mart Stores, Inc. with the 2002 Community Commitment Corporate Award in recognition of community involvement and diversity practices.
- "Wal-Mart received the Hispanic National Bar Association 2002 Corporate Partner of the Year Award for its consistent support and best practices in the area of diversity.
- "The Organization of Chinese Americans appointed Wal-Mart Stores, Inc. to its 2002 Corporate Advisory Board.
- "Wal-Mart received the prestigious 2001 and 2002 Billion-Dollar Roundtable Award for spending more than $1 billion with women and minority-owned suppliers.
- "The American Minority Supplier Development Council named Wal-Mart as the 2001 Minority Business Advocate of the Year.
- "Hispanic Business Magazine named Wal-Mart one of the Top 25 Diversity Recruitment Programs in 2001 for its aggressive program to hire and promote Latinos and Latinas.
- "Wal-Mart Stores, Inc. received a Blue Ribbon Board Award from the organization Catalyst for having two women on its board of directors. Catalyst is a nationally established organization that works with the business sector to advance women."

Our Commitment to Responsible Employment

- "Wal-Mart is recognized as one of the leading employers of disabled people in the nation. In the 2002 annual poll by *Careers for the Disabled* magazine, Wal-Mart was named 1st among all U.S. companies in providing opportunities and a positive working environment for people with disabilities.
- "With more than one million associates nationwide, Wal-Mart Stores, Inc. is the fastest growing and largest private employer in the United States. Both full-time (~70% of Wal-Mart's work force) and part-time associates are eligible for benefits.
- "Since the inception of Wal-Mart's profit sharing plan in 1972 and the inception of Wal-Mart's 401(k) plan in 1997, Wal-Mart has contributed nearly $3 billion toward the retirement funds of its associates.
- "Wal-Mart Stores, Inc. is one of the leading employers of senior citizens in the United States, employing more than 164,000 associates 55 and older." (http://www .walmartstores .com/wmstore/wmstores/Mainnews.jsp?BV_ SessionID=@@@@0511680954.1104 867644 @@@@ &BV_EngineID=cccgadcmilmfdflcfkf cfkjdgoodglg.0&pagetype=news&categoryOID= -8772&catID=-8248&template= DisplayAllContents.jsp) (1/4/05).

REFERENCES

Bakan, J. (2004). *The corporation: The pathological pursuit of profit and power*. New York: Free Press.

Bergdahl, M. (2004). Being the world's biggest target. *Retail Merchandiser, 44*(9), 44.

Bianco, A., Zellner, W., Brady, D., & France, T. (2003, October 6). Is Wal-Mart too powerful? *BusinessWeek, 3862,* 100–108.

Carroll, A. B. (1979). A three-dimensional conceptual model of corporate social performance. *Academy of Management Review, 4,* 497–505.

Carroll, A. B. (1998). The four faces of corporate citizenship. *Business & Society Review, 100–101,* 1–7.

Cavanagh, J., Mander, J., Anderson, S., Barker, D., Barlow, M., Bellow, W., et al. (2002). *Alternatives to economic globalization.* San Francisco, CA: Berrett-Kohler.

Cisco Systems. (n.d.). Retrieved January 10, 2004, from http://www.cisco.com/en/US/ about/ac227/about_cisco_corporate_ citizenship_home.html.

Collins, J. C. (2001). Good to great: Why some companies make the leap—and others don't. New York: HarperBusiness.

Collins, J. C., & Porras, J. I. (2002). Built to last: Successful habits of visionary companies. New York: HarperBusiness Essentials.

Crook, C. (2005, January 20). The good company. *Economist.* Retrieved January 24, 2004, from http://www.economist.com/ displaystory.cfm?story_id=3555212.

Daniels, C. (2004). Wal-Mart's women problem. *Fortune, 150*(1), 14.

Davidson, S. M., & Rummel, A. (2000). Retail changes associated with Wal-Mart's entry into Maine. *International Journal of Retail & Distribution Management, 28*(4/5), 152–169.

Derber, C. (2002). *People before profit: The new globalization in an era of terror, big money, and economic crisis.* New York: St. Martin's Press.

Derber, C. (2004). *Regime change begins at home: Freeing America from corporate rule.* San Fransisco, CA: Berrett-Kohler.

ExxonMobil. (2004). Retrieved January 5, 2004, from http://www.exxonmobil.com/ corporate/Citizenship/Corp_citizenship_ home.asp.

Fishman, C. (2003, December). The Wal-Mart you don't know. *Fast Company, 77,* 68–75.

Frederick, W. C. (1995). *Values, nature, and culture in the American corporation.* New York: Oxford University Press.

Handy, C. (2002, December). What's a business for? *Harvard Business Review,* 49–55.

Hoch, S. J. (2004, October 6). Can Wal-Mart beat history? *Advertising Age, 74*(40), 23.

Holmes, S., & Zellner, W. (2004, April 12). The Costco way. *BusinessWeek, 3878,* 76–77.

Korten, D. (1995). *When corporations rule the world.* San Francisco, CA: Berrett-Koehler.

Korten, D. (1999). *The post-corporate world: Life after capitalism.* San Francisco, CA: Berrett-Koehler.

Malch, S. (2004, October 23). Wal-Mart's mid-life crisis. *Maclean's, 117*(34), 45.

Margolis, J. D., & Walsh, J. P. (2003). Misery loves companies: Rethinking social initiatives by business. *Administrative Science Quarterly, 48,* 268–305.

Mastercard. (2006). Retrieved February 15, 2006, from http://www.mastercardintl .com/corporate/corp_citizen.html.

Microsoft. (2005). Retrieved January 5, 2005, from http://www.microsoft.com/mscorp/ citizenship/.

Multinational Monitor. (2004, January/ February). Taking on sprawl-mart: Sprawl-busting community by community: An interview with Al Norman. *Multinational Monitor,* 30–34.

Novartis. (n.d.). Retrieved January 10, 2004, from http://www.novartis.com/corporate_ citizenship/en/index.shtml.

Orlitzky, M., & Benjamin, J. D. (2001). Corporate social performance and firm risk: A meta-analytic review. *Business and Society, 40*(4), 369–396.

Orlitzky, M., Schmidt, F. I., & Rynes, S. L. (2003). Corporate social and financial performance: A meta-analysis. *Organization Studies, 24,* 403–441.

Pearson, M., & McGee, J. E. (2000). Survivors of "W-Day": An assessment of the impact of Wal-Mart's invasion of small town retailing communities. *International Journal of Retail & Distribution Management, 28*(4/5), 170–180.

Pfizer. (2005). Retrieved January 5, 2005, from http://www.pfizer.com/subsites/corporate_ citizenship/what_is_cc.html.

Rifkin, J. (2004). *The European dream: How Europe's vision of the future is quietly eclipsing the American dream.* New York: Jeremy P. Tarcher (Penguin).

Rowell, A. (2003, October). Welcome to Wal-World: Wal-Mart's inexhaustible march to conquer the globe. *Multinational Monitor,* pp. 13–16.

Sanson, M. (2004, August). Are chain stores ruining the landscape of America? *Retail Hospitality, 88*(8), 10.

Saporito, B., Boston, W., Gough, N., & Healy, R. (2003). Can Wal-Mart get any bigger? *Time, Canada, 161*(2), 26–32.

Strategic Direction. (2004). There's big—and there's Wal-Mart: Winners on a huge scale. *Strategic Direction, 20*(9), 8–11.

Stringer, K. (2004). Wal-Mart's surge leaves dead stores behind. *Wall Street Journal, 244*(53), B1.

Tsao, A. (2002, December 2). Will Wal-Mart take over the world? *BusinessWeek Online,* from Business Source Premier.

Useem, J. (2004, March 8). Should we admire Wal-Mart? *Fortune,* 118–120.

Waddock, S. (2004, March). Companies, academics, and the progress of corporate citizenship. *Business & Society Review, 109,* 5–42.

Waddock, S. (2006). *Leading corporate citizens: Vision, values, value added* (2nd ed.). New York: McGraw-Hill.

Waddock, S. A., & Graves, S. B. (1997a). The corporate social performance—financial performance link. *Strategic Management Journal, 18*(4), 303–319.

Waddock, S. A., & Graves, S. B. (1997b, September). Quality of management and quality of stakeholder relations: are they synonymous? *Business & Society, 36*(3), 250–279.

Wal-Mart. (2005). Retrieved January 4, 2005, from http://www.walmartstores.com/ wmstore/wmstores/Mainabout.jsp.

Wal-Mart Foundation. (2005a). Retrieved January 13, 2005, from http://www .walmartfoundation.org/wmstore/ goodworks/scripts/index.jsp.

Wal-Mart Foundation. (2005b). Retrieved

January 13, 2005, from http://www.walmartfoundation.org/wmstore/goodworks/scripts/AboutUs.jsp.

Weiser, J., & Zadek, S. (2000). *Conversations with disbelievers: Persuading companies to address social challenges.* New York: Ford Foundation.

Wood, D. J. (1991). Corporate social performance revisited. *Academy of Management Review, 16*(4), 691–718.

6

Corporate Social Responsibility in Scandinavia

A Turn Toward the Business Case?

METTE MORSING

ATLE MIDTTUN

KARL PALMÅS

Scandinavian companies have a long history of integrating issues of ethics and social responsibility into corporate strategies, and today these issues seem to appear with a renewed urgency in the wake of globalization. While Scandinavian companies since the 1980s have been exposed to strong environmental regulation and so have integrated environmental concerns into their business strategies for a number of years, many Scandinavian managers also claim that ethics and social responsibilities always have been an inherent way of doing business. Often, the social initiatives have been implemented in an informal and even implicit way as a response to current local expectations and demands. Lately, the corporate social responsibility (CSR) discussions in Scandinavian companies engage a new tone of international concern and call for a systematic and conspicuous corporate commitment as Scandinavian companies experience the consequences of globalization.

In this chapter, we explore the interplay among state, society, and business as we depict how CSR unfolds in Denmark, Norway, and Sweden. First, we briefly outline five analytical approaches to CSR and position the Scandinavian perspectives. Then, we outline some characteristics in the Scandinavian context for CSR initiatives in the small welfare states. Next, we introduce how CSR unfolds in each of the three countries: in what shape it emerged, what stakeholders were involved, and how it is developing today. We follow this with

an outline of selected Scandinavian industries' CSR activities based on an empirical study. We end the chapter with a discussion of future challenges for CSR in Scandinavian companies.

APPROACHES TO CSR

While discussions of CSR and the influence of stakeholders are as old as the concept of the corporation itself (Carroll, 1999), it has developed throughout the twentieth century and engendered many conceptualizations. Across theories of stakeholder relations, there is a shared assumption that stakeholder engagement is critical and that CSR initiatives are needed. We define CSR initiatives as those actions taken to bridge organizational and stakeholder expectations. The stakeholder theories differ, however, in their conceptualizations of the corporate commitment to CSR, but across theories there is a general agreement on the distinction between CSR stemming from a desire to do good, that is, the "normative case," and CSR reflecting an enlightened self-interest, that is, the "business case" (Smith, 2004). In our understanding of the business case, it is a question of companies' attempts to make rational sense of their CSR engagement and so arguing beyond the obligation to society as reason for engaging in CSR activities.

In her book *Value Shift*, Lynn Sharp Paine (2000) at Harvard Business School develops four arguments for the corporate business case and one argument for the normative case. The "business case" is about (1) risk management, that is, companies establishing mechanisms to prevent crisis or scandals to occur; (2) civic positioning, that is, companies depending on civil society's acceptance of them as legitimate stakeholders in society (their "license to operate"); (3) market positioning, that is, companies appearing as socially responsible to attract consumers; and (4) organizational functioning, that is, companies developing attractive and sensitive cultures to attract and maintain the most qualified people as well as to maintain a high alertness toward changes in stakeholder expectations. The fifth argument is the "normative case," in which CSR is driven by a sense of obligation to society. It is often argued that CSR in practice is often driven by a combination of the business case and the normative case, and we also argue that this combination has been the driver for CSR in the Scandinavian countries. However, we find it useful to maintain the distinction between the business and the normative cases, since we find that the Scandinavian companies recently are witnessing a turn toward the business case overshadowing the normative case.

While "social obligation" may seem an appropriate political argument for a CSR initiative in social democratic welfare states, our descriptions and analyses of CSR in Denmark, Norway and Sweden demonstrate that this approach may be downplayed in current corporate strategies. As companies find themselves with professional management teams (taking over after the company's founder) and in the midst of globalization with immense—in fact, endless—demands for social contributions, business managers have to choose their corporate CSR strategies carefully and, not least, to argue and account for them to their professional board of directors. Although the business case and corporate self-interest may have been an argument for corporate CSR initiatives also a hundred years ago, today we find the corporate self-interest far more conspicuously demarcated in arguments and actions of CSR in the Scandinavian companies than we used to only a decade ago. In Denmark, the inclusive labor market strategy has attempted to encourage corporate CSR engagement via appealing to improvement of organizational functioning. In Sweden and Norway, a few, but conspicuous, corporate scandals have given arguments for highlighting risk management as a

reason for improving CSR initiatives. In the final section of this chapter, we discuss future challenges for CSR in the Scandinavian companies.

THE SCANDINAVIAN MODEL

In a study of CSR in Scandinavia, it is worthwhile to take a look at the national cultures of the three countries, that is, those beliefs and values that are widely shared in society at a particular point in time (Ralston, Holt, Terpstra, & Kay-Cheng, 1997). Prior research points to history, religion, proximity, and education as important factors in defining a cultural context (Ronen & Shenkar, 1985), and in these factors, we do find a similar pattern across the Scandinavian countries. The three countries share an historical heritage (they have been united: Denmark and Norway from 1387 to 1814, and Sweden and Norway from 1814 to 1905), the languages are rather similar and understood without translations, the same religion dominates (Lutheran), and for the last 50 years the countries have shared a political ideology based on social-democratic ideas, which have come to be known as the Scandinavian model. According to a professor on Scandinavian management, Tor Greenness (2003, p. 19), the Scandinavian model refers generally to

- stable labor relations, based on two powerful bargaining groups agreeing mutually or bilaterally on how to distribute the results of industrial productivity;
- reforms in working life, introduced and supported through the bargaining system, rather than by legal regulation; and
- strong governments, usually social-democratic, in alliance with the trade unions, strongly committed to an extensive welfare and social security system and with full employment as an absolute objective.

Empirical studies of the similarities of the three countries conclude that Denmark, Norway, and Sweden form a compact cluster in comparison with other nations or regions (Hofstede, 1980; Inglehart, Basanez, & Moreno, 1998). These studies demonstrate that value collectivism, power sharing, and participative modes of decision making characterize the leadership style across the three countries, although differences exist among the three countries and are particularly highlighted as managers from the different countries meet in, for example, Nordea, currently the largest Nordic bank and the result of mergers of many Nordic banks, to discuss corporate strategy, values, and management development. While the Danes are found to take a "no" as a further step in the negotiation process, the Swedes will accept the decision and work systematically to get the work done, and the Norwegians will immediately turn to develop a new proposal, reframing the same suggestion in order to have it accepted as they originally planned it. However, in comparison with people from other European, U.S., African, or Asian countries, the Scandinavians appear to be rather similar. Their shared cultural, political, and societal background has given rise to the description of the particular "Scandinavian management" that is known to encourage flat hierarchies, project management, and a high degree of employee involvement and dialogue in Scandinavian companies. In the following, we explore to what extent issues on ethics and CSR have formed a trajectory of "Scandinavian management" and emerged and evolved in similar patterns in Denmark, Norway, and Sweden.

DOES CSR HAVE A ROLE IN SMALL WELFARE STATES?

Actually, the notion of CSR appears to raise modest expectations in the Scandinavian countries. In principle, incentives to engage in social initiatives seem low. We mention three reasons that corporate CSR initiatives do not seem to enjoy the encouragement and urgency found in many other areas of the world: (1) the role of the state in the Scandinavian countries, (2) the Scandinavian managers' self-perceptions, and (3) the high degree of trust in the Scandinavian civil societies.

The Role of the State in Scandinavian Countries

The state has been the main provider of social services since the 1930s. In Denmark, the first comprehensive social legislation took place in 1933,[1] and in neighboring Sweden, the welfare institutions were also founded in 1933, when the Social Democrats and the Farmers' Party reached a political compromise on social welfare issues. In

Norway, collaborative and constructive relations between labor and capital were institutionalized by the so-called "General Agreement" (i.e., *hovedavtalen*) in 1935 to further industrial development and social welfare.

Denmark is a small country with 5 million people, Norway with 3 million, and Sweden with 9 million. The three countries have, until recently, been characterized by rather stable and homogeneous populations and a long tradition for participatory democracy. Generally, the Nordic welfare model (compared to the Continental, Atlantic and Southern models; Berghmann, 1997) is characterized by citizens being granted extensive social rights. There is a strong emphasis on personal social services organized and financed by local authorities and transfer schemes financed and organized by the state. Local authorities are, by tradition, strong and relatively independent. Although there is an upper limit to municipal taxation, municipalities have the authority to spend local tax in ways they see fit, which provide them with a strong position as opposed to local authorities in other types of welfare models (Lund, 2003). In the Scandinavian countries, welfare expenditure is high. To accommodate these state responsibilities, citizens and companies are exposed to paying some of the world's highest taxes.

Scandinavian Managers' Self-Perceptions

Many Scandinavian company managers claim that acting socially responsibly has always been an inherent part of the company culture. They say that their companies have since their establishment taken into consideration the implications of corporate actions in particular on local communities and other stakeholders that may substantially affect or be affected by the operations of the business. The majority of Scandinavian companies are closely embedded in the local societies in which they operate and originally were founded, and they have historically demonstrated a continuous interest in the "well-being" of those local societies.

In Denmark, such companies as Grundfos, Lego, Danfoss, SparNord, and Novo Nordisk have long histories of contributing to the welfare of their local societies. Within the last 15 years, Danish companies have started to communicate more conspicuously about their CSR initiatives (Morsing, 2003). For example, the world's first ethical accounting statement appeared in 1989 in a collaboration between researchers at Copenhagen Business School and a Danish Bank, SparNord, as the bank's CEO decided not only to engage in supporting the local community in a number of CSR initiatives but also to report on the outcomes of the dialogue in terms of social initiatives, because the company wanted to contribute to development of the local society and to demonstrate this dedication as a supplement to the annual financial report (Giversen, 2003). Novo Nordisk, the world's largest producer of insulin, is another Danish company with a strong reputation for having integrated CSR into its core business strategy. Novo Nordisk was way ahead of environmental legislation in the 1980s and is now taking the corporate lead on social responsibility. The company has won international prizes for its social initiatives and its sustainability reporting.[2] TDC, the largest provider of teleservices in Denmark, has also initiated a number of CSR initiatives on, for example, integration of ethnic minorities to the workplace and promotion of female managers.

In Norway, the largest oil company, Norsk Hydro, is partnering with Amnesty International to develop advanced human rights strategies in their international operations. And Norske Skog, one of the world's largest paper producers, is actively stimulating trade unionization at their plants and organizing "Norwegian-style" dialogue with its employees worldwide to benefit from the constructive cooperation that characterizes Nordic industry–labor relations.

In Sweden, the carmaker Volvo has historically pioneered the concepts of industrial democracy (union representations in the boards of directors and the corporate assembly—*koncernnämnden*, which is compulsory for Nordic companies today, but was like a revolution then) and humanized production in the Kalmar and Uddevalla plants. Another example is the furniture retailer IKEA, which in the early 1990s adopted a systematic approach to managing their environmental impact in the countries where they source raw materials. The company's commitment to forging a "responsible supply chain" has subsequently come to include wider social concerns, notably in the issue of child labor.

Apart from individual companies, networks and associations to promote and assist the development of CSR initiatives have emerged. For example, Green Network was founded in 1994, and today it is a voluntary association of 275 public and private organizations in Jutland with the ambition to promote sustainability. In the late 1990s the Nordic Partnership emerged (Denmark, Norway, and Sweden plus Finland and Iceland) as a nongovernmental organization (NGO) initiative, as the World Wildlife Fund invited some of the largest companies in the Nordic countries to commit themselves publicly to promoting sustainable corporate practices in collaborative partnerships with NGOs and local authorities.

Whether these Scandinavian companies are fully recognized for their CSR initiatives, and whether they engage in these initiatives today as a social obligation to society or for pure corporate self-interest is not the issue here. Rather, the point to make here is that quite a few Scandinavian managers perceive their companies as already rather socially responsible, and although one might object that this perception is based on corporate reputations and managerial opinions rather than on facts and structures, the consequence is that these perceptions do not provide managers with an immediate incentive for further social engagements.

The High Degree of Trust in the Scandinavian Civil Societies

While "trust" is a key issue in current discussions on the drivers for CSR in international business,[3] this does not seem to be an urgent driver of CSR in the Scandinavian companies. In the light of extreme corporate financial power[4] and in the wake of corporate scandals, trust was a main issue at the World Economic Forum in Davos in 2003 and in 2004—or rather, the *lack* of trust toward private companies. However, this skepticism and distrust does not seem to be the case in Denmark, Norway, and Sweden. Yet, for a number of years, the Scandinavian countries have been known to be among the least corrupt countries in the world according to Transparency International; in 2002, Denmark was ranked as number 2 worldwide, Sweden number 3, and Norway number 6 (Zadek, 2003). According to research on national cultures, Scandinavian societies were characterized by a strong sense of egalitarianism and a low power distance (Hofstede, 1980, 1994), which in practice means that there is a perceived relatively small difference between "top" and "bottom" of the Scandinavian organizational hierarchies. The relatively even distribution of income across professions contributes to the picture of an egalitarian society. A recent survey of the Downing Street Strategy Unit (Bibb & Kourdi, 2004) depicts Scandinavians as one of the most trusting people. In the survey people were asked: "Generally speaking, can others be trusted?" Scandinavians were found to be the most trusting, with nearly 70% saying that they trust others, compared to only 30% in the United States, Britain, and France (p. 11).

However, in Sweden, in the wake of corporate scandals related to extraordinary remuneration to top managers, public trust toward corporations has fallen somewhat. Notably, the Skandia affair, in which 200 million euros of pension savings were lost, has dented the confidence in business. Although the Skandia affair and a few other corporate scandals have appeared lately in the Scandinavian business environment, this does not seem to have set off a conspicuous corporate distrust among the Scandinavian citizens when compared with other nations. The relative trust toward managers may also be seen as a reflection of the managerial actions to avoid corporate scandals; for example, in Denmark, a corporate governance guideline was initiated by a group of managers and the Copenhagen Stock Exchange in the wake of a Danish corporate scandal of Nordisk Fjer, which also resulted in development of a corporate governance code, which is referred to as the Nørby Code.[5] In the fallout of the Skandia affair, former Swedish finance minister Erik Åsbrink has led a commission of business representatives to develop a code of conduct for Swedish business. Norwegian industry has also had its recent scandals, with Statoil caught in corruption in Iran, and the large credit company Finance Credit bankrupted following the revelation of extensive fraud. However, while the two episodes have led to extensive consequences for management in the Statoil case (the resignation of the CEO and the chairman of the board) and in the Finance Credit case (the most severe sentence for economic fraud in Norwegian history), there have been no major initiatives to draw strong corporate governance implications, beyond a pretty conventional modernization of the Oslo Stock Exchange corporate governance rules.

We now revisit our initial question: Why should Scandinavian companies want to engage in more CSR initiatives? First, the Scandinavian countries with their participative democracy have strong states to provide social services to their societies;

second, Scandinavian managers perceive themselves as already rather socially responsible; and third, there is no alarming distrust of Scandinavian companies among the general public.

However, although it apparently does not seem urgent for Scandinavian companies to engage in further CSR initiatives, many Scandinavian companies engage in expanding and integrating their CSR initiatives into core business strategies. In the following section, we discuss the history, the drivers, and the perspectives of corporate CSR initiatives in Denmark, Norway, and Sweden.

CSR IN DENMARK

Danish companies seem to be in midstream when it comes to CSR. Traditionally, paternalistic founding fathers of Danish companies have contributed to society with a great deal of CSR initiatives. Lego, Grundfos, Novo Nordisk, Danfoss, and Bang & Olufsen are among the well-known Danish companies built on a set of strong corporate values about ethics and responsibility. Often, the most conspicuous activity was the development of the company's local societies, which was basically argued as part of the corporate social obligation to society. But, as the founders are gradually being replaced by professional management teams, the social obligation toward society does not seem to provide a sufficient answer to this next generation of managers on the question of why Danish companies should be concerned with CSR initiatives. In the public agenda of CSR, corporate benefits in terms of a better working place and improved organizational functioning have been the primary arguments during the last decade, with an emphasis on the inclusive labor market.

Based on a welfare society with a strong state as the main provider of social services since 1933, Danish companies contributed to the development of society as a social obligation to society, decided and controlled by paternalistic founding fathers of wealthy companies. The later development of strong unions imposing demands on companies to ensure employee involvement in boards resulted in advanced labor market legislations, and later, in the 1980s, advanced environmental legislation was imposed to ensure companies practiced environmental protection. The development of these legislations have been resisted by many Danish companies but have also been designed and implemented in a collaboration between government and some of the corporate frontrunners in Danish industry in an acknowledgment of the competitive advantage in terms of product development and new markets, which can be a spinoff from these legislations.

In the 1990s, the Danish welfare model started to come under pressure as it was learned that the Danish state supported almost 25% of the able-bodied population. Rather than legislation or appeals to purely "social obligation," the government sought to encourage companies to engage in CSR initiatives by appealing to improvement of organizational functioning. A large number of people found difficulties in maintaining a stable relation to the labor market, and this created social exclusion of those people who were unable to live up to normal workforce standards, for example, the handicapped, the elderly, ethnic minorities, and socially marginalized people. This meant a major increase in public expenditure and created an unsustainable pressure on the welfare system. In 1995, the Danish minister of social affairs, Karen Jespersen, in the then Social-Democrat government, was the first to call for corporate assistance in meeting the challenge and for constructing a Danish agenda for CSR in what she referred to as "the inclusive labour market strategy." The ideal was social cohesion, and the means were to mobilize private companies and social partners in "social partnerships" to address the problems of unemployment and social exclusion. A comprehensive campaign labeled "It Concerns Us All" was initiated by the social minister in 1994, which tied together labor market and social issues and encouraged partners in the private as well as the public sector to join forces (Socialministeriet, 2000).

Although many Danish company managers will argue that their CSR initiatives concern many other issues, the inclusive labor market strategy has nevertheless been the predominant CSR issue on the Danish public agenda. While the then Social-Democrat government set the agenda around 10 years ago to encourage private companies to engage, state institutions and trade unions have taken up the agenda simultaneously and enlarged it to include also public organizations. Further, a recent study of the two largest business-oriented Danish newspapers' coverage of CSR issues during the last nine years shows the dominance of the inclusive labor market in the public discourse:

28% of all articles on CSR were concerned with the inclusive labor market, while the rest of the articles were scattered on various CSR issues (Morsing, Langer, & Eder-Hansen, 2005).

Partnerships Between State and Private Companies

One outstanding Danish company, Grundfos, inspired Karen Jespersen initially. Grundfos is a major producer of hydraulic pumps and has historically shown a great interest in contributing to the development of the local society, because the founder believed strongly in the corporate interdependence between the company and society and felt a strong moral obligation to give back to society. Grundfos was a typical example of a sound old Danish company that in practice had shown how it contributed to solving societal problems while serving its own agenda. In relation to the CSR approaches to the normative and the business case for CSR outlined in the beginning of this chapter, Grundfos exemplifies a company that integrates both: CSR as a social obligation and as a corporate self-interest. Grundfos has established a number of special workshops for people with reduced capacity that serve to integrate minorities from the local community into the workplace, while contributing to the maintenance of a flexible workforce, and the minister realized that in order to rectify social exclusion, employers had to understand not only their moral obligation but also the advantages in creating special working conditions for this group of people. For a company like Grundfos, a flexible workforce is important in the prospect of a future labor shortage, and for Grundfos there is a profound interest in integrating a larger number of people into the workforce. For Karen Jespersen, it was vital for the inclusive labor market strategy that it be more than an expression of the normative case:

> [T]he companies had to show more than the desire to do good. It was not merely a question of asking companies to do more but of finding ways in which the political system and the companies might join forces in addressing fundamental societal problems. Hence, the point was to build dialogue and co-operation between the political system, the companies and the local authorities. Partnerships were the essence. (Thyssen, 2003, p. 27)

"It Concerns Us All" became the starting point of the Danish government's campaign on CSR, in which social partnerships between private companies and state institutions are central. The campaign built on the argument that CSR could contribute to the organizational functioning of the firm in terms of a flexible work force but had strong tones of CSR being a social obligation from companies. While the campaign encouraged and attempted to motivate companies to see themselves as part of the larger society, there was also a strong concern that the campaign would not meet its goals without the participation and commitment of companies. To highlight the corporate interest in the campaign and to highlight that it was more than a political vision, the minister formed a National Network of Company Leaders as a central element in a functional and symbolic sense. The National Network consisted of company leaders from 16 of the most admired Danish companies.[6] The purpose of the network is to

> contribute to the current debate about corporate social responsibility—to function as an advisory body to the Minister and to help inspire companies to take independent initiatives promoting social welfare among employees as well as in the local community. The primary goal of the National Network is to help limit social exclusion and increase the integration in the labour market. (National Network, 1996)

While the network started a series of systematic and inspiring dialogues between private companies and public institutions, it also carried the message of positive will to contribute to enhancing the national social inclusion from some of the most admired managers in some of the most admired Danish companies, that is, managers and companies known to be setting the agenda in many other areas, as well.

Nevertheless, the campaign met resistance and skepticism from the Danish Employers' Confederation (*Dansk Arbejdsgiverforening*) as well as from the largest employers' organization, the Confederation of Danish Industries (*Dansk Industri*). They were concerned that the campaign was the first move toward regulation of CSR—a notion they were, and are, against. However, from the beginning it was clear that the main idea was that company commitment must be based on voluntary initiatives and efforts. The social ministry, the

network, and the companies emphasized this again and again. Experiences with regulation on CSR from other countries—and even from environmental regulation in Denmark—had shown how companies in many instances would pay their way out. However, Minister Jespersen had higher ambitions. "Social involvement has many different faces," she said, and the overall vision was a long-term shift in the attitude toward new forms of interaction between state and private companies rather than short-term results or regulations, as it targeted redefining social policies as an *investment* rather than as an *expense* for society or a regulation of social behavior.

"Soft Law"

Although regulation was never the Danish state's agenda on CSR, administrative systems and frameworks have been developed as a kind of "soft law" for companies and social partners, which they themselves can interpret and put into practice according to the local context. We emphasize two initiatives: the "social coordination committees" and the recent framework agreement, the "social chapter."

In 1998, the social coordination committees became mandatory for all 269 Danish local authorities. It was the first—and so far only—"soft law" on CSR in Denmark, as the committees were included in the new social legislation. A social coordination committee is a forum of representatives from the Danish Employers' Confederation (*Dansk Arbejdsgiverforening*), the Confederation of Danish Trade Unions, the Public Employment Agency, and other relevant organizations. The role of the local authorities in collaboration with the social partners and private companies is to map the status of unemployment and social exclusion in the local authority and to develop a strategy of how to integrate those socially excluded people into the workforce in private companies. The committees function as an institutionalized framework for the development of partnerships with a minimum of regulation: the committees function as a role model; they must be established, but how the individual committees decide to live up to the broadly defined role is left to individual local agreements. As an indication of the willingness among Danish local authorities to support the campaign, it is interesting to note that 60 of Denmark's 269 local authorities had established these social coordination committees before they became mandatory in 1998.

In 1999, updated and reinforced in 2004, the "social chapter" (www.personaleweb.dk/rum-for-alle) was launched by the National Association of Municipalities (*Kommunernes Landsforening*), the National Association of Counties (*Amtsråds-foreningen*), the Trade Union for Public Servants, and Copenhagen and Frederiksberg municipalities, which formed a "framework agreement" to encourage all Danish local authorities to participate themselves in employing socially excluded people. This was an enlargement of the inclusive labor market strategy because it encouraged local authorities not only to engage in social partnerships but also to employ people who could not enter the workforce in normal conditions. The strategy is called the "social chapter," which refers to the agenda of prevention, retention, and integration on the workplace. The social chapter is, first and foremost, a signal that the central labor market partners agree that not only private companies but also local authorities shall contribute in taking a social responsibility in terms of the inclusive labor market strategy. The social chapter is, like the social coordination committees, articulated in broad terms, leaving it up to individual authorities to develop a strategy that fits the individual local context. It is a framework agreement, and as such, it may be referred to as the "softest" of soft laws. Nevertheless, the current national campaign to promote the social chapter has already gained much interest.

While the Danish campaign on the inclusive labor market strategy is characterized as a success, having had a large impact on social and labor market strategies in society at large and in changing the notion of social responsibility from a peripheral to a mainstream issue discussed at all levels in society, the initial problems that set off the campaign continue to challenge the welfare society. The number of people provided for by the Danish government is still growing. There is a widening gap between strong and weak in society, and new challenges have been posed by a growing immigration rate.

CSR IN NORWAY

As in Denmark, the social democratic tradition in Norway has clearly played a role in codifying a spirit of constructive cooperation to further industrial development and social welfare. In the postwar period, this spirit of cooperation was continued in several forms, ranging from collaboration through sectoral industrial councils to general policy consultation. All these initiatives have contributed to making the term "stakeholder dialogue" a normal concept in Norwegian industry. Corporate social responsibility is regarded as part of the political and social tradition, and environmental protection and environmental legislation have been regarded, as in Denmark and Sweden, as a natural development to respect a sustainable development of society. Trade unions have had a strong position: dialogue between employers, workers, and government lawmakers is part of the industrial tradition and the Scandinavian model has been highly influential and visible in the development of the Norwegian trade unions. The Norwegian industrial tradition is said to create a "dynamic environment where problems can be raised, discussed and dealt with" (McCallin & Webb, 2004). Long periods of labor government and the collective bargaining culture are major influences on Norway's present business structure and its approach to CSR.

Norway has a long-standing tradition of global commitments—whether through its superior levels of development aid or facilitating peace processes in areas of conflict. The so-called Oslo Accord between Israel and the Palestinian authorities and the subsequent nomination of a previous Norwegian minister, Terje Roed Larsen, to lead United Nations negotiations in the region, unfortunately without lasting results, may serve as an example. Norway has worked to further sustainable development and international stability, which is seen by Norwegian corporations as a business advantage. The Norwegian government's work for sustainable development has been particularly profiled through its first female prime minister, Gro Harlem Brundtland, who led the World Commission on Environment and Development that triggered the later Rio and Kyoto processes. Strongly backed by the trade unions' labor rights engagement and a strong tradition for human rights, the Norwegian government has worked to promote human rights issues. Human rights have therefore been a major topic of CSR in Norway. In 1997, the Confederation of Norwegian Business and Industry launched its human rights checklist for Norwegian businesses operating in the south. In 1998, the Ministry of Foreign Affairs launched a discussion forum called *Kompakt* (Consultative Body for Human Rights and Norwegian Economic Involvement Abroad), which also has produced a number of reports and guidelines for Norwegian corporations. The Norwegian petroleum industry, in particular, is actively pursuing human rights issues as well as social welfare issues when expanding globally.

Although quite a number of Norwegian companies, such as the oil company Statoil, the multienergy and electrometals company Norsk Hydro, and the large Nordic retailer company Coop, are known for their advanced CSR practices, triple-bottom-line reporting (annual reporting of the economic, social and environmental outcomes of an enterprise) is still uncommon, and according to insurance company Det Norske Veritas, there are only a few CSR reports. The Norwegian authorities have neither supported nor advocated triple-bottom-line reporting to any extent. Norwegian law mandates only that corporations include in their annual report issues relating to health and safety. Therefore, Norwegian corporations come out on top, exceeded only by U.K. companies, in surveys looking at social/nonfinancial issues in annual reports. Eighty-one percent of the Norwegian annual reports include health and safety issues, but so far only 29% publish stand-alone CSR reports that are separate from the traditional annual reports (KPMG, 2002).

The Norwegian Accounting Act also requires a corporation to include in its annual report its environmental impact when this impact becomes "more than insignificant." Only 35% of the top 100 Norwegian corporations were actually fulfilling the requirements of this "soft law" in 2001 (Ruud & Larsen, 2002), the loophole being the wording "more than insignificant."

In February 2003, a majority in the Norwegian Parliament voted for a new law on "the right to environmental information." The law will make it mandatory for all corporations, and also all public offices, to provide information on certain environmental issues that can lead to "not insignificant" effects on the environment, including foreign distribution or production, and the products being sold.

Norway has experienced an impact in the finance sector, thanks to the early efforts of the life insurance and financial services company Storebrand —a Norwegian pioneer in socially responsible investment. As in most regions, CSR as evaluated by Scandinavian investors grew out of "negative screening" efforts of certain investment funds. Already in 1960, Sweden's *Ansvar Aktie* fund took what at the time was considered an innovative approach to investing, by boycotting companies involved with apartheid regimes in South Africa and with alcohol or tobacco. Environmental issues were added to the "exclusion criteria" during the 1970s. Norway followed with its first environmental fund that also considered social issues (Joly, 2000) and took a pioneering role in launching the first global best-in-class fund, the Storebrand Environmental Value Fund.

The negative screening set off issues on risk management among Norwegian companies as a driver for more CSR activity, and this tendency was supported by the ongoing discussions about the Norwegian Petroleum Fund, a public fund that comes out of the sizable Norwegian petroleum sector. Very recently, the dilemmas arising in the wake of state-owned funds became clear, as the Norwegian government was challenged to account for the investment portfolio of its petroleum fund, which had a value of just around 877 billion NKr (135 billion USD) mid-2003;[7] reports in the media showed how returns were being secured by investing in, among other issues, companies involved in the production of landmines, ammunition, tobacco, alcohol, and gambling. There are also questions about the human rights and environmental records in a number of the companies that the Petroleum Fund invests in. All of these issues collide in some way with Norway's official foreign or national policies, which restrict weapons exports to conflict zones and include strong anti-tobacco and anti-alcohol engagements. Based on the recommendation of a Parliamentary committee, the government now intends to develop clearer guidelines for the fund, demanding active engagement in companies that align with key principles drawn from the Global Compact.

A special feature in some Norwegian companies is the close dialogue between firms and NGOs. The multienergy and electrometals company Norsk Hydro, with extensive global engagements, has signed an agreement with Amnesty International in order to cooperate on issues of human rights to strengthen the company's future efforts. The win–win situation of the partnership is that Norsk Hydro makes a financial contribution to Amnesty International, and in turn, Amnesty International provides expertise when Hydro steps up its in-house training of managers and employees on how to deal with human rights in the company's business operations in different countries. Amnesty International also helps Hydro report on specific cases.

In sum, the debates and actions on CSR in Norway have been strongly influenced by the traditionally close collaborative efforts among companies, local authorities, government, trade unions, and NGOs. As part of the tradition and as a social obligation toward society, Norwegian companies are inherently embedded in the collective bargaining process and are used to taking stakeholders into consideration. The public debate on CSR in Norway includes and invites critical dialogue on existing CSR practices and the perceived lack of CSR practices, which alerts companies to proactively engage in the CSR dialogue. Recently, the appearance of corporate scandals may indicate an even stronger turn to proactive CSR practices in Norwegian countries rather than CSR as a traditional social obligation for companies.

CSR IN SWEDEN

In contrast to Denmark, the Swedish CSR debate of recent years has led to a deviation from the labor market concerns that characterized the postwar economy. Whereas during most of the twentieth century Swedish corporations focused almost solely on employment and worker protection issues, the 1980s and 1990s saw other areas of business practice becoming subject to public debate and contestation: in the 1980s, environmental issues gained greater significance; in the 1990s, issues of global responsibility, corporate ethics, and governance, as well as identity politics, were put on the agenda. As hinted above, the role of globalization has been paramount in this shift, first, as a driver of the dismantling of the Swedish version of the Scandinavian model (during the 1970s and 1980s), and second, as a generator of new frictions between Swedish corporations and surrounding society.

In Sweden, the ethos of socially responsible business is a legacy from the early decades of the twentieth century, when the country was radically transformed from an agrarian society to an economy based on heavy industry. This rapid industrialization was to some degree the result of industrialists who not only strove to build corporations—they saw it as their duty to build welfare for wider society. For instance, in the 1920s and 1930s, the newly established carmaker Volvo explicitly aimed at enrolling stagnant rural steel works into production, thus creating employment and modernizing working life in the wider economy (Hälleby, 1990). Thus, CSR was indeed construed as an obligation toward society.

Another feature of the Swedish industrialist ethos was frugality: in Swedish business (IKEA being the oft-cited example), corporate cultures have traditionally disapproved strongly of extravagant executive perks. Thus, the ambitions of the industrialists went hand in hand with the discourse of Social-Democrat leadership, which at this time started to speak about Sweden as the "people's home" (an inclusive society based on welfare, solidarity, and egalitarian principles).

The people's home was, however, not merely a lofty political ideal. By the 1930s, it had yielded strong ties between business, trade unions, and the polity, and by the 1950s it had materialized into an elaborate macroeconomic model. The political scientist Bo Rothstein (2003) explains this process as an exercise in gradual trust building and institution building between business institutions and labor unions. One key outcome of this process was the 1938 Saltsjöbaden Accord between business and unions, which sealed a 30–year-long truce on the labor market. Another outcome was the Rehn-Meidner model of economic management, including the investment fund policy, which enabled unions and the polity to influence how corporations invested their profits (Erixon, 2003). A third outcome was the development of worker protection expertise, which saw rationalization engineers mediating between capital and labor when bargaining on improvements in working life (De Geer, 1978; Ryner, 2002).[8]

The latter factors came to have a profound influence on the corporation/society relations. Large corporate initiatives to create employment and improve working conditions were made possible by the investment fund policies.[9] Moreover, the worker protection expertise led to working-life-related process innovations—sometimes also in product innovation (Andréasson & Bäcklund, 2000).[10] The Swedish economic framework thus effectively set the CSR agenda on worker protection. In other words, the political economy "framed" the social responsibilities of the corporation (Callon, 1998).

As internationalization of the Swedish economy undermined the nation-state–bound Rehn-Meidner model, the institutions that committed corporations to worker protection started to buckle. Instead, during the 1980s, green issues made their presence felt. Swedish heavy industry was thus subjected to public debate on industrial pollution and waste. Consequently, new business practices were developed within areas such as chemicals charting, life cycle analysis, and environmental accounting.

The 1990s saw a second wave of repercussions from globalization. First, because Swedish industry is based largely on large corporations operating in several countries, debates on responsible practices in developing countries ensued. Corporations such as fashion retailer Hennes & Mauritz and oil company Lundin Oil came under increased scrutiny on such issues as alleged sweatshop labor and cooperation with undemocratic regimes, respectively.

Second, globalization put heavy strains on the solidarity ethos that buttressed the business/society relations. Swedish executives increasingly come to compare their pay, as well as their tax rates, with that of their international peers. The levels of executive pay proved an explosive issue, and the Swedish-Swiss engineering corporation ABB's excessive remuneration to Percy Barnevik (arguably the most admired Swedish business leader of the 1990s) became known to the public. Moreover, as many Swedish firms were sold to (or merged with) foreign firms, the Swedish tax base and source of employment seemed increasingly unreliable. Critics warned that Sweden was becoming a "subsidiary economy," in which the future of the industry increasingly lay in the hands of foreign decision makers with no concern for the country's overall welfare.[11] By this time, many business leaders called for the return of the statesmanlike industrialist business leaders of the past (Ekman, 2003). In this respect, the ideal of CSR as obligation toward society still loomed large.

The discussions on executive pay did, however, open up a wider debate on corporate ethics and corporate governance, which was to intensify in the 2000s, not least in the wake of the scandal around the insurance company Skandia, Sweden's oldest insurance company, and was until 2001 highly admired, ranked by *Fortune* as one of "10

Great Companies in Europe." In 2003, it emerged that the company's top executives had awarded themselves bonuses amounting to 200 million euros, effectively taken from the firm's pension savings. The significance of this crisis can hardly be overstated: in an economic model originally based upon time-tested bonds of trust between business and stakeholders, a crisis in confidence could have grave consequences. Accordingly, a former minister of finance was appointed to lead a commission on how to restore trust in Swedish business. The outcome of this effort—a Swedish code of corporate governance—is currently under review.

The other complex of issues that has emerged on the CSR agenda during recent years concerns how corporations deal with identity politics. In Sweden, as in other Western societies, class-based politics has increasingly given way to a focus on equal opportunity irrespective of gender, ethnicity, sexual preference, and so on (Fraser, 1999). Regarding ethnicity, many Swedish corporations have been reasonably progressive in setting up programs for nonnative Swedes.[12] These initiatives are generally sorted under the umbrella term "diversity," often inspired by the discourse of Anglo-American firms. One example is the Plural Project, which includes, among others, AstraZeneca (pharmaceuticals), the Föreningssparbanken (private banking), IKEA, and TeliaSonera (telecommunications services).

The main identity-politics–related area of discussion is nevertheless gender equality. Although the feminist movement has been strong within Swedish society for some time, it is only in recent years that the spotlight has been directed toward corporate responsibilities. In 2002, the minister of equality decreed that unless Swedish corporations had a 25% female representation on their boards of directors by the end of 2004, obligatory quotas would be introduced. This pending legislation threat sparked intense discussion and put top management focus on how women are to be promoted within organizations.

To recap, CSR of Swedish corporations used to be embedded in the "people's home" ethos of early industrialists, and to some extent "hard-wired" into organizations by the political economy of the country. Corporate social responsibility was thus bound up with normative claims about the obligation toward wider society, predominantly manifested in creating employment and caring for workers. However, as the strong tripartite (state, business, and union) ties of (the Swedish version of) the Scandinavian model have loosened up, new issues of contestation have emerged, and new stakeholders have entered the fray. As a reaction to this, one can notice a shift toward construing CSR as a "risk management" activity. Some professionals (especially those working directly with these issues) also speak of CSR and new social partnerships as a potential generator of novel business opportunities.

Swedish CSR is therefore undergoing a transition. Although the long-termist, statesmanlike, industrialist leadership of the postwar era is still the ideal, today's executives have a completely different situation on their hands: not only have foreign owners and more short-termist financial analysts gained more influence over management, but also there is less of a consensus on what constitutes "social responsibility" and which stakeholders represent "society." Even if it were possible, focusing on worker protection in close collaboration with union bosses and industry ministers is no longer enough.

Looking forward, there are indications that Swedish business may be handling this transition quite well. Stories of how corporations consult with stakeholders for codetermination and coinnovation (e.g., Volvo's collaboration with the Swedish Asthma and Allergy Association) and of how stakeholders' established expertise is used in new ways (e.g., the worldwide certification of computer screens developed by the Swedish confederation of professional employees) may be indication of what is to come. Future Scandinavian models may well be based on harnessing the knowledge embodied in unions, civil society organizations, research institutes, and universities into new social partnerships. The road to such models is—just as during the founding of the twentieth-century Scandinavian model—contingent upon trust between business and stakeholders. From this perspective, the Skandia affair was unfortunate—a blatant demonstration of the collapse of the "people's home" ethos, it may have seriously dented public confidence in business. Fortunately—and again the links to the previous Scandinavian model are striking— the Scandinavian countries have a strong contingent of skilled mediating actors (CSR consultancies, collaboration-seeking NGOs, academics) who may well be able to bridge these gaps of distrust.

SCANDINAVIAN FRONTRUNNERS: INDICATIONS FROM A STUDY OF INDUSTRIES

For a number of years Scandinavian companies have enjoyed a reputation for being particularly concerned with their impact on stakeholders and society in general as well as for designing and implementing advanced CSR practices. It is, however, difficult to give evidence of such reputations, and there is hardly any coherent analysis to validate the reputation, apart from Transparency International's analyses mentioned previously in this chapter. Nevertheless, recent studies have shown that, in comparison with EU15[13] and U.S. economies, Nordic industry scores high on the two leading CSR indexes: the Dow Jones Sustainability Index World (DJSI) and FTSE4Good. With only 2.5% of the Organisation for Economic Cooperation and Development gross national product, but with 8.3% of the DJSI, the Nordic countries are "overweighted" by a factor of 3.25. The same estimation for the European Union gives an overweighting of only 1.46, while the United States is "underweighted" with a factor of 0.54 (see figure 6.1a). The corresponding figures for FTSE4Good are 1.90 for the Nordic countries, 1.37 for EU15, and 0.60 for the United States (see figure 6.1b).

From this comparison, more Nordic companies qualify as CSR avant garde than do EU15 or U.S. companies. However, the Midttun and Dirdal (2004) study also found that there is considerable variation within the Nordic countries, and some variation also across the two indexes. The DJSI lists the Nordic companies with fairly even high scores (see figure 6.2a), but with Finnish companies as the frontrunners. FTSE4Good, however, lists Swedish companies as the Nordic CSR winners ahead of the other Nordic countries (see figure 6.2b). FTSE4Good, in other words, puts Denmark, Norway, and Finland down at the European Union level but still considerably higher than the United States.

CSR Focus and Implementation in Nordic Firms

Behind the high national scores on sustainability indexes are individual strategic decisions in leading Nordic firms. In a review of the 75 largest

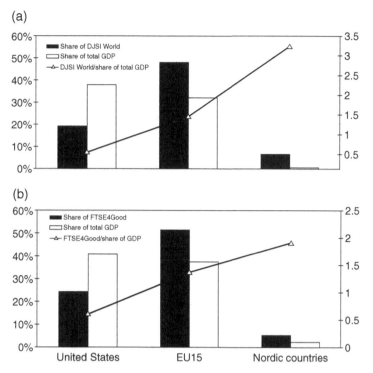

FIGURE **6.1.** The relationship between representation on (a) DJSI World and (b) FTSE4Good (dark shading, left y-axes) and share of total world gross domestic product (GDP; light shading, right y-axes): Nordic countries, United States, and Europe. The line shows the relationship between a region/country's share of the index and the share of total gross domestic product (referring to the scale on the right vertical axis), indicating whether the country or region is over- or underrepresented in the index.

Nordic companies (Midttun & Dirdal, 2004), Nordic industry is demonstrated to integrate rather than separate the frequently argued dilemma between profitability and sustainability (or, in other words, between CSR as enlightened self-interest and as social obligation) by aligning CSR and profit orientation in a mutually supportive way. It is noteworthy, however, that although there is a synergy of the business case and the normative case to be found as argument for CSR in these studies, there is also a clear demarcation of a recent turn toward more business-case–oriented arguments for CSR in these Nordic companies.

In the paper and pulp industry, for example, the integration of life cycle analysis and forest stewardship in the corporate strategies aims at living up to primarily customer expectations in the printing industry and thereby providing a basis for retaining market share in an increasingly environmentally oriented market. In the pharmaceutical industry, the CSR profile is closely tailored to core values and corporate strategies in the health sector: "being there" for somebody. This profiles the pharmaceutical industry as a potential partner with the (in the Nordic countries) *public* health care system on which it is heavily dependent, as well as signaling itself as a trustworthy supplier to patients.

As far as implementation is concerned, Nordic industry is characterized, on the one hand, by a capability to quickly adopt international standards and practices, as the small open Nordic economies from an early stage have fostered extensive international engagement. On the other hand, strong

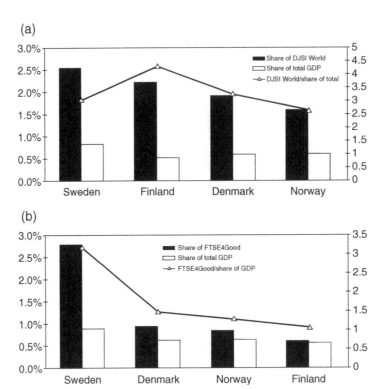

FIGURE **6.2.** The relationship between representation on DJSI World (a) and FTSE4Good (b; dark shading, left y-axes) and share of total world gross domestic product (GDP; light shading, right y-axes): Denmark, Finland, Norway, and Sweden. The line shows the relationship between a country's share of the index and the share of total gross domestic product (referring to the scale on the right vertical axis).

egalitarian values and social-democratic traditions, where "responsible" negotiations between labor and capital interlaced with advanced regulation have created a strong health, environment, and safety basis on which wider CSR issues can also be built. Together, these factors may explain some of the advanced CSR practices that we encounter in Nordic industry. In the following, we briefly look at some of the central industries in the Nordic counties.

The above-mentioned study (Midttun & Dirdal, 2004) found that one of the main strategies for linking CSR and value creation in large Nordic engineering firms seems to be to focus on their customers' sustainability needs. Nordic engineering companies such as the Finnish supplier of process industry machinery Metso, the Swiss-Swedish power and automation technology company ABB, the roller bearing and seals manufacturer SKF, the heat transfer and fluid handling company Alfa

Laval, and the compressor, generator, and industrial tool manufacturer Atlas Copco all seek to work in partnership with customers, not only to live up to stakeholder (i.e., customer) expectations or to manage their technical processes, but also to enhance their life cycle management and material flows.

The alignment of CSR and traditional business values in Nordic pharmaceutical industry is closely linked to the image of care for patients. This is most clearly expressed by the Danish pharmaceutical company Novo Nordisk: CSR is "being there" for patients and other stakeholders. In addition, the pharmaceutical industry is concerned with its relations with public authorities to promote responsible care, as there is a need to search for new venues to explore and expand the research agendas and markets, and therefore there is a need to generate and maintain a "license to operate" among, for example, politicians and the media.

Nordic countries host a prominent pulp and paper industry, accounting for some of the largest pulp and paper companies in the world. Its CSR orientation is strongly focused on large-volume material processing, which motivates responsible life cycle management in response to continuous pressure from the printing industry and other customers. The long-term commitment embedded in the stranded costs of large production facilities also motivates this industry to take a long-term perspective on their operations. Taking a look backward in the value chain, the large pulp and paper producers generally also demand clear environmental commitments from their suppliers. Norske Skog's involvement in environmental issues follows throughout the entire value chain, and the company expects the same high environmental performance from suppliers of goods and services in the value chain as maintained in its own activities. This includes clear objectives and annually set targets supporting both their environmental policy and their strategic vision. Norske Skog is, for example, highly concerned that suppliers use wood harvested only in sustainable managed forests.

With their natural resource endowments, the Nordic countries host an advanced energy industry spanning across the petroleum, hydropower, nuclear, as well as wind and biofuel sectors. This industry is clearly divided into two strands of CSR focus. Companies with a main focus on Nordic and European markets typically concentrate heavily on the environmental dimension, which in some cases is also close to their general commercial profiling. Typical representatives of this group are the Swedish state-owned power company Vattenfall, the Finnish state-owned company Fortum, and the Norwegian state-owned company Statkraft. Companies with broader international/global engagements such as Statoil and Norsk Hydro tend to include and emphasize more strongly the social dimension and stress ethics and governance issues. In addition, Nordic energy companies also typically have in place management systems and often also quantitative information systems to monitor and implement CSR policies, particularly in the environmental field.

The Nordic food industry profiles several CSR-related agendas, depending on their business focus and geographic field of operation. The agenda for the diary industry, with dominantly domestic suppliers and consumers, is predominantly to provide trust and assurance about high quality, that is, health and safety issues. The large retailing chains are also strongly focused on supply chain issues, as they supply goods from all over the world. Specialized suppliers of products with potential health risks, such as alcohol and sugar, are also engaged in compensatory and risk-reducing activities. As for most Nordic countries, there are links among safety, health, environment, and quality.

We have argued that Nordic companies have a reputation for advanced CSR practices, we have pointed out that according to international CSR indices there seems to be some evidence to substantiate this reputation, and we have indicated that a number of industries have emphasized integrating CSR practices into their corporate strategies for a number of years. Nordic companies thus seem engaged and experienced when it comes to CSR. However, this does not mean that there are no future challenges to Nordic companies.

FUTURE CHALLENGES FOR CSR IN SCANDINAVIA

In the midst of our praising of Scandinavian companies, let us remind ourselves that the majority of the Scandinavian companies are not "CSR stars." For example, a study of the 50 largest Norwegian companies compared to international frontrunners showed that more than 60% of them clearly underperformed compared to their international peers (Midttun & Dirdal, 2004). Let us not be naive about the extent to which Scandinavian companies adhere to CSR initiatives. However, the high representation of Nordic firms on the DJSI and FTSE4Good suggests that the situation in most other countries would be worse.

What we find more interesting—and even more promising—is the extent to which Scandinavian companies are prepared for future CSR challenges. In spite of our initial claim about the modest expectations toward CSR in the context of the Scandinavian welfare society, in practice, CSR debates are fairly extensive in Scandinavia. There is a general high degree of critical debate in the media, in academia, and in practice in the three Scandinavian countries. And rather than religious or ethical heritage as argument for the high awareness and action on CSR in Scandinavia, we point to the Scandinavian participative democracy with the state as main provider of social services, managers' openness to social initiatives, and the high degree of trust characterizing the Scandinavian societies as possible arguments. Precisely those same characteristics that were suggested to make CSR superfluous in the beginning of this chapter can also be argued as excellent points of departure for further CSR engagement.

Scandinavian societies seem to provide some of those cultural traits that can drive a CSR agenda forward: a general competence in dialogue, critique, and negotiation; a willingness to engage; and a broad sense of trust are cultural traits sought in the quest for increasing sensitivity toward a variety of stakeholders. The implementation of partnerships across sectors and institutions is also a reflection of these traits. Theories of stakeholder relations have convincingly argued that the challenge of strategic management is about ethics and the need to create a satisfactory balance of interests among the diverse stakeholders, who contribute to or are affected by the organization's actions (Freeman & Gilbert, 1998). It takes democratic discipline and communication skills to create a satisfactory balance between diverse interests. If CSR is about increasing sensitivity toward stakeholders, Scandinavian managers seem to have a good point of departure.

This does not mean that Scandinavian companies are there yet. Corporate social responsibility is a "moving target" also in the Scandinavian countries. What was considered "good" corporate behavior in a Scandinavian context three years ago may no longer be acceptable today. Companies need to perpetually maintain and develop their "sensory organs" toward stakeholder expectations. Although a while ago "social obligation" was a plausible incentive to engage in CSR initiatives—and still is a noble argument—the larger global issues of CSR are entering the Scandinavian debate and requesting a rational business answer to the question: Why do we need to engage in CSR initiatives? Our conclusion is that, although Scandinavian companies are not entirely there yet, they have an excellent point of departure for getting there.

NOTES

1. Former Minister of Social Affairs (from 1929 to 1935) Karl Kristian Steinke implemented the comprehensive Social Reform of 1933, concerning social security for all Danish citizens.

2. For example, in 2002, Novo Nordisk's Sustainability Report was placed as the world's second best report on soft values by United Nations Environmental Programme (after Royal Dutch Shell Group).

3. See, for example, the 2002 Gallup International and Environics International survey of which institutions are trusted to work for the best of society, in which large private and international companies are ranked 11th and 12th after the armed forces (= most trusted!), NGOs, the United Nations, governments, religious institutions, and others. The high level of distrust and skepticism toward companies is seen to be that conspicuous in Denmark.

4. Of the largest economies in the world, 51 are corporations; only 49 are countries (www.globalpolicy.org/socecon/tncs/countries.htm).

5. See the Nørby Code (www.corporategovernance.dk). The Copenhagen Stock Exchange has since 2002 published a set of guidelines for good corporate governance, formulated by a group of Danish CEO managers.

6. In 1996, the founding corporate members of the National Network of Company Leaders were the CEOs of Oticon, Carlsberg, Pressalit, Horsens Gummivarefabrik, Grundfos, Novo Nordisk, Ruko, DSB, Jamo, Post Danmark, Sparekassen Nordylland, Danfoss, Neckelmann, Erik Mainz, Lego, and Falck. Today, the National Network has twelve members. Moreover, there is a number of Regional Networks that work locally across the country. Every year, the National Network awards a prize to a company that has made a special contribution within the field of CSR. For more information, see www.netvaerksprisen.dk

7. See Midttun and Dirdal's (2004) research based on information from the Norwegian *Finansdepartementet*, case number 03/3178, answer from *Finanskomiteen/Senterpartiets fraksjon*, October 10, about the gross national product budget for 2004.

8. A witty satire of how such rationalization engineers permeated Swedish society during this period is provided in the 2003 Norwegian film *Salmer fra Kjökkenet (Kitchen Stories)*, directed by Bent Hamer.

9. The investment fund policy forced corporations to funnel excess profits into a so-called investment fund. Corporations could, if given consent from the government, reclaim these funds for large, socially responsible investments in infrastructure. Thus, the humanized production manufacturing plants built by Saab and Volvo were financed through investment funds.

10. For instance, the seat belt for automobiles was largely the result of the expertise in, and regulation of, worker protection.

11. This argument was summarized in the TV documentary *Jakten på den försvunna skatten* by

SVT (Swedish public service broadcaster) on April 10, 2003.

12. Nevertheless, the issue of whether organizational prejudice and structural discrimination exist is still heavily contested within Swedish business.

13. Midttun and Dirdal (2004) limited their analysis to the old West European Union (EU15), because the new East and Central European member states were found to be very different with respect to political and economic backgrounds and therefore to confound the analysis.

REFERENCES

Andréasson, R., & Bäcklund, C.-G. (2000). *Bilbältet—Svenskt utvecklingsarbete för global bilsäkerhet.* Stockholm: Kulturvårdskommittén.

Berghmann, J. (1997). Can the idea of benchmarking be applied to social protection? *Bulletin Luxembourgeois des Questions Sociales, 4,* 119–130.

Bibb, S., & Kourdi, J. (2004). *Trust matters. For organisational and personal success.* London: Palgrave Macmillan.

Callon, M. (1998). *The laws of the markets.* London: Blackwell.

Carroll, A. B. (1999). Corporate social responsibility: Evolution of a definitional construct. *Business & Society, 38*(3), 268–295.

De Geer, H. (1978). *Job studies and industrial relations.* Stockholm: Almquist & Wiksell International.

Ekman, B. (2003). *Himmel och helvete—om företagande,makt och ledarskap.* Stockholm: Ekerlids Förlag.

Erixon, L. (2003). *Den Svenska Modellens Ekonomiska Politik.* Stockholm: Atlas Akademi.

Fraser, N. (1999). Social justice in the age of identity politics: Redistribution, recognition and participation. In L. Ray & A. Sayer (Eds.), *Culture and economy after the cultural turn* (pp. 25–52). London: Sage.

Freeman, R. E., & Gilbert, D. R. (1998). *Corporate strategy and the search for ethics.* Englewood Cliffs, NJ: Prentice-Hall.

Giversen, J. (2003). The world's first accounting statement. In M. Morsing & C. Thyssen (Eds.), *Corporate values and responsibility: The case of Denmark* (pp. 33–41). Copenhagen: Samfundslitteratur.

Greenness, T. (2003). Scandinavian managers on Scandinavian management. *International Journal of Value-Based Management, 16,* 9–21.

Hälleby, B. (1990). *Så Föddes en Svensk Bilindustri.* Stockholm: Akademiförlaget.

Hofstede, G. (1980). *Cultural consequences.* London: Sage.

Hofstede, G. (1994). *Cultures and organizations. Software of the mind.* London: HarperCollins.

Inglehart, R., Basanez, M., & Moreno, A. (1998). *Human values and beliefs: A crosscultural sourcebook.* Ann Arbor, MI: University of Michigan Press.

Joly, C. (2000). *The role of the financial sector.* Paper presented at the United Nations Conference on Action for a Common Future, Bergen, Norway.

KPMG. (2002). *KPMG international survey of corporate social responsibility reporting. 2002, Environmental social economic.* Retrieved August 5, 2004, from http://www.wimm.nl/.

Lund, J. E. (2003). Partnerships in practice. In M. Morsing & C. Thyssen (Eds.), *Corporate values and responsibility: The case of Denmark* (pp. 179–191). Copenhagen: Samfundslitteratur.

McCallin, J., & Webb, T. (2004, January 25). Corporate responsibility progress in Scandinavia. *Ethical Corporation Magazine.*

Midttun, A., & Dirdal, T. (2004, September 27–28). *Nordic industry and CSR: Frontrunners or discrete societal partners?* Paper presented at the European Academy of Business in Society third annual colloquium in Ghent, Belgium, The challenge of sustainable growth: Integrating societal expectations in business.

Morsing, M. (2003). Conspicuous responsibility: Communicating responsibility—to whom? In M. Morsing & C. Thyssen (Eds.), *Corporate values and responsibility: The case of Denmark* (pp. 145–154). Copenhagen: Samfundslitteratur.

Morsing, M., Langer, R., & Eder-Hansen, J. (2005, December 4–5). *CSR as an act of strategic ambiguity—a longitudinal study of CSR in the media.* Paper presented at the European Academy of Business in Society's fifth annual colloquium, Warsaw.

National Network of Company Leaders. (1996). Retrieved from www .copenhagencentre.org/sw661.asp.

Ralston, D. A., Holt, D. H., Terpstra, R. H., & Kay-Cheng, Y. (1997). The impact of national culture and economic ideology on managerial work values: A study of the United States, Russia, Japan and China. *Journal of International Business Studies, 28*(1), 177–207.

Ronen, S., & Shenkar, O. (1985). Clustering countries on attitudinal dimensions: A review and synthesis. *Academy of Management Review, 10*(3), 435–454.

Rothstein, B. (2003). *Sociala Fällor och Tillitens Problem*. Stockholm: SNS Förlag.

Ruud, A., & Larsen, O. M. (2002). *Miljørapportering i årsberetningen; Følger Norske bedrifter Regnskapslovens pålegg?* (Rapport No. 2/02). Oslo: University of Oslo.

Ryner, J. M. (2002). *Capitalist restructuring, globalisation and the third way: Lessons from the Swedish model*. London: Routledge.

Sharp Paine, L. (2000). *Value shift*. Boston, MA: Harvard Business Press.

Smith, N. C. (2004). Corporate social responsibility. Whether or how? *California Management Review, 45*(4), 52–76.

Socialministeriet. (2000). *Det angår os alle—Status år 2000 for kampagnen om virksomhedernes sociale ansvar*. Copenhagen: Socialministeriet (Danish Ministry of Social Affairs).

Thyssen, C. (2003). Social partnerships—the role of government in Denmark, based on an interview with Karen Jespersen. In M. Morsing & C. Thyssen (Eds.), *Corporate values and responsibility: The case of Denmark* (pp. 25–32). Copenhagen: Samfundslitteratur.

Zadek, S. (2003). A foreigner's view on the case of Denmark. In M. Morsing & C. Thyssen (Eds.), *Corporate values and responsibility: The case of Denmark* (pp. 61–67). Copenhagen: Samfundslitteratur.

7

Corporate Social Responsibility in Asia
A Confucian Context

GLEN WHELAN

While there is now a very extensive literature in the theory and practice of corporate social responsibility (CSR) that has been growing over the last few years, it is still, for the most part, very heavily focused on European and American cultures. This chapter therefore seeks to build upon the still relatively small amount of work conducted on CSR in Asia (e.g., Birch & Moon, 2004) by examining some of the emergent themes and issues that relate, in a fundamental way, to CSR within the region. Of central importance to this chapter is my acknowledgment that the idea of CSR is always embedded within specific social and cultural milieus. Accordingly, I begin the chapter by situating CSR within an Asian context, more specifically, within a Confucian context, for what are often termed Asian values are, in a great many instances, more accurately described as Confucian values (see Birch, 1998). Thus, in the second section, I present a brief overview of Confucian thinking, with specific emphasis on those ideas of most obvious relevance to understanding Asian business.[1] Following this, I show how Confucian thinking can be seen to pervade the activities of business and government throughout the region. With these contextual discussions completed, I then introduce some of the key issues that are currently being discussed in terms of CSR throughout Asia. In the main, these discussions involve issues of corruption, cronyism, and corporate governance. Taken as a whole, these three highly interrelated issues can be termed—in borrowing the title of a work edited by Richter and Mar (2004b)—"Asia's new crisis." Accordingly, I outline the crisis and discuss the manner in which it has called into question the values underpinning the activities of Asian business and government. In concluding the chapter, I highlight some similarities between Asia's new crisis and the corporate accounting scandal that emerged in the United States in 2001–2002. Both events, I suggest, highlight the need for increased attention to be paid to the social, legal, cultural, and moral environment within which corporations exist.

AN ASIAN CONTEXT FOR CSR

Robert Davies, chief executive of the Prince of Wales International Business Leaders Forum, noted while speaking on Corporate Citizenship and Socially Responsible Investment in Hong Kong in 2002 that "business culture and definitions of corporate responsibility must always take account of the local context" (¶ xx). To slightly rephrase this for the present purposes, what one might say is that to have any understanding of the debates surrounding CSR within a given region, one must first understand the culture that infuses business practices within that region. Thus, and with this slight reformulation in mind, it is helpful to refer to Davies once again, who went on to note, in the same speech, that

[i]n most parts of Asia, bonds of family and friendship in economic relations generally account for far more than in the developed Western world where the professionalisation of business, the separation of ownership and control and impact of mobility have diminished the significance of the bonds of friendship and community. Similarly, courtesy and respect, whether for age, wisdom, leadership, neighbours and customs throughout Asia are still striking in comparison. (Davies, 2002, ¶xx)

In making a statement about Asian values, practices, and worldviews, Davies is playing a somewhat dangerous game because Asia is culturally, socially, and geographically an immensely diverse region. In other words, it is far from homogeneous.[2] Nevertheless, and with this substantial disclaimer in mind, Davies is largely correct when he suggests that business practice in Asia, and East Asia most specifically, can be understood to derive from a common Confucian, or early Chinese, heritage. This common Confucian heritage is often used to explain the central importance that many Asians place on bonds of family and friendship, and the respect and courtesy they show for "age, wisdom, leadership, neighbours and customs." As such, it is helpful to recognize, along with Backman (2004), that "Japanese and Korean cultures are partly derivatives of Chinese culture and, when it comes to Southeast Asia, much of that region's business sector is in the hands of overseas Chinese" (p. 10).[3] On this basis, then, I now turn to a, necessarily brief, discussion of Confucianism.

A BRIEF DISCUSSION OF CONFUCIANISM

Confucius lived from 551 to 479 B.C. According to Marinoff (2004), his influence "on Asian cultures is remarkable, and outweighs even that of Aristotle in the West" (p. 21). Nevertheless, and despite "his immense importance in the Chinese tradition, little that is certain is known about Confucius" (Lau, 1979, p. 9). While there is little certain knowledge about Confucius the person, there is no disagreement over the fact that the "origins of Confucianism lie in a collection of sayings known as the *Analects*, attributed to Confucius . . . and in ancient commentaries such as that of his disciple Mencius (372–289 B.C.)" (Richter &

Mar, 2004b, p. 44). The fundamental importance of these two thinkers to the Confucian tradition has been "officially recognized in China for over a thousand years" (Lau, 1970, p. 7) and is nicely reflected by the fact that Meng K'e (Mencius) and K'ung Ch'iu or K'ung Chung-ni (Confucius) are the only two Chinese philosophers who "have the distinction of being consistently known in the West by a latinized name" (Lau, 1979, p. 9).

As Confucius lived more than 2,000 years ago, and given that he has been perceived, and currently is perceived, by many as being one of humanity's preeminent sages, it is not surprising to find Confucianism pervaded by an immense amount of deep, rich, and profound thought. Accordingly, let me explicitly note that, in the discussion that follows, I necessarily concentrate on those elements of Confucianism that I think are of most importance for understanding Asian business practices.

Perhaps the central notion of Confucianism is the idea that "all people maintain a sort of familistic relationship with each other" (Tai, 1989, p. 14). Indeed, "Confucius made the natural love and obligations obtaining between members of the family the basis for a general morality" (Lau, 1979, p. 18).[4] In making the relationships that exist within an archetypal family the basis for a general morality, Confucius was concerned with ensuring the welfare, or harmony, of a given organic whole. As Zhang (1999) has noted, Confucius thought of the "natural and human worlds [as constituting] an organism made up of multitudinous interconnected parts. Each part has its proper position and function in the order of things. If any part falls from its place or is disrupted in its function, the harmony of the whole is impaired" (p. 37). Confucius, then, it might be said, was more concerned with the overall welfare, stability, and harmony of a given society than he was with the welfare of each and every specific individual comprising that society. Thus, it can be strongly argued that this more general and holistic concern is reflected in what Max Weber saw as Confucianism's rejection of all nonutilitarian yardsticks (Zhang, 1999, pp. 1–2).

Confucius made familial relationships the basis of his general morality as he thought a society structured or organized in a manner analogical to that of a family would give rise to the greatest good for the greatest number. In thinking this way, Confucius was in line with Chinese thinking more generally, in the sense that harmony in Chinese society is often thought to depend "on hierarchical organization and on the proper performance of roles from top to bottom. Each individual is expected to follow social norms of conduct" (Zhang, 1999, p. 60). Within Confucianism, these "social norms of conduct" are embodied within five sets of relationships, between ruler and subject, father and son, husband and wife, elder son and younger son, and elder person and younger person (Backman, 1999, p. 10; Tai, 1989, p. 15). Each of these five relationships is, in turn, characterized by a specific set of reciprocal properties or customs. In *The Book of Rites*, "Confucius listed the ethical properties of these relationships: 'Father, kindness; son, filial piety; elder brother, goodness; younger brother, respect; husband, righteousness; wife, compliance; the sovereign, benevolence; the ministers, loyalty'" (Tai, 1989, p. 15).[5]

As the ethical properties of each relationship suggest, the Confucian ethical system is, in addition to being "a pattern or orderly subordination to authority" (Zhang, 1999, p. 75), both personalistic and particularistic (Tai, 1989, p. 15). It is personalistic in that the way in which one acts in relation to a given person will depend on the personal relationship one has with that specific person. And it is particularistic in the sense that one has to treat different people in different ways, as a result of the particular personal relationship one has with these differing people. Such an ethical framework would seem to result in one effectively being obliged to treat most people they know in a different way, and in one being treated in a different manner by nearly every person that knows them. In this regard, Confucianism is starkly different from the "impersonal" and "universal" ethical system of an archetypal Westerner such as Kant.[6]

Now, just as individuals are obliged to relate to those within their families in differing ways, they are also obliged, according to Confucian thought, to relate to those outside of their families in ways that differ from the relationships they have with their family (taken as an abstract whole). This is because Confucianists think it is "unnatural to love all men alike" (Lau, 1970, p. 31), for they think our "obligation towards others should be in proportion to the benefit we have received from them" (Lau, 1979, p. 19). One outcome of such thinking is that

love, and so the obligation to love, decreases by degrees as it extends outwards. Geographically, one loves members of one's own family more than one's neighbours, one's neighbours more than one's fellow villagers, and so on. Socially, one loves members of one's own social class more than those of another class. (Lau, 1979, p. 18)

On this basis, Mencius concluded that love without discrimination was "a denial of one's parents" (Lau, 1970, p. 31).

Thus far, I have commented on the organic, utilitarian, familial, hierarchic, and particularistic elements of Confucianism. Confucianism, I have stated, is organic and utilitarian in that it considers the greatest good for a given community as being the fundamental ethical concern; is familial and hierarchic in that it considers a form of social organization analogous to a hierarchically organized family (e.g., father as benevolent ruler, son and wife as obedient and respectfully ruled) as giving rise to the greatest good for a given community; and is particularistic in that one has different obligations and duties to different people, depending on the personal relationship one has with them.

In addition to these ideas, Confucianism also places great importance on the idea of benevolent and correct behavior and the idea that each and every human has the capacity to learn to act in such a manner. At the risk of being too general,[7] what one might say is that to act benevolently and rightly, or perhaps dutifully and compassionately, is, for Confucianism, to act in a way that is morally correct. Normally, Confucian thought will oppose benevolent action and behavior to narrowly self-interested action and behavior.[8] Thus, while acknowledging the human capacity to act in a narrowly self-interested manner, Confucius also thought that humans had the capacity to act benevolently and rightly, for otherwise, he would not have bothered placing such an emphasis upon these characteristics within his teachings.

Indeed, for Mencius, the capacity to think about "moral duties, about priorities, about the purposes and destiny of man and his position in the universe" (Lau, 1970, p. 15) is what distinguishes humanity from nature more generally, and from animals more specifically. With this in mind, we can find Mencius stating, in book II, part A, chapter 6—a passage Lau (1970, p. 18) considers "justly famous"—that no "man is devoid of a heart sensitive to the suffering of others." He continues:

My reason for saying that no man is devoid of a sensitive heart is this. Suppose a man were, all of a sudden, to see a young child on the verge of falling into a well. He would certainly be moved to compassion, not because he wanted to get in the good graces of the parents, nor because he wished to win the praise of his fellow villagers or friends, nor yet because he disliked the cry of the child. (p. 82)

Basically, Mencius wants to illustrate that the "human heart has built-in moral capacities" (Lau, 1970, p. 28). If the man in the example who is moved by compassion were to act on this compassion and run to prevent the young child from falling into the well, then, according to Confucian thought, the compassionate man could be said to have acted both benevolently and rightly. While acknowledging that these built-in moral tendencies are no more than incipient in the human heart, Mencius also thinks these tendencies "can be developed" (Lau, 1970, p. 28). This, then, is one of the basic reasons for Confucian thought placing central importance on correct learning and proper education, for through these processes, everyone's moral character can be enhanced, and the harmony, stability, and welfare of society along with it.

Before I move on and begin my discussion of the manner in which Confucian thought manifests itself in the activities of business and government throughout Asia, one final, general point needs to be made regarding the pragmatic and undogmatic nature inherent to Confucian thinking. Accordingly, let me refer to Zhang (1999), when he writes: "Few pre-scientific philosophers laid as much emphasis on flexibility: for Confucius, a gentleman should be ready at all times to change according to circumstances. . . . He looked favourably upon compromise since he did not believe that truth and virtue are somehow fixed" (p. 24).

And, it is helpful that I refer to Zhang (1999) once again, this time when he writes:

Confucius did not explicitly provide any general rule or principle to guide one's actions since situations are complex in that they are unpredictable. He taught people that they should consider and understand the impact of their actions rather than memorize some fixed rules. . . . It is often difficult to follow Confucius since he did not provide any fixed rules to follow. (p. 37)

Put succinctly, what this means is that, within Confucianism, greater emphasis is put on rule of virtue than rule of law. This is so for a number of reasons. First, and as Zhang has suggested, rule of virtue is more flexible than rule of law in enabling one to account for any given, specific set of circumstances in their efforts at maintaining the harmony of an organic whole. Second, greater emphasis is placed on rule of virtue than rule of law because the "latter is passive and negative, preventing the people from doing wrong; while the former is active and positive, encouraging people to do good" (Hsu, 1932, p. 172). As discussed further below, this specific, albeit general, element of Confucianism can be found, along with a number of other elements already mentioned, to pervade the activities of business and government throughout the Asian region.

CONFUCIAN VALUES IN ASIAN BUSINESS AND GOVERNMENT

Any talk of business in Asia more generally, or of CSR in Asia more specifically, needs to begin by acknowledging the role played by Asian governments in the commercial sphere. Accordingly, I refer to Robins (2002) when he writes:

Since the 1950s or 1960s, most governments in East Asia have accepted responsibility for the industrialization and accelerated development of their national economies; they have also taken this responsibility seriously. The promotion of economic growth in general, and the establishment of new industries in particular, have been regarded as core responsibilities. . . . Put simply, East Asian governments have accepted a more direct responsibility for growth and given it higher priority than their Western counterparts. They have also shown themselves perfectly willing to "intervene" in the economy in pursuit of these objectives. These policies and actions have given rise to business-government relationships that differ from those in the West. (p. 291)

Importantly, given the discussion of the preceding section, such government intervention is entirely consistent with both Confucianism's organic and utilitarian outlook and its pragmatic and undogmatic approach to benevolent action. As Hsu (1932) has written in this specific regard:

The first principle of benevolent government, according to the sage [Confucius], is that the government should work for the greatest welfare of the people at the greatest economy for the nation. In this principle Confucius would allow the State to undertake any sort of activity so long as such an activity increases the actual welfare of the people and so long as it does not impose upon the people too much financial burden. (p. 106)

Such government intervention is also consistent with Confucianism in the sense that it avoids fixing "one's thought in extremes (yin or yang in popular terms)" (Zhang, 1999, p. 189). Zhang (1999) continues, when "the Confucian mind is concerned with social systems, it will not accept either socialism or capitalism (the two extremes of Western rationalism) as its ideal. The good in reality (not necessarily with regard to intellectual speculation) lies somewhere in between" (p. 189). Given the historical tendency of Asian governments, and East Asian governments in particular, to engage in market intervention,[9] it would seem that the political leaders of such countries would, at the very least, agree with Confucian thinking on this point, even if they would not officially "align" themselves with such a view.

This Confucian pragmatism taken by Asian governments regarding industrial policy and market intervention is also reflected by the manner in which Backman (1999, p. 11) thinks that Asian governments rule *by* law rather than enforce the rule *of* law. He continues: "The law is used as a tool for whatever the ruler's objectives are; it isn't an end in itself. . . . The separation of the judiciary from the government makes little sense in such an environment. . . . Rather than be independent of government, the judiciary is an arm of it" (p. 12). Such practices are consistent with Confucianism in two regards. First, such practices are consistent with the emphasis placed on hierarchic order in Confucian thinking, in that it emphasizes "a pattern of orderly subordination to authority" (Zhang, 1999, p. 75). Second, such practices are consistent with the Confucian preference for rule by virtue over rule by law, for as I have already noted, Confucius "taught people that they should consider and understand the impact of their actions rather than memorize some fixed rules" (Zhang, 1999, p. 37). Regarding this second point, the tendency of Asian governments to rule *by* law, rather than enforce

rule *of* law, is reflected, at the level of business, in the "directive" role that contracts play throughout much of Asia. To refer to Backman (1999) once again:

In the West, contracts, like laws, remain fixed with the passage of time. In Asia, they tend to relate to the prevailing conditions at the time. Should those change, then so too does the legitimacy of the contract. . . . A Western firm might have a contract to sell wheat to a mainland Chinese firm in which the price is fixed at a certain level. However, should market conditions change and the market price move significantly below that specified in the contract, then the Chinese side almost certainly will see this as an opportunity to renegotiate the contract. (p. 14)

With the fixity of government laws and business contracts being less than that of the West, it has been suggested that the importance placed on relationships "in East Asian business . . . is not only cultural; it probably mainly reflects relatively undeveloped legal and regulatory systems that make contract and property right enforcement difficult" (Economic Analytic Unit, 2002, p. 3). But, as I have been suggesting, this is, at least to some extent, to miss the point, for in Confucian thought, the rule of virtue and familial relationships are, when taken together, preferred to rule of law taken by itself. Thus, the undeveloped legal and regulatory systems can be understood in cultural terms, just like the importance placed on relationships.

The importance placed on relationships in Asian business networks and, in particular, the fundamental interconnection that exists between the ideas of family and business throughout much of Asia are perhaps the most obvious way in which a Confucian ideal manifests itself throughout the Asian business world. Regarding this phenomenon, Backman (2004) has highlighted that:

[a] recent World Bank study analysed almost 3,000 publicly traded companies in Hong Kong, Indonesia, Japan, Korea, Malaysia, the Philippines, Singapore, Taiwan and Thailand. It focused on the largest public companies in these countries. It found that outside Japan, families controlled on average at least 60% of the large listed companies. Separation of ownership from family control was also found to

be rare. And that is for listed companies. Family control of unlisted companies is much higher. For many, the family and the firm are synonymous concepts. And that is key to understanding how business in much of Asia works. (pp. 7–8)

With family and business being so closely intertwined, it is not really a surprise that Asian business practices are often thought to differ greatly from Western business practices. Importantly, given that Japan does not have the same correlation between family and business that the rest of Asia does, it needs to be noted that the Japanese business world is often understood, analogically, in terms of the family. In this specific regard, what one might say is that, whereas families tend to establish businesses throughout the rest of Asia, those businesses that are established in Japan tend to become a "family," or behave as if they were a family.[10] Accordingly, the general comments that follow apply to Japanese business just as much as they do to the practice of business in the rest of Asia.[11]

The sense in which business in Asia is closely related to the family, whether literally or metaphorically, has a number of very important implications for understanding the practices thereof. First, it tends to result in the business group, conceived as a community or family, coming to possess an importance in and of itself. This results in individuals being discouraged "from self-seeking pursuits that may jeopardize group cohesion" (Tai, 1989, p. 18). Such self-seeking pursuits are discouraged from an early age, for as Rozman (1991) has recognized, the child is taught, in the "formative years . . . to submerge the self within the group, and to learn to serve the group. He or she learns to conceive of the self not as an abstraction, but in reciprocal terms appropriate to specific relationships" (p. 27). Rozman (1991) continues, in "the countries of East Asia individualism is portrayed negatively, as a cause of selfishness and anarchy— as a barrier to the achievement of the goals of the community or state" (p. 27). The same point was made by Tai (1989) when he wrote:

In Chinese and Japanese societies, individualism as practiced in the West is generally not accepted as a social value. In both societies, individuals seek identity not so much in terms of who they are as in terms of whom they are associated with. Once an individual's group identity is established, the individual will maintain such an identity both within the group and without. And all individuals are supposed to uphold the interest of the group—ranging from the family to the nation—above their own. (p. 17)

Rather obviously, this focus on the group is consistent with the emphasis Confucianism places on the importance of maintaining harmony among, or the welfare of, a given social organism.

With the business enterprise being conceived as a social entity, profits, while not being despised in and of themselves, will, in many instances, not be pursued at the expense of human harmony or group cohesion (Tai, 1989, p. 18). In Japan, for example, employees, along with banks, are normally considered to be the two most important stakeholders (Patrick, 2004, pp. 6–7). This raises an interesting question: If Asian businesses are not necessarily concerned with maximizing shareholder wealth, how do they measure success? In answer to this question, the general consensus is in terms of market share and company size.[12] Importantly, this would seem to be something that both employees and employers can work toward in unison, in the sense that the pursuit of market share and company size would, *at least superficially*, seem to be less likely to result in employees being laid off than would the sole pursuit of shareholder wealth maximization.

Lifetime employment, or the promise of lifetime employment, is another way in which Asian corporations have historically manifested the importance placed on social harmony and enduring relationships.[13] In addition to the importance placed on enduring relationships, such a promise would appear to result from the paternalistic relationship that exists between employer and employee (Tai, 1989, p. 19). This relationship between employer and employee can be equated with that between father and son or ruler and subject. Thus, in line with the Confucian idea of orderly subordination/hierarchization, the employer is meant to act kindly and benevolently toward the employee, and the employee with loyalty and filial piety toward the employer.

The Confucian concern with group harmony and cohesion does not necessarily end at the business firm in Asia. Indeed, it is often suggested that Asian business is better understood in terms of interfirm networks than in terms of individual firms (Hamilton, 1991). Japanese business, for example, is dominated by what are termed *keiretsu*. *Keiretsu* comprises a group of companies that deal with each other on a regular basis and hold shares in each other. These cross-shareholdings tend to be fairly illiquid, in that the various companies rarely, if ever, sell their holdings in each other (Yafeh, 2000). According to Dore (e.g. 1998, 2000), this results in *keiretsu* being somewhat like an extended family or community in which the maximization of short-term profits is not the fundamental aim of all concerned. Rather, *keiretsu* tend to be more interested in the maintenance of the family or community and will take on additional short-term costs in an effort to do so.

And in Korea, the business environment is dominated by massive conglomerates known as *chaebols*. The term

> *chaebol* means "financial house" and is commonly used to refer to conglomerates consisting of many related companies, including a number of companies listed on the stock exchange, which are engaged in a broad range of industrial and services businesses. Most *chaebol* have highly centralized, autocratic management by the founder and his immediate family members. (Black, Metzger, O'Brien, & Shin, 2001, p. 551)

Thus, where the Japanese *keiretsu* demonstrate a concern with group and community harmony between business firms, the Korean *chaebol* demonstrate the concern with a hierarchical order on an interfirm basis. Both traits are, once again, in line with Confucian thought more generally.[14]

As the preceding discussion illustrates, ideals and concepts associated with Confucianism can be found to pervade the activities of both business and government throughout Asia. In particular, the importance Confucianism places on organicism and utilitarianism, familial and hierarchical relationships, and rule by virtue as opposed to rule by law can help explain characteristic features of the organizations, relationships, and networks that comprise the world of Asian business and government. In the following section, I comment on the interrelationship between these characteristic features and Asia's "new crisis."

ASIA'S NEW CRISIS— CORRUPTION, CRONYISM, AND CORPORATE GOVERNANCE

In his foreword to a collection of essays titled *Asia's New Crisis*, Klaus Schwab, executive chairman and founder of the World Economic Forum, noted: "In the late 1990s, corruption, cronyism and poor governance were blamed—rightly or wrongly—for the collapse that led to the Asian financial crisis" (Schwab, 2004, p. viii). Schwab is undoubtedly correct to condition his observation with a strategically placed "rightly or wrongly," because other issues of a more macroeconomic nature have also been posited as giving rise to the massive currency and stock market devaluations that characterized this period.[15] Nevertheless, and as Schwab is suggesting, one cannot deny that many commentators, academics, and pundits more generally have come to see the Asian financial crisis as being intimately related to problems of "corruption, cronyism and poor governance." Going one step further, Richter and Mar (2004a) have suggested that the crisis has resulted in a "dethroning of 'Asian values'" (p. 3). This dethroning has been all the more pronounced in that, during the 1980s most particularly—with this period being prior to both the Asian financial crisis and the bursting of the property and share market bubbles in Japan—Asian values were often championed as giving rise to the "Asian economic miracle."[16]

In the preceding section I noted that certain values consistent with Confucianism can be found to pervade, inform, or help to explain and understand the activities of Asian businesses and governments. Furthermore, I noted, in specific regard to the policies and actions of Asian governments, that the Confucian emphasis on organicism, utilitarianism, orderly subordination, and virtue rather than law were, at the very least, helpful descriptive devices. For one, it was suggested that such ideas manifested themselves in the flexible and pragmatic approach taken by many Asian governments to issues of industrial policy. This flexible approach has meant that Asian governments have had the capacity to encourage or foster the development of certain industries in the name of the commonwealth. Unfortunately, such capacity has also given rise to immense possibilities for government–business corruption.[17] In many instances, such corruption takes the form of business people giving kickbacks to those ministers or public servants responsible for awarding contracts, changing legislation, or granting tax benefits and incentive packages.

It is commonly accepted that such corruption is rife throughout the region. This fact is reflected by the low rankings that many Asian countries receive from nongovernmental organizations such as Transparency International regarding perceived levels of corruption.[18] It is also reflected by the fact that corruption has reached the highest levels of political office. Mohamed Suharto, for instance, the president of Indonesia from 1967 to 1998, is thought to have embezzled up to US$35 billion during his reign (Transparency International, 2004, p. 13). And in South Korea in 2002, President Kim Dae Jung, who had "made fighting corruption a top priority on coming to office in 1997," resigned following a corruption scandal involving two of his sons (Transparency International, 2003, p. 130).

In addition to the flexible approach that many Asian governments take regarding industrial policy, opportunities for corruption throughout the region are increased as a result of weakly developed and poorly enforced legal systems, the subordination of the legal system to state elites, and the fact that policing and judicial functions are often poorly paid (Backman, 1999, p. 23; Backman, 2004, pp. 25–29; Marinoff, 2004, p. 39; Richter & Mar, 2004a, p. 9). Once again, the Confucian ideals of orderly subordination and rule by virtue, as opposed to rule by law, are helpful descriptive devices for understanding such phenomena. Indeed, as Backman (1999) has noted, "Confucianism is sometimes accused of promoting corruption in East Asia" (p. 28). Such accusations are the result of a number of interconnecting elements. First, and as Marinoff (2004) has also noted, "Confucian ethics are often attenuated at the level of the family or community" (p. 21). This attenuation, combined with the fact that Confucianism effectively requires individuals to try to "improve the welfare of their relatives and friends through their influence and contacts," can result in the payment of bribes for favorable treatment by those with the capacity to mete it out (Backman, 1999, p. 28).

Problems that relate to a weak legal framework, and the attenuation of moral responsibility at the level of one's family or "community," have also emerged in the field of Asian corporate governance. In specific regard to this first point,

what needs to be understood is that "[w]hen outside investors finance firms, they face a risk, and sometimes near certainty, that the returns on their investments will never materialize because the controlling shareholders or managers expropriate them" (La Porta, Lopez-de-Silanes, Shleifer, & Vishny, 2003, p. 3).

A strong legal framework that protects outside investors, and most particularly minority investors, can prevent such expropriation. When such a legal framework does not exist or is not properly enforced, expropriation can occur. According to La Porta et al. (2003):

> Expropriation can take a variety of forms. In some instances, the insiders simply steal the profits. In other instances, the insiders sell the output, the assets, or the additional securities in the firm they control to another firm they own at below market prices. Such transfer pricing, asset striping, and investor dilution, though often legal, have largely the same effect as theft. In still other instances, expropriation takes the form of diversion of corporate opportunities from the firm, installing possibly unqualified family members in managerial positions, or overpaying executives. (p. 3)

Given that a strong legal framework that protects outside investors has not existed in many Asian countries,[19] and given that a high level of ownership concentration is a characteristic feature of many Asian corporations, expropriation of this sort has occurred on a fairly regular basis throughout the region. According to Backman (1999, p. 107), one way in which the major shareholders of companies listed on Asia's stock exchanges commonly expropriate from their minority shareholders is by selling an asset that they hold privately to the listed company at an inflated price. Backman (1999) suggests that

> [t]his practice isn't so much endemic to as epidemic in Asia. Indonesia's Salim Group has tried to make ample use of the procedure. On just one occasion, in early 1997, it managed to sell, in one fell swoop, six companies that had been privately held by the controlling family to one of the group's listed arms. . . . (p. 108)

To move on, the attenuation of moral responsibility has also been highlighted as a problem within Japanese corporations. For example, Oki

Matsumoto, the president and CEO of Monex Inc., has stated, in a conversation he had with Karuna Shinsho (2004): "When I see the scandals happening with Japanese corporations these days, whether it's a bank or Tokyo Electric Power, I bet that each individual had strong reservations about doing those bad things. But nobody can say no to the corporation. . . . I think there's a huge gap between individual ethics and those of the corporation"[20] (p. 175). Such moral quandaries for the Japanese employee are further complicated by the fact that, in Japan, corporations have other stakeholders to consider than just their shareholders. As Matsumoto noted in the same conversation, the stakeholders of a corporation in Japan include "the society, employees, clients and shareholders. And the shareholders tend to be ranked lower than other stakeholders" (p. 176).

Joichi Ito, the founder and CEO of Neoteny, a venture-capital firm focused on personal communications and enabling technology, was also party to the same conversation, and as he stated, following on from Matsumoto:

It's very easy to be ethical when your shareholders and customers and your employees are all the same and they're all telling you one thing. But if your shareholders tell you one thing, your partners tell you another thing, the government tells you another thing, and society tells you another thing, then you get into a moral and ethical dilemma. I think one of the key things Japan is experiencing is a disconnect between stakeholders in different sectors of society. For instance, there is foreign money coming into the market, an aging population with a different set of moral values amidst the spread of globalization, and the necessary shifting of resource allocation in Japan from manufacturing to services. (Shinsho, 2004, p. 176)

What Matsumoto and Ito are respectively highlighting, then, are problems that arise when the interests of the group are considered more important than the ethical concern of the individual (or the interests of society at large), and problems that arise when the actions of a corporation are meant to take account of an immense variety of, often highly divergent, interests. Clearly, and once again, such problems can, at the very least, be related to a number of elements of central concern to Confucian thought. Most particularly, they can be related to the emphasis Confucian

thinking places on organicism, hierarchies, and utilitarianism.

In bringing this section to a close, let me state once more that most of the issues surrounding corporate governance and corruption in Asia came to the fore following the Asian financial crisis of 1997–1998. The flight of foreign capital that resulted in substantial currency depreciations and stock market declines throughout the region helped reveal what Richter and Mar (2004b) have termed Asia's "new crisis." Largely, they suggest, the crisis that has emerged is an ethical one, in that "the crisis created an ethical void, marked by the inability of Asia's elites to inspire and propose a new ethical grounding for the region. The void has become more pronounced as some of the elite which provided leadership—or at least prosperity—in the past have been discredited, through scandal, shame or simply lack of vision" (p. 3).

Given the immense importance of Confucianism throughout the region, and the manner in which many of its key ideals manifest themselves in the organizations, networks, and relationships that comprise the interconnected world of Asian business and government, it would seem apparent that these ideals have, at the very least, an explanatory function to play in certain elements of the present crisis. In this, the penultimate section of the chapter, I have suggested as such. Clearly, in making this point, I do not want to suggest that Confucianism is the one and only cause of the present crisis. Indeed, if the teachings of Confucianism, properly conceived, were genuinely heeded, it would seem that many of the problems the region currently faces could have been avoided. For example, while Confucius undoubtedly placed rule by virtue above rule by law, he also recognized that a "system of legal justice . . . is necessary to preserve social order . . . as long as there are people whose moral nature is too low to be regulated voluntarily by the teaching of virtue and *li*" (Hsu, 1932, p. 172).[21] And, as the weak and poorly enforced legal systems that exist throughout much of Asia have demonstrated, this piece of Confucian wisdom is as true today as it has ever been.

CONCLUDING REMARKS

In this chapter, I began by noting, along with Robert Davies (2002), that, in most parts of Asia, great importance is placed on bonds of family and friendship, and respect and courtesy is shown for "age, wisdom, leadership, neighbours and customs." These Asian values, I suggested, are perhaps more accurately described as Confucian values. Accordingly, and given the massive influence early Chinese culture has had throughout Asia, and East Asia most specifically, I provided a brief overview of certain Confucian ideals. Following this, I then noted that these ideals can, at the very least, be used to help describe the organizations, networks, actions, and relationships that comprise the world of Asian business and government. Lastly, I suggested that the Asian financial crisis, and the subsequent "dethroning of 'Asian Values'" (Richter & Mar, 2004a, p. 3), has resulted in a certain malaise settling over the region. In the main, this crisis emerged as a result of weak and poorly enforced legal systems, and certain powerful individuals operating within a severely attenuated moral framework. The net result is that outright stealing has come to characterize the actions of a few too many leading politicians and business people throughout the region.

Importantly, the Asian region is far from alone in suffering from such corruption, cronyism, and poor corporate governance. To pick just one of the better known examples, in December 2001, Enron, a company that "by some turnover measures . . . had been the seventh largest company in the United States," filed for bankruptcy (Gordon, 2004, p. 322). Enron's collapse was part of the "sudden explosion of corporate accounting scandals and related financial irregularities that burst over the financial markets between late 2001 and the first half of 2002" (Coffee, 2004, p. 333). This crisis, it has been suggested, was, much like the Asian crisis, the result of certain individuals operating within a severely attenuated moral framework. This particular crisis in the United States was, however, unlike the Asian crisis in that it was not facilitated by a weak and poorly enforced legal system but, rather, largely arose as a result of a change in executive compensation patterns, a change that was, rather perversely given this turn of events, meant to ensure that corporations were governed with the best interests of shareholders in mind.[22] Nevertheless, once one moves up a level of abstraction, this difference between the two crises disappears, for both crises were facilitated by the legal framework, or lack thereof, within

which certain individuals suffering from a severely attenuated moral framework were operating.

These two crises, I would suggest, are of immense interest to those interested in CSR in Asia, and those interested in CSR more generally, because both crises reveal two factors essential to the continued existence of the corporation as a socio-economic institution. The first factor is the need for a strong and enforceable legal framework that can ensure, as best as possible, that those people who both have a severely attenuated moral framework and manage to reach levels of senior management cannot organize a state of affairs that financially benefits themselves to the severe detriment of their shareholders. Second, it also reveals, I would suggest, a basic need for the majority of managers, and the majority of politicians, to have sufficient levels of moral development to recognize that such basic acts as stealing are wrong.

Without these two conditions being satisfied, the corporation ceases to be a viable instrument with which to organize patterns of production and consumption.[23] And if the corporation ceases to be a viable instrument with which to organize patterns of production and consumption, then there is no point in talking, writing, or simply thinking about "corporate social responsibility." Jaime Augusto Zobel de Ayala II (2004), president and CEO of the Ayala Corporation in the Philippines, is clearly aware of this fact:

> In the midst of the Asian economic miracle in the late '80s and early- to mid '90s, there was a rising trend in corporate Asia towards responsible corporate citizenship. Success made many Asian companies more ready and willing to take on a larger social role. But the Asian financial crisis of 1997 and Japan's deep slide into economic stagnation have stemmed this tide, as attention shifted in most companies toward sheer survival. As crony capitalism was unmasked as one of the culprits behind the crisis, the focus in recent years has been more on corporate-governance issues and how corporations are run than on issues of social responsibility. (p. 165)

While the distinction Zobel de Ayala II is making between corporate-governance issues and issues of social responsibility is slightly mistaken, the sentiment he is communicating is absolutely sound.

To conclude, then, let me note that corporations, much like capitalism more generally, always exist within a specific social, legal, cultural, and moral environment. Certain basic environmental conditions need to be maintained if corporations are to exist at all. If the positives that humanity derives from corporations are to be increased in the future, and the negatives associated with this institutional form correspondingly decreased, there will obviously need to be changes made to this environment. Given that "Asia may become the next long-term custodian of global civilization" (Marinoff, 2004, p. 37), it is of the utmost importance that Asians devote significant energies to these activities. Confucian thinking has a large and important role to play in this regard.

NOTES

In writing this chapter, I have benefited from discussions with David Birch.

1. In concentrating on those "Asian" values that correlate with Confucianism, I concentrate on East Asia at the expense of including India and Central Asia. East Asia includes, among other countries, Japan, South Korea, Taiwan, Hong Kong, Singapore, Thailand, Malaysia, Indonesia, the Philippines, and China. Robins (2002), for instance, includes all these countries in his analysis of industrial policy in East Asia because of their accelerated development.

2. Michael Backman (1999) has made this point by rhetorically asking "what could Singaporean-Chinese bond-trading yuppies—Budweisers in one hand and mobile phones in the other—possibly have in common with the Dani tribesman of Indonesia's Irian Jaya province whose traditional dress is little more than a well-placed gourd?" (p. 9). See also Birch, Schirato, and Srivastava (2001).

3. Backman (1999, p. 207) also provides some figures to back up his claim. These figures show that even though the ethnic Chinese are but a small minority in some East Asian countries, they still manage to control a large proportion of private domestic capital. In Indonesia and the Philippines, for instance, where the ethnic Chinese comprise only 3.5% and 2% of the respective populations, Backman reports that they manage to control 70% and 55% of the respective private domestic capital. The fundamental importance that the Chinese diaspora has played in Southeast Asian business has also been recognized by Dore (2002, p. 17).

4. This is commonly accepted as a central notion. Zhang (1999), for instance, makes the same point with almost exactly the same words when he writes that "Confucius held that the natural affection existing between relatives within one family is the cornerstone of social morality" (p. 32).

5. Tai is citing *The Book of Rites*, which was cited in Fu'ch'uan Chang (1958, p. 22). The translation made is his own.

6. Kant's categorical imperative is a classic instance of such impersonal and universal ethical thinking. The main works in which Kant deals with the idea are *Fundamental Principles of the Metaphysics of Morals*, *Critique of Practical Reason*, and *The Metaphysics of Morals*. Although it is commonly acknowledged that there are various formulations, in *Fundamental Principles* Kant (1785/1988) writes: "There is . . . but one categorical imperative, namely this: *Act on that maxim whereby thou canst at the same time will that it should become a universal law*" (p. 49, emphasis in original). Talcott Parsons (1937, pp. 550–551) thought this distinction a key one between Confucian ethics and Western ethics more generally (see Tai, 1989, pp. 10, 15).

7. See Lau (1979) for a discussion and distinction of the various Confucian virtues.

8. See chapter 1, book 9, of the *Analects*, for instance, where it is written: "The occasions on which the Master talked about profit, Destiny and benevolence were rare" (Confucius, 1979, p. 96).

9. See Robins (2002) for a general discussion of this tendency. More specifically, Robins (2002) defines "intervention" as being

any government action that influences prices. Such actions range from the imposition of bans, quotas and tariffs on trade, through domestic preference mechanisms in public procurement, local content requirements and offset agreements, to the provision of subsidized land and other financial inducements to lure desired foreign investment. It may also embrace such features as export processing zones and concessionary tax provisions. Where designed to achieve specific industry outcomes, rather than simply to raise or for some other nondevelopmental purpose, such actions are normally coordinated and constitute what is commonly referred to as "industry policy." (pp. 291–292).

10. Both Rozman (1991) and Tai (1989) have suggested that, despite the fact that families do not control business organizations to the same extent as they do in the rest of East Asia, much business activity in Japan can only really be understood in terms of the family metaphor. Indeed, Rozman (1991) has suggested that the "classical Chinese family (*chia*) and the modern Japanese enterprise (*kaisha*) popularly epitomize region-wide characteristics" (p. 31).

11. It is worth noting, once again, that in speaking of Asia I do not wish to understate the

many differences that can be found to exist among the diverse peoples of Asia. In specific regard to business in East Asia, for instance, one can turn to Whitley (1992, 1999) and Hamilton (1991) to find discussions of differences that exist among a variety of East Asian countries.

12.   See, for instance, Chen (2002, p. 39) and Backman (1999, pp. 12–13) regarding East Asia more generally. In specific regard to Japan, refer to Bebenroth and Tabuchi (2004, p. 29).

13.   Commonly, life time employment is associated with the Japanese. See, for instance, Patrick (2004, p. 7). Rozman (1991) has also suggested this to be characteristic of East Asian business more generally (p. 30).

14.   Importantly, a major reason for the emergence of both the Japanese *keiretsu* and the Korean *chaebol* was the prohibition the occupying authorities (i.e., Americans) placed on holding companies in both countries after the World War II. In specific regard to Japan, the reason for this prohibition was a result of the occupying forces thinking that the family-owned conglomerates that existed prior to World War II were an important part of the of the Japanese socioeconomic structure that went to war. See Black et al. (2001, p. 551) regarding Korea, and Yafeh (2000, p. 75) regarding Japan.

15.   See Hill (1999, p. 7) for a table that highlights the currency and stock market movements in the western Pacific from July 1, 1997, through September 15, 1998. To give the worst example, Indonesia's currency depreciated 78% over this period against the U.S. dollar, and its stock market dropped 91% in U.S. dollars over this period.

16.   After World War II, a number of East Asian economies enjoyed growth of a previously unforeseen scale and rapidity. Robins (2002) provides a brief overview of this growth.

17.   And, in specific regard to China's history, Zhang (1999) has noted that "not a few politicians have misused" the "flexibility implicit in Confucius' teaching for their own evil purposes" (p. 37).

18.   Japan, Singapore, Hong Kong, and, to a lesser extent, Taiwan and Malaysia generally rank better in Transparency International's *Global Corruption Report*. Indeed, in the Transparency International (2003) Corruption Perception Index, Singapore, Hong Kong, and Japan ranked 5th, 14th and 21st, respectively. For a catalogue of such rankings, see Transparency International's website at http://www.transparency.org.

19.   Johnson, Boone, Breach, and Friedman (2000) have strongly argued that those countries with the weakest levels of protection for minority shareholders experienced the greatest levels of currency depreciation and stock market decline during the Asian financial crisis. Furthermore, it is important to note that, in the financial corporate governance literature, those Asian countries with a common law legal system are normally thought to have stronger levels of protection for minority shareholders than those Asian countries with a civil law legal system. La Porta et al. (2003) give a fairly succinct description of why this is believed to be so.

20.   The Tokyo Electric Power Company was found to have falsified nuclear safety documents in power plants it operated (Richter & Mar, 2004a, fn. 2).

21.   Hsu (1932) has observed that, for Confucius, *li* had a number of:

> important functions. In the first place, *li* furnished a kind of unwritten law in political control. . . . Secondly, *li* is a socializing factor in moral discipline. . . . Thirdly, *li* is a harmonizing factor in arts and literature. . . . While *li* is the builder of personality and character, says Confucius, *yueh* or "music" completes the process; and so *li* and *yueh* go together. (pp. 90–91)

22.   Regarding this changing pattern, Coffee (2004) has noted:

> As of 1990, equity-based compensation for chief executive officers of public corporations in the United States constituted approximately five percent of their total annual compensation; by 1999, this percentage had risen to an estimated 60 percent. Moreover, between 1992 and 1998, the median compensation of Standard and Poor's 500 chief executives increased by approximately 150 percent, with option based compensation accounting for most of this increase. (p. 335)

Basically, this, among other factors (see Coffee, 2004, more generally) acted as a perverse mechanism in that it encouraged chief executives to inflate their share price (in whatever way), because they would significantly benefit from being able to sell shares at an inflated price.

23.   Rather obviously, this is because if shareholders don't think managers will refrain from appropriating monies, or if they don't think the legal structure can satisfactorily protect them from such appropriations (e.g., through acts of corruption), then they will not provide the capital required to establish a corporation in the first place.

REFERENCES

Backman, M. (1999). *Asian eclipse: Exposing the dark side of business in Asia*. Singapore: John Wiley & Sons.

Backman, M. (2004). *The Asian insider: Unconventional wisdom for Asian business*. Basingstoke, UK: Palgrave Macmillan.

Bebenroth, R., & Tabuchi, S. (2004). Corporate governance in Japan: Government regulations. *Osaka Keidai Ronshu, 54*(5), 429–438.

Birch, D. (Ed.). (1998). Asian values; public cultures [Special double edition]. *Social Semiotics, 8*(2).

Birch, D., & Moon, J. (Eds.). (2004). Corporate social responsibility in Asia [Special issue]. *The Journal of Corporate Citizenship, 13*(Spring).

Birch, D., Schirato, T., & Srivastava, S. (2001). *Asia: Cultural politics in the global age.* Sydney: Allen & Unwin.

Black, B., Metzger, B., O'Brien, T. J., & Shin, Y. M. (2001). Corporate governance in Korea at the millennium: Enhancing international competitiveness [Final report and legal reform recommendations to the Ministry of Justice of the Republic of Korea 15 May, 2005 (With an introduction to the report by Bernard Black)]. *The Journal of Corporation Law, 26*(3), 537–608.

Chang, F. (1958). *Tzu-yu ye Jen-ch'uan [Freedom and Human Rights].* Hong Kong: Asia Press.

Chen, M. 2002. Post-crisis trends in Asian management. *Asian Business & Management, 1*(1), 39–58.

Coffee, J. C., Jr. (2004). What caused Enron? A capsule social and economic history of the 1990s. In T. Clarke (Ed.), *Theories of corporate governance* (pp. 333–358). London: Routledge.

Confucius. (1979). *The analects* (D. C. Lau, Trans.). London: Penguin Books.

Davies, R. (2002, June 10). *Corporate citizenship and socially responsible investment: Emerging challenges and opportunities in Asia.* Paper presented at the Association for Sustainable and Responsible Investment in Asia conference, Hong Kong. Retrieved January 10, 2005, from http:// www .corporatecitizenshipasia.net/csr/ crwebassist .nsf/content/fId2b3ar4.html.

Dore, R. (1998). Asian crisis and the future of the Japanese model. *Cambridge Journal of Economics, 22*(6), 773–787.

Dore, R. (2000). *Stock market capitalism: Welfare capitalisms—Japan and Germany versus the Anglo-Saxons.* Oxford: Oxford University Press.

Economic Analytic Unit. (2002). *Changing corporate Asia: What business needs to know: Vol. 1. Main report.* Canberra, Australia: Department of Foreign Affairs and Trade.

Gordon, J. N. (2004). What Enron means for the management and control of the modern business corporation: Some initial reflec-

tions. In T. Clarke (Ed.), *Theories of corporate governance* (pp. 322–332). London: Routledge.

Hamilton, G. (Ed.). (1991). *Business networks and economic development in East and Southeast Asia* (Monograph No. 99). Hong Kong: Centre for Asian studies, University of Hong Kong.

Hill, H. (1999). An overview of the issues. In H. W. Arndt & F. H. Hill (Eds.), *Southeast Asia's economic crisis: Origins, lessons, and the way forward* (pp. 1–15). Singapore: Institute of Southeast Asian Studies.

Hsu, L. S. (1932). *The political philosophy of Confucianism: An interpretation of the social and political ideas of Confucius, his forerunners, and his early disciples.* London: George Routledge & Sons.

Johnson, S., Boone, P., Breach, A., & Friedman, E. (2000). Corporate governance in the Asian financial crisis. *Journal of Financial Economics, 58,* 141–186.

Kant, I. (1988). *Fundamental principles of the metaphysics of morals* (T. K. Abbott, Trans.). New York: Prometheus Books. (Originally published 1785)

La Porta, R., Lopez-de-Silanes, F., Shleifer, A., & Vishny, R. (2003). Investor protection and corporate governance. *Journal of Financial Economics, 58,* 3–27.

Lau, D. C. (1970). Introduction. In Mencius, *Mencius* (D. C. Lau, Trans.; pp. 7–46). London: Penguin Books.

Lau, D. C. (1979). Introduction. In Confucius, *The analects* (D. C. Lau, Trans.; pp. 9–55). London: Penguin Books.

Marinoff, L. (2004). What is business ethics? What are its prospects in Asia? In F.-J. Richter & P. C. M. Mar (Eds.), *Asia's new crisis: Renewal through total ethical management* (pp. 16–40). Singapore: John Wiley & Sons.

Mencius. (1970). *Mencius* (D. C. Lau, Trans.). London: Penguin Books.

Parsons, T. (1937). *The structure of social action.* New York: Free Press.

Patrick, H. (2004). *Evolving corporate governance in Japan* (Working Paper No. 22). Chicago: Centre on Japanese Economy and Business, Columbia University Business School.

Richter, F.-J., & Mar, P. C. M. (2004a). Why Ethics? In F.-J. Richter & P. C. M. Mar (Eds.), *Asia's new crisis: Renewal through total ethical management* (pp. 3–15). Singapore: John Wiley & Sons.

Richter, F.-J., & Mar, P. C. M. (Eds.). (2004b). *Asia's new crisis: Renewal through total ethical management.* Singapore: John Wiley & Sons.

Robins, F. (2002). Industry policy in Asia. *Asian Business & Management, 1*(1), 291–312.

Rozman, G. (1991). Introduction: The East Asian region in comparative perspective. In G. Rozman (Ed.), *The East Asian region: Confucian heritage and its modern adaptation* (pp. 3–42). Princeton, NJ: Princeton University Press.

Schwab, K. (2004). Foreword. In F.-J. Richter & P. C. M. Mar (Eds.), *Asia's new crisis: Renewal through total ethical management* (pp. vii–viii). Singapore: John Wiley & Sons.

Shinsho, K. (2004). Management: New Japanese business culture. In F.-J. Richter & P. C. M. Mar (Eds.), *Asia's new crisis: Renewal through total ethical management* (pp. 174–180). Singapore: John Wiley & Sons.

Tai, H.-C. (1989). The Oriental alternative: An hypothesis on culture and economy. In H.-C. Tai (Ed.), *Confucianism and economic development: An Oriental alternative?* (pp. 6–37). Washington, DC: Washington Institute Press.

Transparency International. (2003). *Global corruption report*. London: Pluto Press and Transparency International. Retrieved December 19, 2004, from. http://www.transparency.org/publications/gcr/download_gcr/download_gcr_2003

Transparency International. (2004). *Global corruption report*. London: Pluto Press and Transparency International. Retrieved December 19, 2004, from http://www.transparency.org/publications/gcr/download_gcr/download_gcr_2004.

Whitley, R. (1992). *Business systems in East Asia: Firms, markets and societies*. London: Sage.

Whitley, R. (1999). *Divergent capitalisms: The social structuring and change of business systems*. Oxford: Oxford University Press.

Yafeh, Y. (2000). Corporate governance in Japan: Past performance and future prospects. *Oxford Review of Economic Policy, 16*(2), 74–84.

Zhang, W.-B. (1999). *Confucianism and modernization: Industrialization and democratization of the Confucian regions*. London: Macmillan Press.

Zobel de Ayala II, J. A. (2004). Leadership—business in society: Leading by example. In F.-J. Richter, & P. C. M. Mar (Eds.), *Asia's new crisis: Renewal through ethical management* (pp. 160–173). Singapore: John Wiley & Sons.

8

Corporate Social Responsibility and Public Relations

Perceptions and Practices in Singapore

KRISHNAMURTHY SRIRAMESH

CHEW WEE NG

SOH TING TING

LUO WANYIN

Long recognized as one of the "Asian Tigers," Singapore (whose name means Lion City and thus the city's Merlion mascot) is one of the leading economic centers in Asia. After becoming a Republic in 1965, the island-state developed rapidly within two generations and currently has the third highest per capita gross domestic product (after Japan and Hong Kong) in Asia. Without resting on its laurels, this country with no natural resources is trying to stay economically competitive through various strategies including attracting greater foreign investment. It is in this context that corporate social responsibility (CSR) is relevant to Singapore. The government, for example, prides itself as being both a promoter and practitioner of CSR (Balakrishnan, 2004). Corporations, too, are allocating more resources to CSR practices (Khanna, 2004a). Tor (2004) remarked that Singaporeans cannot get through the first decade of this millennium without knowing about CSR. The British High Commissioner to Singapore remarked that "the stage is now set for a CSR revolution in Singapore" (Collins, 2004). All these factors served as the rationale for us to conduct the wide-ranging analysis of the status of CSR in Singapore that is the focus of this chapter.

Located just 137 kilometers north of the equator, Singapore is a very cosmopolitan and multiethnic society of 4.24 million (Singapore Department of Statistics, 2004) people living in one main island and about 50 islets covering about 685 km². More than three-quarters of the population are of Chinese ethnicity, while 14% are Malay and 8% Indian. The city-state is also temporary home to almost 800,000 foreign nationals who are not Singaporean citizens or permanent residents. English is the lingua franca in business and educational settings, while Chinese, Malay, and Tamil are the other three official languages.

The Peoples Action Party (PAP) is the only party that has held power since Singapore became a republic in 1965, leading what was a struggling developing country at birth to a robust economy in a matter of two generations. The republic has attracted foreign investment, particularly in high technology, banking, petroleum, and shipping sectors, by developing a robust infrastructure and low corruption in governance. Singapore is currently the 12th largest trading partner of the United States, with whom it began a free trade relationship in January 2005.

However, Singapore is constantly trying to retool itself to remain competitive. The government set up two initiatives—*Remaking Singapore* and *Singapore 21*—in order to meet the challenges of the twenty-first century (Sriramesh & Rivera, 2006). Although it is a parliamentary democracy where it is mandatory for citizens to vote, observers have also criticized it for low levels of political pluralism (e.g., Chua, 1995; Ho, 2000; Yuen, 1999). This is borne out by the fact that the ruling PAP has 82 of 84 parliamentary seats. So, its rapid economic development has also been accompanied by higher levels of social control by the government. As we discuss further below, this plays a role in who drives the development of CSR activities in Singapore in the future. With this brief introduction to Singapore, we focus on the state of CSR in the city-state by first offering a brief review of literature and then presenting the findings of our wide-ranging study.

CSR IN ASIA AND SINGAPORE

The awareness about, and adoption of, CSR practices has so far been generally low in Asia compared to the developed countries of the West. Globalization appears to be the single largest factor that has propelled the CSR movement in Asia (Chambers, Chapple, Moon, & Sullivan, 2003). Rapid globalization also requires that corporations based in Asia keep pace with global standards. As a result, companies that venture into international markets have felt the pressure to improve their CSR standards to measure up to the expectations of their global stakeholders to remain competitive (Khanna, 2004b). The way CSR is perceived and practiced is shaped by culture, religion, political, and socioeconomic conditions. Thus, there are likely to be significant differences in the way CSR is conducted across different countries and regions (Bronn & Vrioni, 2001). We argue later in this chapter that, because of Singapore's unique sociopolitical environment, the drivers of CSR in Singapore may be quite different from other regions of the world.

Singapore has seen an increase in attention to CSR especially after the nonprofit Centre for CSR was established in 2003. However, according to Hung and Ramasamy (2004), overall awareness of the concept is still low among the mass media, academia, government agencies, and corporations in Singapore. Many early studies of CSR in Singapore (e.g., Andrew, Gul, Guthrie, & Teoh, 1989; Foo & Tan, 1988; Tsang, 1998) used the disclosure method, which analyzed corporations' self-reported CSR performances via corporate annual reports or websites. Because CSR can be difficult to quantify, such reports provide a means of determining the quality of corporations' commitment to CSR (Macleod, 2001). A study of Singapore's banking, food, and beverage industries during 1986–1993 (Tsang, 1998) showed that 16 of 33 corporations had no references to social responsibility or community involvement. In the remaining 17, CSR reporting was focused largely on employee matters. Although Tsang's study aimed to stimulate similar studies with the hope of making longitudinal comparisons, we could not find a more recent study to determine whether the situation has changed in the last seven years.

The disclosure method, despite its popularity, has several drawbacks as a measure of CSR practices. For example, corporate social reporting may lag behind actual involvement and might not be an accurate reflection of corporate behavior (Hung & Ramasamy, 2004; Keeler, 2002). This method also may ignore the behavior of smaller corporations that tend to have lower disclosure rates (Andrew et al., 1989). There is also a concern that the information provided by corporations in their annual reports and websites could be driven by publicity motives (Tsang, 1998). After all, social desirability is often a key factor to be considered when one attempts to make extrapolations based on self-reported data.

Recent studies appear to move away from the disclosure method, preferring the stakeholder perspective instead. A study of nine Asia-Pacific countries including Singapore (Edelman, 2004) interviewed different stakeholders such as consumers and corporate executives and found that stakeholders in Asia-Pacific are increasingly (a rise from 29% in 2003 to 36% in 2004) concerned with the needs of the community beyond their own needs. About 65% of the stakeholders interviewed for the study felt that corporations need to be socially responsible, compared with 35% in 2003—almost doubling in just one year. Interviewees ranked community welfare as having the lowest priority and saw offering top-quality products and services as the most important factor. While the study by Edelman provided good insights on stakeholders' perspectives, the findings were not specific to Singapore and did not account for significant differences in economic development and culture across the countries studied. Hung and Ramasamy (2004) also conducted a comparative study of CSR awareness but limited their analysis to only one stakeholder—employees. However, this is consistent with Clarkson's (1995) finding that "stakeholder satisfaction" should be used as a measure when evaluating CSR.

Besides the growing attention from scholars and the media, Singapore has hosted an increasing number of CSR conferences. In 2004, three significant conferences on CSR were held in the city-state involving organizations such as the British High Commission, Centre for CSR, and United Nations Global Compact (2004). The conferences were attended by executives of multinational and domestic corporations, small and medium enterprises (SMEs), and private and public sector organizations. This is indicative of the increasing interest in CSR across a wide spectrum of corporations in Singapore.

At the conference organized by the British High Commission (2004), Nottingham University surveyed the delegates in attendance. More than half said that there was a person in their organization with responsibility over CSR, and more than 80% said that they were required to consider CSR implications when doing their job. We feel these results appear to be highly optimistic possibly because the sample was skewed. We observe that those choosing to attend such conferences can be assumed to have heightened interest and a favorable disposition toward the topic.

The Nottingham University survey also found that in Singapore, customers, shareholders, and employees were recognized as the most important stakeholders while suppliers, competitors, and nongovernmental organizations (NGOs) were the least important. This finding corresponds with the stakeholder approach where corporations are more concerned with primary stakeholders. An inconsistency here would be the perceived lack of primacy of suppliers and business partners among the respondents, although these stakeholders have direct transactions with the corporation. The researchers noted that the respondents may not pay enough attention to the ability of these groups to do harm to the corporation's reputation—a trap Nike fell into when it believed it could keep the sweatshop practices of suppliers and partners away from its doorstep.

For the purposes of this study, we adopted Bowd, Harris, and Cornelissen's (2003) definition of CSR, which was derived from the views of scholars such as Carroll (1999), Wood (1991), Freeman (1984), and Friedman (1970). In addition, Bowd et al. (2003) incorporated recent industry reports such as Commission of the European Communities (2001, 2002) and the *Financial Times* Top 100 Index to present their definition: "CSR is corporations being held accountable by explicit or inferred social contract with internal and external stakeholders, obeying the laws and regulations of government and operating in an ethical manner which exceeds statutory requirements" (p. 19).

Addressing the vagueness of the term "ethical manner," Bowd et al. (2003) offered examples of ethical behavior such as proactive community involvement, philanthropy, corporate governance, and commitment to the environment. This definition also entails a commitment to accountability, where the organization is obliged to measure and audit its CSR strategy, aims, principles, and manifestations, while simultaneously continuing its focus on generating profits for investors. We adopted Bowd et al.'s definition because we believe it is comprehensive and embraces the dominant academic and industry views on CSR. We next conducted a review of literature—a body that we see more as a collection of approaches rather than a coherent theoretical body of knowledge. The lack of a unified body of knowledge is also indicative of the relative novelty of this field. We offer a brief review of the dominant literature in this domain by dividing them into three categories: the business and society approach, economic approach, and stakeholder approach. We then identify the research questions for this study before describing the methodology and the findings.

Business and Society Approach

The view that corporations have an obligation to society developed at a time when corporations were enjoying unprecedented levels of power—especially over citizens—while exercising little social responsibility (Carroll, 1999; Wood, 1991). Carroll's (1979) model of CSR, which came into prominence during the 1970s, framed business responsibilities into four components: economic, legal, ethical, and discretionary. When the author reformulated the model in 1991, he depicted it in the form of a pyramid, with economic performance being the most basic function (depicted at the bottom of the pyramid) and moving up to legal, ethical, and philanthropic (which replaced discretionary) components.

Carroll's (1991) CSR pyramid stated that a socially responsible corporation should simultaneously "strive to make a profit, obey the law, be ethical, and be a good corporate citizen" (p. 43). He specifically distinguished between philanthropic and ethical responsibilities noting that many corporations assume that they are being socially responsible by being good corporate citizens in the community. Interestingly, several scholars and economists have in fact rejected philanthropy as a legitimate corporate action (Friedman, 1970; Lantos, 2001). Carroll himself stated that philanthropy, while highly desirable, is actually less important than the first three components of CSR. It should be noted that even though the four components have been discussed as separate constructs, they are not mutually exclusive.

Building on Carroll's work, Lantos (2001) classified CSR into three forms: ethical, altruistic, and strategic. Lantos saw ethical CSR as the minimal, mandatory fulfillment of a corporation's economic, legal, and ethical responsibilities to its publics. The author argued that strategic CSR, where corporations participate only in those philanthropic actions that will financially benefit them by attracting positive publicity and goodwill, should be practiced over altruistic CSR, which he felt constitutes making philanthropic contributions at the possible expense of stockholders. He contended that altruistic CSR is not legitimate. Despite their different orientations, these scholars have put forth a common notion that corporations do not operate in isolation from the society where they exist. This symbiotic relationship was summarized by Wood (1991): "Business and society are interwoven rather than distinct entities" (p. 695).

Economic Approach

Contrary to the proponents of the business and society approach, classical economists separated social functions from economic functions, asserting that businesses have the basic responsibility of maximizing profits for their owners or shareholders. Noted economist Adam Smith (1863, as cited in Lantos, 2001), was perhaps the first to espouse the market value maximization perspective, arguing that by pursuing profits, corporations produce the greatest social good because the invisible hand of the capitalist market ultimately helps solve society's problems. Lantos (2001) used the term "economic CSR" to refer to profit-oriented CSR activities, which absolves corporations from social contribution because they pay taxes and wages to employees rather than enslaving them (Marcoux, 2000). Some economists have gone as far as to argue that the only social responsibility corporations have is to obey the laws of the land (Carr, 1996).

Like Carr, Nobel laureate economist Milton Friedman offered the dominant and well-known view representing the economic approach separating social functions from business functions, asserting that the "business of business is business" (Klonoski, 2001). However, Friedman (1970) did recognize a spectrum of moral and ethical responsibilities, positing that the social responsibility of corporations is to "make as much money as possible while conforming to the basic rules of the society, both those embodied in law and those embodied in ethical custom" (pp. 32–33).

Stakeholder Approach

The economic approach overlooked the fact that in the effort to maximize profits, corporations do affect multiple stakeholders. The stakeholder approach to CSR viewed the corporation as "a set of interrelated, explicit or implicit connections between individuals and or groups of individuals" (Rowley, 1997) that include anybody who "can affect or is affected by the achievement of the organization's objectives" (Freeman, 1984). This approach distinguishes between primary stakeholders (e.g., employees, customers, and suppliers) and secondary stakeholders (e.g., the media and NGOs) according to their relative impact on the corporation (Clarkson, 1995). It advocates that corporations are responsible for addressing the interests of the various stakeholders—not just those of the owners and shareholders—because these other stakeholders make important nonmonetary investments in corporations, albeit at varying levels depending on the corporation's objectives (Boehm, 2002; Freeman, 1984; Key & Popkin, 1998).

Our review of the relevant literature on CSR led us to conclude that the existing research pertaining to CSR in Singapore consists either of studies that measure social reporting (e.g., Andrew et al., 1989; Foo & Tan, 1988; Tsang, 1998) or comparative studies between CSR in Singapore and other nations (e.g., Edelman, 2004; Hung & Ramasamy, 2004; Welford, 2003). The current body of knowledge fails to provide information on the current status of CSR in Singapore.

We therefore designed this study to assess the current status of CSR among a sample of corporations in Singapore using several research questions to guide our study. The research questions sought to address such things as the current perceptions about CSR, the activities Singaporean corporations conduct in the name of CSR, the motivation behind these CSR practices, the various stakeholders these corporations consider important vis-à-vis CSR, and the decision-making processes behind CSR practices of these corporations, as well as the way corporations communicate CSR-related messages to stakeholders. We also sought to assess how these corporations evaluate their CSR practices and what benefits they have achieved from their CSR initiatives. We used stakeholder analysis rather than the disclosure method because of the deficiencies of self-disclosure that we cited above. To gain a comprehensive understanding of CSR in Singapore, we gathered data from corporations that practice CSR as well as those that reported that they did not engage in CSR activities.

We gathered data from a variety of organizations such as SMEs, large corporations, public and private enterprises, and local, regional, and multinational corporations (MNCs). Although we chose Bowd et al.'s (2003) definition to guide the study, we recognized that CSR may not be perceived similarly by all executives. Therefore, we were cautious in framing our questions so as not to influence the insights of executives who might have had their own definitions and interpretations of CSR. Many corporations (e.g., Microsoft and ExxonMobil) employ the term "corporate citizenship" and often use it synonymously with CSR, especially in the United States and Europe (Munshi, 2004). Indeed, the concept of corporate citizenship overlaps largely with the concept of CSR. Business executives interviewed in a U.S. study (Center for Corporate Citizenship at Boston College, 2004) defined a good corporate citizen as a corporation that makes profit, pays taxes, provides jobs, operates ethically, treats its employees well, produces reliable products, has a good environmental record, and works to improve conditions in the society. The parameters of corporate citizenship identified by the respondents are similar to what CSR encompasses. Because Singapore is home to many American and European MNCs, we decided to use the terms interchangeably during data collection, although we recognize that the two concepts have slightly differing connotations in the literature.

We used a self-administered web-based questionnaire and personal interviews for gathering our data. We invited 288 corporations to participate in the study, 74 of whom sent usable responses (response rate of 26%). The sample consisted of an almost equal number of large corporations (> 200 employees) and SMEs; 39% were domestic and 60% multinational. These corporations represented various industries, although the majority were from the service (20%), information technology (18%), and banking and finance (16%) sectors, in keeping with the economic landscape of Singapore.

Because we also wanted to know the perceptions of individual corporate executives toward CSR that was not necessarily tied to their own organization's philosophy and organization-level practices, we used snowball sampling to elicit responses from 513 additional corporate executives, gathering data over two months. The male-to-female ratio of our sample was balanced (51–49%), with the majority of corporate executives (67%) between 21 and 30 years of age. These executives represented various industries such as service (23%), banking and finance (18%), and information technology (14%). Fifty-three percent of the executives were from large corporations, and 47% were from SMEs, a healthy mix in size of corporations. The majority of executives (60%) worked for regional (Association of Southeast Asian Nations [ASEAN]) or multinational corporations. We reminded participants—through an introductory phone call and cover letter—that we expected them to give their responses even if they had not heard of CSR or their corporations did not, in their view, practice CSR.

After tabulating the survey data, we conducted in-depth face-to-face interviews with 19 corporate executives to seek further insights on their CSR practices. We also interviewed managers of NGOs, community representatives, trade associations, and the mass media. We found the use of these "elite interviews" useful because these senior managers were able to elaborate on the status of CSR in Singapore because of their experience.

FINDINGS

A majority of the corporate executives surveyed displayed a broad understanding of the concept of CSR and were able to recognize that CSR consists of a range of responsibilities covering legal, ethical, and philanthropic aspects as proposed by Carroll (1991). The survey respondents recognized the different parameters (e.g., anticorruption, health and safety, business ethics) listed in the questionnaire as factors that would make a corporation socially responsible. Likewise, interviewees were able to describe CSR comprehensively and viewed CSR as essential to a corporation's sustainability. The discussion of profitability as a parameter of CSR was more controversial, and the respondents were divided on whether generating profits was considered CSR. Many of them, however, felt that a corporation needs to be profitable first before it can consider CSR as important to its corporate agenda.

We believe the high awareness level of CSR (69% of survey respondents) might be attributed to the recent increase in media coverage as well as the launch of several initiatives to promote CSR in Singapore, all of which occurred when we were conducting this study. The sample of corporate executives perceived all the parameters we listed to be significant and the parameters to be relevant in Singapore. In particular, a majority of respondents listed not being corrupt, observing business ethics, observing health and safety issues in the workplace, care for the environment, and observing responsible labor practices as the most significant CSR values. It must be noted here that, as mentioned above, the ruling PAP that has held power since Singapore's birth as a republic has stressed the need to root out corruption in government activities. Likewise, common themes of CSR that emerged during the interviews revolved around observing ethical practices, employee welfare, care for the environment, and "giving back to the society."

Although *profitability* scored the lowest mean among all the parameters, it was still perceived by the sample of corporate executives to be a significant aspect of CSR. The interviewees expressed mixed sentiments toward profitability. A few interviewees did not think that being profitable should be a part of a corporation's social responsibility. One interviewee commented that "being profitable is the basic requirement of any company that exists in the economy." On the other hand, several interviewees felt that profitability is an essential part of CSR. One interviewee from a publicly listed corporation felt that his corporation has to be profitable "to run the company efficiently . . . improve the system . . . be responsible to his [sic] shareholders . . . staff . . . contribute to the community."

The survey data revealed that making charitable contributions and community involvement were the least significant parameters after prof-

itability for our respondents. A number of corporate executives (41%) disagreed that CSR is about making charitable contributions, while 29% took a neutral stand. Similar sentiments were echoed in some interviews, as indicated by one interviewee who said, "[T]here are notions of volunteerism and corporate philanthropy involved, but these are just elements of it [CSR]. The meat of CSR is to mainstream it into the regular business operations."

Interviewees had diverse interpretations of CSR, one stating that the term was a "concept akin to an amoeba." Many interviewees said that the parameters of CSR are relevant to different corporations in varying degrees depending on the nature of the industry and the stakeholders that corporations perceived to be important. A majority of the corporate executives surveyed (83%) disagreed that corporations need not be concerned with society. This suggested that they perceived corporations to have some obligations toward society and viewed business and society as "inter-woven rather than separate entities" (Wood, 1991, p. 695).

More than half (52%) the corporate executives felt that CSR should be recognized as a core business function, while almost three-quarters (74%) agreed that social responsibility should be a consideration when formulating corporate strategies. Further, a majority (63%) perceived CSR to have a positive impact on the financial performance of corporations. These findings suggested that the corporate executives in our sample acknowledged that CSR should be an integral part of business. Yet, nearly half (49%) agreed that CSR is largely a publicity issue. This suggests a discrepancy between how the corporate executives in this sample felt CSR *should be practiced* (normative), as opposed to how they perceived CSR *is practiced* (positive).

With regard to the appropriateness of using CSR to gain publicity, some of our interviewees felt corporations should not leverage CSR activities for publicity purposes, while others felt that the benefits derived from these activities are more important than the intended motives. As for the need to regulate CSR, 46% of the respondents agreed that CSR should be completely voluntary and not governed by any law or regulation. A few interviewees felt that CSR should "come from the heart" and not merely intended to comply with government regulations or legislations. An executive from an MNC felt that CSR is not about what the government sees as right or wrong, saying, "It's not what the government should do but what companies should do. . . . It is not about just operating within the rules." A majority of interviewees perceived profitability as a precondition before their corporations could commit resources to CSR. However, a few interviewees felt that CSR does not necessarily have to come after profitability.

Of the 74 corporations surveyed, 72 reported that they engaged in CSR-related activities, as defined by their own notions of CSR. The most commonly performed activities reported by these corporations were charitable donations (76%), employee welfare and training programs (74%), and community projects (69%). These findings were confirmed by many interviewees who discussed philanthropic activities as CSR efforts before any prompting by the interviewer. Some interviewees felt that CSR is simply a new way to label some of the philanthropic functions that have been traditionally practiced by corporations. Interestingly, some interviewees disagreed that philanthropy should be a major aspect of CSR, even though they acknowledged it as a commonly practiced activity in Singapore. Our interviews also revealed that the type of CSR activities conducted was closely linked with the nature of the corporation. Size and industry of the corporations, too, were considered to be important determinants of the type of CSR activities practiced. One SME interviewee expressed concern over the applicability of the various CSR parameters to smaller corporations that are generally less concerned with community relations and global outreach. Some interviewees also reported that business-to-business corporations have fewer incentives to practice CSR because their clients are unlikely to appreciate their investment in CSR efforts.

The survey findings indicated that the listed motivators to practice CSR were considered important among respondents with the top three motivators being enhance reputation, long-term sustainability, and enhance community trust and support. The only exception was to avoid regulation, indicating that respondents in our sample did not want to practice CSR in order to avoid government regulation. Respondents were divided on whether government regulation should be considered as a CSR motivator. Almost half of them (49%) indicated a neutral stand toward government intervention. It is important to note that the other half of the sample corporations did not consider government regulation as a motivational factor. Interestingly, some of our interviewees believed that the government of Singapore should be instrumental in driving the CSR movement. Their reasons ranged from the government's powerful financial, media, and human resources to the large number of government-linked companies (GLCs, or public sector enterprises) and a vast amount of regulatory power. We return to the power of the government when we discuss these data and offer recommendations further below.

The results suggested that our sample of corporations considered CSR to be vital for a corporation's survival. In addition, the focus on enhancing reputation and community support indicated that the corporations in the sample were receptive to the business and society approach of the literature reviewed above. Interestingly, our interviewees were more inclined to value external and punitive motivators such as "consumer pressure," "government guidelines," and "crisis prevention." Interviewees also generally agreed that corporations should not be considered as being separate from the community, regardless of whether a corporation is local, regional (ASEAN), or multinational. Economic motivators align a corporation's CSR efforts with potential monetary returns. Our respondents listed attracting investors, promoting transactions/partnerships, and increasing profits as economic motivators. The data suggested that most corporations in the sample did not practice CSR for bottom-line reasons. Although most corporations considered all the motivators listed as essential, motivators aligned with corporate agenda ranked among the lowest in importance. Interestingly, some interviewees who were skeptical about certain local corporations' CSR efforts questioned the above survey findings.

We were also interested in knowing who made CSR-related decisions in the sample organizations —the drivers of CSR within a corporation. Our data revealed that the CEO (74%), head of human resources (45%), directors (39%), and the head of corporate communications (38%) most often made CSR-related decisions. Nearly half (45%) of the sample of corporations reported that three or more departments made CSR-related decisions, suggesting an integrated CSR decision-making process. Our data suggested that CSR initiatives are top-down driven in Singapore, with MNCs receiving directives mainly from their regional or global headquarters and the CEOs making decisions for SMEs.

We also sought to understand which stakeholders were perceived as important by corporations in the sample and how corporations in the sample communicated their CSR-related messages to their stakeholders. Corporations in the sample identified the primary stakeholders[1] listed by us as being the most important. The top two stakeholders were customers and employees. This perception of the high importance of employees was consistent with our earlier finding that employee welfare programs constituted a major portion of the CSR activities in the sample corporations. These findings were mirrored by our interviewees, who saw employees and customers as significant stakeholder groups with the power to impact CSR. Some interviewees cited examples in the United States, where consumer advocacy groups pressured corporations to be more CSR conscious by boycotting products.

Within the primary stakeholder group, suppliers were considered by the sample of corporations to be the least important. Some interviewees stressed that there is a growing need for corporations to pay attention to their suppliers' practices. One interviewee believed that the onus is on individual corporations to monitor and investigate the ethical behavior of their suppliers. Interestingly, the least important stakeholders appeared to be NGOs. The representative of one NGO interviewed by us was not surprised with this finding. He explained that NGOs in Singapore play a "facilitator" role rather than that of "community activist." He elaborated that this is due partly to the limited power of NGOs and the relatively low level of activism in most Asian societies, including Singapore, due to cultural and political factors. We refer to these findings further below when we discuss CSR drivers in Singapore.

A majority (89%) of the corporations communicated with their stakeholders about their CSR practices. The stakeholders with whom organizations communicated most frequently were customers and employees, which is not surprising given that these correspond with the stakeholders who were perceived by the sample of corporations to be the most important. The main communication tools employed were company leaflets and posters, websites, and annual reports.

Interestingly, the sample of corporations did not seem to communicate as frequently with the mass media about CSR practices as one would have imagined. Only 37% of the sample corporations reported that they issued press releases, and 32% communicated to the mass media about their CSR activities. It is reasonable to presume that the mass media are not a common tool used by the sample of corporations to disseminate information about CSR and that they are concerned about being perceived as using CSR for publicity purposes.

Almost a quarter of the corporations in the sample (23%) had a department dedicated to CSR activities. About 10% indicated that CSR activities were handled mostly by ad hoc project groups. Annually, about 42% of the corporations allocated a budget specifically for CSR activities. Many interviewees reported that the allocated budget tends to fluctuate according to situational factors such as profit margins and scale of activities. As far as the breakdown of the manpower distribution for CSR activities is concerned, almost half of the sample corporations (49%) had designated staff to plan CSR activities, of which about 40% allocated more than eight members. However, a significant proportion of respondents (30%) were unable to cite specific numbers, suggesting the low level of tracking of manpower allocation. Some interviewees explained that the number of planners varied among projects because of the voluntary nature of the ad hoc committees. Further, CSR planning in some of the corporations spans across several departments, making it difficult to determine the exact number of staff designated for CSR activities.

Evaluation should be a key ingredient of every corporate activity including CSR practices. A majority of the corporations (61%) surveyed indicated that they did not evaluate their CSR practices at all. Likewise, many of the corporate executives interviewed also reported that they did not conduct any evaluation related to CSR. Interviewees attributed this to the novelty of CSR. Further, many of the interviewees stated that their corporations did not specify goals or targets for their CSR initiatives. The standards and methods for evaluation differed widely among survey respondents. This was confirmed in interviews where evaluation techniques ranged from casual and informal methods such as tracking media coverage or simply talking to customers for feedback to more formal methods such as focus groups and surveys. Nevertheless, many interviewees viewed evaluation as an essential step that should be adopted. Problems associated with evaluation, according to interviewees, include the lack of appropriate evaluation instruments, the intangible nature of the results of CSR practices, and the perceived lack of importance given to CSR reporting.

Survey data indicated that verbal feedback was the most common method used by the few organizations that did any CSR evaluation at all. Of the 29 corporations that reported doing CSR evaluation, only five used profit figures to measure the success of their CSR efforts. This result appeared to contradict our earlier finding that profitability is a perceived benefit of CSR. This deviation between the two findings might be due to the difficulty in measuring the relationship between CSR and profitability. While the sample of corporate executives might believe that CSR has a positive impact on financial performance, it might be difficult for corporations to actually measure the impact and link the two variables conclusively. Other evaluation methods used were the number of corporate volunteers, feedback from beneficiaries, and the number of days of leave claimed to serve as volunteers were also used. A quarter of the corporations surveyed were not sure of how data for evaluation were collected. Half of the corporations reported their CSR initiatives either in their annual reports or on their websites.

We also tried to find out what benefits the corporations in the sample had achieved in their CSR initiatives. The most frequently cited benefits were improved customer loyalty (57%), improved organizational culture (53%), and attracting and retaining employees (35%). The top benefits cited by the corporations in our sample were related to customers and employees, who were also the most important stakeholders identified. The interviewees also cited similar benefits. In addition, they reported that their corporations enjoyed a more cohesive workforce, enhanced image, and reduced business costs as a result of CSR practices. It was paradoxical that improved image and reputation (11%) was the least frequently cited benefit of CSR, considering an earlier finding that enhancing reputation was the most significant motivation for corporations to engage in CSR activities. The sample of corporations might have difficulty assessing the impact of CSR on reputation because corporate reputation is hard to measure.

CSR Activities

CSR activities appeared to revolve around philanthropic aspects because most interviewees equated CSR with philanthropic activities such as "em-ployee volunteerism," "corporate donations," and other charitable activities. This could be attributed to the limitation that it is easier for the interviewees to discuss such activities as opposed to legal and ethical activities. We also acknowledge that such community-oriented activities may be preferred by corporations because of their ability to generate better publicity and garner public goodwill. While actual practice appears to lag behind perceptions (which are more comprehensive), this is understandable as the modern concept of CSR was introduced to Singapore less than half a decade ago (Roche, 2003), and it has been gaining popularity only in the last couple of years.

DISCUSSION

In analyzing the above findings, it became clear to us that CSR practices varied widely among our sample of corporations. Interestingly, most of the interviewees cited that a top-down approach is ideal when organizations make decisions about CSR. Likewise, the survey results revealed that almost three-quarters of the CEOs from the sample of corporations made decisions on CSR, thus centralizing such decisions. We found that corporations adopted three major approaches when they practiced CSR: proactive, accommodative, and reactive. *Proactive* corporations are motivated by their corporate values and agenda to implement initiatives on CSR, which are aligned with their corporate strategies. These are typically large corporations and MNCs. *Accommodative* corporations tend to follow existing guidelines and regulations to fulfill minimum CSR criteria. They also may consider feedback from important stakeholders and attempt to meet the CSR expectations of these groups. *Reactive* corporations tend to react to events and conduct CSR activities on an ad hoc basis. We also found that, although evaluation is critical to all organizational activities, it is conducted minimally as far as CSR is concerned. One obstacle that constrains corporations in evaluating their CSR efforts can be the inherent difficulties in measuring CSR, as stated in our literature review. We also discovered from the interviews that some corporations do not set goals prior to implementing their CSR projects. Thus, there is no benchmark for these corporations to evaluate their CSR activities, and as a result, they seem to do very little CSR evaluation.

Based on our quantitative and qualitative data, as well as insights from the literature review, we identified seven stakeholders that are able to influence corporations to practice CSR in Singapore. We refer to these stakeholders as drivers: the government of Singapore, NGOs, mass media, corporations, trade associations, consumers, and employees (see table 8.1).

In order to evaluate the effectiveness of these drivers, we assessed the current activity level of each driver and found that the government and NGOs were currently active in driving whatever CSR activity we were able to unearth.

We also analyzed the potential impact that each driver may have in motivating corporations to practice CSR. Factors that contributed to this analysis include the perceived importance of the driver among the sample corporations and the perceptions about corporate executives toward CSR. Insights and recommendations from our elite interviews, coupled with our understanding of Singapore's political, socioeconomic, and cultural variables, also helped us make informed evaluations. We also offer an arbitrary index to rate the potential impact of each driver consisting of ratings ranging from very weak to very strong. We believe drivers that are rated very weak or weak are unlikely to influence the CSR behavior of corporations to any significant degree. Drivers rated moderate may be able to change attitudes and perceptions among corporation executives but are unlikely to change corporate behavior significantly. Those rated strong and very strong are the drivers with the most potential to lead the CSR movement in Singapore to the next level.

We recognize that the potential impact and current activity level of the drivers can be highly variable, particularly among corporations, consumers and employees. The final rating established is based on an estimation of the average of the aggregate behavior (see table 8.1). Based on our analysis, drivers that featured strongly in both areas of potential impact and current activity level include the government and corporations. This is driven by the fact that some senior government ministers have taken the lead to promote CSR in high-profile seminars targeted at corporations. While our interviewees were divided on whether the government should legislate for CSR, most agreed that the government is in a strong position to raise CSR awareness and performance among corporations, given the nature of political system that exists in Singapore.

Our data suggest that despite their high level of interest and activity, NGOs appear unlikely to bring about significant changes in corporate behavior vis-à-vis CSR. This is not surprising considering that civil activist groups in Singapore are relatively quiet, again owing to the sociopolitical climate of the country. In fact, the interviewees representing two local NGOs recognized the limitations of their efforts to drive CSR. One way to increase the impact of NGOs is for the NGOs to collaborate with trade associations or other drivers to give these organizations the added muscle. An example of one such effort is the setting up of the National Tripartite Initiative (NTI) on CSR in 2004, which consists of volunteers, government representatives, labor unions, a consumer group, and a trade association. Considering that more than 100 corporate members attended its launch, we believe NTI has the potential to contribute to the robust growth of the CSR movement in Singapore. Based on our data, we have rated the mass media, including business publications, as moderate for their potential impact. This is also in line with the nonactivist orientation of most of the mass media in Singapore due to the existing media system.

In effect, we perceive a strong role for the government as the driver of CSR in Singapore and not for NGOs, primarily because of the unique sociopolitical environment of the city-state. Although Singapore is a parliamentary democracy, it is also a corporatist state (Sriramesh & Rivera, 2006). Corporatism (or corporativism) is a malleable concept and lacks a universally accepted definition. Teulings and Hartog (1998) described corporatism as "a type of social organization that is intermediary between capitalism and socialism" (p. 27). We believe that Singapore shares the two dimensions of social corporatism that Pekkarinen, Pohjola, and Rowthorn (1992, pp. 2–3) identified: centralized wage bargaining involving the government, labor unions, and employers, and a level of egalitarianism (what we would like to call communitarianism) where national solidarity is emphasized in sharing the fruits of economic growth. Singapore's system of government involves a strong link between the government, corporations, and labor unions. For example, the National Trades Union Congress (NTUC) is a body representing a majority of the labor force (63 trade unions and 6 labor associations representing 400,000 members). The Secretary General of the NTUC is a member

TABLE 8.1 An analysis of the potential effectiveness of CSR drivers in Singapore

Driver name/description (what driver can do to promote CSR)	Potential impact	Current activity level	Effectiveness	
			Strengths	Weaknesses
Government				
• Legislate and regulate CSR • Set minimum standards that need to be met • Set CSR-friendly laws such as tax exemption on corporate donations	Strong	Active	• Ability to ensure that minimum standards are fulfilled • Authority to get the attention and compliance of corporations	• Preference (among corporate executives surveyed and interviewees) for CSR to be voluntary • Limited ability to be comprehensive and cover all areas • Weak motivation for corporations • Lack of sensitivity to market needs and changes
NGOs				
• Raise awareness among various stakeholder groups • Stimulate discussion on CSR • Establish corporate networks/alliances on a local and global basis to facilitate communication on CSR • Establish standards to assess CSR performance • Establish CSR awards to recognize positive CSR practices	Weak	Active	• Independence from the government and corporations • Possess the desire to change corporate behavior	• Perceived unimportance of NGOs as stake-holders among sample corporations and interviewees • Limited power of civil activists in Singapore
Mass media				
• Expose irresponsible conduct of corporations • Highlight positive CSR practices • Raise awareness of issues and opportunities surrounding CSR • Initiate evaluating systems to assess and publicize CSR performance	Moderate	Aware/ active	• Extensive outreach across different sectors of the society • Ability to act as a watchdog on corporations	• Limited success of existing efforts by media to promote CSR among corporations

TABLE 8.1 (continued)

Driver name/description (what driver can do to promote CSR)	Potential impact	Current activity level	Effectiveness	
			Strengths	Weaknesses
Corporations				
• Communicate with stakeholders about CSR practices to raise awareness • Require that business partners follow certain CSR standards	Strong	Latent/aware	• Groups (e.g. Temasek Holding Companies) and large MNCs have power to influence behavior of business partners • Corporations driven by competition; actions of rival corporations may get more attention than actions of NGO and Media	• Behavior among corporations is highly variable • Difficulty in reaching out to SMEs • Danger of corporations jumping onto the bandwagon without a proper understanding of CSR
Trade associations				
• Regulate CSR practices within the industry • Set industry-specific CSR standards • Identify relevant CSR issues and opportunities • Establish system to recognize corporations that fulfill industry CSR standards • Highlight positive CSR practices	Strong	Latent	• Possess best knowledge of industry needs and issues • Access to corporations in the industry • If membership is important in the industry, potential to use membership criteria to promote CSR practices	• CSR may not be a concern of the trade association • Limited power of trade associations in specific industries • Not all corporations are regulated by their trade associations
Consumers				
• Product and corporation boycotts • Support companies with strong CSR practices • Exhibit willingness to pay more for products by socially responsible corporations	Very strong	Nondriver	• Affect corporations' bottom-lines directly • Perceived importance as a stakeholder among sample corporations and interviewees	• Singaporean consumers are generally apathetic and so minimal activists
Employees				
• Consider CSR when choosing employment • Provide feedback on CSR practices • Participate in CSR activities • Express interest and desire in CSR activities	Very strong	Nondriver	• Affect corporations' bottom-lines directly • Perceived importance as a stakeholder among sample corporations and interviewees	• Singaporean employees generally apathetic • Lack of activist labor union in Singapore

of the cabinet in the Prime Minister's office, which is representative of the co-optation of labor unions by the government. The National Trades Union Congress (2006) itself describes the relationship between these key stakeholders this way:

> What started off as a symbiotic relationship between the NTUC and the government has developed into a tripartite alliance after the labour movement chose, in 1969, to adopt a cooperative, rather than a confrontational policy towards employers. Indeed, tripartism is the driving force behind Singapore's economic and social development.

In addition to this close linkage involving the labor movement, employers, and the government, the government also controls many corporations that are called government-linked companies. Further, although it is a labor union, NTUC itself runs a popular grocery chain and other business ventures most often associated with corporations. This deliberate "blurring of the boundaries" between the government, labor, and at least a large share of corporations is representative of corporatism and atypical of most environments around the world. So when we assess the environment for CSR practices, Singapore offers a rather unique situation, which is why we have proposed the government and corporations as the prime drivers of CSR. In most other parts of the world, one would expect either NGOs or corporations themselves to be the leaders of CSR activities because of the distinct boundaries between these entities and the diverse roles they play owing to the socioeconomic environment.

Alegret (1998) identified four dimensions of corporativism: the ancient guilds' corporatism, traditional or antirevolutionary corporatism, state-controlled fascist-oriented corporatism, and technocratic or neocorporatism. We believe that Singapore is representative of neo- or technocratic corporatism where, according to Alegret, societal decision making is almost exclusively in the hands of technocrats so as to reduce or avoid "open and violent conflict between the different groups of interests . . . while the State reserves for itself the roles not only of judge, but also that of interested party" (p. 6).

In addition to being a corporatist system, Singapore is also communitarian (Sriramesh & Rivera, 2006; Chay, 2003). Garfinkle (2006, n.p.) noted that "Communitarians recognize that a healthy society must have a correct balance between individual autonomy and social cohesion." This description fits everything that the PAP has done since Singapore became a republic. Stressing racial amity in this multiethnic society, for example, is just one of the ways communitarian philosophy has guided government policies. The emphasis given to GLCs (public sector corporations) is another way communitarianism is evident in the society.

In 1999, the government of Singapore started the Singapore 21 program, whose aim was to "strengthen the intangibles of society like social cohesion, political stability and the collective will, values and attitudes of Singaporeans" (Singapore 21 Committee, 2004). This is another example of communitarianism that is summed up aptly by the Institute for Communitarian Policy Studies: "Communitarianism is essentially an optimistic approach to issues of public policy. While mindful of human tendencies to act in self-interested ways, Communitarians believe that it is possible to build a good society based on the desire of human beings to cooperate to achieve community goals that are based on positive values" (Garfinkle, 2006).

Communitarianism also guides the way media in Singapore cover subjects, including CSR. The media are expected to self-regulate and not report on anything that would adversely affect the amity among the multiethnic populace. There is also minimal media competition in this rather small media market, which further inhibits media access to NGOs or activists by providing multiple and competing media outlets.

CONCLUSION

We hope there will be many more comprehensive studies about CSR in Singapore in the future, which should also help the growth of the movement in this city-state. Future researches may select specific variables from the framework (e.g., employees and potential impact) and test their relationship empirically. The Asian tsunami tragedy, which happened in the midst of data collection for this study, has helped raise the awareness of CSR among corporations in Singapore. Because CEOs and top managers were found to be the key decision makers of CSR activities among the corporations in our study, future researchers can conduct a deeper study of the attitudes of these senior managers toward CSR. Another area of study can include investigating the perceptions about consumers and employees, because they were regarded as the most important stakeholders by the sample of corporations in our study. Future research can also examine the potential impact and current activity level of customers and employees, as well as other stakeholders such as NGOs and trade associations, to empirically test our analysis on the various CSR drivers. Another possible research avenue is to explore the distinct CSR issues associated with the different industries so that specific guidelines and recommendations can be formulated. A longitudinal study to uncover any significant trend in executives' perceptions about CSR and corporations' CSR activities over time may also be an interesting area for future research.

NOTE

1.   Clarkson (1995) distinguished between primary and secondary stakeholders. *Primary stakeholders* are those groups or individuals that have direct transactions with the corporation and include owners, suppliers, employees, and customers. *Secondary stakeholders* have a more "distant" even if no less important relationship and include environmental groups, society at large, media, and local community groups.

REFERENCES

Alegret, J. (1998). *Politics and economy: Corporatism and democratic participation in the fishermen's confraries in Catalonia.* Girona: University of Girona.

Andrew, B. H., Gul, F. A., Guthrie, J. E., & Teoh, H. Y. (1989). A note on corporate social disclosure practices in developing countries: The case of Malaysia and Singapore. *British Accounting Review, 21,* 371–377.

Balakrishnan, V. (2004). *Promoter and practitioner: The Singapore government's experience.* Paper presented at the Singapore/UK: Developing Corporate Social Responsibility seminar. Retrieved April 15, 2004, from http://www.mti.gov .sg/public/NWS/frm_NWS_Default .asp?sid=39&cid=1941.

Boehm, A. (2002). Corporate social responsibility: A complementary perspective of community and corporate leaders. *Business and Society Review, 10*(2), 171–194.

Bowd, R., Harris, P., & Cornelissen, J. (2003, July). *CSR—A schools approach to an inclusive definition: Setting the scene for future public relations and communications research.* Paper presented at the 10th International Public Relations Symposium, Lake Bled, Slovenia.

British High Commission. (2004). Singapore/ UK: Developing corporate social responsibility. In *Corporate social responsibility workbook.* Singapore: Author.

Bronn, P. S., & Vrioni, A. B. (2001). Corporate social responsibility and cause-related marketing: An overview. *International Journal of Advertising, 20*(2), 207–222.

Carr, A. Z. (1996). Is business bluffing ethical? In S. B. Rae & K. L. Wong (Eds.), *Beyond integrity: A Judeo-Christian approach.* Grand Rapids, MI: Zondervan.

Carroll, A. B. (1979). A three-dimensional conceptual model of corporate performance. *Academy of Management Review, 4,* 497–505.

Carroll, A. B. (1991, July/August). The pyramid of corporate social responsibility: Toward the moral management of organizational stakeholders. *Business Horizons, 34*(4), 39–48.

Carroll, A. B. (1999). Corporate social responsibility: Evolution of a definitional construct. *Business and Society, 38,* 268–295.

Center for Corporate Citizenship at Boston College. (2004). *The state of corporate citizenship in the US: A view from inside 2003–2004.* Retrieved October 22, 2004, from http://www.bc.edu/centers/ccc/Media/ state_cc_report.pdf.

Chambers, E., Chapple, W., Moon, J., & Sullivan, M. (2003). *CSR in Asia: A seven country study of CSR website reporting* (ICCSR Research Paper Series, No. 09-2003). Nottingham, UK: Nottingham University.

Chay, C. (2003). Becoming professionals: A portrait of public relations in Singapore. In K. Sriramesh and D. Vercic (Eds.), *The global public relations handbook: Theory, research, and practice* (pp. 86–105). Mahwah, NJ: Lawrence Erlbaum.

Chua, B. H. (1995). *Communitarian ideology and democracy in Singapore.* London: Routledge.

Clarkson, M. B. E. (1995). A stakeholder framework for analysing and evaluating corporate social performance. *Academy of Management Review, 20,* 92–117.

Collins, A. (2004, May 26). Developing corporate social responsibility: The British perspective. Retrieved Nov 17 from http://www.fco.gov.uk/Files/kfile/csr%20tripartite%20hc%20speech3.pdf

Commission of the European Communities. (2001). *Promoting a European framework for corporate social responsibility.* Luxembourg: Author.

Commission of the European Communities. (2002). *Communication from the commission concerning corporate social responsibility: A business contribution to sustainable development.* Luxembourg: Author.

Edelman. (2004). *Edelman Asia Pacific stakeholder study: The only way to have a friend is to be one.* Retrieved November 1, 2004, from http://www.edelman.com/image/insights/content/4CoreStakeholder04.ppt#320,2,Slide 2.

Foo, S. L., & Tan, M. S. (1988). A comparative study of social responsibility reporting in Malaysia and Singapore. *Singapore Accountant,* 12–15.

Freeman, E. (1984). *Strategic management: A stakeholder approach.* Boston, MA: Pitman.

Friedman, M. (1970, September 13). The social responsibility of businesses is to increase its profits. *New York Times Magazine,* 32–33.

Garfinkle, N. (2006). *The communitarian vision.* Retrieved April 14, 2006, from http://www.gwu.edu/~icps/vision.html.

Ho, K. L. (2000). *The politics of policy-making in Singapore.* Singapore: Oxford University Press.

Hung, W. T., & Ramasamy, B. (2004). A comparative analysis of corporate social responsibility awareness, Malaysian and Singaporean corporations. *Journal of Corporate Citizenship,* 13, 109–123.

Keeler, D. (2002, May). Spread the love and make it pay. *Global Finance,* 16(5), 20–25.

Key, S., & Popkin, S. (1998). Integrating ethics into the strategic management process: Doing well by doing good. *Management Decision,* 6(5), 331–338.

Khanna, V. (2004a, March 20). It's everybody's business. *Business Times Singapore.* Retrieved June 11, 2004, from Factiva database (http://business-times.asiaone.com/).

Khanna, V. (2004b, March 20). Singapore companies heeding the CSR call. *Business Times Singapore.* Retrieved June 11, 2004, from Factiva database (http://business-times.asiaone.com/).

Klonoski, R. J. (2001). Foundational consider-ations in the corporate social responsibility debate. *Business Horizons,* 34(4), 9–18.

Lantos, G. P. (2001). The boundaries of strategic corporate social responsibility. *Journal of Consumer Marketing,* 18(7), 595–639.

Macleod, S. (2001). Why worry about CSR? *Strategic Communication Management,* 5(5), 8–10.

Marcoux, A. M. (2000, July 24). *Business ethics gone wrong* (CATO Policy Report). Washington, DC: CATO Institute.

Munshi, N. V. (2004). Conversations on business citizenship. *Business and Society Review,* 109(1), 89–93.

National Trades Union Congress. (2006). *NTUC and tri-partism.* Retrieved April 14, 2006, from http://www.ntucworld.org.sg/ntucunions/abt_ntuc_tripartism.htm.

Pekkarinen, J., Pohjola, M., & Rowthorn, B. (1992). Social corporatism and economic performance: Introduction and conclusions. In J. Pekkarinen, M. Pohjola, & B. Rowthorn (Eds.), *Social corporatism* (pp. 363–397). Oxford: Clarendon Press.

Roche, J. (2003). Analysis: Corporate responsibility issues in Singapore. *Ethical Corporation.* Retrieved September 19, 2004, from http://www.ethicalcorp.com/content.asp.

Rowley, T. J. (1997). Moving beyond dyadic ties: A network theory of stakeholder influences. *Academy of Management Review,* 22(4), 887–910.

Singapore 21 Committee. (2004). What is Singapore 21? *Singapore 21 Report.* Retrieved December 2004 from http://www.singapore21.org.sg/menu_flash.html.

Sriramesh, K., & Rivera, M. (2006). E-Government in a corporatist, communitarian society: The case of Singapore. *New Media and Society,* 8(4), 707–730.

Teulings, C.N., & Hartog, J. (1998). *Corporatism or competition: An international comparison of labour market structures and their impact on wage information.* Cambridge: Cambridge University Press.

Tsang, E. W. K. (1998). A longitudinal study of corporate social reporting in Singapore: The case of banking, food and beverages and hotel industries. *Accounting, Auditing & Accountability Journal,* 11(5), 624–635.

United Nations Global Compact. (2004, October). Corporate social responsibility and the Global Compact. Unpublished presentation at United Nations Global Compact Singapore Network Inaugural Workshop, Singapore.

Welford, R. J. (2003). Corporate social responsibility in Europe and Asia: Critical elements of best practices. *Journal of Corporate Citizenship, 13*, 31–47.

Wood, D. J. (1991). Corporate social performance revisited. *Academy of Management Review, 16*, 691–718.

Yuen, C. K. (1999). *Leninism, Asian culture and Singapore*. Retrieved December 2004 from http://www.comp.nus.edu.sg/~yuenck/sing.

9

Corporate Social Responsibility in Mexico

An Approximation from the Point of View of Communication

MARIELA PÉREZ CHAVARRÍA

Over the past few years, the topic of corporate social responsibility (CSR) has captured a great deal of interest, but its development and dissemination have varied from one country to another, taking on the cultural nuances typical of each nation or region. Research on these nuances would still appear to be exiguous, although some studies exist along these lines, such as that of Juholin (2003) in Finland and those of Sanborn (2004), Agüero (2002), and Sánchez (2000) in Latin America, among others, in which the main focus has been to identify the national characteristics presented by CSR.

In Mexico, although the topic has been developed over time, CSR still faces quite a few challenges: What is the significance of CSR? What exactly does it involve? How is it communicated? How can you make it visible? How do you disseminate it so that it can be applied, without it being considered a resource exclusively in the service of company image and public relations? How can it be seen as important, in and of itself, rather than a peripheral activity typical of the portfolios in this discipline? (Frankental, 2001; L'Etang, 1994; Roberts, 2003).

Moreover, as is well known, advances in the Internet have modified organizational communication (Augustine, 2001). In this new interactive context, it is no longer possible to communicate according to a linear model of univocal meanings and unilateral decisions. Today, the challenge in-volves participation and communication in a chaotic, open, interactive milieu that demands dialogue, confidence, and credibility between what is said and what is done (Stroh & Jaatinen, 2001; Tixier, 2003).

Given this panorama, in this chapter I present research that seeks to find out what is communicated on the Internet, insofar as CSR is concerned, by Mexican companies. In particular, I focus on companies with the best reputation in 2004, to wit: "[T]hose recognized for their responsible practices and their commitment to Mexican society" (Transparencia Mexicana y Consulta Mitofsky, 2004). I also attempt to discover the following: What is CSR in Mexico like, from what companies themselves say? What do companies say about themselves regarding this topic? To whom do they send those messages? How do they communicate on the Internet?

This research is important for several reasons. First of all, very little has been studied on the topic—that of social responsibility and communication in Mexico—and therefore, the resulting analysis may shed some light on how companies adjust to global pressure. Second, it may provide evidence on how CSR has developed in Mexico. Above all, it may discover what efforts the business sector has been making so that future research can compare it to similar groups in other countries.

In addition, from the standpoint of communication—which underlies and guides this work—

the research is relevant because it brings up an issue little explored in the analyses of messages over the Internet in Mexico. Still further, it is important in and of itself because I know of no other studies in Mexico tackling this subject from the point of view of communication. There undoubtedly *is* research, but it is not well known or has not yet come forth.

Finally, developing CSR provides new spaces for analysis and reflection regarding organizations and their behavior. Therefore, this research attempts to make a modest contribution to how commitments in the communicative and virtual space of the Internet become explicit. This research does not purport to be exhaustive and is limited to a study of the top 10 companies. They were recognized for their actions involving responsibility and commitment to Mexico in the sole report on reputation published in Mexico to date (Indice Mexicano de Reputación Empresarial, 2004).

OVERVIEW OF CSR IN MEXICO

Beginning the final decade of the twentieth century and up to the present day, Mexico, like all countries around the world, has undergone a series of changes that undoubtedly have had an impact on the practice of CSR. This is particularly true because of the process of opening up that the country went through in the 1990s, which left its mark on all areas of national life.

In the economic sphere, Mexico went from a closed, protected, and paternalistic economy to a free market one with the signing of NAFTA in 1994, an event that fully placed it within the context of a global economy. In the political realm, it democratically changed governing parties after more than 70 years of continual administration by a single party in power, the Institutional Revolutionary Party. In the social sphere, the population continued growing until it reached more than 100 million inhabitants, increasing demands associated with the people's well-being. In this context, marked by economic inequality, the social responsibility of the companies under study was born and grew.

Historical Background and Development to the Present

As a starting point, Mexico has a long tradition of philanthropy, in the sense of help and support,

going back to the time of the Indian cultures and persisting to the present. According to Verduzco (2003), ever since the pre-Hispanic era with the Aztec *capulli*—a form of organization dividing the city into precincts of neighbors with the same lineage who answered to a chief or lord—those living within these neighborhoods had the support of the community, when needed. This could be considered a clear antecedent of social support organizations.

Verduzco (2003) himself points out that, during the Conquest and colonial times (approximately 1510–1800), the presence of the Catholic Church became a decisive factor, both as a source of social aid in protecting the Indians, the poor, and the forsaken and also as a powerful institution that, due to its riches, built schools, hospitals, nurseries, and so forth.

Beginning in 1810, with independence, the power of the Church declined, but certain institutions set up by Catholics continued with the responsibility of attending to the health and education sectors, the poor, and the sick, among other needy groups. Between 1876 and 1910, during the Porfirio Díaz administration, charity got a boost from the creation of the Board on Private Assistance (*Junta de Asistencia Privada*), which still exists. A law on private charity was issued, an event giving legal personality to these institutions and protecting them by exempting them from taxes and allowing other deductions. This permitted them to grow and strengthen their national presence (Verduzco, 2003).

With the Revolution of 1910 came major changes for Mexico. Free lay education was established, thereby limiting the Church. But it was not until 1940 that the state would consolidate itself with a single official party and its positive social policies permit it to counterbalance the weight of the Church's influence. In northern Mexico (specifically, Monterrey), between the end of the nineteenth and the beginning of the twentieth centuries, large companies were founded that were to become the pillars of a good part of the national economy. In Monterrey, states Cerutti (2000), there was an economic linking of the families that founded these companies. However, they would also share a community of principles, since the businessmen of that era distinguished themselves from others by their social concern, leading them to take interest in issues outside the company. For example, quite a bit before social benefits were offered workers by the state (i.e., about 1940), Monterrey's largest companies were concerned about workers' housing, as well as providing them with medical attention through their own clinics, schools, and so on.

This concern, which is notable among northern businessmen but can be seen in other nuances in the rest of Mexico's private sector, distinguished itself by developing a set of activities aimed at supporting social issues, the fruit of a deep-rooted Christian ethic. As Sanborn (2004) pointed out, religious faith provided great motivation for charity and social assistance and influenced the corporate philanthropy that is common in both Mexico and Latin America. Generally speaking, it is not the company but the owner who decides to involve himself in social projects. Therefore, to bring together businessmen in such efforts, the Employers' Confederation of the Mexican Republic (*Confederación Patronal de la República Mexicana*) was founded in Monterrey in northern Mexico in 1929. It was national in scope and conservative in nature.

Then, nurtured by the ideology and objectives of that organization, was born the Social Union of Mexican Businessmen (*Unión Social de Empresarios Mexicanos* [USEM]), which came out of the Union of Catholic Businessmen (*Unión de Empresarios Católicos*), founded in 1957. In 1963, there appeared the Mexican Foundation for Social Development (*Fundación Mexicana para el Desarrollo Social*), created by a group of Catholic businessmen seeking a solution to rural issues through social promotion strategies not involving paternalism or assistance. This institution, together with the USEM, as Verduzco (2003) states, constitutes an example of the actions of businessmen who, ever since that era, have been concerned with the country's social situation. Likewise, during this period, the Coordinating Business Board (*Consejo Coordinador Empresarial*) was founded, an organization bringing together chambers of commerce, industry, and so on, which seeks to "provide guidelines for companies so that they assume social responsibility" (Agüero, 2002, n.p.).

During the 1980s, social and civil organizations grew after the 1985 earthquakes, which shook social consciousness. However, with the Salinas administration (1988–1994), the main effort of nongovernmental organizations (NGOs) was in the economic rather than political realm. In 1988, the National Human Rights Commission (*Comis-ión Nacional de los Derechos Humanos*) was established. Similarly, in that year, the Mexican Center for Philanthropy (*Centro Mexicano para la Filantropía* [CEMEFI]) was created by private initiative. All these organizations began collaborating with the state on social projects, but they also started intervening in public policy issues.

CEMEFI, an institution created by a businessman from the north, deserves particular mention because, at present, it is one of the few national organizations dedicated to strongly encouraging the culture of philanthropy and CSR in Mexico. It is a charitable organization that is "non-profit and unaffiliated with any party, race or religion," (as its webpage describes it). At present, this organization is recognized, both nationally and internationally, as a pioneering entity in the introduction of the concept of CSR (CEMEFI calls it "business social responsibility" or *responsabilidad social empresarial*) throughout the country and, therefore, in promoting and supporting businesses implementing CSR.

Its efforts are laudable because, among other things, CEMEFI has managed to bring together the dispersed efforts of business philanthropy already existing and has tried to find solutions to the issues of responsibility and social imbalances. Moreover, since 2000, it is the only organization issuing "certification" to companies, that is, a special "Socially Responsible Company" (*Empresa Socialmente Responsable*) award. This award is the first of its kind in Latin America and recognizes practices of social responsibility in those companies that voluntarily "measure and compare their own performance in the area of responsibility so as to perfect it" (F. Cajiga, personal interview, December 2004).

Through its efforts, CEMEFI has helped implement, over time, social programs that are consistent with company objectives. It likewise promotes communicating social action so that it serves as an example and motivation for other organizations. More than anything else, it encourages a "strategic philanthropy" model (Sánchez, 2000), a consequence of global competition and of the demand for responsibility that, along with the importance of communication, create the conditions for firmly planting this model as part of company activities. Another of CEMEFI's merits is having "professionalized" the actions of social aid, so that companies and businessmen can lay aside the "altruistic philanthropy" model (Sánchez, 2000) and move on to a strategic one.

MEXICAN BUSINESS CULTURE: PATERNALISM AND SOCIAL RESPONSIBILITY

The scenario of CSR in Mexico would not be complete without including, although in a general manner, a brief review of the importance of the national culture in ethical decision making and in social responsibility. Culture touches everything, as Hofstede (1991) states. Therefore, culture is also present in how CSR is conceived and carried out in each country. Authors such as Agüero (2002) and Sanborn (2004) contemplate this aspect in their research. If we consider Hofstede's four dimensions of culture—(1) power distance, (2) uncertainty avoidance, (3) individualism versus collectivism, and (4) masculinity versus femininity—we can better understand Mexico's business culture.

According to De la Cerda and Núñez (1993), Mexican business organizations and leaders can be characterized by the following:

1. *High index of power distance*, that is, very centralized organizations in which autocratic and paternalistic leadership predominates
2. *High index of uncertainty avoidance*, which explains the preference for well-defined rules
3. *Low index of individualism and therefore collectivism*, a characteristic that explains employees tending to go along with the organization because they value relationships and security
4. *High index of masculinity* due to, among other reasons, weakness and femininity being cultural signs reflecting submission, or due to the social devaluation of Mexican culture

Nicholls, Lane, and Brehm (1999) affirm, for example, that marked paternalism can be seen clearly because management is the one making decisions, setting goals, and resolving conflict, while the workers tend to wait for instructions. For example, workers' decisions are often made based on their role and level. These researchers also talk about a tradition of worshipping the boss (a hierarchical culture with a great deal of power distance), a clear reflection of the very history of a country such as Mexico, as well as of the social, economic, and political life, in which all authority resides with the highest on the totem pole. The boss (father, president, or ruler) has lofty powers

to sanction (a vertical culture) but also the responsibility to provide protection.

To that end, Martínez and Dorfman (1998) observe that, perhaps, because of the influence of the family (a fundamental value in Mexican culture), this model, in which father decides and protects, is the one operating in Mexican organizations. It is a patriarchal-organizational construct in which the boss or owner provides security and protection to the employees in exchange for loyalty. This model generates confidence and solidarity.

> The responsibility of the entrepreneur with regard to the dignity of the worker does not end at the company exit, but encompasses the life of the worker. He should be concerned the worker lives in dignity and we cannot ask him to live with dignity if we do not provide him with the means to live with dignity. Here come together what we already mentioned with regard to his training as a means to increase productivity, which will give him the opportunity to earn a better wage which, in turn, allows him and his family to aspire to more dignified and more humane living conditions. (Milanés, 2003, "Más allá de la empresa," paragraph I)

Therefore, the management style characterizing Mexico's business culture, and likewise Latin America's, presents a marked paternalistic style, which might explain the model of philanthropy and CSR practiced at these latitudes. The immediate boss is *the boss*—a paternalistic figure—who, by protecting and taking care of his employees, obtains the acceptance of the public in general and at the same time obtains sympathy. So the immediate boss helps the community and, this way, manages to be seen as good (image/reputation), but also reinforces and perpetuates his power.

One clear example of this paternalistic behavior is the Sociedad Cuauhtémoc y Famosa, an association created within the Monterrey brewery (Cervecería Cuauhtémoc- Moctezuma). The association was founded in 1918 and is perhaps one of the oldest associations in Mexico dedicated to "promoting the integral development of collaborators and their families" (from the FEMSA webpage). Noteworthy among its original objectives is to provide employees with medical services, savings plans, sports, courses, and scholarships, among other benefits. Also in its installations, it has developed a recreational center with green areas, sports fields, rooms for social events, an open-air theater, swimming pool, cafeteria, discount store, and clinic with medical services ranging from pediatrics, maternity, and family medicine to dental services.

Types of Relationship Between Company and Society

Be it by tradition, by culture, or by religious beliefs, it is clear that in Mexico the private sector has collaborated in the solution of social problems practically from the beginnings of its business activity, as G. Lozano (2003) mentions. Entrepreneurs have been involved in social responsibility in a variety of ways. The reasons for this help may be the personal ones of the company (altruistic) or pragmatic-utilitarian (strategic). One may even speak of social coaction, as Husted and Salazar (2005) do, and of mixed reasons or combinations of them. But independent of the motives, what is noteworthy is that the help does not cease, and new support ties are constantly being developed between the companies and civil society, especially NGOs.

Roitter (1996) distinguishes seven kinds of relationships between companies and society—valid in any country—likewise articulated with the company's economic, commercial, and institutional goals:

1. *Complementary action*: initiatives developed by the company, which are tied to economic-commercial requirements. In addition, they generate benefits for third parties, with training programs for employees and for the public in general, or they recycle materials.
2. *Compensatory action*: measures adopted by the company to neutralize the effects produced on the environment by its activities.
3. *Sponsorship*: supporting a particular event or spectacle in exchange for advertising space.
4. *Marketing with cause*: a strategy relating the marketing of a product to a cause involving social interest.
5. *Patronage*: sustaining longer term cultural activities that are open to the community. It may also involve sustaining or supporting scientific research.
6. *Philanthropy*: beneficial actions, including donations.

7. *Social investment*: types of interaction between the company and its surroundings. It supposes the design and startup of a joint project and likewise implies applying its human resources to a social initiative (corporate volunteerism).

Wymer and Samu (2003, cited in G. Lozano, 2003) mention similar types of collaboration, which range from traditional philanthropy, which persists today, to the following:

- *Corporate foundations*: nonprofit entities created by the company for philanthropic goals
- *Licensing*: agreements with NGOs so that companies can use their names or logotypes in exchange for payment of usage rights
- *Promotions based on transactions*: donating a specific amount, be it money or in kind, in direct proportion to company sales (social marketing)
- *Joint promotions*: promotions by means of which a NGO and the company work together to support a cause
- *Joint beginnings*: agreements in which a NGO and the company work in close collaboration to achieve common goals and develop competitive advantages.

To this list should be added a new type of help called "rounding" (*el redondeo*), which surfaced specifically in Monterrey and which has already spread to other parts of Mexico. It consists of a major company forming a "strategic alliance" with an association, for example, the Red Cross, and for one or two months asking all customers for the excess change on their final bill, which goes to the NGO or organization supported during that time. For example, if the bill was 8.75 pesos, it would be rounded off to 9 pesos and the extra 25 centavos donated. This way, the association obtains funds for its activities and the company looks good in the eyes of the consumers. I should add that this system allows companies to deduct from taxes something that it is *not* given directly by the company, but rather by the consumers. Although it is praiseworthy that others are helped, there is no reason for this action to imply a tax benefit for the company providing the "service." Some critics have called this action something like the "all-around business of rounding" (*el negocio redondo del redondeo*).

Generally speaking, one might think that most of these types of relationships seem to have been designed mainly to boost company economic benefits, reputation, or image, and not to generate in-depth social commitment and involvement. This is shown by the complementary and compensatory actions, the creation of foundations, and all the variant relationships associated with marketing, such as sponsorship, patronage, and licensing, just to name a few that catch the eye of different stakeholders. In addition, one should mention that the abundance of types of relationships does not necessarily imply the existence of planned or strategic programs but, rather, is an example of creativity and good intentions with a wide range of isolated programs, in the majority of cases.

Therefore, the types of relationship between companies and society are varied and abundant and, possibly in the case of Mexico, such types constitute one more manifestation of collectivist and paternalistic culture. It is not possible to determine what actions are those most developed so far, but what can indeed be stated is that the concept of CSR and programs in favor of the community and the environment are already incorporated into many Mexican companies, although there is still a great deal of confusion between philanthropy and true social responsibility.

Dimensions and Development of CSR

In light of the variety of interpretations of CSR and, to understand the issue more in depth, the Mexican Center for Philanthropy (CEMEFI) proposes grouping social responsibility indicators into four categories: (1) business ethics (including values, code of ethics, transparency, compliance with tax liabilities, social security, etc.), (2) quality of life in the company (including programs developing personnel, personal career plans, training, safety, and hygiene), (3) ties and commitment to the community and their development (donations, support for development of suppliers, participation in public life, participation in society's institutions, etc.), and (4) care and preservation of the environment.

In turn, the Instituto Ethos in Brazil proposes a more specific set of indicators than the preceding, involving seven main categories: (1) values and transparency (self-regulation in codes of conduct, transparency in relationships with society), (2) internal public (dialogue and participation, respect for the individual, respect for the worker), (3) environment (handling environmental impact, responsibility vis-à-vis future generations), (4) suppliers (selection of and arrangements with suppliers), (5) consumers/clients (social dimension of consumption), (6) community (relations with the local community, philanthropy/social investment, volunteer work), and (7) government and society (political transparency, social leadership). Although the dimensions are not the same, what is relevant is that CSR implies company action (beyond obligations) vis-à-vis all their stakeholders.

Today, one may also speak of stages or levels of CSR: CSR1, corresponding to a first level, when the notion of responsibility takes hold, and CSR2, or corporate social responsiveness, involving more advanced aspects (Perdiguero, 2003). On this topic, Andriof and Waddock (2002) say that the former belongs to an initial, reactive stage and the latter to a proactive one. In contrast, for Husted (2000), CSR1 alludes to only the obligations companies should have in order to improve their social milieu, while *responsiveness* is oriented toward how to respond; that is, it emphasizes the company's abilities to respond to social pressure.

In this sense of *responsiveness*, Schvarstein (2003) proposes the notion of the social intelligence of organizations, which implies developing competency at an organizational or individual level, aimed at complying with social responsibility. For example, social intelligence might include empathy, the capacity to form relationships with people in a particular context, communication, the capacity to catalyze change, building ties, and the ability to develop group synergies, among others. Social intelligence includes not only integrated capacities but also the resources available to carry out initiatives.

Social Reporting

Another important aspect of CSR is linked with ways of measuring results and social reporting based on three areas: social, environmental, and economic. The importance of reporting lies in the fact that it has become a way for companies to present themselves and, with that, constitutes a means of influencing reputation and good image (Hooghiemstra, 2000). Likewise, it can be considered a decisive tool for showing the transparency currently demanded of companies. It can also contribute to improving credibility and winning confidence, although reporting in and of itself is no guarantee of transparency.

Precisely the biggest criticism made of social reporting is that, while it contains only the positive, its benefit is reduced because, in these reports, organizations put only what they want or what is beneficial to them—not the reality of things. Agüero (2002) pointed out that reporting was positive but did not make reference to the impact of companies on reducing inequality or increasing opportunities. It measures neither improvements in the quality of life within the community or within the company, nor the social cohesion, social capital, and other aspects of social value. However, what these reports contain is important for the relationship and ties with all the stakeholders because, in some way, a public accounting is made of company actions. Since they are self-presented documents, one has to keep in mind the following:

- The type of information divulged (the content's agenda)
- Those receiving the reports and their need for information (e.g., those benefited by the actions taken in said reports)
- The means used to make the reports public (ideally, they should be chosen with a mind toward satisfying the recipients', not the company's, needs for accessibility, but the opposite usually occurs; i.e., the company chooses the means most convenient for it)
- Systems for receiving feedback (this would provide equality and would reflect a bidirectional, symmetrical communications model)
- Independent or external verifiers examining the information
- Systems for following up on social performance, monitoring, and control

Of course, there may be other considerations, but at least this is fundamental and broadens the discussion quite a bit. On the other hand, with regard to the media used to make the reports public, the Internet has emerged as one of the most popular over the past few years, although many companies continue to resort to traditional media and combine them with Internet. For Snaider, Hill, and Martin (2003), the Internet not only facilitates disseminating more information more easily and at lower cost but also permits the public to control the flow of information that the company targets to its different interest groups. Through this medium, it is possible to have access to messages earmarked for other stakeholders.

Benefits and Recognition of CSR

Organizations complying with obligatory norms "are socially responsible by imposition, which does not deny that they can also be by election if they go beyond that" (Schvarstein, 2003, p. 49). But, in countries like Mexico, where it is easy to tread on social rights, it is not strange that many companies build their image proclaiming respect for norms whose compliance is obligatory. Schvarstein (2003) observes: "They sell as virtuous that which is demanded of them" (p. 50) and, even so, they are rewarded with certain benefits such as being exempt from fines, being subject to credit, and even enjoying a certain recognition. But when a company voluntarily elects to be responsible and, with its action, goes beyond what is strictly required of them, then that constitutes ethical conduct. It exercises its social responsibility in a committed manner and, with that, demonstrates not only that it considers itself responsible, but also that it recognizes the importance of the others around it.

Among the major benefits of this type of ethical behavior, the World Bank mentions the following advantages for companies: (1) it generates a social license to function; (2) it provides sustainable development that improves reputation and trademarks, yields more efficient operations, boosts sales and preserves customer loyalty, and provides greater capacity to attract and retain employees; (3) it creates new business opportunities; (4) it attracts and retains investors and partners; (5) it avoids crises from bad conduct; (6) it generates government support; and (7) it creates relational and political capital. Villafañe (2004) mentions, moreover, several other advantages, including the positioning and differentiation of trademarks, greater overall acceptance, better corporate and trademark image, cohesion of corporate culture around company values, and the development of a collaborative work culture.

Other advantages are the awards and prizes that socially responsible companies may earn, such as the Socially Responsible Company award given by CEMEFI, an award that is unique in Mexico. It is based on a self-diagnosis (not verified or measured) done by companies, taking as a basis the four areas CEMEFI recognizes as key indicators of a socially responsible company. The award is "a graphic award granted to companies meeting the *minimum standards* of social responsibility and it may be used for one year on its corporate image, allowing it to be recognized for its commitment and social performance by society in general and particularly by its customers, employees, stockholders and suppliers" (taken from CEMEFI webpage, emphasis added).

THE CSR OF THE 10 TOP MEXICAN COMPANIES: METHODOLOGY

In order to explore and discover what is communicated on the Internet regarding the CSR of the top 10 Mexican companies, according to the first report on reputation published in April 2004 (Indice Mexicano de Reputación Empresarial, 2004), my research is based on the analysis of representative cases or *discretionary examples* (Juholin, 2003). The relevance of this resides in that said cases, because of their characteristics, could be considered a reflection of present-day Mexican thinking regarding the topic at hand.

As the main source of data, the Internet was chosen because, in addition to its ease of access and dissemination of information, researchers such as Augustine (2001), Esrock and Leichty (1998), and Stroh and Jaatinen (2001) consider this medium to have modified the relationship between the organization and its publics. To a certain degree, it has created new scenarios that affect the way and methods of traditional communication (e.g., shortening the power distance between the company and its stakeholders), message content and form (more visual, with graphics and colors), and feedback systems (through chats, e-mails, blogs, etc.). This has favored bidirectional communication and has provided an opportunity for interaction both for the company as well as for the different publics, notwithstanding where the latter are located. In turn, S. McMillan (2000), Snaider et al. (2003), and Maignan and Ralston (2002) contend that, at present, the Internet constitutes an efficient medium and a valid resource for analyzing content in the area of communication, as is shown in their work. Another source of data was in-depth interviews with the heads of communication or CSR in the five companies to which there was access.

Data were collected during May and June 2004 and updated in April, May, and June 2005. It should be pointed out that, although it is true that webpages contain information elaborated by public relations departments, they are ideal for the purposes of this research because they form part of the public discourse that is self-presented by the organizations and reflect their identity (see Cheney & Christensen, 2001). Noteworthy among the advantages offered by the analysis of such sources are that it does not interrupt organizational processes (unintrusive), and that information can be verified, accessed, and fixed in time and space (J. McMillan, 1986), even though the duration is increasingly ephemeral on the Internet.

For the sample, the first 10 companies in reputation were chosen, according to the results published in the *Índice Mexicano de Reputación Empresarial (IMRE)* by the Mitofsky consulting firm (the Mitofsky study of the top ten places showed 11 companies, but two of them—Coca-Cola FEMSA/FEMSA Cerveza—are part of one beverage company, FEMSA, and share the same webpage with no difference in information, so I count them as one company). Apparently, it is the first and only company to publish such measurements in Mexico.[1] For their study, they set up their own methodology, considering eight aspects on which they based their perception of qualified informants, to wit: (1) the company's relationship with its workers, (2) its relationship with suppliers and customers, (3) its respect for the environment, (4) its relationship with stockholders and partners, (5) its relationship with the competition, (6) its respect for the law and current norms, (7) its commitment to the development of Mexico. To that end, the best-reputed organizations included four from higher education (private universities); three beverage companies (among them, two breweries); two food-product companies, and two from the construction sector. (See the appendix for information on each company.)

The greatest challenge in doing the analysis was to find a format or model for the research, and in the absence of one, I opted for developing my own, integrating two fundamental aspects: form and content. For the analysis of external elements (form), I took ideas from a format used to analyze teaching websites, as developed by Pere Marques (2004). For aspects of content, variables were determined taking into account (a) the research query of this study, (b) the variables evaluated by the Mitofsky consulting firm (relationship of the company with its workers, suppliers and customers, community, environment, competition, stockholders, and partners, as well as respect for current laws and norms, and its commitment to the development of the country), and (c) stakeholder theory. Regarding the criteria used to evaluate these variables, I checked to see whether or not they were present. Also considered were which messages were issued and how the relationship between the company and its stakeholders come about.

The process followed in the analysis was as follows:

1. Identify pages for reviewing *aspects of form* (*external ones*), for example:
   (a) *Structure of the milieu*, that is, menus, map for navigating, ease of use (friendly environment), communication, and when updated (evaluated as does/does not exist)
   (b) *Technical-aesthetic aspects*, that is, homogeneous screens, iconicity (presence of graphic elements), images and other multimedia resources, agile link management, clear names, pleasant surroundings (aesthetics) (evaluated as *high, normal, low*, with *high* meaning abundant resources and *low* meaning there are one, two, or none)
2. Do content analysis:
   (a) Review, on each page, the implicit and explicit declarations regarding CSR (mission, values, philosophy, code of ethics, definition of CSR), as well as the ease of accessing the information
   (b) Identify what types of messages are disseminated regarding CSR and to whom, for example, types of programs and areas covered (community, environment, employees, society in general), according to the headings indicated in the Mitofsky consulting firm's evaluation; the ease of accessing information; and the capacity to receive feedback
3. Analyze overall and by sector or industry (higher education, beverage, food product, and construction industries) drawing similarities between the pages vis-à-vis CSR

It is important to clarify that external elements or elements of form were considered so as to explore how these organizations communicate in a medium such as the Internet. In particular, and as a second research goal, I was interested in learning about the *usability* (or ease of navigating pages) and other aspects relative to the attractiveness of the pages (iconicity, homogeneity, multimedia resources, surroundings, etc.), as well as the accessibility of the companies with the best reputation in communicating and receiving feedback from their different publics and from press rooms. In addition, by reviewing these external aspects, it is possible to determine whether the information is easy to locate, whether everyone has access, and how transparent or ambiguous a company is in publicizing social responsibility.

Other questions that came up at the time of research were as follows: What is CSR in Mexico like, based on company websites? What do the companies say about themselves regarding CSR? To whom are the messages targeted? What areas are those most attended? How does culture influence practices and communication? What does CSR mean for these companies?

FINDINGS

General Results

With regard to external aspects or form, the research showed that, on all pages, there is a friendly environment as well as contact with the public, at least by e-mail, but only five (45%) included press rooms with additional information. In technical-aesthetic aspects (iconicity and homogeneity on the screen, aesthetic milieu, and link management), seven of the companies (63.6%) were good, while the pages of the rest rated between normal and poor. I also observed that seven organizations (63%) constantly update their information, while the others do not.

With regard to the content analysis for exploring messages on CSR, I found that 10 of the 11 (90%) companies did make statements or indirect mention of the topic. That is to say, responsibility in some way appears in their mission, vision, or value statement, but only six (54%) directly mentioned social responsibility, and of those, four (34%) provided a definition of the concept. Only one (9%) did so expressly. The same four had a special section on their webpage regarding this point. On the other hand, in other statements, three companies have a code of ethics guiding their actions, although only two (18%) made it available on the Internet.

Insofar as the ease of accessing information on CSR is concerned, seven (63.6%) companies turned out to be easily accessible. Of these, four (36%) had specific programs with clearly identified areas dedicated to the public. In contrast, on the other organizations' pages, information was scattered, semihidden, or so hard to find that only experts would know it dealt with CSR programs. All programs on responsibility could be grouped into areas. Table 9.1 shows the types of programs or target groups, the number of companies having those programs, and the percentage of the total number of companies analyzed that this represented. It is important to point out that, within the community programs, there were matters of public health and poverty, just to mention the most important.

Analysis by Sector or Industry

Higher Education

Four private universities were in the sample. Of them, two made the information quite accessible and had CSR programs for the community clearly identifiable on their webpages. The other two also had such programs, but they were encompassed in other programs. So they had to be inferred because they were not reflected in the Internet communication.

Beverages

Three companies belong to this group. Two are the FEMSA companies and the other is a brewery, Cervecería Cuauhtémoc-Moctezuma. FEMSA made quite a bit of information available, easily

accessible by the public (a special Internet section). In addition, their varied CSR programs covered five areas: community, ecology, employees, culture, and education. The other company, a major beer producer with products in 150 countries, stood out because of its meager information in that area and because its page had one of the poorest designs, with little information.

Food Products

Two companies were in this group. One was recognized in the *IMRE* study (Índice Mexicano de Reputación Empresarial, 2004) as having the best reputation, although its webpage was rated poor in design but outstanding because of the copious CSR information targeting all of its publics. In fact, it was the only company to define the concept of CSR, to have a code of ethics, and to have programs in five specific areas: community, ecology, health/nutrition, sustainability, and education. In contrast, the other company, despite being a worldwide brand (Nestlé), had a Mexican webpage with little information, seemingly there only to prove that they had an Internet page. Its design, quality, and amount of information, as well as no reference to CSR, did not do justice to the company's size or reputation.

Construction

Two companies were included in this group. Both companies had good site design, ease of accessing information, and varied and abundant CSR programs. From the page design and content, both showed a careful, well-planned strategy of communicating by Internet. One of them was the only company in the study to include information on sustainability, exactly as is stipulated by international norms (reporting according to the Global Reporting Iniciative [GRI] format; see http://www.globalreporting.org/ReportingFramework/G3Online/).

DISCUSSION OF FINDINGS

CSR Practices and Motivation in Mexico

In this section, I deal only with for-profit companies (the four universities excluded), since, due to their nature, universities are under greater pressure

TABLE **9.1** CSR-targeted programs

Program target	Companies with these programs	
	Number	%
Community in general (three companies had specific programs for combating poverty)	11	100%
Ecology and the environment	7	63%
Education	7	63%
Promoting art and culture	2	18%
Employees	2	18%
Sports	1	9%

to be socially responsible. Of the seven companies in this study group, five are multinationals, but one of them is not a Mexican company (Nestlé). The other one (Grupo Modelo), although it not multinational, has products in 150 countries around the world. That is, most of the companies most admired are huge organizations in the big leagues of the world marketplace. Another characteristic distinguishing them is that they have been established for some time: FEMSA Cerveza was founded in 1891, CEMEX in 1906, Vitro in 1909, and Grupo Modelo in 1925; Nestlé was established in México in 1930, and the most recent, Grupo Bimbo, came about in 1945. They have therefore witnessed and participated in Mexico's development and are aware of its needs and its shortcomings, and all have programs protecting the environment, as well as local and regional community development in the regions where they operate. However, do their actions respond to a strategy, to their identity, or to their owners' decisions?

From the type of social programs developed by these companies, I found that, in the majority of actions, there is a combination of CSR practices with charity work and donations, as in the cases of Bimbo and Nestlé, for example. The former recognizes this fact: "[F]or 40 years now, we have been supporting schools because the owners saw the need and decided to help," and "they are commitments one already has, to which a percentage of last year's sales are earmarked" (M. Hernández, Bimbo Institutional relations, personal interview, December 2004). Nestlé publishes the fact it donates foodstuffs to 49 food banks.

The donations to food banks is due, possibly, to the fact they are companies specializing in food products, although Grupo Modelo tends toward all types of donations. In turn, Vitro and FEMSA have, since their origins, shown a clear concern for protecting their employees, helping them acquire housing, medical attention, and education. "FEMSA was one of the first responsible companies in Mexico because, for 100 years now, it has been doing this" (L. Solano, public relations director, personal interview, November 2004). Similarly, Vitro was born with a clear social vocation from the very beginning because it always looked to protect its employees. Apparently, the founders of these companies, in addition to family ties, shared this same community of principles prevailing in the other companies, such as Catholicism and a tendency toward charity.

To be sure, there is less charity now, but donations continue on by the decision, preference, or wishes of the founding entrepreneurs and do not follow a plan or strategic program. Analysis clearly shows that, among the motives for CSR, is the combining of altruistic reasons with strategic philanthropy. On the one hand, there are companies whose social action is a clear reflection of their identity. One could posit that they are not reactive in light of global pressure. But there are others in which CSR does constitute a strategic resource used to increase the company's economic benefit, provide legitimacy, and boost their image. This occurs with CEMEX, which developed carefully designed programs in tune with their line of business (cement).

Husted (2000) calls this *philanthropy of safe issues*, because companies obtain clear benefits from supporting popular and politically correct causes, such as children, education, and the marginalized. One representative example is that of programs for the Tarahumara or Mazahua Indians, sponsored by Bimbo. Many other companies see actions earmarked for these groups as a way of putting their social responsibility into practice. From an ethical point of view, the companies seem to exhibit a teleological, rather than a deontological, tendency.

It is also important to mention here what Sánchez (2000) said regarding the very paternalism of Mexican and Latin American business culture, because it may well explain the CSR model practiced in these companies and, generally speaking, in Mexico. The boss or owner decides to participate in social programs, without following a planned strategy. His sole main purpose is to help and protect his employees, ensuring their loyalty, but also obtaining social recognition, power, and prestige.

Moreover, if the social actions of these companies are analyzed in the light of the types of relationships between company and society (Roitter, 1996), one can clearly see that all organizations have programs corresponding to *compensatory actions* (environment and community) by which they neutralize the effects their activities have on the environment (clear examples are Bimbo's reforestation and water care programs and CEMEX's support of environmental programs). They also have compensatory action programs in synch with their own training needs and some that Roitter would term *social-investment programs*, in which company and society design and start up a joint project, as is the case of certain CEMEX programs or the designated-driver program by FEMSA (brewery). The latter seeks to have every group that will be drinking to identify a driver who will refrain from drinking. That person is identified by a bracelet, is provided with nonalcoholic drinks for free in bars in exchange for staying sober all night, and then takes home each of his or her friends who drank.

Finally, among the cases analyzed, there is a whole heterogeneous range of practices and programs whose coverage, scope, or goals are unknown. Therefore, it is possible to think that a few social actions are the result of a careful CSR strategy because among the underlying motivations are mixed reasons for being socially responsible, although those of a personal or altruistic nature prevail. Another outstanding characteristic is that not all the areas or dimensions of responsibility mentioned by CEMEFI are covered, even though the main ones are: environment and community.

On Communication, Internet, and Stakeholders

How do these companies handle communications on the Internet? I explained above that, of the sites analyzed, few show a careful strategy of design and technology. Companies do use the medium but do not take advantage of its interactivity and bidirectionality. So, with the exception of CEMEX and, to a lesser degree, FEMSA, little attention is given to the communication needs of the various stakeholders. The information does indeed exist, but not the connectivity. There is a linear, asymmetrical model of unidirectional communication (Grunig & Hunt, 2003), in which the organization has control of the channel and, of course, the content, showing it only in a positive light. For that reason, Cox and Duprext (n.d.) have pointed out that, to be credible, balance is necessary.

The accessibility of the information varies between excellent and deficient, as in the case of Grupo Modelo, for example. Only one company, CEMEX, offers a detailed report of its activities, exactly as set forth in worldwide GRI standards. However, the company posts this report because, in addition to showing its transparency, it also looks good. This gives it more visibility and recognition before investors and before the rest of its interest groups around the world (CEMEX is worldwide).

With regard to the visibility of social programs in the results, I found that investors and stockholders seem to be the main group targeted, since, among the companies presenting accessible information, most of it is found in the section dedicated to this group. But, why do other companies post so little information? Bimbo follows the philosophy of "the right hand doesn't know what the left hand is doing," and they clearly present a low communicative profile. Leaving aside positions with religious nuances, it seems to be a communicative trend in many Mexican companies. Possibly, culture influences the decision "not to make too much noise" and seek modesty, so as not to call attention to oneself. But such behavior is not very effective in terms of corporate communication because today a company that stays silent, far from reducing the possibility of being the target of controversy, becomes a vulnerable organization. The absence of communication is not "no communication" but, rather, negative communication. In addition, all information vacuums will be filled somehow by different stakeholders. On the other hand, if the so-called responsible actions are not measured and controlled, their effectiveness will not be known. This seems to be the trend in Mexico.

It is certainly not easy to communicate all your activities without running the risk of seeming overbearing. But communicating social commitments and actions tends to lend them more respect, thereby committing companies all the more. Moreover, by bringing together the information in social reports, information on activities is disseminated internally and departments not involved directly with them learn about CSR, and this leads to integration. It would appear, however, that this is not valued highly in Mexico.

Moreover, employees are a major means of communication in companies. Likewise, there is the quality of the products manufactured and other behaviors the community considers in judging. That is why companies are recognized with awards for social responsibility and for having a good reputation. Now, of the top 10 (11) companies analyzed , five have won recognition as Socially Responsible Companies. One may think that the desire for a good reputation can be a factor contributing to making social actions known.

The preceding also seems to apply in the case of codes of ethics. These are publicized because of external pressure and because of the need to have a code in order to be listed on the stock exchange, thereby attracting investment. Such is the case of FEMSA, which did not have a document of this type until 2003. They stated that it was not necessary because they had other instruments defining conduct (see Pérez, 2005). But, suddenly toward the middle of 2004, they put it on the Internet. CEMEX is another example. They did have a code in 2003 but said it was private, unavailable even to researchers that year. In contrast, codes of ethics are now public documents because the stock exchange requires it. Just like social reports, it leads to a good reputation among stakeholders.

In summary, one could say that, without a doubt, a good part of a company's reputation depends on communicating its socially responsible actions and programs. At the same time, these factors are intimately tied to the culture, as has been shown in this research. Mexico, like other countries around the world, has its own voice for speaking about CSR, and this voice, although incipient here, is always contextual. If it were not, it would cease to be social responsibility (J. Lozano, 2006).

CONCLUSIONS

In light of this research, I can affirm that CSR in Mexico is still quite a new topic, with many challenges yet to be faced. Although socially responsible actions are not new, and the tradition of solidarity and help in Mexico is well established, CSR still does not appear as strong in Mexico as in other countries. Nor does there appear to be conceptual agreement on what is understood by CSR or how to differentiate it from philanthropy. All this, together with a dearth of research, makes social responsibility an emerging issue.

As I showed in this chapter, a distinctive feature of Mexican companies is that, generally speaking, most responsible actions are cases of assistance or philanthropy, with reactive programs abounding. In contrast, there are very few companies with a true CSR strategy. The well-known paternalism, characteristic of Mexican business culture as well as that of other Latin American cultures, together with religiosity, seems to be the underlying root motivating charity and social assistance, the most common forms of aid. These models appear to be shifting toward other forms of social action better reflecting the interaction

between company and society. But the process is barely starting, and there is still quite a bit of ground to be covered to go from traditional responsibility (CSR1) to the implications of responsiveness (CSR2).

Another fundamental aspect has to do with the importance of stakeholders and the need to establish and improve relationships with them so as to build permanent ties that seek the common good beyond the goals of marketing or company reputation. From this research, it is evident that many of these stakeholder groups remain unattended. Feedback from and information on webpages are insufficient. There is a need for a good ethical underpinning, missing in the great majority of organizations in Mexico.

On the other hand, as the pivotal point of CSR, communication appears to be a challenge in and of itself. It is no longer enough to be socially active. Now, one has to know how to report these actions because, as shown in this analysis, this is not done adequately in the majority of the companies studied. To date, only two organizations in Mexico publicize their environmental and social responsibility reports as set forth by the GRI (one of them is CEMEX). The rest barely report or prefer silence so as not to draw attention to themselves, because of false modesty or because they consider helping a duty about which no one should boast.

Of the cases studied, although they all allude directly or indirectly to CSR, only half publicize some of their programs or actions. Only four companies (approximately 40% of the sample) discuss them in clearly differentiated sections of their own webpage. This can be interpreted in several ways: (1) there is no communication strategy for this, (2) it is not communicated on the Internet, or (3) CSR is not yet on company agendas as a strategic and priority issue.

Therefore, CSR likewise implies not only doing good, but also learning to communicate that fact. Care must be taken that it does not become a resource for looking good or selling more. In that case, as Roberts (2003) observes, these would be merely cosmetic actions. What is communicated will be an expression of corporate egotism, in which the company demands to be seen not only as powerful but also as good. In this case, the concern is not for others, but for how others see the organization ("the ethics of narcissus"; see Roberts, 2003).

Another conclusion drawn from the study is that the symmetric bidirectional model proposed by public relations theorists is a design for the new era of social responsibility, requiring the constructing of alliances and meanings. Dialogue with the surroundings appears to be an unavoidable condition for action, encouraging initiatives and generating more projects for actors to participate in. However, in all the cases analyzed, an asymmetrical unidirectional model predominates in which no option for dialogue appears to exist. This does not mean it does not exist, just that it is not reflected in the medium analyzed in this research.

One more aspect deriving from the analysis has to do with the Internet's role as a medium for involving all parties interested in the topic of CSR. Based on the formal webpage elements (design, navigation, windows, homogeneity, etc.), as well as access to the amount and quality of information, only 7 of the 11 (10) companies analyzed provided transparent, accessible, and sufficient information. Four barely qualified, and one was quite bad. This leads one to think about the lack of attention given to a resource such as the Internet, which still does not seem to be a space for relationships between organizations and their publics.

In summary, CSR entails a great many implications for communication. I have been able to show that it is necessary to (1) exclude the dilemma of communicating or not, because it is no longer optional—communicating is part of social responsibility and should begin from within the organization; (2) encourage an ethical focus for communication; (3) know how to inform and communicate; (4) seek transparency; (5) promote dialogue for two-way communication; and (6) develop social reporting. In order to be effective, one has to work a great deal to create a communication strategy integrating social concerns with reputation, while seeking a balance between the two, so that spending on communication is no greater than that of the actions themselves.

Moreover, national culture *does* count. After reviewing the literature and the analysis, I can say that CSR is seemingly affected by national and even regional differences. Both local practices and the characteristics of corporate identities (whether they be multinational, traded on the market or not, etc.) have an impact on responsible actions. This variable, as well as the aforementioned regarding communication, opens up new research possibilities on the topic of concern in this study.

Finally, I should underscore the fact that, although the sample analyzed is not representative, in an exploratory study such as this one, based on the companies with the best reputations in the country, the data do allow us to discover ways of studying how it came into existence and how the topic of social responsibility is treated in Mexico. This research is but a small sample of what some big Mexican organizations say about themselves. It is clear that the road ahead is a long one for Mexico. The challenges are enormous and varied, and the needs great, but CSR is an unavoidable imperative encompassing us all.

APPENDIX: COMPANIES WITH THE BEST REPUTATION IN MEXICO IN 2004

Below, I offer some basic information on the companies analyzed. The order follows their ranking. (see http://www.consulta.com.mx/interiores/15_otros_estudios/oe_indicemex0304.html).

Grupo Bimbo

Founded in 1945 in Mexico, today Grupo Bimbo is one of the most important commercial bakery operations in the world because of the positioning of its trademark, production, and sales volume, in addition to being the undisputable leader in its field in Mexico and Latin America. With a presence in 14 countries of the Americas and Europe, it manufactures, distributes, and markets more than 4,500 products and more than 100 well-known brand names. Since 1980, Grupo Bimbo is a public entity listed on the Mexican Stock Exchange. It is made up of six organizations and a holding company, operating companies in the commercial baking and foodstuffs industry in general. Today, the group has 71 plants located in Mexico, the United States, Central and South America, and Europe. It has a fleet of 26,000 units, bringing its products to 1,325,250 points of sale around the world. Its website is located at http://www.grupobimbo.com/.

ITESM

The Instituto Tecnológico y de Estudios Superiores de Monterrey was founded in 1943 by a group of Monterrey businessmen headed by Eugenio Garza Sada. It has a presence throughout Mexico, Latin America, and the world through its Virtual University. At present, it has 33 campuses and offices in Mexico and Latin America. It has academic exchange programs with more than 300 universities in Mexico and abroad. It also has several liaison offices throughout the world that promote the Institute. Its website is located at http://www.itesm.mx.

CEMEX

Cementos Mexicanos, S.A. was founded in 1906. It is the third largest cement company in the world in terms of installed capacity, which at the end of 2003 was approximately 81.5 million tons. In addition, it is one of the largest commercializers of cement and clinker, having sold more than 9 million tons in 2003. As a holding company and through its operational subsidiaries, it deals primarily in the production, distribution, marketing, and sale of cement, ready-mixed concrete, and clinker. It has operations in North, Central, and South America, Europe, the Caribbean, Asia, and Africa, with cement production plants located in Mexico, Spain, Venezuela, Colombia, the United States, Egypt, Philippines, Thailand, Costa Rica, the Dominican Republic, Panama, Nicaragua, and Puerto Rico. At the close of 2003, its worldwide assets totaled approximately $US 16 billion. As of April 30, 2004, its market capitalization was approximately $9.5 billion dollars. Its website is located at http://www.cemex.com/.

Nestlé

Nestlé was founded in 1867 and came to Mexico in 1930. It is the world leader in foodstuffs. It currently has a presence on all continents, with more than 8,500 products, made in 500 factories, located in more than 70 countries, and with more than 225,000 collaborators throughout the world. In Mexico, the Nestlé Group has undergone constant growth, currently with 15 manufacturing centers distributed through 12 states. It provides unique opportunities for development, generating some 7,000 jobs. The website for the Nestlé Group in Mexico is located at http://www.nestle.com.mx/.

Universidad Iberoamericana

The Universidad Iberoamericana follows the educational curriculum of the Company of Jesus, and its mission is to make a firm contribution, in an atmosphere of responsible participation, openness, freedom, respect, and positive criticism. For more than 60 years, the Universidad Iberoamericana has been not only a witness but also an active agent in the Mexico's development. At present, it offers 37 bachelor and 29 graduate programs, designed from the standpoint of a departmental system and under the criterion of curricular flexibility. Its website is located at http://www.uia.mx/.

Grupo Modelo

Founded in 1925, Grupo Modelo is a leader in the manufacturing, distribution, and sale of beer in Mexico. Its domestic and export market share is 62.70% as of December 31, 2002. It has seven breweries in Mexico, with an installed capacity of 46 million hectoliters of beer a year. At present, it has 10 brands, featuring Corona Extra, "the best sold Mexican beer in the world," as well as Modelo Especial, Victoria, Pacífico, Negra Modelo, and others of a regional character. Its website is located at http://www.gmodelo.com.mx/.

ITAM

The Instituto Tecnológico Autónomo de México, formerly the Instituto Tecnológico de México, was founded on March 29, 1946, by the Asociación Mexicana de Cultura. The latter brought together a distinguished group of bankers, industrialists, and merchants, headed by Raúl Baillères, for the purpose of making higher education the engine of the industrial and economic change of Mexico. Its website is located at http://www.itam.mx.

Universidad de las Américas–Puebla

The Universidad de las Américas was founded in Mexico City in 1940, under the name of Mexico City College, a 2-year community college, by Henry L. Cain, the superintendent of the American School Foundation at that time. In 1968, it changed its name to Universidad de las Américas, A.C., and its studies were recognized by educational authorities of the State of Puebla. It grants bachelor and master's degrees, as well as two doctorates. Its website is located at http://www.udlap.mx/.

Vitro

Vitro, S.A. de C.V., through its subsidiary companies, is a major participant in three different lines of business: plate glass, glass containers, and glass kitchen articles. Vitro companies produce articles for multiple markets: automotive and building glass; glass containers for wine, liquor, cosmetics, pharmaceutical, and food and beverages; aluminum containers; and glass articles for the kitchen, industrial, commercial, and end-consumer use. Based in Monterrey and founded in 1909, Vitro has investments with large-scale, world-class producers, providing its subsidiary companies with access to international markets, worldwide distribution channels, and leading-edge technology. Vitro subsidiaries do business throughout the North and South American continents, with installations and distribution centers in nine countries, exporting its products to more than 70 countries around the world. Its website is located at http://www.vitro.com.

FEMSA Cerveza and Coca-Cola FEMSA

FEMSA is the largest beverage company in Mexico and Latin America, exporting to the United States, Canada, and selected countries of Latin America, Europe, and Asia. Begun in 1890 with the founding of the brewery Cervecería Cuauhtémoc, and headquartered in Monterrey, FEMSA operates through the following subsidiaries: FEMSA Cerveza produces and distributes well-known brands of beer such as Tecate, Tecate Light, Carta Blanca, Superior, Sol, Dos Equis Lager, Dos Equis Ambar, Indio, Bohemia, and Noche Buena. Coca-Cola FEMSA is the leading bottler of Coca-Cola products in Latin American and the second largest bottler in the worldwide Coca-Cola system, serving Mexico City and its metropolitan area, southeastern Mexico (the states of Michoacán, Guanajuato, Puebla, Tlaxcala, Tabasco, Chiapas, Oaxaca, and most of Veracruz) and Guatemala, Costa Rica, Nicaragua, Venezuela, Panama, Colombia, Brazil, and Argentina. The company operates a dozen bottling plants in Mexico, four in Central America, six in Colombia, four in Venezuela, three in Brazil, and one in Argentina. Its website is located at: http://www.femsa.com.

NOTES

I am grateful to George Cheney for his support and guidance.

1. For their research, the consulting firm Mitofsky studied 108 companies selected according to the following criteria: (a) sales among the country's top 500, and (b) belonging to one of the 12 areas proposed in the research design: (1) food products and nonalcoholic beverages, (2) higher education, (3) automobiles, (4) pharmaceutical industry, (5) alcohol and tobacco, (6) self-service and department stores, (7) public works and construction, (8) financial services (9) informatics and telecommunications, (10) mass media, (11) tourism and transportation, and (12) the energy sector (see http://www.consulta.com.mx/interiores/15_otros_estudios/oe_indicemex0304.html).

REFERENCES

Agüero, F. (2002). *La responsabilidad social empresarial en América Latina: Argentina, Brasil, Chile, Colombia, México y Perú.* Unpublished manuscript, School of Intenational Studies, University of Miami Grupo RSE-CHILE.

Augustine, I. (2001). Communication style in the information age. *Corporate Communication,* 6(4), 199–204. Retrieved September 19, 2005, from the ABI/INFORM Global Database (Document ID: 149006581).

Andriof, J., & Waddock, S. (2002). Unfolding stakeholder engagement. In J. Andriof, S. Waddock, B. Husted, & S. Sutherland (Eds.), *Unfolding stakeholder thinking.* London: Greenleaf.

Cerutti, M. (2000). *Propietarios, empresarios y empresas en el norte de México: Monterrey, de 1848 a la globalización.* México City: Siglo XXI.

Cheney, G., & Christensen, L. T. (2001). Organizational identity: Linkages between internal and external communication. In F. M. Jablin & L. L. Putnam (Eds.), *The new handbook of organizational communication* (pp. 231–269). Thousand Oaks, CA: Sage.

Cox, S., & Duprext, X. (n.d.). *La responsabilidad social corporativa como aporte a la ética y probidad públicas.* Retrieved June 24, 2004, from http://www.geocities.com/transparenciachile/estudio_sobre_la_responsabilidad.htm.

De la Cerda, J., & Núñez, F. (1993). *La administración en desarrollo: Problemas y avances de la administración en México.*

México City: Instituto Internacional de Capacitación y Estudios Empresariales.

Esrock, S. L., & Leichty, G. B. (1998). Social responsibility and corporate web pages: Self presentation or agenda setting. *Public Relation Review, 24*(3), 305–319.

Frankental, P. (2001). Corporate social responsibility—a PR invention? *Corporate Communications, 6*(1), 18–23.

Grunig, J., & Hunt, T. (2003). *Dirección de relaciones públicas.* Barcelona: Gestión 2000.

Hofstede, G. (1991). *Cultures and organizations: Software of the mind.* London: McGraw-Hill.

Hooghiemstra, R. (2000, September). Corporate communication and impression management—new perspectives: Why companies engage in corporate social reporting. *Journal of Business Ethics, 27*(1/2). 55–68. Retrieved September 19, 2005, from ABI/INFORM Global database.

Husted, B. (2000, September). Is it ethical to use ethics as strategy? *Journal of Business Ethics, 1*(2), 21–31.

Husted, B., & Salazar, J. (2005, January-April). Un estudio exploratorio sobre la estrategia social de empresas grandes ubicadas en México. *Contaduría y Administración UNAM, 215,* 9–23.

Indice Mexicano de Reputación Empresarial. (2004). Retrieved April 29, 2004.

Juholin, E. (2003). *Born again. A Finnish approach to corporate social responsibility.* Jyväskylä: University of Jyväskylä.

L'Etang, J. (1994). Public relations and corporate social responsibility: Some issues arising. *Journal of Business Ethics, 13*(2), 111–123.

Lozano, G. (2003). *México: El sentido de negocio de las alianzas intersectoriales.* Monterrey, Mexico: SEKN.

Lozano, J. (2006). *El contexto, siempre el contexto.* Retrieved March 6, 2006, from http://www.iarse.org/site/modules.php?name=Sections&op=viewarticle&artid=10.

Maignan, I., & Ralston, D. (2002). Corporate social responsibility in Europe and the US: Insights from businesses' self presentation. *Journal of International Business Studies, 33*(3), 497–514. Retrieved September 19, 2005, from ABI/INFORM Global Database (Doc. ID: 195566361).

Marques, P. (2004). *Análisis de web docentes.* Retrieved May 28, 2004, from http://dewey.uab.es/pmarques/webdocen.htm.

Martínez, S., & Dorfman, P. (1998). The Mexican entrepreneur: An ethnographic study of the Mexican empresario. *International Studies of Management and Organization, 2,* 97–124.

McMillan, J. (1986). In search of the organizational persona: A rationale for studying organizations rhetorically. In L. Thayer (Ed.), *Organization—communication: Emerging perspectives* (Vol. 2, pp. 21–45). Norwood, NJ: Ablex.

McMillan, S. (2000). The microscope and the moving target: The challenge of applying content analysis to world wide web. *Journalim & Mass Communication Quarterly, 77*(1), 80–98. Retrieved December 27, 2004, from ABI/INFORM Global database.

Milanés, S. (2003). *Valores éticos y pragmatismo del empresario mexicano.* Retrieved May 15, 2005, from http://www.usem.org.mx/archivos/contenido/articulointeres/valores_eticos_del_empresario_mexicano.pdf.

Nicholls, C., Lane, H., & Brehm, M. (1999). Taking self-managed teams to Mexico. *Academy of Management Executive, 13*(3), 15–25.

Perdiguero, T. (2003). *La responsabilidad social de las empresas en un mundo global.* Madrid: Anagrama.

Pérez, M. (2005). Ética y comunicación interna en las organizaciones: Estudio exploratorio en dos multinacionales de origen mexicano. In A. Castillo (Ed), *Comunicación organizacional. Teorías y estudios.* Málaga, Spain: Clave Aynadamar.

Roberts, J. (2003, May). The manufacture of corporate social responsibility: Constructing corporate sensibility. *Interdisciplinary Journal of Organization, Theory & Society, 10*(2), 249–265.

Roitter, M. (1996). *La razón social de las empresas. Una vinculación entre los vínculos entre empresa y sociedad en Argentina.* Argentina: Centro de Estudios de Estado y Sociedad.

Sanborn, C. (2004). *La filantropía "realmente existente" en América Latina.* Bogotá, Colombia: Departamento de Ciencias Sociales y Políticas, Centro de Investigación de la Universidad del Pacífico.

Sánchez, M. C. (2000). Motives for corporate philanthropy in El Salvador: Altruism and political legitimacy. *Journal for Business Ethics, 2*(4), 363–376.

Schvarstein, L. (2003). *La inteligencia social de las organizaciones.* México City: Paidós.

Snaider, J., Hill, R., & Martin, D. (2003). Corporate social responsibility in the 21st century: A view from the world's most successful firms. *Journal of Business Ethics, 48*(2), 175–187.

Stroh, U., & Jaatinen, M. (2001). New approaches to communication management for transformation and change in organizations. *Journal of Communication Management, 6*(2), 148–165.

Tixier, M. (2003). Note: Soft vs. hard approach in communicating on corporate social responsibility. *Thunderbird International Business Review, 45*(1), 71–91.

Transparencia Mexicana y Consulta Mitofsky. (2004).

Verduzco, G. (2003). *Organizaciones no lucrativas: Visión de su trayectoria en México.*México City: El Colegio de México and CEMEFI.

Villafañe, J. (2004). *La buena reputación: Claves del valor intangible de las empresas.* Madrid: Pirámide.

Wymer, W., & Samu, S. (2003). Dimensions of business and nonprofit collaborative relationships. *Journal of Nonprofit & Public Sector Marketing, 11*(1), 1–22.

III

LEGAL PERSPECTIVES

10

Legal Versus Ethical Arguments

Contexts for Corporate Social Responsibility

MATTHEW W. SEEGER
STEVEN J. HIPFEL

On December 3, 1984, the Union Carbide plant in Bhopal, India, experienced a major crisis, resulting in the leak of 45 tons of methylisocyanate, a toxic chemical used to produce insecticide. As many as 10,000 people died from the disaster with many thousands more suffering long-term physical damage, including blindness, respiratory problems, birth defects, and neurological problems. Union Carbide's initial response was to deny responsibility for the accident. The company did make emergency relief payments and later settled all civil liability for the accident with $470 million. Claiming it had met its legal obligations, Union Carbide began to extricate itself from India. Responsibility for the plant site and for victims was eventually turned over to the Indian government. The company did fund a relief trust and built a clinic to help treat victims, but the legacy of long-term disability, contaminated water, and lingering health effects has remained unresolved.

The Union Carbide Bhopal accident, as well as a number of other both dramatic and mundane examples, illustrates the debate over corporate social responsibility (CSR). Companies such as Exxon Mobil, Wal-Mart, Enron, Merck Pharmaceuticals, Microsoft, American International Group, Royal Dutch Shell, and many others have been accused of hiding behind minimal legal requirements and avoiding larger social responsibilities. This debate has been framed by a variety of competing positions, including practical versus desirable goals, minimal acceptable versus optimal required actions, and ethical versus legal behaviors. This last tension often frames much of the larger debate over CSR because legal restrictions usually carry the most direct consequences for organizations. The law, although bearing some general relationship to larger ethical principles, is comparatively narrow in its dictates and does not account for a broad range of ethical positions or moral obligations. In addition, important arguments have developed around the competing legal versus moral obligations that organizations have to various stakeholders and the ways in which these obligations can be balanced and met. The larger debate over corporate responsibility may also become mired in discussions of specific legalistic requirements or narrow competing values, which avoids larger moral questions and issues.

Here we focus specifically on four forms of CSR that include both legal and ethical dimensions: product responsibility, worker rights, environment responsibility, and communication responsibilities (Metzler, 1996; Seeger, 1997; Werhane, 1985). We first examine the concepts of CSR and responsiveness and then explore the general strictures and obligations posed by legal versus ethical codes. We also explore three views of the relationship between ethics and the law: (1) legal positivism (separate realms model), (2) natural law theory (correspondence model), and (3) the social responsibility model.

Our purpose is not only to compare and contrast the obligations for social responsibility that accrue from legal codes and more general ethical traditions, but also to examine ways in which they function in larger discussions regarding what is a responsible corporation. Legal obligations, although often the minimal moral standards, sometimes become positioned as the organization's *maximum* obligation. In addition, the law and, in particular, fiduciary obligations to shareholders sometimes actually impede the ability of the corporation to act in an ethically appropriate way. We suggest that detailed legal strictures regarding responsibilities, while sometimes desirable, may ultimately limit the corporation's flexibility and ability to be responsive to the dynamic and competing values of stakeholders. A social responsibility model of the law and an organizational responsiveness approach, therefore, are the most appropriate to facilitating CSR.

CORPORATE SOCIAL RESPONSIBILITY

The concept of CSR has been a formal topic in organizational studies since at least the 1930s and can probably be traced back much further to the dawn of the Industrial Revolution (Buchholz, 1990). Even during the most egregious periods of the robber barons and monopolistic corporate exploitations of workers, markets, and the environment in the later nineteenth century, some attention was given to larger social values and needs. Henry Ford, for example, created a sociology department during the early days of the Ford Motor Company. Although paternalistic in its imposition of Ford's own middle class values, it did help educate workers and assist in their physical and social welfare. In many ways, Henry Ford's approach was characteristic of these early efforts at corporate responsibility. Most often, these efforts reflected the owner's personal value system and frequently were associated with religion. Many corporations simply imposed these values on workers and the community through capital's economic leverage.

Because employment is fundamentally a matter of contract law, there were few employer obligations or employee rights in law beyond those mutually agreed to by the parties. For example, absent employer benevolence, there was *no* protection for workers injured or killed on the job prior to state workers compensation statutes, unless they could prove their loss was attributable to employer negligence under tort law. Environmental exploitation and pollution were essentially unregulated.[1] The excesses of corporations in these and other arenas contributed significantly to government intervention to protect public health and safety, preserve national resources, and avoid the potential social upheaval from labor unrest. As concepts of CSR evolved, corporate efforts to address social problems became more formalized and organized, eventually leading to the community-based philanthropic organization known initially as the Community Chest. The Community Chest, and its later version, the United Way, was grounded in a general recognition that organizations had an obligation to help offset some of the harms they created. In addition, these structures made corporate philanthropic activities easier, more systematic, and less risky (Heald, 1970).

Two important arguments have developed around these philanthropic activities (Madsen & Shafritz, 1990). First, some critics suggest that profit-making organizations have no legitimate interest in philanthropy. Solving social problems is the domain of government and social welfare organizations in the third sector, and profit-making organizations are distracted from their principle obligation when they seek to right social problems. Moreover, private organizations simply do not have the resources to solve social problems. A second argument is that corporate philanthropy, in forms like the United Way community-based efforts, seeks to support a very narrow set of social needs and values. Largely, these needs and values are ones that ultimately benefit the corporations offering the support. Other needs, issues, and values go largely unaddressed. Organizations, for example, may fund community beautification projects that are visible and affect the overall attractiveness of a corporation's location, while ignoring unseen issues of water and air pollution that have much wider and potentially long-term impact. Many substantive issues, therefore, are disregarded while corporations promote those values that are in their own best interest.

These arguments have led to a reconceptualization of the concept of CSR. In its traditional manifestation, corporate responsibility means attending to a narrow set of social values and issues, usually through limited philanthropic activities (see Buchholz, 1990). An alternative perspective, called corporate social *responsiveness*, argues that organizations should be more flexible and open in accommodating an evolving and dynamic set of social values and needs (Buono & Nichols, 1995; Sethi, 1987). Corporate social responsiveness emphasizes organizational processes and structures that react to the social needs and values of a wide range of individuals and groups who have an interest in the organization. As such, responsiveness is consistent with both the two-way symmetrical views of corporate communication and the stakeholder model of organizational ethics (Deetz, 1992; Grunig, 2001). These views promote equitable relationships between organizations and stakeholders and encourage the representation of the needs, interests, and perspectives of stakeholders in organizational decisions. Responsiveness concerns the relative permeability of the organization's boundaries and its willingness and ability to anticipate and adjust to society's changing character, needs, and values (Sethi, 1987). In this way, responsive organizations are able to be more socially responsible by virtue of their willingness to hear and respond to social needs, standards, and values. Some organizations, such as the heavy engine manufacturer Cummins Inc., have established long records of attending to social issues, whereas others, such as MacDonald's, have worked to be much more responsive to social issues and concerns, such as environmental issues and the ethical treatment of animals.

THE ROLE OF LAW

Philosophers and legal theorists have long debated the relationships among ethics, morality, and the law, while managers often struggle to find the pragmatic nexus between legal dictates and moral principles (Kratz, 1999; Siegel, 2001). The law, morality, and ethics initially appear to be the same or at least closely related concepts because all three embody codes of conduct. On closer review, however, they differ in significant ways. Morality, in general, is the larger framework of values and beliefs one lives by, while ethics are general provisions, norms, and standards for judging good versus bad, right versus wrong, and desirable versus undesirable. Thus, ethics are used to assess whether actions are moral. Both define what it means to be a good person (Hall, 2002). Law both

mandates and prohibits a range of conduct, but arguably these are minimal standards designed largely to maintain basic social order. Further, many laws are administrative in nature. Speed limits, for example, are not based in some general framework of morality but are necessary to maintain orderly travel. There is also a critical difference in how law, morality, and ethics constrain behavior. Morality and ethics generally lack the formal system of sanctions and penalties that governing institutions use to enforce legal conformity.

Conformity with a code of morality and ethics is dependent on individual conscience, social pressures, and public standards, or fear of God. Accordingly, most people refrain from killing their neighbor because they view such an act as morally repugnant and not necessarily because of any legal prohibition. Even when the law sanctions killing, such as defense of the state in times of war, the conscientious objector will refrain from such behavior because of a personal moral objection. In certain narrow circumstances, some have felt morally compelled to oppose and even violate such laws as the South's Jim Crow racial segregation statutes in the United States. In other instances, civil disobedience has led to incidental violations of the law. During the 1980s, protestors in the United Kingdom regularly trespassed on the Greenham Common military bases as part of a demonstration against the presence of morally objectionable nuclear weapons. This is not to suggest that the law is entirely unrelated to morality and ethics, especially in a theocracy.[2] Adultery, for example, was a crime throughout colonial America, especially where secular government overlapped religious institutions. While many U.S. citizens today consider adultery to be morally wrong, it is largely viewed as a personal matter, and only a few jurisdictions in the United States make it a crime.

While moral principles, ethical frameworks, and legal codes have their own unique traditions, domains, and forms, they clearly intersect at a variety of points. Several descriptions of the relationships among law, morality, and ethics have been offered. Three views have dominated the discussion: separate realms, correspondence, and responsibility.

The separate realms model originates in the legal positivism of legal philosophers such as H. L. A. Hart and John Austin (Edwards, 1967; Hall, 2002; Voakes, 2000). According to legal positivists, the law is a system of clearly defined rules established by a sovereign. The answer to the question of who is sovereign depends on who, in fact, is obeyed. Sovereignty is unrelated to legitimacy or right, which are moral issues. As a result, the law is a creature of politics and bears only a passing or casual relationship to morality and ethics. Ethics and law are, in essence, separate realms. Ethics and law also represent distinct but related realms of discourse, where different assumptions, arguments, and rules apply.

The second dominant description, natural law theory, has been characterized as a correspondence model (Edwards, 1967; Voakes, 2000). According to this view, the law should correspond with more general ethical and moral frameworks. For example, Thomas Aquinas, an early advocate of this description, argued that human conduct is regulated by a general moral order that is reflected in the law (Hall, 2002). The law exists in a relatively close, almost parallel relationship to ethics, in part because ethics and morality are the basis of the legal code. The legal positivist counters this assertion by arguing there is no way to objectively ascertain this moral order, as evidenced by the fact that reasonable minds can differ on what is moral conduct. Additionally, a separation between morality and the law is demonstrated by the fact not all conduct that is illegal, such as speeding, is immoral, and not all immoral conduct, such as failing to keep a promise of fidelity to one's spouse, is illegal.

A third description borrows elements from these two traditional schools of thought and has been characterized as the social responsibility model (Voakes, 2000). United States Supreme Court Associate Justice Oliver Wendell Holmes and other adherents of the American "legal realist" school reflect this hybrid view and part from the legal positivists (Hall, 1992, 2002). They note that if the law were merely a set of clearly defined rules, there would be no need for lawyers to argue issues in dispute or for judicial discretion in the application of the law. According to this view, the law is based on a current of underlying moral principles that dictate how it is applied and a collective willingness on the part of the citizenry to be bound by the law. Therefore, the decisions of juries and judges are affected by a host of factors, including social class, political ideology, and personal values, morals, and ethical perspectives. It is the moral or ethical code and the obligation to be responsible to that code that informs the dynamic interpretation and application of the law.

These views regarding the relationship between ethics and the law manifest in a wide variety of contexts and issues regarding CSR. This includes larger discussions and debates regarding what constitutes responsible corporate conduct. Here we describe four specific domains where the legal and ethical responsibilities of corporations are most strongly felt: product responsibility, worker rights, environmental responsibility, and communication responsibilities.

DOMAINS OF LEGAL AND SOCIAL RESPONSIBILITY

Product Responsibility

The most direct experience many stakeholders have with a company is through its products and services. The nature of an organization's products and services also determines much about the organization's technology, markets, overall business practices, and image. Companies, for example, often use products and services to provide a fundamental social justification for the organization and its activities. Pharmaceutical companies often describe their activities as finding cures for diseases and improving the quality of human life. Morality generally dictates that corporations produce goods and services that have some social value and be socially responsible. The law, however, requires only that corporations use reasonable care to protect consumers from identifiable and avoidable harm caused by the use of their products and services. It is morally objectionable to produce and encourage tobacco products that clearly harm consumer health, but it is not illegal. Further, while social pressure and consumer demand may ultimately result in a less harmful cigarette, the law does not mandate its development. This limited legal responsibility to use reasonable care is reflected in a complex, dynamic, and very old body of law known as tort law.

Although there is a legal obligation to use reasonable care when placing products and services in the stream of commerce, there is a tension between the ancient dictum of the marketplace, *caveat emptor* (buyer beware), and the social policy need to protect the innocent buyer. This is especially the case in a technologically complex society where full consumer knowledge about a product or service may be unrealistic. A company may know its product or service presents risks to the consumer, and it may be argued that failure to eliminate these risks or make full disclosure to the consumer is immoral. The availability of a legal remedy for the resulting harms is addressed by tort law and is contingent on whether the corporation acted negligently. Negligence occurs if the organization has breached its legal duty to use reasonable care. The tort law principle of strict liability has increasingly been applied in product liability cases where there is no corporate negligence but the product or service presents an inherent risk of significant harm. The theory is that the manufacturer or service provider is in the best position to protect the individual from economic loss caused by their product or service by purchasing insurance or spreading out the loss through higher prices. Accordingly, while negligence may implicate ethical issues because it involves the breach of a legal duty, strict liability does not because there is no wrongdoing.

Whether a company is negligent in producing a product or providing a service is a multipart test (Morris, 1953). First, there must be a general duty to act with reasonable care. The next test is whether there was a breach of this duty. If so, the final question is whether the breach of duty was the proximate cause of the injury. What constitutes reasonable care is a difficult question and is based on the "reasonable man" test, the way people should act when exercising due caution and responsibility. Associate Supreme Court Justice Holmes based liability on those harms "an ordinary person would have foreseen" (Hall, 1992, p. 407). The reasonable man, therefore, is not required to act perfectly and avoid all harm. What constitutes reasonable care in the commercial world is often defined by government regulation or generally accepted industry practices, both of which are subject to change in response to political or market pressures. Accordingly, although toys of early periods with jagged or sharp metal corners may have presented real risks and caused actual harm, they were not necessarily negligently designed, given the available materials and manufacturing processes and because they conformed with what was acceptable at the time. In theory, negligence principles are not intended to ensure a perfectly safe world, only the avoidance of foreseeable and avoidable harm.

The natural law theorist (correspondence model) would argue that there is a general moral obliga-tion to avoid putting others at risk, and this is reflected in negligence tort law. The legal positivist (separate realms model) would assert that market factors and not morality motivates the production of increasingly safe products and services, and the purpose of tort law is to compensate for economic loss associated with failing to meet minimal standards based on specific legal rules. But these rules are subject to subjective application based on a number of factors, sometimes rooted in the individual juror's or judge's sense of morality and fairness. The potential subjectivity of tort law application is further complicated by the principles of comparative and contributory negligence, which respectively reduce or negate a negligent party's legal responsibility based on the injured party's conduct. These principles apply when, for example, a product causes harm because it was used improperly or for an unintended purpose. Assigning such degrees of blame for a specific harm is an inherently subjective undertaking that is affected by personal biases and predisposition.

It is also worth noting that there is a growing call for tort reform because of concern that juries disregard the personal responsibility of the injured party in the apparent belief manufacturers should warn against all possible acts, and indemnify even those exercising the poorest personal judgment. Juries are sometimes seen as holding corporations responsible for any harm because of an increasing expectation of a risk-free society. Tort law also recognizes that a negligent party may escape liability if the injured party voluntarily uses a product with full knowledge of the risks. For this reason, a variety of businesses such as health clubs have clients sign releases from liability. Although cigarette manufactures have asserted this principle in cases were individuals choose to smoke despite knowledge of the health risks, this argument is receiving decreasing public support. In fact, some plaintiffs argue that gun and cigarette manufacturers should be held legally responsible for harm caused by their products based on a theory of generic liability (Hall, 2002). This view holds that these specific products are inherently defective even with warnings and in the absence of substitute products or alternative products designs. The application of these tort law principles illustrates that the law in these limited circumstances is increasingly being administered in a context of moral judgments in ways that support the responsibility model of law's relationship to morality and ethics. While it is legally acceptable to produce and market cigarettes, the shifting notion of social responsibility has eroded some of the protections cigarette manufacturers traditionally enjoyed in tort law. Thus, cigarette companies have faced new legal limitation on marketing and promotion, and some of their traditional legal defenses have eroded.

Strict product liability is a tort principle that illustrates that law can be founded in practical and economic terms as opposed to moral consideration because this form of liability applies in the absence of demonstrable wrongdoing. Strict liability can apply, for example, when a plaintiff's ability to prosecute his or her claim is hampered by the manufacturer's exclusive control of essential pertinent information, or because such information has been lost. The manufacturer should *not* benefit from such circumstances. Strict liability has been applied as a social policy tool to induce manufacturers to design a safer product when negligence liability alone has not resulted in product modification. The final purpose, and perhaps most illustrative, is to spread the cost of risk for certain ultrahazardous products and activities across a large economic base (Hall, 2002). This social policy reason for imposing strict liability might appear to violate a basic sense of fairness because the corporation is held liable in the absence of culpability or, at times, even an expectation their specific product or service might cause harm. The theory is that if the cost of insuring against injury is placed on the manufacturer, this cost with be factored into the price of a product or service and passed on to the customer. The pharmaceutical industry is a classic example of where this principle is applied. It is often impossible to ensure drug safety despite extensive testing and preliminary trials because side effects can take years to manifest themselves, or because of unique patient factors. At the same time, drug development and widespread use provide enormous social benefits and should be encouraged. The result of such strict liability is that each customer is effectively buying insurance against the possibility he or she will suffer a catastrophic injury because of the medication.

Worker Rights

As with producing and delivering socially responsible goods and services, a company's legal respon-

sibilities to its employees are not coextensive with any perceived or actual moral obligation. Like product liability, the legal obligation to employees is frequently founded in economic as opposed to moral considerations. Worker compensation and collective bargaining are two examples. The development of workers compensation at the beginning of the twentieth century largely replaced application of tort law in the work place (Hall, 2002). To qualify for workers compensation benefits, an employee needs only to establish a work-related injury and, unlike in tort law, does not have to establish employer fault. In this regard, worker compensation is a form of insurance. In most jurisdictions, employers pay into the program usually based on the number of their employees and number of claims they have filed. Compensation benefits are based on a schedule of injuries and lost wages. The employer benefits from not being subject to potentially large judgments because employees are precluded from suing under the program (Hall, 2002). The employee benefits from receiving benefits regardless of the cause of injury, albeit potentially less than what might be recovered if employer negligence could be established in a lawsuit. Few would argue that an employer has a moral obligation to support employees who cannot work because of injuries they sustain through their own negligence, but even these individuals are afforded protection.

Similarly, the right to unionize and engage in collective bargaining is rooted in economic considerations. United States law has long favored the principle of employment at will, under which both the employer and employee can terminate the employment relationship for good reasons, bad reasons, or no reason at all (Hall, 2002). The employee, however, is often at a disadvantage in negotiating the terms of employment. The ability of employees to bargain with their employer as a group and use their numbers to leverage concessions was often undermined by the legal doctrine of employment at will that allowed an employer to stop such efforts through wholesale or selective firings. The U.S. Congress recognized that this imbalance in negotiating power retarded economic development by keeping wages low and, consequently, the federal National Labor Relations Act (NLRA) of 1935 (2000) was enacted to protect employee rights to bargain collectively. Many viewed the NLRA as an unethical statute at the time of its passage because it constrained the right of contract and limited employer discretion. From a larger public policy perspective, however, it has had enormous social benefits by improving working conditions and wages.

The employment contracts negotiated under the NLRA and similar state statutes often enabled employees to secure benefits and favorable working conditions not mandated by law and have led to generally accepted employment standards and practices that extend to nonunionized companies. Such generally accepted practices include providing retirement packages, promotion opportunities based on objective standards, health benefits, termination notices and outplacement services, and child care, among many others. Adoption of such employment practices by nonunionized companies in large part results from a need to compete for labor with companies whose employees have secured such benefits through collective bargaining. With time, however, these benefits have become social expectations and the earmark of a responsible organization. In this way, the law regarding workers rights has evolved along the lines of a responsibility model in its relationship to larger understandings of morality and ethics.

Environmental Responsibility

There is a growing public consensus that both individuals and businesses have an ethical obligation to conserve and protect the environment as a common inheritance. The problem is that environmentally sound decisions often do not mirror those that optimize corporate profits. The design and production of a less polluting automobile may satisfy a greater social good, but it may be difficult to justify the lost profits associated with research and development until there is a market for such a vehicle. Additionally, undertaking such a financial risk could be considered a breach of the fiduciary obligation to maximize profits that management owes investors. In other words, many organizations will fail to take environmentally friendly actions unless required by law to do so.

Environmental laws reflect this tension and generally establish regulatory schemes to minimize, but not completely prohibit, environmental harms. For example, the federal Endangered Species Act of 1973 (2000) does not necessarily prohibit the "taking" (killing or injuring) of a federally listed species incidental to an otherwise lawful activity. It does, however, require that these

"takings" be permitted so that regulators can protect the overall health of a species through permit restrictions. Similarly, the Clean Water Act of 1977 (2000) and Clean Air Act of 1970 (2000) regulate the introduction of pollutants into the environment through a permitting process. The amount of authorized pollution is based on the current level of pollution and the environment's ability to absorb more and still meet identified environmental quality standards. Accordingly, what constitutes an acceptable level of pollution is largely a value judgment on which reasonable minds might disagree based on individual priorities. Often, these judgments are based on the level of harm to the public health that might occur if the level of a dangerous pollutant reaches some threshold. Mercury, a deadly neurotoxin, may be discharged by organizations as long as the levels found in the food chain are not judged as sufficient to cause harm to the public health.

Permitting, however, is an implicit acknowledgment that pollution is a consequence of an industrial society that can only be controlled and not entirely eliminated. The recent Kyoto Protocol to the United Nations Framework Convention on Climate Change and the refusal of the United States to ratify the agreement is a good example. The protocol recognizes that some level of greenhouse gas emission is inevitable in an industrialized society, but seeks to limit the emission and the resulting harm. The current U.S. administration, however, has argued that these limits would simply place too high a financial cost on American business and industry.

How priorities are balanced in the development of federal environmental law appears to confirm a legal positivist view of the law because these statutes are political in nature. While the environmental activist might claim that it is immoral to kill a single whale, there is currently no way to completely ensure commercial fishing will not result in whale deaths. From a political and public policy perspective, the ethics of protecting whales must be balanced with the practical concerns of encouraging an industry that provides food and employment. This is not to say measures to further minimize the risk of whale deaths are not possible, but these measures often entail significant costs, and the extent to which they are imposed and when are dependent on political will. The United States, for example, is currently pursuing a cap and trade greenhouse gas emission policy that allows regulated sources of emission to continue to pollute but uses market-based incentives to encourage a gradual reduction in emissions.

From another perspective, the legal environmental responsibilities of organizations have shifted to a social responsibility model. This is particularly the case were degradation of the environment is seen to affect human rights (U.S. Environmental Protection Agency, 2004). The environmental justice movement, for example, focuses on the exploitation of natural resources in ways that disrupt traditional cultures and communities, undermines sustainability, or disproportionately affects the health and well-being of a particular group. In this instance, environmental law tends to reflect more general human rights concerns that in turn draw on fundamental moral questions. Of course, the legal positivist might argue that such moral underpinnings are relevant to the law only because a political authority gives them voice. Nevertheless, the fact that the law addresses such moral concerns at all reflects a policy determination that social responsibility warrants the force of law at least in some narrow circumstances.

Communication Responsibilities

A fourth set of legal responsibilities has emerged around the communication obligations of organizations. The traditional view is that corporate information is proprietary, private, and not subject to public disclosure. The legal mandate to disclose previously private information, however, is increasing. In some instances, sound economic policy demands such measures to protect the marketplace regardless of the morality of prohibited practices. The federal laws prohibiting insider trading such as the Federal Securities Exchange Act of 1934 (2000), for example, are intended to encourage stock market investment by promoting a level playing field among investors. Accordingly, only information that is in the public domain can generally be used as a basis for investment decisions. While the violation of these laws may be seen as immoral based on a general proposition that it is wrong to break the law, the attempt to gain some advantage through unique knowledge could be considered good business, and for much of America's history, insider trading was arguably a marketplace expectation. Other legal disclosure mandates, however, bear a clearer relationship to ethics.

The law generally recognizes that a company has a proprietary interest in keeping their product components and production processes private. Such privacy can be essential in a competitive market. Other interests can, however, have precedence. The federal Emergency Planning and Community Right to Know Act of 1986 (2000; EPCRA) establishes requirements for certain classes of companies that manufacture or use hazardous materials to make this information available to the public. In addition, EPCRA requires that covered companies report releases of hazardous materials and develop an emergency response plan in coordination with community emergency response authorities. Similarly, the federal Occupational Safety and Health Act of 1970 (2000; OSHA) includes a hazard communication requirement that employees be given information about hazardous materials in the each work area and training in their safe use and handling. Both EPCRA and OSHA are predicated on the need to provide for public health and safety, but underlying this purpose is the ethical proposition that people have a right to know about risks associated with hazardous materials so they can take appropriate measures to protect themselves.

A company also has a strong interest in keeping its financial information confidential because of the enormous effect this information can have on a company's marketplace standing. Financial information directly affects many business activities such as the ability to borrow money and negotiate with creditors. Investors look to the financial health of a publicly held company as a key factor in deciding whether to invest in the company since it is a good indicator of potential financial return. Accordingly, companies have a significant incentive to mischaracterize their financial condition, and it is often difficult for potential investors to confirm the accuracy of financial data. The corporate financial scandals involving Enron, Arthur Andersen, Tyco, and WorldCom illustrate the enormous financial consequences to individual investors who rely on false representations about a company's financial condition. There is always a fine line, however, between puffery and fraud in the moral ambiguity of the marketplace, in that product claims are almost always exaggerated. Nevertheless, to knowingly misrepresent material facts to induce investment is fraud and unethical. The recently enacted Sarbanes-Oxley Act of 2002 imposes several corporate reporting requirements intended to avoid the circumstances of the cited scandals. Chief executive officers and chief financial officers must now personally certify that financial reports fairly represent a company's financial condition. The Act provides for financial and criminal penalties for violations. Further, the Act requires that a company must disclose "on a rapid and current basis" information the Securities Exchange Commission determines is necessary or useful to investors or where disclosure is in the public interest. The Act tends to support a natural law perspective, to the extent that the Act codifies ethical practices to protect against fraud, because it gives legal weight to the generally held ethical precept that it is wrong to cheat others.

DISCUSSION

As we noted above, discussions of minimal legal responsibilities are often framed as the organization's maximum ethical obligation. Organizations often argue that they are meeting the law with regard to specific activities and therefore have no other obligations to act in a socially responsible manner. In cases of workers rights to notification for job loss, for example, meeting federal, state, and contract requirements is often considered more than sufficient. This notion that the law equals ethics is primarily associated with the correspondence view described above. Efforts to legislate organizational morality, however, have often fallen short. Organizations may exploit loopholes or move their operations to jurisdictions with less strict regulation. In some cases, corporations may determine that it is actually cheaper to continue acting in a socially questionable and even illegal manner and simply pay any fines or penalties as a cost of doing business.

Some critics have argued that efforts to legislate social responsibility have the opposite effect. By limiting the relative degree of choice organizations have over their own conduct, the law encourages managers to take only the minimal actions required and avoid larger moral questions. While the loss of control through excessive governmental regulation is an issue for many managers, it is clear that the opposite approach is likely to see an even greater erosion of CSR.

A second view of social responsibility, associated primarily with the fiduciary obligations of organizations to stockholders, is consistent primarily with the separate realms model. Under this perspective, the organization's primary responsibility is to the owners of the company, the stockholders, and its primary obligation is to maximize wealth. The noted economist Milton Friedman summarized this view when he observed that "the social responsibility of business is to increase its profits" (M. Friedman, 1990, p. 274). Organizations should, accordingly, meet the limits of legal obligations to avoid reducing profits. This view has supported a number of legal efforts to enforce shareholder rights when management is seen as taking actions that are not in the best interests of the shareholder-owners. In addition, proponents of the view also argue that legal and ethical issues are distinct domains or separate realms. Freidman, for example, argues that social responsibility is an individual construct and that a "businesses as whole cannot be said to have responsibilities" (p. 274). Social responsibility is the domain of the individual.

In issues of environmental responsibility described above, for example, an organization meeting its fiduciary obligations to owners might seek to meet the most minimal legal obligations in order to avoid financial penalty. The organization might also exploit any loopholes, such as exporting toxic chemicals to countries with more lax environmental standards. While individual managers or stockholders might make a personal commitment to higher standards of environmental responsibility, there is no obligation for the organization to adhere to such standards, nor could an individual manager or stockholder impose his or her standards on the corporation.

The third theory regarding the relationship between the organization and the law, as noted above, is the social responsibility model. This view is grounded in the notion that larger moral obligations inform the interpretation and application of the law. Social responsibility is most clearly evident in instances where a large body of case law has emerged. In these instances, judges look to precedent, context, and the ways in which various issues have been interpreted to make legal judgments. Questions of morality and ethics, therefore, may help inform legal decisions without the expectation that there is a direct correspondence between the law and the ethics.

A social responsibility approach to the relationship between law and ethics complements a corporate social responsiveness approach to questions of organizational ethics and morality.

Social responsibility points to the larger underlying moral context of the law and acknowledges that the law is dynamic in its development, interpretation, and application. Nevertheless, while the law evolves to address changing societal conditions within a political framework, this is often a very slow and incremental process. Accordingly, social responsiveness suggests that organizations should be sensitive to the larger norms, needs, values, and morality of diverse stakeholders outside the limited context of the law. An ongoing exchange and adaptation of the organization to issues of social concern help ensure that the organization is legitimate and operating in a manner consistent with social norms and values.

Those organizations that take a social responsibility stance with regard to the law may also see themselves as having greater latitude to address ethical and moral deficiencies in their conduct. The law as a system of punitive constraints is sometimes seen as limiting organizational choice, including the ability of the organization to address social wrongs. The opportunity to draw upon larger moral codes and ethical traditions outside the law to explain, justify, and support its actions may enhance the organization's relative freedom regarding these issues. In other words, legal requirements grounded in social responsibility need not constrain organizations from choosing to operate in a manner consistent with larger moral frameworks. Examples of organizations refusing to limit themselves to what is legally required, although rare, do exist. In one such case, the textile manufacturing company Malden Mills, of Massachusetts, was forced to make choices about its workforce after experiencing a devastating fire. Economic reality and the possibility of significant legal liability suggested that the company take a large insurance settlement, close it operations, and leave the community it had been part of for more than 100 years. The CEO, Aaron Feurstein, however, followed his own sense of social responsibility and was responsive to the needs and values of the community. Feurstein committed to continue to pay workers and to rebuild the plant.

The case of Malden Mills also illustrates that those organizations choosing to be responsive to larger moral and ethical frameworks are able to garner widespread social support and are often in a more defensible position. Feurstein received an overwhelming outpouring of support from customers, suppliers, and members of the community.

He was widely touted as an example of corporate ethics in an era where most executives were concerned only about the bottom line.

In a similar example, the food company Schwans of Minnesota was caught up in a controversy over a *Salmonella* outbreak. The company moved quickly to contain the outbreak and offered to test members of the community and pay for their medical treatment. Attorneys for those plaintiffs who chose to sue argued that Schwans was moving too fast and had generated too much good will and that their clients could not receive a fair trial. In essence, the company was able to diffuse at least some of the potential legal harm that might have followed the outbreak by immediately acting in a socially responsible manner.

Responsiveness to the community and decisions that follow larger understandings regarding what is right clearly bolster the organization and place it in a more defensible position, at least in the court of public opinion. This is not to suggest, however, that being responsive is a kind of shield from the law. Corporate social responsiveness does not alleviate an organization of its legal obligations. The law remains a minimal set of obligations to which organizations must adhere. The law does not correspond directly to larger understandings of ethics and morality, however. Organizations cannot claim that meeting legal obligations also satisfies their obligations to be responsive and socially responsible.

CONCLUSION

The law is only one set of contingencies organizations face in determining how to be socially responsible. Community and cultural standards; professional norms; stakeholder views; moral, religious, and ethical traditions; and the value system of the organization and its managers and employees must also be taken into consideration. A stance involving corporate social responsiveness along with a social responsibility view of the law is sufficiently flexible and dynamic to accommodate the wide range of dynamic contingencies organizations face.

Organizations need such flexibility as they seek to balance and accommodate stakeholder needs and values. We suggest that detailed legal strictures regarding responsibilities, while sometimes desirable, may ultimately limit the corporation's flexibility and ability to be responsive to the dynamic and competing values of stakeholders. Moreover, the law cannot accommodate every possible moral contingency and will inevitably be judged as both incomplete and inflexible. A social responsibility model and an organizational responsiveness approach, therefore, are the most appropriate in encouraging corporations to be socially responsible and place questions of ethics and morality on an equal footing to questions of the law.

NOTES

1.   The Rivers and Harbors Act of 1899, often cited as the first American environmental statute because it prohibited the dumping of refuse and debris into U.S. rivers and harbors, was enacted primarily to ensure navigational safety as opposed to promoting water quality.

2.   Although beyond the scope of this chapter, the religiously based moral underpinnings of early American jurisprudence is well documented. This is particularly true with respect to criminal law and theories of punishment, especially as they relate to the imposition of corporal punishment and the death penalty. See Banner (2002) and L. M. Friedman (1993). Whether considering colonial America or a fundamentalist Islamic state, the legal positivist would assert that the moral foundation of the law in these societies results from a political authority giving status of law to religious precepts, and not because the law mirrors the universal morality of the natural law theorist.

REFERENCES

Banner, S. (2002). *The death penalty*. Cambridge, MA: Harvard University Press.

Buchholz, R. A. (1990). The evolution of corporate social responsibility. In P. Madsen & J. M. Shafritz (Eds.), *Essentials of business ethics* (pp. 298–310). New York: Penguin.

Buono, A. F., & Nichols, L. (1995). *Corporate policy values and social responsibility*. New York: Praeger.

Clean Air Act of 1970 (as Amended), 42 U.S.C. § 7401 *et seq.* (2000).

Clean Water Act of 1977 (as Amended), 33 U.S.C. § 1251 *et seq.* (2000).

Deetz, S. A. (1992). *Democracy in an age of corporate colonization*. New York: State University of New York Press.

Edwards, P. (1967). *The encyclopedia of philosophy*. New York: Macmillan.

Emergency Planning and Community Right to Know Act of 1986 (as Amended), 42 U.S.C. § 11001 *et seq.* (2000).

Endangered Species Act of 1973 (as Amended), 16 U.S.C. § 1531 *et seq.* (2000).

Federal Securities Exchange Act of 1934 (as Amended), 15 U.S.C. § 78a–78jj (2000).

Friedman, L. M. (1993). *Crime and punishment in American history*. New York: Basic Books.

Friedman, M. (1990). The social responsibility of business is to increase its profits. In P. Madsen & J. M. Shafritz (Eds.), *Essentials of business ethics* (pp. 273–281). New York: Penguin.

Grunig, J. (2001). Two-way symmetrical public relations: Past, present and future. In R. L. Heath (Ed.), *Handbook of publics relations* (pp. 11–30). Thousand Oaks, CA: Sage.

Hall, K. L. (Ed.). (1992). *The Oxford companion to the Supreme Court of the United States*. Oxford: Oxford University Press.

Hall, K. L. (Ed.). (2002). *The Oxford companion to American law*. New York: Oxford University Press.

Heald, M. (1970). *The social responsibility of business: Company and community 1900–1960*. New Brunswick, NJ: Transaction Books.

Kratz, L. (1999). Form and substance in law and morality. *University of Chicago Law Review, 66*, pp. 566–596.

Madsen, P., & Shafritz, J. M. (Eds.). (1990). *Essentials of business ethics*. New York: Penguin.

Metzler, M. (1996). When laws are not enough: Ethical criteria for risk communication. In J. Jaksa & M. Pritchard (Eds.), *The ethics of technological transfer* (pp. 151–165). Cresskill, NJ: Hampton Press.

Morris, C. (1953). *Morris on torts*. Brooklyn, NY: Foundation Press.

National Labor Relations Act of 1935 (as Amended), 29 U.S.C. § 151 *et seq.* (2000).

Occupational Safety and Health Act of 1970 (as Amended), 29 U.S.C. § 651 *et seq.* (2000).

Rivers and Harbors Act, 33 U.S.C. § 401 *et seq.* (1899).

Sarbanes-Oxley Act, Pub. L. 107–204, 116 Stat. 745 (2002).

Seeger, M. (1997). *Organizational communication ethics: Decisions and dilemmas*. Cresskill, NJ: Hampton Press.

Sethi, S. P. (1987). A conceptual framework for environmental analysis of social issues and evaluation of business response patterns. In S. P. Sethi & C. M. Fable (Eds.), *Business and society* (pp. 39–52). Lexington, MA: Lexington Books.

Siegel, S. A. (2001). John Chipman Gray and the moral basis of classical legal thought. *Iowa Law Review, 89,* 1513–1599.

U.S. Environmental Protection Agency. (2004). *Environmental justice.* Retrieved October 25, 2004, from http://www.epa.gov/compliance/environmentaljustice/.

Voakes, P. S. (2000). Rights, wrongs, and responsibilities: Law and ethics in the newsroom. *Journal of Mass Media Ethics, 15,* 29–42.

Werhane, P. (1985). *Persons, rights, and corporations.* Englewood Cliffs, NJ: Prentice-Hall.

11

Corporate Deception and Fraud

The Case for an Ethical Apologia

KEITH MICHAEL HEARIT

Few ideas are more remarkable than the collective historical amnesia that accompanies a bubble economy. Like the tulip bubble that created a highly speculative financial environment in the seventeenth century in Holland, or the go-go years of the late 1920s on Wall Street, the information technology bubble of the late 1990s brought about stupendously high valuations of companies that had little or no earnings, but because of a valuable Internet domain name (e.g., www.pets .com), such companies were expected to change the nature of commerce in the twenty-first century. Correspondingly, technology firms were projected to dominate this competitive landscape over more traditional "bricks and mortar" businesses, creating all kinds of advertising and revenue "synergies." The example that most accurately supports this point is the failed merger of AOL Time Warner, in which an overvalued Internet service provider with 23+ million subscribers was able to purchase the venerable media giant—the proverbial fish that swallowed the whale. Since the merger, AOL CEO Steve Case has resigned and the company has considered ways to spin off the AOL portion of the business.

Yet the collapse of the bubble economy, and the tremendous sense of financial loss of so many, led Americans (and media) to seek those who were responsible for the failure. To this end, a number of scapegoats were offered: Ken Lay and Jeffrey Skilling at Enron, Dennis Kozlowski at Tyco, Gary

Winnick at Global Crossing, and David Duncan and the entire Arthur Andersen accounting firm. Even America's domestic doyenne, Martha Stewart, was accused of insider trading and subsequently convicted of lying to investigators and obstruction of justice. Each new disclosure, whether it was accounting gimmicks embedded in offshore corporations or old-fashioned insider trading, left the suspicion for many individual investors and holders of 401(k)s (which one commentator had remarked had become 201(k)s by the time it was all over) that the game was rigged; and to reference an old Wall Street story, the Wall Street professionals were buying yachts while individual shareholders had precious few assets to show for their many trades. The underlying causes that connected these disparate cases are the triumph of free market fundamentalism, the cult of the CEO as savior, and the ideological leitmotif that pervades contemporary corporate discourse that suggests that fundamentally new and different approaches to business are necessary if companies are to remain competitive in the new global economy (Conrad, 2003).

At root, there really are only two meta-approaches that account for the social responsibility of the modern corporation. The first, the classical approach, argues that organizations have an obligation only to their shareholders (Friedman, 1962, 1970), and they "do good by doing well." The second, the so-called stakeholder approach (although it has taken a number of different forms, among them the two-way symmetrical model, institutional theory, legitimacy theory, the social demandingness model, and the social activism model), suggests that in exchange for the sacrifices companies require of society (i.e., the consumption of raw materials, the use of labor, the environmental harm, and the favorable tax benefits they receive), organizations have an obligation to act in a socially responsible manner (Brummer, 1991; Metzler, 2001; Pfeffer & Salancik, 1978). Therefore, corporate acts should demonstrate values of honesty, responsibility, and equality, as well as show an ongoing concern for and contribution to the well-being of the communities in which they operate. In other words, organizations should be "good corporate citizens" (Hearit, 1995; Seeger & Ulmer, 2003). Some suggest that this responsibility should go even further and take the form of social activism in which corporations contribute to the positive resolution of social problems (Brummer, 1991). In effect, corporate social responsibility is not simply individual managers being required to make ethically defensible decisions, but instead consists of organizational decisional processes that take into account the values of the wider community (Deetz, 2003; Epstein & Votaw, 1978).

By acting in a socially responsible manner—one that demonstrates a congruence between the organization's values and larger social values—organizations are likely to inoculate themselves from the prospect of a crisis. Conversely, crisis-prone companies are viewed not to take their social responsibility seriously (Coombs, 1999; Dowling & Pfeffer, 1975; Pauchant & Mitroff, 1992).

Yet, the problem that inheres in the social responsibility literature is the assumption that organizations can manage these twin obligations by integrating their business function with an eye toward their social responsibility (and thus prevent crises from developing). These obligations do not always align and, indeed, are often incompatible. To be successful economically, corporations have to privilege stockholder interests over stakeholder interests (e.g., as a by-product of the production process, a manufacturing plant will often emit hazardous chemicals, wastes, and particulates). Subsequently, given the pressures from stockholders for a favorable short-term return on their investments, coupled with the limited legal liability that they face, corporations are emboldened, if not required, to take risks in pursuit of a profitable return—risks that often lead to damaging revelations and shameful outcomes. In such instances, corporations face crises of social responsibility.

Such was the case that occurred with the venerable Wall Street firm Merrill Lynch, which New York Attorney General Eliot Spitzer alleged had an inherent conflict of interest in how it did business. In an effort to maintain the lucrative investment banking business of corporate clients, Merrill Lynch published fraudulent research that it used to encourage individual investors to purchase stocks with inflated by ratings. Examples of e-mails subpoenaed by Spitzer showed Internet and technology analysts recommending the purchase of stocks by investors that they privately called "junk," "crap," "dog," and "disaster" (White, 2002, pp. 1A, 5A). The suit by Spitzer led to a settlement that had Merrill Lynch admitting no wrongdoing but at the same time paying a $100 million fine to the treasury of the State of New York (Hearit & Brown, 2004).

The willingness on the part of Merrill Lynch to pay a $100 million fine but continue to deny that it had done anything wrong illustrates a major concern on the part of companies in the midst of a crisis, and reveals the difficulty of acting in a socially responsible manner: an admission of responsibility is viewed as invitation for lawsuits and is seen by investors to foreshadow huge legal judgments against the institution. Yet not to be conciliatory is seen by publics and media as a reticent company that is unwilling to "do the right thing."

What, consequently, is the ethical response for those companies operating in the new millennium who would seek to uphold stockholder interests but at the same time be socially responsible in their management of corporate crises? This chapter examines the problem of corporate social responsibility, particularly in those contexts in which businesses are accused of wrongdoing and, in attempting to come clean and issue an apologia, must balance stockholder and stakeholder publics. Specifically, I argue that there is an emerging consensus that organizations can indeed act socially responsibly, particularly when it concerns taking blame for their wrongdoing (while at the same time balancing this problem with shareholder interests). To support this thesis, this chapter (1) reviews the discursive status of contemporary organizations, (2) examines and contrasts the twin obligations of corporate officers, (3) notes the complexity of the contemporary legal landscape, and (4) details how companies might manage these twin obligations with the deliverance of an ethical apologia.

THE DISCURSIVE STATUS OF CONTEMPORARY ORGANIZATIONS

The modern corporation is a relatively recent creation and unique in history. Before the rise of the Industrial Revolution, most individuals' experiences with organizations were limited; indeed, with the exception of the Catholic Church, a national military, and, of course, political institutions such as the government, people's lives were characterized by a relative absence of organizational experience.

Yet with the advent of organization, people's lives are now characterized by a hyperorganizational reality. In contemporary terms, William Whyte's (1956) "organizational man" of the 1950s now seems almost quaint. Indeed, most people are no longer anonymous but eponymous, characterized by the many organizations of which they are members, be they work, religious, social service, political, or fraternal.

The nature of the modern organization is unique in its discursive character. Taken together, political, economic, legal, and social factors all work to make such a status possible. This can be seen in the fact that corporations have accrued large amounts of economic capital. As a matter of fact, many companies are so large that they surpass the gross domestic product of many small countries. Indeed, with all the mergers in the financial services industry, the United States now has its first company valued in the trillions of dollars; according to *Forbes* magazine, Citicorp's valuation (the price of its stock times the number of shares) is now $1 trillion (Forbes, 2003). Yet even with this considerable economic footprint, there is little legal regulation; the capitalistic marketplace allows and even encourages corporations to follow the flow of capital, to move at will with little or no regard to the social costs that occur because of this freedom. Such freedom often incurs tremendous social costs on the communities corporations leave behind.

In addition to their large size and accompanying economic clout, organizations are social actors in three distinct ways. First, they are political actors. Through a favorable tax code and the freedom to lobby Congress, organizations regularly participate in and influence the political process. As such, organizations have opinions, and these opinions are specific to the organization *qua* organization, opinions that have been shown to diverge from those of individual executives and employees (Namenwirth, Miller, & Weber, 1981).

Concomitant with this political status, corporations also have a legal status that must, by definition, be different than the traditional conception of a natural person. As Coleman (1974) observes, the past 150 years has witnessed the rise of the "juristic person," a nonpersonal entity such as a church, trade association, or labor union, the primary manifestation of which is the modern corporation. This juristic person can own property and sue; in fact, the juristic person has legal protections that natural persons do not. Corporations cannot, for example, be put in jail; neither can a single corporation be charged with conspiracy, for a juristic person cannot conspire within itself. While a juristic person does not have all the legal rights of natural persons, the direction of court rulings has been toward more rights for organizations, not fewer (Vibbert, 1990). The U.S. Supreme Court, in *First National Bank of Boston, et al. v. Bellotti, Attorney General of Massachusetts* (1978), for instance, ruled that speech that is otherwise protected does not lose its protection because it emanates from a corporate source. Recent Supreme Court rulings have extended the free speech rights of organizations so that, while they still do not have blanket protection, on a practical level companies enjoy most every other free speech right that individuals do.

In addition to their legal status, corporations also have a distinctive social status. This social status results in a form of discursive power, in that corporations are social actors that create persuasive identities. Companies spend a great deal of time, money, and effort on their advertising to construct memorable images. As a result, the general public tends to treat companies with thousands of employees as if they exist in a singular manner. Newspaper and broadcast accounts, for instance, report that "ExxonMobil announced ..." or "General Motors revealed plans to ...," all statements that demonstrate that a company is a distinct and identifiable social actor. In this way, a corporate image is a "real fiction" (Fisher, 1970, p. 132), a singularly distinct social persona that is recognizable to external constituencies (Dionisopoulos & Vibbert, 1983).

Finally, with all these advantages—huge economic power, significant political influence, a unique and powerful legal status, and a discursive social identity—organizations are legally required by law to represent the issues of their shareholders and not the interests of the communities in which they are situated. Said another way, the only social obligation, ensconced in law, is to stockholders and not to stakeholders (Epstein, 1972; Friedman, 1962, 1970).

THE TWIN OBLIGATIONS OF CONTEMPORARY ORGANIZATIONS

It is a safe assertion that tension will always exist between corporations and their stakeholders. On the one hand, communities enjoy the benefits corporations can deliver—achievements that no one man or woman can provide: technological innovation, comfort in the form of a high standard of living, the payment of property taxes, philanthropic support of local institutions, and the like. On the other hand, such capabilities accrue large rewards to corporations, rewards that may result in tremendous amounts of exchange power, power that makes individuals uncomfortable (Sennett, 1980).

For-profit business organizations that operate in the twenty-first century milieu are caught in a difficult and unique double bind, in that they have two obligations, one to their shareholders and the other to their communities. When business is good, most organizations are able to finesse this problem by engaging in public philanthropy with surplus funds. However, when an organization faces a crisis, particularly one of its own making, the polar different obligations come into particularly fine relief. When a corporation is charged with wrongdoing, the charge further exacerbates the natural suspicions of corporations because it claims that the use of exchange power by the corporation is unacceptable, for the company's actions are not congruent with public values (Dowling & Pfeffer, 1975; Hearit, 1995). The charge provides individuals with evidence by which to challenge the

social legitimacy of large corporations and, in some cases, the institution of capitalism as a whole (Habermas, 1975).

Competing Constituencies

In a crisis, the tension between economic and social responsibilities is direct and pronounced. On one side is the social responsibility to community. Stakeholders that make up this side of the equation take the form of consumers, communities, victims, and media. These angered publics criticize organizational actions. They regularly analyze statements by company officials and find them lacking. Furthermore, they often engage in a form of social sanction against the organization, be it some type of protest such as a consumer boycott, direct calls to the company, or a cutting up of credit cards such as Exxon faced after the *Exxon Valdez* oil spill in Prince William Sound (Hearit, 1994).

During a crisis, consumers and media demand a conciliatory response on the part of organizations and expect an apology. Not surprisingly, it is the impulse of many corporate officials to listen to their public relations counsel and respond in an accommodative way to critics and victims. To do so will go a long way to mitigate public anger and hostility. While a company caught in a crisis may not practice full disclosure, the emphasis in this type of response nonetheless is to get the facts out. The motivation for doing so is to make long-term image concerns primary by repairing the damaged reputation of the organization.

Such an approach is illustrated in the stance taken by the Toshiba Corporation in 1987 after disclosures that one of its subsidiaries, the Toshiba Machine Company, had sold top secret milling equipment to the former Soviet Union. Such equipment enabled the USSR to produce dramatically quieter submarines and altered the strategic balance of power between the United States and the Soviet Union. Public outcry against the company was great, and the company received a great deal of negative press attention; even members of Congress got in the act with staged photo-ops that showed them smashing Toshiba computers and boom boxes with sledgehammers. The company responded to public pressure and hostility by directly apologizing for the illegal sales, forcing the resignation of two top Toshiba officials, and going out of its way to differentiate the Toshiba Corporation from the unethical acts of the Toshiba Machine Company (Hearit, 1994).

While it may be the impulse of companies in a crisis to respond in an accommodative way, organizations are highly hesitant to do so, for, in the words of Cooper (1992), "Every word used to persuade the public is a word which may be used to persuade a judge" (p. 40). Because of this, organizational officials must take into account the interests of another key public, that being stockholders. As noted above, responsibility to stockholders is the only responsibility enshrined in law (Epstein, 1972; Friedman, 1962, 1970). As a result, organizations act on the advice of legal counsel that instructs organizations to practice minimal disclosure and say nothing or as little as possible. This is because organizations fear that to apologize is to incur legal liability, largely due to the idea that public statements of corporate officials that take some form of responsibility are proof of organizational guilt. This position is supported by Marcus and Goodman (1991), who argue that when organizations are in the midst of crises, those that issue strong statements of denial find that the valuation of their equities hold firm. Those that offer conciliatory responses, conversely, find that their stock prices suffer, because the markets view an accommodative response to be one in which an organization accepts responsibility. In this type of context, organizations privilege immediate financial concerns over long-term image and reputation ones.

Communicatively, organizations in this position take a stance in which they offer a denial of responsibility. Instead of focusing on long-term reputational concerns, a denial approach privileges short-term legal consequences and views community outrage to be painful but more tolerable than a negative legal judgment. While such a stance may function to preserve a company on a financial level, it tends to perpetuate anger at the consumer level.

This type of legally dictated stance was taken by the Ford Motor Company in 2000–2001 when revelations surfaced that Firestone Wilderness and ATX and ATX II tires were unsafe and prone to fail at suspiciously high rates (Hearit, 2006). Of particular concern was the fact that a large number of the tire failures occurred on Ford Explorers. While the case is complex, and locating where actual guilt lies is difficult, the privileging of short-term legal concerns (specifically, the fear of legal liability) accounts for the fact that Ford officials made no conciliatory public statements other than when CEO Jacques Nasser communicated before Congress in September 2000 that the only thing for which the company was sorry was that it had installed faulty Firestone tires on its trucks and sport utility vehicles (Hearit, 2006). Instead, the company tried to demonstrate its concern for its constituents (and prevent more lawsuits) by replacing the faulty tires as quickly as it could.

In sum, although organizations caught in a crisis respond in many different ways with multiple permutations, at root they really face two distinct sets of choices (a third, unsatisfactory way is discussed below). The first is to deny and side with stockholders, privileging their immediate economic and legal responsibility, but to do so keeps public hostility alive. The alternative is to apologize and identify with victims, privileging the long-term reputation of the company and social responsibility to the community, all the while taking the huge risk of legal action against a company.

THE COMPLEXITY OF THE CONTEMPORARY LEGAL ENVIRONMENT

The primary reason that organizations are loath to take any kind of public responsibility for their actions is due to the difficult and contested legal environment in which they operate. Such an environment is poisonous to an organization that wants to act socially responsibly when accused of wrongdoing. This is due to a number of factors.

First, American culture is a litigious one. People regularly sue in hopes of achieving a large financial settlement. There are a number of examples in the last few years in which juries have awarded significant awards to victims of corporate wrongdoing. Philip Morris is one case. A California jury awarded a victim more than $28 billion dollars, an amount that was later reduced by a judge (New York Times, 2002). Similarly, in the last 10 years juries have awarded large multimillion dollar judgments against Ford, General Motors, and others. In such an environment, to make an accommodative statement puts one in the position that might make it easier to be sued.

These large judgments are rooted in the problem of liability. The first kind of legal responsibility that most businesses face is that of compensatory liability. This means that a victim is compensated for the actual loss or harm. Traditionally, compensatory damages have been assessed in terms of a straightforward calculus that takes into account the time missed from work and the subsequent salary loss. As the September 11th terrorist attacks have shown, determination of such a number in an adult is relatively simple in that it involves a calculus of current earnings and lifespan. While an adult is relatively straightforward, to do the same for a child is much more difficult.

Conversely, it is punitive damage awards that corporations fear, for in punitive damages, a jury punishes an organization for its wrongdoing. That is, in addition to the compensatory damages to pay for the actual harm, punitive damages work on the assumption that an organization knowingly and willfully did wrong and brought about harm and so, as a result, should be punished severely (Davidson, Knowles, & Forsythe, 1998). Although there are ongoing attempts by pro-business forces to limit the size of punitive damage awards, particularly in the area of medical malpractice, one has to suspect that the threat of such awards will continue to be a moderating influence on corporate actions.

What is interesting about the judgments against some of America's largest corporations is that they tend to be the result of legal action taken by so-called superlawyers. These are individual attorneys and firms who have taken it as their business to specialize in one specific type of product such as medical devices or vehicle rollover. To this end, all of their efforts are spent pursuing the one industry. Subsequently, a whole cottage industry of firms (e.g., Safetyforum.com, Safetyresearch.net, and Safetyfocus.net) have sprung up around these attorneys, both as a vehicle by which to locate potential victims and also as clearinghouses of information and technology reconstruction to aid such attorneys in their efforts.

Of course, the real path to riches for attorneys is not to successfully sue a company on behalf of one victim; rather, it is when they are able to develop a class action lawsuit, in which they act as the attorney for an entire class. Judgments in class action lawsuits are even more substantial, in that attorneys typically receive more in compensation than do the individual victims. Research suggests that attorneys who successfully litigate on behalf of a class earn between $5,000 and $25,000 an hour (Seglin, 2002), a powerful incentive to sue.

Only time will tell if efforts by the Bush II administration to reign in abuses in class action lawsuits in the United States will be successful (Morgenson & Justice, 2005).

It should be noted that in this chapter I do not come down on the side of business interests. Indeed, the use of bankruptcy law is a well-known abuse of the system exercised by socially irresponsible corporations to avoid compensating victims (e.g., Dow Corning regarding silicone breast implants and Johns-Manville Corporation regarding asbestos poisoning). Rather, I simply argue that the way in which the legal system is constructed gives attorneys a compelling motivation beyond helping the injured. As such, companies have to build the cost of liability into the products that they sell. Companies operate in a difficult and contested legal environment, one in which there are powerful disincentives for organizations that might desire to behave in a socially responsible way.

THE MANAGEMENT OF THE TWIN OBLIGATIONS OF FIDUCIARY AND SOCIAL RESPONSIBILITY

So, how does a company caught in a crisis respond in such a way as to balance the twin obligations of its social and fiduciary responsibilities? The traditional position is that an organization cannot apologize to its constituencies, for in doing so, it will incur legal liability. The reason for such a position is that if an organization stands up and "does the right thing" by taking responsibility it is, in effect, inviting lawsuits from hungry attorneys who see such an admission of culpability as an invitation for a lawsuits. Fitzpatrick (1995), for instance, notes that the primary component of a strategy designed to minimize liability is to not communicate or, if you must talk, "say as little as possible and release it as quietly as possible" (p. 22). A legal stance also denies responsibility and instead tries to shift the blame elsewhere (Fitzpatrick & Rubin, 1995).

Others have argued that most organizations caught in a crisis try to balance the two demands between their social responsibility to their community and their fiduciary responsibility to their stockholders. They tend to do this by engaging in equivocal communication—communication that is of such a bland and ambiguous nature that it satisfies no one (Tyler, 1997). Unfortunately, to engage in too much equivocality leads consumers to reject a message as insincere. An example of equivocal communication occurs when companies announce that they are sorry that an event happened, but do so in such a way as to not assume any hint of responsibility for the act. This leads to some strange semantic gymnastics, resulting in organizations denying that they did anything wrong but at the same time promising not to do it again (Tyler, 1997).

One such creative use of equivocal communication was crafted by British Petroleum, which was responsible for an oil spill off the coast of San Diego. Perhaps learning too well from the mistakes of Exxon and its spill in Alaska, the company responded: "Our lawyers tell us it's not our fault, but it sure feels like our fault and we'll do everything we can to fix it" (Sandman, 1993, p. 64).

While there is a great deal of complexity to the issue, there does appear to be a growing consensus that organizations should not fear and shy away from apologies completely, but instead, in certain contexts and situations, they can and should apologize (Cohen, 1999, 2002; Patel & Reinsch, 2003). In other words, there are ways in which a strategic organization *can* meet its fiduciary obligation to its stockholders while at the same time meeting its ethical obligations to the communities of which it is a member.

But before articulating the contexts in which one can apologize, it is important to be specific about what is meant by an apology. From a legal perspective, an apology has two parts (Cohen, 1999, 2002). First is the acknowledgment of a harm and an expression of regret. Second is the assumption of responsibility for what has happened.

These two components come out in a variety of ways in terms of how people and institutions deal with the problem of guilt and fraud. The first is of the "I'm sorry *if* anyone was offended" variety. This generalized apology does little by way of effectiveness. Second, is the "I'm sorry it happened" category. Such was the apology offered by Exxon to the people of Prince William Sound after the disastrous oil spill in 1989 (Hearit, 1995). A third type is the "I'm sorry and I'm responsible" variety. A final and most ethical form is "I'm sorry and responsible, and can I provide restitution and compensation in order to make things right?" form. It is the nexus between the second and third

forms with which the remainder of this chapter is concerned.

While not codified in such a way so as to permit sweeping generalizations, contemporary common law is written in such a way that to apologize carefully is not to incur legal liability (Cohen, 1999; Patel & Reinsch, 2003). What is meant by this is that the law allows for a distinction between the apology—"I'm sorry that such and such happened"—and the assumption of responsibility: "We're responsible and guilty for what happened." Such a position allows for organizations the option to deliver apologies, just so that the apologies do not utilize direct and overt assumptions of responsibility.

Situations in Which Organizations Can Safely Apologize

There are a number of situations in which organizations can safely apologize. The first is in those situations in which there is no real victim, specifically in what Hearit (1994, 1995) describes as "media-flap" kinds of crises. These are those situations when liability concerns are minimal or nonexistent, such as faced Chrysler in 1987 when revelations surfaced that the company had unhooked the odometers of cars, drove them for an average of 40 miles, rehooked the odometers, and then sold the cars as new. The company came clean, apologized, and offered extended warranties for customers with the "test-driven" cars (Hearit, 1994). Similarly, AT&T faced a service interruption in 1991 in which it was unable to deliver long-distance service for seven hours. While people were inconvenienced and planes were delayed, there were no harms or injuries. Because of the outage, AT&T apologized and acknowledged, "Apologies are not enough," detailing the corrective action it was taking to ensure that the problem did not recur (Benoit & Brinson, 1994, p. 82). In both the Chrysler and AT&T situations, there were no victims who suffered corporal harm, and while there might have been some financial costs, those costs were such that the damages could be easily calculated (Wagatsuma & Rosett, 1986).

Second, organizations can apologize in those situations in which the harm is in the speech, that is, in those contexts in which the misdeeds take the form of defamation and slander. In such situations, given the fact that slander and libel are offenses of speech, it follows that a primary remedy in such a situation should be in the realm of speech (Wagatsuma & Rosett, 1986).

A third situation in which organizations are wise to apologize is when they are likely to be sued successfully, with or without an apology (Cohen, 1999). Many reject apologizing, claiming that to do so is to invite lawsuits. Yet there are many situations in which an organization has done wrong and will be sued (successfully) regardless of whether or not it offers a statement that assumes responsibility. In those situations, it follows that an organization should use an apology to repair its reputation and preserve its long-term image (Kauffman, Kesner, & Hazen, 1994). In 1993, after a crisis in which *E. coli* caused the deaths of three children in the Pacific Northwest, the Foodmaker Corporation, which operated Jack in the Box restaurants, took an approach (after some initial, failed attempts at denial) whereby it acknowledged its responsibility for the harm it had caused. The company then worked to position itself as a leader in food safety technology while working to pay all medical bills and settle claims made by parents (Ulmer & Sellnow, 2000).

Fourth, an organization should apologize if it can afford to (Cohen, 1999). That is, if an organization has a considerable amount of liability insurance, insurance that would not be violated by an admission of guilt, then it follows that an organization can afford to apologize and should do so (Cohen, 1999). Given the considerable amount of liability insurance the Exxon Corporation carried (close to $1 billion), for instance, it could have afforded to adopt a much more conciliatory approach than it did after the oil spill in Prince William Sound.

Fifth, an organization can and should apologize when its very survival is threatened (Kauffman et al., 1994). Witness the case of Arthur Andersen. Due to liability concerns, the company fought the allegations leveled against it in the Enron debacle. In so doing, it created the conditions that threatened its very survival and eventually brought about its downfall. Had it taken a more conciliatory approach, it might have negotiated a legal settlement that would have enabled the firm to survive.

Finally, and most critically, organizations should consider offering an apology directly to the victims that it has harmed. In particular, the best time to apologize is in the framework of media-

tion, or as part of a legal settlement. Here, the organization and the wronged attempt to come to some sort of resolution for the transgression, and they do so by offering and accepting an apology and compensation (Cohen, 1999). In this way, an organization has an opportunity to apologize in a legally protected context.

CONCLUSIONS

In this chapter I have attempted to reconcile the competing tensions that inhere in a corporation's social responsibility, particularly in those circumstances in which an organization is accused of misconduct, and as a result, the tensions between its legal fiduciary responsibility and its public social responsibility are laid bare. In so doing, I have attempted to isolate and demonstrate the competing counsel, the publics, and the different objectives that organizational officials have to choose among in a crisis context.

At root, it is possible for an organization to act socially responsibly during a crisis situation without necessarily incurring legal liability. This is done by distinguishing between the public and private communication of an organization. To put it another way, an ethical apology occurs when organizations provide a statement of sympathy and concern for public consumption and a private apology to the victim, especially in a context of mediation that includes compensation considerations. This provides a vehicle for ethical communication in which an organization is able to incur no (new) liability for its socially responsible corporate speech and concomitantly is able to respond to the needs of the victim privately. By doing so, a company is able to fulfill its fiduciary responsibilities by not going out of its way to invite lawsuits as well as its moral and ethical ones by doing the right thing in order to mitigate harm and provide restitution for those it hurt.

A company that has engaged in fraud or caused some other form of serious harm will get sued regardless—due to the grievous nature of the wrong. The point in this chapter is that companies are wise to communicate in such a way as to balance the twin requirement of their social and financial responsibility so that they can serve both shareholder interests and the public interest. Astute corporate officers are wise to reflect on a calculus that takes into account the type of the misdeeds, the requests of victims, the amount of media attention, and the possibility that an apology will lessen the possibility of a lawsuit, and make a strategic decision so as to act in a way that honors both obligations.

REFERENCES

Benoit, W. L., & Brinson, S. L. (1994). AT&T: Apologies are not enough. *Communication Quarterly, 42*, 75–88.

Brummer, J. J. (1991). *Corporate responsibility and legitimacy: An interdisciplinary analysis.* New York: Greenwood Press.

Cohen, J. R. (1999, May). Advising clients to apologize. *Southern California Law Review, 72*, 1009–1069.

Cohen, J. R. (2002). Legislating apology: The pros and cons. *University of Cincinnati Law Review, 70*, 819–872.

Coleman, J. S. (1974). *Power and the structure of society.* New York: W.W. Norton.

Conrad, C. (2003). Setting the stage: Introduction to the special issue on the "corporate meltdown." *Management Communication Quarterly, 17*, 5–19.

Coombs, W. T. (1999). *Ongoing crisis communication.* Thousand Oaks, CA: Sage.

Cooper, D. A. (1992). CEO must weigh legal and public relations approaches. *Public Relations Journal, 48*, 40, 39.

Davidson, D. V., Knowles, B. E., & Forsythe, L. M. (1998). *Business law* (6th ed.). Cincinnati, OH: West Educational Publishing.

Deetz, S. (2003). Corporate governance, communication, and getting social values into the decisional chain. *Management Communication Quarterly, 16*, 606–611.

Dionisopoulos, G. N., & Vibbert, S. L. (1983, November). *Re-fining generic parameters: The case for organizational apologia.* Paper presented at the annual meeting of the Speech Communication Association, Washington, DC.

Dowling, J., & Pfeffer, J. (1975). Organizational legitimacy: Social values and organizational behavior. *Pacific Sociological Review, 18*, 122–136.

Epstein, E. M. (1972). The historical enigma of corporate legitimacy. *California Law Review, 60*, 1701–1717.

Epstein, E., & Votaw, D. (Eds.). (1978). *Rationality, legitimacy, responsibility: Search for new directions.* Santa Monica, CA: Goodyear Publishing.

First National Bank of Boston, et al. v. Bellotti, Attorney General of Massachusetts, 435 U.S. 765 (1978).

Fisher, W. R. (1970). A motive view of communication. *Quarterly Journal of Speech, 56*, 131–139.

Fitzpatrick, K. R. (1995). Ten guidelines for reducing legal risks in crisis management. *Public Relations Quarterly, 40*, 33–38.

Fitzpatrick, K. R., & Rubin, M. S. (1995). Public relations vs. legal strategies in organizational crisis decisions. *Public Relations Review, 21*, 21–33.

Forbes. (2003, March 28). The Forbes 500s. Retrieved May 6, 2005, from http://www.forbes.com/2003/03/26/500sland.html.

Friedman, M. (1962). *Capitalism and freedom.* Chicago: University of Chicago Press.

Friedman, M. (1970, September 13). The social responsibility of business is to increase its profits. *New York Times Magazine,* pp. 32–33, 124–125.

Habermas, J. (1975). *Legitimation crisis.* Boston, MA: Beacon Press.

Hearit, K. M. (1994). Apologies and public relations crises at Chrysler, Toshiba, and Volvo. *Public Relations Review, 20*, 113–125.

Hearit, K. M. (1995). "Mistakes were made": Organizations, apologia, and crises of social legitimacy. *Communication Studies, 46*, 1–17.

Hearit, K. M. (2006). *Crisis management by apology: Corporate response to allegations of wrongdoing.* Mahweh, NJ: Lawrence Erlbaum.

Hearit, K. M., & Brown, J. (2004). Merrill Lynch: Corporate apologia and fraud. *Public Relations Review, 30*(4), 459–466.

Kauffman, J. B., Kesner, I. F., & Hazen, R. L. (1994, July-August). The myth of full disclosure: A look at organizational communication during crisis. *Business Horizons, 37*, 29–39.

Marcus, A. A., & Goodman, R. S. (1991). Victims and shareholders: The dilemmas of presenting corporate policy during a crisis. *Academy of Management Journal, 34*, 281–305.

Metzler, M. (2001). The centrality of organizational legitimacy to public relations practice. In R. L. Heath (Ed.), *Handbook of public relations* (pp. 321–334). Thousand Oaks, CA: Sage.

Morgenson, G., & Justice, G. (2005, February 20). Taking care of business, his way. *New York Times*, p. 3–1.

Namenwirth, J. Z., Miller, R. L., & Weber, R. P. (1981). Organizations have opinions:

A redefinition of publics. *Public Opinion Quarterly, 45*, 463–76.

New York Times. (2002, December 19). Smoker's award cut to $28 million, p. A30.

Patel, A., & Reinsch, L. (2003). Companies can apologize: Corporate apologies and legal liability. *Business Communication Quarterly, 66*, 17–26.

Pauchant, T. C., & Mitroff, I. I. (1992). *Transforming the crisis-prone organization.* San Francisco, CA: Jossey-Bass.

Pfeffer, J., & Salancik, G. R. (1978). The created environment: Controlling interdependence through law and social sanction. In *The external control of organizations: A resource dependence perspective* (pp. 188–202). New York: Harper.

Sandman, P. M. (1993). *Responding to community outrage: Strategies for effective risk communication.* Fairfax, VA: American Industrial Hygiene Association.

Seeger, M. W., & Ulmer, R. R. (2003). Explaining Enron: Communication and responsible leadership. *Management Communication Quarterly, 17*, 58–84.

Seglin, J. (2002, December 15). Wanted: More civility, not civil suits. *New York Times,* p. 3–4.

Sennett, R. (1980). *Authority.* New York: Vintage.

Tyler, L. (1997). Liability means never being able to say you're sorry: Corporate guilt, legal constraints, and defensiveness in corporate communication. *Management Communication Quarterly, 11*, 51–73.

Ulmer, R. R., & Sellnow, T. L. (2000). Consistent questions of ambiguity in organizational crisis communication: Jack in the Box as a case study. *Journal of Business Ethics, 25*, 143–155.

Vibbert, C. B. (1990). Freedom of speech and corporations: Supreme Court strategies of the extension of the First Amendment. *Communication, 12*, 19–34.

Wagatsuma, H., & Rosett, A. (1986). The implications of apology: Law and culture in Japan and the United States. *Law & Society Review, 20*(4), 461–497.

White, B. (2002, May 22). Deal may help reform Wall Street. *Bay City Times,* pp. 1A, 5A.

Whyte, W. H., Jr. (1956). *The organizational man.* Garden City, NY: Doubleday.

12

Regulation

Government, Business, and the Self in the United States

JOHN LLEWELLYN

Did you ever expect a corporation to have a conscience, when it has no soul to be damned, and no body to be kicked?
Edward, First Baron Thurlow

As this chapter is being written, the world is coming to grips with a natural disaster of monumental proportions—an undersea earthquake and the tsunamis it spawned. The death toll is 283,000. The initial aid commitment from the U.S. government was $35 million; it was characterized as "stingy" by an official of the United Nations. Then came the announcement by President George W. Bush of an increased U.S. commitment of $350 million and his angry response to the earlier criticism (Sanger & Hoge, 2005). This presidential action (and reaction) is a clear reminder that social responsibility has a fluid definition; it applies to institutions of all sizes and shapes, not merely corporations. This instance also underscores the futility of trying to manage one's reputation only within a given locale (e.g., the United States); regardless of plans and strategies, the wider world can impinge in an instant.

On a less global note, but closer to the thrust of this chapter, are two news items recounting unprecedented actions by corporate directors. The first item is an agreement by 10 former directors of WorldCom to "fork over $18 million of their own money to settle a class-action lawsuit brought by [those parties] who lost hundreds of millions of dollars when the company collapsed in 2002, the largest bankruptcy in history" ("Directors on Notice," 2005, ¶ 1). In the second story, 10 former directors of Enron have agreed "to pay $13 million out of their own pockets as part of a $168

million settlement of a lawsuit brought by onetime shareholders who lost billions of dollars in the company's collapse in 2001" (Eichenwald, 2005, ¶ 1). The fact that both of these items ran in the *New York Times* on the same day may be serendipity, but it is also a clear sign of the depth of public resentment regarding corporate misbehavior and director malfeasance.

This chapter is authored by a communication scholar who studies the rhetoric of institutions. In an earlier lifetime, I practiced public relations for a number of state and local governments. In this role, I worked with the news media, wrote speeches for politicians, and promoted the public image of these agencies. With the background of these experiences, I examine the strategies and ethics of corporate social responsibility (CSR) claims.

One's perspective on corporate regulation—its desirability, efficacy, and extent—benchmarks one's political philosophy. In the United States, the history of the ebb and flow of our sentiments about large corporate entities and their regulation is well known. Wells (2002) observes: "Since the late nineteenth century, Americans have debated what duties large business organizations might have to their workers, customers, neighbors, and the public at large" (p. 77). After the Civil War, urban centers grew and railroads and manufacturing burgeoned. This development was followed by the *laissez faire* approach to economics and the rise of large corporations run by "robber barons." In response came the Progressive Movement and the muckraking journalists who told the story of corporate excesses through the new vehicle of the mass media in the form of popular newspapers and magazines. The Roaring Twenties was an era when business regained its momentum and argued for its autonomy. When the roar faded with the onset of the Great Depression, business was no longer in the power position. Franklin Roosevelt's New Deal ushered in an era of increased federal power over both corporations and citizens.

World War II completed the nation's recovery from the effects of the Depression. The national government was center stage in coordinating wartime manufacturing and managing public opinion regarding the war. The Advertising Council also recognized the need to condition public attitudes about business in hopes of postwar tranquility and public acceptance of the economic order: "The battle for the preservation of American democracy did not end on the last day of the war. One crisis ended. Another began. In peace, as in war, the informed and intelligent cooperation of the people is the priceless ingredient of a working democracy" (War Advertising Council, 1945, quoted in Jackall & Hirota, 2000, p. 45).

At war's end, returning service personnel went to college, earned degrees, married, moved to the newly created suburbs, and spawned the baby boom. Corporations grew to meet postwar demand for deferred goods. After the relative quiet of the 1950s, the 1960s, and early 1970s saw much upheaval as social movements took shape: civil rights, antiwar, environment, women's rights, and consumerism. All of these movements, directly or indirectly, put corporations that were part and parcel of the now troublesome status quo on the spot. Coupled with the Watergate scandal that led to President Nixon's resignation, these social trends put the established order under a great deal of stress. Federal legislation addressed many of these concerns and created responsibilities for corporations in complying.

The corporate takeover glut of the 1980s brought public attention back to questions of CSR as merged companies shed workers and raised public concerns even as stockholders profited. In response, from 1983 to 1993, 29 states passed laws ("corporate constituency statutes") allowing corporate boards to weigh the impact of a proposed takeover on stakeholders (employees, suppliers, and other affected parties) as well as stockhold-

ers (Wells, 2002, p. 127). The next advocates for CSR were from the Progressive Law Movement, which battled a "nexus of contracts" argument that claimed that there was no foundation for CSR activities because there is no real corporation per se, only a web of contracts upon which no special duties (e.g., CSR) can be hung (Greenfield, 2002, p. 591; Wells, 2002, p. 130).

Despite the persistence of this historical activity, Wells (2002) is hardly sanguine about results: "There is a problem with these debates: they rarely seem to go anywhere. Viewed in historical perspective, it is clear that each new round of debate on CSR largely recapitulates the earlier debate in a slightly altered form" (p. 78). Wells distills four enduring tenets from all this talk: CSR applies to giant corporations, not smaller firms; reformers want to alter, not eliminate, corporate power; the issue is always the extent of shareholder primacy—may a board aid nonshareholders; and CSR endures despite social changes. Wells sees an irony in these notions: "Corporate social responsibility is not a novel solution to an unchanging problem; quite the contrary, it is an unchanging solution to an ever-new problem" (p. 81).

LEGITIMACY

The real objective in CSR activities is gaining public acceptance of the corporation's right to exist. The overarching principle is embodied in the term "legitimacy."

The challenge of demonstrating corporate legitimacy in democracies is complicated by the fact that corporate wealth is inequitably distributed. In fact, Jurgen Habermas (1973) has observed that all class societies reproduce themselves by inequitably, yet legitimately, appropriating socially produced wealth (p. 96). In Marxist theory, this distribution process is supposed to result in increasing alienation from capitalism; however, evidence of such systematic alienation is scarce in the United States (Pfeffer, 1985, p. 413). Maintaining popular acceptance of this inequitable distribution mechanism is a fundamental challenge for political and economic elites. To protect their interests, corporations must manage the inherent tension between democratic political values and corporate economic practices. Satisfying business regulations that the public views as credible is an elementary strategy for corporate legitimacy.

In examining organizational legitimacy, Dowling and Pfeffer (1975) explain that organizations can choose one or more strategies from among three: adapting to existing norms, attempting to change social norms, or identifying with socially legitimate symbols, values, or institutions (p. 124). Even adapting to social norms, however, is no guarantee that those norms will not change with time and circumstance; the phenomenon is called "value pluralism" (Hess, 1999, p. 46).

Three features of American belief systems have served to sustain corporate legitimacy in the face of an ever-ready public distrust: public willingness to distinguish positive institutional actions from failures of leaders and members, trust in continued progress that brings personal optimism, and a habit of attributing failure to individual power holders, not institutions (Lipset & Schneider, 1987, p. 384). These features suggest why and how CSR strategies succeed across the years: institutions take credit for successes while individual executives shoulder blame for failure. And yet there are limits. Philip Morris changed its name to Altria as part of a plan to abandon its "bunker mentality." Its earlier confrontational stance was winning no friends, and, in the words of one board member, the company was in danger of "losing permission to exist from society" (Alsop, 2004, p. 27).

LAW AND CSR

There are legal dimensions to the topic of CSR. The compliance with law standards is the most basic of the conceptions of CSR, a sine qua non principle (Hess, 1999, p. 45).

On the face of it, CSR and law are either redundant terms or significantly at odds. One legal scholar describes the linkage this way: "CSR is a function of law and law is a function of CSR" (Ostas, 2001, p. 264). Common sense would suggest compliance with law as the first social responsibility of citizens, whether individual or corporate. And yet, corporate compliance with law is hardly a sure thing despite the fact that most citizens assume it to be certain.

As this passage is written, U.S. pharmaceutical giant Schering-Plough has agreed to pay $346 million in fines and damages for a kickback scheme intended to defraud Medicaid and violate federal law (Schering-Plough settles, 2004). United States Attorney Patrick Meehan said, "This wasn't a mistake. It was a marketing strategy. The result was that programs created to provide health care to the poorest among us were actually paying more for drugs than those who have private health insurance" (¶ 8). A corporate vice president uses a stock phrase from public relations to obscure the charge and its implications: "We are pleased that we are now putting this matter from the past behind us" (¶ 12). This firm was not alone in its illegal actions. Bayer paid $257 million and GlaxoSmithKline $86.7 million to settle similar charges (¶ 15).

This story suggests there is more work ahead for Duncan Burke, Glaxo's vice president of corporate image and reputation:

> I'm trying to get people to think about reputation systematically, to remind them to take it seriously all the time. Big drug companies are seen as pariahs right now because of the issue of access to medicine at a reasonable price. So it's especially important that there's one person in my position to reflect on how the world thinks of Glaxo and how we want the world to see us. (Alsop, 2004, p. 23)

Burke might be relieved to know that these incidents are coded as aberrant: individuals are removed, monies returned, executives rarely do time, and the industry continues business as usual without any examination of systemic defects.

PARAMETERS OF ORGANIZATIONAL SUCCESS

To prosper, organizations need to have success on three distinct performance dimensions: the legal, the responsible, and the profitable. Organizations that are seen to fail the legal test, while claiming to be law abiding, can be headed for trouble. However, as the Schering-Plough vice president illustrates, there are numerous public relations tactics to redirect or minimize corporate illegalities. Negotiated settlements produce a one-day bad news story rather than protracted and notorious public trials like those of O. J. Simpson, Scott Peterson, and Michael Jackson.

Not all organizations are, in fact, law abiding, and the problems are not restricted to the pharmaceutical industry. For example, major cigarette-making corporations have asked a federal appeals court to throw out a $280 million claim against them brought by the U.S. Justice Department ("Cigarette-makers appeal," 2004). The government wants a portion of the industry's profits made since 1971 from illegally selling cigarettes to underage smokers. The companies are arguing that giving over the money would not serve to restrain future unlawful conduct as required by the racketeering statute. The issue being argued here is not whether companies intentionally broke the law in the past but whether this penalty is proper for those offenses.

Organizations want to be seen as socially responsible. They may even want to be socially responsible, but the public perception that they are is the crucial prize (Llewellyn, 1990; Macleod, 2001; Spencer, 2002). So the profession of public relations exists to draw public attention to the alignment of corporate behavior with public expectations. The core challenge in pursuing CSR is to determine what the public's salient values are and how far the public really wants the organization to go in service of those values. Organizations, which are in business for the long haul, nevertheless must seek to adapt minute by minute to the public's sentiments. Witness the perils of corporate advertising after the attacks of September 11, 2001: How long to be sad? How long to praise the firefighters? When to go back to "business as usual"?

In the not-too-distant past, firms in the United States did not offer benefits to same-sex partners. And today? When and how did organizations "learn" to make those changes? Scholars suggest that it may be a case of pluralistic ignorance where legions of dissenters all view themselves as alone when they may actually hold a majority or strong minority position. Once unmasked, the social "taboo" on extending same-sex partnership benefits virtually evaporated: "Since 1992, when Lotus Development Corporation became the first publicly traded company to offer domestic partner benefits, over 7,300 private and public employers have extended such benefits" (Notes, 2004, p. 1978).

The firm's second challenge with CSR is in deciding the extent of its commitment. The defining purpose of any organization is to execute its core technology for a profit. What should such a firm do about supporting public education? Helping the homeless? When does that socially responsible mission begin to compromise the core technology of the firm? When will consumers say, "Enough with helping the rain forests already, I came in for a cup of coffee"?

Finally, while pursuing CSR goals the organization must be profitable. While firms may have deep pockets, they got them by absorbing more energy from the environment than they put back into it. In the final analysis, firms must be sustained by their environment through the importation of energy (read: money and talent). One of the convolutions in studying CSR is the corporate aversion to a clear articulation of the profit motive. Executives prefer to speak of the organization as a "family"; the metaphor has worked well —so well, in fact, that employees of Disneyland ("the kids") vehemently resisted management's restructuring plans in the face of economic downturns (Smith & Eisenberg, 1987). The family metaphor means that breaking regulations is a violation of trust and thus a stain on the corporate character. In a clearly profit-seeking system, a violation might simply be an act of cost–benefit rationality.

For most firms, profit is reducible to money. In some cases, that fact is so essential and so defining that ethical problems seem inevitable (at least in hindsight). The primacy of personal wealth was the goal at Enron. Its 401(k) plan handout for employees featured George Bernard Shaw's observation that "'lack of money is the root of all evil' . . . Houston luxury car dealers knew to come to Enron to exhibit their wares every bonus period" (Prentice, 2003, p. 435).

There is a "default option" whereby the public grants organizations the benefit of the doubt on all three dimensions of success—legality, social responsibility, and profitability—until events dictate otherwise. In the absence of a disaster or a whistleblower, firms have lustrous reputations. New York Attorney General Eliot Spitzer does not share these "see no evil" assumptions. Examining internal processes of Wall Street researchers, the mutual fund industry, and the insurance business, "Mr. Spitzer found dubious industry practices that had been going on for years. But, as he made clear, that didn't make them right" (Morgenson, 2005).

PERSPECTIVES ON CSR

As Wells (2002) has noted, CSR is a topic that is at once perennial and consistently new. So it is with the literature on the subject. This is also a topic on which reasonable people can differ at both philosophical and pragmatic levels.

The discussion starts with Milton Friedman's definition of corporate duty: "to make as much money as possible while conforming to the basic rules of society, both those embodied in law and those embodied in ethical custom" (Friedman, 1970, cited in Ostas, 2001, p. 263). If this position dominated, the subject would be closed. Alice Tepper Marlin (1998) offers a counterstatement:

> Milton Friedman, the prime advocate of the position that the responsibility of business is exclusively to maximize profit for shareholders, has lost the debate. Business leaders who once gave only a recalcitrant response to the feisty demands of activists now have developed an enlightened appreciation of the value of corporate reputation as a competitive advantage. (p. xi)

While the list of CSR concerns is always in flux, McIntosh, Leipziger, Jones, and Coleman (1998) identify eight broad categories: corporate governance, environment, human rights and the workplace, fair trade and ethical investment, arms trade, tobacco, animal welfare and protection, and education (p. vii). In any case, CSR is a growth industry for public relations counselors: "The language of CSR is quite fashionable at the moment, but it's not just a fad," a London public relations executive notes. "There have been some permanent changes in society's expectations of businesses and how they behave" (White, 2002, p. B10).

Ostas (2001) offers a deconstruction of CSR showing that both "law" and "markets" are deeply problematic terms. He challenges the classical construct of the market that "imposes" demands on a robotically responding management. Ostas concludes with a four-step heuristic for management: take business ethics seriously, see markets holistically and test assumptions, embrace legal ambiguities constructively and work to improve the law, and pay close attention to the values of all parties and understand that social gains from CSR need not diminish profit (p. 274).

REGULATORY IMPULSES AND CSR

Spencer (2002) observes that a mix of post-9/11 worries, a go-it-alone sentiment in America, a rise in antiglobalization efforts, and recent corporate scandals may brew a cocktail of public discontent with profound consequences: "Whatever their private wishes, governments will almost certainly feel bound to reregulate the frameworks of market capitalism" (p. 188). The Western world is in a trust drought, he suggests, pointing out that the Roman Catholic Church and the accountancy profession, once paragons of solidity and certainty, are now adrift. He sees CSR as a thin reed in the face of such uncertainty and political pressure. Even with the inevitable rough and tumble of capitalistic practices, Spencer observes, "there may be minimum levels of behaviour below which public faith in the whole system is undermined" (p. 189).

The specific focus of this chapter is regulation and its relationship to CSR. In general, the public expects governmental agencies to write rules to constrain the institutions' improper impulses, especially for-profit enterprises.

One of the powers of a regulation is that it puts actors on notice that they are subject to a behavioral standard: "The very presence of the regulation itself is meant to constrain in some way the otherwise discretionary activities of those to whom it applies" (Brummer, 1991, p. 43). As a practical political matter, laws and regulations to constrain organizations are usually shaped with input and influence from those very organizations. This phenomenon is known as "capture theory." Ostas recounts a sterling example. Ortho Pharmaceuticals Corporation sought approval from the U.S. Food and Drug Administration for a new drug. The Ortho physician, a member of the research team, declined to approve the drug for reasons of safety and ethics. Ortho fired her and argued that the FDA could protect the public's interest. The New Jersey Supreme Court upheld the firing (Ostas, 2001, p. 263).

Lobbyists, politically influential friends, and trade associations work to shape legislation as it moves through its routes: committees, legislative assemblies, and chief executive action. Ostas (2001) explains trade association work: "[It is] designed to present the common interests of the otherwise competing firms. Managing the law and the legislative process has become a tool of competitive strategy" (p. 264). Those organizations have the resources to monitor regulatory processes; average citizens and nonprofit groups usually do not. Consider the November 11, 1998, correspondence between Chairman Ken Lay of Enron and then-governor George W. Bush of Texas. Lay concludes: "Please have your team let me know what Enron can do to be helpful in not only passing electricity restructuring legislation but also in pursuing the rest of your legislative agenda. Again, Linda and I extend our heartiest congratulations! We look forward to working with you and your team as you bring Texas into the 21st century. Sincerely, Ken." Then this hand-written note: "George: Linda and I are incredibly proud of you and Laura. Ken" (Bush-Lay Letters, 2004). Sometimes regulators and the regulated can be inordinately friendly.

After enactment, corporations use lawsuits to stay implementation, overturn, or weaken a law. With a certain irony, corporations point to the very laws they shaped as protections for the public interest. They cite those laws as an affirmative defense to lawsuits. For instance, in the United States, tobacco companies put warning labels on their products and then "successfully argued before the U.S. Supreme Court that the warning relieves the companies of some degree of liability" (Hilts, 1996, p. 35).

ENTER SARBANES-OXLEY

The most direct product of the "trust drought" that Spencer describes is the Sarbanes-Oxley Act passed by Congress and signed into law in July 2002. In the words of the *Harvard Law Review*:

> Arguably the most far-reaching corporate reform legislation since the Securities and Exchange Acts of 1933 and 1934, the Act was designed to increase the transparency, integrity and accountability of public companies and, in turn, to combat the kind of corporate deceit that had given rise to the scandals and financial breakdowns. (Notes, 2003, p. 2123)

An emerging perspective in legal scholarship raises doubts about the success of such measures, however well intentioned. Conventionally, regulations are premised on managing actors who are personally and economically rational. Prentice (2003) sums up the limits of rationality:

> Of course, rational wrongdoers would have been deterred by the civil and criminal provisions already on the books that will likely send

Enron's Michael Kopper and Andy Fastow, WorldCom's Scott Sullivan, Tyco's Dennis Kozlowski, and others to jail. Unfortunately perhaps, it is not a rational world . . . even beneficial legislation like Sarbanes-Oxley offers no panacea. (p. 442)

This criticism is in response to the Chicago School that privileges economic rationality. To support his point, Prentice inventories barriers to rationality: "bounded rationality" based on incomplete information; "satisficing," making "good enough" decisions; seeing what you believe (confirmation bias); recalling information selectively and optimistically; framing issues deceptively; using examples rather than statistics; hanging onto sunk costs; and "bounded willpower": even with understanding (e.g., smoking and health), people may be unwilling to change (Prentice, 2003, p. 426).

These behavioral principles raise serious questions about the rational/economic model of human, and thus corporate, behavior. The Sarbanes-Oxley Act may be cited as a basis for renewed confidence in the markets, but it seems safe to predict now that some corporate leaders, with no interest in rational action, will transgress its terms for reasons that we cannot now anticipate. As Prentice (2003) notes, "According to traditional economic analysis, regulation of Enron was unnecessary because Enron, like other rational actors, would voluntarily act honestly in order to reduce long-term costs of raising capital, and its officers would not derail promising individual careers by engaging in financial fraud" (p. 427).

Perhaps hope is to be found in a new psychological instrument to identify psychopaths. Its developers, psychologists, note that in business such individuals "are prone to being 'subcriminal' psychopaths: smooth-talking, energetic individuals who easily charm their way into jobs and promotions but who are exceedingly manipulative, narcissistic and ruthless" (Psychopathic C.E.O.s, 2004). The frenetic climate of modern business is a perfect fit for the psychopathic style: "If I couldn't study psychopaths in prison, I would go down to the Stock Exchange" (Psychopathic C.E.O.s, 2004).

LAW, CORPORATE GOVERNANCE, AND CSR

One form of regulation that gets much attention, especially in the legal community, is corporate governance. There is a vibrant debate among legal scholars on questions of CSR and its in-house incarnation, corporate governance. The debate ranges across issues of what should be taught, for what reason, and alternate means of reaching those goals. Greenfield (2000) decries the short shrift given to these sorts of issues in many law classrooms: "Professors of corporate law however, neglect broad questions surrounding the role of corporations in society because of perceived time constraints . . . it is impossible, it is said, to spend more than a few class hours on the softer issues of corporate personality, the duty of the corporation to nonshareholder constituencies, and the like" (p. 1012). These omissions, Greenfield contends, preclude students from confronting a pivotal question: Is the corporation too powerful an institution?

Greenfield (2000) underscores this concern. Corporate profits rose at a double-digit rate from 1993 to 1997, while workers' hourly wages, in constant dollars, fell to $1 below 1973 levels. While productivity has risen annually, 30% of workers cannot rise above poverty levels. Of the poor, 70% are working people. Salaries of CEOs are 400 times that of the average worker; two decades earlier, the difference was less than 30 times. CEOs earn the average worker's annual salary in less than one day. Greenfield characterizes these data as flaws in the economic system and adds, "Corporate law is a key part of the economic system. Corporate lawyers and corporate law professors should be participants in the discussion of how to remedy that system's flaws" (p. 1017).

The United States has the highest poverty rate among advanced economies, Greenfield notes, and suggests that students be reminded that societal arrangement, including the status quo, is a choice. He suggests another way to cast the question: "In a society in which many people have nice cars but cannot find a place to park them safely, ought that society not spend less effort on producing cars more efficiently and more effort in trying to create a society that is stable and safe?" (Greenfield, 2000, p. 1020). As an avenue to that awareness, he suggests that fellow professors teach *Local 1330 v. United States Steel Corp* (1980), a case arising from the closing of Youngstown Steel. Although the company lied to the workers, it prevails in this case; the court's ruling privileges shareholders over all other interested parties, but this text serves to highlight the tensions in that position.

Law professor Therese Maynard (2002) points to the Progressive Law Movement as a philosophy that transcends the reliance on law and economics alone to solve modern corporate law problems. She examines the problem of "spinning," or the practice of investment banking firms allocating attractive initial public offering (IPO) shares to individual clients in anticipation of future business arrangements with their firms. The individual then sells the IPO shares after their initial runup and makes a lavish personal profit. Maynard recounts a case in which the client "flipped" the stock and pocketed $2 million (p. 1514). Within a month, his firm used the same investment bank for its IPO.

As an antidote to this sort of behavior, she cites the work of Melvin Eisenberg, who stresses the importance of fiduciary duty law, especially the duty of loyalty, in promoting proper corporate behavior. Eisenberg dichotomizes loyalty: "I will refer to loyalty that is based on an internalized norm . . . as *authentic*, and to loyalty based on reputational concerns as *instrumental*. Instrumental loyalty is good, but authentic loyalty is better" (Eisenberg, 1999, cited in Maynard, 2002, p. 1511). Maynard notes that in addition to loyalty, the employee also has a fiduciary duty of candor. Under this principle, the employee would be obliged to tell the firm of the IPO share offer since failing to do so blocks the firm's right to pursue that profitable avenue. The candor principle also applies when the firm is selecting bankers to handle its IPO; the CEO needs to reveal the earlier business dealing so that the board can scrutinize his advice about bankers with that awareness in mind (Maynard, 2002, p. 1520). Beyond the realm of legal duties, such disclosures also constitute ethical conduct that the market, employees, and other parties should be able to expect from an executive.

Maynard closes with the observation that strict judicial enforcement of these fiduciary duties has a salutary effect on the definition and reinforcement of social norms within corporations. Maynard (2002) explains: "These norms that are internalized into one's character go a long way toward explaining why certain things are simply *not* done, while other things simply *are* done. . . . Progressive corporate law . . . presents the opportunity for corporate law scholars to acknowledge explicitly the importance of *ethics* in the decision-making process in everyday corporate life" (p. 1524).

CHALLENGES OF CORPORATE RHETORIC

Corporations have a fundamental rhetorical difficulty, especially when they wish to act as advocates. The difficulty is that the organization will speak to many specialized audiences—employees, regulators, stockholders, local governments—and yet all these corporate stories must add up. This challenge of articulating a clear and defensible truth to all comers is one of the key duties of management.

There is more than a little bruising of credibility when a critic catches the corporate rhetor promoting two divergent views of reality. For example, corporate reformer Ralph Nader used executives' contradictory statements regarding a "product liability explosion" to suggest their hypocrisy. In public statements, the executives, such as Dow Chemical's CEO Frank Popoff, decried product liability suits: "Our uniquely American legal system imposes an annual tax . . . of $150 billion to $200 billion on all our industries because of the problem. I think it's a killer to our global competitiveness" (Nader, 1995, p. 24). At the time of this statement, Dow faced lawsuits related to its drug Seldane and also silicone breast implants. Nader then quotes the company's 10-K report to investors: "[T]he possibility that litigation of these claims would materially impact the company's consolidated financial statements is remote" (p. 24).

Codes of ethics present another rhetorical challenge for the corporation. The reliance on corporate codes in the reasoning of Sarbanes-Oxley offers only a partial mechanism for regulating corporate behavior. Codes promoted under the legislation offer no recourse when the transgressions are committed at the highest level of the organization: "And a striking similarity among all of the recent corporate scandals is the high level of the major players" (Notes, 2003, p. 2128).

One of the most venerated mechanisms in any CSR discussion is the appeal to—even requirement for—corporate codes of ethics. These calls are important gestures and can even produce meaningful results but the secret lies in the discourse around developing a code. Organizational culture must play a central role in the crafting of codes if they are to be effective. An open discussion of the difficult choices and close calls inherent in business judgments is very useful for organization members. It is that process of conversation and deliberation and the awareness and sensitivity it engenders, rather than a hard copy code, that are valuable.

Enron's code of ethics, known as RICE—respect, integrity, communication, and excellence—has been exposed as a token and a smokescreen: "[D]espite its well-known RICE code of ethics, the real rule was an unwritten one: NO BAD NEWS" (Prentice, 2003, p. 430). Perhaps, in hindsight, this code should be labeled "puffed RICE."

MAKING REGULATION WORK

There are instances of successful self-regulation in American industry. Hemphill (2003) cites the U.S. entertainment industry—motion pictures, music recording, and electronic video games—as a success story in public issue management and self-regulation. This industry has established its own standards and enforced them, thus reducing governmental oversight (p. 341). He defines the elements of successful self-regulation: "clear in their intent, considered legitimate by industry membership, and complied with voluntarily" (Hemphill, 2003, p. 348).

Social compliance stands in contrast to regulation. It focuses on "the monitoring of labor, health and safety, and environmental standards in the workplace" (Blecher, 2004, p. 479). The practice by nongovernmental organizations reflects a view that laws in both developing and developed nations (including the United States) may fail to protect human rights and labor rights. Blecher notes, for instance, that U.S. law does not cap working hours or require paid vacations. Social custom usually means that employees are not abused, but in reality that protection is customary, not legal.

SA8000 is an industry code that business and nongovernmental organizations have jointly developed to assure basic rights: "[It] is increasingly becoming the standard against which U.S. companies monitor their contractors' labor practices" (Blecher, 2004, p. 479). Such a standard is necessary, she notes, because the laws of many nations are weak or easily manipulated.

Assuring supplier compliance with corporate standards is now a major activity for prominent brands and retailers. The Gap has 100 staffers devoted to that subject. Nike has had its program in place since 1992; 80 employees monitor its contractors. A point system measures compliance; contract assignments may be based on those rankings. The effectiveness of these efforts has had little study, although the monitors are often touted in public relations activities (O'Rourke, 2003, p. 10).

The long and flexible supply chains that are facts of life in the apparel industry make monitoring—whether governmental or nongovernmental—very difficult: "The Gap alone sources from 4,000 factories in 55 countries; Disney is estimated to source from over 30,000 factories and Walmart [sic] from even more" (O'Rourke, 2003, p. 21).

GLOBAL RESPONSIBILITIES

United States regulations may solve a problem at the national level, but that action may not be the end of the matter in terms of CSR. The U.S. Environmental Protection Agency (EPA) banned U.S. sales of the pesticide dibromochloropropane, found to cause sterility, in 1979. It was developed by Shell and Occidental in the 1940s. After the EPA action, its use continued in Central America and elsewhere on banana plantations. As a consequence of subsequent exposure, 3,000 Central American fruit workers filed suit in federal court against corporations that are household names in the United States: Shell Oil, Dow Chemical, Occidental Petroleum, Dole Food, Del Monte Fresh Produce, and Chiquita Brands.

Some of these companies settled earlier suits in the countries of use where legal systems are rudimentary at best. The settlements ranged from $1,500 to $2,000 per plaintiff. A more recent suit in Nicaragua led to a verdict of more than $1 million per worker. The companies have refused to pay, and the order will have to go through U.S. courts (Windsor, 2004, p. 744).

DeMott (1997) distills the essential issue in the examination of CSR and regulation: "[I]t is often difficult to explain how duties and rights . . . might be intelligibly applied to a person that is purely the invented creature of compliance with legal form" (p. 39). Legal scholar H. L. A. Hart further parses the issue: "[I]t is not the legal personality but the 'moral' personality that perplexes most" (quoted in DeMott, 1997, p. 39).

CORPORATE AGENCY AND OVERSIGHT

The questions of agency and oversight are central to issues of CSR. DeMott (1997) notes that the crucial mechanism for a corporation is "the incentive structure within which its agents act" (p. 40). It follows that incentives play a large part in shaping organizational culture, and "directors are ultimately accountable for the corporation's culture" (p. 41). When things go wrong, there are inevitably questions about the organization's responsibility for bad acts. DeMott shows that management and directors may face liability not for ordering bad actions but for overseeing an incentive structure that led to them. The converse of this principle underscores the importance of creating incentives for right action within the corporate culture.

Prentice (2003) summarizes the issues of ethics and culture highlighted by Enron and Tyco and by all the unheralded corporations with sound ethics: "When corporate officers only talk the talk and do not walk the walk, codes of ethics are essentially meaningless" (p. 436). Stone (1975) transcends CSR to promote social responsiveness as a corporate stance, not a mere statement of philosophy as social responsibility may be. "Responsiveness" connotes habits of awareness and preparation to act. Consider the highway analogy: the responsible motorist will stop to aid someone in distress while the responsive motorist will as well but will carry a fire extinguisher, flashlight, and first aid kit in the car for the time when the response is needed (Hess, 1999, p. 54).

Hess (1999) advocates social reports as a mechanism for dialogue between the corporation and the public. The information explains the company's practices and allows stakeholders to offer feedback. Social reporting creates an ongoing cycle of interaction. He cites the social reporting practices of The Body Shop International and Ben & Jerry's Homemade as among the most widely publicized.

When all else fails, candor or an expression of apology is sound both ethically and strategically. Stephen Parrish of Altria [*nee* Philip Morris] notes the positive, if challenging, new road the firm is taking: "We still have to keep proving we're sincere and not just trying to reduce the amount of punitive damage in lawsuits brought by cigarette smokers" (Alsop, 2004, p. 27). Similarly, James

Adamson, who took over the parent company of Denny's following racial discrimination charges, gets the message:

> If management had told African-Americans that they were sorry and employees would either be fired or receive diversity training, the company could have avoided a U.S. Justice Department investigation. Sometimes you have to say you're sorry and risk litigation and stand tall and protect your bonds with your customers. But instead, it took a $54 million class action settlement and many years of hard work to see the tide turn with the African-American community. (Alsop, 2004, p. 28)

CORPORATE ACTIONS

In tracing the evolution of issues management as a tool of organizational strategy, Heath (2002) defines the current situation as an opportunity to become proactive in dealing with internal and external challenges. He targets four areas for improvement: strategic business planning, corporate responsibility standards, monitoring issues, and public policy dialogue. He cites the issue monitoring and reacting practices of Enron as exemplary; the firm lacked only one thing: "a commitment to corporate responsibility that truly reflected the reality of sound business practices rather than sheer opportunism" (p. 211). Heath highlights three issues worthy of greater concern from corporate leaders: protecting and enhancing brand equity, understanding the full value of information and goodwill, and providing options through issues management to meet boardroom opportunities and challenges (p. 212).

Macleod (2001) takes a novel approach to issues of communication and CSR. She urges communication professionals within the organization to apply their skills to "persuade shareholders of the reputation-building benefits of CSR" (p. 8). Conventionally, communicators are charged with making the CSR message fly with the broader public, but Macleod recognizes the need for a more deft touch in the long-term interest of the organization: "The challenge is to reveal what a company is doing without making it look too self-interested" (p. 8). Alsop (2004) expresses a similar concern in this fashion: "The trick is to make your corporate citizenship powerful and highly visible

without looking as if you're just out for glory" (p. 24). The additional problem is in characterizing that stance as a trick. These efforts are necessary because the corporation confronts a number of crucial issues: an increasingly stark rich–poor divide, interests in sustainability, and pressures for transparency. Macleod (2001) underscores the essential challenge and the ephemeral dimension of CSR promotion: "Getting the tone right is crucial" (p. 8). Then she adds, "CSR isn't just about PR. It has to have foundations in policy" (p. 9).

In the realm of corporate self-praise there is an important role for rhetorical craft. Alsop (2004) recounts as inartful and ineffective DuPont's text-heavy and self-congratulatory image ad about its efforts to reduce chlorofluorocarbons. In contrast, he profiles a subtle and effective ad for Toyota's gas-electric hybrid vehicle that was light on copy and bore the headline, "Daddy, what's smog?" (p. 25).

REGULATION OF THE SELF

Regardless of documented cases, citizens continue to operate on the assumption that corporations are law abiding. Instances of misbehavior are usually attributed to individuals; the public perceives nothing inherently antisocial in the notion of a corporation. People want to believe that individual ethics will spawn CSR behaviors. However, when individuals enter into social systems—including corporations—they are subject to forces beyond their own values.

Sociologist Robert Jackall (1983) examines the impact of bureaucracy on executive ethics. One executive put the issue in practical terms: "What is right in the corporation is what the guy above you wants from you" (p. 6). Jackall concludes that bureaucracy is always about power and domination, not mere management techniques. He challenges the notion of CSR: "Sooner or later, most managers realize . . . that there are no intrinsic connections between the good of a particular corporation, the good of an individual manager, and the common weal" (p. 198).

On the issue of regulation and the self, the question of new technologies in general and the Internet specifically needs to be raised. Corporations and other powerful institutions have created websites that introduce their offerings and views in cyberspace. The technology is a mild adjunct to all of the conventional ways that firms present and promote their views. In contrast, the World Wide Web has been a revolutionary site for resistance to established power. Roper (2002) profiles Internet activism and predicts "a rise in the power of citizens and a government response to that power that will include regulation to protect social and environmental interests" (p. 113). The Internet has become the town square for the global village, to mix several metaphors. Roper notes that established interests hold global economic summits, but now they are behind fortifications and swathed by security agents, following the counterdemonstrations in Seattle in 1999 associated with the meeting of the World Trade Organization.

To the extent that powerful organized interests dominate issues and agendas, the Internet "deregulates" information and access with a mode of organizing equally available to all comers. This deregulation creates the possibility of meaningful dissent from an otherwise calcified power structure. The interests that promote "free trade" concepts now have to deal with dissenters, who can organize, gather, and publicize their views and official responses without reliance on conventional institutions. This resource questions the legitimacy of corporate actions and repositions dissenters and the public at large. Roper (2002) notes that modern corporate practice accords people significance as consumers—individuals who are recipients of economic choices provided by multinational providers as are governments: "Absent from the model is the role of citizens with the power, essential to democracy, to collectively confer or deny legitimation to governing bodies" (p. 116). Creative use of the Internet, however, recreates the public sphere stressed by Habermas and allows people to function once again as citizens.

RECOMMENDATIONS

Macleod (2001) offers specific steps for greater success in promoting CSR: seek credibility through third-party publicity; be certain that performance supports presentation; use compassionate and enthusiastic spokespeople, ideally the CEO; and promote best practices to other organizations (p. 9). These are all worthwhile suggestions, but they hover around the crucial issue identified by Macleod—public and media skepticism of altruistic claims. The organization and its messengers must walk a fine line.

After contemplating all the issues facing organizational public affairs practice in the current climate, Spencer (2002) suggests a plain standard: "Success, both in business and in public affairs, may come to rest not so much on the adoption of ethical codes, but on the internalization of an ethos of openness and truth that regenerates trust" (p. 189).

The progressive law movement offers a subtle approach to negotiating the interactions of the corporation and society. It provides empowerment to attorneys who want to help the organization do the right thing: "One of the most important messages that I take away from the teachings of the emerging body of work known as progressive corporate law is that it preserves the practice of law as a noble profession" (Maynard, 2002, p. 1528).

There are many reasons to engage in CSR— some noble, some very pragmatic. It was Saul Alinsky (1971) who said, "The fact is that it is not man's 'better nature' but his self-interest that demands that he be his brother's keeper. . . . This is the low road to morality. There is no other" (p. 23).

Martha Stewart, as both her person and her corporation, has taken a beating in the realms of reputation and share value. Alsop (2004) believes that some of that harm could have been mitigated with attention to CSR, but there was none:

A search of the . . . web sites reveals nothing about social responsibility. You will learn on the corporate site about Martha's birth date— August 3—her favorite perfume brands, and the names of her hairdresser and her four dogs and seven cats. She and her company either don't understand or don't care much about what's really of concern to people today. It's not a good thing. (p. 24)

One of the most interesting ideas in improving labor–management relations is the "incomplete contract" as described by Greenfield (2002). These relationships are important for many reasons; for this article, they matter because employees must inevitably be the vehicles for successful corporate action, including meeting regulatory obligations. The essence of the notion is that employee performance is higher in the absence of explicit performance requirements. When both parties meet in an atmosphere of mutual respect, good things happen. In bargaining experiments, "[n]either participant acts selfishly. . . . If the employer offers a high wage, the employee responds with higher effort, even when the employer is unable to penalize the employee for offering less. . . . It may be more profitable for firms to pay higher-than-competitive wages" (p. 626).

As Wells (2002) observed, the topic of CSR has been discussed repeatedly throughout the last century with no clear results. However, there seems to be a sea change with a series of significant scandals, the rise of globalism, the pervasiveness and egalitarianism of the Internet, and the decline of governmental powers in many corners of the world. Perhaps this round of discussion will mark a significant step forward in the relationship between capitalism and the flourishing of human society.

REFERENCES

Alinsky, S. D. (1971). *Rules for radicals*. New York: Vintage.

Alsop, R. J. (2004). Corporate reputation: Anything but superficial—the deep but fragile nature of corporate reputation. *Journal of Business Strategy, 25*(6), 21–29.

Blecher, L. (2004). Above and beyond the law. *Business & Society Review, 109*(4), 479–492.

Brummer, J. J. (1991). *Corporate social responsibility and legitimacy: An interdisciplinary analysis*. New York: Greenwood Press.

Bush-Lay Letters. (2004, July 8). Retrieved January 6, 2005, from http://www.thesmokinggun.com/archive/0708042lay4.html.

Cigarette-makers appeal U.S. racketeering claim. (2004, July 27). *Winston-Salem Journal*, A1.

DeMott, D. A. (1997). Organizational incentives to care about the law. *Law & Contemporary Social Problems, 60*(4), 39–66.

Directors on Notice. (2005, January 8). *New York Times*. Retrieved January 8, 2005, from http://www.nytimes.com/2005/01/08/opinion/8sat2.html.

Dowling, J., & Pfeffer, J. (1975). Organizational legitimacy: Social values and organizational behavior. *Pacific Sociological Review, 18*(1), 122–136.

Eichenwald, K. (2005, January 8). Ex-directors at Enron to chip in on settlement. *New York Times*. Retrieved January 8, 2005, from http://www.nytimes.com/2005/01/08/business/08enron.html

Friedman, M. (1970, September 13). The social responsibility of business is to increase its profits. *New York Times Magazine*, pp. 32–39.

Greenfield, K. (2000). There's a forest in those trees: Teaching about the role of corporations in society. *Georgia Law Review, 34*(2), 1011–1024.

Greenfield, K. (2002). Using behavioral economics to show the power and efficiency of corporate law as regulatory tool. *University of California Davis Law Review, 35*(3), 581–644.

Habermas, J. (1973). *Legitimation crisis* (T. McCarthy, Trans.). Boston, MA: Beacon.

Hart, H. L. A. (1954). Definition and theory in jurisprudence. *Law Quarterly Review 70*(1), 37–55.

Heath, R. L. (2002). Issues management: Its past, present and future. *Journal of Public Affairs, 2*(4), 209–214.

Hemphill, T. A. (2003). Self-regulation, public issue management and marketing practices in the US entertainment industry. *Journal of Public Affairs, 3*(4), 338–357.

Hess, D. (1999). Social reporting: A reflexive law approach to corporate social responsiveness. *Journal of Corporation Law, 25*(1), 41–84.

Hilts, P. J. (1996). *Smokescreen: The truth behind the tobacco industry cover-up*. Reading, MA: Addison-Wesley Publishing Company.

Jackall, R. (1983, September-October). Moral mazes: Bureaucracy and managerial work. *Harvard Business Review, 61*(5) pp. 118–130.

Jackall, R., & Hirota, J. M. (2000). *The imagemakers: Advertising, public relations and the ethos of advocacy*. Chicago: University of Chicago Press.

Lipset, S. M., & Schneider, W. (1987). *The confidence gap: Business, labor, and government in the public mind* (rev. ed.). Baltimore, MD: Johns Hopkins University Press.

Llewellyn, J. T. (1990). The rhetoric of corporate citizenship (Doctoral dissertation, University of Texas). *Dissertations Abstracts International, 52*, 22.

Local 1330 v. United States Steel Corp. 631 F.2d 1264 (6th Cir. 1980).

McIntosh, M., Leipziger, D., Jones, K., & Coleman, G. (Eds.). (1998). *Corporate citizenship: Successful strategies for responsible companies*. London: Financial Times.

Macleod, S. (2001, August/September). Why worry about CSR? *Strategic Communication Management,5*(5) pp. 8–9.

Marlin, A. T. (1998). Foreword. In M. McIntosh, D. Leipziger, K. Jones, & G. Coleman (Eds.), *Corporate citizenship: Successful strategies for responsible companies* (pp. xi–xiii). London: Financial Times.

Maynard, T. (2002). Law matters. Lawyers matter. *Tulane Law Review, 76*(6), 1501–1529.

Morgenson, G. (2005, January 1). The envelopes, please. *New York Times.* Retrieved January 2, 2005, from http://www.nytimes.com/2005/01/01/business/yourmoney/02award.

Nader, R. (May 8, 1995). Double talk on tort reform. *Legal Times,* p. 24.

Notes. (2003). The good, the bad and their corporate codes of ethics: Enron, Sarbanes-Oxley, and the problems with legislating good behavior. *Harvard Law Review, 116*(7), 2123–2141.

Notes. (2004). Finding strategic corporate citizenship: A new game theoretic view. *Harvard Law Review, 117*(6), 1957–1980.

O'Rourke, D. (2003). Outsourcing regulation: Analyzing nongovernmental systems of labor standards and monitoring. *Policy Studies Journal, 31*(1), 1–29.

Ostas, D. T. (2001). Deconstructing corporate social responsibility: Insights from legal and economic theory. *American Business Law Journal, 38*(2), 261–299.

Pfeffer, J. (1985). Organizations and organizational theory. In G. Lindzey & E. Aronson (Eds.), *The handbook of social psychology* (3rd ed., pp. 379–440). New York: Random House.

Prentice, R. (2003). Enron: A brief behavioral autopsy. *American Business Law Journal, 40*(2), 417–444.

Psychopathic C.E.O.s. (2004, December 12). *New York Times Magazine,* p. 90.

Roper, J. (2002). Government, corporate or social power? The Internet as a tool in the struggle for dominance in social policy. *Journal of Public Affairs, 2*(3), 113–124.

Sanger, D. E., & Hoge, W. (2005, January 1). U.S. vows big increase in aid for victims of Asian disaster. *New York Times.* Retrieved January 2, 2005, from http://www.nytimes.com/2005/01/01/international/worldspecial4/01d.

Schering-Plough settles kickback charges. (2004, July 31). *Winston-Salem Journal,* D1.

Smith, R., & Eisenberg, E. M. (1987). Conflict at Disneyland: A root metaphor analysis. *Communication Monographs, 54*(4), 367–380.

Spencer, T. (2002). Truth and public affairs. *Journal of Public Affairs, 2*(3), 186–189.

Stone, C. D. (1975). *Where the law ends: The social control of corporate behavior.* New York: Harper & Row.

Wells, C. A. H. (2002). The cycles of corporate social responsibility: An historical retrospective for the twenty-first century. *University of Kansas Law Review, 51*(1), 77–140.

White, E. (2002, November 13). PR firms advise corporations on social-responsibility issues. *Wall Street Journal,* p. B10.

Windsor, D. (2004). The development of international business norms. *Business Ethics Quarterly, 14*(4), 729–754.

13

Can Corporate Personhood
Be Socially Responsible?

DEAN RITZ

Corporate personhood creates equality before the law that results in inequality in human society. It permits corporate appeals to justice that result in human injustice. These claims—the first legal, the latter moral—appeal to the ideals of human equality before the law and universal participation in the political community, ideals reflected in normative definitions of democracy. If the primary social good of a civil society is democratic self-governance, then privileging a few to deny the democratic rights of the many works in opposition to that primary social good. The direct consequences of corporate personhood unavoidably violate that social good, and so corporate personhood is rightly declared socially irresponsible.

Instead, corporate social responsibility (CSR) efforts should realign and drive towards two ends: first, empowering human communities to resist corporate rights claims that invalidate and deny the inalienable rights of human beings, which could be accomplished by increasing the power and efficiency of genuinely democratic processes; second, eliminating the constitutional rights granted to corporations and thus the anti-democratic powers granted to corporate agents.[1] I begin this chapter by establishing the meaning of the terms and claims. Then in the main body I investigate the claims and consider counterclaims. I then conclude by proposing a response to the situation.

BACKGROUND

Consider two tools of modern society: corporations and a republican form of government. At the most superficial level, *corporations* are "mechanisms by means of which a number of persons unite for the purpose of assembling a fund of capital with which to carry on some business enterprises" (Dodd, 1954, p. 367). In the United States, they are created and dissolved under the authority of individual states, with each corporation a state-created fictional entity possessing a legal existence independent of its shareholders and incorporators. This fictional entity may enter into contracts, hold named title to property, incur tax liability, and be a party to a lawsuit—characteristics also ascribed to natural persons (Millon, 2001, pp. 39–40). State corporation codes now permit corporations to be created for no specific purpose other than providing shareholders with the privileges of incorporation. These privileges include perpetual existence, special tax treatment, the imposition of fines rather than imprisonment of shareholders or corporate employees for corporate violations of law, shareholder liability limited to the value of their investment and no more, and legal personhood with its consequent constitutional rights. This chapter focuses on state-chartered for-profit corporations only.

The other tool of modern society, the *republican form of government*, is by definition subject to the people; that is, the people hold the ultimate power, with the government a formal arrangement through which that power is exercised upon the population. A minimal list of role-related responsibilities includes maintaining a system of laws, keeping the peace, and promoting the good. Maintaining a system of laws includes procedures for their establishment, so the sovereign people may codify their will in law; for their publication, so those subject to them may be adequately informed; for their enforcement, including procedures for dealing with lawbreakers; and for their modification and revocation. A system of laws is a prerequisite for keeping order. Keeping the peace refers to keeping the peace between people and the government as well as between the people themselves. Compared to a totalitarian government, it is considered more benign and likely more efficient to "set limits to the power which the ruler should be suffered to exercise over the community" (Mill, 1998, p. 6). Such an arrangement motivates people peaceably to grant authority to a government, and government officials willingly to accept limits on the power entrusted to them. Each exchanges some liberty for mutual stability and security. A constitutionalized government makes explicit this arrangement by enumerating the basic rules, particularly the responsibilities and the corollary limits on the power of the government, public officials, and other agents of the government.

Consequently, a republican form of government must provide remedies for harms upon the people's sovereignty or infringement upon the people's inalienable rights—particularly when the government is the agent of these harms. Governments can and do act beyond their authority, beyond constitutional limits. When they do, the people's sovereignty collapses in the absence of practical remedies. But who counts as the sovereign people? All of us? Just a few of us? This is where the ideals of democracy arise. The most central democratic ideal is universal participation. The sovereign people should comprise every moral agent in the political community, *moral agents* being individual persons capable of making decisions for which they may be praised or blamed.

The democratic ideal of universal participation adds two more desirable role-related responsibilities to a republican form of government. First, it should distribute rather than consolidate power (Morehouse, 2001, p. 213). Second, it has a responsibility to prevent concentrations of private

power from overwhelming public power, what President Franklin Roosevelt defined as fascism (Roosevelt, 1938). Both are violated when political power is consolidated into the hands of the few. Consolidation results from the establishment of a ruling class or, complementarily, through the abrogation of political rights ostensibly and equally held by all moral agents. Monarchies and plutocracies are examples of the former. The disenfranchisement of 4.7 million felons in the United States is an example of the latter (Felons, 2004). Herein, the term *republican form of government* refers to a republican form of government reflecting democratic ideals.

A republican form of government receives grants of power from the sovereign people—not a sovereign king or queen. The people retain rights against the government, that is, against the government's use of power that is beyond the government's authority. So, a *right* is a type of power, too. Legal philosopher Richard Dworkin, in his book *Taking Rights Seriously* (1977), claims that having a right implies that it is wrong to interfere with it, or at least special justification is required (p. 188). He further identifies and distinguishes two kinds of rights: legal rights and moral rights (p. 185). *Legal rights* are those granted by the government, such as the right to make a right turn at a red light (under specific conditions). These rights are established through the passage of laws, and their revocation or modification is done through the passage of other laws. *Moral rights*, in contrast, exist outside the law and are characterized as those rights that people have independent of any government (p. 184).

What are these moral rights? Thomas Hobbes (1651/1997), a philosopher with a dismal view of human nature, identifies one. He asserts a natural right to protect oneself: "The Right Of Nature . . . is the Liberty each man hath, to use his own power, as he will himselfe, for the preservation of his own Nature; that is to say, of his own life" (p. 72). To say that a right arises from a state of nature is also to say that it exists independent of any government and so, too, may be considered a moral right. *Inalienable rights* are a special class of moral rights. These are those moral rights essential for entering into a social contract, such as establishing a government—particularly a republican form of government. The first inalienable right, then, is the right to establish a republican form of government. This right must exist outside and thus independent of a republican form of government; otherwise, how could we exercise it and establish this government? As a matter of legal fact, "[t]he United States shall guarantee to every State in this Union a Republican Form of Government" (U.S. Const., Art. IV, § 4). This right to form a republican form of government presumes the right to associate with others freely and to enter into social contracts with others, for without these capacities we could never establish this kind of government.

What do these inalienable rights rest upon? What is their foundation? There are those who will argue that we have no inalienable rights, that they are nothing more than an idealistic claim to the "natural rights" philosopher Jeremy Bentham (2002) famously characterized as "nonsense upon stilts." True, violent governmental persecution of persons due to their political, social, or cultural beliefs proves that rights are not always assured. For example, many twentieth-century governments passed laws disenfranchising certain populations in order to subsequently "legally" deny these populations' rights (Arendt, 1976, pp. 276–288). By making these denials of rights legal, the governments claim that no harm is done and thus no remedy required. This practice continues in a similar manner today with "enemy combatants" held by the United States, a status the federal government asserts curtails or eliminates enemy combatants' rights (Priest, 2005). No legal rights, thus no legal harms.

This vulnerability acknowledged, I appeal to inalienable rights in the context of a republican form of government as those a sovereign people minimally expect for themselves in order to maintain sovereignty over their government. In this context, no rational human being would fail to demand and assume these rights, and no government bound to provide a republican form of government, as the U.S. government is bound to do, can justify abrogating them. If they are abrogated, then the republican form of government is lost. And if citizens accept this, then their sovereignty is lost. A sovereign people should not and will not compromise them, nor should their republican form of government. So essential are these rights that not only should they not be given up, they cannot be given up even if we sovereign people wish to do so; this is the very meaning of taking rights seriously (Dworkin, 1977, p. 191).

In summary, our inalienable rights are those rights essential for a sovereign people in the context of a republican form of government: a right to freely associate with others, a right to enter into social contracts with others, a right to form a republican form of government, a right to equality before the law, and a right to universal participation in the political community. A republican form of government has role-related responsibilities to distribute rather than consolidate power, to prevent concentrations of private power from overwhelming public power, and to provide practical remedies to infringement upon inalienable rights—particularly when committed by the government or its agents.

The ideal of universal participation in the political community applies to rights as well. Who gets them? This is central to the question at hand: is it socially responsible for a sovereign people to codify corporations as legal persons and consequently bestow constitutional rights upon them? History has much to offer in substantiating the importance of this inquiry and in answering it. Extending inalienable rights to include more human beings, such as indentured servants, those who did not own real estate, African-Americans, Native Americans, women, and other classes of persons took generations of large-scale effort. In other words, it took genuine social movements where a *movement* is defined as an effort to secure rights—not an effort to regulate harm (R. L. Grossman, personal communication, March 2005). We can look at two of these social movements to expand our appreciation of personhood: the civil rights movement, particularly the efforts of abolitionists, and the women's rights movement. Both sought personhood and thus rights for their respective classes of human beings. Both classes suffered from the government's denials of their inalienable rights due to their status as less than legal persons. Both were forced to submit to the rule of those who denied these rights, denials backed by the full power of the government.

The civil rights movement may be characterized as a struggle for legal recognition of personhood, in this case, the recognition of African-Americans as the legal equals to Caucasians and thus entitled to the same rights and privileges. Essential to this claim is the demand that government cease its efforts to deny the rights of African-Americans, cease pretending that rights denials are harmless because they are legal. The public campaign (as illustrated in figure 13.1) provoked Americans to recognize that rights denials, although legal, are in fact abhorrent harms.

Regarding the earlier struggle against slavery, William P. Meyers (personal communication, January 2001) noted, "Slavery is the legal fiction that a person is property. Corporate personhood is the legal fiction that property is a person." The notion that people may be a form of property is an ancient one, but abolitionists challenged this "peculiar institution" with decades of organizing and resistance efforts, including flagrant violations of law (e.g., the Underground Railroad). These efforts culminated in the passage of the 13th Amendment to the U.S. Constitution in 1865, ending legal slavery. Until then, slaves were defined as property and denied standing in court. They even remained slaves when traveling in free U.S. territories and states, for to grant slaves freedom under such circumstances was considered an unlawful deprivation of their owner's property (*Dred Scott v. Sanford*, 1851). The law, the courts, and the entire apparatus of government engaged in denying rights to slaves—to these human beings.

Abolitionists argued that before these persons were denied their inalienable rights, they were human beings (Graham, 1968, p. 605), and the government was obligated to recognize them as legal persons with full concomitant rights and protections. Abolitionists did not lobby for the establishment of a slave protection agency to regulate when and how a slave master may treat their slave, or ask slave owners to sign voluntary "codes of conduct" (Grossman, 2001, p. 301). Abolitionists did not seek to purchase all the slaves and then give each slave a property title to him or herself. And with the passage of the 13th Amendment, the government did not compensate slaveholders for their loss of property. They did not take these positions because these affirmed the myth that a person may be property. Instead, they sought a fundamental change to the culture and the law: African-Americans are human beings, with the government obligated to recognize their personhood and protect their inalienable rights. As Supreme Court Justice William Brennan wrote regarding government's duties to prevent rights denials:[2]

Government is the social organ to which all in our society look for the promotion of liberty, justice, fair and equal treatment, and the setting of worthy norms and goals for social conduct. Therefore something is uniquely amiss in a society where the government, the authoritative oracle of community values, involves itself in racial discrimination. Accordingly, in the cases that have come before us this Court has condemned significant state involvement in racial discrimination, however subtle and indirect it may have been and whatever form it may have taken. . . . These decisions represent vigilant fidelity to the constitutional principle that no State shall in any significant way lend its authority to the sordid business of racial

FIGURE **13.1.** Civil rights activists blocked by Tennessee national guardsmen and flanked by tanks in Memphis, Tennessee, 1968. © Bettmann/Corbis.

discrimination. (*Adickes v. Kress & Co.*, 1970, pp. 191–192)

The women's movement remains similar in spirit to that of the civil rights movement. It continues to seek full legal personhood, in this case the recognition of women as the legal equals to men and thus entitled to the same rights and privileges. Essential to this claim is the demand that government cease its efforts to deny the rights of women, cease pretending that these rights denials are harmless because they are legal. Throughout the recorded history of patriarchal societies, women received fewer and lesser rights and powers than those granted to men. They were denied the right to own property and thus their own wages; denied public education, access to private schools, and admission to the legal bar; they were denied the right to initiate divorce proceedings; denied medical decision-making authority for their bodies; and, of course, they were denied the right to vote (Freedman, 2002). Women, like slaves, were once considered property, in this case that of their husbands (or fathers or brothers). This is the rationale that in earlier times made it legally impossible for a husband to rape his wife. After all, how can he violate that which he owns?[3] Indeed, like slaveowners, one could argue that a man should be able to own as many wives as he can afford. As with slaves, the law, the courts, and the government engaged in denying rights to women—to these human beings.

American women continue fighting for legal equality. From 1923 until 1972, an Equal Rights Amendment was introduced into the U.S. Congress every year. Section 1 of the proposed amendment states, "Equality of rights under the law shall not be denied or abridged by the United States or by any state on account of sex" (Equal Rights Amendment, 2003). In 1972, the U.S. Congress passed this amendment and forwarded it to the states for ratification, where it then failed in the ratification process. It continues annually to be introduced into Congress but remains unratified, and women remain legal inferiors to men, their full humanity denied.

Why this interest in personhood? Because with its recognition comes the rights and protections afforded the class. Consequently, the government's infringement upon the class's rights is recognized as legal harm, and those harmed now have cause to seek legal remedies. The struggle for civil rights of African-Americans is a struggle for equal rights

under the law, to have their harms recognized and remedies made. The same is true of the women's rights movement. The same is true of the current gay rights movement. These movements drive toward this. And when the law is on your side so is the power of the government. In 1957, President Eisenhower sent the 101st Airborne Division to enforce the rights of nine African-American children and gain their entrance into an illegally segregated public school in Little Rock, Arkansas. In 1963, President Kennedy sent deputy federal marshals, U.S. border patrolmen, federal prison guards, and ultimately, federal troops to force the University of Mississippi to acquiesce and permit James Meredith, a young black man, to matriculate. This is what it means to have the law on your side. When the government or its agents deny rights, as the state governments of Arkansas and Mississippi did, the harms are recognized and the remedies backed by the full force of other branches of government.

Shareholders and incorporators had a movement of their own, the corporate rights movement. It was and is grounded in the recognition of corporations as legal persons. *Corporate personhood* defines corporations as legal persons. Public officials granted constitutional rights to corporations as a direct consequence of this definition. The following list highlights some of the constitutional rights awarded to corporations. They were not awarded by the lengthy constitutional amendment process used by African-Americans and women but by declarations of the U.S. Supreme Court. The year 1886 marks the Supreme Court decision that, "totally without reasons of precedent" (Horowitz, 1992, p. 67), first accepted the theory of corporate personhood in a claim to a federal constitutional right, the equal rights clause of the 14th Amendment (*Santa Clara v. Southern Pacific Railroad Co.*, 1886).[4] Here is a partial list of some consequent constitutional rights awarded by the Supreme Court. They are listed in chronological order (Edwards, 2003; Linzey, Brannen, & Grossman, 2003; Mayer, 1990, pp. 664–667).

- Fourteenth Amendment due process rights (*Minneapolis & St. L. R. Co. v. Beckwith*, 1889): Corporate agents gained a right for judicial review on state legislation that might exceed a state's authority with respect to the authority of the federal government.
- Fifth Amendment due process right (*Noble v. Union River Logging R. Co.*, 1893): Cor-

porate agents gained a right for judicial review for rights infringement on federal legislation.

- Fourth Amendment protections "against unreasonable searches and seizures" (*Hale v. Henkel*, 1906).
- Sixth Amendment right to a jury trial (*Armour Packing Co. v. United States*, 1908).
- Fifth Amendment right to compensation for government takings (*Pennsylvania Coal Co. v. Mahon*, 1922).
- Fifth Amendment right to freedom from double jeopardy (*Fong Foo v. United States*, 1962).
- Seventh Amendment right to a jury trial in a civil case (*Ross v. Bernhard*, 1970).
- First Amendment right to free speech for purely commercial speech (*Virginia Pharmacy Board v. Virginia Consumer Council*, 1976).
- First Amendment right to corporate political speech, particularly protecting the expenditure of money as a form of speech (*First Natl. Bank of Boston v. Bellotti*, 1978).
- First Amendment right against coerced speech, that is, association with speech whose content would compel them to speak in response (*Pacific Gas & Elec. Co. v. Public Util. Commn. of California*, 1986).

Corporations also acquired judicially invented special rights, including that of "managerial prerogative" and the "business judgment rule."[5] Supplementing this extension of corporate power, courts expanded the constitutional doctrine of the Commerce Clause (U.S. Const., Art. I, § 8) and the Contracts Clause (U.S. Const., Art. I, § 10). These extensions further limit the authority of individual states to define the character of economic activity within their jurisdictions; that is, they further privatize economic decision-making authority. Corporate due process rights enable corporate agents to seek judicial nullification of state and federal legislation as beyond the government's authority. Individual states also awarded to corporations many of the rights of their respective state constitutions. With all of these rights at their disposal, corporations, creations of state governments, shifted into the position of vigilant(e) citizens, keeping a disdainful eye on government infringement upon corporate rights claims. Corporate agents bring aggregate assets to bear in pursuit of challenging government infringement. This includes the tax-deductible use of shareholders'

assets, advertising campaigns, the support of corporate and industry associations, and protected political speech including donations. In the end, rights protections for corporations do what rights are supposed to do: they limit the power of government and bring the full force of government to bear in rights protections—even from democratic authority.

What follows are some recent examples of corporate agents exercising the constitutional rights claims of corporations.[6] The point here is not to argue the merits of any particular legislation or case but rather to show concrete examples of how corporate agents exercise corporate rights claims to nullify laws created through democratic processes.

- A Minnesota statute banned the retail sale of milk "in plastic nonreturnable, nonrefillable containers" (Minn. Laws, 1977). The U.S. Supreme Court nullified that statute for violating the Clover Leaf Creamery Company's 14th Amendment constitutional rights claims to equal protection, as well as violating the Constitution's Commerce Clause (*Minnesota v. Clover Leaf Creamery Co.*, 1987).
- A Vermont statute required that "[i]f rBST has been used in the production of milk or a milk product for retail sale in this state, the retail milk or milk product shall be labeled as such" [Vt. Stat. Ann. tit. 66, § 2754 (C) as cited in *International Dairy Foods Association v. Amestoy*, 1996].[7] The U.S. federal court nullified the statute for violating International Dairy Foods Corporation's First Amendment constitutional rights claims to free speech.
- A Massachusetts statute prevented corporate agents from using expenditures to speak on public referenda up for voter approval (Mass. Gen. Laws Annot., 1976). The U.S. Supreme Court revoked the statute for violating the plaintiff corporation's First Amendment constitutional rights claims to free speech and 14th Amendment constitutional rights claims to equal protection (*First Natl. Bank of Boston v. Bellotti*, 1978).
- Reusing a successful tactic from American citizen opposition to apartheid in South Africa, a Massachusetts statute restricted state purchases to exclude companies that do business with Myanmar (Mass. Acts, 1996), a nation controlled by an oppressive military dictatorship. In response to a suit by corporations exercising due process rights claims,

U.S. Supreme Court revoked that statute for violating the Constitution's Supremacy Clause (*Crosby v. National Foreign Trade Council*, 2000).

- The citizens of South Dakota amended their state constitution to prohibit corporations (i.e., excluding precisely defined family farm corporations) from engaging in farming or buying or obtaining an interest in land used for farming in South Dakota (S. Dakota Const., Art. XVII § 21). The U.S. federal court nullified the state's constitutional amendment for violating the Commerce Clause due to its "intent to discriminate" (*South Dakota Farm Bureau, Inc. v. Hazeltine*, 2003).

- Chadds Forth Township, Pennsylvania, denied a zoning variance request by the Omnipoint Communications Enterprises Corporation for the construction of a microwave cell tower. Based on the Civil Rights Act (42 U.S.C. § 1983), passed after the Civil War in order to protect newlyfreed slaves, Omnipoint sued for violation of its civil rights. The U.S. federal court forced the township to comply with the variance request and provide remedies as specified in the Civil Rights Act, that is, reimburse the corporation for its legal expenses (*Omnipoint Communications Enterprises L. P. v. Zoning Hearing Board of Chadds Ford Township*, 1998).

These are tangible consequences of corporate personhood. We are nearly ready to ask and answer the question: Can corporate personhood be socially responsible? *Social responsibility* is an assessment of values based on comparisons, an assessment that some actions and consequences are more worthy of admiration than others. I propose the use of *rule utilitarianism*, a form of utilitarianism developed by Richard Brandt (Snoeyenbos & Humber, 1999, pp. 27–28), to determine whether or not corporate personhood is socially responsible. Rule utilitarianism combines the classic utilitarian rule of "maximize utility" with the premier constraint that actions be compatible with the *moral code* of the community experiencing the consequences. To be compatible means to not violate a value in the moral code except in the case where it is necessary to violate a lesser value to ensure the integrity of a superior value. This is the moral code of individuals living and interacting with other members of the community, not a

moral code of persons stranded outside of human communities. Rule utilitarianism retains one of the classic criticisms of act utilitarianism: the problem of assigning quantifiable values to different consequences, for how else could one know which causal action maximizes utility? We may avoid this particular problem if this analysis clearly shows that corporate personhood violates the moral code of the community experiencing the consequences and so is already determined to be socially irresponsible. This is my intention.

In review, this section defined the following terms: corporations, a republican form of government, inalienable rights, personhood, and social responsibility; it identified the role-related responsibilities of a republican form of government, including its relationship to inalienable rights; it described how personhood clears a path to rights and the significance of rights in the political community; it confirmed that corporations received personhood recognition, listed some of the rights consequently awarded to corporations by the U.S. Supreme Court, and provided examples of the exercise of those rights; and lastly, it proposed the use of rule utilitarianism as the means to judge whether or not corporate personhood is socially responsible.

ANALYSIS

The above background on the consequences of corporate personhood may be summarized in a legally mechanistic way. The possession of legal rights converts some actions into legally recognized harms. Legally recognized harms enable those harmed to seek legal remedies. Claims of harm upon one's rights are strongest when the government causes the harm. So, when citizens act through their government in ways that allegedly infringe on corporate rights claims, as in the above examples, corporate agents possess a strong case for remedies. History shows that legislative laws, ostensibly expressions of a sovereign people through their republican form of government, routinely are nullified by government agents protecting corporate rights claims. As a consequence, corporate personhood results in the denial of the sovereign peoples' right to self-governance. Corporate personhood is antidemocratic. It results in the denial of inalienable rights.

The rule utilitarian analysis of corporate personhood is equally succinct. Rule utilitarian theory first requires that actions comply with the community's moral code. It is quite reasonable to see inalienable rights as the preeminent value in this moral code. To violate the preeminent value is to violate the moral code. Actions violating the code are actions judged as wrong by rule utilitarian theory and thus socially irresponsible. Corporate personhood violates the moral code and so is socially irresponsible. Lastly, failure to comply with the moral code obviates the need to perform a quantitative calculation of utility.

So, what are the options? One option is a middle way of *secondary moral agency* (Werhane, 1985).[8] Under this theory, corporate managers operate the corporation in service of the primary moral agents (i.e., the shareholders) who have provided instructions on the corporation's purpose. The managers use these instructions in compliance with their role-related responsibilities as corporate managers, a condition called "methodological collectivism" (p. 51). Corporations operate as secondary moral agents and, as moral agents, are entitled to secondary rights claims. The important consequence of this theory is that corporate secondary rights claims would be legally inferior to the primary rights claims of primary moral agents. This provides expected normative resolutions in conflict between the rights of natural persons and the rights claims of corporations; that is, a natural person's rights trump a corporation's secondary rights. However, this theory leaves corporations with rights against the government; it leaves corporate agents with the ability to nullify the actions of a republican form of government (or at least meet them head-on if we also considered the government to be a secondary moral agent of the primary moral agent, citizens). The theory of secondary moral agency leaves us with the same socially irresponsible arrangement and thus should be removed from our consideration.

The other option is the elimination of corporate personhood and the consequent grant of constitutional rights. Following the method of rule utilitarian analysis, this option needs to comply with the community's moral code. If it satisfies this requirement—where the other option failed—we should consider this as the socially responsible option without the further step of calculating and comparing utility.

It is not a punishment to corporate shareholders or incorporators that corporations should not possess rights, but rather a protection for the body politic through the protection of the inalienable rights of human beings. Some may consider access to economic opportunities an inalienable right; after all, economic activity, even if only through barter, predated governments. Even if, for argument's sake, we accept access to economic activity as an inalienable right, this does not translate into an inalienable right an ability to incorporate for business activities. Rather, the privilege of incorporation merely demonstrates the community's loose commitment to commerce. Logically, it becomes groundless to claim there is some genuine right for this privilege to then possess rights superior to its creator. This would be "nonsense upon stilts." Recall that human beings create a republican form of government and stand sovereign over their government. Our government then creates corporations and logically remains sovereign over them and thus so do the sovereign people. In both cases, the creators do not bargain away their sovereignty in the act of creation. We can only conclude that the primary harm caused by the elimination of corporate personhood is harm to the expectations of shareholders and incorporators. Disappointing as this may be to them, disappointing others is not an obvious violation of the moral code, or is a weak violation at best (certainly weaker than violating the preeminent value of inalienable rights). The elimination of corporate personhood is compatible with the moral code, and as the only one of the three options that complies with the community's moral code, it is the only socially responsible option.

OTHER CONSIDERATIONS

Even without corporate personhood, economic activity persists. Even without corporate personhood, human incorporators and shareholders still retain their inalienable rights in their human role as individual members of the political and civil community; they are not denied their rights as human beings. Rather, only their property is denied rights. Even without corporate personhood, shareholders and incorporators benefit from tremendous privileges granted to the corporate form, benefits easily acquired by completing a sparse form of one or two pages in length and paying a modest filing fee (just US$175 for the State of Washington, e.g.). The right to trump inalienable rights should not be one of the benefits of incorporation (and certainly not for US$175). This brings us to the last refuge for opposing the elimination of personhood and rights for corporations: the United States and the world cannot afford for political communities to hold sovereignty over their corporate creations. In other words, the economy cannot afford inalienable rights for human beings. Surely, these claimants would argue, we cannot have moral theory hold back economic activity. Instead, we should trust markets to decide what is or is not socially responsible using economic activity as the supreme measure of utility.

This is a claim that we should do what is profitable "though the world should perish." But how does one compare the value of inalienable rights to that of economic activity? Slavery is an excellent means of promoting economic activity and growth. Early U.S. history, as well as that of European global colonization, provides ample empirical proof that slavery generates economic growth and wealth (for some). Pollution also generates economic activity in the expenses of cleanup (when done), and by externalizing some production costs in order to create deceptively affordable products and thus greater market demand. Every new occurrence of cancer in the human population (with money to spend on health care) promotes economic activity and thus expands the gross national product (GNP). Should it then be a national priority to enslave others, to despoil the natural environment, to promote the release of carcinogenic substances into the environment? The answer is an unequivocal "No" because these actions violate the moral code of the community.

Economic utilitarianism, that is, classic act utilitarianism using economic value to quantify utility, has its ethical flaws: first, its inability to price that which is priceless; second, its silence on distribution of benefits and burdens. These flaws rationalize the involuntarily suffering of some (e.g., slaves, people living downstream or downwind) for the overall benefits to the community (measured in GNP). It rationalizes human harms upon people and the natural environment. To contrast, the moral code component of rule utilitarianism better serves our purposes because it honors the highest ideals of the community. Maximizing economic activity alone—economic utilitarianism—simply is not and should not be society's highest value.

It is obvious why corporate agents make corporate rights claims. These claims expand their economic opportunities. When the managers of a cellular phone corporation are able to use civil rights claims to force a township government to site a cell phone tower in opposition to the townspeople, it does so for the purpose of maximizing profit. Is society obligated to provide this path to profit maximization? No, because it comes at the expense of our inalienable rights. The second and more strategic goal of any individual claim to corporate rights is to reinforce the legitimacy of corporate rights claims in general. Corporate managers are simply honoring the adage, "ignore your rights and they'll go away." Corporate rights are profitable to exercise and thus priceless to protect.

THE CULPABLE

A moral agent is someone who may be blamed or praised for an action. Given the preceding assessment of corporate personhood as socially irresponsible, who are the blameworthy moral agents? The blameworthy moral agents are public officials: the elected representatives, political appointees, members of the judiciary—any agent of the government obligated to uphold the U.S. constitutional guarantee of alienable rights. Therefore, these officials have a role-related responsibility to ensure these rights; they do not possess the authority to undermine them. Public officials did restrain themselves from unilaterally extending constitutional rights to certain classes of natural persons, most obviously African-Americans, Native Americans, and women. Yet we should not equate the government's rights denial of human beings with rights denials of corporations. Corporations are not natural persons due the respect, rights, or dignity that civil society currently grants to them. Rather, corporations are legal fictions; they are tools for human use. And yet, due to the actions of public officials, they are a form of property endowed with tremendous legal and economic power to act upon the world. Writing in dissent on a case further extending free speech rights to corporations, U.S. Supreme Court Justice Byron White wrote:

> It has long been recognized, however, that the special status of corporations has placed them in a position to control vast amounts of economic power which may, if not regulated, dominate not only the economy but also the very heart of our democracy, the electoral pro-

cess. . . . The State need not permit its own creation to consume it. (*First Natl. Bank of Boston v. Bellotti*, 1978, p. 809)

A republican form of government not only "need not permit its own creation to consume it"; its role-related responsibilities prohibit it. This prohibition extends to its creations, as well. Public officials are not authorized to grant its creations (e.g., corporations) permission to do that which the state is explicitly forbidden to do. Rather, public officials' role-related responsibilities require they protect our rights.[9] History and logic show us that public officials have failed to do so.

The difficulty some will have in this assessment likely reflects the success of the neoliberal claim equating democracy with unregulated markets, that political liberation depends upon liberated markets. And for those who fail to value political liberation as reason enough, the claim also appeals to self-interest; that is, your material well-being and your job depend upon liberated markets. The lore tells us that there is no other way; there is only one successful model, and we have reached the end of history. The lore itself makes clear analysis difficult to accept because it blurs the lines between various sectors of modern society: public law (i.e., political law) and private law (i.e., corporate law), economics and politics, business and government, and our individual professional roles and our role as individual human beings in a human community. This market-based democracy claim debases democracy and aggrandizes markets. With this blurring of sectors, it is not surprising that public officials act in what should be forbidden ways; that is, they act to advance economic interests at the cost of inalienable rights. It is not surprising that a people claiming self-governance and fetishizing democracy would fail to recognize the legal and cultural specifics that undermine both.

PROPOSAL

The CSR movement implicitly recognizes how corporate agents exert tremendous power upon the world. Often, this power legally brings about very real harms upon human health, human society, political governance, and the natural environment. The growing documentation daily appears in nearly every newspaper. The question CSR presumes to be the right inquiry regarding these harms is this: What should we natural persons do in order to influence corporate agents to reduce or eliminate these harms? This is a misleading question because it presumes corporations are beyond civil authority. This presumption is false. Instead, we can ask a different and more empowering question when we realize that corporations are not the superiors to governments and should not act in the capacity of governments: How should we define the capacities of business organizations to meet essential needs without dishonoring community values? The answer may simply be that corporations are narrowly defined entities, or perhaps subservient and operationally transparent partners in the operation of government programs. The particular and critical point is that specific answers must be arrived at through the exercise of our inalienable rights. To do this, corporate influence on political governance must not be regulated; rather, it must be eliminated.

Perhaps some persons still hold out hope for other, less drastic measures than reasserting democratic authority over corporate agents' powers. These include advocates of CSR and the regulatory agency regime. The U.S. regulatory agency regime, exemplified by the Environmental Protection Agency (EPA) and the Occupational Safety and Health Administration, among others, represents one alleged attempt to mitigate corporate harms. It serves to define "harm" and "danger" as parts per billion, in the amount of radiation exposure workers must be willing to accept if they want to work, and the smokestack release of mercury if we want electricity. The regulatory regime permits these harms, with only modest means for correcting violations, one at a time, after violations happen. This mechanism keeps human beings on the defensive, subjects them to harms, and directs citizens down a narrow and expensive path for the award of limited remedies. The regulatory regime gives corporations a tremendous voice in setting these regulations, in defining what is harmful and what is not, in resisting democratic authority. Does the regulatory regime work? Well, it depends upon whom it is supposed to work for.

One representative and well-documented example of the regulatory regime in action occurred in 2001 when the U.S. EPA revoked safety regulations introduced in the 1990s pertaining to rat poison (Eilperin, 2004; Hotz, 2004; Kurlantzick, 2005), what the EPA euphemistically calls "rat control toxins." The revoked regulations originally required the inclusion of bitter taste and soluble dye coloring into rat poison. The bitter taste reduces the likelihood of children eating it (because rat poison is left where rats and children can find it—on the floor). The dyes give parents and caregivers a visible sign that a child has touched and possibly eaten rat poison. The chemical industry, operating through its Rodenticide Registrants Task Force, successfully lobbied the EPA to roll back these regulations (Kurlantzick, 2005, p. 19). The result has been a near tripling of reported incidents of children sickened by rat poison to a number that reached 50,000 in 2004 (Hotz, 2004, p. A21). In light of corporate influence upon the regulatory regime, and the inefficiency of human beings deliberately limited to responding to harms one at a time and only after they happen, and then forced through the narrow, drawn-out, and expensive regulatory process, we should recognize the primary purpose of the regulatory regime as regulating what people may do to protect themselves or implement other visions for their communities. In other words, the regulatory regime is designed to regulate democracy (Morris, 2001b).

The CSR movement represents another approach. It promotes voluntary actions by corporate agents to do more than the law requires. What would characterize a typical CSR response to the rat poison regulations described above? Ask corporations voluntarily to change their product to reduce dangers to children? Ask corporate agents to demand stricter regulations (e.g., those they asked be revoked by the EPA)? Asking corporate agents to adhere to the law is not much of an advance in preventing harm, especially when corporations are able to use their constitutional rights to define the law and to resist local communities who would rather eliminate the harm than regulate and legalize some amount of it. Clearly, the law fails us when we have to ask for voluntary compliance, when we must wait for the harm to happen and then expend tremendous effort to win a remedy. This is not a model for how a sovereign people should act or how a republican form of government honors its responsibilities.

This consequently leads to two categories of suggestions for advancing democratic authority over the corporate form: those pertaining to the law, and those pertaining to the lore of culture. Regarding the law, the possibilities are presented in the order of actions at the level of local govern-

ment, then state government, and then the national government. At the local level, township governments can adopt ordinances that revoke corporate personhood in their township; two towns in the state of Pennsylvania already have done so (DiStefano, 2003). They can challenge corporate rights claims when the exercise of these rights abrogates their citizens' inalienable rights (Linzey et al., 2003). They can enact ordinances that focus on the actor rather than the act, such as revoking operating authority for businesses with multiple violations of law or whose manner of operation simply violates community standards (e.g., large-scale factory "production" of animals).[10]

At the state level, the codes of corporate governance could be changed to enhance local control and democratic authority. Corporate anthropologist Jane Anne Morris (2001a) offers a glimpse of these possibilities: define shareholders as having greater control over the management and policies of the corporations; require that a percentage of shareholders live within the state of incorporation; prohibit corporate groups, that is, corporate ownership of stock in other corporations, a technique commonly used to create firewalls of limited liability between parent corporations and their subsidiaries; prohibit charitable donations beyond those specified in corporate bylaws; prohibit political donations to candidates, political parties, political actions committees, and referenda before the voters; require recycled content in the production of products, or the use of some amount of renewable energy (Morris, 2001a, pp. 86–87). Additionally, citizens can elect state attorneys general willing to pursue involuntary dissolution of habitual corporate criminals. Citizens can elect legislators willing to revoke state laws that preempt local control in the guise of being "business friendly" at the expense of inalienable rights. Eventually, citizens should amend state constitutions to eliminate corporate personhood as it pertains to rights in each state's constitution.

At the national level, laws can be changed to keep corporate legal actions in state courts rather than federal ones. Laws that preempt state authority over issues of corporate governance can be repealed. Long-range goals include amending the federal constitution to revoke corporate personhood, nullify corporate rights claims, and expand the protection and scope of inalienable rights for human beings. Corporate social responsibility efforts should, at the least, avoid investing in efforts that presume corporations have the capacity to act in the roles of government, that presume the superiority of corporations to governments. Rather, CSR efforts should assist the global movement working to secure the inalienable rights of human beings.

Of course, legal challenges to these will come from corporate managers exercising existing claimed rights against the government and their influence on legislatures and the larger political and cultural communities. Political parties dependent on the support of corporate shareholders and managers will resist sanctioning candidates whose positions they find threatening. But even when such attempts fail in courts and legislatures they serve the purpose of popular education and help drive changes in culture in order to drive changes in law. Realizing these changes necessarily requires and deserves their broad public discussion and consensus. Those who struggled to end slavery and secure voting rights for women have shown us what this takes: a reconsideration of the myths that legalize injustice. For the task at hand, these myths are two: first, that property deserves rights; second, that property interests are superior to human rights.

In reconsidering the myth that property deserves rights, we must distinguish between the rights deservedly accorded natural persons from the rights they may desire for their property. This is not about a person's right to possess property or to do with it what he or she wishes (provided its use complies with the community's moral code). The term "property rights" does not refer to the property possessing rights but rather refers to the owner's claim for the benefits of ownership. At the core of this claim is the right to exclude others from access, to exclude others from these benefits—whatever they might be (Cohen, 1933, pp. 45–46; Singer, 2000, pp. 2–3), a claim backed up by police power. But these benefits are not unlimited. Zoning ordinances control what we may build on our private property (Singer, 2000, p. 8). Ownership of a gun does not entitle you to fire it at will, such as within a city that forbids the discharge of firearms. "A murderer cannot claim innocence on the grounds that he owned his gun and that, as an owner, he was entitled to do what he wanted with his property" (Singer, 2000, p. 3). Nor do we claim that the gun has free speech rights, that the gun, in being discharged, was expressing itself. These examples illustrate how the government may enforce limits upon the benefits of ownership. They show that rights are not for the objects we human beings control but rather only for the human beings themselves.

There also exist many legal and ethical limits to the benefits of property ownership. Consider the following scenario. In the United States, patent title grants its owner with monopoly rights on the commercialization of the patent. Should this right mean that if someone patents a cure for AIDS but refuses to allow its commercialization, that our society should let tens of millions die prematurely in order to honor the patent right? What if the patent in question is a patent on a particular plant created not in a laboratory but by nature? How does the title of the patent entitle its owner with a right to let others die through the exclusionary characteristic of title to property? At the very least, the government is permitted to take this private property for public benefit, compensating owners for the deprivation of their benefits of ownership (U.S. Const., 5th Amend.), although it is hard to comprehend how these benefits can include causing unnecessary suffering and premature death. The benefits of property ownership have limits, both practical and moral. This has obvious implications for corporate governance and the privileges sovereign people grant or deny corporate shareholders, incorporators, and managers.

CONCLUSION

Corporate personhood has brought about our current political predicament whereby corporate agents exercise government-backed rights to undermine the will of citizens working through democratic processes to protect their families, their communities, their natural environment, and their republican form of government. In practice, this is a form of minority rule. History provides us models for expanding membership in political communities, thereby helping human beings realize majority visions for human communities. Historian Lawrence Goodwyn (1978) describes the psychology that built the U.S. populist movement in the late nineteenth century (what he characterizes as the largest democratic mass movement in U.S. history). Goodwyn writes that they "demonstrated how intimidated people could create for themselves the psychological space to dare to aspire grandly—and to dare to be autonomous in the presence of powerful new institutions of economic concentration and cultural regimentation" (p. 295). In responding to claims of corporate personhood we, like the populists, should aspire grandly for our inalienable rights and the ideals of democratic self-government. When morality, reason, and tremendous necessity compel action, it is incumbent upon moral agents such as ourselves —human beings who claim self-governance—to rise to the challenge.

NOTES

1. Corporate agents include shareholders, incorporators, and corporate managers, and so forth, that is, people authorized to direct the use of corporate assets.

2. The words of the U.S. Supreme Court are not the words of authorities beyond the human. So, they are not quoted with the intention of reverence but simply because these particular words say something of relevance to this inquiry.

3. "About half of the states treat spousal rape differently from other types of rape," providing lesser penalties for conviction for a spousal rapist than a nonspousal rapist (Roberts, 2005). This would seem a vestigial remnant of a husband's property claims upon his wife.

4. One recently published claim argues that the personhood precedent set in *Santa Clara* resulted from a clerical error (Hartmann, 2002). Willful deceit by counsel is another claim skillfully explored in the literature around this case (Graham, 1968).

5. Managerial prerogative declares as private nearly all of the decisions made by corporate managers even when they have substantial impact upon the public, for example, manufacturing plant relocation or closure, the selection of methods of toxic or benign means of production, and the kinds of waste that will be produced. The business judgment rule protects corporate officers from personal liability when they act with ignorance or incompetence.

6. There are hundreds of such examples, and likely thousands of disbanded attempts to pass federal, state, and municipal laws due to the chilling effect of corporate constitutional rights claims (R. L. Grossman, personal communication, March 2005).

7. Recombinant bovine somatotropin (rBST) is a synthetic growth hormone approved in 1993 by the U.S. Food and Drug Administration for use in dairy cows producing milk for human consumption (*International Dairy Foods Association v. Amestoy*, 1996, p. 69).

8. An expanded exploration of this was published previously as part of Ritz (2003).

9. Further, there existed alternatives to their unilateral acts. Those seeking the extension of constitutional rights to corporations could have sought it through the democratically driven constitutional amendment process (i.e., the same process used to end slavery and to extend voting rights to African-Americans and women). But this option, too, is problematic because, as I earlier explained in the discussion of rights, inalienable rights not only should not be given up, but cannot be given up even if we sovereign people wish to do so. That is a characteristic of being inalienable. We cannot separate ourselves from them even if we wish to do so. Thus, it is irrational and thus immoral even to try to give them up. A constitutional amendment proposing the establishment of corporate personhood asks us, then, to do the irrational.

10. The work of the Community Environmental Legal Defense Fund provides one model for this approach at the level of local and state governments (see http://www.celdf.org).

REFERENCES

Adickes v. Kress & Co., 398 U.S. 144 (1970).

Arendt, H. (1976). *The origins of totalitarianism.* New York: Harcourt Brace & Company.

Armour Packing Co. v. United States, 209 U.S. 56 (1908).

Bentham, J. (2002). *Rights, representation, and reform: Nonsense upon stilts and other writings on the French Revolution.* Oxford: Oxford University Press.

Cohen, M. (1933). *Law and the social order.* New York: Harcourt, Brace & Company.

Crosby v. National Foreign Trade Council, 530 U.S. 363 (2000).

DiStefano, T. (2003, March 25). Licking says corporations don't have "people" rights. *Clarion News.* Retrieved April 2, 2005, from http://www.theclarionnews.com/ General_News/11676.shtml.

Dodd, E. M. (1954). *American business corporations until 1860: With special reference to Massachusetts.* Cambridge: Harvard University Press.

Dred Scott v. Sanford, 60 U.S. 393 (1851).

Dworkin, R. (1977). *Taking rights seriously.* Cambridge, MA: Harvard University Press.

Edwards, J. (2003, May). Corporate personhood timeline. *New College Law Review,* 4(1), 51–76.

Eilperin, J. (2004, April 15). Rat-poison makers stall safety rules: EPA had drafted regula tions to protect children, animals. *Washington Post*, p. A3.

Equal Rights Amendment, S.J. Res. 11 (2003).

Felons and the right to vote [Editorial]. (2004, April 11). *New York Times.* p. 4–12.

First Natl. Bank of Boston v. Bellotti, 435 U.S. 765 (1978).

Fong Foo v. United States, 369 U.S. 141 (1962).

Freedman, E. B. (2002). *No turning back: The history of feminism and the future of women.* New York: Ballantine Books.

Goodwyn, L. (1978). *The populist moment.* New York: Oxford University Press.

Graham, H. (1968). *Everyman's constitution.* Madison: State Historical Society of Wisconsin.

Grossman, R. (2001). Revolutionizing corporate law. In D. Ritz (Ed.), *Defying corporations, defining democracy* (pp. 300–303). New York: Apex Press, for POCLAD.

Hale v. Henkel, 201 U.S. 43 (1906).

Hartmann, T. (2002). *Unequal protection: The rise of corporate dominance and the theft of human rights.* New York: Rodale Books.

Hobbes, T. (1997). *Leviathan.* New York: Norton. (Originally published 1651)

Horowitz, M. (1992). *The transformation of American law, 1870–1960: The crisis of legal orthodoxy.* New York: Oxford University Press.

Hotz, R. L. (2004, November 14). Collateral damage in the war on rats: Activists suing the EPA say children are at risk because safety rules on poison were revoked. *Los Angeles Times*, p. A21.

International Dairy Foods Association v. Amestoy, 92 F.3d 67 (2d Cir 1996).

Kurlantzick, J. (2005, January/February). The rat pack. *Mother Jones, 30*(1), 18–19.

Linzey, T., Brannen, D., & Grossman, R. (2003). *Draft brief of amici curiae.* Retrieved February 1, 2005, from http://www.ratical.org/corporations/demoBrief.html.

Mass. Acts 239, ch. 130 (1996).

Mass. Gen. Laws Ann., ch. 55, 8 (1976).

Mayer, C. J. (1990). Personalizing the impersonal: Corporations and the Bill of Rights. *Hastings Law Journal, 41*(13), 580–667.

Mill, J. S. (1998). On liberty. In J. Gray (Ed.), *On liberty and other essays* (pp. 5–130). Oxford: Oxford University Press.

Millon, D. (2001). The ambiguous significance of corporate personhood. *Stanford Agora: An Online Journal of Legal Perspectives, 2*(1), 39–58. Retrieved December 12, 2004, from http://agora.stanford.edu/agora/cgi-bin/article2_corp.cgi?library=millon.

Minneapolis & St. L. R. Co. v. Beckwith, 129 U.S. 26 (1889).

Minnesota v. Clover Leaf Creamery Co., 449 U.S. 456 (1987).

Minn. Laws, ch. 268, Minn. Stat. § 116F.21, 1978 (1977).

Morehouse, W. (2001). We the people: Building a truly democratic society. In D. Ritz (Ed.), *Defying corporations, defining democracy* (pp. 211–216). New York: Apex Press, for POCLAD.

Morris, J. A. (2001a). Corporations for the seventh generation: Changing the ground rules. In D. Ritz (Ed.), *Defying corporations, defining democracy* (pp. 82–88). New York: Apex Press, for POCLAD.

Morris, J. A. (2001b). Sheep in wolf's clothing. In D. Ritz (Ed.), *Defying corporations, defining democracy* (pp. 99–103). New York: Apex Press, for POCLAD.

Noble v. Union River Logging R. Co., 147 U.S. 165 (1893).

Omnipoint Communications Enterprises L.P. v. Zoning Hearing Board of Chadds Ford Township, PA, UCS Bi, 98–2295, November 1998 (1998 WL 764762, E.D. Pa.).

Pacific Gas & Elec. Co. v. Public Util. Commn. of California, 475 U.S. 1 (1986).

Pennsylvania Coal Co. v. Mahon, 260 U.S. 393 (1922).

Priest, D. (2005, January 2). Long-term plan sought for terror suspects. *Washington Post*, p. A1.

Ritz, D. (2003). When rights collide: Free speech, corporations, and moral rights. *Ethical Space, 1*(1), 39–45.

Roberts, M. (2005, February 7). *Groups challenge Arizona spousal rape law.* Associated Press. Retrieved February 7, 2005, from http://news.yahoo.com/news?tmpl=story&u=/ap/20050208/ap_on_re_us/spousal_rape.

Roosevelt, F. D. (1938, April 29). *Message to Congress on the concentration of economic power.* Retrieved January 20, 2005, from, http://publicpolicy.pepperdine.edu/academics/faculty/lloyd/projects/newdeal/fr042938.htm.

Ross v. Bernhard, 396 U.S. 531 (1970).

Santa Clara v. Southern Pacific Railroad Co., 118 U.S. 396 (1886).

Singer, J. (2000). *Entitlement: The paradoxes of property.* New Haven, CT: Yale University Press.

Snoeyenbos, M., & Humber, J. (1999). Utilitarianism and business ethics. In R. E. Frederick (Ed.), *A companion to business ethics* (pp. 17–29). Oxford: Blackwell Publishing.

S. Dak. Const. Retrieved February 13, 2006, from http://legis.state.sd.us/statutes/ConstitutionArticleList.aspx.

South Dakota Farm Bureau, Inc. v. Hazeltine, 340 F.3d 583 (8th Cir., 2003).

U.S. Const. Retrieved February 13, 2006, from http://www.gpoaccess.gov/constitution/browse2002.html#2002.

Virginia Pharmacy Board v. Virginia Consumer Council, 425 U.S. 748 (1976).

Werhane, P. H. (1985). *Persons, rights and corporations*. Englewood Cliffs, NJ: Prentice-Hall.

IV

ECONOMIC PERSPECTIVES

14

How to Read Milton Friedman

Corporate Social Responsibility and Today's Capitalisms

JAMES ARNT AUNE

[I]f the lion had a consciousness, his rage at the antelope
he wants to eat would be ideology. . . .
    Theodor W. Adorno, *Negative Dialectics*

Scholars of rhetoric and organizational communication (Aune, 2001; Cheney, Christensen,
Conrad, & Lair, 2004) have drawn our attention
to the role of communication in constituting a
range of economic discourses that enable or constrain organizational actions. The dominant economic discourse in Western democracies since the
mid-1970s emphasizes the power of unregulated
markets to deliver prosperity. Free market economists (in Chicago School, Austrian, and other
varieties) are distinguished by their use of what
Kenneth Burke (1969a) calls a "metonymic" reduction of human motivation to rational cost–
benefit calculation of the likelihood of a "narrowly
defined economic well-being" (J. Buchanan, 1984,
p. 13).[1] As George Stigler (1975) wrote, "There
is, in fact, only one theory of human behavior, and
that is the utility-maximizing theory" (p. 140).
This metonymic reduction of the scope of human
action paradoxically relies on two noneconomic
forms of utility: the aesthetic and cognitive appeal
of parsimonious explanations of human behavior,
and the psychological need to appear "realistic"—
a mature, nonromantic observer of the human
condition (Aune, 2001, pp. 38–56).

Rhetorical strategies—grounded in the fundamental nature of human beings as symbol-using
animals (Burke, 1968)—thus precede and constitute the rational calculation beloved by neoliberal
economists. As the prominent labor historian
William H. Sewell, Jr. (1993) wrote, neoliberal
economists' emphasis on rational choice ignores
two other important motivating factors in human
life: meaning (determined by culture) and power
(determined by politics). Neoliberal economists
foreground scarcity as an explanation of human
action and neglect the role of cultural meanings
and political power in shaping scarcity itself. For
example, the ratio of executive salaries to average
worker salaries is dramatically higher in the United
States than in Japan or Western Europe. Neoliberal economists would contend that the executives are being paid their market value, and yet
market value alone cannot explain the extreme
disparity. Something else must be going on—a
cultural shift in how work is valued in the United
States. The net effect of foregrounding scarcity and
rational choice alone is to close off inquiry into
meaning and power—a rhetorical move that
masks the existence of unjust power relations.

It is important to look carefully at the unexamined assumptions and rhetorical strategies of
neoliberal economics in order to improve public
discourse about political economy in general and
about corporate social responsibility (CSR) in
particular. The classic statement of conservative
political economists' rejection of CSR is Milton
Friedman's 1970 essay "The Social Responsibility of Business Is to Increase Its Profits."[2] Friedman's position has become even more influential
after the decline of social democracy and the
Keynesian consensus among Western industrial

nations since 1975. Economists such as Henderson (2001) continue to rely on Friedman's core arguments, while adapting them to the new context of a globalized economy. Organizations such as the Competitive Enterprise Institute (Gupta, 2005) and the Free Enterprise Action Fund (Kudlow & Co., 2005) recently have gone on the attack against CSR, arguing that it is a smokescreen for leftist assaults on capitalism; Henderson (2001), for example, refers to CSR as "a new variation on a standard collectivist theme" (p. 143). This chapter examines the rhetoric of Friedman's essay, contending that its appeal stems largely from the simple formalism of what Perelman and Olbrechts-Tyteca (1969) refer to as a "quasi-logical appeal." The undefended major premise of Friedman's argument is that any government or corporate interference with the natural workings of the market prevents resources from flowing to their most valued uses. Government intervention, beyond punishing fraud, introduces unnecessary "friction" into the natural and smooth workings of the market. As in David Ricardo's (1817/1996) original formation of the theory of comparative advantage and Ronald Coase's (1960) theory of transaction costs, society is better off when goods flow freely across national borders, when government does not impose regulations to attend broadly "social" ends, and when resources freely flow to those who value them most financially. Questions of cultural meaning and power are thus rendered irrelevant to the analysis of the flow of commodities.

Although the simplicity and seemingly lawlike character of this argument are appealing to certain kinds of audiences, the argument as a whole is an ideological distortion, for four main reasons developed in this chapter: (1) Friedman, the major architect of positivism in economics, covertly introduces individualist and utilitarian ethical standards into his scientific argument, largely without any evidence or reasoning to support the choice of these standards; (2) Friedman, like other neoliberal economists, refuses to engage the possibility that the economy is "embedded" in society and culture (what sociologists sometimes refer to as the "economist's elision"); (3) Friedman's rhetorical style denigrates the process of democratic deliberation by his recurring straw man characterization of his opponents as "socialists" and as lacking in "realism"—what I refer to here as Friedman's "realist style"; and (4) even on its own terms, the antisocial responsibility argument fails by privi-

leging short-term over long-term wealth enhancement, both for the firm and for society as a whole. The current debate over global warming is perhaps the best example: the United States is unwilling to cut back on energy consumption and oil company profits even if current consumption levels hurt the atmosphere. I focus on another example in the conclusion of the chapter: the tendency of U.S. corporations to work against U.S. foreign policy interests by trading with nations that sponsor terrorism. I suggest that the traditional conservative emphasis on patriotism and national self-interest may be the best rhetorical wedge for progressive intervention into the corporate responsibility debate. The apparent triumph of conservatism in 2004 rests on a very shaky coalition between libertarians and social conservatives. If, say, Halliburton's (a petroleum, energy, and construction contractor formerly headed by Vice President Dick Cheney) investments in Iran or Saudi Arabia run counter to the democratic aims of U.S. foreign policy in the Middle East, the insistence that Halliburton become "socially responsible" ceases to be an argument associated with the "wimpy" and "unrealistic" Left.

The chapter proceeds in four parts: first, I provide a close reading of Friedman's 1970 essay, identifying specific tactical rhetorical maneuvers in the text; second, I identify the underlying ideological narrative presupposed by his essay, at the level of what I call "deep rhetorical invention," in its rational choice assumptions about human action; third, I continue the ideological analysis by interrogating the "realist style" of Friedman's argument; and, finally, I examine empirical aspects of the social responsibility debate after globalization in order to show problems with the anti-CSR position.

RHETORICAL ANALYSIS OF FRIEDMAN ON CSR

My focus in this chapter is on the rhetoric of CSR. As practiced since Aristotle and Cicero, and refined by twentieth-century theorists such as Chaim Perelman and Lucie Olbrechts-Tyteca (1969), Kenneth Burke (1968, 1969a, 1969b), and Richard McKeon (1987), the rhetorical analysis works at two levels:

1. Examining the tactical maneuvers executed in the presence of an adversary: how audiences are

selected and addressed; how opposing positions are represented; how evidence is marshaled; how terms are defined; how language, especially metaphor, is deployed; how specific argument patterns familiar to the audience are used. The goal of such textual analysis is to identify points of weakness in an argument and to facilitate democratic discussion and debate by making all of an advocate's premises open to public inspection. Everyone seems to agree that rhetorical analyses of political speeches, courtroom arguments, and advertisements are appropriate; however, convincing practitioners of academic discourse, especially in the sciences, that they, too, are engaged in rhetorical activities is often a harder sell, although some of the most widely read work in rhetoric in the 1990s made a powerful case for the study of disciplinary rhetoric (e.g., Edmundson, 1984; Gross, 1990; Nelson, Megill, & McCloskey, 1987; Simons, 1990).

2. At a more abstract level, in ways largely unconscious to the advocate, is what might be called the study of deep invention. The first canon of classical rhetoric was invention: the process of coming up with arguments in presenting a political or legal case. Classical invention drew on a stock of existing commonsense generalizations in order to develop strategies. Contemporary rhetorical theorists have drawn our attention to "deep invention": how disciplinary projects or ideologies make fundamental representations of reality itself, or of the domains of their research and argument; how society, culture, politics, economics, ethics, and law are configured and defined; how the process of reasoned argument itself is represented. In Condit's (1990) terms, what are the underlying characterizations and narratives of an ideological position? What are the "deep figures" (Jameson, 1990, p. 256)—metaphors, images, patterns of argument—that recur in key ideological texts?

Throughout this section of the chapter, I identify specific textual moves in Friedman's argument against social responsibility and then move to a more abstract level by analyzing the patterns of deep invention underpinning his ideology.

The Audience

The first question typically asked in rhetorical analysis is how the rhetor constructs his or her implied reader, or target audience. The immediate audience here is "businessmen" and, perhaps, given the essay's long afterlife in business school

discussions of ethics, students of business administration. As Kenneth Burke (1969b) wrote, rhetoric proceeds by *identification* and *division*. Friedman (1970) shrewdly divides his potential audience into businessmen and their enemies. The strategy polarizes the audience immediately: this text is directed to people who already think like Friedman and to people in business who may need talking points in dealing with advocates of CSR. There is no effort to "adapt" to the beliefs or values of opposing members of the audience: they are all already "socialists" by even raising the issue of CSR. Friedman begins the essay by expressing astonishment that businessmen refer to the "social conscience" of business. Such talk is "pure and unadulterated socialism." Businessmen who refer to the social responsibility of business are "unwitting puppets of the intellectual forces that have been undermining the basis of a free society these past decades." No one wants to be a puppet, especially someone in a profession that prides itself on entrepreneurial vision and self-reliance.

Sliding Down the Slippery Slope

It seems a little odd at first to characterize a business executive who discusses CSR as somehow equivalent to, say, Fidel Castro, but Friedman's essay is actually organized around this notion of equivalence, grounded in a slippery slope argument. Any effort to direct business in socially responsible directions is "already" socialism. Like a fundamentalist who views any nonliteral interpretation of the Bible as destroying faith, or an NRA member who views any registration of firearms as tantamount to confiscation of firearms, the smallest effort to consider the social impact of corporate actions is already a surrender to the enemy. Slippery slope arguments occur in a highly polarized rhetorical climate, in which the other side is viewed as an evil enemy rather than, as in normal politics, simply mistaken. Friedman (1970) treats his opponents as, at best, naive and, at worst, part of a vast left-wing conspiracy to destroy capitalism as we know it. A shrewd rhetorical tactician, Friedman wisely does not frame his implied audience as including his opponents; they are already beyond redemption. He instead, much like a religious preacher, directs his audience to examine their consciences for signs of temptation by the enemy.

The oversimplification and polarization in Friedman's (1970) essay are essential to his strategy, and yet they do raise a number of potential problems—problems that so far have tended to blunt the ideological force of the "pure" ideological project of libertarianism generally. The core problem is when and by what moral standards we refuse to let certain policies be left to the "market." Markets value efficiency and, over time, increase aggregate wealth, and yet human beings seldom make important decisions about their lives on the basis of efficiency or aggregate utility. There is something vaguely creepy about allowing the market to allocate organ transplants or children for adoption (but see Epstein, 1997). Because our cultural values shape our view of children or body organs as commodities, most of us happily allow centralized government agencies to make decisions about their distribution (no matter how much such a procedure smacks of a Soviet "command" economy). Also, reformers from Benjamin Disraeli to Franklin Delano Roosevelt to John Kerry have proposed to restrict the dominion of the market, not in order to destroy capitalism, but to blunt the potentially revolutionary force of its tendency to exacerbate class divisions.

Friedman further claims that social responsibility becomes a lightning rod for regulation. The actual experience of Western capitalist societies in the late twentieth century suggests otherwise. Even within the framework of neoliberal economics, there are always potentially negative "externalities" to two-person contracts. Corporate misbehavior, whether by polluting or by failing to pay employees a living wage, does in fact impose costs on society. Wal-Mart, for example, displaces the costs of health insurance onto the states (see Walmart Watch, 2005). Much of the rationale for governmental regulation has in fact been the prevention of future corporate misbehavior. The "rational" corporate executive would thus use CSR strategies in order to forestall government regulation.

Although Friedman (1970) ruthlessly consigns morality to the private realm, it appears that this fundamental question of political economy—when should we let the market decide?—is in fact a public moral decision itself. It is based on Friedman's smuggling in of moral principles *not* widely accepted outside the community of neoliberal economists, libertarians, and disciples of novelist-philosopherAyn Rand. Once a fundamentalist invokes the slippery slope argument, it is always possible to outflank the advocate to the right; some of the most vicious attacks made by Austrian

economists, for example, at the von Mises Institute at Auburn, are made against Friedman and the Chicago School for not being sufficiently zealous about government intrusion into the market (see North, 1992).

How Rational Deliberation Is Modeled in the Text

Friedman (1970) thus radically polarizes his audience and constrains the range of acceptable policy alternatives through the slippery slope argument. Another, more global, tactic for constituting his target audience and stigmatizing his opponents is the use of the realist style, which functions, as suggested above, at the level of deep rhetorical invention. The general strategy is something like this: accuse the opposition of fuzzy thinking, and present oneself as a model of intellectual clarity. As Friedman wrote, the whole discussion of the social responsibility of business lacks "rigor." Only individuals have responsibilities. Corporations are only artificial persons. So what responsibilities do individuals in corporations have? "In a free-enterprise, private-property system," the primary actor is the corporate executive, and his responsibility is to make as much money as possible while conforming to principles of law and ethics. Some corporations, of course, may be designed for charitable purposes, in which case the manager has a responsibility to render certain services. The manager as private individual may feel compelled to donate to charity, refuse to collaborate with unethical corporations, or join the military. These may be "social responsibilities," but they are incurred in the manager's own time, and not that of the owners of the business.

The brief mention of "ethics" in this section of the essay is worth noting: the executive or manager must follow "the basic rules of the society, both those embodied in law and those embodied in ethical custom." "Ethics," here, is synonymous with custom and thus has no further grounding other than social convention—a point of view consistent with Friedman's other work on "positive" methodology in economics. Even Friedman's opposition to socialism appears to rest on purely conventional grounds: socialism is antithetical to the law and ethical custom of a "free society." His argument also rests on a bright line between private conduct and conduct as a corporate agent, suggesting that "private" ethics is a matter of taste, while the public ethics of a manager is constrained by social custom. Later on in the essay, Friedman's amoralism becomes explicit: "In a free society, it is hard for 'evil' people to do 'evil,' especially since one man's good is another's evil." At a more abstract level, Friedman polarizes his audience around two competing views of language. Note that the first move is to identify a mismatch of language and reality: corporations are not persons. Supporters of CSR are "analytically loose" and "lack rigor." They do not know how the "real world" works. Once this realist move is made, the pejorative invocation of the term "rhetoric" is seldom far behind: "What does it mean to say that the corporate executive has a 'social responsibility' in his capacity as businessman? If this statement is not pure rhetoric, it must mean that he is to act in some way that is not in the interest of his employers." Friedman's rejection of rhetoric is the hallmark of what Hariman (1995) has called the "realist style." Friedman, like neoliberal economists in general, speaks and gestures in a recognizable *style*, as you can see from the distinct examples given here. In the words of Adam Smith (1776/1976):

> It is not from the benevolence of the butcher, the brewer, or the baker, that we expect our dinner, but from their regard to their own interest. We address ourselves, not to their humanity but to their self-love, and never talk to them of our own necessities but of their advantages. Nobody but a beggar chuses to depend chiefly upon the benevolence of his fellow citizens. (p. 18)

A more recent example is Judge Richard Posner's (1988) use of the "no free lunch" principle:

> [T]he economic approach to human behavior insists on just the sort of gritty realism that the New Criticism taxed some Romantic poetry with trying to evade. In its insistence on the centrality of self-interest (and hence of incentives) in motivating human action, in its insistence that everything has a cost—that there is no such thing as a free lunch—and in its consequent skepticism about Utopian projects, economics is revealed as a bastion of Enlightenment values. The absence of Romantic uplift is precisely what makes economics—the rejection of Romanticism in the sphere of government—so repugnant to the heirs of Romanticism. (p. 312)

These arguments are *styled* in a "realistic" way. They constitute an audience that is pleased with itself for "seeing through" the pretensions of poets, dreamers, and Romantics. They reflect the commonsense assumption that decisions are best made by leaders who rely on hard facts rather than soft emotions. Hariman demonstrates how realism is both a commonsense attitude and also a political *style*.

Hariman (1995) wrote that successful politicians know intuitively that political success involves "conventions of persuasive composition that depend on aesthetic reactions. . . . In a word, our political experience is *styled*" (pp. 2–3). We come to recognize a distinctive *political style* as "a coherent repertoire of rhetorical conventions depending on aesthetic reactions for political effect" (p. 4). Hariman identifies four types of political style: realist, republican, courtly, and bureaucratic. He analyzes the rhetoric of Machiavelli and Henry Kissinger as masters of realism who created "a characteristically modern political style that crafts an aesthetically unified world of sheer power and constant calculation" (p. 13). The discursive practice of realism asserts simultaneously an epistemology, a political theory, and a rhetoric. Realists profess to see the world clearly. They assume that international politics is a competition among states and that domestic politics is a competition among interest groups. Participants in this competition pursue power through rational calculation; they presume that attending to issues other than power (e.g., "values" or "morality") is a distraction (Beer & Hariman, 1996, p. 6). Finally, they use an antirhetorical rhetoric that favors the plain style and avoids verbal ornament. They denigrate opponents as "rhetorical," too caught up in their own textuality to serve rational calculation (Hariman, 1995, p. 17). Realist rhetoric thus is configured within the master trope of *metonymy*: the reduction of political life to a calculus of power. Rhetoric is reduced to transparent exchange of information. The political actor suffers a reduction as well:

> Only a person of a certain type will survive in a world of hard realities and sovereign powers. When reality is defined against textuality, one is sublimating the sociality of politics. If a discourse is a true representation of its subject because it is devoid of ornament (that is, because it is not directed to please others), then it must stand independently of a social situa-

tion, free of social motives such as the quest for higher status. Once one discovers the vectors of power in a field of material forces, there is no need to understand social practices, regulations, or entertainment except as they are manipulated. (Hariman, 1995, p. 30)

Friedman, as a consummate practitioner of the realist style, "sees through" the "rhetoric" of advocates of social responsibility and constitutes his audience as tough-minded, practical *men* (on the gendered character of traditional economics, see Ferber & Nelson, 2003).

To summarize, the economic realist style works in the following ways:

1. *Human nature is defined downward.* It is safest to concentrate on self-interest as the fundamental human motivation. Those who do not are hopelessly "romantic" or "utopian." Language and cultural and political power are simply irrelevant features of human behavior.

2. *Political, governmental processes are redefined as exclusively social.* As Sheldon Wolin (1960, 1989) has argued, the classical economists eroded the concept of the distinctively political. Politics became associated with "government." Society was a spontaneous, self-adjusting order, with no need for a principle of authority other than the pressure of social conformity, guaranteed by the presence of Adam Smith's "impartial spectator" within each human breast.

3. *Efficiency is defined as a default norm, including efficiency of information exchange.* The economic realist reduces all questions of value to individual taste: "*de gustibus non est disputandum,*" as Gary Becker and George Stigler (1996) emphasized in a famous article. "Tastes are the unchallengeable axioms of a man's behavior: he may properly (usefully) be criticized for inefficiency in satisfying his desires, but the desires themselves are *data*" (p. 24). The only common ground for communication between people is agreement on individual tastes or else the good of efficiency.

Friedman's Internal Inconsistency

My goal thus far has been to foreground those rhetorical choices by Friedman (1970) that his own theory suggests are irrelevant to the "realistic" business of utility maximization. Serious public economic debate cannot proceed until neoliberal economists are questioned about their unexamined cultural and communicative assumptions. Yet even on its own terms, Friedman's argument lacks rigor. The boundaries between moral and social responsibility are never made clear. Even if business, as an institution, does not have moral responsibilities in the way an individual actor does, it does not necessarily follow that business corporations lack social responsibilities. Note that Friedman has already admitted that the corporation has a moral responsibility: to increase the wealth of shareholders; yet shareholders are interested in making profits and fulfilling social responsibilities, from the minimum requirement of a safe workplace to refusal to do business with racist or terrorist states. Friedman thus, in a curiously paternalistic way, insists—without argument—that his definition of corporate values must trump any social values held by shareholders.

Here Friedman introduces a powerful analogy: the manager who reduces profit for social ends such as reducing pollution or hiring members of disadvantaged groups takes over the functions of government, because he is in effect imposing taxes and deciding how to spend the proceeds. The corporate executive thus becomes a civil servant, a public employee. The result is thus full-blown socialism, the rejection of market mechanisms in favor of political mechanisms. There may be instances where a corporation may contribute to charity or do other good works in a community, but let's not "rationalize" these as exercises of "social responsibility." They are simply efforts to generate goodwill through self-interested expenditures, a reasonable option in the face of widespread aversion to capitalism, profits, and the "soulless corporation." Michael Porter and Mark R. Kramer (2002), for example, refer to "strategic philanthropy." These efforts are in fact "hypocritical window dressing." Here again, Friedman's clear-eyed realism sees through the "rhetoric."

Friedman makes the claim that social responsibility necessarily comes at the expense of the interests of employers or shareholders. Note again the avoidance of any empirical analysis by Friedman; he does not research the actual impact of socially responsible policies on business. Here is one example: after the 1990s activist assault on Nike for maintaining sweatshop conditions in its overseas suppliers, it has emerged as a leader in progressive work practices (Zadek, 2004). Oddly enough, Friedman does not seem to imagine an audience of consumers who might desire to purchase commodities grown, manufactured, or distributed under ethical conditions—thus suggesting an inherent contradiction of sorts in his view of capitalism. Market capitalism, according to Friedman, works by satisfying shareholders and consumers alike—yet he wishes to exclude questions of social justice from the market, even if social justice is an essential part of the utility many consumers or shareholders may wish to maximize. The seemingly neutral quality of the term "utility" (part of its rhetorical, hardheaded appeal) disappears, replaced simply by increased income and decreased monetary expenditure.

Dissociative Argument

Friedman's final strategy relies on what Perelman and Olbrechts-Tyteca (1969) call "dissociation." A dissociative argument works by introducing a division into a concept the audience previously regarded as a single entity. For example, when arguing against creationism, an advocate might contend, "Genesis is a *religious* document, not a *scientific* document." At a more abstract level (what I have been calling "deep invention"), all philosophical or ideological systems represent reality through dissociation. The general dissociation works like this: divide the domain of knowledge into term I (which represents mere appearance) and term II (which represents the underlying reality). This is the fundamental philosophic pair out of which the others proceed: rhetoric/dialectic, *nomos/phusis* in ancient Greece; ideology/science or bourgeoisie/proletariat in classical Marxism; *langue/parole* or competence/performance in linguistics. Term II in these examples reflects both a division of a previously undifferentiated realm of appearance and an identification of the "real" underlying that appearance.

Just as I have shown that Friedman strongly dissociates the moral and the social, the public and the private, he does this to politics and economics, as well. Economics always functions as term II, its underlying reality trumping the illusions of term I, politics. He wrote that market mechanisms rest on unanimity, that no individual may coerce another, and that all cooperation is voluntary. Political mechanisms, however, rest on conformity. If you lose the vote, you still have to con-

form to what the majority wants. If, however, it could be demonstrated that dominant actors in the market disproportionately influence political mechanisms to their own ends, in opposition to the general interest of the majority, what becomes of Friedman's argument? The general strategy, finally, of the whole essay is to proceed deductively from a set of rigid dissociations between capitalism and socialism, markets and government, and then provide the reader (and the rhetor) the formal satisfaction of a geometric proof. Undergirding Friedman's realist style is the persistent use of what Perelman and Olbrechts-Tyteca call "quasi-logical" arguments. By applying the logic of the syllogism to the fuzzy and imperfect world of human action, advocates can preempt the necessity of reasoned judgment by the audience. Like the slippery slope, quasi-logical arguments are the staple of fundamentalism of all varieties.

The "purity" of Friedman's premises relies centrally on an invisible strategy: substitute formal premises or models for historical or empirical inquiry—two core problems with neoclassical economics in general. What, for example, was an employer to do, circa 1910, about child labor? If he declined to hire workers younger than 16, he would have been imposing a "tax" on the profits of his shareholders (assuming that child labor was profitable—something I've never seen measured in the historical and legal literature on the practice). Yet "social customs" over the course of the twentieth century came to reject child labor. Does the manager then need to wait until some ideal "tipping point" to decide not to hire child labor, or is he allowed to predict, like an "alert" entrepreneur, where social customs are going?

Politics by its very nature is denigrated as the realm of authoritarianism, not the common good. A pure night watchman state is very attractive, given the captivity of the state by special interests, but there remains what Marxists used to call the "problem of the transition": Friedman has nothing to say about the disproportionate influence of corporations in government, from the oil industry to the credit card industry. These corporations act in their interests, that is, through lobbying and targeted campaign contributions. Further, even though corporations are not individuals, it is possible increasingly to identify the actions of corporations with the actions of individuals. The Bush family's enduring relationship with the House of Saud over the years and Dick Cheney's consistent support of the interests of Halliburton are but two examples (Unger, 2004). Writing from an Austrian perspective, Richard W. Wilcke (2004) rightly criticizes Friedman for ignoring the way business leaders influence government, through lobbying and targeted campaign contributions, in order to obtain various forms of corporate welfare. The free market system can only work, morally, if all participants in the market start from a position of equality (as in Nozick's [1974] famous *Anarchy, State, and Utopia*). Wilcke wrote, "Business leaders seeking an ethical standard consistent with the free market should look elsewhere, however, because Friedman's essay seems to exculpate a practice antithetical to the free market—*corporate* lobbying for special government favors" (p. 187). It would appear, then, that Friedman is not arguing from a universal, rational standpoint, but rather from the narrow interests of the business class.

To summarize, Friedman makes the following four rhetorical moves in his essay: (1) He polarizes his audience into misguided friends and evil enemies. (2) He uses slippery slope arguments to reinforce the polarization. (3) He frames himself and his audience as hardheaded, realistic, and nonrhetorical. (4) He uses dissociative and quasilogical arguments to denigrate politics and exalt market forces.

The mythic underpinning of Friedman's (1970) social responsibility argument depended heavily upon a Cold War narrative: the virtuous, free market United States battling the evil, collectivist East. Reaching its apotheosis in Ronald Reagan's presidency, the merging of patriotic nationalism with free market ideology became a powerful political force. What happens, however, when the quest for corporate profits appears to undercut the national interest? The increasingly global character of the economy since Friedman wrote makes this contradiction clearer.

The persistent use of polarizing and dissociative strategies potentially reminds the critical reader of anthropological studies of myth, with their focus on binary oppositions. As Marshall Sahlins (1976) wrote, the unique feature of bourgeois society is the structurally determining role of economic symbolism. Primitive society based its myths on kinship relations, while capitalist society bases its core myth on market exchange. Sahlins wrote that the economist's elision of culture misses core questions any economic science

would need to solve. For example, Karl Marx spends a lot of time in *Capital I* explaining why a certain quantity of wheat exchanges for X hundredweight of iron: "While the answer to the rate of equivalence in terms of average necessary labor time is brilliant, it does not tell us why wheat and why iron—why certain commodities are produced and exchanged and not others" (Sahlins, 1976, p. 149). One needs a theory of culture in order to explain why wheat and iron are exchanged rather than puppies and lead. Friedman's (1970) argument has a similar problem: its *ideological* rather than scientific character. Ideology, in the Marxian sense, is the insistence that historically constructed and hence transitory social arrangements are somehow natural and somehow eternal. Friedman universalizes his defense of *laissez faire* capitalism without investigating the historical and cultural roots of this particular vision of human nature and the economy.

CSR SINCE GLOBALIZATION

At the time Friedman wrote his essay, the major concerns related to CSR included environmental and racial issues. The actual concept dates back more than 100 years, when late nineteenth century U.S. drug companies created codes of conduct designed to preserve both profit and public health. Beginning with the divestiture movement in South Africa, however, the CSR debate began to take a global turn. In 1977, the Reverend Leon Sullivan proposed a human rights code for companies doing business in South Africa, known as the "Sullivan Principles."

Efforts by Starbucks and other firms in the coffee industry to institute "fair trade" standards in relation to coffee growers also appear to have paid off with consumers (Argenti, 2004). After criticism by environmentalists, Chiquita Brands obtained independent certification for its 119 banana farms in Central and South America and upgraded its operations to reduce the use of chemicals (Werre, 2003). Shell Oil's effort to improve its environmental and CSR image after a crisis in 1995 has made the company more profitable and appealing to investors (Guyon, 2003). It initiated a $50 million annual social investment program in Nigeria. Following criticism of its labor practices in El Salvador and elsewhere, Gap established a code of vendor conduct for its contract manufacturers and hired 80 compliance officers to oversee labor, health, and safety issues in its contract operations around the world (Dahle, 2004). The most balanced recent account of CSR is probably David Vogel's (2005) *The Market for Virtue*, which concludes that CSR is best understood as a business strategy for companies with highly visible brands whose reputations have been threatened by activists. My overall point here is that the Friedman (1970) account of CSR simply cannot account for changing preferences among consumers that may affect the corporate bottom line. What happens when corporations maximize profits by trading with enemy nations during wartime?

Trading With the Axis of Evil

Economic sanctions and export regulations passed by the U.S. Congress bar U.S. citizens and companies from trading with Iran, North Korea, Libya, and the Sudan. Because of a legal loophole, however, companies can trade through foreign subsidiaries that employ no U.S. citizens. Hewlett-Packard, Kodak, and Procter & Gamble, for example, simply ship their products to Dubai, where their foreign subsidiaries then "reexport" the goods to Iran (Scherer, 2003). According to Michael Scherer (2003):

> General Electric is providing four hydroelectric generators to expand a dam on the Kurun River through a Canadian subsidiary called GE Hydro and is also supplying pipeline compressors and gas turbines for Iran's burgeoning oil sector through an Italian unit called Nuovo Pignone. Not far from the Iraqi border, a subsidiary of Halliburton is helping to build a $228 million fertilizer plant, one of the world's largest. Another Halliburton division based in Sweden is providing the Iranian National Oil Co. with a $226 million semi-submersible drilling rig, while other subsidiaries operate in Libya. A British subsidiary of ConocoPhillips helped Iran survey its Azadegan oil field, and ExxonMobil only recently sold its Sudanese gas subsidiary based in Khartoum.

Such trading with the "Axis of Evil" has in fact been encouraged by the Bush administration itself:

> As CEO of Halliburton, Dick Cheney lobbied to lift U.S. sanctions against Iran and Libya, saying they hurt business and failed to stop terrorism. As vice president, Cheney has initiated a "comprehensive review of sanctions" as part of the National Energy Review, suggesting that sanctions against oil-producing nations should be relaxed to improve "energy security." (Scherer, 2003)

Public scrutiny of U.S. corporations' evasion of the sanctions has increased in recent years. In January 2003, a bill was introduced in Arizona requiring state pension funds to disclose their dealings with sanctioned countries. Fund managers for public employees in New York City, California, and Colorado have urged shareholders of General Electric, Halliburton, and ExxonMobil to pass resolutions disclosing contracts with state sponsors of terrorism, such as Iran and Syria (Blumenthal, 2002). From Friedman's standpoint, these corporations are doing nothing wrong, as long as their activities are legal and as long as they increase profits for their shareholders. And yet the examples illustrate another inherent contradiction in the neoliberal position on CSR: not only are consumers' preferences for ethical business practices subordinated to the profit motive, but the "free society" sustained by the free market must surrender its own national interests to the interests of corporations. The logic is inexorable, if you start with Friedman's assumptions. If all that matters is wealth maximization, then even the nation-state must yield before the relentless flow of resources to their most valued uses. From the standpoint of practical politics, here is the most vulnerable point of corporate capitalism: when profits trump patriotism, patriotism will always win in the mind of the democratic public. Yet what happens when global capitalism also threatens the security of U.S. workers?

Can a Capitalist Be Patriotic?

Perhaps the most class-conscious rhetoric in recent historical memory is being uttered by the prominent American conservative Patrick Buchanan. In his 1998 book *The Great Betrayal*, he wrote, in language one might also have heard from John Sweeney (the head of the AFL-CIO) or the late Paul Wellstone (Democratic senator from Minnesota):

> America is no longer one nation indivisible. We are now the "two nations" predicted by the Kerner Commission thirty years ago. Only the

dividing line is no longer just race; it is class. On one side is the new class, Third Wave America —the bankers, lawyers, diplomats, investors, lobbyists, academics, journalists, executives, professionals, high-tech entrepreneurs—prospering beyond their dreams. . . . On the other side of the national divide is Second Wave America, the forgotten Americans left behind. White-collar and blue-collar, they work for someone else, many with hands, tools, and machines in factories soon to be hoisted onto the chopping block of some corporate downsizer in some distant city or foreign country. (p. 7)

Buchanan goes on to describe his epiphany when he visited the James River paper mill in New Hampshire in 1991, while he was campaigning for the U.S. presidency. On that very day, news of more layoffs had reached the workers, and he stood waiting to shake workers' hands as they stood in line to get their Christmas turkeys. Buchanan walked over to one "hard-looking worker about my own age who was staring at the plant floor. I grabbed his hand and told him who I was; he looked up, stared me in the eye, and said in an anguished voice, 'Save our jobs!' It went right through me." The next day Buchanan learned that the U.S. Export-Import Bank, a government agency, was financing a new paper mill in Mexico. "*What are we doing to our own people?* I asked myself" (p. 19).

The last part of *The Great Betrayal* provides a blueprint for a "new nationalism," in which Patrick Buchanan attempts to marry "the patriotism of Theodore Roosevelt to the humane vision of Wilhelm Roepke" (a German economist who was a major architect of the Christian Democrats' "social market" economy in West Germany after World War II), who contended:

The market is not everything. It must find its place in a higher order of things which is not ruled by supply and demand, free prices, and competition. It must be firmly contained within an all-embracing order of society in which the imperfections and harshness of economic freedom are corrected by law and in which man is not denied conditions of life appropriate to his nature. (Roepke, 1960, p. 91, as cited in P. Buchanan, 1998, p. 288)

Buchanan proposes goals of full employment, high levels of worker compensation (refusing to put "U.S. free labor . . . into Darwinian competition

with conscript labor"), high tariffs, a simpler and fairer tax code, and greater controls on the movement of capital across national boundaries (p. 301).

By raising the example of Buchanan, I do not intend to endorse his blanket rejection of free trade, but rather to suggest that, along with the problem of corporate trading with the Axis of Evil, the displacement of American foreign policy and economic interests by corporate profit represents an important starting point for crafting progressive arguments. Derailed by identity politics for the last 20 years (deemphasizing class-based economic issues in favor of an emphasis on race, gender, and sexual orientation), the American Left now has the opportunity to craft anticorporate arguments and build political coalitions based on appeals to American self-interest rather than abstract principles of justice. It remains unclear whether American business is capable of continuing current trends toward greater CSR, or if Marxists are correct that the entire system of global capitalism must collapse before human values take precedence over profits. My more modest effort in this chapter has been to undermine the major barrier faced by advocates of greater social responsibility by business: Friedman's enduring myth of the realistic, profit-centered corporation, as justified by the formalistic rhetoric of neoliberal economics. Whether reform or revolution is on the global horizon depends on the future of democratic discussion and debate about economic issues. Economics is far too important to leave to the quasi-logical, formalistic rhetoric of Friedman and his ilk. It remains to be seen whether a "kinder, gentler" capitalism may emerge out of the CSR debate, but in the meantime we need to insist that opponents of CSR argue for their assumptions as well as their conclusions.

NOTES

1. "Metonymy" is a "realistic" metaphor, the substitution of one word for another with which it is associated, for example, substituting "White House" for "Bush administration." According to Burke (1969a, pp. 503–517), scientific explanations of human motives reduce the scope of human motivation, for example, by focusing on reward/punishment, as behaviorist psychologists do, or rational calculation of profit, as neoclassical economists do.

2. Friedman's essay is widely available online. See http://www.colorado.edu/studentgroups/libertarians/issues/friedman-soc-resp-business

.html (downloaded September 1, 2005). Since the essay is quite short, I have not supplied page numbers for individual quotations, but I follow their original sequence in the essay.

REFERENCES

Argenti, P. A. (2004). Collaborating with activists: How Starbucks works with NGOs. *California Management Review, 47*, 91–116.

Aune, J. A. (2001). *Selling the free market: The rhetoric of economic correctness.* New York: Guilford Press.

Becker, G. S., & Stigler, G. (1996). De gustibus non est disputandum. In G. L. Becker (Ed.), *Accounting for tastes* (pp. 24–50). Cambridge, MA: Harvard University Press.

Beer, F., & Hariman, R. (1996). *Post-realism: The rhetorical turn in international relations.* East Lansing: Michigan State University Press.

Blumenthal, R. (2002, October 7). Under scrutiny. *Barron's, 82*(40), 23–24.

Buchanan, J. (1984). Politics without romance: A sketch of positive public choice theory and its normative implications. In J. Buchanan (with R. Tollison) (Ed.), *The theory of public choice* (Vol. 2, pp. 11–22). Ann Arbor: University of Michigan Press.

Buchanan, P. (1998). *The great betrayal: How American sovereignty and social justice are being sacrificed to the gods of the global economy.* Boston, MA: Little, Brown.

Burke, K. (1968). *Language as symbolic action.* Berkeley: University of California Press.

Burke, K. (1969a). *A grammar of motives.* Berkeley: University of California Press.

Burke, K. (1969b). *A rhetoric of motives.* Berkeley: University of California Press.

Cheney, G., Christensen, L. T., Conrad, C., & Lair, D. J. (2004). Corporate rhetoric as organizational discourse. In D. Grant, C. Hardy, C. Oswick, & L. Putnam (Eds.), *The Sage handbook of organizational discourse* (pp. 79–103). London: Sage.

Coase, R. H. (1960). The problem of social cost. *Journal of Law and Economics, 3*, 1–44.

Condit, C. (1990). *Decoding abortion rhetoric: Communicating social change.* Urbana: University of Illinois Press.

Dahle, C. (2004, September). Gap's new look: The see-through. *Fast Company, 86*, 68, 71.

Edmundson, R. (1984). *The rhetoric of sociology.* London: Macmillan.

Epstein, R. (1997). *Mortal peril.* Reading, MA: Addison-Wesley.

Ferber, M. A., & Nelson, J. A. (Eds.). (2003). *Feminist economics today: Beyond economic man.* Chicago: University of Chicago Press.

Friedman, M. (1970, September 13). The social responsibility of business is to increase its profits. *New York Times Magazine*, pp. 32–33, 122–126.

Gross, A. (1990). *The rhetoric of science.* Cambridge, MA: Harvard University Press.

Gupta, P. (2005, January 19). Arthur Laffer: Corporate social responsibility detrimental to stockholders. *New York Sun*, p. 11.

Guyon, J. (2003, November 10). From green to gold. *Fortune, 148*(10), 226.

Hariman, R. (1995). *Political style.* Chicago: University of Chicago Press.

Henderson, D. R. (2001). *Misguided virtue: False notions of corporate social responsibility.* London: Institute of Economic Affairs.

Jameson, F. (1990). *Late Marxism.* London: Verso.

Kudlow & Co. (2005, March 28). Steven Milloy of the Free Enterprise Action Fund discusses his organization's work against corporate social responsibility [News transcript]. CNBC. Retrieved from Lexis-Nexis Academic Universe website October 25, 2006.

McKeon, R. (1987). *Rhetoric: Essays in invention and discovery.* Woodbridge, CT: Ox Bow Press.

Nelson, J., Megill, A., & McCloskey, D. N. (Eds.). (1987). *The rhetoric of the human sciences: Language and argument in scholarship and public affairs.* Madison: University of Wisconsin Press.

North, G. (1992). *The Coase theorem: A study in economic epistemology.* Tyler, TX: Institute for Christian Economics.

Nozick, R. (1974). *Anarchy, state, and utopia.* New York: Basic Books.

Perelman, C., & Olbrechts-Tyteca, L. (1969). *The new rhetoric: A treatise on argumentation* (J. Wilkinson, Trans.). Notre Dame, IN: Notre Dame University Press.

Porter, M., &. Kramer, M. R. (2002). The competitive advantage of corporate philanthropy. *Harvard Business Review, 80*(12), 57–68.

Posner, R. (1988). *Law and literature: A misunderstood relation.* Cambridge, MA: Harvard University Press.

Ricardo, D. (1996). *Principles of political economy and taxation.* Buffalo, NY: Prometheus Books. (Originally published 1817)

Sahlins, M. (1976). *Culture and practical reason.* Chicago: University of Chicago Press.

Scherer, M. (2003, July/August). Sidestepping sanctions. *Mother Jones*. Retrieved August 30, 2005, from http://www.motherjones.com/news/outfront/2003/07/ma_45201.html.

Sewell, W. H., Jr. (1993). Toward a post-materialist rhetoric for labor history. In L. R. Berlanstein (Ed.), *Rethinking labor history: Essays on discourse and class analysis* (pp. 15–38). Urbana: University of Illinois Press.

Simons, H. W. (1990). *The rhetorical turn.* Chicago: University of Chicago Press.

Smith, A. (1976). *The wealth of nations.* Chicago: University of Chicago Press (Originally published 1776)

Stigler, G. J. (1975). The theory of economic regulation. In G. J. Stigler, *The citizen and the state: Essays on regulation* (pp. 114–141). Chicago: University of Chicago Press.

Sullivan Principles for Social Responsibility (1977). Retrieved October 25, 2006, from http://www.globalsullivanprinciples.org/principles.htm.

Unger, C. (2004). *House of Bush: House of Saud.* New York: Scribner.

Vogel, D. (2005). *The market for virtue.* Washington, DC: Brookings Institution Press.

Walmart Watch. (2005). Retrieved from http://walmartwatch.com/home/pages/healthcare February 15, 2005.

Werre, M. (2003, May). Implementing corporate social responsibility: The Chiquita case. *Journal of Business Ethics*, 44(2/3), 247–260.

Wilcke, R. W. (2004). An appropriate ethical model for business and a critique of Milton Friedman's thesis. *Independent Review*, 9(2), 187–209.

Wolin, S. (1960). *Politics and vision.* Boston, MA: Little, Brown.

Wolin, S. (1989). *The presence of the past.* Baltimore, MD: Johns Hopkins University Press.

Zadek, S. (2004, December). The path to corporate responsibility. *Harvard Business Review*, 82(12), 125–132.

15

Corporate Social Responsibility as Oxymoron

Universalization and Exploitation at Boeing

DANA L. CLOUD

> *At some point in this brave new business world, the concerns of the people should be placed first. . . .*
> Keith Thomas, *Weight Plus Friction Equals Wear*

Since 1997, I have been studying the situation of workers at the Boeing Company in Wichita, Kansas, and the Puget Sound area (Everett and Seattle, Washington). Drawing from about 40 hours of interviews with dissident unionists at this company, my project has focused mainly on ordinary workers' experience of and resistance to layoffs, outsourcing, benefits reduction, and the implementation of "new" management models. I tell the story of worker resistance not only to the company but also to a top-heavy and conservative union leadership. This project shows that many workers at Boeing understand corporate responsibility in ways that could inform and deepen corporate social responsibility (CSR) research.

Consider the following instances of corporate conduct at Boeing over the last several years. Which among them are the more irresponsible?

- March 2005: CEO Harry Stonecipher was forced to resign after an office affair that, according to company statements, was "causing embarrassment to Boeing" ("The End of the Office Affair?" 2005).
- February 2005: Toronto-based investment firm Onex purchased Boeing's Wichita manufacturing facility for $1.2 billion, displacing or laying off as many as 10,500 workers (McCormick, 2005). On May 23, 2005, Wichita journalists Lefler and McMillan (2005) reported that workers are waiting to

reapply for their jobs and have no voting rights on a proposed union contract cutting wages by 10% and eliminating hospitalization insurance entirely. The company is offering free mental health services to displaced workers.

- May 2004: Boeing implemented lean production practices in its operations for the new 7E7 jumbo jet, cutting the number of workers needed for the project from 5,000 to 1,000 and offloading most of the work to overseas and nonunion workplaces (Feldstein, 2004, p. C1; "The 7E7 Difference," 2004).
- 2003: Then-CEO Phil Condit resigned after it was revealed that under his watch, Boeing had made questionable deals with the Pentagon, including an $18 billion Pentagon purchase of a hundred 767 tankers. Pentagon official Darleen Bruyun allegedly tipped Boeing off that Airbus had come in with a lower bid for the aircraft. After the alleged tip, Boeing manager Michael Sears offered Bruyun a management position at the company (Holmes, 2003).
- 2001–2003: Boeing laid off 11,000 workers in Wichita. According to the *New York Times*, the lives of many Wichita families "unraveled" (Kilborn, 2003).
- 2001–2002: Boeing engaged in mass layoffs, firing more than 30,000 workers across all of its facilities (Schultz, 2001). In 2002,

Boeing earned $54 billion, with net earnings of $2.6 billion, the second highest amount since 1999 (Boeing Company, 2003). In December 2001, Boeing Commercial Division chief Alan Mulhally justified both enormous executive salaries and outsourcing, saying, "We have got to get everybody to share the risk of this huge enterprise" (Song, 2001).

- March 2001: Offered $60 million in incentives from Chicago and the state of Illinois, Boeing announced the relocation of its corporate headquarters (minus half of headquarters employees) from Seattle, Washington, to Chicago, Illinois. CEO Phil Condit said the move was a "strategic decision" to "maximize shareholder value" (Verhovek, 2001). A number of workers saw the move as a desertion of a community Boeing was preparing to "trash," without having to look workers and their families in the face (Barboza, 2001). Confirming this impression, the *New York Times* quoted Condit as saying that the headquarters had to be physically separate from any of Boeing's operations so that the company could make objective decisions about where to add and cut jobs (Verhovek, 2001).

In popular media, corporate misconduct means scandal at the top, and the 2003 and 2005 Pentagon and sex scandals were front-page news, bringing widespread attention and criticism to Boeing's shady dealings. In contrast, layoffs, speedups, and the move of corporate headquarters, covered most often in the business pages, have been framed as sound business decisions. To win workers' participation in these "sound business practices," corporations effect rhetorical strategies aimed not at winning public opinion but at making workers party to decisions that are against their own class interests.

This analysis depends on a definition of interests as the material stakes workers have in material improvements in their work conditions and standard of living. I embrace the Marxist view that, ultimately, workers' fundamental interests lie in making a world without profit-driven corporate work life. Thus, workers' interests are antagonistic in the short and long term to the interests of executives and stockholders (see Eagleton, 1991, pp. 212–217; Eagleton, 2003, pp. 174–207). Although everyone involved in an enterprise is a stakeholder, it is important to call attention to how those stakes are profoundly unequal. As an aside, it is worth noting that the language of "stakeholding" often participates in the ideological universalization of corporate interests across all the categories of "stakeholders" without adequate attention to class differences and conflict-based relations in the corporate firm.

Universalization is one of the most common and dominant strategies of capitalist ideology. Eagleton (1991) wrote that, in universalization, "values and interests which are in fact specific to a certain place and time are projected as the values and interests of all of humanity" (p. 56). He explains that universalizing strategies are successful when one class of people can convince others of the plausibility of the unity of their interests. "It is a question, in other words, of how the group or class describes itself to itself, not just of how it sells itself to others" (p. 57).

Ultimately, the goal of universalization is to make sectional interests invisible as such. This process is not always malign: In social movement coalitions, for example, universalizing discourse can bring diverse groups into mutually beneficial activity (ideally without suppressing difference) in common cause. However, when the discourse of company owners exhorts workers to identify with their interests, it is attempting to mystify the very real material divide between the lives and standards of living of owners, on the one hand, and workers, on the other.

In this chapter, I focus on two prominent universalizing strategies employed by bosses and managers at Boeing. First, the discourse of management in the era of the high-performance work organization (HPWO) justifies mass layoffs and pressures on workers toward efficiency and new standards of productivity (Cushman & King, 1997; Obloj, Cushman, & Kozminski, 1995). Second, Boeing's own belabored public and internal discourse about corporate and employee conduct substitutes the interests of executives and shareholders and makes workers accountable to corporate and shareholder interests without reciprocal accountability. These two discourses share the strategy of universalization.

An analysis of these strategies is important to CSR because it exposes how a corporation can "universalize" an ethical position in order to quell labor unrest, co-opt various stakeholding groups, including union leadership, and maintain a favorable public image even in times of economic trouble or scandal. In the study of corporate responsibility, we need to look as closely at the internal practices directed toward employees as we do at the external stances of the corporation toward the community and the environment. Inside the corporation, the exhortation to universal investment in the company's success often wins workers' cooperation with actual relations of exploitation, defined as the expropriation of value produced by workers, a process necessary to corporate profitability. As in the manufacture of a corporation's public image, internal communication often pays lip service to social responsibility. Thus, as Cloud (2005) argues, we must attend not only to the communicative dimensions of labor relations (see Dawkins, 2004) but also to the material exploitation of workers as a regular feature of corporate conduct.

Before turning my attention to the analysis of the HPWO and statements of corporate ethics at Boeing, I provide some background on the company and its labor relations. Importantly, the 1990s were not the first years Boeing tried to quell worker resistance with the rhetoric of humanistic management, nor were they the first years when such efforts were in vain, as workers struck the company for gains beyond the lip service to cooperation and shared interests.

LEAN AND MEAN AT BOEING: SOME BACKGROUND

The Boeing Aircraft and Aerospace Company got its start in the 1910s, when Bill Boeing built his first plane, incorporated his company as the Pacific Aero Products Company, and won a series of Navy contracts during World War I. Changing the company's name to The Boeing Company, Bill Boeing and his engineers built their first plant in Seattle, where they designed and produced the historic seaplanes the Bluebill and the Mallard (Serling, 1992, pp. 1–13). Since that time, Boeing has become the largest manufacturer of aircraft and the largest defense contractor in the world.

Staving off challenges from rival aircraft manufacturer McDonnell Douglas, and weathering economic crises in the 1930s and 1970s, Boeing led production of aircraft for the United States in both world wars (Serling, 1992, pp. 13–37). During the arms race, Boeing developed missiles and entered the aerospace field, while increasing its share of passenger jet development (pp. 80–120). Meanwhile, the Boeing Company expanded its operations, purchasing Vertol Aircraft in Philadelphia, the eventual maker of the Osprey. During the Vietnam War, this plant produced the Chinook and Comanche helicopters. The Philadelphia plant was organized by the United Auto Workers and was notorious for conflicted labor relations (pp. 180–240).

Strikes rocked the company throughout its history. In response to labor unrest, management at a Boeing subsidiary plant in Philadelphia implemented the company's first quality management program in 1974 (well before the 1990s proliferation of total quality management, workplace team programs, lean manufacturing, etc.): the "Pride in Excellence Campaign." Explicitly, this program was designed to reduce union militancy by giving workers a voice in production and by imposing an ideology of quality over workers' rights, which became a matter of individual rather than collective merit (Serling, 1992, pp. 210–215).

Throughout the post–World War II period, Boeing was shaken by economic crisis and labor conflicts. A corporate crisis in 1969–1970, during which orders dried up, resulted in the reduction of the workforce from 101,000 to 38,000. In Seattle, the unemployment rate hit 17% as Boeing integrated its production facilities in Washington State. Despite a bounce back to profitability (based on 727 sales) later in the decade, wages and benefits for workers remained stagnant. In 1974, Boeing stock was selling at $12 per share, and it split six times over 16 years, resulting in stockholder equity soaring from $995 million to $8 billion between 1974 and 1999 (Serling, 1992, p. 399).

In the recession of the 1980s, Boeing's diversification into military and aerospace products proved an asset in spite of some scandals in the 1980s about price gouging in foreign and government contracts. Other problems plagued Boeing during these years, however, including huge safety and health problems resulting from worker illness from fiberglass, graphite, and phenol-formaldehyde poisoning at the Auburn, Washington, plant. Doctors later dubbed the nausea, lung problems, and other symptoms exhibited by workers the "aerospace syndrome" (Serling, 1992, p. 435).

From a conservative, business–union stance, the International Association of Machinists and Aerospace workers (IAM) District Lodge President, Tom Baker, called on workers to "calm down" while he negotiated safety improvements with the company. As Buhle (1999) noted, the history of

American labor is, in part, a history of "business unionism" in which union leadership becomes aligned with management. Pushing against a co-opted union leadership, ordinary workers on the shop floor were also concerned with the growing trend of mandatory overtime. In 1989, the union had 57,000 members in Seattle and Wichita. In their victorious 48–day strike in 1989, they won both wage increases and a reduction in mandatory overtime. The company claimed that they were strapped for cash, "only marginally profitable" (Serling, 1992, pp. 436–437).

The strike also resulted in the second of Boeing's labor–management "persuasion" strategies: the Quality Through Training Program, which, according to some Boeing workers, meant an institute that trained and rewarded workers for performing multiple jobs, enabling layoffs, or becoming the equivalent of company managers (Serling, 1992, pp. 449, 458). Also at this time, the union and management collaborated on the joint IAM/Boeing Health and Safety Institute, designed to reduce union grievances over occupational hazards. In 1990, the continuous quality improvement program was "implemented as a way of life," and 100 Boeing executives traveled to Japan to learn how to motivate workers and avoid labor action (p. 458).

This shift in managerial strategy, paralleled in a number of other industries including auto manufacturing, represents an offensive against workers both materially and rhetorically. Implementation of management–labor teams, quality through training, and high-performance flow models represent attempts to invest workers in the profitability of the company, even as the company ramps up layoffs, outsourcing, and workload (see Alvesson, 2000; Reed, 1996). Since President Ronald Reagan's firing of striking air traffic controllers in 1981, the union movement has been on the decline even as employers have ratcheted up demands on the workforce. Ordinary people's standard of living has been stagnant, and their work conditions have become more demanding. American workers are on the job for more hours per week than ever in U.S. history (Economic Policy Institute, 2004–2005b). Meanwhile, average executive pay has skyrocketed to more than 300 times the average earnings of workers (Economic Policy Institute, 2004–2005a). At Boeing, mass layoffs have been accompanied by accelerating profits, rising stock prices, and soaring executive compensation.

It used to be that the rhetoric of the lean and mean corporation was patently mean. Jack Welch at General Electric is perhaps the most emblematic example of a CEO who employed the stick rather than the carrot to motivate workers. Notably, his successor, Jeffrey Immelt, has taken on a different, kinder persona, exhorting workers to identify with the corporate interest in profit and to see themselves as participants in corporate decision making (Useem, 2004). In no way does this shift in tone represent a scaling back of the lean production process. A number of other major corporations have implemented leaner production processes (thus laying off workers) while at the same time preaching employee involvement in the company (through quality through training, team programs, etc.). At Boeing, mass layoffs accompanied the rhetoric of the HPWO, which incorporated workers into quasi-management positions in safety and performance teams in an attempt to make workers stakeholders in corporate profits.

THE ILLUSIONS OF THE PARTICIPATORY WORKPLACE

Participatory management models encourage identification across class lines in the workplace. For example, when workers take on quasi-managerial roles, their demands for fair economic participation may fall by the way. Participation generally entails only symbolic information sharing among workers and managers, and even that sharing is encouraged for the benefit of company profitability, not workers' empowerment. Stohl and Cheney (2001) explain this contradiction as a paradox of identity: "Be *self*-managing to meet *organizational* goals" (p. 360). Allegedly humanistic workplace reforms enable regimes of "concertive control" (Barker & Cheney, 1994; Tompkins & Cheney, 1987) in which employees are charged with managerial tasks (e.g., supervising other workers) while receiving none of the material benefits of being a company manager (see also Mumby & Stohl, 1991; Papa, Auwal, & Sighal, 1997).

A number of other scholars have recognized the contradictions of allegedly humanizing or democratizing trends in corporate management. For example, Cheney (1995) calls our attention to how the "push for productivity" in the context of globalization euphemizes layoffs as "right sizing" and lays more work on fewer employees in the name of "empowerment" (p. 168). Continuous quality improvement, joint management–union safety and production teams, and the involvement of workers in the HPWO are hailed as exemplary of an allegedly new management style of some corporations, yet as Cloud (1998) argues, strategies of worker voice, empowerment, and emotional support have characterized capitalist workplaces in the United States since the Hawthorne studies of 1927–1932, in which a team led by Elton Mayo studied the effects of illumination, interview procedures, fatigue and monotony, handling of complaints, and employee social organization on organizational efficiency and worker satisfaction. (Roethlisberger & Dickson, 1934, pp. 35–47). As I have argued elsewhere, these studies introduced into the workplace therapeutic discourses designed to address anxieties about industrialization and increasing worker unrest in psychological terms rather than redress material grievances (Cloud, 1998, p. 38).

To one degree or another, most critical organizational communication scholarship valorizes workers' voices in formulating an organization's values (see Cheney, 1995, p. 171; compare Cheney, 1999). Some overestimate the extent to which power relations in organizations are amenable to democratic symbolic reconstruction (see Cooren, 2004; Taylor & Robichaud, 2004; but compare Conrad, 2004). Thus, if workplace democracy is a matter of both economic and symbolic justice, competition and the imperative to profit mean that true material and participatory democracy in corporate organizations is always incomplete (Cloud, 2005). Reed's (1996) work demonstrates that many justice and participation models of workplace organization stress the move to participatory democracy on a moral basis, rather than conceiving democracy also in economic terms (p. 34; see also Reed, 1998).

As Mats Alvesson (1982, 2000) has similarly argued, humanistic values are limited in their capacity to influence the formal structures and economic inequities of most corporate workplaces. As Alvesson (1982) explains, humanistic organization theory "gives the false impression that the economic laws of capitalism, and the system's pressure for efficiency are accompanied by a marked trend toward better and more equal working conditions" (p. 126). Chiapello and Fairclough (2002) have updated this critique in their article calling attention to the disingenuousness of new management ideologies that proclaim worker integrity and agency while instituting downward pressure on wages, new forms of meritocracy, and the privatization of retirement, health care, and other benefits (p. 189).

In light of this research, one can regard the implementation of participatory lean production models as ideological mystifications of class antagonism, attempts to blur the lines between the contending interests of employers and workers. For example, a 1992 *New York Times* article covered a visit by new U.S. Steel CEO Thomas Usher with unionized workers in Gary, Indiana. The event was notable because "[o]ther heads of U.S. Steel would never have dreamed of being in the same room with the union people" (Hicks, 1992). While Usher's predecessors had emphasized the "mean" in "lean and mean," Usher represented "a significant shift in relations between management and labor . . . a historic changing of the guard at Big Steel" (Hicks, 1992). Usher is credited with improving efficiency and quality and the creation of team spirit. "The carefully drawn line between management and labor, which existed for generations, is beginning to blur." He is "committed to getting everyone involved in the process of quality." Usher is quoted as saying:

> Our long-term interests are exactly the same. . . . Whether you are a manager or a member of the union, everyone wants to do a good job, and they want to provide for their families. But I think there is a growing realization that we are not going to make it without the union and the union is not going to make it without us. (Hicks, 1992)

This statement suggests that a worker's struggle to provide for her family is of the same qualitative nature as the manager's needs; therefore, everyone has an equal interest in pulling together. The statement, "Our long-term interests are exactly the same," encapsulates in direct form the key universalizing message of new management models.

Usher seems to admit to the ideological function of this move: "As a culture in this company, we have asked a lot of people's backs, but not enough of their minds" (Hicks, 1992). The language of team spirit, lean production, and quality is part of the battle for workers' minds in justification for taking the labor of their backs. Asking more of their minds will not entail asking less of their backs. On the face of it, the language of quality can just as easily refer to pressure on workers to do more, better, as it does to worker empowerment of any sort.

HIGH PERFORMANCE: MAKING BELIEVERS OUT OF WORKERS

Discourse of the HPWO is one ideological expression of the Toyota-ization (Cushman & King, 1997, p. 129) of manufacturing, in which the implementation of lean initiatives are framed in terms of employee pride in performance. Donald Cushman and his colleagues have been leading advocates of "continuously improving an organization's performance" through high-speed management (Cushman & King, 1997). They argue that because of shifts in technology, the global economy, and the business climate, corporations must do a number of new things; these include to "stay close to their customers and competitors," engage in creative and quick retooling and product design, and "cannibalize" old products and "retrench" workers (p. 7):

> It is important to notice in this summary that the corporations need not stay close to their workers; it is the customers and competitors whose interests determine the process of change. Indeed, the book's index includes no references to workers, employees, or labor, and one of the only times the book mentions workers is in the context of how management should communicate the already-determined changes in the workplace to a potentially resistant workforce. (p. 143)

The only other invocation of workers is in the discussion of teamwork, where the necessity of collaboration in the production process is defended as promoting the "growth and personal well-being of the team members" (Cushman & King, 1997, p. 106). Teamwork also leads to faster production and higher quality in "output," satisfying customers. In addition, it teaches workers (team members) to work interdependently in the future, enabling the company to use management more efficiently (p. 106). Barker and Cheney (1994) and Mumby and Stohl (1991) call attention to how group members in work teams took on control functions sometimes more rigid than those in a traditional managerial setting. In a book advocating the HPWO, Obloj et al. (1995) wrote, "Managers

cannot force workers to form QCs [quality circles], but may skillfully use peer pressure and rewards to encourage workers" (p. 44). Thus, as Stohl and Cheney (2001) note, participatory practices are often paradoxical, when involvement of workers in day-to-day decision making leads to their identifying with management and a reduced voice in longer term corporate decision making and values (p. 351).

This discourse positions workers ("team members") as tools in the process of satisfying customer and managerial interests. There is absolutely no mention of what might be in the workers' best or material interest (see also Obloj et al., 1995, pp. 54–112). Mary Jo Feldstein of the Lean Enterprise Institute (LEI) notes the contradictions: "The concept asks companies to cut waste across the production process. Too often, chief executives use a few lean initiatives as a way to downsize rather than convert employees into believers. . . . Chief executives need to take their excitement to the shop floor" (Feldstein, 2004). At the LEI, training documents encourage managers to implement optimum continuous flow. Nowhere on the website are workers or unions mentioned as contributing to or affected by this process. In this statement, Feldstein also reveals the importance of ideology in winning workers to labor on behalf of someone else's profit: workers must be converted into "believers," into the language of high performance in a leap of faith that belies their real interests.

Likewise, an article celebrating workplace change at Lockheed-Martin dates the invention and widespread implementation of the HPWO and related programs to the early 1990s. At that time, Lockheed began to form joint partnerships with the electrical workers to redesign work flow in the new,

> high performance work system [that] seeks to enhance organizational performance by combining innovative work and management practices with reorganized work flows, advanced information systems, and new technologies. Most important, it builds on and develops the skills and abilities of frontline workers to achieve gains in speed, flexibility, productivity, and customer satisfaction. (Jarboe & Yudken, 1997, pp. 65–66)

A similar rhetoric emerges from the American Society for Training and Development ("The Top

24," 2004), whose reports on worker-friendly companies hail corporate cultures that engage workers in new priorities and strategies. The goal of such programs is to improve workers' "understanding of how their own jobs and contributions were connected to the new company's strategy" (p. 42). The rhetorical motive of this statement is evident if it is worded in the reverse, to say that the company should understand how its actions contributed to the workers' goals. This patently improbable reformation calls attention to how commitment in the corporation is not reciprocal. Notably, the point of new performance models is to enhance the companies' profitability, not to share profits or other gains with the workers whose engagement is solicited in these discourses.

The American Society for Training and Development hails such companies as Hewlett-Packard, in which workers acquire and share knowledge (but not profits). Companies whose workers get 12 days off for community service (not vacation) garner kudos. Likewise, the group celebrates quality of work life movements as humane correctives to the "slash-and-burn economics of the 1970s and 1980s, which generated a workforce strongly antagonistic to certain corporate policies" (Chalofsky & Griffin, 2005, p. 45). Again, it is clearly articulated here that the goal of the new humanism is to reduce worker antagonism. The authors do not acknowledge that the new rhetoric of quality of work life has paralleled an intensification of slash-and-burn corporate policies.

"WEIGHT PLUS FRICTION EQUALS WEAR," OR, GETTING THE JOINT AT BOEING

At Boeing, lean manufacturing resulted in unrest and anxiety among workers, leading to strikes in 1989 and, against the leadership of the union, in 1995. In 1990, it took 150 mechanics to complete a plane, whereas in 2003 that number was down to 56. One staffer of the IAM commented, "They have a functioning moving line now; they've cut flow days; they're saving money. If only we could get them to take some of those savings and keep people working, we'd really have something going" (Gates, 2003).

Boeing introduced lean manufacturing and HPWO together in the 1990s, alongside a new rhetoric of joint union–management participation in safety teams and worker training. A writer in *BusinessWeek* called these efforts a "touchy-feely" invocation of worker empowerment. Even the article's title suggests that the appeal to empowerment is a cover for lean measures: "When the Going Gets Tough, Boeing Gets Touchy-Feely" (D. J. Young, 1994). Confirming this suggestion, workers I have interviewed recognized these programs as Trojan horses. David Clay, a democratic unionist in Everett, Washington, commented to me,

> What happens with jointness is that the union membership's getting the joint. They get people in positions, political appointments from the union for those who helped the current leadership get elected. In the process, a pseudo-union–management position gets created. And in those relationships, the terms of work get negotiated outside of union contracts. (personal communication, August 1999)

Similarly, Keith Thomas, a union activist in Wichita, noted that jointness programs turned union workers effectively into company managers in an attempt to obscure the differences in interests between workers and management (personal communication, April 1998). Both Clay and Thomas believe that such programs are signs of retreat on the part of unions in the face of relentless downsizing. Yet, as the union member quoted above noted, the scaling down of the work process has never resulted in job protection. An IAM strike in 1995 won significant gains for workers, but in 1999 and 2002, the union made concessions and the contracts included increased participation in joint programs—as Boeing laid off 30,000 workers.

Regarding HPWO and lean manufacturing models, Thomas (2002) called attention to the effects of speedup, longer shifts and mandatory overtime, and pressure for ever greater productivity on the human body:

> The human body is a beautifully designed machine. When it comes to human beings, though, there are limitations as to what can be repaired and replaced. . . . What I don't see in all these "new" proposed worker management teams, whether proposed by a union or a company, is recognition of the human condition. . . . The continual drive to increase production does not take into the account the limitations and tolerances of joints, repetitive movements, lifting

capacity, bones, tissue, fatigue, the heart and soul. . . . They push for the maximum production possible. (¶ 44)

In this letter to the unionized workers of the IAM, Thomas calls on workers to refuse cooperation with lean manufacturing, because "*It is not something that can be fixed down the road, because the physical damage will already have been done*. . . . *At some point in this brave new business world the concerns of the people should be placed first*" (¶ 12, emphasis original). As Chong, Emmett, and Sikula (2001) argue, continuous improvement and quality programs do not empower workers: "Americans today are treated as pieces of machinery or inventory. We are becoming 'just-in-time' inputs where the ultimate goal is productivity and profit" (p. 33; see also Hillard, 2001).

The HPWO exhorts workers to create and share ideas that ultimately lead to their own demise. This contradiction could be mobilized against the universalizing assumptions of the high-performance system. As another layer of cover for exploitation, codes of conduct such as the one produced by Boeing attempt yet again to render corporate interests as universal and inclusive of workers.

A CODE OF ETHICS FOR EVERYONE (?) AT BOEING

Boeing's 2004 *Ethical Business Conduct Guidelines*, available on the company website, begins with a photo collage of workers on the job—working with circuitry, shaping airplane wings, discussing important matters at a conference table, welding, making tools, examining lights, and performing clerical work. Only one image, that of two older white men (who may or may not be managers or executives) seated at a gleaming boardroom table, indicates that the document addresses or concerns management or executives. CEO Harry Stonecipher's cover letter of the document, addressed "To the people of Boeing," exhorts workers to "execute your piece of the business plans" (Boeing Company, 2004b) It is evident in this statement that Stonecipher would like workers to see themselves as contributing as part of a corporate whole to a business plan in which, ostensibly, they share fundamental interests with Stonecipher and other executives and shareholders.

This page is followed by a one-page summary of "Our Values." These include leadership, integrity, quality, customer satisfaction, people working together, a diverse and involved team, good corporate citizenship, and enhancing shareholder value, which, importantly, comes last on the list so that the other values build up to it. The use of the first-person plural pronoun suggests that workers, management, and executives together share an interest in executing the company's business plan so that shareholders will profit.

Notably, none of the values described on this page refers to valuing labor and respecting workers' rights. Only the customer and the shareholder appear here as constituencies to which Boeing workers (alongside owners and managers) are accountable. Good corporate citizenship is directed at external constituencies, emphasizing community service and environmental protection. As noted above, "quality," information sharing, and teamwork are buzzwords of HPWO, to which workers contribute talent and knowledge but from which they receive only harder work and uncertain futures.

Intriguingly, Boeing's ethics documents, in which the company talks to itself about itself, universalize interests across owner, management (but see Rodin, 2005), and labor as united in the service of customers and shareholders. While workers in the pages of the guidelines are expected to be loyal and accountable to the profitability of the business, the corporation itself is not positioned as reciprocally accountable to the workers. Instead, the corporation is accountable only to customers and owners of stock.

The universalization strategy is apparent in the "Boeing Code of Conduct," the first major section in the *Ethical Business Conduct Guidelines*. The code warns employees against engaging in any conflict of interest or behaviors that might embarrass the company. These include insider trading, inappropriately disclosing proprietary information, and using company property for personal gain. While the first two items clearly refer to executive managerial ethics, the latter incorporates nonmanagement employees. By referring to all of these categories without distinction as for "employees," the document puts insider trading on a par with a worker's carrying off of tools or pens. All workers in 2004 were asked to sign the code of conduct, basically pledging allegiance to corporate profitability. Union leaders encouraged workers to do so. Union activist Keith Thomas in

Wichita refused to sign the document. He was suspended for five days as a result of his refusal. About the code, Thomas (2004) wrote (in an open letter to the senior vice president):

> The Boeing Code of Conduct is an *economic* Code of Conduct. It comes from the nature of business in general. Boeing Management maintains that we have a business culture, not a family culture. I couldn't agree more. Business exists to profit. No profit—no business. Since Boeing is in business to profit, it is no doubt sound business practice that would dictate the basic rules of the company code. (¶ 19)

Thomas argues that such a code has no moral content at all, since it is "developed by business to assist the company with the exploitation of workers on a global scale" (Thomas, 2004, ¶ 21). He also notes a number of contradictions in the code: while workers are called corporate citizens, they do not have the right of free speech. The company sold airplanes to the apartheid regime in South Africa while announcing it was opposed to apartheid. Thomas wrote, "This was at a time when Nelson Mandela was in prison and South African Death Squads were killing their opposition, including children" (¶ 27).

The company laid workers off immediately following the September 11, 2001, terrorist attacks, while proclaiming the need to keep the economy going. Thomas (2004) wrote, "The Boeing Management got this company into its current mess of scandal, charges, fines, ridicule, lawsuits, and loss of prestige and credibility. Yet Boeing employees are the ones given the choice of signing or being terminated" (¶ 10).

The major ethical breach Thomas calls attention to, however, is that the company engages in practices that harm and even kill workers. In the letter, he recounts the story of his friend and co-worker Joe Cauley, who in 1988 died as a result of exposure to toxic chemicals in the plant:

> One incident that got me to thinking about the ethics and integrity of the people running the Boeing Company was when one of my best friends, Joe Cauley, was carried out of the Wichita plant, never to return. That was February 5, 1988. I can still see his sweet face through the ambulance window as he smiled and waved goodbye to me for what turned out to be the last time. He was 34 years old, healthy, full of life, a good provider for his family and a good worker for Boeing, who left behind a young wife and two small children. The company fought his widow in court for eight years over culpability in his death. In the end, she won the battle. (Thomas, 2004, ¶ 2)

Belying these events, Boeing attempts to construct a public image of virtue and responsibility. Thus, the Boeing board of directors has a code of conduct specific to itself, prohibiting conflicts, breaches of proprietary confidentiality, abuse of corporate opportunities, and illegal behavior. Yet the *Ethical Business Conduct Guidelines* is a universal code; there is one single unified statement of ethical business conduct policy at Boeing that "applies to all employees of The Boeing Company, including subsidiaries, contingent labor, consultants, and others acting for the company ('employees')" (p. 5). The definition of everyone involved as acting (not just working) for the company is the basic maneuver of this universalizing discourse.

In the space of a few pages, the guidelines address whether an employee may surf the Internet on company computers during lunch break (yes, within reason), whether a Boeing representative may offer jobs and other benefits to relatives (no), and whether an executive may exploit trade secrets (absolutely not). The rest of the guidelines provide detailed ethics scenarios and information about how to report ethics violations at any level; again, there is only one "ethics line" to call to report any kind of misconduct at any level of the company, conflating corporate accountability and worker accountability. The ethical decision-making flow chart and hypothetical scenarios walk employees through potential conflict of interest situations, again equating sharing of trade secrets with taking ballgame tickets from a supplier. The irony, of course, is that the document itself enacts and mystifies a fundamental conflict of interest between the company's drive for profit and the workers' standard of living. When faced with a concern, a worker is told to approach management with it. If management *is* the concern, there is nowhere to go.

Understanding corporate wrongdoing in terms of individual high-level scandal operates in tandem with discourses about organizational culture. Both obscure what should be brought into the arena of ethical consideration: the regular exploitation of the worker. Chong et al. (2001) argue that "the effects of continuous improvement, downsizing, and reengineering; part-time workers, lessened loyalty and commitment, early retirement, and virtual work all weaken an ethical treatment of workers" (p. 33).

CONCLUSION: ETHICS OR POLITICS? RESPONSIBILITY OR JUSTICE?

To whom must a corporation have responsibility? In the context of constraining global capitalist competition and the priority of profit, to whom *can* a corporation have responsibility? If one puts labor at the center of accounts of CSR, business as usual comes into relief as a system of routine and necessary misconduct toward workers. Workers, who turn inert, worthless materials into saleable commodities, are always paid less than their product's actual value. In addition, employers must put intensifying downward pressure on wages and benefits to maintain profitability, since other costs of production are less malleable. The squeezing of profit from workers constitutes the basic relationship of exploitation in every capitalist firm (Marx, 1847, 1865, 1867a, 1867b). As Chong et al. (2001) put it, "People, not property, are every organization's primary provision. Manpower, not money, is every institution's main material" (p. 36).

From this perspective, there is no such thing as a nonexploitative capitalist workplace. When metal is mined to make aircraft, when workers fashion engines and wings in dangerous chemical-laden, hot environments, and when other workers put the aircraft together, a commodity worth millions of dollars rolls onto the runway. No executive performed this labor, perhaps instead spending part of each day organizing and planning the distribution of the profits from the airplane's sale. To ask a corporate board to stop exploiting workers would be akin to asking a shark to stop swimming. Each action would kill its agent.

In this light, the bulk of literature on CSR is limited in its ability to evaluate corporate conduct. While there are indeed a range of economic, political, and social commitments pursued under the rubric of CSR, the general tendency of the academic and popular treatments of the idea is to prescribe contained or even token responses by the business community to challenges from outside—whether from government agencies, competitors,

critics, or consumers (see Baker, 2005; Monks, Miller, & Cook, 2004; Starck & Kruckeberg, 2005). For example, in developing countries, a measure of CSR is how corporations respond to economic crisis and pollution with token philanthropic aid and minimal environmental redress (Hamann, 2004; R. Young, 2004).

A focus on corporate responsibility to *external* constituencies is actually part and parcel of ideological universalization. Supporters of CSR portray the corporation as a holistic entity that contains workers, managers, and bosses acting in concert, potentially for the public good. Little CSR scholarship considers labor as a separate constituency at all (but see Korczynski, 2003; Murray, 2004). While CSR advocates in the business world disapprove of businesses that "screw the poor and the environment to make their obscene profits" (Baker, 2005), they have little to say about employers who "screw" the workers to "make their obscene profits."

However, there is a growing critical scholarly literature on CSR. A number of scholars have pointed out that externally oriented CSR is often more a matter of manipulating a corporation's public image than actually doing good for others (Fineman, 2001; Roberts, 2003). Blowfield (2004) questions the fundamental assumption that business can do good in environmental and international development projects driven by capital (see also Acutt, Medina-Ross, & O'Riordan, 2004). I add to this series of criticisms the argument that an organization's treatment of workers may be the most concrete and, perhaps, the most telling measure of its commitment to social responsibility.

During periods of massive layoffs, Boeing increases its charitable giving to local food pantries. Workers who have just been fired are encouraged to volunteer in community service. Blind to such contradictions, the dominant discourses of corporate responsibility in popular and corporate culture universalize responsibility and individualize blame. Allegedly inclusive managerial schemes pass for ethical labor relations, and universalizing corporate ethical codes invoke no responsibility whatever for the well-being of workers.

As throughout the history of labor struggles, however, acknowledgment of the obvious inconsistencies—between the rhetoric of teamwork and the moving of a company's headquarters to get distance from workers, between soaring profits and mass layoffs, between a discourse of quality and the reality of speedup, between a code of conduct that prohibits theft and the daily theft of workers' labor—may break through the illusions of universality. The presence of voices such as David Clay's and Keith Thomas's suggests that at such moments, the impetus for workplace justice can redefine ethical corporate conduct in terms of accountability to workers rather than to profiteers.

It is unlikely that recognition of antagonism and the limitations of existing frames for corporate responsibility will happen in executive suites or commercial mass media. Thankfully, however, ordinary workers have resources for consciousness raising in their own experience of exploitation and in the counterdiscourses of agitators within unions. To the extent that union officialdom has given ground to the rhetoric of high performance, joint interests, and lean production, it will take a revitalization of the democratic union movement to reinvent and circulate a discourse of corporate conduct that underscores questions of ethical, political, and economic justice for workers.

This democratic union movement is the subject of my broader research project about Boeing workers and is beyond the scope of this chapter. However, it bears saying that full reciprocity and accountability are, on a Marxist argument, unsustainable in a world dominated by corporate competition. Irresponsibility is not just the province of the new business world of high performance and lean production. If we take seriously Marx's (1867b) idea that labor produces value without attendant and proportional material reward for workers, we must then recognize the fundamental and routine misconduct necessary to all business in capitalism throughout its history.

Any consideration of CSR that includes the real interests of workers will come up against the basic injustices of capitalism, not only to workers but also to the environment, the poor, and victims of often-profitable wars. We must not see responsibility only in terms of a company's externally oriented benevolence while companies such as Boeing routinely sacrifice workers on the altar of profit. The capitalist firm is not a moral entity but rather a political one; it is materially invested in perpetuating necessarily unequal relations of power, both internal and external. Thus, critics of CSR must concern themselves with politics, moving from a discussion of ethics and responsibility to a discussion of justice. This shift poses a new challenge: to imagine and create a different kind of world entirely.

REFERENCES

Acutt, N., Medina-Ross, V., & O'Riordan, T. (2004). Perspectives on corporate social responsibility in the chemical sector: A comparative analysis of the Mexican and South African cases. *Natural Resources Forum, 28,* 302–317.

Alvesson, M. (1982). The limits and shortcomings of humanistic organization theory. *Acta Sociologica, 25,* 117–131.

Alvesson, M. (2000). Varieties of discourse: On the study of organizations through discourse analysis. *Human Relations, 53,* 1125–1149.

Baker, M. (2005). *Arguments against corporate social responsibility.* Retrieved May 18, 2005, from http://www.mallenbaker.net.

Barboza, D. (2001, May 11). Chicago, offering big incentives, will be Boeing's new home. *New York Times,* p. C1.

Barker, J. R., & Cheney, G. (1994). The concept and practices of discipline in contemporary organizational life. *Communication Monographs, 62,* 19–43.

Boeing Company. (2003). *Boeing reports fourth quarter and full-year 2003 results.* Retrieved April 25, 2005, from http://www.boeing.com/companyoffices/financial/quarterly.htm.

Boeing Company. (2004b). *Ethical business conduct guidelines.* Retrieved January 22, 2006, from http://www.boeing.com/companyoffices/aboutus/ethics/.

Blowfield, M. (2004). CSR and development: Is business appropriating global justice? *Development, 47,* 61–69.

Buhle, P. (1999). *Taking care of business.* New York: Monthly Review Press.

Chalofsky, N., & Griffin, M. G. (2005, January). It takes a community. *TD: Training and Development,* 43–48.

Cheney, G. (1995). Democracy in the workplace: Theory and practice from the perspective of communication. *Journal of Applied Communication Research, 23,* 167–200.

Cheney, G. (1999). *Values at work: Employee participation meets market pressure at Mondragon.* Ithaca, NY: ILR Press.

Chiapello, E., & Fairclough, N. (2002). Understanding the new management ideology: A transdisciplinary contribution from critical discourse analysis and new sociology of capitalism. *Discourse and Society, 13,* 185–208.

Chong, W. K., Emmett, D., & Sikula, A. (2001). Employee relations, ethics, and the changing nature of the American workforce. *Ethics and Behavior, 11,* 23–38.

Cloud, D. L. (1998). *Consolation and control in American culture and politics: Rhetorics of therapy.* Thousand Oaks, CA: Sage.

Cloud, D. L. (2005). Fighting words: Labor and the limits of communication at Staley, 1993 to 1996. *Management Communication Quarterly, 18,* 509–542.

Conrad, C. R. (2004). The illusion of reform: Corporate discourse and agenda denial in the 2002 "corporate meltdown." *Rhetoric and Public Affairs, 7,* 311–338.

Cooren, F. (2004). Textual agency: How texts do things in organizational settings. *Organization, 11,* 373–393.

Cushman, D. P., & King, S. S. (1997). *Continuously improving an organization's performance: High-speed management.* Albany, NY: State University of New York Press.

Dawkins, J. (2004). Corporate responsibility: The communication challenge. *Journal of Communication Management, 9,* 108–114.

Eagleton, T. (1991). *Ideology: An introduction.* London: Verso.

Eagleton, T. (2003). *After theory.* London: Verso.

Economic Policy Institute. (2004–2005a). CEO Pay. Retrieved May 18, 2005, from http://www.epinet.org/books/swa2004/news/swafacts_ceopay.pdf.

Economic Policy Institute. (2004–2005b). State of the working American. Retrieved May 18, 2005, from http://www.epinet.org/subjectpages/labor.

The end of the office affair? (2005, March 12). *Economist,* p. 64.

Feldstein, M. J. (2004, April 16). Lean and mean. *St. Louis Post Dispatch,* p. C1.

Fineman, S. (2001). Fashioning the environment. *Organization, 8,* 17–31.

Gates, D. (2003, February 21). Toeing the line at Boeing. *Seattle Times,* p. C1.

Hamann, R. (2004). Corporate social responsibility, partnerships, and institutional change: The case of mining companies in South Africa. *Natural Resources Forum, 28,* 278–291.

Hicks, J. (1992, April 3). The steel man with the kid gloves. *New York Times,* p. D1.

Hillard, M. (2001). Paperworkers' response to work reorganization efforts. *Review of Radical Political Economics, 33,* 287–293. Retrieved March 19, 2005, from EBSCO Academic Search Premier database.

Holmes, S. (2003, December 15). Boeing: What really happened. *Newsweek,* pp. 32–43.

Jarboe, K. P., & Yudken, J. (1997). Time to get serious about workplace change. *Issues in Science and Technology, 13* (http://www.issues.org/13.4/jarboe.htm). Re-

trieved March 13, 2005, from EBSCO Academic Search Premier database.

Kilborn, P. (2003, April 16). Slump in plane travel grounds Wichita. *New York Times,* p. A14.

Korczynski, M. (2003). Communities of coping: Collective emotional labor in service work. *Organization, 10,* 55–79.

Lefler, D., & McMillan, M. (2005, May 22). *Two letters later, no more job.* Retrieved May 23, 2005, from http://www.kansas.com/mld/kansas/news/local/11707750.htm.

Marx, K. (1847). *Wage, labor, capital.* Retrieved April 15, 2005, from http://www.marxists.org/archive/marx/works/1847/wage-labour/index.htm.

Marx, K. (1865). *Value, price, and profit.* Retrieved April 15, 2005, from http://www.marxists.org/archive/marx/works/1865/valueprice-profit/index.htm.

Marx, K. (1867a). Commodities and money. *Capital* (Vol. 1, part I, chap. 1). Retrieved April 15, 2005, from http://www.marxists.org/archive/marx/works/1867-c1/ch01.htm.

Marx, K. (1867b). The labor process and the process of producing surplus value. *Capital* (Vol. 1, part III, chap. 7). Retrieved April 15, 2005, from http://www.marxists.org/archive/marx/works/1867-c1/ch07.htm.

McCormick, M. (2005, February 24). Separation anxiety: Boeing sale to be completed today. Retrieved April 25, 2005, from http://nl.newsbank.com/nl-search/we/Archives?p_action=list&p_topdoc=11.

Monks, R., Miller, A., & Cook, J. (2004). Shareholder activism on environmental issues: A study of proposals at large US corporations (2000–2003). *Natural Resources Forum, 28,* 317–331.

Mumby, D. K., & Stohl, C. (1991). Power and discourse in organization studies: Absence and the dialectic of control. *Discourse and Society, 45,* 313–332.

Murray, J. (2004). Corporate social responsibility discussion paper. *Global Social Policy, 4,* 171–196.

Obloj, K., Cushman, D. P., & Kozminski, A. K. (1995). *Winning: Continuous improvement theory in high-performance organizations.* Albany, NY: State University of New York Press.

Papa, M. J., Auwal, M. A., & Sighal, A. (1997). Organizing for social change within concertive control systems: Member identification, empowerment, and the masking of discipline. *Communication Monographs, 64,* 219–249.

Reed, M. (1996). Organizational theorizing: A historically contested terrain. In S. R. Clegg, C. Hardy, & W. R. Nord (Eds.), *Handbook of organization studies* (pp. 31–56). London: Sage.

Reed, M. (1998). Organizational analysis as discourse analysis: A critique. In D. Grant, T. Keenoy, & C. Oswick (Eds.), *Discourse and organization* (pp. 193–213). London: Sage.

Roberts, J. (2003). The manufacture of social responsibility: Constructing corporate sensibility. *Organization, 10*, 249–265.

Rodin, D. (2005). The ownership model of business. *Metaphilosophy, 36*, 163–182.

Roethlisberger, F. J., & Dickson, W. J. (1934). *Management and the worker: Technical vs. social organization in the industrial plant.* Boston, MA: Harvard University Press.

Schultz, K. (2001, September 17). Layoff roundup. *The Daily Deal.* Retrieved April 25, 2005, from LexisNexis database.

Serling, R. J. (1992). *Legend and legacy: The story of Boeing and its people.* New York: St. Martin's Press.

The 7E7 Difference (2004, May 21). *Seattle Times*, p. C1.

Song, K. M. (2001, December 15). CEO of Boeing commercial airplanes faces the firing line on talk radio. *Seattle Times.* Retrieved March 21, 2005, from LexisNexis database.

Starck, K., & Kruckeberg, D. (2005). Ethical obligations of public relations in an era of globalization. *Journal of Communication Management, 9*, 29–41.

Stohl, C., & Cheney, G. (2001). Participatory processes, paradoxical practices. *Management Communication Quarterly, 14*, 349–408.

Taylor, J. R., & Robichaud, D. (2004). Finding the organization in the communication: Discourse as action and sensemaking. *Organization, 11*, 395–413.

Thomas, K. (2002). *Weight plus friction equals wear.* Retrieved April 22, 2005, from http://www.keith-thomas.info/boeing_page.htm.

Thomas, K. (2004). *An open letter regarding the Boeing Company's Code of Conduct.* Retrieved April 22, 2005 from http://www.keith-thomas.info/boeing_page.htm.

Tompkins, P. K., & Cheney, G. (1987). Coming to terms with organizational identification and commitment. *Central States Speech Journal, 38*, 1–15.

The Top 24. (2004). *TD: Training and Development, 58*, 28–67. Retrieved March 19, 2005, from EBSCO Academic Search Premier database.

Useem, J. (2004, April 5). Another boss, another revolution. *Fortune, 149*, 112.

Verhovek, S. H. (2001, March 21). Boeing, jolting Seattle, will move headquarters. *New York Times*, p. A3.

Young, D. J. (1994, January 17). When the going gets tough, Boeing gets touchy-feely. *BusinessWeek*, 65–68.

Young, R. (2004). Dilemmas and advances in corporate responsibility in Brazil: The work of the Ethos Institute. *Natural Resources Forum, 28*, 291–302.

16

Toward an Accounting for Sustainability

A New Zealand View

STEWART LAWRENCE

Accounting is a ubiquitous social practice—it touches each of us, every day, in our personal and professional lives. No matter what occupation we take up, there will be no escaping financial responsibility and accountability. Even outside of paid employment, individuals need to be financially responsible and accountable: in families, in social clubs, and in any kind of group activity where resources are acquired and consumed. For centuries, the practice of accounting was limited to providing information relating to the stewardship of financial resources. Increasingly, accountability is expanding beyond that of the stewardship of financial resources to include social and environmental responsibilities. New types of accounting may be needed in the future if we are to guarantee the sustainability of our limited resources for future generations. The nature and extent of these accountings are being widely debated in the academic accounting literature. The study of accounting is sociopolitical in the sense that the way we account both reflects and constitutes the sort of societies we live in. To understand accounting practice is also to understand the nature of the entities for which accounting is performed and the social relations within and between them, that is, who is accountable to whom, for what, and why.

In this chapter, I provide an understanding of accounting that goes beyond technique and that explicitly recognizes the sociopolitical. The first part of the chapter concerns how accountants contribute to the perception of objective reality through their universally applied measurement techniques. The possibility of expanding the representations beyond financial considerations to those of social and environmental concerns is then discussed. It is important to understand the traditional concept of accountability and how this concept is being challenged. The underpinning theoretical models are examined as a precursor to identifying the potential role of accountants and their objectifying techniques in moving toward sustainable development. A change of consciousness from the maximizing "self" with all its attendant calculus to an outward-looking concern for "the Other" may be a precursor to sustainable practices.

ACCOUNTING AND SOCIAL REALITY

Accountants have long been acknowledged as experts in creating a sense of order. Their view of the world is generally accepted as objective, true, and fair and is indeed a skilled accomplishment. The accountant's job has traditionally been viewed as that of providing an objective and truthful representation of some underlying reality. Traditional mainstream accounting practice and research took for granted that there was an externally existing reality (Chua, 1986). Both practice and research were based on a belief in an economic reality that existed independently of the accountant's measurements of it. Because of this basic assumption, the concept of truth has had an important place in the discourse of accountants. Goldberg (1980) argued that when accountants deviated from the presentation of truth, they were no longer acting as accountants:

> The accountant is thus concerned primarily with ascertaining and presenting the truth. . . . The accountant, qua accountant, is not directly concerned with either propaganda or prudence . . . to the extent that he [*sic*] is concerned, he is widening his responsibility beyond his primary and principal task of the ascertainment and presentation of truth. (p. 5)

The traditional self-image of accountants as presenters of fact and as purveyors of truth has come under increasing scrutiny and questioning from academics (Chua, 1986; Gambling, 1985; Hines, 1988; Lowe, 2004; Morgan, 1988). According to the alternative view, the economic reality that accountants communicate is a product of the interpretive schemes employed. The interpretive schemes called upon in daily activity by practitioners may not be apparent even to the practitioner. The professional training and socialization of an accountant ensure that the interpretive schemes do not depend on personal conviction, but on the weight of opinion and authority encapsulated and communicated through accounting standards. The practitioner's job is to apply them, not question them. Deviations to standard procedures are greatly discouraged and can result in an auditor's qualification in the annual report. Managers of companies also have expectations that accountants will abide by well-articulated rules and procedures that eliminate any subjective influence.

The notion of objectivity is important both in accounting and in the routines of everyday life. The problem faced by accountants is a specific example of a more general feature of everyday life. We all employ objectifying procedures that work. They work as long as we do not question them too closely. Much of the social environment that appears to us as objective is not objective in the sense that it consists of concrete objects, but rather is procedurally objectified; that is, it assumes a social objectification. Accounting plays its part in

that it is both an invention of the human mind and a means of objectifying human thought.

There are two opposing views about creativity in accounting. That accounting practice has a creative element is viewed with concern by many accountants. The term "creative" is used in accounting in a particular sense to imply an intention to distort or misrepresent, rather than to objectively reflect, an underlying reality. In contrast to this conservative perspective, there is an increasingly popular view that all accounting is necessarily creative (Hines, 1988). Here, the term "creative" is used in the sense that accounting practices play a vital role in the construction and reproduction of society. It is a paradox that accountants have to believe that there is an objective reality in order to play their part in its social construction. The rules and conventions are necessary for "objectivity," but the objectivity is a partial representation of a complex reality. It is a paradox that, by following generally accepted accounting practices, accountants are engaged in constructing a subjective, one-sided representation of reality. Accounting is often stated to be the language of business, and conducting business would be inconceivable without a method of communicating its results. Accounting concepts are transmitted by the use of language that objectifies subjective processes.

Accountants have institutionalized business reporting practices and, in doing so, have produced a language for communicating about business phenomena. This language and the interpretive schemes surrounding the accounting craft require some examination.

THE LANGUAGE OF BUSINESS

Language is one of our most important institutions for creating a sense of order and stability. It is through language that we create a sense of common understanding and ordered reality. We create typifications and generalizations that form common sense or common understandings of everyday reality. Ethnomethodologists study this phenomenon—how speech establishes and maintains the reality of the everyday world. It is through language that social events become *accountable*. The argument is that what we take to be the objective features of speech, and of social life in general, are objective because we express them in objective terms, that is, in terms of their common or intersubjective properties, not because of their unique or context-specific features. All explanations and accounts render unique specific events or objects in terms of their generality or typicality. For example, if the word "tree" is used, it conjures up myriad specific examples, each of which is unique, yet each of which is understood only as a member of a general category.

In the same way, accounting procedures generate reports of unique, context-specific features that are in a generalized form. A general rule is applied to a wide diversity of assets that in no way attempts to capture the specific, unique circumstances of each asset. Practical accounting procedures are used to present objective reports, but the objectivity is a result of procedures that are designed to create an acceptable illusion, an image rather than a true representation, but an image that enables people to get on with their everyday practical projects. The chaos of daily events is routinely recorded by accountants under a set of consistent categories, and accounting procedures are used to achieve a sense of tidiness, order, and stability in organizations and in society. This notion is encapsulated in Cooper's (1983) parent–child dialogue:

> Daughter: Daddy, why do things get in a muddle?
> Father: What do you mean, "things" . . . "muddle"?
> Daughter: Well, people spend a lot of time tidying things, but things seem to get in a muddle all by themselves and then people have to tidy them up again. (p. 269)

The orderliness achieved by accounting systems is not a natural phenomenon; it is a human imposition on an otherwise chaotic world. The order is the result of applying a categorical paradigm. Both positive and normative accounting theories are articulated through categorical paradigms. The uniqueness of events is *represented* using the generality of a priori account headings. In conventional accounting, a mass of chance and disparate events is transformed through classifications and associated recording and reporting procedures and made to appear consistent and orderly. An important theoretical construct facilitating this process is that of the *market*—the abstract mechanism that is assumed to rationalize chaos. Accounting practices take for granted the existence of such markets (Hines, 1989, pp. 62–65).

Markets are strongly advocated as a means of allocating society's scarce resources in the most efficient way. Price signals and accounting cost data are used as information devices to direct resources to their most profitable, that is, most efficient, use. But these price signals are impersonal, and those without resources play no part in setting prices and determining what should be produced—they are excluded from the markets. This has been the argument of those calling for more government interference in markets and for an ethical approach to business decision making that might result in a better, or more equitable, distribution of income and wealth.

EXPANDING CONCEPTS OF ACCOUNTABILITY—SOCIAL RESPONSIBILITY REPORTING

It was the view of the economy as an ordered and self-regulating mechanism tending toward equilibrium prevalent in the 1980s that prompted the advocacy of a more limited role for the state, and the free play of market forces. But markets are not natural phenomena existing independently of social activities. Markets are the construct of human beings. The failing of unregulated markets to provide a decent lifestyle for millions of the world's population has brought increasing calls for more state interference in the play of markets and a more socially responsible approach from businesses. Increasingly, businesses are expected to be responsible not only for making profits, but also for their more general social, economic, and environmental impacts. Accountants have responded to the need for different kinds of reporting on firms' activities. John Elkington (1997) popularized the concept of the triple bottom line (TBL), that is, an expansion of the traditional company reporting framework to take into account environmental and social performance in addition to financial performance. This concept has been taken up and expanded upon worldwide. The Global Reporting Initiative (2002) provides voluntary guidelines for business reporting on human and environmental impacts of business activities. Reporting on the social and environmental impacts of operations is now a requirement of businesses belonging to the World Business Council for Sustainability. The guidelines are comprehensive and detailed, requiring new forms of accounting. For most small and medium-sized firms, however, which make up 98% of firms in New Zealand, the requirements may be incompatible with their resources.

Much of the research on company reporting began to question the reasons for the production of disclosures, since reporting is voluntary. The self-interested corporation has to appear "legitimate" in the sense that its pursuit of self-interest can be shown to align with the interests of its various stakeholders. It is perhaps one of the paradoxes of recent years that the increased emphasis on principal–agency theory[1] and greater demands for increased shareholder value have occurred at the same time as an increased interest in business ethics, corporate social responsibility, and corporate citizenship. The argument that the sole responsibility of business was to make a profit (Friedman & Friedman, 1962) was widely accepted in a period when social objectives were assumed to be the responsibility of the nation state. Since then we have witnessed a period in which the nation-state has been in retreat, both in the East and in the West. The state has reduced its welfare role and its offering of social services under the pressure of global capitalism and fiscal crises, and societies have seemed to be overtaken by forces that no one could control (Smith, 1999, p. 49). In many places, the power to affect social conditions and welfare of the general population seemed to have shifted from nation-states to the large transnational corporations. Such was their apparent power and autonomy that there emerged an interest in business ethics and corporate citizenship. Businesses were seen as the only organizations with the resources, technology, and global reach to make a difference (Hart, 1997).

Much literature in accounting deals with the reactions of large firms to outside influences on their practices and reporting in relation to social and environmental impacts. It is assumed that, without such pressure from the outside, firms will not act other than self-interestedly. The outside pressure is necessary to combat the systemic forces of capitalism. The corporate response has been varied, but most have responded by having explicit and public codes of ethics and principles of conduct (even Enron had these) and began to publish environmental and social reports. Concern for the environment and sustainability of society (including business operations) has encouraged a movement in business corporations toward TBL reporting. According to Elkington (1999), "To refuse the challenge implied by the TBL is to risk extinction" (p. 75).

Yet there is a sense that the big firms have produced a public relations machinery to gloss over the risks and continue with "business as usual" (Milne, Owen, & Tilt, 2001). Their codes of conduct and social and environmental reports may be viewed as knowing and cynical attempts to be seen as ethical and to counter problems of corporate image. It is all "the ethics of narcissus" (Roberts, 2004), a view of corporate self with a new narrative of responsibility without requiring anything new or different beyond the work of a few public relations people at the head office. It is not that executives are morally corrupt, but that they are part of a system that does not allow any expression of generosity to others. This is the paradox of "ethical" business practice. It is an oxymoron, at least under conventional assumptions underlying principal–agency theory, the theory underpinning the traditional corporate accountability model.

Evidence shows that the vast majority of enterprises in New Zealand do not have any formal reporting of their social and environmental practices. Fewer than 5% of the firms in the category of "small and medium" (fewer than 100 employees) have any kind of formal report, and among the larger firms (more than 100 employees), only 27% had a reporting activity (Lawrence & Collins, 2003). Whether firms should be accountable to outsiders for social and environmental impacts is still controversial. In the following sections, I present a review of the theoretical underpinnings of the concept of "accountability." I examine the underlying assumptions about human behavior of conventional principal agent approaches and argue that they may not apply to small and medium-sized firms, giving reasons and drawing implications.

The notion that firms are responsible and accountable to a wider stakeholder group than their owners or shareholders is still rejected (Henderson, 2001). Corporate social responsibility reflects an ever-expanding concept of accountability. Principal–agency theory has been a core element underpinning accountability in finance and accounting literature. It resulted in an almost universal set of techniques and practices designed to control the conduct of executives and managers both internally and externally (Walsh & Seward, 1990). The conventional concept of accountability involves a high degree of monitoring of executive performance and decision making. Accounting practices are employed to support transparency through detailed disclosures, mainly about financial performance.

The basic assumption of principal–agency theory is that human beings are utility-maximizing individuals and that their behavior is driven by self-interested opportunism (Jensen & Meckling, 1976). Based on this assumption, the aim of control mechanisms is to align the interests of managers (agents) with those of shareholders (principals). According to Roberts (2004), attempts to constrain and align managerial self-interest with investor interests has had the effect of producing, or at least promoting, the very self-interested opportunism that it attempted to avoid. The whole theory is a-ethical. It takes without question the sovereignty of shareholders and their property rights to govern corporate behavior. It creates, according to Roberts (2004), an individualistic subjectivity, one contrary to wider concerns of ethical conduct.

Recent examples of opportunistic behavior that have caused the collapse of major corporations have simply reinforced the perceived need for greater monitoring and reporting as reflected in the U.S. Sarbanes-Oxley Act (2002), the Australian Corporate Law Economic Reform Programme (2004), and the U.K. Higgs Report (2003). According to Roberts (2004), such reports and legislative reforms accept the assumption of self-interested behavior, an acceptance that he argues is the cause, not the solution, to the problems of ethical conduct in organizations.

Stakeholder theory is an extension of the perceived need to have accountability to shareholders for management actions, with the recognition that there are other "interests" that had to be taken into account in corporate decision making. The stakeholder approach acknowledges that there are multiple interested parties in any organization's activities. These stakeholders are entitled to know how the decisions by management affect their interests. The need for transparency and accountability is thus extended to a broader constituency. Reporting is encouraged still on the basis that those removed from decision-making roles within organizations need to be suspicious of the motives and consequent actions of executives of companies. The latter have to justify their actions on the grounds that the entire organization is acting "ethically"—by which is meant not self-interestedly at the expense of the various identified stakeholders. As yet, there are no

reporting standards against which auditors could be employed to judge the veracity of any reports produced.

An interesting finding of a survey of firms in New Zealand (Lawrence & Collins, 2003) was that many small and medium-sized firms engage in socially responsible and environmentally protective practices but do not report these. The reasons for such actions cannot be easily explained in terms of traditional models of accountability and transparency based on principal–agency theory. The practices are not reported and are generally invisible. The responses indicated that practices are undertaken for ethical reasons that go beyond self-interest, at least of the managers. Explanations provided for actions (recorded on the survey instrument) included, "It is the right thing to do," "It is our values," and "It's just right." Such comments suggest that there are reasons other than self-interest at work.

How then can we explain the social practices of small firms? The exclusive focus on self in utility-maximizing models may need to be reevaluated. We need another approach to understanding what business ethics is all about. One approach is to recognize that humans cannot escape being ethical, that they feel an inescapable responsibility to neighbors; that is, they are not as essentially individualistic as the economic theories imply (Roberts, 2004). According to Roberts, the problem of ethics in business is not about how to get ethics back into business but rather of exploring how our ethical sensibility (caring for others) is routinely blunted.

It may be possible to learn from prominent business people who oppose conventional ways of doing business, such as the New Zealander Dick Hubbard. The founder of a cereal manufacturing firm that bears his name, he was also the founder of a network called Business for Social Responsibility that has since merged into the Sustainable Business Network. Hubbards Foods Ltd. produced a triple bottom line report in 2001. As explained in its website, the report revolves around:

> Social and people responsibilities; Planet and environmental responsibilities; Profits and financial responsibilities.

Basically, it recognises that a company cannot be judged by profits alone. Although this report was written in 2001, the Triple Bottom Line concept is still a key part of both current and future business strategy. (Hubbards Foods Ltd., 2001)

What is surprising is that his firm has abandoned TBL reporting from 2002 onward. I sought an explanation. I was referred to the founder's often-stated conviction that TBL was becoming a part of corporate public relations designed for public recognition and that more important were the behind-the-scenes, undisclosed, ethical acts—almost following the biblical recommendation: "Beware of practicing your piety before men in order to be seen by them" (Matthew 6:1).

Truly ethical behavior comes from a sense of moral obligation toward others and is not done for self-glorification. It comes from an openness to the Other, which is denied in utilitarian approaches. It is not instrumental. It is compelled by a sense of nonindifference to others. It is done against self-interest. According to Bauman (1993), morality cannot be rule based. Following rules allows us to comply minimally and turn away. Rules are mechanisms for switching off our moral capacity, not a means of activating or fulfilling it. An issue for business ethics is how to activate such moral capacity.

Instead of legislating for and controlling the activities of small and medium-sized firms, it may be better to allow greater freedom and autonomy. Yet the consequences are difficult to accept—a kind of moral anarchy. Surely, there is a need for some centralized government direction to foster sustainable activities.

A COMMUNITARIAN APPROACH TO ACCOUNTING FOR SUSTAINABILITY

Increasing awareness of the earth's limited resources to meet everyone's needs has persuaded many people of the need to conserve and protect the environment instead of exploiting it for profit. Yet we still do not have a theory of accountability that would support the overwhelming need for an accounting to the Other rather than to self-interest (Shearer, 2002).

New forms of accounting involving communitarian principles may be required in the future (Lehman, 1999). From a communitarian perspective, the community is the starting point for any kind of analysis. It implies that the use of environ-

mental assets is a subject for deliberations in the public sphere. In this section, I suggest a new form of business accountability, based on the communitarian approach and using an example to illustrate the practicality of the idea. The example relates specifically to the natural environment in New Zealand and is referred to as the Lake Taupo project. It is an example of a community that has agreed a set of overriding values that will guide decision making. At the top of the list of communal values was an ecological concern—preserving the water quality in Lake Taupo. The strategy set out in the 2020 *Taupo-nui-a-Tia Action Plan* (Environment Waikato, n.d.) sets goals for the community:

> The purpose of the project is to provide a framework for the management of Lake Taupo and its catchment that incorporates scientific knowledge with the values and aspirations of iwi and hapu (Ngati Tuwharetoa), and the wider community. The strategy is intended to influence not only environmental decisions that may affect the sustainability of the lake and its catchment, but also economic and social decisions. We envisage the strategy being implemented through the activities of statutory management agencies, iwi, businesses, and community groups.

The strategy recognizes the need to incorporate scientific knowledge with values and aspirations of the community. It recognizes that ecological concerns must be taken into consideration as well as social and economic concerns.

If the concerns of business extend beyond self-interest to social justice and the preservation of natural habitats, we are forced to reconceptualize the concept of accountability in a way that recognizes the communal imperative or common good. Mechanisms for incorporating business decisions within community values are being worked out. Generally, there is a need for mechanisms to allow the engagement of various stakeholder groups with businesses. The provision of accurate and verified reports of business activities is a necessary precursor. It involves more than reporting the impacts of past activities, whether financial, social, or environmental. It involves the giving of reasons for one's actions, giving an account. Schweiker (1993) states that giving an account of one's actions is a means of creating self-identity and by which individuals are constituted as moral agents:

"Giving an account is one activity in which *we come to be* as selves and particular kinds of communities through forms of discourse that shape, guide and judge life regarding concern for the common good, human solidarity and basic respect" (p. 235, emphasis in original). It opens up the possibility of self-regulation when there is a conflict of interest between self and Other. But when livelihoods are at stake, it could well be that self-regulation is insufficient to achieve an outcome that benefits others. If that is the case, how should regulation operate, if not by centralized government? We may need democratic ways of decision making, a bottom-up (communitarian) rather than a top-down control mechanism. It has to be done concretely, on a case-by-case basis.

Lake Taupo provides an example where the community, including farmers, agreed in principle through a broad-ranging consultative process to a list of values that would guide community sustainable development. At the top of the list was the preservation above all else of water quality. Securing agreement in principle has proved to be easier than getting action. Scientific evidence suggests the most likely cause of degradation is the many small farms around the lake. Leaching of chemicals and discharges of animals into the streams, rivers, and the lake itself are affecting (and even if stopped today would continue to affect for the next 50 years) the lake's water quality. This, in turn, affects social and economic opportunities for all those engaged in the district. People live in the district mainly because of the access to recreational and economic opportunities afforded by the lake. Naturally, individual farmers are reluctant to give up their livelihoods, even in the knowledge of the scientific findings.

Despite the community explicitly stating its commitment to sustainability, and a concrete goal being established, agreeing to individual responsibility and action is problematic. The local authority, Environment Waikato, has raised a dedicated tax for action. A 2004 rate demand notice contained an entry for an individual's contribution to "protecting Lake Taupo." It was $9 in 2004 and doubled in 2005. The government has matched its earmarked tax with a central grant. It is proposing a tax on excessive application of nitrogen to the farmlands. This would require farmers to report their use of fertilizers.

Thus, bottom-up community values have been expressed and small business operations have been exposed as creating environmental dangers. Community support for action has led to a combined government, local authority, and community strategy for changing land use. A fund to support those affected will prevent the burden from falling only on those whose livelihoods, such as farmers, are threatened by community action. Social justice and environmental concerns can be expressed and taken into account in business activities.

Such an approach suggests a way forward along the lines of a communitarian model of accountability (Lehman, 1999). In such an approach, businesses are not separate from their "environments" but an integral part of them. Business enterprises are an integral part of civil society. Decisions of civil society require firms to supply adequate information for a participatory democratic process. Such processes are evident but far from commonplace. The freedom given to firms to operate is conditional on being an active participant in communal decision making based on explicit criteria about what is acceptable economic activity. This may be an illustrative example of what the New Zealand parliamentary commissioner for the environment (2002) meant by his recommendation that we must "redesign our socio-political-economic system in ways that reintegrate the dependencies between people and our underpinning ecological systems."

CONCLUSION

Modern societies are complex arenas for the discussion and settlement of conflicting interests. Accounting is a means of helping resolve those disputes in ways that reflect general community standards of fairness and equity, as well as efficiency and effectiveness. Increasingly, environmental and social considerations are being recognized, and accounting may play a role in making visible the wider societal impacts of various courses of action. That managers of firms have a responsibility for those wider impacts is still controversial, and the boundaries of accountability are being debated. Until we have an accounting that recognizes and represents social and environmental impacts, managers will be entitled to restrict their accountability and act as agents for their shareholding owners. More and more, there is a recognition that the activities of firms affect many constituencies and that the reporting to only one is damaging to sustainable practices. The economistic models underpinning accounting and finance theory are based on individual utility maximization. This set of behavioral assumptions may not be adequate to reflect the complexity of modern decision making that increasingly requires recognition of "external" social and environmental effects. Increasingly, those effects are not regarded as "external" but as part of integrated networks of community and natural life systems. A communitarian approach is being debated. Still, the mechanisms for communal accountability have not yet been established. Theoreticians and practitioners are working toward a more inclusive accounting, one that recognizes social equity and environmental protection. It may still be an anthropocentric view of accountability of human activities, but it is a move in the right direction.

NOTE

1. Principal-agency theory is a theory based on self-interested rational choices in which the principal compensates the agent for performing acts that are beneficial to the principal and costly to the agent. It involves the design of incentive schemes so that agents act in a way that principals wish.

REFERENCES

Bauman, Z. (1993). *Postmodern ethics.* Cambridge: Polity Press.

Chua, W. F. (1986). Radical developments in accounting thought. *Accounting Review, 61,* 601–632.

Cooper, D. (1983). Tidiness, muddle and things: Commonalities and divergencies in two approaches to management accounting research. *Accounting Organizations & Society, 8*(2–3), 269–286.

Corporate Law Economic Reform Programme. (2004). Audit Reform and Corporate Disclosure Act. Retrieved January 13, 2005, from http://www.austlii.edu.au//cgi-bin/disp.pl/au/legis/cth/consol_act/clerpracda2004727/sch1.html.

Elkington, J. (1997). *Cannibals with forks: The triple bottom line for 21st century business.* Oxford: Capstone Publishing.

Elkington, J. (1999). Triple bottom line revolution—reporting for the third millennium. *Australian CPA, 69*(11), 75–76.

Environment Waikato. (n.d.). *The 2020 Taupo-nui-a-Tia action plan: An integrated sustainable development strategy for the Lake Taupo Catchment.* Environment Waikato and Tuwharetoa Maori Trust Board. Retrieved June 13, 2004, from http:// www.ew.govt.nz/policyandplans/taupo/documents/index3.pdf.

Friedman, M., & Friedman, R. D. (1962). *Capitalism and freedom.* Chicago: University of Chicago Press.

Gambling, T. (1985). The accountant's guide to the galaxy, including the profession at the end of the universe. *Accounting, Organizations & Society, 10*(4), 415–424.

Goldberg, L. (1980). *An inquiry into the nature of accounting.* New York: Arno Press.

Global Reporting Initiative. (2002). *Sustainability reporting guidelines.* Retrieved December 15, 2003, from http://www.globalreporting.org/guidelines/2002.asp.

Hart, S. (1997). Beyond greening: Strategies for a sustainable world. *Harvard Business Review, 75*(1), 66–76.

Henderson, D. (2001). *Misguided virtue: False notions of corporate social responsibility.* Wellington: New Zealand Business Roundtable.

Higgs Report. (2003). *Review of the role and effectiveness of non-executive directors.* Retrieved June 14, 2004, from www.dti.gov.uk/cld/non_exec_review.

Hines, R. D. (1988). Financial accounting: In communicating reality, we construct reality. *Accounting, Organizations & Society, 13*(3), 251–261.

Hines, R. D. (1989). The sociopolitical paradigm in financial accounting research. *Accounting, Auditing & Accountability Journal, 2*(1), 52–76.

Hubbards Foods Ltd. (2001). *Triple bottom line report.* Retrieved November 4, 2004, from http://www.hubbards.co.nz/TBL01.pdf.

Jensen, M., & Meckling W. (1976). Theory of the firm: Managerial behavior, agency costs and ownership structure. *Journal of Financial Economics, 13,* 305–360.

Lawrence, S. R., & Collins, E. (2003). Sustainable practices of businesses in New Zealand. Retrieved March 23, 2004, from http://www.wms-soros.mngt.waikato.ac.nz/NR/exeres/56B828A5–DAC7–4B75–88F8–03C3C18DA25F.htm.

Lehman, G. (1999). Disclosing new worlds: A role for social and environmental accounting and auditing. *Accounting, Organizations & Society, 24,* 217–241.

Lowe, A. D. (2004). Post-social relations: Toward a performative view of accounting knowledge. *Accounting Auditing & Accountability Journal, 17*(4), 604–628.

Milne, M., Owen D., & Tilt, C. (2001).

Corporate environmental reporting: Are New Zealand companies being left behind? *University of Auckland Business Review, 3*(2), 24–36.

Morgan, G. (1988). Accounting as reality construction: Towards a new epistemology for accounting practice. *Accounting, Organizations & Society, 13*(5), 477–485.

Parliamentary Commissioner for the Environment. (2002, August). *Creating our future: Sustainable development for New Zealand.* Retrieved March 15, 2004, from http://www.pce.govt.nz/reports/allreports/1_877274_03_8.shtml.

Roberts, J. (2004, June 28–30). *Agency theory, ethics and corporate governance.* Paper presented at the Corporate Governance and Ethics Conference, Sydney.

Schweiker, W. (1993). Accounting for our-selves: Accounting practice and the discourse of ethics. *Accounting Organizations & Society, 18*(2/3), 231–252.

Shearer, T. (2002). Ethics and accountability: From the for-itself to the for-the-other. *Accounting Organizations & Society, 27,* 541–573.

Smith, D. (1999). *Zygmunt Bauman: Prophet of postmodernity.* Cambridge: Polity Press.

Sarbanes-Oxley Act. (2002). An Act to protect investors to improve the accuracy and reliability of corporate disclosure made pursuant to the securities laws, and other purposes. Pub. L. No. 107-204, 116 Stat. 745.

Walsh, J., & Seward, J. (1990). On the efficiency of internal and external corporate control mechanisms. *Academy of Management Review, 15*(3), 421–458.

17

Consumer Activism and Corporate Social Responsibility

How Strong a Connection?

BRENDEN E. KENDALL

REBECCA GILL

GEORGE CHENEY

CONSUMERISMS IN THE TWENTIETH CENTURY AND BEYOND

The Reframing of Consumption as a Primary Goal

"Consumerism was the twentieth century's winning 'ism'" (Gopnik, 1997, p. 80). With this bold and deliberately ironic statement, a writer for the *New Yorker* magazine made the point that whatever other movements rose and fell in the past 100 years or so, the force of consumerism is with us. Indeed, it is now so common to speak of "consumer society," to substitute the term "consumer" for "citizen," and to speak of nations like China as "emerging markets of consumer power," that in everyday talk consumption has ceased to be an object of attention. For people in industrialized societies, regardless of their position on the political spectrum, consumption is not just a means to live but a way of life (Miles, 1998). And nowhere perhaps is this truer than in the contemporary United States.

But, how did we get here? At the turn of the twentieth century, "consumption" referred primarily to use, to waste, and to the disease of tuberculosis. That is, the term had negative and neutral meanings, but not particularly positive ones. With the advent of lifestyle advertising (and indeed, the notion of lifestyle choice itself) in the 1920s, the rise of mass production technologies from the 1910s onward, and especially through the creation of the marketing discipline in the 1950s, consumption became elevated beyond need and desire to a fundamental pursuit (see the critical history in Ewen, 1976).

By the mid-1970s, most neo-Marxist theorists and writers agreed that the focus of a contemporary critique of capitalism must shift from production to consumption, in recognition of the nexus of images of individual success, material comfort, and even transcendent "salvation" that accompany late-twentieth-century consumption practices (Baudrillard, 1980).

The 1960s and early 1970s, of course, gave voice to consumer activism (e.g., Nader, 1965) just as the period featured broader movements reacting against material indulgence and the traditional emblems of success in capitalist democracies. This consumer activism centered, first, on awareness of issues such as safety and integrity of products/services, extending to demands for information under the banner of "consumer protection." Today's Simple Living movement (see http://www.simpleliving.net/) is to some extent the successor to the back-to-basics and counterculture "return to nature" of that earlier period.

What is especially interesting for our purposes is how that so-called "radical" period also gave rise to—or at least was trumped by—an even more thoroughly consumptive culture and the almost complete redefinition of the citizen in terms of consumption-oriented images and practices. At the same time that marketing assumed preeminence over its corporate cousins of production, sales, public relations, and advertising, in the 1990s, the cultures of North America, Western Europe, the Pacific Rim, and Australasia became completely saturated by a notion of the consumer with individual rights but few or no responsibilities to the commonwealth (Cheney, 2005).

"Consumption" and "Consumerism" as Contested Terms

Still, we would not want to position consumption or consumerism as univocal expressions or as singular activities or movements. As anthropologists (e.g., Douglas & Isherwood, 1979) and anthropologically inclined marketing scholars (e.g., Belk, Wallendorf, & Sherry, 1989) have demonstrated so well, the practices and meanings of consumption are as diverse within societies as between them.

The consumption of technology is one example. Consumers' relationships to technology are complex and manifold. For some people, technology occupies a strictly instrumental role in their lives: finding and using what is needed to accomplish tasks. The prevailing image here is that of a tool. For others, technology today represents a means of connection, a route to staying current, even a basis for social or intellectual community. For still others, technology and its consumption are so wedded to notions of progress and forward movement that they cannot even see the root metaphor for much of technological advertising: the running of an endless race (see Cheney, Christensen, Zorn, & Ganesh, 2004). Moreover, when you ask people about their specific technologies in the home or office, some will be materially transparent to them; that is, they will in effect look right through them as windows on the world. Thus, our landfills are now full of old computers, and their toxic components are invisible to most consumers of technology—in more ways than one.

The point is that, however critical we may be of consumer society, we should not presume it to be monolithic or static. In fact, the ambiguities surrounding consumption can be exploited for a variety of ends. In the interest of promoting more material consumption, Visa commercials play on the idea that "There are some things money can't buy." The subtext for such advertisements is, "But, you can and should buy a helluva lot!" Collective consumer energies can be harnessed for support of brand loyalty (as when Coca-Cola tried to change its "classic" formula in 1985), in the interest of community (as with conventions of Saturn car owners), and, as we discuss in this chapter, political action against a corporation.

(Re)Politicizing Consumption

Probably the best single book on the multiple expressions of the consumer and consumerism is Gabriel and Lang's (1995) *The Unmanageable Consumer*. After reviewing the historical development of modern consumerism, Gabriel and Lang move through a series of metaphors for the consumer, with each highlighting certain practices and potentialities for the life of consumption. Among these crystallizing images are chooser, communicator, explorer, and hedonist, but also victim, rebel, activist, and citizen. The overall message of this book is that contemporary consumption practices are confused, volatile, and fragmented. Still, it is the second cluster of metaphors that are of greatest interest to us here. We want to consider specific forms of political-personal expression by the consumer—that is, those directed not only against corporations but as leverage for positive social change. This expression is what might be called "conscientious consumption" (Cheney, 2005). Within the context of this volume on multiple approaches to corporate social responsibility (itself, of course, a contested term), we consider some current consumer activist campaigns targeted at prominent multinational corporations.

In the remainder of this chapter, then, we first examine a history of consumer rights and responsibilities. Second, we provide examples of the range of consumer options today for affecting corporate policy and behavior (from traditional boycotts to bioregionalism) Then, we examine the features of six notable and global cases, some of which have been ongoing for decades, and all of which have received extensive media coverage since the 1990s. Finally, we trace some implications for communication and persuasion.

CONSUMER RIGHTS
AND RESPONSIBILITIES

Consumer rights and consumer responsibilities are terms whose meanings are established and challenged by individual and collective activists, corporations, governments, nongovernmental organizations (NGOs), and other interest groups. Consumer protection legislation in the United States and other countries, as well as the contemporary consumer movement, however, have defined consumer *rights* while leaving consumer *responsibilities* somewhat more difficult to pin down.

March 15, 1962, marked President John F. Kennedy's endorsement of the Consumer Bill of Rights, making Kennedy the first U.S. president to acknowledge the need for consumer protection. Kennedy announced the following consumer rights: the right to choose, the right to safety, the right to be informed, and the right to be heard. Kennedy called upon government agencies such as the Federal Trade Commission and the Federal Communication Commission to support the Consumer Bill of Rights in their interactions with consumers, and also established the Consumer Advisory Council. The council, however, apparently did not accomplish much and turned out to be "little more than window dressing" (Creighton, 1976, p. 43). Likewise, President Johnson's Consumer Advisory Council remained largely ineffective. Creighton ascribes the inability of the Johnson council to implement changes to the lack of "presidential backing or the pressure of an effective consumer lobby," suggesting that mere acknowledgment of consumer rights is not enough to create change and that consumers themselves must get involved in ensuring their rights (p. 44).

March 15, 1983, saw the first World Consumer Rights Day, commemorating President Kennedy's establishment of the Consumer Bill of Rights. Since then, the global organization Consumers International has added four more items to the Consumer Bill of Rights: the right to satisfaction of basic needs, the right to redress, the right to education, and the right to a healthy environment. Table 17.1 defines each consumer right.

The United Nations has also taken up the consumer protection torch. The *United Nations Guidelines for Consumer Protection*, adopted by the United Nations General Assembly in 1985, embraces all eight consumer rights in some form or another (Consumers International, 2000; Overby, 2002) and encourages governments to use the guidelines "in formulating and strengthening consumer protection policies and legislation" (United Nations, 2004, Background, ¶ 1). In 1999, the United Nations added issues of sustainable consumption to the guidelines, introducing important

TABLE 17.1 Consumer rights

Consumer right	Description
The right to choose	To be able to select from a range of products and services, offered at competitive prices with an assurance of satisfactory quality
The right to safety	To be protected against products, production processes, and services that are hazardous to health or life
The right to be informed	To be given the facts needed to make an informed choice, and to be protected against dishonest or misleading advertising and labeling
The right to be heard	To have consumer interests represented in the making and execution of government policy, and in the development of products and services
The right to satisfaction of basic needs	To have access to basic, essential goods and services: adequate food, clothing, shelter, health care, education, public utilities, water, and sanitation
The right to redress	To receive a fair settlement of just claims, including compensation for misrepresentation, shoddy goods, or unsatisfactory services
The right to consumer education	To acquire knowledge and skills needed to make informed, confident choices about goods and services, while being aware of basic consumer rights and responsibilities and how to act on them
The right to a healthy environment	To live and work in an environment which is nonthreatening to the well-being of present and future generations

Source: Consumers International (2000).

environmental and social elements of consumer rights (Overby, 2002; United Nations, 2004) and again placing the burden of protecting and policing customers onto governments and "national policy making" (United Nations, 2004, Background, ¶ 4).

Governments, however, are not always willing and/or able to take on these responsibilities. It is in this light, then, that scholars and activists have called for widespread consumer activism (Creighton, 1976). For example, according to Creighton, Nader sees "the need for personal involvement and personal commitment," calling for a "new kind of citizenship" where citizens seek to educate themselves and maintain consumer vigilance (p. 60). Despite these early calls for consumer awareness and activism, an explicit bill or code of consumer responsibilities has yet to emerge, often leaving consumer responsibility an overlooked component of consumer protection and ethical consumption. However, there are a few sources that explicitly discuss the ideal role of the consumer. The Consumer Protection Branch of the Government of Saskatchewan, for example, offers six consumer responsibilities on its website (Consumer Protection Branch, 2005; see Table 17.2).

Such consumer responsibilities stress that consumers, as well as corporations, play a role in the market and in consumption practices, and that consumers need to be aware, educated, and respectful. Political scientist Michele Micheletti (2003) notes that contemporary consumers not only are more aware of how they contribute to negative consumption practices but are also more willing to participate in collective action in the marketplace. In fact, Micheletti identifies recent consumer action as *political consumerism*, where citizens create political issues out of their personal choices, such as what coffee to drink, what clothing to buy, and whether to purchase local or global goods. Consumer responsibilities, indeed, now encompass a new sphere of politically, socially, and ethically motivated decisions and choices. Such decisions, however, can be made only by those who buy into the responsibilities of the consumer in the first place and, as such, are aware of the issues at hand and of their options for making informed purchasing decisions and for sending messages to corporations and affecting corporate social responsibility.

CONSUMER OPTIONS FOR AFFECTING CORPORATE BEHAVIOR AND POLICY

Citizen-consumers who choose to "fight back" (Bloomstein, 1976) or to engage in conscientious consumerism (Cheney, 2005) have various discursive options for affecting corporate behavior and policy, regardless of political intent. Consumer advice manuals from earlier decades often advise individual action in the form of phone calling and letter writing (e.g., Bloomstein, 1976; Eiler, 1984). As electronic information technology becomes nearly ubiquitous, the ways in which consumers can send messages to corporations and organizations are becoming more varied and accessible.

TABLE 17.2 Consumer responsibilities

Consumer responsibility	Description
The responsibility to beware	To be alert to quality and safety of goods and services before you buy
The responsibility to be aware	To gather all the information available about a product or service and keep up-to-date on changes and innovations in the marketplace
The responsibility to think independently	To make decisions on real needs and wants
The responsibility to speak out and complain	To inform businesses and other consumers in a fair and honest manner of your dissatisfaction or satisfaction with a product or service and to communicate to manufacturers and governments your expectations of the marketplace
The responsibility to be an ethical consumer	To not engage in dishonest practices that cost all consumers money
The responsibility to respect the environment	To avoid waste, littering, and contributing to pollution

Source: Consumer Protection Branch (2005).

Today, we often see consumers taking larger scale, community-based action and making extensive use of the Internet. In this section, we briefly discuss the discursive strategies that consumers can and have used to bring about changes in corporate policies and practices.

Recognizing that there are many strategies for consumer activism, we address several here: phone calls, letter writing, and petitioning; creating alternative venues for consumption; participating in boycotts and buycotts; developing local and bioregional alliances; staging demonstrations such as protests and marches; embracing critical pop culture and media; performing violence/violent action; and aligning with established social movements.

Phone Calls and Letter Writing

On an individual level, there are a variety of options for speaking up against corporate irresponsibility and for conscientious consumption. Phone calling and writing letters are two such options in addition to seeking advice from consumer protection manuals and handbooks that instruct consumers on making smart purchases and lodging compelling complaints. Such individual options, however, have evolved with technology. Phone calls and letters are now often replaced with emails to the company, completion of Internet feedback surveys, and Internet petitions. What we find most compelling is the ease with which consumers can now add their voices to the fray: consumers can send faxes and letters to corporations and politicians through a few key activist organizations, via the Internet, and on an issue-by-issue basis. For example, in 2000 and 2003, consumers could send postcards, sign petitions, and send faxes to Starbucks Coffee all through the Global Exchange and Organic Consumers Association (OCA) websites; the 2003 OCA campaign facilitated more than 2,000 faxes from consumers to the corporation (Organic Consumers Association, n.d.). Such armchair activism is convenient and inexpensive and requires little commitment.

Creating Alternative Venues for Consumption

The Internet has rapidly become a vehicle for individual-to-individual sales, for promotion of small and independent retailers. Sites such as Worldstock .com offer an avenue for consumers to circumvent big business and for artisans in developing countries to more directly market their goods via the Internet. Similarly, market communities on the Internet such as eBay (http://www.ebay.com) and CraigsList (http://www.craigslist.com) allow consumers, artisans, and entrepreneurs to negotiate directly with one another in order to reuse and recycle, essentially side-stepping the quintessential "corporate middleman." The Freecycle Network (http://www.freecycle.org) creates local groups in which community members reduce waste and consumption of new goods by sharing and trading unwanted items for free.

Boycotts and Buycotts

Boycotts have a long and rich history in consumer activism, although the term did not arise until the 1870s in England (Micheletti, 2003). Friedman (1995) defines boycotts as attempts "by one or more parties to achieve certain objectives by urging individual consumers to refrain from making selected purchases in the marketplace" (pp. 198–199). In refusing to purchase products on a large-scale basis, consumers have a voice in effecting corporate change. Historical and contemporary examples of boycotts abound, with some being recurring or ongoing. Exemplifying this point, one can see ExxonMobil boycotts as cyclical and trace boycotts of Coca-Cola back to the early 1900s. Boycotts, however, are not without their dilemmas. During his work on the Wal-Mart/Kathie Lee Gifford scandal, labor activist Charles Kernaghan insisted that both an absolute consumer boycott of Wal-Mart and Wal-Mart's boycott of the Honduran factory that produced Gifford's clothing line would actually harm Honduran workers (Dicker, 2004).

Buycotts, on the other hand, "encourage people to purchase goods following an established set of criteria" (Micheletti, 2003, p. 50). Buycotts often take the form of labeling schemes where consumer groups identify products that "make the grade." Developed by Florence Kelly of the National Consumers League, the White Label scheme is of particular historical significance. An early version of a fair trade label, the White Label scheme (1898–1919) required manufacturers to open their doors to inspections and regulations in order to be considered worthy of the White Label. A considerable success, the label forced manufacturers to change "factory workplace conditions and [improve] the situation of workers" (Micheletti, 2003, p. 51).

One contemporary study (Prasad, Kimeldorf, Meyer, & Robinson, 2004) showed that many consumers will select labeled products over unlabeled counterparts. Today, consumers and groups such as the Worker Rights Consortium demand that companies such as Nike and Gap make their manufacturing chains and practices transparent and undergo independent monitoring of their factories.

Labeling schemes are also played out writ large in actual retail companies. The store Ten Thousand Villages (www.tenthousandvillages.com), for example, follows the principles set forth by the International Fair Trade Association (IFAT) in obtaining all of their merchandise from around the world. The IFAT principles are sevenfold and include transparency in manufacturing practices, a commitment to the environment, and gender equity. Such a retail store provides a watchdog function and a guarantee of fair trade throughout the global supply chain.

Internet-based opportunities for buycotts are plentiful. Quite recently, we have even seen a directly political association with consumer decision making. Websites such as BuyBlue (http://www.buyblue.org) and Shop Right (http://www.shopright.org) are dedicated to demonstrating connections between corporations and political parties so that consumers can make buying decisions in line with their political affiliation, blue (Democratic) or red (Republican).

Localism and Bioregionalism

In the past 30 years, numerous examples of consumer power on the local and regional level have appeared around the world. These range from consumer cooperatives surrounding organic farms (e.g., in many parts of North America), to alternative trade systems across borders (e.g., between Bangladesh and India), to local exchange trading systems (LETS). While these examples vary in terms of their political interests and commitments, all of them share a concern for local control over production, distribution, and access.

LETS involve interdependence between and among producers and consumers. Some of these systems are more avowedly anticorporate than others. Similar to an age-old barter system but more systematized, LETS usually produce their own currency. Local subscribers include individuals as well as businesses and other organizations. The Ithaca (New York) HOURS (see http://www.ithacahours.com/home.html) is one of the best-known and most developed LETS systems, and it has recently been studied by the governments of China and Japan.

Demonstrations, Protests, and Marches

Demonstrations, protests, and marches invite consumers to join in collective action and civil disobedience to send a message. Public on-site protests accomplish several tasks. First, they provide evidence of a united front against a particular organization or activity. Second, they create an undeniable physical presence that constrains corporate response and can resist containment of an issue. Third, because marches and other demonstrations bring together vocal collectivities, they can provide the ground for arguments from transcendence (Burke, 1969, as cited in Stewart, Smith, & Denton, 2001). In protest rhetoric, corporations or governments are often portrayed monolithically and the protesters as a united group formed of many individuals and subgroups.

It is often the purpose of protests, rallies, and marches to mobilize concerned citizens and, when published or broadcast in media outlets, to articulate the identities of consumers in opposition to the marketers and manufacturers of the products they consume (Egan, 1998). Juxtaposition is a rhetorical strategy that "contextualizes different forms of knowledge about the situation, altering the dynamics of certainty and uncertainty surrounding the situation" (Schwarze, 2003b, p. 315). Demonstration organizers will often incorporate those directly harmed by corporate malfeasance into public actions, as United Students Against Sweatshops (USAS) has recently done in an anti–Coca-Cola rally at the United Nations. Such strategies manifest the effects of alleged misconduct, "giving them a face," as the saying goes. Protests, marches, and other public events can challenge the everyday consumer's experience of a product with the narratives of those harmed in or outraged by its production, distribution, or marketing (Pezzullo, 2003).

Critical Pop Culture and Media

Activist groups and savvy purveyors of media are spreading consumer awareness through mass media outlets, inviting consumers to rethink the role that corporations play in contemporary society. One of the most talked about examples of this at our university, the University of Utah, is the *South Park* episode (Parker, 2004) that depicts "Wall-Mart" as a soul-stealing, disembodied being that threatens to economically and spiritually destroy the small town of South Park, Colorado. Contemporary singer-songwriters and groups such as Ani DiFranco, Public Enemy, Bruce Springsteen, and Rage Against the Machine speak out against corporate and government (mis)behavior in their lyrics and personal politics, echoing the protest songs of Woody Guthrie, Joan Baez, and John Lennon. For example, the punk group Anti-Flag's (2001) song "Seattle Was a Riot" thoughtfully questions how citizens can expect to have their voices heard and criticizes the institutions that ignore human suffering, referencing the 1999 World Trade Organization protests.

Various documentaries also critically assess the role that big business plays in contemporary society. For example, the award-winning film *The Corporation* (Achbar & Abbott, 2003) incorporates the voices of corporate executives, social activists, scholars, and economists into a discussion of corporate social responsibility. Much like Morgan Spurlock's popular documentary *Super Size Me* (Spurlock, 2004), *The Corporation* invites viewers to consider their own complicity in corporate (mis)behavior as well as the ramifications of corporate (in)action. Likewise, we note the recent release of Robert Greenwald's documentary *Wal-Mart: The High Cost of Low Price* (Gilliam, Greenwald, & Smith, 2005). This documentary is unique in that Greenwald solicited stories and footage from consumers. The documentary was also financed without corporate contributions—rather, grants and donations supported the production—and the film opened in independent theaters, in public venues, and at parties in private residences throughout the United States.

Such media operates to question corporate responsibility on a large scale and introduces and maintains activist sentiments among the public/audience. The power of activist media is apparent: according to a *Newsday* article, Starbucks Coffee refuses to sell Bruce Springsteen's newest album in their stores partly because of its clear anticorporate sentiments ("Boss Isn't Starbucks' Cup of Tea," 2005). And, with Greenwald's film we have a salient example of how consumers can go beyond being audience members and become involved in the creation and distribution of critical media.

Violence and Militant Acts

Extreme or violent action gains the attention of government, business, and media, and activists may engage in what are often labeled "terrorists acts" to that end. Often, the purpose of a particular activist strategy is to stimulate media attention and corporate or state response. Another purpose can be to challenge audiences of public discourse to rethink the relationships between viewers, activists, and targets of anticorporate campaigns. DeLuca (1999) calls actions of this nature, attuned to the digital age, "image events."

DeLuca and Peeples (2002) suggest that symbolic violence, "acts directed toward property, not people, [are] designed to attract media attention" (p. 137). They note that the WTO demonstrations in Seattle, where a faction of protesters attacked Starbucks cafes and Niketown, garnered media coverage of police violence and brutality, while the largely orderly protests at Washington, DC's International Monetary Fund/World Bank conference in 2000 did not. Certainly, peaceful activists will often claim that violent acts do not represent the whole of a movement and its strategy. But, striking attacks against property can serve to counter institutions' maintenance of control through refusal to acknowledge a social movement's existence (Bowers, Ochs, & Jensen, 1993).

Social Movement Alignment

Consumers wishing to use their voices and to enact change can also find outlets in established national and global social movements such as the anti-globalization, antisweatshop, and student movements. Nascent and established social movements often address issues with which conscientious consumers sympathize. In addition, aligning consumer action with social movement organizations has the potential to offer alternative consumer identities, represent a broad and concerted voice in the interest of pro-social change, and change the course of movement activity.

United Students Against Sweatshops (USAS) exemplifies the coordination of conscientious consumers and social movement activists (see http://

www.studentsagainstsweatshops.org). Student representatives at a 1998 conference established USAS as a coalition of universities and students committed to the adoption of efficacious codes of conduct for apparel sourcing on college campuses. Student consumers concerned about the origins of the products emblazoned with their university's logo provided the impetus and structure for USAS. Later, USAS helped to start the Worker Rights Consortium, a group dedicated to independent investigation and monitoring of global production facilities. USAS has played essential roles alongside labor and women's rights groups such as Global Exchange and UNITE! in campaigns targeting Nike, Gap, the Kathie Lee brand, and Coca-Cola. In less than a decade, USAS has become a formidable voice for (student) conscientious consumers and a major player in the antisweatshop and labor rights movements.

So often, attempts to induce socially responsible activity in corporations address myriad issues. Norman's (2004) *The Case Against Wal-Mart*, for example, provides 13 counts of antisocial behavior against the world's largest retailer—from labor rights violations, to unfair trade practices, to disregard for property rights. In instances where corporate misdeeds are so numerous or so caught up in "the way things are done," consumer and social movement organizations alike can benefit from strategic alliances. Radical groups can dramatically expose or force discussion of important issues, and more institutionalized groups can work to effect material changes in corporate practice (M. M. Cooper, 1996). The paramount obstacle to effecting pro-social change in corporations is establishing productive dialogue between disparate groups and concerned consumers (Carty, 2002; M. M. Cooper, 1996).

Summary

The various options for both individual and collective conscientious consumption have, in many instances, proven to be successful in effecting corporate change. In fact, several cases of consumer activism and corporate change have taken on a global character. To put into context the feasible options for consumer activism described above, we next discuss the various dimensions of such cases, including the ensuing action (if any) taken by the corporation in the name of (or under the guise of) corporate social responsibility.

SOME NOTABLE CORPORATE CASES OF CONSUMERISM AND ACTIVISM

In this section and in the appendix we provide accounts of six cases—Coca-Cola, Shell, Texaco, Wal-Mart, Nike, and Starbucks Coffee—in which conscientious consumption figures prominently. The cases have been selected because they involve multinational or global corporations, highlight many of the consumer options detailed above, have been featured prominently in U.S. news media, and have occurred within the last decade. For each case, we trace seven themes: (1) central issues addressed by or concerning consumers, (2) the origins of consumer awareness and the genesis of the case, (3) the nature and extent of consumer involvement, (4) specific strategies utilized by consumer activists and turning points in the case, (5) corporate responses or actions in the case, (6) the extent of interaction and coalition development between consumers, corporations, governments, and NGOs, and (7) outcomes and implications we anticipate for the specific cases and consumer activism more broadly. We expect the cases described in the appendix to speak for themselves in many ways, but in this section we draw out common themes and implications for links between consumer activism and corporate social responsibility.

From our range of cases, several patterns emerge. Widespread consumer awareness of exigencies stems from news media stories and investigative journalism in several instances. In the cases of Nike and Wal-Mart, specific news stories or series helped touch off waves of interest in and antagonism toward corporate misdeeds. In cases such as those of Starbucks Coffee and Shell Oil, extensive media coverage of significant events— WTO protests in Seattle in 1999, and the planned sinking of the Brent Spar platform, respectively— augmented interest in (anti)corporate campaigns already underway. Popular entertainment media can further buoy public interest in consumer issues, as with *Doonesbury*'s scathing series on Nike in 1997.

Consumers seem to take one of three roles in the cases. First, consumers can be the target audience of specific campaigns. Two examples are how residents in a particular city were encouraged to not shop at any Wal-Mart store after the company announced plans for a redundant Super Wal-Mart, and the encouragement of Starbucks patrons to buy the chain's fair-trade–certified coffees. Second, consumers can organize as a group. Third, consumer identities can play a lesser role in antagonistic organizations. Groups clearly representing consumers (e.g., USAS) play a role in some cases, while many groups get portrayed in public talk as being composed of "activists" rather than "consumers" (e.g., Rainforest Action Network), although we would argue that this is in some ways a false dichotomy.

The preference a group might have for one approach over another depends largely upon their goals for systemic change (reformist or radical) and which tactics the group considers best serves those ends. For example, consumers in 1985 were in an uproar over New Coke and considered letter writing, phone calling, and media use the most appropriate ways to send their message to Coca-Cola. However, we see an entirely different reaction with the Guatemalan Coca-Cola unrest, where union workers for a bottling plant were being terrorized, beaten, and brutally murdered. In this case, consumers and activists utilized drastically different tactics, including sending a gruesome photo of a murdered union organizer to Coca-Cola constituents, engaging in mass protests and demonstrations, and developing the visceral Stop Killer Coke campaign. Clearly, in these two situations with the same company, consumer activists developed their approaches in order to best send a message to the corporation and relevant governments and to meet their unique end goals. Consider further the span of these cases and which (if any) serve as promising, progressive examples of consumer activism.

Finally, conscientious consumption, in concert with a number of forms of activism, can effect real, if limited, change. Nike was the first apparel company to disclose the name and location of *all* of its contracted factories, a requirement of its affiliation with the Fair Labor Association and a persistent demand from the Worker Rights Consortium. Nike has also ensured wage increases for factory laborers in several cases. Shell Oil has agreed to work with the World Conservation Union (IUCN) to inform their development of an oil pipeline in an area inhabited by gray whales. Starbucks Coffee now offers organic milk (at an increased price) and fair trade coffee and has established a division devoted to community development and social responsibility. Furthermore, Starbucks coffee shops offer various consumer-oriented brochures designed to inform and reassure the consumer, such as *Commitment to Origins*, *Living Our Values*, and *Help Restore a Costa Rican Rainforest*. Of course, all of the cases demonstrate the conservative and obstinate nature of transnational corporations, as well as the need for ongoing, public, and perhaps recalcitrant responses on the part of consumers, activists, and other corporate antagonists. Most of the concessions won in these cases resulted from intense and prolonged work. If we are to see further pro-social responses from any of these companies, it will be incumbent upon conscientious consumers to keep the central issues of these cases alive in public discourse and impossible for companies to ignore (Raymond, 2003).

DISCUSSION: LESSONS FOR CONSCIENTIOUS CONSUMERS AND IMPLICATIONS FOR PERSUASION

Political norms and values drive conscientious consumption. That is, individuals or collectivities engaging in conscientious consumption most often make salient, hold companies to account for, and take responsibility for the political and social history of the products or activities with which they are concerned. Such engagement necessarily goes beyond rational calculation of the economic benefits of consumption by isolated consumers (Creighton, 1976). Micheletti (2003) highlights the interconnectivity of consumer conscientiousness and political citizenship:

> Consumer responsibility-taking . . . entails the practice of judgment, autonomy, and solidarity, which many scholars agree are three main aspects of citizenship. Practicing judgment, autonomy, and solidarity requires that consumers be empowered with resources and civic skills. They must have both product knowledge and experience and the ability to assess both product quality and the values embedded in products. (p. 17)

Utilizing consumption as an arena for political action—by affecting consumers' decision making, persuading corporations and governments to alter or adopt policies, or establishing communities of like-minded consumers—is no easy task. As Micheletti makes clear, one must develop the capacity to exercise informed judgment, be free to make independent decisions, and be able to create persuasive communities for change, dimensions we address below.

While Micheletti (2003) links these capacities to citizenship, Gabriel and Lang (1995) caution that connections of the citizen and consumer in everyday talk stem from divergent interests. They explain that the Left "has stretched the idea of consumer in the direction of citizen," whereby consumers make morally defensible choices mindful of social needs (p. 176). The Right, on the other hand, "has sought to incorporate the citizen into its image of the consumer by using the spurious concept of 'votes' and ballots" so that "the marketplace becomes a surrogate for political discourse" (p. 176). The concept of conscientious consumption risks the pitfalls of both the Left and Right articulations of citizen-consumers. However, Micheletti's three aspects of citizenship provide a useful framework for discussing the implications of persuasion and social action on the part of consumers that "confront the implications of one's choices, their meaning and their moral value" (Gabriel & Lang, p. 174).

Practicing Judgment

The first aspect of politicized consumption involves consumers developing and utilizing a capacity for discrimination and judgment of products, corporations, and prevailing social conditions. Politically minded consumption requires that avenues be open for consumers to research products, industries, and regulatory policies. In this view, primarily developed by the U.S. consumer movement during the 1960s and 1970s, consumers are empowered to make decisions when provided adequate information by transparent institutions. Such a duty is reflected in the consumer rights and responsibilities tenets discussed above.

We should step back, however, and consider why and at what point consumers might begin to act and buy conscientiously. Vatz (1973) argued that "utterance strongly invites exigence" (p. 159). That is, persuasive, pragmatic communication can generate the awareness and sense of immediacy of an issue to compel people to action and change. Consumers cannot induce corporations to adopt and remain accountable to socially responsible practices if ignorant of pressing concerns, threats, or cases. Schwarze (2003a) writes that the trouble

in the case of the exposure of Libby, Montana, mine workers and residents to harmful asbestos—as in many instances of corporate irresponsibility—was not that the workers' and residents' plight "fell through the cracks" but that "the cracks in the system were not large enough" to allow for public knowledge about and deliberation on the mine, the products it helped produce, and their associated risks (p. 629). At the very least, to make informed political choices regarding certain products, companies, or industries, consumers must be made aware of an issue and convinced of its significance and connection to their social-economic behavior.

Exercising Autonomy

We demonstrated above that political documentaries, critical news coverage, and the like are often the key stimulants to broad social discussion and concerted consumer efforts. However, the social force and relative autonomy of consumers, even those committed to conscientious consumption, are matters of ambiguity and contention.

In terms of broad social agendas, discourses of free market economics that disparage the inefficiency of public and regulatory bodies have achieved widespread dominance (Aune, 2001). Under a pure model of neoliberal economics, consumers exercise their autonomy by voting with their dollars, as explained above. Of course, consumers acting only this way are denied the fruits of collective action and collaboration, and those consumers with more money effectively have more votes. In any case, weakened public institutions provide little guard against wealthy private interests—as has become clear in recent years.

Further, some argue that the extensive and deep connections fostered between corporations, consumers, and the public sector through new forms of marketing and advertising make consumer autonomy impossible (Creighton, 1976; Ruskin & Schor, 2005). This brand of thinking about consumer movements and consumer society suggests that consumerism is so deeply entrenched in contemporary culture that alternative forms of, or alternatives to, consumption are obscured for individuals who always already have a stake in the status quo. Consider the consequences of recent developments in marketing. Some marketers now provide incentives for everyday consumers to drop positive talking points about a specified product or brand into otherwise normal conversations with friends, family, coworkers, and others, afterward documenting their interactions. This sort of marketing effectively turns ordinary consumers into willing reproducers of corporate messages. Strikingly, many participants in these schemes claim that they get and stay involved not just for incentives and awards, but because they like feeling "like a part of something" or that they are working for a higher purpose (Walker, 2004).

Yet another perspective holds that consumption and consumer identity are decidedly fragmented. Gabriel and Lang (1995) assert that consumerism is in its "twilight" and that "consumers will lead precarious and uneven existences" in the future (p. 190). Much of the social movement literature in communication treats leadership and individual empowerment as a central element of movement lifecycles (see, e.g., Stewart et al., 2001). Ganesh, Zoller, and Cheney (2005) submit that such treatment has led to the absence of leaderless activism, undirected convergences, and alternative forms of activism and protest in communication scholarship (for a discussion of these forms of action, see T. Jordan, 2002). It remains undetermined whether the generally marginalized state of conscientious consumption is a result of a lack of superempowerment of traditional leaders; the demonstration of minimal efficacy of individualized, autonomous consumers; the signals of emerging new forms of activism and networking; or some other situation.

Establishing Solidarity

What is more certain, however, is that advocates for corporate change and conscientious consumption have won victories in cases by heightening public consciousness and influencing companies through collective initiative. Obdurate corporate entities and relatively stable social systems are most effectively challenged when "the stakeholder group in question will be motivated to pressure the target . . . out of its own self interest" (Manheim, 2004, p. 108). The key is that stakeholder groups, such as consumers, perceive themselves as a group. The production of social solidarity, of peoples and publics, is an effect of rhetoric (Biesecker, 1989; Charland, 1987; McGee, 1975). Establishing solidarity among disparate stakeholders is an important task for corporate antagonists and conscientious consumers alike.

Manheim (2004) defines the broad outlines of rhetorical strategies designed for (anti)corporate campaigns:

> At the abstract level of social-value pronouncements, everyone has a common purpose and everyone wins. But at the concrete level of policy formulation, purposes diverge and some gain advantage over others. . . . It follows that it is to the advantage of corporate antagonists to argue their case to the public at the abstract level, using the broad support for pro-social values—justice, fairness, dignity, responsibility—as leverage, while it is to their advantage to negotiate with the company at the specific level where the real benefits reside. (p. 96)

When Manheim states that "everyone wins" with statements that invoke abstract values and key terms with social traction, he might be interpreted from a communication perspective to say that certain terms, tropes, or strategies tend to encourage people to see their program as righteous, and themselves as a coherent public, centered on that righteous aim. What rhetoricians call ideographs accomplish the interconnection and distinction of people. McGee (1980) clarifies the term:

> An ideograph is an ordinary-language term found in political discourse. It is a high-order abstraction representing collective commitment to a particular but equivocal and ill-defined normative goal. It warrants the use of power, excuses behavior and belief which might otherwise be perceived as eccentric or antisocial, and guides behavior and belief into channels easily recognized by a community as acceptable and laudable. (p. 15)

Such can be seen in the demand that Nike ensure that its laborers receive a "living wage." While Nike capitulated to activists on several occasions —raising Indonesian workers' wages, investigating mistreatment in Mexican factories, disclosing the locations of its subcontracted factories, and so on— activists and consumers continued to press for "wage justice" and "living wages" across the board. Consequently, Nike antagonists developed a concerted call for change, won concrete changes in Nike and gains for production workers, and maintained pressure and vitality in their corporate campaign.

Ultimately, concerted social organizing has to bring communal and normative pressure to bear in order to realize immediate potentials of conscientious consumption. Ganesh et al. (2005) argue that the nascent movement against global capitalism and corporatism demonstrates "creative inventions of social, political, and economic relations and identities" among participants and between participants and the greater global society (p. 180). Articulating interconnectivity between consumers of different classes, genders, and races is a rhetorical accomplishment, as Laclau and Mouffe (1985) demonstrate, and will naturally come before organized resistance or change.

New forms of organizing and networking and the utilization of new information communication technologies (ICTs) are facilitating the rapid, ad hoc development of myriad groups that organize politically minded consumers (Wolf, 2004). Additionally, social movements of today are both lampooning and co-opting practices traditionally reserved for the for-profit sector (Klein, 1999; Wolf, 2004), strategies fueled by the creative use of new ICTs (Carty, 2002). The possibilities for immediate, widespread mobilization of consumers and activists should compel organizations targeted by campaigns or threatened by alternative forums for consumption to seriously consider the steps they can take to forestall crisis (Nichols, 2003). Yet as Loeb (1999) notes, "social involvement converts us from detached spectators into active participants" (p. 29). Civic action and conscientious consumption inevitably involve some elevated degree of vulnerability and responsibility for understanding and defending one's actions.

POSSIBILITY AND PARADOX: THE ROLES OF CONSCIENTIOUS CONSUMERS

Writes Schwarze (2003a): "The most egregious examples of corporate irresponsibility are best interpreted as situations coproduced by corporations and the state" (p. 628). Corporate social responsibility is best enacted as a collective engagement of consumers and players in civil society, state institutions, and corporations. Consumers who diligently study their options, assert their ideological commitments, and appropriately engage others implicated in their consumption—whom we have been calling conscientious consumers—have an important role in keeping companies and governments accountable and socially responsible. At the same time, corporate social responsibility rhetoric can veil the ultimate purpose of corporations: to make money for shareholders (Crook, 2005). Corporate social responsibility posturing can mask otherwise untoward behavior, as in Fannie May's fall from *Business Ethics Magazine*'s "Top 100" list in 2005 ("100 Best Corporate Citizens," 2005). Similarly, responsibility talk can amount to narcissism, where the organization remains more committed to the legitimacy of its image than to its accountability to various publics (Ganesh, 2003).

So, is it enough to demand that corporations be "socially responsible"? We think it is the burden of conscientious consumers to demand information and institutional relationships that enable unencumbered access to and discussion of information and perspectives on products, practices, and ethics—what Ulmer and Sellnow (1997) call significant choice. One demand is surely that there be countervailing forces to the transnational corporation and its support network that today includes many functions of government. And of course, conscientious consumers have a role in exposing questionable social conditions and persuading corporations to affect pro-social change. But, there's a puzzle: At what point does an active, conscientious consumer become an activist? Can, and should, consumers be activists? Are consumers outright struggling against the injustices of sweatshop labor, environmental destruction, and union busting simply anticorporate globalization, environmental, and labor rights activists? Do the distinctions matter?

Important questions for those concerned with communication revolve around the construction of messages that negotiate the effectiveness, scope, and predominant values of conscientious consumption. Those who urge consumers to just vote with their dollars also limit the range of options and richness of voice consumers have to effect change. People may also be convinced that, given the rise of conscientious consumption in everyday talk, thoughtful consumption *suffices* as activism. One of our students, for instance, said with sincerity: "It's nice to know that I don't have to go out and chain myself to something to make a difference; I can just buy things that represent my values."

Consumer activism of the 1960s and 1970s allowed consumers greater confidence to pass judgment on corporations and their products. One might argue advances of that movement made possible the demand for socially responsible products (e.g., sweat-free and free trade) and companies (e.g., Patagonia and The Body Shop). Consumer activism and conscientious consumption present rich possibilities for change. For, as Schwartz and Gibb (1999) write: "When corporations do behave responsibly, they can be important transmitters of knowledge and skills as well as sources of the societal wealth required to create jobs, entrepreneurial opportunities, and family security" (p. 106). The extent to which consumers capitalize on those possibilities for genuine change and social good is variable. Of course, many affiliated with new social movements allege that consumerism itself is the central obstacle to a more just world (Carty, 2002).

We began this chapter by noting that consumerism pervades contemporary life. Love them or hate them—see them as new sites for creative activism and social change, or as central to societal inequality and injustice—consumerism and consumption are concepts with which scholars, activists, and citizens must grapple. Simultaneously, some predict (e.g., Rucht & Neidhardt, 2002) that contemporary societies provide grounds ripe for the emergence and development of an array of social movements deeply embedded in social institutions. Let us not dismiss the possibilities for political action presented here, or promote "activistism," the unilateral and problematic preference for "action" over "reflection" (Featherstone, Henwood, & Parenti, 2004). Conscientious consumerism has important, if unsettled and paradoxical, roles in the debate over corporate social responsibility.

APPENDIX: SIX NOTABLE CORPORATE CASES OF CONSUMERISM AND ACTIVISM

Coca-Cola Company

Case time line	Early 1900s to present
Central issues	Human rights Consumer choice Union busting and labor organizing
Origins of consumer awareness	Early 1900s: Cocaine in Coca-Cola, an ingredient until 1903, spurs criticism of the budding
	1970s: Environmentalist consumers irritated with the waste and pollution caused by Coca-Cola.
	1975: Guatemala City workers unionize; violence and intimidation ensues.
	1978: General Romeo Lucas Garcia takes power in Guatemala, union organizers and members murdered and terrorized, often while doing Coca-Cola business. Former general secretary of the union informs Coca-Cola at annual stockholders meeting.
	1985: Coca-Cola presents New Coke, later labeled the "marketing blunder of the century."
Nature and extent of consumer involvement	1970: Earth Day protestors heap nonreturnable bottles in front of Coca-Cola headquarters.
	1980s to present: International Union of Food and Allied Workers' Associations (IUF) sponsors boycott; consumer activism escalates. Amnesty International organizes letter-writing campaign; protests against slayings, terrorism, and threats in Guatemala, Colombia, India, Europe, etc.; Coca-Cola protests occur worldwide, even today.
	1985: Consumers protest New Coke, stage letter-writing campaign (40,000 letters), lodge 8,000 phone calls per day. Media features negative reaction to New Coke. Alabama church prays for soul of local bottler.
Specific strategies and key moments	1912: *Good Housekeeping* cartoon warns against Coca-Cola's drug effects. Filmmaker produces moral tale about woman addicted to the soft drink beverage "Dopokoke."
	1980: IUF mails gruesome photograph of murdered union organizer to Coca-Cola affiliates, effecting global work stoppages.
	1985: ABC's Peter Jennings interrupts programming to announce return of Coca-Cola Classic.

	2001:	United Steelworkers of America and the International Labor Rights Fund sue on behalf of Colombian union. In 2003, U.S. District Court dismisses case, citing lack of factual evidence and ruling that jurisdiction is in Colombia.
	2002:	Health Global Access Project and others target Coca-Cola with multifaceted campaign—petitions to protests—for unfulfilled promises of health coverage for HIV/AIDS-positive employees in Africa. University campuses host Kick Coke Off Our Campus campaigns.
	2003:	Interorganizational Stop Killer Coke campaign launched to pressure company.
	2004:	New York City council member leads a fact-finding journey to Colombia, cites violations of human rights. He identifies all U.S. citizens as Coca-Cola shareholders through our "consumer dollars."
	2005:	Colombia Solidarity Campaign publishes *Anti-Coke Manifesto* documenting labor intimidation in Colombia and pollution in India. United Students Against Sweatshops (USAS), with others, holds International Day of Protest Against Coke.
Responses from the corporation	1970:	Coca-Cola weakly promotes recycling.
	1978:	Coca-Cola president states, "While lamenting the problems in Guatemala, we also must respect the laws and processes of other nations" (Pendergrast, 1993, p. 321). Coca-Cola still cites lack of "proof" that violence is connected to the corporation through the Guatemalan bottling plant.
	1980:	Coca-Cola announces it will not renew Guatemalan franchise manager's contract, but bloodshed continues; manager eventually bought out by union men and chaos subsides.
	1985:	Coca-Cola announces return to "Classic Coke" formula within months of response to New Coke.
	2001:	Company announces at United Nations its intention to cover treatment costs for African employees with HIV/AIDS.2005: Coca-Cola commissions a review of Colombian bottling facilities. Present: Company maintains website dedicated to its presence in Colombia, India, etc. (http://www.cokefacts.org).
Interaction and coalition development	1979:	Amnesty International and the IUF are among those protesting Coca-Cola's *laissez fare* attitude toward Guatemala and Colombia.
	1980s to present:	Coordination between student and human rights, labor, and health care activists for global boycotts and protests.
	1985:	Coca-Cola listens to its various customers' demands to reinstate "classic" formula.
Short-term and (anticipated) longer term effects		Overwhelmingly, Coca-Cola shows reluctance to take responsibility (even if only indirectly) for its franchisers in South America, Africa, and other regions. The company continues to downplay the connections between union organizing and terrorism at their bottling plants in South America. By many accounts, the company has proceeded with a minimal implementation of their HIV/AIDS coverage program, which requires restrictive monetary commitment on the part of workers. Coca-Cola has dismissed or resisted numerous campaigns and boycotts over the years, making only small, specific advances in areas of social responsibility. Unfortunately, but perhaps tellingly, the most successful consumer campaign against this company to date was the 1985 response to the change in the classic formula.

Sources: Baran (2003), Colombia Solidarity Campaign (2005), Damouni (2004), Frundt (1987), Gutkin (1994), Leith (2005), McQueen (2003), Pendergrast (1993), and Health Global Access Project (2002).

Shell Oil Company

Case time line	1958 to present
Central issues	Human rights
	Environmental justice
	Animal rights

Origins of consumer awareness	1958: Shell pollutes the Niger Delta in Nigeria (spilling six million liters of oil); gas flares cause acid rain, and levels of water pollution are 360 times higher than allowed in Europe.
	1992: Ken Saro-Wiwa begins the Movement for the Survival of Ogoni People (MOSOP).
	1994: Public outcry when Shell plans to sink the Brent Spar storage buoy off the coast of the United Kingdom.
	1994 to present: A Shell-led gas project threatens gray whales in the Sakhalin Island region of Russia's far east; gas pipes are to be routed through the ocean. International Whaling Commission warns that energy exploration could kill off the 100–whale population.
Nature and extent of consumer involvement	Citizens, consumers, and activist organizations petition and protest Shell Oil. In 1995, citizens of Nigeria and activists complain about Shell to the Nigerian government (it is argued that this led to the hanging of nine human rights activists, Ogoni activist Ken Saro-Wiwa included), and millions of citizens in the United Kingdom boycott Shell due to the Brent Spar fiasco. In 1998, Nigerian consumers boycott Shell and other oil companies working in the Niger Delta again, and demonstrators seize pumping stations; Federated Niger Delta Izon Communities threaten Shell foreign workers' safety. Shell has also come under fire by organizations such as Amnesty International, who point to Shell's size and wealth as a reason for Shell to claim larger responsibility for human and environmental rights; the people of Nigeria's destitution is noted, despite Nigeria being Africa's largest exporter of oil.
Specific strategies and key moments	1995: Saro-Wiwa labels Shell's activities "environmental racism," which is picked up by activists and writers to characterize the Nigerian situation. Greenpeace lands helicopter on the Brent Spar buoy to prevent its sinking.
	1997: Earth Culture demonstrates with 70–75 bicyclists circling pumps of New Jersey gas station.
	1998: Demonstrations on May 14 mark annual shareholders meeting. Keynote speaker labels Shell's activities "environmental terrorism."
	2005: World Wildlife Federation urges European Bank for Reconstruction and Development to withhold funds for Sakhalin project.
Responses from the corporation	1990–1995: Shell requests Nigerian military protection (results are brutal military action against Ogoni people); Shell admits "some fault" but blames citizens for sabotage, as well as deforestation and population growth, and leans on claims that it funded education and cleanup programs. In 1993, Shell suspended Ogoniland region operations. Shell continues to drill in Nigeria.
	1997: Shell announces "change of heart" and will to take better care of environment.1998: Enters negotiation with Nigerian communities.
	2004: Shell chairman, Lord Ronald Oxburgh, admits he fears for the planet because oil companies are partly responsible for global warming effects. Greenpeace demands action over talk.
	2005: Shell claims the Sakhalin project is "unambiguously" going ahead, but with precautions for routing pipes through whale habitats, and sought an independent report from the World Conservation Union. Shell announces that it will enter reconciliation talks with the Nigerian government and Ogoniland representatives.
	Present: Company addresses criticism on their website but dodges responsibility in states such as Nigeria.
Interaction and coalition development	Environmental and human rights movements work together extensively: • American Friends Service committee and a U.S. chapter of MOSOP organize 1998 conference on Shell's activities in Nigeria. • Rainforest Action Network and Project Underground release independent report of Shell activities. • More than 50 NGOs formed coalition to change Shell's Sakhalin Island project.

	• Shell agrees to heed World Conservation Union advice and to take necessary precautions (although the report insists that the most precautionary route would be to halt project and gather more data).
Short-term and (anticipated) longer term effects	It has only been since the mid-1990s or so that Shell has acknowledged the need for corporate social responsibility in their global projects, although activists have claimed that Shell's wrongdoing dates back to 1958. Along with this, consumer complaints and action have continuously been levied against Shell, despite the company's rhetorical commitments to human rights, sustainable development, and the environment. Thus, we can conjecture that the short-term effects have been and will continue to be merely Band-Aid solutions and that long-term effects are a long time coming. In 2005, boycotts of and protests against Shell are global.

Sources: Adam (2004), "After Shell's Climbdown" (1995), Goodman and Scahill (1998), "Hollow Shell" (1995), D. Jackson (1995), G. Jordan (2001), Lewis (1995, 1996), Malcom (1998), "Nigeria, Shell Oil Assailed by WCC" (1997), "Nigerian Youths Seize 9 Oil Pumping Stations" (1998), "Opposition Groups in Nigeria Threaten Foreign Oil Workers" (1998), Oster (2005), Rainforest Action Network (1997), "Risk of Extinction to Grey Whales If Shell Project Continues" (2005), Schwartz and Gibb (1999), Shell Nigeria (n.d.), "Shell on the Rocks" (1995), Soper (1997), and "Unrest in Nigeria Hurts Oil Production" (2005).

Texaco

Case time line	1964 to present
Central issues	Human rights; Race and hiring practices; Civil rights; Environmental justice
Origins of consumer awareness	1992: Texaco pulls out of Ecuador: study estimates 16 million gallons of crude oil spilled and billions of gallons of toxic wastewater dumped during 1964–1992, polluting the land and water, creating health problems and defects among humans and animals, and displacing indigenous communities.
	1996: Racist remarks by Richard Lundwall, Texaco Senior Coordinator of Personnel Services, caught on tape and leaked; 1,400 black employees sue Texaco for racial discrimination.
Nature and extent of consumer involvement	1993 & 1999: Ecuadorian rainforest Indians sue Texaco for "environmental racism" and cultural genocide. 1993 lawsuit thrown out of a New York court, because the (former) Ecuadorian government insisted the trial be carried out in Ecuador. Indigenous peoples and activists sue again in 1999.
	1993 to present: General international boycott of Texaco's actions in Ecuador.
	1996: Ecuadorians march to presidential palace with photographs of recent Texaco oil spill. Demands made for Ecuadorian government support of lawsuit against Texaco (see above, 1993 & 1999). African-American drivers threaten boycott. Texaco's stock drops $1 billion.
Specific strategies and key moments	1994: Rainforest Action Network urges boycott of Texaco products, asking consumers to send shredded Texaco credit cards to the company.
	1996: Rev. Jesse Jackson and other civil rights leaders call for national boycott and changes in Texaco policy toward employees of color.
	1999: Ecuadorian activists sponsor media advertisement campaign accusing Texaco of "racial discrimination, chapter 2," claiming that "Texaco does not create this level of devastation near white people" (quoted in McCool, 1999, ¶ 3).
Responses from the corporation	1994–1995: Texaco negotiates and donates $40 million toward Ecuador cleanup. Allegations hold that only select sites were cleaned and that $10 million went missing from project.
	1996: Texaco fires Lundwall and settles out of court for $176.1 million in the civil rights lawsuit (Lundwall was acquitted of the charges). Texaco promises to encourage equality and sets goals to promote minorities and held diversity workshops for employees.
	1999: Texaco's spokeswoman claims: "Texaco acts and operates responsibly wherever we are in the world. And we acted responsibly in Ecuador" (quoted in McCool, 1999, ¶ 5).

Interaction and coalition development	1996:	Coalition of Ecuadorian indigenous people and farmers march on the Ecuadorian presidential palace.
	1999:	U.S.-based groups such as Amazon Watch, Rainforest Action Network, and Friends of the Earth support the Ecuadorian activists' "racism 2" media campaign.
Short-term and (anticipated) longer term effects		In the short term, Texaco seems to have a grasp on making necessary changes, such as donating $40 million to Ecuador. (Those "donations" released the company of responsibility for further cleanup.) However, it is argued that this amount of money does not cover all of the necessary expenses for cleanup, and oil spills, pollution, and severe health problems and birth defects persist. Likewise, Texaco has made many immediate promises to quell racism and promote equality, although it is difficult to tell if such changes are mere lip service. That watchdog groups and Ecuadorian activists are still boycotting Texaco indicates that Texaco has not completely committed to sincere corporate social responsibility.

Sources: "Alexander Cockburn's America" (1996), Belfield (1996), "Boycott Texaco" (1994), Bryant (1997, 1998), Eichenwald (1996), Hutchinson (1996), Markels (1999), "Massive Amazon oil spill" (1992), McCool (1999), Rainforest Action Network (1996a, 1996b), Schwartz and Gibb (1999), and Talbot (1999a, 1999b).

Wal-Mart

Case time line	1987 to present
Central issues	Union busting and labor organizing Manufacturing labor (sweatshop) conditions Exploitive global trade Sprawl and community development
Origins of consumer awareness	1992: *Dateline NBC* documents foreign sweatshop and child labor production of items labeled "Made in the USA."
	1995: National Labor Committee exposes the sweatshop manufacture of Kathie Lee Gifford brand clothing, sold only at Wal-Mart.
	2004: *New York Times* publicizes alleged systematic labor law violations (see Greenhouse 2003, 2004a, 2004b, 2004c, 2004d; Greenhouse & Hays, 2004).
Nature and extent of consumer involvement	Numerous cities vote, lobby, and protest to prevent the establishment of Wal-Mart stores (see Norman, 1999, p. 237).
	Consumer reaction to sweatshop production of Wal-Mart products featured in many television and print news exposés.
	Consumers target audience in United Food and Commercial Workers International Union (UFCW) information campaigns.
Specific strategies and key moments	1987–1989: Steamboat Springs, Colorado, planning commission votes to keep out Wal-Mart. Television and print exposure follows. Wal-Mart abandons development plans after public outcry.
	1989 to present: UFCW and AFL-CIO campaign against Wal-Mart's job outsourcing, use of child labor, union busting, etc.
	1991: UFCW begins campaign to end Wal-Mart's sourcing of apparel from Bangladesh. Mother's Day press conferences held.
	1993: Al Norman leads effort to keep Wal-Mart out of his Massachusetts town. Norman is now a leading anti–Wal-Mart activist.
	1995: National Labor Committee brings sweatshop worker to United States for press conferences, congressional testimony, and meeting with Gifford and Wal-Mart. Antisweatshop movement gains national attention.
	2003: *South Park* episode about retail giant, "Wall-Mart," that decimates town's economy and controls minds of townsfolk with low prices.
	2004: The UFCW successfully unionizes Wal-Mart in Quebec, Canada. (See response, below.) *Dukes vs. Wal-Mart*, largest U.S. class-action lawsuit ever. "The suit alleges unequal wage and promotion policies for women" (Dicker, 2004, p. 106).

	2005: UFCW and Center for Community and Corporate Ethics establish activist websites (http://www.wakeupwalmart.com and http://www.walmartwatch.com). Robert Greenwald produces documentary *Wal-Mart: The High Cost of Low Price*, financed by donations; created with amateur footage, it premiered in more than 3,000 independent venues (see http://www.walmartmovie.com).
Responses from the corporation	1980s to present: Litigation against cities that attempt to ban store or super-store development.
	1985: "Buy American" campaign begins, ostensibly to recover outsourced manufacturing jobs.
	1990s: Kathie Lee Gifford participates in Clinton administration task force for sweatshop prevention measures.
	2004: Wal-Mart closes a Quebec store, under much media attention, that had voted to unionize under UFCW; helps prevent passage of California's Proposition 72, an attempt to increase health care costs covered by employers.
Interaction and coalition development	UFCW and AFL-CIO collaborate on Wal-Mart campaigns.
	Negotiations take place between Honduran workers, National Labor Committee, Kathie Lee Gifford, and Wal-Mart.
	Al Norman continues to coordinate efforts to stop planned Wal-Mart stores.
	Academics, labor activists, and consumers interact at conferences to assess Wal-Mart's influence and discuss resistive strategies (see Greenhouse, 2004b, 2004c).
Short-term and (anticipated) longer term effects	Despite a long history of local resistance from communities slated for Wal-Mart expansion, information campaigns, labor organizing efforts, and embarrassments over sweatshop labor, Wal-Mart continues to grow and dominate retail markets. For many consumers, Wal-Mart serves as the evil corporation prototype, but record numbers shop at the stores for low prices. While Wal-Mart might serve as a flashpoint for debate or a minimum standard for boycotters who say, "At least I won't shop *there*," consumers seem to be a small problem for the company.

Sources: Dicker (2004), Greenhouse (2003, 2004a, 2004b, 2004c, 2004d), Greenhouse and Hays (2004), Norman (1999, 2004), and Ortega (1998).

Nike

Case time line	1990 to present
Central issues	Manufacturing labor (sweatshop) conditions
	Race and hiring practices
	Corporate branding
Origins of consumer awareness	1990: Operation Push announces Nike boycott, insisting Nike's hiring and banking practices demonstrate racial bias.
	1992: Ballinger writes a *Harper's* exposé, arguing Nike's global business model exploits ever-cheaper labor markets.
	1995: Enloe's *Ms.* article spotlights Nike's flight from South Korea after workers won better conditions, unionization, and higher pay, connects plight of female workers to marketing campaigns supporting women athletes and associations. CBS's *48 Hours* produces investigative report into working conditions at a Vietnamese factory.
Nature and extent of consumer involvement	Limited consumer response to Operation Push's Nike boycott. Thuyen Nguyen formed Vietnam Labor Watch in response to a CBS *48 Hours* show on Nike. Nike sponsored Nguyen's tour of subcontracted facilities in Vietnam. Nguyen coordinated with Global Exchange to publish in the *New York Times* after Nike refused to release findings. Consumers form an audience for NGO Global Exchange and USAS protests, demonstrations, and boycotts.
Specific strategies and key moments	1996: Global Exchange brings female Indonesian factory worker, fired for organizing, to United States for tours, politician meetings, and

	unannounced visit to Nike headquarters. Vietnam Labor Watch visits and condemns Nike contracted facilities.
	1997: Michael Moore's film *The Big One* debuts, featuring Nike CEO Phil Knight interview. *Doonesbury* mocks Nike in cartoon series.
	1998: USAS forms, spreads rapidly, and demands universities not purchase apparel and other items made in sweatshops.
	1997–1998: Global Exchange, USAS, and UNITE! coordinate numerous protests.
	1999: The Worker Rights Consortium (WRC) founded in competition with Fair Labor Association (FLA).
	2001: USAS and WRC successfully pressure Nike, Reebok, and the contracted Mexican KukDong factory to reinstate workers illegally fired for organizing.
Responses from the corporation	Nike dismissed early charges of illegal and immoral labor contracting.
	CEO Phil Knight participated in Clinton administration antisweatshop task force, which created the FLA.
	1996: Nike refuted Vietnam Labor Watch's damning findings and commissioned another report.
	1999: Nike agrees to pay Indonesian workers more than minimum wage and back pay to Vietnamese labor.
	2001: Nike produces its first corporate responsibility report, and quietly stifles a "Truth Tour" organized by students that targeted various Niketown stores.
	2005: Nike discloses identities of all contract factories—first apparel company ever to do so. The action is mandated by Nike's involvement with the FLA.
Interaction and coalition development	1990s: Global Exchange assists relatively unknown Vietnam Labor Watch in publishing report. Global Exchange collaborates with USAS and WRC for a number of protests against Nike.
	1997: The Fair Labor Association is chartered, active by 2003. FLA consists of multinational apparel companies, NGOs, and universities.
	1999: USAS established to support student voices in university apparel sourcing. USAS is affiliated with UNITE! and helps create WRC.
Short-term and (anticipated) longer term effects	After a low point in 1998, Nike has grown considerably and demonstrated consistent, increasing profitability. Nike's participation in the FLA and disclosure of subcontracted facilities set a strong standard for competitors and emulators. The lawyer in a suit against Nike calls the FLA "an excellent vehicle for Nike to further develop its corporate responsibility efforts and allow interested consumers to measure the performance of Nike and other companies" (Egelko, 2003, ¶ 13).

Sources: Ballenger (1992), Egelko (2003), Enloe (1995), J. E. Jackson and Schantz (1993), Manheim (2004), Schwartz and Gibb (1999), and Shaw (1999).

Starbucks Coffee

Case time line	1999 to present
Central issues	Antiglobalization, community destruction, and corporate branding
	Fair-trade practices
	Genetically modified versus organic foods
Origins of consumer awareness	1999: Global Trade Watch and others plan protest of Seattle WTO conference; protesters and rioters single out corporations such as Starbucks and Nike as representatives of corporate globalization and greed.
	1999: Fair-trade coffee movement, led by Global Exchange, requests Starbucks halt use of "sweatshop coffee."
	2001: Organic Consumers Association (OCA) criticizes Starbucks' lack of organic options and nonsupport for organic farming.
Nature and extent of consumer involvement	1999: WTO civil disobedience turns into vandalism of Starbucks stores, 600 protesters arrested, $3 million in property damage. The 2000 "anniversary" sees vandalism of nine Starbucks stores.

	2000:	Eighty-four organizations sign Global Exchange's Open Letter petition; hundreds of individuals fax letters or send postcards from the Global Exchange website protesting sweatshop coffee.
	2003:	Individuals send more than 2,000 faxes on behalf of organic foods and farming through OCA to Starbucks during annual shareholders meeting.
Specific strategies and key moments	1999/2000:	Global People's Tribunal issues citizen's arrests for trade leaders of industrialized countries. Mostly peaceful protesting led to police brutality and to vandalism and rioting; Starbucks windows shattered and stores vandalized.
	2000:	Global Exchange capitalizes on ABC report of low wages at Guatemalan coffee plantations, plans 30 Roast Starbucks demonstrations on April 13.
	2002–2004:	OCA and other critics demonstrate outside Starbucks offices and stores during annual shareholders meeting.
Responses from the corporation	2000:	Starbucks signs with TransFairUSA, a fair-trade coffee certifier, and establishes a Department of Corporate Social Responsibility within the organization.
	2001:	Starbucks donates $1 million to developing country coffee farmers, promises to buy 1 million pounds of organic coffee in 12–18 months, begins publishing the Corporate Social Responsibility Annual Report.
	Present:	Starbucks advertises their fair-trade practices and commitment to sustainability through in-store brochures; offers organic milk for $.40 extra; website heralds commitment to corporate social responsibility.
Interaction and coalition development	1999:	WTO protests saw activists groups working together, including the Raging Grannies, the Sierra Club, the Humane Society, the Global People's Tribunal, Friends of the Earth, and Global Trade Watch.
	2000:	Starbucks signs with TransFairUSA and begins to promote fair-trade coffee awareness; features fair-trade coffee in conjunction with TransFairUSA as its Coffee of the Week during May 3–9, 2004 (coinciding with World Fair Trade Day on May 8).
	2004:	OCA and Global Exchange team up in demonstrations during the Starbucks annual shareholders meeting.
Short-term and (anticipated) longer term effects		Starbucks responded quickly to accusations of globalization, corporate branding, and community and small business destruction by creating the Department of Corporate Social Responsibility and to fair-trade issues by signing with TransFairUSA. These changes have had short-term effects that ostensibly benefit farmers in developing countries and also allow Starbucks to tout their commitments to corporate social responsibility. However, Global Exchange and OCA charge Starbucks with greenwashing and failing to offer fair-trade coffee on a daily basis, suggesting that long-term effects are too far in the future. Despite this, Starbucks comes across as making the most proactive corporate social responsibility commitments of all the cases.

Sources: Box (2003), H. Cooper (1999), Cray (2000), Global Exchange (2005), Gorman (2000), Gorov (1999), Organic Consumers Association (n.d.), and "Starbucks Will Buy Beans at Premium" (2000).

NOTE

We thank Trish Stuhan for her contributions in the early development of this project.

REFERENCES

Achbar, M. (Producer/Director), & Abbott, J. (Director). (2003). *The corporation* [Motion picture]. Vancouver, British Columbia, Canada: Big Picture Media Corporation.

Adam, D. (2004, June 17). Oil chief: My fears for the planet. *Guardian*. Retrieved September 28, 2005, from http://www.guardian.co.uk/uk_news/story/0,3604,1240496,00.html.

After Shell's climbdown. (1995, June 24). *Economist*, p. 16.

Alexander Cockburn's America. (1996, November 26). *New Statesman, 125*, 26.

Anti-Flag. (2001). Seattle was a riot. On *Fat*

music: Vol. 5. Live fat, die young. San Francisco, CA: Fat Wreck Chords.

Aune, J. A. (2001). *Selling the free market: The rhetoric of economic correctness.* New York: Guilford Press.

Ballenger, J. (1992, August). The new free-trade heel. *Harpers, 285,* 46–47.

Baran, M. (2003, November/December). Stop killer Coke! *Dollars & Sense, 250,* 10–15.

Baudrillard, J. (1980). *For a critique of the political economy of the sign.* London: Telos Press.

Belfield, R. (1996, December 6). The net. *New Statesman, 125,* 43.

Belk, R. W., Wallendorf, M., & Sherry, J. F., Jr. (1989). The sacred and the profane in consumer behavior: Theodicy on the Odyssey. *Journal of Consumer Behavior, 16,* 1–38.

Biesecker, B. A. (1989). Rethinking the rhetorical situation from within the thematic of difference. *Philosophy & Rhetoric, 25,* 351–364.

Bloomstein, M. (1976). *The consumer's guide to fighting back.* New York: Dodd/Mead.

Boss isn't Starbucks' cup of tea. (2005, May 9). *Newsday,* p. A10.

Bowers, J. W., Ochs, D. J., & Jensen, R. J. (1993). *The rhetoric of agitation and control.* Prospect Heights, IL: Waveland Press.

Box, D. (2003, July). Starbucks. *Ecologist, 33,* 22–23.

Boycott Texaco. (1994, April). *Progressive, 58.* Retrieved September 27, 2005, from EbscoHost Databases.

Bryant, A. (1997, Nov 2). How much has Texaco changed? *New York Times,* p. C1.

Bryant, A. (1998, May 13). 2 in Texaco case found not guilty. *New York Times,* p. A1.

Carty, V. (2002). Technology and counter-hegemonic movements: The case of Nike Corporation. *Social Movement Studies, 1,* 129–146.

Charland, M. (1987). Constitutive rhetoric: The case of the "Peuple Quebecois." *Quarterly Journal of Speech, 73,* 133–150.

Cheney, G. (2005, March). *The United Consumers of America. Or, is there a citizen in the house?* Paper presented at the 2nd annual Humanities Lecture, University of Utah, Salt Lake City.

Cheney, G., Christensen, L. T., Zorn T. E., Jr., & Ganesh, S. (2004). *Organizational communication in an age of globalization: Issues, reflections, practices.* Prospect Heights, IL: Waveland Press.

Colombia Solidarity Campaign. (2005). *The anti-Coke manifesto.* Retrieved October 10, 2005, from http://www.tmcrew.org/ killamulti/cocacola/dossier/anticokefinal1 .pdf.

Consumer Protection Branch, Saskatchewan, Canada. (2005). *Rights and responsibilities.* Retrieved July 9, 2005, from http:// www.saskjustice.gov.sk.ca/cpb/rightsrespon .shtml.

Consumers International. (2000). *World Consumer Rights Day.* Retrieved July 9, 2005, from http://www .consumersinternational.org.

Cooper, H. (1999, July 16). Will human chains and Zapatistas greet the WTO in Seattle? *Wall Street Journal,* p. A1.

Cooper, M. M. (1996). Environmental rhetoric in the age of hegemonic politics: Earth First! and the Nature Conservancy. In C. G. Herndl, & S. C. Brown (Eds.), *Green culture: Environmental rhetoric in contemporary America* (pp. 236–260). Madison: University of Wisconsin Press.

Cray, C. (2000, May). A sweeter cup. *Multinational Monitor, 21.* Retrieved September 26, 2005, from EbscoHost Databases.

Creighton, L. B. (1976). *Pretenders to the throne: The consumer movement in the United States.* Lexington, MA: Lexington Books.

Crook, C. (2005, January 22). The good company. *Economist, 374,* 3–4.

Damouni, N. (2004, February 2). City council delegation to Colombia reports on human rights claims against Coca-Cola. *New York News Network.* Retrieved October 10, 2005, from http://www.laborrights.org/ press/coke_council_0204.htm.

DeLuca, K. M. (1999). *Image politics: The new rhetoric of environmental activism.* New York: Guilford Press.

DeLuca, K. M., & Peeples, J. (2002). From public sphere to public screen: Democracy, activism, and the "violence" of Seattle. *Critical Studies in Media Communication, 19,* 125–151.

Dicker, J. (2004). *The United States of Wal-Mart.* New York: Penguin.

Douglas, M., & Isherwood, B. (1979). *The world of goods.* London: Routledge.

Eichenwald, K. (1996, November 13). Calls issued for boycott of Texaco. *New York Times,* p. D1.

Eiler, A. (1984). *The consumer protection manual.* New York: Facts on File Publications.

Egan, T. (1998, September 13). The swoon of the swoosh. *New York Times Magazine,* pp. 66–70.

Egelko, B. (2003, September 13). Nike settles suit for $1.5 million: Shoe giant accused of lying about workers' treatment. *San*

Francisco Chronicle. Retrieved April 23, 2005, from http://www.sfgate.com/cgi-bin/article.cgi?file=/chronicle/archive/2003/09/13/BU47505.DTL&type=business.

Enloe, C. (1995, March/April). The globe-trotting sneaker. *Ms., 6,* 36.

Ewen, S. (1976). *Captains of consciousness: Advertising and the social roots of consumer culture.* New York: McGraw-Hill.

Featherstone, L., Henwood, D., & Parenti, C. (2004, November/December). Beyond activism: Why we need deeper thinking in our protests. *Utne Reader,* pp. 72–75.

Friedman, M. (1995). On promoting a sustainable future through consumer activism. *Journal of Social Issues, 51,* 197–215.

Frundt, H. J. (1987). *Refreshing pauses: Coca-Cola and human rights in Guatemala.* New York: Praeger.

Gabriel, Y., & Lang, T. (1995). *The unmanageable consumer: Contemporary consumption and its fragmentations.* Thousand Oaks, CA: Sage.

Ganesh, S. (2003). Organizational narcissism: Technology, legitimacy, and identity in an Indian NGO. *Management Communication Quarterly, 16,* 558–594.

Ganesh, S., Zoller, H., & Cheney, G. (2005). Transforming resistance, broadening our boundaries: Critical organizational communication meets globalization from below. *Communication Monographs, 72,* 169–191.

Gilliam, J., Greenwald, R., & Smith, D. (Producers), & Greenwald, R. (Director). (2005). *Wal-Mart: The high cost of low price* [Motion picture]. Los Angeles: Brave New Films.

Global Exchange. (2005). *Starbucks campaign.* Retrieved September 25, 2005, from http://www.globalexchange.org/campaigns/fairtrade/coffee/starbucks.html.

Goodman, A., & Scahill, J. (1998, November 16). Drilling and killing. *Nation,* pp. 6–7.

Gopnik, A. (1997, August 4). Trouble at the tower. *New Yorker,* p. 80.

Gorman, M. (2000, November/December). A cuppa justice. *Utne Reader,* p. 78.

Gorov, L. (1999, November 30). The varied foes of the WTO unite in Seattle protests. *Boston Globe,* p. A1.

Greenhouse, S. (2003, February 16). Wal-Mart faces lawsuit over sex discrimination. *New York Times,* p. 22.

Greenhouse, S. (2004a, November 19). Lawsuits and change at Wal-Mart. *New York Times,* p. A25.

Greenhouse, S. (2004b, May 12). Some critics of Wal-Mart joining forces to change it. *New York Times,* p. C4.

Greenhouse, S. (2004c, April 17). Wal-Mart, a nation unto itself. *New York Times,* p. B7.

Greenhouse, S. (2004d, January 18). Workers assail night lock-ins by Wal-Mart. *New York Times,* p. 1.

Greenhouse, S., & Hays, C. L. (2004, June 23). Wal-Mart sex-bias suit given class-action status. *New York Times,* p. A1.

Gutkin, S. (1994, January 24). Rebels bomb Mormon churches and Coca-Cola bottler to protest U.S. presence. *Associated Press.* Retrieved October 10, 2005, from LexisNexis database.

Health Global Access Project. (2002). Treat Your Workers campaign. Retrieved October 10, 2005, from http://www.healthgap.org/camp/campaigns.html.

Hollow Shell. (1995, June 24). *Economist,* p. 76.

Hutchinson, B. (1996, November 16). Texaco settles racial suit for $ 176M; Decision comes after oil chief, Hub civil rights group confer. *Boston Herald,* p. 1.

Jackson, D. (1995, November 15). Our thirst for oil fuels terror in Nigeria. *Boston Globe,* Op-ed, p. 19.

Jackson, J. E., & Schantz, W. T. (1993). Crisis management lessons: When push shoved Nike. *Business Horizons, 36,* 27–35.

Jordan, G. (2001). *Shell, Greenpeace and Brent Spar.* New York: Palgrave.

Jordan, T. (2002). *Activism! Direct action, hacktivism, and the future of society.* London: Reaktion Books.

Klein, N. (1999). *No logo.* New York: Picador.

Laclau, E., & Mouffe, C. (1985). *Hegemony and socialist strategy: Towards a radical democratic politics.* London: Verso.

Leith, S. (2005, April 14). Coke's Columbian controversy: Activists, students claim company is complicit in anti-union violence. *Atlanta Journal-Constitution.* Retrieved October 10, 2005, from LexisNexis Academic database.

Lewis, P. (1995, November 11). Rights groups say Shell Oil shares blame. *New York Times,* p. A6.

Lewis, P. (1996, February 13). After Nigeria represses: Shell defends its record. *New York Times,* p. A1.

Loeb, P. R. (1999). *Soul of a citizen: Living with conviction in a cynical time.* New York: St. Martin's Press.

Malcom, T. (1998, March 27). Oil blight lingers for Ogoni. *National Catholic Reporter 34.* Retrieved September 26, 2005, from EbscoHost Databases.

Manheim, J. B. (2004). *Biz-war and the out-of-power elite: The progressive-left attack on the corporation.* Mahwah, NJ: Lawrence Erlbaum.

Markels, A. (1999, May/June). Texaco's crude legacy. *Mother Jones, 24*, 65–66.

Massive Amazon oil spill. (1992, fall). *Earth Island Journal*, 7. Retrieved September 27, 2005, from EbscoHost Databases.

McCool, G. (1999, September 23). Ads by Ecuadorian plaintiffs accuse Texaco of racism. *Reuters*. Retrieved September 28, 2005, from http://www.ran.org/news/newsitem.php?id=372&area=oil.

McGee, M. C. (1975). In search of "the people": A rhetorical alternative. *Quarterly Journal of Speech, 63*, 235–249.

McGee, M. C. (1980). The "ideograph": A link between rhetoric and ideology. *Quarterly Journal of Speech, 66*, 1–16.

McQueen, H. (2003). *The essence of capitalism: The origins of our future*. New York: Black Rose Books.

Micheletti, M. (2003). *Political virtue and shopping: Individuals, consumerism, and collective action*. New York: Palgrave Macmillan.

Miles, S. (1998). *Consumerism as a way of life*. London: Sage.

Nader, R. (1965). *Unsafe at any speed: The designed-in dangers of the American automobile*. New York: Grossman.

Nichols, N. (2003). Stopping the activist attackers. In S. John & S. Thomson (Eds.), *New activism and the corporate response* (pp. 137—151). New York: Palgrave Macmillan.

Nigeria, Shell Oil assailed by WCC. (1997, January 22). *Christian Century, 114*. Retrieved September 27, 2005, from EbscoHost Databases.

Nigerian youths seize 9 oil pumping stations. (1998, October 8). *New York Times*, p. A11.

Norman, A. (1999). *Slam-dunking Wal-Mart! How you can stop superstore sprawl in your hometown*. Atlantic City, NJ: Raphel Marketing.

Norman, A. (2004). *The case against Wal-Mart*. Atlantic City, NJ: Raphel Marketing.

100 best corporate citizens for 2005: Companies that serve a variety of stakeholders with excellence and integrity. (2005, Spring). *Business Ethics Magazine Online*. Retrieved April 20, 2005, from http://www.business-ethics.com/whats_new/100best.html.

Opposition groups in Nigeria threaten foreign oil workers. (1998, October 12). *New York Times*, p. A5.

Organic Consumers Association. (n.d.). *Starbucks fair trade campaign*. Retrieved September 25, 2005, from http://www.organicconsumers.org/Starbucks/index.htm.

Ortega, B. (1998). *In Sam we trust: The untold story of Sam Walton, and how Wal-Mart is devouring America*. New York: Times Business.

Oster, S. (2005, May 31). Shell to start talks with Nigeria, Ogoni activists. *Wall Street Journal*. Retrieved October 10, 2005, from LexisNexis Academic database.

Overby, B. (2002). Contract, in the age of sustainable consumption. *Journal of Corporation Law, 27*, 603–630.

Parker, T. (Writer, Director). (2004, November 3). Something Wall-Mart this way comes [Television series episode]. In T. Parker, M. Stone, A. Garefino, & F. Agnone (Producers), *South Park*. New York: Comedy Central.

Pendergrast, M. (1993). *For God, country, and Coca-Cola: The unauthorized history of the great American soft drink and the company that makes it*. New York: Charles Scribner's Sons.

Pezzullo, P. C. (2003). Resisting "National Breast Cancer Awareness Month": The rhetoric of counterpublics and their cultural performances. *Quarterly Journal of Speech, 89*, 345–365.

Prasad, M., Kimeldorf, H., Meyer, R., & Robinson, I. (2004). Consumers of the World Unite: A market-based response to sweatshops. *Labor Studies Journal, 29*(3), 57–80. Retrieved November 30, 2005, from http://muse.jhu.edu.

Rainforest Action Network. (1996a, June 20). *Ecuadorian citizens protest Texaco's Amazon oil pollution* [Press Release]. Retrieved September 28, 2005, from http://www.ran.org/news/newsitem.php?id=245&area=oil.

Rainforest Action Network. (1996b, November 14). U.S. court supports Texaco's environmental racism abroad [Press Release]. Retrieved September 28, 2005, from http://www.ran.org/news/newsitem.php?id=233&area=oil.

Rainforest Action Network. (1997, March 23). *Shell Oil drills on indigenous lands; student activists take over Greensboro station*. Retrieved September 26, 2005, from http://www.ran.org/news/newsitem.php?id=226&area=oil.

Raymond, D. (2003). Activism: Behind the banners. In S. John & S. Thomson (Eds.), *New activism and the corporate response* (pp. 207—227). New York: Palgrave Macmillan.

Risk of extinction to grey whales if Shell project continues. (2005, February 16). *Milieukontakt Oost-Europa*. Retrieved September

27, 2005, from http://www.milieukontakt
.nl/activity_more.php?activity_id=279.

Rucht, D., & Neidhardt, F. (2002). Towards a
"movement society"? On the possibilities
of institutionalizing social movements.
Social Movement Studies, 1, 7–30.

Ruskin, G., & Schor, J. (2005). Every nook and
cranny: The dangerous spread of commer-
cialized culture. *Multinational Monitor, 26,*
20–24.

Schwartz, P., & Gibb, B. (1999). *When good
companies do bad things: Responsibility
and risk in an age of globalization.* New
York: John Wiley & Sons.

Schwarze, S. (2003a). Corporate-state irresponsibility, critical publicity, and asbestos
exposure in Libby, Montana. *Management
Communication Quarterly, 16,* 625–632.

Schwarze, S. (2003b). Juxtaposition in environmental health rhetoric: Exposing asbestos
contamination in Libby, Montana. *Rhetoric & Public Affairs, 6,* 313–335.

Shaw, R. (1999). *Reclaiming America: Nike,
clean air, and the new national activism.*
Berkeley: University of California Press.

Shell Nigeria. (n.d.). *Shell Oil Corporation.*
Retrieved September 27, 2005, from http://
www.shell.com/home/Framework?siteId=
nigeria.

Shell on the rocks. (1995, June 24). *Economist,*
p. 57.

Soper, L. (1997). Investing with a conscience:
The Ogoni story. *Herizons, 11,* 8–9.

Spurlock, M. (Producer/Director). (2004). *Super size
me* [Motion picture]. New York: The Con.

Starbucks will buy beans at premium. (2000,
April 11). *New York Times,* p. C2.

Stewart, C. J., Smith, C. A., & Denton, R. E.
(2001). *Persuasion and social movements*
(4th ed.). Prospect Heights, IL: Waveland
Press.

Talbot, D. (1999a, August 29). Petroleum waste
taints village life. *Boston Herald,* p. 6.

Talbot, D. (1999b, August 29). Rain forest pays
the price of oil: Suit claims Texaco polluted
Ecuador. *Boston Herald,* p. 1.

Ulmer, R. R., & Sellnow, T. L. (1997). Strategic
ambiguity and the ethic of significant
choice in the tobacco industry's crisis
communication. *Communication Studies,
48,* 215–233.

United Nations, Production and Consumption
Branch. (2004). *United Nations guidelines
for consumer protection.* Retrieved July 9,
2005, from http://www.uneptie.org/pc/
sustain/policies/consumser-protection
.htm.

Unrest in Nigeria hurts oil production: Shell
shuts in volumes. (2005, August 19).
International Oil Daily. Retrieved September 27, 2005, from LexisNexis Academic
database.

Vatz, R. E. (1973). The myth of the rhetorical
situation. *Philosophy & Rhetoric, 6,* 154–
161.

Walker, R. (2004, December 5). The hidden (in
plain sight) persuaders. *New York Times
Magazine,* 68–75.

Wolf, G. (2004, September). Weapons of mass
mobilization. *Wired,* pp. 131–137.

V

SOCIAL PERSPECTIVES

18

Corporate Governance, Corporate Social Responsibility, and Communication

STANLEY DEETZ

Both corporate social responsibility (CSR) and corporate governance have become major international issues. Many of the reasons for this appear in this volume. Only a few are reviewed here. The more central interest is in showing the intertwined nature of governance, responsibility, and the quality of social and economic choices. Arguably, corporate governance reform provides the best hope for addressing the problems of our times and providing a synergistic relation between CSR and economic viability. But different reforms provide different hopes and possibilities. These differences are of concern here. Any analysis has to remain relatively abstract given the complex differences arising from industries, national laws and policies, and specific historical exigencies. Nonetheless, some general directions can be given that might focus the development of specific contextualized responses.

The flow of the argument of this chapter is thus: contemporary concerns with both corporate governance and CSR have arisen from organizational failures and negative social consequences that appear to be systemic in nature. The systemic quality is created by corporate governance structures and processes that enable the exaggerated representation of some values and interests and the omission of others. Organizational decisions are inevitably interested and value laden rather than simply economically rational, but the various conflicting values and interests in society have not been given an equal opportunity to influence decision making. Significant public decisions are made in the corporate site, creating systematic distortions in social and economic developments and posing important moral and political questions.

Traditional governance models have counted on some combination of managerial stewardship, governmental regulation, and consumer choices to make operant wider social values. For a variety of well-documented reasons, these have each become less effective in providing guidance (Deetz, 1995a; Kelly, 2001; Schmookler, 1992). Whether based on rights or need for performance, getting social values and interests into the decisional premises, processes, and routines has become an ever more pressing problem. Stakeholder collaboration becomes one promising alternative. The central questions—Whose objectives should count? How much should they count? How will they be accounted for?—arise in all modern organizations. Beyond the political aims of a new form of governance, evidence suggests that the presence of diverse values can aid creativity, constituent commitment, workplace coordination, and product and service customization, and that these are especially important for the competitiveness of postindustrial societies and in the more knowledge-intensive industries where forms of social and intellectual capital are central.

Stakeholder governance models offer possible political and economic benefits. Still, stakeholder collaboration remains fairly underdeveloped and often ineffective. Part of this arises from limited stakeholder inclusion, strategic management of stakeholders or co-optation of stakeholder involvement by managerial groups. Perhaps a bigger but more hidden problem has been the lack of serious attention to models of communication in decision making. Participation models have largely been evaluated as if they are all alike, without careful attention to the models and skills of communication present. Clearly, communication concepts and practices embedded in public/state democratic processes are rarely useful for the types of collaborations that are most effective. More productive concepts and practices can be developed from consideration of innovative communication processes based on conflict rather than consensus models. Good communication rests not in the finding of common ground but in assuring requisite diversity and contestation coupled with the ability to invent creative options that sustain mutual commitment, difference, and mutual accomplishment of diverse goals.

FORCES BEHIND RETHINKING GOVERNANCE

Issues of corporate governance have been long term. Over the years, different societies have struggled with shareholder rights and various processes for representing other stakeholders, principally employees. While some have followed more radical political agendas, most of these were attempts to make adjustments within the context of the more general owner rights/managerial prerogative model whenever specific social problems arose. While within academic circles larger discussions regarding political rights maybe of concern, outside of this the interest is primarily in making adjustments to better manage the immediate social and economic problems (see, e.g., Organisation for Economic Co-operation and Development, 2004; Sarbanes-Oxley Act of 2002). In the contemporary context, both external social issues and internal economic ones have reinvigorated this discussion.

The increased attention to governance by those traditionally defined as outside the organization appears generated by four core problems. All of these have strong social and economic implications for the wider society, but the first three are rarely expressed in CSR terms. From the standpoint of general social interests, any discussible governance solution would need to address each of these in some fashion: (1) scandals and the financial disruptions created by these scandals; (2) the dominance of short-term decision making and subsequent lack of organizational development and socially beneficial growth; (3) managerial self-interests that have run counter to productivity and development; and (4) the general decline of CSR.

Scandals and Financial Market Disruption

The various scandals at Enron, WorldCom, and so forth have in many ways demonstrated fundamental weaknesses in governance processes. Of primary concern in most discussions has not been the loss of employee jobs and retirement accounts in the specific scandals but rather the exposure of systemic weaknesses in accounting and control processes that potentially cut across all companies and countries. While in the United States the media and public attention may continue to focus on the personal characteristics and failures of corporate leaders, around the world, and in Europe specifically, the focus has been on the system breakdown and the consequences for financial markets (Deetz, 1995c). As the Organisation for Economic Co-operation and Development (2004) leads its own report: "The dramatic collapse of major companies over the past few years has focused the minds of governments, regulators, companies, investors, and the general public on the weaknesses in corporate governance systems and the associated threat posed to the integrity of financial markets" (p. 3). And, in an even more narrow sense, the 2002 Sarbanes-Oxley Act, while heralded as a fundamental shift in governance, focuses most directly on financial oversight and auditing with the hope of increasing the confidence of financial investors.

Concern with Growth and Development

While scandals may have gotten everyone's attention and focused the governance discussion, several other changes that affect economic health have been of more long-term concern. The increased centrality of the quarterly report, return on investment measures, and short-termness poses problems flowing from current governance processes. The use of the return on investment in the buying and selling of stock rather than company worth and growth as the measure of value has tended to favor financial manipulations and cost-containment strategies over building companies. The growing dominance of institutional investors also has consequences. Institutional investors, un-like traditional owners, are often more concerned about overall return than the health of any spe-cific company. This invites short-term strategies (see Deal & Kennedy, 1999). Further, as resources are held by institutional investors, individuals are less able and likely to know much about the practices of the companies their funds are invested in (Or-ganisation for Economic Co-operation and Devel-opment, 2004, pp. 64–66).

The dominance of short-term decision making and subsequent lack of growth is a concern to most European societies. Few doubt the need for profits to keep companies viable, but when man-agement sees profit as their product rather than a byproduct of good business choices, long-term consequences to the business and society result. In an analogous way, a person needs oxygen to live, but living for oxygen can lead to less than healthy choices.

Managerial Self-Interests

At least since Chandler's (1977) work, we have known that managerial capitalism functions differ-ently from idealized models of capitalism. Mana-gerial self-interests and control attempts have always had a major impact on corporate decisions. But a number of things are new and more prob-lematic. The growth of executive salaries, espe-cially in the United States, has been startling to say the least. Upper level executives have acted less like citizens and have deployed a somewhat rawer eco-nomic logic with less consideration of the conse-quences for the organization, other employees, and host societies. Personal agendas and identity needs have more greatly influenced product development and takeover and merger strategies. And standard decisional routines increasingly run counter to real growth in productivity and development.

CSR and Social
Value Representation

While all three of the above issues might be loosely referred to as issues of CSR, a much wider range

of CSR issues are present that focus primarily on social value representation. Corporate social re-sponsibility and value representation are often discussed in contrast to an economic-only view of organizations. This is, of course, misleading. Or-ganizational decisions are inevitably value laden. Beliefs and values fill the gaps between what can be known and the need to act. Assumptions about people, fairness, and business practices matter. And organizational practices based in wider value systems endlessly direct choices. Values are em-bedded within standard accounting practices and knowledge production activities. But we tend to talk about them as values only when they arise from nonmanagerial groups, and then, mostly only when there is some specific harm to the larger society. Corporate social responsibility and value representation concerns are not about *whether* values, but *whose* and *what* values, are represented in business decisions.

No one familiar with the international business situation today needs to be told that contempo-rary issues of responsibility are complex and criti-cal. They range through important issues such as human rights, environmental protection, equal opportunity and pay for women and various dis-advantaged minorities, and fair competition. Such broad issues become instantiated in activities such as using prisoners as workers, moving operations to environmentally less restrictive communities, offering and taking bribes and payoffs, creating environmentally unsound or wasteful products, closing of economically viable plants in takeover and merger games, growing income disparity, de-clining social safety nets, malingering harassment, maintaining unnecessary and unhealthy controls on employees, and advocating consumerism.

In such a context, value/moral/ethical/aesthetic considerations are taking on additional signifi-cance. Few today see business as either socially benign or benevolent. Still, the growing popular-ity of such discussions is easily co-opted into more or less responsible "green" and "social" market-ing. And, the discussion often uses traditional con-ceptions of policies and individual responsibility that may be of limited value. In contrast, broader concerns draw our attention less to reactive issues of law and ethics and more to proactive issues of morality and social good.

Much of the discussion of CSR has focused on the morality or ethical principles of corporate lead-ers and how these become embedded in the culture and practices of organizations (e.g., Treviño & Weaver, 2003). Attention is often directed to the character of these leaders and their qualities as citizens of national, regional, and world communities (MacIntyre, 1984). This orientation treats CSR problems as arising from individual defects rather than governance and decisional structures and the solution as policies and standards rather than better processes of making business decisions. Much can be gained by focusing more on the decisional processes and responsive choices internal to organizations.

THE RESPONSE TO THESE PROBLEMS

Various mechanisms exist to address problems with scandals and managerial choices as well as for social value representation. Wider social concerns affect business decisions primarily through governmental regulation, consumer choices, and managerial goodwill and stewardship (often supported through hopes of economic gain or diminished regulation). Each has clear weaknesses, and even in combination, these processes are limited in their ability to represent social values well (see Deetz, 1995a, 1995b).

In general, the European Union and United States have each responded to these contemporary problems with sets of new guidelines and regulations, on the one hand, and increased enticements for voluntary compliance (comply or explain obligations and encouraged with the threat of further regulation), on the other (Organization for Economic Co-operation and Development, 2004, p. 40). The types of initiative as well as relative success and failure are carefully documented in two recent Organisation for Economic Co-operation and Development (OECD) documents (*Corporate Responsibility*, 2001, and *Corporate Governance*, 2004). While many initiatives can be identified, OECD assessment across countries shows major changes in decisional processes and voluntary compliance to be less than encouraging (Organisation for Economic Co-operation and Development, 2004, pp. 52–3). Certainly, shareholder protection through greater financial transparency and reformations in boards has been achieved (pp. 58–79), but little more than this. Much the same could be said regarding the Sarbanes-Oxley Act in the United States. The focus has been heavily on financial

oversight, generating a further layer of internal bureaucracy and initiating an entire industry of compliance consultants rather than concern with the larger public or with producing a viable external surveillance. Rather than a governance change, those in the industry describe it perhaps best as "no accountant left behind." Rarely has any group benefited so much by its failure. Perhaps more important, such an approach has given more financial transparency and mechanisms to assure the following of standard accounting practices, but the significant CSR questions focus more on the values embedded in standard accounting practices, and these remain unexplored.

While the relation of governmental interventions and corporate decisions is not developed here, a brief list of problems can show why state intervention, while important, can only be a part of the solution. Even though regulation and incentives can influence system choices, most significant choices will remain within corporations themselves. Even if they wanted to, governments cannot micromanage companies. Further, the effects of their enticements are uneven at best (see Ring, Bigley, D'Aunno, & Khanna, 2005) and "monitoring of compliance is in general underdeveloped" (Organisation for Economic Co-operation and Development, 2004, p. 11) or weak (pp. 52–53).

Governments lack both the popular legitimacy and capacity to make or require more proactive corporate choices, governmental policy is largely influenced by corporate leaders and lobbyists, and rarely do public agencies have enough information soon enough to participate actively in corporate processes to make them more publicly accountable. Additionally, regulation inevitably leads to a costly double bureaucracy—a public one to establish guidelines and monitor compliance for public good, and a private one that struggles to keep up with the paperwork, find loopholes, and avoid regulation. The application of endless bureaucratic rules constantly runs counter to good situational judgments and common sense, and the costs are matched by the energy and imagination used by corporate managers in pursuing narrow self-interests at the expense of public health, public information, and positive social development. Globalization provides for an even larger set of potentially competing values. Yet, with globalization of business, governmental powers are weakened in the ability to support the inclusion of social values, and further, international trade agreements often outlaw social value representation (Organisation for Economic Co-operation and Development, 2001, p. 31).

The prospect of consumer choices leading to more responsible businesses and wider value representation is not great, either. The concept is clear enough. Multiple value systems could be integrated into business choices through strategic consumption. If stakeholders were not happy with managerial decisions, they could eventually vote with their feet or dollars. Unfortunately, in this formulation, social and political relations are reduced to economic relations, democracy is reduced to capitalism, citizens to consumers, and discussion to buying and selling. These transformations have costs. The translation of values into the economic code entails a constraining of people's capacity to make decisions together and reduces potential human choices to choices already available in the system as controlled by others. The marketplace does not work well as a way of representing social values. Marketing and advertising, ability to exclude or externalize social and environmental costs, the complexity and length of the chain of decisions, the difficulty of translating some values into economic terms, and inequitable distribution of money all weaken the ability of consumption to represent values. Yet those who endeavor to resist such forces often find countercultural movements co-opted into market capitalism (J. Heath & Potter, 2004). As many have shown, free market capitalism was never intended to represent the public well; it was intended to describe how to make a return on financial investment (Kelly, 2001). The idea that market choices accomplish representation, and money measures it, is a misleading fiction. Markets are value laden rather than neutral representation processes, but the values are rarely explored (see Schmookler, 1992).

Government regulation, consumer choices, and corporate good will offer very weak mechanisms for value representation and virtually no support to communication processes that create win–win situations where multiple stakeholders—including shareholders—can successfully pursue their mutual interests (Deetz, 1995a). Perhaps more important, they do not enable or stimulate creative decisions whereby corporate economic objectives and social good are synergetic rather than competing interests. Ultimately, the best hope rests in getting wider values into the decisional premises,

processes, and routines rather than to trying to direct from the outside.

THE NONINEVITABILITY OF CONTRADICTIONS BETWEEN SOCIAL AND BUSINESS CONCERNS

A common public conception, promoted often by business leaders, is that the inclusion of social concerns is costly and that a basic contradiction exists between doing good and doing well. Available evidence across specific firms and industries is not always clear as to whether doing social good leads necessarily to better economic performance, or the causal direction between doing good and doing well. But plenty of support suggests that there is no necessary contradiction (Clarkson, 1995; de Jong & Witteloostuijn, 2004; Lawler, 1999; McLagan & Nel, 1995; Organisation for Economic Co-operation and Development, 2004, pp. 77–78). The differences in relationships appear to be linked to external conditions and manner of value inclusion rather than to any essential tension.

The value addedness of inclusion does not appear to come simply from goodwill or reduced litigation and regulation. The principal value may come from the breaking of standard managerial decision routines that are not economically sound. This was detailed in the outcomes of various decisional impasses in the comanagement process in the early days at Saturn before they returned to a more standard General Motors model (Rubinstein, Bennett, & Kochan, 1993). Even more generally, this can be seen in the failure to meet objectives in most cost-containment and layoff strategies implemented by managers in economic downturns. Opposition and difference are essential to assessing existing decision routines and inventing new ones. The knowledge economy's dependence on human capital produces additional economic pressure. Even those often critical of various forms of participation as a way of including wider social concerns often see it as positive in the more knowledge-intensive industries (Kerr, 2004).

From a business (although not necessarily managerial) standpoint, the primary justification for widespread inclusion is that diverse group participation in organizational decisions will lead to better decisions than are currently being made.

Evidence supports that people can make good collaborative decisions if given the chance, but participation and inclusion cannot be assessed in the abstract. They must be linked to specific objectives and processes of inclusion. Inclusion seems most valuable when four types of business outcomes are important: creativity in product development and decision making, increased employee commitment, enhanced coordination, and greater product customization.

Several well-accepted claims advance this position that are in no way unique to my argument: diversity can enable greater creativity. As Kerr (2004) showed in his analysis of the value of diverse inputs at Hewlett-Packard and Southwest Airlines, participation "will contribute positively to an organization's performance where . . . the organization's output must be diverse and original" (p. 91). Further, the use of distributed expertise can lead to faster, higher quality decisions. Members at the point of the business activity are often in a better position to innovate and improve processes. The presence of valued social and intellectual capital makes employee retention and commitment essential. Decisional involvement correlates positively with different dimensions of commitment affecting productivity, recruitment, and retention, for example. Given the cost of control and surveillance, especially in knowledge industries, coordination through shared values and personal commitments is often more effective than supervision. And, finally, higher valued products often results from product customization that is linked to diverse group and value inclusion.

Despite the sometimes weak models and inadequate implementation, evidence on decisional quality, effectiveness, and efficiency consistently favors participatory decisional forms over traditional hierarchical alternatives (Cheney, 1995; Cheney et al., 1998; Lawler, 1999; McLagan & Nel, 1995; Seibold & Shea, 2001). Where participation programs have been less successful, the lack of managerial acceptance and inadequate participation processes appear to have been largely responsible (Cotton et al., 1988).

Bottom line: Ultimately, new governance conceptions and practices can reduce the opportunity for scandals, encourage growth and long-term thinking, balance managerial self-interest, and make decisions more responsive to wider social values while at the same time encourage greater creativity in product development and decision making, increase employee commitment, enhance coordination, and enable greater product customization. A tall order, on the one hand, but interestingly, when looked at holistically, all are advanced by similar transformations.

Workplaces could be positive social institutions providing forums for the articulation and creative resolution of important social conflicts regarding the use of natural resources, the production of desirable goods and services, the development of personal qualities, distribution of income, and the future direction of society.

In some ways, the workplace could be a better site for public decision making than the traditional political process, given the close connection between decisions made there, their public consequences, and the speed of adjustment. Steering from the inside may be more effective than the carrot and stick given the complex pressures that guide decision making in corporations today. In a wide number of circumstances, companies have been more progressive and less ideologically directed than their elected counterparts. In many cases, companies, unlike governments and their agencies, simply cannot afford to be disconnected from external realities (or to build fantasies about them) or to allow irrational responses to diversity in their ranks.

But, by focusing primarily on measuring narrow, contrived economic outcomes, like return on investment, the broader issues of corporate health and social and economic effects of business decisions have not been carefully assessed or evaluated. Systems of diverse interest representation have only occasionally been developed. And we have been less likely to develop more creative (and profitable) work processes. If we are to steer from the inside, a wider range of values and people need to be inside.

Meeting social and economic goals requires a transformation of organizational governance and decision-making processes to include more decisional voices representing social and economic values and generating explicit value contestation as part of the business decision process. Such representation and contestation can enhance creativity, productivity, economic performance, and greater fulfillment of social good. Accomplishing this requires new models of corporate governance focusing on stakeholders rather than shareholders and new models of communication enabling more productive discussions and decision processes.

THE STAKEHOLDER GOVERNANCE MODEL

New concepts of governance and processes of decision making are necessary to realize this potential. Given the difficulties of existing hopes and interventions, stakeholder models have come to the fore as offering a new set of directions. Clearly, not all stakeholder conceptions are alike. They range from discussion of how to strategically manage stakeholder groups, to voluntary process of consultation in employment and environmental issues, to much more expansive conceptions of reforming concepts of ownership and governance (Donaldson & Preston, 1995; Reed, 1999). Stakeholder governance conceptions nearly always involve both social and business concerns. Most agree that concern with stakeholders varies to the extent that "capital (human and physical) and other rights are tied to a given enterprise and therefore subject to possible losses from the action of, inter alia, management" (Organization for Economic Co-operation and Development, 2004, p. 70). Organisation for Economic Co-operation and Development standards represent this well, reflecting both social well-being issues and benefits to business but, like most, reflects mostly on issues of trade-off and balance rather than the creativity that can come with conflict among stakeholders. And, perhaps as important, they reflect only on the presence or absence of inclusion with no attention to communication and decision processes once stakeholders are present.

Certainly many over the years have recognized the existence of multiple stakeholders with legitimate claims (e.g., Carroll, 1999; Donaldson & Preston, 1995; Freeman, 1984). Labor unions, supplier cartels, and consumer groups are ways by which some stakeholders have attempted to acquire the size and clout necessary to be represented in corporate decisions. But as we know from other collaborative decision-making contexts, creativity and mutual satisfaction are based on commitment to a codeterminative process rather than just having a place to argue out self-interests (e.g., Gray, 1989). In most discussions of stakeholder models, management has been left as oppositional to other stakeholders rather than as a group that could and should have a commitment to mutual accomplishment.

In a fully developed stakeholder model, management's function would need to become the coordination of the conflicting interests of stakeholders rather than the managing or controlling of them. The logic is not one of containing stakeholder interests, but trying to accomplish them through corporate activity. In a fully developed model, management would be hired by all stakeholders and work to optimally coordinate the meeting of all interests as if they were interests of the corporation, thus seeking the most creative codetermination for the benefit of all stakeholders.

Thus far, the stronger versions of this model have mostly been developed in quasi-public enterprises and in environmental collaborations. While some of these have become venting and/or buy-in mechanisms and others ploys for green marketing, others have offered creative and beneficial solutions. For example, Lange (2003), building on insights from bona fide group theory (Putnam & Stohl, 1990), has detailed the functioning of ecosystem management following the Clinton Forest Plan beginning in 1994 (Gorte, 1993). But for-profit companies have not overlooked stakeholder inclusion opportunities. de Jong & van Witteloostuijn (2004) showed how the Dutch Breman Group's structures and processes of participation, while partly restricted to works councils, helped to "develop and sustain organizational adaptation and learning" (p. 54). Employee participation of various forms is common today in most successful companies. The resistance to and finally embracing of employee involvement may be instructive in looking to the potential of including other stakeholders. Philosophically, the concept of stakeholder is taking hold. Johnson & Johnson, as well as other major companies, has as a part of its credo the belief that, if management attends to stakeholder interests, profits will result, rather than the other way around. Some of this has clearly translated into positive corporate choices.

Stakeholder inclusion is not for the balancing of power and advancing self-interests but is essential for the processes of creativity that can advance both social and economic interests rather than trade them off against each other. Such a juxtaposition of goals is a critical feature of any attempt to move to creativity and innovation. Such a model begins with a determination of who has legitimate stakeholder interests, some determination of what those interests are, and a determination of how interest diversity advances responsiveness and creativity.

Many questions remain to be answered in the development of advanced stakeholder governance. Basic ones are little different from those for participation more generally: Which stakeholders should be involved? Where and how should they be involved? Who should speak on behalf of a stakeholder group? Will stakeholders, when involved, understand and effectively articulate their own interests? How to keep potential cost of participation down?

These issues continue to be productively worked out in other contexts. But an additional, relatively hidden issue remains that significantly hinders the acceptance and practice of stakeholder governance. This issue may derail even the most positive move to stakeholder governance: What is to be the nature of the stakeholder interaction in the decision-making process? This issue is most often overlooked, even in fairly complete reviews of participation processes. The biggest task may not be overcoming the autocratic tendencies of many managers and the communication structures, principles, and practices fostered by this, but rather in providing new ways to think about and practice communication in places where participation is genuinely favored.

MODELS OF STAKEHOLDER COMMUNICATION

The—what might appear to be benign—communication conceptions and practices have tremendous impact on the success and viability of stakeholder governance programs. The form and practices of participation, not just its existence, matter. Communication is an integral part of any form of participation. Having a right and a place to say something and having a process to positively affect decisions are often very different. This is developed below in looking at alternative understandings of communication, democracy, conflict, and dialogue.

The issues of communication are not simple and best not simply left to trainers and practitioners. The so-called linguistic turn in management studies and extensive work on organizational discourse has focused attention on human interaction but has remained relatively abstract and concerned with rather large cultural formations rather than considering the critical issues of how collaboration in decision making is accomplished.

Concerns with the representation of social values and economic success are rarely necessarily contradictory and are most often mutually supportive, especially in the long term. A careful look at communication practices, however, is critical to positive outcomes. Even in countries with strong codetermination models and structures such as Germany, Sweden, and Denmark, the communication model and practices may be fairly traditional and greatly reduce the impact and benefits of participation.

Native communication concepts and practices have been largely treated as unproblematic, thus leading to a focus on developing participation *forums* and higher levels of involvement with uneven consequences for decision processes. Much of this results from dominant "enlightenment" conceptions of communication that overlook critical aspects of interaction processes whereby meanings and interests are produced. The production of personal meanings in communication is overlooked with attention to their expression. Managerially driven forms of participation based in these older conceptions are often strategic attempts to increase loyalty and commitment or decrease resistance rather than to seek genuine decisional input. The lack of *voice* even with appropriate *forums* results from constrained decisional contexts, inadequate or distorted information, socialization and colonization activities, and the solicitation of "consent" where stakeholders "choose" to suppress their own needs and internal value conflicts (see Deetz, 1998). Even team-based decision making is often filled with self-generated limits to open participation (Barker, 1999). Overcoming these problems requires a collaborative constitutive view of communication, based in conflict rather than consensus models.

Most managers' approach to communication grows out of specific concepts of hierarchy and control. Business schools more often require public speaking, presentation, and message design skills rather than listening and negotiation skills. "Leadership" training is still primarily conceived in the form of directing or taking charge of others (Calás & Smircich, 1991; Chrislip & Larson, 1995). Theories of control, persuasion, and motivation are treated more centrally than cooperation, facilitation, and group creativity. Even the renewed interest in ethics in business schools directs attention to the individual's character and compliance rather than normative ideals in communication. Corporate communication is often simply another word for strategic communication. Directives and compliance gaining characterize the communication relation to internal groups; advertising and public relations, to external ones. Clearly, such conceptions and skills of communication cripple rather than aid participation.

Thus, not only are managers hesitant to include even employees, let alone other stakeholders, in crucial decisions by disclosing information, sharing power, or granting autonomy, but also they lack the concepts and skills necessary to do so even if they wanted to. Clearly, managers lack the critical skills of democratic communication necessary for coordinating divergent interests, let alone the ability to facilitate interaction that can lead to creative, mutually satisfying outcomes. This certainly affects their perceptions of cost of participation, how those costs compare to control costs, the likelihood of economic viability, and so forth.

But what models would they need? Several models exist arising with the increased use and talk about team decisions, dialogue, and forms of participation generally. Often, however, these alternatives have not been theoretically or empirically investigated and have been presented in a vague unproblematic way as simply "democratic" communication or "dialogue" (see Isaacs, 1993). And frequently, dialogue and democratic communication have been seen as requiring little training or development: if we build a trusting team, members will communicate well; if we develop participatory attitudes, appropriate skills will spontaneously arise.

But all democracies and dialogues are not alike, and native intuitions and skills can be less than positive (Deetz & Simpson, 2004). Anyone hanging around most corporations will hear a lot more complaint about the endlessness and frustrations of meetings than the lack of opportunity to participate. This results from the inability to participate well, not just from the limited nature of participation tasks. Often, the problem of meetings, and communication more generally, results from the borrowing of liberal democratic communication models from state processes with the concurrent humanist commitments to representation and consensus rather than more participatory communication models committed to diversity, conflict, and creativity.

Corporate organizations are not like state democracies. As Kerr (2004) argued, they lack "accountability of the governed, right of participation, free exchange of information, and right of representation" (p. 81). But even if these could be assured, common views of democracy and communication used for state processes were never designed to accomplish the type of participation that can deliver on the promises laid out above. Common native understandings are largely based in an enlightenment conception of "liberal democracy" as institutionalized and advanced by Western state institutions. Barber (1984) provided one of the more complete analysis of the consequences for state practices and decisions given this view in contrast to more participatory forms of democracy (see also Bachrach & Botwinick, 1992). While he focused more on issues of structure and representation than on forms of communication, his initial distinction between liberal and participatory democracies is instructive to understanding the limits of productive participation in the workplace even when it is desired.

Liberal democracy is core to the justification of contemporary forms and institutions of communication (see fuller discussion in Deetz, 1992; Deetz & Brown, 2004). The weakness of its communication conceptions may partly account for the poor regard people have for political processes and the general cynicism in many societies. Unsurprisingly, an eighteenth-century model of democracy and communication—based in different conceptions of human experience, forms of power, and contexts of decision making—does not work well in a twenty-first century world. No other social science, nor the practices they engender, could survive their eighteenth-century models.

Critical theories of communication originating primarily from Habermas (1979, 1984) have revived discussion of communication in public decision making. The description of an ideal speech situation provides a heuristic for determining the minimal conditions for stakeholder involvement in decision-making discussions. Most of these are familiar. At the minimum, we might expect reciprocity of opportunity for expression; some equality in expression skills; the setting aside of authority relations, organizational positions, and other external sources of power; the open investigations of stakeholder positions and "wants" to more freely ascertain their interests; open sharing of information and transparency of decision processes; and the opening of fact and knowledge claims to redeterminization based on contestation of claims and advantaged modes of knowledge creation (e.g., accounting processes; see Deetz, 1992). Such concepts have also been developed by Forester (1989, 1999) for public planning processes. Much of this work is directly applicable to stakeholder decision making. And much work has shown how organizational talk can be analyzed to discover the retention and protection of hidden values and ideology (e.g., Fairclough, 1992) and the presence of various forms of discursive closure (Deetz, 1992; Thackaberry, 2004). Pearce and Littlejohn (1999), from a somewhat different perspective, show how to develop communication processes for engaging even moral conflicts where deep cultural differences produce what would appear to be intractable conflict. Barge and Little (2002) have shown how a Bakhtinian conception of dialogic communication can help develop contingent and situated practices that enhance responsiveness to conflicting stakeholder values.

Social responsibility and increased economic health is found in fostering particular communicative micropractices in everyday work contexts. Communication difficulties arise from communication practices that preclude value debate and conflict, substitute images and imaginary relations for self-presentation and truth claims, arbitrarily limit access to communication channels and forums, and then lead to decisions based on arbitrary authority relations. Critical theories have been useful because they identified the key problem as the nature of the discussion itself rather than the profiles of the participants.

But Habermasian concepts of communicative competence and warranted claims, like theories of dialogue advanced by Senge, Issacs, and others, are based more on finding common ground and a deeper prior consensus than in producing a future beyond current cultural constraints (Deetz & Simpson, 2004; Isaacs, 1993). And further, most of these theories are aimed at participants understanding each other rather than the need to make decisions together. (See this developed in Benhabib's [1992] critique of Habermas's ideal speech situation.) Critical theory alone does not offer a theory or practice of dialogue embracing difference and facilitating decision making on the part of stakeholders (Wolin, 1996; Young, 1996).

Appropriate concepts and practices of communication are required to move beyond mere mutual understanding to making quality decisions together. Continuing research across sites at the University of Colorado (R. Heath, 2005; MacDonald, 2004), and that summarized by Lange (2003) regarding environmental collaborations, suggests a few basic insights: First, pro-

grams that focus on stakeholders jointly making decisions are of much greater value than those that simply give stakeholders a say. Second, membership based on the diversity of interests of those at the table and discussion processes that encourage emergent solutions are of greater value than those whose members represent external groups and are committed to maintaining positions held by those not at the table. Third, as shown for years by people working with conflict, focusing on outcomes and interests in the interaction is of greater value than focusing on problems and wants and bargaining over preferred solutions. This is especially the case when problems are defined by stakeholders as the absence of their preferred solutions. And, finally, maintaining conflicts and differences as a positive energy toward creativity is of greater value than seeking common ground and value consensus.

Development of these concepts and practices requires an enriched theory of communication. Such a theory focuses on understanding the cultural politics of experience and processes of domination in interaction, has a strong conception of "Other" and "Otherness," and is grounded in conflict theories. Such a theory helps turn these insights in positive practices. Such a theory shows how difference or "distantiation" enables exploring of alternatives and producing creative decisions. Such a theory works against native views focused on similarity, consensus, and finding common ground in showing how requisite diversity and contestation coupled with the ability to invent creative options can sustain mutual commitment and mutual accomplishment of interests, thus including diverse social values.

Stakeholder governance, with appropriate collaborative communication practices, can generate more creativity, effecting new product development, greater efficiency and effectiveness in personal and organizational goal accomplishment, higher levels of mutual commitment, and greater product and service customization. Interaction modeled on collaboration grounded on the embracing of difference has great potential.

Clearly, a reformed "stakeholder" conception of workplaces can be enhanced by the application of a conflict-based communication theory to the workplace for the sake of greater responsibility and more effective production. Such a conception can (1) provide a communication-based understanding of the complex processes of organizational life, (2) direct the evaluation of existing organizational forms and activities, and (3) provide guidance for the education of members and redesign of organizational structures and practices. Corporate social responsibility can be made possible by the inclusion of multiple social values into the decisional premises, processes, and routines and the development of communication processes that use the situations of conflict and difference to generate creative win–win responses.

REFERENCES

Bachrach, P., & Botwinick, A. (1992). *Power and empowerment: A radical theory of participation*. Philadelphia, PA: Temple University Press.

Barber, B. (1984). *Strong democracy*. Berkeley: University of California Press.

Barge, J. K., & Little, M. (2002). Dialogical wisdom, communicative practice, and organizational life. *Communication Theory, 12*, 375–397.

Barker, J. (1999). *The team makes the rules: Culture and control in self-managed teams*. Thousand Oaks, CA: Sage.

Benhabib, S. (1992). *Situating the self: Gender, community, and postmodernism in contemporary ethics*. New York: Routledge.

Calás, M., & Smircich, L. (1991). Voicing seduction to silence leadership. *Organization Studies, 12*, 567–602.

Carroll, A. (1999). Corporate social responsibility. *Business & Society, 38*, 268–295.

Chandler, A. (1977). *The visible hand: The managerial revolution in American business*. Cambridge, MA: Harvard University Press.

Cheney, G. (1995). Democracy in the workplace: Theory and practice from the perspective of communication. *Journal of Applied Communication Research, 23*, 167–200.

Cheney, G., Straub, J., Speirs-Glebe, L., Stohl, C., DeGooyer, D., Whalen, S., et al. (1998). Democracy, participation and communication at work: A multidisciplinary review. In M. E. Roloff (Ed.), *Communication yearbook 21* (pp. 35–91). Thousand Oaks, CA: Sage.

Chrislip, D., & Larson, C. (1995). *Collaborative leadership: How citizens and civil leaders can make a difference*. San Francisco, CA: Jossey-Bass.

Clarkson, M. (1995). A stakeholder framework for analyzing corporate social performance. *Academy of Management Review, 20*, 92–117.

Cotton, J., Vollrath, D., Froggatt, K., Lengnick-Hall, M., & Jennings, K. (1988). Employee participation: Diverse forms and different outcomes. *Academy of Management Review, 13*, 8–22.

Deal, T., & Kennedy, A. (1999). *The new corporate cultures: Revitalizing the workplace after downsizing, mergers, and reengineering*. Reading, MA: Perseus Books.

Deetz, S. (1992). *Democracy in the age of corporate colonization: Developments in communication and the politics of everyday life*. Albany: State University of New York Press.

Deetz, S. (1995a). *Transforming communication, transforming business: Building responsive and responsible workplaces*. Cresskill, NJ: Hampton Press.

Deetz, S. (1995b). Transforming communication, transforming business: Stimulating value negotiation for more responsive and responsible workplaces. *International Journal of Value-Based Management, 8*, 255–278.

Deetz, S. (1995c). Character, corporate responsibility and the dialogic in the postmodern context. *Organization: The Interdisciplinary Journal of Organization, Theory, & Society, 3*, 217–225.

Deetz, S. (1998). Discursive formations, strategized subordination, and self-surveillance: An empirical case. In A. McKinlay & K. Starkey (Eds.), *Managing Foucault: A reader* (pp. 151–172). London: Sage.

Deetz, S., & Brown, D. (2004). Conceptualising involvement, participation and workplace decision processes: A communication theory perspective. In D. Tourish & O. Hargie (Eds.), *Key issues in organizational communication* (pp. 172–187). London: Routledge.

Deetz, S., & Simpson. J. (2004). Critical organizational dialogue: Open formation and the demand of "Otherness." In R. Anderson, L. Baxter, & K. Cissna (Eds.), *Dialogic approaches to communication* (pp. 141–158). New York: Lawrence Erlbaum.

de Jong, G., & van Witteloostuijn, A. (2004). Successful corporate democracy. *Academic of Management Executive, 18*, 54–66.

Donaldson, T., & Preston, L. (1995). The stakeholder theory of the corporation: Concepts, evidence and implications. *Academy of Management Review, 20*, 63–91.

Fairclough, N. (1992). *Discourse and social change*. Cambridge: Polity Press.

Forester, J. (1989). *Planning in the face of power*. Berkeley: University of California Press.

Forester, J. (1999). *The deliberative practitioner: Encouraging participatory planning processes*. Cambridge, MA: MIT Press.

Freeman, R. E. (1984). *Strategic management: A stakeholder approach*. Boston, MA: Pitman.

Gray, B. (1989). *Collaborating: Finding common ground for multi-party problems*. San Francisco, CA: Jossey-Bass.

Gorte, R. (1993, July 16). *The Clinton Administration's Forest Plan for the Pacific Northwest* (CSRReport 93–664 ENR). Washington, D.C.: Congressional Research Service, Library of Congress.

Habermas, J. (1979). *Communication and the evolution of society* (T. McCarthy, Trans.). Boston, MA: Beacon Press.

Habermas, J. (1984). *The theory of communicative action: Vol. 1. Reason and the rationalization of society* (T. McCarthy, Trans.). Boston, MA: Beacon.

Heath, J., & Potter, A. (2004). *Nation of rebels: Why counterculture became consumer culture*. New York: Harper Business.

Heath, R. (2005). *Interorganizational collaboration: Implications for democracy in community models of communication and problem solving*. Unpublished doctoral dissertation, University of Colorado, Boulder.

Isaacs, W. (1993). Taking flight: Dialogue, collective thinking, and organizational learning. *Organizational Dynamics, 22,* 24–39.

Kelly, M. (2001). *The divine right of capital: Dethroning the corporate aristocracy*. San Francisco, CA: Berrett-Koehler.

Kerr, J. (2004). The limits of organizational democracy. *Academic Journal of Management Executive, 18,* 81–95.

Lange, J. (2003) Environmental collaboration and constituency communication. In L. Frey (Ed.), *Group communication in context* (pp. 209–234). Hillsdale, NJ: Erlbaum.

Lawler, E. (1999). Employee involvement makes a difference. *Journal for Quality & Participation, 22,* 18–20.

MacDonald, J. (2004). *Public involvement in dispersing public funds: Values, native communication theories and collaboration*. Unpublished doctoral dissertation, University of Colorado, Boulder.

MacIntyre, A. (1984). *After virtue: A study in moral theory* (2nd ed.). Notre Dame: University of Notre Dame Press.

McLagan, P., & Nel, C. (1995). *The age of participation: New governance for the workplace and the world*. San Francisco, CA: Berrett-Koehler Publishers.

Organisation for Economic Co-operation and Development. (2001). *Corporate responsibility: Private initiatives and public goals*. Retrieved June 14, 2005, from www.SourceOECD.org.

Organisation for Economic Co-operation and Development. (2004). *Corporate governance: A survey of OECD countries*. Retrieved June 14, 2005 from www.SourceOECD.org.

Pearce, W. B., & Littlejohn, S. (1999). *Moral conflicts*. Thousand Oaks, CA: Sage.

Putnam, L., & Stohl, C. (1990). Bona fide groups: A reconceptualization of groups in context. *Communication Studies, 41,* 248–265.

Reed, D. (1999). Stakeholder management theory: A critical theory perspective. *Business Ethics Quarterly, 9,* 4523–583.

Rubinstein, S., Bennett, M., & Kochan, T. (1993). The Saturn partnership: Co-management and the reinvention of the local union. In B. Kaufman & M. Kleiner (Eds.), *Employee representation: Alternatives and future directions* (pp. 339–370). Madison, WI: Industrial Relations Research Association.

Sarbanes-Oxley Act. (2002). Pub. L. No. 107–204.

Schmookler, A. (1992). *The illusion of choice: How the market economy shapes our destiny*. Albany: State University of New York Press.

Seibold, D., & Shea, B. C. (2001). Participation and decision making. In F. Jablin & L. Putnam (Eds.), *The new handbook of organizational communication* (pp. 664–703). Thousand Oaks, CA: Sage.

Thackaberry, J. A. (2004). Discursive opening and closing in organizational self study: Culture as the culprit for safety problems in wildland firefighting. *Management Communication Quarterly, 17,* 319–359.

Treviño, L. K., & Weaver, G. (2003). *Managing ethics in business organizations: Social scientific perspectives*. Stanford, CA: Stanford University Press.

Wolin, S. (1996). Fugitive democracy. In S. Benhabib (Ed.), *Democracy and difference: Contesting the boundaries of the political* (pp. 31–45). Princeton, NJ: Princeton University Press.

Young, I. (1996). Communication and the other: Beyond deliberative democracy. In S. Benhabib (Ed.), *Democracy and difference: Contesting the boundaries of the political* (pp. 120–136). Princeton, NJ: Princeton University Press.

19

Corporate and Institutional Responses to the Challenge of HIV/AIDS

The Case of South Africa

GRANT SAMKIN

STEWART LAWRENCE

A THREAT TO SUSTAINABILITY

Threats to global sustainability are increasingly evident. A glaring example today, in South Africa and much of the developing world, is that of human immunodeficiency virus (HIV) and acquired immunodeficiency syndrome (AIDS). The extent of the threat to humanity from this epidemic is apparent, for example in the barometer showing cumulative AIDS deaths in South Africa since the start of the HIV epidemic (http://www.redribbon.co.za), while at the end of 2003, the Joint United Nations Programme on HIV/AIDS estimated that 37.8 million people were living with HIV/AIDS, with the highest concentrations in the sub-Saharan continent (http://www.redribbon.co.za/home/default.asp?access_page=5825). This chapter examines the organizational and institutional responses to a major challenge to business and social sustainability in South Africa.

According to Koelble (2004, p. 71), the South Africa government has adopted an approach that involves minimal direct interference in the economy. This policy is comparable to the "third way" (Giddens, 1998)—an approach that accepts that it is no longer possible for social democrats to assume the state has the capacity to compete with market forces to provide security for all of its citizens. It appears that the government has decided that the transformation of its society cannot be achieved without the support of capital,

both international and local. Business firms have been charged with a large part of the desired societal transformation.

This chapter examines the conduct of business in the changed political and social conditions of South Africa and the possibility of transforming society through business. It is based on evidence collected through multiple research methods, including focus groups, intensive interviews, and field site visits. It tells the story of a developing consciousness and the associated business practices and accountabilities evident in postapartheid South Africa. In an interconnected global community, the problems evident in South Africa are symptomatic of more widespread challenges to global sustainability. There are shifts in consciousness that may provide new structural possibilities and accountabilities.

A general issue is that of business accountability. What are the limits to firms' accountability when the government is unable or unwilling to tackle serious threats to a sustainable society? The concept of corporate social responsibility is becoming widely accepted. But as the distinction between the firm and its "external environment" is blurred, the extent of social obligations is debatable, and subject to voluntary definition. In this chapter, the shifts in consciousness are shown to be captured in the influential report in South Africa of the Institute of Directors in Southern Africa (IODSA) King Committee on Corporate Governance for Southern Africa (Institute of Directors in Southern Africa, 2002), which insists on corporate social responsibility based on the South African concept of *Ubuntu* (humanity). The 2002 IODSA King report (referred to as King II) advised the adoption of policies and practices recommended in the Global Reporting Initiative (2002) *Sustainability Reporting Guidelines*. South African contributions to the Global Reporting Initiative are reviewed, in particular, the development of a resource document on the reporting of HIV/AIDS. Finally, the extent of reporting and practices relating to the pandemic is presented. Although there have been surveys of reporting, this chapter provides more in-depth evidence of actual practices through case studies of several organizations. The evidence suggests that, although a changing consciousness on the part of individual enterprises in South Africa is taking place, little state activity to coordinate efforts either to prevent or to treat the disease seems to be occurring.

BACKGROUND TO THE HIV/AIDS PANDEMIC

The first AIDS cases were identified in South Africa in 1985 in the cities of Johannesburg and Cape Town, with a few cases being discovered in Pretoria and Durban (Smith, 2000). In all cases, those infected were young, white, homosexual males. The profile of those infected led to the disease being perceived as a "gay disease." It was this incorrect perception that Makgoba (2001, p. 3) argues has contributed significantly to the explosion of HIV/AIDS in Africa:

> When AIDS was first wrongly linked to homosexual practice many Africans promoted the notion that homosexual practices were "unAfrican," thus sowing the seeds for denial to justify why AIDS would not be prevalent in their communities. This denial predictably became the first African public response to AIDS and swept across the continent as country after country became engulfed in the HIV/AIDS epidemic. The AIDS denial was later compounded by stigmatisation, chauvinism, the distortion of scientific information and ignorance.

The reasons for the spread of HIV/AIDS in South Africa are both numerous and complex. They have been considered by Smith (2000) and in more detail by Barnett and Whiteside (2002). In order to appreciate the complexities associated with HIV/AIDS, it is instructive to review certain factors that contribute to the spread of HIV/AIDS.

Migrant Policies

As with any environment in which social unrest exists, the apartheid period created a context for the rapid spread of HIV/AIDS. Its associated migrant labor policies contributed. Black labor was forced to migrate from their "homeland," and the absence of male role models from the nuclear family contributed to the risk of breakdown of family structure, resulting in dysfunctional families (Smith, 2000). Many men joined the ranks of migrant labor and worked for a significant portion of the year in the Gauteng province. While they are away, these men, who often live in single-sex hostels, have their sexual needs assuaged on a commercial basis by sex workers. In a study of the mining town of Carletonville, reported on by Barnett and Whiteside (2002), 60% of adolescent girls in the study area were infected with HIV/AIDS, and 50% of the women admitted to being commercial sex workers. When the men return home, sexually transmitted infections and HIV/AIDS are transmitted to their partners. It is this migration and mobility, Barnett and Whiteside (2002) explain, that creates patterns of sexual behavior and mixing that are perfect for the spread of sexually transmitted diseases.

Infrastructure

South Africa possesses a comprehensive infrastructure of main highways that link the major sea ports, Durban, Cape Town, and Richards Bay, with the industrial hub of the country—Johannesburg in the Gauteng province. From there, access to East and Central Africa is also relatively straightforward. Smith (2000) explains that these truck routes have been documented as contributing to the HIV epidemic.

Poverty and Inequitable Wealth Distribution

Extreme poverty and inequality have also contributed to the spread of HIV/AIDS (Barnett & Whiteside, 2002; Smith, 2000). Following the collapse of apartheid, the establishment of a democratically elected government, and the relaxation of certain of laws previously in place, large informal settlements, or squatter camps, developed on the periphery of major towns. In addition, the majority of the country's wealth remains in an exclusive and small number of hands, with some estimates being 10% of the population controlling 80% of the wealth. A significant number of black South Africans continue to experience homelessness, degraded neighborhoods, and unemployment. In September 2002, Statistics South Africa placed the unemployment rate at 30.5% (Kingdon & Knight, 2004, p. 199; StatsSA, 2003). A number of analysts, however, believe that the unemployment rate is higher than that published. In addition to the unemployed, a significant number of individuals are underemployed and uneducated.

Crime and Violence

Crime and gang violence is endemic in South Africa. Barnett and Whiteside (2002, p. 154) claim that rape and gang rape are potent methods of spreading HIV. They provide figures of 54,310 sexual crimes officially reported in 1998. Rape is an efficient means of HIV/AIDS transmission because of the trauma it inflicts. Barnett and Whiteside (2002, p. 153) suggest that the violence that accompanied the end of apartheid also contributed to a widespread philosophy of fatalism:

> This perception that "what will be, will be" in turn diminished individual worth, responsibility and accountability. The feeling is still prevalent and makes people live for today without valuing tomorrow. It can be summed up in a shrug of the shoulders and the response: "If AIDS kills me in five years' time, so what?" (p. 153)

IMPACT ON SOUTH AFRICAN SOCIETY

It is clear that HIV/AIDS affect South African society both in the short and long term, and this impact is likely to be significant. Some commentators (e.g., Dorrington, Bradshaw, & Budlender, 2002) consider that in South Africa the HIV/AIDS epidemic is entering its mature phase. In a worst-case scenario, with no changes in behavior and no interventions, the Actuarial Society of South Af-

rica model estimates that 6,558,628 people were infected with HIV/AIDS on July 1, 2002. For an epidemic to reach its peak, the number of new infections must slow because those who are infected are dying. Dorrington et al. (2002, p. 2) suggest that the number of new infections peaked in 1998 and has since begun to decrease (although Whiteside [2003] does not believe that HIV infections have peaked). The number of individuals dying from AIDS on an annual basis has only recently started to increase. Dorrington et al. (2002) argue that without interventions to reduce mortality, the number of deaths will peak in 2010, with one of its consequences, the number of children who are orphaned, peaking in about 2015.

A significant feature is that, of the approximately 6.5 million people living with HIV/AIDS, 6.1 million (95.1%) are in the 18–64 age group: the age group that is productive and is responsible for raising the next generation. It is the extent of the potential problem that has enabled Bell, Devarajan, and Gersbach (2003) to argue that "by killing off mainly young adults, AIDS also seriously weakens the tax base, and so reduces the resources available to meet the demands for public expenditures, including those aimed at accumulating human capital, such as education and health services not related to AIDS" (p. 9). The enormity of the social impact poses severe problems and possible new responsibilities for business.

THE SOCIAL RESPONSIBILITY OF BUSINESS

Faced with a fragmented approach by central government to tackling HIV/AIDS, private initiatives by corporations were imperative. Koelble (2004) quotes from the website of the South African Foundation (http://www.safoundation.org.za/fhome .html), whose members include the largest and most influential corporations in the country:

> The membership of the South African Foundation represents the major sectors of the South African economy. They account for a large party of employment in the formal sector, make significant contribution to tax revenue and engage in extensive social responsibility programs to the benefit of society as a whole with an emphasis on the disadvantaged. (p. 63)

The acknowledged social responsibility is reflected in influential documents produced in the South African context—the Institute of Directors in Southern Africa (1994) King I report and the King II report—and in the social reporting requirements, especially in relation to HIV/AIDS, of the Global Reporting Initiative (2003a, 2003b), both of which are discussed below.

Acceptance of Corporate Social Responsibility—The King Report

The IODSA King reports on corporate governance are very influential documents in South Africa and internationally. They were developed with input from a variety of stakeholders and acknowledge that a novel concept of corporate governance that recognizes the increasing involvement of previously excluded black citizens in business and society would be required in the new democratic South Africa. The King I report was issued in 1994, and the revised version, King II, was published in 2002. King II argues that an inclusive approach to corporate governance requires that the purpose of the company be defined and the values by which the company will carry on its daily life should be identified and communicated to all stakeholders. The report expresses in a uniquely South African way the basic purpose of corporate activities. The report includes the following words at the beginning of the section on integrated reporting:

> *Umuntu Ngumuntu Ngabantu*
> I am
>   because you are;
>   you are
>   because we are.
>
> Institute of Directors in Southern
> Africa, 2002, § 4, p. 96)

These words express the sense of the interdependence and interconnectivity of humanity. King II reflects on South African values and culture, especially that of *Ubuntu*, which means "being human," "humanness," or what it means to be human. It involves such qualities as cooperation, supportiveness, togetherness or solidarity, and interdependentness and interconnectedness. What matters most is the quality of our relationships with others. This idea of interdependence and quality of relationships is used in a corporate con-

text. What a truly human business organization would have as its purpose is articulated in the report as follows: "Corporate citizenship is the commitment of business to contribute to sustainable economic development, working with employees, their families, the local community and society at large to improve their quality of life" (p. 96).

King II recommends that every organization should take into account all threats to the health of stakeholders, including that of HIV/AIDS. It imposes a responsibility on directors of companies to ensure that they understand the economic impact of HIV/AIDS on business activities and have a strategy in place to manage the impact. Moreover, it advises that companies monitor and measure performance and report to stakeholders on the health and well-being of employees on a regular basis.

A possible criticism of King II is that is has no regulatory backing.[1] Few companies may be persuaded by its call to humanity and inclusiveness. King II itself notes (p. 117) that the corporate community had offered little by way of public accounting and reporting on its strategies and actions for combating the social and economic impacts of HIV/AIDS. Consequently, there was little evidence of measures taken to promote business sustainability in the face of HIV/AIDS. A recommended way forward was that companies report in accordance with the Global Reporting Initiative, for which South Africa has been requested to develop a resource document on reporting on HIV/AIDS.

Global Reporting Initiative

The Global Reporting Initiative (GRI) was first published in June 2000 (Global Reporting Initiative, 2002, p. 65; http://www.globalreporting.org/AboutGRI/WhatWeDo/OurHistory/OurHistory.htm). It represents an international cooperative effort to establish sustainability reporting guidelines for voluntary use by organizations worldwide. It develops ways of reporting on economic, environmental, and social dimensions of companies' activities, products, and services. In an interview for this study in June 2003, a representative of GRI in South Africa stated that the general principles of GRI are "to ultimately make social and ecological reporting as normal and in a sense as expected as financial reporting."

The mission of the GRI is to provide a framework for disclosure that will result in a new level of accountability and transparency. Among the driving forces for the development of the GRI has been the expansion of a global capital market and developments in information technology. Public demonstrations have drawn attention to problems of governance and the capacity of existing national and international institutions to govern or regulate corporate activity. There is a need for borderless governance structures to ensure that corporate activity results in environmental and social as well as economic benefits. Global standards of reporting are needed, as represented by the GRI.

Increasingly, such corporate accountability is now not just expected for multinationals but has become a broader movement for all sizes of organizations around the world. Companies of all sizes are facing new expectations from informed consumer groups for sustainability practices. The news media and other information technologies make people more aware of such issues. Financial markets are recognizing the long-term benefits of sustainability practices and placing a premium on companies with sound environmental and social strategies and policies (Spiller, 2000). New measures of "social responsibility" are emerging, and linkages between corporate sustainability practices and brand image, reputation, and future asset valuation are capturing the attention of mainstream financial markets. Sustainability reporting according to an internationally accepted framework, such as the GRI, would assist the better understanding of such linkages. The movement to harmonize financial accounting standards now encompasses the broader reporting of an integrated set of performance indicators.

The GRI is an evolving set of guidelines. The contribution of South Africa has been to develop a set of guidelines for a particular set of social performance indicators, specifically on HIV/AIDS reporting. The guidelines are as yet incomplete and not yet ready for global use. By November 2003, the pilot edition of *Reporting Guidance on HIV/AIDS: A GRI Resource Document* had been issued for public use and feedback.

The GRI's general guidelines on social reporting drew heavily on the International Labour Office (ILO) *Tripartite Declaration Concerning Multinational Enterprises and Social Policy* (http://www.ilo.org/public/english/employment/multi/tripartite/declaration.htm) and the Organisation of Economic Co-operation and Development's *Guidelines for Multinational Enterprises* (Global Reporting Initia-

tive, 2002, p. 51). More controversial than environmental disclosure, many of the social issues are nonquantifiable. This has resulted in indicators often being of a qualitative nature, dealing with measures of the organization's systems and operations, such as the existence of policies, procedures, and management practices.

And so it is with the HIV/AIDS. The guidelines take an incremental approach recognizing that organizations face different operational situations, reporting capacities, and stakeholder pressures. Thus, it is acknowledged that different amounts of disclosure will be relevant to different organizations. The guidelines provide a full and detailed suite of reporting recommendations, from very broad to very specific. The aim is to allow experimentation by reporting entities.

There are a set of basic-level indicators, and a very much more detailed decomposition of the basic indicators for those wishing to engage in full disclosure. As a representative of the Durban Chamber of Commerce said in a July 2003 interview for this study: "You have got to achieve a balance between making sure those requirements (for reporting) help that individual business in managing HIV/AIDS, and doesn't overwhelm it with just copious amounts and screeds and screeds of reports that never ever get put into action, and never result in anything." Several interviewees expressed similar views concerning the amount of detail required. A common view was that level one, the barest qualitative information about the existence of relevant policies and practices, is the most valuable. A financial analyst and adviser to GRI said, "One approach I did like is the incremental approach, saying. Well, here's the first stage. A company should start somewhere; just go through the first basic-level indicators" (July 2003 interview).

The basic-level indicators provide a starting point for those entities reporting for the first time, or low-capacity organizations. Other than requiring entities to estimate costs associated with their various HIV/AIDS programs, the basic-level indicators require no quantitative information. Organizations are asked if they have explicit policies and strategic plans to manage HIV/AIDS, and whether such policies have been developed with the relevant stakeholder groups. Does the company know its prevalence rate, and does it have awareness/education and training programs? Does the organization have programs to assist workforce members who have AIDS? Does the organization provide antiretrovirals to HIV-positive employees, or those who have AIDS?

Introducing these basic-level indicators recognized that the incremental approach needed a low base from which to commence. The more detailed performance indicators were developed in a multi-stakeholder process to ensure that disclosure across the entire spectrum of public interest occurred, from financial to social concerns. Within each recommended disclosure are a further number (between 2 and 10) of detailed instructions and specific indicators that companies wishing to comply with full reporting requirements should consider and report on. For example, under measuring, monitoring, and evaluation, firms are requested to indicate current and projected future HIV/AIDS prevalence and incidence rates among relevant populations, current HIV/AIDS-associated costs and losses to the organization, and total assumed future HIV/AIDS-associated costs/losses. Such analysis and reporting requires factual evidence and skills beyond those of traditionally trained accountants.

The extreme challenge of HIV/AIDS means no uniform solution is possible. Disclosure requirements being developed recognize that organizations face different operational situations, reporting capacities, and stakeholder pressures. It is acknowledged that different amounts of disclosure will be relevant to different organizations. The guidelines provide a full and detailed suite of reporting recommendations, from very broad to very specific. The aim is to allow experimentation by reporting entities and to encourage a phased approach to reporting for those organizations that do not have the capacity to implement the full disclosure guidelines. The extent of corporate reporting has been a subject of interest to public accountants as well as academic researchers. Some information is available about the reporting practices of major corporations, as indicated in the following section.

THE CORPORATE RESPONSE— EVIDENCE OF PRACTICE AND REPORTING

A 2001 KPMG survey of sustainability reporting in South Africa indicated that 57% of the top companies report to some extent on sustainability issues. However, HIV/AIDS is one of the issues least reported (across all sectors, an average of 32% of companies mention HIV/AIDS in their annual reports). There are companies that have reported in accordance with the full GRI requirements. Anglo Gold, a subsidiary of Anglo American, is one of the few companies that does so. It reports a prevalence rate of 30% among its South African workforce. It calculates, based on (different) actuarial estimates, that by 2009 the expenses associated with HIV/AIDS would amount to between 8% and 17% of the payroll. Anglo Gold's 2003 budget for a workplace and community intervention program was US$2.6 million, which equates to US$58 per employee. The company offers antiretroviral drugs to infected employees and their immediate families. The cost of highly active antiretroviral drugs is reported as US$244 per patient per month (US$2,928 per year). The company reports that there were 410 patients in 2002, and this number was expected to rise to 820 by December 2003 (DeYoung, 2003, p. 2).

Anglo Gold is an exception rather than the norm. Our interviewees had mixed responses to full reporting, but the vast majority indicated that the detail of reporting required was possibly too revealing for external reporting, although useful for internal management purposes. There is evidence of internal managerial and workforce changes. A survey by Bendell (2003) found wide variations in corporate policies and programs and the extent of coverage provided to employees and their dependents. According to his results, most companies do not consider how their normal operations and strategies affect poverty, and thus HIV/AIDS. This is despite the United Nations General Assembly Declaration of Commitment on HIV/AIDS, which emphasizes the importance of poverty and unsustainable development for the spread and impact of HIV/AIDS. He concludes that the limited scope and scale of corporate action on HIV/AIDS suggest a lack of wholesale and comprehensive engagement on this matter by even the largest companies, and even in the most affected areas, such as South Africa.

To find evidence of the extent of actual practices, several firms were visited in Kwa-Zulu-Natal, the part of South Africa with the highest prevalence rates, and findings are reported below. We visited three organizations, with differing ownership structures: a wholly owned subsidiary, a joint venture with an overseas company, and a locally owned company operating in Durban.

Case 1—A Wholly Owned Subsidiary

The first company visited was a wholly owned subsidiary of a major international company. It did not report fully, but used information on HIV/AIDS internally to provide educational and medical support to employees and their families.

M Ltd. was incorporated in 1967 and is located near the Indian sector of Chatsworth, Durban. It is involved primarily in the forestry, paper, and packaging industries and operates through a number of divisions. It is a major South African and global supplier of paper products. Approximately one-third of this output is exported, mainly to customers in Australasia, South America, India, Europe, and Africa.

M Ltd. has approximately 1,100 employees. Most of the unskilled jobs are contracted out, and there are currently approximately 500 permanent contractors on site. The nurse at M Ltd. indicated that when prevalence testing was first conducted among employees, the company had a voluntary participation of approximately 80% and a low prevalence rate of 4.5%. A slightly higher rate was found among independent contractors. When the tests were repeated two years later, the rate was slightly above 5%. From this, the company was able to estimate that they have approximately 60 HIV-positive employees. This relatively low incidence rate probably reflects the close familial ties of the Indian community and strict supervision of younger people. Currently, 22 employees are on treatment. M Ltd. has a sophisticated education and training clinic with full-time medical staff, which has been running on site for approximately 16 years.

There is an extensive education program that includes HIV-positive individuals talking at the company and an annual drive to highlight HIV/AIDS. Local celebrities are also used to talk directly to the staff. On the day of our visit, Naveen Singh, a presenter at East Coast Radio, was touring the plant encouraging staff to be tested for HIV. It was noted that several members of the groups were already sporting their "I know my status" badges. The previous week, the former world boxing champion Baby Jake Matlala had been on site. When reporting on this visit in *The Natal Mercury*, Leeman (2004) quoted the CEO as saying, "Knowing your status means that steps can be taken to ensure the best quality of life pos-

sible. We are offering free counselling and testing to all employees and their families. Access to treatment, education programs and support groups will also be provided." Regular visits by an Industrial Theatre group that makes use of humor and everyday experiences aims to educate through entertainment.

The message is simple: HIV/AIDS is a personal responsibility. This is in line with the government's approach, which emphasizes individual responsibility rather than collective action.

Case 2—Partly Owned Joint Venture

The second company (BA) visited was a joint venture with an overseas company. The South African company did not report externally in accordance with the GRI guidelines. They did not have an accounting system that could identify HIV/AIDS-related costs, even direct costs. Privacy of those coming forward for testing and treatment is a major consideration in their data gathering and reporting procedures.

BA is a member of a group of companies that operates from premises situated in Pinetown, 15 kilometers from the east coast city of Durban. It is a joint venture between a local company and an American company, the largest producer worldwide of paper machine clothing and engineered industrial fabrics. In South Africa, BA consists of a paper machine clothing division that manufactures forming fabrics, dryer fabrics, shrink covers for drums, deckers, and filter segments, and an industrial products division that manufactures filter fabrics and bags for dry filtration, wet filtration, accessories and woven substrates for conveyor belting, and needle-punched automotive and filtration felt.

The Durban manufacturing unit employs 251 people (the group has approximately 650 employees). Like other parts of the textile industry, the group has faced heavy competition since deregulation and removal of protective tariffs for local manufacturers. However, it operates within a very specialized part of textiles and employs relatively skilled people earning 40% above industry average wages.

The group has a proactive stance regarding HIV/AIDS, employing a nursing sister and an occupational nurse between 7:00 A.M. and 4:30 P.M. each workday. The nursing sister is licensed to dispense a restricted list of medications. There is also a wellness program, which includes the provision of vitamins and supplements, and a pathway for the various levels of medication for those testing positive. Because of privacy, the nurse could not reveal to us, or to the management, exactly how many people were on medication for HIV/AIDS. The nursing sister and management were aware that few employees had taken up the offers for testing. Despite encouragement from management and the trade unions, fewer than 20 people had volunteered for voluntary counseling and testing (VCT). The operations manager felt that the main reason was mistrust. The workers could not accept that management would not discriminate against those testing positive or that their status would not be made known within the community. The nursing sister had more personal explanations, such as embarrassment at admitting what she called "shenanigans" that went on between workers in the factory, especially those on the night shift.

There are many reasons for refusing to be tested, and the operations manager suspected basic human denial and not wanting to know. He estimated there may be 20 or so employees who may be positive but had not come forward for testing. He explained why HIV/AIDS was not especially problematic for this company, at least so far. The records from the time and attendance system linked to payroll indicated that absenteeism had been stable for a long period at between 2.5% and 3%. In March, it had risen to 3.5%, but investigations revealed that was due to a seasonal factor rather than HIV/AIDS. The manager was aware that the company was losing people to AIDS, but as he said in an August 2004 interview, "We are losing people, but we had to downscale. We were carrying too many people, in the industry, and in our firm. So the impact has not been felt yet."

Also, under the government's *Skills Development Act, No. 97 of 1998*, the company had taken on "learners," that is, long-term unemployed people for upskilling. Through appropriate training, the company had been able to replace people with the trainees. Out of eight learners taken on, seven had been given full-time employment. However, the nursing sister expressed concern about the potential of these long-term unemployed individuals providing a potential new source of HIV/AIDS infections. In spite of these concerns, the introduction of learners and the multiskilling of

employees were important in finding cover for absentees.

Although prevalence rates were suspected to be higher than at M Ltd., the management at BA was still not experiencing major production problems. There was evidence of a proactive health policy for their employees and support for those testing HIV positive. The trade union representatives were aware and appreciative of management's desire for more staff to be tested.

Case 3—Locally Owned

The third company (R) visited is a family-owned and controlled firm. It did not report on HIV/AIDS externally but was very proactive in use of information inside the firm. It operates a website, disclosed detailed information on the ethnic makeup of workers and management, and reported on its efforts to assist historically disadvantaged individuals belonging to ethnic groups identified by the African National Congress government as being disadvantaged under the previous apartheid regime.

The company employs 48 designers, 36 sales and service staff, and 460 production staff. It is now in the hands of the third generation of the family. The firm has joint managing directors who are both committed to employment equity and occupational health. This commitment was evidenced through discussions and providing access to all public documents and any staff member chosen.

R has an affirmative action and equity policy, with a commitment to develop those people excluded from the mainstream of economic activity. By uplifting and empowering the 270 historically disadvantaged individuals in its employ, the management sees a ripple effect to members in the community as each employed individual supports an extended family. It monitors the progress of individuals and responds to personal social requirements. The company aims to provide specific opportunities, especially for black employees, to develop skills they may be lacking. The overall racial profile of the company is 34% Black, 3% Colored, 42% Indian, and 21% White.[2] Attempts to employ more black people in the design department have been hampered by a lack of available skilled individuals. To overcome this lack of qualified black designers, the company has selected a number of black employees to put through an intensive in-house training program. The company has sent some to other countries to visit and tour similar production facilities and to get a better understanding of production processes, including England, Turkey, Russia, Poland, United States, Dubai, and Saudi Arabia. From these visits, new ideas for improving production at R have resulted. The management profile is 15% Black, 65% Indian and Colored, and 20% White. In accordance with a staff suggestion, the company is investigating the establishment of a student exchange program with companies in the United Kingdom (where the company has a sales facility) and in Turkey (where the company has a production facility). The company has, since the beginning of 2004, begun to implement a black economic empowerment policy to attempt to reach the targets in the government's Balanced Scorecard. This scorecard measures three core elements of black economic empowerment (BEE). These are:

- Direct empowerment through ownership and control of enterprises and assets
- Human resource development and employment equity
- Indirect empowerment through preferential procurement and enterprise development (Department of Trade and Industry, 2003, p. 14 [http://www.thedti.gov.za/bee/complete.pdf])

The scorecard achieves two main purposes. First, it facilitates the process of setting measurable targets for BEE, and second, it enables government departments, state-owned enterprises, and other public agencies to align their own procurement practices and individual BEE strategies.

According to the company's policy statement: "There is no restriction on the Skills Development Budget from Management." In terms of procurement, the company already lists the black-owned and black-empowered companies from which it receives services and supplies. It is close to the targets in the government's BEE scorecard.

HIV/AIDS has had an impact on the firm. In attempting to explain the difficulties facing the firm, the operations manager, in an August 2004 interview, attempted to articulate the issues facing him on a daily basis as follows:

I don't believe that as a company we understand the ramifications of the HIV/AIDS prevalence. I don't. We, as a company, are just plodding along. I am probably the closest to the absenteeism caused by it and the illnesses

that go with it which don't allow people to come to work. I am still learning to understand what is AIDS. Do I go hammer and tongs and dismiss a guy because he has not come to work, or do I take a lenient approach and nurse him along because he has a life-threatening disease?

Although there are confidentiality issues surrounding HIV/AIDS and there is no compulsion for HIV-positive employees to disclose their status to their employees, the operations manager was able to estimate the number of HIV/AIDS deaths that has occurred in the company. This he described in his interview as follows: "Over the last two years, R has lost between 8 and 12 staff members each year to what I would term AIDS. They weren't shot, they weren't run over by a car. They were all young people and they died. For us, as a close family business, it has hit us seriously."

Unlike M, R does not employ full-time medical staff. Approximately one year ago, the company made the decision to provide medical services to their factory staff. This was part of a three-pronged initiative to improve the quality of life for its employees, by ensuring that every staff member had access to a reasonable standard of housing, reliable transport to get to work safely, and decent health care. A doctor and a nurse are employed to make regular twice-weekly visits to the company. A private clinical psychologist visits the company once a week to conduct counseling sessions as part of a VCT program.

R has encouraged employees to attend VCT, but to date only 15 employees have done so, despite requests from management and medical staff to come forward. The procedure an employee goes through is shown in figure 19.1. The reporting of prevalence rates in accordance with the GRI requirements is problematical for many firms due, in part, to low participation, meaning that any statistic quoted is potentially misleading. A statistic about the possible percentage of the workforce that is HIV positive is therefore secondary to ensuring that appropriate support structures are in place. This was confirmed by R's doctor, who thought companies should not concern themselves at this time with issues such as prevalence rates. For him, this fell into the category of distracting, as opposed to useful, information. Of more importance was the process and policies followed by the firm. In an August 2004 interview, he articulated the approach he believed firms should incorporate:

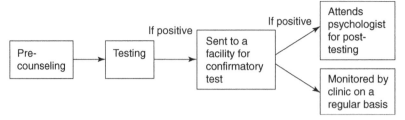

FIGURE **19.1.** Procedure for VCT attendance.

Do you have voluntary counselling and testing? Do you have a health education programme? Do you have peer educators? Are condoms available? Are you making people aware? Is there access to chronic monitoring? Are we making people aware of when there is an AIDS day or a condom week? Do you have a good ill health retirement process? Have you trained your line managers to deal with absenteeism, and production issues? Do you have a good monitoring system that looks at giving you data on who is absent, and which department is being affected? Are you following the Labour Relations Act, Employment Equity Bill in dealing with those people who have productivity and absenteeism issues? Only once you have all the above in place are you able to target the problem areas.

Interestingly enough, the structures that R's doctor believed should be considered by firms before they focused on their individual prevalence rates were the same issues the GRI focused on in its depth/quality/sustainability of HIV/AIDS program indicators (Global Reporting Initiative, 2003a, 2003b).

The doctor also believed that HIV/AIDS should not be treated differently from any other chronic disease. A normal process of diagnosis of illness followed by the well-known treatment protocols could remove the stigmatization and reluctance of people to secure appropriate treatment. State provision of medications, if available, would also encourage voluntary testing. Those tested privately could secure faster access to the state's clinical facilities and medications; the testing and diagnosis procedure itself is expensive and not readily available in the state system.

REFLECTIONS AND CONCLUSION

The issue of HIV/AIDS in the company workplace means that companies have had to rethink workplace health strategies. Virtually every interviewee was of the opinion that there needed to be more central leadership. In a July 2003 interview, the representative from the Durban Chamber of Commerce said businesses were doing "their bit" but stated his concern: "We are concerned about the perceptions of HIV/AIDS on business and foreign investment. Of particular concern is the impact that unfavorable information on prevalence rates may impact the motor industry. This may result in capital flight, a lack of new investment, and job losses."

Many explanations are possible for the inaction of the South African government toward the pandemic (Koelble, 2004, p.57). One of the legacies of apartheid has been that there is insufficient state capacity to deliver the kinds of policies the African National Congress government might wish to implement. Whether in the fields of education, housing, social, or health policy, the capacity of the state is hindered by both administrative and financial constraints. There are concerns about the ability of the state health sector to implement the distribution and oversee the use of medications even if they were to be provided free of charge.

Some commentators have suggested that the Mbeki administration has followed the advice of a powerful group of domestic financial institutions, export-oriented manufacturers, and mining companies at the expense of its traditional allies and partners in the antiapartheid movement (Koelble, 2004, p. 59). The importance of international reactions and, in particular, the flight of capital is ever present. According to Koelble (2003, p. 69), several banks, such as Morgan Chase, hold vast quantities of South African currency (US$400 billion in the case of Morgan Chase), so much that overnight they could devastate the value of the currency and adversely affect the South African economy. Yet, Bendell (2003) argues that it is the financial interests of major financial institutions that may be a source of possible assistance to corporate South Africa:

> However, one possible route forward emerges from the analysis, involving the financial community. The argument is made that HIV/AIDS may pose significant risks to current and future corporate financial performance, so that the financial community should increasingly be interested in whether the companies they invest in are attuned to that risk and managing it accordingly. Moreover, it is argued that this risk cannot be managed effectively by individual corporate action, but requires an economy-wide response. Therefore joint action from the financial community may help institutionalize corporate responses, while sensibly extending the risk management approach to include the risks to economies and societies as a whole.

Companies also are anticipating greater involvement of government in health provision. Companies (e.g., R and BA) are waiting for the government to provide antiretrovirals so that they can set in place better management systems. This is especially important for these smaller companies because they do not have the resources to provide antiretrovirals themselves. However, their employees are fortunate because the companies do provide opportunities for VCT and initial treatment. These firms have policies in place to assist employees with basic health, transport, and accommodation.

There are signs of shifts in consciousness that could provide new structural possibilities. In an interconnected global community, the problems of South Africa are symptomatic of more widespread challenges to global sustainability. The response locally provides a basis for international action. It requires a transformation in thinking on the part of the drivers of economic and social and environmental impacts—international financiers and South African businesses large and small. The GRI

provides guidelines that are voluntary. From our research in South Africa, it seems the most significant aspect of the GRI is that it raises awareness of social and ecological issues among senior management of companies. The incremental approach encourages companies to self-reflect on the policies and programs they have in place for dealing with a potential threat to their long-term sustainability. Reporting internally is the first step. External reporting need not be quantitative but could be used to inform interested stakeholders and potential investors of the preparedness of the company to tackle the problems they confront through the HIV/AIDS pandemic. The GRI guidelines allow an incremental approach, starting with self-awareness. They stand on the premise that corporations worldwide need to rethink their activities and encompass a new vision of purpose.

Corporations are the only organizations with the resources, technology, and global reach to facilitate sustainability (Cooperrider & Dutton, 1999). Companies may have to rethink their prevailing views about strategy, competition, and cooperation if the world's resources are to be sustainable. This is reflected in the Global Compact initiative of the United Nations launched in the new millennium (http://www.unglobalcompact.org/), together with other cooperative agreements in addition to the GRI, such as the Institute of Social and Ethical Accountability's Accountability 1000 (http://www.accountability.org.uk) and the International Organisation for Standardisation's ISO 14001 (http://www.iso1400.com). There is the international agreement concerning climate change: the Bonn agreement on the Kyoto protocol. The financial markets are drawing attention to the need for sustainable practices, witnessed by the U.K. FTSE4Good Index (http://www.ftse.com/Indices/FTSE4Good_Index_Series/index.jsp) and the U.S. Dow Jones Sustainability Index (http://www.sustainability-indexes.com/). In South Africa, KPMG is developing a sustainability index for rating and ranking South African companies (KPMG, 2001). International investors, it is expected, will be attracted to companies that report active social and environmental programs to enhance the well-being of their communities and employees.

It is significant that, in the study of practices concerning the corporate response to HIV/AIDS in South Africa, one of the most influential documents, King II, speaks of corporate governance in human rather than economic terms. Economic performance is important, but it is a means, not an end. There is a need for a more inclusive approach. There, the crisis represented by the HIV/AIDS disease has forced a rethinking of corporate governance. Although actions are still embryonic, a change in consciousness is evident. The inclusive philosophy of corporate governance reflected in King II is a start. The new revisioning of corporate purpose implicit in the GRI is another major influence. The Global Compact incorporates a new ethic. It is timely to suggest a rethink about the utility maximizing calculus of the self that underlies most accounting and finance models. An accounting that captures the effect on the Other, as an ethical imperative, is needed. Examples indicating progress on the path are required. Some aspects of the corporate response to a crisis in South Africa can be illuminating even though still embryonic. The hope is that international investor confidence will generate economic growth and growing prosperity for the population of South Africa. However, the hands-off approach of the government creates unequal access to health care and growing disparities between the skilled and semiskilled in full-time employment and the unemployed.

NOTES

1. Certain of the principals enunciated in King II have been incorporated into the Johannesburg Securities Exchange listing requirements.
2. The terminology used in this chapter is consistent with the terminology used to classify people in South Africa.

REFERENCES

Barnett, T., & Whiteside, A. (2002). *AIDS in the twenty-first century: Disease and globalisation.* New York: Palgrave Macmillan

Bell, C., Devarajan, S., & Gersbach, H. (2003, June). *The long-run economic cost of AIDS: Theory and an application to South Africa* (World Bank Report). Retrieved October 5, 2004, from http://www1.worldbank.org/HIV_aids/docs/BeDeGe_BP_total2.pdf.

Bendell, J. (2003). *Waking up to risk: Corporate responses to HIV/AIDS in the workplace.* Retrieved October 5, 2004, from http://www.unrisd.org/80256B3C005BCCF9/(search)/8836D5E635B2D234C1256DD6004EE8C1?Opendocument&highlight=2,bendell&fromsearch=yes&query=bendell.

Cooperrider, D. L., & Dutton, J. E. (1999). *Organizational dimensions of global change.* Thousand Oaks, CA: Sage.

Department of Trade and Industry. (2003). *South Africa's economic transformation: A strategy for broad-based black economic empowerment.* Pretoria: Author (http://www.thedti.gov.za/bee/complete.pdf).

DeYoung, P. (2003). Global health initiative—private sector intervention: Case example—using a direct service model to provide workplace prevention, care, support and treatment. Geneva: World Economic Forum (http://www.weforum.org/en/initiatives/globalhealth/Case%20Study%20Library/AngloGold).

Dorrington, R., Bradshaw, D., & Budlender, D. (2002). *HIV/AIDS profile in the provinces of South Africa—indicators for 2002.* Rondebosch: Centre for Actuarial Research, Medical Research Council, and the Actuarial Society of South Africa.

Giddens, A. (1998). *The third way: the renewal of social democracy.* London: Polity Press.

Global Reporting Initiative. (2002). *Sustainability reporting guidelines.* Amsterdam: Author.

Global Reporting Initiative. (2003a, February). *Reporting guidance on HIV/AIDS: A GRI resource document* (8th draft for public comment). Amsterdam: Author.

Global Reporting Initiative. (2003b, November). *Reporting guidance on HIV/AIDS: A GRI resource document* (Pilot edition for public use and feedback). Amsterdam: Author.

Institute of Directors in Southern Africa. (1994). *King report on corporate governance.* Johannesburg: Author.

Institute of Directors in Southern Africa. (2002). *King report on corporate governance for Southern Africa—2002.* Johannesburg: Author.

International Labour Office. (2001).Tripartite declaration of principles concerning multinational enterprises and social policy. Geneva: Author.

Joint United Nations Programme on HIV/AIDS (UNAIDS). (2004). 2004 Report on the global AIDS epidemic. Geneva: Author (http://www.redribbon.co.za/home/default.asp?access_page=5825).

Kingdon, G. G., & Knight, J. (2004). Race and the incidence of unemployment in South Africa. *Review of Development Economics, 8*(2), 198–222.

Koelble T. A. (2004). Economic policy in the post-colony: South Africa between Keynsian remedies and neoliberal pain. *New Political Economy, 9*(1), 57–78.

KPMG. (2001). *Survey of sustainability reporting in South Africa* (4th ed.). Johannesburg: Author.

Leeman, P. (2004, September 2). Baby Jake leads AIDS drive. *The Natal Mercury,* p. 1.

Makgoba, W. M. (2001). [Preface]. In R. Dorrington, D. Bourne, D. Bradshaw, R. Laubscher, & I. M. Timaeus, *The impact of HIV/AIDS on adult mortality in South Africa* [Technical report]. Tygerberg: Burden of Disease Research Unit, Medical Research Council.

Organisation for Economic Co-operation and Development. (2000). The OECD Guidelines for Multinational Enterprises. Paris: Author (http://www.oecd.org/document/28/ 0,2340,en_2649_201185_2397532_1_1_1_1,00 .html).

Skills Development Act (South Africa). (1998). No. 97.

Smith, A. (2000, June/July). HIV/AIDS in Kwa Zulu-Natal and South Africa. *AIDS Analysis Africa, 11*(1), 6–9.

Spiller, R. (2000). Ethical business and investment: A model for business and society. *Journal of Business Ethics, 27,* 149–160.

StatsSA. (2003). *Labour force survey: September 2002, statistical release PO210.* Pretoria: Statistics South Africa (http:// www.statssa.gov.za/publications/ statsdownload.asp?PPN=P0210&SCH=1498).

Whiteside, A. W. (2003, January). *Health, economic growth, and competitiveness in Africa.* Paper originally developed for the African Growth and Opportunity Act Forum (AGOA) meeting, Mauritius.

20

Business, Society, and Impacts on Indigenous Peoples

MARCUS BREEN

Indigenous peoples today stand at the crossroads of global-ization. In many ways, indigenous peoples challenge the fun-damental assumptions of globalization. They do not accept the assumption that humanity will benefit from the construc-tion of a world culture of consumerism. Indigenous peoples are acutely aware, from their own tragic experience over the past 500 years, that consumer societies grow and prosper at the expense of other peoples and the environment.

E.-I. A. Daes, *The Impact of Globalization on Indigenous Intellectual Property and Cultures*

Businesses that continue the historical goal of creating capital affect the global ecosystem. These businesses produce modes of globalization that enhance profits while having a direct impact on indigenous people who live as trustees of con-tinents, islands, and archipelagos. They are the human embodiment of ecosystems. But they are not passive subjects of globalization. Indeed, in-digenes have been demanding a dual life within and outside globalism's capital creation. They ex-pect, even demand, a share of the profits. In so doing, their actions define how corporate social responsibility (CSR) is structured as they take their place at the table to negotiate their roles in glo-bal business activity. They also demand to be left alone, drawing on the knowledge they have acquired from the practice of corporate social *irresponsibil-ity*. Having been subjected to the deepening of glo-balization and its increasingly frictionless networks of social interaction, they are caught within an in-ternational system of unfolding corporate and insti-tutional rule making (Hoogvelt, 2001, p. 125).

Indigenes—numbering up to 450 million people —are demanding new definitions of themselves as part of their identity-making rights (Pritchard, 2004). Yet they are caught in a rapidly shifting context, where the boundaries of corporate profit making combine with and compete against pub-lic policy to create the shifting sands of diffused interests. Like those shifting sands, the ethics as-sociated with indigenous people are realigning themselves. Consequently, the boundaries defin-ing how corporations treat indigenous people are in need of adjustment because corporate interests increasingly stretch over indigenous land. Indig-enous people also operate in an ethical space through their engagement in debate and dialogue that often escalates to outright warfare with a mix of corporations, governments, and institutions. If we describe this set of social interactions as the political economy of indigenous people, it can be seen as an intensified domain of multiple overlap-ping boundaries, reflecting an interdisciplinary convergence of social relations, cultural theory, and economic practice.

The range of factors incorporated into this po-litical economy is wide. Here are some examples. In Australia, Aborigines with a 60,000–year history have to contend with mining companies and gov-ernment allies making demands on their land, while profits do little to sustain the traditions of the people. In the Amazon, ancient tropical pharmaceuticals are being exploited that demand the involvement of highly skilled legal teams with knowledge of intellectual property rights (IPRs). When IPRs produce licensing revenue for indigenes, how is monetary wealth absorbed into traditional cultural life? Just east of Papua New Guinea on the island of Bougainville, indigenous people took up arms against a copper mining company, closing the mine in 1989, thereby gaining a peace agreement that includes progressive moves toward autonomy after 2004. In the Chiapas area in southern Mexico, a number of indigenous groups joined forces and conducted both military and communications warfare against their federal and state governments, with positive results. All these cases vary, and with each case, a variety of issues require engaged considerations of justice in order to responsibly study how to manage the change. The question always remains, however, change in whose interest?

TERRITORIAL STRUGGLES

The previously existing space or "home" of the indigenes, the forests and deserts, the streams and rivers of their ecosystem, becomes the territory on which struggles over CSR take place. In applying a critical perspective to these struggles, it is necessary to define the deepening erritorial spaces in which indigenes live. In so doing, CSR includes all advanced world structures and institutions that affect their ecosystem. This includes less tangible matters such as developed first-world cultures and values that are introduced by Westernized anthropologists as well as air-born pollutants brought by earth-moving equipment and factory ships to otherwise pristine environments. Home still exists, but for indigenes the struggle is to find ways to survive and work with corporations and international, regional, and national policy agencies to make CSR a reality.

It is not only corporations that need to consider responsibility. For example, the controversy following the publication in 2000 of Patrick Tierney's book *El Dorado: How Scientists and Journalists Devastated the Amazon* highlighted unethical treatment by anthropological researchers and misconduct toward Yanomami people in Venezuela and Brazil. Tierney's book serves as a humbling reminder that apparently benign researchers and scientists are engaged in reproducing a complex

system of relations that invades and corrupts the ecosystem just as much as corporate polluters. Just as corporations are included in this discussion, so are academics and researchers. The spectrum of issues reflects the interwoven public and private concerns that emerge when working with indigenes (Cantwell, Friedlander, & Tramm, 2000).[1] Indeed, indigenes do not "want to remain the object of science, they want to speak with their own voices and have their own institutions of authority," thereby establishing the integrity of their own ecosystems even as the global ecosystem incorporates them (Muecke, 1996, p. 252).

In order to make sense of CSR in the indigenous context, I suggest in this chapter the Instrumental Policy Behavior Process model, which provides a methodology for conceptualizing a set of actions that meet fundamental ethical concerns. The approach is based on the principle of a moral "duty of assistance" to help indigenes establish their dignity within their own evolving ecosystem and their relationship with deepening globalization (Rawls, 2004, as quoted in Singer 2004, p. 179). Furthermore, this approach follows the question asked by Peter Singer (2004, p. 193): "What policy will produce the best consequences?" The answer is in a set of strategic behavioral propositions that prescribe how corporations should behave toward indigenes.

MAPPING CONNECTIONS

Walter Truett Anderson (2001) suggested that the magnification of globalization is due to the speed with which international interactions take place. An appreciation of the intensity of the depth of globalization confirms the fact that the reach of capitalism can selectively access indigenes given the needs of capital to exploit them and their ecosystems. Anderson (2001, pp. 8–9) has proposed six categories in which the processes of globalization have occurred:

1. Human mobility: mass migration, population growth
2. Information technology: computation for information generation
3. Communications technology: convergence technologies that bring telephone, television, satellite, and computer communications into a worldwide network

4. Genetic information: genomics producing new vaccines, therapies, diagnoses, pesticides, crops, energy, and industries
5. Organizations: more corporations, governments, and nongovernmental organizations
6. International trade and investment: increases in technological and institutional infrastructures that facilitate continuous international integration

These elements of the global ecosystem require the creation of new macroarticulations of *reliability* and *dependability* for business. These linkages are part and parcel of a set of globalizing activities that have been features of political economy reaching back to Adam Smith, Karl Marx, and the classical economists. What differs now is that the decade of 1992–2003 saw the emergence of powerful vested interests that sought to push through trade and administrative agreements and treaties with a multilateralism (some argue a unilateralism on behalf of the United States) that had unanticipated consequences.

Characterized as "globalizing system-opening processes" by Anderson (2001), these changes have had far-reaching effects on indigenous people. They have unevenly absorbed and engaged indigenous people through a mix of trade-related protocols, agreements, and treaties such as the Declaration on the Right to Development (United Nations, 1968), the General Agreement on Tariffs and Trade (United Nations, 1947), various trade-related treaties within the World Trade Organization, (1994), the North American Free Trade Agreement (NAFTA) (between the governments of the United States, Canada, and Mexico, 1994), and free trade agreements generally. Often devised and signed at a high level by national and regional political leaders and constitutional officials, such agreements affect indigenous people most profoundly, after the fact.

This is nothing new. The processes associated with "system opening" have been underway from the earliest days of Europeanization. Take, for example, Howard Zinn's (1995) telling of the Spanish conquest of the Americas, when Pizarro, following closely on the heels of Christopher Columbus, went about massacring Aztecs because of a

> frenzy in the early capitalist states of Europe for gold, for slaves, for products of the soil, to pay the bondholders and stockholders of the expeditions, to finance the monarchical bu-

reaucracies rising in Western Europe. To spur the growth of the new money economy rising out of feudalism. . . . These were the violent beginnings of an intricate system of technology, business, politics and culture that would dominate the world for the next five centuries. (p. 12)

Given this scenario, pressure on indigenous people has been a feature of the story of expansion driven by the need to accumulate capital. This pressure is not new. However, it is more gargantuan then previously considered, which is why it can be characterized by reliability and dependability: basic features of capitalist production in a powerful supply chain. These macroarticulations are manifested by corporations that seek out precise sites for exploitation of natural resources. Sustainable or not, reliability and dependability of resources continue to work over time, as the accumulation of capital is defined by a process that grows deeper in its quest for raw products that are processed to maximize returns. Thus, the rainforests of the Amazon are logged not only because they are vast, but because they offer low-cost, readily exploitable natural resources where weak and politically unorganized indigenous people traditionally live. This kind of scenario has been historically reproduced around the planet and is now intensifying in resource-rich environments.

Corporate social responsibility in relation to indigenes is caught in the contradiction of demand from first-world consumers for raw materials embedded in indigenous territory that are part of the traditions of the circulation of indigenous social and cultural life. So Tiffany can implement a "chain of custody" for the diamonds the company buys on the world market, thereby setting an ethical standard for responsible mining and environmental behavior associated with the origination of its products (Tiffany & Co., 2004). And while the custody standard promotes social and environmental fairness, it says nothing about economic justice for Africans associated with the collection of diamonds. It also says nothing about the principle of capital accumulation based on the exploitation of natural resources owned by indigenes who see much of their dignity taken from them in the quest by corporations to harvest low-cost resources.

One solution to the creation of capital through the combined exploitation of low cost labor and raw resources is sustainability. But what is sustainability? This chapter cannot address this subject in any detail, except to say that it is a pressing matter that has been addressed by numerous authors with increasingly energy (Barry, Dunphy, & Baxter, 2004; Dobson, 1999; Josephson, 2005). Nevertheless, sustainability includes a complex set of forces that establishes the ground rules for a discussion of CSR. It can be used to address the fundamental ethical issues of corporate behavior toward indigenes whose perspective on sustaining nature through time and space is part of the "inside-nation needs" where values and ideas have a salience related to their "inside-cultural pace" (Rÿser, 2004). The question arises of how feasible it is to match surplus value with sustainability in the indigenous territory. The answer goes to the heart of contemporary capitalism but is more pressing in the indigenous context. One answer can be found in diverse definitions of capital.

THE QUESTION OF CAPITAL ASSUMPTIONS

Corporate social responsibility has to accept changing definitions of capital, which in turn are defined by new concepts of the market, goods and services, and value itself. While I am not about to open the Pandora's box of these shifting definitions, I want to work through some of the assumptions that need to be broached to help define the indigenes' capital challenge.

First among these assumptions is the fact that capital is a financially defined value. That is, western ideas of money-value dominate most definitions of capital. With the deepening of globalization, there are "two potentially opposing forces: the global marketing of goods and the global marketing of ideas. Indigenous peoples are rich in ideas and stories; it has always been their principal form of capital" (Daes, 2004). The fundamental resource of indigenes is the intellectual capital associated with their way of life. These concepts about the survival of ideas cannot necessarily be quantified, although that is happening, for example, in places where traditional forest remedies associated with pharmaceuticals are exploited for first-world solutions to disease. When capital is defined in ways that rely on nonfinancial considerations, the idea of profit has to alter, as well.

If profit is no longer a fundamental tool for measuring capital, the foundations of surplus value and capitalism itself require reconsideration. Few tools are adequate to this task. "Situatedness" does, however, help to provide a conceptual framework whereby the unique characteristics of the impact of globalization on indigenous sites and people's can be effectively analyzed (Harvey, 1996). This term, derived from discussions about the postmodern condition, means that there are a variety of methods that can be used to comprehend the formation of contemporary capital in specific situations and thus more accurately reflect its emerging meaning and value. This includes an appreciation of "distinct forms of capitalism" manifested through different institutional arrangements, varied systems of economic organization, and mutually related business systems. Expanding tolerance for an appreciation of the "situatedness" of spatially specific formations within this organically evolving business value structure will encourage alternative forms of profit to be incorporated into the value chain (Whitley, 1999). An example of this may be delivery of health services by private corporations in return for access to traditional lands and resources. Similarly, provision of HIV/AIDS drugs could be provided in a capital-valued exercise that operates outside the profit–loss capital mentality of Western organizations—this is simply the reinvention of public good.

The second assumption relates to the suitability of capitalism when applied to indigenes. Exploitation of intellectual property and the intangibles therein are subjected to valuations from capitalist centers that reward noncapitalists with money. This in itself is an injustice, given that money has little to no value due to its irrelevance to the everyday lives of indigenes who live outside the purview of consumption. The propensity of corporations to monetize all their considerations—labor, resources, profits, productivity—limits the scope of possibilities for alternative systems of value. The incessant push to convert all corporate activities into a money value limits the range of options available for indigenes and reflects the shortage of creative thinking among corporations in responding to indigenous needs. Where the accumulation of capital is possible due to the monetization of indigenous intellectual property or natural resources, only one means of engaging in a transaction is possible—that defined by capital. The assumption that capital is suited to indigenes needs to be interrogated.

A similar form of interrogation is required to evaluate the assumption that globalization will produce benefits for indigenes. Evidence that global financial resources will flow to undeveloped people is not easy to prove. Rather, the trend is against capital redistribution taking place in an ethical way. Among the world's poorest people, the evidence is disturbing. The Scorecard on Globalization, a 20–year measure resulting from research undertaken by the Center for Economic and Policy Research (2004), based in Washington, D.C., showed a consistent drop in positive results. Commenting on economic growth, the report notes:

> The fall in economic growth rates was most pronounced [of all measured categories] and across the board for all groups or countries. The poorest group went from a per capita GDP growth rate of 1.9 percent annually in 1960–80, to a *decline* of 0.5 percent per year (1980–2000). For the middle group (which includes mostly poor countries), there was a sharp decline from an annual per capita growth rate of 3.6 percent to just less than 1 percent. Over a 20-year period, this represents the difference between doubling income per person, versus increasing it by just 21 percent. The other groups also showed substantial declines in growth rates.

While it may be too early to say what this means for indigenous peoples, there is no adequate way of measuring the impact of globalization on their unique communities, except through the economic lens of growth and development.

A fourth assumption is that capital can work through some form of CSR delivered to indigenes and the poor. Hernando De Soto (2000) has examined what makes capitalism work in capitalist societies and its continual failure in emerging and transitional ones. His research led to the conclusion that a "formal property system" that documents ownership, transactions, and value is the foundation stone for unlocking capital in poor nations (p. 47). Such an infrastructure—in effect, another form of capital developed over hundreds of years through legal processes and documentation—has to be created and mobilized before wealth can be made to work (as capital). This important and very persuasive set of insights offers another means of conceiving of a set of concrete activities that creates a "systematized body of laws" that reflect the ownership rights of indigenes (p. 164).

A variety of concerns—most important, government and state interests—have to create the flexibility in specific locales to manage the growth of legal systems of ownership. It is highly unlikely that corporations will work on this effort without acting out of self-interest. Equally, there is no guarantee that governments will equitably represent indigenes, where those same governments are frequently captured by vested interests from the corporate world. Corporations may participate in establishing such systems, but the real issue is finding a method whereby disinterested third parties can represent indigenous interests, free of preconceptions about capital formation. An approach to governance that includes a framework of global civil society as an open and democratic system of inclusion promoted by world organizations will play a major role in this reconfiguration, as I suggest further below (Hewson & Sinclair, 1999, p. 15).

Another assumption is that communications technologies will resolve the power imbalance of indigenes in their relations with contemporary capitalism. This is an extension of the assumption that capitalism will work if good people help indigenes with aid projects, in a fairytale-like scenario of all-around self-congratulatory success. There is reason to believe that the anticipated benefits of new information and communication technologies (ICTs) will produce a knowledge economy or an information society for indigenes, as proposed in first-world centers. However, this appears to not be the case, with some minor exceptions. Differentiated models of development are required, along with expectations for what can realistically be achieved through the use of ICTs (Breen, 1992).

For example, the World Summit on the Information Society (WSIS) held December 10–12, 2003, in Geneva offered a number of propositions for advancing the global development agenda through active implementation of ICTs. From the indigenous perspective, an early comment (not reflected in the final declaration) clarified the position of indigenous peoples.

> "The concerns of 370 million indigenous people are not reflected in the Summit's outcome documents," said Forum Member Mililani Trask at the press briefing, adding that not even a paragraph in the Summit's draft Declaration and Action Plan addresses the concerns of indigenous

communities. Previous paragraphs addressing specific indigenous concerns—human rights and fundamental freedoms, cultural diversity and local content, and the right of free prior informed consent on the exploitation of indigenous resources—were deleted from the Summit's outcome documents, Ms. Trask said, as had happened at previous United Nations conferences. (United Nations, 2003)

The sticking point in the final WSIS Declaration (World Summit on the Information Society, 2003) was not so much the failure to mention indigenous needs as it was the more fundamental disarticulation between indigenous rights to protect knowledge and how ICTs would redefine knowledge in an informational mode when transmitted through new technologies. As global capitalism moves deeper into indigenous territory, the disembodiment inherent in ICTs may serve only to mislead and confuse indigenous people in their efforts at comprehending capital's quest for enlargement.

A sixth, but by no means final, assumption is the belief that capitalism and democracy always work as consensual partners. This issue has been raised in the debate about the "democracy deficit" in the global capitalist enterprise ("The FP Interview," 2000). "Democracy deficit" was used by Lori Wallach to argue that the global market-opening strategies of organizations such as the World Trade Organization (WTO) took place against a backdrop of undemocratic activities premised on the unaccountability of the WTO and first-world governments that are directly involved in its policy-making activities. While this is not the place to debate the merits or otherwise of this opinion, we need to remember that corporations influence policy-making institutions in ways that create benefits primarily for the influencers, not the indigenes (Nye, 2003).

Wallach's argument is that market facilitation was enforced by the strong and their representative agencies, especially the WTO, the Organization for Economic Co-operation and Development, the International Monetary Fund, and the World Bank. Weak or ill-prepared nations operate in something of an enclosure of interests, where public interest has been constrained by market interests, which dominate the policy-making process. In summary, the argument suggests that a global commitment to corporate market opening is aligned with the unrepresentative national political interests of the world's most developed nations in the current phase of capitalist expansion within globalization.

The belief that a change in the decision-making and participatory processes must occur was given salience at the WTO Doha Round of ministerial negotiations held in Cancun, Mexico, in September 2003. Leading up to this event, various groups of developing world nations—in some cases least developed nations or developing nations with large indigenous populations such as Brazil—established coalitions aimed at creating strategies to defend their emerging economies. Seeking "special and differential treatment" for national development goals, these nations rejected claims for "effective market access to all members" and demanded "due regard" for their export interests (World Trade Organization, 2003). At Cancun, these same nations refused to sign the Ministerial Declaration that imposed demands on their often nascent economies. While indigenous people were not a feature of these meetings, national ministerial representatives carried their interests and, as such, pushed back against the democracy deficit.

INSTRUMENTAL POLICY BEHAVIOR PROCESS

Given the state of CSR *apropos* indigenous people, a model needs to be built that describes the historical and emerging situation and what ought to be achieved. The proposed model is the Instrumental Policy Behavior Process (IPBP), which encapsulates the eight R's of indigenous life, described below. The eight R's provide the descriptive foundations on which to build a more substantive theory of possibilities for CSR, based on the principle of linking transnational corporations with global institutions and systems of production (Bove, 1996).

The IPBP is instrumental because it establishes a direct, causal relationship between corporate behavior, attitudes, and values and indigenous people. It is instrumental because it insists on policy action in cases where there is either (a) an absence of CSR or (b) unethical behavior touted as CSR. In both cases, the result produces public policy responses that are intended to achieve more than the amelioration of corporate excesses (Breen, in press). Clearly, corporations can be engaged in CSR through their internal governance processes, as well as by proactively creating and supporting public policy making that benefits them. Alternatively, they can be subjected to prescriptive public policy injunctions due to their failure to meet acceptable ethical standards in their treatment of indigenes. There is really no clear entry point, as we are already in history. There are, however, situated entry points depending on the context and the historical development of indigenous people's interactions with corporations and governments.

The IPBP begins with repression and moves through a series of transition phases that mobilize instrumental CSR responses. I have characterized these transition phases as the eight R's of indigenous life:

1. Repression
2. Revolt
3. Reform
4. Resource
5. Regulation
6. Review
7. Recoup
8. Reinvent

The ideal is to move indigenous peoples into the latter phases of contemporary reinvention, where they are able to consciously decide how they live and under what conditions. Such decision making will necessarily lead to change. However, it will not lead to a first-world–imagined utopia where a mystical past of pure nativization interacts with corporate and capitalist-creating institutions.

The experience of everyday life for many indigenous peoples is repression. Indeed, repression is the prevailing historical experience of indigenous people in their relation with CSR. This may take many forms, but in the limited scope of CSR, it includes the fundamentals of ethical or unethical treatment of indigenes. Defining repression includes a wide spectrum of activities. For this exercise, I include any shift in territory that affects the previously held autonomy of the indigenes. The purpose of this definition is to raise the threshold to its maximum level of tolerance, in keeping with the view within liberalism that personal/individual/collective freedom to live is a fundamental quality of the ideal existence. Threshold activities that qualify under the repression definition would range from a foreign person entering the space of the indigene to a direct invasion and takeover of sovereign land. The result is a change in behavior. A company moving into a wilderness area where Aboriginal people have lived since time immemorial and refusing to respect the heritage and meaning of the land is a form of repression. Shooting, poisoning, relocating, or denying the people an opportunity to learn how to express their opinion would be forms of repression.

There are two instrumental responses to repression: revolt or reform. They may or may not occur simultaneously and will end either in decimation for one side—usually the indigenes—or some type of resolution that becomes formalized as public policy reform. Revolt manifests itself as violence in keeping with revolutionary movements, ranging from all-out warfare to guerilla skirmishes and the inconvenience of everyday life for the nonindigenous repressors or those associated with them.

There are alternative responses to repression. The reform response can produce a cascading public policy effect. Within the emerging field of governance theory, the "myriad techniques and practices" of the public policy-making apparatus necessarily invoke complex relationships between states and a growing array of para-state agencies with responsibility for social and economic management, which indeed creates a cascading public policy effect (Purvis, 2002, p. 31). While I do not have the space to explore this set of institutional interactions, it is helpful to provide a contemporary example of the cascading public policy effect, within the IPBP.

Consider the protests against the construction of a liquefied natural gas pipeline by Bolivians of indigenous descent ("A Political Awakening," 2004). The largely nonviolent protests coalesced around an action group, the Confederation of Indigenous Nationalities of Ecuador (La Confederación de Nacionalidades indígenas del Ecuador [CONAIE]), which carried forward the aspirations of indigenous people in Latin America in the late 1980s and continue up to today. Their activism led to a reform movement and a model of governance that shifted from the local to the international policy-making environment. CONAIE worked through the International Labor Organization (ILO) to create a governance rule book (or convention) that established a reform climate for the treatment of indigenes in Bolivia, Colombia, Ecuador, Peru, and elsewhere.

The cascading public policy effect is evident in the way the ILO's Convention 169 committed governments to guarantee indigenous people equal rights, as well as encouraging their participation in formulating policies affecting them, respect for their institutions, customs, law and culture, and health and education: "Recognising the aspirations of these peoples to exercise control over their own institutions, ways of life and economic development and to maintain and develop their identities, languages and religions, within the framework of the States in which they live" (International Labor Organization, 1989).

These principles were then included in the constitutions of the nations where CONAIE was coordinating opposition efforts: Bolivia, Colombia, Ecuador, and Peru. Moreover, these nations included in their updated national constitutions declarations about the "pluri-ethnic" or multicultural composition of their nations. Attentive critics will note that an ILO document that was signed in 1989 has brought limited success in terms of equal rights for indigenes in the nations concerned. In fact, as recently as January 2005, armed revolt emerged in Peru when a group seeking to establish a nationalist indigenous movement modeled on the ancient Inca Empire briefly took over a remote police station (Vecchio, 2005). Despite the Shining Path and Tupac Umaru—Peruvian revolutionary groups that drew their motivation from indigenous people—the ILO declarations and constitutional reforms have yet to produce day-to-day change. Nevertheless, despite the wide variations in response to repression, the ILO initiative points to the history of political organization that indigenous people have used to appeal to supranational institutions like the ILO, thereby bringing pressure on national governments to control corporations' treatment of indigenous populations.

This example indicates how the cascading public policy effect can be orchestrated to create an environment where instrumental actions occur. Therefore, the result that ought to emerge from principled statements is reform. A key aspect of reform includes resource allocation. This is the basis for all state-based power—tax collection, rents, and their distribution among citizens—as Adam Smith noted in the eighteenth century and classical economists have argued ever since. Claims that reform instrumentally generates or redirects resources should not be taken for granted. In fact, reform may be a political, yet cynical, act of apparent goodwill, with no intention of recognizing indigenous needs (another R of indigenous life that accompanies revolt) or reform producing material benefits through

resource allocation. More commonly, lip service is given by policy makers to distributive resource mechanisms that benefit indigenes. Conversely, as noted above, private corporations and governments may also use capital and finance-based resource allocation reward mechanisms as a type of CSR when it is *not* appropriate.

Clearly then, resource allocation is a struggle. It includes political battles over sustainability between nations and peoples within nations and regions (e.g., California's claim to Colorado River water is disputed by Colorado and the five other states that make up the Colorado River Basin states—Nevada, New Mexico, Wyoming, Utah, and Arizona—as well as Mexico). National governments work within the emerging governance arrangements that are brought to bear on them by indigenous groups collaborating with transnational policy-making bodies such as the United Nations and the ILO. On the other hand, agreements to allocate taxation revenues, rainforest wood sales income, mineral and extractive industry resource returns, or intellectual property license fees to indigenes involve fraught political decisions. The capital associated with resource allocation can solve nothing for many indigenous people who require a nuanced bureaucracy and infrastructure to make the finance make sense. This means that finance may not in fact be money capital, but access to and participation by indigenes in decisions about resource allocation and everyday life. Resource allocation demands detailed attention because, if paired with informed public policy making to include financed infrastructures, it may represent genuine social and economic progress. If resources are provided in the context of social responsibility activism, the consequences can be positive. Thus, the cascading public policy effect can be seen to become operational in a contingent sense.

Once the reform and resources initiatives are in play, regulation of the relationship between the state, corporations, and indigenes becomes part of the continuing engagement. (Note that I envision a complex model of regulation for all participants in the relationship.) At this point, the institutional apparatus or infrastructure necessarily follows, whereby regulation of corporate and state interests is formalized through laws, bureaucracy, management systems, and research. The associated structural changes mark the new relationship both materially and symbolically.

As the state's structures mesh with indigenous needs, they will also link with global and regional policy-making bodies (e.g., ILO and CONAIE). Regulation becomes a management tool that controls the interactions between indigenes, corporations, the state, and global institutions. Regulation is really nothing more than the realization of the legal structures that control CSR. If governments and corporations lack commitment to indigenes, the regulations will falter and fall away, leaving CSR a mere shadow of possibilities.

An example of this type of failed reform is the San Andreas Accords, signed in 1996 between the Zapatistas and the Federal Mexican Government. This bill promoted the free development of Indian cultures, indigenous rights of access to natural resources, independent indigenous media, and unbiased courts (Mexico's Law, 1998). As I show below, this reform did little to assist the indigenous people in the Chiapas region, as much because of the entrenched problems in that area as the lack of commitment to regulate the accords on the part of the government of the day. Soon enough—in a reversal of the IPBP—revolt became official in that region of Mexico, as the reforms failed to resolve the historical repression of the indigenes through an absence of institutions and regulatory and infrastructural systems of implementation.

Once regulation is established as a process within the cascading public policy effect, review of the policies must follow. As globalization pressures and falling standards of living for the world's poorest continue to create challenges, existing and new policies will be required. Instrumentally, what follows is the opportunity for the indigenes to recoup rewards from their lands. Alternatively, indigenous people may decide not to reap financial benefits. The preservation of the frozen Alaskan oil fields is a case in point. Inuit do not need oil money, and a case can be made that gas guzzling American automobiles ultimately represent a kind of curse on indigenous life in the Arctic. Following Federal legislative changes in 2006, oil drilling is likely to happen in the Arctic National Wildlife Refuge (ANWR) in the near future. The question will be how the money capital that is considered by Washington politicians to be a reward for Inuit peoples will be allocated and for what purpose. An answer to that question characterizes the perpetual dilemma facing indigenes wherever they are plagued by the wealth of natural resources on their land.

In establishing policy settings, corporations have to negotiate with the state, global institutions, and indigenous peoples to establish governance standards in a constant review cycle. If indigenes choose not to exploit their resources, the policies will reflect that decision as clearly as decisions to exploit their resources for profit and capital creation.

As these activities take place, indigenous people may reinvent themselves. That is, they will make decisions about their changing identity, their place in the world, their lifestyles, and cultural preservation. This is the biggest challenge because it can be positively or negatively influenced by private-sector interests whose position of power allows them to choose social responsibility models to create the rules of engagement.. In fact, a key aspect of this challenge is that indigenes may have no choice to reinvent themselves, because change may be forced upon them by the unavoidable pressure of globalization.

The question at this point is multidimensional. It is about the transparency of the policy-making process, the commitment of governments to public interest obligations and regulatory responsibilities, and the ethical role supranational institutions have to enforce governance. It is also about how resources are invested in indigenous survival. The fact remains that with contemporary globalization there is little or no chance of going back to an earlier indigenous identity free of the complexities of contemporary trade and commerce.

From this vantage point the process involved in IPBP is dynamic and multifaceted. Corporate social responsibility will be played out in diverse ways, with numerous competing interests. The question is how to provoke the most positive outcomes of the process, whereby the anticipated cascading effect will produce benefits. The results are political and will be resolved in each situation depending on the equity of the participants. As Jeremy Rifkin (2004) recently argued, if the rugged individualism of the capital accumulation model of corporate America is given priority, then the model will likely collapse into revolt. If the cooperative public policy orientation of the Europeans is given priority, then, in Rifkin's view, positive social and economic outcomes will follow. Given these kinds of choices, the IPBP offers a way of understanding the policy options available to make decisions that are based on justice and human development goals.

SOME CASE STUDY OBSERVATIONS: ZAPATISTA POWER

The indigenous people have always lived in a state of war because war has been waged against them and today the war will be in their favour.
Subcomandante Marcos, 1994 Interview

It would be obscene to pretend that researchers and academics from the developed world could undertake a summary of CSR and indigenous peoples without stating that violent force and warfare play a significant role in the history of development. Revolutionary fervor emerges as an act of desperation and as the result of ideological and political education, when, among other things, even a semblance of CSR is absent. In the case of the Chiapas region of Mexico, the local movement by indigenous people to claim their dignity resulted from a long history of degradation and a commitment to organize politically on the part of a small group of educated Mexicans. The formation of the Zapatista National Liberation Army (EZLN) offers students of social movements, globalization, and corporate and state governance a view into the emerging system of indigenous mobilization within CSR models.

More precisely, the rise of the EZLN can be seen as part of a global transition to an organizational form that reflects new concepts of communication and power. Instead of traditional vertical centralized structures of power, their movement is characterized by horizontal network organizations that decenter and undercut hierarchical military authority. When the San Andreas Accords failed to curtail the degradation of indigenes in the Chiapas region, the mobilization of the EZLN followed their commitment to democratic systems of decision making. Armed and organized revolt grew out of the failure of the reforms. This was obvious to the indigenes who had been educated about the state of war in which they lived their everyday lives (Hardt & Negri, 2004, pp. 85, 89).

Perhaps there is no reason to know about the Tzotziles, Tzeltles, Choles, Tojolabales, Mames, and Zoques, the major ethnic groups of the Chiapas region. However, when organized, these groups became a force that matched their everyday experience of violence with a response that was traditional in its warlike characteristics while

reflecting new organizational and communication system practices. Peasants from these groups worked together after recognizing that despite reform rhetoric from the Mexican federal government, their rights would continue to be suppressed. In the poorest region of Mexico, they realized that the large-scale public policy initiatives—such as those identified above in ILO Convention 169, undertaken in world capitals, and promoted by national politicians—would trickle down to them far too slowly, if at all. They realized that the United Nations, the European Union, corporations, and governments could hatch plans that would do little to change their deplorable treatment. Consequently, a social movement emerged that recognized the slow-moving rational structures of administrative reform as proposed by international and national organizations. In Chiapas, failed reform was replaced with revolt.

In so doing, the Zapatista movement took indigenous issues to the forefront of international discussion. This revolutionary effort linked indigenous interests to social responsibility. It mobilized revolt in keeping with the unethical treatment of the people as described by the chief strategist and political theorist of the EZLN Subcomandante Marcos (1994): "The repression on the indigenous population has been present for many years. The indigenous people of Chiapas suffer 15,000 deaths per year that no one mourns. The great shame is that they die of curable diseases and this is denied by the Department of Health." The Zapatista movement drew attention to the limitations of a corporate focus on social responsibility and extended it to the ideological foundations of the entire social and political apparatus. Subcomandante Marcos noted: "In Mexico, the entire social system is based upon the injustice in its relations with the Indians. The worst thing that can happen to a human being is to be Indian, with all its burden of humiliation, hunger and misery."

The Zapatista movement was mobilized through the barrel of a gun, in tandem with profoundly well-argued positions on justice that were no more and no less than demands for access to Mexican citizenship and the rights to self-management, balanced with participation in Mexican society. Claims to be treated with dignity highlighted the role government plays in the delivery of social services, while reinforcing claims to resource reallocation to Chiapas from more affluent parts of Mexico. This story was publicized in

Mexico and around the globe. In a world where societies are linked through capital relations, media, and advanced technologies, abused indigenes like those in the Chiapas regioncan pressure governments to create policies that directly affect the allocation of public funds and private investment in underresourced areas. Furthermore, the lesson learned from Chiapas is that where there is a high incidence of degradation and labor exploitation, governments, acting in collaboration with corporations or by regulating them, should respond with models of social responsibility, or expect revolutionary consequences (Cleaver, 1998).[2]

Beyond the national reform and revolt focus, the Zapatista revolt attracted worldwide attention by insisting on policies that reflect the IPBP in action. The articulation of the Zapatistas' struggles to regionalization and globalization was seen in the way the Zapatistas drew attention to "multinational institutions governing global economies" (Irr, 2003, p. 238). For example, the signing of NAFTA led to the rapid devaluation of the Mexican currency (the peso) in 1994 and the commensurate "increase in international oversight of remote areas" such as the Chiapas region: this was an extension of the "pace and structure of global policing" (p. 248). In a dialectical sense, NAFTA and emerging technologies such as the Internet provided the world with an eye and an obligation to see Chiapas as a region where pressing social injustices had to be remedied. In other words, while people in Chiapas suffered from the devaluation of the peso and the prospect of being subjugated by foreign business in a free trade context, they were also connected and empowered by newly invigorated links with NAFTA partners and global media to the north.

Famously, the Internet was used by Subcomandante Marcos and his international supporters to draw attention to the issues in Chiapas and to stage the revolt with detailed statements and claims coming from the front lines. This high-tech element of the Zapatista movement affirms the internationalization of war by indigenes, where the global reach of the Internet creates links between everyday concerns such as nonexistent health treatment by national governments or faux reforms that cynically buy time for corporations or governments seeking to avoid resource allocation and the stages of development that follow the ethical demands of the IPBP. The Internet extended and amplified the eight R's of indigenous life: "We

expect a favourable reaction from Mexican society towards the reasons which give birth to this movement because they are just. You can question the method of struggle, but never its causes" (Subcommandante Marcos, 1994).

CONCLUSION

History shows that the struggle for social and economic progress throws into relief the best and worst of human nature. Capital's quest for expanding markets and access to resources incorporates all possibilities. For the world's sensitive ecosystem, the direct impact of capital production by corporations magnifies the extremes when viewed together with the lives of indigenous people. As deepening globalization is carried by corporations to every corner of the planet, the impact on indigenes grows more profound. The forces at work demand that fresh approaches to CSR be invented in keeping with the new international political economy. Some of these inventions will involve new ways of thinking both within and beyond the territory defined by capital. Meanwhile the forces at work need to be deeply informed by each situation where indigenes are affected.

As the range and variety of indigenes, their institutions, and their interests expand, corporations cannot act as free agents. Rather, they need to be included in equitable public policy-making processes with governments, nongovernmental organizations, and supranational organizations working to produce responsible governance. Failure by corporations and governments to engage in the pursuit of justice will not produce capital or even human benefits but rather revolt by indigenes in *their* pursuit of justice. From the indigenes' perspective, positive results can result by engaging with emerging public policy ideas about CSR. These ideas will grow within a broad, international public discourse, often created by indigenes themselves. The approach proposed here suggests that positive effects flow from the Instrumental Policy Behavior Process as a result of comprehending the direct relationship between the behavior of indigenous peoples in their responses to repression. The answer to the question of what policy will produce the best consequences will necessarily be multidimensional, reflecting the evolving needs, demands, and situations of indigenes everywhere.

NOTES

1. A variety of ethical concerns for anthropologists have been mapped, including uses of research results, bioethics, the role of governments and professional bodies in controlling and evaluating the results of the research, cooperation among different nations and indigenous organizations, confidentiality, subject security, effects on remote communities, informed consent, professional human rights, and public policy.

2. Chiapas has been an integral part of Mexican and global capitalism for a long, long time. The workers of Chiapas have provided the rest of Mexico and the world with agricultural exports such as lumber, coffee, and beef and their own labor power through migration north. For quite some time, they have also been providing hydroelectric power and oil, essential components of "modern" Mexican industrialization. Locally, they have labored in that most contemporary sector of postindustrial society—the tourist industry—providing the services required and coming into constant contact with people from all over the world.

REFERENCES

Anderson, W. T. (2001). *All connected now: Life in the first global civilization*. Boulder, CO: Westview Press.

A political awakening: Indigenous movements and democracy in the Andean countries. (2004, February 24). *Economist*, pp. 35–37.

Barry, J., Dunphy, R., & Baxter, B. (Eds.). (2004). *Europe, globalization and sustainable development*. London: Routledge.

Bove, P. A. (1996). Afterword: Memory and thought. In R. Wilson and W. Dissanayake (Eds.), *Global, local: Cultural production and the transnational imaginary* (pp. 372–387). Durham, NC: Duke University Press.

Breen, M. (1992). Desert dreams, media and interventions in reality: Australian aboriginal music. In R. Garofalo (Ed.), *Rockin' the boat: Mass music, mass movements* (pp. 149–170). Boston: South End Press.

Breen, M. (in press). Popular music policy making and the instrumental policy behavior process. *Popular Music*.

Cantwell, A.-M., Friedlander, E., & Tramm, M. (2000, December). Introduction, ethics and anthropology: Facing future issues in human biology, globalization and cultural property. *Annals of the New York Academy of Sciences, 925*, vii–xx.

Center for Economic and Policy Research. (2004). *The scorecard on globalization*. Retrieved October 15, 2004, from http://www.cepr.net/globalization/scorecard_on_globalization.htm.

Cleaver, H. (1998). *The Zapatistas and the electronic frontier of struggle*. Retrieved May 1, 2005, from http://www.eco.utexas.edu/faculty/Cleaver/zaps.html.

Daes, E.-I. A. (2004, May). [Lecture] *The impact of globalization on indigenous intellectual property and cultures*. Lecture presented at the Museum of Sydney, Australia. Retrieved October 15, 2004, from http://www.hreoc.gov.au/speeches/social_justice/indigenous_ip.html.

De Soto, H. (2000). *The mystery of capital: Why capitalism triumphs in the west and fails everywhere else*. New York: Basic Books.

Dobson. A. (Ed.). (1999). *Fairness and futurity: Essays on environmentalism and social justice*. New York: Oxford University Press.

The FP Interview: Lori's War. (2000). *Foreign Policy, 118*, 37–47.

Hardt, M., and Negri, A. (2004). *Multitude: War and democracy in the age of empire*. New York: Penguin.

Harvey, D. (1996). *Justice, nature and the geography of difference*. Oxford: Basil Blackwell.

Hewson, M., & Sinclair, T. (Eds.). (1999). *Approaches to global governance theory*. Albany: State University of New York.

Hoogvelt, A. (2001). *Globalization and the postcolonial world: The new political economy of development*. Baltimore, MD: Johns Hopkins University Press.

International Labor Organization. (1989). *Indigenous and tribal people's convention. Database of international labor standards, C169*. Retrieved May 1, 2005, from http://www.ilo.org/ilolex/english/convdisp1.htm.

Irr, C. (2003). All published literature is World Bank literature or the Zapatistas' storybook. In A. Kumar (Ed.), *World Bank literature*. Minneapolis: University of Minnesota Press, pp. 237–252.

Josephson, P. (2005). *Resources under regimes: Technology, environment and the state*. Cambridge, MA: Harvard University Press.

Mexico's law to solve Chiapas. (1998, March 21). *Economist*, pp. 38, 41.

Muecke, S. (1996, March). Cultural studies and anthropology. *Oceania, 66*(3), 248–259.

Nye, J. (2003). *The "democracy deficit" in the global economy: Enhancing the legitimacy and accountability of global institutions* (Triangle Papers No. 57). Washington, DC: Trilateral Commission.

Pritchard, S. (2004). Defining indigenous:

Between culture and biology. *Cultural Studies Review, 10*(2), 51–61.

Purvis, T. (2002). Regulation, governance, and the state: Reflections on the transformation of regulatory practices on late-modern democracies. In N. Sargeant & P. Swan (Eds.), *Law, regulation and governance* (pp. 28–53). Ontario: Oxford University Press.

Rifkin, J. (2004). *The European dream: How Europe's vision of the future is quietly eclipsing the American dream.* New York: Penguin Group.

Rÿser, R. (2004). Editorial. *Lukanka, Fourth World Journal.* Retrieved October 15, 2004, from http://www.cwis.org/fwj/51/lukank51.html.

Singer, P. (2004). *One world: The ethics of globalization.* New Haven, CT: Yale University Press.

Subcomandante Marcos. (1994). *Interview.* Retrieved December 12, 2004, from http://www.revolutionarydemocracy.org/rdv1n2/marcos.htm.

Tierney, P. (2000). *El Dorado: How scientists and journalists devastated the Amazon.* .New York: Norton.

Tiffany & Co. (2004). *A case study in diamonds and social responsibility.* Wharton Business School, Business Ethics, University of Pennsylvania. Retrieved December 20, 2004, from http://knowledge.wharton.upenn.edu/article/1074.cfm.

United Nations. (1947). General Agreement on Tariffs and Trade. Geneva: Author.

United Nations. (1968). *Declaration on the right to development.* Geneva: Author (http://www.unhchr.ch/html/menu3/b/74.htm).

United Nations. (2003). *Global forum adopts declaration, action program on indigenous peoples and information society, documents to be submitted to WSIS* [Press release (HR 47/17 PV1544)]. Retrieved December 12, 2005, from http://www.un.org/News/Press/docs/2003/hr4717.doc.htm.

Vecchio, R. (2005, January 2). Peru Nationalists vow to end siege. *Boston Globe* (Associated Press), p. A8.

Whitley, R. (1999). *Divergent capitalisms: The social structuring and change of business systems.* Oxford: Oxford University Press.

World Summit on the Information Society. (2003, December 8). *Shaping information societies for human needs: Civil society declaration.* Geneva: Author. Retrieved November 12, 2004, from http://www.itu.int/wsis/docs/geneva/civil-society-declaration.pdf.

World Trade Organization. (2003, 13 September). *Services negotiations* (Draft Cancun Ministerial Text, 2nd rev.). Retrieved 20 December, 2005, from http://www.wto.org/english/thewto_e/minist_e/min03_e/draft_decl_rev2_e.htm.

Zinn, H. (1995). *A people's history of the United States: 1492–present* (rev. ed.). New York: Harper Perennial.

21

Activism, Risk, and Communicational Politics

Nike and the Sweatshop Problem

GRAHAM KNIGHT

By the late 1990s, Nike, the global sportswear giant, had acquired a reputation not only for marketing success based on creative advertising and celebrity athletic endorsements but also for producing its merchandise in third-world sweatshops. This second half of Nike's reputation was due in no small measure to the efforts of a growing, transnational social movement mobilized against sweatshop labor practices, particularly in the global apparel and footwear industries. Activism against Nike and other brand-name retailers in the apparel and footwear industries is part of a larger social movement critical of the growth of corporate power, and neoliberal globalization generally, that has developed since the late 1980s. The movement against corporate globalization represents not only the emergence of a new field of social activism but also, more fundamentally, a reconfiguration of the relationship between the economic and political systems, on the one hand, and the sociocultural life-world, on the other. In light of these changes, in this chapter I examine the antisweatshop movement from the perspective of late modernity as a risk society in which social practices and processes are becoming increasingly reflexive. The chapter begins with an overview of the antisweatshop movement, and its focus on Nike in particular, in the context of both economic restructuring and the growth of new social movement activism, or what Ulrich Beck (1997) has called *subpolitics*. This is followed by a critical

assessment of the argument that social movements such as the antisweatshop movement represent a value shift in the developed, affluent countries of the global North from materialist concerns with the redistribution of economic goods to postmaterialist concerns with the ethics and aesthetics of lifestyle and identity. The theses of postmaterialism and identity politics are one-sided conceptualizations of late modernity inasmuch as they overlook the development of reflexivity, uncertainty, and risk that accompany the growth of social contingency characteristic of late modernity. This critique is used as the basis for developing an alternative analysis of the antisweatshop movement that uses the risk society thesis to explain the way that subpolitics accentuate the communicational aspects of anticorporate activism, and how this has contributed to a shift in corporate communication practices with the development of issues management strategies and the movement for corporate social responsibility (CSR).

NIKE'S SWEATSHOP PROBLEM

Although sweatshop labor conditions in third-world apparel and footwear factories started to become an object of criticism in the late 1980s and early 1990s, particularly on the part of human and labor rights activists, it was not until the mid-1990s that the issue gained substantial publicity in North America. Although the initial burst of attention was not directed specifically against Nike, by 1997 the company was at the center of the media spotlight (Greenberg & Knight, 2004). The following year, Nike's cofounder and then CEO, Phil Knight, acknowledged that the company's brand name had become "synonymous with slave wages, forced overtime, and arbitrary abuse" (Dionne, 1998) and announced "new initiatives to further improve factory working conditions worldwide and provide increased opportunities for people who manufacture Nike products" (Nike, 1998). Wage levels, forced overtime, and arbitrary abuse were only some of the problems for which Nike and its competitors in the global sportswear and casual apparel industries were being criticized. Other problems included nonpayment of wages, excessive working hours, violation of local minimum wage and working age laws, dormitory conditions for migrant workers, sexual harassment of female workers, the lack of workplace health and safety measures and worker education about workplace hazards, disregard for local environmental impacts, denial of worker rights to form independent unions and engage in collective bargaining, the lack of formal grievance procedures, and the intimidation and harassment, including dismissal, of workers for union organizing (see, e.g., Connor, 2001, 2002).

Moreover, many activists and researchers questioned whether managerial practices were as arbitrary as Knight had implied. Assertive, confrontational managerial practices are common in low-skilled, labor-intensive industries where workers are directly responsible for the rate of output and productivity depends primarily on intensifying the labor process through direct pressure to speed up production while maintaining product quality (a particular issue for prominent brand-name companies such as Nike). Rather than being exceptional, direct, high-pressure forms of managerial control are typical for the kind of labor process found in the apparel and footwear industries where gender hierarchies—female workers and male supervisors—are readily mobilized as an additional dimension of pressure and control in the form of verbal, physical, and sexual harassment. Compounding all these problems was the fact that Nike and other prominent brand-name companies in the sportswear industry had been increasingly sourcing their products from factories located in countries that had not only low-wage labor markets but also governments that were generally hostile to in-

dependent unions, unwilling or unable to enforce their own labor and environmental laws, and quick to use repressive measures to quell signs of social discontent. Nike's preference to source its production from countries with strong governments was acknowledged by the investment community as part of the company's corporate identity, an identity that was reinforced as Nike relocated production from countries such as South Korea and Thailand, not only as wage levels rose but also as democratization spread (Jardine Fleming Research as cited in Campaign for Labor Rights, 2004).

Although Nike was by no means the only object of antisweatshop criticisms and activism, it became the most prominent target, at least in the late 1990s, for four main reasons. First, many of the initial complaints, particularly about abusive management practices, came from workers in factories producing Nike products. Second, activists recognized that it was important to pick a company that was profitable and economically successful enough to be able to afford any additional costs that eliminating sweatshop working conditions would incur without significant risk to its financial viability. Third, Nike is the leading company in the global sportswear industry (based on annual revenue), and activists believed that targeting the market leader would be the best way to put pressure on the entire industry to resolve the sweatshop problem (Global Exchange, 2004).

The final reason was that Nike owed much of its market success to a business model that put a high premium on corporate identity together with a promotional strategy that integrated diverse elements of publicity and communication as key to marketing success. As part of its corporate identity and promotional strategy, Nike claimed to be a socially responsible and responsive company that championed the disadvantaged, particularly women and racial minorities, in the area of sport and physical fitness. Its CSR practices, however, had often been closely associated with its response to problems and controversies, and this created grounds for suspicion about the company's real intentions. Nike's Participate in the Lives of American Youth (PLAY), for example, was introduced in 1994 on the heels of bad publicity associated with media reports of a wave of "sneaker crimes," youths being mugged and even killed for their sports shoes (Cole, 1996; Stabile, 2000). Nike's claims to CSR provided an opportunity for antisweatshop activists to question not only the company's labor practices but also its ethical sincerity, credibility, and reliability. Nike's legitimacy was disputed on two levels: it was charged with a performance gap for failing to meet acceptable labor standards and respect workers' rights, and with a credibility gap for failing to live up to its own self-promotional claims to ethical responsibility. Activists argued that the very groups Nike championed in its consumer market, women and people of color, were those it exploited and oppressed in the workplace. Nike was painted as a hypocrite as well as a bad employer (Shaw, 1999).

THE SWEATSHOP CONTROVERSY IN CONTEXT

The growing controversy over sweatshop labor practices can be situated at the intersection of two structural changes—economic and political—that have been gaining momentum since the 1970s. On the economic level, the deindustrialization of the affluent economies of the global North has seen manufacturing—product fabrication and assembly—move to developing countries, notably in Asia. Particularly in buyer-driven commodity chains such as sportswear, where low-skilled, labor-intensive work and direct forms of managerial control are common, the relocation of production has been accompanied by a radical restructuring of corporate practices in the form of subcontracting and outsourcing (Gereffi, 1994). Transnational companies such as Nike do not own the factories in which their branded products are made. They are in this sense increasingly hollowed-out, virtual organizations. The earlier system of corporate ownership and control is being replaced by the more differentiated and complex system of export processing or triangle production. Production facilities are owned and operated by third-party manufacturers, often headquartered in South Korea, Taiwan, and Hong Kong and located in lower wage countries such as Indonesia, China, Vietnam, Mexico, and Honduras. The transnationals retain direct control over operations related to product consumption, such as styling, design, research and development, marketing, advertising, and other forms of promotional communication, where the value-added process is greatest. Their presence at the point of production is mainly in the form of buyers and quality control supervisors.

The effect of the triangle system is that product supply chains become more extended, and this intensifies cost pressures as more links in the chain result in more points at which profit is extracted. The manufacturing workforce is at the bottom of the chain where cost-cutting pressure accumulates, despite the fact that manufacturing labor costs represent only a very small proportion of the final retail price of the product. The downward pressure on wages and working conditions is reinforced on both sides of the capital–labor relation. Particularly in poorer, less developed third-world countries, workers, especially women workers, lack alternative, higher wage sources of employment; the alternatives are often agriculture or the informal sector where conditions are usually more precarious (Kabeer, 2004). In the absence of strong unions, this seriously reduces workers' bargaining power in the labor market (Mandle, 2000). On the part of the northern-based transnationals, the appeal of export processing supply chains is that they increase merchandisers' bargaining power with subcontractors over supply costs and increase their flexibility with respect to short-term fluctuations in their consumer markets. Manufacturing contractors are in often fierce competition with one another for orders from high-profile transnationals, and this adds to downward price pressure. Unpredicted increases in demand allow brand-name merchandisers to open up new supply conduits or put pressure on existing suppliers to increase production at little or no notice—hence the issue of excessive working hours. Similarly, sudden downturns in demand allow merchandisers to cancel or reduce orders at a moment's notice, which results in layoffs, shorter working hours, and lower pay. At least in the early years of the antisweatshop movement, the subcontracting system also gave Nike and other brand-name merchandisers the pretext for disavowing responsibility for sweatshop conditions because they claimed to be simply the buyers of products made in factories owned and operated by others.

On the political level, the growth of the antisweatshop movement speaks to a shift in the way social issues are formed and politicized as objects of debate, advocacy, contention, and resolution in postindustrial or postmodern society. This change is captured in the ongoing expansion of subpolitics and the concomitant emergence of new social movements. "Subpolitics" refers to a broad range of political activism and contention that originate outside the formal sphere of institutionalized party politics (parliamentarianism and interest group lobbying) but also underlie it in the sense that the substance of subpolitics usually bears on the concerns, values, and interests of the sociocultural life-world. Subpolitics is very much the field of what has been termed "life politics" (Giddens, 1991) and "lifestyle politics" (Bennett, 1998). It is oriented to the way that everyday life is problematized and politicized as the interests and contradictions of the private sphere are transformed into a topic for public debate, decisionmaking, and action. Given what Habermas (1984) has called the increasing "colonization" of the sociocultural life-world by the political and economic systems, this means that the contents of subpolitics often concern the issues and problems people face as clients of the state and consumers in the marketplace. Antisweatshop activism is in many ways paradigmatic of this focus inasmuch as it is oriented tactically to what Micheletti (2004) calls *political consumerism.*

Social movements are the principal actors in the field of subpolitics, and institutional power centers, the large corporation and the state, are the principal focus of contention and challenge. While the field of subpolitics has a long history, it has taken on an increasing social and cultural prominence over the past 30 years since the late 1970s, particularly in the global North as the relationship between older social movements, notably the labor movement, and institutional party politics has begun to erode. The weakening of the labor movement and the rightward shift of social democratic political parties have opened up a space for new social movements such as the peace and environmental movements, second- and third-wave feminism, the movement for sexuality rights, movements for equality and autonomy on the part of ethnic and racial minorities, and the anticorporate/antiglobalization movement. These new movements are distinctive in two senses. First, they are movements that are concerned more with rights relating to social autonomy, self-determination, social participation, and social identity than with the redistribution of material social goods or social and legal emancipation from arbitrary state oppression. Following Foucault (1982), the history of modern society can be seen schematically in terms of three types of struggle—against domination, exploitation, and subjectification—that correspond broadly to three generations of rights (Hernandez-Truyol & Gleason, 2002). Although

the three types of struggle and rights often overlap and intermix in specific, concrete situations, one type tends to predominate as the focal point of social movement ideology and activism. The struggle against domination involves claims to political and civil rights to protect individuals from arbitrary state power. Struggles against exploitation invoke second-generation social and economic rights to material protection and security to counter the precariousness of the labor market. The development of new social movements in the later part of the twentieth century marks a shift to struggles against subjectification—"the submission of subjectivity" (Foucault, 1982, p. 213)—that entails third-generation cultural and personal rights to autonomy, social recognition, and equitable "participation in social life" (Fraser, 1999). Second, these are movements that often have an altruistic focus in the sense that they are oriented toward benefiting society as a whole or those other than their own members and supporters. They are movements that function in terms of value rationality rather than instrumental rationality, and this has accentuated the role that ethical claims making plays in the construction of collective movement identities and collective action frame as well as in the frame alignment process (Benford & Snow, 2000; Melucci, 1996).

In sociological terms, these diverse movements represent a broader redefinition of social cleavages and conflicts in terms of status group as well as class inequalities. For this reason, new social movements have often been defined in terms of contention over symbolic rather than material social goods. The forms of political activism in which they engage have been represented as a *postmaterialist* politics or a *politics of recognition* that departs from the older, openly materialist *politics of redistribution* in which the labor movement and other class-determined movements engaged (Bennett, 2004). The concepts of postmaterialism and recognition politics imply the evolution of a new type of modernity in which (sub)politics is increasingly oriented to cultural and ethical values resulting from the growing individualization of social life. Social action and social relations are detraditionalized and opened up to conscious decision making and choice rather than left to custom and convention. Invoking and following tradition becomes just one more way of making choices and decisions. For new social movements, this represents a change not only of focus and direction but also of structure. The pluralization of problems and issues around which postmaterialism and recognition politics coalesce has meant that the centralized, bureaucratic model of organization and activism adopted by the labor movement has been replaced by a more fluid, network model of affiliation and coordination (Castells, 1997). In this respect, new social movements tend to mirror the same processes of organizational decentralization, flexibility, and virtualization characteristic of the hollowed-out transnational corporation.

The theses of postmaterialism and identity/recognition politics have not gone without criticism (see, e.g., Barker & Dale, 1998). In the case of the antisweatshop movement, in particular, activism is motivated by and oriented to decidedly materialist values inasmuch as the goal of the movement is to improve the working conditions, self-organizing capacity, and remuneration of workers in developing countries. This is not to deny that much of the movement's activist focus is directed at northern consumers, both individual and institutional, and that participation in the movement has a strong ethical dimension. With the exception of the union movement, the different segments of the antisweatshop movement—local citizens groups, faith communities, established nongovernmental organizations (NGOs) and international NGOs such as Oxfam, and campus-based student groups—do not have a strong material self-interest at stake in their struggle. If anything, they may stand to lose in this respect insofar as the costs of improving the work lives and life chances of third-world workers may result in higher costs for brand-name consumer goods. But the motives of antisweatshop activists and the means of antisweatshop activism do not detract from the fact that the movement's goal is the same as that of other labor struggles, the material well-being of workers. The antisweatshop movement is a continuation of the moral politics of the nineteenth century when, for example, the movements against slavery and cruelty to children attracted primarily conscience constituents whose energies were mobilized to serve the interests of others. Nor is this kind of collective altruism and the focus on the ethical mobilization of consumer pressure new to the struggle against sweatshops. In an article aptly titled "The Morals of Shopping" published in 1900, John Graham Brooks made it clear that "(t)o buy products made by labourers working in unwholesome surround-ings is to help perpetuate those evil conditions" (p. 401).

The antisweatshop movement is a hybrid, part old social movement oriented to materialist issues of socioeconomic security and precariousness that reflect the class relations of production, part new social movement concerned with postmaterialist questions of social justice related to identity, social recognition, and the sphere of consumption. It is a movement that ethicizes the status relations of consumption in one context as leverage to serve material class interests in another. The relationship between its members and supporters in the global North and its intended beneficiaries in the South is better characterized as a politics of identification rather than identity, a recognition of the rights and conditions of a social other rather than the social self (Maffesoli, 1996). Identity politics is directed primarily to creating distinctions as the basis for claims to loyalties, status, and/or rights. The promotional practices of brand-name merchandisers are a form of identity politics. Their goal is to distinguish products in terms of symbolic values and motivate interest and attachment on the basis of those values. Recognition and valorization are at the heart of corporate promotionalism (O'Neill, 1999). Identity politics presupposes individualization inasmuch as they offer a means to streamline complexity and simplify choices and decisions. The politics of identification, on the other hand, are more fluid, transitional, and contingent (Maffesoli, 1996). They are concerned with traversing differences and distinctions without collapsing or effacing them. What the politics of identification presupposes is the possibility of being able to see a part of oneself in someone else who is otherwise quite different. This possibility is realized in the way that societal ethics and personal emotions become fused and mutually referential. This is especially critical for any movement in which the material self-interest of members does not play a significant role.

The economics of triangle or export processing manufacturing and the subpolitics of new social movements intersect in the growing importance of communication in the public sphere as the means by which economic value is realized and accumulated, on the one hand, and institutional power is challenged and disputed, on the other. Brand-name merchandisers such as Nike depend on a broad array of promotional communication —logoed product design, advertising, marketing, celebrity endorsements, philanthropic initiatives, company reports, press releases, public relations statements, corporate architecture, and other forms of "corporate writing" (Boje, 2000)—to sell what are essentially parity products in a saturated, competitive marketplace. It is in communication of one form or another that Nike invests most heavily. Similarly, for the antisweatshop movement, communication constitutes the core of its activity. Internally, the network structure of the movement means that communication is essential to ensure the distribution of information and co-ordination of messages and actions. As Bennett (2003, 2004) has argued, the Internet and electronic communication have had a major impact on new social movements not only in the sense that they are relatively cheap and instantaneous, but also because they have become critical to the reproduction of networked structures whose organization and functioning are looser, more decentralized, and more contingent. Externally, all aspects of the framing process—diagnosing the problem, defining and arguing for solutions, encouraging support, and aligning these frames to resonate with news media agendas and public opinion in an issue-competitive environment—rely heavily on a range of communicational practices and media.

COMMUNICATIONAL POLITICS AND THE RISK SOCIETY

The postmaterialism and identity recognition theses shed light on only one side of antisweatshop activism because they only capture one side of the structural and semantic changes occurring in modern society. Modernization entails an accelerating process of social differentiation affecting meanings and identities on all levels of social organization. The effect of this is twofold. First, by extending the chain along which the consequences of social action ramify, differentiation opens up and expands the field of contingency. Courses of action are opened up to individualized choice and decision making as the necessity of tradition or convention is weakened. Increasingly individualized life-worlds with their own semantics become more common. This is the side of modernization that gives rise to postmaterialism and identity politics. Second, greater differentiation also increases social complexity by making social pro-

cesses increasingly reflexive; processes begin to apply to themselves before reaching what would otherwise be their terminus (Beck, 1997; Luhmann, 1995). From a systems frame of reference, reflexivity helps to stabilize social processes by doubling the reproduction of system reality (Luhmann, 1995). From an action frame of reference, however, reflexivity feeds the expansion of contingency and complicates the determination of courses of action in the form of latent side effects that may manifest as problems elsewhere or later on. Contingency introduces not only the possibility of individual choice and decision making into social action but also greater risk as the reflexive growth of possibilities increases uncertainty, insecurity, and doubt. The risk society and reflexive modernity are the obverse of postmaterialism and postmodernism.

The development of the risk society has depended not only on structural changes that have intensified the production of problematic side effects but also on ideological changes represented by the growing hegemony of neoliberalism. Economically and politically, neoliberalism has contributed to the weakening of the principal institutional apparatuses of social security and protection, Fordism, and the Keynesian welfare state.[1] As a system of regulating labor relations, Fordism is being increasingly replaced by more flexible, decentralized, and contingent modes of labor market and workplace organization, of which the triangle or export processing model is one example. Similarly, at the political level, the dismantling of Keynesian demand management policies and the assault on the benefits and entitlements of the welfare state have reintroduced dimensions of risk and uncertainty into the distribution of social goods and life chances. As Beck (1997) has argued, the distribution of "bads" has replaced the distribution of "goods" as the focus of political contention, and avoiding or reducing risk has become a dominant social rationality.

The risk society thesis has a number of implications for understanding the sweatshop controversy. First, as Beck (1997) points out, the risk society dispels the logic of exclusionary binary choices that characterized earlier forms of modernity. Risk society is a society of both/and rather than either/or possibilities. Sweatshop labor practices do not cease being an economic solution once they are defined as a social and ethical problem. The two sides coexist in negotiation with one another, and this makes the problematic character of sweatshops doubly complex. In the field of sub-politics, the materialist as well as postmaterialist dimensions of new social movements such as the antisweatshop movement are able to coexist without necessarily contradicting one another or without one dimension taking permanent precedence over the other. The values of social security and social justice are both involved in new social movement struggles, and while these values are interrelated, neither is reducible to the other. Second, the risk society accentuates the communicational character of politics inasmuch as concern with risk and the distribution of "bads" focuses attention away from credit claiming and onto the management—avoidance, deflection, and displacement—of blame as the critical issue in political relations (Pierson, 1994). Blame management not only requires greater communicational energies and resources than credit claiming, but also changes the structure of political semantics. Blame is more overtly normative than credit inasmuch as it implies harm or adversity of some kind, and this speaks to political relations that are antagonistic rather than simply competitive. Blaming plays a critical role in social movement framing by concretizing the attribution of causal or remedial responsibility for a given problem in an ethically resonant and publicly relevant way. As the antisweatshop movement's preoccupation with Nike demonstrates, blaming allows grievances to be concentrated and communicated more effectively and consistently. Subpolitics require enemies.

Third, risk makes politics communicational because risk is a simulation or virtual object rather than a real one. Risk is an extrapolation from current conditions and tendencies to future possibilities; it is a concept without an extant concrete referent. The social ontology of risk consists in the media used to measure, assess, and communicate it as a possibility marked by uncertainty (Ericson & Doyle, 2003). Risk is a conceptual tool that otherwise resource-poor social movements can use to confront powerful opponents such as governments or transnational corporations by publicly challenging the legitimacy of their performance and credibility. Questioning the legitimacy of institutional power centers introduces uncertainty into their environments and makes the calculation of risk an important aspect of how responses to these challenges are determined. The principal means by which social movements make life riskier for the powerful is the strategic use of events. Con-

tingency puts a premium on events as the way in which risk is identified and communicated, and the generation of events is a principal resource that social movements can mobilize. In the case of antisweatshop activism, this often takes the form of discursive political consumerism in which movement-generated events are designed to draw attention to brand-name corporations as the link between labor practices in the global South and consumer practices in the global North (Micheletti, 2004). The most obvious example of this kind of communicational politics is the public protest against sweatshop conditions geared to attracting broader media attention (Sage, 1999). This kind of tactic carries its own risks, however. Demonstrations and protests often receive negative coverage as the media dwell on the disruptiveness of the event itself as opposed to the message it is intended to convey (Smith, McCarthy, McPhail, & Augustyn, 2001). In the case of antisweatshop activism, culture jamming has also become a popular way to garner public and media attention without necessarily disrupting public space in a way that creates inconvenience or negative reaction. Culture jammers use humor as a way to mock and ridicule the symbolism and hypocrisy of corporate power. In the campaign against Nike, the saga of Jonah Peretti has become the most celebrated case of culture jamming (Peretti, 2003; Micheletti, 2004). When Nike offered consumers the opportunity to customize a new pair of sneakers with a personal name, Peretti ordered his with the term *sweatshop* on them. Nike refused his order, and the ensuing e-mail exchange between Peretti and Nike rapidly circulated over the Internet, reaching an estimated audience of more than 10 million people (Peretti, 2003).

What has also become a significant dimension of the antisweatshop movement's communicational politics is the research report documenting and exposing the realities of working conditions, managerial practices, wage levels, and obstacles to unionization and collective bargaining. The antisweatshop struggle has evolved into a battle of reports, studies, surveys, and other documentary forms of evidence and argument reaffirming the extent of the problem on the part of movement activists, and disputing activist claims and/or reasserting good intentions and efforts on the part of targeted corporations. Antisweatshop activism has become evidence-centered activism in which meanings and interpretations are being constantly contested. In large measure, the struggle over meaning is intensified by the relative invisibility and dispersion of the problem from the perspective of consumers and investors in the global North where much of the activism is directed. Karl Marx's "hidden abode of production" is doubly hidden by the geographical as well as social separation of work and consumption that results from the export processing system (Marx, 1887/1967, p. 176). For northern publics, the realities of sweatshop conditions are constructed and mediated by activist networks, corporate public relations professionals, and communications media rather than directly experienced. This complex process of mediation not only opens up the space for meanings to be contested, but also makes it imperative for the protagonists to reiterate and substantiate their basic claims on a recurrent basis.

In addition to generating events, social movements also attempt to exploit relevant events and situations as they arise in order to frame the central problems being addressed. Risk plays a critical role in the framing process inasmuch as it is a means to transform episodic events into evidence of problems that are continuous and systemic rather than isolated and aberrant (Knight & Greenberg, 2003). An example of this was the 2001 strike by workers at a Nike contract factories, the Kukdong (later renamed Mexmode) facility in Atlixco, Mexico. Antisweatshop activists quickly mobilized to portray the strike as evidence that Nike was not serious in its claims about improving labor standards and respecting labor rights. Several reports about the dispute quickly appeared, confirming labor rights violations and recommending reforms (Alcalde, 2001; Korean House for International Solidarity, 2001; Verité, 2001; Worker Rights Consortium, 2001a; see also Worker Rights Consortium, 2001b). Faced with the risk of more adverse publicity, Nike eventually pressured Kukdong to recognize the workers' right to free collective bargaining.

Events become risky not only because they disrupt norms and expectations, but also because they contain the potential to confirm and amplify existing problems or set new precedents. It is this potential that activists have to make more or less explicit in order to translate events into problems, and situate self-contained occurrences in broader, ongoing processes. Transforming events into problems means defining them in crisis terms, and this is a common tactic used by social movements to register their presence on the media and public agendas. Crises are important because they imply an urgent need for remedial intervention and because they plant the seed of doubt as to the risk of recurrence and amplification (Knight & Greenberg, 2003). Risk establishes uncertainty about the future, and it is this uncertainty that acts as the basis for rationalizing the seriousness and continuity of problems beyond the lifespan of the particular events or local situation in which they come to light. Regardless of how exceptional they may be in terms of past experience, events can take on generalized significance as the harbinger of new developments once they are successfully defined in terms of recognizable hazards or threats. The success of the definitional process then becomes reflexively self-reinforcing: recognizing new risks means recognizing the risk of new risks.

When social movements use events to introduce risk and uncertainty into institutional environments, they challenge the legitimacy of power centers by altering the relationship between the two dimensions of that legitimacy: performance and credibility. Although the primary focus of the antisweatshop movement has been Nike's performance gap—the disparity between workplace standards and practices—what becomes strategically important for both Nike and the movement is the credibility gap that opens up with respect to Nike's claims. The credibility gap subsumes the performance gap as specific instances of sweatshop abuse are subsumed by the discursive construction of an ongoing, systemic problem. Sweatshop abuses take on their meaning and symbolic power in terms of the way that they reinforce the overall image of Nike as unreliable, untrustworthy, and hypocritical. The credibility gap reflects more strongly the ethical dimensions of Nike's corporate reputation than the performance gap. Nike factories may or may not be bad places to work, but for the consumer audience being targeted by northern activists, it is more important that Nike be seen as ethically suspect because it cannot be trusted to practice what it preaches. The performance gap does not cease to be important; rather, it takes on the role of serving the reproduction of the credibility gap. Further instances of sweatshop abuses come to demonstrate first and foremost that Nike is not sincere in its claims to social responsibility. The credibility gap is more damaging to Nike's reputation than the performance gap because it questions the company's ethical reliability at the level of communication, and this goes to the heart of Nike's dependence on a strategy of pro-motionalism as the basis for continued market success. The credibility gap feeds skepticism about Nike that creates uncertainty, and it is uncertainty rather than a negative image per se that is ultimately troubling to centers of institutional power. As sociological research on social stigma has long recognized, negative labeling can become self-fulfilling because it undermines trust. Once trust is thrown in doubt, it is very difficult to restore, precisely because it becomes risky to do so, particularly when those casting doubt form a loosely connected network of different actors rather than a single unified voice.

FROM PROBLEMS TO ISSUES: THE CORPORATE RESPONSE

When confronted with claims of systemic problems, corporations (and increasingly governments too) respond by attempting to transform these problems into issues, and they do this on both an institutional and communicational level. To transform a problem into an issue is to play down its problematic character while acknowledging that there is something—a topic or question—that needs to be addressed, especially discursively. Issues are problems that have been neutralized to some extent by making them into matters of common interest and concern, amenable to negotiation and reform. Turning problems into issues is a semantic process, but one that has concrete, practical implications for how the parties involved will engage in negotiation and undertake reform. The language of issues has stronger consensual connotations than the language of problems, and the effect of this is to depoliticize the focus of contention to some extent. Issues imply relations of difference rather than antagonism.

Issues management is an area of corporate communication and public relations that has grown in importance since the 1970s. Its initial growth can be seen as both a reaction to the increasing inadequacy of previous public relations practices, particularly those associated with crisis reaction, and as an aspect of the communicational politics of neoliberalism. Issues management developed out of the long established business practice of lobbying governments with respect to fiscal, legislative, and regulatory intervention. It is about influencing, if not controlling, government intervention in a way that preserves and enhances corporate interests and autonomy. The development of issues management not only has expanded corporate attempts to influence governmental decision making in light of new complexities fostered by neoliberal globalization, but also has refocused business initiatives in a more proactive way. Issues management has taken on the task of thinking about future challenges to corporate interests and autonomy in an increasingly interconnected and complex environment. It is a response to the growth of uncertainty and risk that are the side effects of structural changes designed to promote and extend corporate power.

The continuing growth of issues management is now closely tied to another development in the field of corporate communication, the movement for CSR. Although the CSR movement draws proponents from government and civil society, it is also being increasingly embraced by the corporate sector itself. Corporate social responsibility involves a reworking of traditional forms of business philanthropy and civic engagement in terms of a less overtly hierarchical and moralistic ideology. Corporate social responsibility defines itself as socially inclusive, and its stated terms of reference are the community and the environment. The language of accountability, transparency, sustainability, business ethics, corporate citizenship, and triple bottom line (social and environmental as well as financial impact) reporting permeates CSR discourse about the social role of corporate activities and corporate relations with a globalizing civil society. If issues management represents the shift in corporate lobbying practices with the growth of neoliberalism, then CSR represents the shift in corporate relations with civil society concomitant with the growth of subpolitics and social movement activism. The success of neoliberalism in restricting the interventionist role of government has created not only the space for subpolitics but also the need for the organized capital to deal directly with the social movement actors that are filling that space. The recasting of the state's role from intervener to facilitator has reduced the capacity and rationale of the state to act as a buffer between business interests and the sociocultural life-world. Business has to deal directly with social movements as well as the state, and CSR is one of the principal strategies that business is deploying in those dealings.

Neither issues management nor CSR figured in

a significant way in Nike's initial response to anti-sweatshop criticism. The initial response tended to take the traditional form of reactive crisis management, with an emphasis on denial of responsibility, evasion, blame displacement, attacking critics, and the use of internal auditing reports to counteract movement claims about the seriousness and pervasiveness of the problem. Although the company introduced its own workplace *Code of Conduct* in 1992, it did little to implement and enforce it while pointing to the code as evidence of its good intentions (Boje, 1999; Bullert, 1999). These responses only served to worsen Nike's credibility gap without addressing in a substantial way its performance gap. Perhaps because Nike had been so successful in the use of creative advertising and marketing (Goldman & Papson, 1998), it seemed slow to recognize the seriousness of the sweatshop problem and the inadequacy of its response to criticism. The situation began to change as media coverage and adverse publicity peaked in the mid to late 1990s (Bennett, 2003; Greenberg & Knight, 2004). The media strategy adopted by key elements of the antisweatshop movement, particularly the labor and human rights NGO Global Exchange, had been to cultivate relations not only with news reporters covering the sweatshop controversy but also with current affairs columnists on agenda-setting U.S. dailies such as the *New York Times* (Bullert, 1999; Shaw, 1999). Columnists play a critical role in interpreting events and issues, and they have the latitude to take ethical stances that news reporters do not normally enjoy. The strategy paid off, as Bob Herbert (see, e.g., 1996a, 1996b, 1997) of the *New York Times* wrote a series of columns in 1996 and 1997 that were openly critical of Nike. It was in this context of critical publicity that Nike began to shift its public relations response on both an institutional and communicational level.

Since the peak years of bad publicity, Nike has become involved in a number of institutional initiatives around the sweatshop issue and CSR more broadly. Its initial move was to become involved in the Apparel Industry Partnership (AIP), sponsored by the U.S. President Clinton's administration to bring major actors in the sweatshop controversy together to work out a long-term solution in the form of a voluntary code of labor conduct that apparel merchandisers would implement and oversee in their contract manufacturing operations. The AIP subsequently gave rise to the

Fair Labor Association (FLA), of which Nike was a charter member. The FLA is a voluntary monitoring and reporting organization whose affiliates include prominent apparel and footwear merchandisers as well as NGOs and Canadian and American colleges and universities that license the use of their name and logo on collegiate goods such as clothing. In addition to the FLA, Nike is also involved in the Global Compact, a United Nations initiative to mobilize corporate participation in the promotion of human, labor, and environmental rights; the Global Reporting Initiative (GRI) to develop a common set of guidelines for companies to report publicly on the "economic, environmental, and social dimensions of their activities, products, and services" (Global Reporting Initiative, 2004); and the now defunct Global Alliance for Workers and Communities, an NGO-like organization cofounded by Nike whose mission was "to improve the lives and future prospects of workers involved in global production and service supply chains" in cooperation with corporate, state, and civil society actors (Global Alliance for Workers and Communities, 2004). Nike has also undertaken its own CSR initiatives, such as the Nike Foundation, whose goal echoes one of the tenets of identity recognition politics, namely, to give "the world's most disadvantaged girls an opportunity to participate more fully in life" (Nike, 2004a).

These Nike initiatives share two major characteristics. First, they are multilateral: they involve partnerships with other organizations spanning the corporate world, the state sector, and civil society. Multilateralism is a strategy for dispersing causal and remedial responsibility for problems. While it implies that problems are systemic rather than isolated, multilateralism also offers an opportunity for blame to be managed in a collective, institutional fashion and for companies to display their commitment to problem resolution of a long-term, sustainable kind. Multilateralism is a way of sharing in the problem by sharing in its solution, and this tends to dilute the concentration of blame on any one actor. Second, these and other initiatives encompass problems in procedurally oriented methods of debate and resolution. Problems are "proceduralized" by establishing institutional mechanisms in which different actors with different interests and perspectives are brought together to discuss questions of measurement, investigation, assessment, verification, reporting, remedial alternatives, and so on. Questions of legitimacy—performance and credibility—tend to be recast in procedural rather than ethical terms. The value rationality on which the problematization of labor standards and rights was first based is gradually displaced by the procedural rationality of methodology.

Multilateralism and proceduralism institutionalize problems in the name of solutions, and the effect of this is to turn those problems into issues of semantics. Discussion, deliberation, debate—in short, talk—are the substance of issues management and much of what passes for CSR. Material problems are transformed into issues of communication, reflecting the subsumption of performance by credibility. A recent debate between Jeff Ballinger, a leading antisweatshop activist, and two Nike representatives illustrates this transformation well. In contrast to Ballinger, who was calling for such steps as better wages and the development of unions, the Nike representatives stressed their company's commitment in areas such as "reaching out to nongovernmental organizations," "assessing/getting workers' feedback," "design(ing) sensitivity training" for managers, and, in the absence of unions, developing "parallel processes so that our management would really sit down with workers and hear their needs and perspectives" (Wokutch, 2001, pp. 213, 221). For activists, the material conditions of the workplace and Nike's performance as an employer remain the central point of contention. For Nike, on the other hand, the workplace is defined, at least in the public sphere, as a postmaterialist context of issues whose relevance bears ultimately on corporate reputation and credibility.

The transformation of the sweatshop problem into a manageable issue has occurred primarily through the *Code of Conduct* as the paradigmatic instrument for specifying and monitoring labor standards and provisions. The *Code of Conduct* represents not only an institutional change in the governance of labor conditions, namely, the effective substitution of a stakeholder-centered system of voluntary monitoring and reporting for a state-centered system of binding regulation, but also a semantic change. The language of binding regulation is that of conformity and violation; the language of voluntary codes, on the other hand, is one of compliance and noncompliance. By representing instances of sweatshop conditions in terms of what the latest FLA report calls "noncompliance

issues," what is constructed semantically is not a situation of violation or transgression for which a penalty is due, but rather a situation of falling short in which an ongoing attempt to improve requires renewed effort in order to make the grade (Fair Labor Association, 2004). Voluntary codes replace rules with a test. The language of regulation draws legitimacy from the way its frame of reference is taken up with the rights of those in a position of social disadvantage or dependency. This focus on rights effectively disappears from the language of compliance. Codes are framed in terms of employer standards and requirements rather than worker rights; as even observers sympathetic to Nike have noted, the company's code eschews explicit reference to worker rights (Murphy & Mathew, 2001). The subject of every "core standard" in Nike's *Code of Conduct* is the "contractor" or "member of the supply chain," not the worker (Nike, 2004b). The language of codes specifies maximal responsibilities without reference or relation to rights. It is the language of reassurance that addresses uncertainty generated out of controversy and contention by severing the relationship between responsibilities and rights. Codes are defined in such a way that they can easily function as the elusive terminus of a continuous journey of effort, self-recognition, and commitment, rather than as a point of departure for enforcing and enhancing rights.

CONCLUSION

If issues management and CSR represent the way corporations are attempting to negotiate the contentiousness of both conventional politics and activist subpolitics, for social movements they also represent a form of risk. Social movements continue to be faced with the perennial strategic dilemma between confrontation with and distance from their opponents or engagement with them in institutional structures of conflict resolution. Both courses of action carry risks—marginalization in the first case, co-option in the second—and the looser, network form of organization and mobilization of movements such as the antisweatshop movement can be seen as a way to allow confrontation and institutional engagement to coexist to a greater extent than would be the case for more hierarchical, bureaucratic forms of organization. When Medea Benjamin of Global Exchange gave credit to Nike for efforts to improve working conditions, for example, divisions over strategy became evident and Global Exchange received strong criticism from other participants in the antisweatshop movement, but the movement itself did not collapse (Bullert, 1999).

What this incident also demonstrates is that the antisweatshop movement mirrors its corporate opponents inasmuch as its legitimacy and effectiveness also depend on the relationship between practical performance and public credibility. Global Exchange had been particularly effective in bringing public relations skills to the movement, but this had, in the view of some other activists, run the risk of making Nike per se the center of attention at the expense of the working conditions and life chances of third-world workers (Bullert, 1999, p. 14). The communicational politics that characterize global risk society exert pressure on both institutional power centers and those who challenge them to subsume practical performance under credibility and reputation. For the antisweatshop movement, this pressure generates a tension between achieving movement goals and reproducing movement identity and salience. What complicates this tension is the social and cultural separation and distance between the worlds of production and consumption that the antisweatshop movement have to traverse, and the contingent nature of the politics of identification that connect the ethical concerns of northern consumers to the material working conditions and life chances of southern workers. Just as the movement for CSR effectively occludes attention to worker rights in its attempt to put an ethical face on corporate intentions, antisweatshop activism gravitates toward the ethical concerns of affluent consumers as the focus of its communicational politics. The challenges facing the antisweatshop movement are diverse, but managing political distance—between confrontation and engagement, the interests of producers and consumers, performance and identity and credibility—remains central to all of them.

NOTE

1. Fordism refers to a system of socioeconomic regulation based on some form of corporatist settlement between the state, business organizations, and organized labor. At the level of work organization, Fordism is characterized by mass production, semi-skilled labor processes, and a regime of relatively high wages and benefits determined through institutionalized collective bargaining. Fordism's political counterpart is the Keynesian welfare state based on the state's management of macroeconomic forces through a policy of demand management. In concrete terms this meant the expansion of public sector service provision in areas such as schooling, health care, housing, and social welfare support.

REFERENCES

Alcalde, A. (2001). *Opinion presented by Arturo Alcalde Justiani regarding the case of "Kuk Dong International."* Retrieved on February 6, 2006, from http://www .laborrights.org/projects/sweatshop/ kukdong.html.

Barker, C., & Dale, G. (1998). Protest waves in western Europe: A critique of "New Social Movement" theory. *Critical Sociology, 24*(1&2), 65–104.

Beck, U. (1997). *The reinvention of politics: Rethinking modernity in the global social order* (M. Ritter, Trans.). Cambridge: Polity Press.

Benford, R. D., & Snow, D. A. (2000). Framing processes and social movements: An overview and assessment. *Annual Review of Sociology, 26*, 611–639.

Bennett, W. L. (1998). The uncivic culture: Communication, identity, and the rise of lifestyle politics. *PS: Political Science and Politics, 31*(4), 41–61.

Bennett, W. L. (2003). Communicating global activism: Strengths and vulnerabilities of networked politics. *Information, Communication & Society, 6*(2), 143–168.

Bennett, W. L. (2004). Branded political communication: Lifestyle politics, logo campaigns, and the rise of global citizenship. In M. Micheletti, A. Follesdal, & D. Stolle (Eds.), *Politics, products, and markets* (pp. 101–125). London: Transaction Publishers.

Boje, D. (1999). Is Nike Roadrunner or Wile E. Coyote? A postmodern organization analysis of double logic. *Journal of Business & Entrepreneurship, 2*, 77–109.

Boje, D. (2000). Nike corporate writing of academic, business and cultural practices. *Management Communication Quarterly, 14*(4), 507–516.

Brooks, J. G. (1900, December 22). The morals of shopping. *Woman's Journal*, p. 401.

Bullert, B. J. (1999). *Strategic public relations, sweatshops, and the making of a global movement* (The Joan Shorenstein Center on the Press, Politics and Public Policy, Working Paper Series No. 2000–14). Cambridge, MA: John F. Kennedy School of Government, Harvard University.

Campaign for Labor Rights. (2004). *Nike likes a "strong government."* Retrieved February 6, 2006, from http:// www.ksg.harvard .edu/presspol/Research_Publications/ Papers/Working_Papers/2000_14. PDF.

Castells, M. (1997). *The information age: Vol. 2. The power of identity.* Oxford: Blackwell.

Cole, C. (1996). American Jordan: P.L.A.Y., consensus and punishment. *Sociology of Sport Journal, 13,* 366–397.

Connor, T. (2001). *Still waiting for Nike to do it.* San Francisco, CA: Global Exchange.

Connor, T. (2002). *We are not machines.* Oxfam Community Aid Abroad. Retrieved February 6, 2006, from http://oxfam.org .au/campaigns/nike/report/machines/ notmachines.pdf.

Dionne, E. J. (1998, May 15). Bad for business. *Washington Post,* p. A27.

Ericson, R., & Doyle, A. (2003). Risk and morality. In R. Ericson & A. Doyle (Eds.), *Risk and morality* (pp. 1–10). Toronto: University of Toronto Press.

Fair Labor Association. (2004). *Fair Labor Association year two annual public report.* Retrieved on February 6, 2006, from http:// www.fairlabor.org/2004report/print.html.

Foucault, M. (1982). The subject and power. In H. Dreyfus & P. Rabinow (Eds.), *Michel Foucault: Beyond structuralism and hermeneutics* (2nd ed., pp. 208–226). Chicago: University of Chicago Press.

Fraser, N. (1999). Social justice in the age of identity politics: Redistribution, recognition and participation. In L. Ray & A. Sayer (Eds.), *Culture and economy: After the cultural turn* (pp. 25–52). London: Sage.

Gereffi, G. (1994). The organization of buyer-driven commodity chains. In G. Gereffi & M. Korzeniewicz (Eds.), *Commodity chains and global capitalism* (pp. 95–122). Westport, CT: Praeger.

Giddens, A. (1991). *Modernity and self-identity: Self and society in the late modern age.* Stanford, CA: Stanford University Press.

Global Alliance for Workers and Communities. (2004). *About Global Alliance.* Retrieved October 29, 2004, from http://www .theglobalalliance.org/partners.htm.

Global Exchange. (2004). *Nike campaign: Frequently asked questions.* Retrieved February 6, 2006, from http://www .globalexchange.org/campaigns/sweat-shops/nike/faq.html.

Global Reporting Initiative. (2004). *GRI at a glance.* Retrieved February 6, 2006, from http://www.globalreporting.org/about/ brief.asp.

Goldman, R., & Papson, S. (1998). *Nike culture: The sign of the swoosh.* London: Sage.

Greenberg, J., & Knight, G. (2004). Framing sweatshops: Nike, global production, and the American news media. *Communication & Critical/Cultural Studies, 1*(2), 151–175.

Habermas, J. (1984). *The theory of communicative action: Vol. 2. Lifeworld and system: A critique of functionalist reason* (T. McCarthy, Trans.). Boston, MA: Beacon Press.

Herbert, B. (1996a, June 24). From sweatshops to aerobics. *New York Times,* p. A15.

Herbert, B. (1996b, June 12). Trampled dreams. *New York Times,* p. A27.

Herbert, B. (1997, March 28). Brutality in Vietnam. *New York Times,* p. A29.

Hernandez-Truyol, B., & Gleason, C. (2002). Introduction. In B. Hernandez-Truyol & C. Gleason (Eds.), *Moral imperialism: A critical anthology* (pp. 1–16). New York: New York University Press.

Kabeer, N. (2004). Globalization, labour standards, and women's rights: Dilemmas of collective (in)action in an interdependent world. *Feminist Economics, 10*(1), 3–35.

Knight, G., & Greenberg, J. (2003). Events, issues, and social responsibility: The expanding terrain of corporate public relations. In D. Demers (Ed.), *Terrorism, globalization and mass communication* (pp. 215–231). Spokane, WA: Marquette Books.

Korean House for International Solidarity. (2001). *Public report on the labor dispute of Kukdong International Mexico S.A. de C.V.* Retrieved on February 6, 2006, from http://daga.dhs.org/atnc/archives/report/ publicreportonthelabordisputeofkukdong international.pdf.

Luhmann, N. (with Baecker, D.). (1995). *Social systems* (J. Bednarz, Trans.). Stanford, CA: Stanford University Press.

Maffesoli, M. (1996). *The time of the tribes: The decline of individualism in mass society* (D. Smith, Trans). London: Sage.

Mandle, J. R. (2000). The student anti-sweat-shop movement: Limits and potential. *Annals of the American Academy of Political & Social Science, 570,* 92–103.

Marx, K. (1967). *Capital: A critique of political economy: Vol. 1. The process of capitalist production* (S. Moore & E. Aveling, Trans.) (F. Engels, Ed.). New York: International Publishers. (Originally published 1887)

Melucci, A. (1996). *Challenging codes: Collective action in the information age.* Cambridge: Cambridge University Press.

Micheletti, M. (2004, April). *Just clothes? Discursive political consumerism and political participation*. Paper presented at the 2004 European Consortium for Political Rresearch Joint Sessions, Workshop 24, Uppsala, Sweden. Retrieved February 6, 2006, from http://www .essex.ac.uk/ecpr/events/jointsessions/ paperarchive/uppsala/ws24/Micheletti.pdf.

Murphy, D. F., & Mathew, D. (2001). *Nike and global labour practices: A case study prepared for the New Academy of Business Innovation Network for Socially Responsible Business*. Retrieved February 6, 2006, from http://www.new-academy.ac.uk/ publications/keypublications/ documents/ nikereport.pdf.

Nike. (1998). *Nike chairman and CEO Phil Knight new labor initiatives*. Retrieved July 5, 2001, from http://www.nikebiz.com/ labor/speech_trans.html.

Nike. (2004a). *Nike names new VP of corporate responsibility*. Retrieved February 6, 2006, from http://www.nike.com/nikebiz/ news/pressrelease.jhtml?year=2004& month=10&letter=g.

Nike. (2004b). *Code of conduct*. Retrieved on February 6, 2006, from http://www .nike.com/nikebiz/nikebiz.jhtml?page=25 &cat=code.

O'Neill, J. (1999). Economy, equality, and recognition. In L. Ray & A. Sayer (Eds.), *Culture and economy: After the cultural turn* (pp. 76–91). London: Sage.

Peretti, J. (with Micheletti, M.). (2003). The Nike sweatshop email: Political consumerism, Internet, and culture jamming. In M. Micheletti, A. Follesdal, & D. Stolle (Eds.), *Politics, products, and markets* (pp. 127–142). London: Transaction Publishers.

Pierson, P. (1994). *Dismantling the welfare state? Reagan, Thatcher, and the politics of retrenchment*. Cambridge: Cambridge University Press.

Sage, G. (1999). Justice do it! The Nike transnational advocacy network: Organization, collective actions, and outcomes. *Sociology of Sport Journal, 16*, 206–235.

Shaw, R. (1999). *Reclaiming America: Nike, clean air, and the new national activism*. Berkeley: University of California Press.

Smith, J., McCarthy, J. D., McPhail, C., & Augustyn, B. (2001). From protest to agenda building: Description bias in media coverage of protest events in Washington, D.C. *Social Forces, 79*(4), 1397–1423.

Stabile, C. (2000). Nike, social responsibility, and the hidden abode of production. *Critical Studies in Media Communication, 17*, 186–204.

Verité. (2001). *Comprehensive factory evaluation report on Kukdong International Mexico, S.A. de C.V.* Retrieved June 27, 2001, from htp://www.nikebiz.com/media/ nike_verite_report.pdf.

Wokutch, R. (2001). Nike and its critics. *Organization & Environment, 14*(2), 207–237.

Worker Rights Consortium. (2001a). *WRC investigation re complaint against Kukdong (Mexico): Preliminary findings and recommendations*. Retrieved January 21, 2005, from http://www.workersrights.org/ Report_Kukdong_1.pdf.

Worker Rights Consortium. (2001b). *WRC investigation re: Complaint against Kukdong (Mexico) report and recommendations*. Retrieved January 21, 2005, from http://www.workersrights.org/Report_ Kukdong_2.pdf.

VI

ENVIRONMENTAL PERSPECTIVES

22

Corporate Environmentalism

CONNIE BULLIS
FUMIKO IE

As we consider the environment and corporate responsibility, we might recall ecofeminist Ynestra King's (1990) commentary when she suggested:

> The piece of the pie that women have only begun to sample as a result of the feminist movement is rotten and carcinogenic, and surely our feminist theory and politics must take account of this, however much we yearn for the opportunities that have been denied to us. What is the point of partaking equally in a system that is killing us all? (p. 106)

Although King's comments were directed largely to the feminist movement, we might well heed her thoughts as we approach issues of corporate responsibility. As we consider the social contracts under which corporations operate, King reminds us that it is pointless to focus solely on the social system without considering how that system is related to the natural system. Elsewhere she has commented that people are utterly dependent on nature (King, 1989), a dependence often forgotten in our understandings of social systems as distinct from natural systems. As corporations are more responsive to multiple stakeholders, including customers, employees, governments, people who live in places where they do business, and so forth, they need to include the natural environment as a central consideration.

Two general assumptions undergird this exploration. First, the state of the natural environment is so degraded that the quality of human life is threatened. Environmental problems pervade the earth, so much so that speculation continues over the "end of nature" and many writers express concern with whether humans have so devastated the earth's systems that it will be unable to continue to support life. With the grave projections regarding natural systems, and the future of human life itself, we might argue that any contemporary consideration of social responsibility is, at best, incomplete without the inclusion of ecological considerations. At most, we might argue that a concern with environmental responsibility must be the foundation of any understanding of social responsibility because the potential for the death of (human) life itself makes the environmental imperative primary.

Second, because corporations are such central players in terms of economic force, world scope, political power, and environmental degradation, clearly, we cannot adequately understand environmental concerns without considering the crucial roles corporations hold. A concern for the state of the environment cannot be adequately examined without considering corporations. Corporations have been cast in the role of villain in some cases and in that of hero in other instances. As environmental concerns have evolved over the years, many corporations have been heavily involved in determining how to adapt to the natural environment or, more specifically, to the pressures they perceive regarding their environmental stances. A variety of stances are evident with elements of both villainy and heroics. Given the importance of organizational actors, it is valuable to consider these varied stances and what might be expected of organizations in the future.

Here, we first give a very brief overview of the relevant recent historical context. Next, we consider some stances corporations are taking toward the environment and how they are related to social responsibility. We report results of an examination of corporate websites in the year 2000 designed to analyze how corporations communicate their environmental stances or present themselves through one significant medium, and speculate what trajectories we might anticipate.

RECENT HISTORICAL CONTEXT

In the United States, the reaction to Rachel Carson's *Silent Spring* (1962) marked the initiation of serious environmental concerns as related to corporate practice. Her rhetorically adroit description of the environmental damage wrought by chemicals resulted in a number of major environmental laws (Frankel, 1998) during the two decades following publication, including such crucial laws as the Clean Air Act of 1970, the Clean Water Act of 1977, and the Superfund (Comprehensive Environmental Response, Compensation, and Liability Act of 1980). These laws changed the ways in which corporations could legally operate. In 1984, a more significant event brought further attention to corporate responsibility. The chemical leak in Bhopal, India, that killed 1,500 people and injured thousands more brought international attention both to the uses of toxic chemicals and to how large multinational companies operate in developing countries. Irrespective of legal issues, Union Carbide faced international scrutiny. Corporations in general, and the chemical industry in particular, responded with voluntary changes to reduce harmful emissions, better release information regarding toxic emissions (some of which was required by the 1986 Superfund Amendments and Reauthorization Act) and work more closely with communities.

In these cases, the intersection of human health and environmental destruction is very clear, yet social responsibility and environmental concerns have not always been considered in an integrated way. Instead, social responsibility and environmental performance have often been considered separately.

A further historical marker was the United Nations–sponsored Earth Summit in 1992. At this historical gathering, governments, corporations, and nongovernmental organizations from around the world met to develop plans for addressing planetary environmental problems. The Earth Summit resulted in a recognition of the United Nations' earlier definition of sustainability. The United Nations World Commission on Environment and Development, chaired by Gro Brundtland, published its report, *Our Common Future*, in 1987. The 1987 Brundtland report is widely credited as proffering the general definition of sustainable development that is widely acknowledged. It defined *sustainable development* as development that meets the needs of the current generation without compromising the ability of future generations to meet their needs (World Commission on Environment and Development, 1987). Since then, critics have dubbed sustainable development an oxymoron, praised the term for its rhetorical ambiguity and range of potential to adapt to varying local conditions (Peterson, 1997), and discussed it widely. While being highly ambiguous, this definition clearly emphasizes the significance of the long-term future. By focusing on the long-term future, important questions are enabled. For example, sustainability issues include how to conserve resources for the future, how to include resources in accounting and planning processes, and how to be responsive to the trends sprouted out of this general concern. As these kinds of questions and issues have become more commonplace, corporations are pressured to participate in these concerns.

The 1992 Earth Summit also resulted in the charter for business within Agenda 21 and the formation of the Business Council for Sustainable Development. A number of leaders of major corporations formed the Business Council for Sustainable Development, which sought to involve business in sustainable development by encouraging voluntary change in businesses around the world. The chairman of the group, Stephan Schmidheiny, wrote *Changing Course: A Global Business Perspective on Development and the Environment* (1992). This book was a strong indictment of business and a compelling call for voluntary change. In 2002, as the 2002 Earth Summit approached, the renamed World Business Council for Sustainable Development published an updated version, *Walking the Talk: The Business Case for Sustainable Development* (Holliday, Schmidheiny, & Watts, 2002).

Several cases of corporate wrongdoing have generated international attention and simultaneously provided strong incentives for corporations to attend to environmental concerns. As corporations and industries strive to remain competitive, profitable, and in good favor with the public and host communities, many perceive a need to show environmental concern but also prefer to avoid added legal constraints. Voluntary changes and environmental programs have often resulted.

While corporate responses to environmental concerns are individualized, theorists have nonetheless conceptualized descriptive themes to group corporate responses in to general stances. These general approaches aim to describe how corporations position themselves, or what stances they adopt. These sets of stances are arranged hierarchically, somewhat historically dynamic, and also conceptualized in stages or phases ranging from more modest approaches to more serious approaches. Here we integrate and summarize a set of descriptive stances, considering the feasibility, potential ironic uses (and abuses), and intersection with social responsibility of each stance. The identified stances also provide a framework through which to examine corporate practices and/or corporate discourse. However, if a descriptive framework is to be empirically useful, it needs to be empirically validated. Certainly, in part at least, corporations explain their environmental stances as they communicate about themselves. One important means of presenting themselves is through corporate websites. We report the results of a field test in which we tested the usefulness of the phase distinctions by applying the framework to how organizations present themselves on their websites.

CORPORATE STANCES TOWARD ENVIRONMENTAL CONCERNS

There are a number of hierarchically conceptualized descriptive frameworks that identify several phases or approaches (see Cannon, 1994, p. 229). Here, we draw most heavily on Dunphy, Griffiths, and Benn's (2003) hierarchically arranged stances, although some of their descriptions are adapted both to more sharply distinguish among phases and to integrate additional models. We may view these as historically dynamic, although certainly there are corporations that fit into each of the phases, and it is unclear whether corporations will evolve toward the stronger ecologically sensitive phases. Dunphy et al. distinguish six phases and discuss their intersections with social responsibility: rejection, nonresponsiveness, compliance, openness, integration, and collaboration.

Rejection entails a singular focus on immediate economic gain. In this approach, exploitation of any available resources (employees, the natural environment, government regulations, and communities) should be maximized to enhance profit. There is a conscious rejection of any obligation that does not enhance profit. Although this view may seem somewhat anachronistic, it is warranted from at least one widespread point of view. This approach is sensible and obligatory from the often-cited Milton Friedman (1970/2005) neoliberal economic stance. In this view, corporations or, more realistically, corporate executives are obligated to owners and must act in owners' interests. Corporations are responsible for only one social responsibility, which is maximizing the profits of shareholders (while acting within the relevant legal and ethical societal customs). To the extent that they do not marshal available resources toward this important end, they are not functioning optimally or ethically. In this view, a focus on the environment is considered as illegitimate taxation, taxes being imposed on owners, employees, and customers and then spent on social goods. Such taxation and social expenditure are the proper role not for private enterprise in a capitalist system but rather for government. Friedman (1970/2005) even likens corporate interest in social responsibility such as concern for pollution to socialism.

At first glance, this view may seem somewhat extreme. However, we encounter this perspective routinely as applications of the "bottom line" and "efficiency." In fact, this ideology undergirds practices such as our collective fascination with the stock market, accounting practices, and the way companies survive or fail. As David Korten (1995, 1999) has argued, no single organization can simply radically change its ways. Rather, individual companies exist within a context that requires profitability. As individual corporations adapt to the trends and pressures they face, certainly their most ubiquitous and significant focus is the pursuit of profit. As long as external practices and reward structures encourage an exclusive or even a strong central focus on profit, it is feasible and practical for corporations to adopt this stance and to remain in this phase.

In its most pure form, clearly corporations uniquely pursuing maximized profits reject social responsibility as they reject environmental responsibility. People, like the natural environment, are viewed as resources. The routine use of terms such as "human resources," the common assumption that employees can "steal" time from companies, and the encouragement to "market" oneself are simple examples of how corporations may be encouraged to adopt rejection as a sensible, feasible stance.

As Friedman (1970/2005) noted, however, corporations need to operate within legal and ethical societal customs. Friedman's position, then, is compatible with stances other than rejection, depending on the operative legal and ethical customs. As the legal and ethical milieu evolves, corporations often adapt accordingly. Corporations are increasingly adopting the less oblivious stances described below. By understanding this need to be compatible with legal and ethical societal customs, then, we can understand how corporations can be encouraged to adopt more environmentally responsible stances while acting in the best interests of owners.

Nonresponsiveness is characterized by a lack of awareness of interests other than immediate financial viability. Rather than actively rejecting a concern for the environment, this stance entails a benign negligence. Rather than an active embrace of Friedman's argument, this stance is characterized by a taken-for-granted assumption that it is only natural that both a compliant work force and a community can be valuable. Environmental consequences, like consequences of corporate behaviors for people, are simply outside the scope of the corporation and not on the corporate agenda.

Like rejection, nonresponsiveness is a reasonable stance in situations where corporations are competitive and profitable and thus rewarded for nonresponsiveness. The legal and ethical environments enabled this response prior to the advent of environmental laws, well-known environmental problems such as the *Exxon Valdez*, and external pressures from public interest groups. Once more,

environmental laws and societal ethical interests began to develop following some of the events summarized above. Corporations, too, turned increased attention to the environment. However, to the extent that laws are not enforced and/or noncompliance does not affect profit, and an unchallenged industry ethos supports nonresponsiveness, this remains a feasible stance. This is particularly significant in smaller companies that are not required by law to comply with environmental regulations. The logic that culturally supports nonresponsiveness is that restrictions should not apply to those smaller companies that cannot afford to comply. Here, the ability to make a profit must be treated as most important. The same logic precludes smaller companies from having to comply with laws we might consider socially responsible legislation. For example, smaller companies are not required to comply with the Family and Medical Leave Act of 1993.

The rejection and nonresponsiveness stances are grounded in organizational traditions of taking the natural environment for granted. Resources have traditionally not been accounted for, and these stances assume that there will be no change. Moreover, it is a significant investment to change. The move toward the next phase, compliance, requires attention to information systems and may require additional positions, change in culture, added technology, and change in how people perform their duties.

Compliance involves an awareness that negative sanctions can be harmful to the corporation's bottom line. Organizations adopting this approach respond to threats such as bad publicity, community action, and/or legal sanctions. Compliance may involve both adapting to external pressures and attempting to control those pressures. Companies that are compliant, then, follow legal constraints. Moreover, they attempt to adapt to stakeholder expectations to avoid undue criticism.

At a minimum, compliance is encouraged through the desire to avoid the financial cost of noncompliance. Perhaps more important, the reputational cost of noncompliance may be quite high with consumers, suppliers, and shareholders. A now-classic example is the *Exxon Valdez*. The ship spilled 10.8 million gallons of crude oil into the Prince William Sound in Alaska, killing hundreds of thousands of birds and animals along a thousand miles of coast. Exxon was given the largest fine in U.S. history for an environmental crime and suffered enormous reputational costs. The case now serves as an impetus toward compliance for many companies.

Compliance need not be seen entirely as negative. Porter suggests that well-designed regulation can be responded to with increased innovation, helps create predictability, and helps corporate awareness (Dunphy et al., 2003, p. 46). In turn, this creates better measurement and assessment. Enforcement needs to go hand in hand with regulation to provide the motivation for corporations to change from nonresponsiveness to compliance.

Environmental and social responsibility intersect in that another cost of noncompliance, in a context in which stakeholders value compliance, may be that irresponsible companies have to pay employees more to work for them, while compliance translates into more willing potential employees.

Compliance became increasingly important as environmental laws evolved and public opinion shifted following the publication of *Silent Spring* (Carson, 1962). This continues to be an important stance for organizations to adopt. Compliance, especially with clear legal requirements, would seem to be a minimal stance organizations would adopt toward environmental issues. And this is generally the case, especially with larger corporations (Frankel, 1998). However, to the extent that laws and customs are inadequate to prevent further deterioration of the earth's life-sustaining systems, compliance is an inadequate response. As corporations seek to minimize their costs, they influence governments to minimize legal constraints. Many environmental and employment laws do not pertain to smaller organizations and hence are irrelevant to a large portion of companies and employees.

While it may seem surprising that some organizations would not adopt a stance of compliance, it makes sense that unless enforcement is expected and compliance is rewarded, a company might find that the costs of compliance far outweigh the benefits. Often, compliance minimally entails adding compliance specialists to the payroll, and those specialists are empowered to create change in the organization. For larger corporations, responsibility for a full supply chain and for the product's life cycle and disposal creates the need for more substantial structures such as committees, departments, information systems, and cultural values that encourage compliance. This is very costly for corporations.

Openness connotes a sense of a need to both achieve an environmental record and to share information with external stakeholders. In part, this information sharing is mandated by law. For example, Title III of the Superfund Amendments and Reauthorization Act of 1986 requires some publication of emissions information. However, as companies adapted to this public accountability mandate, some went beyond what was required by law (Frankel, 1998). In this way, stakeholders may be less inclined to distrust the organization, and consequently, by sharing information, organizations may avoid legal action as well as informal difficulties such as distrust. Companies may find openness, then, to be feasible as they adapt to their legal and ethical contexts. Monsanto led the chemical industry in voluntarily disclosing its emissions. More and more companies are publishing environmental reports or incorporating environmental performance into their annual reports. With increasing scrutiny, companies may benefit from warding off distrust from potential critics. In doing so, they also increase openness among employees as information sharing becomes more prevalent.

As organizations adopt the stances or phases just described, the environment and associated constraints are implicitly, and often explicitly, assumed to be a problem, a cost, and/or an enemy (Frankel, 1998). Adapting to the environment, from these perspectives, is difficult and intrudes on the purpose of business. More recently, many corporations have adopted stances, or moved into phases, in which concern for the environment becomes an opportunity, a saving, and/or a friend. We turn now to these stances.

Integration is adopted as corporations assume that social and environmental responsibility can pay either immediately and directly, or perhaps in the long run and indirectly. This stance represents a shift from a more defensive posture to an assumption that an environmental focus can be a positive benefit for the organization. Rather than viewing an environmental focus as a cost or imposition, through efficiency savings, a company can realize positive gains from its environmental attention. This is, then, a win–win proactive stance. By attending to the pressures to be more environmentally sensitive, companies can gain in their reputation and ability to operate within customary legal and ethical expectations while benefiting financially as well. A company adopting this stance, then, gains by adapting to environmental needs. This approach has the advantage of drawing on a long history of organizational interest in efficiency, traceable at least to Frederick Taylor's (1911) scientific management and continuing through the twentieth and into the twenty-first century. This framework provides a comfortable fit, then, with pervasive managerial history and culture. Companies are able to incorporate a new environmental and social focus within a familiar framework, accomplishing the transition from defensive posture to familiar opportunity and challenge. Efficiency can be gained in part by examining energy use and changing wasteful practices. This approach often evolves to a more systemic process through which continuous improvement and redesign are emphasized, leading to changes in operations, organizational design, and product design. These ongoing changes focus on efficiency as it conserves natural resources and ecosystem health as well as organizational cost savings and human benefits in the long run.

Many organizations adopted this stance during the 1990s as environmental management systems were promoted and found to be successful in many instances. Corporations realized dollar savings as waste was reduced and efficient systems introduced. Total quality environmental management could be readily adopted by organizations that were familiar with total quality management systems. ISO 14000 voluntary certification was widely adopted. Organizations, then, found many isolated opportunities for savings. For example, by plugging holes in water pipes, adding heating insulation to buildings, or purchasing more fuel-efficient vehicles, companies were able to save resources and money. They also began to adopt more comprehensive systems to yield greater efficiencies. Clearly, this phase is feasible for organizations to the extent that they are able to identify and benefit from opportunities to improve efficiencies. They are able to continually improve their use of energy, waste, and operations so that the natural environment and their profits both benefit. As more companies in more industries reap these benefits, the stance becomes increasingly desirable and necessary among competitors, suppliers, and customers. The approach can lead to major changes in technologies, cultures, organizational structures, and operations. The feasibility is predicated on the familiar framing of efficiency. Some user pay policies toward pollution as well as increased

competition, familiarity with continuous improvement systems, and the obvious benefits encourage the efficiency stance. As efficiencies are gained, it may become limiting to continue to identify and benefit from increased efficiencies. In other words, it becomes increasingly difficult to continue to become continuously more and more efficient because the simplest and most cost-effective changes have been identified. Added efficiencies are often less feasible and less cost-effective.

As organizations adopt these environmental management systems, the inherent link between environmental and social issues becomes increasingly evident. After finding isolated areas for improved efficiency, organizations often find they are more successful when environmental systems are integrated with training, empowerment, teamwork, and reward systems. Dunphy et al. (2003) point out that to attain maximum ecological efficiency, a positive use of human resources is necessary. Committees, teams, organizational cultures need to implement participative systems that integrate human and environmental concerns with bottom line efforts. Moreover, internal and external groups need to work together through an ongoing process to identify and implement improvements.

This trend toward a win–win and integrated systems approach to efficiency requires and animates change in the social system. As organizations strive for integration, environmental concerns may be moved further into the central core of the organization. This suggests that environmental concerns are integrated into strategy. For example, rather than focusing on efficiencies in the production process, a strategic approach sometimes entails considering whether a different product should be produced. In other cases, a company may strategize to position itself as an environmental leader. British Petroleum strategically adopted the term "beyond petroleum" as one facet of its strategic positioning. Awareness of planetary limits, global warming, and resource exhaustion can be turned into strategic business opportunities and competitive advantage. Corporations that have successfully integrated environmental management systems have realigned human systems to fully benefit from participatory engagement.

Corporate citizenship, advanced human resource strategies, and innovative and environmentally benign products are treated as profitable strategic choices. They also become integral to a corporation's identity. Environmental considerations become integral to strategic positioning. Here, the sense that environmental consideration can be a benefit rather than a cost is extended. Organizations may include environmental concerns into their mission and vision statements. They then consider the environment throughout their operations as they bring operations into alignment with mission and vision. This may entail positioning the company as an industry leader in environmental concern. For example, BP successfully positioned itself as the leader in the petroleum industry. Companies may develop innovative services or products for new evolving markets. This stance entails understanding ecological threats and opportunities as resources for competitive advantage. It involves more risk taking and investment in the future. Here measurement systems are aligned with goals. Performance indicators for all aspects of the organization are included.

Integration as strategic proactivity has become increasingly meaningful as corporations attend to evidence suggesting that customers in some markets want to see corporate environmental performance. A PriceWaterhouseCoopers 1999 Millennium Poll showed that two of every three citizens wanted companies to go beyond their traditional goal of maximizing shareholder value to consider broader societal goals (cited in Dunphy et al., 2003, pp. 39–40). This response revealed that the cultural environment is clearly conducive to corporate sustainability practices. Some corporations have benefited from this by adopting product differentiation strategies to adapt to these particular markets. There are inherent limits here as industries shift and product differentiation becomes difficult when everyone is doing it the same way.

Again, a company adopting the integration stance incorporates environmental concern into its basic purpose and direction. In implementing its strategy, environmental concern is integrated into its operations, decision-making, and measurement systems. This stance may well entail an environmental management system but incorporates this system into its strategic direction. Adopting an integration stance, then, may range from considering environmental management systems, to integrating environmental concern with human systems, to integrating environmental concerns into strategic direction. For some corporations, a stronger awareness of the importance of partnerships and cooperative external relationships may encourage a stronger stance—collaboration.

Collaboration may be developed through any number of processes. However, it is logical to anticipate that, in the process of developing strategy, the vision and mission statements are involved, and in implementing strategy, corporations often need to consider their relationships not only with employees, but with their external stakeholders. As they adopt a stance that is strategically proactive, then, they may go further by advancing stakeholder relationships. These collaborative relationships take many forms such as partnerships, committees, project collaboration, marketing to the green consumer sector, encouraging environmental and social responsibility among suppliers, citizen advisory groups, or various suggestion systems.

A corporate interest in efficiency often evolves into cooperative relationships with suppliers and consumers as stewardship of the product life cycle is examined. Industrial ecology approaches include a variety of organizations that operate symbiotically to benefit all. Following the 1984 Bhopal disaster, chemical companies often created community councils as a means of better cooperating with the local communities in which they operated. Companies may form partnerships with nongovernmental organizations, collaborate to provide community resources such as green spaces, cooperate with regulating agencies, or employ any variety of collaborative forms.

The six phases just described are highly consistent with Friedman's perspective. Rejection and nonresponsiveness assume that environmental concerns are irrelevant to organizational purposes. Compliance, openness, integration, and collaboration attend to the legal and societal context within which an organization must operate. Integration and collaboration maximize the organization's interests in profit by adapting to internal and external interests in environmental concerns. Although there is a general trend moving from rejection toward collaboration, all of these phases are currently feasible, and various organizations do align themselves with each phase.

Nevertheless, many observers articulate an urgent sense that these approaches are insufficient to avert coming disaster. As long as growth is primary, one can imagine an end of needed natural resources or a point where the lack of clean air, water, and food brings about a collapse of human societies. Therefore, we summarize a seventh more radical approach below.

The transition to sustainability implies a truly different set of assumptions about the corporation and its role in the world. Moving to more of a systems-based approach and the need to consider how actors affect each other leads to an approach where the best interests of single corporations are not the sole focus. Instead, an understanding of the implications of the environmental crisis leads to an understanding that the well-being of all people, and the biological systems that support them are mediated through organizational activities. For example, Donaldson (2005) claims, "It seems reasonable in such instances, then, to place the responsibility not upon a single class of agents, but upon a broad collection of them, including governments, corporate executives, host-country companies and officials, and international organizations" (p. 132).

Sustainability may be described as the most ideal of the approaches. This phase suggests an internalized ideology of working for an ecologically sustainable world, often by promoting positive practices in society generally. Commitment includes support for a viable planet and a just, equitable social world as well as human fulfillment. The primary focus becomes sustainability with the more technical aspects of environmental problems serving this focus. A more holistic sustainability approach also includes social concerns, corporate citizenship, reputation, and performance as defined through a sustainability lens (Laszlo, 2003). As Laszlo explains, "Managers will need to experience the world differently, as human beings connected to the world around them and not only as professional managers" (p. 27). Organizations are considered to be moral entities with significant roles to play in maintaining ecological integrity.

Here, corporations become aware of the importance of adopting a broader role in moving toward a sustainable world. Callenbach, Capra, Goldman, Lutz, and Marburg (1993) contrast environmental management (which is consistent with the previously described stances above) with sustainability when they suggest that

[e]nvironmental management is associated with the idea of coping with environmental problems for the benefit of the company. It lacks an ethical dimension and its main motivations are legal compliance and improvement of the corporate image. Ecomanagement (which we have labeled sustainability), by contrast, is motivated by an ecological ethic and by a concern for the well-being of future generations. (p. 62)

They go on to clarify, "Shallow environmentalism tends to either accept by default or positively endorse the ideology of economic growth. Deep ecology replaces the ideology of economic growth with the idea of ecological sustainability" (p. 62). As corporations move toward sustainability, they recognize that "unlimited economic growth on a finite planet can only lead to disaster" (p. 63). They see themselves as part of an interdependent ecological system where each organization may be most important and meaningful in its role of participating and facilitating the health of the whole and of the long term. This stance, then, adopts a different vision and assumption. It represents (or can represent) a shift from neoliberalism and calls for transformation more than incremental shifts. From this view, economic value for shareholders is not the dominant purpose of corporations. One commonly touted exemplar here is Ben & Jerry's, widely known as a company that espouses product, social, and economic missions (with the environmental mission incorporated into the social mission).

While corporations adopting (or trending toward) this stance may engage in many of the practices associated with compliance, openness, integration, and collaboration, sustainability implies an enhanced understanding of environmental concerns as a systemic issue that needs to be addressed in new ways. Typically, sustainability entails partnerships and interactions with a wide variety of stakeholders (e.g., Global Forest Watch gives information to Ikea to facilitate Ikea's interest in purchasing wood products from companies that harvest trees sustainably). There is a fundamental reconsideration of products and production processes (e.g., Interface is well known for having substituted the newer service of maintaining floor coverings for the older product—carpets). Sustainability requires a transformation of operations involving stakeholder participation. Both internal and external stakeholders are far more involved as organizations are realigned to focus on sustainability. Organizations are often developed into learning organizations. Organizations not only advocate transparency but also create meaningful alliances and partnerships with a wider array of stakeholders. Ecological sustainability is treated as a key criterion for all business activities. Full cost accounting, in which the environmental and human costs are incorporated into accounting systems, is another key change. This may entail creating different products, a new industry, and/or collaborating with a variety of organizations to create an interdependent community to enhance sustainability. Industry, government, and communities evolve through collaborating for sustainability. At best, human and natural systems are necessarily integrated.

These descriptive phases are heuristically valuable in identifying corporate responses to environmental issues. It remains to be seen whether they are empirically useful. If so, they may be valuable for examining corporate practices and discourse, understanding how corporations adopt environmental interests, tracking shifts over time, and considering ways in which environmental and social stances do and do not intersect in practice. Here, we report an initial examination of corporate discourse as evident on corporate websites conducted in part to explore whether the stances described are empirically identifiable in corporate discourse. Another purpose was to begin to explore the relative proportions of companies expressing the various stances. Finally, we were interested in testing the common assertion that larger companies are able to attend more to environmental concerns while smaller companies are not, due to lower compliance requirements and fewer resources.

AN EXPLORATORY EXAMINATION OF CORPORATE DISCOURSE

In this examination, we empirically identified how organizations that are directly related to environmentally hazardous businesses express or do not express their concern about the environment through company webpages. We chose energy-related companies because energy is indispensable for our life, and in order to produce energy we have to use natural resources including, but not limited to, petroleum, natural gas, coal, water, and wind. Not only the ways we consume energy (e.g., emission of exhaust gas) but also the consumption of the natural resource itself is harmful to the natural environment to some extent. Because we cannot live without energy in our civilized societies, it is necessary for us to understand the importance of the relationship between the natural environment and the companies that provide energy. The organizations dealing with energy are responsible for acknowledging and diffusing this understanding. Here we examine how they exhibit their stance toward environmental concerns through the company webpages.

Websites provide a relatively easy and financially reasonable method to offer information to a wide audience. Along with increasing private use of computers, more and more companies use websites to present themselves to multiple audiences. The company webpages often include company profiles, activities, and financial information, which seem to be primarily for convenience of their stakeholders. Webpages, then, have become an important medium through which companies express themselves. We examined websites with several questions in mind.

First, we asked whether there is a relationship between company size and the expression of environmental concerns. Second, we sought to describe how companies comment on the environment. Specifically, we sought to determine whether the environmental stances identified above are identifiable on webpages and, if so, how prevalent is each stance. Finally, we sought to discern to what extent companies follow their stated stances with actual behaviors, or environmental action.

Methodology

Sample

Companies were systematically selected from the *Standard & Poor's Register of Corporations, Directors, and Executives* (Standard & Poor's Corporation, 1999). Companies were selected from an index of Standard Industrial Classification (SIC) numbers, which refer to particular industrial categories. The SIC indexes used for this study were 4911 (electric services), 4922 (natural gas transmission), 1382 (oil and gas field exploration services), and 1311 (crude petroleum and natural gas). Some companies are indexed with two or more SIC numbers according to their multiple business fields. Those companies' names appear under all the SIC category indexes in which they are involved.

For each SIC number, companies are listed in alphabetical order. The fifth company from the top of each list was selected. From there, every fifth listing was selected. For those companies that were selected and did not mention a web address, a researcher telephoned the company and asked for the web address. If a company reported not having a website or did not respond, the next company on the list was selected. Ninety-one web addresses were collected (16 from the list for SIC 4911, 5 from 4922, 12 from 1382, and 58 from 1311). Seven companies among the 91 total companies were not analyzed due to technical problems such as printing failure or access problems. A total of 84 company webpages were examined.

The demographic data of each company, such as location, businesses in which they are involved, annual sales, and number of employees, were collected from Standard & Poor's Corporation (1999, vol. 1), which listed these data under each corporation's title. Because one of the purposes of our inquiry was to explore the relationship between company scale and concern about the environment, the number of employees, sales results, and the number of SIC numbers were noted. Since each SIC number represents a business category, the companies with more SIC categories are involved in broader activities. This could be indirectly interpreted as another measure of the size of the company.

The companies examined were located in 25 U.S. states and four foreign countries (Canada, Scotland, Australia, and Switzerland): Texas ($N = 21, 25\%$), Canada ($N = 10, 11.9\%$), Colorado ($N = 7, 8.3\%$), California ($N = 6, 7.1\%$), Oklahoma ($N = 5, 6.0\%$), and Utah ($N = 4, 4.8$); three (3.6%) companies each in Illinois and Alabama; two (2.4%) companies each in Wyoming, Michigan, Pennsylvania, and Louisiana; one (1.2%) company each in Hawaii, Kansas, Connecticut, Arizona, Kentucky, Delaware, West Virginia, South Dakota, North Carolina, Missouri, Nevada, Ohio, Massachusetts, Indiana, Scotland, Australia, and Switzerland.

Coding

To develop a coding scheme, first we distinguished companies that mentioned the environment in some way from those that did not mention it at all. Second, their points of reference to the environment were examined and categorized as primary (main concerns) or secondary (indirect or implicit mention, e.g., environmental protection as a facet of corporate social responsibility or products as environmentally safe).

Third, the stance, or posture, with respect to environment was coded. We assumed that rejec-

tion and nonresponse were indicated by no mention and did not differentiate between these two stances. Compliance was coded by some mention of abiding by legal regulations concerning the environment. Openness was identified by the inclusion of environmental information such as emission information, or by hazard acknowledgment. Integration was evident when a company mentioned its practice of considering the financial bottom line and environmental commitment to be integrated. Some also included a social interest in such statements. At a minimum, these websites expressed a win–win orientation toward the company's interests and environmental concerns. Collaboration was evident when projects or partnerships with environmental groups, communities, or government were included. Sustainability was identified by appeals to a planetary ethic, a long-term outlook, or a recognition that past or even current policies may not be enough for a better future. This includes environmental concern beyond surrounding communities and at a global scale. When websites evidenced more than one of the stances, we coded the website as fitting the strongest of the stances that were represented. Finally, in order to examine whether companies provided evidence of actions taken in conjunction with their environmental stances, each website was coded for whether or not an environmental action was specified.

Procedures

Two researchers independently examined and then coded webpages. When differences were identified, researchers discussed the coding and reached consensus. The one difference that occurred regarding environmental mention was resolved by one researcher agreeing she had missed a mention that was on a website. Two differences in coding whether mention was primary or secondary were resolved through discussion. The five differences on stance were more difficult to resolve and, with one exception, were categorized as Other. In other words, coders agreed that several of the webpages were not appropriately coded into any of the stance categories.

Results

Of the 84 websites analyzed, 39 (46.4%) mentioned the environment in some way and 45

(53.6%) did not. Of those websites that mentioned the environment, 28 (71.8%) treated the environment as a primary subject, and 11 (28.2%) treated the environment secondarily or indirectly.

In order to examine the relationships between company size and expression of involvement in environmental issues, company size was analyzed by considering sales, number of employees, and number of SIC categories. Each of these indices was related to whether or not the environment was mentioned. Descriptive results are displayed in table 22.1. These results indicate that on all three indices, in general, companies that mention the environment are larger than those that do not.

Because the distributions were non-normally distributed, Mann-Whitney's nonparametric test was employed to examine the relationship between size and expression of environmental concern. This test ranks the observed values and compares the mean ranks of the two groups. The higher the mean rank, the larger the values are. However, in the sense that it does not include the amount of difference in values, it is not influenced by the non-normal distribution of values. The mean ranks and statistical results are displayed in table 22.2. All differences are significant at or below the .01 level. These results indicate that larger companies more often mention the environment in their websites.

We tested for a relationship between size and whether the environment is treated as primary or secondary. Table 22.3 displays the descriptive statistics for sales, number of employees, and the number of SIC categories in relation to whether

TABLE 22.2 Mean ranks for mention or not mention of the environment by size

Environmental mention	N	Mean rank	Sum of ranks	Mann-Whitney
Sales				441.50*
No mention	42	32.01	1344.50	
Mention	37	49.07	1815.50	
Number employees				411.50*
No mention	43	31.57	1357.50	
Mention	36	50.07	18.02.50	
SIC number				605.00*
No mention	45	36.44	1640.00	
Mention	39	49.49	1930.00	

*$p < .01$.

the companies expressed direct or indirect concern about the environment. Due to the non-normal distribution of values, the Mann-Whitney nonparametric test was used to test for differences. These results, displayed in table 22.4, indicate that companies that mention the environment in an indirect or secondary way are generally smaller than companies that mention the environment as a primary issue on their websites.

We probed the websites that mentioned the environment further to examine the stances portrayed. Results are displayed in table 22.5. Given the small number of company websites that could be clearly and reliably interpreted using our framework, inferential statistics were not computed. The proportions illustrate that, in general, in this very

TABLE 22.1 Sales, number of employees, and number of SIC categories by mention of the environment

	Mention	Not mention
Sales		
Mean	3,343.82	265.23
Median	276.32	33.45
Number of employees		
Mean	14,754.08	657.79
Median	995.50	50.00
Number of SIC categories		
Mean	3.31	2.00
Median	1.82	1.00

TABLE 22.3 Sales, number of employees, number of SIC categories by primary/secondary environmental mention

	Primary mention	Secondary mention
Sales		
Mean	4,203.54	211.18
Median	447.37	70.68
Number of employees		
Mean	19,385.50	458.22
Median	2,270.50	170.00
Number of SIC categories		
Mean	3.85	2.18
Median	2.00	2.00

TABLE **22.4** Ranks and Mann-Whitney statistics for primary or secondary mention

Primary/secondary mention	N	Mean rank	Sum of ranks	Mann-Whitney
Sales				
Primary mention	26	21.75	565.50	
Secondary mention	11	12.59	137.50	
Number of employees				53.5*
Primary mention	27	21.02	567.50	
Secondary mention	9	10.94	98.50	
Number of SIC categories				122.5
Primary mention	28	21.13	591.50	
Secondary mention	11	17.14	188.5	

*$p < .02$.

small sample of companies that mention the environment in one industry, there is some evidence that the stronger stances are more common than the weaker stances.

For some organizations, the environmental stance was further supported by environmental actions. Twenty-two (57.9%) reported at least one environmental action they had taken (for example, designating and developing acres for wildlife protection). Sixteen (42.1%) did not mention any actions while 1 was not codable.

Discussion

These results suggest that a slight majority of energy-related businesses that had websites did not mention the environment. Further, they support common contentions that larger companies more commonly express their concerns about the environment. In addition, larger companies generally

TABLE **22.5** Environmental stances portrayed on websites

Stance	N	%
Compliance	5	12.8
Openness	2	5.1
Integration	8	20.5
Collaboration	7	17.9
Sustainability	9	23.1
Other	8	20.5

comment on the environment more directly while smaller companies tend to mention the environment more indirectly. These findings suggest that larger companies are more likely to take advantage of the opportunity to portray a positive image of themselves by expressing their concern for and involvement in environmental protection.

The stages or stances described here are only partially identifiable empirically in corporate self-presentations on websites. Of those websites examined, 20% included environmental self-presentations that were not entirely consistent with the stances theorized as evidenced in our "Other" category. This suggests a far broader array of actual corporate expressions than the framework suggested. We infer that corporations are creative, face unique situations, and address those situations with unique perspectives.

The results presented here also demonstrate that the level of concern for the environment is quite high among those that articulate an environmental concern. Only approximately 13% expressed their involvement in a passive way, or as compliance. More than 20% actually expressed an environmental stance that indicated a sustainability focus, the most ideal of the stances. The integration and collaboration stances are indicative of organizations that have turned the corner in terms of considering the environment as an opportunity rather than a cost. It appears that, of those companies that do express their environmental interests, most adopt perspectives consistent with stronger stances rather than merely with compliance and openness. In the future, it will be important to track changes over time in corporate stances and practices. Here we have provided one description of how a sample of mainly U.S.-based companies in energy-related fields described themselves through one medium in the year 2000. Future research should revisit these companies while also observing more general trends. By tracking general trends, we can both monitor changes over time and provide a positive impetus for corporations to change.

As scholars develop the ability to systematically analyze web discourse, we can overcome some of the limitations of the empirical work reported here. In our development of a category system to systematically code websites, we privileged environmental stances in our framework and thereby failed to fully examine one of our key claims—that corporations' environmental and social responsibility are inextricably related. Our category system also failed to account for a high percentage of our data. Clearly, more comprehensive frameworks need to be employed so that the data are accounted for and so that environmental and social responsibility may be empirically examined together. Method triangulation will be valuable in better understanding how corporations enact their stated stances and how they produce the discourse that is analyzed by examining websites. It will be useful to systematically analyze and compare discourses of social and environmental responsibility across several variables such as industry, national location, reputation, performance, and so forth. Although systematically coding and comparing is valuable, scholars also need to attend to the particular situations and practices better identified through in-depth case studies.

FUTURE TRAJECTORIES

It seems clear from contemporary writings on corporate environmentalism, from past case studies, and from our examination of corporate websites in the energy field that corporate stances toward the environment are varied.

As several authors have noted, stances such as rejection and nonresponsiveness are prevalent among corporations and also evident in an absence of commentary on environmental matters in more than half of our sample of energy-related company websites. There appears to be a relationship between company size and whether and how company interest in the environment is expressed. Both regulations and public pressure have focused almost exclusively on larger companies. One key future consideration is how a wider range of companies can be encouraged to enhance their environmental awareness and response. Clearly, this is difficult within an assumptive base that adopts profitability as the single overriding interest because the prevailing logic holds that smaller companies cannot afford to be environmentally responsible. Where environmental concerns are costly, this assumption is sensible. By attending to opportunities for integration or efficiency gains, smaller companies may be able to identify ways to adopt more environmentally friendly stances. Simultaneously, the regulatory environment could encourage more active engagement.

The evidence generated from our examination of websites is consistent with current claims regarding corporate interest in, and specific stances

toward, the environment. A sizable portion of the websites we examined did address environmental concerns. Of those, the majority addressed the environment in a positive way rather than simply as a necessary cost. Some corporations are, it appears, engaging in integrative, win–win strategies while others are adding collaborative relationships to enhance their environmental records. Finally, a portion of corporations articulated visionary sustainability statements. This is particularly encouraging and suggests that the stages identified in the literature on corporate environmental stances may be useful as a means of describing and comparing corporate self-representations. More important, it suggests that some corporations are speaking in ways that may facilitate modes of adaptation beyond the confines of Freidman's profitability imperative.

Caution is, of course, warranted because corporations may well exaggerate or even misrepresent themselves through their self-presentations upon which researchers depend. Our examination also revealed that 60% of the websites that included the environment also included reports of actual actions or behaviors in support of their environmental claims whereas 40% did not (unpublished data). This suggests that a sizable minority of companies making environmental claims did not also describe specific behaviors to support their claims, calling the veracity of their environmental talk into question. Of course, there may be contradictions between claimed behaviors, actual behaviors, and patterns of behavior that contribute to a particular environmental stance. Nevertheless, by asserting environmental claims, organizations certainly expect to be pressured to act consistently with their assertions. As more organizations articulate stances that more closely approximate sustainability and grapple with new approaches, we can anticipate ongoing efforts to continue to shift toward more sustainable ways of operating. As described by Dunphy et al. (2003), the stronger environmental stances are inextricably dependent on more equitable and humane internal and external social practices. The integration, then, of social responsibility and environmental responsibility should become increasingly evident.

Given evidence regarding importance of organizations as actors and the variety of (villainous and heroic) stances they have taken vis-à-vis both environmental and social concerns, it seems clear that increased attention and encouragement should continue to result in creative and valuable adaptations as social systems and natural systems continue to coevolve largely through processes mediated by organizations. David Korten (2005) joins a procession of visionaries who identify alternatives to the status quo. He contrasts what he calls the "suicide economy" with "economies for life." In his view, because there have been so many cases of corporate corruption within the global profit-driven economy in which ownership and power are decoupled from obligations to people and place, a shift toward local economics is beginning. These new economies are based on personal responsibility, local ownership and markets, and values that encourage equity and democracy. His description makes clear that sustainability requires a change in the basic economic structure because, as he has argued (Korten, 1995, 1999), individual corporations must adapt to the economic structure within which they operate. As long as the economic structure rewards the destruction of people and the environment by rewarding profit and delinking owners from the destructive practices that corporations engage in, progress toward social and environmental improvement will be incremental and inadequate. By linking owners with the full consequences of their decisions, argues Korten, life-enhancing values would guide financial decisions. His provocative description of life-sustaining economies embedded in local communities provides a guideline for transforming the "rotten and carcinogenic" pie Ynestra King warns us about.

It also reminds us that the trend toward sustainability is a realistic potential future trajectory that is sought by a variety of current initiatives. Corporations will take on very different forms as sustainability initiatives continue. However, as the stances organizations take toward environmental concerns shift toward the sustainability end of the continuum, the trajectory toward sustainability is encouraged.

NOTE

We thank George Cheney for his participation in developing the coding scheme for this study.

REFERENCES

Callenbach, E., Capra, F., Goldman, L., Lutz, R., & Marburg, S. (1993). *EcoManagement: The Elmwood guide to ecological auditing and sustainable business*. San Francisco, CA: Berrett-Koehler.

Cannon, T. (1994). *Corporate responsibility*. London: Pitman.

Carson, R. (1962). *Silent spring*. Boston, MA: Houghton-Mifflin.

Clean Air Act. 42 U.S.C. § 7401 *et seq.* (1970).

Clean Water Act. P.L. 95–217 (December 27, 1977).

Comprehensive Environmental Response, Compensation, and Liability Act. 26 U.S.C. §§ 4611–4682 (1980).

Donaldson, T. (2005). Moral minimums for multinationals. In S. Collins-Chobanian (Ed.), *Ethical challenges to business as usual* (pp. 129–141). Upper Saddle River, NY: Pearson/Prentice-Hall.

Dunphy, D., Griffiths, A., & Benn, S. (2003). *Organizational change for corporate sustainability*. London: Routledge.

Family and Medical Leave Act. 29 U.S.C. § 2601 *et seq.* (1993).

Frankel, C. (1998). *In earth's company*. Gabriola Island, BC: New Society Publishers.

Friedman, M. (2005). The social responsibility of business is to increase its profits. In S. Collins-Chobanian (Ed.), *Ethical challenges to business as usual* (pp. 224–229). Upper Saddle River, NJ: Pearson, Prentice-Hall. (Reprinted from *New York Times Magazine*, pp. 32–33, 122–126, September 13, 1970)

Holliday, C. O., Schmidheiny, S., & Watts, P. (2002). *Walking the talk: The business case for sustainable development*. San Francisco, CA: Berrett-Koehler.

King, Y. (1989). The ecology of feminism and the feminism of ecology. In J. Plant (Ed.), *Healing the wounds: The promise of ecofeminism* (pp. 18–28). Philadelphia: New Society Publishers.

King, Y. (1990). Healing the wounds: Feminism, ecology, and the nature/culture dualism. In I. Diamond & G. Orenstein (Eds.), *Reweaving the world: The emergence of ecofeminism* (pp. 106–121). San Francisco, CA: Sierra Club Books.

Korten, D. (1995). *When corporations rule the world*. West Hartford, CT and San Francisco, CA: Kumarian Press and Berrett-Koehler.

Korten, D. (1999). *The post-corporate world: Life after capitalism*. West Hartford, CT and San Francisco, CA: Kumarian Press and Berrett-Koehler.

Korten, D. (2005). Economies for life. In S. Collins-Chobanian (Ed.), *Ethical challenges to business as usual* (pp. 573–581). Upper Saddle River, NJ: Pearson, Prentice-Hall.

Laszlo, C. (2003). *The sustainable company.* Washington, DC: Island Press.

Peterson, T. R. (1997). *Sharing the earth: The rhetoric of sustainable development.* Columbia: University of South Carolina Press.

Schmidheiny, S. (1992). *Changing course: A global business perspective on development and the environment.* Cambridge, MA: MIT Press.

Standard & Poor's Corporation. (1999). *Standard & Poor's Register of Corporations, Directors, and Executives.* New York: Author.

Superfund Amendments and Reauthorization Act. 42 U.S.C. § 9601 *et seq.* (1986).

Taylor, F. (1911). *The principles of scientific management.* New York: Harper Bros.

World Commission on Environment and Development. (1987). *Our common future.* Oxford: Oxford University Press.

23

Greening of Corporations?

Eco-talk and the Emerging Social Imaginary of Sustainable Development

SHARON M. LIVESEY

JULIE GRAHAM

CORPORATE ECO-TALK AND THE PERFORMANCE OF SUSTAINABLE DEVELOPMENT

A new form of corporate eco-communication emerged in the late 1980s and early 1990s, distinct from the crisis communication arising out of environmental disasters such as the poisonous gas leak at Union Carbide's plant in Bhopal, India, or the nearly 11 million gallon oil spill of the *Exxon Valdez* in Alaska's pristine Prince William Sound. Now companies found themselves responding to controversies caused not by their wrongdoing or negligence but by society's changing expectations. Changing social values had made unacceptable the narrow economic calculus by which they had conventionally operated, forcing them into public debates with their critics where new values were articulated and performed.

The new corporate eco-talk involved businesses in adopting and adapting emerging concepts of sustainable development. A number of companies moved beyond debate to dialogue with a wide range of stakeholders, including social advocacy groups; in a few cases, they ventured further, entering into eco-collaborations with nongovernmental organizations (NGOs) dedicated to protecting the natural environment and human rights. Such efforts could be taken simply as public relations maneuvers or cynical attempts by businesses to avoid regulation or deflect criticism without changing their practices in any substantial respects. We take a different view. Whatever the original instrumental intent, language and symbolic action may have constitutive effects beyond what any particular agents—corporate communication departments, CEOs, other corporate rhetors, or their critics—can control. Corporate eco-talk participates in (re)creating the firm and (re)constructing its relationship to nature, while opening up novel possibilities of understanding and action at the societal level. In the cases we document here, new forms of corporate behavior and relationships with internal and external stakeholders emerged. These were integral to and constitutive of what can be perceived as a society-wide shift toward corporate social responsibility, enacted through such practices as environmental and social reporting, stakeholder dialogue, and NGO–business partnerships.

In this chapter, we focus primarily on a rhetorical contest between the Royal Dutch/Shell Group and critics of its environmental and human rights record in Nigeria. Our analysis foregrounds the performative effects of discourse, as evidenced first in ruptures and shifts in social values and norms that threatened traditional modes of development and their ability to sustain Shell's social license to operate. We then demonstrate the performativity of Shell's own eco-talk, focusing on the new organizational practices that emerged out of its rhetorical engagements with its critics. We also discuss more briefly two cases involving other sectors—the fast-food industry and rice agriculture in the United States—where shifts in social values contributed to the emergence of collaborations between businesses and NGOs. This innovative institutional form exemplified win–win environmentalism, embodying a particular understanding and performance of sustainable development.

Taken together, these three local examples both reflected and consolidated particular meanings of sustainability. We do not want to suggest, however, that corporate eco-talk or the innovative practices that flowed from it necessarily signify unidirectional corporate progress toward sustainability, for we do not see sustainable development as a fixed goal or set of technical outcomes. Rather, it is a value that informs ongoing ethical practice. As such, it must (and will) be continually defined and redefined in local skirmishes and political contests both within and outside the corporation, struggles that have transforming effects on corporate identities, values, and modes of operation. We argue that this is how sustainability is actually performed—in other words, how it is made a reality at the level of the corporation, and how it potentially becomes hegemonic (although necessarily contested) at the level of society as a whole.

FRAMING THE CONTEST: LANGUAGE/PERFORMANCE/ ENVIRONMENT/ DEVELOPMENT

In 1995, the Royal Dutch/Shell Group, one of the largest petroleum products companies in the world, was the target of international protests and threatened with consumer boycotts because of its failure to publicly oppose the Nigerian government, Shell Nigeria's local business partner,[1] when it executed nine Ogoni activists. Among the nine was Ken Saro-Wiwa, an internationally acclaimed journalist and writer who had spearheaded the environmental protest against Shell. The incident precipitated a complex set of debates between Shell and its critics over corporate responsibility for the natural environment and human rights. The Movement for the Survival of the Ogoni People (MOSOP), Greenpeace, the Sierra Club, Amnesty International, Human Rights Watch, the media, and other stakeholders in Shell's sociopolitical milieu introduced dissident voices that disrupted Shell's institutionalized practices and beliefs. The

shocks to Shell's image challenged its modernist rationality and provoked what Shell itself called a "transformation" in its corporate culture (Knight, 1998, p. 2).[2] The company moved from the taken-for-granted language and practices of economic development toward a cautious commitment to sustainable development. Moreover, as Shell attempted to balance its economic, environmental, and social responsibilities, it opened itself to such potentially democratizing communication practices as stakeholder engagement, dialogue, and "social" or triple-bottom-line reporting, which combined accounts of corporate economic, environmental, and social performance (Elkington, 1998).

By examining contrapuntal texts of Shell and its critics, we demonstrate the dynamics of Shell's corporate identity transformation and, perhaps more important, trace a particular corporation's emerging practice of sustainable development. This temporary and local fixing of meaning is both an instance of the performativity of discourse (in that Shell remade its identity in line with its understanding of broad social and environmental imperatives) and of the (re)constitution of discourse through everyday practice (in that the meaning of sustainable development was embodied in and transformed by Shell's language and actions). The language employed in the contests between Shell and its critics was not just an aspect of Shell's culture and its external environment narrowly conceived. Rather, the language here was a reflection of, and a shaping force in, larger sociopolitical understandings of the ecological problematic and of corporate responsibility for the environment (Hajer, 1997; Peterson, 1997).

Shell's Green Talk as Corporate Discursive Performance

The eco-talk that emerged in Shell's struggle over Nigeria can be seen as involved in producing "systems of shared meanings that facilitate organized action" (Smircich & Stubbart, 1985, p. 724)—in other words, as constitutive of the corporation itself and, ultimately, of an emerging social imaginary of sustainable development. In particular, its representations of nature affected the way the firm conceived of its relationship to the natural world, which in turn engendered new practices of corporate environmental responsibility (Clark & Jennings, 1997; Livesey, 2002). As the firm's environmental practice changed, so did its relationships with external stakeholders and its conception (and self-perception) of corporate accountability. In this way, the public eco-talk of corporations such as Shell can be seen as performative (Cheney & Christensen, 2000; Weick, 1995), constituting or consolidating the dominance of society-wide beliefs and values as well as the behavioral possibilities and patternings they afford (Fairclough, 1992).

Shell's changing relations to nature and to stakeholders, however, must be seen as formatively tied to the shifting fates of certain historically evolved discourses or socioeconomic paradigms. To contextualize Shell's eco-meaning making, we offer a simplified and schematized outline of shifts among the discourses of development, environmentalism, and sustainable development over the past 50 years.

Changing Social Discourses of Development and Environment

While discourses incorporate widely accepted understandings, social practices, and institutional forms (Fairclough, 1992), they are neither simple nor unambiguous. Instead, they harbor competing or conflicting elements, and actors located within particular discursive domains derive their positionings from a range of meanings, practices, and norms. Coupled with the fact that dominant discourses are always contested, this discursive dispersion means that organizations, like other actors, must ceaselessly strive to reproduce particular commitments and identities, to sustain their stories and their definitions of, for example, progress and development, and to (re)constitute their notions of the boundaries and legitimate activities of the firm (Butler, 1993; Gibson-Graham, 1996; Hajer, 1997). The contradictory and spotty individual and organizational performances can be seen, over time, as consolidating the dominance of one discourse and undermining that of another. It is this process of consolidation that is invoked when we say that discourse is performative, bringing into being certain types of institutions and practices, enactments and enforcements, mainstreams and deviations. Hindsight is the appropriate perspective from which to view this "performation," in this case of different regimes of environmental/societal interaction.

According to Hajer (1997), *the* central question in modern society is how the current ecological "crisis" is to be understood. Across a spectrum of social groups and institutions, the natural environment has become a site of discursive struggle arising out of alternative representations of the nature/society interface. Among these, the traditional discourse of development, which postulates social progress measured in terms of economic indicators such as gross domestic product, is perhaps the dominant social paradigm (Egri & Pinfield, 1996). Employing a utilitarian, anthropocentric view of nature as resource and sink, developmentalism treats the environment as separate, knowable, and susceptible to control. Its confident stance is grounded in a modernist, technocratic ethos that privileges expert knowledge, the methodologies of hard science, and the bureaucratic procedures through which expert determinations are accepted and enforced (Peterson, 1997).

Discourses of radical environmentalism began to disrupt the dominant development discourse beginning in the 1960s, when the environmental movement was galvanized by the publication of Rachel Carson's (1962) *Silent Spring*. Using scientific evidence to mobilize public awareness of the toxic side effects of industrial progress, Carson showed the connection between environmental and human health and the risks of unproblematic commitment to economic development. Over time, green advocacy groups positioned themselves as "relentless critics" of business (Krupp, 1986, p. 1), and industrial failures such as Chernobyl, Bhopal, and Three Mile Island magnified the impact of their critique.

As the environmental movement burgeoned in the 1980s, groups promoting a more ecocentric view of nature demanded radical changes in patterns of production and consumption (Dowie, 1995). At the same time, however, alternative discourses of sustainable development began to surface in the public arena. Sustainability was given wide currency by *Our Common Future*, a report produced by the United Nations World Commission on Environment and Development (1987) and more informally known as the Brundtland Report. Brundtland called for an integrated, global approach to environmental problems and offered the possibility of consensus by balancing human development needs against environmental well-being. But it defined sustainability in broad and vague terms, conceptualizing sustainable development simply as "meet[ing] the needs of the present without compromising the ability of future generations to meet [theirs]" (p. 43), and as "promot[ing] harmony among human beings and between humanity and nature" (p. 65). This led to continuing debate over the meaning (or meaninglessness) of the term,[3] a debate that some have interpreted as indicating the concept's lack of viability. From our perspective, however, lack of initial specification is a quality common to all universals, including "freedom," "democracy," "community," and "environment," that must be defined and redefined through particular local enactments (Gibson-Graham, 2006; Gladwin, Kennelly, & Krause, 1995).

The shifting fortunes of these discourses of development, environment, and sustainable development, so smoothly narrated here, play out much more complexly and confusingly in the agonistic interactions of corporate social engagement. Shell's transformation—its move away from a narrow economic conception of its corporate responsibility toward a particular enactment of sustainability—was brought about through public debate with its critics. In what we are calling Shell's discursive crisis in Nigeria, all three of these discourses were at play, prompting and sustaining intense conflict among the actors. The texts of that conflict document the company's transformation, allowing us to see the micro-leveltwists and turns that ultimately perform/institute sustainable development (at least in one of its guises).

CONTENDING VOICES IN NIGERIA

Shell's early Nigerian controversy offers a wealth of materials that are publicly available from the company and its critics. Among other things, the company's senior executives discussed its evolving social and environmental sensitivity with unusual frankness. While Shell's environmental communication and, indeed, the conflict over the proper role of Shell in Nigeria, are ongoing, we focus primarily on company texts published between 1995 and 1997, as well as earlier and contemporaneous texts of critics that deal with Shell's problems in Nigeria. The corporate texts illustrate the company's early and middle-stage responses to the issue of environmental and social responsibility, and anticipate the symbolically important moment of publication of the Shell Group'sfirst annual social report, *Profits and Principles—Does There Have To Be a Choice?* (Knight, 1998).[4]

Ecological Warfare or Development in the Niger Delta?

Shell's local exploration and production company, the Shell Petroleum Development Company of Nigeria (SPDC, often referred to as Shell Nigeria), operated in a joint venture with the Nigerian government and two European oil companies, which were minority partners. The Nigerian government derived 80% of its federal revenues and 90% of its foreign exchange from royalties and taxes provided by multinational oil companies such as Shell, which was the country's largest producer. SPDC also contributed significantly to Shell's bottom line, accounting for about 14% of the company's total oil production worldwide. In 1995, about 80% of Nigerian oil came from the Niger Delta (Lawrence, 1999a).

Conflict between Shell and its critics stemmed from their fundamentally different understandings of corporate responsibility, of the human relationship to nature, and of the basis of rights to natural resources. According to the critics, weak environmental regulation meant that indigenous peoples, such as the Ogoni farmers and fishermen who lived in the Niger Delta, suffered severe economic, ecological, and health impacts from oil production while gaining little or no benefit from the oil that came from their land. Shell's activities also had more general environmentally deleterious effects. In Nigeria in 1995, for example, 75% of gas byproducts from oil drilling were flared—burned off in the open air—as compared to a world average of less than 5%, and less than 1% in the United States. Flaring caused some of the worst local environmental pollution as well as contributing adversely to global warming (Essential Action & Global Exchange, 2000, n. 7). Between 1982 and 1992, 40% of Shell's total oil spills worldwide had been in Nigeria, suggesting that Shell's standards for environmentally responsible performance in Nigeria were particularly slack (Rowell, 1994, n. 38, citing *Oil Spill Intelligence Report*). Oil spills threatened farming and fishing, which were the primary means of sustenance for the local communities, and also harmed the Delta's mangrove swamps, one of the largest and most ecologically sensitive wetlands in the world (SPDC, 1997a).

For Saro-Wiwa and MOSOP as well as other tribal chiefs in the Delta, oil company devastation of the land amounted to "ecological war" against the people (e.g., MOSOP, n.d.a , ¶ 2; Saro-Wiwa,

1995a, p. 131).[5] Oil production activities threatened not only the land but also the "extinction" of the Ogoni themselves (MOSOP, n.d.b, ¶ 5; Saro-Wiwa, 1995a, p. 132). Beginning in the early 1990s, joined by global NGOs and the media, Saro-Wiwa, MOSOP, and others began to publicize the environmental degradation and inequity stemming from Shell's presence in Ogoniland. Graphic descriptions of environmental devastation emerged.

In one newspaper story, for instance, Ogoniland was described as existing in a "hydrological vice grip: impure rain water, impure stream water, but no pipe born water" (Niboro, 1993, ¶ 15), with night skies lit "like one huge torch" as a result of flaring (¶ 12). At the World Conference of Indigenous Peoples on Territory, Environment and Development at the Rio de Janeiro Earth Summit in 1992, the Niger Delta Rivers chiefs pictured their communities as engulfed by ecological calamity:

> Air pollution . . . emissions and flares day and night, producing poisonous gases that are silently and systematically wiping out . . . and otherwise endangering the life of plants, game and man himself . . . widespread water pollution and soil/ land pollution . . . agricultural lands contaminated with oil spills. (Dappa-Biriye et al., 1992, quoted in Rowell, 1994, ¶ 30 and n. 44)

In a film produced by environmentalists and cited on an NGO website, a chief from the village of Korokoro explained:

> When crude oil touches the leaf of a yam or cassava, or whatever economic trees we have, it dries immediately. It's so dangerous. And somebody who was coming from . . . Shell was arguing with me. So I told him that you're an engineer. . . . I did not go to the university, but I know that what you have been saying in the university sleeps with me here. So you cannot be more qualified in crude oil than myself who sleeps with crude oil. (Chief GNK Gininwa, quoted in Essential Action, n.d., ¶ 7 and n. 6)

Expressing here the immediacy of the connection between his people and nature, Chief Gininwa sets the evidence of his body against engineering and economics to resist the arguments and assurances of expertise. Similarly, Chief Dappa-Biriye links human to plant and animal suffering: all local species are endangered. This is the discourse of grassroots environmentalism, powerful and persuasive in its intimate familiarity with local environments and the harsh realities its speakers endure (see Peterson, 1997).

The local critics also highlighted the vast inequities in wealth and concomitant distortions of tribal life produced by the Ogoni's unauthorized insertion into an international market economy. They believed that the land was their "ultimate heritage," grounding not only their identity but also their right to its sustenance (Saro-Wiwa, 1995b, ¶ 1). By their estimates, $30 billion of oil had been pumped from Ogoni territories by 1990, but the Ogoni themselves saw little or no return in the form of royalties, local development of the economy, or community support structures (MOSOP, n.d.a; Niboro, 1993). This situation, where legal ownership rather than historical co-presence determined the flow of nature's benefits, struck the Ogoni as bitterly ironic. Their "wealth had become a nightmare" (Ake, 1994, ¶ 1). "Black gold" had become "a curse for them while feeding others fat" (Ekeocha, 1993, ¶ 2)—including most prominently Shell and its local partners.

The arguments for a fairer and more immediate share of nature's benefits surfaced the contradictions in the progress myth by making immediate and visible the environmental harm caused by oil production and by juxtaposing the costs to the poor against the benefits to the rich. Using an alternative logic, Saro-Wiwa and MOSOP claimed "Ogoni (like hundreds of other small ethnic groups in Nigeria) deserves to control its own resources, environment, and the right to rule itself" (MOSOP, n.d.b, ¶ 11). Saro-Wiwa himself often employed the powerful and pointed language of international political economy, representing collusion between oil companies and the corrupt Nigerian regime as the determining factor in Ogoni dispossession. In Saro-Wiwa's (1994) words, relationships such as that between Shell and the Nigerian government were "[T]he root of the Nigerian malaise and must be rooted out if coming generations are to find peace and progress. The union between international capitalist and local oppressors which denigrates our people must now be broken" (¶ 14; see also Saro-Wiwa, 1995a). Here the "union" with corporate capital does not bring progress, but rather positions some Nigerians as their brothers' "oppressors."

Following Saro-Wiwa, others used the metaphor of "heartless exploitation" to characterize the situation in Ogoniland (e.g., Ake, 1994, ¶ 4). This metaphor inverted the "head and heart" hierarchy that Shell typically used to frame its rhetorical struggles over the environment and environmental justice (see, e.g., Wybrew, 1995). Whereas Shell valued scientific reason, painstaking evaluation, and thoughtful consultation over what they saw as undisciplined emotion, to the Ogoni these "values of the head" seem unconscionable, elevating profits and conventional business performance above responsible care for environment and community. The language in these instances reflects pre-Brundtland political debates over competing rights of North and South and the meanings of "progress" and "development" in the context of emerging economies.

In 1993, MOSOP had organized a massive nonviolent public protest in Ogoniland against Shell, in which two thirds of the people participated. This had led the company to withdraw its staff and close its Ogoniland operations (SPDC, 1997b). Angry at MOSOP's impact on Shell's most valuable production sites in Ogoni and afraid of the unsettling precedent for other Niger Delta tribes, General Sani Abacha, the Nigerian dictator, looked for ways to crack down on MOSOP leaders. In 1994, Saro-Wiwa and other MOSOP leaders were arrested on charges of conspiracy to murder four Ogoni chiefs. On November 10, 1995, Saro-Wiwa and nine other Ogoni were executed following a kangaroo court–style military tribunal.

Abacha's intent to silence Shell's critics backfired, for the executions became an international cause célèbre, powerfully symbolizing the deadly effect of Shell's presence in Nigeria (MOSOP, n.d.b). Although the company maintained that it had pursued quiet diplomacy with the Nigerian government, MOSOP, international environmental and human rights groups, and progressive companies (most prominently, The Body Shop) insisted that Shell could have intervened more forcefully. Joined by churches, writers' groups, and socially responsible investor funds, they protested against Shell at its London headquarters, urging Shell to divest its Nigerian holdings. The widespread attention precipitated a number of investigative studies of the Nigerian situation.[6] There were increasingly strong demands that Shell revise its corporate structure, implement new policies related to environmental management and reparation, develop procedures to safeguard human rights, and expand reporting practices to make

corporate social and environmental performance more transparent. As pressure increased, the calls for Shell boycotts began to take effect. The World Bank withdrew funding for an important natural gas project, the Metro Toronto Council rejected a contract with Shell, and certain charitable organizations refused to accept Shell's contributions.[7]

Shell responded to Saro-Wiwa's martyrdom and related criticism by expressing "shock" and "sadness" over his execution (Knight, 1998, p. 2; SPDC, 1997b, p. 7). Not surprisingly, however, the company still minimized and displaced blame for the political and ecological problems in Nigeria. The booklet published by Shell Nigeria in 1997 is representative of its initial public posture (SPDC, 1997b). As suggested by its title, *Nigeria Brief: Ogoni and the Niger Delta*, the report was legalistic and defensive. SPDC posited that it had been "unfairly used to raise the international profile" of the MOSOP campaign against the Nigerian government (inside front cover). Acknowledging but downplaying environmental problems, it attributed to sabotage two thirds of all company oil spills that took place in Nigeria in 1996. It admitted that corporate facilities needed upgrading but argued that Ogoni allegations of environmental "devastation" were grossly exaggerated (pp. 8–9). It cited journalists' conclusions that, of the huge damage to the Delta "routinely claimed by campaigners," Shell's geographically limited operations contributed only a tiny "fraction" (*The Independent*, November 8, 1996, cited in SPDC, 1997b, p. 6).

Shell bolstered its position by referencing World Health Organization and World Bank reports that downplayed the link between health and gas flaring or other forms of oil pollution. These authorities said that poverty-related issues, including population growth, deforestation, erosion, and over-farming, were the primary causes of the Ogoni's problems (SPDC, 1995; SPDC, 1997b, p. 8).[8] Using a tactic familiar in corporate environmental disputes, Shell claimed a lack of "evidence" linking such problems as asthma and skin rashes to oil company activities (p. 10). Shell further rationalized its practices by arguing that "responsible citizenship" in cases of environmental degradation was demonstrated by legal reparation agreements "signed by all parties" (p. 11).[9] It also employed a "common practice" defense, arguing that outdated technologies in use in Nigeria were "acceptable" in the 1960s and 1970s when its facilities were built (p. 14). These points, of course, ignored the power relations encoded in institutional norms and procedures (see Human Rights Watch, 1998).

As to questions of human rights and demands for environmental justice, the company expressed sympathy with Ogoni concerns but argued that they were outside the domain of its authority. While acknowledging "some influence" with the government, Shell Nigeria emphasized the limits of that influence, stating that it would be "dangerous and wrong" for Shell to yield to campaigners' demands that it seek to have Saro-Wiwa's verdict overturned (SPDC, 1995, p. 1). Shell Group Chairman Cor Herkströter (1996a) argued similarly that the company lacked "license" to interfere in politics or the sovereign mandate of government (¶¶ 69–70; see also Herkströter, 1996b). Given the corporation's economic hold over the Nigerian government, such claims were as unpersuasive to Shell's NGO and international critics as they were to the local people. Moreover, Shell had failed to address the fact that it was clearly advantaged by the government's choices.

A July 1997 speech by Group Managing Director Phil Watts at the Fourth African–African American Summit in Harare, Zimbabwe, reflects the influence of traditional developmentalism among Shell's executive leadership at the time. Watts (1997a) argued that "development is the key challenge for the people of this continent. Supporting this development is a major challenge for the world community" (¶ 1). Economic liberalization—the opening of markets—is important to attract "capital flows—and associated transfer of skills—which have been so important for progress elsewhere" (¶ 3). In this vision, economic development, enhanced by Shell's charitable giving and skill transfer, constituted the primary cure for poverty and social deprivation. Such development would both emerge from, and be the basis of, "long-term partnership with the peoples and governments [of Africa]—creating companies that are rooted in African society" (¶ 33). Environmental problems, on the other hand, involved "no easy choices or instant solutions" but rather demonstrated the need to "make constant trade-offs" (¶ 36)—trade-offs that, not surprisingly, often favored economics over environment.

Watts's generic prescriptions, the justifications in the Shell Nigeria report, and Chairman Herkströter's exculpating rationales contrast starkly with the immediacy of the Ogoni story of a ruined nature and community. They reflect a bureaucratic discursive mode that compartmentalizes and fragments knowledge to fit institutional forums and formulas (Fairclough, 1992; Peterson, 1997). They render "reality" in terms of expert categories, proofs, and limits on corporate jurisdictional powers that seem far removed from the felt "reality" of the executions and everyday life in the Niger Delta—the downside of "progress" and development. More generally, these texts reveal Shell's predilection, shared with corporations generally, for representing itself as apolitical (Cheney & Christensen, 2000)—that is, as a subject and neutral party rather than a powerful agent in the political order and in the marketplace. Historical arguments (e.g., that such have been the costs of development historically) and promises of future progress (e.g., present poverty will eventually yield to the comforts of a consumer society) shield the corporation from blame for present harms.

CORPORATE REFLEXIVITY AND CHANGE

Despite this evidently defensive posture, sustained controversy and public relations crises[10] ultimately prompted reflexivity and culture change at Shell (Lawrence, 1999b). The company began to use outsider perspectives to interpret itself to itself (see Cheney & Christensen, 2000); it drew upon market research and stakeholder consultation to discover how stakeholders perceived the company, and what kinds of environmental and social performance were expected by society at large. Shell's investigations generated cognitive dissonance and a far-reaching sense of disturbance within the corporation, leading to conversations and ultimately to programs designed to produce and support change: "We looked in the mirror and we neither recognised nor liked some of what we saw. We have set about putting it right" (Knight, 1998, p. 2).

Of course, Shell's move toward acceptance of greater social and environmental responsibility was neither immediate nor uniform; it occurred at varying rates and to various degrees across different parts of the company and, indeed, was hardest to achieve in Nigeria (Wheeler, Fabig, & Boele, 2002). In fact, Shell's sustainability consultant John Elkington, who ultimately shaped Shell's triple-bottom-line reporting, initially refused Shell's request for help. In his two-page contribution to Shell's first social report (Knight, 1998),

Elkington noted that his refusal had been based on his feeling that many Shell executives were "in denial" and that the mission of his "values-led consultancy" would be better served by continuing to "leverage change [at Shell] from the outside" (p. 37). The Shell Group chairman, however, showed significant leadership in publicly acknowledging his company's failures and its commitments to change. In a remarkably candid speech, Herkströter (1996a) blamed Shell's "stumblings" on its inability to recognize newly emerging social values and noted that the "vacuum" of moral authority had been filled by NGOs because "the more traditional structures [of business and government had] failed to adapt" (¶ 45). He saw this failure to be the result of "technological arrogance" (¶ 58), which he attributed to the company culture and to the scientific and technical backgrounds of its people. "For most engineering problems," he continued, "there is a correct answer. For most social and political dilemmas there is a range of possible answers— almost all compromises" (¶ 59). In hindsight, Herkströter recognized that problems of the natural environment and human rights could not be contained by technical expertise or the conventions and structures of bureaucracy. Rather, they were *ethical* problems, requiring social negotiation and dialogue. As he acknowledged, "[A]lone we could never have reached the right approach. . . . [W]e should have discussed [these issues] in a more open and frank way with others in order to reach acceptable solutions" (Herkströter, 1996a ¶ 2).

The company's slowly and differentially changing values and practices were reflected even in 1997 speeches by Watts, where more traditional views of development were mixed with the language of sustainability. In his speech at Harare, for instance, although defining progress primarily in terms of economic liberalization and markets, he couched the discussion within a broader claim that development in Africa must be "sustainable" in order to provide "long-term value" (Watts, 1997a, ¶ 2). Both at Harare and later that year, he explicitly referenced the Brundtland Report when defining sustainable development for Shell in terms of "three essential pillars—economic development, human development and environmental sustainability" (Watts, 1997a, ¶ 4; see also Watts, 1997b, ¶¶ 53–56). This reference reflects a significant corporate event—the fact that early in 1997 the Shell Group had revised its general business principles to incorporate Brundtland and the notion of sustainability. By embracing this concept, even in terms that express tension, ambivalence, resistance, and contradiction, Shell seemed to acknowledge that the narrow economic terms of the progress myth and the development paradigm were no longer adequate and that it had to define its environmental and "social" obligations in new ways. Overall, Shell began to accept that its technical problem solving was inextricably tied to ethical practice.

Shell modified its behavior as well as its language. In fact, the company was at pains to emphasize that its actions had to match its words (see, e.g., Knight, 1998). It began to work with a new breed of sustainability consultants such as Elkington. In Nigeria, Shell put in place and publicized plans to track and report environmental problems, to upgrade its facilities, to reduce flaring, and to minimize the impacts of its future exploration activities (see Knight, 1998; SPDC, 1997a, 1998). Globally, in addition to expanding its general business principles to incorporate commitments to sustainable development and the United Nations Declaration of Human Rights, the company implemented changes in its corporate structure, developed environmental policies and programs, and adopted policies to protect human rights. Along with BP, Shell broke from the U.S. industry–led anti-Kyoto Global Climate Coalition in 1997 (Knight, 1998).

In terms of communication, Shell's leaders overtly espoused socially and environmentally responsible corporate citizenship in public forums around the globe. This was one of many steps in a larger plan to transform the company's traditionally secretive and inward-focused culture and make its operations more transparent. Shell promised that it would report on its social and environmental performance, hold dialogue with a wider range of stakeholders, listen better to critics' concerns, and experiment with new, unfamiliar, and potentially democratizing communication venues. For instance, company websites were developed to provide information and opportunity for debate on a variety of issues including Shell's role in Nigeria, corporate environmental responsibility, human rights, and global warming. Critics' comments were posted on the website together with answers by Shell spokespeople. In Camisea, Peru, Shell initiated dialogue with indigenous groups during the planning stages of a gas development project in the rainforest (Knight, 1998). Overall, to use Shell's words, its decision processes had been transformed from DAD—decide, announce, deliver—to DDD: dialogue, decide, deliver (Rothermund, 1998). It should be recognized, however, that these moves did not represent the adoption of an "environment-centered" vision of sustainable development. Rather, the company was explicit about its plan to tell its own story better—and to revitalize the discourse of development within the discourse of sustainability (see, e.g., Knight, 1998).[11]

FROM DIALOGUE TO ECO-COLLABORATION: ODD ALLIANCES OF SUSTAINABLE DEVELOPMENT

In the typically laggard extractive industries, Shell's innovative communication practices distinguished the company from many of its industry counterparts. In other industries, however, especially consumer-oriented industries in the United States, a number of firms were already pursuing an even more adventurous strategy, embarking on collaborations and partnerships with environmental NGOs. Whereas Shell used dialogue with outsiders and consultants to transform itself, these firms established *new organizational forms*, institutionalizing a distinctive type of environmentalism and of corporate social responsibility. Eco-collaboration between businesses and advocacy groups involved what became known as win–win environmentalism. In this model, sustainable development is fostered by greening corporations through market incentives (Krupp, 1986; Livesey, 1999). Environmentally responsible behavior simultaneously improves the company image and benefits the corporate bottom line through the development of innovative products and processes that reduce costs, increase productivity, or offer other competitive advantages in the marketplace (Waddell, 2000).

Eco-collaboration differed from other manifestations of corporate environmental action. Prior to 1990, companies had typically donated to green advocacy groups or causes, acted unilaterally to lessen the environmental impacts of their operations, or, at most, cooperated with like-minded people in related private enterprises or industry associations to develop environmental performance standards.[12] By contrast, environmental partnerships directly engaged critical outsiders in companies' internal decision making. Creating

alliances with former "enemies" meant working on business problems across divides of difference in order to find and implement solutions. In part, this required *using* difference to imagine innovative alternatives.

Two precedent-setting examples of eco-collaboration involved the fast-food giant McDonald's and California rice producers.[13] McDonald's joined with the ostensibly hostile environmental group Environmental Defense Fund (EDF)[14] in 1990 to establish a joint Waste Management Task Force that explored options to reduce the ecological impacts of McDonald's packaging. Before partnering with EDF, McDonald's had already attempted to green its image by taking a high-profile stance on the environment, exemplified by its 1989 annual report, which was formally dedicated to the environment and resembled an Audubon Society publication more than a typical corporate report. In addition, the company had sponsored environmental education programs for children and displayed a wealth of literature in its restaurants explaining its position on a number of environmental issues ranging from ozone depletion to preserving the rainforest to waste disposal. In New England, it had introduced recycling of its polystyrene clamshell packaging, and on Earth Day 1989 it committed $500 million to buying recycled materials for its restaurants as a way of boosting demand for products made from recyclables. These moves, however, had not deterred its critics. Eco-advocates continued to target McDonald's support for America's "throw-away society" where convenience outweighed environmental concerns. The company's famous clamshell packaging was a particular bone of contention because of its nondegradability, toxicity, and harmful effects on the ozone layer. Seeing an opportunity to develop alternative packaging options that would save costs for McDonald's and better protect the earth, EDF approached McDonald's to propose what became a precedent-setting collaboration between an NGO and a large, influential corporation.

The California Rice Industry Association (CRIA), which represented Sacramento Valley rice farmers, formed the Ricelands Habitat Partnership (RHP) together with environmental author/activist Marc Reisner and two waterfowl conservation groups—Ducks Unlimited and the California Waterfowl Association. Like McDonald's, prior to joining the RHP, the rice industry in California had faced mounting criticism from environmentalists. Postharvest practices of burning rice stubble were polluting the air over Sacramento, and rice was seen as consuming too much of California's scarce water. A six-year drought beginning in 1987 exacerbated the already intense competition among water users, including agricultural producers, urban and suburban developers, commercial salmon fishermen, and environmentalists. Although initially a critic, Reisner was persuaded that, with appropriate support and changes in certain practices, rice fields could serve environmental interests and help prevent the loss of farmland to suburban tract development. He became rice's advocate and a central force in the formation of the RHP. The waterfowl NGOs and Reisner worked with farmers to develop a project to flood rice fields in winter, which turned them into good compromise habitat for threatened waterfowl species migrating from Canada to Mexico and provided an alternative technique for farmers to rid their fields of rice stubble. The project gave farmers the opportunity to attract federal and state program funds designed to encourage eco-friendly agricultural practices. Plus, of course, the industry's environmental image was enhanced.

Although different from the Shell case in terms of outcome, the McDonald's–EDF and RHP cases resembled that of Shell in one important respect: the corporate moves toward eco-collaboration were triggered by discursive shifts—or, in Shell's words, changing social expectations—that had made certain taken-for-granted businesses practices unacceptable. In the United States, such changes were reflected in laws passed in response to public protest. McDonald's, for example, faced local regulations over its use and disposal of its polystyrene clamshells (Livesey, 1999). Similarly, Sacramento Valley rice farmers were threatened by environmental legislation, including soon-to-be-implemented bans on rice-stubble burning and federal laws to protect wildlife habitats by cutting back on agricultural water allocations.

In the McDonald's and RHP cases, solutions engendered under the partnerships addressed both business and environmental problems. At the symbolic level, as an institutional form that joined together business and eco-advocates, the eco-collaborations powerfully communicated the potential of win–win environmentalism and the viability of integrating economic and environmental interests. Because they united traditionally antagonistic groups, business eco-partnerships also represented new and daring public commitments—for both the

firms and the NGOs—on the "question of what the organization 'is' or 'stands for' or 'wants to be'" (Cheney & Christensen, 2000, p. 232), particularly in terms of environmental responsibility and sustainable development.

Symbolic results were matched by changes in behavior "on the ground," including innovative business practices that had positive environmental effects: less garbage, less smoke, more bird-sustaining habitat. Although the most widely publicized result of the McDonald's–EDF partnership was the company's eleventh hour decision to dump its clamshell packaging, in fact the partnership led to a 42-step corporate action plan to reduce behind-the-counter waste as well as customer garbage. Notions of what might constitute appropriate action by NGOs to protect the environment were changed, too; the RHP, for example, helped to gain acceptance for new concepts and practices such as "compromise habitat" and "dual use" of land (for economic and environmental purposes). The RHP also produced some surprising results. For example, rice producers acknowledged that they had entered into the collaboration out of self-interest (e.g., one commented, "We figured we could hug a duck; he'd save us" [rice farmer II, tr., p. 15]).[15] Yet, they found that the project ultimately gave them "linkage to . . . [many other] environmental issues through waterfowl" (rice farmer III, tr., p. 15). Eco-collaboration, in other words, had performative effects that exceeded the intentions of its participants.

Stories and story-telling about the win–win results of these collaborations were integral to their enactment and extended their constitutive effects. The McDonald's case was much publicized in the popular press (see Livesey, 1999) and in scholarly articles and books (e.g., Bendell, 2000; Wasik, 1996). In the case of the RHP, the participants themselves recognized the performative effects of story-telling about their partnership. As one farmer put it:

> The RHP [was] the first [collaboration] as a farm group. And when we tossed that stone, it was like a pool in the morning . . . and it's still rippling out there. . . . I got to tell the President of the United States about the Rice Habitat Partnership on national television . . . when we were writing the Farm Bill. And they used this whole partnership thing to implement national farm policy . . . because USDA [United States

Department of Agriculture] sees these partnerships as the only way to accomplish these environmental goals in the future. (rice farmer III, tr., p. 12)

Via story-telling, local initiatives were converted into exemplars that legitimized and institutionalized eco-collaboration and win–win environmentalism as a form of sustainable development (Bendell, 2000).

Of course, below the surface of the win–win story of eco-collaboration were the tensions likely to be felt in an alliance of former adversaries. These were expressed as rhetorical ambivalence and sometimes in outright conflict between the parties. For example, at a joint national press conference to announce the McDonald's–EDF partnership, EDF's leader, Fred Krupp, talked about preserving his organization's right to "bring out the heavy artillery" of litigation, lobbying, and public exposure of corporate wrongdoing (see Livesey, 1999). In the RHP, the rice farmers and the conservation groups fought about their different understandings of "truth." The conservationists wanted to proceed only on the basis of their "data" and scientifically proven hypotheses; they found CRIA too preoccupied with public relations. On the other hand, the farmers believed the conservationists to be too narrowly focused on waterfowl and insensitive to fish. Since the rice industry's idea of eco-community was shaped by the pragmatics of water politics in California, the farmers' focused on the need for consensual truth. Paradoxically, this gave them a view of the ecosystem that was sometimes broader and more flexible than that of the waterfowl scientists.

Expressions of difference and the heterogeneity of the groups produced identity strains, yet also served the partners' needs to remain recognizable to themselves and their primary stakeholders (compare Westley & Vredenburg, 1991). They also opened up space for personal and institutional change. Further, as the RHP example shows, difference sometimes served the partnerships' wider purposes of sustainable development by bringing alternative perspectives to bear. Finally, whether or not the partnerships succeeded or survived, the story that emerged from them contributed to the greater familiarity and potency of the discourse of sustainability.

PERFORMING SUSTAINABILITY: RHETORIC/DISCOURSE/ CONFLICT/TRANSFORMATION

Public relations theory has traditionally relied on classical rhetoric to explain the processes involved in the firm's symbolic management of its external environment through issue advocacy or crisis management (Cheney & Vibbert, 1987). This approach conceptualizes firms as managing or controlling their publics by creating, or restoring, goodwill.[16] Though suggestive, such theories do not fully capture the reflexive and constitutive nature of corporate discourse. Moving beyond classical rhetoric, Cheney and Christensen (2000) hold that the social reality of the organization is created and maintained through language and symbolic action. We understand this constitutive process as involving a dynamic interaction between broad social narratives (or discourses) and local enactments (including the stories they produce). Our interest is in the performativity of discourse at the levels of the firm *and* of society and in the complex interaction between corporate talk and social transformation(s).

In the case of Shell, because of evolving discourses of corporate social responsibility, the company had to defend its image and prove its trustworthiness, to account not just for the production of goods and services but also for the risks and harms resulting from its activities (Beck, 1992). By adopting and adapting the language of sustainable development, Shell both served its own identity needs and contributed to revising the progress myth that underpins modern corporations and a capitalist economy.

Discursive shifts also affected the U.S. fast-food and rice-producing industries, where changes in social norms led to environmental laws that threatened their conventional modes of operation. In these cases, the companies did not simply listen to their critics, but engaged them in their decision making through eco-collaborations designed to find solutions that simultaneously addressed business and environmental problems. Stories about the partnerships were integral to their ability to broaden their impacts on the wider society through the communication and legitimation of this emergent form of environmental problem solving. In these stories, green partnering both embodied and symbolized win–win environmentalism, a particular enactment of sustainable development.

We have emphasized that the language practices of Shell, McDonald's–EDF, and RHP participants have effects extending well beyond their impacts on local corporate and NGO identity, or even on the broader environmental movement. The narratives, conversations, and other texts produced by these actors are constitutive not just of the firm and the NGO but of discursive hegemony and larger patterns of institutional practice. Here we have drawn upon Butler's (1993) concept of performativity, understood as the "reiterative and citational practice by which discourse produces the effects that it names" (p. 2). In their everyday, often agonistic, sometimes banal iterations, corporate eco-talk and eco-collaborative storying bring into being the world of which they speak, revealing the power of "discourse to produce the phenomena that it regulates and constrains" (p. 2). This does not mean that sustainable development will ever be fully or permanently realized—all performance is subject to interruption and requires continual reenactment. Rather, it is to suggest that it matters what we think and say and the contexts and contests in which we say it.

In this light, like other scholarly research, our chapter constitutes a story with potential to shape understandings of sustainable development. We hope that it may help practitioners and researchers understand sustainable development as a contingent political and ethical practice rather than a goal or technology with measurable indicia that can be routinely described and universally applied. Perhaps our work will also encourage others to embrace a vision of the ethical and political effects of story-telling (including their own).

NOTES

We thank Cathy L. Hartman and Edwin R. Stafford of Utah State University for giving us access to transcripts of their interviews of participants in the Ricelands Habitat Partnership. We are also grateful to the *Journal of Business Communication* for permission to use previously published material and to the editors of this volume for their patience, insights, and helpful suggestions.

1. Shell operates through local companies (e.g., Shell UK, Shell Nigeria) that are owned by parent companies (Royal Dutch Petroleum Company and the "Shell" Transport and Trading Company), which in turn hold shares in the Royal Dutch/Shell Group of Companies (the Shell Group). The parent companies and the Group have overlapping executive committees.

2. Earlier in 1995, Shell had confronted an environmental crisis over its decision to sink the *Brent Spar*, an obsolete oil platform and rig in the North Atlantic. *Brent Spar* and Nigeria together promoted intense internal reflection and debate, ultimately leading Shell to transform its corporate culture. In this article, we focus on Shell's Nigerian troubles. For a fuller description of the *Brent Spar* controversy and its relationship to Nigeria, see Livesey (2001).

3. Brooks (1992) reported that a minimum of 40 working definitions of "sustainable development" had appeared within five years of the publication of Brundtland (cited in Hajer, 1997, p. 1; see also Meadowcroft, 2000; Peterson, 1997).

4. We include in the analysis here segments from corporate reports and "briefs," executive speeches, journal articles, media reports, and other materials publicly available from the external affairs departments and websites of the Shell Group, Shell UK, and Shell Nigeria and from NGO websites, particularly Greenpeace, MOSOP, and Human Rights Watch, which were Shell's chief critics on environmental matters. Citations in Shell's literature to particular groups guided our choice of texts critical of the company. For background inrmation, we relied on prior scholarly research and case studies, especially Lawrence (1999a, 1999b).

5. In Ogoni language, the same word is used for the "land" and the "people" (Saro-Wiwa, 1995a, p. 2).

6. See, for example, Human Rights Watch (1998), Manby (1999), Project Underground and Rainforest Action Network (1997), the Unrepresented Nations and Peoples Organization (1995), and the World Council of Churches, as cited in Lawrence (1999a).

7. In 1997, a nonprofit shareholder group put forward a resolution at Shell's annual general meeting demanding measures to increase corporate environmental and social responsibility (Lawrence, 1999b).

8. On this count, Shell attempted to show its good faith through its sponsorship of a Niger Delta Environmental Survey, funded by the oil industry (SPDC, 1997b, p. 10), but because of the funding, the Ogoni viewed the survey with suspicion, and its key representative quit the panel (MOSOP, n.d.a; see also SPDC, 1995).

9. Shell Nigeria provided a figure of $16.6 million for oil spill compensation, aggregated for all Nigeria and paid between 1992 and 1996, but no data as to the average compensation amounts paid in Ogoni (SPDC, 1997b, p. 9).

10. See note 2.

11. In Nigeria, the company's transformation was constrained by its polarized position and the

political context there, including ongoing popular opposition. Although Shell Nigeria committed to, and did, significantly reduce gas flaring and took other steps to improve its environmental and social performance, its relationship with the Ogoni community has remained contentious (see Wheeler, Fabig, & Boele, 2002). For evidence of Shell's transformation, therefore, we need to look primarily at its behavior and communication in other settings.

12.   E.g., formulation of standards such as the chemical industry's Responsible Care program (see Livesey, 1999).

13.   For more complete accounts of these eco-collaborations, see Livesey (1999) and Hartman (2001).

14.   Environmental Defense Fund subsequently changed its name to Environmental Defense.

15.   Interviews conducted in 1995 with participants in the RHP were confidential. Hence, interviewees are designated generically; e.g., rice farmer I, rice farmer II, etc. Page numbers refer to typed transcripts of oral interviews.

16.   Recent theorists distinguish strategies that defend the firm against outside claims (e.g., denial/buffering) from those that promote identification between the corporation and its publics (e.g., bolstering/bridging) (see Ice, 1991; Meznar & Nigh, 1995). Buffering protects against outside pressures and secures the firm's legitimacy, while bridging may "promote internal adaptation to changing external circumstances" (Meznar & Nigh, 1995, p. 977).

REFERENCES

Ake, C. (1994, July 25). Nightmare of state violence. *Tell.* Retrieved April 19, 2000, from http://www.mosopcanada.org/text/info/mosop0245.html.

Beck, U. (1992). *Risk society: Towards a new modernity.* London: Sage.

Bendell, J. (Ed.). (2000). *Terms for endearment: Business, NGOs and sustainable development.* Sheffield, UK: Greenleaf.

Butler, J. (1993). *Bodies that matter: On the discursive limits of "sex."* New York: Routledge.

Carson, R. (1962). *Silent spring.* New York: Houghton Mifflin.

Cheney, G., & Christensen, L. T. (2000). Identity at issue: Linkages between "internal" and "external" organizational communication. In F. M. Jablin & L. L. Putnam (Eds.), *New handbook of organizational communication* (pp. 231–269). Thousand Oaks, CA: Sage.

Cheney, G., & Vibbert, S. L. (1987). Corporate discourse: Public relations and issue management. In F. M. Jablin, L. L. Putnam, K. H. Roberts, & L. W. Porter (Eds.), *Handbook of organizational communication: An interdisciplinary perspective* (pp. 165–194). Newbury Park, CA: Sage.

Clark, V. J., & Jennings, P. D. (1997). Talking about the natural environment: A means for deinstitutionalization? *American Behavioral Scientist, 40,* 454–464.

Dowie, M. (1995). *Losing ground: American environmentalism at the close of the twentieth century.* Cambridge, MA: MIT Press.

Egri, C., & Pinfield, L. (1996). Organizations and the biosphere: Ecologies and environments. In S. Clegg, C. Hardy, & W. Nord (Eds.), *Handbook of organization studies* (pp. 459–483). London: Sage.

Ekeocha, O. (1993, May 17). A cry for justice—or drum beats of treason? *African Guardian.* Retrieved April 19, 2000, from www.mosopcanada.org/text/info/mosop0245.html.

Elkington, J. (1998). *Cannibals with forks: The triple bottom line of 21st century business.* Gabrioloa Island, BC: New Society Publishers.

Essential Action. (n.d.). *Shell in Nigeria: What are the issues?* Retrieved May 30, 2000 from http://essentialaction.org/shell/issues.html.

Essential Action & Global Exchange. (2000, January 25). *Oil for nothing: Multinational corporations, environmental destruction, death and impunity in the Niger Delta* [Report]. Retrieved April 19, 2000, from http://www.essentialaction.org/shell/report/index.html.

Fairclough, N. (1992). *Discourse and social change.* Cambridge: Polity Press.

Gibson-Graham, J. K. (1996). *The end of capitalism (as we knew it): A feminist critique of political economy.* Oxford: Blackwell Publishers.

Gibson-Graham, J. K. (2006). *A post-capitalist politics.* Minneapolis: University of Minnesota Press.

Gladwin, T. N., Kennelly, J. J., & Krause, T. (1995). Shifting paradigms for sustainable development: Implications for management theory and research. *Academy of Management Review, 20,* 874–907.

Hajer, M. A. (1997). *The politics of environmental discourse: Ecological modernization and the policy process.* Oxford: Clarendon Press.

Hartman, C. L. (2001). Catalyzing environmental collaborations: The role of green alliance entrepreneurs. In M. Moore & R. Moore (Eds.), *Proceedings of the Annual*

Conference of the Academy of Marketing (pp. 80–86). San Diego, CA: Academy of Marketing Science.

Herkströter, C. (1996a, October 11). *Dealing with contradictory expectations—the dilemmas facing multinationals* [Speech]. Retrieved November 21, 1999, from http://www.Shell.com/library/speech/0,1525,2424,00.htm.

Herkströter, C. (1996b, November 25). *Challenge and change: Making a contribution in historic times* [Speech]. Retrieved November 21, 1999, from http://www.shell.com/library/speech/1525,2322,00.html.

Human Rights Watch. (1998, February). *The price of oil* [Report]. Human Rights Watch/Africa. Retrieved March 31, 2000, from http://www.hrw.org/hrw/reports/1999/nigeria/Nigew991–01.htm.

Ice, R. (1991). Corporate publics and rhetorical strategies: The case of Union Carbide's Bhopal crisis. *Management Communication Quarterly, 4,* 341–362.

Knight, P. (1998). *Profits and principles—does there have to be a choice?* [Report]. London: Royal Dutch/Shell Group.

Krupp, F. (1986, November 20). New environmentalism factors in economic needs. *Wall Street Journal,* p. 34.

Lawrence, A. (1999a). *Shell Oil in Nigeria* [Online case study]. Council for Ethics in Economics. Retrieved January 26, 2000, from http://www.i-case.com/cases/shella/docs/contents.htm.

Lawrence, A. (1999b). *The transformation of Shell, 1994–1999* [Online case study]. Council for Ethics in Economics. Retrieved January 26, 2000, from http://www.i-case.com/cases/shellb/docs/contents.htm.

Livesey, S. M. (1999). McDonald's and the Environmental Defense Fund: A case study of a green alliance. *Journal of Business Communication, 36,* 5–39.

Livesey, S. M. (2001). Eco-identity as discursive struggle: Royal Dutch/Shell, *Brent Spar,* and Nigeria. *Journal of Business Communication, 38,* 58–91.

Livesey, S. M. (2002). The discourse of the middle ground: Citizen Shell commits to sustainable development. *Management Communication Quarterly, 15,* 309–343.

Manby, B. (1999, May). Nigeria: Crackdown in the Niger Delta [Report]. *Human Rights Watch World Reports, 11*(2A). Retrieved April 5, 2000, from http://www.hrw.org/reports/1999/nigeria2/Ngria993.htm.

Meadowcroft, J. (2000). Sustainable development: A new(ish) idea for a new century? *Political Studies, 48,* 370–387.

Meznar, M. B., & Nigh, D. (1995). Buffer or bridge? Environmental and organizational determinants of public affairs activities in American firms. *Academy of Management Journal, 38,* 975–996.

MOSOP (Movement for the Survival of the Ogoni People). (n.d.a). *The role of Shell in Ogoni.* Retrieved January 26, 2000, from http://www.mosopcanada.org/text/shell.html.

MOSOP (Movement for the Survival of the Ogoni People). (n.d.b). *The story of the Movement for Survival of the Ogoni People (MOSOP).* Retrieved January 26, 2000, from http://www.mosopcanada.org/text/shell.html.

Niboro, I. (1993, October 4). Death on a sea of oil. *African Guardian.* Retrieved April 19, 2000, from http://www.mosopcanada.org/text/info/mosop0030.html.

Peterson, T. R. (1997). *Sharing the earth: The rhetoric of sustainable development.* Columbia: University of South Carolina Press.

Project Underground & Rainforest Action Network. (1997). *Shell's independent annual report: Human rights and environmental operations information on the Royal Dutch/Shell Group of Companies 1996–1997* [Report]. Berkeley, CA: Rainforest Action Network.

Rothermund, H. (1998, April 23). *Dialogue, decide, deliver* [Speech]. Retrieved on October 25, 1999, from http://www.shell.co.uk/news/speech/spe_dialogue.htm.

Rowell, A. (with A. Goodall). (1994). *Shell-shocked: The environmental and social cost of living with Shell in Nigeria* [Report]. Retrieved April 15, 2000, from http://archive.greenpeace.org/comms/ken/hell.html.

Saro-Wiwa, K. (1994, August 8). Message from prison. *The News.* Retrieved April 19, 2000, from http://www.mosopcanada.org/text/info/mosop0245.html.

Saro-Wiwa, K. (1995a). *A month and a day: A detention diary.* London: Penguin.

Saro-Wiwa, K. (1995b). *Closing statement to the Nigerian military appointed tribunal.* Retrieved May 10, 2000, from http://www.Greenpeace.org/~comms/ken/.

Smircich, L., & Stubbart, C. (1985). Strategic management in an enacted world. *Academy of Management Review, 10,* 724–736.

SPDC (Shell Petroleum Development Company of Nigeria Ltd.). (1995, October 31). *Verdict on Mr Ken Saro-Wiwa and others* [Press release]. Retrieved October 27, 2006, from http://www.shell.com/home/Framework?siteId=nigeria&FC2=&FC3=/nigeria/html/iwgen/news_and_library/

press_releases/1995/1995_3110_01031127
.html.

SPDC (Shell Petroleum Development Company of Nigeria Ltd.). (1995, November 19). *Clear thinking in troubled times* [Press release]. Retrieved October 20, 2006, from http://www.shell.com/home/Framework? siteId=nigeria&FC2=&FC3=/nigeria/html/ iwgen/news_and_library/press_releases/ 1995/1995_1911_01031142.html.

SPDC (Shell Petroleum Development Company of Nigeria Ltd.). (1997a). *People and the environment: Annual report 1997.* Lagos, Nigeria: Author.

SPDC (Shell Petroleum Development Company of Nigeria Ltd.). (1997b, August). *Nigeria Brief: Ogoni and the Niger Delta* (Booklet). Lagos, Nigeria: Author.

SPDC (Shell Petroleum Development Company of Nigeria Ltd.). (1998). *People and the environment: Annual report 1998.* Lagos, Nigeria: Author.

United Nations World Commission on Environment and Development. (1987). *Our common future* [Brundtland Report]. Oxford: Oxford University Press.

Unrepresented Nations and Peoples Organization. (1995, February). *Ogoni: Report of the UNPO mission to investigate the situation of the Ogoni in Nigeria.* Retrieved March 31, 2000, from http://www.unpo .org/member/ogoni.html.

Waddell, S. (2000). Complementary resources: The win-win rationale for partnership with NGOs. In J. Bendell (Ed.), *Terms for endearment: Business, NGOs and sustain-* *able development* (pp. 193–206). Sheffield, UK: Greenleaf.

Wasik, J. (1996). *Green marketing and management: A global perspective.* Cambridge, MA: Blackwell.

Watts, P. (1997a, July 24). *A developing contribution—Shell companies in Africa.* Speech given at the Fourth African-African American Summit, Harare, Zimbabwe. Retrieved October 25, 1999, from http:// www.shellnigeria.com/info/info_display .asp?ID=10.

Watts, P. (1997b, November 18). *Contributing to sustainable development* [Speech]. Retrieved November 22, 1999, from http: //www.shell.com/library/speech/ 0,1525,2302,00.html.

Weick, K. E. (1995). *Sensemaking in organizations.* Thousand Oaks, CA: Sage.

Westley, F., & Vredenburg, H. (1991). Strategic bridging: The collaboration between environmentalists and business in the marketing of green products. *Journal of Applied Behavioral Science, 27,* 65–90.

Wheeler, D., Fabig, H., & Boele, R. (2002). Paradoxes and dilemmas for stakeholder responsive firms in the extractive sector: Lessons from the case of Shell and the Ogoni. *Journal of Business Ethics, 3,* 297–318.

Wybrew, J. (1995, July). *Brent Spar*—a "public relations disaster?" *Journal of the UK Institute of Public Relations.* Retrieved November 18, 1999, from www.Shellexpro .brentspar.com/shell/brentsapr/analysis/ 1995/199550700-000000.

24

Discourses of Sustainability in Today's Public Sphere

TARLA RAI PETERSON
TODD NORTON

At the risk of being essentialist, we ground this chapter in the claim that the tradition of identifying human society and the natural environment as mutually exclusive is the most fundamental challenge facing decision makers—indeed, any stakeholders—who seek sustainability (Agyeman, Bullard, & Evans, 2003; Busch, 1996; Latour, 2004; Leopold, 1949; World Commission on Environment and Development, 1987). That is, sustainability can develop only when humans begin to understand themselves as part of, rather than apart from, nature and use this rearticulated relationship to foster Aldo Leopold's (1949) expanding community of ethical responsibility. The concept of sustainable development (SD) was intended to facilitate this integration, but has fallen short (McGoldrick, 1996; T. R. Peterson, 1997). Given the expanding political power of the corporate sector in the twenty-first century, Leopold's expanded community cannot begin to develop without significant contributions from the public, private, and third sectors.

Sustainability is a systemic concept for suggesting how society might enable all beings to meet their needs and express themselves while preserving diversity, both within the human species and beyond it. In this chapter, we define sustainability as the careful nesting of human needs and desires within natural flows and processes of the biosphere so as to improve the quality of human life while conserving the vitality and diversity of the earth. Our definition is drawn largely from the International Union for the Conservation of Nature and Natural Resources (see *Caring for the Earth*, 1991). Currently, many corporate practices block attempts toward sustainability by rendering nature a wedge between social elites and the disenfranchised. As it matures, the corporate social responsibility (CSR) movement may enable a shift toward sustainability by encouraging both scholars and administrators to focus on problems that occur in the "space between" humanity and nature (Latour, 2004), the material and the symbolic (T. R. Peterson, 1997; Pezzullo, 2003a, 2003b), and the subject and object (Bradbury & Lichtenstein, 2000). That is, CSR could motivate critical examination of contemporary relations among individual humans, across human cultures, and between those cultures and the earth. For example, CSR should approach the conundrum created by the modern society's investment in technology that enables control over nature, while simultaneously degrading the earth's capacity to support human life. A responsible business should question the appropriateness of relying on myriad human bodies while simultaneously engaging in activities that objectify those bodies. It would appear that humans and their creatures, including, but not limited to, corporations, function both materially and symbolically and are both subject and object. Sustainable practice cannot afford to ignore these spaces.

Haraway (1991, 1997) argues that "socio-techno-bio bodies" shape our existence into strange creatures such as cyborg, "Femaleman," and "Oncomouse." While it makes little sense to reduce human actors to the biological realm of genetic determinism, neither is it useful to reduce them to the symbolic. We are not suggesting that students of the symbolic are wrong to argue that material reality matters only to the degree it has symbolic significance. Rather, material reality has an uncanny ability to intrude into our symbolic constructions; subjects and objects have an annoying propensity to trade places, and the earth's pollution can no longer be contained. As Beck (1992) notes, human health risks resulting from late modern industrial production are not limited to factory workers and poor neighborhoods. For example, in relatively wealthy nations, citizens who can pay the price have avoided air pollution by living above the inversion or upwind of the factory or toxic waste site. They avoid water pollution by living upstream from where toxic plumes from active and decommissioned military bases enter the water table. However, even the wealthy have run out of places to hide and are reduced to battling each other in their efforts to avoid environmental damage to their personal spaces and bodies. A socially responsible corporate sector has the potential to facilitate critical examination of the spaces between traditional answers to environmental problems. If, on the other hand, business-as-usual interests highjack the concept of CSR, the potential to encourage creative approaches to building inclusive yet diverse communities will be lost.

Although the results of human-induced damage to the environment have become difficult for anyone to avoid, both unsustainable development and social injustice are acute problems in spaces undergoing rapid change. Examples include borderlands between more and less affluent nations (e.g., the United States and Mexico) where economies are fueled by high migration rates, or regions that have recently experienced disasters such as Hurricane Katrina along the U.S. Gulf Coast in 2005. In these spaces, long-time residents and newcomers are prone to differential treatment, differential access to political systems, and differential conceptions of justice. The challenge of sustainably developing in these relatively unstable regions has growing implications in a globalizing world where communication, transportation, and associated technologies dramatically alter the trajectories of permeability between locales.

Our primary goal in this chapter is to suggest possibilities for enhancing sustainability by integrating social responsibility, which is typically thought of as socioeconomic practice, and healthy ecosystems, which are typically thought of as material (or physical) processes. We begin with a review of the literature on SD and follow with a brief discussion of contemporary (and potential) points of convergence between SD and CSR, especially as related to the environmental justice (EJ) movement. Third, we explore perceptions of development elicited from conversations with residents of the U.S.–Mexican border to illustrate the relationship between development and the corporate sector, and the implicit potential for CSR to contribute to SD. We conclude by arguing that appropriately integrated public and private spheres can facilitate SD, while a wholly private system focused on short-term benefits for the few can effectively block sustainability of any sort.

SUSTAINABLE DEVELOPMENT: PANACEA OR PANDORA'S BOX?

No concept associated with environmental protection has enjoyed more widespread public legitimacy than SD, something conservation biologists have long advocated in an attempt to encourage careful use of natural resources (Allen & Hoekstra, 1993; Leopold, 1949). During the last decade of the twentieth century, virtually everyone supported it. With the publication of *Our Common Future* by the World Commission on Environment and Development in 1987, the idea was imported into the popular lexicon. An explosion in publications utilizing the term soon followed (Aguirre, 2002; World Commission on Environment and Development, 1987). The concept became a centerpiece for global development policy following the 1992 United Nations Conference on Environment and Development in Rio de Janeiro and the 2002 World Summit on Sustainable Development in Johannesburg (Agyeman et al., 2003). This social shift was legitimized by science and capitalized on the residual uncertainty inherent to the World Commission's definition of SD as meeting "the needs of the present without compromising the ability of future generations to meet their own needs" (World Commission on Environment and Development, 1987, p. 43; M. N. Peterson, Peterson, & Peterson, 2005).

The definition's greatest strength, as well as its most damning weakness, is its ambiguity. Although communities embracing SD must subscribe to a direct link between sustainability and development, as well as intergenerational and international equity, those communities also create their own terms of implementation, or operational definitions (T. R. Peterson, 1997). For example, some advocates for indigenous groups use SD to argue that because such groups have always used their natural resources, they should not be denied access to them by those who would protect wilderness, while others use the same concept to argue that such groups should not be denied the right to protect natural resources from those who would spur economic development (Amnesty International & Sierra Club, 2000; Nabhan, 1995). Agyeman et al. (2003, p. 5) have suggested a modified definition of SD that includes the clause "in a just and equitable manner," but this definition has yet to attain popular currency.

The conflicting values and beliefs associated with the confusing array of perspectives toward SD should surprise no one. Given a definition that "allows proponents to simultaneously endorse both environmental protection and economic development, governments, private industry, natural resource agencies, conflict resolution professionals, and many environmental advocacy groups wholeheartedly embraced SD" (T. R. Peterson & Franks, 2006). Multiple meanings evolved as sustainability advocates rooted the concept in their personal moral sentiments without making the values and politics associated with those sentiments explicit (Lélé & Norgaard, 1996). Powerful business interests joined in the attempt to co-opt the meaning and use of the term. For example, business interests have colonized SD for use in marketing campaigns designed to convince the public that purchasing certain high-end brands of building materials, food, toiletries, and other products will eliminate environmental problems associated with the consumer society epitomized by the United States (Stauber, 1994; Woollard & Ostry, 2000). As a case in point, Origins, a company "promoting beauty and wellness through multi-sensory products and feel-good experiences" (Origins, 2005), says it also is committed to

> preservation of earth, animal and environment. . . .
>
> We do whatever we can to protect the earth and its resources. We use no aerosols. We opt

for recycled materials including papers, cartons and packing materials. And we always favor packaging that's easily recyclable. So you can feel free to indulge in and enjoy our products without hesitation. . . . So what are you waiting for? Twist off a cap. Flip up a top. Inhale a wonderful aroma. Sweep on a delicious cream. Dabble in some Sensory Therapy. Lather up and feel tingly clean. Play with nature's colors. Take serious care of yourself. Have serious fun and feel great doing it. (¶¶ 11–13)

For about $30, anyone can buy a small container containing 15 milliliters (just more than half an ounce) of moisture treatment for the eyes, enriched with silver tip white tea, mica, vitamin A, and white birch extract, all of which have been harvested in a sustainable manner. And, since the tiny plastic container is packaged in a dainty white box made from recycled paper, the consumer is doing her part to sustain the earth.

Many advocates of SD discarded the concept when they discovered SD was "code for perpetual growth . . . force-fed to the world community by the global corporate-political-media network" (Willers, 1994, p. 1146). Rhetoric from the U.S. Department of Energy (DOE) illustrates the mainstream application of SD that has led to this hostile view. Its National Energy Policy Office encourages SD in the form of "reliable, affordable and environmentally responsible production, delivery and use of energy"; responsibilities include "assur[ing] a secure and sustainable energy future" and "implementing the Efficient Energy for Sustainable Development Partnership" (U.S. Department of Energy, n.d.). In response to redevelopment needs prompted by Hurricane Katrina in September 2005, the DOE approved bids for the sale of 11 million barrels of crude oil from the Strategic Petroleum Reserve. Secretary Bodman proclaimed that the sale "ensures that refineries have the petroleum they need to keep gasoline and diesel fuel flowing to American consumers while production facilities in the gulf region regain their capacity. As we move forward, we will continue to monitor the overall supply of petroleum available and the needs of the nation as we determine next steps" (U.S. Department of Energy, 2005, ¶ 2).

Deep ecologists eventually rejected the World Commission's definition for its implicit anthropocentrism, and many environmental ethicists rejected SD in favor of "ecosystem sustainability"

(Callicot & Mumford, 1997; Jacob, 1994). When the competing views of SD and its failure to meet the expectations of its advocates became apparent, "it fell from grace among ecologists nearly as rapidly as it had become popular" (M. N. Peterson et al., 2005, p. 264). Critical evaluation of SD as a conceptual framework for environmental management can be summed up in the claim that, at best, it is an unproven concept and, and at worst, it has failed to slow the inexorable degradation of environments needed to preserve environmental health for humans and other species.

LINKING CSR WITH SUSTAINABLE DEVELOPMENT

Explicit connections between SD and CSR have only recently begun to develop (Agyeman, 2005; Agyeman et al., 2003; Waterman, 2002). For this chapter, we begin with the World Commission on Environment and Development's (1987) now classic definition of SD as "development that meets the needs of the present without compromising the ability of future generations to meet their own needs" (p. 47). We also accept the general consensus of development scholars, agencies, and consultants, that SD requires at least healthy communities, economies, and environments. Our concept of CSR is clearly explained by Article 13, a U.K. company specializing in consulting on corporate social responsibility (Article 13, 2002), which defines a socially responsible company as one that

- recognizes that its activities have a wider impact on the society in which it operates; and that developments in society in turn impact on its ability to pursue its business successfully;
- actively manages the economic, social, environmental and human rights impact of its activities across the world, basing these on principles which reflect international values, reaping benefits both for its own operations and reputation as well as for the communities in which it operates;
- seeks to achieve these benefits by working closely with other groups and organisations— local communities, civil society, other businesses and home and host governments. (¶ 4)

Although, at some level, CSR is simply a defensive reaction to scandals, market disruption, and international development disasters, it has the potential to move beyond this reactive stance. Sustainable development and CSR are integrated to varying degrees through sets of operational principles identified by companies claiming to be socially responsible and committed to sustainability. Several semiofficial certification organizations have emerged to promote CSR and legitimize (or not) corporate claims of responsible sustainability. These include Article 13 (http://www .article13 .com/default.asp), Business in the Community (http://www.bitc.org.uk/index.html), Ceres (http://www.ceres.org/), CSR Europe (http:// www .csreurope.org/), Natural Step (http://www .naturalstep.org/), the World Business Council for Sustainable Development (http://www.wbcsd.org/), and many others.

The ethos of these organizations varies considerably. The World Business Council for Sustainable Development, which was founded in 1995, has based its case for SD on the argument that SD is good for business and has achieved credibility across a broad spectrum of interests. It has developed coalitions representing environmental and industry concerns, working with groups ranging from the World Resources Institute to the International Council of Forest and Paper Associations Partners in various initiatives. It has achieved credibility among groups focusing on environmental protection by supporting the Kyoto Protocol and working toward the development of a Green House Gas Protocol. Its credibility in the private sector comes from its membership and from such programs as training in how to use SD to build customer/client trust and create competitive advantage through brand innovation. Natural Step is widely recognized as offering a new development model that responds directly to the growing realization that the earth's resources are finite and that human economic activity can be destructive, benign, or beneficial.

These organizations have begun sponsoring certifications and awards for socially responsible businesses. For example, Ceres, whose mission is to "move businesses, capital, and markets to advance lasting prosperity by valuing the health of the planet and its people," has a program to award outstanding sustainability reporting by Canadian, Mexican, and the United States companies (Ceres, 2005, ¶ 2). Their awards are intended to (a) encourage companies to thoroughly report on sustainability, economic, environmental and social performance; (b) reward best practices; (c) provide models for companies new to sustainability reporting; and (d) encourage transparency between companies and stakeholders (¶ 3). Perhaps one day businesses will have a standardized sustainability certification process similar to that available to agriculturalists who certify as organic growers, sanctioned by political entities ranging from states and provinces to international coalitions. For now, opportunities to validate claims of CSR remain relatively nonsystematic.

Given the relative power and influence of multinational corporations in the twenty-first century, CSR is essential to achieving SD. At the same time, without a broad grounding in sustainability, CSR has little chance of moving beyond the realm of greenwashing. This relationship, along with the need to pursue CSR globally, leads us to identify closely with the operating principles of Natural Step, which maintains separate, yet linked, offices in 12 countries. It assists governments and businesses in "creating new ways for people to live and thrive—while keeping the planet's ecosystems and the global social tissue healthy and able to sustain us and future generations" (Natural Step, 2003a, ¶ 4). Its sustainability principles are as follows:

In a sustainable society, nature is not subject to systematically increasing:

1. concentrations of substances extracted from the earth's crust;
2. concentrations of substances produced by society;
3. degradation by physical means

and, in that society . . .

4. human needs are met worldwide (¶ 6).

Natural Step recommends the following *practices* for applying their sustainability *principles*:

- Eliminate our contribution to systematic increases in concentrations of substances from the earth's crust. This means replacing certain minerals that are scarce in nature with others that are more abundant, using all mined materials efficiently, and systematically reducing dependence on fossil fuels.
- Eliminate our contribution to systematic increases in concentrations of substances produced by society. This means systematically replacing certain persistent and unnatural

compounds with ones that are normally abundant or break down more easily in nature, and using all substances produced by society efficiently.

- Eliminate our contribution to systematic physical degradation of nature through over-harvesting, depletion, foreign introductions and other forms of modification. This means drawing resources only from well-managed ecosystems, systematically pursuing the most productive and efficient use both of those resources and land, and exercising caution in all kinds of modification of nature.
- Contribute as much as we can to the goal of meeting human needs in our society and worldwide, going over and above all the substitution and dematerialization measures taken in meeting the first three objectives. This means using all of our resources efficiently, fairly, and responsibly so that the needs of all people on whom we have an impact, and the future needs of people who are not yet born, stand the best chance of being met. (Natural Step, 2003b)

ENVIRONMENTAL JUSTICE AS LINK

Environmental justice (EJ) provides an important link between SD and CSR. McGoldrick (1996) argues that SD's most critical challenge is to develop a "credible and accepted normative hierarchy" (p. 818). Here we follow Agyeman's (2005) definition of EJ as "community reaction to external threats to the health of the community, which have been shown to disproportionately affect people of color and low income" (p. i). Environmental justice could provide both theoretical and practical bases for evaluating that hierarchy in action. McGoldrick's statement harks back to our concern with the spaces between, described above. It is entirely possible to develop a sustainable society that conceptualizes human laborers as objects for producing capital and justifies this objectification by a discourse about the material benefits for society to be gained by the sacrifice of a few insignificant individuals. In such a society, rational use of information regarding human anatomy and physiology would determine the appropriate ratio of energy intake (in terms of calories), energy output (in terms of work), and energy renewal (in terms of sleep) to achieve maximum efficiency. Human objects would be provided with food, sleep, and work tasks necessary to ensure efficient production, but with nothing else that might interfere with production. Although most advocates for SD hold implicit normative beliefs that lead them to find historical examples of such societies reprehensible, contemporary society continues to abuse both its human and other resources. In the name of national security and protection of its citizens, for example, the nuclear powers of the world designate national sacrifice zones where plutonium production, testing, and storage contaminate the land too badly for human inhabitation. The conceptual complexity of these symbolic/material intersections is that corporate use of land and resources is based largely on a symbolic scarcity principle which functions as a self-justifying motivator to use resources at a greater clip than nature can renew them. Ironically, few people seem willing to object when their or the lives of their children, whose original right to life was raucously demanded, are sacrificed to short-term economic development (Kozol, 1996).

Critics of the EJ movement claim that it has no basis in scientific fact, but rather is a mask for efforts of minorities and other disenfranchised groups to gain political power (Bowen & Wells, 2002). They note that, although poor and minority communities often are located in or near environmentally degraded areas, few if any studies have demonstrated a causal relationship between decisions to locate a polluting facility and either the income or ethnicity of local residents (Bryant & Mohai, 1992; Commission for Racial Justice, 1987; General Accounting Office, 1983; Mennis, 2002). In other words, it is difficult to document a phase of the decision process during which corporate managers explicitly state, "Let's dispose of our toxic waste in this neighborhood because it is inhabited by [some category of disenfranchised] people." Rather, such decisions are cloaked in the language of economic expedience and utility.

Claims that the EJ movement is grounded in political aspirations, rather than scientific fact, ironically reveal its potential for linking social responsibility with sustainability. The U.S. Environmental Protection Agency's (EPA) definition of EJ mandates "fair treatment" and "meaningful involvement" of all potentially affected groups (U.S. Environmental Protection Agency, 2005). The EPA version of EJ defines "fair" as equal (i.e., no group receives a disproportionate share of negative environmental consequences). Data from numerous studies demonstrate that different socioeconomic groups bear differential shares of negative environmental impacts. Further, if minorities and those from lower income brackets must struggle to gain political power in the environmental decision-making arena, then they probably find their current involvement insufficiently meaningful. Given the current socioeconomic situation, it would be difficult to justify a claim that benefits and costs of corporate practices are fairly/equally distributed or that access to political structure is broadly shared.

At base, EJ has been concerned with *distribution*, which can be a difficult construct to operationalize. Walzer's (1983) categorization scheme of free exchange, need, and deserts is a widely used descriptive system that explains several past and current approaches to distributive justice. For instance, if all people received an equal environmental quality level for a given investment of time or money, free exchange justice would exist. This version of EJ might preclude disparities rooted in ethnicity, but not income. It would be "just" for all poor humans to live in pressboard shacks, with open sewers, in the shadow of landfills filled with toxic waste from plants producing luxuries for wealthier humans. In contrast, EJ rooted in the need version of justice would mandate expending exceptional efforts for those living in degraded environments. Wealthy communities would be expected to provide the revenue needed to supply indoor plumbing with hot and cold running water for their poor neighbors. The third option, rooted in the merit system, might require residents to earn the right to protection from exposure to toxic waste (regardless of who benefits from that waste) by contributing a predetermined amount of resource (e.g., money or time) to the local sheriff's reelection campaign. Although it should be clear that none of these versions of justice is adequate in all circumstances or cultures, and each version has different implications for EJ, they provide a useful starting point in the attempt to move beyond mandated equality in the distribution of harm.

Agyeman et al. (2003) argue that equal treatment is necessary but insufficient for EJ, adding that "access to the decision-making and policy-making processes" also is required (p. 3). Although it should be clear that EJ can be defined in multiple ways, excluding some people from access to the very community that distributes justice is unjust by any definition. The lifeboat ethics proposed by Hardin (1968, 1993), wherein the developed world avoids the environmental degradation imposed on, or imposed by, the world's poor by keeping them out of the boat, perpetuates the dangerous illusion that sustainability can be achieved without developing an inclusive community. Beating back those who attempt to clamber into the lifeboat not only masks environmental injustice but also perpetuates a dysfunctional and unsustainable community. Within such divided communities, the environmental degradation of spaces and bodies remains an externality for some, including powerful elites.

Even institutional access is insufficient to attain justice within liberal democratic contexts scattered across the earth, where justice must address the democratic paradox (Mouffe, 2000; M. N. Peterson, Allison, Peterson, Peterson, & Lopez, 2004). This paradox refers to the intrinsic conflict between individual liberty and equality. Briefly, attempts to maximize individual liberty do so at the expense of political equality, while attempts to maximize political equality similarly curtail individual liberty. The complex interaction between concerns for equality and individual freedom create difficult problems. For example, protection of individual liberty maintains differences in decisions that influence exposure to environmental hazards and the ability to act on those decisions. I may prefer to live far from a toxic waste dump, yet my income may be insufficient for me to obtain a home anywhere other than near the dump. Although it may be physically possible for me to take a second job that augments my income sufficiently to enable purchase of a home far from the dump, I may choose not to do so. Finally, we should note that all of these approaches to justice are limited by their focus on end products (or states), rather than the means of production.

CORPORATE RESPONSIBILITY: TO WHOM?

The potential value of CSR depends largely on to whom we assume the corporation owes responsibility. If we define the object of that responsibility narrowly, CSR is minimally helpful in enhancing SD. If, on the other hand, we define that object broadly, CSR becomes fundamental to SD. In fact, the practice of CSR could provide an effective complement to the EJ movement.

Both EJ researchers and advocates have tended to concentrate on the results of environmental

injustice as compared to the physical processes and social practices that create it. Large-scale projects have focused on the spatial relationship between pollution sources and disenfranchised people (Bryant & Mohai, 1992; Commission for Racial Justice, 1987; General Accounting Office, 1983; Mennis, 2002). A few studies have begun to identify the everyday cultural politics leading to environmental injustices and delve into the practices that exclude disenfranchised voices from the decision-making process itself. For example, Maantay (2002) demonstrates how zoning practices lead to less healthy living environments for certain segments of the population, and Pezzullo's (2003a) critique of National Breast Cancer Awareness Month argues that it is an effective means of diverting resources and attention away from the relationships between environmental toxins and breast cancer. Another need is the exploration of appropriate responses to current injustices. Agyeman et al. (2003) note the paucity of research toward solutions, suggesting that it may stem from the relative ease of reactive, as opposed to proactive, behavior. Further, to have political weight, those solutions must integrate socioeconomic practice with material process (Latour, 2004). Pezzullo's (2003b) analysis of "toxic tours" in Louisiana responds to this need with an ethnographic account of how material bodies perform EJ as a social movement and bring awareness of its significance to a broad audience.

If EJ is to move beyond a unitary focus on the currently inequitable distribution of environmental harms, it must grapple with differences among different concepts of justice, as well as differences between advocates for social justice and sustainability. Some critics find EJ and SD fundamentally incompatible. Dobson (2003) exemplifies the argument against the notion that EJ and the drive toward sustainability need each other, arguing that "rapprochements [between them] will only ever be temporary and transient" (p. 83). We find this concern about the transitory nature of potential success largely irrelevant, however, because we assume no solutions to this dilemma will be anything but temporary and transient. Sustainability is not a final state of things. Rather, it is a process that is shaped and guided by social practice. For example, essential ecological processes and life-support systems can be strengthened or destroyed by international trade practices.

Given the overwhelming influence corporate interests exert on contemporary socioeconomic practice, we will not get far without including corporate behaviors in our calculus. Without the cooperation from the corporate sector, we cannot begin to explore the most significant socioeconomic practices that contribute to degraded environments. Unless we critically examine these practices, we have no hope of addressing unsustainable development associated with environmental injustice. Given its increasingly global influence on development policy, the corporate sector must participate in this exploration to enable discovery of how the material that constitutes bodies and habitats interacts with political practices, and how those practices might be changed.

SPACES AND BODIES
ON THE EDGE

Both unsustainable development and environmental injustice are chronically acute at the boundaries between comparatively affluent and poor nations, such as the United States and Mexico, where longtime residents and mushrooming immigrant populations are prone to differential treatment, differential access to political systems, and differential conceptions of justice. Although social, technical, and material dimensions are linked in any form of development, these linkages become especially problematic at the boundaries between poverty and affluence. Borderlands and border people are locked into a positive feedback loop of degradation catalyzed by infusion of global society's discards. In this sacrifice zone, the earth can neither protect nor provide for its inhabitants, and the humans drawn there can neither protect nor provide for the earth. The disabled, the elderly, and the unemployed flock to borders where they can survive with little or no financial capital. This context has growing implications in a globalizing world where so-called free trade political structures enable multinational corporations to use communication, transportation, and associated technologies to enhance the mechanistic interchangeability of resources, including human labor.

Although it remains essential to respect the concept of individual agency, it is critical to realize that people do not make decisions in a social vacuum, nor can they easily escape environmental degradation. Further, escape is nearly impossible. We interviewed approximately 400 residents along the U.S. side of the southeast border between the United States and Mexico during the summer of 2005. Most of our informants lived along the southern edge of Cameron and Hidalgo counties, were legal residents, and lived on less than US $10,000 annually. They were able to survive by constructing a strong support network with friends and relatives in similar circumstances. While this network provided needed support, it also bounded their options. For example, Alejandra told of how grateful she was to have relatives in this region, because they had enabled her to move from her home in Buttonwillow, California, to escape the horrors of "toxic chemicals and brainless babies" (M. N. Peterson, Peterson, & Peterson, 2006). Yet social ties and economic circumstances had drawn her to another sacrifice zone. Her close friend's baby had been part of cluster of infants with neural tube birth defects born and buried in Buttonwillow in 1992, near the same time health professionals in Cameron County reported an unusual spike in the same type of birth defects to the Texas Department of Health and to the U.S. Centers for Disease Control and Prevention. Both the Buttonwillow and Cameron County cases drew national attention from public health professionals, biological science researchers, mainstream media, and environmental rights advocates (Cole & Foster, 2001; T. R. Peterson, 1997). Official reports played down the seriousness of the outbreaks, vaguely blamed them on individual lifestyle choices such as diet, bemoaned the lack of sufficient data, and found no evidence that these specific births were related to the pregnant mothers' exposure to industrial wastes such as xylene and toluene (California Birth Defects Monitoring Program, 1993; Texas Department of Health, 1992). In 2005, Alejandra was living directly downwind from the *maquiladoras* in Matamoros and downstream from those in Reynosa.

Maquiladoras are assembly plants in Mexico, especially along the border between the United States and Mexico, to which materials and parts are shipped and from which the finished product is returned to the original market, usually in the United States. Corporations operating *maquiladoras* in these border towns include General Motors, AT&T, Fisher Price, Nike, *QuimicaFlor* (a venture supported by DuPont), and Stepan Chemical. Corporate executives and company spokespersons proudly proclaim that, although advocates for public health and EJ have been filing lawsuits against them for more than 20 years, the general trend has been to establish no conclusive link between the factories and local health problems, such as the birth defects mentioned above. Community activists and some government officials from both the United States and Mexico caution against this sanguine perspective, noting that chemicals such as xylene (a known cause of birth defects) have been found in soil samples at up to "53,000 times acceptable levels." Antonio Zavaleta, a medical anthropologist, explains that public participation in governance has historically been minimal in the region. The economic promise of industrialization enabled corporations to "put industrialization on top of an old system of politics . . . and so there were some notable abuses" (Minaya & Downing, 2001). Dissenters also point out that, despite demonstrated disparities between the documented amounts of hazardous waste produced and disposed of, going back to the mid-1980s, hazardous waste remains difficult to track. Large portions produced in border towns such at Matamoros and Reynosa never make it to licensed disposal facilities in Mexico or the United States. Although nobody seems to know what happens to the waste, the laws of physics indicate that its disappearance does not translate into nonexistence. Weak freedom-of-information laws in Mexico, combined with the public information implications of recently expanded definitions for national security in the United States, further complicate efforts to document the disposal of hazardous waste (T. R. Peterson, 1997; Queral, 2001).

Other community organizers focus on the environment inside the plants, claiming that, although industry causes severe environmental damage to the region, "the greatest damage is being done [is] not outside of the plants, but inside" (Minaya & Downing, 2001). For example, a 1998 study by *Universidad Autónoma Metropolitana* found that 83% of workers received inadequate safety gear; 60% worked in environments contaminated with unsafe levels of chemical emissions, dust, or noise; and more than 4% had borne a child with a birth defect (Minaya & Downing, 2001). Of course, political and socioeconomic structures make it impossible to verify these findings. The difficulties associated with verifying allegations of environmental injustice, as well as the national security ramifications, prompted the EPA to commission a study of justice issues related to development in the U.S.–Mexico border region by the National Environmental Justice Advisory Council (NEJAC). The report includes recommendations for improving public participation, broadening environmental protection programs, establishing cross-border enforcement mechanisms, and ensuring that SD and EJ are explicitly linked (National Environmental Justice Advisory Council, 2003). When considering possibilities for practice, however, we should note that NEJAC works in an advisory capacity only, and it depends on the EPA to renew its charter annually. There is, at the time of this writing (2005), no record of official EPA acceptance of NEJAC's report.

FACILITATING/INHIBITING DISCOURSES OF SUSTAINABILITY

At least two groups of people have direct, but very different, experiences with the material aspects of environmental degradation. Scientists measure the concentrations of toxic substances in the air and water with machines. Border residents measure these concentrations with their bodies. The citizens of the earth's borderlands bring the interstices between current socioeconomic practices and ecological processes into sharp relief and offer wisdom to those of us who have stubbornly resisted awareness of a profound choice facing humanity. On one hand, we can continue to rush about with little thought for our bodies, or those of other beings, ignoring conflicts over social justice and sustainability. Unhindered by a global sense of responsibility, our failure to develop in sustainable ways will continue coalescing into a degraded biosphere, shared by all surviving species. On the other hand, we may slow down and expand our visions of the earth, hear its voices, and stretch the temporal and spatial scales of our social concern to the frontiers of EJ and beyond to the global ecological processes that sustain us. Expanding the frontiers of our concern to broader vistas of time and space opens the way to sustainability.

As mentioned above, sustainability refers to an evolving process, rather than to a static end-state. That evolution is influenced by social practice that is the subject of discourse, and community members must be capable of participating in the discourse. In a world ordered largely for and by multinational corporations that engage in synchronous communication at will, it is difficult to conceptualize how to open participation in the discourse of SD in any meaningful way. Further, we must discover how to include both human and nonhuman bodies in our communities of concern. Peters (1999) suggests that a notion of discourse grounded in open dissemination offers the most appropriate model for contemporary social interaction. Although this messy and imprecise vision of communication may inspire chaotic visions of scattered, impersonal, one-way missives, it also encourages us to understand every being as capable of making choices that have material consequences. It also encourages us to respect others without dismissing their Otherness. Understanding and acting on disseminated communiqués from businesses, people, animals, or rivers require interpretation of texts by unintended receivers—not an easy task, but an essential one. Dissemination of thoughts and feelings among material beings opens the possibility for conceptualizing a just society that includes all of us. Although such a society does not guarantee sustainability, its absence guarantees the continuation of unsustainable practices.

We are not suggesting that corporations can or should do this alone. In fact, CSR holds the most promise when it encourages business to cooperate with other private and public bodies to establish and enforce regulations that seem reasonable to responsible corporate citizens. Thus, if it is to contribute to sustainability, CSR must encourage corporations to demonstrate an increased commitment to democratic governance and to play a leadership role in development and enforcement of environmental regulations.

As human cultures have become increasingly aware of environmental issues and have expressed a desire to participate in the regulatory process, the problem of constructively incorporating public interests has become a central concern for many government agencies, private corporations, and interest groups. Numerous nations have laws requiring stakeholder involvement in addressing significant environmental issues. Although the jurisdiction of the National Environmental Policy Act (NEPA) is limited to the United States, "NEPA's influence has been far-reaching, with its progeny in the statute books of 19 states and over 130 of the world's nations" (Salzman & Thompson, 2003, p. 275). Regulatory agencies in nominal democracies throughout the world are now required to identify and invite members of the interested public to provide comment on significant actions that will affect the environment.

One reason that public participation has been so central to environmental governance is that it is considered a critical component of democratic society (Steelman & Ascher, 1997). Supporters of broad participation in decisions regarding environmental development posit that the public can best judge and represent its own interests and that participation will further enhance the public's ability to participate in democracy, reduce public feelings of powerlessness and alienation, and increase the legitimacy of the governing body (Fiorino, 1990). Thus, broad public participation in development decisions is assumed to benefit society by creating policy that reflects public values and that nurtures individual and group empowerment. Similarly, organizational research indicates that enabling broad participation in organizational governance can be justified because diverse participation in organizational decisions will lead to better decisions than are made solely by managers (Cheney et al., 1998; de Jong & van Witteloostuijn, 2004; Organization for Economic Co-operation and Development, 2004, pp. 77–78).

Expectations for public participation in decision-making activity suggest that, if it provides an adequate opportunity for participants to examine scientific and technical information, it is more likely to result in well-informed decisions that are generally accepted. As it applies to development policy, public participation is much more likely to be competitive than collaborative. The existence of scarce, and sometimes fragile, nonrenewable resources combined with the negotiation structure of most processes lead to disputes "centered around the distributive allocation of a fairly fixed set of resources" rather than the pursuit of mutually beneficial and satisfactory decisions for all stakeholders" (Walker & Daniels, 1996, p. 80). For this reason, wholly voluntary approaches to development issues are unlikely to achieve sustainable results. Although we agree with Susskind, Levy, and Thomas-Larmer's (2000) claim that today's complex environmental conflicts require consensus building, we do not see that as the most critical challenge. In fact, management by consensus is dangerous because the attempt to placate everyone risks the attenuation of any impetus for change and reifies the status quo (Mouffe, 2000; M. N. Peterson et al., 2004). Prevailing values, economies, and politics have thoroughly demonstrated their inability to nurture either a just or a sustainable society.

Although people and organizations can alter their behavior when they believe it will lead to improvements, inertia is strong. People cling to the status quo, especially when they perceive that change threatens their power. Because governments have to balance the gains of change against the inevitable costs of upheaval, they develop policies through a slow succession of cautious steps. Corporate regulation along the lines suggested by the CSR movement has the advantage of leveling the playing field between businesses that choose to behave in a sustainable manner and those that do not. Appropriate regulatory frameworks provide socially responsible corporations with an opportunity to encourage development approaches that are consistent with EJ and sustainability, while maintaining economic viability.

Pragmatically, environmental regulation is consistent with current political practice, thereby facilitating more immediate implementation of SD initiatives. Governments have demonstrated their ability to successfully manage development by increasing costs. For example, the U.S. Congress enacted the Coastal Barrier Resources Act of 1982 at least in part to increase the cost of constructing and/or maintaining buildings in the coastal margins of the United States. The Act simply eliminates federally subsidized mortgages, loans, and insurance for development in the coastal margins. Despite recent attempts by political conservatives to co-opt environmental regulations, they remain generally compatible with existing social norms. Accordingly, these regulations are likely to have a positive impact for mitigating unsustainable development.

An openly just society can promote sustainability by bridging the gap between the needs of material bodies and social practices. We can design and inhabit democratic societies in which people, as well as corporations, have defensible rights. Similarly, we can design and inhabit societies that are simultaneously just and sustainable. Life scientists can help by discovering how to represent the earth's voices in forms that corporate executives can hear. And supporters of the move toward CSR can help by grappling directly with the challenges posed by socioeconomic structures that place humans at odds with others, even members of the same species.

The move toward CSR has the potential to significantly alter current practices that mitigate against the possibility of learning how we might live in a more sustainable manner. It can begin to realize that potential by cooperatively enhancing national and international regulatory regimes and by expanding opportunities for genuine democratic governance among corporate stakeholders. Our material existence, no less than our socioeconomic life, depends increasingly on competence to understand and nurture practices that enable large-scale decisions reflecting deliberation, debate, and conflict over both direct and indirect observations of the physical world.

REFERENCES

Aguirre, B. E. (2002). "Sustainable development" as collective surge. *Social Science Quarterly, 83,* 101–118.

Agyeman, J. (2005). *Sustainable communities and the challenge of environmental justice.* New York: New York University Press.

Agyeman, J., Bullard, R. D., & Evans, B. (Eds.). (2003). *Just sustainabilities: Development in an unequal world.* Cambridge, MA: MIT Press.

Allen, T. F. H., & Hoekstra, T. W. (1993). Toward a definition of sustainability. In W. W. Covington & L. F. Debano (Eds.), *Sustainable ecological systems: Implementing an ecological approach to land management* (pp. 98–107). Fort Collins, CO: Rocky Mountain Forest & Range Experiment Station.

Amnesty International & Sierra Club. (2000). *Environmentalists under fire: 10 urgent cases of human rights abuses.* Retrieved May 28, 2004, from http://www.sierraclub .org/human-rights/amnesty/report.pdf.

Article 13. (2002). Corporate social responsibility, business advice UK, sustainable development. Retrieved September 25, 2005, from http://www.article13.com/ CSR.htm.

Beck, U. (1992). *Risk society: Towards a new modernity* (M. Ritter, Trans.). Newbury Park, CA: Sage.

Bowen, W. M., & Wells, M. V. (2002). The politics and reality of environmental justice: A history and considerations for public administrators and policy makers. *Public Administration Review, 62,* 688–698.

Bradbury, H., & Lichtenstein, B. M. (2000). Relationality in organizational research: Exploring "the space between." *Organization Science, 11,* 551–564.

Bryant, B., & Mohai, P. (Eds.). (1992). *Race and the incidence of environmental hazards: A time for discourse.* Boulder, CO: Westview Press.

Busch, L. (1996). Bringing nature back in: Principles for a new social science of nature. *Centennial Review, 40,* 491–501.

California Birth Defects Monitoring Program. (1993). *Neural tube defects in Kern County: Buttonwillow area cluster investigation.* Retrieved August 20, 2005, from http://www.cbdmp.org/pdf/buttonwillow.pdf.

Callicott, J. B., & Mumford, K. (1997). Ecological sustainability as a conservation concept. *Conservation Biology, 11,* 32–40.

Caring for the earth: A strategy for survival. (1991). Gland, Switzerland: International Union for the Conservation of Nature and Natural Resources, United Nations Environmental Programme, and World Wide Fund for Nature.

Ceres. (2005). *Sustainability reporting.* Retrieved September 25, 2005, from http://www.ceres.org/sustreporting/reporting_awards.php.

Cheney, G., Straub, J., Speirs-Glebe, L., Stohl, C., DeGooyer, D., Whalen, S., et al. (1998). Democracy, participation and communication at work: A multidisciplinary review. In M. E. Roloff (Ed.), *Communication yearbook 21* (pp. 35–91). Thousand Oaks, CA: Sage.

Coastal Barrier Resources Act. 16 USC 3501 *et seq.* (1982).

Cole, L. W., & Foster, S. R. (2001). Buttonwillow: Resistance and disillusion in rural California. In L. W. Cole, and S. R. Foster (Eds.), *From the ground up: Environmental racism and the rise of the environmental justice movement* (pp. 80–102). New York: New York University Press.

Commission for Racial Justice. (1987). *Toxic wastes and race in the United States: A national report on the racial and socio-economic characteristics of communities with hazardous waste sites.* New York: United Church of Christ.

de Jong, G., & van Witteloostuijn, A. (2004). Successful corporate democracy. *Academic of Management Executive, 18,* 54–66.

Dobson, A. (2003). Social justice and environmental sustainability: Ne'er the twain shall meet? In J. Agyeman, R. D. Bullard, & B. Evans (Eds.), *Just sustainabilities: Development in an unequal world* (pp. 83–95). Cambridge, MA: MIT Press.

Fiorino, D. J. (1990). Citizen participation and environmental risk: A survey of institutional mechanisms. *Science, Technology, & Human Values, 15,* 226–243.

General Accounting Office. (1983). *Siting of hazardous waste landfills and their correlation with racial and economic status of surrounding communities.* Washington, DC: Resources, Community, and Economic Development Division.

Haraway, D. J. (1991) *Simians, cyborgs, and women: The reinvention of nature.* New York: Routledge.

Haraway, D. J. (1997). Modest_witness@ second_millenium. *Femaleman©_meets_ OncoMouse™ Feminism and techno-science.* New York: Routledge.

Hardin, G. (1968). Tragedy of commons. *Science, 162,* 1243–1248.

Hardin, G. (1993). *Living within limits: Ecology, economics, and population taboos.* New York: Oxford University Press.

Jacob, M. (1994). Sustainable development and deep ecology: An analysis of competing traditions. *Environmental Management, 18,* 477–488.

Kozol, J. (1988). *Rachel and her children: Homeless families in America.* New York: Crown Publishers.

Kozol, J. (1996). *Amazing grace: The lives of children and the conscience of a nation.* New York: Harper Perennial.

Latour, B. (2004). *Politics of nature: How to bring the sciences into democracy* (C. Porter, Trans.). Cambridge, MA: Harvard University Press.

Lélé, S., & Norgaard, R. B. (1996). Sustainability and the scientist's burden. *Conservation Biology, 10,* 354–365.

Leopold, A. (1949). *A Sand County almanac and sketches here and there.* London: Oxford University Press.

Maantay, J. (2002) Zoning law, health, and environmental justice: What's the Connection? *Journal of Law, Medicine & Ethics, 30,* 572–593.

McGoldrick, D. (1996). Sustainable development and human rights: An integrated conception. *International & Comparative Law Quarterly, 45,* 796–818.

Mennis, J. (2002). Using geographic information systems to create and analyze statistical surfaces of population and risk for environmental justice analysis. *Social Science Quarterly, 83,* 281–297.

Minaya, Z., & Downing, J. (2001). *Matamoros: Toxic legacy.* Retrieved September 26, 2005, from http://journalsm.berkeley.edu/projects/border/matamoros/html.

Mouffe, C. (2000). *The democratic paradox.* New York: Verso.

Nabhan, G. P. (1995). Cultural parallax in viewing North American habitats. In M. E. Soule & G. Lease (Eds.), *Reinventing nature: Responses to postmodern decon-struction* (pp. 87–101). Washington, DC: Island Press.

National Environmental Justice Advisory Council. (2003, May 5). *Unheard voices from the border: A report on environmental justice in the US-Mexico border region from the past to the future.* Retrieved September 20, 2005, from http://www .epa.gov/compliance/resources/publications/ ej/nejac/nejac-ej-border-report.pdf.

Natural Step. (2003a). .The Natural Step international gateway. Retrieved September 25, 2005, from http://www.naturalstep.org/ com/nyStart/.

Natural Step. (2003b). Principles. Retrieved September 25, 2005, from http://www .naturalstep.org/learn/principles.php.

Organization for Economic Co-operation and Development. (2004). *Survey of corporate governance developments in OECD countries.* Retrieved September 20, 2005, from http://www.oecd.org.dataoecd/58/27/ 21755678.pdf.

Origins. (2005). Welcome to Origins. Retrieved September 20, 2005, from http://www .origins.com/about.tmpl.

Peters, J. D. (1999). *Speaking into the air: A history of the idea of communication.* Chicago: University of Chicago Press.

Peterson, M. N., Allison, S. A., Peterson, M. J., Peterson, T. R., & Lopez, R. R. (2004). A tale of two species: Habitat conservation plans as bounded conflict. *Journal of Wildlife Management, 68,* 243–261.

Peterson, M. N., Peterson, M. J., & Peterson, T. R. (2005). Conservation and the myth of consensus. *Conservation Biology, 19,* 762–767.

Peterson, M. N., Peterson, M. J., & Peterson, T. R. (2006). Moving toward sustainability through integration of social practice and material process. In R. Sandler & P. C. Pezzullo (Eds.), *Environmental justice and environmentalism: The social justice challenge to the environmental movement.* Cambridge, MA: MIT Press.

Peterson, T. R. (1997). *Sharing the earth: The rhetoric of sustainable development.* Columbia: University of South Carolina Press.

Peterson, T. R., & Franks, R. R. (2006). Environmental conflict communication. In J. G. Oetzel & S. Ting-Toomey (Eds.), *The Sage handbook of conflict communication: Integrating theory, research, and practice* (pp. 419–449). Thousand Oaks, CA: Sage.

Pezzullo, P. C. (2003a). Resisting National Breast Cancer Awareness Month: The rhetoric of counterpublics and their cultural performances. *Quarterly Journal of Speech, 89,* 345–365.

Pezzullo, P. C. (2003b). Touring Cancer Alley, Louisiana: Performances of community and memory for environmental justice. *Text & Performance Quarterly, 23,* 226–252.

Queral, A. (2001). Border lines: Issues in the lower Rio Grande Valley. *J Times: The Sierra Club Environmental Justice Newsletter, 2*(1), 11–13.

Salzman, J., & Thompson, B. H. (2003). *Environmental law and policy.* New York: Foundation Press.

Stauber, J. C. (1994). Going . . . going . . . green! *PR Watch, 1*(3), 1–3.

Steelman, T. A., & Ascher, W. (1997). Public involvement methods in natural resource policy making: Advantages, disadvantages and trade-offs. *Policy Sciences, 30,* 71–90.

Susskind, L., Levy, P. F., & Thomas-Larmer, J. (2000). *Negotiating environmental agreements: How to avoid escalating confrontation, needless costs, and unnecessary litigation.* Washington, DC: Island Press.

Texas Department of Health. (1992). *An investigation of a cluster of neural tube defects in Cameron County, Texas.* Austin, TX, and Atlanta, GA: Texas Department of Health and the Centers for Disease Control and Prevention.

U.S. Department of Energy. (2005, September 14). *Secretary Bodman announces sale of 11 million barrels of crude oil from the nation's strategic petroleum reserve* [Press release]. Retrieved September 17, 2005, from http://www.energy.gov/news/1713 .htm.

U.S. Department of Energy. (n.d.). *Spotlight on the Office of National Energy Policy.* Retrieved September 17, 2005, from http:// www.energy.gov/engine/content.do? PUBLIC_ID=13581&BT_CODE=AD_AP& TT_CODE=SPOTLIGHTDOCUMENT.

U.S. Environmental Protection Agency. (2005). *Environmental justice.* Retrieved August 31, 2005, from http://www.epa.gov/ compliance/environmentaljustice.

Walker, G. B., & Daniels, S. E. (1996). The Clinton administration, the Northwest Forest Conference, and managing conflict: When talk and structure collide. *Society & Natural Resources, 9,* 77–91.

Walzer, M. (1983). *Spheres of justice: A defense of pluralism and equality.* New York: Basic Books.

Waterman, P. (2002). The call of social movements of the Second World Social Forum, Porto Alegre, Brazil, 31 January–5 February, 2002. *Antipode, 34,* 625–632.

Willers, B. (1994). Sustainable development: A new world deception. *Conservation Biology, 8,* 1146–1148.

Woollard, R. G., & Ostry, A. S. (2000). *Fatal consumption: Rethinking sustainable development.* Vancouver: University of British Columbia Press.

World Commission on Environment and Development. (1987). *Our common future.* Oxford: Oxford University Press.

25

Green Marketing and Advertising

WORAWAN YIM ONGKRUTRAKSA

About a decade ago, *environmental marketing* began to boom. We entered the age of environmental marketing as firms started to set their green marketing strategies in plain view:

Under fire from environmentalists for its disposable diapers, Procter & Gamble pledges to spend $20 million per year to help develop a composting infrastructure.
L'Eggs, a subsidiary of Sara Lee Corp., redesigns its famous plastic egg, making it far more environmentally benign.
Coca-Cola starts using recycled plastic in its 2-liter soda bottles.
McDonald's makes a $100 million recycling commitment to its consumers. (Coddington, 1993, p. 1)

It is obvious that notable corporate giants deem it a must to promote corporate images that reflect their environmental awareness and involvement.

Today's world is now facing enormous environmental problems and challenges. Environmental problems caused more than 2,000 people to perish in Europe in 2003 due to a heat wave, while storms and floods sporadically killed people in many parts of the world the following year. The 2004 tsunami in the Indian Ocean killed more than 186,000 people in South and Southeast Asia, making it one of the deadliest disasters in modern history. The 2005 hurricane Katrina killed more than 1,800 in the southern United States. The $200 billion in damages made Katrina the most destructive and costly natural disaster in the history of the country. The devastating aftermath of hurricanes Katrina and Rita should force President Bush to face up to the threat of climate change and international cooperation on the issue.

Natural disasters are only one type of environmental issue that proves that, at the beginning of the new millennium, we should further emphasize the importance of environmental marketing. Consumers, for example, are now more concerned about environmental problems than ever. According to a recent survey, North American consumers believe that companies should take greater steps to deal with environmental issues—35% in 1996, up from 29% in 1993 (Lawrence, 1998). Roper's national opinion poll on attitudes toward the environment shows that the majority of Americans regard a number of issues as "very serious" (Roper Starch Worldwide, 1996), including industrial water and air pollution, destruction of ozone and rain forests, industrial accidents, oil spills, and hazardous waste. Further, many people are convinced that businesses should play a major role in confronting these issues, as evidenced by a national Cone/Roper survey on cause-related marketing (Cone Communications, 1994), which found that the quality of the environment ranked second only to crime among issues businesses need to improve upon.

Public concern over environmental issues produced a dramatic increase in the number of "green" product introductions between 1985 and 1990 (Drumwright, 1994). Furthermore, evidence reveals that more marketers are making environmental claims about their products. They recognize that environmental responsibility is a potential source of marketing advantage for companies. Many firms are engaged in environmental activities, despite consumer skepticism about their environmental claims and the Federal Trade Commission's attempts to regulate their use in the last few years (Banerjee, 1999). For example, Mayer, Cude, Gray-Lee, and Scammon's (1995) audit of grocery store products across the United States uncovered environmental product or package claims, either explicit or implied, for 66% of the 397 brands they audited. Green marketing grossed $9.18 billion in 1995, while the growth of the green marketing industry was expected to continue to reach $30 billion between years 2000 and 2001 (Bahn & Wright, 2001). As a global corporation, General Electric expects to allocate a substantial portion of its $90 million corporate advertising budget to express its eco-stance, its biggest marketing push since the launch of its "Imagination at Work" positioning in 2003. "GE doesn't harm the environment when it brings good things to life" is the message that will underpin a massive companywide business initiative to push its environmentally friendly products (Creamer, 2005, p. 7).

In order to illustrate the big picture of green marketing, this chapter first explores definitions of environmental marketing, green organization, green consumer, and green advertising. Second, I review previous green advertising studies. The review suggests that green advertising, without environmental substance in other operations, leads to what may be called "greenwashing," which suggests that consumers cannot trust the content of green advertisements. In addition, I examine the development and features of green advertising in Japan, Thailand, and China. Finally, I discuss the future of green marketing and advertising.

A CLOSER LOOK AT GREEN MARKETING

We lead our lives in so-called "complex environments" such as found in extreme capitalism. Now, the world has become more global and, in certain economic respects, less diverse. We find ourselves in the marketing environment that makes us be either or both product providers or consumers. In the past 15 years or so, the world's most populous country, China, has undertaken the most rapid rate of industrialization the world has ever seen. In fact, China's cheap and abundant labor has helped to create a world market more intensely competitive. In order to survive in this competitive world environment, product providers need to create innovative marketing strategies and attention-getting persuasive efforts.

As a result, marketers (mostly of Western origin) have been viewed as the source of persuasive innovations relevant to the environmental problems we face today. Marketers invented "environmental marketing" or "green marketing." Polonsky (1994) proposed the following definition of green or environmental marketing: "all activities designed to generate and facilitate any exchanges intended to satisfy human needs or wants, such that the satisfaction of these needs and wants occurs, with minimal detrimental impact on the natural environment" (p. 391).

Another definition that may cover all related aspects is from the American Marketing Association (2004), which defines green marketing as

the marketing of products that are presumed to be environmentally safe[retailing definition], the development and marketing of products designed to minimize negative effects on the physical environment or to improve its quality [social marketing definition], and the efforts by organizations to produce, promote, package, and reclaim products in a manner that is sensitive or responsive to ecological concerns. (¶ 1)

These definitions reflect the concept of how marketers can transform a crisis into an opportunity. Marketers use this green marketing philosophy and theory in their market strategy and apply it to their communication tools. They also position themselves as "green organizations."

Some of the literature suggests reasons why firms might increase their use of green marketing. Polonsky (1994), for example, states that organizations perceive green marketing to be an opportunity to achieve their objectives, and they believe they have a moral obligation to be more socially responsible. In addition, governmental bodies are forcing firms to become more responsible. Competitors' environmental activities also pressure firms to strengthen their environmental marketing activities. Finally, cost factors associated with waste disposal or reductions in material use force firms to modify their behavior.

However, firms must be very cautious when they employ green marketing. Regardless of the reasons a firm uses for green marketing, a number of potential problems must be overcome (Polonsky, 1994). Firms using green marketing must ensure that their activities do not mislead consumers or industries and do not breach any of the regulations or laws dealing with environmental marketing. Therefore, green marketing claims must clearly state environmental benefits. They must explain environmental characteristics that are beneficial. Marketers also must ensure that comparative differences are justified and negative factors are considered. Moreover, green marketing must use only meaningful terms and pictures.

Green marketing requires new marketing and management strategies that can effectively address key challenges relating to "how we define green, how we develop green products that customers will like, and how we communicate our commitment and initiatives with credibility and impact" (Ottman, 1993). If customers are environmentally conscious and want to make choices supporting sustainable development, a company can transform these environmental concerns into business opportunities. Competitive advantage based on environmental friendliness requires integrating environmental perspectives into all aspects of marketing planning, especially into marketing strategies but also into basic structures and functions. For example, one of the tools for the forest industry is the use of third-party certificate to ensure a sustainable forest management (Hansen & Juslin, 1999). In another example, McDonald's has introduced a number of well-publicized environmental initiatives through the years, such as unbleached paper carryout bags and replacing polystyrene foam sandwich clamshells with paper wraps and light-weight recycled boxes (Kotler & Keller, 2006).

ENTER THE "GREEN CONSUMER"

If there is a seller, there must be a buyer. If there are green marketers, there must be green consumers. "Green consumers" are people who realize

that they currently live in a time of environmental crisis. They have the courage to act upon these problems. They started the three Ts—think, talk, take action—for protecting the world and their children who will inherit this endangered planet from their shameful and irresponsible ancestors. They are people who are sensitive to new trends and act upon their beliefs. Green consumers have an image of being active. A 1991 survey by Mintel International Group Ltd. found that 50% of consumers would switch their brand to one that is "greener." The survey also found that 20% of the U.S. population are active green consumers, willing to pay on average 7% more for green products, although half of this group thought green products to be overpriced and of inferior performance.

Numerous studies have addressed the characteristics of green consumers, or ecologically conscious consumers, as a focus of investigation or as a secondary issue. The majority of these studies have found demographic variables associated with self-report measures of environmental commitment, behavioral indicators of environmental commitment, or psychometric scales measuring environmental consciousness. Several studies have attempted to identify psychographic correlates of green attitudes and behaviors. Although these studies have not investigated psychographic variables in as exhaustive a manner as the research into demographics, they do provide some interesting insights into the nature of the green consumer. Typical psychographic characteristics include political orientation, altruism, and perceived consumer effectiveness; the premise is that consumers' attitudes and responses to environmental appeals are a function of believing that individuals can positively influence the outcome to such problems (Straughan & Roberts, 1999).

The Roper organization developed the best-known segmentation of consumers' environmental attitudes in 1990 for the consumer goods company S.C. Johnson & Son, Inc. (based in New York City), identifying five categories of consumers (Coddington, 1993). The first group, "true-blue greens," contains the most proactive green U.S. citizens. For these people, being environmentally aware is not an on-again, off-again activity; it is a way of life. They are the recyclers, composters, and volunteers but are still a decided minority in most communities, making up 10% of the American adult population, down slightly from the 11% in 1990. Second, the "greenback greens" are only moderately active in environmental causes in general. Their allegiance is faltering, having declined from 11% of adults in 1990 to 5% in 1996. They are the group most likely to hold white-collar jobs. Third, the "sprouts" are former greenback greens; they still care but are less willing to pay premiums. Sprouts make up 33% of the adult population, up from 26% in 1990. They have embraced environmentalism somewhat slowly. Fourth, the "grousers" are erstwhile greenback greens who view the environment as someone else's problem. They care about the environment to some extent, but not enough to go out of their way to do anything about it. Grousers say they are too busy to shop green, or they complain about product cost and quality. Finally, the "basic browns" simply do not believe individuals can make a difference in solving environmental problems; indeed, they do not even wish to make an effort (Coddington, 1993).

THE RISE OF GREEN ADVERTISING

To guide green messages effectively to the target, the green consumers, green marketers must be familiar with and clearly understand the promotional tools they use as a green medium. Specifically, they want direct access to the mass public and, therefore, they must learn how to effectively communicate through the advertising media. Advertising is a powerful tool because it has the ability to manipulate green consumers (Coddington, 1993; Iyer, Barnerjee, & Gulas 1995). As stated above, firms are targeting the environmentally conscious consumers. This has become quite evident in the nature of the advertising messages of commercial firms (Carlson, Grove, & Kangun, 1993). More specifically, Procter & Gamble has begun using refillable containers and bottles made with less plastic for many of its household products (Reitman, 1995). McDonald's, which has been criticized for its environmentally unsound food packaging practices, has replaced some polystyrene containers with paper, initiated a recycling program for those polystyrene containers still used, and has begun using napkins, towels, and boxes made of recycled paper (McDonald's Corporation, 1990, pp. 532–539). New products are positioned on the basis of environmental appeal, and green advertising is on the rise as more manufacturers are informing their consumers about the pro-

environmental aspects of their products and services. Although the volume of green advertising has increased dramatically, environmental claims are relatively new in advertising (Iyer et al., 1995).

Iyer et al. (1995) define environmental or green advertising as including any ad that meets one or more of the following criteria: explicitly or implicitly addresses the relationship between a product/service and the biophysical environment, promotes a green lifestyle with or without highlighting a product/service, or presents a corporate image of environmental responsibility.

The International Chamber of Commerce (ICC) *Code of Advertising Practice* (see International Chamber of Commerce, 1991) is an international code of green advertising adopted by the ICC. It is widely accepted as the basis for promoting high standards of ethics in advertising by self-regulation against a background of national and international law. The code recognizes social responsibilities toward the consumer and the community and is primarily an instrument for self-discipline. The *ICC International Code of Environmental Advertising Publication* (International Chamber of Commerce, 1991) is an extension of the ICC *Code of Advertising Practice*, which therefore remains applicable on any aspect not specifically dealt with in the environmental code. The environmental code is also read in conjunction with the other ICC codes of marketing practice: marketing research practice, sales promotion practice, direct marketing practice, and direct sales practice. The environmental code applies to all advertisements containing environmental claims in all media. It thus covers any form of advertising in which explicit or implicit reference is made to environmental or ecological aspects related to the production, packaging, distribution, use/consumption, or disposal of goods, services, or facilities (collectively termed products).

The basic principles of the environmental code maintain that all green advertising should be legal, decent, honest, and truthful. Green advertising should be consistent with environmental regulations and mandatory programs and should conform to the principles of fair competition, as generally accepted in business. No advertisements or claims should be such as to impair public confidence in the efforts made by the business community to improve its ecological performance.

Another organization that plays an important part for corporations addressing environmental problems is the Global Ecolabelling Network

(2006), a nonprofit association of third-party, environmental performance labeling organizations founded in 1994 to improve, promote, and develop the "ecolabeling" of products and services. Ecolabeling is a voluntary method of environmental performance certification and labeling practiced around the world. An ecolabel identifies overall environmental preference of a product or service within a specific product/service category based on life cycle considerations. In contrast to green symbols or claim statements developed by manufacturers and service providers, an impartial third party—in relation to certain products or services—independently determines environmental leadership criteria awards.

Many different voluntary (and mandatory) environmental performance labels and declarations exist. The ISO identifies three broad types of voluntary labels, with ecolabeling fitting under the type I designation:

> Type I: a voluntary, multiple-criteria based, third-party program that awards a license that authorizes the use of environmental labels on products;
> Type II: informative environmental self-declaration claims;
> Type III: voluntary programs that provide quantified environmental data of a product, under preset categories of parameters set by a qualified third party and based on life cycle assessment, and verified by that or another qualified third party. (Global Ecolabelling Network, 2006)

Further, the ISO has identified that these labels share a common goal:

> through communication of verifiable and accurate information, that is not misleading, on environmental aspects of products and services, to encourage the demand for and supply of those products and services that cause less stress on the environment, thereby stimulating the potential for market-driven continuous environmental improvement. (Global Ecolabelling Network, 2006)

The roots of ecolabeling are found in a growing global concern for environmental protection on the part of governments, businesses, and the public. As businesses have come to recognize that environmental concerns may be translated into a market advantage for certain products and services, vari-ous environmental declarations/claims/labels have emerged on products with respect to services in the marketplace (e.g., natural, recyclable, eco-friendly, low energy, and recycled content). While these have attracted consumers looking for ways to reduce adverse environmental impacts through their purchasing choices, they have also led to some confusion and skepticism on the part of consumers. Without guiding standards and vigorous investigation by an independent third party, consumers may not be certain that the companies' assertions guarantee that each labeled product or service is an environmentally preferable alternative. This concern with credibility and impartiality has led to the formation of both private and public organizations providing third-party labeling. In many instances, such labeling has taken the form of ecolabels awarded to products approved by an ecolabeling program operated at a national or regional (i.e., multicountry) level.

The scope of green codes and labeling reflects the great effort of organizations that try to make the green movement more sustainable in mainstream societies, in both the national and international arenas. However, the guidelines concerning the scope of green marketing are not widely adopted or practiced (Coddington, 1993; Kotler et al., 2005). Nevertheless, despite the fact that not many marketers practice the criteria, this situation is far better than having no criteria at all.

A growing number of researchers have sought to analyze and critique the "dark" side of green marketing. Scholarship on green marketing is discussed in the following section.

SCHOLARLY INVESTIGATIONS OF THINGS GREEN

Content Analyses of Media

The evidence of previous literature that used a content analysis method shows that in the early period of such content analysis study (1991–1995), most researchers attempted to comprehend the nature of green ads in various media. In the next period of study (1995–2000), researchers looked for the functional dimension of green ads and suggested that there might be greenwashing, which means that consumers cannot trust the content of green advertisements. A review of several significant content analyses on green ad studies follows.

A study conducted by Peterson (1991) compared the percentage of commercials that referred to environmental responsibility in 1979 with the percentage in 1989. A sample was collected from commercials appearing on three American television networks, one local station, and five cable companies on two randomly chosen days of each month over two years, recorded between 8:00 A.M. and 12:00 P.M. Data coders looked for commercials that directly advocated ecological responsibility, that is, those that showed an ecologically responsible participant in a favorable light, and those that favorably illustrated a goal of an ecologically responsible issue. Research results indicated an increase between 1979 and 1989 from 5.8% of environmental advertisements to 6.9%. Although there was no change in the percentage of the ads having direct ecology themes, all of the environmentally related categories were more frequently represented in 1989 than in 1979.

Several years later, scholars were interested in finding out the nature of green advertising by analyzing and identifying the different types. Carlson et al. (1993) took samples from all issues of print ads between 1989 and 1990 that appeared in 18 popular press and environmental magazines. Eventually, 100 samples were included in the study. These researchers were interested in categorizing the ads in terms of (1) environmental claims and (2) misleading/deceptive claims. Five types of environmental claims were identified: product orientation, process orientation, image orientation, environmental fact (i.e., a statement, ostensibly factual, about the environment), and their combinations. Four types of misleading/deceptive claims were detected: vague/ambiguous ads, claims that omitted important information necessary to evaluate the ads' truthfulness, false ads, and ads that contained more than one misleading element.

In addition to content analysis of print ads, Iyer and Barnerjee (1993) did a content analysis of a "convenience sample" of 95 television ads. They identified three types of green ads, based on (1) the types of ad sponsors (profit vs. nonprofit organization), (2) the foci of ads (corporate image focused vs. product oriented), and (3) the depth of ads (shallow vs. moderate). Iyer and Barnerjee recommended that future researchers deploy every resource necessary to obtain probability samples to further the goals of empirical research.

After the period of exploring the nature of green ads, scholars explored deeply the functional dimension of green ads. McGowan (2000) attempted to determine whether environmental advertisers provided consumers with informational cues such as whether marketers provide consumers with an environmentally "pretty picture" of their product, service, or organization (e.g., value-expressive appeals) or whether they are trying to inform consumers of the key benefits of their "green" product, service, or organization (e.g., utilitarian appeals). McGowan's content analysis of 100 environmental ads in the United States revealed that the majority are product related that provide consumers with utilitarian claims, which focus on key product benefits. However, it is unclear whether those advertisers have consistently followed the Federal Trade Commission guidelines when making their environmentally related product-benefit claims.

Following McGowan (2000), Kärnä, Juslin, Ahonen, and Hansen (2001) focused on the relationship between the companies' environmental activities and their environmental advertising campaigns. Green advertising, without an environmental emphasis and an appropriate connection between marketing strategies and operations, would lead to greenwashing. From the researchers' standpoint, greenwashing is a misuse of the principles of environmental marketing, which means that consumers cannot trust the content of advertisements. This study tested the proposition that green advertising reflects environmentally sound strategic and operational-level decisions. The empirical data for the study were collected from the Finnish forest industry, including advertising programs used by the industry. More than half of the 167 ads contained environmental aspects.

The previous examples explore the nature and functions of green ads in various media. Some scholars have become suspicious about the superficial use of green ads and refer to it as a greenwashing process. Obviously, the work of the green academic world is not complete; there is a great need for further investigations and especially for international comparative analyses. For example, it would be very instructive to compare green ads in developing or industrializing nations with those in the Western industrialized world.

Survey and Experimental Approaches to Green Advertising

Although there have been some significant studies of what categories of environmental issues and which types of green messages exist in the media (e.g., see Cornwell & Schwepker, 1992; Weaver-Lariscy & Tinkham 1992), much less research has been conducted on how people *respond* to environmentally persuasive messages (Thorson, Page, & Moore, 1995). Nevertheless, one type of literature focuses on the identification of variables that predict which types of consumers will be "environmentally concerned." Schwepker and Cornwell (1991) reviewed this literature in detail. A particularly relevant study is Balderjahn's (1988) conceptualization of how certain personality variables and attitudes about the environment relate to environmentally responsible patterns of consumption. Balderjahn showed that German consumers' attitudes toward pollution relate to their attitudes toward ecologically conscious living; those attitudes, in turn, served as predictors of three dependent variables: energy conservation behavior, environmental concern, and recycling. In addition, consumers' belief in their own effectiveness and control corresponded to the same three dependent variables. Using U.S. consumers as their subjects, Schwepker and Cornwell (1991) replicated Balderjahn's study and showed that consumers with a higher internal locus of control—who were concerned about litter, who believed there was a pollution problem, and who had a favorable attitude toward ecologically conscious living—were more inclined to report buying ecologically packaged products. They suggest that as people become more aware of the problem of solid waste, their attitudes and purchases change correspondingly.

The evidence suggests that motivating consumers to express their concerns through actual behavior is, to some extent, a function of increasing their perception that individual actions do make a difference. Ellen, Wiener, and Cobb-Walgren's (1991) research on "the role of perceived consumer effectiveness in motivating environmentally conscious behaviors" (p. 102) found a positive relationship between perceived self-efficacy and participation in some environmentally conscious behaviors. Their study demonstrated that perceived consumer effectiveness was distinct from environmental concern and contributes uniquely to the prediction of certain pro-ecological behaviors.

Besides consumer's attitude toward green ads, scholars are interested in the development of green products, especially with green labeling. Scammon and Mayer (1993) stated that environmental labeling programs administered by private organizations and government agencies have been, or are being, developed in countries around the world. Even in countries where such programs are not yet in place, marketers have increasingly made environmental claims in their advertising of consumer products. Although the goal of both third-party labels and seller environmental claims is to provide consumer information, each approach has its own particular strengths and limitations. Scammon and Mayer's (1993) study briefly examined some of the issues in administering environmental labeling programs and regulating environmental claims. It compared environmental labels and claims in terms of their value to consumers. Survey results focused on consumers' understanding of terminology dealing with recycling, a common theme in environmental claims and labeling programs.

Green products and green labeling relatively reflect green corporations. Davis (1994) provided empirical direction for marketers contemplating the development and presentation of environmentally themed corporate advertising. He showed how consumers' current perceptions of a company's environmental concerns interact with the type of corporate environmental activity communicated in the advertising to influence consumers' attitudes toward the corporate advertiser and its products, and their intent to purchase its products. This research demonstrated that environmentally themed corporate advertising does have the potential to improve corporate images or product benefits as a means of increasing consumer purchase intent if the focus of the environmental ad reflects the nature of consumers' current perceptions of the corporation.

In the following period of green advertising study, advertising scholars gave strong attention to green advertising when they published several significant surveys and experimental studies on green ads in 1995. At that time, the Journal of Advertising dedicated a special issue to green advertising. One of the pioneers in experimental methods for studying green ads was Obermiller (1995), who performed two experiments, recruiting 95 adults for the first study and 205 for the second. In both instances, as is common with experimental work, he used convenience-sampling methods to obtain subjects. The purpose was to determine which kinds of appeals are the most effective for consumers when the communication goal relates to social marketing. Obermiller considered positive and negative strategies for achieving this social objective and labeled these strategies as the "sick-baby" and the "well-baby" approaches. The sick-baby strategy uses a message that emphasizes the severity of the problem (e.g., "We have only enough energy resources to last for 20 more years, given current rates of consumption"). The well-baby strategy uses a message that emphasizes the importance and potential effectiveness of individual action (e.g., "Only you can prevent forest fires"). Obermiller concluded that the sick-baby appeal might offer advantages when dealing with problems that people are relatively unaware of, and that the well-baby appeal should be used with issues for which increasing concern is not a reasonable communication objective. Also, Obermiller found that communication effectiveness varies by situation. That is, it is difficult to identify a generic communication strategy that will work for all audiences and all product categories.

Schuhwerk and Lefkoff-Hagius (1995) conducted a study comparing consumer response to different print advertisements for a green laundry detergent. The results showed that, for those consumers who are highly involved with the environment, there were no significant differences in purchase intent, attitude toward the ad, and support arguments between appeals. However, for the less involved consumers, the green appeal was significantly more persuasive than the nongreen appeal in terms of the same variables.

Scholars also eagerly sought the most effective tool for measuring the effectiveness of green ads. Mohr, Eroglu, and Ellen (1998) looked at the development and testing of a measure of skepticism toward environmental claims in marketers' communications. An investigation of how consumers' skepticism affects the response to green marketing claims would benefit from a reliable and valid measure of skepticism. The report describes a two-stage research project and the resulting four-item measure of skepticism toward environmental claims made in advertising and on packaging.

Two studies examine green consumers' attitude and their demographics. The first study, Straughan and Roberts (1999), looked at the future of green marketing and examined the dynamic nature of ecologically conscious consumer behavior. The study also provides a method of profiling and segmenting college students based upon ecologically conscious consumer behavior. Findings indicate that, despite a significant amount of research at-

tention, demographic criteria are not that useful a profiling method as psychographic criteria. Consistent with past findings, the study indicates that perceived consumer effectiveness provides the greatest insight into ecologically conscious consumer behavior (i.e., a function of consumers' belief that individuals can positively influence the outcome to such problems). Further, the inclusion of altruism to the profile appears to add significantly to previous efforts. Additional constructs suggest that environmental segmentation alternatives are more stable than past profiles that have relied primarily on demographic criteria.

The second study (Trent, 2000) identifies factors that determine attitudes toward an environmental advertisement and its sponsoring company. Through an experimental design, the study sought to examine whether demographic variables influence attitudes, involvement, or participation in the environmental arena. Three hypotheses and three research questions were developed to address different aspects of the effects of news stories on audiences. Trent concluded that source credibility does not influence attitudes to the extent researchers first believed.

We can deduce that survey and experimental approaches to green advertising have been designed mainly to determine consumers' attitudes toward green ads (e.g., do consumers like them, hate them, or support them?). Some research by "green scholars" has searched for the best green advertising forms and structures (Obermiller, 1995; Schuhwerk & Lefkoff-Hagius, 1995) by testing a variety of appeals. However, no remarkable study stands out that shows any deep influence of green advertisements. What would be useful in advancing the practical environmental benefits of green advertising would be research into methods of making green advertising more effective and appealing. Given the rapid rise of environmental problems and of consumerism in non-Western contexts, environmental advertising needs to be more effective globally.

GREEN ADS IN JAPAN, THAILAND, AND CHINA

Advertising and promotion are important parts of the marketing program of firms competing in the global marketplace (Belch & Belch, 2004). Green management and green marketing are well-developed global issues in industrialized nations (Wasik, 1996). Green advertising has expanded in many countries as part of corporations' global advertising strategy. Nearly 90% of the money spent on advertising products and services around the world is concentrated in the industrialized countries of Western Europe and the Pacific Rim, including Japan, South Korea, and Australia.

However, countries that have never made the top 10 global market ad-spending rankings—China is a primary example—are now making a difference. Chinese advertising spending is increasing rapidly (Koranteng, 2000). In addition, Thailand has the fastest growing ad industry in Southeast Asia. The Thai advertising industry has always been one of the more vibrant and creative in Southeast Asia, and perhaps even Asia as a whole, liberated from some of the more strict regulations that apply in Singapore and Malaysia (Asian Market Research News, 2002).

Japan, following a number of high-profile incidents (e.g., the Minamata mercury disaster), introduced strict pollution control regulations and invested heavily in environmental technology, much of it transferred from the United States and Europe. (AsianEnviro, 2006). Thus, Japanese advertisers gradually applied green advertising in their ad strategy. In 1990, Volvo's print advertisement, published in the Nikkei newspaper, received an annual advertising award from the Japan Eco-Life Center and from Nihon Keizai Shimbun. This was the first monumental step for green advertising to advance in Japan (Nihon Keizai Shimbun, 1994). While attracting tremendous attention and creating strong awareness, the 1992 Earth Summit challenged the Japanese advertising industry to employ more environmental themes in their advertising processes. For example, Dentsu, Inc. the largest advertising agency in billing in Japan (Frith, 1996), released a report on the results of its "Green Consumer" Awareness Survey (Dentsu News, 1998). The report analyzes and compares the results of the latest survey conducted in October and November 1997 on consumer awareness of the environment as well as on environment-friendly products and corporate communications that employed an environmental theme; similar surveys were conducted in 1991, 1992, and 1993.

According to Dentsu's report, a rapid increase in the number of green consumers has begun to produce a profound effect on corporate marketing decisions and communication. Green consumers are not perceived as having a particularly unusual awareness of environmental issues and represent a very ordinary grouping of consumers. Although environmentally friendly products are perceived as expensive, there has been a sharp rise in the number of people who accept the higher cost. *Advertising Age* (1998) reported that Dentsu itself has scored a big hit with its "Eco-project" advertising for Toyota. The campaign highlights Toyota products and efforts that help the environment. The Toyota Prius, using emission-reducing gasoline and an electric engine, has enjoyed robust sales since it first hit the Japanese market.

In Thailand, the boom of green advertising, which started in the late 1990s, has continued to be one of the most important marketing strategies for firms (Saereerat, 1995). Generally recognized for a long period, Thailand's pollution problems—most notably air pollution in the urban areas—have been critical to the emergence of green advertising there (Saereerat, 1995). To help promote public awareness of such problems, multinational oil companies such as Caltex, Shell, and the Petroleum Authority of Thailand, along with automobile companies with assembly plants such as Mercedes Benz and Honda (with catalytic converter engines), have substantially invested in a series of green advertising campaigns (Saereerat, 1995). Siam Motors assembles and markets Nissan vehicles in Thailand and has also launched its own "Think Earth" campaigns, which won the eighth annual Thailand Marketing Award (social support section) in 1991–1992, a huge success similar to that of the Save Thai Sea project, also an award winner (Thailand Marketing Award Proceeding, 1992). Retail department store giants such as Central Holdings contribute by using bags that are more environmentally friendly ("UV and degradable" and "UV and biodegradable").

In China, rapid economic expansion and continued reliance on coal will likely double the country's carbon dioxide emissions by 2010. Consequently, China will likely become the world's largest emitter of greenhouse gases sometime between the years 2010 and 2025. However, official policy offers little hope for remedial action (Hudson, 1997). As a result, Chinese firms such as Shanghai Volkswagen Automotive Company and Chinese government have been using green advertising more frequently.

Despite the fact that, for the last decade, green advertising has been widely used in Thailand and China, green advertising in these two countries still is in a beginning stage. A content analysis of green advertisements from Japanese, Thai, Chinese, and American newspapers (Ongkrutraksa, 2003) showed that for green ads in Thailand and China, environmental images of an organization are likely to be considered misleading or deceptive. This study supported the finding of the previous research by Iyer et al. (1995) and Carlson et al. (1993). The study showed that the majority of advertisers in Thailand and China sought to use mostly green messages (promotion of a green company image) and attempted to project a green corporate image, rather than focus on the environmental benefit of their product or service. This might lead to greenwashing because it is green advertising without environmental substance in other operations; as a result, consumers cannot trust the content of green advertisements.

In relation to advertising appeals, Ongkrutraksa (2003) suggested that green advertisements from Japan were mostly "soft sell." The results support Lin's (1993) study that shows the Japanese ads take a "softer sell" approach. Japanese green ads heavily used positive emotional appeal (consisting of messages that use reward appeal or a positive point of view). As Japan is regarded as a "high-context society," specific comparative or logically based appeals may not be needed or desired (Lin, 1993). On the other hand, Thai green ads used highly negative emotional appeal (consisting of messages that use a fear appeal or a negative point of view). For Thai ads, the results have been replicated with Obermiller (1995) as Thailand is still in the developing state of environment awareness. Negative emotional appeal may be more effective among lower awareness consumers.

GREENWASHING AND THE FUTURE OF GREEN ADVERTISING

Environmental responsibility is a potential source of marketing advantage for companies. However, green advertising is not only about simply transferring facts—it is also about building social confidence, capabilities, and empowerment. From my perspective, green marketing's potential may best be described as enormous if the marketers use it smartly and honestly. Companies must be alert to the fact that, to practice green marketing policies, their whole structures must be integrated. That is,

no more dressing up the green ad with just birds and trees, but giving information of how companies are incorporating environmental values into manufacturing processes, products, packaging, and every aspect of the corporate culture. Businesses should continue to pursue sustainability in serious ways. Green advertising without environmental substance in other operations leads to the appearance or the reality of greenwashing. *Macmillan Dictionary* (2006) defines "greenwash" as "to try to convince people that you are doing something which is good for the environment by being involved in small, environmentally friendly initiatives, especially as a way of hiding your involvement in activities which are damaging to the environment" (¶ 1). Most consumers are now very socially conscious and well informed to the degree that they know that greenwashers use green ads only as gimmicks. More and more consumers voluntarily monitor and reveal greenwashers to the entire world. One of the most active environmental nonprofit organizations, Green Life (2005), describes greenwashing on their website as follows:

In the marketplace, media and politics, greenwash serves several purposes, among them: fooling environmentally conscious consumers into buying environmentally destructive products; generating positive press about a company's environmental commitment; and resisting government environmental regulation through preemptive voluntary policies within an industry. Collectively, greenwash's goals maintain the status quo of unsustainable consumption by deceiving and appeasing progressive parties.

Every year for the past decade, the watchdog group Green Life has released a report titled *Don't Be Fooled*. The report calls attention to the year's 10 worst greenwashers: the 10 companies that have made the most misleading claims about the environmental benefits of their products and industries. Their list for 2005 (Green Life, 2006) was as follows:

America's 10 Worst Greenwashers

1. Ford Motor Company
2. BP
3. United States Forest Service
4. ChevronTexaco
5. General Motors
6. Nuclear Energy Institute

7. Alliance of Automobile Manufacturers
8. TruGreen ChemLawn
9. Xcel Energy
10. National Ski Areas Association (¶ 1)

Below is an example that Green Life considered the "worst greenwasher":

Vehicle for vehicle, GM today is the auto-industry's worst emitter of smog-forming pollutants and ranks only ahead of Ford in producing heat-trapping emissions. Judging from their maturation to date, the vehicles of the future are either too disappointing or too distant to distinguish themselves from their predecessors: Hybrid Power to the People features gas-electric pickup truck models—of which GM will produce just 2,500 in 2005—offering a modest 10 percent mileage improvement on their conventional counterparts; similarly, the hybrid transit buses of All Aboard the Magic Bus boost fuel efficiency over non-hybrid models by just 10–20 percent, far short of the advertised 60 percent upgrade that a GM executive acknowledged was overstated; and Who's Driving the Hydrogen Economy? suggests that children today will drive "cleaner cars," though hydrogen still may be yielded by fossil fuels decades from now. The trio is backed by GM's $3 billion advertising budget, the largest in the United States. (¶ 4)

GM should ensure the accuracy of its environmental claims by stating only what it knows to be true. That criterion affects its focus on hydrogen in their ad, which seems to project unrealistic expectations.

Another green advertiser that was criticized is BP (a global oil, gas, and chemicals company headquartered in Britain). BP's advertisements in the International Herald Tribune in November 2000 asserted, "Beyond . . . means being a global leader in producing the cleanest burning fossil fuel" (see BP case study at Sourcewatch, 2005, ¶ 5). However, BP was criticized by the Earth Summit Business Academy, the producers of the Green Oscars. They gave an award in 2002 for "Best" greenwash to BP for their Beyond Petroleum rebranding campaign (Friends of the Earth, 2002). BP brags about investing US$200 million in solar energy, roughly the price of the redesign of its logo and related advertising. At the same time, it spends billions of U.S. dollars buying up more energy companies and exploring for oil (Terra Viva, 2005). The trap for companies such as BP is that big-spending promotional campaigns often raise expectations that the organization is incapable of meeting.

Frank O'Donnell, president of Clean Air Watch, a nonpartisan, nonprofit organization, also criticized General Electric. As noted above, the firm allocated $90 million corporate advertising budget to back its eco-stance in 2003: General Electric, the conglomerate whose environmental legacy has been dominated by its poisoning of the Hudson River with PCBs—and its reluctance to clean up the damage—is turning over a green new leaf. Or so the company claims. But even while GE was hosting a glitzy cocktail reception to roll out a new pro-environmental public relations and ad campaign, the company was working behind closed doors in Congress to secure another delay in cleaning up the Hudson—a cleanup that is supposed to cost the company half a billion dollars (Tompaine, 2005).

These are legitimate criticisms from consumers, which green advertisers should take seriously. For advertisers to avoid being called a greenwasher, critics recommend steps to reconcile expressed claims with actual policy. The recommendations do not necessarily represent bold environmental reform but are typically modest measures designed to convey a company's identity. Advertising is one way of getting across the commitment to helping customers find environmental solutions to problems. Thus, green advertisers must take their green movement cautiously. Moreover, in order for consumers to trust environmental claims, advertisements must reflect genuine environmental performance by companies. It is important to expend the effort to really understand the audience's situations, needs, and perceptions.

In addition, in terms of international green advertising, the message will have to be adapted to the local market, and advertisers will have to discover new ways of reaching local, green consumers (Butler & Kraisornsuthasinee, 1999). Therefore, this chapter agrees with Polonsky and Mintu-Wimsatt (1995) that still more challenges in green marketing research for marketing practitioners and theorists lie ahead. The rise of green marketing has stimulated the most research in the area of consumer behavior. Future green advertising research for practitioners could explore how consumers integrate green issues into the decision-making process. Moreover, the trends in government legislation also indicate increasing environmental consciousness. Can governments protect the environment and simultaneously stimulate the economy? This is a major question, and one that will continue to challenge any government and its constituents.

Research on green advertising needs to acknowledge its dual role: in conducting faithful empirical analysis of green claims and support by industry and in conducting informed and penetrating advocacy. Just as there is a powerful persuasive dimension to advertising itself—overall, if not always with respect to individual messages—so, too, there can be strategic impacts from research.

A CALL TO AWARENESS AND ACTION

We are running out of time; the world is going to suffer dramatically due to environmental problems if we continue to ignore them. We, as consumers, should support green movements. Consumer watchdogs should become even more vigilant in their surveys and more sophisticated in their strategies for drawing attention to inconsistencies between corporate preaching and practice. The academic world should focus more on what determines the most effective green ads and strategies in a globally diverse context and urge corporations to adopt such strategies. Green marketers should be honest in presenting their full array of policies and programs, thereby ensuring they do not merit the title of greenwasher.

REFERENCES

Advertising Age. (1998). *Green consumers' influence grows. Dentsu reports.* Retrieved February 21, 2006, from http://www.adage.com/paypoints/buyArticle.cms/login?newsId=12838&auth=.

American Marketing Association. (2004). *Marketing glossary dictionary.* Retrieved October 14, 2004, from http://www.marketingpower.com/live/mg-dictionary-view1332.php.

AsianEnviro. (2006). *Japan environmental review.* Retrieved February 21, 2006, from http://www.asianenviro.net/content/jer_sample.htm.

Asian Market Research News. (2002). *Thailand Advertising Spend at 8 to 10% Annual Growth.* Retrieved February 21, 2006, from http://www.asiamarketresearch.com/news/000184.htm.

Bahn, K. D., & Wright, N. D. (2001). A model of green product purchase behavior. *Academy of Marketing Studies, 4,* 74–79.

Balderjahn, I. (1988). Personality variables and environmental attitudes as predictors of ecologically responsible consumption patterns. *Journal of Business Research, 17*(1), 51–56.

Banerjee, S. B. (1999). Corporate environmentalism and the greening of strategic marketing. In M. Charter & M. J. Polonsky (Eds.), *Greener marketing: A global perspective to greening marketing practice* (pp. 16–40). Sheffield, UK: Greenleaf.

Belch, G., & Belch, M. (2004). *Advertising and promotion: An integrated marketing communications perspective* (6th ed.). Chicago: McGraw-Hill/Irwin.

Butler, J., & Kraisornsuthasinee, S. (1999). Green strategies in developing economies. In M. Charter & M. J. Polonsky (Eds.), *Greener marketing: A global perspective to greening marketing practice* (pp. 338–350). Sheffield, UK: Greenleaf.

Carlson, L., Grove, S., & Kangun, N. (1993). A content analysis of environmental advertising claims: A matrix approach. *Journal of Advertising, 22*(3), 28–39.

Coddington, W. (1993). *Environmental marketing: Positive strategies for reaching the green consumer.* Washington, DC: McGraw-Hill.

Cone Communications. (1994). *Cone/Roper benchmark survey on cause-related marketing.* Retrieved October 22, 2000, from http://www.conenet.com/website/crm/report.htm.

Cornwell, T. B., & Schwepker, C. H., Jr. (1992). Attitudes and intentions regarding ecologically packaged products: Subcultural variations. In L. Reid (Ed.), *Proceedings of the 1992 conference of the American Academy of Advertising* (pp. 119–121). Athens, GA: Grady College of Journalism and Mass Communication, University of Georgia.

Creamer, M. (2005, May 9). GE sets aside big bucks to show off some green; print, TV blitz part of plan to double revenue from eco-safe offerings. *Advertising Age, 76,* 7.

Davis, J. J. (1994). Consumer response to corporate environmental advertising. *Journal of Consumer Marketing, 11*(2), 25–37.

Dentsu News. (1998). *Green consumer survey report* [in Japanese]. Retrieved February 14, 1998, from http://www.dentsu.co.jp/DHP/DOG/greenconsumer/b3.html.

Drumwright, M. E. (1994, July). Socially responsible organizational buying: Environmental concern as a non-economic buying criterion. *Journal of Marketing, 58*, 1–19.

Ellen, P. S., Wiener J. L., & Cobb-Walgren C. (1991). The role of perceived consumer effectiveness in motivating environmentally conscious behaviors. *Journal of Public Policy & Marketing, 10*(2), 102–117.

Friends of the Earth. (2002). Press release. Retrieved February 14, 2006, *from* http://www.foe.co.uk/resource/press_releases/20020823130012.html.

Frith, K. T. (Ed.). (1996). *Advertising in Asia, communication, culture and consumption.* Ames: Iowa State University Press.

Global Ecolabelling Network. (2006). *What is ecolabelling?* Retrieved February 21, 2006, from http://www.gen.gr.jp/eco.html.

Green Advertising. (1995). Special issue. *Journal of Advertising 24*(2).

Green Life. (2005). *What is green wash?* Retrieved September 27, 2005, from http://www.thegreenlife.org/greenwash101.html#2.

Green Life. (2006). *Don't be fooled.* Retrieved February 21, 2006, from http://www.thegreenlife.org/dontbefooled.html.

Hansen, E., & Juslin, H. (1999). *The status of forest certification in the ECE region* (Geneva Timber and Forest Discussion Paper ECE/TIM/DP/14). New York: United Nations Publications.

Hudson, C. (1997). *The China handbook.* Chicago: Fitzroy Dearborn Publishers.

International Chamber of Commerce. (1991). *ICC international code of environmental advertising publication.* Retrieved February 21, 2006, from http://www.iccwbo.org/home/statements_rules/rules/1991/envicod.asp.

Iyer, E., & Barnerjee, B. (1993). Anatomy of green advertising. *Advances in Consumer Research, 20*, 494–501.

Iyer, E., Barnerjee, B., & Gulas, C. (1995). Shades of green: A multidimensional analysis of environmental advertising. *Journal of Advertising, 24*, 21–31.

Kärnä, J., Juslin, H., Ahonen, V., & Hansen, E. (2001). Green advertising: Greenwash or a true reflection of marketing strategies? *Greener Management International, 33*(Spring), 59–70.

Koranteng, J. (2000, May). Ranking the top global ad markets. *Advertising Age International, 17*, 17–20.

Kotler, P., Armstrong, G., Ang, S.-H., Leong, S.-M., Tan, C.-T., & Tse, D. (2005). *Principles of marketing: An Asian perspective.*Singapore: Prentice-Hall.

Kotler, P., & Keller, K. (2006). *Marketing management* (12th ed.). New York: Prentice-Hall.

Lawrence, M. (1998). *Nation's first cause-related marketing trends report finds consumers more responsive to strategic CRM campaigns.* Retrieved February 21, 2006, from http://www.celf,net/iprex/news.

Lin, C. (1993). Cultural differences in message strategies: A comparison between American and Japanese TV commercials. *Journal of Advertising Research, 33*(3), 40–48.

Macmillan Dictionary. (2006). *Greenwash.* Retrieved February 21, 2006, from http://www.macmillandictionary.com/New-Words/050110-greenwash.htm.

Mayer, R. N., Cude, B. J., Gray-Lee, J., & Scammon, D. L. (1995). Trends in environmental marketing claims since the FTC guides: Two-year auditing results. In K. F. Fox (Ed.), *Consumer interests annual: Proceedings of the annual conference of the American Council on Consumer Interests* (pp. 161–166). Columbia, MO: American Council on Consumer Interests.

McDonald's Corporation. (1990). *McDonald's and the environment.* Oakbrook, IL: Association for Consumer Research.

McGowan, C. L. (2000). *Utilitarian and value-expressive claims in environmental advertising: A content analysis.* Unpublished doctoral thesis, Wayne State University, Detroit.

Mintel International Group Ltd. (1991). *The green consumer report.* London: Author.

Mohr, A. L., Eroglu, D., & Ellen S. P. (1998). The development and testing of a measure of skepticism toward environmental claims in marketers' communications. *Journal of Consumer Affairs, 32*(Summer), 25–30.

Nihon Keizai Shimbun, Advertising Section. (1994). *Read business from newspaper advertising.* Tokyo: Nihon Keizai Newspaper Publishing.

Obermiller, C. (1995). The baby is sick/the baby is well: A test of environmental communication appeals. *Journal of Advertising, 24*(2), 55–70.

Ongkrutraksa, W. (2003). Content analysis: Green advertising in Japan Thai, China and American studies. *Asia Pacific Advances in Consumer Research, 5*, 120–126.

Ottman, J. A. (1993). *Green marketing: Challenges and opportunities for the new marketing age.* Lincolnwood, IL: NTC Business Books.

Peterson, R. T. (1991). Physical environment television advertisement themes: 1979 and 1989. *Journal of Business Ethics, 10*(3), 221–228.

Polonsky, M. J. (1994). An introduction to green marketing. *Electronic Green Journal, 1*(2). Retrieved February 21, 2006, from http://gopher.uidaho.edu/1/UI_gopher/library/egj/.

Polonsky, M. J., & Mintu-Wimsatt, A. T. (1995). The future of environmental marketing: Food for thought. In M. J. Polonsky & A. T. Mintu-Wimsatt (Eds.), *Environmental marketing: Strategies, practice, theory and research* (pp. 389–391). New York: Haworth Press.

Reitman, V. (1995, May 10). Green product sales seem to be wilting. *Wall Street Journal, 220,* 135–148.

Roper Starch Worldwide. (1996). *The green gauge reports.* New York: Author.

Saereerat, S. (1995). *Marketing for environment.* Bangkok: Pattanasueksa Publishing.

Scammon, D. L., & Mayer, R. N. (1993). Environmental labeling and advertising claims: International action and policy issues. *European Advances in Consumer Research, 1,* 338–344.

Schuhwerk, M. E., & Lefkoff-Hagius, R. (1995). Green or non-green? Does type of appeal matter when advertising a green product? *Journal of Advertising, 24*(2), 45–54.

Schwepker, C. H., & Cornwell, T. B. (1991). An examination of ecologically concerned consumers and their intention to purchase ecologically packaged products. *Journal of Public Policy & Marketing, 10*(2), 1–25.

Sourcewatch. (2005). *BP.* Retrieved September 27, 2005, from http://www.sourcewatch.org/index.php?title=BP#BP.27s_rebranding_as_a_.27green.27_company.

Straughan, R. D., & Roberts, J. A. (1999). Environmental segmentation alternatives: A look at green consumer behavior in the new millennium. *Journal of Consumer Marketing, 16*(6), 558–575.

Terra Viva. (2005). *Greenwashing awards unearth the dirt.* Retrieved September 27, 2005, from http://www.ipsnews.net/riomas10/2708_4.shtml.

Thailand Marketing Award Proceeding. (1992). *The list of award recipients in the 8th Thailand marketing awards proceedings.* Bangkok.

Thorson, E., Page, T., & Moore, J. (1995). Consumer response to four categories of "green" television commercials. *Advances in Consumer Research, 22,* 243–250.

Tompaine. (2005). *GE's greenwashing.* Retrieved September 27, 2005, from http://www.tompaine.com/articles/20050513/ges_greenwashing.php.

Trent, J. H., Jr. (2000). *Environmental advertising: A study of the development of attitudes toward "greenwashing" advertising.* Unpublished master's thesis, University of Nevada, Reno.

Wasik, J. (1996). *Green marketing and management: A global perspective.* Cambridge, MA: Blackwell Publishers.

Weaver-Lariscy, R. A., & Tinkham, S. F. (1992). Knowledge and opinions as predictors of recycling behavior: Implications for environmental advertising strategy. In L. Reid (Ed.), *Proceedings of the 1992 conference of the American Academy of Advertising* (p. 45). Athens, GA: Grady College of Journalism and Mass Communication, University of Georgia.

26

Sustainable Development Discourse and the Global Economy

Promoting Responsibility, Containing Change

SHIV GANESH

The very publication of this book both presupposes and establishes the proliferation of discourse about corporate social responsibility (CSR), so it is not my aim to rehearse the contours of this trend. Rather, I wish to expand the scope of such collective assessment of CSR discourse by examining it with reference to other dominant discourses in late industrial global capitalism that attempt to connect issues of economic growth with social and environmental concerns. While in many senses all discourse implicitly serves to establish relationships between economic and social domains—indeed, for Foucault, the very distinction between economy and society is discursive—I focus on another dominant discourse of our times, that of sustainable development, which since the early 1980s has become the main referent of any discussion about international and global economic development (Escobar, 1995; Ganesh, 2005). In doing so, I hope to aid in furthering our collective understanding of how CSR discourse is related to sustainable development discourse, and how conventional understandings of this discourse might serve to contain change rather than engender radical structural transformation. In concluding, I discuss how we might productively begin to reenvision the relationship between CSR and sustainable development.

Accordingly, this chapter is divided into three substantive sections. First, by way of a detailed introduction, I briefly describe a history of global sustainable development discourse and examine the nature of the relationship between this discourse and CSR. Second, in the body of the chapter I unpack three key assumptive bases of conventional sustainable development discourse. Third, by way of an extended conclusion, I examine the issue of accountability as an alternative referent for the relationship between CSR and sustainable development.

A BRIEF HISTORY OF SUSTAINABLE DEVELOPMENT DISCOURSE

"Development" is not a singularly coherent system of ideas and beliefs. That is, it is hard to think about development as a unified ideological scheme, and as Hilhorst (2002) demonstrates in her study of a Philippine Igorot village, the concept of development can easily have multiple meanings and various implications even within a single community. If "development" at a local level can mean different things, then it is reasonable to argue that the notion of global development does not have a straightforward relationship with liberal politics or even, disturbingly, with democracy at large. This is illustrated by such contemporary global trends as recent policy shifts in "developing" nations toward liberalization and the diminishing of the idea of state responsibility (Chakravartty, 2004), as well as the emergence of fundamentalist groups that articulate their own visions of what counts as development. In contemporary India, for example, the term is used differently by different groups, and in every case the formulation of the idea of development has represented the interests of specific groups of people, whether it is the political elite, industry, the middle class, or the peasantry (D'Souza, 1990; Omvedt, 1995).

In spite of the evident polysemy of the term, it is equally clear that development does function as a discourse in the Foucaultian sense. That is, it serves to establish and articulate finite relationships between people and things. Arturo Escobar's (1995) influential arguments about the wide discursive span of development, for example, demonstrate how it identifies and constructs third-world poverty as something that has to be problematized, strategized, acted upon, changed, and brought into line with global economic prescriptions. For Escobar, sustainable development, despite its eco-friendly credentials, has emerged as a dominant development discourse not because it offers something completely new, but rather because it has pasted environmental managerialism upon the classical concern of development economics, that is, poverty.

How and when did the term "sustainable development" come to occupy such a prominent place in global discussions about development? Its circulation in international circuits of development discourse can be traced not to the much-maligned Brundtland Commission, but further back to 1972, at the United Nations Conference on the Human Environment in Stockholm, where its relevance was underscored by the United Nations Development Programme's Stockholm declaration (Roy, 1995). However, as the wording of the declaration itself demonstrated, the term "conservation" was a defining factor in the relationship between environmental and developmental discourse (United Nations Development Programme, 1972). The term "sustainable development" continued to gain currency throughout the 1970s and gained serious momentum in 1980 when the World Conservation Strategy, devised by the International Union for the Conservation of Nature and Natural Resources in conjunction with the United Nations Environmental Programme (UNEP), zeroed in on the term in an attempt to promote the idea that conservation and development were interdependent rather than antithetical (United Nations Environment Pro-

gramme, 1980). Importantly, the strategy marked a key move on the part of the United Nations away from the then predominant notion of conservation as being antigrowth, and launched a new era of global advocacy that environmental conservation could be achieved by modifying rather than transforming systems of transnational capitalist production.

In 1987, the World Commission on Environment and Development, led by Gro Harlem Brundtland, defined sustainable development during the Tokyo declaration by using a line that has since become a slogan or a cliché, depending on your point of view: "development that meets the needs of the present without compromising the ability of future generations to meet their own needs (p. 1). The publication of *Our Common Future* (referred to as the Brundtland report) is often cited as the single most important moment in the ascendancy of sustainable development discourse and, indeed, was a critical event that signaled the coming of age of this discourse. The Brundtland report made the unprecedented move of subsuming, within a single overarching term, both economic and social development. The Tokyo declaration called for all nations to explicitly adopt the objective of sustainability as the goal and the test for national and international policy. The report went on to recommend a set of principles to integrate the idea of sustainable development into *all* national goals.

Conceptually, then, the notion of sustainable development can be said to be far broader than any other formulations and definitions of development that preceded it. Since the 1980s, the notion of sustainable development has become integrated with and now inseparable from all forms of social activity that involve the term "development." This broadest possible formulation was advanced at the Earth Summit at Rio de Janeiro in 1992 (United Nations Conference on Environment and Development, 1992) and has been evident since then in such global conferences such as the Earth Summit Plus Five in New York in 1997 and the World Summit for Sustainable Development (WSSD) in Johannesburg in 2002.

Following from such breadth is, of course, ambiguity. As I indicated above, it is evident (and significant) that there is considerable debate and varied articulation of what counts as sustainable development practice (Peterson, 1997). This variation in specific formulation of what does or does not count as sustainable development is not necessarily apparent from the official history presented above. Still, the existence of such variance stands to reason, given the broad reach of the Brundtland report's formulation as well as the subsequent semantic expansion of the term. It is equally significant that a diversity of practices—from agriculture to family planning—find themselves rubbing shoulders under the sustainable development umbrella. Probably as important is the fact that in the last 5–10 years, practitioners and researchers in the area of sustainable development have increasingly begun to refer to CSR as a means of achieving sustainable development.

Corporate social responsibility is now commonly advocated as a means to achieve sustainability, both by practitioners in the development apparatus (Frame, 2005) and by researchers (Young, 2004). In its crudest form, such advocacy is articulated as a plea for corporate organizations to behave responsibly and pursue sustainable development goals, but most renditions of the relationship between CSR and sustainable development are not so coarse. In fact, there are more and more complex ways of measuring issues of sustainability in business (Labuschagne, Brent, & von Erck, 2005). For instance, in 1997, UNEP launched the now popular and increasingly criticized Global Reporting Initiative (see www .globalreporting.org) that aims to accumulate impact data in social, environmental, and economic dimensions.

Moreover, the connection between the two discourses sometimes transcends the "means to an end" relationship visible in both popular and academic discourse. Overall, in discursive terms, the overlap between CSR and sustainable development is clearly becoming more and more substantive as they begin to shape each other. For example, the World Business Council for Sustainable Development, established in 1991, which now counts more than 170 companies in its membership, *defines* CSR in terms of sustainable development in its mission statement, as "the commitment of business to contribute to sustainable economic development, working with employees, their families, the local community and society at large to improve their quality of life" (World Business Council on Social Development, 2005). Here, CSR is not merely a method; it is a *commitment* and an *ethos*, interpreted in sustainable development terms.

In other instances, sustainable development is interpreted in CSR terms. This is reflected in some sustainable development measures that focus as much upon internal organizational process as they do upon external organizational impact. For example, the Wuppertal sustainable development indicator framework follows the United Nations Commission on Sustainable Development in assessing institutional aspects of sustainability, stipulating that institutional indicators of sustainable development include the degree to which the organization employs participatory structures and pays attention to issues of justice and gender balance (Labuschagne et al., 2005).

The global dominance of sustainable development discourse and its increasing association with CSR discourse has received a fair amount of critique and assessment, both by scholars and by practitioners. For example, a recent special issue of *Development* asked whether CSR is rewriting development (Harcourt, 2004). Essays in that issue tackle critical issues about whether the notion of CSR is hollowing out notions of public development altogether either by explicitly advocating or implicitly assuming that public structures are bankrupt and that private and corporate sectors are the only means by which real development and change can occur (Blowfield, 2004; Fox, 2004). Additionally, some nongovernmental organizations (NGOs) have become increasingly vocal about their opposition to CSR and have begun to point out that several corporations use CSR as window dressing. For example, in a recent report, U.K.-based Christian Aid activists used internal e-mails, memos, and letters to British American Tobacco (BAT) to demonstrate that BAT's use of CSR rhetoric was purely a greenwashing strategy intended to ensure the failure of the United Nations's Framework Convention on Tobacco Control (Christian Aid, 2005), given that they had not actually instituted any measures to ensure that their products did not reach minors.

Clearly, then, it is critical that we take seriously the extent to which these discourses have come together as well as the impact that such an alliance might have for our collective notions of progressive global social change. One means of accomplishing such an assessment is to examine in more detail three assumptive bases of conventional sustainable development discourse. Given the self-evident polysemy of sustainable development discourse, I follow David Korten (1996) and distinguish between conventional versus "emergent alternative" renditions of sustainable development.

For Korten, conventional (and powerful) wisdom on sustainable development is professed by such institutions and actors as the United Nations, World Bank, International Monetary Fund, and the General Agreement on Tariffs and Trade. While Korten outlines differences between these two perspectives in the form of a slew of prescriptions in areas such as lifestyles, poverty, population, and trade, I present three assumptive bases that underlie conventional prescriptions in particular. The first of these assumptions of sustainable development discourse lies in its invocation of the metaphor of a single human family. The second lies in its advocacy of environmental care as a goal that is achievable within the parameters of current economic growth, and the third lies in the relationship between states and civil society that sustainable development discourse envisages. I address these three issues in turn.

SUSTAINABLE DEVELOPMENT DISCOURSE AND METAPHORS OF FAMILY

While environmental politics have emerged as a staging ground for conflict between the rich countries of the North and the poor countries of the South (Ganesh, Zoller, & Cheney, 2005; Gupta, 1998), conventional rhetoric about sustainable development has moved us toward quite another set of assumptions about the basis for global interaction. The very title of the 1987 Brundtland report—*Our Common Future*—invoked the metaphor of a single humanity working together as a family. This created the grounds for the suggestion that the problem of the environment was something that all inhabitants of the planet could work out together by engaging in similar forms of social activity. Since then, the recurring notion of one Earth, a fragile ecosystem suspended in space, has been captured by the visual image of the globe. The globe has been a prominent motif at various United Nations conferences, most recently at the WSSD in 2002, where the summit logo itself was a globe carried on the wings of what one assumes is a dove of peace.

As Meister (1999) argues, such imagery serves to focus on warm and fuzzy themes of human protection and comfort. This is further evidenced by the pomp and circumstance of the formal opening of the 1992 United Nations Conference on Environment and Development (UNCED). The official opening consisted of a ship full of children from all over the world sailing into Rio de Janeiro bearing the banner "Keep The Promise . . . For a Better World for All the Children" (Stephens, 1992). And at the 2002 Johannesburg conference, the predominant theme at the opening concert was global friendship, evident in joint performances by local musicians and Western mainstream pop acts.

Some religious organizations have also, in the last decade or so, begun to make explicit connections between their notions of spirituality and the notion of sustainable development. The trope of a single human family evident in sustainable development discourse helps us to understand how and why this has become possible. A 1994 statement by the National Spiritual Assembly of the Baha'is of the United States (1994) serves as a useful illustration in this regard:

Patterns of sustainable development, however, will not emerge without systematic changes in the underlying ethos of societal institutions, and this in turn requires changes in the values and attitudes of individuals. Recognition of the fundamental interdependence between human life and the biosphere is only the first step toward creating this new consciousness. An ecologically sustainable civilization . . . involves both an internal and external reordering, and such a reordering can only occur when the human heart is transformed. The path toward sustainable development can only be built upon the deep comprehension of humanity's spiritual reality—a reality that lies at the very essence of human beings. . . . In considering the connection between the spiritual dimension of human existence and sustainable development, it is helpful to recall how the world's great religious systems have guided humanity in the past. The moral code of the Ten Commandments and the Golden Rule (that we should treat others as we ourselves wish to be treated)—both of which find their expression in nearly every religious tradition—serve both as ethical guidelines and a summons to spiritual achievement. (¶ 4–6)

It is evident that this statement suggests that a metaphysical, singular spiritual human nature must be understood and harnessed in order to achieve sustainable development. What is really interesting about the association is the simultaneous secularization of religious discourse (in this case, the Baha'i faith) and the evangelization of the secular discourse of sustainable development. This dual move is made possible by the trope of a single humanity already present in both sustainable development and Baha'i discourse. Similar moves are visible in other religions, as well, notably in several Christian churches, including the Catholic Church and the Anglican Church. For instance, in a statement issued just before the 2002 Johannesburg summit on sustainable development, the Global Anglican Congress on the Stewardship of Creation made the following statement in a declaration to the Anglican Communion:

> Our planetary crisis is environmental, but more than that, it is a crisis of the Spirit and the Body, which runs to the core of all that we hold Sacred. . . . Transformation is, at its heart, a spiritual matter; it includes every aspect of our lives. As members of the Anglican Communion, at all levels of its life, we must play our part in bringing about this transformation toward a just, sustainable future. Now is the time for prayerful action based on the foundation of our faith. (Tuatagaloa-Matalavea, 2002, ¶ 6)

Again, one witnesses the yoking together of environmental and religious discourse in terms of a singular unified spirituality. That this large unified vision declares oneness in the face of other evidence is clear not only from the upsurge (one might say construction) of global religious fundamentalism (Giddens, 2000) but also from the fact that cause-and-effect relationships in environmental problems vary drastically all over the world. In the North, for instance, one of the root causes of environmental degradation over the last century and a half has been industrial pollution and waste disposal, whereas in the South, historically the chief problems have stemmed from an overexploitation of the natural resource base, which preceded the industrial pollution problems that face it today (Thomas, 1992). Consequently, it stands to reason that what should have been done (or is yet to be done) to achieve sustainable development really ought to vary tremendously not only horizontally, across the globe, but also vertically, within a particular political economy. None of this is evident in either secular or religious articulations of a singular human family in the context of sustainable development.

It is also worth mentioning that scholars have established that, more often than not, this unified vision of humanity evident in sustainable development discourse invokes the category "nature" as a fragile femininity that needs protection (Shiva, 1989, 1991). In this respect, that sustainable development discourse urges the family of humanity to care for and work together in the race to save the planet makes it an unreservedly masculinist, patriarchal discourse with a conservative and predominantly heterosexist view of family. Eventually, as others have argued, that this "family of nations" might have senior and junior members, parents and children, and masculine and feminine roles is glossed over by conventional sustainable development discourse (Gupta, 1998; Malkki, 1994).

Given all of this, it should not come as a surprise that an increasing number of organizations call for a return to conservative family values as a means of achieving sustainable development. For example, a Christian NGO that calls itself Family Unity for Sustainable Development Foundation works on communication and health promotion campaigns in Nigeria, on the manifest supposition that improving the health of the family regarding tuberculosis prevention can be accomplished by educating women homemakers. This, in turn, serves to further privatize the role of women within the family by making them, rather than men, primarily responsible for family health. In the North, the United States, in particular, has increasingly lobbied for platforms for conservative pro-family NGOs at international meetings, as evidenced by the consultative role that conservative Christian organizations such as the Family Research Council and the World Family Policy Center (a Latter Day Saints NGO based at Brigham Young University) played leading up to the 2002 Johannesburg Summit (Butler, 2002). These recent moves serve to underscore the latent conservatism that lies behind articulations of "a single humanity" in conventional sustainable development discourse.

RELATIONSHIPS BETWEEN ECONOMY AND ECOLOGY IN SUSTAINABLE DEVELOPMENT DISCOURSE

The universalizing scope of current conventional sustainable development discourse is accompanied by a self-evident ambiguity as to what specific development projects might be considered sustainable or not (Ganesh, 2005). In addition, it advocates the idea that sustainability can be achieved, not by containing economic growth, but simply by modifying it (McMichael, 1996; Meister & Japp, 1998). As I detailed above, the term was popularized in the 1980s by the United Nations apparatus in an effort to move away from the notion of environmental conservation, which was seen as unrealistic and antigrowth. It is worth mentioning that Christine Oravec (1984) in a much-cited essay demonstrates how, in the early-twentieth-century United States, the term "conservation" itself came to replace the term "preservation" in environmental discourse for precisely the same reason that preservation was construed as being antipublic and antieconomy, whereas conservation was not.

It is evident, then, that from its outset, conventional sustainable development discourse has carried the assumption that the spread of an eco-friendly transnational capitalism can take care of the environmental externalities of current modes of production. Paul Hawken's work, for example, represents a sophisticated exposition of this position. Over the years, Hawken has sketched out his vision of a "natural" capitalism, maintaining that if capitalist systems attribute adequate value to natural resources and reduce their dependence on metals, fuels, and other minerals, capitalist systems can stabilize themselves and prepare for long-term stability (Hawken, 1994; Hawken, Lovins, & Lovins, 1999; Lovins, Lovins, & Hawken, 1999).

This argument, though, has received criticism from several quarters; indeed, it could be said that critics of sustainable development discourse have, over the years, tended to focus more on this assumption than any other (Hove, 2004). Even so, the criticism itself is not univocal and reflects a variety of positions. Some critics approach the issue through a postcolonial lens. For example, Vandana Shiva (1991) maintains that arguments in favor of eco-friendly global capitalism serve to mask fundamental tensions between Western capitalist expansion and local ethics of environmental care. For the former, an ever-increasing natural resource base is a precondition for its existence, and for the latter, the heart of the issue is the retention of the symbiotic relationship between human beings and the worlds in which they live. Other postcolonial critiques include the idea that the very concept of sustainable development is

Western and is set up in such a way as to blame environmental degradation caused by third-world poverty and population displacement as the chief culprit behind unsustainable economic growth, rather than unsustainable patterns of consumption in the West itself (Banerjee, 2003; Munshi & Kurien, 2005).

Another criticism of the "eco-friendly" or "natural capitalism" view comes from explicitly socialist positions. From this point of view, there exists a basic contradiction between capitalist industrial expansion and environmental protection not accounted for by sustainable development discourse (Hove, 2004). John Bellamy Foster (2003) also points toward this contradiction in his critique of Hawken's work. In particular, Foster critiques Hawken for underestimating a capitalist economy's need for energy and resources, citing as evidence energy consumption data from the United States and Japan and demonstrating the inability of these countries to engage in efficient consumption of energy, even within the parameters of economic efficiency defined by their respective economies. Eventually, as Saurin argues, a critical analysis of sustainable development has to see environmental crises as an intrinsic part of capitalist accumulation (Saurin, 1996). Indeed, for him, the category "environment" itself has to be seen in terms of the values, interests, and power behind the international division of labor instead of being taken as a given base upon which world economies run.

In sum, it might be said that the tendency to discuss sustainable development in terms of the ecological stress on economic endeavors rather than on the ecological impact of the economy reflects a key assumption of conventional sustainable development discourse: that environmental crises are solvable within the limits of the current global political economy. And in doing so, it serves to contain rather than revolutionize various collective visions of the future.

SUSTAINABLE DEVELOPMENT DISCOURSE AND STATES, MARKETS, AND CIVIL SOCIETY

The third assumptive base of conventional sustainable development discourse lies in its depiction of relationships between states, markets, and civil society and is related to its assumptions about the nature of capitalist growth. How such discourse conceives of the relationship between states and markets can be seen in the declarations of various conferences sponsored by the United Nations in the last 12 years or so, from UNCED to WSSD. Primarily, these documents position the market as the key engine that drives sustainable growth, with the task of the nation-state being to facilitate such growth.

The idea that the market is a key base for sustainability was made explicit in UNCED's Agenda 21 at Rio:

> Sustainable development cannot be achieved worldwide while massive poverty persists. Wealth created by trade, along with continued economic reforms and a substantial increase in the transfer of financial resources and technology from rich to poor countries, is an essential means to achieving this end. . . . Domestic and international environmental policies are of paramount importance for all aspects of sustainable development. As such policies become more effective, the risk that economic activities—including trade and development—may contribute to environmental degradation is reduced. . . . Barriers to trade can create impediments to the achievement of sustainable development, particularly for developing countries, and trade liberalization is an important component of progress toward sustainable development for all countries. (United Nations Conference on Environment and Development, 1992, p. 2)

In other words, free and unregulated trade (not, as the slogan goes, "fairly regulated" trade) is the vehicle that will carry sustainable development across the world. Another United Nations report, based on the proceedings of the 1995 World Summit on Social Development held in Copenhagen, is also saturated in the discourse of sustainable development: the term appears on virtually every page of the report. Here, the virtues of a free market are touted once again. The report in fact advocates that the role of nation-states should merely be to facilitate the development of free markets. For instance, the report says that "the task of nation-states is to promote dynamic, open, free markets, while recognizing the need to intervene in markets, to the extent necessary" (World Summit on Social Development, 1995, p. 6). And finally, the 2002 WSSD in Johannesburg also contained rhetoric that promoted free trade as a prime means of realizing sustainability. A report

from the summit states: "At the Summit, governments agreed that opening up access to markets is key to development and committed themselves to support the phase-out of all forms of export subsidies" (World Summit for Sustainable Development, 2002, p. 3).

Whereas these reports unsurprisingly restrict themselves to large statements about the direction that economic change should take, it is also important to note that they prescribe key roles for other organizations, notably NGOs. For example, the accordance of an increasingly important role for NGOs in promoting sustainable development has been visible at the International Institute for Sustainable Development (IISD) in Canada, which spells out its principles in its *Summary of IISD's Principles for Trade and Sustainable Development* (1995). The document says that, in order for international cooperation on the environment to occur, "Non-government institutions and agencies must take a leadership role in realizing the principles of sustainable development by enacting sustainable livelihoods" (p. 1).

It is easy enough to locate examples of NGO discourse that position NGOs as prime movers behind sustainable development efforts. More interesting is the United Nations's increasing willingness in the 1980s and 1990s not only to work in partnership with NGOs but also to work *through* them (Butler, 2002), as well as the fact that governments themselves have publicly begun to refer to NGOs as primary actors in sustainable development. It has become commonplace for public government figures to invoke the term *partnership* when referring to NGOs and the leadership role that these organizations play. For example, British Prime Minister Tony Blair said, in his speech at the release of his government's third annual report on Sustainable Development in 2003:

> I pay tribute to the hard work of the UK team . . . and to the enormous efforts made by business, community groups and NGOs. We agreed [on] action on areas such as sanitation and water, renewable energy, biodiversity, and oceans . . . in partnership with governments, businesses and NGOs, we are working to find new ways of removing barriers to investment in these [climate change] technologies. (¶ 28)

The idea that governments should work through NGOs, in partnership with them, is also evidenced in the more specific policies of international development institutions. For example, the U.S. Agency for International Development (USAID), in a document titled "USAID's Strategy for Sustainable Development: An Overview" (1995), argues that:

> the United States in particular has an historic opportunity: to serve our long-term national interests by applying our ideals, our sense of decency, and our humanitarian impulse to the repair of the world . . . the United States must articulate a strategy for sustainable development. It must forge a partnership with the nations and the people it assists. It must focus on countries where its help is most needed and where it can make the most difference . . . Thus, the fundamental thrust of USAID's programs, whether in democracy building, environment, economic growth, or population and health, will aim at building indigenous capacity, enhancing participation, and encouraging accountability, transparency, decentralization, and the empowerment of communities and individuals. Our projects will involve and strengthen the elements of a self-sustaining, civic society: indigenous non-governmental organizations (NGOs), including private voluntary organizations . . . , productive associations, educational institutions, community groups, and local political institutions. (p. 2)

In other words, the United States as a nation-state has an especially unique obligation. It must, according to USAID, promote democracy and "repair a ravaged world" by developing "local organizations and communities" rather than by making explicit commitments to supporting democratic nation-states themselves. This approach, in fact, has characterized the vast majority of USAID's work throughout the world, where it channels funds, with the permission of governments, to national and regional NGOs, sometimes resulting in creating privileged networks instead of engendering social change (Henderson, 2002).

In sum, conventional understandings of sustainable development can be said to invoke neoliberal understandings of the relationships among states, markets, and civil society. Neoliberal prescriptions, in particular, involve such political moves as economic deregulation, privatization, and the relinquishing of overt government control and responsibility in civil domains. Such politics are especially evident in the way in which a conventional discourse of sustainable development conceives of states, markets, and civil society, which is to enthrone the market and see NGOs rather than states as central mobilizers in civil society.

REVISITING THE CSR CONNECTION: PROMOTING ACCOUNTABILITY

Three summary observations about these three assumptions of conventional sustainable development discourse are in order. First, these assumptions demonstrate that, in many ways, conventional sustainable development discourse is a global discourse *par excellence*. It travels by invoking the metaphor of the universal family, masking potential local contradictions between economy and ecology, and addressing itself to the development of markets and the support of NGO work. This journey, or border crossing, is accomplished precisely by the argument that there are, in fact, no borders at all.

Second, many scholars, such as Aihwa Ong (1999) and Nikolas Rose (1996) have argued that neoliberalism is not only an economic doctrine but also a political and therefore moral ideology. In this light, conventional sustainable development discourse can be seen as bringing a moral dimension to contemporary neoliberalism, inasmuch as it brings together, albeit loosely, conservative notions of family with issues of privatization and the primacy of the market. Moreover, given the overt espousal of environmental care in sustainable development rhetoric, it might not be a stretch to speculate that such discourse could be said to represent the key morals of neoliberalism itself.

Third, these three assumptions taken together can be said to contain radical change as much as engender it. To be sure, even conventional understandings of sustainable development (when implemented) have the potential to effect some beneficial material changes in the form of emission reductions, alternative forms of energy generation, and recycling. However, the vision of social change that it presents to us is truncated inasmuch as we are unable to cogently articulate visions of social change that lie beyond late capitalism, or express possibilities for collective communal organizing beyond those that it argues are key, namely, markets, governments, and NGOs. Other forms of organizing, including unions, social movements, public protests, and the like, are not presented as viable means to achieve sustainable development. Moreover, the single humanity motif and the visions of family in the discourse are, as I have discussed, easily appropriated (some might even say engendered) by conservative forces themselves.

Having spent a considerable amount of space unpacking sustainable development discourse, it now remains to revisit the relationship between CSR and sustainable development. At the outset, it is worth mentioning that there is evidence that there is an increasing disjuncture between discursive and material realities. That is, even as discourse about CSR is proliferating, there is some evidence that CSR practices have not in fact been adopted on a large scale and still exist at the margins of business practice, and even those on the frontlines of CSR implementation acknowledge this. As Frame (2005), for instance, says:

> However, it is widely accepted that progress [in implementing CSR practices] has been slow among OECD [Organisation of Economic Cooperation and Development] countries despite the proliferation of national, regional, and local policy statements. Indeed . . . CSR is being used by some corporations "merely as a branch of PR" and that "rhetoric and the reality are simply contradictory." (p. 423)

While there are a number of explanations as to why CSR might not be working as well as it could, one in particular bears mention here: the voluntary nature of CSR. Some scholars have maintained that the voluntary nature of targets in CSR does not work because CSR foregrounds responsibility rather than structures of accountability (Lund-Thomsen, 2005). Accordingly, they argue for structures of regulation to govern environmental risk. Others, for example, C. K. Prahalad (2004) take contrary firm-oriented perspectives, arguing that while big business has to be involved in eradicating poverty, CSR by itself can not accomplish this task because the achievement of sustainability is seen as an add-on to the bottom line and is distinct from the mission of the corporation, which is purely to make a profit. Implicit in Prahalad's view is the idea that CSR is voluntary because the corporation does not have to engage in it in order to be profitable. Instead, Prahalad says, big business can work from the bottom up, by framing sustainability itself as profitable, working in undeveloped markets and realizing margins there

and, in that way, turning impoverished communities themselves into consumer groups.

Given the voluntary nature of the notion of corporate responsibility, some scholars have argued that, in the context of environmental governance in particular, CSR can be actualized only within a context of accountability (Hamann, Acutt, & Kapelus, 2003; Lund-Thomsen, 2005; Shrivastava, 1995). Given that conventional sustainable development discourse and conventional understandings of CSR go hand in hand, it becomes acutely important for those activists interested in articulating emergent alternative discourses of sustainability to discuss corporate ethics explicitly in terms of corporate accountability rather than responsibility. For Lund-Thomsen (2005), the notion of corporate accountability "is associated with international NGO alliances and community-based organizations that demand stricter regulation of corporate behavior by national governments and the enactment of an international corporate accountability convention to prevent corporate misconduct" (p. 620).

However, a regulatory framework needs to be complemented with movements in civil society. Indeed, as Schwarze (2003) argues, citizens are often subject to corporate–state *irresponsibility* and consequently cannot rely on government regulation alone to ensure corporate accountability, and instead have to take recourse to what he calls a "critical publicity," understood as a public questioning of power. In this regard, some scholars have pointed toward the efficacy of radical NGOs and social movements as "civil regulators" (Palacios, 2004). Such civil regulation, in general, includes campaigns, boycotts, public pointing out of misconduct, and melodramatic protests.

Accordingly, if we are to meaningfully generate emergent alternative discourses of sustainability, then activists have to not only centralize the issue of a translocal structure of accountability but also develop critical watchdog roles for activists and local communities regarding issues of economic and environmental justice, social inequities, and grassroots democracy. Indeed, this chapter provides a template through which this might be accomplished and assessed. That is, if we are to ensure a full structure of accountability, understood in terms of both state and civil regulation, in the context of sustainable development issues, a critical public awareness of the key assumptions of conventional sustainable development discourse is a must. Such awareness would be constituted by efforts to articulate grounded, local and alternative notions of family instead of the transcendental version offered by conventional discourse, by articulations of visions of economic systems that provide correctives to neoliberalism, and by movements that argue for democracy and public organization, in addition to (or perhaps in lieu of) economic and private actors as key factors in achieving sustainability. Ensuring that we construct space for such voices is pivotal in enriching our understanding of potential futures for the planet and its irrevocably diverse people.

NOTE

I am grateful to George Cheney, Sara Hayden, Steve Schwarze, and Heather Zoller for their suggestions and commentary during various iterations of this chapter.

REFERENCES

Banerjee, S. B. (2003). Who sustains whose development? Sustainable development and the reinvention of nature. *Organization Studies, 24,* 143–180.

Blair, A. (2003, February). *Sustainable development helps the poorest.* Retrieved January 22, 2006, from http://www.labour.org.uk/output/p3073.asp.

Blowfield, M. (2004). CSR and development: Is business appropriating global justice? *Development, 47*(3), 61–69.

Butler, J. (2002). New sheriff in town: Christian right nears major victory at United Nations. *Public Eye, 16*(2), 14–19.

Chakravartty, P. (2004). Telecom, national development and the Indian state: A postcolonial critique. *Media, Culture & Society, 26*(2), 227–249.

Christian Aid. (2005). *BAT in its own words: Behind the mask of corporate social responsibility.* Retrieved July 18, 2005, from http://www.christian-aid.org/indepth/504/bat.

D'Souza, V. (1990). *Development planning and structural inequalities: The response of the underprivileged.* New Delhi: Sage.

Escobar, A. (1995). *Encountering development: The making and unmaking of the third world.* Princeton, NJ: Princeton University Press.

Foster, J. B. (2003). A planetary defeat: The failure of global environmental reform. *Monthly Review, 54*(8), 4–8.

Fox, T. (2004). Corporate social responsibility and development: In quest of an agenda. *Development, 24*(3), 29–37.

Frame, B. (2005). Corporate social responsibility: A challenge for the donor community. *Development in Practice, 15*(3/4), 422–432.

Ganesh, S. (2005). The myth of the non-governmental organization: Governmentality and transnationalism in an Indian NGO. In G. Cheney & G. Barnett (Eds.), *Organization—communication: Emerging perspectives* (Vol. 7, pp. 193–219). Creskill, NJ: Hampton Press.

Ganesh, S., Zoller, H. M., & Cheney, G. (2005). Transforming resistance, broadening our boundaries: Critical organizational communication studies meets globalization from below. *Communication Monographs, 72*(2), 169–191.

Giddens, A. (2000). *Runaway world: How globalization is reshaping our lives.* London: Routledge.

Gupta, A. (1998). *Postcolonial developments: Agriculture in the making of a modern India.* London: Duke University Press.

Hamann, R., Acutt, N., & Kapelus, P. (2003). Responsibility vs. accountability: Interpreting the World Summit for Sustainable Development for a synthesis model of corporate citizenship. *Journal of Corporate Citizenship, 9*(10), 20–36.

Harcourt, W. (2004). Is CSR rewriting development? *Development, 47*(3), 1.

Hawken, P. (1994). Mind your eco-business. *New Statesman & Society, 7*(306), 29–30.

Hawken, P., Lovins, A., & Lovins, H. (1999). *Natural capitalism: Creating the next industrial revolution.* Boston, MA: Little, Brown.

Henderson, S. (2002). Selling civil society: Western aid and the nongovernmental organization sector in Russia. *Comparative Political Studies, 35*(2), 139–167.

Hilhorst, D. (2002). Village experts and development discourse: "Progress" in a Philippine Igorot village. *Human Organization, 60*(4), 401–413.

Hove, H. (2004). Critiquing sustainable development: A meaningful way of mediating the development impasse? *Undercurrent, 1*(1), 48–54.

International Institute for Sustainable Development. (1995). *Summary of IISD's principles for trade and sustainable development.* Toronto: Author.

Korten, D. (1996). *Sustainable development: Conventional versus emergent alternative wisdom.* Washington, DC: Office of Technology Assessment.

Labuschagne, C., Brent, A. C., & von [van] Erck, R. P. G. (2005). Assessing the sustainability performances of industries. *Journal of Cleaner Production, 13*, 373–385.

Lovins, A., Lovins, H., & Hawken, P. (1999). A road map for natural capitalism. *Harvard Business Review, 77*(3), 145–150.

Lund-Thomsen, P. (2005). Corporate accountability in South Africa: The role of community mobilizing in environmental governance. *International Affairs, 81*(3), 619–633.

Malkki, L. (1994). Citizens of humanity: Internationalism and the imagined community of nations. *Diaspora, 3*(1), 41–68.

McMichael, P. (1996). *Development and social change: A global perspective.* Thousand Oaks, CA: Pine Forge Press.

Meister, M. (1999). "Sustainable development" in visual imagery: Rhetorical function in the Jeep Cherokee. *Communication Quarterly, 45*(3), 223–234.

Meister, M., & Japp, P. (1998). Sustainable development and the global economy: Rhetorical implications for improving the quality of life. *Communication Research, 25*(4), 399–421.

Munshi, D., & Kurien, P. (2005). Imperializing spin cycles: A postcolonial look at public relations, greenwashing, and the separation of publics. *Public Relations Review, 31*(4), 513–520.

National Spiritual Assembly of the Baha'is of the United States. (1994). *Unity and consultation: Foundations of sustainable development.* Retrieved September 10, 2005, from http://www.bcca.org/services/lists/noble-creation/bic-5.html.

Omvedt, G. (1995). The search for sustainable development: An alternative development model. *Catalyst* (Spring), pp. 1–3.

Ong, A. (1999). *Flexible citizenship: The cultural logics of transnationality.* Durham, NC: Duke University Press.

Oravec, C. (1984). Conservationism vs. preservationism: The "public interest" in the Hetch-Hetchy controversy. *Quarterly Journal of Speech, 70*(3), 444–458.

Palacios, J. J. (2004). Corporate citizenship and social responsibility in a globalized world. *Citizenship Studies, 8*(4), 383–402.

Peterson, T. R. (1997). *Sharing the earth: The rhetoric of sustainable development.* Columbia: University of South Carolina Press.

Prahalad, C. K. (2004). *The fortune at the bottom of the pyramid: Eradicating poverty through profits.* Philadelphia, PA: Wharton School Publishing.

Rose, N. (1996). Governing "advanced" liberal societies. In A. Barry, T. Osborne & N. Rose (Eds.), *Foucault and political reason: Liberalism, neo-liberalism and rationalities of government* (pp. 37–64). Chicago: University of Chicago Press.

Roy, M. (1995). *The emergence of sustainable development—a chronological perspective.* Ontario: International Institute for Sustainable Development.

Saurin, J. (1996). International relations, social ecology and the globalization of environmental change. In J. Vogler & M. Imber (Eds.), *The environment and international relations* (pp. 77–98.) London: Routledge.

Schwarze, S. (2003). Corporate-state irresponsibility, critical publicity, and asbestos exposure in Libby, Montana. *Management Communication Quarterly, 16*(4), 625–632.

Shiva, V. (1989). *Staying alive.* New Delhi: Kali for Women.

Shiva, V. (1991). *Ecology and the politics of survival: Conflicts over natural resources in India.* New Delhi: United Nations Press.

Shrivastava, P. (1995). Industrial/environmental crises and corporate social responsibility. *Journal of Socio-economics, 24*(1), 211–228.

Stephens, S. (1992). "And a little child shall lead them": Children and images of children at the UN Conference on Environment and Development. Dragvoll, Norway: Norwegian Center for Child Research.

Thomas, C. (1992). *The environment in international relations.* London: Royal Institute of International Affairs.

Tuatagaloa-Matalavea, T. F. (2002). *The Global Anglican Congress on the Stewardship of Creation: Declaration to the Anglican Communion.* Retrieved September 9, 2005, from http://www.aco.org/un/steward_01.html.

United Nations Conference on Environment and Development. (1992). *Agenda 21.* New York: United Nations Press.

United Nations Development Programme. (1972). *Declaration of the United Nations Conference on the Human Environment.* New York: United Nations.

United Nations Environment Programme. (1980). *World conservation strategy.* New York: United Nations Environment Programme, Worldwide Fund for Nature, & World Conservation Union.

U.S. Agency for International Development. (1995). *USAID's strategy for sustainable development: An overview.* Washington, DC: Federal Information Exchange.

World Business Council on Social Development. (2005). *WBCSD on corporate social responsibility*. Retrieved on July 10, 2005, from http://www.wbcsd.org.

World Commission on Environment and Development. (1987). *Our common future*. London: Oxford University Press.

World Summit for Sustainable Development. (2002). *The road from Johannesburg*. New York: United Nations.

World Summit on Social Development. (1995). *Copenhagen declaration on social development: Part C. Commitments*. Copenhagen: United Nations.

Young, R. (2004). Dilemmas and advances in corporate social responsibility in Brazil. The work of the Ethos Institute. *National Resources Forum, 28*, 291–301.

27

The Behavior of Corporate Species in Ecosystems and Their Roles in Environmental Change

DOUGLAS CRAWFORD-BROWN

The scientific study of ecosystems and environmental change focuses on the ways in which species produce, use, and transform material and energy, as well as the roles they play in environmental processes. The behavior of species, in turn, may be viewed as having two components: a purely biophysical component explainable by principles of biology, chemistry, and physics, and a social component related to the decisions that lead to behaviors influencing material and energy use. Understanding this latter component clearly becomes more important as focus shifts from plant species to animal to human, with corporations being among the most complex human organizations. This chapter provides a framework for analyzing the role of corporations in the material and energy flows that govern the environment, and for understanding how that role is in part controlled by the balance of principles from the emerging concept of sustainable enterprise: economic vitality, social justice, and environmental quality. It uses methods of ecological analysis to trace the environmental impacts of corporate behavior, relating this behavior to concepts of precaution in the face of uncertainty, product stewardship, environmental citizenship, and sustainable development.

AN ENVIRONMENTAL PRIMER

Global climate change, conservation of species, impacts of ozone on human health, and myriad other challenges facing society share a common root: the role of the environment in affecting key human values, and the role of human institutions and behavior in governing that environment. Environment, however, is a topic that easily spreads out to encompass all aspects of the world; essentially everything is part of our environment in some sense. And yet it is impossible to imagine everything all at once in assessing the environmental behavior of an organization. So a framework is needed to focus attention onto those aspects of the world that are most central to environmental study. As with any framework, one can start at any point and work in all directions from there. This chapter begins with the science of the environment, or at least the parts of the environment studied by the sciences. It is from this vantage point that the more social issues, including the behavior of corporations and their role in environmental change, are viewed.

The theme advanced here is that corporations may be viewed as part of an ecosystem and studied much as we would a herd of elephants or field of corn. It is necessary to view corporations, or any other part of human behavior, not as separate from ecosystems or the environment, but rather as structural and functional parts of that ecosystem. Doing so moves corporations toward a philosophy of earth system management, as has been proposed by Graedel and Allenby (2003) in their thoughts on industrial ecology. It moves society toward a view of corporations as participants in the management of the environment, rather than as the "enemy" to be fought by explicitly environmental organizations. Viewed from this perspective, the myriad environmental challenges mentioned above are not all isolated, disparate, phenomena, each requiring mastery of a new, and potentially arcane, language and set of methodologies. They are instead all manifestations of one underlying set of principles that control how the behavior of corporations (and individuals and governments) produces the environmental change that may lead in the end to either decrements or improvements in climate, species diversity, human health, and so forth. The overall framework for the following discussion is shown in figure 27.1: material or energy flows from the infrastructure into the environmental system (dashed box), in turn affecting both climate and health (Crawford-Brown, 1999).

To begin, the environment is an environment *for* something: humans, spotted owls, and so on. It is the set of conditions that affect the evolution of these species and their well-being, however broadly conceived this might be. This is shown as the box labeled "Health" in figure 27.1. While health might be considered for any species, the overwhelming majority of environmental decisions are based on changes in human health, and so the examples used throughout this chapter consider the impact of environmental change on the health of humans.

But the environment is not *all* of the conditions affecting health. It is those conditions that seem to work primarily through the system of environmental compartments shown in the dashed box of figure 27.1. It is the quality of the air, the water, the soil/rocks, and the biosphere. Again, not just any quality, but those particular qualities that make life possible, that affect the evolution and well-being of species. They are qualities of the concentration of pollutants in the compartments, the density of plant life, and so forth. Each of these environmental qualities is in turn caused by processes that move and transform material and energy in environmental systems. So, environmental phenomena invariably involve some form of change, or cycling, in the material or energy flowing through the environmental system.

If we consider these phenomena, we need to ask whether the biosphere plays a role in them. Do any species affect the movement of carbon through the environmental system, the availability of nutrients

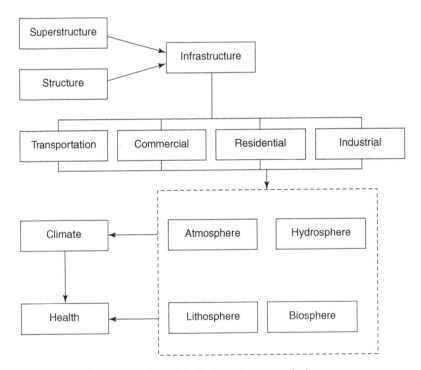

FIGURE **27.1.** A conceptual model of all environmental phenomena.

in soil, the ways in which pollutants reach human populations? The answer clearly is yes, and so environmental phenomena involve species not only as organisms affected by the environment, but as fundamental components of that environment. But which aspects of these species? Presumably, those aspects that affect, or perturb, the processes that move and transform material and energy in environmental systems.

As ecology shows us, to understand the role of species in the larger environmental system, we need to understand both their biological properties (their cells, organs, etc.) and their structural properties. We need to understand the structural roles played by species in cycles, such as the roles of producers, consumers, and decomposers in taking carbon dioxide from the atmosphere, converting it to organic carbon to build bodies, and ultimately returning it to the atmosphere as carbon dioxide. A theme explored further below is the role of humans—including corporations—in producing material and energy, in consuming material and energy, and in decomposing or recycling material and energy.

We could treat humans as a black box, with material and energy going in and material and energy coming out—somewhat changed. If all we want to do is to say how humans affect environmental processes, this may be all we need. Leaving humans as a black box, though, seems unsatisfactory. If we do not know what things look like inside the box, we are missing untold opportunities to bring about changes to that box. So, tearing open the box seems important in understanding environmental phenomena. What is inside the box? There are parts of society that use material and energy: our transportation systems, our industries, our homes, our businesses, and so on. This is shown in figure 27.1 as "Infrastructure." If we look a little more deeply, we see that these uses do not spring from thin air. They are guided by very real organizations, making decisions that serve a variety of human needs. The utility provides electricity so that elementary school students can learn to read; the automotive industry provides vehicles so people can travel from their homes to work; the chemical industry provides herbicides so weeds do not choke crops needed to feed the hungry. There are, of course, many ways to supply these needs; it is not necessary that travel to work be by an automobile. But something is left out of our understanding of corporate behavior if we examine only

the products they produce and ignore the needs those products serve.

Let us call this aspect of society the "structure" (economic, legal, social, political, etc.). These organizations are run by individuals who have their own way of thinking about human needs and environmental quality and the balance that must be met in satisfying the many demands we place on our organizations and on our lives. These individuals are in turn guided by their "superstructure," or system of beliefs and rituals (scientific, religious, philosophical, etc.). So, if we are serious about understanding the black box containing human systems, it is necessary to understand how human needs arise, how they are translated into organizations with the goal of meeting those needs, how those organizations make their decisions, and how those decisions produce changes in the ways in which material and energy flow through our infrastructure.

This leads to a picture of environmental phenomena, and the role of organizations such as a corporation, that looks something like the following definition:

> Environmental processes involve changes in the flow and transformation of material or energy (e.g., pollutants) within the environmental system at levels sufficient to cause significant changes in the health and well-being of humans and other species. Environmental behavior is any effect of beliefs (superstructure) or social organization (structure) on the infrastructure of society, such as to cause changes in the use of material and energy on a scale that significantly perturbs environmental processes. An environmental problem, as distinct from an environmental phenomenon, is a change in material or energy processes that is sufficiently large to cause a decrease in health and well-being of some species—usually, but not necessarily, humans.

This definition points us toward a particular way of viewing environmental challenges and locating solutions. It directs us to look closely at the ways in which corporations extract, transform, and release material and energy in environmental systems. With this definition in mind, we can begin to consider how corporations might be viewed as components of an ecosystem, asking how the infrastructures, structures, and superstructures of those corporations ultimately affect the corporation's participation in the flow of material and energy around the globe (Hawken, 1993). Hawken draws from this vantage point to propose a series of innovations in which individual corporations, or entire industries, "close the cycle" of flow of materials such as toxins, essentially "renting them out" to users and then collecting them back together for a radical form of recycling that mimics the way nutrients flow through an ecosystem (p. 49).

CORPORATIONS AND SUSTAINABILITY

There has been a sea change in the ways in which environmental behavior by corporations is viewed in the United States. European nations, spurred by the practices of the European Commission, have for some time made environmental decisions through the collective discussion of the social partners (Lauber, 2000). These partners include government, environmental nongovernmental organizations (NGOs), labor, industry, and a few other groups that depend on the specific issue. Such discussions bring to the table a vast range of considerations, with the recognition that rational decisions require a balancing of values. To take but one example, conservation of land calls for reflection on the value of species diversity (and protection of their habitats), of new and affordable housing in response to population growth, of economic development stimulated by construction of new industries, and on through a list of values that rarely coincide in a single organization.

By contrast, U.S. environmental decisions grew from a tradition established in the early days of the U.S. Environmental Protection Agency (EPA). The environmental governmental organization (generally the EPA) identifies an evident problem. The Cuyahoga River catches fire and anyone, even a nonscientist, can understand that water should not be catching fire. There is a clear perturbation in the environmental system, and the link to corporate behavior (the lack of pollution prevention) is evident. The solution is to hit the polluter with a regulatory hammer until the behavior stops. This is the model—command and control—that has dominated the environmental arena in the United States since the early 1960s. As time has passed, two things have changed. First, either the straightforward environmental problems have been dealt with, or the regulatory hammers needed to deal with them are in place. The remaining environmental problems tend to be less evident to the senses and less easily traced to the behavior of a single segment of society. It is less clear how specific environmental effects (e.g., changes in the incidence of asthma) are related to specific causes (e.g., emissions of particles into the air). Cutting pollution in the Cuyahoga River by controlling the waste pipes from industries caused an immediate decrease in the public health threats from that river. It is much less clear whether specific cuts in emissions of particles will produce a measurable change in poor health such as asthma.

Second, there has been increasing recognition that the more intractable environmental problems such as climate change are related not to an isolated source, but rather to systemic factors in society. Global climate change, if it is caused by human sources of carbon dioxide, is rooted in fundamental characteristics of a modern lifestyle. Each person in the United States produces about 25 tons of carbon dioxide per year (eight hot air balloons), spread across the four sectors of the infrastructure shown in figure 27.1. Figure 27.2 shows the relative contributions to annual carbon emissions from the four sectors in North Carolina, with a fifth category (utilities) related not to the end use but rather to the source of generation of the energy consumed in the other four sectors. Note that corporate behavior, captured largely by the industrial, commercial, and utility sectors, contributes about 60% of the carbon emitted annually, suggesting that such behavior is a key component in the effects of society on at least this one perturbation of an environmental cycle—the cycle of carbon.

Corporations play a role in this material and energy use, but they are responding in large part to market demands caused by individuals who get up in the morning and choose to drive rather than walk, to purchase a gas guzzler, to leave on a light when not in the room, and so on. These individuals, in turn, are responding to community designs in which work, home, and play are far apart; where public transit is nonexistent or inconvenient; and where social values seem to make ownership of large SUVs preferable to the less dramatic Prius. At most, corporations are enablers rather than the root cause of such environmental problems, except to the extent that they create these demands for goods and services through manipulation of the marketplace.

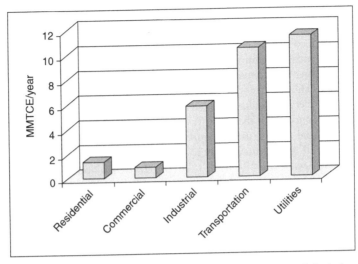

FIGURE **27.2.** The contribution of the four components of the infrastructure, plus utilities, to annual carbon emissions in North Carolina. The units are million metric tons of carbon (equivalent) per year (MMTCE/year). These values must be multiplied by approximately 4 to estimate million metric tons of carbon dioxide per year. Data are from D. Warmuth, Appalachian State University (personal communication, June 2004).

In this setting, it simply is not fair, or even particularly effective, to saddle corporations with the full burden of solving such problems. The solutions are much more societal ones, tackling all of the aspects of infrastructure, and the underlying structure and superstructure, that play such important roles in causing the problems. And since the evidence for a causal link between any one proposed solution and the actual change in health is less than it has been when command and control solutions were preferred, there is a good argument to be made for increasing reliance on more voluntary measures, and measures that are shared by a larger cross section of society.

Within this new complexity of environmental problems, there is a greater need to balance values in ways that are much closer to the European Union model than to the older U.S. model. The mantra of this balancing act is sustainability—the balancing of goals related to environmental quality (and hence health), social justice, and economic vitality. Imagine again the ecosystem described above, in which there are producers (plants), consumers (animals), and decomposers (microbes). No scientist would complain that the animals were not doing their fair share of producing organic

carbon from the atmosphere; that simply is not the role of the consumers in the ecosystem. Each species has a particular role in the cycling of material and energy, with the entire system ensuring that the cycle is maintained.

Human communities can be envisioned as having an analogous structure, similar to that used in the European Union deliberations. Some organizations are responsible for producing human needs, some are responsible for satisfying those needs, and some are responsible for placing boundaries on the ways in which that satisfaction is achieved. In such a model, corporations might be viewed as simply having the role of identifying and then satisfying human needs, with the additional goal of increasing economic vitality. It might be argued that society can no more complain about a corporation failing to meet the goals of environmental quality or social justice than it can complain about animals not being producers of organic carbon. Corporations may well have a specialized role in the larger ecosystem. Leave it to the city planners to design communities that do not require so much transportation. Leave it to the EPA to develop regulatory limits on carbon dioxide releases. This, at least, is an argument for allowing corporations to focus on the economic vitality leg of sustainability. It treats sustainability as a property of entire communities, with corporations occupying a specialized ecological niche that brings them to the table as a social partner when environmental decisions must be made. This same model calls for other components of society to bring competing and equally important concerns to the table (environmental quality, social justice) and to work with corporations to craft a community that together brings sustainability.

There is, however, an alternative view, and corporations themselves have been at the forefront of developing it. That view is one of sustainable enterprise—the development of new industries, or new ways of conducting old industries, that reflect internally the three goals of sustainability (Hart, 1997). To understand the superstructure leading to this view, consider a number of ways in which corporations might view their contribution to the emissions of a pollutant such as particles and ultimately to respiratory disease in some individuals:

1. The corporation might simply ignore it, either through lack of knowledge or through the belief that it is up to other parts of society to worry about that. In that case, sustainability simply is not an issue.
2. The corporation might understand the effects, and recognize the existence of regulatory limits on emissions, but treat the fines that come from exceeding those limits as normal operating costs. In that case, sustainability is an issue, but one addressed largely at a higher level of social organization than the corporation. A sustainable business practice is one in which fines incurred in ignoring environmental change do not significantly erode profits.
3. The corporation might perform a calculation of the net profit, taking into account the health effects in its workers. It might, for example, calculate the lost productivity of the work force due to days of work lost, and the increased health care costs due to hospital visits, and subtract this from its profit stream. In that case, sustainability is being considered internally in the corporation, with "sustainable" practices being those where the emission of particulates is sustainable if the health care costs and lost productivity—and perhaps any fines—do not outweigh the profits.

4. The corporation might perform a kind of macroeconomic analysis, considering the full impact of its activities on the health of the national population and the state of the economy, and designing its practices so the overall health of society is optimized. (A sustainable business practice is one that balances fully the goals of sustainability in the larger society.)

The fourth option may be a bit much to ask of corporations, suggesting as it does the willingness to give up some internal economic performance to optimize the overall health of the social ecosystem in which the corporation is embedded. It may be too altruistic to satisfy either the corporation or its investors. But it points to the model espoused in sustainable enterprise. In that model, corporate decisions simultaneously reflect at least a concern for economic vitality, environmental quality, and social justice, with the goal of optimizing the ecosystem. It is a form of constrained optimization: optimize the three legs, but within some boundaries of economic vitality (profit) that are needed to ensure the survival of the corporation in the first place. Corporations can be altruistic, but they cannot be expected to be suicidal!

That brings us full circle, since this strong view of sustainable enterprise must be set within a community in which each actor makes his or her contribution and is willing to perform a similar balancing of values. If the corporation is willing to consider environmental quality and social justice, others—such as the NGOs—must bring economic vitality into their own internal discussions. If corporations are willing to admit that some level of particulate emissions is simply unsustainable, creating an unacceptably high number of health effects, others—such as the EPA—must admit that there is a flip side: that there is some level of emissions that *is* sustainable, that does not constitute an unhealthy perturbation to natural systems. Pushing below this level may be detrimental to the overall picture of a sustainable community. To see this flip side, one need only look at the nations of the former Soviet Union. Maps of environmental devastation and collapsed economies lie almost directly over each other. And if corporations create products that are environmentally and socially preferable, others—the consumers—must choose these products even if they cost more or are less convenient.

CORPORATE DECISION POINTS

Figure 27.3 shows a cycle of corporate decisions in the chemical industry, and their relationships to regulatory programs, developed by the EPA's National Pollution Prevention and Toxics Advisory Committee (NPPTAC). This diagram is being used by the NPPTAC members—consisting of representatives from industry, government, NGOs, and academia—to identify strategies to adjust corporate behavior through a mixture of regulatory and voluntary programs. It is founded on three methodologies or perspectives: life cycle analysis, green chemistry, and product stewardship.

Life cycle analysis brings the tools of ecological assessment to the forefront in corporate and societal decisions. Figure 27.3 shows the cycle through which any chemical product passes. A need is identified in society (e.g., a need for sofas that are flame retardant), and the corporation conducts research and development to create a chemical whose function will satisfy that need. This chemical then is manufactured and transported to a secondary manufacturer that will use it to create the final product (the sofa). The sofa then is transported to the commercial sector and sold to the consumer. At the end of a useful life, the consumer disposes of the product, and the cycle begins again. At each point in the cycle, one can imagine material and energy flowing into that step—needed to manufacture that component—and material and energy flowing out either as product or as waste.

Corporations might view their roles as being confined to the steps from research and development through to a step immediately before consumer use. If that is the case, then ecological concerns of the corporation are restricted to issues having to do with the efficiency of material and energy use during the manufacturing and transportation processes. By analogy with the views on sustainable enterprise, the possible views on these life cycle issues are as follows:

1. The corporation might ignore life cycle issues, simply living with the inefficiency of material and energy use, as well as the environmental impacts of this inefficiency. The waste generated then becomes the responsibility of other parts of society, whose role in the ecosystem is to mitigate the effects on health.

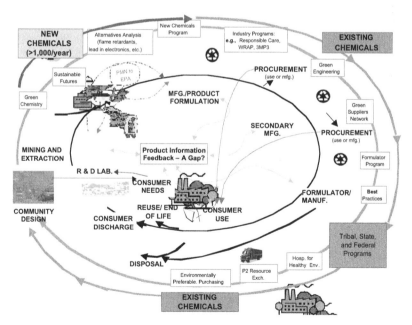

FIGURE **27.3.** The cycle of development, manufacturing, distribution, and use of chemical products in the United States (inner ring), with their relationship to specific U.S. Environmental Protection Agency programs (outer ring).

2. The corporation might use life cycle methods to help increase their internal efficiency of material and energy use. This reduces waste (the higher the efficiency, the lower the waste stream and, hence, perturbation of environmental processes), but with the sole goal of reducing operating costs. Cogeneration facilities, for example, ensure that waste heat generated from electricity production goes back into the manufacturing process to drive some of the needed chemical reactions. The result is a form of pollution prevention through closing material and energy cycles within the corporation. Closing the cycle decreases waste, decreases pollution, and increases profit—or at least increases profit if the cost of process changes needed to close the cycle does not exceed the savings in efficiency.

3. The corporation might use life cycle methods to help reduce the overall environmental impact of the cycle from research and development through to manufacturing and distribution. In these cases, groups of corporations—for example, the manufacturers of the flame retardant and of the sofas—collocate and share facilities so that material and energy use is minimized. Still, the consumer use and disposal aspects of the cycle in figure 27.3 are outside the loop of corporate decisions. This option for corporate behavior is where *green chemistry* has found its home—the development of alternative chemicals that perform the same function in a product, but do so with reduced environmental impacts. The goal there is not to change the behavior of society in either product demand or consumer use, but to change the process and products leading to satisfaction of that demand and use.

4. The corporation might adopt a cradle-to-grave concept of *product stewardship*. In this system, a corporation assumes responsibility for all stages of the life cycle of a product, from creation to use to disposal. Such systems have been developed successfully in Europe, especially in the Netherlands, with respect to electronic goods. The justification given is either that the manufacturer *ought* to be responsible in this way, or that having the manufacturer be responsible is simply a more efficient and effective way of ensuring that the overall environmental impact will be minimized. In the latter case, it is assumed that the corporation has the resources and skills needed to deal effectively with proper disposal, whereas the consumer is less likely to act responsibly when disposing of the product, through ignorance, poor choices, or lack of resources.

The cradle-to-grave view is increasingly popular but suffers from several drawbacks. First, it is difficult to perform a complete life cycle analysis for a product. Even if energy and material used in various steps of the process can be estimated—and this alone is a challenge—it is not clear where to draw the ecological boundaries in the calculation. Does the overall perturbation of environmental processes by the sofa creation include the manufacturing facility? (Clearly it does.) Does it include hauling the cotton fabric to that facility? (Probably.) Does it include growing the cotton? (Perhaps.) Does it include clearing the land to create the field to grow the cotton? (Well. . . .) It simply is not clear where to draw the boundary in attributing environmental impacts to a particular product. If the cotton from the field were not used in the sofa, it might have been used elsewhere in society, such as in manufacturing clothes. So why is the sofa industry charged with the environmental impacts of the cotton field? These may not be intractable problems, but they have proven immensely problematic so far.

Second, we can reintroduce the idea that corporations are but one part of the ecosystem. It may not be their legitimate role, or responsibility, to take care of products from conception to birth to death. They are taking on a large task when they agree to do this. What is the incentive? A possible argument is that the marketplace does not properly reflect the cost of products or corporate activity. The cost of a sofa does not reflect the environmental impacts of the manufacturing process or the impacts of disposal. By making the manufacturer more responsible for all steps in the life cycle, it can be argued that the true costs of perturbations in the environmental system will begin to be reflected in the cost of products.

Methods are slowly developing to perform the tasks of environmental accounting called for above (Cairncross, 1995), although they remain controversial. It is difficult enough to determine how money is allocated to environmental protection within a complex corporation. Even this side of the ledger sheet can be clouded with uncertainty. It is more difficult to assess the costs of environmental change that may accompany use of materials and energy by a corporation. This is in part due to the significant uncertainty in the relationship between environmental change caused by a specific corporation's activities and any quantifiable impact on human or ecosystem health. Environmental systems generally are able to withstand some minimal level of perturbation to their material and energy cycles without effect; below this level, feedback mechanisms mitigate the effect of the change to bring the system back to its original condition. Above this level of perturbation, the adverse effects certainly are found, but the size of the change needed to move the system off its original position often is highly uncertain.

And even if the change is demonstrated, quantifying the debit side of the ledger has proven difficult at best. Direct human health effects can at times be quantified through costs of health care and lost worker productivity, issues dealt with routinely in a corporation's accounting. Issues such as the economic value of more generalized notions of "quality of life" become more problematic. And attributing economic value to key ecosystem services that might be lost through large environmental change has been a virtual battleground since at least 1990. While it is clear that ecosystems perform services such as purification of groundwater or buffering of human populations from disease (Daily, 1997; Koren & Crawford-Brown, 2004), it is far from clear whether the worth of these services is found in the intrinsic value of the parts of the ecosystem providing the service, or in the cost to society if those services must be replaced by new infrastructure such as a water purification plant to replace the filtering services of a lost wetlands area when a corporation builds a new facility. The behavior of corporations is beginning to reflect thinking on cradle-to-grave issues (Dow and DuPont come to mind as examples of corporations that have been particularly forward looking), but there is merit in the claim that full accounting must take place in the society at large rather than being placed on the shoulders of the corporations.

An alternative position is that corporations are a part of society with unusual resources to bring to bear on the problems of environmental change. Their participation in cradle-to-grave (or cradle-to-cradle programs in which products are com-pletely recycled) may not be required but should be strongly encouraged and then facilitated by other actors. The EPA's Office of Pollution Prevention and Toxics has a variety of programs designed to help industry move toward a reduction in the overall environmental impact of their products (see the outer ring in figure 27.3). The programs in green chemistry, sustainable futures, green supplies network, and so on, all provide support for good corporate behavior, by providing information on how corporations can bring life cycle analysis and sustainable practices to their operations, celebrating and rewarding best practices, creating infrastructures needed to transfer best practices, and so on. Such programs recognize that corporations are a key part of the material and energy processes created by society, and hold a unique position in those processes, but that they need the resources of the entire community to satisfy their internal needs (economic vitality) while simultaneously selecting material and energy processes that will reduce the perturbations to essential environmental processes.

PRECAUTION AND RISK

Consider the concepts of risk and the precautionary principle as these relate to corporate decisions. The preceding sections focus largely on aspects of the infrastructure and structure underlying environmental behavior. A clear relationship is assumed between specific behaviors in a corporation and measurable indicators of environmental quality or health. This section focuses on environmental decisions and how corporations might better reflect philosophical positions on the relationship between reasonable evidence, risk, and behavior. These issues arise because the impact of specific changes in behavior on environmental indictors never is clear, with significant uncertainty in the extent to which risk is reduced through these changes. As such, the issue is one related to the superstructure of corporations.

The regulatory world encounters risk in a setting of decision making under uncertainty, with the acceptable level of perturbation to an environmental system being only poorly defined in most cases. Strategies have been developed to factor this uncertainty into the selection of allowed limits on perturbations (e.g., limits on emissions of particles), with most of these strategies being rooted in the idea of a *margin of safety*. The underlying argument has several steps:

- There is a level of risk to human or ecosystem health deemed unacceptable by some criterion (e.g., an unacceptably high probability of cancer).
- There is some best estimate of the level of perturbation to an environmental system needed to produce this risk.
- Even though this is a best estimate, there is still significant scientific uncertainty as to the level of perturbation that must be avoided to stay below this risk.
- To reflect this uncertainty, individuals or organizations are not allowed to produce the perturbation suggested by the best estimate; instead, they are restricted to a perturbation below this level. The difference between the best estimate and the allowed limit represents a margin of safety, providing some assurance to society that, even if scientists are wrong, there will not be an unacceptable risk produced by the corporate activity.

This use of margins of safety is not different in nature from the ways in which corporations make use of concepts from insurance and the investment world to deal with economic risk. Most corporations, however, follow a rather strict interpretation of cost–benefit analysis in negotiating environmental positions, following the practices of the Office of Management and Budget, with whom they share economic and political leanings. Under this interpretation, expectation values of the number of predicted effects are compared against expectation values of costs, and behaviors are chosen such that the marginal cost of an increasingly protective behavior (protective in the sense of a smaller environmental risk) is more than offset by the marginal gain in health benefit.

Such an approach is rooted in a concern for public health rather than individual rights. This is an honored philosophical tradition founded in utilitarianism (Sunstein, 2002), but somewhat at odds with the rights-based tradition of the regulatory community. It raises a question as to how (or even whether) a margin of safety will be reflected in such a utilitarian calculation, and how large this margin of safety must be in balancing the goals of sustainability. The larger the margin of safety, the greater the confidence that environmental risk is being reduced below unacceptable levels, but at greater cost and, hence, reduced profit and economic activity.

Environmentalist organizations push strongly for strict application of the precautionary principle: when faced with uncertainty, choose the risk estimate that is likely to overstate the risk (better safe than sorry). Their argument is that such applications will tend to push risk lower in the long run, which they take to be an unmitigated good. Corporations, by contrast, note that higher margins of safety result in more stringent environmental regulations, which result in more costly control measures, which reduce profit. Apart from an argument that their role in society is to generate profit, they point to the inefficiency of this use of resources. If the margin of safety is large, and the risk turns out to be much less than suggested, money will have been wasted on control measures that were not needed to reach the environmental goal of sustainability. This money could, they argue, have been spent on other measures to reduce risk in society or to increase social justice through spreading the wealth to the poor (Wiener & Graham, 1995). The argument from corporations is that unreflective application of the precautionary principle leads to less sustainable societies. The argument from the opposing side is that failure to reflect uncertainty and apply a margin of safety is not socially responsible behavior in the face of effects that may be quite large even if poorly understood.

There is no correct margin of safety to invoke in resolving this dispute. As a result, there is no external scientific body to which society can turn to find the answer. This leaves the margin of safety subject to manipulation, or to capture by the strategic interests of an actor. Want an economic activity stopped? Raise the required margin of safety high enough to effectively ban all such activities. Want the activity to proceed? Lower the required margin of safety.

Corporations have encountered this strategic use of the precautionary principle at the international scale through their global activities, finding their products allowed in one area of the world but not in another. Both the European Commission and the World Trade Organization have weighed in on these issues (Commission of the European Communities, 2000; Crawford-Brown, Pauwelyn, & Smith, 2004), searching for a middle ground that better reflects the tendency, mentioned above, for environmental behavior to be governed by the collective decisions of social partners in the European Union. The European Union position is clarified in four principles that should be applied in all cases of application of the precautionary principle:

- *Proportionality*: Measures should be proportional to the desired level of protection. Corporations must meet this desired level, but the measures should not force them below this level through inappropriately large margins of safety.
- *Nondiscrimination and consistency*: Comparable situations should be treated comparably. If a margin of safety that is large (or small) is applied in one circumstance by a corporation or regulatory authority, that same margin should be applied in all comparable circumstances.
- *Examination of the benefits and costs of action and lack of action*: This principle contains two parts. First, the precautionary principle should not simply prevent a corporate activity based on a concern over its risks. It is necessary to ask what societal need that activity was serving, and the benefits of meeting that need. Second, it requires that a decision be based on a comparison of the costs and benefits in a world both with and without the activity. There may well be a risk from the activity, but it might be more than outweighed by the risk if that activity does not take place.
- *Examination of scientific developments*: The margin of safety, or regulatory measure, should be in place only until the science needed to quantify risk improves to the point where these measures can be changed (increasing or decreasing the regulatory control depending on the implications of this improvement in science).

These principles do not prevent the strategic application of the precautionary principle by the players in environmental disputes, but they do place rational constraints on attempts to justify those positions. The World Trade Organization has taken a similar tack (Crawford-Brown et al., 2004). It argues that an organization (corporation, government, NGO, etc.) should have flexibility in performing a risk assessment and applying either a cost–benefit or precautionary approach, but that the argument justifying a position must be transparent, consistent with previous decisions by that organization, and supported by the available science.

There is a need for corporations to reconcile, or perhaps integrate, the perspectives of cost–benefit analyses and application of the precautionary principle. This will not be easy, because they stem from two very different philosophical positions on the reasons for corporate behavior to reduce risks. The cost–benefit approach locates this reason in the ability of specific corporate behaviors (pollution prevention) to yield benefits that outweigh the costs of the action. The precautionary approach locates this reason in the fact that corporations use a shared environmental system to produce profit, and should "ante in" to a pool of societal resources needed to generate confidence that health is maintained. While combining these two perspectives may be difficult, there are some promising first steps being taken in corporate–government collaborations: (1) including the costs of externalities in the cost–benefit calculations, (2) producing uncertainty distributions on cost–benefit ratios and using percentiles in the tails of these distributions to select appropriate actions, and (3) optimizing on the marginal cost–benefit ratio while using individual rights and precaution as constraints on this optimization. Taken together, these advances should yield a common ground on which corporate and regulatory decisions can be discussed and negotiated in the movement toward sustainability.

CLOSING COMMENTS

Corporations constitute significant components of the environmental system, producing as they do material and energy flows that perturb natural systems in ways that hold the potential to decrease human health. The extent of this perturbation depends on decisions reached within corporations on the degree to which environmental sustainability is considered an internal property of the corporation or an external property of the larger society. Understanding the magnitude of this perturbation, its relationship to material and energy use in corporations, and the role of community members in driving this use is central to developing effective strategies to reduce the environmental impacts of corporate behavior.

Producing greater sustainability will require several key adjustments to the structure, superstructure, and infrastructure of society as these relate to corporations. Infrastructure changes are exemplified by decisions leading to green chemistry or pollution prevention. Without these changes, all of the ISO-14000 filings (ISO-14000 is an environmentally oriented management system dem-onstrating that a corporation has put in place administrative structures needed to oversee material and energy use) or green marketing campaigns imaginable will not produce more sustainable business practices. Structural changes are exemplified by movements toward life cycle analysis and the integration of activities from diverse organizations involved in the cycling of materials and energy from mining to manufacturing to transportation to use and disposal or recycling. Finally, changes in the superstructure are exemplified by the willingness of corporations to use full environmental accounting in pricing goods, or to apply the precautionary principle in choosing target levels of perturbations in the environment.

A big move forward is the increasing trend in corporations to consider the triple bottom line of sustainability—environmental quality, social justice, and economic vitality—simultaneously in pursuing profit. For this movement to succeed, however, sustainability must be recognized as a function of entire communities in which corporations are embedded, with new structures needed to form partnerships among industry, regulators, NGOs, community planners, and consumers. These structures will link the organizational species of the ecosystem through practices reflecting a concern for life cycle analysis, environmental accounting, cradle-to-grave responsibility, and recognition of corporations as legitimate social partners in the design of sustainable communities.

REFERENCES

Cairncross, F. (1995). *Green, Inc.: A guide to business and the environment*. Washington, DC: Island Press.

Commission of the European Communities. (2000). *Communication from the commission on the precautionary principle*. Brussels, Belgium: COM 2001 (1).

Crawford-Brown, D. (1999). *Risk-Based environmental decisions: Methods and culture*. Dordrecht: Kluwer.

Crawford-Brown, D., Pauwelyn, J., & Smith, K. (2004) Environmental risk, precaution and scientific rationality in the context of WTO/NAFTA trade rules. *Risk Analysis, 24*, 461–469.

Daily, G. (Ed.). (1997). *Nature's services: Societal dependence on natural ecosystems*. Washington, DC: Island Press.

Graedel, T., & Allenby, B. (2003). *Industrial ecology*. Upper Saddle River, NJ: Prentice-Hall.

Hart, S. (1997). Beyond greening: Strategies of a sustainable world. *Harvard Business Review, 75*, 66–76.

Hawken, P. (1993). *The ecology of commerce: A declaration of sustainability*. New York: Harper Business.

Koren, H., & Crawford-Brown, D. (2004). A framework for the integration of ecosystem and human health in public policy: Two case studies with infectious agents. *Environmental Research, 95*, 92–105,

Lauber, V. (2000). The political and institutional setting. In A. Mol, V. Lauber, & D. Liefferink (Eds.), *The voluntary approach to environmental policy* (pp. 62–103). Oxford: Oxford University Press.

Sunstein, C. (2002). *Risk and reason*. Cambridge: Cambridge University Press.

Wiener, J., & Graham, J. (1995). Resolving risk tradeoffs. In J. Graham & J. Wiene (Eds.), *Risk vs. risk: Tradeoffs in protecting health and the environment* (pp. 226–272). Cambridge, MA: Harvard University Press.

VII

COMMENTARY ON CORPORATE SOCIAL RESPONSIBILITY

The Contributions of Communication and Other Perspectives

28

Is Sustainability Sustainable?

Corporate Social Responsibility, Sustainable Business, and Management Fashion

THEODORE E. ZORN
EVA COLLINS

While we share the enthusiasm of many of our fellow authors in this volume for corporate social responsibility (CSR) and sustainable business, we are simultaneously unnerved when we see some of the corporations responsible for the most grievous acts against humanity and the environment flying the flag of sustainability (e.g., Palazzo & Richter, 2005). The rapidly filling bandwagon leads us to question whether CSR and sustainable business are simply the "thing to do" for businesses or whether, as we hope, there is a sincere and "sustainable" trend toward businesses acting with a moral consciousness.

The focus of this chapter is to examine the extent to which the current interest in CSR and sustainable business is the latest in a long line of management fads and fashions (e.g., Abrahamson, 1996; Jackson, 2001), or whether these ideas are instead more stable and permanent elements of doing business. The question of whether CSR and sustainable business fit the criteria for management fashions is important far beyond simply applying a label to them. At issue is whether practices that have the potential to create more effective organizations and, more important, positive contributions to societies are subject to the "here today, gone tomorrow" mentality that has been experienced with other well-known business practices such as management by objectives (MBO), quality circles, total quality management (TQM), and business process reengineering (BPR) or, alterna-

tively, whether these practices can be permanently woven into the fabric of organizational and societal life.

Thus, this chapter builds on literature addressing the diffusion of management practices and the social construction of management knowledge. This literature has been concerned with deconstructing management thought and practice such that the modernist view of management as a more or less linear progression of increasingly sophisticated knowledge of organizational reality and increasingly effective ways to manipulate and control that reality is recast as discursive conceptions that are constructed and continually renegotiated to produce meaningful accounts of organizational practice (Parker, 1992). As du Gay, Salaman, and Rees (1996) argued, "The dispositions, actions and attributes that constitute 'management' have no natural form, and for this reason must be approached as a series of historically specific assemblages" (p. 264). Thus, management practices such as CSR/sustainable business are seen as normative belief structures, the diffusion of which are influenced by social and political pressures rather than simply the logical or march of progress or "rational" advance of knowledge (e.g., Fiss & Zajac, 2004).

As the editors suggest in the overview to this volume, both CSR and sustainable business are part of a cluster of terms that includes sustainable development, socially responsible business, green management, corporate citizenship, and ethical business. While some see CSR and sustainable business as synonymous (see, e.g., FAQs, 2004; Laine, 2005), others distinguish them. The New Zealand Sustainable Business Network website defines sustainable business as "the integration of economic growth, social equity and environmental management, both for now and for the future" (Sustainable business network, n.d.). The British government's CSR website defines CSR as "the voluntary actions that business can take, over and above compliance with minimum legal requirements, to address both its own competitive interests and the interests of wider society" (What Is CSR? 2004).

Thus, both concepts highlight the notion of balancing interests—economic versus social and environmental interests, and the current versus future generations' interests. Both encourage businesses to adopt tools such as triple bottom line (TBL) accounting and social reporting. Foot and Ross (2004) argue that sustainability or sustainable business can be viewed as a broader concept compared to CSR; sustainability "embraces a wider, time-dependent definition of a benefit to society (such as social capital) and focuses on results rather than standards of behaviour" (p. 113). In chapter 24, Peterson and Norton state that "CSR is essential to achieving SD [sustainable development]." In addition, sustainable business tends to have a more explicit emphasis on the natural environment. As Allen (2004) reported, one member of the now defunct New Zealand Businesses for Social Responsibility (NZBSR) objected to the name "Sustainable Business Network" (the organization into which NZBSR merged) on the grounds that it suggested too much emphasis on the environment; he preferred "Businesses for Social Responsibility" because he argued that it suggested a more balanced approach.

We do not need to resolve this debate for our purposes here—nor could we. The two terms overlap with each other and with other, similar terms. As Ganesh argues in chapter 26, CSR has been defined in terms of sustainability, and at the same time, sustainability has been defined in terms of CSR. It is enough for our purposes to recognize that both are highly popular "banners" that organizations are using both to make real changes as well as to convey particular identities to stakeholders. Thus, while we discuss CSR and sustainability separately here, we treat them as different

terms that describe essentially the same underlying set of concerns, values, and practices.

In what follows, we document the rise of CSR and sustainable business in terms of scholarly attention and corporate adoption; identify the nature and characteristics of management fads and fashions, including the negative consequences of such fashions; assess the degree to which CSR and sustainability fit the criteria for management fashion; and finally, discuss the implications of their "faddishness" for CSR and sustainability.

THE RISE OF CSR AND SUSTAINABLE BUSINESS

The concept of CSR has been discussed, practiced, and studied for decades. Seeger and Hipfel note in chapter 10 that CSR has been around since the 1930s. Others (e.g., Wilson, 2003) trace it as far back as ancient Greek society. One of the seminal works in the CSR literature is Howard Bowen's *Social Responsibilities of the Businessman* (1953). Bowen introduced the basic idea underlying CSR: corporations have an obligation extending beyond economic performance. In addition, he argued that the pursuit of profit is not incompatible with ethical conduct and the assumption of social responsibilities.

Milton Friedman is one of the most-cited critics of CSR (see Aune, chapter 14, for a detailed critique of the rhetoric of Friedman). Friedman (1970) argued that shareholders have entrusted company managers with their funds to increase their return, not for a general social interest. Business, Friedman asserted, best serves society by operating efficiently, employing workers, paying taxes, and increasing shareholder return. *The Economist* has continued that line of argument in more than 30 articles attacking CSR, sustainable business, and related initiatives (Guthey, Langer, & Morsing, 2006).

In spite of Friedman's argument, the adoption of CSR practices gained traction with many businesses. Allen (2004) describes an uneven but continual development of CSR initiatives from the 1950s to today. The last 15 years in particular have seen an explosion of interest and activity, with the formation of multiple national and international associations and rapidly increasing attention by academics (de Bakker, Groenewegen, & den Hond, 2005). Businesses for Social Responsibility in the United States was formed in 1992 and CSR-Europe in 1996.

Not coincidentally, the past 15 years have also witnessed the emergence and rapid growth of sustainability initiatives. Ganesh, in chapter 26, argues that sustainable development entered the global discourse in 1972 at the United Nations Conference on the Human Environment in Stockholm. Most sustainability literature references the 1987 Brundtland report from the World Commission on Environment and Development, titled *Our Common Future*, as the major impetus for the sustainability movement. That report gives what is perhaps the most commonly accepted definition of sustainable development as progress that "meets the needs of the present without compromising the ability of future generations to meet their own needs" (p. 43). Since then, many different definitions have emerged for sustainability, sustainable business, and sustainable development (e.g., Murcott, 1997, lists 57 differing definitions of sustainable development). Ganesh (chapter 26) and Peterson and Norton (chapter 24) detail the impact of this ambiguity. Suffice it to say that sustainability has become a contested concept invoked to support numerous political and social agendas by businesses, governments, and public interest groups.

The business community in Europe took up the sustainability banner in 1991 by forming the Business Council for Sustainable Development. The original mandate for the founding 50 CEOs was to provide business input to the 1992 Earth Summit in Rio de Janeiro (Origins, n.d.). Since then, sustainability has continued to gain traction in the business community. The original organization has grown into the *World* Business Council for Sustainable Development, with 175 international member companies (Origins, n.d.).

Both CSR and sustainable business efforts are apparently gathering strength. In 2003, PriceWaterhouseCoopers's global survey of CEOs found that concerns over concepts of sustainability were continuing to gather momentum in the business community. Today, many of the CSR and sustainable business associations and organizing bodies make little effort to distinguish CSR and sustainable business. For example, the United Kingdom's government website addresses this issue as on their FAQ webpage:

> How does CSR differ from sustainability or responsible business practice or sustainable development or any of the other terms used? Different terms are used, for example CSR, corporate responsibility/citizenship or sustainability. The common factor is that we are talking about how a company operates, taking account of its social and environmental as well as economic and financial impacts. (FAQs, 2004)

In a similar vein, the World Business Council for Sustainable Development treats CSR as one of its "cross-cutting themes" (Origins, n.d.).

Thus, the past 15 years have seen the surge of interest in CSR and sustainable business among businesses and academics. "Why now?" is an interesting question. Most analysts (e.g., Waddock, chapter 5) suggest that expectations of societies for business practice have changed such that businesses are expected to do more than merely comply with the rules for ethical practice, but to take responsibility for proactively addressing perceived social inequities and environmental degradation. Thus, one answer to the question "Why now?" is that businesses have responded pragmatically to a change in societal expectations.

In part because of such changes in expectations, businesses expect instrumental benefits to accrue from adopting CSR and sustainability—or at least being perceived to do so. Certainly many businesses have been persuaded to signal their alignment with CSR/sustainability because doing so is perceived as a way to increase profits. Increased profitability might come from innovative companies developing new products and services that society needs, with the result that both society and business benefit. Examples include the emergence of eco-tourism, eco-shopping (e.g., www.ecomall.com), and technologies that clean the environment.

In addition, good CSR practices may increase profitability by avoiding the liability and loss of market share from a widely publicized scandal. The accusations that Nike used sweatshops to produce goods, or the experience of Shell in Nigeria being tarred with support for a corrupt government discussed by Livesey and Graham in chapter 23, or the many other examples cited in this volume, have all captured the attention of corporate executives. A recent survey in the United States suggested that "82% of executives agree that operating responsibly benefits the bottom line" (Rochlin, Witter, Monaghan, & Murray, 2005, p. 5). A global survey found that 79% of CEOs agreed that "Sustainability is vital to the profitability of any company," an increase from 69% on the same survey one year earlier (PriceWaterhouseCoopers, 2003, p. 26).

Researchers have also demonstrated an interest in whether a socially responsible strategy leads to increased profits. More than 100 studies have explored the relationship between virtue and profit, and the results have been mixed, with some studies showing a positive impact on profit, and others the reverse (Simpson & Kohers, 2002). The most accurate conclusion, at this time, appears to be that socially responsible firms perform no worse and perhaps better than non-socially responsible firms (Steiner & Steiner, 2005).

In addition to profitability, marketing, image, and staff retention played a key role when considering reasons that companies adopt CSR/sustainability practices. Many CSR/sustainable business associations tout such benefits in making the "business case" for adopting CSR/sustainability (e.g., About BSR, n.d.). One survey found that "79 percent of CEOs said reputation and brand have considerable or extensive impact on their approach to sustainability, while 69 percent named attractiveness to employees, and 63 percent, improved shareholder value" (PriceWaterhouseCoopers, 2003, p. 28)

Whether CSR/sustainable business is a management fashion is open to debate. What is undeniable, however, is that such initiatives have grown enormously in popularity in recent years. One of the indications of the popularity of CSR/sustainable business programs is the rise of "social investing." These funds have now exceeded $2.1 trillion and "between 1995 and 1999, such funds grew three times as fast as the broader universe of all professionally managed investment portfolios" (Lynn, 2001).

Another indication is the rise of academic programs addressing these concerns (Meglio, 2005; Utne, 2004). Universities are being assessed by their ability to provide business students with sustainability education. The World Resources Institute publishes a well-known annual survey, *Beyond Grey Pinstripes*, ranking business schools' environment and social content in MBA programs (Beyond Grey Pinstripes, n.d.). Meanwhile, business graduates are being assessed on whether they are "sustainability literate." For example, a recent survey in the United States suggested that "77% of corporate recruiters think it important to hire students that are aware of social and environmental issues" (Benn & Bubna-Litic, 2004, p. 83).

In the next section, we explore the characteristics of management fads and fashions as applied to CSR and sustainability.

THE NATURE AND CHARACTERISTICS OF MANAGEMENT FADS AND FASHIONS

A number of streams of research have called attention to the transitory nature of certain management practices. For example, research emanating from institutional theory has empirically documented how practices become established as a result of pressures from various sources to be seen as legitimate members of a particular organizational field (Scott, 1991; Tolbert & Zucker, 1983; Van de Ven & Hargrave, 2004). These include "mimetic" pressures, or the perceived need to imitate the practices of other organizations. Similarly, management fashion theory (Abrahamson, 1996, 1997; Abrahamson & Fairchild, 1999; Jackson, 2001; Rolfsen, 2004) and guru theory (Clark & Salaman, 1998) have identified the tendency of organizations to adopt the latest popular management programs (e.g., TQM, BPR, knowledge management) and then to gradually discard these programs in favor of newer ones. Finally, discourse theorists (Thompson & Davidson, 1995; Zorn, Christensen, & Cheney, 1999; Zorn, Page, & Cheney, 2000) have explained how being immersed in sociocultural discourses promoting particular values and practices leads managers to draw on these discourses as resources in developing and selling strategic organizational changes and leads staff to see such changes as logical "best practice."

These perspectives all point to the notion that, rather than seeing current management practices as the culmination of knowledge that has resulted in steady improvements or progress, contemporary practices reflect transitory beliefs influenced by social pressures and discourses, including a substantial amount of hype by management "gurus," the popular press, consulting firms, and business schools. The notion of management *fashion* has been proposed to highlight certain dimensions of management trends. Like any metaphor, it foregrounds certain features while masking others. Management fashions have been defined as "transitory collective beliefs that certain management techniques are at the forefront of management progress" (Abrahamson, 1996, p. 254) and as "transitory beliefs that if certain management techniques and practices are pursued, organizational performance will increase" (Spell, 2001, p. 358).

Of course, to label something a management *fashion* is to frame it in a particular way. As Benders and van Veen (2001) argue, terms such as "fad" and "fashion" are used mainly pejoratively. Connotations of fashion suggest frivolousness, an emphasis on aesthetics (particularly superficial or surface aesthetics), a concern with image over substance, emotive or nonrational decision making, and short-term or temporary changes rather than long-term, permanent or stable changes. Contrast the label of management fashion with alternative ways of framing newly adopted practices: management knowledge (or wisdom), best (or leading-edge) practice, industry standards, or new paradigm. Thus, our attempt to consider sustainable business and CSR as fashions could be seen as an attempt to disparage these movements. While certainly we intend to cast a critical eye over organizational practice, we do so in the hope that our efforts will encourage integrity and endurance of these movements.

Since our interest is to identify whether in fact sustainable business and CSR have characteristics of management fashions, we need to identify the criteria for management fashions. Spell's (2001) definition, cited above, suggests one criterion: a belief that if the concept is adopted, organizational performance will increase.

Jackson and Rigby (2000), based on a review of the literature, identified five criteria for a management fashion: (1) "It has a management technique, practice or concept at its heart" (p. 4). (2) "There is a collective belief that it is at the forefront of management progress" (p. 4). (3) The new idea is "has its own distinctive lexicon and signifiers" (p. 4). (4) "Over time it demonstrates a bell-shaped adoption or popularity life cycle" (p. 4). This refers both to adoption of the practice by organizations as well as to the pattern of publications about the concept. That is, as the concept comes into vogue, more and more articles are written about it, resulting in a peak, and then a steady decline as it is replaced by other fashions. (5) A fashion is actively disseminated by the management fashion industry—that is, business schools, consultants, gurus, and the media. An important means by which they are disseminated is the universalization strategy that Cloud discusses in chap-

ter 15. That is, the management fashion industry promotes practices that appear to have had success in a small number of situations as applicable universally to all organizations. In turn, managers in firms adopting a fashion often universalize the values and interests underlying a fashion (e.g., the importance of quality or service excellence) to all stakeholders.

Rolfsen (2004) added to our understanding of management fashions by identifying the criteria for *successful* fashions. While not claiming that all are necessary, her list is telling and suggests other typical management fashion characteristics. (1) Following other authors, she identified *timing* as the most important requirement—specifically, that the management idea must resonate with problems and concerns that are particularly prominent in an era (see Guillen, 1994; Huczynski, 1993). (2) Rolfsen suggested that a successful management fashion must present the alternative to adopting the concept in an unfavorable way. The idea is presented as imperative to prevent disaster or crisis that may be expected from not adopting it. (3) The concept should be easy to remember, for instance, in memorable abbreviations of three letters (e.g., TQM, BPR, and MBO). (4) A successful management fashion must provide a "concrete recipe for action" (p. 124). (5) In spite of the apparent clarity and specificity of the previous two criteria, management fashions should be "vague and ambiguous" (p. 125). Strategic ambiguity (Eisenberg, 1984) enables the concept to promote "unified diversity"; for example, we can rally around the abstract principle, label, or concept (e.g., quality or service) and still maintain flexibility in the specific actions taken. (6) Rolfsen suggests that successful management fashions "appear to be academic" (p. 125), with research to support their effectiveness. (7) Perhaps most controversially, she argued that successful management fashions are typically launched on the U.S. East Coast, in particular, by professors from Harvard or MIT.

Of course, to say that a concept has characteristics of a management fashion does not mean that it is necessarily wrong, "fluff," or lacking in usefulness. Management tools become successful fashions in part because they contain ideas that are appealing and sensible. Regarding TQM, for example, who can argue against the idea of improving the quality of products and services by continuously examining and improving them?

In the next section, we consider whether sustainable business and CSR have the characteristics of management fashions.

ARE CSR AND SUSTAINABLE BUSINESS MERELY FASHIONS?

In the one published study that we have identified that has addressed this question, Fineman (2001) considered whether "organizational greening"—a construct conceptually similar to CSR/sustainable business—constitutes a management fashion and concluded that while it has some similarities, it differs in several important ways from accepted criteria for management fashions. Specifically, he argues that, unlike other management fashions, greening (1) does not appeal to productivity or profit; (2) is not coherent, but is a mix of ideas rather than a single idea; and (3) does not offer a reassuringly simple and secure solution to ambiguous problems.

However, while we agree with Fineman that there are noteworthy differences between CSR/sustainable business compared to many other management fashions, we are not so quick to dismiss the fashion appeal of these concepts. Let us consider Fineman's specific arguments. First, regarding the argument that CSR/sustainable business does not appeal to profit, we argue that, on the contrary, many writers and consultants advocate the "business case" for CSR and sustainability (see, e.g., The Business Case, 2004), and many researchers have investigated the relationship between CSR/sustainable business adoption and profits (e.g., Simpson & Kohers, 2002), and most CEOs believe there is a positive correlation (PriceWaterhouse-Coopers, 2003). The World Business Council for Sustainable Development states this explicitly:

> The starting point for the WBCSD's work is based on the fundamental belief that a coherent CSR strategy, based on sound ethics and core values, offers clear business benefits. In other words, that acting in a socially responsible manner is more than just an ethical duty for a company, but is something that actually has a bottom line pay-off. (Business Role, n.d., ¶ 1)

Plus, there is little question that many businesses have taken on these notions in the hope of differentiating themselves from competitors—and ulti-

mately increasing profits as a result. In line with this rationale, *Fortune Magazine*'s annual Accountability Rating, which ranks the world's largest 100 companies on the extent to which they have integrated CSR practices, is presented as "a business rating, not a moral one. It looks at the world's biggest corporations and asks . . . are they . . . prepared to maximize the opportunities of our changing world?" (Zadek, 2005).

Second, we agree with Fineman that CSR and sustainable business are not completely coherent and that they contain a mix of ideas and even labels. However, the same could be said about most other successful management fashions. Total quality management, for example, is actually one of a group of labels for quality management programs (e.g., continuous quality improvement and business process improvement) that are often used interchangeably, and there are many varieties of TQM programs, such as Deming's version, Juran's, and the International Standards Organization certification programs. As Zbaracki (1998) found in his empirical investigation, what organizations actually do when they claim to have implemented TQM also varies significantly. Similarly, Zorn and Taylor (2004) argued that there are at least four distinctly different meanings for knowledge management, one of the latest management fashions.

Finally, Fineman's third argument for distinguishing greening from other management fashions is that it does not offer a reassuringly simple and secure solution. Again, we would argue that the distinction is not obvious. As Waddock (chapter 5) argues, many organizations have seemingly found self-identifying as socially responsible or sustainable a simple and secure way to deflect criticism and bolster their reputation with customers and other stakeholders, while going about doing business as usual.

Table 28.1 provides a summary of the major features of management fashions, and sample evidence regarding CSR/sustainable business that corresponds to these features. As table 28.1 shows, there is ample evidence that CSR/sustainable business have most of the characteristics associated with management fashions. Most notably, the rate of adopting CSR/sustainability by businesses has escalated rapidly in recent years, as has research publications on the subject. Adopting such initiatives is encouraged by a "fashion industry" (Jackson & Rigby, 2000) that includes business schools, consultants, and the business press. While the specif-

TABLE 28.1 Management fashion features of CSR and sustainable business

Management fashion feature	Applicable to CSR/ sustainable business?	Sample evidence
Has a management technique, practice, or concept at its heart	Yes	Concepts: Triple bottom line (TBL) accounting and (or sustainability) reporting (Krajnc & Glavic, 2005; Livesey, 2002), stakeholder collaboration (Steurer, Langer, Konrad, & Martinuzzi, 2005), waste reduction.
Believed that, if adopted, it will increase organizational performance	Yes	A majority (82%) of executives agree that operating responsibly benefits the bottom line (Rochlin, Witter, Monaghan, & Murray, 2005). Proponents consistently argue the "business case" for CSR/sustainable business (e.g., Brady, Thomas, Clipsham, & Smith, 2005) and the bottom-line benefits of adoption (e.g., del Mar Garcia de los Salmones, Crespo, & Rodriguez del Bosque, 2005; Simpson & Kohers, 2002), including competitive advantage (see About BSR, n.d.).
Has a bell-shaped popularity life cycle	Not yet clear	Rapid growth in recent years of social reporting, TBL accounting, sustainability and CSR associations. Academic publications on CSR rose rapidly from 1990 to 2002, possibly declining in 2003 (de Bakker et al., 2005; Guthey et al., 2006).
Believed that it is the forefront of management progress	Yes	"Corporate sustainability can be viewed as a new and evolving corporate management paradigm" (Wilson, 2003, p. 1). "In the last three or four years the term [TBL] has spread like wildfire. The Internet search engine, Google, returns roughly 25,200 webpages that mention [it]" (Norman & MacDonald, 2004, p. 244).
Has its own distinctive lexicon and signifiers	Yes	TBL, corporate citizenship; employee well-being, social reporting; stakeholder engagement; social investing
Is actively disseminated by management fashion industry	Yes	Consultants who specialize in sustainability (e.g., SustainAbility) as well as global consulting firms such as PriceWaterhouseCoopers, tracking sustainability trends and currently boasting "400 global experts working with social and environmental issues" (PriceWaterhouseCoopers, 2005). Business press recognizing top performers (e.g., *Fortune*'s annual Accountability Rating). Rapidly increasing academic programs focused on CSR/ sustainable business (Aspen Institute, 2005).
Resonates with prominent concerns of the time (timing)	Yes	Climate change, peak oil, work–life balance, corporate accounting scandals; increasing gap between rich and poor; dramatically increased CEO salaries; failure of neoliberal policies to improve well-being of the poor; distrust of multinational corporations.
Describes the alternative in an unfavorable way	Yes	For example, Elkington (1999) states that, "To refuse the challenge implied by the TBL is to risk extinction" (p. 75).
Has easy-to-remember terms	Yes	CSR, TBL.
Provides concrete recipe for action	Somewhat	Specifics vary, but almost all involve waste reduction, stakeholder engagement, TBL, and social reporting.
Is vague and ambiguous	Yes	Wide range of definitions for both CSR and sustainable business (e.g., http:///Murcott, 1997; see also Fergus & Rowney, 2005; Laine, 2005).
Appears to be academic	Yes	Extensive research that has increased dramatically since 1991 (de Bakker et al., 2005). Increasing number of business schools require courses in CSR/sustainable business (Aspen Institute, 2005).
Launched in the East Coast of the United States	Somewhat	The Brundtland report was commissioned by the United Nations, which is headquartered in New York. John Elkington, originator of TBL concept and perhaps the premiere sustainability "guru," is based in London.

ics of CSR/sustainable business initiatives vary greatly, there are some simple, concrete recipes for action that businesses may take. Specifically, the business that wants to jump on the bandwagon will typically (1) engage with one or more stakeholder groups to identify priorities, (2) identify specific waste reduction opportunities, (3) adopt TBL accounting to measure its performance, (4) produce a social report (or incorporate social reporting into its annual report) to trumpet its achievements, and (5) join an association of businesses with a stated commitment to CSR/sustainable business. As with other management fashions, actual day-to-day company practices may or may not change significantly when an organization claims to have adopted CSR/sustainable business, but the organization gains status and legitimacy by being able to claim adoption of a "leading-edge" practice.

However, a crucial characteristic—the bell-shaped curve in popularity—is yet to be seen. That is, the popularity of CSR/sustainable business has undoubtedly been on the rise for the past decade and a half, but we are yet to see a drop in its popularity, as would be necessary to see it as a fashion. This is critical, since the proponents of CSR/sustainable business—and we consider ourselves among them—hope to see a steady increase and eventual leveling off (as it becomes the norm) of adoption and interest.

IMPLICATIONS OF FASHION FOR CSR/SUSTAINABLE BUSINESS

There are a number of dangers arising from the fashionlike qualities of CSR/sustainability. Some of these are reflected in what Waddock refers to as the "dark side" of CSR/sustainability in chapter 5. In particular, she mentions an overly narrow focus on explicitly doing good that masks day-to-day practices that create substantial harm, and she describes the gap between the rhetoric and reality of many companies' corporate citizenship efforts.

Both of these dangers are exacerbated by the faddishness of CSR/sustainable business. That is, the broad appeal of a currently "hot" fashion increases the reputation-enhancing potential of adopting an otherwise positive practice. Recall that management fashions are by definition hyped by the fashion industry—particularly consultants, business schools, and the business press—and that

they resonate with prominent concerns and values of the era in which they are popular. In addition to whatever inherent merits the practice may have, the adopter may also garner kudos for addressing the most pressing concerns of the era by a means persuasively recommended by those considered to be experts.

Thus, building on Waddock's arguments in chapter 5, we suggest that adopting a fashionable practice such as CSR/sustainable business presents a relatively easy, but potentially superficial, path to enhancing the company's reputation: make a relatively minor effort to "do good" and then subsequently trumpet the company's CSR/sustainability commitments and achievements. Also, the faddishness of a particular practice increases the likelihood that the company's rhetoric will not match the reality of their implementation. That is, given the goodwill to be gained from claiming to embrace a fashionable practice and the ambiguity surrounding what it means to actually implement the practice, there is a strong temptation to claim to be "doing it" while actually doing very little. Zbaracki (1998) found that even companies that had been singled out as exemplars of TQM success in some cases had made only minimal changes in their management practices. More relevant to our analysis, Sellwood's (2005) study of CSR practices in Brazil found a significant gap between companies' rhetoric and actual practices. Thus, a risk is that CSR/sustainability may be adopted for the wrong reasons—that is, as a public relations exercise rather than a commitment to substantive change. However, as Livesey and Graham argue in chapter 23, even adopting such practices for the "wrong reasons" has promise: "Whatever the original instrumental intent, language and symbolic action may have constitutive effects beyond what any particular agents . . . can control. Corporate eco-talk participates in (re)creating the firm and (re)constructing its relationship to nature, while opening up novel possibilities of understanding and action. . . . " Thus, while we have no doubt that many companies adopt CSR/sustainable business in large part because it is fashionable to do so, we remain hopeful that there may be positive consequences from their efforts.

CONCLUSION

CSR/sustainability clearly has many of the characteristics of a management fashion. There seems little doubt to us that many organizations are adopting CSR/sustainability in part because it is fashionable. Some fashions last longer than others, however, with some even becoming relatively permanent fixtures. Fashions grounded in practicality and utility can make a permanent mark on our culture.

Thus, adopting sustainability because it is fashionable is not entirely a bad thing. It does not, for example, necessarily follow that adoption of a fashion means that it will have no substantial impact. Total quality management, for instance, maintains enough academic interest for its own journal (*Total Quality Management and Business Excellence*), and quality management initiatives still generate substantial consultancy business for organizations such as the Juran Institute and the "Big Five" consulting firms. Total quality management can also be seen to have morphed into currently popular programs such as International Standards Organization certification and Six Sigma management.

Perhaps more to the point, whereas the popularity of the TQM label and the enthusiasm for the concept as a panacea for organizational maladies have waned, many argue that quality management has simply become standard practice—a given rather than a novel idea. As Glover and Noon (2005) argued recently, "Whereas in the 1980s quality management was considered a competitive advantage, now it is seen by managers to be a competitive necessity" (p. 728). Whether or not we regard CSR/sustainable business as a fashion, a similar fate may be in store.

An important distinction between businesses' embrace of TQM compared to sustainable business is the paradox that sustainability presents to business. That businesses have a significant role to play in contributing to sustainability goals is not in doubt, given their centrality to the root of many environmental problems and issues related to social equity. However, many current business practices seem incompatible with notions of sustainability, particularly the obsession with continued growth (Hamilton, 2003). It is a bit like a dictator leading the charge for democracy.

A number of commentators suggest that radical changes in business practices, and even the capitalist system, are required for CSR/sustainable business to be effective and sustainable. (Ehrenfeld, 1999; Hawken, 1993; Welford, 2000). Several authors in this volume come to similar conclusions. Cloud (chapter 15), for example, agrees with Fried-

man (1970) that the corporation is inevitably a profit-seeking enterprise at the expense of all other interests. However, whereas Friedman does not believe corporations have authority from shareholders to engage in CSR, Cloud concludes that CSR can perpetuate harmful "business as usual" practices, particularly related to workers. She argues: "Any consideration of CSR that includes the real interests of workers will come up against the basic injustices of capitalism, not only to workers but also to the environment, the poor, and victims of often-profitable wars." She seems to imply that CSR efforts by individual companies are doomed to failure because of their inability to address the deeper contradictions of capitalism.

Breen (chapter 20) is equally critical of the injustices perpetuated by the capitalist system, particularly related to indigenous peoples. But unlike Cloud, Breen puts CSR forward as an opportunity to redress fundamental injustices of the capitalistic system. He argues, "Corporate social responsibility has to accept changing definitions of capital, which in turn are defined by new concepts of the market, goods and services, and value itself." Only in this way, Breen asserted, can the evolving needs and demands of indigenous peoples be addressed.

Furthermore, Deetz (chapter 18) offers us a way to inject interests beyond the profit motive. Ultimately, for CSR/sustainability initiatives to succeed, corporate decision making must include voices driven by other motives. Otherwise, concurring with Cloud, CSR/sustainability initiatives are doomed to failure. Thus, stakeholder governance models offer a way to provide a check on short-sighted practices that may be unethical or unsustainable and to ensure that creative means of attaining goals that benefit both the organization and the wider society are surfaced.

We agree with Breen that CSR/sustainable business is an opportunity and one that business may feel compelled to participate in. Adoptions that may initially have been fashion driven may ultimately be driven by the necessities of survival and, as a result, become a permanent way of life.

Thus, we are optimistic about the prospects for CSR/sustainable business as "sustainable" business practices. Climate change, finite resources, rising income inequality, and population demographics are likely to move sustainability from passing fashion to unquestioned priority. As we see it, the public is increasingly likely to demand responsible practices, and businesses are increasingly likely to see that they have no other choice.

Our conclusion is not the harsh indictment of CSR that Cloud presents in chapter 15. We highlight the danger rather than the inevitability that the biggest risk of CSR/sustainable business being merely fashionable is that it may encourage and legitimize incremental change rather than radical change.

REFERENCES

About BSR (n.d.) Retrieved December 10, 2005, from http://www.bsr.org/Meta/About/index.cfm.

Abrahamson, E. (1996). Management fashion. *Academy of Management Review, 21*(1), 254–285.

Abrahamson, E. (1997). Technical and aesthetic fashion. In B. Czarniawska & G. Sevon (Eds.), *Translating organizational change* (pp. 117–137). Berlin: Walter de Gruyer.

Abrahamson, E., & Fairchild, G. (1999). Management fashion: Lifecycles, triggers, and collective learning processes. *Administrative Science Quarterly, 44*(4), 708–740.

Allen, C. (2004, May 5–8). *A rose by any other name? A discursive typology of the terms business social responsibility and sustainability in New Zealand.* Paper presented at the First International Critical Discourse Analysis Conference, Valencia, Spain.

Aspen Institute. (2005). *Beyond grey pinstripes: Preparing MBAs for social and environmental stewardship.* Retrieved December 29, 2005, from http://www.beyondgreypinstripes.org/pdf/2005_beyond_grey_pinstripes.pdf.

Benders, J., & van Veen, K. (2001). What's in a fashion? Interpretative viability and management fashions articles. *Organization, 8*(1), 33–53.

Benn, S., & Bubna-Litic, D. (2004). Is the MBA sustainable? Degrees of change. In C. Galea (Ed.), *Teaching business sustainability: Vol. 1. From theory to practice* (pp. 82–94). Sheffield, UK: Greanleaf.

Beyond Grey Pinstripes. (n.d.). Retrieved December 10, 2005, from http://www.beyondgreypinstripes.org/index.cfm.

Business Role (n.d.) Retrieved December 10, 2005, from http://www.wbcsd.org/templates/TemplateWBCSD5/layout.asp?type=p&MenuId=MTE0OQ&doOpen=1&ClickMenu=LeftMenu.

Bowen, H. (1953). *Social responsibilities of the businessman.* New York: Harper.

Brady, K., Thomas, W., Clipsham, J., & Smith, M. (2005). *Corporate social responsibility: Lessons learned.* Ottawa: Canadian Interdepartmental Working Group on Corporate Social Responsibility.

Clark, T., & Salaman, G. (1998). Telling tales: Management gurus' narratives and the construction of managerial identity. *Journal of Management Studies, 35*(2), 137–161.

De Bakker, F. G. A., Groenewegen, P., & Den Hond, F. (2005). A bibliometric analysis of 30 years of research and theory on corporate social responsibility and corporate social performance. *Business & Society, 44*(3), 283–317.

del Mar Garcia de los Salmones, M., Crespo, A. H., & Rodriguez del Bosque, I. (2005). Influence of corporate social responsibility on loyalty and valuation of services. *Journal of Business Ethics, 61,* 369–385.

du Gay, P., Salaman, G., & Rees, B. (1996). The conduct of management and the management of conduct: Contemporary managerial discourse and the constitution of the "competent" manager. *Journal of Management Studies, 33*(3), 263–282.

Ehrenfeld, J. R. (1999). Cultural structure and the challenge of sustainability. In K. Sexton, A. A. Marcus, K. W. Easter, & T. D. Burkhardt (Eds.), *Better environmental decisions: Strategies for governments, business and communities* (pp. 223–244). Washington, DC: Island Press.

Eisenberg, E. (1984). Ambiguity as strategy in organizational communication. *Communication Monographs, 51,* 227–242.

Elkington, J. (1999). Triple bottom line revolution: Reporting for the third millennium. *Australian CPA, 69*(11), 75–76.

FAQs. (2004). Retrieved December 10, 2005, from http://www.societyandbusiness.gov.uk/faqs.shtml.

Fergus, A. H. T., & Rowney, J. I. A. (2005). Sustainable development: Lost meaning and opportunity? *Journal of Business Ethics, 60,* 17–27.

Fineman, S. (2001). Fashioning the environment. *Organization, 8*(1), 17–31.

Fiss, P. C., & Zajac, E. J. (2004). The diffusion of ideas over contested terrain: The (non)adoption of a shareholder value orientation among German firms. *Administrative Science Quarterly, 49,* 501–534.

Foot, D. K., & Ross, S. (2004). Social sustainability. In C. Galea (Ed.), *Teaching business sustainability: Vol. 1. From theory* to practice (pp. 107–125). Sheffield, UK: Greenleaf.

Friedman, M. (1970, September 13). The social responsibility of business is to increase its profits. *New York Times Magazine*, pp. 32–33, 122–126.

Glover, L., & Noon, M. (2005). Shop-floor workers' responses to quality management initiatives: Broadening the disciplined worker thesis. *Work, Employment & Society, 19*(4), 727–745.

Guillen, M. F. (1994). *Models of management.* Chicago: University of Chicago Press.

Guthey, E., Langer, R., & Morsing, M. (2006). Corporate social responsibility is a management fashion. So what? In M. Morsing & S. C. Beckman (Eds.), *Strategic CSR Communication* (pp. 39–60). Copenahgen: Djøf.

Hamilton, C. (2003). *Growth fetish.* Sydney: Allen & Unwin.

Hawken, P. (1993). *The ecology of commerce.* New York: Harper Collins.

Huczynski, A. (1993). *Management gurus: What makes them and how to become one.* London: Routledge.

Jackson, B. (2001). *Management gurus and management fashions: A dramatistic inquiry.* London: Routledge.

Jackson, B., & Rigby, D. (2000, November 14). *Bringing e-business to New Zealand: The role of the "big five" management consulting firms.* Paper presented at the European Institute for Advance Studies in Management, Brussels.

Krajnc, D., & Glavic, P. (2005). How to compare companies on relevant dimensions of sustainability. *Ecological Economics, 55*, 551–563.

Laine, M. (2005). Meanings of the term "sustainable development" in Finnish corporate disclosures. *Accounting Forum, 29*, 395–413.

Livesey, S. M. (2002). The discourse of the middle ground: Citizen Shell commits to sustainable development. *Management Communication Quarterly, 15*(3), 313–349.

Lynn, B. (2001, 15 March). Going green in shades of gray. *American Way Magazine.*

Meglio, F. D. (2005, July 15). *It's getting easier being green.* Retrieved September 2, 2005, from http://www.businessweek.com/bschools/content/jul2005/bs20050715_9296_bs001.htm.

Murcott, S. (1997). Definitions of sustainable development. Retrieved December 10, 2005, from http://www.sustainableliving.org/appen-a.htm.

Norman, W., & MacDonald, C. (2004). Getting to the bottom of the triple bottom line. *Business Ethics Quarterly, 14*, 243–262.

Origins of the WBCSD. (n.d.). Retrieved December 10, 2005, from http://www.wbcsd.ch/templates/TemplateWBCSD2/layout.asp?type=p&MenuId=NDEx&doOpen=1&ClickMenu=LeftMenu.

Palazzo, G., & Richter, U. (2005). CSR business as usual? The case of the tobacco industry. *Journal of Business Ethics, 61*, 387–401.

Parker, M. (1992). Post-modern organizations or postmodern organization theory. *Organization Studies, 13*, 1–17.

PriceWaterhouseCoopers. (2003). *6th annual global CEO survey: Leadership, responsibility, and growth in uncertain times.* Retrieved December 28, 2005, from http://www.pwc.com/gx/eng/ins-sol/survey-rep/ceo6/pwc_6_ceo_survey.pdf.

PriceWaterhouseCoopers. (2005). *Sustainability/CSR reporting.* Retrieved December 29, 2005, from http://www.pwc.com/extweb/service.nsf/docid/d0c36bf56dbfd3ba85256d890080e377.

Rochlin, S., Witter, K., Monaghan, P., & Murray, V. (2005). Putting the corporate into corporate responsibility. *AccountAbility Forum 5*, 5–13.

Rolfsen, M. (2004). The tyranny of trends? Towards an alternative perspective on fads in management. In D. Tourish & O. Hargie (Eds.), *Key issues in organizational communication* (pp. 112–129). London: Routledge.

Scott, W. R. (1991). The organization of societal sectors. In W. W. Powell & P. J. DiMaggio (Eds.), *The new institutionalism in organizational analysis.* Chicago: University of Chicago Press.

Sellwood, J. (2005). Strategy for sustainability: Pioneerism or survival? Recent experiences from Brazil. *AccountAbility Forum, 5*, 14–20.

Simpson, W. G., & Kohers, T. (2002). The link between corporate social and financial performance: Evidence from the banking industry. *Journal of Business Ethics, 35*, 97–109.

Spell, C. S. (2001). Management fashions: Where do they come from, and are they old wine in new bottles? *Journal of Management Inquiry, 10*(4), 358–373.

Steiner, G. A., & Steiner, J. F. (2005). *Business, government, and society: A managerial perspective* (11th ed.). New York: McGraw-Hill.

Steurer, R., Langer, M. E., Konrad, A., & Martinuzzi, A. (2005). Corporations, stakeholders and sustainable development I: A theoretical exploration of business-society relations. *Journal of Business Ethics, 61,* 263–281.

Sustainable Business Network (n.d.). Retrieved December 10, 2005, from http://www .sustainable.org.nz/about.asp.

The Business Case for CSR. (2004). Retrieved December 10, 2005, from http://www .societyandbusiness.gov.uk/businesscasecsr .shtml.

Thompson, P., & Davidson, J. O. C. (1995). The continuity of discontinuity: Managerial rhetoric in turbulent times. *Personnel Review, 24*(4), 17–33.

Tolbert, P. S., & Zucker, L. G. (1983). Institutional sources of change in the formal structure of organizations: Diffusion of civil service reform, 1880–1935. *Administrative Science Quarterly, 28,* 22–39.

Utne, L. (2004, May/June). The green M.B.A. *Utne Reader,* 28–29.

Van de Ven, A. H., & Hargrave, T. J. (2004). Social, technical, and institutional change: A literature review and synthesis. In M. S. Poole & A. H. Van de Ven (Eds.), *Handbook of organizational change and innovation* (pp. 259–303). New York: Oxford University Press.

Welford, R. J. (2000). *Corporate environmental management 3: Towards sustainable development.* London: Earthscan.

What Is CSR? (2004). Retrieved December 10, 2005, from http://www.societyandbusiness .gov.uk/whatiscsr.shtml.

Wilson, M. (2003, March/April). Corporate sustainability: What is it and where does it come from? *Ivey Business Journal,* pp. 1–5.

World Commission on Environment and Development. (1987). *Our common future* [Brundtland report]. Oxford: Oxford University Press.

Zadek, S. (2005). *Global accountability: Responsibility isn't a blame game.* Retrieved October 1, 2005, from http:// www.fortune.com/fortune/global500/ articles/0,15114,1107344,00.html.

Zbaracki, M. J. (1998). The rhetoric and reality of total quality management. *Administrative Science Quarterly, 43,* 602–636.

Zorn, T. E., Christensen, L. T., & Cheney, G. (1999). *Do we really want constant change?* San Francisco, CA: Berrett-Koehler.

Zorn, T. E., Page, D., & Cheney, G. (2000). Nuts about change: Multiple perspectives on change-oriented communication in a public sector organization. *Management Communication Quarterly, 13*(4), 515–566.

Zorn, T. E., & Taylor, J. R. (2004). Knowledge management and/as organizational communication. In D. Tourish & O. Hargie (Eds.), *Key issues in organisational communication* (pp. 96–112). London: Routledge.

29

Corporate Social Responsibility and Public Policy Making

CHARLES CONRAD
JÉANNA ABBOTT

Governments create corporations, much like Dr. Franken-
stein created his monster, yet, once they exist, corporations,
like the monster, threaten to overpower their creators. . . .
Though the movement against corporate rule would be im-
possible, even senseless, without robust nongovernmental
institutions, community activism, and political dissent, the
belief these can be a substitute for government regulation,
rather than a necessary complement to it, is dangerously
mistaken. . . . [A]fter all, what many business leaders want
[is] replacement of government regulation of corporations
with market forces, perhaps shaped by the oversight of
nongovernmental organizations. . . . In this scenario, cor-
porations get all the coercive power and resources of the
state, while citizens are left with nongovernmental organi-
zations and the market's invisible hand—socialism for the
rich and capitalism for the poor.

J. Bakan, *The Corporation*

Getting the most out of capitalism requires public interven-
tion of various kinds, and a lot of it: taxes, public spend-
ing, regulation in many different areas of business activity.
It also requires corporate executives to be accountable—
but to the right people and in the right way.

C. Crook, "The Good Company"

Can corporations ever be expected actually to make altruistic decisions in the public interest (as they see it) at their
own long-term expense? *Yes, on occasion; it is, however,*
easier and more natural to make believe. . . . Corporations
disguise motivations skillfully, attributing to themselves be-
nevolence whenever they change strategies, even though the
change also increases long-term gains or reduces long-term
losses.

M. Bronfenbrenner, "The Consumer"

Our initial reaction to the chapters that form this collection was that, while there is very little debate in the traditional sense of point–counterpoint, there clearly are two voices. One voice, clearest in the chapters that make up parts I and V, offers narratives of progress, a movement toward the global dominance of what Jeremy Rifkin (2004) has called the "European dream," a vision that

> emphasizes community relationships over individual autonomy, cultural diversity over assimilation, quality of life over the accumulation of wealth, sustainable development over unlimited material growth, deep play over unrelenting toil, universal human rights over property rights, and global cooperation over the unilateral exercise of power. (p. 3)

Through organized, sometimes brilliant, informal social/economic pressures and education, advocacy by consumer, labor, and religious groups has led corporate executives to voluntarily engage in socially and environmentally responsible action.

A second voice simultaneously celebrates these developments but tells a more cautionary tale. It suggests that voluntary moves toward corporate social responsibility (CSR) and social democracy (SD) often seem to be fleeting (see Deetz, chapter 18; Breen, chapter 20; Peterson & Norton, chapter 24; Samkin & Lawrence, chapter 19). Even widely touted examples of exceptionally responsible societies (Morsing, Midttun, & Palmås, chapter 6) and corporations—Ben & Jerry's, The Body Shop, Malden Mills—eventually seem to lose their CSR/SD commitments with changes in leadership or adaptation to globalized markets (see most of the chapters in parts III, IV, and VI; also see Bakan, 2004; Cheney, 1999; Seeger & Ulmer, 2002). Friedmanites (see Aune, chapter 14) and CSR/SD advocates seem to agree that competitive pressures make it difficult for individual corporations to invest in CSR/SD activities, even if doing so makes financial sense in the long term, when they are competing with firms that refuse to do so. For every Shell Oil attempting to get its house in order, there is an ExxonMobil excusing its record profits, refusing to contribute to heating funds for poor Americans, returning to federal appeals courts multiple times in an effort to avoid paying a decade-old legal judgment for the *Exxon Valdez* oil spill

(Cook, 2006; Zarembo, 2003). For every negotiated settlement of water use rights that respects the interests of multiple stakeholders (Lawrence, chapter 16), there are instances of intractable conflicts, failed negotiation, and imposition of inequitable outcomes through political power (Putnam & Peterson, 2003). With no external mechanism for ensuring corporate accountability, the kind of internal resistance to CSR/SD that Livesey and Graham (chapter 23) observed at Shell Oil often dominates decision making, particularly over issues of "externalities" (see Deetz, chapter 18; Ganesh, chapter 26; McMillan, chapter 1). Advocacy is crucial to voluntary CSR/SD, but sustaining sufficient pressure over the long term, even with the coordination provided by electronic communication technologies, is very difficult (see Breen, chapter 20; Kendall, Gill, & Cheney, chapter 17; Knight, chapter 21; McMillan, chapter 1). When executives attempt to balance the two sets of pressures, it is not surprising that relatively few privilege CSR/SD in their decision making (see Bullis & Ie, chapter 22; Waddock, chapter 5). Neither is it surprising that, when they do consider CSR/SD, they do so in terms of a very narrow set of social problems, and their organizations are often the primary beneficiaries (see Cloud, chapter 15; Deetz, chapter 18; Seeger & Hipfel, chapter 10). Some of these voices (Breen, chapter 20; Deetz, chapter 18; Ganesh, chapter 26; Hearit, chapter 11; Livesey & Graham, chapter 23; Llewellyn, chapter 12; Samkin & Lawrence, chapter 19; Waddock, chapter 5) have even argued that governmental controls over the actions of multinational corporations (MNCs) are absolutely necessary supplements to informal advocacy, in part because governmental policies often play a crucial role in cases of corporate social *ir*responsibility.[1] As voters in the world's largest economies rush to elect or re-elect U.S. President George W. Bush's neoliberal ideological siblings—in Australia, Britain, Germany, and Canada, among others—and as the United States moves to increase neoliberal influence on major international nongovernmental organizations, the continued dominance of America's "incoherent empire" (Mann, 2003, esp. chap. 2) seems assured.[2]

In this chapter, we hope to move the CSR debate farther in the latter direction. We begin with the observation that, in spite of welcome and significant progress in many parts of the world, advocates (and the primary beneficiaries) of the American dream, with its focus on material advancement grounded in the individualism and isolation of the frontier experience (Rifkin, 2004), still possess exceptional symbolic capital, financial resources, and functional control of the most powerful political-economic-military system on the planet (Johnson, 2004). That control is exercised through conscious, agile, strategic manipulation of public policy making by corporate elites. We argue that it is only through careful examination of the ways in which corporate elites influence the *process* of public policy making that we can fully understand the barriers to achieving widespread CSR. Our focus is on policy making in the United States. While we acknowledge this serious limitation (and discuss it at more length in the final section of the chapter), our goal is to encourage CSR/SD scholars throughout the world to focus their attention on public policy making. To do so, we have to start somewhere, and given the global reach of American policies, the United States seems to be an appropriate place.

THE CYCLICAL HISTORY OF CSR IN THE UNITED STATES

As Wells (2002) and Ostas (2001; also see Hearit, chapter 11; Llewellyn, chapter 12; Seeger & Hipfel, chapter 10) have argued at length, the history of CSR in the United States has been a cyclical one—corporate executives strategically exploit sociopolitical situations and new organizational "technologies"[3] and legitimize their efforts through symbolic action that articulates, reinforces, and redefines dominant cultural values. Eventually, the resulting maldistribution of power, privilege, and wealth leads to a legitimation crisis (Habermas, 1975). In some cases—the "trust-busting" era at the turn of the twentieth century, the New Deal, and the Great Society—the backlash is so intense and extensive that it simply overwhelms corporate advocates. Public opinion is mobilized sufficiently to elevate issues of CSR to the policy agenda. If advocates are able to get legislators to take an identified problem seriously, forge a winning coalition among legislators with "diverse interests and perceptions," *and* overcome the arguments and political influence of corporate opponents, public opinion actually may generate progressive public policies (Wilson, 1974, pp. 137, 149–152). Their efforts are aided by the backlash that accompanies socially responsible policies. The increased costs of CSR policies can lead to cartelization and price fixing as the entry of new competitors is made more difficult; executives can respond to the increased costs by reducing the production of low-profit-margin "poor man's goods"; executives can push for (and usually receive) increased government protectionism and/or financial assistance (directly through "corporate welfare" or indirectly through "tax relief"); and executives become increasingly vulnerable to pressure from stockholders whose returns are reduced (Bronfenbrenner, 1974; Rothenberg, 1974; Schelling, 1974). Elites, including corporate executives, steadfastly oppose these policies while they are being enacted and implemented, primarily in private, and redouble their efforts once progressive policies are enacted. Their counterattacks in a variety of venues and through a wide range of symbolic and structural strategies "outflank" advocates of CSR and culminate in the enactment of organizationally supportive public policies (Bakan, 2004).

With each iteration, the advocates of neoliberal economics have become more sophisticated in their rhetoric (Aune, 2001), more precise in their arguments, and more skilled in the use of available media. Since the beginning of the Reagan era, they have created a vast network of institutional arrangements that provide evidence to support their rhetoric and networks to coordinate their activities (Aune, 2001; Mooney, 2005).[4] The cycle has led to an increased influence for corporate executives over public policy making, transforming the state from the primary mechanism of restraining corporate/executive power to the primary ally of those interests. Canadian sociologist Joel Bakan (2004) observed:

> Economic globalization and deregulation have diminished the state's capacity to protect the public interest (through, for example, labor laws, environmental laws, and consumer protection laws) and have strengthened its power to promote corporations' interests and facilitate their profit-seeking missions (through, for example, corporate laws, property and contract laws, copyright laws, and international trade laws). Overall, however, the state's power has not been reduced. (p. 154; also see Kain, 1974, pp. 231, 234)

Strategies, Tactics, Rhetorical Cunning, and Organizational Outflanking

The concept of "rhetoric" occupies a very small place in contemporary organizational theory. When scholars have focused their attention on symbolic action, it has been more often through the multiple lenses of "discourse" analysis perspectives that highlight the "talked" and "textual" nature of everyday interaction in organizations (Conrad, 2004b). The distinction is an important one for understanding debates about CSR because "rhetorical" perspectives foreground the intentional, strategic use of social-linguistic structures to produce, reproduce, and legitimize structures of privilege and domination: "rather than the discourse-driven subject, the subject may be a politically conscious language user, telling the right kind of stories to the right audiences at the right moment" (Alvesson & Karreman, 2000, p. 1132; also see the discussions of discourse and material relationships provided in Aune, chapter 14; Cloud, chapter 15; Ganesh, chapter 26; McMillan, chapter 1). In short, rhetorical perspectives invite analyses of organizational/executive persuasion, including "lies, and the lying liars who tell them," to coin a phrase (Elliott & Schroth, 2002).

This imbalance may stem, at least in part, from the perspectives taken by advocates of rhetorical perspectives. In general, that work has been grounded in an "old rhetoric" of Aristotle and his successors (see Cheney, Christiansen, Conrad, & Lair, 2004). While popular histories laud Athens during and immediately after the "golden age" as the cradle of democracy and the origins of reason, its democracy was limited to a largely homogeneous racial, gender, and economic elite, even during its most democratic decades. As Jeffrey Walker (2000) points out, Aristotle's conception of rhetoric was oriented toward the most elite segment(s) of the Athenian population: "Aristotle's preferred term for 'deliberative' discourse is *symbouleutikon* . . . which is better translated as 'advisory,' . . . suggest[ing] that Aristotle's image of an ideal speech situation is a relatively small group of councilors, or magistrates—not the popular Assembly, nor the popular jury-courts, of the Athenian democracy" (p. 14).

This recognition of the inadequacies of Aristotelian rhetoric has led many to return to the fundamental debates of the classical era and to rediscover the Sophistic tradition. Aristotelian rhetoric is appropriate to what Michel de Certeau (1984) has called "strategic" practices—those in which "a subject of will and power (a proprietor, an enterprise, a city, a scientific institution)" employs force grounded in control of spaces in which relationships can be managed and dominated (pp. xx, 36). It reflects a *"triumph of place over time.* It allows one to capitalize acquired advantages, to prepare future expansions, and thus to give oneself a certain independence with respect to the variability of circumstances" (p. 35). It relies on surveillance (what de Certeau calls, after Foucault, "panoptic practices") and the ability to "define the *power of knowledge* by this ability to transform the uncertainties of history into readable spaces" (p. 36). For Aristotle's mentor Plato, it was *techne,* "a kind of professional knowledge, directly opposed to the *paidea* of the freeman" (Atwill, 1998, p. 55). It underlies, and reproduces, a "sovereign" conception of power, one that Stewart Clegg (1989) argues was reinvigorated in Thomas Hobbes's *Leviathan* and introduced to modern social theory by political theorist Robert Dahl and his successors. Of course, the advantages built into strategic practices do not guarantee positive outcomes for elites; the possibility of resistance always is present. Sovereign power is limited spatially and temporally. Peripheral areas are more difficult to control than power centers. In addition, its use *reproduces* existing rules and resources of domination, undermining its ability to innovate and adapt to new contingencies (Clegg, 1989, pp. 170, 219–220; also see Mann, 1986). Strategic action also must continually be legitimized, and an Aristotelian rhetoric of "political, economic, and scientific rationality" is designed precisely for this purpose (de Certeau, 1984, pp. ix). Ironically, the greatest threat to "strategic" action is its visibility.

Athens also was a stable, even static, elite democracy (Garver, 1994; Hill, 1983), and thus fundamentally different than the "rhetorical situation" of the postmodern (or late postmodern [Anthony Giddens] or post-postmodern [Rifkin]) condition of the early twenty-first century. For our era, the very different rhetoric of the Sophists is more appropriate (Ballif, 1998; Jarrett, 1991; Neel, 1988; Poulokas, 1995). Citing Carl von Clauswitz, de Certeau notes that "the more a power grows, the less it can allow itself to mobilize part of its means in the service of deception. . . . Power is bound by its very visibility. In contrast, trickery is possible for the weak" (p. 37). Hence, strategic action must be hidden or disguised, either symbolically or structurally.

Sophistic rhetoric is "tactical":

It allows agents to insinuate themselves into spaces that they do not control. It depends on time; it is always on the watch for opportunities; always searching for ways to win everyday battles through clever tricks, knowing how to get away with things, "hunter's cunning," maneuvers, polymorphic simulations, joyful discoveries, poetic as well as warlike. The Greeks called these "ways of operating" *metis*. (de Certeau, 1984, p. xix)

The closest English translation for the term *metis* probably is "cunning," but explaining it is difficult because the Greeks did not provide a comprehensive examination (Murphy, 2002; also see Ballif, 1998; Detienne & Vernant, 1978). It is the antithesis of Aristotelian *techne*; it is symbolized by Prometheus's attempts to deceive Zeus and by the Trojan horse. Unlike the philosophical *nous*, which is constant and unchanging, it is the intelligence of the fox, in which the weaker takes the stronger by surprise. It is a momentary conquering of situations that are transient, shifting, disconcerting, ambiguous, and porous (Atwill, 1998; Detienne & Vernant, 1978). It lies between magic and rule-governed, strictly deducible thought. "Trickery is possible for the weak" (de Certeau, 1984, p. 37) and is taught through the stories of "ordinary folk" (Atwill, 1998, p. 82).

But, tactical practices and cunning also are vulnerable. First, they are exhausting. The process of constant maneuver is exhilarating, creating a unique form of joy, but "whatever it wins, it does not keep" (de Certeau, 1984, p. xix). Second, they are susceptible to hegemonic processes. Extending sovereign power over space and time requires the development of disciplinary power and "the diffusion of disciplinary techniques" (Clegg, 1989, p. 219). Tactical practices are impeded by both knowledge and ignorance. Knowledge includes understanding of what needs to be done, but also understanding the potential costs of resistance and the likelihood (often quite low) of success. Ignorance may be

of matters of strategy, such as assessing the resources of the antagonist, of routine procedures, rules, agenda setting, access, of informal

conduits [of power] as well as formal protocols, of the style and substance of [sovereign] power. It is not that they do now know the rules of the game; they might not recognize the game, let alone know the rules. (Clegg, 1989, p. 221; also see Mann, 1986, p. 7)

Ignorance also may result from isolation, from not knowing the identities of potential allies, who to form networks with among resistors, or how to coordinate complex actions over time and space. Elites, of course, have incentives to employ all of the symbolic and structural strategies available to them in an effort to minimize interactions among potential resisters, to undermine their solidarity, and to guide resistance in approved directions.

Michael Mann has argued that, historically, elites have been able to "outflank" resistance by "constituting a stable organizational field of extensive, coherent, and solidaristic alliances and nodal points" (quoted in Clegg, 1989, p. 223).[5] The central challenge elites face is organizational—control, logistics, and communication (Mann, 1986, p. 2). They do so through four interrelated sources of power: ideological, economic, political, and military (defined broadly to encompass all police powers). The role of the state is to mediate among these modes of power (p. 417). Through *strategic* (using de Certeau's definition) manipulation of "circuits of praxis," elites are able to institutionalize "the laws and norms of the social group in which both [elites and the masses] operate" (p. 6). Because relatively stable institutionalized structures are necessary for *tactics* of resistance, they are insulated from attack: "institutionalization is necessary to achieve routine collective goals; and thus . . . social stratification, also becomes an institutionalized feature of social life" (p. 7). The ability to influence the development and institutionalization of multiple social structures creates three strategic options for elites. First, it allows them to move among circuits of power in a search for the optimal configuration in particular cases— if workers strike, the army (or Pinkerton agents) can be called in to "restore order" or take over air traffic control (military circuit); "permanent replacements" can be hired to return idled plants to operation (economic circuit); evangelists can be hired to persuade workers that their pain is the result of their own sins (ideological circuit); the courts can be used to jail or execute resistance leaders, bankrupt union treasuries, or strictly regulate the conditions under which resistance takes place (e.g., the 1935 U.S. National Labor Relations Act; political circuit).

Second, elites can alter the institutional configurations themselves. Capitalism and industrialization, Mann argues, changed power configurations in a number of ways. Perhaps the most important was that the four circuits became progressively more intertwined and mutually supportive (Mann, 1993). Others have suggested that the latter half of the twentieth century transformed Weber's *observations* of a link between the ideological (religious) and economic realms into a fulfilled *prophecy* as free market fundamentalism emerged as a central religio-political-economic ideology (Aune, 2001; Kuttner, 1996; Soros, 1998). Like any ideology, its rhetorical power stems from its ability to "put together in a single explanation and organization a number of aspects of existence that have hitherto been marginal, interstitial to the dominant institutions of power" (Mann, 1986, p. 21). Ironically, elites identify the institutional changes that they need to make by monitoring and interpreting successful *tactical* action by nonelites. Some of the elites' adaptations will fail—there is no reason to attribute omniscience to them—and in other cases nonelites will quickly create/learn tactics that exploit the new institutional arrangements. But, tacticians will always be "playing catch up," and elites will always be modifying the rules of the game.

Finally, elites also can engage in *tactical* action by acting within and among existing circuits of praxis.[6] As Clegg and de Certeau have noted, this approach is risky because it can foster at least momentary alliances among nonelites. However, tactical action by elites can easily be disguised rhetorically through denial, universalizing sectional interests, and a host of other well-practiced rhetorical moves. More important for this chapter, elite tactical action can be hidden from public view through processes of privatizing public policy making.

Outflanking and the Development of the "American System"

Charles Perrow's *Organizing America* (2002) provides a highly accessible summary of the ways in which corporate elites strategically managed the fragmented U.S. political structure and an emerging neoliberal political-economic ideology to construct the "American system" of large, weakly regulated, and politically powerful corporations. This developmental process is deeply ironic because it emerged in a society that was extremely distrustful of concentrated power. It also is a tribute to the power of unintended/unanticipated consequences and the ability of concentrated interests to maneuver around those consequences through a complex maze of interstitial networks.

By 1830, the doctrines of *laissez faire* capitalism had triumphed (Mann, 1993). Supportive structural arrangements soon would follow. Prior to that date, corporations could exist only after receiving highly restrictive charters that were granted only when applicants could demonstrate that doing so would meet *public* needs that could not efficiently be met though direct public action. For this reason, and because large, centralized, interstate organizations had not yet developed, the crucial U.S. Supreme Court decisions of 1819—the *Dartmouth* decision establishing corporate "personhood," decisions establishing limited liability for officers of corporations, and a group of decisions giving federal laws precedence over state statutes—did not *seem* to be threatening (see Ritz, chapter 13). The latter decisions were crucial because the federal government was much weaker than the governments of the largest states—it was not until the New Deal that this power imbalance was reversed (Mann, 1993; Perrow, 2002).[7]

This does not mean that the decisions were not highly political.[8] At every step, "easy incorporation" had to be justified. Some justifications were grounded in Jeffersonian-Jacksonian populism—corporations "would offset the centralized state and prevent the concentration of wealth in the hands of the few who would have the economic and political clout to secure charters" (Perrow, 2002, pp. 38–39)—and others were the outgrowth of Whig classism, that the wisdom of educated judges should take precedence over the emotionality of the unschooled masses (p. 44). Still other justifications were early echoes of today's neoliberal ideology (for summaries, see Aune, 2001; Hirschman, 1991). Entrepreneurs must take risks, and it is in the public's interests to limit those risks in order to facilitate economic growth and prosperity (Perrow, 2002, pp. 42, 45). Indeed, governments would be wise to form partnerships with entrepreneurs in order to encourage, assist, and protect them (p. 127). Furthermore, regulating corporations infringed on *private* liberties and rights of *private property* (p. 113). Incorporation offered a means of addressing public needs that is inherently more economically efficient than government ever can be (p. 118), especially since when government does attempt to regulate, its efforts usually "backfire" (p. 184).

Perrow's analysis ends with the 1920s because by then the "American system" was in place—the wave of consolidation that started during the Depression of 1898 was over by 1902. In only four years, the aggregate value of stocks and bonds of large corporations had increased eightfold, from approximately US$1 billion to almost US$8 billion (Roy, 1997, p. 5). Even critics of the corporate form had largely accepted the notion of "shareholder primacy"; economists and the general public lauded the benefits that economies of scale offered to consumers; a series of U.S. Supreme Court decisions that size alone was insufficient grounds for antitrust litigation gave large corporations additional legal legitimacy; and the rapid economic growth of the 1920s combined with much wider ownership of stocks to broaden popular support (Wells, 2002).[9]

Corporate rhetoric celebrated a new "welfare capitalism." It was motivated by a "rational" concern for increasing customers' disposable income so that they could purchase corporate-made products, and rendered credible by citing highly publicized examples of "corporate social responsibility." The new CSR rhetoric was so pervasive that Theodore Levitt (1958) complained that it was no longer fashionable to talk about making money, but only about how to "serve the public."[10] Even the staunchest critics were reformist rather than radical. Calls for eliminating the corporate form disappeared, and the incentive system that encouraged managers to favor their own interests over those of other stakeholders went largely unchallenged (Horowitz, 1992; Seligman, 2003). Armed with their newly constructed legitimacy, corporate executives continued the process of creating legal havens at the state level (with Delaware and Connecticut occupying the pro-corporate, pro-executive extremes that they still hold) through legislation and litigation.

The social and economic dislocations of the Great Depression revived public debate about the advantages and limitations of the American system, the most important of which was the one between A. A. Berle, an economist who helped draft the banking and securities laws of the New Deal, and Harvard Law School professor E. Merrick Dodd (Wells, 2002). In response to public loss of confidence in the ability of "private enterprise" to manage the economy on its own, the size and regulatory role of the federal government increased significantly. Corporate charitable contributions were made legal and encouraged, and new power blocs—unions, farmers, and so on—formed and grew in power. Suddenly, executives became responsible for mediating multiple stakeholder interests, not just controlling organizational operations for the benefits of stockholders (McKie, 1974b). But, with the economic explosion accompanying the end of World War II and the pressure on countervailing power blocs that emerged from the Red Scare, pressure on executives once again waned.

By the time Harry Truman was elected president, a clear, cyclical pattern had emerged. During times of strong economic growth, critics express concern/fear about increasing corporate/executive power. Executives counter with a rhetoric of CSR and create a number of programs that demonstrate the social consciousness of captains of industry and the adequacy of *voluntary* efforts: "at least in public pronouncements, few corporate leaders failed to make a nod to their firms' 'social responsibilities'" (Wells, 2002, p. 16). In public organizational and economic discourse, executives and their actions are foregrounded, while the fortuitous roles of exogenous market forces are minimized (Ostas, 2001). Economic growth is cast as the gift of "secular saviors," to use Ron Kuhrana's (2002) term, and their political allies:

> A usable ideology makes one's own group both the epic hero of economic development and the noble victim of exploitation. . . . The businessman has at various times adopted the congenial doctrines of laissez-faire, Social Darwinism, rugged individualism, "Less government in business and more business in government," and "what's good for General Motors is good for the country." He tells dread tales of the confiscatory tax collector and the predatory trade unionist. (Bronfenbrenner, 1974, p. 170)

Academics provide ideological support for these assertions and counter the "vague and unspecific" criticisms offered by opponents (Wells, 2002).[11] Buoyed with favorable public opinion sustained by an ongoing economic boom, executives press for legislation and judicial precedents to increase their freedom of action and reduce government interference in the marketplace (Conrad, 2003a). This rhetoric at least temporarily increases public trust in executives and reduces public support for government, an effect that seems to last across economic cycles (McKie, 1974a).

During periods of economic decline, critics of corporate/executive power become more active, credible, and influential, and public esteem for its secular saviors declines (McKie, 1974a). In response, corporate rhetors focus on the need to free corporations from government restraint and provide public financial support for their activities so that they can make the difficult but rational decisions necessary to revive the economy. Market forces and government interference are foregrounded; executives are cast as tragic heroes fighting against almost insurmountable odds (Chen & Meindl, 1991). The combination of supportive rhetoric and executive cunning—careful movement among available venues (courts, state governments, federal government, multinational agencies) and modifying those structures—revives corporate hegemony.

Contemporary Public Policy Making as Organizational Outflanking

Influencing public policy making is central to corporate management of the CSR cycle. In general, elites prefer to construct public policy in private. Open public policy conflicts are risky. They can lead to the formation of coalitions among low-power actors that may upset political power balances and may even undermine the psychological processes that generate deference to elites (Vogel, 1989). In addition, making policy in public forces elites to engage in rhetoric justifying their preferences. Although they have a number of influential strategies available, rhetorical acts are inherently risky. *Private* policy-making processes do not require justification of actions/preferences, and policy outcomes are more easily controlled. Of course, the simplest means of privatizing public policy making is to press for laws and political structures that allow corporations to hide information about their operations. This can be done directly, as in the petrochemical industry's success in 2006 in persuading the U.S. Environmental Protection Agency to allow firms to release up to

5,000 pounds of toxic chemicals—DDT, PCBs, and so on—into the environment (a 10-fold increase over the current limit) without disclosing their actions (Gormley, 2006). It also can be done indirectly, by reaching negotiated settlements with regulators, or out-of-court settlements with plaintiffs, in which information gathered during legal proceedings is sealed from the public view. However, especially with the advent of new communication technologies, suppressing information is becoming increasingly difficult. Fortunately for corporate elites, public policy conflicts can still be privatized, even after damning information is made public. Tactical options range from direct suppression of dissent through the power of the state, to manipulating formal rules so that public decisions are made in private, to quietly implementing policies in ways that violate their publicly avowed purposes (Deetz, 1992; Schattschneider, 1960; Stone, 1988), to displacing the conflict to other issues. For example, for decades in the United States a "cozy triangle" composed of the U.S. Department of Agriculture, farm interests, and cigarette companies has quietly controlled federal tobacco policy. Consumer groups, health care interests, and the Food and Drug Administration were, in comparison, unorganized and powerless to challenge the iron triangle's stranglehold on policy (Kingdon, 1995). As the primary growth market for U.S. tobacco products has shifted to Asia, federal trade agencies have been added to the mix, but the process has changed little. In theory, nonelites also can engage in these "tactical" actions, but the byzantine structure of the Washington lobbying "circuit," combined with inferior financial resources and knowledge of the bureaucracy, puts them at a disadvantage.

Sustaining Policy Monopolies

Once corporate elites establish policy monopolies, they are sustained through three processes: (1) cultivating images of expertise, (2) manipiulating the structure of public policy making, and (3) articulating a supporting ideology. Claiming distinctive expertise is easiest for topics with high levels of technical complexity (e.g., genetic engineering). But any interest group can solidify its position by claiming that its interest area is technically complex (for examples, see the analysis of managerialism in Deetz, 1992; see also the discussion of the legacy of scientific management in Cheney &

Brancato, 1993). The views of policy experts are particularly difficult to challenge when they seem to be based on objective measurements, rules, and procedures. This culturally sanctioned preference for the trappings of science has led to the proliferation of right (and left) wing "think tanks" whose primary function is to generate "research" that supports their ideological biases and the interests of their corporate sponsors (Aune, 2001; Mooney, 2005; Rich, 2004; Zarembo, 2003). Much of this effort focuses on arcane and seemingly inconsequential regulatory rules and procedures. But institutionalized rules inevitably have important policy consequences (Kriebel, 1991). For example, Mahon and McGowan (1997) demonstrate that claims of complexity/expertise long have allowed the accounting industry in the United States to avoid government regulation or oversight (also see Riker, 1980). During times of policy quiescence, the "hidden clusters" of career bureaucrats spend their time assessing conditions, issuing mandated reports, and devising and revising possible "solutions" to those conditions (Kingdon, 1995). It is at this level that professional lobbyists have the greatest impact by maintaining constant contact with and influence over the "hidden cluster" of policy makers. The number of registered lobbyists in Washington, D.C., has exploded —up by a factor of 10 since Ronald Regan's election and by a factor of 2 since George W. Bush became president. Many (250) are former congresspersons or their aides. Comparable growth has occurred in the capitals of the largest U.S. states. Secrecy rules make it difficult to assess the scope of state-level lobbying, but in 2004 more than $1 billion was spent in the 42 states that require detailed reporting; the pharmaceutical industry alone spent more than $48 million on state lobbying (Broder, 2006; Saul, 2006). Almost all represent the interests of corporations or collections of corporations.

Career bureaucrats/lobbyists may labor over a particular issue for years before they find ways to successfully manipulate political "openings" and enact pet proposals outside of the glare of the public spotlight. For example, accelerated depreciation of business capital expenditures was advocated as a means of reducing the governmental "burden" on the private sector during the Reagan era, of increasing organizational productivity during the boom years of the 1990s, and eventually was enacted as a means of reversing the Bush II

recession. Similarly, during the 1960s when it was politically viable to advocate expanding social service programs, advocates of health maintenance organizations (HMOs) touted them as a means of increasing access to care by the poor. Later, when the Nixon administration focused on cost containment, HMO advocates argued that health care cost increases were driven by the fee-for-service payment system and could be controlled by increased reliance on managed care. Still later, when the public health community sought to focus on preventative care, HMOs were touted as a solution to that problem, as well (Stone, 1988). Similarly, for years corporate think tanks have touted medical savings accounts as a solution to virtually any health care problem (Kingdon, 1995). Since only one company, a major Ohio contributor to Republican candidates, offered the plans, and since the primary beneficiaries are higher income individuals with substantial employer contributions to their health insurance, it was difficult to mobilize support for them. A pilot program was established during the first Bush administration; it was expanded after the demise of the Clinton health plan in order to show that Congress was doing *something* about health care costs and again in the 2005 Medicare Reform Act. The financial industry continued to ignore the plans, which they viewed as a health care issue, until White House officials began to meet with lobbyists during 2005. Once they understood that the plans could be used as tax-free investment vehicles, their interest skyrocketed. An official lobbying group, the H.S.A. Coalition, was formed and now is pressing for increases to, or elimination of, limits on the amount of money that can be deposited in the accounts. With financial industry advertising, and continued administration backing, the number of Americans enrolled in health savings accounts is predicted to rise by a factor of 5 by 2010 (Dash, 2006).

In some cases, hidden processes actually reverse the intent of legislation. An outgrowth of the Enron/ WorldCom scandal was popular pressure to reverse a trend for U.S. corporations to incorporate in offshore locales (primarily Bermuda) in order to avoid U.S. taxes. In public, corporate advocacy groups and the bill's sponsors touted it as a step that would protect American jobs and increase fairness of the tax code. But, as the bill was debated, the House of Representatives quietly inserted tax credits that actually encourage U.S.

firms to shift their offices offshore. Their net effect was to reduce corporate taxes by $60.8 billion, 10 times the size of the Bermuda loophole. George Washington Law School's Bob Peroni noted that this "is not reform, but loophole replacement" (Johnston, 2002, p. 1). Organizations had long lobbied for each of these provisions without success.

Hidden processes also disadvantage workers. For years, Federal Express pressured the Tennessee congressional delegation to find a way to exempt it from federal labor laws. Their desires were finally granted when the delegation attached a rider to the 1998 extension of minimum wage benefits that effectively achieved their objectives. Organized labor long sought to have federal contracts withheld from firms that have been convicted of violating federal labor laws, finally succeeding via a Clinton executive order, which was summarily reversed after the Bush II administration took office.

The sheer complexity of policy proposals, particularly omnibus tax or spending bills, means that few legislators have fully read *anything* they vote on, and the availability of last-minute amendments means that corporate allies eventually will be able to quietly insert preferred policy changes into an attractive bill, sometimes literally in the middle of the night. During 2004 alone, more than 14,000 such "earmarks" were added, more than 10 times as many as in 1995. A total of 6,376 were added to the 2005 transportation bill alone (Levine, 2006; Roth, 2006). Virtually all were responses to corporate lobbying.[12] Earmarking has multiplicative effects, because

> by the time appropriation bills reach the House or Senate floor, passage by a lopsided margin is virtually assured because every member who got earmarks is obligated to vote for the entire bill. Further the scope of debate is substantially narrowed, with even partisan arguments that would occur otherwise hushed as Republicans and Democrats find common cause: protecting their pork. . . . Solving the earmark problem will require transparency—a requirement that earmarks be included in the actual text of legislation (where they can be seen and challenged) rather than hidden in committee or conference papers. (Flake, 2006)

Even bills with overwhelming popular support can be strategically undermined. On June 23, 2005, the U.S. Supreme Court ruled that state and local governments can use "eminent domain" to transfer ownership of private property to corporations in order to increase tax revenue. The outcry, from across the political spectrum, was immediate and intense. Opinion polls indicated that 90% of Americans wanted the decision to be reversed; politicians at state and federal levels engaged in a contest of comparative outrage and promised immediate action. Given its historical obsession with private property rights, it was not surprising that Texas was the first state to act. Faced with intense public opposition, the development lobby could not act in public. Instead, they quietly persuaded legislators to omit key definitions from the bill. Governments still will be allowed to condemn "blighted" property, and existing case law defines the term very broadly, including "faulty street layout" (houses on a dead-end street or cul-de-sac) and relative "economic liability" (more tax money would be generated by using the land for shopping mall or toxic waste dump)—the issue raised by the Supreme Court decision in the first place. But, legislators did take action, as they had promised, and sins of omission (not defining key terms in legislation) are very difficult to attack (Berliner, 2005; also see Berliner, 2003). Federal legislation on the issue was expected during 2006.

Of course, nonelite groups also have an interest in establishing a monopoly on public understandings of a policy area and in creating institutional arrangements that perpetuate that monopoly (Kingdon, 1995; Redford, 1969).[13] But pro-business groups and those representing the interests of upper class citizens should be more effective. They are more tightly organized than are groups that represent other interests, have greater money and prestige, are better able to exploit the decision processes of legislative bodies, are better equipped to obtain and use private information provided by politicians, and are able to exaggerate their political power in the minds of policy makers (Wilson, 1974). When elites' interests are threatened, they are able to quickly mobilize these resources to keep undesirable proposals off of the public agenda. For example, during the frenetic debate over the Sarbanes Accounting Reform proposal during July 2002, Senators McCain and Levin offered an amendment that would have required corporations to report the value of stock options paid to their employees as expenses on their quarterly and annual reports. Under intense pressure from Silicon Valley firms operating as the Stock Options Coalition and by the Business

Roundtable, the (Democratic) leadership of the Senate manipulated rules in a way that kept the proposal from even being discussed, burying the bill the day after Alan Greenspan described unexpensed options as "avenues to express greed" (Wayne, 2002). Senator Byron Dorgan offered an amendment that would have required executives to return any performance bonuses they had received during the six months prior to their firms declaring bankruptcy. This amendment, too, was rejected (within minutes) without being discussed. In one sense, both amendments represented a failure in elite control because they were proposed in public. But the fact that they never reached the formal agenda illustrates Baumgartner and Jones's (1993) conclusion that, "when interests are well-mobilized on one side of an issue and poorly organized on the other, conflict and political debate are unlikely" (p. 190; also see Stone, 1988; Wilson, 1973, 1974).

Finally, monopoly control of the policy-making process is strongest when it can be defended through references to a supporting ideology that is tightly linked to the dominant values of the society, for example, belief in the sanctity of the "free market" (Aune, 2001; Baumgartner & Jones, 1993; Kingdon, 1995; Riker, 1980, 1982). The more nonrational a decision process is, the more central is organizational rhetoric to its function and outcomes. Goals, core values, actors, interests, and issues all are contested terrain, and policy making depends on the capacity of various spokespersons to create plausible narratives about public organizational/economic policies. Even the "purest" CSR/SD, "multiple-stakeholder" discourse can be co-opted by corporate rhetors (see Aune, chapter 14; Cloud, chapter 15; Ganesh, chapter 26; Peterson & Norton, chapter 24; Stohl, Stohl, & Townsley, chapter 2). Public policy is a web of dilemmas and paradoxes, enigmas that are constructed, revised, and reconstructed through symbolic processes (Conrad & Millay, 2001). Political structures, economic systems, and societal ideologies create the "space" within which rhetoric functions. When the structures are fluid, the systems are fragmented, and the ideologies are replete with tensions and contradictions, the space is enlarged, and the importance of organizational rhetoric is magnified.

Consequently, the most important question raised by organizational influence on public policy making may be under what circumstances discourse, organizational or otherwise, significantly influences the decision-making process. In some cases, influence is exercised in private, and public discourse is irrelevant. In these cases, public discourse is relevant only after the policies has been made and is focused on justifying/legitimizing the decisions that have been made and/or the process itself.[14] Invariably, those justifications assert that the policy was designed to benefit all citizens, not just a privileged few:

> A favored course of action benefits society as a whole and imposes costs on no one in particular. . . . [T]he maximum total welfare criterion of the rational model [of decision making] can be seen as a highly desirable costume with which people try to dress their proposals. In the guise of numbers and the seeming logic of "maximizing welfare" (who could be against that?), the criterion appears as an irrefutable, unassailable, and even innocent way of deciding. In fact, the decision was made long before the criterion was invoked. (Stone, 1988, p. 205)

Thus, the primary function of public policy discourse is not to make decisions, but to develop compelling justifications of decisions that have already been made. Indeed, the privatization of public decision making is already a significant barrier to representative democracy (Held, 1996), and its importance has steadily increased during the past two decades (Greider, 1997).

Snatching Victory from the Jaws of Defeat

If organizational actors fail, and a problem does reach the public agenda, they have a number of strategies available to (1) keep it from being placed on the *policy* agenda, (2) prevent unwanted policies from being enacted in a form that threatens the organization, and (3) prevent enacted policies from being implemented.[15] The first two goals are achieved through public discourse designed to influence the way in which "problems" are defined and policy questions are framed, influence public opinion on the issue, and define the terms of the public policy debate (Baumgartner & Jones, 1993). If policy initiatives are enacted, corporate rhetors return to private influence processes with the "hidden cluster" of government bureaucracies. The goal of blocking strategies is to "contain" an issue or limit its popular appeal. Opponents prefer using the lowest cost strategies that can succeed in blocking a policy initiative (Cobb & Ross, 1997, esp. chaps. 1, 2, 12), particularly if policy initiators have a high level of social legitimacy. Low-cost strategies include refusing to acknowledge that a problem exists, denying knowledge of the problem (the response that Hilts [1994] notes characterized the tobacco industry's treatment of the health effects of smoking for more than 50 years), or undermining the legitimacy of groups that are pushing for policy change. One of the most sophisticated low-cost strategies is "anti-patterning" (Ibarra & Kitsuse, 1993), arguing that a problem is an isolated incident. The strategy is most effective when media coverage of an issue is "episodic," focusing on individual instances rather than continuous focusing on the systems that created/allowed a problem to persist (Iyengar, 1991). The "just a few bad apples" response to the 2002 "corporate meltdown" provides a paradigm case of antipatterning (Conrad, 2003b, 2004a).

Should low-cost (or high-cost) strategies fail, and they usually do (Cobb & Ross, 1997), policy opponents can engage in a variety of "middle-cost" strategies. They may launch ad hominem attacks on initiators or resort to "symbolic placation." Disputing the initiators' evidence (e.g., global warming), discrediting them (e.g., labeling them "tree huggers" or "radical environmentalists"), or casting oneself as a "victim" of the initiators' actions are the simplest form of attacks. For example, during 1994 the Clinton administration briefly considered a casino tax to pay for part of its welfare reform proposal; Nevada's governor flew to Washington to join lobbyists hired by the casino industry claiming that casinos were being unfairly singled out and were victims of a political fight that did not involve them: "What do casinos have to do with welfare reform?" The appeal worked and the proposal was never introduced in Congress (De Parle, 1994). More sophisticated attacks include arguing that the "problem" is a "private-sector" concern, not a matter for public policy. Hall and Jones (1997) show that this strategy has been especially effective in blunting calls for increased regulation after periods of business malpractice. By arguing that the private sector/free market has a built-in self-corrective mechanism, the Securities and Exchange Commission (SEC) has repeatedly been able to avoid taking a more active role. Finally, opponents can raise public

fears about the impact of a policy proposal. The astonishing success of the "Harry and Louise" ads during the debate over the Clinton health care plan in 1993–1994 made it abundantly clear that organizational rhetors, in the guise of "public interest" campaigns, can significantly influence the development of public policy by using media buys to directly mold public opinion (Beauchamp, 1996; Hacker, 1997; Skocpol, 1996). Although reforming the U.S. health care financing system was a high-priority item for the American people, and large majorities initially supported the general outline of the Clinton plan, its complexity made it easy for opponents to create the impression that the result of the reform might be to weaken the U.S. health care system. The ads depicted a woman explaining the more anxiety-producing parts of the plan to her woefully uninformed husband, without mentioning that other parts of the plan were designed to balance the impact of the target aspect in order to prevent negative effects. As doubt and confusion increased, support for the plan fell.

Middle-cost strategies are conceptually quite simple—organizational rhetors draw on culturally sanctioned assumptions (*topoi*) to frame policy proposals in ways that make them seem objectionable. As Aristotle argued, some of those *topoi* are grounded in assumptions held by the populace in general, for example, the inherent superiority of free market capitalism over any other economic system, and the inevitable futility and perversity of government "interference" in the free market system (Aune, 1994, 2001). Other *topoi* are situation or industry specific. For example, health care reformers long have been confronted with claims that the United States has the best health care system in the world, a claim that can be supported only by a very careful definition of "best" and very selective presentation of supporting evidence.

Similarly, the pharmaceutical industry has successfully argued—in spite of compelling evidence to the contrary—that continued high drug costs for U.S. consumers are necessary to sustain their active research and development programs (which in turn ensure the continuation of America's rightful place as the best drug developer in the world), in spite of abundant evidence that undermines that claim. Until Republicans captured control of both houses of Congress, insurance company (HMO) rhetors were less successful in their argument that government regulations and "runaway lawsuits" have driven up health care premiums, although there is no question that they are persistent in using that strategy (Boyle, 2002; Vibbert & Bostdorff, 1993). In 2005, Congress passed the strict restrictions on class-action suits that the industry had long been seeking. The Bush II administration made additional "tort reform" a high legislative priority in 2006, abandoning the effort only after the president's poll numbers plummeted.

Eventually corporate rhetors and friendly policy makers coincide to develop a coherent rhetorical position. For example, tobacco industry rhetors initially found that standard *topoi* failed to mollify palpable hostility to the industry, both in the Senate and among the public. However, they eventually were able to reframe the debate from an issue of industry behavior to a question of government interference. They were able to use opponents' arguments that the industry covered up the addictive properties of nicotine to define smokers as innocent victims. Since the funding mechanisms in the bill relied on increased tobacco taxes, they were able to frame the bill as a tax bill in disguise, one that penalized precisely those poor and middle class victims that the bill's proponents had demonstrated were incapable of shaking their addiction. Furthermore, by creating and funding purportedly "grass roots" organizations, the industry was able to distance itself from the process while adding credibility to its claims. Once the appeal started to influence public attitudes, pro-industry policy makers began to rely on the appeal almost exclusively in their public discourse. In short, corporate attack discourse serves two primary functions. First, it draws on those assumptions to influence and/or legitimize particular policies, either alone or thorough a symbiotic relationship with the discourse of pro-industry policy makers. Second, it reproduces and reinforces the cultural assumptions on which it is based.

Corporate rhetors also can block policy initiatives through strategies of "symbolic placation," which serves to diffuse the emotional intensity that motivates and unites policy initiators. Placation always involves some acceptance of the reasonableness of proponents' claims. It may be wholly symbolic, as when U.S. senators engaged in a competition in comparative outrage after the Enron bankruptcy (Krugman, 2002a; Cohen, 2002; "Reformers All," 2002). Six months, and hundreds of hours of Congressional testimony and senatorial press conferences later, no corrective proposals had emerged from any of those commit-

tees. Indeed, the only systematic bill, sponsored by Paul Sarbanes, was stuck in committee (Oppel, 2002b). Only after the even larger Worldcom bankruptcy, combined with a number of similar actions by smaller firms, did Congress move to pass the Sarbanes-Oxley reform bill. But placation also may involve the presentation of alternative policy proposals that create the illusion that the initiators' concerns are being addressed, but fail to make meaningful changes (and may even exacerbate the underlying problems). The U.S. House of Representatives combined its outrage at the Enron bankruptcy with a bill on 401K plans that rolled back some existing protections and "does practically nothing to protect [workers] from an Enron-type fiasco" (Henry, 2002, p. 1A) and corporate accounting that critics aptly labeled the "Ken Lay Protection Act" (Oppel, 2002a). Fortunately, the bill failed in the U.S. Senate. Hall and Jones (1997) note that the history of the SEC includes multiple cases in which it responded to complaints that it had been inactive in dealing with corporate corruption by increasing the number of reporting releases dealing with disclosure and filing requirements. Consequently, Cobb and Ross (1997) conclude, "although this activity did not deal with the main concerns of critics, it gave the impression that the SEC was an activist agency pursuing solutions to problems in the financial marketplace" (p. 215).

Placation also may involve claims that policy proposals will have disastrous consequences or violate cherished social values. In economic policy disputes, the most common claims are that the policy constitutes an unwarranted and dangerous government intrusion into a free market that has sufficient corrective processes in place (Aune, 2001). This argument has been the basis of repeated efforts to block national health insurance and other forms of health policy reform (Harkey, 1997). In the United States, claims that proposals are unpatriotic, socialistic/communistic, or a violation of individual rights also are common and effective. This rhetoric of "symbolic reassurance" ensures that "tangible benefits continue to go to the organized and powerful" (Cobb & Ross, 1997, p. 214) while the resources of policy initiators and the emotional impetus underlying their activism are depleted.

Finally, policy opponents may define a problem in ways that limit its scope and political appeal. Once the 1964 Democratic landslide made it obvious that Medicare would pass in some form, opponents (led by the American Medical Association) sought to attach a means test to the bill, limiting its scope to nonwealthy seniors. Their goal was to define the proposal as a "welfare" proposal rather than an extension of more positively perceived "social security," thereby reducing its popular appeal especially among politically influential wealthy and upper middle-class seniors (Marmor, 2000). During the post-Enron policy debates of 2001 and 2002, opponents of substantive change have successfully reduced problems of "corporate government," first by defining it as an "investments crisis" (which makes it irrelevant to the 50% of Americans who have no stock exposure), then to an "accounting crisis," and then to a problem of insufficient penalties for corporate securities fraud. In the process, the CEO incentive system that generated Enron-like behaviors was defined out of the equation (Krugman, 2002b; Machiz, 2002; Nichols, 2002). Through strategic definition and redefinition, public "problems" were contained to a small range of issues, supported by an increasingly smaller range of advocates, calling for a set of increasingly minor policy changes (Conrad, 2004a).

In the unlikely event that opponents' policy-blocking strategies fail, their attention turns to the implementation process, which takes place in private where organizational rhetors have their greatest advantages. In some cases, implementation blocking involves persuading government officials to simply not enforce policies, or to do so in a way that minimizes their impact. For example, the Bayh-Dole Act (Arno & Davis, 2001) is a provision of the U.S. patent law that requires pharmaceutical firms that develop new drugs through research supported by federal funds (about 80% of the drugs developed in the United States) to make those drugs available at a reasonable price. However, the law has never been enforced (although the Bush II administration did threaten to enforce it against any firms that sold the "abortion pill" RU-486 in the United States) because the industry has successfully described it as an anticompetitive price control measure (Arno & Davis, 2002). In other cases, regulators can be persuaded to implement policies but to do so in ways that undermine their intent. For example, within hours after the signing of the 2002 Corporate Accountability Act (Sarbanes-Oxley Act), the Bush administration announced that it would interpret its whistleblower protection provisions as narrowly as possible (Bumiller, 2002), and most subsequent whistleblower claims have been settled in the companies' favor. Of more than 300 complaints filed between 2002 and 2005, only three have been settled in favor of the plaintiffs (Fulcrum Financial Inquiry, 2005). The SEC slowly watered down other Sarbannes-Oxley requirements (Fulcrum Financial Inquiry, cited in Bakan, 2004, p. 171, fn. 8), eventually deciding to exempt almost all foreign firms operating in the United States and U.S. firms with market values of less than US$100 million. U.S. firms with values between $100 million and $700 million (80% of U.S. corporations) have been exempted from the requirement of the Sarbanes-Oxley Act that they have auditors certify the effectiveness of their internal controls (Norris, 2005b). Post-Enron court decisions have made it clear that members of boards of directors cannot be held financially liable for rubber stamping fraudulent financial reports (Norris, 2005a). Finally, the executive branch can be persuaded to not provide the funds necessary to implement objectionable policies. SEC funding was increased by 300% in the Sarbannes-Oxley Act, but still is lower than it was in 1990 (Conrad, 2004a).

In August 2005, New York's (Republican) Governor George Pataki signed a law requiring the state to create an easily used website that consumers could use to compare prescription drug prices across the state. The pharmaceutical industry had tried to block the bill, but because the notion of rational choice based on accurate information is central to free market ideology, it was difficult to develop a persuasive public rhetoric. They were not even able to complain about the costs of the system because the state had sufficient funds on hand as the result of successful litigation against a drug company for price fixing. The bill passed both houses of the New York legislature unanimously. Five months later, Pataki inserted a provision that would repeal the law "deep in one of the budget bills" that he proposed. When the reversal became public, the governor's office quickly backed off, but the outcome still is in doubt and the website still does not exist (Cooper, 1996).

Recently, a third system has emerged—when regulators actually do try to regulate the industries they oversee, corporations go "over their heads" to legislators. On three different occasions during the 1990s, the Financial Accounting Standards Board (FASB, the private-sector agency that establishes accounting principles for the U.S. industry), in conjunction with the SEC, attempted to tighten regulations on corporate practices. On all three issues—stockholder rights to sue in cases of fraud (1991), the expensing of stock options (1994), and limiting consulting contracts by auditors (2000)— Congressional threats to reduce the power or funding of regulatory agencies led them to pull back (A. Levitt, 2002). So common are these processes that "regulatory capture" has become a taken-for-granted element of modern American political science (for examples, see Breyer, 1984; Gerety, 1984; Kuttner, 1996; Ritti & Silver, 1986; Wilson, 1974).

Policy Monopolies Go Global

The dominating role that the alliance between the U.S. government and U.S.-based MNCs plays in the global economy and in the nongovernmental organizations that control it is widely recognized (see, e.g., almost anything written by George Soros or George Stiglitz during the past decade). Although this is not a new development—the United States has been able to appoint directors of the World Bank and has had a bloc vote large enough to veto any International Monetary Fund policy initiative since the inception of those organizations—it has become increasingly important with the globalization of capital markets and the advent of regional trade agreements (Greider, 1997; Mann, 2003). Not only is the United States positioned to negotiate favorable terms during treaty formation, but also its recent history is one of selective, and strategic, compliance with such treaties. As analyses of globalization generally acknowledge, these developments have significantly eroded the national sovereignty of developing and even developed countries.

As important for our purposes, globalization creates new venues through which the executives of MNCs can move strategically. For example, since the inception of the NAFTA treaty, the Canadian softwood industry has been trying to force the United States to abide by its relevant terms. After losing multiple cases before the court established as part of the trade agreement, the U.S. Department of Commerce, on the behest of U.S. manufacturers, sought a ruling by the World Trade Organization—the only such effort that led to a pro-U.S. decision. After finding that the NAFTA decisions would take precedence, the industry moved to another venue, the U.S. courts, and sued

to force changes in the agreement itself and in the makeup of the NAFTA court. As the maneuvering continues, illegal U.S. duties stay in place, duties that have cost Canadian producers more than CDN$5 billion ("U.S. Lumber Industry," 2006).[16] Multinational corporations have the advantage of being able to act in all venues simultaneously, that is, to employ "synchronous communication at will" (Peterson & Norton, chapter 24), or to focus their resources on the optimal venue at a given point in time/place. CSR/SD advocacy groups simply do not have the resources and network connections that are needed to employ cunning in this way.

CONCLUSION

One of the most important, complex, and controversial topics in contemporary social and organizational theory involves the relationship between dominance and resistance. A number of analytical frameworks have suggested that power-resistance relationships are multidimensional, composed of interrelated processes that are separated by time, space, and venue. Each of these frameworks notes that, while power holders have an advantage because they are able to define the contexts within which relationships are negotiated, low-power actors can resist—and sometimes even alter the structural and ideological constraints/enablements they face—through "cunning." Social structures/ideologies are replete with fissures and contradictions, interstitial places through which potential resisters can move tactically and symbolically.

In this chapter, we suggest that the advantages available to elites are even more extensive than these models suggest. Like nonelites, they, too, can move tactically, as well as strategically. The key to their doing so is the process of making public policy. Using the United States as a case study, we argue that corporate elites can move quietly and rapidly through the fragmented public policy-making network (Offe, 1996; Swan, 2002), focusing their resources and activities on the optimal locale (local, state, federal, or international), the optimal level (electing friendly politicians; influencing the "hidden cluster" of career policy makers, the public policy agenda, and the public agenda), and the optimal time (long-term policy development, overt policy making, policy implementation, and regulation). Armed with superior financial, and usually technical, resources, corporate elites can act tactically within existing structures/ideologies while simultaneously acting strategically to revise those guidelines/constraints in preferred directions. As Schwarze (2003) points out, the "most egregious examples of corporate irresponsibility are best interpreted as situations coproduced by corporations and the state" (p. 628, as cited in Kendall et al., chapter 17).[17] What more could the proverbial English gentleman want?

Limitations, And Directions

Like all of the contributors to this volume, we celebrate those examples of successful moves toward increased CSR/SD, congratulate the thousands of people who worked tirelessly to achieve those victories, and hope that the "European dream" really is the key to the present and the wave of the future. But, like many contributors, we also are concerned that, in celebrating successful voluntary efforts, we may excessively deemphasize the structural and ideological advantages that MNCs and their executives have in undermining CSR/SD. Like a few, we are concerned about the possible appropriation of CSR/SD discourse by its opponents. Robert Kuttner (1996) observes that the triumph of free market fundamentalism in the United States resulted only in part from neoliberal rhetors' persuasive skills and structural advantages. Equally important was their opponents' inadvertent legitimation of the assumptions on which their rhetoric was based—their tendency to assume the primacy of communitarian values without articulating a case for them, accepting the assertion that individualism and communitarianism are mutually exclusive, accepting a dichotomy between efficiency and equality (instead of affirming their interconnectedness), and implicitly accepting the notion that a libertarian "free market" and a state-controlled economy are the only options available to capitalist societies. As Ganesh (chapter 26) and Stohl et al. (chapter 2) point out, the discourse of CSR/SD can readily be exploited to justify neoliberal ideology or undermine solidarity among dissenting groups.

We also believe that a comprehensive understanding of the CSR/SD debate must focus on corporate colonization of public policy-making processes. We have focused on the United States simply because we have no expertise on similar processes in other societies. Our hope is that, by describing corporate influence on public policy, we will encourage scholars in other counties to conduct systematic analyses of those relationships in their political systems. It is only through multiple, society-specific analyses of corporation–state alliances—the kind of research that Morsing et al. report in chapter 6—that we can fully understand existing barriers to CSR/SD, or identify the tensions, contradictions, and fissures through which resistance to can be most successful. The executives of MNCs are positioned to both understand policy-making processes in all of the countries in which their organizations operate, and to strategically move among those venues. Unless scholars work together to understand the corporatization of policy making in their countries, and the complex interrelationships that exist across national boundaries, advocates of CSR/SD will always be "playing catchup."

NOTES

1. As Wells (2002) has shown, even one of the most influential defenders of *voluntary* social responsibility, E. Merrick Dodd, shifted from celebrating "welfare capitalism" in the Unites States as compelling evidence that voluntary action by civic-minded executives was sufficient, to the conclusion that "only government action . . . could impose on corporate management the responsibilities he believed they owed [society]" (Wells, 2002, p. 15). Drawing on Max Weber's concept of "booty capitalism," Michael Mann (1993, esp. chap. 3) notes that the impact of government–MNC alliances has been easiest to observe in the "extractive industries." For a contemporary assessment, see the *New York Times* series on the gold industry (Perlez & Bergman, 2005; Perlez & Bonner, 2005; Perlez & Johnson, 2005; Leith, 2002).

2. We realize that many Canadians will take issue with our decision to include them in this group, but on a wide variety of issues, particular those related to neoliberal economics, "a conservative party government is expected to be more in line with Bush administration policies" (Duff-Brown, 2006). Or, as National Democratic Party Leader Jack Layton was wont to remind Canadians during the recent election campaign, when Canada's two conservative parties merged at the beginning of the new century, they became more powerful, *and* dropped the word "progressive" from their name. The most recent evidence of increasing neoliberal influence over nongovernmental organizations is Paul Wolfowitz's decision to replace career employees of the World Bank with appointees with close ties to the Bush administration—Robin Cleveland, Kevin Kellems, and

Suzanne Rich Folsom—or who have supported key Bush policies (e.g., Ana Palacio, who was Spain's foreign minister when that country chose to contribute troops to the invasion and occupation of Iraq [Blustein, 2006]).

3. We define the term "technology" in its broadest possible sense, including organizational structures, modes of operating, and practices, as well as the narrower, more common definition. We also will use the terms "executive" and "executivism" where most writers would use the term "manager" and "managerialism" because it is a more precise term. The issue is not "managerial" power or "managerial privilege" but rather the power and privilege of the occupants of executive suites —the Enron debacle had nothing to do with the actions, attitudes, or power of the manager of its shipping division, but everything to do with the occupants of the executive suite(s).

4. Corporation-friendly politicians strengthen the rhetorical power of the evidence created by think tanks by silencing dissenting voices.

5. Mann (1986) defines classes in terms of economic power, not wealth or income, "that is, in persons' ability to control their own and others' life chances through control of economic resources —the means of production, distribution, and exchange" (p. 216).

6. As far as we know, neither Mann nor de Certeau (1984) takes this position explicitly. In fact, Mann (1993) subsequently abandons the concept of "circuits of praxis," although Clegg (1989) expanded and refined it in his model of "circuits of power." We believe our extension is consistent with their overall arguments, but it is our extension of them.

7. Breen (chapter 20), Waddock (chapter 5), and Stohl et al. (chapter 2) provide contemporary instances of MNCs searching for, and manipulating, weaker governments.

8. In many cases the policies resulted from blatant power politics. For example, Chief Justice John Marshall carefully delayed hearing the *Dartmouth* case until the court had a pro-corporation majority. In a related action, Henry Clay, faced with a populist Kentucky House of Representatives that was ready to close down the Bank of Lexington (in which Clay held stock and served as legal counsel), threatened to have the state Senate immediately foreclose on all state-backed loans to small farmers (Perrow, 2002, pp. 46–47). Kentucky Progressives capitulated.

9. As John Kenneth Galbraith (1997) points out, only a minority of Americans owned stock during the 1920s. However, it was not the number of people who owned stock that was important, it was "the way it became central to the culture" (p. 83).

10. For a similar critique of the current CSR movement, see Crook (2005).

11. During the 1950s and early 1960s, pro-corporate academics included A. A. Berle, Peter Drucker, Eugene Rostow, and David Rockefeller; critics included Galbraith, C. Wright Mills, and Robert Heilbroner.

12. This process also suggests that the argument offered by opponents of campaign finance reform that money "only buys access, not votes" is misleading. It is because elites have greater access to policy makers than do nonelites that they are able to dominate private and quasi-private policy-making processes.

13. Political scientists have studied policy monopolies in a variety of settings and have used a number of different terms to describe them—*iron triangles*, *policy whirlpools*, and *subsystem politics* are the most common. The classic study of health care policy-making triangles is Starr (1982, 1994).

14. Ironically, these justifications typically focus on the rationality of privatizing public policy making—to minimize distractions, ensure the availability of unbiased and complete information from policy experts (e.g., the Bush II administration's defense of its energy policy taskforce, and the Clinton administration's defense of its health policy group), allow decision makers to thoroughly discuss complex policy issues, or protect "national security" (e.g., Halliburton's Iraq contracts).

15. Of course, organizations may want to initiate new policies as well as block policy initiatives. For example, there was substantial corporate support for President Bush's tax reform package during 2001. But large corporations were so successful in enacting desired policies from 1975 through 2001 (Greider, 1992; Kuttner, 1996; Phillips, 2002) that their primary concern today is with blocking policy.

16. Canada's new conservative government has settled the dispute, allowing the U.S. to retain USD $1 billion of the disputed funds. For an analysis of the impact of NAFTA on the Canadian pharmaceutical policy, see Fuller (1998); on the Mexican concrete industry, see Hensel (2006); and on the Argentine honey industry, see Mann (2003).

17. For modern examples, see Livesey and Graham's (chapter 23) analysis of Shell's operations in Nigeria, Stohl et al.'s (chapter 2) analysis of Enron's non-U.S. operations, and Breen's (chapter 20) summary of MNC–government complicity against the interests of aboriginal peoples in Mexico, Australia, and New Guinea.

REFERENCES

Alvesson, M., & Karreman, D. (2000). Varieties of discourse: On the study of organizations through discourse analysis. *Human Relations, 53,* 1125–1149.

Arno, P., & Davis, M. (2001). Why don't we enforce existing drug price controls? *Tulane Law Review, 75,* 631–700.

Arno, P., & Davis, M. (2002, April 17). Why don't we enforce existing drug price controls? *Houston Chronicle,* p. 27A.

Atwill, J. (1998). *Rhetoric reclaimed.* Ithaca, NY: Cornell University Press.

Aune, J. (1994). *Rhetoric and marxism.* Boulder, CO: Westview Press.

Aune, J. (2001). *Selling the free market.* New York: Guilford Press.

Bakan, J. (2004). *The corporation.* Boston, MA: Free Press.

Ballif, M. (1998). Writing the third-sophistic cyborg. *Rhetoric Society Quarterly, 28,* 51–74.

Baumgartner, F., & Jones, B. (1993). *Agendas and instability in American politics.* Chicago: University of Chicago Press.

Beauchamp, D. (1996). *Health care reform and the battle for the body politic.* Philadelphia, PA: Temple University Press.

Berliner, D. (2003). *Public power, private gain.* Washington, DC: Institute for Justice.

Berliner, D. (2005, October 7). When push came to shove, legislature let Texas down. *Houston Chronicle,* p. 19A.

Blustein, P. (2006, February 9). World bank staff worries surface. *Houston Chronicle,* p. D3.

Boyle, L. (2002, May 14). Insurers, heal latest malpractice "crisis" thyselves. *Houston Chronicle,* p. 23A.

Breyer, S. (1984). *Regulation and its reform.* Cambridge, MA: Harvard University Press.

Broder, J. M. (2006, January 24). Amid scandals, states overhaul lobbying laws. *New York Times on the Web.* Retrieved on January 24, 2006, from www.nytimes.com.

Bronfenbrenner, M. (1974). The consumer. In J. McKie (Ed.), *Social responsibility and the business predicament* (pp. 169–190). Washington, DC: Brookings Institution.

Bumiller, E. (2002, August 1). Bush criticized by lawmakers on corporate governance. *New York Times on the Web.* Retrieved on August 1, 2002, from www.nytimes.com.

Chen, C., & Meindl, J. (1991). The construction of leadership images in the popular press. *Administrative Science Quarterly, 36,* 521–551.

Cheney, G. (1999). *Values at work.* Ithaca, NY: Cornell University Press.

Cheney, G., & Brancato, J. (1993). *The rhetoric of scientific management.* Unpublished manuscript, University of Colorado at Boulder.

Cheney, G., Christiansen, L., Conrad, C., & Lair, D. (2004). Organizational rhetoric as organizational discourse. In D. Grant, C. Hardy, C. Oswick, & L. Putnam (Eds.), *The handbook of organizational discourse* (pp. 79–104) Thousand Oaks, CA: Sage.

Clegg, S. (1989). *Frameworks of power.* Newbury Park, CA: Sage.

Cobb, R. W., & Ross, M. H. (Eds.). (1997). *Cultural strategies of agenda denial.* Lawrence: Kansas University Press.

Cohen, A. (2002, February 11). Making political sense of the committees making political sense of Enron. *New York Times on the Web.* Retrieved on February 11, 2002, from www.nytimes.com.

Conrad, C. (2003a). Setting the stage. *Management Communication Quarterly, 17,* 5–19.

Conrad, C. (2003b). Stemming the tide. *Organization, 10,* 549–560.

Conrad, C. (2004a). The illusion of reform. *Rhetoric & Public Affairs, 7,* 311–338.

Conrad, C. (2004b). Organizational discourse analysis: Avoiding the determinism-voluntarism trap. *Organization, 11,* 427–439.

Conrad, C., & Millay, B. (2000). Confronting free market romanticism: Health care reform in the least likely place. *Journal of Applied Communication Research, 29,* 153–170.

Cook, L. (2006, January 22). Exxon profits hit record $36 billion. *Houston Chronicle,* p. 1A.

Cooper, M. (2006, January 20). New prescription pricing law faces repeal in Pataki budget. *New York Times on the Web.* Retrieved January 20, 2006, from www.nytimes.com.

Crook, C. (2005, January 2). The good company. *Economist, 37,* 41–31.

Dash, E. (2006, January 27). Savings accounts for health costs attract Wall Street. *New York Times on the Web.* Retrieved on January 27, 2006, from www.nytimes.com.

de Certeau, M. (1984). *The practice of everyday life.* Berkeley: University of California Press.

Deetz, S. (1992). *Democracy in an age of corporate colonization.* Albany, NY: State University of New York Press.

De Parle, J. (1994, May 9). Casinos become big players in the overhaul of welfare. *New York Times,* pp. A1, A9.

Detienne, M., & Vernant, J.-P. (1978). *Cunning intelligence in Greek culture and society* (J. Lloyd, Trans.). Sussex, UK: Harvester Press.

Duff-Brown, B. (2006, January 19). Conservatives pick up steam as Canadian elections near. *Houston Chronicle,* p. A18.

Elliott, A. L., & Schroth, R J. (2002). *How companies lie.* New York: Crown Business Books.

Flake, J. (2006, February 9). Earmarked men. *New York Times on the Web.* Retrieved on February 9, 2006, from www.nytimes.com.

Fulcrum Financial Inquiry. (2005, March). *SOX whistleblower claims have been resolved in employers' favor . . . but this may change.* Retrieved on February 2, 2006, from fulcrumfinancial.com.

Fuller, C. (1998). *Caring for profit.* Vancouver: New Star Books.

Galbraith, J. K. (1997). *The great crash of 1929.* New York: Mariner Books.

Garver, E. (1994). *Aristotle's rhetoric.* Chicago: University of Chicago Press.

Gerety, T. (1984). Why good lawyers make bad Marxists. In J. R. Pennock & J. W. Chapman (Eds.), *Marxism* (pp. 116–138). New York: New York University Press.

Gormley, M. (2006, January 22). Bid to cut pollution reports criticized. *Houston Chronicle,* p. A6.

Greider, W. (1992). *Who will tell the people?* New York: Simon & Schuster.

Greider, W. (1997). *One world, ready or not.* New York: Simon & Shuster.

Habermas, J. (1975). *Legitimation crisis.* Boston, MA: Beacon Press.

Hacker, J. (1997). *The road to nowhere: The genesis of President Clinton's plan for health security.* Princeton, NJ: Princeton University Press.

Hall, B., & Jones, B. (1997). Agenda denial and issue containment in the regulation of financial securities. In R. W. Cobb & M. H. Ross (Eds.), *Cultural strategies of agenda denial* (pp. 40–69). Lawrence: Kansas University Press.

Harkey, J. (1997). Agenda denial and the Clinton Plan. In R. W. Cobb & M. H. Ross (Eds.), *Cultural strategies of agenda denial* (pp. 1124–167). Lawrence: Kansas University Press.

Held, D. (1996). *Models of democracy.* Stanford, CA: Stanford University Press.

Henry, J. (2002, April 12). Pension security measure ok'd out of Enron's ashes. *New York Times on the Web.* Retrieved on April 12, 2002, from www.nytimes.com.

Hensel, B., Jr. (2006, January 20). Move may end cement battle. *Houston Chronicle,* pp. D1, D4.

Hill, F. (1983). The rhetoric of Aristotle. In J. J. Murphy (Ed.), *A synoptic history of classical rhetoric* (pp. 19–76). Davis, CA: Hermagoras Press.

Hilts, P. J. (1994, May 7). Tobacco company was silent on hazards. *New York Times,* pp. A1, A11.

Hirschman, A. (1991). *The rhetoric of reaction.* Cambridge, MA: Belknap Press.

Horowitz, M. (1992). *The transformation of American law, 1870–1960.* New York: Oxford University Press.

Ibarra, P. R., & Kitsuse, J. I. (1993). Vernacular constituents of moral discourse. In G. Miller & J. A. Holstein (Eds.), *Constructionist controversies* (pp. 113–146). New York: Aldine de Gruyter.

Iyengar, S. (1991). *Is anyone responsible?* Chicago: University of Chicago Press.

Jarrett, S. (1991). *Rereading the Sophists.* Carbondale, IL: Southern Illinois Press.

Johnson, C. (2004). *Blowback.* New York: Henry Holt & Company.

Johnston, D. C. (2002, July 17). Bill closing Bermuda loophole also includes tax breaks. *New York Times on the Web.* Retrieved on July 17, 2002, from www.nytimes.com.

Kain, J. (1974). Urban problems. In J. McKie (Ed.), *Social responsibility and the business predicament* (pp. 217–246). Washington, DC: Brookings Institution.

Kingdon, J. (1995). *Agendas, alternatives and public policies.* Boston, MA: Little Brown.

Kriebel, K. (1991). *Information and legislative organization.* Ann Arbor: University of Michigan Press.

Krugman, P. (2002a, May 21). Enemies of reform. *New York Times on the Web.* Retrieved on May 21, 2002, from www.nytimes.com.

Krugman, P. (2002b, July 2). Everyone is outraged. *New York Times,* p. A21, col. 16.

Kuhrana, R. (2002). *Searching for a corporate savior.* Princeton, NJ: Princeton University Press.

Kuttner, R. (1996). *Everything for sale.* New York: Alfred Knopf.

Leith, D. (2002). *The politics of power.* Manoa: University of Hawaii Press.

Levine, S. (2006, 19 January). Texas lawmakers are mixed about reforms. *Houston Chronicle,* p. A9.

Levitt, A. (2002, June 30). Interview. *Frontline.* Retrieved July 1, 2002, from http://www.pbs.org/wgbh/page . . . e/shows/regulation/interviews/levitt.html.

Levitt, T. (1958, September–October). The dangers of social responsibility. *Harvard Business Review, 66,* 40–48.

Machiz, M. (2002, March 6). Bush's remedies to Enron are beside the point. *Houston Chronicle,* p. 31A.

Mahon, J. F., & McGowan, R. A. (1997). Making professional accounting accountable. In R. W. Cobb & M. H. Ross (Eds.), *Cultural strategies of agenda denial* (pp. 70–85). Lawrence: Kansas University Press.

Marmor, T. (2000). *The politics of medicare* (2nd ed.). New York: Aldine de Gruyter.

Mann, M. (1986). *The sources of social power*, Vol. 1. Cambridge: Cambridge University Press.

Mann, M. (1993). *The sources of social power*, Vol. 2. New York: Cambridge University Press.

Mann, M. (2003). *Incoherent empire*. London: Verso.

McKie, J. (1974a). Changing views. In J. McKie (Ed.), *Social responsibility and the business predicament* (pp. 17–41). Washington, DC: Brookings Institution.

McKie, J. (1974b). The issues. In J. McKie (Ed.), *Social responsibility and the business predicament* (pp. 1–16). Washington, DC: Brookings Institution.

Mooney, C. (2005). *The Republican war on science*. New York: Basic Books.

Murphy, J. (2002). Cunning, rhetoric, and the presidency of William Jefferson Clinton. In L. Dorsey (Ed.), *The presidency and rhetorical leadership* (pp. 231–251.). College Station, TX: Texas A&M University Press.

Neel, J. (1988). *Plato, Derrida, and writing*. Carbondale, IL: Southern Illinois University Press.

Nichols, J. (2002, July 15). Bernie Sanders: It's about a lot more than accounting. *Nation Online*. Retrieved on July 16, 2002, from www.thenation.com.

Norris, F. (2005a, August 12). Inept boards need have no fear. *New York Times on the Web*. Retrieved on August 12, 2005, from www.nytimes.com.

Norris, F. (2005b, December 15). Moves at S.E.C. to loosen rules on many companies. *New York Times on the Web*. Retrieved on December 15, 2005, from www.nytimes.com.

Offe, C. (1996). *Modernity and the state: East, West*. Cambridge, MA: MIT Press.

Oppel, R. (2002a, April 25). G.O.P. bill on auditing clears House. *New York Times on the Web*. Retrived on April 25, 2002, from www.nytimes.com.

Oppel, R. (2002b, July 14). A point man on corporate change. *New York Times on the Web*. Retrieved on July 14, 2002, from www.nytimes.com.

Ostas, D. (2001). Deconstructing corporate social responsibility. *American Business Law Journal, 38*, 261–299.

Perlez, J., & Bonner, R. (2005, December 27). Below a mountain of wealth, a river of waste. *New York Times on the Web*. Retrieved on December 27, 2005, from www.nytimes.com.

Perlez, J., & Johnson, K. (2005, October 24). Behind gold's glitter: Torn lands and pointed questions. *New York Times on the Web*. Retrieved on October 25, 2005, from www.nytimes.com.

Perlez, J., & Bergman, L. (2005, October 25). Tangled strands in fight over Peru gold mine. *New York Times on the Web*. Retrieved on October 25, 2005, from www.nytimes.com.

Perrow, C. (2002). *Organizing America*. Princeton, NJ: Princeton University Press.

Phillips, K. (2002). *Wealth and democracy*. New York: Broadway Books.

Poulokas, J. (1995). *Sophistical rhetoric in classical Greece*. Columbia, SC: University of California Press.

Putnam, L. L., & Peterson, T. R. (2003). The Edwards Aquifer dispute. In R. Lewicki, B. Gray, & M. Elliott (Eds.), *Making sense of intractable environmental conflicts* (pp. 107–142). Washington, DC: Island Press.

Redford, E. S. (1969). *Democracy in the administrative state*. New York: Oxford University Press.

Reformers all. (2002, February 2). *New York Times on the Web*. Retrieved on February 2, 2002, from www.nytimes.com.

Rich, A. (2004). *Think tanks, public policy, and the politics of expertise*. New York: Cambridge University Press.

Rifkin, J. (2004). *The European dream*. New York: Penguin.

Riker, W. H. (1980). Implications from the disequilibrium of majority rule for the study of institutions. *American Political Science Review, 74*, 432–46.

Riker, W. H. (1982). *Liberalism against populism*. Prospect Heights, IL: Waveland Press.

Ritti, R. R., & Silver. J. A. (1986). Early processes of institutionalization. *Administrative Science Quarterly, 31*, 25–42.

Roth, B. (2006, February 3). Reformers taking aim at shadowy earmarks. *Houston Chronicle*, pp. A1, A10.

Rothenberg, J. (1974). The physical environment. In J. McKie (Ed.), *Social responsibility and the business predicament* (pp. 191–216). Washington, DC: Brookings Institution.

Roy, W. (1997). *Socializing capital*. Princeton, NJ: Princeton University Press.

Saul, S. (2006, January 21). In the newest war of the states, forget red and blue. *New York Times on the Web*. Retrieved on January 21, 2006, from www.nytimes.com.

Schattschneider, E. E. (1960). *The semi-sovereign people*. Hinsdale, IL: Dryden Press.

Schelling, T. (1974). Command and control. In J. McKie (Ed.), *Social responsibility and the business predicament* (pp. 79–108). Washington, DC: Brookings Institution.

Seeger, M., & Ulmer, R. (2002). A post-crisis discourse of renewal. *Journal of Applied Communication Research, 30*, 126–142.

Seligman, J. (2003). *The transformation of Wall Street* (3rd ed.). New York: Aspen Publishers.

Skocpol, T. (1996). *Boomerang*. New York: W.W. Norton.

Soros, G. (1998). *The crisis of global capitalism*. New York: Public Affairs Press.

Starr, P. (1982). *The social transformation of American medicine*. New York: Basic Books.

Starr, P. (1994). *The logic of health care reform*. New York: Penguin.

Stone, D. (1988). *Policy paradox* (2nd ed.) New York: W.W. Norton.

Swan, P. (2002). Governing at a distance. In M. MacNeil, N. Sargent, & P. Swans (Eds.), *Law, regulation, and governance* (pp. 1–27). Don Mills, Ontario: Oxford University Press.

U.S. lumber industry challenging free-trade dispute process. (2006, January 18). Retrieved January 18, 2006, from www.canada.com.

Vibbert, S., & Bostdorff, D. (1993). Issue management and the "lawsuit crisis." In C. Conrad (Ed.), *The ethical nexus* (pp. 103–120). Norwood, NJ: Ablex.

Vogel, D. (1989). *Fluctuating fortunes*. New York: Basic Books.

Walker, J. (2000). *Rhetoric and poetics in antiquity*. New York: Oxford University Press.

Wayne, L. (2002, July 20). Tighter rules for options fall victim to lobbying. *New York Times on the Web*. Retrieved on July 20, 2002, from www.nytimes.com.

Wells, C. A. H. (2002). The cycles of corporate social responsibility. *Kansas Law Review, 51*, n.p.

Wilson, J. Q. (1973). *Political organizations*. New York: Basic Books.

Wilson, J. Q. (1974). The politics of regulation. In J. McKie (Ed.), *Social responsibility and the business predicament* (pp. 135–168). Washington, DC: Brookings Institution.

Zarembo, A. (2003, December 7). Controversy spills from Exxon-funded jury research. *Houston Chronicle*, p. 47A.

30

The Case of the Subaltern Public

A Postcolonial Investigation of Corporate Social Responsibility's (O)Missions

DEBASHISH MUNSHI

PRIYA KURIAN

Corporate social responsibility (CSR) has been, for the most part, a catch-all term that businesses use to trumpet concepts as wide ranging as ethical governance, sustainable development, environmental sensitivities, and profit generation with a conscience. Yet, the theory and practice of the term fall far short of its professed goals of equity and justice because of its glaring omissions: "corporate" overlooks the many proxies of corporations, including states and financial institutions; "social" ignores the political, including issues of gender and diversity; and "responsibility" glosses over accountability.

More significantly, what is missing in the discourse on CSR is the voice of the subaltern—described by Gramsci (1988) as a group that is deliberately marginalized by the hegemony of the ruling elite and elitist texts. Despite CSR's feel-good rhetoric, it does not adequately represent what postcolonial scholars call the "Other"—people "who lie outside the influential inner circle of power" (Munshi, 2005, p. 60).

Our study on the use of CSR in the theory and practice of public relations (see Munshi & Kurian, 2005) makes the point that corporate image is managed through processes that have a distinct hierarchy of publics ranging from Western shareholders and global consumers at the top to Western activists somewhere in the middle, First World workers and Third World workers below them, and finally, the nonconsumer citizens of the Third

World at the bottom of the heap. The nonconsumer citizens together constitute the subaltern "Other," although clearly power differentials mark even this large and heterogeneous group.

Drawing on postcolonial approaches that endeavor to learn from "insurgent knowledges that come from the subaltern, the dispossessed, and seek to change the terms and values under which we all live" (Young, 2003, p. 20), we find the CSR discourse to be elitist—self-serving at its worst when it feeds into marketing campaigns, and limiting even when it embarks on a mission "to save the planet/natives" without compromising in any way on its profit orientation. For example, BP's campaign to rebrand itself in a more "enviro-friendly" way by adopting the slogan "Beyond Petroleum" can be read primarily as a marketing tool to give it an edge over its competitors. The rebranding campaign was, as a case study by Michael Fox of Ogilvy Public Relations (in Lattimore, Baskin, Heiman, Toth, & van Leuven, 2004) reveals, "targeted at, in order, BP employees, its business partners, and opinion leaders" (p. 365). Even when seemingly well intentioned, attempts at "social responsibility" could smack of simple-minded paternalism. When "cereal king" Dick Hubbard, owner of New Zealand–based Hubbard Foods Ltd., took his workers to a free holiday in Samoa to celebrate the company's 10th anniversary in 1998, he believed it was CSR. But given that the decision precluded consultation with the workers to decide whether such a holiday was, in fact, the most appropriate reward for them, it could be seen by some as a paternalistic step (Walker & Monin, 2001).

Our critique is not meant to dismiss CSR either as a theoretical concept or as a practical tool, for it has indeed reshaped some businesses and pushed them toward more ethical and sustainable practices. Rather, our critique aims to add a new dimension to the robust theorizing of CSR in this volume by looking at CSR through the eyes of subaltern publics. This is important because most authors in this volume (with a few exceptions, notably Stohl, Stohl, & Townsley, chapter 2) tend to focus on corporate functioning in the context of elite publics, be they stakeholders in the West or activist groups everywhere, including in the Third World. Little attention is paid to perspectives of those in the margins who do not have either the purchasing power or the lobbying clout of elite publics. The subaltern studies project led by Guha and Spivak (1988), among others, gives ordinary people a chance to "speak within the jealous pages of elitist historiography and, in doing so, to speak for, or to sound the muted voices of, the truly oppressed" (Gandhi, 1998, p. 2). By providing a "subaltern lens" to view CSR, we hope to identify some of the omissions in the discourses of CSR that consolidate the privileging of certain powerful publics and the marginalization of others.

CORPORATE PROXIES

The underplaying of the nexus between powerful corporations and states in much of the CSR discourse is the first omission we examine. While discussions on CSR tend to concentrate on the activities of corporations, there is no doubt that "some of the most egregious examples of corporate irresponsibility are best interpreted as situations produced by corporations and the state" (Schwarze, 2003, p. 627). Tsing (2005) points out how in the context of the "militarization of the Third World and the growing power of corporate transnationalism . . . entrepreneurs and armies were able to disengage nature from local ecologies and livelihoods, 'freeing up' natural resources that bureaucrats and generals could offer as raw materials" (p. 28). Big businesses, thus, invariably team up with the state to get their profit-generating machines to grind along.

It is this logic of capitalics—a politics fueled by global capital (Munshi & Kurian, 2005)—that also allows corporations to seduce or coerce Third World states to loosen or ignore their environmental and social regulations either through the allure of big bucks for foreign direct investment or through "their structural power and threat of relocation" (Clapp, 2005, p. 24). Cash-starved states then bend over backward to appease multinational corporations by granting them precious resources such as land, water, and power. A chain reaction sets in where states not only forfeit their obligation to provide basic needs to their citizens but also turn violent if citizens come in the way of their objectives, as was evident in the struggles over water privatization efforts in Bolivia, for example. When the residents of the Bolivian city of Cochabamba rose in protest in 2000 against the high cost of privatized water levied by Aguas del Tunari, a subsidiary of the transnational corporation Bechtel, the government sided with the company and unleashed terror on its citizens (Shultz, 2005). It was only in the face of sustained public protests and rebellion that the government was forced to cancel the contract (Olivera, 2004).

Although the insidious corporate–state nexus is evident in both developed and developing nations, the implications and repercussions of such a nexus are often experienced differently by the publics/citizens of the First World and the Third World. In most cases, the worst impacts are reserved for Third World subaltern publics—whether it is the thousands of slum dwellers who died in one of the world's worst industrial disasters at the Union Carbide plant in Bhopal, India (Munshi & McKie, 2001), or the many indigenous peoples, for example, the Ogoni in Nigeria (Rowell, 1996), the Brazilian Kayapo (Turner, 1999), or the Meratus Dayaks of Indonesia (Tsing, 1993, 2005)—who are at the receiving end of environmental havoc and social upheaval caused by explorations for oil, timber, and minerals on their lands.

Trade in toxic waste is yet another area that illuminates the nexus among First World states and transnational corporations, on the one hand, which have increasing amounts of wastes to be disposed of, and Third World states, on the other hand, that seemingly have the facilities to treat the wastes. In February 2006, the French Navy's decommissioned aircraft carrier *Le Clemenceau*, destined for Alang in India, Asia's largest maritime graveyard, was ordered back to France after protests and a court challenge by environmentalists, who argued that Alang had no facilities to deal with the asbestos-riddled ship. For Alang workers, however, the ship-breaking contract represented a chance of at least short-term economic security (McDougall, 2006; see also Langewiesche, 2000). This episode is but the latest in a longer saga of the French efforts to get rid of the *Clemenceau*. In 2003, the ship was returned to France after a company breached its contract to dismantle it in Spain and towed it instead to Turkey (Bremner, 2006).

More than anything else, the tussle over *Le Clemenceau* illustrates the limits of the Basel Convention on Control of Transboundary Movement of Hazardous Wastes and Their Disposal (1989). The French decision to recall the ship came after France's highest court was advised by its judicial adviser that the "stripped-down vessel" was to be considered "waste, rather than as a warship" and hence subject to the Basel Convention (Bremner, 2006). Yet the fact that the ship nearly made it to the shores of India shows that its recall by France had less to do with the effectiveness of the Basel Convention than with the outcry raised by Greenpeace and other environmental activists (see Greenpeace, 2006).

The reality is that despite attempts to ban the trade in toxic wastes, a "brown realism" (Narain, 2006) prevails, whereby a new global system using the poor as "the shield of the rich" now functions. This global system has as its protagonists First World and select Third World states and the corporations that buy the toxic wastes, all of which profit from the labor of the marginalized workers, many of them casual, for whom toxic wastes serve as a means to survival. For these subaltern publics to be *meaningfully* heard, states with some measure of real autonomy (and thus able to resist the powerful clout of the transnational corporations) would need to be brought into the discussion of CSR. As Ritz (chapter 13) argues, democratic governments "should distribute rather than consolidate power" and have "a responsibility to prevent concentrations of private power from overwhelming public power. . . ."

Another key element of the dominant coalition of the capitalics system is the powerful financial sector. The capitalics system tends to see the free market as its pivot and yet it thrives on the "rules of the game" set by international economic institutions such as the International Monetary Fund,

World Bank, and World Trade Organization, which serve the interests of privileged publics "in more advanced industrialized countries—and particular interests within those countries—rather than those of the developing world" (Stiglitz, 2002, p. 214). Aiding the international economic institutions are private-sector financial powerhouses, including transnational banks and accounting firms. A well-documented dossier of seven case studies put together by the Corporate Responsibility Coalition (2005) highlights the ways in which the finance sector

> provides a haven to siphon off much-needed tax revenues from cash-strapped developing countries . . . ; is a primary conduit for bribery and corruption . . . ; regularly undermines human rights protection by financing projects which pose a threat to the implementation of human rights laws in developing countries, in breach of some companies' own codes of conduct; often fails to assess adequately the environmental impacts of projects and to address issues raised before releasing project finance, yet continues to reap the reputational benefits of participation in voluntary CSR initiatives. (p. 1)

That financial institutions continue to reap such "reputational benefits" (Corporate Responsibility Coalition, 2005) despite their actions points to the hierarchies of publics they have in their scheme of things. The publics that matter are the shareholders in the developed world. As a United Nations Conference on Trade and Development (UNCTAD) press release of October 14, 2005 (cited in the report by the Corporate Responsibility Coalition, 2005), reveals: "In fact, profits from the extraction of oil or iron ore or bauxite were frequently spirited out of developing countries and back to corporations in the industrialised north."

For these institutions, the subaltern publics, who bear the social, political, economic, and ecological brunt of the projects managed by corporations with the blessings of obsequious states, do not count. For example, Amnesty International (2005) voiced its concern about the potential threat to the human rights of such subaltern publics in two countries of Central Africa—Chad and Cameroon—where a consortium of transnationals such as ExxonMobil, Chevron, and Petronas were extracting oil in projects agreed to by governments, the World Bank, and financial institutions. Amnesty International's (2005) concern is that "the project agreements could encourage the governments of Chad and Cameroon to ignore their human rights obligations, by claiming that the agreements prevent them from taking measures that would destabilise the financial equilibrium of the project."

Clearly, the nexus between corporations, states, and financial institutions constitutes a dominant coalition that undermines subaltern publics. While states have largely forfeited powers of economic governance to corporations and financial bodies, they do maintain direct political control over their citizens through instruments of force such as police and military structures (Jessop, 1994; Jones, 2003). As Jones (2003) speculates, we are probably in a situation where "the state is becoming the primary disciplinary mechanism for global capital" (p. 268) while shedding its social equity functions (see also McMillan, chapter 1). In such a situation, poor nonconsumer publics are forced to accept a world order that effectively excludes them. Such exclusions are already visible in many cities where key publics of the "techno-economy" live and work in secure, fortified spaces while the "downgraded members of the grunge economy" are not only kept apart socially and spatially but are also subject to intense police (read state) surveillance (Jones, 2003, p. 268). Deliberate and discriminatory exclusions in turn push those in the margins toward social unrest.

Given the intricate ways in which states, financial institutions, and corporations combine to further the politics of exclusion, CSR will remain vacuous unless processes are set in place that eliminate "corporate influence on political governance" (Ritz, chapter 13). Effective CSR should ensure that companies conduct their business in settings that allow states to fulfill their role of providing social, cultural, and political safety and sustenance to all their citizens.

POLITICAL REALITIES

The political angle brings us to the second omission in the CSR discourse. The limited way in which CSR discourse defines "social" responsibility disregards the political dimensions of the world of capitalics. The limited vision of "social," too, is designed to serve elite publics. Mirroring the civilizing mission of imperial regimes, CSR initiatives

of transnationals using Third World labor tend to focus on measures geared to assuage the guilt in consumers of the North who are appalled by the poor working conditions of workers, including children, in textile and carpet sweatshops. The silent subaltern publics remain in the margins as CSR ignores the political contexts of the less privileged South. The contradictions and complexities evident in such situations are captured by this question posed by Vogel (2005): "Is Union Oil acting responsibly by improving working conditions on its pipeline construction project in Burma or irresponsibly by continuing to do business in a country with a repressive military government?" (p. 5).

A similar contradiction is evident in the continued presence of countless small carpet factories in Mirzapur, Varanasi, and Bhadohi in northern India, notorious for their use of child labor, which flourish because of an ever-increasing demand for hand-made Indian carpets and rugs in the Western market. The example of companies that proudly showcase their CSR by proclaiming that they ensure that the rugs supplied to them are not made with child labor miss the political and economic imperatives of local contexts. While the use of children in factories and mills is abhorrent, abolition of such a practice can hardly be achieved by merely sourcing products from factories without children. In the context of India, for instance, many of the child workers come from economically and socially disadvantaged segments of the population such as the scheduled castes and tribes. Shutting them out of employment without a proper plan to rehabilitate and educate them would only push them and their families to the edge of despair. In fact, as Vogel (2005) argues, "some firms have undermined the welfare of poor families—and of poor children in particular—by attempting to prohibit child labor" (p. 5). A social worker of the British charity Oxfam told the *Economist* ("Human Rights," 1995) that thousands of child workers, who were sacked by textile factories in Bangladesh in the mid-1990s because of market pressures, ended up in far more reprehensible professions such as prostitution (also cited in Vogel, 2005). There are, in fact, meaningful alternatives to a sudden and outright ban on child labor. For instance, as voluntary organizations in India, such as Child Relief and You, have focused on, much more can be done to ensure that children have mandatory access to schooling, alongside the creation of humane working conditions. This would allow children to gain education critical to their future well-being while contributing to their own immediate survival and that of their families (for a discussion of ways to eliminate child labor, see also Bellamy, 1997).

Acknowledging such socioeconomic and political imperatives is essential for the creation of a sustainable society. Some scholars, including several in this volume, have argued that CSR and sustainable development are linked by their potential commitment to the broad goals of social and ecological sustainability (see, e.g., Bullis & Ie, chapter 22; Ganesh, chapter 26; Livesey & Graham, chapter 23; Peterson & Norton, chapter 24). In a sense, the assertion that "CSR is essential to achieving SD [sustainable development]" (Peterson & Norton, chapter 24) may not be a contradiction, given the largely symbolic nature of the two terms. But if we were to ask if CSR can help make any *fundamental* change to the "deep structure of world politics" (Conca, 1993), the answer is likely to remain an emphatic *No!* Conca (1993) cites Robert Cox to identify the three dominant tendencies of the world system: economic globalization, the sovereign state system, and the hegemony of modernity. He then describes the emergence of what he calls "explicit" and "implicit" environmental politics, the former characterized by overt attempts to address environmental problems and the latter by those efforts that lie outside the areas currently labeled as environmental (pp. 309–314). For Conca (1993), "the patterns of explicit environmental politics reflect a marked tendency toward *re*structuring (in the sense of reproducing), rather than restructuring (in the sense of fundamentally altering) the modern, sovereign, capitalist features of the current world order" (p. 310). If CSR is, at least in part, a response to global environmental change, then to what extent is it changing the nature of the deep structure?

Following Conca (1993), we would argue that just as the text of sustainable development, captured in the now classic *Our Common Future* (World Commission on Environment and Development, 1987), has a subtext of capitalism, modernity, and sovereignty, so too does CSR. As long as corporations, the building blocks of the global capitalics system, engage in their primary task of enhancing profits through the exhaustion of nature/natural resources and the creation of new consumers and new desires, neither ecological sustainability nor social responsibility is likely to

materialize (see McMillan, chapter 1). Both elide any meaningful commitment to those who have always remained on the margins of the capitalist world—the subaltern publics who have little say in corporate decisions and who remain mostly absent or silenced in the "mainstream" discourses of consumerist society, whose anxieties CSR now tries to allay.

Even if we were to assume capitalism, modernity, and sovereignty as givens in the current globalized world of capitalics, the fundamental issue of justice still remains. In placing the question of justice at the center of the investigation, postcolonial approaches can help highlight some of the deficiencies of CSR. With justice in mind, then, we can revisit the CSR efforts of those corporations that have been at the receiving end of negative publicity—Shell, for instance. Livesey and Graham (chapter 23) talk about a "society-wide shift toward corporate social and environmental responsibility" among such corporate bodies. But we need to scrutinize carefully exactly how Shell's dealings with the Ogoni people and the indigenous people of Peru (two examples cited by Livesey & Graham) have changed. What material changes have in fact taken place in the conditions in which these subaltern publics live? As Boele, Fabig, and Wheeler (2001a, 2001b) point out in their study of Shell Nigeria and the Ogoni, despite significant changes adopted by the Royal Dutch/Shell Group —including the explicit recognition of human rights post-1995—"many of the issues raised by the Ogoni (such as the need for locally sustainable development, distribution of oil wealth, community projects, and environmental issues) have yet to be addressed" (p. 75)—although they see "reconciliation" with the Ogoni as possible (Wheeler, Rechtman, Fabig, & Boele, 2001, p. 193).

Similarly, we may well applaud Shell for consulting the indigenous people of Peru and taking better steps at preventing human rights abuse and minimizing pollution (see Chatterjee, 1997), but it may be more pertinent to ask whether it would have dropped its plan for pumping natural gas in Peru if these consultations revealed major opposition from local groups. Indeed, as Breen (chapter 20) points out: "Corporate social responsibility in relation to indigenes is caught in the contradiction of demand from First World consumers for products that are embedded in indigenous territory as well as being part of the traditions of the circulation of indigenous social and cultural life."

The omissions in the "social" aspect of the CSR discourse include, most centrally, any recognition of the impacts of economic globalization and ecological degradation on Third World women. The many challenges that women in the Third World face—poverty, unemployment, and the consequences of environmental destruction such as the greater distances to be walked to get clean water, fodder, and firewood (Bhavnani, Foran, & Kurian, 2003)—are greatly exacerbated, if not necessarily always created, by the actions of corporations, in conjunction with state-sponsored development efforts. In Nigeria, the Niger Delta Women for Justice (2004) have this poignant quote on their website:

> Egi women are farmers, fisherwomen and hunters. With all the flaming and pumping oil into our swamp areas they have denied us every living thing. Today we have no hope while they are making billions of naira with our gifts from God. They don't care or hear our cry. When we cry the oil companies will only throw tear gas on us and beat us and drive us out of our land.

Yet, "the women of the Third World are not merely victims. As 'subaltern counterpublics' . . . women in the Third World meet these challenges and confront them actively" (Bhavnani et al., 2003, p. 2), often incurring the wrath of the state. In Dabhol, India, women were at the forefront of protests against the Dabhol power plant (a joint venture between three U.S.-based multinational corporations: Enron, General Electric, and Bechtel) and became the particular target of police brutality. Amnesty International (1997) cites a report by the People's Union for Civil Liberties fact-finding team that investigated the arrest of 26 women and 13 men on June 3, 1997, which concluded: "The police targeted mainly women, some of whom were minors, and the arrests were made violently, in violation of the legal, constitutional and humanitarian principles."

Yet, CSR discourses rarely acknowledge the gender-specific political and material consequences of the very presence of corporations in the Third World. If, as Waddock (chapter 5) says, it is the "paradox," the "dark underbelly" of corporate citizenship, that the more successful a corporation is, the more likely it is to have negative impacts on "the societies and communities in which [it is] embedded," then we would go further and point out that these impacts are also gender and class specific. For us, CSR can be meaningful if it acknowledges political realities and stays in tune with sociopolitical movements for social equity, political enfranchisement, and justice.

FRAMEWORKS FOR ACCOUNTABILITY

This brings us to the third omission in the CSR discourse: accountability. The term "responsibility" has strong undertones of the civilizing mission of the colonial era when imperialists sought to colonize territories as part of their responsibility to civilize the "savage natives" but concealed their real motive of political, social, cultural, and, most important, economic domination.

Corporate social responsibility, by most accounts, is a strategic process that is primarily concerned with managing the image of corporations and countering any real or potential criticism of the social impacts of profit-driven businesses on the lives and values of people. In the course of such image management, it takes upon a projected role of responsibility through a guided philanthropy that is quickly publicized to the publics that count. The target publics of CSR is evident in the fact that CSR

> is now an industry in its own right, and a flourishing profession as well. Consultancies have sprung up to advise companies on how to do CSR, and how to let it be known that they are doing it. . . . Most multinationals now have a senior executive, often with a staff at his disposal, explicitly charged with developing and co-ordinating the CSR function. In some cases, these executives have been recruited from NGOs. There are executive-education programmes in CSR, business-school chairs in CSR, CSR professional organisations, CSR websites, CSR newsletters and much, much more. ("The good company," 2005)

Subaltern publics are not in the range of CSR's vision. "When commercial interests and broader social welfare collide, profit comes first" ("The good company," 2005). It is noteworthy that corporations most prominent in donating large sums to social and environmental causes in the name of CSR often continue to be involved in activities that jeopardize the lives of subaltern publics. Activists such as Srivastava (2006) say that Coca-Cola was one of the major sponsors of the World Water Forum held in Mexico in 2006 (see http://www.worldwaterforum4.org.mx/home/genwwf.asp?lan=), although "Coca-Cola's abuses in India are being challenged vigorously by communities all across India." According to Srivastava (2006), the company's water extraction has led to "sharp drops in groundwater levels, resulting in severe water shortages" as well as pollution of the scarce remaining groundwater and the soil because of the discharge of wastewater into farmlands. There have, in fact, been protests in India against transnational beverage companies, including both Coca-Cola and Pepsi (BBC News, 2005). A journal published by the Centre for Science and Environment in India, *Down to Earth*, also documented in 2003, and again in 2006, how the soft drinks manufactured by the two Cola giants had levels of pesticide in them that were much higher than what is considered safe for humans: "The sum of all pesticides in the PepsiCo brands added up to 0.0180 mg/l, 36 times higher than the European Union's limit (EEC) for total pesticides. Coca-Cola brands had 0.0150 mg/l of all pesticides, 30 times more than the same EEC limit" (Narain, 2003; see also Centre for Science and Environment, 2006).

According to Beder (2002), "Companies with poor reputations in the area of human rights" often try to "gain a good environmental reputation to offset their human rights record" through cultivated image management (p. 66). From a postcolonial perspective, managing the image of corporate reputations through philanthropic aspects of CSR is much like the way in which the empires of the colonial era talked about their "benevolent" acts in building institutions such as courts, railways, and universities in the colonized world. If the courts made sure that justice was dispensed in a manner that was culturally appropriate to the Western colonizers, the railways ensured that natural resources from colonized territories could be effectively transported to the ports for onward dispatch. The imperial network of universities established by the British had a "strongly stated civilizing mission" and served a "pivotal function in organizing locally relevant theoretical justifications for globalization" as well as in vesting in the hands of the colonial elites the control of ideas and knowledge (Ma-Rhea, 2002, pp. 208–209).

To make a move toward any meaningful corporate citizenship, then, we have to begin with the acknowledgment that "the capitalist firm is not a moral entity but rather a political one; it is materially invested in perpetuating necessarily unequal relations of power, both internal and external" (Cloud, chapter 15). Indeed, the legal "personhood" of corporations is "antidemocratic" and "results in the denial of the sovereign peoples' right to self-governance" (Ritz, chapter 13). Responsible behavior, especially that which takes into account the Third World publics, will not evolve "naturally" from the good intentions of companies. Clapp (2005), for instance, cites a key study by UNCTAD, which "found that the most influential motivating factor for TNCs [transnational corporations] to develop corporate environmental policies was government-based laws and regulations" (p. 27).

Although Seeger and Hipfel (chapter 10) note that the "law cannot accommodate every possible moral contingency," we would argue that good corporate citizenship can only begin to be realized by the creation and enforcement of regulatory frameworks that are embedded with the norms of planetary sustainability and sensitive to the rights and values of *all* publics. Morsing, Midttun, and Palmås (chapter 6) discuss the notion of CSR in the context of Sweden where the Swedish nation is seen as "'the people's home' (an inclusive society based on welfare, solidarity, and egalitarian principles)." Similarly, McMillan (chapter 1) discusses the idea of "*ethos*" that "not only constructs a safe and hospitable 'dwelling place' . . . but also invites us into *participation* in that social space." Genuine commitment to CSR would perhaps mean extending the context of the "people's home" and "safe dwelling place" to the planet as a whole. Creating systems of accountability requires an acknowledgment that "sustainable societies" must embrace diversity, heterogeneity, and difference—what is good for the shareholding public, in other words, is not necessarily good for the subaltern public. As Stohl et al. (chapter 2) state: "A global CSR is responsive to the multiple cultures, value sets, and communicative practices of different nations while recognizing that (inter)organizational contexts are no longer bounded by the nation-state."

Central to this process of making corporations accountable is the role that citizens and civil society movements can play (see Ganesh, chapter 26; Kendall, Gill, & Cheney, chapter 17; Knight, chapter 21). "Corporate antagonists and conscientious consumers" (Kendall et al.) are, of course, among the key players in this process of creating an ethos and an effective politics that help keep issues of social and environmental justice at the center of the search for a sustainable and diverse world. But so are several relatively unnoticed movements in the Third World that have been trying to mobilize subaltern publics into fighting back against the onslaught of state–corporation tyranny. Subaltern publics include not just the many unseen residents of Cochabamba who forced the Bolivian government to cancel the contract of privatized water awarded to a Bechtel subsidiary, or the poor villagers of Dabhol in India whose protests headed the challenge to Enron in the country, or groups that have stood up to Shell in the Niger Delta, but also people who have not caught the attention of either activists or the media but who live to survive in many "out-of-the-way places" (Tsing, 1993, p. 27) of the globe and wage a relentless struggle against the consequences of a capitalics system.

CONCLUDING REFLECTIONS

Postcolonial perspectives on CSR provide agency to subaltern voices and clear the path for these voices to be factored into the mainstream discourses on CSR. In other words, such perspectives urge CSR to look beyond the upper caste publics of the First World stakeholders and consumers and to take note of the needs of the subaltern publics at the geographical as well as discursive periphery.

To be equitable and just, CSR would need to change its terms of reference. It would have to go beyond appropriating the lexicon of sustainability and empowerment from the realm of activists for strategic corporate gain. It would need to acknowledge the corporation-state-financial institution nexus more clearly and call for a tighter regulatory regime that would make it harder for corporations to ignore the voices of the subaltern publics; it would need to factor in the political along with the social; and it would need to call for accountability to all publics, including especially the subaltern ones.

None of this is straightforward or easy. The rhetoric of CSR deals with universalized principles, which may well be a good starting point. But it is when these universalized notions of what is responsible or sustainable encounter the specific political, economic, and cultural contingencies of the subaltern women and men in places beyond the gaze of scholars, activists, and the media that CSR can be freshly theorized and implemented. For such fresh understandings of CSR, we would need to step back from structured formulations and acknowledge instead the complex interplays between ethics and the law; society, culture, and politics; and responsibility and accountability. It is finally the shifting and contingent alliances that spring up among the subalterns, activist groups, ethical consumers, progressive institutions, and civil society movements that offer the most potential for realizing the diverse visions of an equitable, just, and sustainable world.

NOTE

We thank George Cheney and Robert V. Bartlett for their comments and helpful suggestions on an earlier draft of this chapter.

REFERENCES

Amnesty International. (1997). *India: The Enron project in Maharashtra—protests suppressed in the name of development.* Retrieved February 26, 2006, from http://web.amnesty.org/library/Index/engASA200311997.

Amnesty International (2005). *Contracting out human rights: The Chad-Cameroon pipeline project.* Retrieved February 26, 2006, from http://www.amnestyusa.org/business/document.do?id=ENGPOL340122005.

Basel Convention on Control of Transboundary Movement of Hazardous Wastes and Their Disposal. (1989). Retrieved February 27, 2006, from http://www.basel.int/text/documents.html.

BBC News. (2005, January 20). *Cola companies told to quit India.* BBC News Online edition. Retrieved February 26, 2006, from http://news.bbc.co.uk/2/hi/south_asia/4192569.stm.

Beder, S. (2002). Environmentalists help manage corporate reputation: Changing perceptions not behaviour. *Ecopolitics: Thought + Action, 1*(4), 60–72.

Bellamy, C. (1997). *The state of the world's children 1997.* New York: Oxford University Press. Retrieved February 27, 2006, from http://www.unicef.org/sowc97/.

Bhavnani, K.-K., Foran, J., & Kurian, P. (2003). An introduction to women, culture and development. In K.-K. Bhavnani, J. Foran, & P. Kurian (Eds.), *Feminist futures: Re-imagining women, culture and development* (pp. 1–21). London: Zed Books.

Boele, R., Fabig, H., & Wheeler, D. (2001a). Shell, Nigeria and the Ogoni. A study in unsustainable development: I. The story of Shell, Nigeria and the Ogoni people—environment, economy, relationships: Conflict and prospects for resolution. *Sustainable Development, 9*(2), 74–86.

Boele, R., Fabig, H., & Wheeler, D. (2001b). Shell, Nigeria and the Ogoni. A study in unsustainable development: II. Corporate social responsibility and "stakeholder management" versus a rights-based approach to sustainable development. *Sustainable Development, 9*(3), 121–135.

Bremner, C. (2006, February 16). Humiliation for France as court sinks toxic ship's passage to India. Retrieved February 27, 2006, from http://www.timesonline.co.uk/article/0,,3-2042564,00.html.

Centre for Science and Environment (2006). CSE releases new study on pesticides in soft drinks. Retrieved 27 September 2006 from http://www.cseindia.org/misc/cola-indepth/cola2006/cola-index.htm

Chatterjee, P. (1997, May). Peru goes beneath the Shell. *Multinational Monitor*. Retrieved February 27, 2006, from http://www.thirdworldtraveler.com/Transnational_corps/Peru_Shell_MNM.html.

Clapp, J. (2005). Global environmental governance for corporate responsibility and accountability. *Global Environmental Politics, 5*(3), 23–34.

Conca, K. (1993). Environmental change and the deep structure of world politics. In R. Lipschutz & K. Conca (Eds.), *The State and Social Power in Global Environmental Politics* (pp.309–330). New York: Columbia University Press.

Corporate Responsibility Coalition. (2005). *A big deal? Corporate social responsibility and the finance sector in Europe*. Retrieved February 27, 2006, from http://www.foe.co.uk/resource/reports/big_deal.pdf.

Gandhi, L. (1998). *Postcolonial theory: A critical introduction*. Sydney: Allen & Unwin.

"The Good Company." (2005, January 22). *The Economist* (Leaders), p. 12.

Gramsci, A. (1988). *An Antonio Gramsci reader: Selected writings, 1916–1935* (D. Forgacs, Ed.). New York: Schocken Books.

Greenpeace. (2006). *Shipbreaking*. Retrieved March 16, 2006, from http://www.greenpeaceweb.org/shipbreak/.

Guha, R., & Spivak, G. (Eds.). (1988). *Selected subaltern studies*. Oxford: Oxford University Press.

Human rights. (1995, June 3). *The Economist*, pp. 58–59.

Jessop, B. (1994). Post-Fordism and the state. In A. Amin (Ed.), *Post-Fordism* (pp. 251–279). Oxford: Blackwell.

Jones, M. T. (2003). Globalization and the organization(s) of exclusion in advanced capitalism. In R. Westwood & S. Clegg (Eds.), *Debating organization: Point-counterpoint in organization studies* (pp. 252–270). Malden, MA: Blackwell.

Langewiesche, W. (2000, August). The ship-breakers. *Atlantic Monthly*, pp. 31–49.

Lattimore, D., Baskin, O., Heiman, S. T., Toth, E. L., & van Leuven, J. (2004). *Public relations: The profession and the practice* (4th ed.). New York: McGraw-Hill.

Ma-Rhea, Z. (2002). The economy of ideas: Colonial gift and postcolonial product. In D. Goldberg & A. Quayson (Eds.), *Relocating postcolonialism* (pp. 205–216). Oxford: Blackwell.

McDougall, D. (2006, February 11). Battle on high seas over "toxic" ship. Retrieved February 27, 2006, from http://www.timesonline.co.uk/article/0,,3-2034937,00.html.

Munshi, D. (2005). Through the subject's eye: Situating the other in discourses of diversity. In G. Cheney & G. Barnett (Eds.), *International and multicultural organizational communication* (pp. 45–70). Creskill, NJ: Hampton Press.

Munshi, D., & Kurian, P. (2005). Imperializing spin cycles: A postcolonial look at public relations, greenwashing, and the separation of publics. *Public Relations Review, 31*(4), 513–520.

Munshi, D., & McKie, D. (2001). Different bodies of knowledge: Diversity and diversification in public relations. *Australian Journal of Communication, 28*(3), 11–22.

Narain, S. (2003, August 15). The pesticide is the point. *Down to Earth*. Retrieved February 26, 2006, from http://www.downtoearth.org.in/editor.asp?foldername=20030815&filename=Editor&sec_id=2&sid=1.

Narain, S. (2006, February 19). Desperately seeking waste. *Down to Earth, 14*(19): 1–2. Retrieved February 26, 2006, from http://www.downtoearth.org.in/cover_nl.asp?mode=2.

Niger Delta Women for Justice. (2004). Home page. http://www.ndwj.kabissa.org/. Retrieved February 27, 2006.

Olivera, O. (2004). *Cochabamba! Water rebellion in Bolivia* (tr. T. Lewis). Cambridge, MA: South End Press.

Rowell, A. (1996) *Green backlash: Global subversion of the environmental movement.* London: Routledge.

Schwarze, S. (2003). Corporate-state irresponsibility, critical publicity, and asbestos exposure in Libby, Montana. *Management Communication Quarterly, 16*(4), 625–632.

Shultz, J. (2005, January 28). The politics of water in Bolivia. *The Nation.* Retrieved February 26, 2006, from http://www.thenation.com/doc/20050214/shultz.

Srivastava, A. (2006, March 8). Coca-Cola and Water. *India Resource Center.* Retrieved March 6, 2006, from http://www.indiaresource.org/campaigns/coke/2006/cokewwf.html.

Stiglitz, J. (2002). *Globalization and its discontents.* London: Penguin.

Tsing, A. L. (1993). *In the realm of the diamond queen.* Princeton, NJ: Princeton University Press.

Tsing, A. L. (2005). *Friction: An ethnography of global connection.* Princeton, NJ: Princeton University Press.

Turner, T. (1999). Indigenous right, environmental protection and the struggle over forest resources in the Amazon: The case of the Brazilian Kayapo. In J. Kerr-Conway, K. Keniston, & L. Marx (Eds.), *Earth, air, fire, water* (pp. 145–169). Amherst, MA: University of Massachusetts Press.

Vogel, D. (2005). *The market for virtue: The potential and limits of corporate social responsibility.* Washington, DC: Brookings Institution Press.

Walker, R., & Monin, N. (2001). The purpose of the picnic: Using Burke's dramatistic pentad to analyse a company event. *Journal of Organizational Change Management, 14*(3), 266–279.

Wheeler, D., Rechtman, R., Fabig, H., & Boele, R. (2001). Shell, Nigeria and the Ogoni. A study in unsustainable development: III. Analysis and implications of Royal Dutch/Shell Group strategy. *Sustainable Development, 9*(4), 177–196.

World Commission on Environment and Development. (1987). *Our common future.* New York: Oxford University Press.

Young, R. (2003). *Postcolonialism: A very short introduction.* Oxford: Oxford University Press.

31

The Discourse of Corporate Social Responsibility

Postmodern Remarks

LARS THØGER CHRISTENSEN

A book like this, entitled *The Debate over Corporate Social Responsibility*, should be scrutinized and challenged for its own language(s), its own linguistic enactment(s) of the notion, and the phenomenon of corporate social responsibility (CSR). Dedicated to, among other things, explaining and demonstrating the "merits of a communication-based perspective for analyzing the history, development, and future of CSR," as described in the overview, the editors Cheney, Roper, and May undoubtedly welcome such a challenge so that the book becomes the impetus for further debate and development rather than containing the debate. It is the humble ambition of this chapter to contribute to this challenge and to help move the debate beyond the boundaries of this volume.

Following a request from the editors, my commentary proceeds largely from a *postmodern* perspective. To some readers, such a perspective entails a cynical approach insensitive to, or at least critical of, hopes for social betterment—with or without the involvement of corporations. As several of the chapters in this volume demonstrate, however, cynicism is not the exclusive attitude of postmodern theories. While some postmodern writers clearly promote such views, cynicism is not the perspective I take here. I employ the postmodern perspective to highlight ironies or paradoxes associated with the discourses of CSR, to stimulate a sensitivity to the language we use when discussing the contribution of business to social betterment, and, most of all, to demonstrate the limitations of (at least some) grand narratives of modernity when discussing the prospects for corporations to be involved in social responsibility programs. Beginning with the last issue, my commentary is organized in three overall sections discussing, respectively, the construction of the corporation as the adversary, the communicative challenges of doing good, and, finally, some preliminary requirements for a renewed discourse on CSR.

CONSTRUCTION OF THE CORPORATION

The Corporation as Adversary

With some notable exceptions, most chapters in this volume seem skeptical if not outright unsympathetic to the idea that social responsibility become programs of corporate initiative and patronage. And while the rhetoric and the arguments vary considerably, a significant number of the book's authors seem to subscribe to the view that big (and, in particular, U.S.-based) business is immoral and that no matter what individual corporations do, they cannot be trusted. Moreover, while most authors acknowledge the significance of CSR, several seem to reserve the right to label anything corporations do under the banners of CSR, sustainable development, green management practices, and so on, as "greenwashing" or otherwise cheap public relations gimmicks.

Chapter 1 by McMillan sets the tone by quoting J. Roberts's view that corporations are incapable of anything like true responsibility. Although the modern organization, according to McMillan, stepped into the vacuum of social responsibility left by the ongoing separation and individuation of modernity, it is "unfit as a harbinger of social responsibility" and "inherently incapable of taking society's interests into account." Without specifying precisely what a modern organization is, McMillan is not hesitant to conclude that the modern corporation is ill suited to be a socially responsible player in the world of today. Similarly, chapter 5 by Waddock takes the view that, since the incentives of companies focus on short-term profitability and share price, they tend to ignore the interests of other stakeholders (and nature). While her chapter claims to cover both the "business does bad" and "business does good" cases, the latter position does not receive equal voice here. Rather, it is constantly overshadowed by a frequently aired suspicion that business cannot be trusted (on this point, see also Peterson & Norton, chapter 24).

In line with McMillan, both Cloud (chapter 15) and Lawrence (chapter 16) describe CSR as an *oxymoron*. While the chapter by Lawrence does not rule out the possibility that business firms can expand their socially responsible activities and become accountable to interest groups other than shareholders, Cloud's chapter conveys a fundamental distrust in the ability and willingness of corporations to do good—especially vis-à-vis their own workers. Although her call for CSR scholars and managers to look *inside* the organization to include the conditions of employees is very well argued and articulated (a point to which I return further below), Cloud's initial position seems to prevent her from acknowledging CSR initiatives as anything other than "ideological mystifications of class antagonism." Subscribing to a version of Marxism, according to which the fundamental or "real" interests of workers lie in "making a world without profit-driven corporate work life," Cloud is able to conclude that corporate misconduct is a necessary routine in all business under capitalism. Given their initial positions and statements, it seems that Cloud and others are caught in a discourse that closes in on itself to the effect that their conclusions, to a large extent, are given in advance.

Chapter 26 by Ganesh displays a different version of this same tendency. Proceeding from an initial distinction between conventional and alternative renditions of sustainable development, Ganesh suggests that all conventional understandings of sustainable development invoke the key "morals" of neoliberalism—morals that favor global capitalism. Without citing any details of the document, Ganesh claims that even the Brundtland report *qua* its name—*Our Common Future*—represents a conventional understanding of sustainable development and, thus, "an unreservedly masculinist, patriarchal discourse with a conservative and predominantly heterosexist view of family." Ganesh does not specify what an alternative discourse on sustainable development entails, yet his generalizations endorse a polarization of perspectives that at once discards all environmental initiatives with corporate involvement as neoliberal and preserves the "alternative" discourse and its promise of "radical change" from criticism.

Given the sociohistorical context of this book, conceived as it is in the aftermath of the "corporate meltdown," the suspicion aired in these chapters toward big corporations is understandable—if not particularly productive or enlightening. Most of the characteristics ascribed to big corporations in these chapters—short term, profit oriented, irresponsible, antidemocratic, and so on—are wellknown and often-used attributes in the academic community and do not contribute much to our understanding of the potentials of business to be wholeheartedly involved in future projects of social responsibility. The authors of these particular chapters seem to use past corporate behaviors of a few iconic firms (or highly visible brands) to justify and confirm their initial views rather than discussing the possibilities for corporations to overcome some of the systemic and structural limitations to responsible behavior. Chapter 1 by McMillan, in particular, represents this tendency to reject the notion of CSR based on the reading of a few select scandals. Following right after her important and precise critique of Enron (a critique found in a few other chapters as well; compare Stohl, Stohl, & Townsley, chapter 2), McMillan proceeds to the following conclusion: "So not only has the modern corporation failed to act in ways that qualify it as a harbinger of social responsibility, its voice has been inconsistent with the task, as well."

Sliding from a critique of Enron to "the modern corporation" in general represents a case of what Aune (chapter 14) calls a "slippery slope argument." Aune's interesting rhetorical analysis of Milton Friedman's classical 1970 essay thus could easily be applied to McMillan (chapter 1), Waddock (chapter 5), Cloud (chapter 15), and Ganesh (chapter 26). Just like Friedman, these authors seem to construct the "enemy" by polarizing the audience through identification and division. Accordingly, it is tempting to suggest, as Aune does with respect to Friedman, that these chapters are written to people who already think like their authors—thus "saving the saved." Consequently, other readers of these chapters may only be confirmed in their initial perception that the CSR discourse is nothing but "a smokescreen for leftist assaults on capitalism" (see Aune, chapter 14). And that is highly unfortunate. There is too much at stake in terms of pressing human, social, and environmental issues to maintain such a polarizing discourse.

The Modernist Heritage

Although the chapters cited thus far represent the suspicion toward the corporate actor most explicitly, other chapters confirm the impression that trust in business corporations is at an all-time low (see, e.g., Ritz, chapter 13). The fact that we are experiencing what Llewellyn (chapter 12) calls a "trust drought" can clearly be attributed to the wave of scandals and multiple cases of misconduct that flooded the corporate landscape, in particular, corporate America, at the turn of the twenty-first century. Suspicion and lack of trust toward business corporations, however, is not a recent phenomenon. As I argue below, it represents a modernist tradition from the Enlightenment—a tradition upheld and celebrated in particular in the academic community—to question and challenge everything we take for granted, for example, face-value accounts, privileged perspectives, or a sacrosanct version of reality.

According to modernist epistemology, the world is not what it seems and rarely what it claims to be. In the vocabulary of modernity, society is a *spectacle* (Debord, 1983)—a scene with a front stage, to which the general audience has access, and a back stage, whose secrets and illusions are usually hidden from view. Through the use of reason and rationality, the promise of modern thought is to help the spectator move behind the "curtain," uncover the truth behind its fancy fa-

cades and seductive appearances, and eventually emancipate the spectator from the superstitions and repressions of authoritative regimes. Hegel's distinction between *Schein* (skin or appearance) and *Wesen* (essence)—a distinction reproduced in the works of Marx—represents the modern notion of revealing and exposing the truth concealed by the glitter and images of the world. Modernity, in other words, represents the ideal of absolute (self)transparency—an ideal reflected in positive science, and notions of open and unrestricted discussion (see, e.g., Vattimo, 1992).

In this volume, the modernist perspective is evident not only in the above-mentioned chapters that claim to have access to the truth behind the images of CSR or the workers' "real interests" but also in sophisticated discussions of CSR development that presuppose an increasing level of (self)-transparency in business corporations and society in general. Without at all suggesting that chapter 2 by Stohl et al. represents a simplistic distinction between the world as it seems and the world as it *really* is, I note that their globally focused third-generation level of CSR presumes a growing level of self-awareness and self-transparency on the part of corporations and an increased insight and knowledge on the part of consumers and society. While our awareness and understanding of processes of procurement, production, consumption, and disposal from cradle to grave have been growing in some respects, it would be a mistake to assume that corporations have generally become more transparent to themselves or their different stakeholders (Christensen, 2002)—an observation, however, that does not negate the *goal* of more insight and knowledge.

In his book *The Transparent Society*, the Italian philosopher Gianni Vattimo (1992) discusses the advent of postmodernity, a social condition he terms "the society of communication." According to Vattimo, we live today in a society of generalized communication, a society of the mass media in which virtually everything is expected to become an immediate object of communication. The mass media of postmodernity, Vattimo continues, has made the modern ideal of self-transparency technically possible. By offering information in "real time" about practically everything that happens on the globe, the mass media, according to Vattimo, could be seen as "a concrete realization of Hegel's Absolute Spirit: the perfect self-consciousness of the whole of humanity, the coincidence between what happens, history and human knowledge" (p. 6). This potential of the mass media, however, has not materialized. While the privileged perspective assumed by modern thought has been eroded by developments in modern science and philosophy itself—including the scientific discoveries by Bohr, Heisenberg, and Einstein at the beginning of the twentieth century—the mass media has facilitated what Vattimo calls "a general explosion and proliferation of *Weltanschauungen*, of world views" (p. 5). With the increase in information about possible forms of reality, the notion of one single perspective or reality becomes impossible to sustain (see also Lyotard, 1984). Within this context, Vattimo claims, the realization of the modernist ideal of self-transparency is not within reach, principally because it has led to an intensification of modernity's proclivity for questioning rather than to more stable answers or truths (compare Castoriadis, 1987).

Vattimo's arguments are radicalized in the writings of Baudrillard. According to Baudrillard (1988), modernity has been obsessed with meaning, with an overdetermination of causes, effects, and answers, to the effect of producing an amount of information that eliminates our conventional notions of alienation and transparency. According to Baudrillard, the current level of information production is obscene:

> Obscenity begins when there is no more spectacle, no more stage, no more theatre, no more illusion, when every-thing becomes immediately transparent, visible, exposed in the raw and inexorable light of information and communication. *We no longer partake of the drama of alienation, but are in the ecstasy of communication.* . . . It is no longer the obscenity of the hidden, the repressed, the obscure, but that of the visible, the all-too-visible, the more-visible-than-visible; it is the obscenity of that which no longer contains a secret and is entirely soluble in information and communication. (Baudrillard, 1988, pp. 21–22)

One does not have to subscribe to Baudrillard's declaration that alienation has been eliminated or his implicit assumption that the obscene level of information has produced clarity or insight to appreciate that his notion of communication ecstasy calls for us to revise the modernist notion that we find in some of the chapters reviewed above, of uncovering a single or univocal reality behind the appearances of CSR, sustainable development, and other dimensions of contemporary corporate communications. In the vocabulary of Baudrillard, corporate scandals and misconduct have been exposed in the raw and inexorable light of information and communication for decades without producing a marked increase in our ability to see through the complexities of corporate behavior and its interdependency with consumption and social life in general. The feeling that such exposition rarely uncovers any secrets hidden to the general populace indicates that perhaps we are caught in our own language game of revealing the truth behind the appearances of spectacles, stages, images, and displays (Lyotard, 1984; Murphy, 1988).

CORPORATE SOCIAL RESPONSIBILITY AS COMMUNICATION

Whereas modernist epistemology emphasizes the importance of moving behind appearances, postmodernity invites us to step into *the reality of appearances themselves*, to understand the interplay and polysemy of signifiers and the creative (or destructive) force of communication itself (e.g., Murphy, 1988). For example, consider the notion of "development." As Ganesh (chapter 26) points out, development is a polysemic term with discursive qualities. Moreover, in contrast to the modernist notion of "progress" that specifically refers to patterns of Western development—patterns to be emulated by other societies—development has become an autonomized signifier without a clear external goal (or *telos*), in other words, a signifier that refers primarily to itself. Although the notion of development invokes a host of other signifiers—free-market enterprise, low inflation, high gross national products, and so forth—it has lost the clear direction or teleology of progress and become its own referent, a referent that we often relate to as self-explanatory. This section takes a closer look at CSR and sustainable development as communicative practices.

Communication as Emergence

Taylor and van Every (2000) argue that organizations emerge in communication. Communication and organization, they claim, are *equivalent* terms. Inspired by, for example, phenomenology, speech-action theory, and conversational analysis, Taylor and van Every show how an organization comes into being through the ways its leaders and members speak about and account for its actions and activities. Speech, in other words, *is* action just as our acts simultaneously speak. Accordingly, it is not possible to distinguish in a meaningful way between what an organization says and what it does. This, however, is not to suggest a simple one-to-one correspondence between what an organization says and what it is. Obviously, an organization that describes its corporate communication activities in terms of, for example, "dialogue" does not emerge as an excellent communicator simply by talking this way. Nor would dialogue, of whatever type, become all that the organization is. What the perspective does imply is that the ways organizations talk about themselves and their practices are not neutral undertakings, but constitutive activities that contribute—through the articulation of ideals, values, and horizons—to the continuous enactment of organizational reality (Weick, 1979). This, for example, is clearly the case when organizations subscribe to notions such as "integrated communications" or "one-voice company." Although it may be impossible for organizations to integrate all their messages at once, the ambition of speaking with one voice across different audiences is so powerful in the current business environment that contemporary organizations increasingly impose systems of control on everything employees say or do (e.g., Christensen & Cheney, 2005).

Rather than being something distinct and separate from the organizational practice, communication, thus, is the "essential modality," as Taylor and van Every (2000) put it, for organizational life. If we accept the proposition that *communication has organizing properties* that shape and generate our organizations (Cooren, 1999), we need to pay careful attention to the ways organizations talk about their visions, ideals, and practices. Folded into such visions and ideals are definitions of organization that guide the behaviors of managers and employees far beyond message creation and message handling per se (see, e.g., Putnam, Phillips, & Chapman, 1996).

Politics as Communication

Although Knight, in chapter 21 on Nike and the problem of sweatshops, is critical of the tendency

for social, political, and environmental problems to be redefined as issues of *communication* management, he acknowledges the increased role communication plays in defining new political spaces, subpolitics, outside the formal and institutionalized party system. The increased investment in communication, which characterizes both corporations and their adversaries, both Nike and the antisweatshop movement, creates a world of "communicational politics"—a world more focused on the management of opinions than on the resolution of material problems.

Communicational politics is manifested, for example, in "blame management" which, according to Knight, plays a key role in the efforts of social movements to attribute causes and responsibilities for a particular problem. Using risk as a conceptual tool, resource-poor social movements are able to challenge the legitimacy and performance of powerful corporations and governments and force them to rethink and redefine their practices in terms of risk management. Highlighting well-known corporate brands, social movements are able to generate events discursively in ways that mobilize the interest of the media and public opinion and potentially amplify existing problems and define new precedents.

Knight cites two discursive initiatives by business corporations to counter these strategies of social movements: multilateralism and proceduralism. Multilateralism is, in the words of Knight, "a strategy for dispersing causal and remedial responsibility for problems"—a strategy that implies that problems are systemic and collective rather than specific to a particular corporation and that, as a consequence, tends to spread blame to more than one corporate actor. Proceduralism refers to the practice of establishing *institutional* mechanisms for dealing with problems—mechanisms such as investigations, assessments, verifications, reporting, and so forth. Together such mechanisms have a tendency to reduce real problems to issues of procedures and semantics. Knight's chapter, in other words, is instrumental in demonstrating the transformative power of communication in shaping our perceptions of reality.

Talk and the Emergence of New Organizations

Chapter 23 by Livesey and Graham presents a somewhat more optimistic account of how corporate communication potentially influences an organization to change its behaviors to become more socially responsible or, as in this case, more environmentally conscious. In line with the works of Taylor and van Every (2000) and Cooren (1999) cited above, Livesey and Graham (chapter 23) illustrate how eco-talk emerged in the Royal Dutch/Shell Group and how this talk became a creative force in shaping the corporation's renewed identity. Rather than seeing eco-talk and other corporate initiatives in the area of sustainable development as simply public relations maneuvers, Livesey and Graham chose to focus on the performative, pragmatic dimensions of language and communication:

> Whatever the original instrumental intent, language and symbolic action may have constitutive effects beyond what any particular agents —corporate communication departments, CEOs, other corporate rhetors, or their critics—can control. Corporate eco-talk participates in (re)creating the firm and (re)constructing its relationship to nature, while opening up novel possibilities of understanding and action at the societal level.

Shell's many clashes with social movements and interest groups throughout the 1990s, especially the critique of its involvement in Nigeria, shocked its modernist rationality, according to Livesey and Graham, and provoked the corporation to transform its corporate culture. Through an examination of select texts by Shell and its critics, Livesey and Graham demonstrate the transformation of Shell's identity toward more sustainable practices. Simultaneously, they show how its new eco-talk at once reflected *and* shaped the understandings of environmental responsibility in society at large. In this case, the adoption of a new way of talking about responsible and sustainable practices influenced the wider array of choices made by the corporation and was ultimately internalized—at least to some degree.

Without suggesting that social discourse is univocal or ignoring competing and conflicting positions within discursive domains, Livesey and Graham make the case that the talk of large corporations has the potential to transform not only the perceptions but also the actual practices of different social actors, including themselves. Stimulating discursive shifts, changing social expectations, and moving toward new environmental

practices—for example, various kinds of "eco-collaboration"—have gradually served to revise the modern myth of progress in which economic interests are at odds with the interests of the environment. Livesey and Graham, thus, insist that what we think and say about sustainability and other dimensions of social responsibility—even when our utterances are occasionally contradictory, banal, or agonistic—matters in the process of shaping and adapting to new situations in our social and natural environments.

Acknowledging the formative power of corporate communications and its potential influence on the emergence of new environmental practices, of course, should not blind us to cases where corporations cynically co-opt the language of sustainability in the interest of colonizing the environmental issue for marketing campaigns (Peterson & Norton, chapter 24). Such "greenwashing" practices (see also Ongkrutraksa, chapter 25) will probably continue to coexist as the dark side of corporate social and environmental responsibility initiatives. As several authors point out, CSR is being used by some corporations as merely a branch of public relations (e.g., Ganesh, chapter 26; compare Llewellyn, chapter 12, and Aune, chapter 14).

A similar observation, however, can be made about our democratic ideal of "dialogue." Dialogue is frequently co-opted by organizations to describe virtually every type of interaction they maintain with their internal and external audiences. Without defending or justifying such practices, it is possible to argue—following Livesey and Graham—that the language of sustainability (and dialogue), even when co-opted, continues to shape management practices through the ideals and prescriptions infolded in its rhetoric. Indeed, just as "dialogue" is not simply empty talk in contemporary organizations but a powerful signifier that can be used by both management and employees to demand more interactive types of communication and participation, CSR is not a dead metaphor—even when the activities described under its banner are not seen as consistent with its name.

Much talk about CSR centers around the notion of *consistency*. The call for consistency between words and action (including other words) is understandable and sympathetic in a complex world of uncertainty and risk. And it corresponds well with contemporary notions of political correctness—not least in areas such as social and environmental responsibility. Corporate managers, thus, are increasingly expected to "walk their talk," that is, to practice what they preach. As Weick (1995) points out, however, the relationship between words and action is more complex. Based on his notion that people act in order to think (see also Weick, 1979), Weick argues that the type consistency prescribed by the walk-the-talk imperative seriously limits the possibility of discovering new solutions or ideas for which the previous words are inadequate: "When told to walk their talk, the vehicle for discovery, the walking, is redirected. It has been pressed into service as a testimonial that a handful of earlier words are the right words" (Weick, 1995, p. 183).

The goal behind the ideal of letting one's actions follow one's words, of course, is to reduce hypocrisy. Like politicians, corporations and corporate leaders are seriously worried about being perceived as hypocritical. As a consequence, decision makers will have a tendency to orient their actions toward the past.

Yet organizations and their leaders may not be able to escape some level of hypocrisy. As Brunsson (2003) argues and illustrates well, most organizations of today face an increasing number of conflicting goals and demands from their many different stakeholders—goals and demands that can rarely be satisfied simultaneously (see also Brunsson, 1989). If all stakeholders (including shareholders and customers) were expecting and demanding the same things, it would be easy for corporations to act consistently and thus be regarded as ethical (as observed by a manager quoted in Whelan, chapter 7). This, however, is almost never the case. To maneuver in a world of conflicting demands, organizations need—at least temporarily—to compensate action in one direction with talk and decisions in the opposite. As even Aristotle (1954) observed, the adaptation of a message to more than one audience is nothing new. Interestingly, as Brunsson points out, this perspective implies that talk, decisions, and actions are mutually "coupled" rather than "decoupled," as often assumed by critics of corporate communications, mutually interdependent rather than disconnected. Far from justifying deception or dishonesty, Brunsson argues that the practice of splitting words and action may constitute a temporary solution to the problem of differing and incompatible demands and goals. And, since talk is action, too, such solutions may sometimes be regarded as adequate by some stakeholders—especially in situations where symbolic responses are highly valued (see also Pfeffer, 1981).

Many of us would regard the practice of separating words and action as unethical—at least when applied consciously to programs of CSR or environmental sustainability. However, Brunsson shows that organizational hypocrisy often arises without anyone having intended it, as a result of a conflict. To reject hypocrisy in the interest of eliminating all inconsistency would be to ignore the complexity of most decision situations of contemporary organizations. As March (1988) argues, hypocrisy—defined as inconsistency between words and action—is a necessary transitional practice in an environment that changes. (Compare Whelan's account of the Confucian context of CSR in chapter 7, regarding how a gentleman must change in accordance with circumstances.) The fact that organizations often have difficulties living up to their own ideals or publicized intentions should not imply, according to March, that organizations must refrain from claiming these ideals and intentions as their own. In line with the view expressed in chapter 23 by Livesey and Graham, March ascribes a highly creative force to language and the relatively unrestricted articulation of ideals. As he points out, a bad person with good intentions *can* be a person who experiments with the possibilities of becoming a good person. Accordingly, he continues, it would be more sensible to prompt and actuate such experiments rather than to discard them, for example, by allowing them to talk about their ideals and good intentions without constantly reminding that their behavior leaves much to be desired. Applied to the topic of this book, this line of argument suggests that although we should continue to be critical of what organizations say or do with respect to social responsibility and sustainability, we should simultaneously allow them to experiment with the ways they communicate about these issues. Such latitude not only allows them to find new solutions for themselves and their own organizational practices, but also—as Livesey and Graham suggest—helps society at large discover new ideals, goals, and productive discourses on responsibility and sustainability. By listening to what corporations say about CSR and related issues outside the typical public relations or publicity context, rather than telling them what to say, we may come across significant insight usually ignored by the media, insight that allows us to adjust our expectations and demands of the corporate actor.

TOWARD A RENEWED DISCOURSES ON CORPORATE SOCIAL RESPONSIBILITY?

Acknowledging that language and reality are closely intertwined (Lyotard, 1984; Murphy, 1988), how should we then talk about CSR? How should our ideals, hopes, and wishes be articulated? And what can we possibly ask corporations, governments, and citizens (or consumers) to do? These are not simple questions and are addressed only in a cursory manner here. In the remainder of this commentary, I discuss and problematize three concepts often linked to discussion of CSR: regulation, responsiveness, and involvement. I argue that although they all are indispensable dimensions of a CSR program, limitations (paradoxes or ironies) are associated with each. An understanding of these limitations, I believe, is necessary for a renewed discourse on CSR.

Regulation or Responsibility— or Both?

What I hope to have demonstrated above is the limits of approaching the issue of CSR with an initial premise that the economic system is "irresponsibility developed into a system" (McMillan, chapter 1). We may agree that much economic activity, as practiced hitherto, seems to prevent or even contradict responsible corporate behavior and that managerial discourse on social responsibility in many instances is one-dimensional and thus inadequate to lead our search for more responsible and sustainable practices. Yet, for the reasons outlined above, it would be a serious mistake to determine once and for all what economic activity is and to decide a priori what corporations can and should say about their future intentions.

To benefit from the voices (and insights) of corporate actors, should corporate participation in and contribution to social responsibility initiatives and programs be regulated more strictly? Perhaps, but this is not an issue around which this book provides much consensus. While some chapters explicitly call for enhancements of regulatory regimes (e.g., Peterson & Norton, chapter 24)—

regimes that have proved valuable in many instances in the European Union—other chapters are concerned that such legislation might actually *limit* social responsibility, that rules and regulations might become excuses for corporations to avoid being fully involved, and thus responsible, social actors (Aune, chapter 14; Seeger & Hipfel, chapter 10). As Lawrence formulates it in chapter 16, "Rules are mechanisms for switching off our moral capacity, not a means of activating or fulfilling it."

Morsing, Midttun, and Palmås (chapter 6) report that managers in Scandinavia, where social responsibility traditionally has been regarded as a state issue funded by high taxes, typically perceive their companies as being already socially responsible—a perception that does not provide them with incentives for further social engagements. Although Scandinavian corporations increasingly take on some of the responsibilities previously ascribed to the state, the opinion that social responsibility is a societal issue will probably persist for many years to come. The challenge, in Scandinavia and elsewhere, is finding some balance between regulation and possibilities for corporations to maintain and develop their individual adaptive capacities.

Responsiveness or Responsibility—or Both?

Since minimal legal responsibilities are often framed as the corporation's maximum ethical obligation, as Seeger and Hipfel argue in chapter 10, we should focus instead on the social *responsiveness* of corporations. Responsive organizations, they continue, "are able to be more socially responsible by virtue of their willingness to hear and respond to social needs, standards, and values." Emphasizing corporate responsiveness, thus, means highlighting the organization's communicative capabilities —its ability to listen, of course, but also its ability to develop its own language of social responsibility.

There is one caveat, however. Seeger and Hipfel's notion of responsiveness concerns the organization's willingness and ability to anticipate and adjust to changing needs and values in society. Their view is consistent with the two-way symmetrical view on corporate communication developed by Grunig and colleagues (e.g., Grunig, 1992). While this may well be the case, it is arguable whether responsiveness in this shape facilitates truly socially responsible behavior among corporations, as Seeger and Hipfel seem to assume. Cheney and Christensen (2001a), for example, argue that the growing ability of many corporations to respond to their stakeholders' interests and demands—response*ability*—does not necessarily imply a growing level of authentic or serious social or environmental responsibility:

> In contemporary "market-oriented" society where corporations demonstrate social responsibility by being open and responsive to claims made by organized publics, the central question is still how such maneuvers correspond with the pursuit of "the overall good." . . . In the writings of scholars who promote the idea of a symmetrical dialogue between organizations and their publics, one senses the implicit assumption that organizations are behaving in a socially responsible manner as long as they adapt to the will of the general public. (pp. 261–262)

As Shell's *Brent Spar* case of 1995 indicated, it can sometimes be more responsible to be true to one's own principles than to adapt to the needs, wishes, and demands of shifting audiences. Shell's bending to the pressure from Greenpeace and European consumers implied that *Brent Spar* was scrapped in a Norwegian fjord—a solution potentially far more harmful to the environment than sinking it in the ocean (see also Cheney & Christensen, 2001b). The procedural correctness of the two-way symmetrical model of communication, in other words, may not always be adequate to stimulate a sufficient sensitivity to the complexity of the social and natural environment (see also Deetz, chapter 18).

Involvement and/ or Responsibility?

Deetz (in chapter 18 and elsewhere) argues that good communication is a matter not of finding common ground or securing consensus between different interests, but of establishing and maintaining a variety of perspectives and assuring that established positions can be contested on a continual basis. Requisite diversity and contestation, Deetz points out, are necessary to stimulate creative solutions and assure a mutual commitment among the involved parties, even when opinions, ideals, and goals differ. Deetz's perspective on CSR, thus, is a *processual* perspective—a perspective focused on participation rather than sacro-

sanct solutions. As a consequence of his emphasis on participation and involvement, he is skeptical toward government regulation, consumer choices, and corporate good will as primary devices for providing social responsibility. Such devices, he points out, "will offer very weak mechanisms for value representation and virtually no support to communication processes that create win–win situations" where multiple stakeholders are involved. His notion of decisional involvement makes good sense in a complex world where many voices must be heard (and respected) to fully comprehend all dimensions and consequences of a decision. Yet it is tempting to object that such a type of involvement and participation presupposes a level of mutual trust that may be difficult to obtain in contemporary society. As several chapters in this book indicate, trust and mutuality vis-à-vis the business environment are not prominent attitudes of today. In addition to the issue of trust, the notion of *equal* participation may be problematic as well. In spite of these difficulties, we have to realize that involvement is a prerequisite for social responsibility.

Our notions of involvement, however, are often limited, unable to account for the many sources of influence and responsibility at play in each social or environmental situation. We ask for corporate involvement in issues of sustainability, but expect corporations to acknowledge primary guilt. We want consumer involvement in conflicts about waste disposal, but rarely extend their responsibilities to the consequences of the decisions made. We demand worker involvement in corporate values, but do not involve them in the deliberations that lead to the formation of those values. As a result, involvement is increasingly regarded as disconnected from responsibility, as an autonomized sphere that does not extend beyond the meeting, the choice, the demonstration, or the vote.

Toward a Broader Focus

Chapter 27 by Crawford-Brown invites us to conceive of responsibility in a broader context of mutuality and interdependency, to acknowledge that corporations are participants in an ecosystem rather than external forces that impose themselves on (or disturb) the system from the outside. Without downplaying the responsibilities of corporations when operating in their particular ecosystems, Crawford-Brown emphasizes that our understanding of corporate behavior is limited if we examine the products they produce without including an understanding of the needs the products serve: "It simply is not clear," he writes, "where to draw the boundary in attributing environmental impacts to a particular product." To fully account for causes and effects of products and production—and devise proper solutions and remedies to the problems they engender—we need macroanalyses at the level of society at large.

In line with this view, chapter 17 by Kendall, Gill, and Cheney emphasizes that consumers have responsibilities as well as rights. Although practices of consumption always operate within a space delineated by systems of production, they are not reducible to what du Gay (1996) calls "the grid of production." Consumption practices, therefore, need to be included in our discussions and critique of social responsibility. Kendall et al. discuss the possibility of "conscientious consumption" and urge us to conceive of consumer involvement in a far broader sense than the notion of "voting with one's dollars" suggests. Such notions, they claim, reduce the citizen to a consumer (see also Deetz, chapter 18) and limit the range of options for involvement and the type of voice that consumers have to effect change.

Finally (at least as far as this chapter goes), we need to extend our notion of involvement to the people who work in the corporations. As Cloud (chapter 15) argues, it is absurd that workers are described as corporate citizens but do not have the right to free speech. Under the impact of the marketing philosophy, corporations increasingly talk about the importance of understanding and staying close to consumers. At the same time, their employees are often ignored. Ironically, they are expected to be involved without being involved (Christensen & Cheney, 2000), to express loyalty and commitment—and thus lack individuality, critical voice, and personal insight—to organizations that increasingly describe their *external* audiences, in particular, the consumers, as individual, critical, and independent. To fully embrace social responsibility, to become forums for the articulation and resolution of important social conflicts regarding issues of environmental and social good (e.g., McMillan, chapter 1; Deetz, chapter 18), corporations need not only to open themselves to their surroundings, but also to look internally, to

become self-reflective, aware of their own practices as well as their own communication.

NOTE

I thank George Cheney for helpful comments to an earlier draft of this chapter.

REFERENCES

Aristotle. (1954). *The rhetoric* (Trans. W. R. Roberts). Cambridge, MA: Modern Library.

Baudrillard, J. (1988). *The ecstasy of communication*. New York: Semiotext(e).

Brunsson, N. (1989). *The organization of hypocrisy: Talk, decisions and actions in organizations*. Chichester: John Wiley & Sons.

Brunsson, N. (2003). Organized hypocrisy. In B. Czarniawska & G. Sevón (Eds.), *The northern lights: Organization theory in Scandinavia* (pp. 201–222). Copenhagen: Copenhagen Business School Press.

Castoriadis, C. (1987). *The imaginary institution of society*. Cambridge, MA: MIT Press.

Cheney, G., & Christensen, L. T. (2001a). Organizational identity. linkages between "internal" and "external" organizational communication. In F. Jablin & L. L. Putnam (Eds.), *The new handbook of organizational communication* (pp. 231–269). London: Sage.

Cheney, G., & Christensen, L. T. (2001b). Public relations as contested terrain. A critical response. In R. Heath & G. Vasquez (Eds.), *Handbook of public relations* (pp. 167–182). Newbury Park, CA: Sage.

Christensen, L. T. (2002). Corporate communication: The challenge of transparency. *Corporate Communication: An International Journal, 7*(3), 162–168.

Christensen, L. T., & Cheney, G. (2000). Self-absorption and self-seduction in the corporate identity game. In M. Schultz, M. J. Hatch, & M. H. Larsen (Eds.), *The expressive organization* (pp. 246–270). Oxford: Oxford University Press.

Christensen, L. T., & Cheney, G. (2005, July 4–6). *The corporate anatomy of integrated communications: Challenging the "bodily" pursuit.* Paper presented at the Critical Management Conference, Cambridge, UK.

Cooren, F. (1999). *The organizing property of communication*. Amsterdam: John Benjamins.

Debord, G. (1983). *The society of the spectacle*. Detroit: Black & Red.

du Gay, P. (1996). *Consumption and identity at work*. London: Sage.

Grunig, J. E. (1992). *Excellence in public relations and communication management*. Hillsdale, NJ: Lawrence Erlbaum.

Lyotard, J.-F. (1984). *The postmodern condition: A report on knowledge*. Minneapolis: University of Minnesota Press.

March, J. G. (1988). *Decisions and organizations*. Oxford: Basil Blackwell.

Murphy, J. W. (1988). Making sense of postmodern sociology. *British Journal of Sociology, 4*, 600–614.

Pfeffer, J. (1981). Management as symbolic action. The creation and maintenance of organizational paradigms. In Y. Cummings & Z. Staw (Eds.), *Research in organizational behavior* (Vol. 3, pp. 1–52). Greenwich, CT: JAI Press.

Putnam, L. L., Phillips, N., & Chapman, P. (1996). Metaphors of communication and organization. In S. R. Clegg, C. Hardy, & W. R. Nord (Eds.), *Handbook of organization studies* (pp. 375–408). London: Sage.

Taylor, J. R., & van Every, E. (2000). *The emergent organization: Communication as its site and surface*. Mahwah, NJ: Erlbaum.

Vattimo, G. (1992). *The transparent society*. Cambridge: Polity Press.

Weick, K. E. (1979). *The social psychology of organizing*. Reading, MA: Addison-Wesley.

Weick, K. E. (1995). *Sensemaking in organizations*. Thousand Oaks, CA: Sage.

32

Corporate Social Responsibility/Corporate Moral Responsibility

Is There a Difference and the Difference It Makes

PATRICIA H. WERHANE

I am honored to be included in this collection of challenging chapters on corporate social responsibility (CSR). Each offers insights that are important in this new century of corporate corruption and moral challenges, and I cannot do justice to any these worthwhile chapters by responding to each in detail. Rather, I shall take up the gauntlet in another way by asking a few questions. First, just what do we mean by CSR? Is it sometimes a fig leaf to distract us from investigating corporate misconduct? Does the term serve as an umbrella term to cover a number of related corporate relationships and alliances? Or is, in fact, the term referring to what I take to be the greatest challenge for companies today: the moral responsibility to create economic, environmental, social, and moral added value in an age of distrust and disillusionment about business?

THE FIG LEAF

Let us begin by tracing some early definitions of CSR. According to Davis and Blomstrom (1975), two of the early thinkers in this field, "[Corporate] social responsibility is the obligation of decision makers to take actions which protect and improve the welfare of society as a whole along with their own interests" (p. 23). A. B. Carroll (1979), often cited in this regard, expands this definition: "The social responsibility of business encompasses the economic, legal, ethical and discretionary expectations that society has of organizations at a given point in time" (p. 500; see also Waddock, 2004, for a thorough summary of this literature).

The problems with the Davis and Blomstrom/Carroll early definitions[1] are twofold. First, there is an almost exclusive focus on business–society relationships, neglecting corporate relationships to their employees, customers, suppliers, and shareholders who directly account for and depend on company success or failure. Second, given these definitions, CSR has been sometimes misidentified with corporate *discretionary* responsibilities to the communities in which companies operate (e.g., philanthropy, charity, or community public relations). Companies that engage in such practices aim to be considered "socially responsible" despite what they do commercially in the marketplace. Enron, for example, was a large donor to the city of Houston and to a number of religious institutions to which its executives belonged. HealthSouth and its CEO were, and perhaps still are, the largest donors to city projects in Birmingham, Alabama. The Rigas family, founders of Adelphia Communication, gave millions of dollars to the city of Coudersport, Pennsylvania, its corporate headquarters while "borrowing" money from Adelphia after it was publicly traded. In every instance, these gifts covered up or sidetracked what these companies and their executives were doing: lying, cheating, and stealing from their shareholders and, as a result in Enron's case, from employee pensions. Worse, they gave away what were allegedly corporate profits while running these companies badly.

During 2005, the parent company of United Airlines was in bankruptcy (chapter 11) and declared its pension fund bankrupt, thus destroying promised pensions for many of its retired, highly paid pilots and managers.[2] During this period, United was one of the largest corporate donors to the Lyric Opera in Chicago. I would argue that this kind of "generosity" is an illustration of CSI, corporate social *irresponsibility*. Companies do have responsibilities to the communities in which they operate just as ordinary citizens and residents do. But philanthropy and charity are discretionary options, both for individuals and for corporations. A company's primary responsibilities are to its employees, customers, suppliers, and shareholders and to the communities in which it operates. A company's primary responsibilities to these communities have to do with how it affects and is affected by those communities. So, for example, when a company is engaged in coal mining, it is responsible for the effects of mining on that landscape, water, and air. United Airlines and the Lyric Opera have little impact on each other. When employees are being laid off and lose their pensions, it is the airline's responsibility, its primary *moral* responsibility, to address and redress that set of problems first, because these are issues that have to do with its operations, management, and profitability, the reasons for its being an airline in the first place. Thus, in the analysis and discussions of CSR, one must take care that the requirement focuses on what companies are morally obligated to do, not merely on discretionary community gifts, particularly when they are used to distract from these obligations.

THE UMBRELLA: CORPORATE SOCIAL RESPONSIBILITY AND CORPORATE MORAL RESPONSIBILITY

One of the strengths of most of the chapters in this collection is that they have, by and large, avoided a huge misnomer, that of limiting CSR to discretionary external relationships between companies and society. In this volume, CSR has been expanded from the original Davis and Blomstrom/Carroll definitions to include "the responsibility of a company for the totality of its impact" (Chandler, 2001, quoted in Stohl, Stohl, & Townsley, chapter 2) including corporate governance, diversity, environmental and legal concerns, social perspectives, and global impact. CSR may encompass responsibilities to one's primary stakeholders—employees, customers, suppliers, and shareholders—as well as to almost any other individual, institution, culture, or society that a company may affect or be affected by, obligations to the natural environment and the ecosystem, relationships with the public sector, governments, and nongovernmental organizations (NGOs), and its global impact, broadly construed. Thus, CSR turns into an umbrella term to cover almost every possible obligation, concern, effect, or responsibility that an organization might encounter, including externalities resulting from corporate behavior or neglect of behavior.

As part of this extensive coverage, in this volume CSR is often linked to or identified with corporate *moral* responsibility (CMR). In the recent past, however, these two, CSR and CMR, have been somewhat distinguished, as the Davis & Blomstrom/Carroll quotations illustrate. Initially, CSR referred to corporate community responsibilities, in the primarily external relationships between a company and society. Corporate *moral* responsibility, then, referred to obligations a firm has as a result of its existence, its reasons for existence, scope and nature of operations, and its various interactions. Sometimes moral responsibility has been interpreted merely as fiduciary responsibilities to shareholders, the providers of capital to the firm (Friedman, 1970). More often, these obligations are formulated as obligations a company *should* have to those whom it affects and who make a difference in the company: its primary stakeholders, one of which, of course, is its shareholders, as well as its employees and managers, customers, and suppliers, and secondarily its obligations to communities in which it operates. Note that these are normative obligations—they spell out what a company *should* do, how it should respect its stakeholders and create added value, how it should not create harms to communities or to the environment, and how and in what ways it should or is not obliged to promote further social, economic, and environmental well-being.

There is nothing wrong with embracing CMR as part of CSR, as long as one is aware of these distinctions, and as long as one does not confuse descriptions of what companies actually do with what companies should do, all things considered. The fear of the conflation is twofold, however: that by adapting a CSR stance we will expect too much of corporations, or that in focusing primarily on CMR we will neglect societal effects and obligations. I say more about this further below.

If companies have all these responsibilities I described above, and I do not challenge that assumption although I do qualify it, I suggest that these responsibilities are of several varieties. First, there are legal responsibilities as spelled out by the constitution and laws of the countries in which companies operate. Most authors have been careful not to confuse CSR with corporate legal obligations as prescribed by law. Second, there are fiduciary responsibilities to shareholders for a return on their investment, to employees and suppliers for fair treatment and adequate remuneration, and to customers to deliver what they paid for. Interestingly, in many of the chapters, fiduciary obligations to shareholders are not always weighed equally with other obligations to other stakeholders or to the environment. This is interesting, if not a weakness, since those obligations still weigh heavily upon managers and are justified in our legal system. Third, CSR implies that companies have further responsibilities, to respect the dignity and rights of their stakeholders, to respect the cultures and societies in which they operate, and to preserve, if not to improve, the ecosystem. But what is the nature and extent of these? Are these all moral *obligations*; that is, do they spell out what a company, or at least a good company, should do? Are they required? Or do they merely spell out exemplary discretionary standards of some exemplary companies? As long as a company is not creating more harm that good, it could be argued that these are nice things to do, and that they exemplify good citizenship, but companies that are not deliberately socially proactive are not necessarily evil.

The question of the extent and scope of CSR and CMR leads me back to two prior issues. First, outlining CSR as many of the chapters in this collection have done and referring to corporate responsibilities that go beyond legalities makes an implicit assumption: that we can hold institutions such as corporations responsible, morally and socially responsible, just as we hold individual people morally and socially responsible. Second, even if we can make a case for institutional respon-

sibility (and I try do to so in the following section), we then have to address the extent of that accountability. Are pharmaceutical companies manufacturing HIV/AIDS drugs responsible for their distribution throughout all of sub-Saharan Africa to the 40 million or more infected victims? Are oil companies responsible for political unrest in the countries in which they drill? Are clothing retailers responsible for the outsourcing of their goods manufactured, for example, whether or not they were made under sweatshop labor conditions? Using some specific examples, I address how one might think about those responsibilities in ways that are both imaginative and not prohibitive to corporate survival and well-being.

CORPORATE MORAL "PERSONHOOD" AND MORAL RESPONSIBILITY

As Dean Ritz summarized in chapter 13, some years ago I defended a modified version of corporate moral personhood, arguing that corporations are secondary moral agents. As Ritz argues succinctly in his chapter, while corporations are by and large treated as legal persons under the law, this is wrongheaded, and these laws should be changed. I agree. Such legal largesse extends to corporations the same rights as individual (human) persons. Because many companies wield a great deal of economic and sometimes political power, this legal contention that corporations are legal persons extends to them *more* in the way of rights than to individual persons.

My arguments for corporate secondary moral agency, however, were not an attempt to bolster the legal position on corporate personhood. Rather, the argument I defended and still defend is that, whatever their legal status (and that may differ from country to country), corporations are secondary moral agents (Werhane, 1985). These arguments are defended on two grounds. Corporations are created by, are made up of, and depend upon individuals and groups of individuals for their existence and legal charter. They also depend on human individuals for capital, property ownership, contracts, management, sales, productivity, supplies, marketing, market share, clients, customers, and so forth. Companies function, and can only function, as a result of human interactions. At the same time, in our ordinary language we speak of corporate responsibilities just as we speak of individual responsibilities. To use some quotations from chapters in this volume, "Wal-Mart, Starbucks, Microsoft, Home Depot, and CVS . . . [have] a dark side to their successes" (Waddock, chapter 5), "Boeing introduced lean manufacturing" and "Boeing's shady dealings" (Cloud, chapter 15), "Shell Oil's effort to improve its environmental and CSR image" (Aune, chapter 14; see also Livesey & Graham, chapter 23), "Some organizations, such as . . . Cummins Inc., have established long records of attending to social issues" (Seeger & Hipfel, chapter 10), "McDonald's joined with the ostensibly hostile environmental group" (Livesey & Graham, chapter 23), "Nike and the Sweatshop Problem" (Knight, chapter 21), among many others. So we tend to hold corporations as well as individuals morally responsible.

We are left with two temptations, both of which are questionable. The first is to ascribe to companies full moral personhood parallel to their legal personhood (French, 1979). But this is erroneous, because unlike rational adult persons, companies cannot act on their own. They cannot come to dinner, shake hands, deliberate, make choices or change their minds, feel guilty or innocent, or even be brought to trial on their own without the concerted activities of those human agents managing and affecting the corporate activities. There is no autonomous moral phenomenon, The Corporation, despite legal incorporation and extensive legal rights. Corporations are created by, function because of, and are destroyed by human beings, usually massive groups of human beings in complex interrelated activities. So corporations are not full-fledged moral persons.

On the other hand, and this is the second temptation, it is equally suspect to ascribe and distribute all corporate activities, good deeds, or wrongdoing to the individuals who manage and affect their operations (Velasquez, 1983). This is because at least large companies act as collectives. What they do is a result of their mission, their operating principles, and activities of thousands of groups of employees and managers. As a result, it is difficult, at best, even in a small company, to trace the source of all activities back to the instigators of the ideas and thus to ascribe praise or blame. For example, Shell Oil has been highly criticized for its operations in the Nigerian Ogoniland oil fields. Shell's management has acknowledged these criticisms and has tried to remedy some of these problems.

They did not and could not dismiss all those responsible because the Ogoniland drilling was a result of a long chain of corporate decisions, a collective set of actions, and one cannot trace back to all the individual culprits. Their remedy has been to revamp mission statements and codes of ethics. People have left, not because of what they did or did not do in Ogoniland, but because they had not signed on to the newly formulated mission (Stohl et al., chapter 2). Note that this is different from, say, the Tyco case, where the CEO, Dennis Kozlowski, and the CFO, Mark H. Swartz, were pretty much individually directly responsible for their misuse of funds. In the Tyco case we have real live individual culprits, and we do not want to let them "off the moral hook," either.

To conclude this section, I observe that we do hold institutions such as corporations as well as individuals morally responsible. This is not just rhetoric. They act as collectives because "*not all actions of corporations are redescribable merely as individual actions*" (Werhane, 1985, p. 31, emphasis added). Collective action is often secondary action, a result of a complex set of actions, often in response to stated or implicit corporate mission, goals, and corporate culture. As a result, employees, managers, legal experts, and others often act as agents on behalf of the company, sometimes bracketing their own desires, interests, and moral belief systems.[3] When there are a series of iterations and variations of these actions, the result, what a company does, cannot be traced back to specific individuals. The individual perpetrators become anonymous, yet the result is corporate activity, for example, drilling in Ogoniland, contracting with manufacturers who use sweatshop labor for clothing and shoes, underpaying employees, creating environmentally sustainable goods, and so forth. Thus, corporations and other collectives are secondary moral agents. While not being independent agents, they are nevertheless responsible for their actions, even when we cannot find the initiating company individuals to praise or blame.

CORPORATE MORAL OBLIGATIONS

Individuals and, secondarily, companies are held morally responsible (a) when they make choices, rather than when they are coerced; (b) when they intend a certain result to occur (even if it does not) or cause an action to occur out of their own choices even sometimes when the result was involuntary; (c) when, within their abilities and capacities, they could have prevented harm or, sometimes, improved a situation; or (d) when, with adequate information, they are faced with more than one alternative and thus could have made another choice. And (e) companies are usually held responsible for outcomes of their actions, as well. Attributing corporate *social* responsibility is sometimes more difficult, I suggest. Sometimes we expect too much of companies, because of their economic largesse; other times we let them off when we perhaps should not. These expectations or lack thereof are particularly true when we focus only on corporate external social responsibilities, or when we confuse moral obligations with more discretionary responsibilities.

To analyze these confusions, let me begin with a few grandiose examples, referred to in other chapters in this volume, and try to generalize from them. I begin with Shell Oil in Ogoniland, Nigeria (see Stohl et al., chapter 2). I do not reiterate the case, but only point out some of the obvious critiques of that set of operations, critiques that Shell itself acknowledges. The drilling operations have created environmental degradation, and the company paid royalties to the formerly corrupt Nigerian government. It engaged in some but allegedly inadequate investment in the Ogoni communities, it hired mostly expatriate labor, and it did not intervene in the Ogoni Ken Saro-Wiwa's political crisis that led to his military tribunal trial and hanging (along with eight other codefendants; Newburry & Gladwin, 2002).

All of these outcomes are bad, very bad. But let us step back from the horrors of these outcomes and evaluate the extent and scope of Shell's moral responsibilities. One wants to argue that Shell is responsible for the environmental degradation resulting from its drilling. True, but is it also responsible for the environmental degradation resulting from Ogoni and other dissidents who tapped into the pipelines, thus creating increased massive spills and fires? One must take care here not to attribute *all* environmental destruction in that region to Shell. Shell should have invested more heavily in the communities in which it drilled, thus preempting possible pipeline violence. True, but . . . how much should Shell have done? What are the limits of its obligations to the Ogoni, as opposed to the re-

sponsibilities of the Nigerian government? And when does community involvement become paternalism or, worse, interference with national sovereignty? The Nigerian government at the time of this case was notoriously corrupt. So, it could be argued, Shell should not have dealt with them; it should not have drilled in Nigeria or pulled out. True, but—and here is an example of what I have called elsewhere "moral risk" (Werhane, 2004; Werhane, Velamuri, & Boyd, 2006)—is it better for a company to do business in a developing economy even when its government is corrupt, or to abstain? Finally, Shell's intervention in the Ken Saro-Wiwa case might have saved his life. Shell's abstention in this case is often considered morally reprehensible. But again, such involvement would entail an enormous moral risk, although it is a risk, I would contend in this instance, that they should have undertaken. When, and in what circumstances, should a company interfere with national sovereignty, particularly around issues of patriotism and dissident behavior?

My point in this example is that thinking about this case in terms of CSR may push us to ask too much of Shell, holding it liable for all the Ogoniland problems. But to ignore Shell's moral behavior is to ask too little. Rather, one should frame these issues in terms of Shell's moral obligations. What is the extent of its obligations to a region and a community in which it operates? What is it capable of doing and achieving? When, and in what ways, would Shell be overextending its responsibilities and interfering with a sovereign nation such as Nigeria? And when should it simply withdraw from a region altogether? These are difficult questions that have no simple answers. But asking them pushes companies such as Shell to think through their moral responsibilities, capabilities, and liabilities. Simply to say that they are or should be "socially responsible" and/or engage in "environmentally sustainable operations," I conclude, does not frame the issues in ways that both extend and limit Shell's obligations.

Let me now turn to the example of Wal-Mart, the ethicists' current favorite *bête noir*. Wal-Mart provides its customers with good quality at the cheapest prices in the country, thus allowing low-income families (and the rest of us) opportunities to purchase more goods from limited budgets. Yet it produces almost none of what it sells, and much of its merchandise is furnished by offshore suppliers who use nonunion sweatshop labor. Wal-Mart does not allow unions to organize its labor force, and it has been accused of various employee mistreatments at its stores in this country. It puts constant pressure on its suppliers to lower their prices (Fishman, 2003; Waddock, chapter 5). If one looks at Wal-Mart from the shareholder perspective, on the other hand, it does very well. It also engages in a great deal of philanthropy (last year it gave away $17 million, most of it to local communities), its managers and executives are paid very well, and its mission statement reads like an ethics thesis.[4] From the perspective of those who work in Wal-Mart locations that take advantage of their employees, of those working in offshore sweatshops without benefits and are often not paid for overtime and paid below a living wage (National Labor Committee, 2003), and of its suppliers, all of whom are constantly pressured to lower their costs of goods, Wal-Mart looks different. Thus, as Waddock exclaims in chapter 5, this creates a paradox of low prices, low costs, shareholder largesse, and supplier and employee suffering. How can one resolve this paradox? What is the extent of this company's obligations, particularly to sweatshop workers who are not Wal-Mart employees, but work instead for a manufacturer who sells to Wal-Mart? What are the limits, if any, to Wal-Mart's obligations, and how and in what ways can we hold them accountable? How can they meet customer and shareholder demands and raise wages?

Let us examine a third example: the HIV/AIDS pandemic in sub-Saharan Africa and, in particular, in South Africa. According to the best data, between 25% and 30% of all South Africans are HIV positive. This population is primarily black, poor, and uninsured. There are a number of political reasons why this epidemic was not addressed early on, as Samkin and Lawrence relate in chapter 19. But now HIV is being recognized as the cause of AIDS, and the epidemic is being addressed. We also now know that, thanks to scientific advancement, those who are infected can be put in remission by daily doses of an AIDS "cocktail," a combination of two or three drugs administered throughout the day. The cost of this cocktail on the Western market is about $15,000–20,000/year (U.S. dollars). According to Marcia Angell, however, the same cocktail can be delivered for as little as $300/year if manufactured generically. Doctors Without Borders contends that this price, $300, can be further cut in half (Angell, 2004, pp. 207–208; Medicins sans Frontieres, 2006).

Who should take the lead in attacking this disease? Even when the disease is recognized and prevention measures are promoted, South Africa does not have enough money to provide drugs for most of its infected indigent population. Samkin and Lawrence relate examples of companies in South Africa that are addressing this problem with their infected employees, in some cases providing funds for drug treatment as well as counseling and other remedies. But dealing with this pandemic as more and more employees become infected (and that is a high probability) will be very costly, perhaps prohibitive. Doctors Without Borders has limited funds as well as a limited medical staff to handle this crisis. A number of Western pharmaceutical companies that contend that their mission is to cure disease[5] claim that, by themselves, they cannot furnish enough doses without going bankrupt. And there are other difficulties. Even if pharmaceutical companies forgo profits and quit worrying about patent copying, companies dealing with such countries as South Africa cannot simply give away HIV drugs—because there are few distribution channels, few medics to administer and monitor the drug use, and little in the way of adequate delivery and follow-up systems in most of South Africa. If the drugs reached the ill, without medical assistance they likely will be misused. Giving away the drugs without monitoring is dangerous, because often these drugs get into the black market. These drugs are often diluted and then resold in developed country markets at discount prices. Worse, insufficient dosages of an antiretroviral drug (either because of dilution or lack of compliance with the prescribed protocol) encourages HIV mutation, causing more harm than simply not administering the dosage.[6]

Surely the countries in which this disease flourishes have responsibilities to their citizens to address this problem, but they cannot. Pharmaceutical companies that manufacture HIV/AIDS drugs did not start or perpetuate the HIV epidemic; why and in what ways are they accountable? Faced with what appear to be overwhelming challenges, these companies could follow the easy path of doing nothing, which in fact is what has happened until recently. But given the mission of pharmaceutical companies, the overwhelming extent of this epidemic, the pressure of their researchers and public opinion to address the HIV epidemic, the hopelessly poor countries in which the epidemic is prevalent, and the efficacy of HIV drugs, this option appears to be morally irresponsible.

All of these examples illustrate corporate dilemmas. Even if we assume, for the sake of the argument, that these companies care about these dilemmas, are they trapped in catch-22 situations? How, and in which ways, are these companies obligated to remedy these situations, or are these instances of corporate discretionary responsibility? I suggest not, but the reasons are complicated and have to do with systems thinking.

SYSTEMS AND SYSTEMS THINKING

I said above that one of the critiques of nondiscretionary CSR is that it sometimes asks too much of companies, particularly in their societal relationships. On the other hand, another critique of a CMR approach is that it is too narrow, preoccupied with primary stakeholder relationships without developing a robust understanding of the complex networks of relationships that unavoidably exist between a company and its communities (Painter-Morland, forthcoming). A systems approach is one possible antidote to both these questions.

A system is "a complex of interacting components together with the relationships among them that permit the identification of a boundary-maintaining entity or process" (Laszlo & Krippner, 1998, p. 51).

> A truly systemic view thus considers how . . . [a company] . . . operates in a system with certain characteristics. The system involves interactions extending over time, a complex set of interrelated decision points, an array of actors with conflicting interests, . . . and a number of feedback loops. . . . Progress in analyzing . . . can only be made with a full understanding of the systemic issues. (Wolf, 1999, p. 1632)

Systems are connected in ways that may or may not enhance the fulfillment of one or more goals or purposes: they may be micro (small, self-contained with few interconnections), mezzo (within organizations and corporations), or macro (large, complex, consisting of a large number of interconnections). Corporations are mezzosystems embedded in larger political, economic, legal, and cultural systems. Global corporations are embedded in many such systems. These are all examples of "complex adaptive systems," open interactive systems that are able to change themselves and affect change in their interactions with other systems (Plsek, 2001). What is characteristic of all types of systems is that any phenomenon or set of phenomena that are defined as part of a system have properties or characteristics that are altered, lost, or at best, obscured when the system is broken down into components. For example, in studying corporations, if one focuses simply on its organizational structure, or merely on its mission statement, or only on its employees or customers, one obscures if not distorts the interconnections and interrelationships that characterize and affect that organization in its internal and external relationships.

A system consists of networks of relationships between individuals, groups, and institutions. How any system is construed, how it operates, affects and is affected by individuals, just as corporations are. The character and operations of a particular system or set of systems affect those of us who come in contact with the system, whether we are individuals, the community, professionals, managers, companies, religious communities, or government agencies. An alteration of a particular system or corporate operations within a system (or globally, across systems) will often produce different kinds of outcomes. Thus, part of CMR is incurred by the nature and characteristics of the system in which it operates (Emanuel, 2000). For example, how Wal-Mart contracts with its suppliers affects those suppliers and their employees, as well as Wal-Mart's customers and shareholders.

What companies and individuals functioning within these systems focus on, their power and influence, and the ways values and stakeholders are prioritized affect their goals, procedures, and outcomes as well as affecting the system in question. On every level, the way individuals and corporations frame the goals, the procedures, and what networks they take into account makes a difference in what is discovered or neglected. These framing mechanisms will turn out to be important normative influences of systems and systems thinking (Werhane, 2002).

Systems Thinking

What do we mean by "systems thinking" or a "systems approach"? For purposes of this chapter, systems thinking presupposes that most of our thinking, experiencing, practices, and institutions are interrelated and interconnected. Almost everything we can experience or think about is in a network of interrelationships such that each element of a particular set of interrelationships affects some other components of that set and the system itself, and almost no phenomenon can be studied in isolation from other relationships with at least some other phenomena.

Adopting a systems approach, Mitroff and Linstone (1993) argue that any corporate action needs to be analyzed from what they call a multiple perspective method. Such a method postulates that any phenomenon, organization, or system or problems arising for or within that phenomenon should be dealt with from a variety of disparate perspectives, each of which involves different worldviews where each challenges the others in dynamic exchanges of questions and ideas (see Mitroff & Linstone, 1993, their chapter 6). A multiple perspectives approach takes into account the fact that each of us individually, or as groups, organizations, or systems, creates and frames the world through a series of mental models, each of which, by itself, is incomplete. While it is probably never possible to take account all the networks of relationships involved in a particular system, and surely never so given that these systems interact over time, a multiple perspectives approach forces us to think more broadly and to look at particular systems or problems from different points of view. This is crucial in trying to avoid problems such as Shell's in Ogoniland, to address the Wal-Mart paradox, or to deal with the HIV/AIDS pandemic, because each perspective usually "reveals

insights . . . that are not obtainable in principle from others" (Mitroff & Linstone, 1993, p. 98). It is also invaluable in trying to understand other points of view, even if eventually one disagrees or takes another tactic (Werhane, 2002).

In analyzing the Shell/Ogoniland case, I tried to place Shell in a network of relationships: with the Ogoni, the Nigerian environment, the Nigerian government, and Ken Saro-Wiwa, as well to its primary stakeholders. Each time, however, I raised the question as to the nature and scope of Shell's responsibility, noting how those with whom Shell interacted were not morally exempt, either. But there is one more piece to this sort of analysis, one that is not always dealt with by either the CSR or the CMR literature. If a company is to truly take the perspective of its stakeholders, it needs to take a truly multiple perspective approach to stakeholder analysis, and draw and redraw its stakeholder maps.

Figure 32.1 illustrates a standard stakeholder map with the company, Shell, in the middle (Freeman, 2002, p. 42). This is logical because the figure refers to corporate relationships and responsibilities. But what happens if I redraw that map, putting the Ogoni in the middle (figure 32.2)? I suggest that, at a minimum, our attention is redirected, that we think more seriously about the Ogoni as people with rights and needs. In contrast, if we place the then corrupt Nigerian government in the center, their corruption and power is more starkly illuminated (figure 32.3). Similarly, putting Bangladesh sweatshop workers at the center of a stakeholder map helps us to

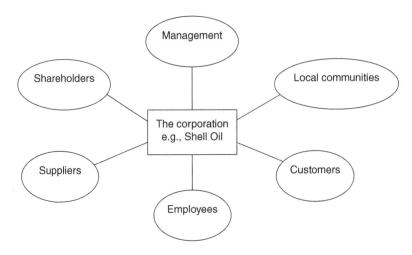

FIGURE **32.1.** Stakeholder map. From Freeman (2002).

6

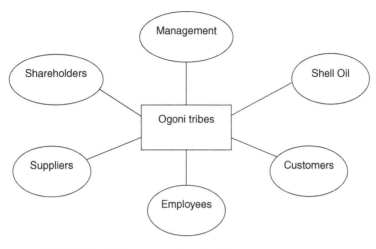

FIGURE 32.2. Stakeholder map—Ogoni tribes.

rethink Wal-Mart marketing and supply chains from a different mental model.

So a multiple perspectives approach is, in part, a multiple stakeholder approach, but with many configurations and accountability lines. It is also an attempt to shake up our traditional mindsets without at the same time ascribing too much in the way of obligation to companies (figure 32.4).

CMR IN A SYSTEMS CONTEXT

But what companies take a multiple perspectives approach; how does this differ, if it does, from a CSR approach; and what are the implications? To

illustrate, I now turn to three new examples that parallel Shell, Wal-Mart, and the business perspective of HIV/AIDS in South Africa. The first is ExxonMobil's exploration of oil in Chad and the development of a pipeline through Cameroon. Chad and Cameroon are two of the poorest and most corrupt countries in the world; Transparency International (2005) listed Chad as the most corrupt country in the world (Cameroon was not listed at all in 2005). For example, Exxon's 2001 revenues were $190 billion; Chad's yearly gross domestic product was $1.4 billion. However, ExxonMobil, in partnership with ChevronTexaco and Petronas, is investing $3.5 billion in drilling in Chad and in building a 600-mile pipeline through Cameroon.

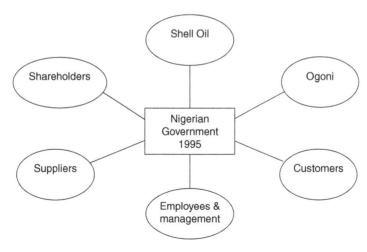

FIGURE 32.3. Stakeholder map—Nigerian government.

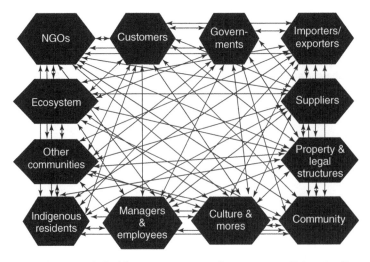

FIGURE 32.4. Stakeholder systems network. Courtesy of Tara Radin.

The project should generate $2 billion in revenues for Chad and $500 million for Cameroon over the 25-year projected drilling period (World Bank, 1999). Still, from ExxonMobil's perspective, carrying out this project is morally risky since, as *Fortune* speculates, the president of Chad, Idriss Déby, who "has a flair for human rights abuses, . . . could 'pull a Mobutu'" (Useem, 2002). (Mobutu was an infamous leader in Zaire (now the Congo) who became an absolute dictator, hanging most of his alleged political enemies and creating a cult around his personality.)

ExxonMobil is a company created by the merger of Exxon and Mobil, and prior to the merger, each was a multibillion dollar oil company. Exxon was best known for the *Exxon Valdez* oil spill, and Mobil, according to *Forbes*, in the early 1990s, became involved with a certain James Giffen, known as a "fixer." It is alleged, but not yet proven, that Giffen, in collaboration with a Mobil executive, was engaged in a questionable payment scheme with the Kazakh government in order to get access to Kazakhstan's oil fields (Fisher, 2003, p.84). There is a perception, at least partly true, that until very recently (and this still sometimes occurs) oil companies simply went into a region with a team of expatriate "foreigners," drilled, dug pipelines, pumped oil, and left.

Given that perception and ExxonMobil's spotty past, what is interesting about the Chad–Cameroon project is ExxonMobil's approach. It has created an alliance with the Chad and Cameroon governments, the World Bank, a number of NGOs, and indigenous populations in the region. Before approving the project, the World Bank created a series of provisos to ensure that there is sound fiscal management of the revenues received by Chad and Cameroon, set up strict environmental and social policies, and consulted with a number of NGOs to protect the rights and welfare of indigenous people in these regions (World Bank, 2002).

By the middle of 2002, the project employed more than 11,000 workers, of whom at least 85% were from Chad or Cameroon. Of these local workers, more than 3,700 have received high-skills training in construction, electrical, and mechanical trades, and 5% of the local workers have supervisory positions. In addition, local businesses have benefited from the project to a total of almost $100 million. The World Bank has developed microlending projects accompanied with fiscal and technical training. The aim is to establish permanent microlending banks in Chad and Cameroon. In partnership with ExxonMobil, the World Bank has created new schools and health clinics, provided HIV education and vaccines against tuberculosis and medical staff to monitor the distribution, distributed thousands of mosquito nets for protection against malaria, and provided farm implements and seeds to develop indigenous agriculture. NGOs have worked with local Pygmy and Bantu tribes to alleviate disruption from the pipeline installation. The Chad and Cameroon governments, in turn, have pledged to use the profits they receive from the venture to improve the standard of living of their citizens (Useem, 2002; World Bank, 2002). This approach is aligned with, although somewhat different from, that suggested by Marcus Breen in chapter 20. This is not a public policy approach, and to date it has not encouraged substantive input from the various indigenous tribes in the region. Nevertheless, it is an attempt to take the interests of the Pygmy and Bantu tribes into account, and that, surely, is a positive step.

It would appear that, at least on the surface, ExxonMobil is attempting to apply a systems approach to this drilling, with some success. Its approach, then, is holistic, envisioning the company as part of an alliance that takes into account and is responsible to multiple stakeholders, not merely shareholders and oil consumers (figure 32.5). Note that there is no individual, tribe, or institution in the center of the graphic in figure 32.5.

The idea is that each of these stakeholders (and there are others I have left out) has a stake in this project; each is responsible—not just ExxonMobil—for the outcomes of this project, and each is accountable.[7] This involvement by all stakeholders and their places in an alliance model distinguishes this approach from some of the CSR approaches that place the primary onus of responsibility on the corporation.

Using a similar approach, I shall focus an aspect of the Wal-Mart paradox: its suppliers' use of nonunionized sweatshop labor. Nike, as Graham Knight writes in chapter 21, had a similar sweatshop problem. Nike owns almost no factories; rather, it buys its goods from numerous manufacturers around the world. So it would appear that what these manufacturers do to get Nike goods to market has nothing to do with Nike. Often, Nike had little knowledge of what went on in the plants that produced its shoes and other products. This changed, of course, when the media began to focus on the working conditions, pay, and safety in plants producing Nike products. Still, why is Nike, rather than these plants, responsible? And what is the extent of that responsibility? As a result of public pressure, Nike began to "look in the mirror" at its mission and corporate image and challenged itself to think about extending the scope of its responsibilities, engaging in what has

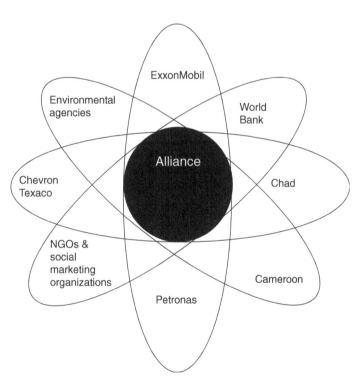

FIGURE **32.5.** ExxonMobil's alliance model. Courtesy of Mary Ann Leeper (Chief Operations Officer, Female Health Company).

become a concerted effort to improve conditions in all sweatshops, not merely in the factories from which it buys but also with the suppliers to those factories.

But Nike did not see this problem as merely *its* problem; rather, it has taken a systems perspective. That is, it sees its responsibilities as extending beyond its own employees, to the system in which its products are produced. It not merely developed a strong code of conduct; it has expanded its influence, its employee standards, and monitoring system to its franchises and, gradually, to their suppliers, as well (Arnold & Hartman, 2003). In this sort of case, one might think of Nike's scope of responsibility in terms of gradually widening concentric circles: first to its employees, customers, and shareholders; second to its contracted suppliers; and third to the suppliers of materials for those suppliers. But Nike does not see its responsibilities in this way. Rather it sees itself in an alliance with all those stakeholders, and is working through all of them, even the suppliers of its suppliers, to make sure materials for its products, as well as its products, are not developed under sweatshop conditions. Figure 32.6 best depicts those relationships.

Nike cannot monitor everything—it is not and cannot be responsible for everything that goes on in the countries in which it has suppliers, but because of its buying power, it can leverage influence and affect supplier conduct. Not to do so would be obligation avoidance.

The HIV/AIDS pandemic invites a model for the distribution of moral responsibilities similar to the ExxonMobil model. This pandemic is embedded in a complex network of relationships, themselves embedded in a complex set of systems and subsystems, including the diverse cultures and practices of indigenous peoples throughout South Africa, distribution issues, financing and funding, pressures from shareholders and NGOs, and the ever-present worry by Western pharmaceutical companies about protection of patents from generic manufacture. The responsibilities for arresting this disease cannot lie merely with the South African government, since it is fiscally incapable of delivering drugs to the infected; it cannot lie merely with companies that employ infected people, simply because, again, the fiscal burden may be too great. Pharmaceutical companies making HIV drugs, too, are not the only ones responsible both for fiscal reasons and because they did not cause the pandemic in the first place.

The model I propose engages companies, donor organizations, NGOs, local villages, and countries in a systemic networking approach to this problem. This is a multistakeholder model to attack and work to alleviate the pandemic by distributing (but not avoiding) the risks and responsibilities. This model was developed by Dr. Mary Ann Leeper, chief operations officer of the Female Health Company (FHC), a for-profit publicly traded company that distributes female condoms

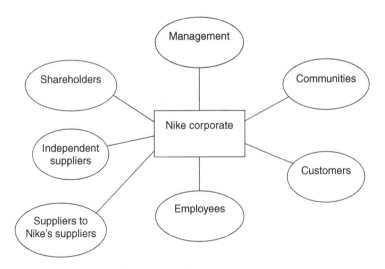

FIGURE 32.6. Stakeholder map—Nike.

to protect women against HIV infection to more than 100 less developed countries, including South Africa. The dilemma for this small company was obvious. They had a fine product, a large customer demand for the female condom, and adequate supplies. But the customer base is penniless and, as mentioned above, governments in less developed countries with high infection rates have little or no funds for this or any other product. So Dr. Leeper began finding donor organizations to support this product. She solicited monies from the Joint United Nations Programme on HIV/AIDS (UNAID), U.S. Agency for International Development (USAID), the United Kingdom Department for International Development (DFID), social marketing organizations that deeply discount products such as condoms, and other international organizations (figure 32.7). But even with money for the product, the company was faced with a second challenge: getting governments in these countries to support the distribution of the product. And there was a third difficulty: training villagers and local health personnel on how to use the

product and how to instruct others. By working with local governments and international nongovernmental organizations (NGOs), the company is gradually overcoming this problem through training and education, village by village in the 100 countries where the FHC distributes it product (Yemen & Powell, 2003).[8]

The FHC alliance model shown in figure 32.7 requires thinking of this enterprise as a program, not merely as delivering a product, just as ExxonMobil has tried to rethink its approach to drilling operations through an alliance model, and as Nike has expanded its stakeholder accountability relationships. Employing this model requires proactive corporate initiatives and the adoption of a systems approach to their operations.

Still, we must ask, why would any company engage in this program? These programs take a great deal of time, effort, and ingenuity, and positive outcomes are slow to be realized. ExxonMobil may not be successful in dealing with the Chad government; Nike has not "converted" all its suppliers to a gentler work environment; Doctors

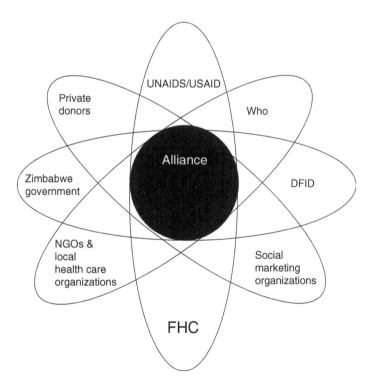

FIGURE 32.7. The Female Health Company (FHC) alliance model. Courtesy of Mary Ann Leeper (Chief Operations Officer, Female Health Company).

Without Borders has had only limited success in South Africa and other regions, due primarily to a paucity of funds, medical staff, and government support. Other companies that are engaging in these processes are also finding that this enterprise is enormously difficult.

There are a number of good reasons why a systems approach is worthwhile. First, and most obviously, with the globalization of capitalism, for better or worse, corporations are now required to take into account all their primary internal *and* external stakeholders. Many companies have always done so. The difference, using this model, is the adaptation of multiple perspectives, trying to get at the mindset of each set of stakeholders from their points of view. From the point of view of rights and justice, an alliance model brings into focus the responsibilities as well as rights of various stakeholders, not merely the corporation. Third, in the case of HIV/AIDS, this is a worldwide pandemic that endangers all of us. So even from a self-interested perspective, companies and countries that can, should help alleviate this disease, if only for their own long-term interests. Fourth, if C. K. Prahalad (2005) is correct, global marketing to what he calls "the bottom of the pyramid," the less economically developed but most populous countries, is critical for the survival and well-being of global companies. Only a systemic approach will be successful in those markets.

CONCLUSION

The explosion of the CSR literature raises awareness of the myriad of ethical and social issues facing today's companies, particularly as they expand in global markets. But the term has been used so broadly as to dilute its impact. Moreover, some of the CSR literature does not parse out carefully the range and limits of CSR and moral obligation. While multinational corporations today are perhaps one of the most powerful sets of economic engines in the global political economies, they are, allegedly at least, *economic* engines with limited goals and means. The interlocking obligations and responsibilities of companies, citizens, NGOs, civic societies, traditions, culture, and even religion should not be overlooked when we focus on CSR. But we should be careful what we wish for. A systems approach, I have argued, that focuses primarily on moral obligations takes into account what each party brings to the table, in terms of both claims and capabilities, and holds each to some measure of accountability. Extending corporate responsibilities too broadly for everything they might even peripherally be involved in also extends their power base and influence far beyond the reasons they were chartered in the first place. One should recall the East India Company that was allowed almost unlimited privileges. The deleterious effects it created for the Asian subcontinent we now call India, Pakistan, and Bangladesh are still evident. That is a mistake worth not repeating.

NOTES

1. Carroll has considerably expanded his thinking since this quoted definition (see Carroll, 1993).
2. These pensions are now rolled into the government's Pension Benefit Guarantee Corporation (PBGC). But according to their website, the maximum pension benefits PBGC pays out for plans ending in 2005 is $45,613.68/year per claimant for those retiring at 65. The amount is lower for early retirees and more for those who retire after 65. How does that affect employees? Ken Bradley, a retired United Airlines pilot who had a six-figure pension, had to retire at 60, the maximum flying age for pilots. Now Bradley will receive only $29,649 from the PBGC (Rose, 2005).
3. That this can be problematic is obvious. Sometimes managers act on behalf of their companies in ways that they would not condone in their own personal behavior. Scott Sullivan, the former CFO of WorldCom, claims his accounting malpractices were done to save the company and preserve shareholder value.
4. "In everything we do, we're driven by a common mission: To improve the quality of life for everyday people around the world" (Wal-Mart, 2006).
5. Merck recognizes this in their mission as stated by George Merck, son of the company's founder: "We try never to forget that medicine is for the people. It is not for the profits. The profits follow, and if we have remembered that, they have never failed to appear. The better we have remembered it, the larger they have been" (Bollier, Weiss, & Hanson, 1991, p. 3). Similarly, Abbott Laboratories' stated mission is "to develop breakthrough health care products that advance patient care for diseases with the greatest unmet medical need" (Abbott Laboratories, 2003).
6. For instance, according to one report, as much as two thirds of the AZT now virtually given away in many African countries by GlaxoSmithKline finds its way back to Europe through black

markets (Friedman, den Besten, & Attaran, 2003, p. 241).

7. This approach does not always guarantee moral success, however. A recent report cites Chad's government as withdrawing from its agreement with the World Bank to channel its oil revenues into poverty alleviation (Polgreen, 2005).

8. A similar model has been adapted by Merck and the Gates Foundation, which they used in attacking HIV in Botswana. Merck has partnered with the Botswanan government and the Gates Foundation in its HIV project in Botswana. It could not merely give its HIV drug, Crixivan, away, even if it had the financial resources and will to do so. Although Botswana has better medical facilities and government than most of the rest of sub-Saharan Africa, its complex culture is such that education, medical infrastructures, and monitoring are not adequate, nor are tribal traditions aligned with modern medical treatment. Without a systems approach, Merck's and the Gates Foundation's attempts to work at the HIV crisis in this country and other less developed countries will fail, whether or not intellectual property rights and patents are preserved. (Weber, Austin, & Bartlett, 2001) In Tanzania, the Abbott Laboratories Fund has partnered with the Tanzanian government and the Axios Foundation (a U.S. NGO) in a multiyear, multimillion dollar project to upgrade and improve the medical care infrastructure, train health care professionals, and expand access to treatment for HIV-infected citizens (Abbott Laboratories, 2003).

REFERENCES

Abbott Laboratories. (2003). Tanzania care. Retrieved September 5, 2004, from http://sitesearch.abbott.com/result_globalCare.jsp?coll=WEB_ABBOTT_Global_Care&paging=1&lang=&dispLeft=true&dispHeader=true&queryText=tanzania&currentPage=3&searchFormType=&queryParser=Internet_AdvancedWeb&dispFooter=true&sourceQuery=&perPage=10.

Angell, M. (2004). *The truth about drug companies.* New York: Random House.

Arnold, D., & Hartman, L. (2003). Moral imagination and the future of sweatshops. *Business & Society Review, 108,* 425–461.

Bollier, D., Weiss, S., & Hanson, K. O. (1991). *Merck and Co.* Harvard University Graduate School of Business Administration Case #9-991-021. Boston: Harvard Business School Press.

Carroll, A. B. (1979). A three-dimensional conceptual model of corporate social performance. *Academy of Management Review, 4,* 497–505.

Carroll, A. B. (1993). *Business and society: Ethics and stakeholder management* (2nd ed.). Cincinnati, OH: South-Western Publishing.

Davis, K., & Blomstrom, R. (1975). *Business and society: Environment and responsibility.* New York: McGraw-Hill.

Emanuel, L. (2000). Ethics and the structures of health care. *Cambridge Quarterly, 9,* 151–168.

Fisher, D. (2003, April 28). Dangerous liaisons: Selling oil means cutting deals with dictators. Nobody does it better than ExxonMobil. *Forbes,* p. 84.

Fishman, C. (2003). The Wal-Mart you don't know. *Fast Company, 77,* 68–70.

Freeman, R. E. (2002). Stakeholder theory of the modern corporation. In T. Donaldson, P. Werhane, & M. Cording (Eds.), *Ethical issues in business* (7th ed., pp. 38–49). Upper Saddle River, NJ: Prentice-Hall.

French, P. (1979). The corporation as a moral person. *American Philosophical Quarterly, 16,* 207–15.

Friedman, M. (1970, September 13). The social responsibility of business is to increase its profits. *New York Times Magazine,* pp. 28–25.

Friedman, M. A., den Besten, H., & Attaran, A. (2003). Out-licensing: A practical approach for improvement of access to medicines in poor countries. *Lancet, 361,* 341–344.

Laszlo, A., & Krippner, S. (1998). Systems theories: Their origins, foundations and development. In J. Scott Jordan (Ed.), *Systems theories and a priori aspects of perception* (pp. 47–74). Amsterdam: Elsevier.

Medicins sans Frontieres [Doctors Without Borders]. (2006). *HIV/AIDS treatment in South Africa proves success in the poorest conditions.* Retrieved March 5, 2006, from http://www.msf.org/msfinternational/ HIV%2FAids+treatment+ in+South+Africa+ proves+ success +in+the+poorest+condi& imgSearch.x=38&imgSearch.y=18, p. 3.

Mitroff, I. I., & Linstone, H. (1993). *The unbounded mind.* New York: Oxford University Press.

National Labor Committee. (2003). *The hidden face of globalization: What the corporations don't want us to know* [Video documentary]. New York: Crowing Rooster Arts.

Newburry, W. E., & Gladwin, T. N. (2002). Shell and Nigerian oil. In T. Donaldson, P. Werhane, & M. Cording (Eds.), *Ethical issues in business* (7th ed., pp. 522–540). Upper Saddle River, NJ: Prentice-Hall.

Painter-Morland, M. (forthcoming). Rethinking

corporate accountability from a global perspective. *Business Ethics Quarterly*.

Plsek, P. (2001). Redesigning health care with insights from the science of complex adaptive systems. In Institute of Medicine, *Crossing the quality chasm: A new health system for the 21st century* (pp. 310–333). Washington, DC: National Academy Press.

Polgreen, L. (2005, December 13). Chad backs out of pledge to use oil wealth to reduce poverty. *New York Times*, p. A15.

Prahalad, C. K. (2005). *The fortune at the bottom of the pyramid*. Upper Saddle River, NJ: Pearson Education.

Rose, B. (2005, January 30). Unkept promises hit retirees. *Chicago Tribune*, § 5, pp. 1, 4.

Transparency International. (2005). Retrieved, September 22, 2005, from http:// www .transparency.org/policy_research/surveys_ indices/cpi/2005, p. 2.

http:///Useem, J. (2002, April 15). Exxon's African adventure. *Fortune*, pp. 102–114.

Velasquez, M. (1983). Why corporations are not morally responsible for anything they do. *Business & Professional Ethics Journal*, 2, 1–18.

Waddock, S. (2004). Parallel universes: Companies, academics, and the progress of corporate citizenship. *Business & Society Review*, 109, 5–42.

Wal-Mart. (2006). Home page. Retrieved May 4, 2006, from http://www.Wal-Martstores .com.

Weber, J., Austin, J., & Bartlett, A. (2001). *Merck global health initiatives (B): Botswana*. Graduate School of Business Administration: Case #9–301–089. Boston: Harvard Business School Press.

Werhane, P. H. (1985). *Persons, rights and corporations*. Englewood Cliffs, NJ: Prentice-Hall.

Werhane, P. H. (2002). Moral imagination and systems thinking. *Journal of Business Ethics, 38*, 33–42.

Werhane, P. H. (2004). The principle of double effect and moral risk: Some case-studies of US transnational corporations. In L. Bomann-Larsen & O. Wiggen (Eds.), *Responsibility in world business* (pp. 105–120). Tokyo: United Nations University Press.

Werhane, P. H., Velamuri, R, & Boyd, D. E. (2006). Corruption and moral risk in business settings. In M. Epstein & K. O. Hanson (Eds)., *The accountable corporation, Vol. 2* (pp. 00–00). Westport CT: Praeger.

Wolf, S. (1999). Toward a systemic theory of informed consent in managed care. *Houston Law Review, 35*, 1631–1681.

World Bank. (1999). *Chad, Cameroon—petroleum development and pipeline project: Environmental assessment. Vol. 1.* Retrieved February 3, 2002, from www-wds.worldbank.org/external/default/main?pagePK= 64193027&piPK=631879.

World Bank. (2002). Chad: Community based integrated ecosystem management project. Retrieved February 23, 2003, from http:// www.worldbank.org/afr/ccproj/project/ pro_overview.htm.

Yemen, G., & Powell, E. (2003). *The Female Health Company (A) and (B)* (UVA-BC-0182-3). Charlottesville, VA: University of Virginia Darden Business Publishing.

Index

AA1000S. *See* Sustainability management systems assurance
ABB, 97, 100
Abbott, JéAnna, 4
Abbott Laboratories, 472*n*5
Abolitionists, 192–193
ACCA. *See* Association of Certified Chartered Accountants
AccountAbility, 45, 63, 66, 68
Accountability, 19, 20–21, 25, 61, 233, 275
  capital, 70
  CSR and, 386–388
  social responsibility reporting and, 234–237
  subaltern publics and, 443–445
  theoretical underpinnings of, 235
Accounting, 181, 232
  objectivity and, 233
  orderliness from, 234
  social reality and, 232–233
  sustainability and, 237–238
ACLU. *See* American Civil Liberties Union
Acquired immunodeficiency syndrome (AIDS), 39, 68, 70, 201, 254*t*, 295, 461, 464, 466, 467, 470, 472
  corporate response to, 284–288
  GRI and, 283–284
  history of, 280

South African societal impact of, 281
  spread of, 280–281
  sustainability and, 279–281
Act utilitarianism, 196
  economic, 198
Action Aid, 64
Activism
  environmental, 48
  Internet, 187, 310
  social, 168
Actuarial Society of South Africa, 281
Adams, Roger, 49
Adamson, James, 185–186
Adecco, 39
Adelphia, 7, 459
Adorno, Theodor, 207
Advertising Age, 373
Advertising Council, 178
Aerospace syndrome, 221
AFL-CIO, 65, 215, 257*t*, 258*t*
African National Congress, 286, 288
Agenda 21, 322, 385
Aguas del Tunari, 439
AIDS. *See* Acquired immunodeficiency syndrome
AIP. *See* Apparel Industry Partnership
Airbus, 219
Alfa Laval, 100
Alien Tort Claims Act, 40
Alliance Capital, 17
Alliance model, 469*f,* 471*f*

Alliance of Automobile Manufacturers, 375
Altria, 179, 185
Alvesson, Mats, 223
Amazon Watch, 257*t*
American Civil Liberties Union (ACLU), 5
American Friends Service, 255*t*
American International Group, 155
American Minority Supplier Development Council, 84
American Revolution, 42
American Society for Training and Development, 224–225
Amnesty International, 32, 53, 65, 70, 90, 95, 254*t*, 337, 440–441, 443
  International Business Group of, 34
Analects (Confucius), 106
Anderson, Walter Truett, 293
Angell, Marcia, 464
Anglo Gold, 284
Annan, Kofi, 48
Ansvar Aktie, 95
Anti-Flag, 247
Antipatterning, 428
ANWR. *See* Arctic National Wildlife Refuge
AOL Time Warner, 167
Apparel Industry Partnership (AIP), 314
Aquinas, Thomas, 158

Arctic National Wildlife Refuge (ANWR), 300
Aristotle, 23, 106, 208, 420, 428, 454
Arthur Andersen, 7, 17, 20, 31, 32, 162, 167, 174
Article 13, 354
Artificial personality, 49, 50
Åsbrink, Erik, 91
ASEAN. *See* Association of Southeast Asian Nations
Asia's New Crisis (Schwab), 111
Association of Certified Chartered Accountants (ACCA), 49
Association of Southeast Asian Nations (ASEAN), 123, 125
AstraZeneca, 97
Atlas Copco, 100
AT&T, 173
Attention economy, 53
Attribution, 20–21
Audubon Society, 344
Australian Corporate Law Economic Reform Programme, 236
Authoritarianism, 213
Ayala Corporation, 114
AZT, 472*n*6

Baez, Joan, 247
Bakan, Joel, 49, 83
  on globalization, 419
Baker, Tom, 221
Ballinger, Jeff, 315
Bang & Olufsen, 91
Bankruptcy law, 172
BankTrack, 70
Barnes & Noble, 81
Barnevik, Percy, 97
Barthes, Roland, 52
Basel Convention on Control of Transboundary Movement of Hazardous Wastes and Their Disposal, 440
Bayer, 179
Bayh-Dole Act, 430
BBC, 46, 53
Bechtel, 31, 439, 443, 445
Beck, Ulrich, 305
Becker, Gary, 212
Behavior change, 48
Ben & Jerry's, 185, 328, 418
Benjamin, Medea, 316
Bentham, Jeremy, 192
Beyond Grey Pinstripes (World Resources Institute), 408

Bhopal disaster, 155, 322, 327, 336, 439
The Big One, 259*t*
bin Laden, Osama, 53
Bioregionalism, 246
Blair, Tony, 385
Blame management, 311, 452
Blogging, 41
Board of Private Assistance, 136
The Body Shop International, 185, 253, 341, 418
Boeing, Bill, 221
Boeing Company, 219–222, 225–227, 229
  code of ethics of, 226–228
  history of, 221
  lean production and, 225
Boeing Health and Safety Institute, 222
Bona fide group theory, 273
Bonn agreement, 289
The Book of Rites (Confucius), 107
Borders, 81
Bowen, Howard, 5, 406
Boycotts, 245–246
BP. *See* British Petroleum
BPR. *See* Business process reengineering
Braithwaite, John, 62
Brancato, Carolyn, 18
Brandley, Ken, 472*n*2
Brands. *See also* Rebranding
  equity of, 186
  global, 52
  impact of, 54
  integrity of, 45–46, 51–54
  super, 52
Brandt, Richard, 196
Braun, Tom, 52
Breman Group, 273
Brennan, William, 193
Brent Spar, 7, 45, 65, 248, 255*t*, 347*n*2, 456
British American Tobacco, 381
British Petroleum (BP), 67, 173, 326, 374, 375, 438
Brooks, John Graham, 309
Brundtland, Gro Harlem, 94, 322, 380
Brundtland report. *See Our Common Future*
Bruner, Emil, 18
Bruyun, Darleen, 219
BT, 49
Bubble economy, 167
Buchanan, Patrick, 215–216
Built to Last (Collins and Porras), 78

Burke, Duncan, 179
Burke, Kenneth, 207, 208
Bush, George W., 177, 182, 418, 425
Business Case for Corporate Citizenship, 47
Business Council for Sustainable Development, 322, 407
Business decision making, 5–6
Business ethics, 9
Business Ethics Magazine, 252
Business for Social Responsibility, 8, 236
Business in the Community, 354
Business judgment rule, 195
Business, language of, 233–234
Business process reengineering (BPR), 405
Business reporting practices, 233
Business Roundtable, 426–427
Business social reponsibility, 15
BuyBlue, 246
Buycotts, 245–246

Cain, Henry, 149
California Rice Industry Association (CRIA), 344, 346
California Waterfowl Association, 344
Caltex, 373
Campaign financing, 62, 433*n*12
Candor principle, 183
Cape, 65
Capital accountability, 70
Capital, definitions of, 295–297
Capital I (Marx), 214
Capitalics, 439, 440
Capitalism, 5, 6, 17, 33, 442
  alienation from, 178
  managerial, 269
  market, 213, 214
  Marxism v., 241
  natural, 384
  power and, 422
  power configurations and, 422
  social movements against, 59
  social progress v., 46
  sustainable, 47
  welfare, 432*n*1
  workplace and, 228
Capture theory, 181
Carbon Disclosure Project, 70
Care work, 41

Careers for the Disabled (magazine), 84
Carroll, Archie, 6
Carson, Rachel, 338
The Case Against Wal-Mart (Norman), 248
Case, Steve, 167
Castro, Fidel, 209
Catalyst, 84
Cauley, Joe, 227
Celebrex, 79
CEMEFI. *See* Mexican Center for Philanthropy
Cementos Mexicanos (CEMEX), 145–147, 149
Center for Economic and Policy Research, 296
Central Holdings, 373
Centre for CSR, 120, 121
Ceres, 354
CERES Principles, 45
de Certeau, Michel, 420, 422, 433*n*6
Certification schemes, 66
Cervecería Cuatémoc-Moctezuma, 138, 144
Chaebol, 111, 116*n*14
Chandler, Geoffrey, 30, 34
Changing Corporate Value (New Consumer), 54
Changing Course (Schmidheiny), 322
Charitable giving, 74
Cheney, Richard, 208, 213, 215
Chevron, 440
ChevronTexaco, 374, 467
Child labor, 33, 68, 213, 257*t*, 441
Child Relief and You, 441
China, market model of, 6–7
Chiquita, 65, 185, 214
Chrysler, 173
Cicero, 208
Cisco, 78
  corporate citizenship statement of, 75
Citicorp, 169
Citizenship, 8
Citroen Pallas DS, 52
Civic positioning, 88
Civil disobedience, 157
Civil regulation, 67
Civil Rights Act, 196
Civil rights movement, 192, 194
Civil society, 59
  definition of, 60
  tactics for, 64–66
Civil War, 177

Class action lawsuits, 172
Clay, David, 225, 229
Clean Air Act, 161, 322
Clean Air Watch, 375
Clean Water Act, 161, 322
Clegg, Stewart, 420, 422
Le Clemenceau, 439–440
Climate change, 59, 70, 365, 391, 394, 411*t*
  commercial impact of, 68
Clover Leaf Creamery Company, 195
CMR. *See* Corporate moral responsibility
Coalition Against Bayer-Dangers, 61
Coase, Ronald, 208
Coastal Barrier Resources Act, 361
Coca-Cola, 40, 51, 242, 245, 246, 248, 249, 365, 444
  consumer activism and, 253–254
Coca-Cola FEMSA, 142, 150
Codes of conduct, 39, 66, 77, 214, 314–315
Codetermination, 274
Coke, 46, 52, 53
Cokewatch, 40
Colgate, 52
Collective bargaining, 96, 160
Collective control, 222
Collins, Jim, 78
Comic Relief, 63
Commission of the European Communities, 121
Communication responsibilities, 162–163
Communicational politics, 310–313
Communications technology, changes in, 41, 47, 54, 61, 79, 244–245, 296–297
  CSR in Mexico and, 135–136, 146–147
  EZLN and, 302
  social movements and, 310
Communications warfare, 293
Communicative competence, 276
Communism, 6
Communitarianism, 128, 131
  sustainability and, 237–238
Community Chest, 156. *See also* United Way
Compensatory damages, 172
Compensatory liability, 171–172
Competition law, 65
Competitive Enterprise Institute, 208

Complexity theory, 53
Comprehensive Environmental Response, Compensation, and Liability Act (Superfund), 322
CONAIE. *See* Confederation of Indigenous Nationalities of Ecuador
Condit, Phil, 219, 220
Confederation of Danish Industries, 93
Confederation of Indigenous Nationalities of Ecuador (CONAIE), 298–300
Confederation of Norwegian Business and Industry, 94
Confucian values, 105
Confucianism, 106–108, 454
  corruption and, 112
  government and, 108–111
Confucius, 106–108, 109
ConocoPhillips, 215
Conrad, Charles, 4
Conscientious consumption, 242, 249–252
  roles of, 252–253
Conservation International, 63
Consultative Body for Human Rights and Norwegian Economic Involvement Abroad, 95
Consumer activism, 241, 244, 252
  notable cases of, 248–249
  strategies for, 244–248
Consumer Advisory Council, 243
Consumer autonomy, 250–251
Consumer Bill of Rights, 243
Consumer Product Safety Commission (CPSC), 5
Consumer responsibilities, 243–244, 244*t*
Consumer rights, 243–244, 243*t*
Consumerism, 241, 242, 248–249
  political, 244, 308
Consumers Association, 54
Consumers International, 243
Consumption, 241
  conscientious, 242, 249–253
  definitions of, 242
Continuous quality improvement, 223
Contract law, 156
  corporations and, 178
Contracts, 109
Coop, 95

Coordinating Business Board, 137
Copenhagen Stock Exchange, 91
Corona Extra, 149
Corporate accountability, 63, 66
Corporate Accountability Act, 430. *See also* Sarbanes-Oxley Act
Corporate agency, 185–186
Corporate agents, 190, 202*n*1
Corporate citizenship, 8, 47–48, 66, 69, 168, 326, 328, 411*t*. *See also* Corporate accountability
  distrust in, 18, 21
  image and, 186
  initiatives for, 46
  rhetoric v. reality of, 75, 77, 79
Corporate Citizenship (McIntosh), 47
Corporate colonization, 16–17
Corporate ecology, 25
Corporate environmentalism, 333
  assumptions underlying, 321–322
  historical context for, 322–323
Corporate Europe Observatory, 64
Corporate governance, 91
  in Asia, 111–113
  law and, 182–183
  rethinking, 268–270
  ROI and, 268–269
  short-term decision making and, 268–269
  stakeholder collaboration in, 267–268
  traditional models of, 267
Corporate hegemony, 17
Corporate law, 183
Corporate misconduct, 220, 227
Corporate moral responsibility (CMR), 460–461
Corporate personhood, 190, 193, 201, 422
  consequences of, 195–196
  development of, 194–196
  moral, 461–462
  rule utilitarian analysis of, 196–197
Corporate philanthropy, 122, 124–125, 139, 156
Corporate power, 59, 61–64
  economic cycles and, 424
  impact of, 18

perspectives on, 63–64, 67
tactics for dealing with, 64–66
Corporate Religion, 52
Corporate Responsibility Coalition, 440
Corporate social responsibility (CSR), 15, 418
  accounting and, 386–388
  activities involved in, 127
  approaches to, 87–88, 127, 167–168
  benefits of, 141–142
  business and society approach to, 121–122
  business case for, 88
  categories of, 181
  collective engagement and, 252
  as communication, 451–455
  communications of, 123, 140–141, 155, 186–188
  contemporary model of, 22–26
  cooptation of, 3
  criticism of, 228, 381, 449
  in Denmark, 91–94
  disclosure method for analyzing, 120
  drivers of, 119*t*–130*t*
  economic approach to, 122
  environmental justice and, 355–357
  evaluation of practices for, 126–127
  as failed antidote, 81–82
  financial markets and, 69–70
  forms of, 122, 155
  generations of, 31, 35–41
  global perspective on, 34–35
  globalization and, 120, 214–216
  as good business practice, 37, 45
  history of, 4–7, 156, 419, 459–460
  HIV/AIDS and, 281–284
  indicators for, 140
  indigenes and, 294
  law and, 158–163, 179
  legitimacy of, 178–179
  management fashions and, 410–412
  in Mexico, 135–136, 146–147
  motivations for, 125
  neoliberal position on, 215
  in Norway, 94–96
  perspectives on, 180–181
  profitability and, 47–48, 78, 124, 180

public relations and, 3
pyramid model for, 121–122
regulation and, 125, 181–182, 455
reporting of, 140–141
responsiveness v., 455–456
Scandinavian model for, 88–89, 96, 98
as social obligation, 92
stakeholder approach to, 120–123
subaltern publics and, 439
sustainable development and, 354–355, 381, 406–408, 442
in Sweden, 96–98
terminology of, 7–9
undermining of, 432
value representation and, 269–270
Corporate social responsiveness, 157
Corporate Sunshine Working Group, 69
Corporate welfare, 214
Corporation(s)
  as adversary, 448–450
  as caretaker, 23
  consumer influence on, 244–248
  credibility of, 21
  decision points for, 397–399
  due process rights of, 195
  environmental issues and, 323–329
  HIV/AIDS and, 284–288
  legal status of, 169
  media and, 62–63
  multinational, 76
  nature of, 16, 50–51, 61–62, 178, 190, 422–423
  political activities of, 62, 169
  regulation influenced by, 199–200
  responsibility and, 16, 228–229
  society's relationship with, 139–140
  stakeholders and, 60
  sustainability and, 394–396
  sustainable, 51
  as systems, 465
  transnational, 17, 60, 62, 309
The Corporation (Bakan), 83
The Corporation (film), 37, 49, 247
Corporatism, 128–129
Corporativism, 129, 131
CorpWatch, 64

Correspondence model, 155, 159. *See also* Natural law theory
Corruption, 74, 91, 111–113
Confucianism and, 112
Costs, externalization of, 64, 76
Coutts Bank UK, 49
Cox, Robert, 442
CPSC. *See* Consumer Product Safety Commission
CraigsList, 245
Credibility gap, 312
Credit Suisse First Boston, 17
CRIA. *See* California Rice Industry Association
Crises as transforming events, 312
Crisis management, 346
Crixivan, 473n8
Cronyism, 111–113
Crook, Clive, 37
CSR. *See* Corporate social responsibility
CSR Wire, 37
Culture
dimensions of, 138
social responsibility and, 148
Culture jamming, 311
Cummins, 157, 462
Cushman, Donald, 224
CVS, 74, 76, 462

Dabhol Power Company, 31–32, 443
Dahl, Robert, 420
Dale, David, 30
Danfoss, 89, 91
Danish Employer's Conference, 93
Dateline NBC, 257t
Davies, Robert, 105–106
Davis, Keith, 5
De Soto, Hernando, 296
DeBeers, 35
Déby, Idriss, 468
Declaration of Independence, 33
Declaration of the Rights of Man, 33
Declaration on the Right to Development, 294
Deep invention, 209, 213
Deforestation, 68
Del Monte Fresh Produce, 185
Demand management, 316n1
Democratic deficit, 297
Demonstrations, 246
Dentsu, 373
Depression of 1898, 423

Deregulation, 6, 419
China and, 7
Det Norske Veritas, 95
Developmentalism, 338
DFID. *See* United Kingdom Department for International Development
Dialogue, 275, 276
eco-collaboration from, 344–346
Díaz, Porfirio, 136
DiFranco, Ani, 247
Disney, 51, 185
Disneyland, 180
Disraeli, Benjamin, 210
Dissociation, 213–214
Distantiation, 276
Distraction effect, 67
Dixon, Frank, 70
Doctors Without Borders, 464, 471–472
Dodd, E. Merrick, 423, 432n1
Doe I v. Unocal Corp., 40
Dole Food, 185
Don't Be Fooled (Green Life), 374
Doonesbury, 248, 259t
Dorgan, Byron, 427
Dove, 46, 52, 53
Dow Chemical, 184, 185, 399
Dow Corning, 172
Dow Jones Sustainability Index, 47, 98f, 99f, 100f, 101, 289
Downing Street Strategy Unit, 91
Drahaus, Peter, 62
Ducks Unlimited, 344
Dukes v. Wal-Mart, 257t
Duncan, David, 167
DuPont, 186, 399
Durban Chamber of Commerce, 283, 288
DVLINK, 22
Dworking, Richard, 191

Earmarking, 426
Earth Culture, 255t
Earth Rights International, 65
Earth Summit, 322, 323, 380, 407
Earth Summit Business Academy, 375
Earth Summit Plus Five, 380
eBay, 245
Ebbers, Bernard, 17
Eco-collaboration, 344–346, 453
Ecolabeling, 369
Ecological warfare, 339

Ecomanagement. *See* Sustainability
Economic liability, 426
Economic liberalization, 342
Economic utilitarianism, 198
Economics
Austrian, 207, 214
Chicago School of, 182, 207
free market, 207
globalization and, 4
laissez faire, 6, 7, 214, 422
neoliberal, 3, 6, 7, 41, 62, 199, 207, 210, 215–216, 310, 313, 323–324
Rehn-Meidner model of, 96–97
"Third Way," 7
Economizing, 76
Ecosystem management, 273, 391–394
Eco-talk, 336–337, 453
Shell and, 337–338
EDF. *See* Environmental Defense Fund
Efficient Energy for Sustainable Development Partnership, 353
Eisenberg, Melvin, 183
El Dorado: How Scientists and Journalists Devastated the Amazon (Tierney), 293
Elkington, John, 8, 54, 234, 342–343, 411t
Emergency Planning and Community Right to Know Act, 162
Eminent domain, 426
Employer's Confederation of the Mexican Republic, 137
Employment, 156
at will, 160
Endangered Species Act, 161
English Bill of Rights, 33
Enhanced Analytics Initiative, 70
Enron, 7, 17, 22, 30–32, 42, 49, 78, 114, 155, 162, 167, 174, 177, 180, 182, 185, 186, 235, 268, 425, 429, 443, 445, 449, 459
RICE principles of, 19, 21, 184
Enron: The Smartest Guys in the Room, 37
Environment Waikato, 238
Environmental activism, 48
Environmental collaboration, 276
Environmental Defense Fund (EDF), 344–347

Environmental justice, 254*t*–256*t*, 342
  sustainable development and CSR linked by, 355–357
Environmental law, 161–162
Environmental management systems, 326, 328
Environmental marketing, 365. *See also* Green marketing
Environmental Protection Agency (EPA), 5, 185, 199–200, 359, 394, 397, 424. *See also* National Pollution Prevention and Toxics Advisory Committee
  environmental justice definition of, 356
  Office of Pollution Prevention and Toxics of, 399
Environmental racism, 255*t*
Environmental responsibility, 161–163
  communication of, 329–333
  corporate stances towards, 323–329
Environmental systems, 391–394
EPA. *See* Environmental Protection Agency
Equal Opportunity Commission, 5
Equal Rights Amendment, 194
Ericsson, 39
Escobar, Arturo, 380
Ethical Business Conduct Guidelines (Boeing Company), 226–228
Ethical Consumer, 54
Ethical responsibility, 351
Ethical Trading Initiative, 61
Ethical workplace management systems certification (SA8000), 46, 184
Ethics
  bureaucracy and, 186–187
  business, 9
  codes of, 184, 226–228
  law and, 155, 157–158
  moral obligation and, 237
Ethos, 23–24
European Academy of Business in Society, 8
European Bank for Reconstruction and Development, 255*t*
Evans, Warren, 49
Executive pay, 222
Export processing, 307, 309

Expropriation, 112
Extractive Industries Transparency Initiative, 70
Exxon, 170, 173, 174, 324
Exxon Valdez, 79, 170, 324, 336, 418, 468
ExxonMobil, 123, 155, 169, 215, 245, 418, 440, 467, 468, 469, 471
  corporate citizenship statement of, 79
EZLN. *See* Zapatista National Liberation Army

Fair Labor Association (FLA), 259*t*, 314, 315
Fair Pensions Campaign, 70
Fair trade standards, 214
Family and Medical Leave Act, 324
Family Research Council, 383
Family Unity for Sustainable Development Foundation, 383
Fannie May, 252
FASB. *See* Financial Accounting Standards Board
Fascism, 191
Fastow, Andrew, 182
FCC. *See* Federal Communications Commission
FDA. *See* U.S. Food and Drug Administration
Federal Communications Commission (FCC), 5, 243
Federal Express, 426
Federal Securities Exchange Act, 162
Federal Trade Commission (FTC), 5, 243, 366
  environmental marketing guidelines of, 370
Feldstein, Mary Jo, 224
Female Health Company (FHC), 470–471
FEMSA, 138, 142, 144, 146, 147
FEMSA Cerveza, 142, 145, 150
Feurstein, Aaron, 164
FHC. *See* Female Health Company
Fiduciary duty law, 183
Fiduciary responsibility, 461
  social responsibility v., 172–174
Filartiga v. Pena-Irala, 40
File sharing, 41
Finance Credit, 91

Financial Accounting Standards Board (FASB), 430
Financial markets
  disruption of, 268
  role of, 69–70
  short-term emphasis of, 76–77
  sustainability benefits and, 283
Financial Times, 121
Firestone, 171
First National Bank of Boston v. Bellotti, 169
FLA. *See* Fair Labor Association
Flash mobs, 53
Foodmaker Corporation, 174
Forbes, 169
Ford, Henry, 156
Ford Motor Company, 156, 171, 374–375
Fordism, 310, 316*n*1
Föreningssparbanken, 97
Forest Stewardship Council, 61, 66
Fortum, 101
Fortune, 19, 31, 80, 97
48 Hours, 258*t*
Foster, John Bellamy, 384
Fox, Michael, 438
Franklin, Benjamin, 80
Fraud, 174
Frederic W. Cook & Company, 18
Free Enterprise Action Fund, 208
Free trade, 59
Freecycle Network, 245
Freeman, R. Edward, 6
French Revolution, 42
Friedman, Milton, 5–6, 7, 16, 19, 30, 33, 122, 163, 181, 207–216, 406, 450
  on boycotts, 245
  environmental issues and, 323–324, 327, 333
Friedman, Thomas, 37–38
Friends of the Earth, 64, 257*t*, 260*t*
FTC. *See* Federal Trade Commission
FTSE4Good, 98*f*, 99*f*, 100*f*, 101, 289
Full cost accounting, 329
Fussler, Claude, 48

Gabriel, Yiannis, 242
Galbraith, Kenneth, 50
The Gap, 38, 65, 184–185, 246, 248
  code of vendor conduct of, 214–215

Garcia, Romeo Lucas, 253*t*
Gates Foundation, 473*n*8
GATT. *See* General Agreement on Tariffs and Trade
Gay rights movement, 194
GE. *See* General Electric
Gender equality, 97
General Agreement on Tariffs and Trade (GATT), 294
General Dynamics, 68
General Electric (GE), 31, 51, 215, 366, 375, 443
General Motors, 169, 171, 271, 374–375
Generic liability, 159
Genomics, 294
Giffen, James, 468
Gifford, Kathie Lee, 245, 257*t*, 258*t*
GlaxoSmithKline, 179
Global Anglican Council on the Stewardship of Creation, 383
Global cities, 38
Global Climate Coalition, 343
Global connectivity, 79
Global consciousness, 36
Global Crossing, 17, 167
Global Ecolabelling Network, 368
Global Exchange, 65, 245, 248, 258*t*–260*t*, 314, 316
Global Forest Watch, 328
Global participation, 36
Global People's Tribunal, 260*t*
Global Reporting Initiative (GRI), 45, 61, 66, 144, 146, 147, 234, 280, 284, 289, 314, 381. *See also* *Sustainability Reporting Guidelines*
  history of, 282–283
  HIV/AIDS and, 283–284
Global Sullivan Principles of Social Responsibility, 39
Global Trade Watch, 259*t*–260*t*
Global warming, 39, 208, 339
Global Witness, 65
Globalization, 4, 8, 17, 30, 36, 42, 60, 88, 113
  CSR and, 214–216
  as driver of CSR, 120
  humanizing, 46
  indigenes and, 292
  policy monopolies and, 431
  processes of, 293–294
  protests against, 74, 247
  regulation and, 419
  social capital and, 38

social movements against, 59
social value representation and, 270–271
Sweden and, 97
Glocalization, 36–38
Glorious Revolution of 1688, 41–42
GolinHarris, 18
Good to Great (Collins), 78
Goodwyn, Lawrence, 201
Government intervention, 108–109, 115*n*9, 208, 270
Government regulators, 5
  CSR and, 125
The Great Betrayal (Buchanan), 215–216
Great Depression, 4, 178, 423
Great Society, 419
Green advertising, 368–369, 370, 373–374
  approaches to, 370–372
  future of, 374–376
Green chemistry, 398
The Green Consumer Guide, 54
Green consumers, 367–368
Green Life, 373–374
Green marketing, 3, 366–367
Green Network, 90
Greenness, Tor, 88
Greenpeace, 7, 70, 255*t*, 337, 440, 456
Greenspan, Alan, 427
Greenwald, Robert, 247, 258*t*
Greenwashing, 260*t*, 366, 374–376, 453
GRI. *See* Global Reporting Initiative
Griffiths, Nigel, 30, 33
Groupthink, 21
Grundfos, 89, 91, 92
Grupo Bimbo, 145, 146, 148
Grupo Modelo, 145, 146, 149
Guthrie, Woody, 247

Habermas, Jurgen, 178
Hailes, Julia, 54
Halliburton, 208, 214, 215
Hamilton, Alexander, 19
Hanson Plc., 49
Hawken, Paul, 384
Health Global Access Project, 254*t*
Health maintenance organizations (HMOs), 425, 428
HealthSouth, 17, 459
Hennes & Mauritz, 97
Herbert, Bob, 314
Herkströter, Cor, 342, 343

Hesiod, 23
Hewlett-Packard, 215, 225
High-performance work organization (HPWO), 220, 222–225
Hispanic Business Magazine, 84
Hispanic National Bar Association, 84
HIV. *See* Human immunodeficiency virus
HMOs. *See* Health maintenance organizations
Hobbes, Thomas, 191, 420
Holmes, Oliver Wendell, 158, 159
Home Depot, 74, 76, 81, 462
Homer, 23
Honda, 373
HPWO. *See* High-performance work organization
HSA Coalition, 425
Hubbard, Dick, 236, 438
Hubbard Foods, 236–237, 438
Human immunodeficiency virus (HIV). *See also* Acquired immunodeficiency syndrome
  GRI and, 283–284
  sustainability and, 279–281
Human rights, 3, 31, 46, 74, 77, 184, 253*t*–254*t*, 269, 342, 468
  evolution of, 33–34, 308
  standards for, 42
Human Rights Watch, 32, 337
Humane Society, 260*t*
Hurricane Katrina, 36, 76, 352
Hurricane Rita, 365

IAM. *See* International Association of Machinists and Aerospace Workers
IBM, 51
ICC. *See* International Chamber of Commerce
ICC Code of Advertising Practice, 368
ICC International Code of Environmental Advertising Publication, 368
ICTs. *See* Information communication technologies
Identity politics, 216, 309, 310
Ideograph, 251
IFAT. *See* International Fair Trade Association

IISD. *See* International Institute for Sustainable Development
IKEA, 90, 96, 97, 328
ILO. *See* International Labor Organization
IMF. *See* International Monetary Fund
Immelt, Jeffrey, 222
Inalienable rights, 191–192
Incentives, 185
Inclusion, 271–272
Índice Mexicano de Reputación Empresarial, 142, 144
Industrial democracy, 90
Industrial ecology, 391
Industrial location, 62
Industrial Revolution, 4, 156
Industrialization, 33
power and, 422
Information communication technologies (ICTs), 252, 296
Innovest Social Investors, 70
Insider trading, 167
Institute for Social and Ethical Accountability, 45
Institute of Directors in Southern Africa, 279, 282
Institute of Social and Ethical Accountability, 289
Institutional Revolutionary Party, 136
Instituto Ethos, 140
Instituto Tecnológico Autónomo de México, 149
Instituto Tecnológico y de Estudios Superiores de Monterrey (ITSEM), 148–149
Instrumental Policy Behavior Process (IPBP), 293, 297–300
Integrity, definition of, 50
Intel, 51
Intellectual property rights, 293, 295
International Association of Machinists and Aerospace Workers (IAM), 221–222, 225–226
International Baby Food Action Network, 61
International Chamber of Commerce (ICC), 368
International Council of Forest and Paper Associations Partners, 354
International Dairy Foods Corporation, 195

International Fair Trade Association (IFAT), 246
International Institute for Sustainable Development (IISD), 385
International Labor Organization (ILO), 298–300, 301
International Labor Rights Fund, 254*t*
International Monetary Fund (IMF), 6, 59, 247, 297, 431, 440
International Right to Know campaign (IRTK), 65
International Standards Institutes (ISO), 39, 369, 410, 413
International Union for the Conservation of Nature and Natural Resources, 351, 380
International Union of Food and Allied Workers' Associations (IUF), 253*t*
International Whaling Commission, 255*t*
Internet activism, 187, 310
IPBP. *See* Instrumental Policy Behavior Process
Iranian National Oil, 215
"Iron Law of Responsibility," 5
IRTK. *See* International Right to Know campaign
ISO. *See* International Standards Institutes
ISO 14000, 326, 402
Issue advocacy, 346
Issue monitoring, 186
Issues management, 186, 313–315
"It Concerns Us All," 92–93
Ithaca HOURS, 246
Ito, Joichi, 113
ITSEM. *See* Instituto Tecnológico y de Estudios Superiores de Monterrey
IUCN. *See* World Conservation Union
IUF. *See* International Union of Food and Allied Workers' Associations

Jack in the Box, 174
Jackall, Robert, 186
Jackson, Jesse (Reverend), 256*t*
Jackson, Michael, 179
Japan
green advertising in, 373–374
market model of, 6

Japan Eco-Life Center, 373
Jefferson, Thomas, 80
Jennings, Peter, 253*t*
Jespersen, Karen, 92–93
Jobs, cost of, 38
Johns-Manbille Corporation, 172
Johnson, B. M., 21
Joint United Nations Programme on HIV/AIDS, 279
Jones, Hannah, 68
Jones, Thomas, 6
Journal of Corporate Citizenship, 47
JPMorgan Chase, 17
Juran Institute, 413
Juxtaposition, 246

Kathie Lee, 248, 257*t*
Keiretsu, 111, 116*n*14
Kelley, Florence, 245
Kennedy, John F., 17, 243
Kernaghan, Charles, 245
Kerner Commission, 215
Kerry, John, 210
Keynesism, 207, 310, 316*n*1
Kickbacks, 112, 179
Kim Dae Jung, 112
King Committee on Corporate Governance for Southern Africa (King I, King II), 279–280, 282, 290
King, Michael, 47
King, Ynestra, 321, 334
Kissinger, Henry, 211
Knight, Phil, 259*t*, 306
Knowledge management, 410
Kochan, T. A., 21
Kodad, 215
Kopper, Michael, 182
Korten, David, 323, 334, 381–382
Kozlowski, Dennis, 17, 167, 182, 462
KPMG, 47, 284, 289
Kramer, Mark, 212
Krugman, Paul, 31
Krupp, Fred, 346
Kuhrana, 423
Kukdong, 312
Kunde, Jesper, 52
Kyoto Accord, 94, 161, 289, 354

Labeling schemes, 245–246
Labor practices, 124
Labor relations, 88, 187
Labor rights, 184
Labor standards, 46, 74

Laissez faire economics, 6, 7, 214, 422
Lang, Tim, 242
Language, business and, 233–234
Larsen, Terje Roed, 94
Law
    bankruptcy, 172
    communications and, 162–163
    competition, 65
    contract, 156
    corporate, 183
    corporate governance and, 182–183
    environmental, 161–162
    ethics and, 155, 157–158
    fiduciary duty, 183
    managing, 181
    moral standards and, 156–158
    patent, 430
    product responsibility and, 158–160
    purpose of, 191
    religion and, 165*n*2
    social responsibility and, 158–163, 179
    soft, 93–94, 95
    tort, 159–160
Lay, Kenneth, 19, 20, 22, 30, 167, 182
Lean Enterprise Institute (LEI), 224
Lean production, 219, 223
    anxiety caused by, 225
    IAM and, 225–226
Learning organizations, 328
Learning platforms, 46
Leeper, Mary Ann, 470–471
Legal positivism, 155, 157–158, 159
Legal rights, 191
L'Eggs, 365
Legitimacy, 178–179
Legitimation, 4, 419
Lego, 89, 91
LEI. *See* Lean Enterprise Institute
Leisinger, Klaus, 50
Lennon, John, 247
Leopold, Aldo, 351
Leviathan (Hobbes), 420
Levinas, Emmanuel, 24
Levitt, Theodore, 423
Liability
    apology and, 171
    compensatory, 171–172
    economic, 426
    generic, 159

minimizing, 172–174
    strict, 159–160
Liberal democracy, 275
Libertarianism, 210
Life cycle analysis, 397–398
Lifestyle advertising, 241
Lifestyle politics, 308. *See also* Subpolitics
Litigation, 171–172
Living wage, 31, 33, 251
Lobbying, 69
Local 1330 v. United States Steel Corp., 183
Local exchange trading, 246
Localism, 246
Lockheed, 35
Lockheed Martin, 68, 224
Lotus Development Corporation, 180
Lovemarks, 52
Lundin Oil, 97
Lundwall, Richard, 256*t*

Machiavelli, 211
Magna Carta, 33
Malden Mills, 164, 418
Management by objectives (MBO), 405
Management fashions
    characteristics of, 408–410
    CSR and, 410–412
    sustainable development and, 410–412
Managerial discourse, 18–22
Managerial language, 22
Managerial prerogative, 195, 202*n*5
Managerial self-interest, 269
Managerialism
    definition of, 19
    narcissism and, 22
    qualities of, 19–22
Mandela, Nelson, 227
Mann, Michael, 421–422, 432*n*1, 433*n*5, 433*n*6
Maquiladoras, 358
Marchand, Roland, 4
Marcos (Subcomandante), 301–302
Margin of safety, 400
Market capitalism, 213, 214
The Market for Virtue (Vogel), 215
Market models, 6–7
Market positioning, 88
Market-based democracy, 199
Markovitz, Steven, 17
Marlboro, 51
Marlin, Alice Tepper, 54, 181
Marques, Pere, 142

Marx, Karl, 4, 214, 229, 294, 312, 450
Marxism, 178, 213, 220, 229, 449
    capitalism v., 241
Massey, Doreen, 50
MasterCard, 78
Matsumoto, Oki, 112–113
Maynard, Therese, 183
Mayo, Elton, 223
MBO. *See* Management by objectives
McDonald's, 38, 40, 51, 52, 61, 157, 344, 346, 347, 365, 367, 368
McDonnel Douglas, 221
McKeon, Richard, 208
McSpotlight, 40, 61
Meaning, 207, 208
Media, corporations and, 62–63
Mediation, 174
Medicaid, 179
Medical malpractice, 172
Medicare Reform Act, 425
Médicins Sans Frontières, 64. *See also* Doctors Without Borders
Meehan, Patrick, 179
Mencius, 106–108
Mercedes, 52, 373
Merck, 79, 155, 472*n*5, 473*n*8
Merck, George, 472*n*5
Meredith, James, 194
Merrill Lynch, 17, 168
Methodological collectivism, 197
Metonymy, 211, 216*n*1
Metso, 100
Mexican Center for Philanthropy (CEMEFI), 137, 140, 141
Mexican Foundation for Social Development, 137
Mexican Revolution of 1910, 136
Mexmode, 312
Meyers, William, 193
Micheletti, Michele, 244
Microlending, 468
Microsoft, 51, 52, 65, 74, 76, 81, 123, 155, 462
    corporate citizenship statement of, 79
Mitofsky, 142–143
M&Ms, 46
Mobil, 468
Mondragon, 21
Monex, 113
Monks, Robert, 50
Monologue, 21–22

Monsanto, 52, 65, 325
Moore, Michael, 259t
Moral agency, 197, 198, 461
Moral agents, 191
Moral authority, 17
Moral obligation, 462–465
  ethics and, 237
Moral rights, 191
Moral standards, law and,
  156–158
Morality, 157
"The Morals of Shopping"
  (Brooks), 309
Morgan Chase, 289
Morris, Jane Anne, 200
MOSOP. See Movement for the
  Survival of Ogoni People
Movement for the Survival of
  Ogoni People (MOSOP),
  255t, 337, 339–341
Mulhally, Alan, 220
Multilateralism, 315, 452
Multinational corporations
  (MNCs). See
  Corporation(s)
MutualFunds.com, 68

Nader, Ralph, 184, 244
NAFTA. See North American
  Free Trade Agreement
Nasser, Jacques, 171
The Natal Mercury, 285
National Action Network, 84
National Association of
  Counties, 94
National Association of
  Municipalities, 94
National Consumers League, 245
National Energy Policy Office,
  353
National Energy Review, 215
National Environmental Justice
  Advisory Council
  (NEJAC), 359
National Environmental Policy
  Act, 360
National Hispana Leadership
  Institute, 84
National Human Rights
  Commission, 137
National Labor Committee,
  257t, 258t
National Labor Relations Act
  (NLRA), 160–161
National Network of Company
  Leaders, 93
National Pollution Prevention
  and Toxics Advisory
  Committee (NPPTAC),
  397

National Ski Areas
  Association, 375
National Spiritual Assembly of
  the Baha'is of the United
  States, 382–383
National Trades Union
  Congress (NTUC), 128,
  131
Natural capitalism, 384
Natural law theory, 155, 158,
  159, 165n2
Natural rights, 192
Natural Step, 354, 355
Negative Dialects (Adorno),
  207
Negligence, 159–160
NEJAC. See National
  Environmental Justice
  Advisory Council
Neoliberal economics, 3, 6, 7,
  41, 62, 199, 207, 210,
  216, 310, 313
  CSR and, 215
  environmental issues and,
  323–324
Neoteny, 113
Nestlé, 145, 149
New Coke, 249, 254t
New Consumer, 54
New Criticism, 211
New Deal, 178, 419, 422, 423
New Zealand Businesses for
  Social Responsibility
  (NZBSR), 406
New Zealand Sustainable
  Business Network, 406
Newbold, Yve, 49
Newell, Peter, 60, 67, 69
NGOs. See Nongovernmental
  organizations
Nguyen, Thuyen, 258t
Niger Delta Women for Justice,
  443
Nike, 38, 40, 65, 67–69, 81,
  185, 212, 246, 248, 251,
  258t–259t, 305, 311, 407,
  452, 469–471. See also
  Participate in the Lives of
  American Youth
  code of conduct of, 314, 315
  marketing mechanisms of,
  309–310
  sweatshops and, 305–307
Nike Foundation, 314
Niketown, 259t
Nikewatch, 40
Nikkei, 373
Nissan, 373
NLRA. See National Labor
  Relations Act

Nokia, 51
Nongovernmental
  organizations (NGOs), 32,
  37, 74, 248
  CSR opposed by, 381
  in Mexico, 137
  in Scandanavia, 90
  Singapore and, 121, 126,
  128, 129t
Nonprofit sector, 60
Nørby Code, 91, 102n5
Nordea, 89
Nordic Partnership, 90
Nordic welfare model, 89
Nordisk Fjer, 91
Norman, Al, 248, 257t, 258t
Normative case, 88
Norrköping model, 39
Norsk Hydro, 90, 95
Norske Skog, 90, 101
North American Free Trade
  Agreement (NAFTA), 38,
  136, 294, 431
  impact of, 433n16
  peso devaluation and, 302
Norwegian Accounting Act, 95
Norwegian Petroleum Fund, 95
Novartis, 78
  corporate citizenship
  statement of, 75
Novartis Foundation, 50
Novo Nordisk, 89–91, 100
NPPTAC. See National
  Pollution Prevention and
  Toxics Advisory
  Committee
NTUC. See National Trades
  Union Congress
Nuclear Energy Institute, 374
Nuovo Pignone, 215
NZBSR. See New Zealand
  Businesses for Social
  Responsibility

Objectivity, accounting and,
  233
OCA. See Organic Consumers
  Associaiton
Occidental Petroleum, 185
Occupational Safety and
  Health Act, 162
Occupational Safety and
  Health Administration
  (OSHA), 5, 199
O'Donnell, Frank, 375
OECD. See Organization for
  Economic Co-operation
  and Development
Offshoring, 37, 38
Ogilvy Public Relations, 438

Olbrechts-Tyteca, Lucie, 208, 213
Olympic Games, 53
Omnipoint Communications Enterprises Corporation, 196
Onex, 219
Ong, Aihwa, 386
Open Society Institute, 65
Operation Push, 258t
Oravec, Christine, 384
Organic Consumers Association (OCA), 245, 259t
Organization for Economic Co-operation and Development (OECD), 49, 268, 270, 273, 297, 387
Organization of Chinese Americans, 84
Organizational citizenship, 8
Organizational culture, 184
incentives and, 185
Organizational identity, 19, 22
Organizational legitimacy, 178–179
Organizations. See also Corporation(s)
discursive status of, 169–170
learning, 328
obligations of, 170–171
as places, 50
value systems of, 164
Organizing America (Perrow), 422
Origins, 353
Ortho Pharmaceuticals, 181
OSHA. See Occupational Safety and Health Administration
Oslo Accors, 94
Oslo Stock Exchange, 91
The Other Side of Offshoring, 37
Our Common Future (WCED), 322, 338, 343, 352, 380–382, 407, 442, 449
Outsourcing, 37, 38, 78
Overfishing, 68
Oversight, 185–186
Owen, Robert, 30
Oxburgh, Ronald (Lord), 255t
Oxfam, 46, 61, 65, 70, 309, 441

Paine, Lynn Sharp, 87
PAP. See Peoples Action Party
Parmalat, 49
Parrish, Stephen, 185
Participate in the Lives of American Youth (PLAY), 306

Participation models, 268, 272
Participatory workplace, 222–224
Partnership, 46
Patagonia, 253
Pataki, George, 430
Patents, 201, 430
Patriotism, profits v., 215
Peck, Jules, 69
Pension Benefit Guarantee Corporation, 472n2
Peoples Action Party (PAP), 119, 124, 131
"People's home" concept, 96–98
People's Union for Civil Liberties, 443
Pepsi, 52, 444
Perelman, Chaim, 208, 213
Peretti, Jonah, 311
Peroni, Bob, 426
Perrow, Charles, 422
Peterson, Scott, 179
Petroleum Authority of Thailand, 373
Petronas, 440, 467
Pfizer, corporate citizenship statement of, 79
Philanthropy
corporate, 122, 124–125, 139, 156
in Mexico, 136–137
strategic, 137
types of, 139
Philip Morris, 171, 179. See also Altria
Pizza Hut, 38
Plato, 420
PLAY. See Participate in the Lives of American Youth
Plural Project, 97
Polarization, 214, 450
Policy monopolies, 424–427
globalization of, 431
Political consumerism, 244, 308
Pollution, 156, 198
user pay policies towards, 326
Popoff, Frank, 184
Porras, Jerry, 78
Porter, Michael, 212
Posner, Richard (Judge), 211
Postmaterialism, 308–309, 310
Poverty, 70
HIV/AIDS and, 280–281
in United States, 183
Power, 208
capitalism and, 422
corporate, 18, 59, 61–64

deception and, 420
industrialization and, 422
politics and, 207, 211
sources of, 421
Precautionary principle, 399–401
Prince of Wales International Business Leaders Forum, 105
Principal-agency theory, 235–236, 239n1
Private sector
public sector boundaries with, 40–41, 71
public sector partnerships with, 92
Privatization, 6, 38
China and, 7
Proceduralism, 315
Procter & Gamble, 215, 365, 368
Product life cycle, 325
Product responsibility, 158–160
Product stewardship, 398
Profit
CSR and, 47–48, 78, 124, 180
maximization of, 80
motive, 6
patriotism v., 215
social responsibility and, 408
sustainability v., 99
Profits and Principles–Does There Have To Be a Choice? (Royal Dutch Shell), 339
Program on Corporations, Law, and Democracy, 64
Progressive Era, 4, 178
Progressive Law Movement, 178, 183, 187
Project Underground, 255t
Property rights, 201
Prudential Securities, 17
Public Enemy, 247
Public interest groups, 5
Public policy implementation, 430–431
Public policy making, 424
Public relations, 180. See also Crisis management; Issue advocacy
social responsibility and, 148
sustainable development and, 346
Public sector
private sector boundaries with, 40–41, 71
private sector partnerships with, 92

Publish What You Pay, 65
Punitive damages, 172
Putnam, Robert, 15

Al Qaeda, 53
Quality circles, 224, 405
Quasi-logical argument, 213
Quattrone, Frank, 17
Qwest Communications, 18

Racketeering, 180
Rage Against the Machine, 247
Raging Grannies, 260*t*
Railtrack, 64
Rainforest Action Network, 249, 255*t*, 256*t*, 257*t*
Rainforest Alliance, 63
Rand, Ayn, 210
Rationality
    bounded, 182
    economic, 182, 207
Rawls, John, 24
rBST. *See* Recombinant bovine somatropin
Reagan, Ronald, 214, 222, 425
Realist style, 210–212, 214
Reasonable care, 159
Rebranding, 18
Recognition politics, 308–309
Recombinant bovine somatropin (rBST), 195, 202*n*7
Red Cross, 139
Red Scare, 423
Reflexivity, 310, 342–344
Regulation, 270–271
    civil, 67
    corporate influence on, 199–200
    CSR and, 125, 181–182, 455
    environmental, 394
    history of, 177–178
    responsibility v., 455
    risk and, 399–400
    self-, 184, 186–187
    social responsibility and, 210
    state, 67
    subaltern publics and, 444
Rehn-Meidner model, 96–97
Reification, 19
Reisner, Marc, 344–345
Remaking Singapore, 119
Reporting Guidance on HIV/ AIDS (GRI), 283
Republican form of government, 190–192
Responsibility standards, 186

Responsiveness, 140, 157, 164
    responsibility v., 455–456
Return on investment (ROI), 268–269, 272
Rheingold, Thomas, 53
Rhetorical analysis, 208–209
RHP. *See* Ricelands Habitat Partnership
Ricardo, David, 208
Ricelands Habitat Partnership (RHP), 344–346
Rifkin, Jeremy, 300, 418
Right(s)
    civil, 192, 194
    consumer, 243–244, 243*t*
    definition of, 191
    due process, 195
    human, 3, 31, 33–34, 42, 46, 74, 77, 184, 253*t*–254*t*, 269, 342, 468
    inalienable, 191–192
    intellectual property, 293, 295
    labor, 184
    legal, 191
    moral, 191
    natural, 192
    property, 201
    shareholder, 268
    to unionize, 160
    women's, 192, 194
    worker's, 160–161
Right sizing, 222
Rio Accord, 94
Rio Tinto Zinc, 37
Risk, 399–401
Risk management, 88, 95
Risk society, 310–313, 316
Rivers and Harbors Act, 165*n*1
Roberts, Kevin, 52, 53
Robertson, Roland, 36
Rodenticide Registrants Task Force, 200
Roepke, Wilhelm, 216
ROI. *See* Return on investment
Romanticism, 211
Ron Brown Award, 84
Roosevelt, Franklin Delano, 178, 191, 210
Roosevelt, Theodore, 216
Rose, Nikolas, 386
Rothstein, Bo, 96
Rounding, 139
Rowe, Jonathon, 62
Royal Dutch Shell, 7, 34, 155, 336, 452
    boycotts of, 337
    eco-talk and, 337–338
    Nigeria and, 337, 339–342

Ruggie, John, 46
Rule utilitarianism, 196–197
Ryterbank, Dan, 18

SA8000. *See* Ethical workplace management systems certification
Saatchi & Saatchi, 52, 53
Sachs, Wolfgang, 47
Sacrifice zones, 356, 358
Sada, Eugenio Garza, 148
Sahlins, Marshall, 214
Salim Group, 112
Saltsjöbaden Accord, 96
Sam's Club, 83
San Andreas Accords, 301
Sara Lee, 365
Sarbanes Accounting Reform proposal, 426. *See also* Sarbanes-Oxley Act
Sarbanes, Paul, 429
Sarbanes-Oxley Act, 18, 162–163, 182, 184, 236, 268, 270, 429
Saro-Wiwa, Ken, 7, 40, 45, 255*t*, 339–340, 466
Satisficing, 182
Saturn, 242, 271
Save Thai Sea project, 373
Save the Children, 63
Scandinavia
    managers' self-perceptions in, 89–90
    role of state in, 89
    trust in, 89–91
    unions in, 91
Scandinavian model, 88–89, 96, 98
Scherer, Michael, 215
Schering-Plough, 179
Schmidheiny, Stephan, 322
Schwab, Klaus, 111
Schwans, 164
Scorecard on Globalization, 296
Sears, Michael, 219
"Seattle Was a Riot" (Anti-Flag), 247
SEC. *See* Securities and Exchange Commission
Secondary moral agency, 197
Securities and Exchange Acts, 182
Securities and Exchange Commission (SEC), 17–18, 69, 163, 428
Security of Employment Act, 39
Separate realms model, 155, 159. *See also* Legal positivism

Settlements, negotiated, 179
Sewell, William, 207
Shanghai Volkswagen Automotive Company, 373
Shareholder primacy, 423
Shareholder resolutions, 79
Shareholder rights, 268
Shaw, George Bernard, 180
Shell Nigeria, 40, 337, 339, 342, 442, 445
Shell Oil, 34, 40, 45, 49, 65, 185, 248, 254t–256t, 373, 407, 418, 456, 462, 463, 467. *See also* Royal Dutch Shell
Shining Path, 299
Shinsho, Karuna, 113
Shiva, Vandana, 384
Shop Right, 246
Short-term thinking, 76–78, 268–269
"Should We Admire Wal-Mart?" (Useem), 80
Siam Motors, 373
Sierra Club, 5, 65, 260t, 337
Silent Spring (Carson), 325, 338
da Silva, Luiz Inácio Lula, 51
Simple Living movement, 241
Simpson, O. J., 179
Singapore, 121, 126, 128, 129t
Singapore 21, 119, 131
Singer, Peter, 293
Situatedness, 295
Six Sigma, 413
Skandia, 91, 97, 98
SKF, 100
Skilling, Jeffrey, 20, 30, 167
Skills Development Act, No. 97 of 1998, 286
Sklair, Leslie, 62
Slavery, 193, 198
Slippery slope argument, 209–210, 213, 214
Smith, Adam, 122, 212, 294, 299
Social Accountability International, 39
Social activism, 168
Social capital, 15, 16
   globalization and, 38
Social coaction, 139
Social compliance, 184
Social contracts, 321
Social moral authority, 17
Social movement alignment, 247–248
Social obligation, 15, 88
   corporate social responsibility as, 92
Social Reform of 1933, 102n1

Social Responsibilities of the Businessman (Bowen), 406
Social responsibility, 16
   crisis situations and, 174
   fiduciary responsibility v., 172–174
   law and, 158–163, 179
   obligation of, 168
   profit and, 408
   regulation and, 210
   reporting and, 234–237
Social responsibility model, 155, 158
"The Social Responsibility of Business Is to Increase Its Profits" (Friedman, M.), 5, 207
   dissociative argument in, 213–214
   intended audience of, 209
   rational deliberation in, 210–212
   realist style in, 210–212, 214
Social solidarity, 251–252
Social Union of Mexican Businessmen (USEM), 137
Socialism, 5, 208, 210, 212
Sociedad Cuauhtémoc y Famosa, 138
Soft law, 93–94, 95
Sophistic rhetoric, 420–421
Soros, George, 17, 431
South African Foundation, 281
South Park, 247, 257t
S&P 500 Index, 68
SparNord, 89, 90
Spinning, 183
Spitzer, Eliot, 168, 180
Springsteen, Bruce, 247
Spurlock, Morgan, 247
Stakeholder Alliance, 63
Stakeholders, 6, 454
   communication with, 274–277
   CSR analysis and, 120–123
   governance including, 267–268, 273–274
   importance of, 126
   map of, 466f, 467f, 470f
   relations with, 147
   systems network of, 468
   theory of, 60, 167–168, 236
   types of, 122, 128, 132n1
   value to, 52
Stakeholding, 46, 220
Standard Fruit, 65
Staples, 81
Starbucks, 74, 76, 81, 245, 247, 248, 249, 259t–260t, 462
   fair trade standards and, 214

Statkraft, 101
Statoil, 91, 95, 101
Steinke, Karl Kristian, 102n1
Stewardship, 232
Stewart, Martha, 167, 187
Stigler, George, 207, 212, 431
Stock Options Coalition, 426
Stonecipher, Harry, 219, 226
Stop Killer Coke, 249
Storebrand, 95
Storebrand Environmental Value Fund, 95
Strategic Petroleum Reserve, 353
Strategic philanthropy, 137
Strategic positioning, environmental considerations and, 327
Strict liability, 159–160
Students Against Sweatshops UNITE, 40
Subaltern publics, 440, 442
   accountability and, 443–445
   CSR and, 439
   definition of, 438
   regulation and, 444
Subcontracting system, 307
Subpolitics, 305, 307–308, 311, 313
Suharto, Mohamed, 112
Sullivan, Leon (Reverend), 39, 214
Sullivan Principles, 39, 214
Sullivan, Scott, 182, 472n3
Super Size Me, 247
Superbrands, 52
Superfund. *See* Comprehensive Environmental Response, Compensation, and Liability Act
Superfund Amendments and Reauthorization Act, 325
SustainAbility, 47
Sustainability, 7–9, 31, 232
   accounting and, 237–238
   communitarianism and, 237–238
   corporations and, 394–396
   definition of, 351
   ecological, 77
   financial markets and benefits of, 283
   HIV/AIDS and, 279–281
   profit v., 99
   transition to, 328
Sustainability management systems assurance (AA1000S), 45, 46
Sustainability Reporting Guidelines (GRI), 280

Sustainable Business Network, 236

Sustainable development, 7–9, 48, 418
civil society and, 384–386
CSR and, 354–355, 381, 406–408, 442
definition of, 322, 347*n*3, 351, 352–354
discourses on, 359–361
eco-talk and, 336–337
environmental justice and, 355–357
family metaphors and, 382–383
history of discourse on, 379–382
management fashions and, 410–412
markets and, 384–386
perspectives toward, 353
public relations and, 346
religious organizations and, 382–383
Shell and, 344–346
undermining of, 432

Swartz, Mark, 462

Sweatshops, 33, 40, 78, 212, 247, 257*t*, 305, 407, 452, 462, 469
historical context of, 307–310
Nike and, 305–307
risk society and, 311–312

Swedish Asthma and Allergy Association, 98

Sweeney, John, 215

Swift, Tracey, 63, 66

Symbolic placation, 428, 429

System, definition of, 465

Systems thinking, 465–467

Taking Rights Seriously (Dworkin), 191

Taylor, Frederick, 326

TDC, 90

TeliaSonera, 97

Ten Thousand Villages, 246

Texaco, 248, 256*t*–257*t*

"Third Way" economics, 7

Thomas, Keith, 225–227, 229

Thor, 65

"Three Basic Beliefs" (Walton), 82

Tierney, Patrick, 293

Tokyo declaration, 380

Tokyo Electric Power Company, 113, 116*n*20

Tort law, 159–160

Tort reform, 159, 429

Toshiba, 170–171

Total quality environmental management, 326

Total quality management (TQM), 405, 409, 410, 412, 413

Toyota, 51, 53, 186, 224, 373

TQM. *See* Total quality management

Trade Union for Public Servants, 94

Transaction costs, 208

TransFairUSA, 260*t*

Transnational corporations (TNCs). *See* Corporation(s)

Transparency International, 39, 90, 98, 112, 467

The Transparent Society (Vattimo), 450

Trask, Mililani, 296–297

Triangle production, 307, 309

Triangle Shirtwaist Factory fire, 35

Triple bottom line reporting, 75, 78, 95, 234–237, 337, 342, 411*t*

TruGreen ChemLawn, 375

Truman, Harry, 423

Trust, in Scandanavian societies, 89–91

Tupac Umaru, 299

Tyco, 7, 17, 162, 167, 182, 185, 472

UAW. *See* United Auto Workers

UFCW. *See* United Food and Commercial Workers International Union

U.K. Higgs Report, 236

UNAID. *See* United Nations Programme on HIV/AIDS

UNCED. *See* United Nations Conference on Environment and Development

UNCTAD. *See* United Nations Conference on Trade and Development

UNEP. *See* United Nations Environment Programme

Unilever, 52, 53

Union busting, 257*t*

Union Carbide, 37, 155, 322, 336, 439

Union of Catholic Businessmen, 137

Union Oil, 441

Unions, 65
decline in U.S. of, 222
human rights and, 3
right to form, 160
in Scandinavia, 91
in Singapore, 128
trade, 94
Wal-Mart and, 81

UNITE!, 248, 259*t*

United Airlines, 460, 472*n*2

United Auto Workers (UAW), 221

United Food and Commercial Workers International Union (UFCW), 257*t*–258*t*

United Fruit, 65

United Kingdom Department for International Development (DFID), 471

United Nations, 46, 53, 63, 94, 299, 301
charter of, 32, 34
consumer protection and, 243–244

United Nations Commission on Sustainable Development, 381

United Nations Conference on Environment and Development (UNCED), 352, 382, 385

United Nations Conference on the Human Environment, 380, 407

United Nations Conference on Trade and Development (UNCTAD), 440, 444

United Nations Declaration of Human Rights, 343

United Nations Development Programme, 380

United Nations Environment Programme (UNEP), 47, 380, 381

United Nations Framework Convention on Climate Change, 161

United Nations Framework Convention on Tobacco Control, 381

United Nations General Assembly Declaration of Commitment on HIV/AIDS, 284

United Nations Global Compact, 39, 45, 48, 49, 53, 95, 121, 289–290, 314

United Nations Global Compact Leaders Summit, 51
United Nations Guidelines for Consumer Protection, 243
United Nations Millennium Goals, 48
United Nations Programme on HIV/AIDS (UNAID), 471
United States Forest Service, 374
United Steelworkers of America, 254*t*
United Students Against Sweatshops (USAS), 246, 247–248, 258*t*–259*t*
United Way, 156
Universal Declaration of Human Rights, 34, 42
Universal participation, 191–192
Universalization, 220, 226, 228
  management fashions and, 409
Universidad de las Américs-Puebla, 149
Universidad Iberoamericana, 149
The Unmanageable Consumer (Gabriel and Lang), 242
Unocal, 64
U.S. Agency for International Development (USAID), 386, 471
U.S. Conference Board, 18, 49
U.S. Constitution
  Commerce Clause of, 195, 196
  Contracts Clause of, 195
  Supremacy Clause of, 196
U.S. Department of Agriculture, 424
U.S. Export-Import Bank, 216
U.S. Food and Drug Administration (FDA), 181, 202, 424
U.S. Steel, 223
USAID. *See* U.S. Agency for International Development
USAS. *See* United Students Against Sweatshops
Useem, Jerry, 80
USEM. *See* Social Union of Mexican Businessmen
Usher, Thomas, 223
Utility, 207
Utility-maximizing theory, 207, 236

Value pluralism, 179
Value Shift (Paine), 87
Value, whole-systems theory of, 70
Vattenfall, 101
Vattimo, Gianni, 450–451
"Veil of Ignorance" (Rawls), 24
Vertol Aircraft, 221
Vietnam Labor Watch, 258*t*–259*t*
Vioxx, 79
Virtual communities, 53
Visa, 242
Vitro, 145, 150
Vogel, David, 215
Voluntary standards, 67
Volunteerism, 74
Volvo, 90, 98, 373
von Clauswitz, Carl, 420
von Mises Institute, 210

Wachovia, 17
Walker, Jeffrey, 420
Walking the Talk (World Business Council for Sustainable Development), 323
Wallach, Lori, 297
Wal-Mart, 40, 74, 76, 80–84, 155, 185, 245, 248, 257*t*–258*t*, 462, 463, 465–467, 469
  Good Works program of, 82–83
  unions and, 81
Wal-Mart: The High Cost of Low Price, 247, 258*t*
Walmartwatch, 40
Walton, Sam, 81–82
Warranted claims, 276
Waste Management Task Force, 344
Watergate, 178
Watkins, Sherron, 22
Watts, Phil, 342, 343
WCED. *See* World Commission on Environment and Development
Weber, Max, 106, 432*n*1
Weick, Karl, 24
Welch, Jack, 222
Welfare capitalism, 432*n*1
Welfare, Nordic model for, 89
Wellstone, Paul, 215
White, Byron, 198
White Label, 245
Whyte, William, 169
Wilcke, Richard, 214

Windfall profits, 5
Winnick, Gary, 167
Wiwa v. Royal Dutch Petroleum Co., 40
Wolin, Sheldon, 212
Women's rights movement, 192, 194
Worker Rights Consortium, 246, 248
Worker's compensation, 156, 160
Worker's rights, 160–161
Working conditions, 31
Workplaces
  capitalism and, 228
  health and safety in, 124
  value debate and, 24
World Bank, 31, 48, 59, 109, 141, 247, 297, 341, 431, 440, 468
World Business Council for Sustainability, 234, 410
World Business Council for Sustainable Business, 48
World Business Council for Sustainable Development, 8, 323, 354, 381
World Commission on Environment and Development (WCED), 94, 322, 338, 352, 354, 380, 407
World Conference of Indigenous Peoples, 340
World Conservation Union (IUCN), 249, 255*t*, 256*t*
World Consumer Rights Day, 243
World Development Movement, 64
World Economic Forum, 47, 90, 111
World Fair Trade Day, 260*t*
World Family Policy Center, 383
World Health Organization, 341
World Resources Institute, 354, 408
World Summit on Sustainable Development (WSSD), 352, 380, 382, 385
World Summit on the Information Society (WSIS), 296–297
World Trade Organization (WTO), 3, 59, 187, 247, 259*t*, 294, 297, 400, 401, 431, 440

World War I, 4, 42
World War II, 4–5, 42, 178,
    216, 423
World Water Forum, 444
World Wide Fund for Nature
    (WWF), 61, 69, 70
World Wide Web, 36
World Wildlife Federation, 255*t*
World Wildlife Fund, 90
WorldCom, 7, 17, 78, 162,
    177, 182, 268, 425, 429,
    472*n*3

WSIS. *See* World Summit on
    the Information Society
WSSD. *See* World Summit on
    Sustainable Development
WTO. *See* World Trade
    Organization
Wuppertal Institute, 47
Wuppertal sustainable
    development indicator,
    381
WWF. *See* World Wide Fund
    for Nature

Xcel Energy, 375

Youngstown Steel, 183

Zadek, Simon, 68
Zapatista National Liberation
    Army (EZLN), 300–302
Zavaleta, Antonio, 359
Zinn, Howard, 294
Zobel de Ayala II, Jaime
    Augusto, 114
Zoning ordinances, 201

Lightning Source UK Ltd.
Milton Keynes UK
UKOW07f1649130915

258527UK00011B/137/P